The Oxford Companion
to American Theatre

The Oxford Companion to

AMERICAN THEATRE

THIRD EDITION

GERALD BORDMAN
THOMAS S. HISCHAK

New York   OXFORD UNIVERSITY PRESS   Oxford
2004

Oxford University Press

Oxford   New York
Auckland   Bangkok   Buenos Aires   Cape Town   Chennai
Dar es Salaam   Delhi   Hong Kong   Istanbul   Karachi   Kolkata
Kuala Lumpur   Madrid   Melbourne   Mexico City   Mumbai
Nairobi   São Paulo   Shanghai   Taipei   Tokyo   Toronto

Library of Congress Cataloging-in-Publication Data
Bordman, Gerald Martin.
The Oxford companion to American theatre/Gerald Bordman, Thomas S. Hischak.—3rd ed.
p.   cm.
ISBN 0-19-516986-7 (alk. paper)
1.   Theatre—United States—Dictionaries.
2.   Theatre—United States—Biography—Dictionaries.
I.   Hischak, Thomas S.   II.   Title.
PN2220.B6   2004
792'.0973'03—dc22

9   8   7   6   5   4   3   2
Printed in the United States of America
on acid-free paper

Other Books by

Gerald Bordman

American Musical Comedy: From Adonis *to* Dreamgirls
American Musical Revue: From The Passing Show *to* Sugar Babies
American Musical Theatre: A Chronicle
American Operetta: From H. M. S. Pinafore *to* Sweeney Todd
American Theatre: A Chronicle of Comedy and Drama, 1869–1969 (3 volumes)
Days to Be Happy, Years to Be Sad: The Life and Music of Vincent Youmans
Jerome Kern: His Life and Music

Thomas S. Hischak

The American Musical Film Song Encyclopedia
The American Musical Theatre Song Encyclopedia
American Theatre: A Chronicle of Comedy and Drama, 1969–2000
Boy Loses Girl: Broadway's Librettists
Enter the Players: New York Actors in the 20th Century
Film It with Music: An Encyclopedic Guide to the American Movie Musical
Stage It with Music: An Encyclopedic Guide to the American Musical Theatre
The Theatregoer's Almanac
The Tin Pan Alley Song Encyclopedia
Word Crazy: Broadway Lyricists from Cohan to Sondheim

Foreword

by Harold Prince

In the 1930s, it was standard procedure for upper-middle-class Jewish parents to take their children to Broadway matinees every Saturday during the season, and during the summer to one of hundreds of theatres, which thrived in barns and local high schools on a menu of popular pot-boilers, light comedies, and the occasional serious play by Sidney *Kingsley, Marc *Connolly, or Lillian *Hellman. I imagine Hellman is the name that lingers—possibly as much for the myth she so diligently created with the help of Mary McCarthy. Kingsley, Connolly, Howard *Lindsay, Russel *Crouse, Robert *Sherwood (heroes of mine), and too many other accomplished playwrights, the meat and potatoes of that busy and golden period on Broadway, may well have been forgotten.

As a child, I was perhaps inexplicably initiated to the glamour of live theatre at a *Mercury Theatre production of *Julius Caesar in modern dress, directed by Orson *Welles. He was twenty-two years old. I was nine. Subsequently, I saw Helen *Hayes in Victoria Regina, the young Robert Morley as Oscar Wilde, Laurence *Olivier and Katharine *Cornell in S. N. *Behrman's *No Time for Comedy, and *Porgy and Bess, played by Todd *Duncan and Etta Moten.

By the time I was twelve, I was going to the theatre alone and purchasing cut-rate tickets in the basement of a drugstore on 42nd Street and Seventh Avenue. *Leblang's Ticket Office was dominated by a huge blackboard reached by a man on a ladder. In those days, matinees were at 2:30 p.m. So, from noon on, buyers gathered to watch the board. As curtain time approached, prices for available tickets were erased and replaced, until, by 2:30, what remained went for fifty cents.

As it was curtain time, I would dash through traffic to a theatre. If it was on 44th or 45th Street, I probably made it before the curtain went up. If it was on 52nd Street (then the Alvin Theatre—now the Neil *Simon), I had missed the first ten minutes. But it was worth it.

It was this way, usually for half a buck, that I saw *Life with Father in the gorgeous old *Empire Theatre on 40th and *Broadway. I saw Joseph *Schildkraut, descendant of a famous Austrian theatre dynasty, opposite Eva *Le Gallienne, heiress to a similar American dynasty, in the thriller *Uncle Harry. And I saw Walter *Huston in *Knickerbocker Holiday, with a libretto by Maxwell *Anderson and music by Kurt *Weill. Later, at only slightly higher prices, I sat in the balcony to see Moss *Hart and Weill's *Lady in the Dark and Laurette *Taylor in Tennessee *Williams's The *Glass Menagerie.

Running parallel with my visits to the theatre were those to the New York Public Library on 42nd Street. The scholar George *Freedley administered the *Theatre Collection behind glass partitions on the third floor. At least once a week, I would visit the collection, riffle through file cards, randomly requesting copies of Joseph *Jefferson's reviews of *Rip Van Winkle, or scrapbooks of Norman *Bel Geddes, a designer of epic brilliance and patriarch of yet another theatre dynasty, or the complete history of the *Provincetown Playhouse. The librarian would process my requests and in time got to know me as I got to know the other familiar faces pouring over the treasures in the collection.

History was always my favorite subject in school. The accumulation of historical facts bordered on obsessive. So, it is little surprise that I chose a life in the theatre.

And to fuel that life, to prepare it, I harbingered information, charting the names, places, the history of an art form, and the tradition of the theatre. Looking backward at that tradition, I hoped to see the future with a place in it for me.

Strange, isn't it, that if this is truly "The Information Age," so much of what bombards us is trivial, disposable, often worthless. Have the "fifteen-second attention span" and "fifteen minutes of fame" permanently altered our priorities?

I suppose by definition I have always been a "groupie." So, doesn't that put me in league with the kids who follow rock bands, who spend their parents' hard-earned money on digital games, who live in and for chat rooms?

Well, of course I don't think so. Because the purpose of celebrating tradition, of studying the past and present so that you can inform the future, is the commitment I shared with my contemporaries in this trade—one that I find lacking in a generation, which is at base as gifted, courageous, and capable of driving our theatre into the future as we and our predecessors were.

Which brings me to *The Oxford Companion to American Theatre*. This revised edition, the first in fourteen years, written by Gerald Bordman and updated by Thomas Hischak, contains material on plays and musicals, authors, composers, actors, directors, choreographers, producers, designers, theatre companies, and theatre movements. And theatres. You will find in the 2004 volume reference to creators, to their material, and to new movements in theatre, all relatively unknown in 1992 when the last revised edition was published. And just in case you were wondering why I asterisked these references in my foreword, it was so that you could easily access them in this extraordinary resource.

Just imagine, had the *Oxford Companion* existed in 1936, what time I would have saved the librarian at the New York Public Library.

But then again, this volume is aptly named your companion. Take it with you and journey on.

Preface to the Third Edition

Among the challenges one faces in updating and expanding Gerald Bordman's masterly *Oxford Companion to American Theatre* is the unbending law of physics that makes it impossible to add material without increasing the size of the book. We have tried to bend this law by changing format and page layout to use the space more practically, and some entries have been combined to avoid the repetition of some information. But one cannot get away from the necessity of cutting something in order to add something else and still keep the *Companion* to one volume. Rather than cut entries in toto, we have decided to edit and condense within the entry whenever possible. In this way the wide scope of the original book is not diminished and new material can be added to maintain the integrity and thoroughness of the first two editions. One of the most distinctive features of the *Companion* is its attention to plays and people of the distant past. We have strived to maintain that unique quality even as attention must be given to names, works, and movements that have proven noteworthy since the last editions were published. The goal has been to expand without growing unwieldy.

In addition to more plays, musicals, and people, the third edition includes new entries on such subjects as Asian American theatre, feminist theatre, gay and lesbian theatre, the redevelopment of 42nd Street, performance art, Hispanic-American theatre, solo performances, road tours, AIDS and the American theatre, Off Off Broadway, participatory theatre events, and various New York theatre companies. Also new are entries on every Broadway theatre, some Off-Broadway houses, additional historic theatres outside of New York, and dozens of regional theatres across the country. All of the Tony Award, Pulitzer Prize, and New York Drama Critics Circle Award-winning American plays are now included (the last now indicated by "NYDCC Award" in the text). Finally, some people and works from the not-so-recent past have been included in our efforts to highlight theatre notables that have proven to be important in the long run.

The following points bear repeating for the reader. The symbol * preceding a name or title indicates the existence of an individual entry for that figure or work. Dates are sometimes open to question. Unfortunately, birth and occasionally death dates can be uncertain or unknown. Where sources give conflicting dates and we could not resolve the problem we placed a question mark after the date given. In a few instances we have fallen back on indicating the period during which a figure flourished with the abbreviation fl. When performance dates are given they apply to New York City unless the entry states otherwise. For plays before 1894 we have used several sources to determine length of run, but primarily Odell's *Annals of the New York Stage*. Also, as in the past, complete credits that are available are given for American plays and musicals while foreign works that were popular in New York are described in an abbreviated format.

I must point out that the editing of the text and the addition of new material was done with Gerald Bordman's blessing but, in the end, the specifics of the process came down to my own decision. He is not responsible for any editorial changes, omissions, or shortcomings one might find in the new edition. Much of the *Companion* remains as Gerald Bordman first wrote it, but every entry has been affected somewhat by the editing and condensing process.

Acknowledgment must be made of the staffs at the Cortland Free Library and the Cortland Memorial Library at SUNY Cortland as well as my editors at Oxford University Press. I would also like to publicly thank three other people: my wife Catherine for her extensive help on the manuscript (and on much else in my life), my research assistant Mark Robinson who collected the information on nonprofit theatres across the country, and Gerald Bordman who had the trust and courage to turn over to me such an important project of his, allowing me to take something that was a long labor of love for him and change it without interference or disapproval.

T. S. H.
Cortland, N.Y.
October 2003

From the Preface to the First Edition

"Companion" is such a likable word, connoting something or someone so welcoming and comfortable, that it has been a special pleasure to bring it hand in hand with two more words that have long suggested admirable qualities and good times, "American" and "Theatre." We can only hope, then, that this *Oxford Companion to American Theatre* will prove delightful, useful company, whether habitually or for particular occasions. Perhaps focusing first on "Companion" is slightly unfair, since the real emphasis here might rather be on "American." After all, for many years theatre lovers have had recourse to the *Oxford Companion to the Theatre*, a basic reference book designed to cover theatre the world over. Both *Companions* cover some of the same matter and readers are urged to compare entries since often material has been approached differently.

An important difference is the inclusion here of entries for plays themselves—several hundred of them. We trust that no American play of major importance has been omitted, but our aim has not been merely to offer plays of enduring aesthetic or historical significance. Rather, we have attempted to give a broad picture of the popular American stage, so we have included as many commercially successful plays as practicable, regardless of the fact that they now may be totally forgotten or have no claim to permanence. To this end, we have offered entries for all non-musical American plays (except for some farce-comedies that straddled the fence between straight play and musical) which achieved a New York run of 100 or more performances before the end of the 1908–09 season, a run indicative in those years of substantial contemporary appeal. Thereafter, as longer runs became more common, the numbers were raised, so that, as an instance, between mid-1909 and 1920 a play had to survive 200 performances to be given an entry. Because hit musicals have almost always run considerably longer than non-musicals we employed even more demanding figures for their inclusion. Of course, numerous plays with shorter runs have been included when they are deemed to have some special interest. (In early years many shows were booked in New York for only limited runs prior to a national tour, and this, too, has been considered.) In play entries, the number of performances is the one assigned by the *Best Plays* series. Although different sources give different figures, the numbers rarely disagree by more than a handful of performances. Students of particular plays of course might want to go back to primary sources to determine the precise count. For plays before 1894 we have used several sources to determine length of run, but primarily Odell's *Annals of the New York Stage*. We have listed producers only where it was deemed to be of interest. In play entries, PP represents Pulitzer Prize, while NYDCCA stands for New York Drama Critics Circle Award. In the latter case only winners of the over-all best play category, established in the 1962–63 season, are acknowledged from that season on.

We have also included a number of foreign plays which had long careers on American stages or which influenced American theatre significantly. Here, however, our choice has been a little arbitrary and the form of the entry is different.

We believe that we have discussed all the giants among our actors, authors, producers, and other theatrical notables. Below this top level we have, of necessity, again had to be a bit arbitrary, but we hope that we have included more than a representative cross section, covering not only all aspects of the theatre, but all years and, where possible, all important theatrical centers. Two difficulties did arise. Among certain artists, especially designers and directors, facts were dismayingly hard to secure as one went back in time, so that a few deserving figures may have been denied an entry for lack of sufficient information. Moreover, material is often equally hard to unearth for figures who were important away from New York, especially in the 19th century. Such towering artists as Boston's Mrs. Vincent or William Warren might present no problem but many other cities had permanent stock companies whose leading figures now appear to be little more than names mentioned in old theatrical memoirs. We can only hope that local theatrical historians will fill in these gaps so that in future editions of this *Companion* such now shadowy figures will once again stand in the limelight.

We have tried, albeit not at the same length or depth, to look at more than legitimate theatre. Minstrelsy, vaudeville, circuses, wild west shows, tent shows, and other instances of live theatre have been allotted as much treatment as space permitted. Film careers of figures and plays have been mentioned only briefly, if at all. Fuller information on these can be found in the *Oxford Companion to Film* and elsewhere.

G. B.
Yellow Wood Farm,
Kirk's Mills, Pa.
June 1984

The Oxford Companion
to American Theatre

A

AARONS, Alfred E. (1865–1936), composer and producer. After beginning his career as a theatrical callboy in his native Philadelphia, Aarons became the manager of New York's Standard Theatre and *Koster and Bial's. He next turned to composing and inserted songs such as "Rag Time Liz" into Broadway musicals. Soon he was producing musicals for which he wrote the scores, including *Mam'selle 'Awkins* (1900) and *The Military Maid* (1900), both of which starred his wife, Josephine Hall. He also produced Ivan *Caryll's *The Ladies' Paradise* (1901) at the Metropolitan Opera House, *His Honor the Mayor* (1906), *Magnolia* (1923), *Tell Me More* (1925), and *$25 an Hour* (1933). His son was **Alex[ander] A. AARONS** (1891–1943), who produced *La La Lucille* (1919), the first of his many shows with George *Gershwin. Aarons joined forces with Vinton *Freedley in 1923 and presented such shows as *Lady, Be Good!* (1924), *Tip-Toes* (1925), *Oh, Kay!* (1926), *Funny Face* (1927), *Here's Howe* (1928), *Hold Everything!* (1928), *Spring Is Here* (1929), and *Girl Crazy* (1930). In 1927 they built the Alvin Theatre (named after the two of them) as a showcase for their musicals, but lost it in the Great Depression. They dissolved their partnership in 1933, and Aarons retired from active production.

ABBEY, Henry [Edwin] (1846–96), manager. Characterized by *Odell as "a restless genius of far-reaching vision and managerial astuteness," he was born in Akron, Ohio, the son of a clockmaker and jeweler. A practice of the time was to sell theatre tickets at jewelry stores, so he began his career as a ticket seller, later doing the same at the Akron Opera House, which he was managing two years later. After running theatres in Buffalo and Boston, Abbey assumed the reins of the *Park Theatre in New York City, then also Booth's and Wallack's. He brought great players under his aegis, including Edwin *Booth, E. A. *Sothern, and Otis *Skinner, and was the first to pair William H. *Crane and Stuart *Robson when he presented them in *Our Boarding House* (1877). Abbey was equally instrumental in bringing to America many great foreign companies and performers, and for several seasons he ran the Metropolitan Opera. In 1893 he built Abbey's Theatre on Broadway,

bringing over Henry *Irving and Ellen *Terry to open the house. His early death cut short a remarkable career. Some sources give his middle name as Eugene.

ABBEY THEATRE. See International Theatre Companies Visiting America.

ABBOTT, George [Francis] (1887–1995), director, playwright, and producer. Born in Forestville, New York, he studied with Professor George Pierce *Baker in the famous *47 Workshop. Some of his early plays were mounted by the *Harvard Dramatic Club by theatres in Boston, and in 1913 he made his acting debut in New York in *The Misleading Lady,* continuing to perform until the mid-1920s. Thereafter his onstage appearances were rare, although in 1955 he played Mr. Antrobus in an important revival of The *Skin of Our Teeth. Apart from helping to rewrite *Lightnin'* in 1918, he did not resume serious playwriting until 1925 when he collaborated with James *Gleason on The *Fall Guy and with Winchell *Smith on *A Holy Terror.* Abbott scored a huge hit with *Broadway* (1926), which he wrote with Philip Dunning and which he also staged. His lean, taut direction, followed by his forceful staging in the same season of another hit, *Chicago,* established him as a master of swift-paced melodrama. That reputation was consolidated when he collaborated on and directed two more popular pieces, *Four Walls* (1927), written with Dana Burnett, and *Coquette* (1927), with Ann Preston Bridgers. Turning to farce, he triumphed with his staging of *Twentieth Century* (1932), *Three Men on a Horse* (1935), which he wrote with John Cecil Holm, *Boy Meets Girl* (1935), *Brother Rat* (1936), *Room Service* (1937), and *What a Life* (1938). Meanwhile he also turned his talents to directing, and sometimes writing, musical comedy, at first working often with Richard *Rodgers and Lorenz *Hart. He staged, among others, *Jumbo* (1935), *On Your Toes* (1936), The *Boys from Syracuse* (1938), *Too Many Girls* (1939), *Pal Joey* (1940), *On the Town* (1944), *High Button Shoes* (1947), *Where's Charley?* (1948), *Call Me Madam* (1950), A *Tree Grows in Brooklyn* (1951), *Wonderful Town* (1953), The *Pajama Game* (1954), *Damn Yankees* (1955), *Fiorello!* (1959), and *A*

Funny Thing Happened on the Way to the Forum (1962). Between 1932 and 1954, he produced many of the shows he wrote or directed. He was librettist and director of the failed musical *Music Is* (1976), then at the age of ninety-five co-produced and staged yet another revival of *On Your Toes* in 1983. In 1987 he directed a revival of *Broadway*, but the mounting was a quick failure. Abbott's last hurrah was a successful Broadway revival of his *Damn Yankees* in 1995 in which he nominally served as artistic consultant. Exceptional in his ability to keep his shows moving, while never seeming heavy-handed or forced, Abbott was a strict, somewhat formal disciplinarian. Lehman *Engel wrote of him, "He always wore a necktie and never removed his jacket at rehearsal. What he said was positive and absolute." Autobiography: *Mister Abbott*, 1963.

ABE LINCOLN IN ILLINOIS (1938), a play in three acts by Robert E. *Sherwood. [*Plymouth Theatre, 472 perf.; Pulitzer Prize.] In a log schoolhouse, Abe Lincoln (Raymond *Massey) first learns about sectionalism and other barriers to "Liberty and Union" and resolves to do something about it. After his fiancée Ann Rutledge (Adele Longmire) dies, Lincoln marries Mary Todd (Muriel Kirkland), whose fiercely possessive, shrewish nature foreshadows her eventual madness. He then runs for Senator from Illinois against the proslavery Stephen Douglas (Albert Phillips). Before long, Lincoln is a presidential candidate, but somehow his victory at the polls gives him no cause for elation. Mary's behavior and the country's divisive sectionalism have both grown worse. As he leaves for Washington, he tells those who have come to see him off of his hopes that fatalism will not reign in America. The first production of the newly formed Playwrights' Company, the play was extolled by most critics, Richard *Watts Jr. of the *Herald Tribune* calling it "Not only the finest of modern stage biographies, but a lovely, eloquent, endearing tribute to all that is best in the spirit of democracy." The drama was revived in 1963 by the *Phoenix Theatre with Hal *Holbrook as Lincoln, and Sam *Waterston starred in a commendable 1993 Broadway revival.

ABEL, Walter (1898–1987), character actor. Equally effective in both Eugene *O'Neill dramas and drawing-room comedies, Abel appeared on Broadway for more than five decades. He was born in St. Paul, Minnesota, and studied acting at New York's *American Academy of Dramatic Arts before making his professional debut as a lieutenant in *Forbidden* (1919). Although he later became a much-recognized screen character actor,

Abel returned to the New York stage often, most memorably as the befuddled stepfather in *The Pleasure of His Company* and the grumpy old stuffed shirt Sir William in the 1975 *Lincoln Center revival of *Trelawny of the Wells*.

ABIE'S IRISH ROSE (1922), a comedy by Anne Nichols. [Fulton Theatre, 2,327 perf.] Because of their fathers' strong religious prejudices, Abie Levy (Robert B. Williams) and Rose Mary Murphy (Marie Carroll) have been secretly married by a Methodist minister. When Abie first introduces her to his father (Alfred Wiseman) as Jewish Rosie Murpheski, the father arranges for a Jewish ceremony. Rose Mary invites her father (John Cope) to the wedding, telling him her fiancé's name is Michael Magee. But when her father arrives with his friend, Father Whalen (Harry Bradley), the truth emerges, as well as explosions of ill feeling. Only the rabbi and priest are understanding. To appease Murphy, Father Whalen weds the couple for a third time. Matters are satisfactorily resolved a year later when Rose Mary has what Solomon calls "twinses": Patrick Joseph Murphy Levy and Rebecca Levy. The grandchildren reconcile the grandfathers. Throughout all the battles and reconciliations, a neighbor, Mrs. Cohen (Mathilde *Cottrelly), chatters on about her operation. Most reviews were kind, if unenthusiastic. However, some of the sharper critics, such as *Benchley, *Broun, and *Nathan, were scathing. At first playgoers were unenthusiastic as well, so producer-playwright Anne Nichols turned to a notorious gangster, Arnold Rothstein, and to *Leblang's Ticket Office for help. Rothstein underwrote losses until the play caught on and the comedy eventually established a new Broadway long-run record, as did many of its road companies. One modern critic, Howard Taubman, in his retrospective assessment of the play, observed, "Its plot is childish, its characters puerile, and even its ear for Jewish and Irish dialects monstrously false." **Anne NICHOLS** (1891–1966) was born in Dales Mills, Georgia, and began her career as an actress. She churned out many touring plays for Augustus *Pitou but, aside from her libretto for *Linger Longer Letty* (1919), she never had another New York success.

ABORN, Milton (1864–1933), producer. Born in Marysville, California, he began his career as a stage manager and actor, and for several years worked with B. F. *Keith in Boston. He joined with his brother Sargent (1867?–1956) to produce popular-priced productions of favorite musicals, and within a few years they had no fewer than six companies touring the country. Milton supervised the artistic end; Sargent, the financial side. The brothers split in the early 1920s and Milton opened a school of opera and operetta. In 1922 Sargent took over the A. W. Tams Music Library, later merging it with the Witmark Music Library. The Tams-Witmark Music Library remains a principal source for licensing musicals for production.

ABRAHAM, F[ahrid] Murray (b. 1939), character actor. The craggy-looking performer was born in Pittsburgh and raised in El Paso, Texas, where he attended the University of Texas. He studied with Uta *Hagen at the Berghof Studio before making his New York debut in 1966 as a replacement in *The *Fantasticks*. Abraham later shone in several supporting roles onstage, usually playing villains or broad farcical characters. After finding fame in Hollywood, he returned to Manhattan and played leading roles in classic works, such as Bottom in *A *Midsummer Night's Dream* and *King Lear*, and in modern plays, memorably Pozzo in the 1988 revival of *Waiting for Godot*.

ACCENT ON YOUTH (1934), a comedy by Samson *Raphaelson. [*Plymouth Theatre, 229 perf.] Steven Gaye (Nicholas Hannen), a successful middle-aged playwright, has written a play about a middle-aged man in love with a young girl, but the actors are unhappy with it until Gaye's young secretary, Linda Brown (Constance Cummings), shows them its virtues. She then assumes the leading role herself, falls in love with her leading man (Theodore Newton), and marries him. Left alone, Gaye finds himself unable to write more plays. Suddenly Linda arrives, announcing she is disillusioned with her handsome but vacuous husband, and Linda and Gaye realize that despite differences in age they are in love. That thought awakens Gaye's little muse, so he begins to dictate a new play to Linda: "Act One . . . Scene One . . . A penthouse apartment in New York City . . . change that—The Bedroom of a Castle in Spain." Critics divided on the merits of the work, Brooks *Atkinson taking a middle ground and finding it too long and contrived, but "lightly good-humored and pleasantly insane." It remained a favorite in summer stock for many years.

ACROSS THE CONTINENT; or, Scenes from New York Life and the Pacific Railroad (1871), a melodrama by James J. McCloskey (revised by Oliver Doud *Byron). [Wood's Museum, 42 perf.] In the depths of New York's most fetid slum, Five Points, a bedraggled widow (Lizzie Safford) begs callous, greedy barroom owner John Adderly (Charles Waverly) for pennies to feed her starving children, for her husband has spent his last cent at Adderly's gin mill. When Adderly refuses, she curses him and his heirs, then goes out in the snow to die. Twenty years later, Adderly has framed a good-hearted gambler, Joe Ferris or "The Ferrit" (Byron), unaware that the noble Joe is the widow's son. Adderly is also attempting to destroy a rich merchant, Thomas Goodwin (Joseph Sefton), at the same time he is seeking to marry Goodwin's daughter Louise (Annie Firmin). Joe escapes from prison, entraps Adderly, and sees him go to jail. Five years later Joe has renounced the city and gambling and taken a job as stationmaster for the Union Pacific in Indian territory. The Goodwins detrain at the station, only to have it attacked by Indians who have been goaded into action by Adderly, recently escaped from jail. As the raid begins, Joe desperately telegraphs for soldiers, who arrive by train just as Louise rushes into his arms. Although the work was dismissed by most critics with terms such as "claptrap," "rubbish," and "purely sensational," Byron's tour de force performance and the clever employment of such newsworthy features as telegraphy and the then equally new Union Pacific Railroad gave the piece a special excitement for audiences and provided Byron with a profitable vehicle for many seasons. The Canadian-born playwright **James J. McCLOSKEY** (1825–1913), who went west in the California gold rush of 1849, performed with almost all of the great actors of his day before turning to writing. He wrote dozens of plays, many recounting his California experiences, among them: *Daring Dick* (1870), *Rory of the Hills* (1870), *The Far West* (1870), *The Trail of the Serpent* (1871), *Poverty Flat* (1873), *For Lack of Gold* (1873), *Life or Death* (1874), *Arabs of New York* (1875), *Buff and Blue* (1876), *Nuggets* (1880), and *The Bowery Boys* (1881), but *Across the Continent* was his only major hit. Ironically, McCloskey made no money on the play, having sold the rights to Byron. For brief periods he managed the Marysville Theatre in California and the Park Theatre in Brooklyn, then spent his last years as a court clerk in New York.

ACTING COMPANY, THE. Founded in 1972 by John *Houseman and Margot Henley, it was an offshoot of special productions mounted by students of the drama division of the Juilliard School and was originally known as the City Center Acting Company. Since that time the company has toured the country, sometimes playing in regular legitimate houses but emphasizing university theatres and art centers. Thus it serves not merely as a training ground for young performers, but also as a practical seminar for students of the theatre. Its repertory consists primarily of classics, interspersed with new plays of interest. While it has met with success in its interpretations of Shakespeare, Marlowe, Sheridan, Shaw, and others, its most popular work has proved to be the musical *The Robber Bridegroom* (1975). Each founder served as artistic director for a time, and Zelda Fichandler ran the touring troupe in the 1990s. Celebrated alumni from the company include William Hurt, Kevin *Kline, Patti *LuPone, Christopher Reeve, David Ogden Stiers, and Jeffrey Wright.

ACTORS' EQUITY ASSOCIATION. Founded in 1912, following the dissolution of the *Actors' Society of America, it had its constitution and bylaws formalized in 1913 with Francis *Wilson elected as its first president. In 1910 the Actors' Society president Thomas *Wise had remarked, "The motto of the Actors' Society is 'equity.' It is their desire to establish an equitable contract, equitable for the actor and equitable for the management." The need for "equity" arose from the gross abuse of performers by much callous management. Actors often had been stranded far from home, had been forced to rehearse for weeks without pay, and frequently had been given little other consideration. The growth of the *Theatrical Syndicate, or Trust, had only aggravated matters. Making but small headway, the actors struck in August 1919, closing virtually all Broadway shows. Performers held a number of benefits to draw financial support, and the public, looking on the actors as friends and aware of the indignities they had suffered, responded wholeheartedly. George M. *Cohan, himself a beloved performer, and the *Producing Managers' Association organized a rival organization, the Actors' Fidelity Association, enlisting many distinguished, more established performers into their camp. But numbers told, so Equity prevailed. With the coming of the New Deal and its support of organized labor, Equity sometimes grew brazen and destructive. For example, its refusal to allow Eva *Le Gallienne and her *Civic Repertory to offer Sunday performances probably doomed that fine group. Always sensitive to foreign (read British) actors taking jobs away from American performers, Equity refused to allow Jonathan Pryce to re-create his London performance in *Miss Saigon* (1991) on Broadway until producer Cameron *Mackintosh threatened to cancel the entire production. In recent years the minimums and bonds demanded by this and other unions have been a factor in stifling production, shrinking the road, and forcing musicals to perform in auditoriums that are really too large for live performances, although the avarice of producers has played no small part in this last absurdity.

ACTORS' FIDELITY ASSOCIATION. See Actors' Equity Association.

ACTORS' FUND OF AMERICA. This organization assists needy performers and others who have worked professionally in the theatre. In 1881 Harrison Grey *Fiske and his *Dramatic Mirror* began to campaign for a fund modeled on England's Actors' Benevolent Fund. Beginning with a benefit in 1882 by M. B. Curtis in his starring vehicle, *Sam'l of Posen*, special performances were given all across the country to help establish the charity. The act of incorporation was passed into law by the New York State legislature later in 1882 and Lester *Wallack was elected the first president. The organization quickly became preeminent among theatrical charities, aiding in many quiet ways as well as establishing a home (now in Englewood, New Jersey) for retirees and opening special cemetery plots. Currently the Fund raises money through special performances of regularly scheduled Broadway shows.

ACTORS' ORDER OF FRIENDSHIP. A fraternal order for performers chartered in Philadelphia in 1849, its first lodge was called the Shakespeare Lodge. In 1888 a New York City branch, the Edwin Forrest Lodge, was established by Louis *Aldrich, John *Drew, and Otis *Skinner, among others. While the Philadelphia branch was active in providing comradeship and charity for nearly half a century, the order eventually gave way to the more efficient and richer *Actors' Fund of America.

ACTORS' SOCIETY OF AMERICA. An organization formed in 1895, partially in reaction to the practices of the *Theatrical Trust, it attempted to regulate and, wherever possible, to standardize contractual obligations between performers and producers. Led by Louis *Aldrich, the group had only minimal influence, and declined in membership after Aldrich's death in 1901. An attempt was made to incorporate it into the *Actors' Fund of America, but when that failed, the group was dissolved in 1912.

ACTORS STUDIO, INC. The preeminent workshop for professional actors, it was founded in 1947 by Cheryl *Crawford, Elia *Kazan, and Robert *Lewis. Membership is limited to those invited after an audition. In 1948 Lee *Strasberg joined the group and soon became its prime mover as the Studio evolved into the leading proponent of "method" acting, a school of performing that encouraged actors to respond as much to their own deepest feelings as to the requirements of the text or dramatic effectiveness. The style of acting developed into a major force in contemporary theatre. Among its proponents were Geraldine *Page and Kim *Stanley, while such Hollywood stars as

Marilyn Monroe, Paul Newman, and Joanne Woodward sometimes came east to study with the group. In the late 1950s and early 1960s the Studio established special units for playwrights, for directors, and for production. This last unit mounted several noteworthy offerings, including a fine 1963 revival of *Strange Interlude. Since Strasberg's death in 1982, its directors have included Ellen Burstyn, Al *Pacino, and Frank Corsaro. Well-known alumni of the Studio include Marlon *Brando, James Dean, Montgomery Clift, Dustin *Hoffman, and Robert DeNiro.

ACTORS' THEATRE. See Equity Players.

ACTORS THEATRE OF LOUISVILLE (Kentucky). A professional resident theatre founded by Richard Block and Ewel Cornett in 1964, it began to achieve major recognition after Jon Jory became its producing director in 1969; he would remain for three decades and make the company one of the most respected American resident theatres. Although the company offers a repertory that includes many classic plays and a Classics in Context Festival, it has become best known for its promotion of new native work. The annual Humana Festival of New American Plays, which now incorporates its former one-act play festival called Shorts, has made the company a leading advocate of contemporary playwriting. Among the dramas to receive trial productions there were *Crimes of the Heart, *Getting Out, Agnes of God, Extremities, and The *Gin Game. Originally located in a loft, then in an abandoned Illinois Central railroad station, the company now performs in three playhouses: the 637-seat Pamela Brown Auditorium, the 319-seat arena-style Bingham Theatre, and the 159-seat Victor Jory Theatre. The troupe has performed on numerous international stages and in 1980 won a *Tony Award for outstanding nonprofit resident theatre.

ACTOR'S WORKSHOP, THE. Founded in 1952 by two professors from San Francisco State College, Herbert Blau and Jules Irving, it rapidly became the city's leading regional theatre. The use of the singular in the name was a conscious decision since it was the founders' intention to offer "a place where each individual could pursue his craft." After two years in a loft and a highly praised mounting of Lorca's Blood Wedding, the troupe moved to an abandoned warehouse. A year later it took over the Marines' Memorial Theatre. Although the company occasionally presented classics, it was best known for its interpretation of modern avant-garde and politically oriented works. Among its noteworthy productions were Mother Courage, The Caucasian Chalk Circle, The Birthday Party, and *Waiting for Godot. It gave performances at the Brussels and Seattle World's Fairs and initiated a workshop for prisoners at San Quentin. After Blau and Irving left in 1965 to head the new theatre at *Lincoln Center, it fell apart, despite sporadic attempts to keep it going.

ADAIR, Jean [née Violet McNaughton] (1873–1953), character actress. With her pinched face and spinsterish appearance, Adair excelled in both comic and tragic roles, usually playing mothers and elderly aunts. She was born in Hamilton, Ontario, Canada, and learned her craft in touring stock companies before making her Manhattan debut in 1922. Adair is most remembered for creating the sweet murderess Aunt Martha in *Arsenic and Old Lace (1941). Her other notable performances include the nagging Mother in the expressionistic *Machinal (1928), the feisty mother-in-law, Mrs. Fisher, in The *Show-Off (1932), the moralizing Aunt Demetria in *On Borrowed Time (1938), the small-town gossip Cora Swanson in *Morning's at Seven (1939), and the modern-day witch Miss Holroyd in *Bell, Book and Candle (1950). Adair's last Broadway performance was as the aged, saintly Rebecca Nurse in the original The *Crucible (1953).

ADAM AND EVA (1919), a comedy by Guy *Bolton, George *Middleton. [*Longacre Theatre, 312 perf.] James King (Berton Churchill), who has made a fortune in rubber, is fed up with his extravagant family, who live beyond even his very ample means, and he longs to escape. When Adam Smith (Otto *Kruger), manager of King's Brazilian estates, visits and says he longs for noise, people, and outstretched arms of family, King hits upon the expedient of changing places for a year with Adam, although he warns the younger man he'll find not outstretched arms but outstretched hands. Taking over with authority, Adam quickly requires the Kings to live within their allowances. Furious, they threaten to hock their jewelry to pay for their high life, so Adam arranges to have all their jewels "stolen." Sensing that the two men who are courting King's unmarried daughter, Eva (Ruth Shepley), are fortune hunters, Adam goes a step further. He announces that King has lost his entire fortune and that the family will have to roll up its sleeves and find gainful employment. To his surprise, they do, even running a successful chicken farm in New Jersey. Eva realizes she is falling in love with Adam; and when King returns to find a changed family, Adam and Eva prepare to wed, but not before Eva has offered Adam a token of her love— an apple. Coming after the hiatus created by the bitter *Actors' Equity strike, the comedy produced by F. Ray *Comstock and Morris Gest was eagerly embraced by Broadway. Burns *Mantle called it "a characteristic comedy of American home life." For years it remained a stock and little theatre favorite.

ADAMS and STROUSE, songwriting team. Lee [Richard] Adams (b. 1924) was born in Mansfield, Ohio, and studied journalism at Ohio State University and at Columbia before writing lyrics with composer Charles [Louis] Strouse (b. 1928) for revues on the summer circuit. New York native Strouse studied at the Eastman School of Music and with Aaron Copland and Nadia Boulanger. Ben *Bagley first brought their songs to Off Broadway in his *Shoestring Revues and in The Littlest Revue (1956), but their reputation was firmly established with *Bye Bye Birdie (1960). Although two years later their excellent songs could not save All American (1962), they found success with a musical version of *Golden Boy (1964) featuring Sammy Davis Jr. Their 1966 effort, It's a Bird It's a Plane It's SUPERMAN, delighted many, but failed commercially. Adams and Strouse's longest-running musical was Applause (1970), another show whose extended New York stand could be attributed in good measure to a star, in this case Lauren *Bacall. Two later shows, A Broadway Musical (1978) and Bring Back Birdie (1980), had only the briefest of stays. Adams also failed when he teamed up with Mitch Leigh on Ain't Broadway Grand (1993). Strouse had a major hit without Adams with *Annie (1977), though working with others he stumbled badly with Dance a Little Closer (1983), Rags (1986), Nick and Nora (1991), and Annie Warbucks (1992). Both men are fundamentally traditional in their work but wide-ranging and inventive, their scores often superior to their unfortunate librettos.

ADAMS, Edwin (1834–77), actor. Born in Medford, Massachusetts, he made his debut in Boston in 1853 in The *Hunchback, then worked in Baltimore, Philadelphia, and New York, serving some of his apprenticeship under Joseph *Jefferson and E. A. *Sothern. Adams's first important New York appearance was in 1862, playing Clifford in Kate *Bateman's production of The Hunchback. With her company he also essayed Charles Surface in The School for Scandal and Macduff in *Macbeth. He began to tour on his own as a star in 1864—he jokingly called himself a "war star"—but met with ill luck when he was booked to open at *Ford's Theatre in Washington two nights after Lincoln's assassination. His playing caught the eye of Edwin *Booth, who selected Adams to play opposite him at the opening of Booth's Theatre in 1869, playing Mercutio to Booth's Romeo and Iago to

Booth's Othello. The Times savaged his performance as Iago, stating, "It is certainly Mr. Adams' worst interpretation. He is utterly deficient in subtlety and guile." That same year Adams gave his first New York performance as Enoch Arden, who returns home after being written off as dead, a role he returned to regularly and with which he is most identified. His last performance was as Iago in San Francisco, playing opposite John *McCullough. Sothern gave a number of benefits to provide for young Adams's widow. Jefferson praised Adams for "the animation of his face, the grace of his person, and, above all, the melody of his voice . . . a born actor, a child of nature if not of art, swayed by warm impulse rather than premeditation."

ADAMS, HOUGH, and HOWARD, songwriting team. Frank R. Adams (1884–1963) began writing lyrics and librettos while a student at the University of Chicago, collaborating with writer Will M. Hough (1882–1962) on the musical His Highness the Bey (1904). The composer of the team was Joe [Joseph E.] Howard (1867–1961), a New Yorker who began as a boy soprano and grew up to write the music for such hits as "Goodbye, My Lady Love" and "Hello, My Baby." Over the next several seasons the trio offered Chicago some of its most successful musical comedies, including The Isle of Bong Bong (1905), The *Umpire (1905), The Girl Question (1906), The *Time, the Place and the Girl (1906)—which established a long-run record for the city—The Land of Nod (1907), Honeymoon Trail (1908), A Stubborn Cinderella (1908), The Prince of Tonight (1909), The Golden Girl (1909), The Flirting Princess (1909), The Goddess of Liberty (1909), and Miss Nobody from Starland (1910). Their songs had a down-to-earth directness and a slanginess not unlike that of George M. *Cohan. Although several of these shows toured successfully after their Chicago runs, none was successful in New York. Thereafter Adams spent most of his time as a journalist, novelist, and early Hollywood screenwriter, while Hough collaborated with others on such shows as the Chicago hit The Girl at the Gate (1912). Howard was involved in an infamous lawsuit years later when it was revealed that he had not written the music for the standard "I Wonder Who's Kissing Her Now," as he had claimed. He returned to performing and was on the stage until the age of ninety-four.

ADAMS, John Jay (1798?–1839), actor. A New Yorker who apparently had enjoyed some success as a businessman, he abandoned his mercantile interests to make his debut as Hamlet in 1822. His repertory also included such standard roles as Othello and Rolla in *Pizarro. Apart from a two-year retirement beginning in 1824, he continued to perform until drink and general dissipation brought about his early death. Despite the brevity of his career, his Hamlet was recalled as one of the finest of his era.

ADAMS, Maude [née Kiskadden] (1872–1953), actress. One of the most beloved of all American performers, she was first carried onstage by her actress mother, Annie Adams, who was in a Mormon stock company in Salt Lake City where she married James Kiskadden and where her daughter was born. Her husband proving a poor provider, Annie Adams soon resumed her career and encouraged her daughter to follow in her footsteps. Adopting her mother's maiden name, Maude Adams played in small theatres in California before settling in San Francisco. She won her first important notices at the age of five as Little Schneider in *Fritz, Our Cousin German*. A few years later, Charles *Frohman witnessed one of her performances and told her mother she might make a good actress if she could rid herself of her western accent. She moved east in a play called *The Paymaster,* making her New York debut in 1888, then came to the attention of E. H. *Sothern, who cast her as Jessie Deane in *Lord Chumley*. After appearing in *A Midnight Bell* (1889) and *All the Comforts of Home* (1890), Adams played Dora in *Men and Women* (1890), created especially for her at the request of its producer Charles Frohman, who had by now reconsidered his earlier rejection. Within a year he had paired her with John *Drew, beginning with *The Masked Ball* and continuing until *Rosemary* in 1896. For some time Frohman had been urging James M. *Barrie to dramatize his novel *The Little Minister*. Watching Adams in *Rosemary,* Barrie realized he had found his Lady Babbie, so he agreed. The play opened at the *Empire Theatre in 1897 with Adams in a starring role for the first time. In 1899 she essayed a highly praised Juliet opposite William *Faversham's Romeo, and two years later she was the original American Phoebe in *Quality Street*. In 1905 she first played the role written with her in mind and with which she always was identified thereafter, the title part in Barrie's *Peter Pan*. An unhappy William *Winter called it "a tolerable performance, in a vein of grotesquerie, pleasantry, impulse and vim," but most critics agreed with another colleague who said the star was "true to the fairy idea, true to the child nature, lovely, sweet, and wholesome." After briefly portraying Viola in *Twelfth Night* (1908), she scored again in yet another Barrie play, as Maggie in *What Every Woman Knows*. A major disappointment was her failure in the title role of *Rostand's *Chantecler* (1911), which had opened to much ballyhoo and a

huge advance sale. Her last important new role was Miss Thing in Barrie's *A Kiss for Cinderella* (1916). Once coming under Frohman's aegis, she never left him. But after his death in 1915, her relations with his firm began to deteriorate. When matters came to a head in 1918, she announced her retirement, although she was still unquestionably one of the theatre's most popular stars. Over the years many important playwrights, Philip *Barry for example, wrote plays with her in mind, hoping to lure her back to the stage. She resisted many offers, returning only twice. During the 1931–32 season she toured as Portia in *The Merchant of Venice* but refused to bring the play into New York. In the summer of 1934 she played Maria in *Twelfth Night* in summer stock. Unlike many stars, Maude Adams shunned the limelight. Away from the theatre she was the most private of people, and for much of her later life lived quietly with a woman friend. But she was generous and high principled. She sometimes raised salaries of fellow players out of her own pay and gave thoughtful gifts to kind stagehands. Once, when a theatre owner doubled the cost of gallery tickets because he knew her name would guarantee a sold-out house, she made him refund the difference before she would perform. "Graceful as a kitten," she had a small, pointed nose, straight, pale hair, and gray-green eyes. The noted Chicago drama critic Amy *Leslie wrote of her, "She is direct and graceful and alive with the finer, more soulful emotions, so that she sighs and melts and droops with supine pleasantness. She is brightly intelligent and reads . . . with much charming intuition and feeling." Biography: *Maude Adams, An Intimate Portrait*, Phyllis Robbins, 1956.

ADDAMS, Augustus A. (d. 1851), actor. No precise records survive to show when or where this star-crossed performer was born, although in or near Boston is generally accepted. He first called attention to himself when he played William Tell in Philadelphia in 1831, then four years later made his New York debut as Damon in *Damon and Pythias,* followed by his Othello. *Knickerbocker Magazine* stated, "This young American actor bids fair to attain distinguished rank as a native tragedian. Physically, he is liberally endowed. His frame is well-knit, and his port commanding. His features, too, are full of expression, and susceptible, in an eminent degree, of sudden and powerful change. His voice also is deep and full. His personation of Othello was the best we have witnessed since we saw Forrest." He also won acclaim as Lear, Shylock, Jaffier, Virginius, Hamlet, Rolla, and Macbeth. In 1835 Robert T. *Conrad wrote the play *The Noble Yeoman* for him, but its first night was canceled when Addams was too drunk to perform, and a delayed premiere was botched because he was still inebriated. Addams's last New York performance was in 1848 as Carwin in *Thérèse*. Thereafter, unreliability stemming from his alcoholism hurt his career and kept him off major stages. T. Allston *Brown noted, "Had he let drink alone, he would have become the greatest actor ever seen in this country."

ADDING MACHINE, THE (1923), a tragedy by Elmer *Rice. [*Garrick Theatre, 72 perf.] On the 25th anniversary of his employment by the Firm, Mr. Zero (Dudley *Digges) is told by the Boss (Irving Dillon) that modern adding machines have replaced him. In a blind fury, Mr. Zero kills his employer. Mr. Zero's harridan wife, Mrs. Zero (Helen *Westley), offers him no consolation as he is tried and then executed. After death Mr. Zero haunts a graveyard and the Elysian Fields, rejecting the company of those who would lure him from his narrow but purposeful ways. His only comforter becomes Daisy Diana Dorothea Devore (Margaret *Wycherly), his onetime co-worker, who has killed herself to be with him. In heaven, Mr. Zero briefly finds satisfaction operating a gigantic adding machine, until he is ordered to return to Earth. He refuses to go back until he learns that he has been doing just that for many incarnations and will continue to do so until he is a totally crushed soul doomed to "sit in the gallery of a coal mine and operate the super-hyper-adding machine with the great toe of his right foot." Many of New York's most perceptive critics agreed with John *Corbin, who wrote that the *Theatre Guild's production of *The Adding Machine* was "the best and fairest example of the newer expressionism in the theatre, that it has yet experienced." Along with a fine cast and the superb direction of Philip *Moeller, the original production offered Lee *Simonson's imaginative sets. The bars and railings in the courtroom set were distorted, Mr. Zero's fury was suggested by large numbers whirling across the stage, and in heaven there was that huge adding machine, which Mr. Zero could walk on. This last piece nearly prevented the show from being seen, when an internal union disagreement erupted over whether it was a set or a prop. For all its excellence, *The Adding Machine* had only a modest Broadway run, but it remained popular for years with college and experimental theatres and established Rice as a major playwright.

ADE, George (1866–1944), playwright. An American humorist most popular in his own day for what he called his "Fables in Slang," he was born in Kentland, Indiana, and was also active in journalism and as a librettist and playwright. His librettist debut, *The Night of the Fourth* (1901), was a failure, but he found success with *The *Sultan of Sulu* (1902), which started the rage for musicals about Americans abruptly transplanted to exotic places, and *Peggy from Paris* (1903). Turning his hand to straight plays, Ade had two hits with the comedies *The *County Chairman* (1903) and *The *College Widow* (1904), which added a new expression to the language. But none of his later plays enjoyed long runs, although *Just Out of College* (1905) and *Father and the Boys* (1908) were by no means failures. He had more luck with his librettos for *The Shogun* (1904), *The Fair Co-ed* (1909), and *The Old Town* (1910). Ade was a master at employing contemporary vernacular, especially the slang of the youth of his day. His comedy was always wholesome and not a little innocent. However, his heavy reliance on quickly forgotten slang and his uncritical views of life make his plays seem puzzling and naïve to a more cynical era.

ADLER and ROSS, songwriting team. Richard Adler (b. 1921) was born in New York, the son of Clarence Adler, a concert pianist and music teacher. Rejecting his father's interest in classical music, he studied at the University of North Carolina with the intention of becoming a writer. An interest in songwriting soon surfaced, but Adler had little success until he met up with Jerry Ross [né Jerrold Rosenberg] (1926–55), another composer-lyricist who was born in the Bronx and had appeared in Yiddish theatre productions as a child. Their work impressed Frank *Loesser, who signed them to an exclusive contract, and, after providing songs for *John Murray Anderson's Almanac* (1953), the team had two hits in a row with *The *Pajama Game* (1954) and *Damn Yankees* (1955). The collaboration was unusual in that Adler and Ross each wrote both music and lyrics, and their songs were melodic, adventurous, and witty. After Ross's premature death, Adler's luck turned sour, although his songs for the flops *Kwamina* (1961) and *Music Is* (1976) were highly praised. In 1973 Adler co-produced a commendable but unsuccessful revival of *The *Pajama Game* and three years later produced Richard *Rodgers's failed *Rex*, but much of his later career was in television and writing concert pieces. Autobiography: (Adler): *You Gotta Have Heart*, 1990.

ADLER, Jacob P. (1855–1926), actor and manager. The preeminent figure of the Yiddish-American theatre, Adler turned to acting in his Russian homeland after dabbling in business and working briefly as one of the few Jews in the Russian civil service. When edicts directed at Jews made performing difficult in Russia, Adler immigrated to London, then came to America in 1887. Two years later he was in New York and heralded as "Greater Than Salvini." His first appearances in *The Beggar of Odessa* and *Under the Protection of Sir Moses Montefiore* were not propitious; but Adler's luck changed when he played *The Russian Soldier*, and his reputation grew when he followed that work with *La Juive*, in which he played Eleazar. For several months he toured with Boris *Thomashefsky, but professional rivalry, a personal scandal, and Adler's distaste for the operettas in the repertory soon drove the men apart. Determined to offer a loftier theatre, Adler took over the Union Theatre, established the Independent Yiddish Art Company, and commissioned a play from Jacob *Gordin, the best of the Yiddish playwrights. The result was *The Yiddish King Lear* (1892), not a Yiddish translation of Shakespeare but a free use of the story. The hero was Dovid Moishele, a rich merchant, whose daughters were viciously selfish housewives. "Shenkt a neduve der Yiddisher Kenig Lear" (Alms for the Yiddish King Lear), Moishele pleads at the curtain. The role remained an important part of Adler's repertory for the rest of his career. Another successful Gordin play followed, *The Wild Man*, in which a self-important father destroys his children. In 1901 Adler brought out a Yiddish translation of *The *Merchant of Venice*. So impressive was his Shylock that it was brought to Broadway in 1903 and 1905, with Adler performing in Yiddish, his fellow actors in English. Gordin's last play, *Elisha ben Avuya*, gave Adler another lifelong success, as did Tolstoy's *The Living Corpse*. A stroke in 1920 forced him to retire. Despite an often-scandalous private life and some questionable business practices, Adler was adored by his special public. An emotional rapport between actor and playgoer enlivened Yiddish performances long after American performances and audiences had become far more restrained. When Dovid Moishele was denied a bowl of soup by one of his monstrous daughters, a voice from the gallery rang out, "Leave those rotten children of yours and come home with me. My wife is a good cook. She'll fix you up." Aware that Adler is German for eagle, his followers saw in the actor's piercing glance, his strong profile, and his commanding presence a natural and appropriate symbol personified. Biography: *Bright Star of Exile*, Lulla Rosenfeld, 1977.

ADLER, Luther (1903–84), actor. The son of Jacob *Adler, he was born in New York, where he made his earliest appearance in Yiddish theatre, then acted with the *Provincetown Players. His Broadway debut was as Leon Kantor, the young violinist with a self-sacrificing mother, in *Humoresque* (1923). His other memorable performances include Sam, the law student, in **Street Scene* (1929); Don

Fernando in *Night Over Taos* (1932); the vicious, ambitious Sam Ginsburg in *Success Story* (1932); Julian Vardaman, the radical professor, opposite Katharine *Cornell in *Alien Corn* (1933); Dr. Gordon, the steadfast, middle-aged physician, in **Men in White* (1933); and Moe Axelrod, the crippled war veteran, in **Awake and Sing!* (1935). His most important role may well have been Joe Bonaparte, who abandons a promising career as a violinist to make money as a fighter, in **Golden Boy* (1937). Many of his later assignments were as replacements to original stars, such as Joseph *Schildkraut in **Uncle Harry* and Zero *Mostel in **Fiddler on the Roof*.

ADLER, Stella (1902–92), actress. The daughter of Jacob *Adler, she first performed with her father in Yiddish Theatre, and for many years moved back and forth between Broadway and Yiddish playhouses. Her best Broadway role may have been that of Bessie Berger, the dominating mother in **Awake and Sing!* (1935). She directed a number of plays, and for many years ran the Stella Adler Conservatory of Acting, which she founded in 1949. Her book *The Technique of Acting* (1988) and others are still widely used by schools and professionals.

ADONIS (1884), a "burlesque nightmare" by William F. Gill (book). [Bijou Theatre, 603 perf.] The sculptress Talamea (Lillie Grubb) creates a statue of Adonis so beautiful that she falls in love with it and, helped by the goddess Artea (Louise V. Essing), brings it to life. Unfortunately, she has sold the statue to the Duchess (Jennie Reiffarth), who is equally taken by the living, wickedly winking beauty, and who insists that Adonis (Henry E. *Dixey) is hers. Adonis is unmoved by all the attention and prefers to play the field, so he runs away to the country, where he promptly falls in love with a simple country girl, Rosetta (Amelia Summerville). The sculptress, the goddess, and the Duchess pursue him there and in the end make life so hectic for him that Adonis begs the goddess to turn him back into stone. She does. The music was by Beethoven, Audran, Suppé, Arthur *Sullivan, Planquette, *Offenbach, Mozart, Haydn, David *Braham, John Eller, and, as Gill wrote, by "many more too vastly numerous to individualize, particularize or plagiarize." Sullivan provided the evening's most popular musical moment when "A Most Susceptible Chancellor" became "A Most Susceptible Statue." Gill's text and E. E. *Rice's production offered not merely an adroit spoof of the Pygmalion-Galatea legend, but of contemporary dramatic and musical theatre mannerisms as well. Thus, the constant rejection of Rosetta by her father was a travesty of a famous scene in the then-popular *Hazel Kirke*. Nevertheless, it was young Dixey's brilliant tour de force that won the most applause and was the chief attraction. The public flocked to the theatre in such numbers that *Adonis* enjoyed the longest run in Broadway history up to its time, and Dixey played it off and on for twenty years.

ADREA (1905), a play by David *Belasco, John Luther *Long. [*Belasco Theatre, 123 perf.] Adrea (Leslie *Carter), a 5th-century princess on an Adriatic isle, has been passed over in the line of inheritance because she is blind. As a result she is deserted by her betrothed, Kaeso (Charles A. Stevenson), who marries her sister Julia (Edith Crane) instead. The wicked Julia, however, tricks Adrea into marrying the court jester, Minus the Echo (J. Harry *Benrimo), by telling her the groom is Kaeso. Adrea learns of Kaeso's disloyalty and Julia's treachery when she regains her sight and becomes queen. She kills Kaeso but then blinds herself again and puts Kaeso's son by Julia on the throne. Sculley Bradley has compared *Adrea* with Belasco and Long's collaboration of two years before, The *Darling of the Gods, noting that both "are romantic tragedies in each of which a beautiful high-born woman, in revolt against the outrages of society and fate, gives all for love and counts the world well lost. Both of these plays present a never-never world, while their language, though passionate and often poetic, is so highly stylized as to intensify the sense of unreality." Many critics felt Adrea was Carter's finest performance. Apart from some revivals that immediately followed, it marked her last association with Belasco, as it did for Long.

ADULATEUR, THE (1773), a satire by Mercy Otis *Warren. Published in 1773 but apparently never acted, it was described on its title page as "a Tragedy, As it is now acted in Upper Servia." It ridiculed the hypocrisies of Governor Thomas Hutchinson of Massachusetts, who pretended to favor the colonists while actually working against them. In the play, Hutchinson was personified as Rapatio, and his sycophantic brother, Foster, as Meagre. Rapatio attempts to undermine the plans for the freedom of Brutus, Cassius, Junius, and Portius (read James Otis [Mrs. Warren's brother], John Adams, Samuel Adams, and John Hancock). In his last soliloquy, Rapatio recognizes the baseness and hollowness of his actions and wails, "I dare not meet my naked heart alone." Despite its never being acted, the play was widely circulated and read by an appreciative audience.

AFRICAN AMERICANS IN THE AMERICAN THEATRE. During much of the colonial era, African Americans' lack of social position and the concomitant prejudices denied them any place in the earliest American theatre. Similarly, because virtually all dramatic entertainment during these years was of English origin, they were rarely presented as characters in plays seen in the colonies. The most notable exception was, of course, Othello, who was always performed by a white actor. Later Thomas Southern's *Oroonoko*, reputedly based on the real story of an African prince sold into slavery during the time of Charles II, was briefly popular. In 1769 the *John Street Theatre saw the American premiere of Isaac Bickerstaffe and Charles Dibdin's comic opera *The Padlock*, which had first been presented the year before at Drury Lane and which introduced the comically drunk, profane character of Mungo, who nonetheless suggested the plight and bitterness of his race as he lamented, "Me wish to de Lord me was dead!" This duality of the illiterate, shiftless yet sometimes shifty buffoon and of the shamefully downtrodden appeared frequently in characterizations of blacks for the next hundred or more years, although it was the comic stereotype that prevailed. Lewis *Hallam Jr. was the first American Mungo. The popularity of Defoe's *Robinson Crusoe* led to numerous stage versions, such as *Robinson Crusoe and Harlequin Friday* (1786) and *The Bold Buccaneers; or, The Discovery of Robinson Crusoe* (1817), which offered a similarly clowning Friday. However, minor black characters did begin to appear in American plays at this time. The figure of Ralpho in *The Candidates*, a play written before 1770 but possibly never mounted, could well be the first African American depicted in American drama. Inevitably, as the free black community grew in the North, some took to the stage. In the 1820s an actor named James *Hewlett apparently headed a small company in New York that performed such works as *Richard III* and *Othello*. The first black actor of distinction, Ira *Aldridge, served behind the scenes with some white companies and acted with black troupes, but, unable to find work commensurate with his abilities, spent most of his career in Europe. As a rule only white men played black characters. Actresses, out of prejudice or vanity, long demurred, and even Edwin *Forrest, failing to convince any leading lady to play in blackface opposite him in *The Tailor in Distress* (1823), drafted an African-American washerwoman for the role. The stereotyped Negro was given widespread popularity by T. D. *Rice in the 1830s. His great song-and-dance turn, "Jim Crow," besides reinforcing the standard stage picture of the African American, presaged the imminent rise of the *minstrel show and was a harbinger of the importance of blacks and black music to the

American lyric stage. So was the dancing of William Henry *Lane, who performed as Master Juba, and who helped evolve the Irish jig into contemporary black stepping.

Within a few years of the rise of minstrelsy and the growing abolition sentiment in the North, a number of protest dramas were spawned. By far the most famous and effective was the dramatization of Harriet Beecher Stowe's *Uncle Tom's Cabin, which from 1852 on was for many years the most successful contemporary American play. Although in retrospect its characterizations betray much of the condescension toward blacks long patent, it was a cogent argument for freedom, if not real equality, for slaves. Another extremely popular work of the time, Dion *Boucicault's The *Octoroon, took an equivocal stance, depicting slavery and the Southern viewpoint with some approbation, but decrying the plight of an innocent half-breed. In the very late 1870s and in the 1880s, Edward *Harrigan's portraits of African Americans were among the best known and most interesting on the American stage. Although all of Harrigan's figures verged on caricatures—and these included his Germans, Italians, Jews, and fellow Irishmen—they were all drawn with a compassion and depth of understanding unique for the day. Thus, one of his most famous figures was Mrs. Welcome Allup, or Rebecca Allup, a sassy but wise maid, who was always played in blackface by Harrigan's great partner, Tony *Hart. Indeed, Harrigan created a whole society of memorable Negro figures. As Harrigan's career was closing, African Americans began to develop a theatre of their own, largely musical. After the Civil War they organized their own minstrel troupes and later turned to writing black musicals, patterned after contemporary white musicals and originally offered only in theatres catering to black audiences. When ragtime entered our musical mainstream, these black songs began to be heard by highly receptive white audiences, and before long shows, both written and performed by blacks, were mounted in regular theatres. The first of these was an afterpiece called The Origin of the Cake Walk (1898), more popularly known by its subtitle, *Clorindy. However, the most popular black musical comedies were those starring Bert *Williams and his partner George Walker. They included *In Dahomey (1903), Abyssinia (1906), and Bandanna Land (1908). The *Johnson brothers, Will Marion *Cook, and Paul *Dunbar were among the leading writers. In 1910 Williams joined the *Ziegfeld Follies, becoming the first African-American entertainer to receive equal billing with whites in a Broadway show. The vogue for these "Negro" musicals quickly passed, and not until the 1920s did black artists truly begin to make a

mark on Broadway. Eugene *O'Neill had employed black characters in some of his early one-act plays, but his *Emperor Jones (1920), with Charles *Gilpin playing the memorable title role, created the first important African-American figure in original American dramatic literature. He later wrote an interesting study of an interracial marriage, *All God's Chillun Got Wings (1924). Other important black plays of the era, all written by whites, included *In Abraham's Bosom (1926) and *Porgy (1927). Whatever their authorship, these plays allowed theatregoers to see the finest African-American actors of the day (Charles Gilpin, Paul *Robeson, Rose *McClendon) in significant roles. But logical casting of black roles was not yet prevalent. Many such characters in contemporary plays were performed by whites in blackface, one of the most notable being Lenore *Ulric, who assumed the title part of the black prostitute in *Lulu Belle (1926).

The 1920s also saw a revival of interest in black musicals, sparked by the runaway success of *Shuffle Along (1921), whose songs were written by the African-American team of Noble *Sissle and Eubie *Blake. But these musicals still trafficked in stereotypes that had been a theatrical stock-in-trade for two centuries and in plots very like those employed in the Williams and Walker shows. Many, like the *Blackbirds series, were plotless revues. A few musicals written by whites, such as Deep River (1926), Show Boat (1927), and Great Day (1929), attempted to look at the black predicament with fresh eyes, though even *Show Boat used a white actress to portray one of its leading black figures. But the lyric for that musical's "Ol' Man River" expressed sentiments not unlike those of Mungo's 160 years before. The 1930s saw a number of prominent African Americans play roles on Broadway, but usually in all-black productions or in specialty numbers. Ethel *Waters was a major song-and-dance figure, but she starred mainly in revues with white casts where her numbers could be separated from the rest of the show. Only in *Cabin in the Sky (1940) did she have a role in a plotted musical, this time with an all-black cast. Twice in her later career—in Mamba's Daughters (1939) and in The *Member of the Wedding (1950)—she gave memorable performances in dramas. Bill *Robinson was the most famous African-American song-and-dance man of the period, but he was relegated to the all-black Blackbirds revues, and later to a *Gilbert and *Sullivan parody, The Hot Mikado (1939).

Many of the period's experimental operas and musicals made use of all-black casts. The Virgil Thomson–Gertrude Stein opera Four Saints in Three Acts (1934), in a controversial production, featured a cellophane set and a cast of African-American singers recruited from New York black churches. *Porgy and Bess (1935), George *Gershwin's lyric and compassionate "folk opera" based upon *Porgy, attracted only small audiences at first on Broadway and was only really recognized as the classic it is in its 1942 revival and in subsequent Broadway productions in the 1950s and 1970s. Later musicals, also written by whites, such as *Carmen Jones, which Oscar *Hammerstein II derived from Bizet's Carmen, attempted new perspectives. The period also saw the production of a large number of protest plays, many concerned with the conditions of African Americans; the *Federal Theater Project and its offshoots were especially active. Many of these plays were too strident for most playgoers' tastes. Stevedore (1934) told of a black longshoreman framed for a crime he didn't commit. John Wesley's They Shall Not Die (1934), produced by the *Theatre Guild, depicted the Scottsboro Trial about some Alabama black youths accused of rape. The African-American poet Langston Hughes wrote a dozen plays of various types and lengths during the decade. *Mulatto (1935), describing the plight of half-castes, with Rose *McClendon as the black mistress of a white plantation owner, had a long run, while Do You Want to Be Free? (1938) ran on weekends for many weeks at the Harlem Suitcase Theater. By far the most successful black-acted, albeit white-written, play of the era was The *Green Pastures (1930). Away from Broadway, in Harlem, the *Lafayette Theatre featured black casts in black-related plays. The Federal Theater sponsored a Negro Theatre group that produced a version of Macbeth set in Haiti, with a mixed white and black cast. From this base producers John *Houseman and Orson *Welles later presented the most distinguished black drama of the period, *Native Son (1941), Richard Wright's adaptation of his novel. The outstanding African-American actor of the time, Paul *Robeson, was outside America during much of the 1930s but returned as Othello (1943) with José *Ferrer and Uta *Hagen.

World War II helped create greater interest in the problems of black America. The dramas continued to be written largely by whites and tended to be protest plays, albeit with more balance and less radical rhetoric. One such play, *Deep Are the Roots (1945), enjoyed a long run. One popular attraction, *Anna Lucasta (1944), was written by a white about white people but it was cast with black actors when no producer would mount it with a white cast. During this decade several producers attempted to cast blacks in roles that did not specifically call for them, such as one of the policemen in *Detective Story (1948). Broadway musicals, such as *Finian's Rainbow (1947) and South Pacific (1949), dealt with racial prejudice. Kurt *Weill's Lost in the Stars (1949) adapted Alan Paton's novel Cry, the Beloved Country, about (Patron wrote more than one novel) South African blacks. Much more significant, however, were the efforts of white songwriter Harold *Arlen, who wrote several musicals featuring black casts and calling in the talents of major African-American performers: Pearl *Bailey, Juanita *Hall, Lena Horne, and Diahann Carroll. Starting with two specialty numbers for Dooley Wilson in *Bloomer Girl (1944), Arlen created shows about black life with appropriate jazz-derived music. St. Louis Woman (1946) deals with a high-stepping black society in St. Louis around a racetrack in 1898, while *House of Flowers (1954), with a book by Truman *Capote, describes a trade war between two brothels on a West Indian isle and had one of Arlen's most exquisite scores. Later musicals included a 1964 adaptation of Clifford *Odets's famous *Golden Boy, with Sammy Davis Jr. as the prizefighter, and *Purlie (1970), which Ossie *Davis adapted from his comedy *Purlie Victorious (1961), about a preacher's encounter with Southern prejudice. African-American entertainers now had the chance to star in interracial casts, such as Leslie Uggams in *Hallelujah, Baby! (1967) and Diahann Carroll as a black model in an interracial romance in *No Strings (1962). The emergence of African-American playwrights on Broadway gathered momentum in the 1950s with such plays as Louis Peterson's Take a Giant Step (1953), a failure, and Lorraine *Hansberry's A *Raisin in the Sun (1959), a success. Other notable plays included Martin Duberman's In White America (1963) and James Baldwin's Blues for Mister Charlie (1964). During this time black performers not only occasionally played roles that were not specifically "Negro" in character, but even some that were specifically white. An example of the former was Diana Sands in The Owl and the Pussycat (1964); the most heralded example of the latter was Canada *Lee as de Bosola in The Duchess of Malfi (1946), a role he played in white makeup. Joseph *Papp's *New York Shakespeare Festival gave African Americans a chance to play other classic roles, notably James Earl *Jones as King Lear. Jones also played Othello (1982) on Broadway opposite Christopher *Plummer but gave his most powerful performance in The *Great White Hope (1968), in which he portrayed the black boxing champion Jack Jefferson.

The civil-rights revolution of the 1960s gave great impetus to an increased black presence on every level of the theatre, particularly Off Broadway. There was a whole new wave of protest plays, this time all written by blacks, including those like Leroi Jones's (later Imamu Amiri *Baraka) The Slave (1965) and The Toilet (1965) and Ed Bullins's The Taking of Miss Jamie, which included direct physical assaults on whites onstage. Jones's The Dutchman (1964), about a white woman seducing and then killing a middle-class black on a subway, was his most effective play and captured the complexity of the race problem in America perhaps better than any other work of the period. Another important development was the foundation of the *Negro Ensemble Company (NEC), sponsoring plays written by blacks and played by black casts. During its existence the NEC had many noteworthy new works, some of which transferred to Broadway.

In the last half of the 1980s, August *Wilson emerged as an important new dramatist. While too many African-American playwrights made a big splash with a powerful work and were rarely heard from again, Wilson has managed for two decades to present a series of critically acclaimed plays, which often found success on Broadway. In the last decades of the 20th century, African Americans onstage have been most visible in musicals. While most Broadway shows feature African Americans in the cast, there have been many successful musicals that were predominantly black, such as The *Wiz (1975), *Dreamgirls (1981), *Ain't Misbehavin' (1978), Eubie! (1978), *Sophisticated Ladies (1981), Black and Blue (1989), Five Guys Named Moe (1992), *Jelly's Last Jam (1992), Bring on da Noise, Bring on da Funk (1996), and The *Lion King (1997). By the millennium African Americans were noticeably visible in all aspects of American theatre, whereas in the past they were primarily performers only. George C. *Wolfe runs the *Public Theatre and other nonprofit theatres across the country, which have African Americans in management, directing, and designing. And while theatre companies with a racial agenda still exist, almost every theatre in America is sometimes a vehicle for African-American artists of all kinds.

AFTER THE FALL (1964), a play by Arthur *Miller. [ANTA, Washington Square Theatre, 208 perf.] Quentin (Jason *Robards Jr.) is a middle-aged lawyer who attempts to bring his life into focus by examining his past. Clearly the women in his life have been pivotal. They were his troubled Mother (Virginia Kaye); his first wife, Louise (Mariclare Costello), who valued her independence above all; and his prospective third wife, Holga (Salome Jens), still scarred by her life in Nazi Germany. But most of all there was his second wife, Maggie (Barbara Loden), a beautiful but insecure actress who ultimately committed suicide. Many critics saw the play as an autobiographical shriving, with the main action centered on Miller's failed marriage to actress Marilyn Monroe. The play was the first production of the *Repertory Theatre of Lincoln Center, but was mounted at a specially constructed theatre pending the completion of the *Vivian Beaumont Theatre. *After the Fall* was revived Off Broadway in 1992 with Frank *Langella as Quentin.

AH SIN (1877), a play by Bret Harte, Mark Twain. [*Fifth Avenue Theatre, 35 perf.] Broderick (Edmund K. Collier), a "knave through circumstances over which he ought to have control," attacks Uncle Billy Plunkett (P. A. Anderson), "the Champion Liar of Calaveras," leaving him for dead and attributing the attack to mill owner York (Henry Crisp). Just as a lynch mob is about to hang York, the wily Chinaman Ah Sin (Charles T. *Parsloe) solves the crime by connecting an incriminating coat to Broderick. The Augustin *Daly production, developed from a character in Harte's poem, was a failure, but it is remembered because of the speech Mark Twain, dressed in white, gave at the end that many critics claimed was better than anything in the play. Sensing a poor reception, Mark Twain began by wryly telling the audience that the play was "intended rather for instruction than amusement" and suggesting, as an example, that "for the instruction of the young we have introduced a game of poker."

AH, WILDERNESS! (1933), a comedy by Eugene *O'Neill. [Guild Theatre, 289 perf.] In "a large small-town in Connecticut," almost the whole Miller family is preparing to celebrate July 4th, although to their teenage son, Richard (Elisha Cook Jr.), they are all slaves of the capitalistic system and the holiday is "a stupid farce." If young Richard's misguided political enthusiasms merely amuse his tolerant father, Nat (George M. *Cohan), another of his passions, reading, seriously concerns his mother, Essie (Marjorie Marquis). Politics, poetry, and prose are scarcely enough to claim all of Richard's youthful ardor. The real love of his life is Muriel McComber (Ruth Gilbert), to whom Richard has been sending letters filled with the same ardent poetry that angers Muriel's father (Richard Sterling). He demands that Richard no longer see his daughter, and if Richard disobeys he'll remove his advertisements from Nat's paper. In adolescent desperation Richard heads for a local bar, where he meets up with a "tart" and gets hopelessly drunk. Luckily his family is understanding and forgiving. Even Muriel would like to continue their romance, so Richard promises he will write and remain loyal when he leaves for Yale in the fall. George Jean *Nathan, to whom O'Neill dedicated the play, proclaimed it "the tenderest and most amusing comedy of boyhood in the American Drama," while Burns *Mantle noted, "It goes back in the American theatre scene to such homely old hits as The *Old Homestead and *Shore Acres." The *Theatre Guild production of O'Neill's only comedy was also praised for Cohan's fine-tuned performance. *Ah, Wilderness!* was given commendable Broadway revivals in 1975, 1988, and 1998, but none of them enjoyed a long run. The play is the source for the musical *TAKE ME ALONG* (1959) with a book by Joseph *Stein and Robert Russell, and lyrics and music by Bob *Merrill. The fine cast included Walter Pidgeon (Nat), Robert *Morse (Richard), Una Merkel (Essie), and Jackie *Gleason as the boozy Uncle Sid. Although the adaptation was remarkably faithful and Merrill's score was both delicate and enjoyable, only the title song enjoyed much popularity. David *Merrick produced the musical at the *Shubert Theatre, and it ran for 448 performances.

AHRENS and FLAHERTY, songwriting team. Lynn Ahrens (b. 1948), the lyricist and librettist member of the duo, was born in New York and studied journalism at Syracuse University. She wrote television commercials and for children's shows before meeting composer Stephen Flaherty (b. 1960) at a BMI Musical Theatre Workshop in 1983. He was born in Pittsburgh and studied music at the Cincinnati College Conservatory of Music. The team's first effort was the musical farce *Lucky Stiff* (1988), followed by the Caribbean fable *Once on This Island* (1990) and *My Favorite Year* (1992), about the early days of television. Ahrens provided lyrics only for Alan *Menken's music in *A Christmas Carol* (1994), then reteamed with Flaherty for *Ragtime* (1998), *Seussical* (2000), and *A Man of No Importance* (2002). The songwriting team is known for their acute sense of pastiche, strong melodic lines, and polished integrated scores.

AIDA (2000), a musical play by Linda Woolverton, Robert *Falls, David Henry *Hwang (book), Elton John (music), Tim *Rice (lyrics). [*Palace Theatre, still running.] Only the basic story of Verdi's celebrated opera is retained in this soft-rock version of the tragic romance between the slave-princess Aida (Heather Headley) and the Egyptian prince Radames (Adam Pascal). *Notable songs*: Every Story Is a Love Story; Elaborate Lives; My Strongest Suit. Bob Crowley's creative, anachronistic sets and Natasha Katz's dazzling lighting contributed greatly to the musical's modern temperament, and Headley's Tony Award–winning performance certainly helped. Generally trounced by the critics, the *Disney production was an audience favorite from the start. **Elton JOHN** [né Reginald Kenneth Dwight] (b. 1947) was born in Pinner, England, and educated at London's Royal Academy of Music. Since 1970 he has been an internationally famous rock star who performs his own music (usually with lyrics by Bernie Taupin). John's first theatre venture was writing additional songs for his movie score for *The Lion King* when it was adapted for Broadway in 1997.

AIDS AND THE AMERICAN THEATRE. Acquired Immune Deficiency Syndrome (AIDS) has made a major impact on the American theatre in two ways: the loss of creative talent and the proliferation of dramas about people affected by the disease itself. When first diagnosed in the early 1980s, AIDS was considered a homosexual disease. Since a large percentage of the theatre community (both artists and audience) has always been gay or lesbian, the effect of AIDS was considerable. Famous, promising, and undiscovered actors, writers, designers, and producers died at an alarming rate in the early 1990s, altering the direction the American theatre might have taken. Since concern over the disease was all encompassing in the theatre world, many plays and musicals were written and presented as a way of dealing with the epidemic. The first two notable works on the subject were Larry Kramer's *The Normal Heart* (1985), which took an angry, political stance, and William M. Hoffman's *As Is* (1985), which explored the more personal aspects of relating to the disease. Subsequent works fell in line with one or the other of these approaches. But many bitter, preachy plays, as well as sentimental dramas wallowing in self-pity, followed and not until the late 1980s and 1990s did the best plays and musicals about AIDS come to light. Among the many noteworthy examples were *Eastern Standard* (1988), *Zero Positive* (1988), *Falsettoland* (1990), *The Destiny of Me* (1992), *Angels in America* (1993), *Jeffrey* (1993), *Pterodactyls* (1993), *Love! Valour! Compassion!* (1994), and *Rent* (1996). In many ways the AIDS epidemic has united the theatre community, resulting in programs to counsel, house, and care for victims of the disease, and organizations, such as Broadway Cares, which hold benefits and actively pursue fundraising programs.

AIKEN, GEORGE L. See *Uncle Tom's Cabin*.

AIN'T MISBEHAVIN' (1978), a revue in two acts with music by Thomas "Fats" Waller. [*Longacre Theatre, 1,604 perf.] Murray Horowitz and Richard *Maltby Jr. conceived the musical retrospective, with various lyricists, using the songs written by the African-American composer-entertainer Waller (1904–43). Only a few of the songs had been created for Broadway, most notably the title number, which had first been sung in the 1929 revue *Hot Chocolates*. Considered the best of the compilation revues of the era, the five-character piece was such a critical and popular success at the *Manhattan Theatre Club that it moved to Broadway for a long run. The show also inspired other retrospective revues, such as the Eubie *Blake tribute *Eubie* (1978), and the Duke Ellington revue *Sophisticated Ladies* (1981). *Ain't Misbehavin'* was successfully revived on Broadway with the original cast in 1988.

AKALAITIS, Joanne (b. 1937), director. One of the American theatre's most controversial artists, she has worked with many different groups over the years, often inciting praise and outrage at her unconventional approach to staging new and classic plays. She was born in Cicero, Illinois, and educated at the University of Chicago and Stanford. In 1970 Akalaitis cofounded *Mabou Mines, and in 1991 she briefly ran the *Public Theatre. Among her many notable productions were *Endgame* (1984) at the *American Repertory Theatre, *The Screens* (1989) at the *Guthrie Theatre, both parts of *Henry IV* (1991), *In the Summer House* (1993) at the Public, and *Arts and Leisure* (1996) at *Playwrights Horizons.

AKINS, Zoë (1886–1958), playwright. She was born in Humansville, Missouri, and made her professional writing debut with the one-actor *The Magical City* (1916). Many critics saw great promise in *Papa* (1919), her comedy about a father who attempts to save his faltering fortune by marrying off his daughters; but her reputation was established by the success of *Déclassée* (1919), about a woman who abandons home and husband. Akins met with varying success with such plays as *Daddy's Gone A-Hunting* (1921), which depicted the consequences of a man's desertion of his family; *The Varying Shore* (1921), the history of a courtesan told in flashbacks in reverse chronological order; *The Texas Nightingale* (also known as *Greatness*) (1922), about the troubled life of an opera singer; *A Royal Fandango* (1923), in which a promiscuous princess is brought to her senses; and a series of adaptations of foreign plays: *The Moon-Flower* (1924), *First Love* (1926), *The Crown Prince* (1927), *The Love Duel* (1929), and *South of Siam* (1929). A bawdy comedy about gold-digging ex-Follies girls, *The Greeks Had a Word for It* (1930), was a huge success; and she won a *Pulitzer Prize for her dramatization of Edith Wharton's *The *Old Maid* (1935). Thereafter, however, her adaptations and such original plays as *O Evening Star* (1936) and *Mrs. January and Mr. X* (1944) met largely with indifference. While many of her early plays shocked audiences by their candor, changing moral codes have dulled their sharpness. Nevertheless, her works can be perceived as urbane, with a superior flare for dramatic situations.

ALABAMA (1891), a play by Augustus *Thomas. [*Madison Square Theatre, 37 perf.] A quarter-century after the Civil War, Colonel Preston (J. H. *Stoddart) is still an unrepentant Confederate, still advocating slavery and condemning the North for destroying his way of life. When the hated Northern-owned railroads come to set tracks along his property, Preston at first fails to recognize that the engineer is his son, Captain Davenport (Maurice *Barrymore), who had gone off as a young man to fight for the Union and who had not been home since. Davenport puts his father's failing estate in order and frees his old sweetheart (May Brookyn) and her son (Henry *Woodruff) from the clutches of a villainous brother-in-law (Walden Ramsay). Thomas's plot, though it confronted still festering sectional differences, was secondary to his studies of various homespun types such as Squire Tucker, "a large baby of fifty . . . tied for life to the apron strings of his mother." The play was produced by A. M. *Palmer in what was perceived as a highly realistic manner, even to sending magnolia perfume wafting through the theatre during a scene in a magnolia grove. Previous commitments forced Palmer to take *Alabama* on the road while it was still drawing large houses in Manhattan. Business on tour was so poor at first that Palmer, suffering from a succession of New York failures, was forced to relinquish the Madison Square Theatre, and so ended his career as one of New York's most distinguished producers. Ironically, *Alabama* eventually caught on with hinterland audiences and remained popular for more than a decade.

ALABAMA SHAKESPEARE FESTIVAL (Montgomery). The premiere producer of classics in the South, the festival began in a high school auditorium in Anniston, Alabama. The company relocated to Montgomery in 1985, where it now operates in the Carolyn Blount Theatre, a facility consisting of a 750-seat festival stage and a 225-seat octagon space. The repertory includes Moliere, Shaw, and Chekhov, as well as Shakespeare, and new works are presented alongside American classics. The company claims to be the sixth-largest Shakespeare festival in the world.

ALBEE, E[dward] F[ranklin] (1857–1930), manager. The scion of an old and wealthy Maine family, he ran away from home to join a circus, serving first as a common roustabout and then as principal ticket seller. On a visit to Boston in 1885, he stumbled on a shabby variety house being managed by B. F. *Keith. Business was poor, but under Albee's guidance the house flourished, offering variety at cut-rate prices. Keith and Albee quickly began buying and restoring old theatres in New England, then building his first new house in Philadelphia. Within a short time, Albee was effectively running the Keith circuit, with Keith remaining loftily behind the scenes. For a while Albee succeeded in monopolizing booking arrangements and on several occasions broke performers' attempts to form unions, at one point establishing an in-house union. By vaudeville's heyday in the first quarter of the 20th century, the Keith chain dominated Eastern vaudeville. Albee was forced out a year before his death by Joseph P. Kennedy, who merged the then faltering Keith and Orpheum circuits into a motion picture theatre chain.

ALBEE, Edward [Franklin, III] (b. 1928), playwright. The adopted grandson of the vaudeville magnate E. F. *Albee, he was born in Washington, D. C., and suffered an unhappy youth, which included being enrolled and removed from a number of schools, briefly attending Trinity College, and assuming a series of odd jobs that ranged from Western Union delivery boy to salesclerk. When early attempts at writing poetry were unrewarding, he turned to playwriting at the suggestion of Thornton *Wilder. His first play, The *Zoo Story, was initially produced in Germany in 1959, then in America a year later. In The Sandbox (1960), he tells how an exasperated Mommy and Daddy leave Grandma on a beach to await the coming of Death in the guise of a young boy. The *American Dream (1961), in which parents kill their disappointing child, and The Death of Bessie Smith (1961), a dramatization of the singer's last hours, were well received. His study of a troubled marriage, *Who's Afraid of Virginia Woolf? (1962), was roundly praised and won the *New York Drama Critics Circle Award, and the next year saw his adaptation of Carson McCullers's The Ballad of the Sad Café reach Broadway. Critics and audiences alike were baffled by *Tiny Alice (1964), in which the richest woman in the world seduces and destroys a Catholic lay brother. In 1966 his dramatization of a novel, Malcolm, and his libretto for Breakfast at Tiffany's were unfavorably received, but A *Delicate Balance had a modest run. A series of interesting failures followed: Everything in the Garden (1967), All Over (1971), *Seascape (1975), The Lady from Dubuque (1980), and The Man Who Had Three Arms (1983). Albee's career took a positive turn with the award-winning *Three Tall Women (1994), followed by the well-received The Play About the Baby (2001) and The *Goat (2002). Albee's plays have dealt with his unique miasma of fantasy and reality, and his figures' inability to come to terms with this sometimes frightening combination. His bent has been largely confrontational and philosophic, but beneath his work lies a dis-turbed sexuality. Biography: Edward Albee: A Singular Journey, Mel Gussow, 2000.

ALBERT [BROWN], Ernest (1857–1946), scenic designer. The Brooklyn-born set artist was a prizewinning student at the Brooklyn Institute School of Design before beginning an apprenticeship in 1877 under Harley Merry, who created scenery for New York's *Park Theatre and *Union Square Theatre. After setting up design firms in St. Louis, Chicago, and Cedar Rapids, Albert settled in New York where he worked primarily for *Klaw and *Erlanger and for Charles *Frohman. Among the many productions that displayed his work were An American Beauty (1896), The Idol's Eye (1897), The Reverend Griffith Davenport (1899), *Ben-Hur (1899), Sapho (1900), The Casino Girl (1900), The *Climbers (1901), The Little Duchess (1901), The *Virginian (1904), and George Washington, Jr. (1906). Many critics considered his spectacular sets for Ben-Hur the high point in his career, one noting, "Nothing approaching it in pictorial display and mechanical ingenuity has ever before been seen in the country." One of his fortes both as a painter and set designer was autumn and winter scenery, and his winter landscape for the "Flirting in St. Moritz" number in the *Hippodrome's Hip Hip Hooray! (1915) was advertised as the largest watercolor ever contrived for the American stage, at 243 feet wide and 70 feet high.

ALBERTSON, Jack (1907–1981), character actor. The tall, thin performer was born in Malden, Massachusetts, and went into vaudeville as a song-and-dance man, also working as a burlesque comic. Albertson made his Broadway debut in 1940 in the revue Meet the People and went on to perform in other revues and in secondary roles in plays. Acting in movies from 1938 and much later as a star on television, he didn't find himself in a stage hit until the 1964 drama The *Subject Was Roses, in which he portrayed the troubled father of a returning war vet. His other memorable Broadway part was the cranky old vaudevillian Willie Clark in The *Sunshine Boys (1972).

ALDA, Alan [né Alphonso D'Abruzzo] (b. 1936), actor. The genial, lightweight leading man brings a slightly sarcastic tone to all his performances, making him ideal in thoughtful comedy. He was born in New York, the son of actor-singer Robert Alda, and educated at Fordham University before studying with Paul Sills's Improvisational Workshop. Alda acted at the *Cleveland Playhouse and on television before making his Broadway debut in 1959, not getting much attention until 1964 when he played the writer Felix who befriends a prostitute-model in The Owl and the Pussycat. He was featured in three major roles in the musical *The Apple Tree,* then went into films and, even more successfully, television. He did not return to Broadway for twenty-six years, and his vehicle, Neil *Simon's mediocre *Jake's Women,* ran only because of Alda's many fans from television. He had much better material as the critical Parisian Marc in *Art (1998) and as the playful, brilliant physicist Richard Feynman in *QED* (2001). His father, **Robert ALDA** [né Alphonso Giovanni D'Abruzzo] (1914–86), was born in New York, the son of a barber, and studied architecture at New York University before going into show business. His only notable stage role was his Broadway debut as the romantic gambler Sky Masterson in the original *Guys and Dolls* (1950).

ALDREDGE, Theoni V[achliotis] (b. 1932), costume designer. The Greek-born artist first gained fame for her work with the *Goodman Theatre in Chicago. Later she designed costumes for many of the *New York Shakespeare Festival revivals, as well as for such diverse hits as *Sweet Bird of Youth (1959), *Mary, Mary (1961), *Who's Afraid of Virginia Woolf? (1962), *Any Wednesday (1964), *Cactus Flower (1965), *Little Murders (1967), A *Chorus Line (1975), *Annie (1977), Barnum (1980), *42nd Street (1980), Woman of the Year (1981), *Dreamgirls (1981), *La Cage aux Folles (1983), Blithe Spirit (1987), The *Secret Garden (1991), The *Time of the Cuckoo (2000), and *Follies (2001). In addition to more than 150 Broadway productions, she has designed extensively for film as well.

ALDREDGE, Tom (b. 1928), actor. Although he is hardly known outside of Manhattan, Aldredge was one of the New York theatre's busiest and most admired performers from the 1960s into the 1990s, especially for his many performances with the *Public Theatre and in Central Park productions. He was born in Dayton, Ohio, educated at the University of Dayton, and studied acting at the *Goodman Theatre School in Chicago. He performed for the *New York Shakespeare Festival for the first time in 1960, returning most summers and playing in contemporary dramas at the Public other times. Among Aldredge's many fine performances were the foppish Sir Andrew Aguecheek in *Twelfth Night (1968), the ineffectual father Ozzie in *Sticks and Bones (1971), the Fool to James Earl *Jones's King Lear in 1973, the cranky senior citizen Norman Thayer in *On Golden Pond (1978), the sickly husband Horace Giddens in the 1981 revival of The *Little Foxes, the Narrator and Mysterious Man in *Into the Woods (1987), writer Washington *Irving in Two Shakespearean Actors (1992), the Italian military physician Dr. Tambourri in *Passion (1994), and

the self-righteous Rev. Jeremiah Brown in the 1996 revival of *Inherit the Wind.* His wife is costume designer Theoni V. *Aldredge.

ALDRICH, Louis [né Lyon] (1843–1901), actor. Born in a village called Ohio State Line, he made his first appearance, as a child prodigy, in 1855 at the Cleveland Academy of Music playing the title role in *Richard III. Using such stage names as Master Moses and the Ohio Roscius, he toured the Midwest playing Macbeth, Shylock, and similar parts, later touring Australia and New Zealand with the Marsh Juvenile Troupe. As an adult Aldrich acted with a stock company at the Boston Theatre, then in 1873 accepted Mrs. John *Drew's offer to be leading man at her celebrated *Arch Street Theatre in Philadelphia. Later in New York he performed with the company at Wood's Museum, and his role as the Parson in The *Danites (1877) brought him widespread fame, playing it nearly six hundred times in the following two seasons. Another brilliant success followed when he produced and starred in *My Partner (1879), which he toured in for six years. Aldrich enhanced his popularity when he produced and starred as Shoulders, the boozy, vengeful swamp rat, in The Kaffir Diamond (1888) and as Col. Hawkins, the rugged Arizona newspaperman on a visit to New York, in The Editor (1890), although neither play was especially profitable. While appearing in Syracuse in the latter play, he sustained serious injuries in the Leland Hotel fire, injuries that for a while seemingly affected his mental stability. His acting was erratic thereafter. However, his personal problems did not prevent him from serving from 1897 until his death as president of the *Actors' Fund. He is generally credited with establishing that organization's home for aging actors. A heavyset man, often gruff and blustering onstage, in private he was quiet, dependable, and much admired.

ALDRICH, Richard S. (1902–86), producer. Born in Boston, he served as president of the *Harvard Dramatic Club and shortly after graduation founded an early summer stock group, the Jitney Players. In 1926 he became general manager of the American Laboratory Theatre, and two years later co-produced his first New York show, *La Gringa.* For several seasons he was co-producer, often uncredited, with Kenneth *MacGowan, of several more shows. In 1933 he joined forces with Alfred *de Liagre Jr., and, after several failures, found success with *Petticoat Fever* (1935). With Richard *Myers he co-produced the well-received plays *Margin for Error (1939) and *My Dear Children* (1940). Aldrich married Gertrude *Lawrence in 1940 and later produced a successful revival of

Pygmalion (1945) for her. *Goodbye, My Fancy* (1948), The *Moon Is Blue* (1951), and The *Love of Four Colonels* (1953) were all postwar successes of his, as were highly praised revivals of *Caesar and Cleopatra* (1949) and The *Devil's Disciple* (1951). For many years he operated the Cape Playhouse in Dennis, Massachusetts, and also ran the *National Theatre in Washington in conjunction with Myers.

ALDRIDGE, Ira [Frederick] (1804?–67), actor. He was often called the first great African-American actor, although he did virtually none of his performing in the States. Believed to have been born in Africa (although some sources say New York and give the year as late as 1807), he is said to have accepted menial jobs at New York theatres while performing leading roles in *Romeo and Juliet* and *Pizarro* with a small Negro ensemble. Prejudice and the practice of having Negroes played by whites in blackface denied him opportunities at major theatres. Dissatisfied, he left America permanently in 1826, settling in England but playing across the Continent. Biography: *Ira Aldredge: The Negro Tragedian*, Herbert Marshall and M. Stock, 1968.

ALEXANDER, Jane [neé Quigley] (b. 1939), actress. The tall, stately leading lady was born in Boston and educated at Sarah Lawrence College and the University of Edinburgh in Scotland. She was successful in regional theatre, particularly at the *Arena Stage in Washington, before making her Broadway debut in 1968 as the white mistress Eleanor Bachman to the African-American prizefighter Jack Jefferson in The *Great White Hope*. Her subsequent roles in New York were as different as they were accomplished, including the apartment-hunting New Yorker Anne Miller in *6 Rms Riv Vu* (1972), the wife Jacqueline Harrison discovering her husband's homosexuality in *Find Your Way Home* (1974), the liberal Supreme Court Justice Ruth Loomis in *First Monday in October* (1978), the cancer victim Joy Davidman in *Shadowlands* (1990), the vengeful millionairess Claire Zachanassian in The *Visit* (1992), and the international banker Sara Goode dealing with romance and her Jewish heritage in The *Sisters Rosensweig* (1992). In the 1990s Alexander served as the chairwoman of the National Endowment for the Arts.

ALIAS JIMMY VALENTINE (1910), a play by Paul *Armstrong. [*Wallack's Theatre, 155 perf.] Lee Randall (H. B. *Warner) is a trusted bank employee who is engaged to Rose Lane (Laurette *Taylor). What neither Rose nor his employers know is that he was once a professional safecracker and is an escaped convict. Detective Doyle (Frank Monroe) knows, but he lacks the proof that will allow him to arrest Randall, so he dogs Randall's footsteps in hope of evidence. When Rose's young niece, Kitty (Alma Sedley), is accidentally locked in the bank's vault, Randall is caught in a dilemma. Deciding the youngster's life is worth more than his freedom, he jimmies open the vault. He then walks toward the detective to give himself up, but Doyle turns away and walks out of his life. A fast-moving, if transparent, melodrama, based on O. Henry's *A Retrieved Reformation,* the show toured for many seasons and was revived on Broadway in 1921. Armstrong is reputed to have written it at the suggestion of producer Theodore *Liebler and to have completed it over a single weekend.

ALICE, Mary [née Smith] (b. 1941), actress. A versatile African-American leading lady who spent much of her career Off Broadway playing challenging characters in contemporary black plays, Alice was born in Indianola, Mississippi, and educated at Chicago State before working as a teacher in public schools. She turned to acting in the 1960s and trained at the *Negro Ensemble Company, the company where she would later give such riveting performances as the grieving mother Rachel Tate in *Zooman and the Sign* (1981). Alice's finest Broadway roles were the durable wife Rose raising her husband's illegitimate daughter in *Fences* (1987) and the 101-year old dentist Bessie Delany in *Having Our Say* (1995).

ALIEN CORN (1933), a play by Sidney Howard. [*Belasco Theatre, 98 perf.] Although Elsa Brandt (Katharine *Cornell) is a superb young pianist, she is forced to drudge for a living as a teacher in a dreary school in order to support her crippled, widowed father (Siegfried Rumann) and make ends meet. Elsa is courted by two young men: Julian Vardaman (Luther *Adler), a radical English teacher, and Harry Conway (James Rennie), a suave, rich married man who wants Elsa for a mistress. After she rejects them both, Julian kills himself. The ramifications of the scandal that will probably ensue allow Elsa to decide her future. When the investigating policeman asks if this is her home, she replies, "No. Vienna." Howard's story was replete with the coincidences and foreshadowings that were the stock in trade of older melodrama. For example, early on Julian brandishes his gun and talks of shooting practice, in a moment not unlike that in *Hedda Gabler.* But for all his melodramatic devices, Howard's writing was subdued, giving the play a modern, civilized air. Nevertheless it was largely on the strength of Cornell (who also produced the drama) and her luminous performance that the play found its small audience.

ALISON'S HOUSE (1930), a drama by Susan *Glaspell. [*Civic Repertory Theatre, 41 perf.; Pulitzer Prize.] Alison Stanhope was a spinster who lived in her brother's house and who wrote poetry, which was not published until after her death, bringing her posthumous fame. Now, eighteen years after her death, her brother (Donald Cameron) is selling the home, and the family has gathered to claim keepsakes. Even Mr. Stanhope's daughter Elsa (Eva *Le Gallienne) appears, although she has been ostracized by the family for running off with a married man. The excitement proves too much for another of Mr. Stanhope's spinster sisters, Agatha (Alma Kruger), who tries to burn down the house lest her sister's dark secret be discovered, but who dies from a heart attack. The secret is finally revealed: Alison, like Elsa years later, was in love with a married man. Unlike her niece, she sublimated her yearnings by writing poetry about her romance. The family agrees in the end to release these poems. The basic story was suggested by the life of Emily Dickinson, but Glaspell set her version in her native Iowa. The play was indifferently received by the critics, who found it too literary, and was given only twenty-five performances in the regular repertory season. When, unexpectedly, it was awarded the *Pulitzer Prize, the *Shuberts hastily moved the play uptown, but it lasted only two weeks more.

ALL GOD'S CHILLUN GOT WINGS (1924), a play in two acts by Eugene *O'Neill. [Provincetown Playhouse, 43 perf.] Although the black Jim Harris (Paul *Robeson) and the white Ella Downey (Mary Blair) have known each other since childhood, Ella drifts away from their relationship as her awareness of racial prejudice grows, but Jim still loves her passionately. Ella takes up with a local ruffian and has a child by him, only to have him desert her and the child die. In desperation she marries Jim. But her racial prejudices continue to bedevil her, finally driving her over the brink of sanity. Dealing with her problems causes Jim to fail his bar exams, but he remains loving and devoted. In her dementia Ella becomes like a child, yet she retains enough basic sense to recognize she has hurt Jim. She begs forgiveness and asks him to play marbles with her. "I'll play right up to the gates of Heaven with you!" Jim responds. Critics were sharply divided on the play's merits. Heywood *Broun dismissed it in the *World* as "a very tiresome play," while in the *Telegram-Mail* Robert Welsh predicted that it was "likely to take a permanent place in the American theatre." Many found this serious, understanding treatment of miscegenation offensive. No one was surprised when the Ku Klux Klan issued threats to O'Neill,

who replied that he had written not a "race problem play" but "a study of two principal characters, and their tragic struggle for happiness." However, attempts at repression came from less-expected sources. Disturbed by rumors that a black man kisses a white girl onstage, the New York City license commissioner threatened to shut down the theatre if the play was produced; and just before the first performance began, police served an injunction forbidding the use of child actors in the play. The players got around these problems by reading from the manuscript and cutting the children's minor roles. Furious at this evasion, District Attorney Joab H. Banton promised to bring charges of obscenity and he did—against a later O'Neill play, *Desire Under the Elms.

ALL MY SONS (1947), a drama by Arthur *Miller. [Coronet Theatre, 328 perf.; NYDCC Award.] Joe Keller (Ed Begley) is a manufacturer who has sold defective airplane parts to the government during the recent war and, as a result, a number of young pilots lost their lives in plane crashes. However, Keller has let the lion's share of the blame fall on his partner, who has been convicted and put in jail. Joe's son, Larry, was engaged to Ann Deever (Lois Wheeler), the partner's daughter, but Larry, a pilot, has been reported missing. A letter from him, written before he disappeared, is uncovered saying that he learned from the papers what his father has done and was so ashamed that he has decided never to return from his next mission. Chris (Arthur *Kennedy), Keller's other son, shows the letter to his father, who recognizes that he has not only prompted his son's death but has killed the other pilots as well. Keller understands that in Larry's eyes "they were all my sons," and in grief and guilt he shoots himself. Critical reaction to the Harold *Clurman–Elia *Kazan production was mixed, conservative critics like Howard Barnes writing in the *Herald Tribune* that the piece displayed "more indignation than craftsmanship . . . the offering merely stammers to a climax." On the other hand, Louis *Kronenberger, writing in the more liberal *PM*, spoke for others when he felt the play allowed Miller "to stand easily first among our new generation of playwrights." A 1974 Broadway revival failed, but a 1987 mounting was a critical success, as was an Off-Broadway production in 1997.

ALL THE WAY HOME (1960), a play by Tad Mosel. [*Belasco Theatre, 334 perf.; Pulitzer Prize; NYDCC Award.] Although Jay Follet (Arthur *Hill) is a country boy and relatively indifferent to religion, he has made a happy marriage with his devoutly Catholic, city-bred wife, Mary (Colleen *Dewhurst). Their life with their young son Rufus

(John Megna) is all the richer for their many visits to their extended family. However, Jay is disturbed by Mary's refusal to explain to Rufus that she is pregnant. So when Jay goes off to visit his dying father and is killed in an auto accident, Mary is left to question her religious beliefs and to prepare Rufus for the new baby. Based on James Agee's novel *A Death in the Family*, the drama received major awards in a weak season for American works. "Though hardly a play," Louis *Kronenberger noted, "it often proved vividly playable." [George Ault Jr.] **Tad MOSEL** (b. 1922), a native of Steubenville, Ohio, was educated at Amhurst College, Yale, and Columbia. He wrote many television dramas but his only other theatre contribution of note was an excellent biography of Katherine *Cornell.

ALLEGRO (1947), a musical play by Oscar *Hammerstein (book, lyrics), Richard *Rodgers (music). [*Majestic Theatre, 315 perf.] Joseph Taylor Jr. (John Battles) is born in a typical American town in 1905, the son of a general practitioner who is happily married and content with his lot in life. When Joe grows up and goes off to college and medical school, he remembers to return and marry his high school sweetheart Jenny (Roberta Jonay). But Jenny is the pushy kind, demanding Joe do something more than remain a small-town doctor. She pushes him right into a big-city medical practice, where everything moves at a fast pace, and Joe grows more unhappy the higher he rises in the world. Only his loyal, affectionate nurse Emily (Lisa Kirk) sees how miserable he is. After he discovers that Jenny has been unfaithful, Joe gives up his large city practice and returns to his small-town roots with Emily. *Notable songs*: So Far; The Gentleman Is a Dope; A Fellow Needs a Girl; Allegro. A sentimental chronicle, its action was commented on by a singing chorus and some innovative staging by director Agnes *De Mille. The most venturesome departure from tradition by Rodgers and Hammerstein, the *Theatre Guild production was also the team's first commercial failure. Coming after *Oklahoma! and *Carousel, it consolidated their reputation as musical theatre experimenters, but it was their last truly off-beat musical.

ALLEN, Fred [né John Florence Sullivan] (1894–1956), comedian. The baggy-eyed, deadpan comic with a marked nasal delivery was most widely known for his successful radio comedy program, but for many years was a favorite both in vaudeville and on Broadway. His Broadway appearances were in The *Passing Show of 1922, Vogues of 1924, Polly (1929), The *Little Show (1929), and Three's a Crowd (1930). It was in The Little Show

that he performed in George S. *Kaufman's famous sketch "The Still Alarm." Autobiography: *Much Ado About Me*, 1956.

ALLEN, Viola (1867–1948), actress. The daughter of actors, she was born in Huntsville, Alabama, and made her first New York appearance in 1882 as Annie *Russell's replacement in the title part of *Esmeralda. In the following seasons she played important roles opposite John *McCullough, W. E. *Sheridan, and Tommaso *Salvini, and she won plaudits as Gertrude Ellingham in *Shenandoah (1889) and as Lydia Languish in The Rivals (1889), showing that she was as adept in comedy as she was in tragedy and melodrama. Allen joined Charles *Frohman's celebrated stock company at the *Empire Theatre in 1893 and might have remained there indefinitely had she not left to essay her most famous role, Glory Quayle, the strong-headed, worldly girl converted by her clergyman lover, in The *Christian. Between appearances in such contemporary plays as *In the Palace of the King (1900), Caine's The Eternal City (1902), and Clyde *Fitch's The Toast of the Town (1905), she successfully played such Shakespearean roles as Viola, Hermione, Perdita, Cymbeline, Rosalind, Lady Macbeth, and Mistress Ford. Thereafter she appeared largely in plays of little significance, relying on her acting and appeal to lure audiences. Lewis C. *Strang wrote of the wide-eyed, round-faced, somewhat sad-miened beauty, "Miss Allen acts mentally rather than emotionally. Her conception of a part is always intelligent, comprehensive, and logical. One catches her meaning instantly."

ALLEN, Woody. See *Play It Again, Sam*.

ALLEY THEATRE (Houston). Founded as an amateur group in 1947 by Mr. and Mrs. Robert Altfeld and by Nina Vance, who rapidly assumed sole leadership, the company began producing plays a year later in a former dance studio located at the end of an alley. In 1949 it moved to an abandoned fan factory and began using professional actors. To overcome continuing financial problems, the company became fully professional in 1954 and started hiring stars to bolster receipts. With increasing recognition and substantial grants, in 1968 it constructed a new complex of two theatres, one with an 824-seat thrust stage and an arena-style space with 310 seats. Repertory leaned heavily toward popular modern plays but later began to emphasize classics and original musicals. The company also enjoys a unique exchange program with British theatres, presenting American premieres of new English works. Among the notable productions to transfer to New York were

Edward *Albee's *The Play About the Baby*, Tennessee *Williams's "lost" drama *Not About Nightingales*, and the musicals *The Civil War* and *Jekyll and Hyde*. One of the pioneers in the regional theatre movement, the Alley won a special *Tony Award in 1996.

ALLIANCE THEATRE (Atlanta). Begun as the Alliance Stage in 1968, the company was part of the Atlanta Arts Alliance, which included ballet and opera as well as live theatre. Two years later it adopted its present name and began offering an eclectic mix of new and classic works. The largest regional theatre in the Southeast, the Alliance is housed in the Robert W. Woodruff Arts Center, consisting of the 800-seat Alliance Stage and the 200-seat Hertz Stage. Two of its successful productions to transfer to New York and become hits were *The *Last Night of Ballyhoo* and *Aida*.

ALSWANG, Ralph (1916–79), designer. The Chicago-born artist studied at the *Goodman Theatre, the Chicago Art Institute, and under Robert Edmond *Jones. He was first represented on Broadway with sets for *Comes the Revelation* (1942). His later designs include *Winged Victory* (1943), *Home of the Brave* (1945), *Strange Bedfellows* (1948), Louis *Calhern's *King Lear* (1950), *The *Rainmaker* (1954), *Time Limit!* (1956), *The Tunnel of Love* (1957), *Sunrise at Campobello* (1958), and his last work, an Off-Broadway revival of *The Lesson* (1978). On a few occasions he co-produced plays and sometimes directed and costumed them as well. In 1970 he worked with the architects of the new Uris Theatre in designing that house, now called the *Gershwin Theatre. Unlike several of his contemporaries whose work was so strikingly original or poetic that it instantly called attention to itself, Alswang was content to create quietly comfortable backgrounds. He excelled at homey, realistic designs. Critics sometimes passed over his work entirely in their reviews or acknowledged it much the way Lewis Nichols did in his notice for *Home of the Brave*, when he observed merely "the settings—good ones—are by Ralph Alswang."

ALTON [Hart], **Robert** (1897–1957), choreographer. Born in Bennington, Vermont, he began his career as a chorus boy in *Take It from Me* (1919), then moved up in the ranks by assisting other choreographers, first creating his own dances for *Hold Your Horses* (1933). His choreography was seen in such successful musicals as *Ziegfeld Follies of 1934*, *Life Begins at 8:40* (1934), *Anything Goes* (1934), *Ziegfeld Follies of 1936*, *Leave It to Me!* (1938), *One for the Money* (1939), *Du Barry Was a Lady* (1939), *Two for the Show* (1940), *Panama Hattie* (1940), *Pal Joey* (1940), *Son's o' Fun* (1941), *By Jupiter* (1942), *Ziegfeld Follies of 1943*, and *Early to Bed* (1943). He also served as director for *Early to Bed*, the 1952 revival of *Pal Joey*, and for his last show, *The Vamp* (1955). Brooks *Atkinson hailed his work in the original *Pal Joey* as "wry and wistful." Alton is given much of the credit for breaking up the regimented platoons of dancers that had dominated Broadway in the 1920s. He split his choruses into smaller groups and often allowed his dancers brief solos.

AMADEUS (1980), a play by Peter *Shaffer. Shaffer's version of the Mozart-Salieri story, told from Salieri's point of view, was done in London in 1979 and first offered to Broadway in 1980, winning the *Tony Award and running just short of three years. Ian McKellen was the original American Salieri and Tim Curry was Mozart, under the careful direction of Peter *Hall. An acclaimed London revival failed to run when brought to Broadway in 1999.

AMBASSADOR THEATRE (New York). The *Shuberts built the musical house in 1921 on West 49th Street to house musicals, and its inaugural production was the operetta *The Rose Girl*. The theatre occupies a narrow piece of property, so designer Herbert J. *Krapp placed the auditorium at a diagonal in order to squeeze in 1,100 seats. The musical *Blossom Time* was the house's first major hit, yet the theatre was often occupied by plays as well. In 1935 the Ambassador reverted to showing films and being used as a radio and television studio. But it returned to legit standing in 1956 and continues so today under the ownership of the Shuberts.

AMBERG, Gustav (1844–1921), manager. Within two years of his coming to America from his native Prague during the Civil War, he was managing German-language theatres in Detroit and Cincinnati. In 1879, along with Mathilde *Cottrelly and Heinrich Conried, he refurbished the historic old *Bowery Theatre, renamed it the Thalia, and presented there what one historian has called "the most brilliant sequence of stars and plays ever given here in German." Amberg gave the American premieres of many contemporary Berlin and Viennese operettas and also presented such great German performers as Marie Geistinger, Antonie Janisch, Heinrich Bötel, Ernst Possart, and Gertrud Giers. In 1888 he built the Amberg Theatre (later the Irving Place), but a succession of poor seasons cost him the house in 1891, so his last active years were spent working for the *Shuberts.

AMERICAN ACADEMY OF DRAMATIC ARTS (New York). The oldest ongoing American school of acting, it was founded in 1884 as the Lyceum Theatre School for Acting by Franklin Haven Sargent after Harvard, where he was a member of the faculty, rejected his plea to open a drama school there. Steele MacKaye, Lawrence Barrett, Charles and Daniel *Frohman, and David *Belasco were among its early associates. At first the curriculum was based on the conservative theories of François Delsarte, which were soon displaced, and the school pioneered in its student productions of *Ibsen, *Strindberg, and Maeterlinck. For a time it used the name New York School of Acting. The theories of its second director, Charles Jehlinger, were similar to those of *Stanislavsky. Francis Fuller and then George Cuttingham succeeded Jehlinger. In 1974 the school opened a West Coast branch in Pasadena, with Michael Thomas as director. Among the school's famous graduates are Edward G. *Robinson, Spencer *Tracy, Lauren *Bacall, Robert Redford, Anne *Bancroft, Hume *Cronyn, Ruth *Gordon, Margaret *Wycherly. Doris *Keane, Jason *Robards Jr., Elizabeth *Franz, and Judd *Hirsch.

AMERICAN AIRLINES THEATRE (New York). Producer brothers Arch and Edgar *Selwyn had the intimate theatre built on 42nd Street in 1918 and named it after themselves. George Keister designed the Italian Renaissance-style house with only 1,051 seats, and it was a favorite for intimate plays. The opening production was a failed vehicle for Jane Crowl called *Information Please,* but over the years the Selwyn had many hit plays and small musicals. The theatre switched to films in 1934 and remained a movie house into the 1990s when the house was returned to legitimacy under the *42nd Street Redevelopment plan. It reopened in 2000 as the American Airlines Theatre, the airline corporation providing a large contribution to the nonprofit *Roundabout Theatre, who made it its permanent Broadway house. Redesigned (and mostly rebuilt) as a 750-seat house, the spacious, modern theatre opened with a revival of *The *Man Who Came to Dinner* starring Nathan *Lane.

AMERICAN BUFFALO (1977), a play by David *Mamet. [*Ethel Barrymore Theatre, 135 perf.; NYDCC Award.] Don Dubrow (Kenneth McMillan), the owner of a junk shop, his "gofer," Bobby (John Savage), and the small-time crook Walter "Teach" Cole (Robert Duvall) plan to rob a customer they believe to have a valuable coin collection. Instead they get to fighting among themselves, and the burglary never takes place. Critical reaction may have been divided about the script and its colorful dialogue filled with expletives, but the razor-sharp performances were generally lauded, as was Santo *Loquasto's set filled with appliances,

furniture, and equipment piled high and creating a cavelike atmosphere. A 1981 revival featuring Al *Pacino as Teach was a hit on Broadway and returned in 1983, but a London production with William H. Macy in the role was less successful Off Broadway in 2000.

AMERICAN COMPANY, THE. The most famous and long-lived troupe of traveling professional actors in our early history was headed initially by David *Douglass; his wife, the former Mrs. *Hallam; and his stepson, Lewis *Hallam Jr. The name, prompted to some extent by growing anti-British sentiments of the day, seems to have been used first in 1763 while the company was touring Virginia and the Carolinas. Constant travel was necessary when the company was formed not only because no American city could yet sustain a full season of theatricals, but also because puritanical movements frequently succeeded in closing playhouses for intervals. Despite all the traveling, Douglass supervised the building of several important early American playhouses, including New York's *John Street Theatre where the troupe eventually was based. After Douglass's departure, the company was run by Hallam Jr., John *Henry, John *Hodgkinson, and William *Dunlap who moved the company to the new *Park Theatre in 1798. By this time the troupe was known affectionately and officially as the Old American Company. The name remained until 1805, when Dunlap went bankrupt and Thomas Abthorpe *Cooper assumed the reins at the Park. During its forty-plus years, virtually every important performer in America appeared with the troupe at one time or another. Most of its repertory consisted of the popular English pieces of the era, but to the company goes credit for being the first professional ensemble to mount native drama when it presented Thomas *Godfrey's The *Prince of Parthia* in 1767.

AMERICAN CONSERVATORY THEATRE (San Francisco). Popularly known as ACT, the company was founded in Pittsburgh in 1964 by William *Ball, who remained its general director until 1986. The company moved in 1965 to Stanford University, then a year later took up residence at the 1,040-seat Geary Theatre in San Francisco, its home ever since. For a time, beginning in 1968, it added a second San Francisco house, the small Marines' Memorial Theatre. After the 1990 earthquake, which severely damaged the Geary, the company performed in the nearby Palace of Fine Arts Theatre while repairs were made. Offering a full season in true repertory fashion (that is, different plays every night or two), the troupe mounts seven or eight major works a year, ranging from Greek classics to the latest European successes. Under Ball's successor, Edward Hastings, the policy has been to bring out at least one new American play per season and to hold a "Plays in Progress" workshop. More recently, the ACT has presented the American premieres of new British works, most memorably plays by Tom *Stoppard. The company also operates a widely respected conservatory-style school that has trained such actors as Annette Bening, Danny Glover, Winona Ryder, and Denzel Washington. Among its most acclaimed productions have been superior revivals of The *Taming of the Shrew, Misalliance, *Cyrano de Bergerac, and *Saint Joan. Its productions and training program were honored with a *Tony Award in 1979.

AMERICAN DRAMATIC AUTHORS' SOCIETY. See Dramatists Guild.

AMERICAN DRAMATIC FUND ASSOCIATION. Established in New York in 1848 and patterned to a large extent after Philadelphia's General Theatrical Fund, which it eventually absorbed, its purpose was "To raise by subscription from the members thereof, by voluntary donations and bequests from members and others—by Public Donors and Theatrical Benefits—a stock or fund for making a provision, by way of annuity, for aged and decrepit Members, and such provision for the Nominees' Widows and Orphaned Children of Members and also for Funeral Expenses." In essence the Association combined characteristics of a fraternal organization and life insurance group. One irony of the arrangement was that often the most needy were denied benefits because their subscriptions had lapsed. This, coupled with poor management, eventually led to cries for a sounder, more compassionately constructed charity, pleas answered with the founding of the *Actors' Fund of America.

AMERICAN DRAMATISTS CLUB. See Society of American Dramatists and Composers.

AMERICAN DREAM, THE (1961), a one-act play by Edward *Albee. [York Playhouse, 370 perf.] Mommy (Jane Hoffman) is a domineering middle-class wife, and Daddy (John C. Becher) is a henpecked, acquiescent husband, whose only son (Ben Piazza) fails to live up to the dream they have of his becoming a typical American young man. In despair and fury they emasculate the boy. Although on its surface the play seemed a detached, intellectualized exercise, it proved to be effective theatre. Much of Albee's dialogue seemed surrealistic, as when Mommy asks a newly arrived guest, "Won't you take off your dress?" The potent little play has been produced hundreds of times over the years in college theatres.

AMERICAN MUSEUM, THE (New York). Originally opened in Chambers Street in 1810 by John Scudder, it found, even in its early history, that its lecture room was given over frequently to variety performers, and entertainment quickly vied with the regular exhibits for popularity. The idea that it was a museum and the entertainment was "moral lectures" allowed many otherwise puritanical citizens to patronize the establishment. The Museum was moved several times and was housed at Broadway and Ann Street when P. T. Barnum took charge in 1842. Although Barnum never changed the institution's name, it quickly became accepted simply as Barnum's Museum. He also retained the practice of presenting variety acts, but added evenings of minstrelsy and drama as well. For the most part, the plays he mounted were claptrap popular melodramas or classics, frequently in curious productions. Thus the *Bateman sisters, child prodigies, appeared playing principal Shakespearean roles. In mid-1850 Barnum remodeled the lecture room into a full-fledged theatre seating nearly three thousand. The opening attraction at the renovated auditorium was The *Drunkard, which ran for more than a hundred performances, setting a long-run record for the time. The theatre and museum were destroyed by fire in July 1865. Barnum quickly opened a new combination playhouse and museum, only to sell it a year later. The newer building was also destroyed by fire in 1868. Apart from the somewhat freakish success of The Drunkard and olio appearances by the likes of Tom Thumb, the theatre of the American Museum contributed little to the course of drama in New York. Yet, possibly because of Barnum's name, it continues to be remembered as "one of the most celebrated playhouses in the city's history." P[hineas] T[aylor] **BARNUM** (1810–91) is best remembered as a colorful circus impresario and for his statement "there's a sucker born every minute." He first made his name by running a touring troupe of freaks and curiosities. In addition to presenting melodramas at the American Museum, Barnum brought famous European artists to America, most memorably the singer Jenny Lind. He is recognized as the first American master of ballyhoo, promoting his attractions with little care for honesty or the truth. He was the subject of the popular musical Barnum (1980). Autobiographies: Autobiography, 1854; The Humbugs of the World, 1865; biography: P. T. Barnum: The Legend and the Man, A. H. Saxon, 1989.

AMERICAN NATIONAL THEATRE AND ACADEMY (ANTA). Chartered by Congress in

1935, it was to provide a "people's" self-supporting national theatre. The word "self-supporting" allowed Congress to refuse financial assistance. The commercial theatre, bucking the Great Depression, displayed little interest in supporting the undertaking. Enthusiasm or distaste for the concurrent *Federal Theatre Project also held back development. After World War II the organization was reorganized with a new board that included representatives from all important facets of the theatre. However, for several seasons its work consisted largely of offering encouragement and advice. In 1950 it purchased the Guild Theatre, renamed it the ANTA, and began to produce a series of revivals and new plays, starting with The *Tower Beyond Tragedy. Although several of the mountings, notably a brilliant revival of *Twentieth Century and Mrs. McThing, were successful, the series soon petered out. In 1963, while the *Vivian Beaumont Theatre at *Lincoln Center was under construction, ANTA built a temporary theatre on Washington Square for use by the company that was planned as the Center's repertory ensemble. With time ANTA simply leased its theatre to commercial productions, while retaining offices in the house. However, with growing financial difficulties and some sense of purposelessness, the theatre was sold in 1981. Working with the Denver Center, in 1984 it established the National Theatre Conservatory in the Colorado city. The Conservatory is a performing arts school that, at long last, is supposed to act as "the final 'A' in ANTA." ANTA West was established as a West Coast branch, while in the 1990s principal offices began the move from New York to Washington.

AMERICAN PLACE THEATRE. Founded in 1963 by Wynn Handman and Sidney Lanier to promote new American plays, it was originally housed at St. Clement's Church, where its first production was Robert Lowell's The Old Glory. In 1971 it moved to a new space on West 46th Street with three theatres. The bunkerlike arts complex was constructed in the bowels of a new building and was made possible by an ordinance allowing tax benefits to developers whose high-rises included public amenities. Remaining loyal to its original aims, it has offered works by such growing native talents as Ed Bullins, Ronald Ribman, Sam *Shepard, Joyce Carol Oates, Bill *Irwin, and Eric *Bogosian. The group also promoted a special project to encourage women dramatists, but this has since been spun off as a separate entity called The Women's Project.

AMERICAN PLAY COMPANY. See Samuel French, Inc.

AMERICAN REPERTORY THEATRE. Two notable theatres have used this name, one in New York after World War II and the current one in Cambridge, Massachusetts. The first American Repertory Theatre was created in 1946 with Cheryl *Crawford, Eva *Le Gallienne, and Margaret *Webster as directors. The company stated its purpose was to "be for the drama what a library is for literature or a symphony orchestra for music." Besides Le Gallienne and Webster, its roster of distinguished performers included Philip Bourneuf, Walter *Hampden, Victor Jory, and Ernest *Truex. It was hoped that with time the organization might develop into the New York equivalent of London's *Old Vic or Paris's *Comédie Française. The schedule for the first season offered King Henry VIII, What Every Woman Knows, John Gabriel Borkman, Androcles and the Lion, Pound on Demand, Yellow Jack, and Alice in Wonderland. The company was housed in an old theatre on Columbus Circle, far from the theatrical center, and disbanded at the end of its first season, which had elicited a disappointing response from both critics and public. Robert *Brustein and Robert J. Orchard cofounded the second American Repertory Theatre in 1980, located at Harvard University's Loeb Drama Center. The company differs from most regional theatres in that it maintains a resident acting company and is known for its controversial productions, such as works by Robert *Wilson and the experimental mounting of Endgame in 1985 that even playwright Samuel *Beckett thought was too extreme. The American Repertory Theatre has also introduced some new native works, such as the drama 'night, Mother and the musical Big River. The company operates an international training conservatory in association with Harvard. In 1986 it won the regional theatre *Tony Award.

AMERICAN SHAKESPEARE FESTIVAL THEATRE AND ACADEMY (Stratford, Connecticut). Conceived in 1950 by Lawrence *Langner, it was later incorporated as a nonprofit organization. A theatre, loosely suggested by surviving drawings of Shakespeare's Globe but fully enclosed and employing the finest modern conveniences and equipment, was opened in 1955 on a site along the Housatonic River with *Julius Caesar, and over the next twenty or so years numerous Shakespearean works were staged. Beginning in 1959 special spring performances for students were initiated. As interest and the quality of production waned, non-Shakespearean plays were added to the programs. The name of the organization was shortened in 1972 to the American Shakespeare Theatre. The theatre saw fewer and fewer productions, most critical and public failures, and bankruptcy followed. In 1988 the property was reincorporated as the nonprofit American Festival Theatre, but little has happened to bring it back to life since then. Although the organization stands as a testament to poor management and the perils of relying on external funding, for the many who enjoyed the pseudo-Shakespearean playhouse in its heyday it remains a high point in American theatregoing.

AMERICAN SOCIETY FOR THEATRE RESEARCH. Founded in 1956 and incorporated in 1967 as a tax-exempt organization under New Jersey law, its purpose is "to serve the needs of theatre historians in the practice of their profession, and to foster the increase of knowledge of the theatre in America." It publishes the *ASTR Newsletter,* the *Theatre Survey,* and books of special interest in its field.

AMERICAN SOCIETY OF COMPOSERS, AUTHORS, AND PUBLISHERS (ASCAP). Founded in 1914 by Victor *Herbert and a number of other distinguished writers and publishers, and known popularly as ASCAP, it was designed to protect and license performing rights of musical compositions. A rival group, Broadcast Music, Inc., or BMI, was founded in 1940. Virtually all major composers and lyricists of the American stage have been members of these associations; neither group deals in dramatic rights.

AMERICAN THEATRE. See Theatre Communications Group.

AMERICAN THEATRE CRITICS ASSOCIATION (ATCA). Founded in 1974 by some of the most distinguished of American drama critics, it has among its stated purposes: 1) "To make possible greater communication among American theatre critics"; 2) "To encourage absolute freedom of expression in theatre and theatre criticism"; 3) "To advance standards of theatre by advancing standards of theatre criticism"; and 4) "To increase public awareness of the theatre as a vital national resource." The ATCA annually recommends a *Tony Award to be given to an outstanding regional theatre and offers special events and luncheon lectures. Affiliated with the Association Internationale des Critiques de Théâtre, it played an important role in the release of two South African actors from imprisonment.

AMERICAN THEATRE WING. This organization was established in 1939 at the behest of Rachel *Crothers and other theatrical women, many of whom had been active in the earlier *Stage Women's War Relief. Shortly thereafter it established the *Stage Door Canteen, which entertained servicemen during World War II. After the war it organized important seminars on all aspects of the theatre, enlisting the best talents to lead the seminars. It has also made numerous scholarship grants. In 1974 it sponsored the First American Congress of Theatre (FACT). Playgoers know it best for its Antoinette Perry (*Tony) Awards, named for a former director.

AMERICA'S LOST PLAYS. The celebrated anthology was first published in a series of twenty volumes by Princeton University Press in the early 1940s, under the general editorship of Barrett H. *Clark. The anthology dealt with the work of such early playwrights as William *Dunlap and James A. *Herne and, with few exceptions, the plays included had never before been published. The research was accomplished with the aid of the Rockefeller Foundation under the auspices of the *Dramatists' Guild of the Authors' League of America. The set has been republished by Indiana University Press.

AMES, Robert (1889–1931), actor. Born in Hartford, Connecticut, he served an apprenticeship with stock companies in New England before catching New York's attention opposite Ruth *Chatterton in *Come Out of the Kitchen* (1916). The boyish-looking Ames was best known as Billy Wade, the high-principled hero of *Nice People* (1921), the unprincipled central figure of The *Hero (1921), the pathetically overreaching husband of *It's a Boy!* (1922), and the black sheep, Ben, in *Icebound* (1923).

AMES, Winthrop (1870–1937), producer, manager, and director. The scion of a wealthy New England family, he was born in North Easton, Massachusetts, and studied art and architecture at Harvard before turning to the theatre. Ames leased Boston's famous Castle Square Theatre in 1904, and for several seasons ran a stock company that changed bills weekly. After a protracted tour of European playhouses, he returned to America and was appointed manager of the ambitious *New Theatre in New York, where he mounted a series of notable productions, mostly of the classics. For a number of reasons, the theatre was a failure, so Ames built two more centrally located and smaller houses, the Little Theatre in 1912 and the *Booth in 1913. Among his most memorable productions were *The Affairs of Anatol* (1912), *The Pigeon* (1912), *Prunella* (1913), *A Pair of Silk Stockings* (1914), *Pierrot the Prodigal* (1916), *The Green Goddess* (1921), *Will Shakespeare* (1923), *Beggar on Horseback* (1924), *Minick* (1924), *Old English* (1924), *White Wings* (1926), and *Escape* (1927). During the

1920s, when *Gilbert and Sullivan's popularity had waned, he rekindled interest with gorgeously mounted revivals of *Iolanthe, The *Mikado,* and *The *Pirates of Penzance.* Ames directed a number of the plays he produced and was considered by many critics to be a leading director of his day. A dignified, reticent man, he was in his demeanor and other respects remarkably different from most of his contemporary rivals. Ames retired in 1932; and when he died penniless, it was discovered that he had given not merely his time, his talent, and his love to the theatre, but his great fortune as well.

ANDERS, Glenn (1890–1981), actor. Born in Los Angeles, he began his career with a hometown stock company then later toured with E. H. *Sothern and Julia *Marlowe. After his first important New York appearance in 1919 in *Just Around the Corner,* the handsome, versatile actor quickly became one of the theatre's busiest, most-sought-after performers. Among his notable roles were Andy Lowry, the heroine's excitable brother, in *Hell-Bent fer Heaven* (1924); Joe, the farmhand who fathers the heroine's child, in *They Knew What They Wanted* (1924); Reuben Light, who makes a god of modern technology, in *Dynamo* (1929); Pat Farley, the heroine's suicidal beau, in *Hotel Universe* (1930); Victor Hallam, whose wife saves him from his domineering mother, in *Another Language* (1932); Bill Blake, the alcoholic lawyer, in *Skylark* (1939); Alexander Craig, the amused observer of other people's problems, in *Soldier's Wife* (1944); and Carleton Fitzgerald, the effeminate director, in *Light Up the Sky* (1948). Writing of his performance in *They Knew What They Wanted,* Stark *Young noted "Glenn Anders steps well out ahead of his past achievements. He understands exactly the kind of shiftless integrity in such a character . . . and brings to the part his singular gift for casual naturalness in his readings and inflections and for a varied tempo in his cues."

ANDERSON, John Murray (1886–1954), director and producer. Coming to New York from his native Newfoundland, he started his career as a ballroom dancer, but before long he was serving as compère in cabaret revues and shortly thereafter began staging his own productions at Paul Slavin's Palais Royal. With Slavin's financial backing, he produced the first *Greenwich Village Follies* in 1919, with subsequent editions following each year through 1924. Anderson also produced and directed several other highly praised revues, notably *What's in a Name* (1920) and *John Murray Anderson's Almanac* (1929 and 1953). He served as lyricist for *What's in a Name* and all his *Follies*

except the last, to which he contributed sketches. Among the many musicals he directed were the *Music Box Revue* (1924), *Dearest Enemy* (1925), *Ziegfeld Follies of 1934, Life Begins at 8:40* (1934), *Jumbo* (1935), *Ziegfeld Follies of 1936, One for the Money* (1939), *Two for the Show* (1940), *Ziegfeld Follies of 1943, Three to Make Ready* (1946), and *New Faces of 1952.* Robert Baral has observed in his study, *Revue,* "John Murray Anderson achieved ravishing stage effects by stressing Simplicity and Taste, which on occasion rivaled Ziegfeld's opulence. Even burlap became exotic when he sprayed it with paint." Anderson subtly created movement by coordinating color and design, and by experimenting with such innovations as revolving stages and treadmills. Autobiography: *Out Without My Rubbers,* 1954.

ANDERSON, Judith [née Frances Margaret Anderson-Anderson] (1898–1992), actress. Coming to New York after gaining her earliest theatrical experience in her native Australia, she played with the stock company at the 14th Street Theatre, then toured with William *Gillette in *Dear Brutus* in 1920. She first called attention to herself in New York with her clawing Elsie Van Zile in *Cobra* (1924), followed by recognition as the spoiled, unstable Antoinette Lyle in *Behold the Bridegroom* (1927), succeeding Lynn *Fontanne as Nina Leeds in *Strange Interlude* (1928), and playing the Unknown One in *As You Desire Me* (1931). After touring as Lavinia Mannon in *Mourning Becomes Electra* (1931), Anderson enjoyed a *succès d'estime* as the Woman in *Come of Age* (1934), and a year later played Delia Lovell, who raises her sister's illegitimate child, in The *Old Maid.* In 1936 she was Gertrude opposite John *Gielgud's Hamlet, and her Clytemnestra in A *Tower Beyond Tragedy* (1940), Lady Macbeth in 1941, and Olga in *The Three Sisters* (1942) further enhanced her reputation. Her greatest performance was probably in *Medea* (1947). Writing in *Theatre Arts,* Rosamund *Gilder observed, "Her Medea is pure evil, dark, dangerous, cruel, raging, ruthless. From beginning to end she maintains an almost incredible intensity, yet she varies her moods so constantly, she moves with such skill through explored regions of pain and despair that she can hold her audience in suspense throughout the evening." In 1953 Anderson was the domineering mother Gertrude in *In the Summer House,* stumbled badly as Hamlet in 1971, then triumphed as the Nurse in a 1982 revival of *Medea.* One critic described the dark, hard-faced actress as a "diminutive woman, burning with passion, [who] gave heroic performances." In 1984 an Off-Off-Broadway theatre on Theatre Row was named after her.

ANDERSON, Mary [Antoinette] (1859–1940), actress. Born in Sacramento, California, but raised in Louisville, she made her hometown debut at the age of sixteen as Juliet. After seasons in Louisville, St. Louis, and San Francisco, she first appeared in New York as Pauline in *The Lady of Lyons* in 1877. Hailed as a promising but unfinished performer, she went on to play Juliet, Lizzie in *Evadne*, the title part of *Meg Merrilies*, and Parthenia in *Ingomar*. When critics attacked her Julia in *The Hunchback*, several important playwrights, including Dion *Boucicault, wrote her warm, encouraging letters. She was considered by many the most beautiful actress on the stage, and her good looks and fervor instantly won over the public, if not the critics. By 1882 she had taken on, among others, the title role in *Ion* and of Galatea in W. S. Gilbert's *Pygmalion and Galatea*. After spending several seasons in England, Anderson returned to America in 1885, a mature actress, offering Rosalind, Clarice in W. S. Gilbert's *Comedy and Tragedy* (a part written expressly for her), and Juliet. Later she was the first actress to double in the parts of Hermione and Perdita in *The Winter's Tale*. In 1889, at the height of her fame, she announced she would marry and retire from the stage. To the surprise and disappointment of her many admirers, she kept her word. She did, however, help with the successful dramatization of *The Garden of Allah* (1911). To convey something of her radiant good looks to its readers, the *Herald* described her as "Tall, willowy and young, a fresh, fair face, short and rounded, a small finely chiselled mouth, large, almond shaped eyes of dark gray or blue, hair of a light brown, a long white throat," and on her retirement, William *Winter wrote, "She filled the scene with her presence, and she filled the hearts of her audience with a refreshing sense of delightful, ennobling conviction of possible loveliness and majesty of the human soul." Few performers were so affectionately remembered. Autobiography: *A Few Memories*, 1896.

ANDERSON, [James] Maxwell (1888–1959), playwright. Born in Atlantic, Pennsylvania, and educated at the University of North Dakota and at Stanford, he became a playwright only after careers as a schoolteacher and a journalist. His first produced play, *The White Desert* (1923), a study of the tragic consequences of marital jealousy, was a failure, but success followed when he collaborated with Laurence Stallings on the war drama *What Price Glory?* (1924). After several other less satisfactory collaborations with Stallings, he again found acclaim with his picture of white-collar married life, *Saturday's Children* (1927). Anderson's first attempt to dramatize the

Sacco-Vanzetti case, *Gods of the Lightning* (1928), written with Harold Hickerson, won little attention; but later in the same season his examination of a mercurial, unstable flapper, *Gypsy* (1929), won some high praise. He turned to blank-verse drama for his recounting of the Elizabeth-Essex story, *Elizabeth the Queen* (1930), and its success prompted him to write many of his subsequent dramas in similar blank verse, making him the only major 20th-century American playwright to do so. His subsequent highly lauded plays include *Night Over Taos* (1932), about the Spanish resistance to American advances in early 19th-century New Mexico; the political satire *Both Your Houses* (1933); *Mary of Scotland* (1933), centering on Mary Stuart; *Valley Forge* (1934), dealing with Washington's struggles in the Revolutionary War; *Winterset* (1935), another play based on Sacco and Vanzetti and the first work to win the *New York Drama Critics Circle Award; *Wingless Victory* (1936), a story of a doomed interracial marriage; and the fantasy *High Tor* (1937). His 1937 verse play about the Mayerling incident, *The Masque of Kings*, failed, but was followed by *The Star Wagon* (1937), a fantasy about a couple who return to their youth to reconsider their lives. More verse plays followed: *Key Largo* (1939), dealing with the Spanish Civil War; *Journey to Jerusalem* (1940), a story of the young Jesus; and *Candle in the Wind* (1941), an antiwar play. *The Eve of St. Mark* (1942) depicted a family farm during the war, *Storm Operation* (1944) centered on the North African campaign, and *Truckline Cafe* (1946) told of an ex-soldier's search for his unfaithful, shamed wife. *Joan of Lorraine* (1946) succeeded largely on the appeal of Ingrid *Bergman in the title role. He used historical personages Anne Boleyn in *Anne of the Thousand Days* (1948) and Socrates in *Barefoot in Athens* (1951), and adapted William March's novel about a vicious child, *The Bad Seed* (1954). Anderson also wrote the book and lyrics for two Kurt *Weill musicals: *Knickerbocker Holiday* (1938), which included "September Song," and *Lost in the Stars* (1949). His frustration with producers led him to cofound the *Playwrights' Company in 1938, and he often railed against the drama critics, once calling them "a sort of Jukes family of journalism" and adding, "It is an insult to our theatre that there should be so many incompetents and irresponsibles among them." John Mason *Brown recalled him as "a great, shy bear of a man, rich in humility and conscience, haunted by a high vision of tragedy, a better dramatist than poet, needing actors to lift his verse into poetry but bravely trying to bring back the music of language to a tone-deaf stage." Biography: *The Life of Maxwell Anderson*, Alfred S. Shivers, 1983.

ANDERSON, Robert [Woodruff] (b. 1917), playwright. Born in New York and educated at Harvard, he won the National Theatre Conference's prize for his 1944 play *Come Marching Home.* His first Broadway success was *Tea and Sympathy* (1953), one of the first American plays to approach the topic of homophobia. Anderson's other long run was his bill of one-acters, *You Know I Can't Hear You When the Water's Running* (1967). His other works include *All Summer Long* (1954), *Silent Night, Lonely Night* (1959), *The Days Between* (1965 and 1979), *I Never Sang for My Father* (1968), and *Solitaire/Double Solitaire* (1970). On the strength of *Tea and Sympathy* he was made a member of the *Playwrights' Company, but his early promise was never realized. Anderson also wrote many scripts for radio and screenplays.

ANDRÉ (1798), a tragedy by William *Dunlap. [*Park Theatre, 3 perf.] Major André (John *Hodgkinson) has been captured and condemned to die for being a British spy. His friends, including patriotic Americans, admire him enough to attempt to save him. First among these friends is Bland (Thomas Abthorpe *Cooper), whom André once had released from a British prison. Bland's mother (Mrs. *Melmoth) also has good reason to plead André's cause, for the British are holding her husband as hostage against the Major's safety. André's English sweetheart, Honora (Mrs. Johnson), comes from England to plead for clemency. But all their efforts are in vain, and, as he goes to his execution, André remarks "I think your country has mistook her interests." While the play was well constructed, the poetry of its blank verse was pedestrian and derivative. In an era when ill feelings against England remained strong, Dunlap's attempt to be evenhanded in his characterizations disturbed some playgoers. The first night was also beset with problems: the set by *Ciceri was incomplete, and Cooper had not learned his lines and had to ask the prompter for help. Five years after its premiere Dunlap revived the work and presented it as a musical extravaganza, *The Glory of Columbia.* The historical Major John André (1751–80) was a British spy in the Revolutionary War, his winning personality endearing him to many of his enemies, and his execution aroused much disapproval, even among loyal Americans. During his brief stay in America, André is said to have engaged in theatricals, designing and building the scenery and costumes for a performance of General Burgoyne's play, *Meschianza.* André's story was dramatized several times, including this version by Dunlap and one by Clyde *Fitch.

ANDREWS, Julie [née Julia Elizabeth Wells] (b. 1935), actress and singer. The attractive English performer was born in Walton-on-Thames and found acclaim as a child soprano in variety and pantomime. She came to New York's attention playing Polly in *The Boy Friend* (1954) then became a bona fide Broadway star when she created the role of Eliza Doolittle in *My Fair Lady* (1956), followed by her Guinevere in *Camelot* (1960). After many years in films, Andrews returned to the New York theatre in the Off-Broadway revue *Putting It Together* (1993) and won plaudits on Broadway as the cross-dressing title characters in *Victor/Victoria* (1995), which had a long but unprofitable run. She brought to her roles, as Stanley *Green has noted, an "air of patrician innocence and her cool, clear voice." Biography: *Julie Andrews*, Robert Windeler, 1997.

ANDROBOROS (1714), a "biographical farce" by Robert Hunter. Established as the first American play to be printed, it has left no records of any performance. Hunter published the work in 1714 as an oblique attack on his adversary, the colonial administrator Francis Nicholson. He depicted Nicholson as Androboros (Man Eater), a militaristic hothead determined to war against the Mulomachians (the French). Androboros persuades an all-too-docile senate to pass a resolution praising his bravery. When asked to explain its action, the senate suggests it praised Androboros before the battle, since there might be no reason to afterward. The play also attacked the officials of Trinity Church, who opposed Hunter after his refusal to grant land to the parish. The title page claimed the book was printed in Moronopolis (City of Morons). **Robert HUNTER** (d. 1734) was governor of New York and New Jersey from 1710 to 1719 and later served as governor in Jamaica from 1729 until his death. He was an author of some contemporary repute, his works having been singled out for praise by Jonathan Swift.

ANGEL STREET (1941), a play by Patrick Hamilton. [*John Golden Theatre, 1,295 perf.] This English thriller about a man's attempt to drive his wife insane was first done in London as *Gas Light* in 1939 and, under its American title, it opened on Broadway two nights before the attack on Pearl Harbor. Concern about our entry into World War II hurt business initially, but trade soon perked up, and the show chalked up 1,295 performances, making it the longest-run foreign drama in Broadway history. Judith *Evelyn and Vincent Price played the wife and husband, while Leo G. *Carroll was the helpful detective. New York revivals in 1948 and 1975 were both unsuccessful.

ANGELS IN AMERICA (1993) a drama in two plays by Tony Kushner. [*Walter Kerr Theatre,

Part I: 367 perf.; Pulitzer Prize, Tony Award; Part II: 216 perf; Tony Award.] This ambitious panorama of America during the age of AIDS took two long full-length plays to tell its sweeping and often surreal story. In *Millennium Approaches*, HIV patient Prior Walter (Stephen Spinella) loses his male lover, the Jewish activist Louis (Joe Mantello), to the conservative Joe Pitt (David Marshall Grant), a Mormon lawyer who works for the bombastic and infamous legal whiz Roy Cohn (Ron Leibman). Joe refuses to leave his mentally unstable wife Harper (Marcia Gay Harden) but confesses his homosexuality to his mother, the unsentimental Mormon Hannah (Kathleen *Chalfant) who leaves Salt Lake City to talk some sense to her Manhattan-based son. As the play builds, various characters experience visions: the drugged Harper converses with Mr. Lies (Jeffrey Wright), Cohn berates the Jewish "spy" Ethel Rosenberg (Chalfant) whom he helped execute decades before, and Prior sees an angel (Ellen McLaughlin) break through the ceiling of his bedroom and announce the coming of a new age. Part II, called *Perestroika*, followed the various relationships that develop between these varied characters, such as the torrid romance between Louis and Joe and the unlikely friendship between Hannah and Prior. Cohn, a closet gay though he vehemently denies it, is dying of AIDS and bribes the drag queen-turned-male-nurse Belize (Wright) to get him the rare drug AZT. But he dies (as Ethel Rosenberg looks on) and Belize uses the drug to (temporarily) save Prior. Louis leaves Joe when he discovers his politics, and years later the survivors gather to reflect on the end of the cold war and the arrival of a new century. The lengthy saga, which had been produced first in London and at the *Mark Taper Forum, was highly praised by the press, Jack Kroll in *Newsweek* calling it "the broadest, deepest and most searching American play of our time." Yet *Angels in America* was not a financial success on Broadway. Part II opened at the Walter Kerr five months after the first part premiered, the two halves playing in repertory for ten unprofitable months. **Tony KUSHNER** (b. 1958), a native New Yorker who grew up in Lake Charles, Louisiana, was educated at Columbia and New York University and began writing plays in the 1980s. His other works include *A Bright Room Called Day* (1991), *Slavs!* (1994), adaptations of Corneille's *The Illusion* (1988) and *The Dybbuk* (1995), and *Homebody/Kabul* (2001).

ANGLIN, Margaret (1876–1958), actress. Born in Ottawa, where her father was Speaker of the Canadian House of Commons and her brother later the country's Chief Justice, she came to New York to train at the Empire Dramatic School, which Charles *Frohman ran in conjunction with his *Empire Theatre. Impressed by her work, Frohman offered her the part of Madeleine West in *Shenandoah,* in which she made her first New York appearance in 1894. She then toured with James *O'Neill and with E. H. *Sothern, performing in such varied pieces as *The *Count of Monte Cristo, Lord Chumley,* and *Hamlet. She won plaudits in 1898 for her Roxane opposite Richard *Mansfield's Cyrano, followed by her Mrs. Dane, the foredoomed woman with a past, in *Mrs. Dane's Defense* (1900) and the wrongly suspected Dora in *Diplomacy* (1901). However, Anglin felt most of Frohman's offerings were too insubstantial, so in 1903 she joined forces with Henry *Miller, and the two toured together with a repertory that included *The *Devil's Disciple* and *Camille. She gave one of her most memorable portrayals as Ruth Jordan, the traditional New Englander who finds love with a rough-hewn Westerner, in *The *Great Divide* (1906) and she enjoyed long runs in *The Awakening of Helen Richie* (1909) and *Green Stockings* (1911). In the 1910s Anglin turned her attention to revivals, appearing in the principal woman's roles in *As You Like It, *Twelfth Night, The *Taming of the Shrew, *Antony and Cleopatra,* and *Lady Windermere's Fan.* She also essayed a number of classic Greek roles, mounting some of the first important professional productions of the school, including *Antigone, Electra, Hippolytus,* and *Medea.* She scored major hits as Vivian Hunt, the long-suffering, faithful wife in *The Woman of Bronze* (1920); Clytemnestra in *Iphigenia in Aulis*; and Joan in *The Trial of Joan of Arc.* Anglin's last New York appearance was as the impoverished but resourceful Lady Mary Crabbe in *Fresh Fields* (1936), although she played several of her old roles in summer stock thereafter. Of her Katherine, Walter Prichard *Eaton wrote, "She herself is the best Shrew since Ada Rehan. . . . She is brilliantly vitriolic, edged like a saber, and she is properly and convincingly subdued, but only after a tussle that kindles the blood." Biography: *Margaret Anglin, A Stage Life,* John Le Vay, 1989.

ANIMAL KINGDOM, THE (1932), a comedy by Philip *Barry. [*Broadhurst Theatre, 183 perf.] Tom Collier (Leslie *Howard) has summoned his father (Fredrick Forrester) and his friend Owen Arthur (G. Albert Smith) to his home to announce his intention to marry Cecelia Henry (Lora Baxter). Owen insists Tom and Cecelia have not one thing in common and information slips out about Tom's longtime mistress Daisy Sage (Frances Fuller). When Tom visits Daisy to tell her of his wedding plans, Daisy is pained but understanding. Studying a picture of Cecelia, Daisy warns Tom, "Look out for that chin." After the marriage, Cecelia becomes possessive and intrusive. She forces Tom to fire his houseman (William Gargan), whom she doesn't like, and interferes in his business affairs. When she doesn't get her way, she has convenient headaches or even locks the door against her husband. Taking his rehired houseman with him, Tom leaves Cecelia. He tells his houseman, "I'm going back to my wife." Of course, he means Daisy. In his preface to Barry's collected plays, Brendan Gill wrote that *The Animal Kingdom* "is a comedy simple in theme and economic in plot . . . the dialogue is at once the wittiest and most natural-seeming that Barry had yet achieved."

ANNA CHRISTIE (1921), a drama by Eugene *O'Neill. [Vanderbilt Theatre, 177 perf.; Pulitzer Prize.] At Johnny-the-Priest's waterfront saloon, where Chris Christopherson (George *Marion) whiles away the hours he is not on his coal barge, a letter arrives for him from his daughter, Anna (Pauline *Lord), announcing she is coming back to New York. Chris has not seen her since she was a youngster, for his wife and Anna went to live with relatives on a farm in Minnesota, and after his wife's death, as Chris explains, "Ay tank it's better Anna live on farm, den she don't know dat ole davil sea, she don't know fader like me." When Anna appears, however, it is obvious to everyone but Chris that Anna has known devils of her own. She was seduced by her cousin when she was sixteen, and, running away to St. Paul, became a prostitute. When the powerful, rough sailor Mat Burke (Frank Shannon) meets and falls in love with Anna, she tells Mat and her father of her history. The men go out, get drunk, and sign on a ship that will take them to Africa. Before they leave, however, they are reconciled with Anna. She promises to await their return and "make a regular place for you to come back to." Chris is uncertain of what that means. "Only dat ole davil sea, she know!" he responds. Burns *Mantle called *Anna Christie* "one of the big dramas of the day, soundly human, impressively true in characterization and, in its bigger moments, intensely dramatic." While the Arthur *Hopkins–produced drama may be more commercially slanted than many other O'Neill plays, it has remained eminently theatrical and has enjoyed a number of revivals, including Broadway productions with Celeste Holm in 1952, Liv Ullman in 1977, and Natasha Richardson in 1993. The play was also turned into the musical **NEW GIRL IN TOWN** (1957) with a book by George *Abbott and songs by Bob *Merrill. With Gwen *Verdon cast as Anna, the role became a dancing one, and Bob *Fosse's choreography was quite ingenious. Cameron Prud'homme was Chris, George Wallace was Matt, and Thelma Ritter often stole the show as the earthy barfly Marthy. The Hal *Prince production played at the 46th Street Theatre for 431 performances. *Notable songs*: It's Good to Be Alive; Flings; Sunshine Girl.

ANNA IN THE TROPICS (2002), a play by Nilo Cruz. [New Theatre (Coral Gables, Florida); Pulitzer Prize.] In the 1930s in Ybor (read Tampa), Florida, a Cuban family of cigar makers struggles with personal problems as the nation around them deals with the Great Depression. When a "lector" entertains the factory workers with a reading of *Anna Karenina*, it serves as a catalyst to breed discontentment and dreams of a better life. The domestic drama won the Pulitzer before it was produced in New York (or any other major city), the first Hispanic-American play to be so honored. Productions at the *Victory Gardens Theatre, the *McCarter Theatre, and the *South Coast Repertory soon followed. **Nilo CRUZ** (b. 1960) was born in Cuba and emigrated to the "Little Havana" section of Miami with his family when he was ten years old. His plays, which blend realism with a romantic sense of nostalgia, include *Night Time to Bolina, A Park in Our House, Dancing on Her Knees, Two Sisters and a Piano*, and *Beauty of the Father*. Cruz is on the faculty at Yale.

ANNA LUCASTA (1944), a drama by Philip Yordan. [Mansfield Theatre, 957 perf.] The African-American beauty Anna Lucasta (Hilda Simms) has been thrown out of her Pennsylvania home and has become a prostitute in Brooklyn waterfront dives. When she tries to give up this life by returning home and rehabilitating herself, she falls in love with Rudolph (Earle *Hyman), a young boy from the South. They marry, but then her past is exposed. Anna flees, returning to her old Brooklyn haunts, but Rudolph follows her there and assures her that the past means nothing to him. Many critics saw *Anna Lucasta* as a latter-day *Anna Christie*. Although the basic story is similar, O'Neill had concentrated on his three principal characters, while the effectiveness of Yordan's drama came from richly drawn minor figures. The Chicago-born **Philip YORDAN** (1914–2003) had been a successful film writer, and this was his only Broadway success. He originally conceived the principals as Poles, but when he failed to find a producer, he gave the play to the American Negro Theatre Company to mount. It was their production that was brought to Broadway.

ANNALS OF THE NEW YORK STAGE. This virtually complete record of the New York stage from its beginnings until mid-1894, written by George C. D. *Odell, was published by the Columbia University

Press in fifteen volumes between 1927 and 1948. The books are distinguished not merely for their completeness, but also for their accuracy and readability. Odell wrote with an obvious affection for the period he was covering, viewing, wherever possible, a theatre season from the eyes of its contemporaries. The set was republished in 1970 by AMS Press.

ANNE OF THE THOUSAND DAYS (1948), a verse drama by Maxwell *Anderson. [*Shubert Theatre, 288 perf.] Henry VIII (Rex *Harrison) is tired of both his wife, Queen Catherine, and his mistress, Mary Boleyn. He lusts after Mary's younger sister, Anne (Joyce Redman), so he decides he will divorce Catherine and marry Anne, even if he must split with the Church of Rome to do so. At first, however, his most stubborn opponent is not the Church, but Anne herself. She would marry Percy, Earl of Northumberland (Robert Duke), so the determined Henry callously forces Percy to marry someone else. Percy dies shortly after the marriage, and though Anne blames Henry for his death, she nevertheless finds herself falling in love with the king. The marriage begins happily enough. Only when Anne gives birth to a daughter does Henry's love sour. Deciding another queen would more likely give him a male heir, Henry confronts Anne with the choice of exile or death. So that her baby, Elizabeth, may someday sit on the English throne, Anne elects to die. When she is dead Henry realizes that his feelings for her still run deep. "It would have been easier," he muses, "to forget you living than to forget you dead." Critics were divided about the merits of the blank verse drama produced by the *Playwrights' Company, though the majority sided with the *Sun*, which hailed it as "a robust and vivid play." That New York's critics liked it at all surprised many, for in tryouts *Anne of the Thousand Days* had been written off as a hopeless failure.

ANNIE (1977), a musical comedy by Thomas *Meehan (book), Charles *Strouse (music), Martin Charnin (lyrics). [Alvin Theatre, 2,377 perf.; Tony Award.] In the midst of the Great Depression little Annie (Andrea McArdle) has been left at an orphanage run by the harridan spinster Miss Hannigan (Dorothy Loudon), who makes life miserable for her and the other girls. A secretary to billionaire Oliver Warbucks (Reid Shelton) comes looking for a waif who can spend Christmas at the Warbucks mansion, and Annie is selected. Warbucks takes an instant liking to her and invites Annie to live with him. He also takes her to Washington, where she meets the president, and he advertises on radio to find her real parents. The broadcast brings a deluge of fraudulent claimants

(including Hannigan's crooked brother) before the FBI learns that Annie's real parents are dead. So Daddy Warbucks adopts her, along with another waif she has befriended—a dog named Sandy. *Notable songs*: Tomorrow; It's the Hard Knock Life; Maybe; Little Girls; Easy Street. The Mike *Nichols–produced musical, which was first done at the *Goodspeed Opera House, was suggested by Harold Gray's famous comic strip, "Little Orphan Annie." Reflecting the view of several critics, Martin *Gottfried in the *Post* condemned the show for its "greasepaint sentimentality," "mawkishness," "cheap nostalgia," and "unabashed corniness," only to conclude, "the damn thing works." *Annie* was popular with families at a time when there were few such shows on Broadway, and "Tomorrow" was the last show tune for many years to achieve widespread popularity. A sequel, *Annie II*, closed out of town in 1990, a rewritten version of it called *Annie Warbucks* (1993) struggled Off Broadway, and a 1997 revival of the original failed on Broadway. Nevertheless, *Annie* remains one of the most frequently produced musicals in amateur theatre.

ANNIE GET YOUR GUN (1946), a musical comedy by *Herbert and Dorothy *Fields (book), Irving *Berlin (music, lyrics). [*Imperial Theatre, 1,147 perf.] Annie Oakley (Ethel *Merman) is an uneducated but happy country girl who is an infallible shot, an asset that lands her in Buffalo Bill's Wild West Show. She falls in love with a rival sharpshooter, Frank Butler (Ray Middleton), but when Annie's popularity soars, the romance is soured. After separating for a time, a shooting match is arranged between Annie and Frank, and Sitting Bull (Harry Bellaver) takes her aside to counsel that she can win her man only by losing the match. So she swallows her pride, loses the match, and gets Frank. *Notable songs*: They Say It's Wonderful; There's No Business Like Show Business; I Got the Sun in the Morning; Doin' What Comes Natur'lly; I Got Lost in His Arms; Moonshine Lullaby; You Can't Get a Man with a Gun; My Defenses Are Down. Berlin's biggest Broadway hit also boasted more song standards than any of his (or just about anyone else's) other scores. Jerome *Kern was scheduled to compose the songs, but when he died before he could begin work, producers *Rodgers and *Hammerstein approached Berlin, who hadn't written for Broadway for six years. The show remains a popular favorite, while "There's No Business Like Show Business" has become a theatrical anthem. A 1999 Broadway revival, with an altered book by Peter *Stone, managed a long run by featuring a series of stars (Bernadette *Peters, Cheryl Ladd, Reba McIntyre, Crystal Bernard) in the title role. The real **Annie OAKLEY** [neé Phoebe Ann Moses] (1860–1926) became famous as a sharpshooter in the circus and, after beating Frank Butler in a shooting match, married him. The couple then joined Buffalo Bill's Wild West Show. The Ohio-born Oakley was reputed to be a shy woman and a homebody. One of her most celebrated stunts was to shoot holes in tickets that were thrown up into the air. Later, free theatre tickets that were punched with a hole became known as Annie Oakleys. Biography: *Annie Oakley of the Wild West*, Walter Havighurst, 1954.

ANOTHER LANGUAGE (1932), a play by Rose Franken. [*Booth Theatre, 348 perf.] Mrs. Hallam (Margaret *Wycherly) has dominated her four sons. Only Stella (Dorothy *Stickney), the wife of the youngest son Victor (Glenn *Anders), has the courage to object to this domination. Stella's battle requires her to use many ploys, such as insisting that the family's traditional Tuesday night dinners not always take place at Mama's. But Stella brings matters to a head when she has an affair with Mrs. Hallam's oldest grandson and her own nephew, Jerry (John Beal). Disclosure of the affair sets off a furious confrontation, but at the same time succeeds in revealing to Victor how blindly clannish he has been. At least he and Jerry will no longer be under Mrs. Hallam's thumb. Gilbert Gabriel of the *American* found the play "steadfastly authentic . . . constantly wise and interesting." Opening with no advance sale, the play turned into a hit with good reviews and fine word-of-mouth. The Texas-born **Rose FRANKEN** [née Lewin] (1894–1988) was also the author of *Claudia* (1941) as well as such less-successful plays as *Outrageous Fortune* (1943), *Soldier's Wife* (1944), and *The Hallams* (1947). Sometimes dismissed as women's plays meant only for the matinee crowd, Franken's domestic dramas are unsentimental and sometimes brutal examinations of family life. Autobiography: *When All Is Said and Done*, 1963.

ANOTHER PART OF THE FOREST. See *The Little Foxes*.

ANOUILH, Jean (1910–87), playwright. Often called the leading French dramatist of his day, he observed both the lighter and darker sides of life with an essentially rueful wit. Unfortunately he was not always well served by his American translators and producers. Among the American mountings of his work were *Antigone* (1946), *Ring around the Moon* (1950), *Mademoiselle Colombe* (1954), *Thieves' Carnival* (1955), *The Lark* (1955), *Waltz of the Toreadors* (1957), *The Fighting Cock* (1959), and *Becket* (1960).

ANSPACHER, Louis K. See *Unchastened Woman, The*.

ANTA. See American National Theatre and Academy.

ANTHONY, Joseph [né Deuster) (1912–93), director and actor. He was born in Milwaukee and educated at the University of Wisconsin and the *Pasadena Playhouse before beginning an acting career that saw him in productions by the *Federal Theatre Project and on Broadway in the 1950s. Anthony began directing in 1948 and soon established a reputation for being an "actor's director" for his insightful work in character plays, but he also staged comedies and musicals with success. His many New York productions include The *Rainmaker* (1954), The *Most Happy Fella* (1954), The *Best Man* (1960), *Mary, Mary* (1961), *110 in the Shade* (1963), and *Finishing Touches* (1973).

ANTONY AND CLEOPATRA, a tragedy by William Shakespeare. The play has had a fitful record in America. New Orleans saw it in 1838 with Ellen *Tree and William Hield. Its first New York presentation seems to have come surprisingly late, not until George *Vandenhoff and Mrs. Bland assumed the title roles in 1846. Infrequent subsequent mountings included those featuring Edward *Eddy and Mme. *Ponisi in 1859 and Joseph Wheelock and Agnes *Booth in 1877. Spectacle was as important to these mountings as was drama. Interest flared in the play in the late 19th and early 20th century. For an 1889 revival headed by Kyrle *Bellew and Mrs. *Brown-Potter, the critics twitted another sort of spectacle, the spectacle of two performers unsuited for their roles, and gave only cursory praise to Philip *Goatcher's lavish settings. In 1909 the *New Theatre opened with a physically sumptuous production of the play and with the *Marlowe-*Sothern team giving their lushly poetic readings. Later notable 20th-century revivals have been Katharine *Cornell's 1947 production with Godfrey Tearle as her leading man and the Laurence *Olivier–Vivien Leigh presentation in 1951. Vanessa Redgrave made a luminous queen in a misguided 1997 production Off Broadway.

ANTOON, A[lfred] **J**[oseph] (1944–92), director. Long associated with the *New York Shakespeare Festival where he did some of his finest work, Antoon was a very promising director of the 1970s, but his career faltered in the 1980s and he died of AIDS after staging *Song of Singapore* (1991). He was educated at Boston College and soon after graduation was directing in New York, staging two outstanding productions in 1972: *That Championship Season* and the turn-of-the-century America setting for *Much Ado About Nothing*, both shows transferring to Broadway. Antoon's other credits include *Subject to Fits* (1971), *The Dance of Death* (1974), *The Art of Dining* (1979), *The Rink* (1984), and popular Central Park productions of *A *Midsummer Night's Dream* (1988) and *The *Taming of the Shrew* (1990).

ANY WEDNESDAY (1964), a comedy by Muriel Resnik. [*Music Box Theatre, 982 perf.] John Cleves (Don Porter) is an arrogant, lecherous, hopelessly spoiled business tycoon who, every Wednesday, meets with his oddball mistress, Ellen Gordon (Sandy *Dennis). Naturally his loyal wife, Dorothy (Rosemary Murphy), knows nothing about his affair as she continues to pamper his childishness, letting him go first in every silly game they play, and ignoring mistakes he makes. When Cass Henderson (Gene Hackman), a lowly employee he treats like dirt, discovers that Cleves writes off Ellen as a tax deduction, the cat is out of the bag. Cleves's puerile, petulant reaction alienates both his wife and his mistress and he realizes that if he cheats at any game from now on, that game will be solitaire. Henry *Hewes of the *Saturday Review* dismissed the play as "slight" but "amusing" and most critics concurred. Yet *Any Wednesday* represented the sort of trivial, if slick, comedy that often keeps theatres lit and profitable between more ambitious plays. Coming to New York with little praise and advance sale, the comedy proved one of the "sleepers" that make for legend on Broadway.

ANYTHING GOES (1934), a musical comedy by Guy *Bolton, P. G. *Wodehouse, Howard *Lindsay, Russel *Crouse (book), Cole *Porter (music, lyrics). [Alvin Theatre, 420 perf.] Reno Sweeney (Ethel *Merman), an evangelist turned nightclub singer, gets such a kick out of Billy Crocker (William *Gaxton) that she boards a Europe-bound liner to dissuade him from pursuing Hope Harcourt (Bettina *Hall). Although Billy pines for Hope, she is determined to marry an English peer, so Billy, who stowed away on the ship, is forced to adopt a number of disguises. Also aboard is a wistful little man, the Reverend Dr. Moon (Victor *Moore), whom J. Edgar Hoover has branded "Public Enemy 13." Moon's ambition is to rise to the top of Hoover's list. On landing, Hope discovers she has become an heiress, so she drops her Englishman and consents to marry Billy. The Englishman turns his attention to Reno, while Moon, learning he has been judged harmless and dropped from the FBI list, walks away muttering nasty things about Hoover. *Notable songs*: All Through the Night; Anything Goes; Blow, Gabriel, Blow; I Get a Kick Out of You; You're the Top. Praised by Brooks *Atkinson as "a thundering good song and dance show," with time this work came to be perceived as the quintessential American musical of the 1930s: brassy, lighthearted, contemporary, and more or less topical. Porter's score was considered his best before *Kiss Me, Kate* (1948). A disaster almost scuttled the show: Bolton and Wodehouse's original libretto dealt with a shipwreck, but just before the musical went into rehearsal, the *Morro Castle* sank with a huge loss of life. Bolton and Wodehouse were out of the country, so producer Vinton *Freedley enlisted Lindsay and Crouse to write a new story, thus initiating one of Broadway's more successful partnerships. There have been two rewritten but popular revivals of *Anything Goes* in Manhattan: an Off-Broadway production in 1962 featuring Eileen Rodgers and Hal *Linden and a lively 1987 version with Patti *LuPone and Howard McGillin.

APA. See Association of Producing Artists.

APOLLO THEATRE (New York). Harlem's most famous theatre, it was built in 1914 on 125th Street as a burlesque house, but by the 1930s it had become home to African-American bands, singers, comics, and hoofers in a variety format. The management featured an amateur night every Wednesday and many later-famous black artists got their start there. The 1,700-seat house closed in 1977, then was a television studio for a while. The Apollo was named a historic landmark in 1983 and since then has housed special events, including the Wednesday talent nights. George C. *Wolfe presented a variety program called *Harlem Song* in 2002 that celebrated the old theatre's history in song and dance. [This theatre is not to be confused with the Apollo Theatre on 42nd Street; see *Ford Center for the Performing Arts.]

APPLAUSE (1970), a musical play by Betty *Comden, Adolph *Green (book), Charles *Strouse (music), Lee *Adams (lyrics). [*Palace Theatre, 896 perf.; Tony Award.] Theatre fan Eve Harrington (Penny Fuller) is so starstruck with Broadway leading lady Margo Channing (Lauren *Bacall) that she is soon her assistant and personal secretary. But it turns out that Eve is really an ambitious actress who worms her way into Margo's life and manages to steal her stage role, her author, and almost her lover. *Notable songs*: Applause; Welcome to the Theatre; Who's That Girl?; But Alive. Skillfully adapted from the celebrated 1950 film *All About Eve*, the musical was a smashing vehicle for Bacall who shone despite her limited singing and dancing talents.

APPLE BLOSSOMS (1919), an operetta by William Le Baron (book, lyrics), Victor Jacobi, Fritz

Kreisler (music). [Globe Theatre, 256 perf.] Nancy Dodge (Wilda *Bennett) thinks she loves Dickie Stewart (Percival Knight), while Philip Campbell (John Charles *Thomas) is sure he loves Anne Merton (Florence Shirley). But when Nancy and Philip are pressed into marriage by their families, they agree to wed with the understanding that after the marriage each is free to go his or her own way. They soon resume their old flirtations only to find at a masked ball that they have come to love each other. Dickie and Anne, old flames, also decide to marry. *Notable songs*: Little Girls, Goodbye; Who Can Tell?; You Are Free. The Charles *Dillingham production is mostly remembered because it gave a handsome leg up to the careers of its chief dancers, Fred and Adele *Astaire. Much of the music by Kreisler, the renowned violinist, was later used in his 1932 Viennese operetta *Sissy*, while his melody for "Who Can Tell?" was given yet a third set of lyrics in 1936 and became popular as "Stars in Your Eyes."

ARBUCKLE, Maclyn (1863–1931), actor. Born in San Antonio, Texas, he gave up a burgeoning law career to try his hand at acting. After making his debut in 1888 in Shreveport, Louisiana, he spent several seasons touring before making his New York bow in 1900, calling attention to himself the next year as the Earl of Rockingham in **Under Two Flags*. Arbuckle portrayed Antonio in *The *Merchant of Venice* (1901) but found his true métier as the folksy, wise George Washington Skipper in *Skipper and Co., Wall Street* (1903). His most memorable role was Jim Hackler in *The *County Chairman*, a part that kept him busy for the next four seasons. Thereafter he met with varying degrees of success depicting similar homespun characters in *The *Round Up* (1907), *The Circus Man* (1909), and *The New Henrietta* (1915). In 1919 he headed a road company of *The Better'Ole*, and, before retiring, the pudgy, friendly miened actor participated in two all-star revivals mounted by The *Players, playing Anthony Absolute in *The Rivals* (1923) and Stingo in *She Stoops To Conquer* (1924).

ARCH STREET THEATRE (Philadelphia). Built by a syndicate financed from New York but led locally by W. B. *Wood, it was based on designs by John Haviland, one of the leading architects of his day, and opened in 1828 as a rival to the *Chestnut Street Theatre and *Walnut Street Theatre. At first it was unsuccessful, but after William Forrest, brother of Edwin *Forrest, took over its management in 1830, it quickly became one of the city's major playhouses. Most of Edwin Forrest's best vehicles were played there when he was in his prime, and several were given their premieres at the theatre. William *Burton took over the house

in the 1840s, giving it some of its greatest hits, including *A Glance at Philadelphia*, his localized version of Benjamin A. *Baker's *A *Glance at New York*. After Burton left, William *Wheatley ran the house. The theatre's heyday is generally considered to have begun in 1861, when Mrs. John *Drew assumed the reins and quickly established one of the greatest of all American stock companies. The house remained under her control for thirty-one years. During the administrations of Forrest, Burton, and Drew, virtually every great performer in America appeared on its stage at one time or another. The decline of the playhouse commenced with Drew's withdrawal in 1892. Another stock company failed, so under Charles E. *Blaney the theatre initiated a policy of popular melodramas. In later years the theatre offered musical comedy stock companies, Yiddish plays, and burlesque before it was demolished in 1936.

ARENA STAGE (Washington, D. C.). Founded in 1950 by Zelda Fichandler, Edward Mangum, and others, the company gave its first performances arena style in an old movie house called the Hippodrome, then moved to a converted brewery. In 1961 the company moved to its current complex where, over the years, it established three performance spaces: the 827-seat arena house called the Fichandler, the 514-seat proscenium Kreeger; and a small basement semicabaret, the Old Vat. Its repertory has balanced classics with new plays, among them premieres of several works that later moved to Broadway, including *The *Great White Hope*, *Indians*, **Moonchildren*, *K-2*, and *Tintypes*. The company toured the Soviet Union under State Department aegis in 1973, and later performed in Hong Kong. In 1976 it was the first regional theatre to receive a *Tony Award for services to its community. Fichandler served as artistic director for forty years, succeeded by Douglas C. Wager who took over in 1991. The Arena is not only the largest nonprofit theatre in the Washington area, it remains one of America's oldest and most consistently outstanding theatre organizations.

ARENA-STYLE THEATRE (Theatre-in-the-Round). Although some hailed the proliferation after World War II of arena-style playhouses, in which audiences surround the stage, as a revolutionary departure, others saw it as the extension of the more open, thrust-stage playhouses that had characterized many Elizabethan and Jacobean theatres before the proscenium-style auditoriums took over at the time of the Restoration. Still others saw such staging merely as an adaptation of standard circus practice to the presentation of more traditional drama. Advocacy of such staging had arisen earlier. Surprisingly, none of the great artists, such as Mrs. *Fiske and Sarah *Bernhardt, who were forced by their rejection of the *Theatrical Syndicate, or Trust, to perform in circus tents at the turn of the century, apparently carried the opportunity to its logical conclusion, preferring to convert the tents into something resembling proscenium auditoriums. In this they were following the practice of most *tent shows that were long popular in American backwaters. But by the 1920s such progressive designers as Robert Edmond *Jones were toying with the idea, which began to achieve worldwide testing a decade later. A major American experimenter was Professor Glenn Hughes of the University of Washington. In 1932 he converted the penthouse of an old hotel into a theatre-in-the-round seating sixty patrons. His success was such that by 1935 his "Penthouse Theatre" had moved to larger quarters in a lodge near the campus, and in 1940 he built a more permanent, somewhat elliptically shaped arena theatre on campus. By that time other cities ranging in size from St. Paul to Lewistown, Montana, had tried similar enterprises with varying success. World War II temporarily halted the spread of the movement, but with peace, arena stages began to appear in many places. Some of the first were the summer *stock tents, cheaper and easier to erect than standard playhouses. Regional theatres were also in the vanguard, with Margo *Jones's Theatre 47 in Dallas, Washington's *Arena Stage, and New York's *Circle in the Square among the most noteworthy. Except for this last space, Broadway theatres are all proscenium and retain the traditional audience-actor spatial relationship. Yet on occasion efforts have been made to turn a Broadway proscenium stage into arena, as witnessed by the productions of *Candide (1974), *Equus (1974), and Copenhagen (2000), which put part of the audience onstage.

ARIZONA (1900), a play by Augustus *Thomas. [Herald Square Theatre, 140 perf.] Captain Hodgman (Walter Hale) of the 11th Cavalry, for all his charm and good looks, is an immoral scoundrel. He has fathered an illegitimate child by Lena Kellar (Adora Andrews) and tries to seduce Estrella Bonham (Jane Kennark), his colonel's wife. Lieutenant Denton (Vincent Serrano) discovers that Estrella plans to elope with Hodgman, to whom she has given her jewels. He talks her out of her plan and recovers the jewels, but Col. Bonham (Edwin Holt), discovering Denton with the jewels, accuses him of theft. Denton renounces his commission but remains near at hand to be with his fiancée, Bonita Canby (Eleanor *Robson), Estrella's sister. When Hodgman is shot, Denton is suspected. To exculpate the devoted Denton, Estrella must confess her attempted infidelity. She

tells Bonham she now truly loves him. At first he is icy, but sensing how much his own rigid behavior had led Estrella to seek affection elsewhere, he picks up a rose that Estrella has dropped on the floor and thrusts it in his shirt. Bernard Sobel, in The Theatre Handbook, described Arizona as "an example par excellence of well constructed melodrama of the type popular at the turn of the century." The play, produced by Kirk *LaShelle and Fred Hamlin, was successfully revived several times, and made into an unsuccessful musical, The Love Call (1927). But its importance lies far more in its direct and indirect influences than in any contemporary excellence. The play is generally credited with starting the rage for "Westerns" in the American theatre. Booked at the failing Herald Square Theatre, which the young *Shubert brothers had taken over as their first New York base, its success allowed them to start their climb to theatrical heights.

ARIZONA THEATRE COMPANY (Tucson and Phoenix). Begun in 1966 as the Arizona Civic Theatre, the company went professional and took its new name in 1978. The troupe is unique in that it serves two major cities with the 664-seat Temple of Music and Art in Tucson and the 695-seat Herberger Theatre Center in Phoenix, its productions playing in both venues. Its two-city operation is a model for arts cooperatives and was cited with a presidential commendation by Ronald Reagan in the 1980s. Sandy Rosenthal cofounded the company and served as its artistic director for many years. The repertory is an eclectic mix of classic and modern plays, musicals, and original works.

ARKANSAS REPERTORY THEATRE (Little Rock). Beginning in 1976 in a former Methodist church, the company has grown to present a full season in its 1988 downtown facility as well as touring productions, outreach programs in schools, and a unique participation with prisons in drama workshops. The company, under the artistic direction of Robert Hupp since 1998, offers a variety of new and classic plays and musicals in its 354-seat MainStage and its 100-seat SecondStage theatres on Little Rock's Main Street.

ARKIN, Alan (b. 1934), actor and director. He was born in Brooklyn and educated at Los Angeles City College and Bennington College before working as a stand-up comic in clubs and with improv groups. As a member of the touring Second City troupe from Chicago, Arkin caught the eye of producers who put him in Off-Broadway comedy revues, some of which he scripted. He made a striking Broadway debut as the hapless would-be actor David Kolowitz in *Enter Laughing* (1963) and the next year was again praised for his portrayal of the unfortunate would-be suicide victim Harry Berlin in *Luv*. The odd, low-key comic actor turned to directing in the 1960s, staging *Eh?* (1966), *Little Murders* (1969), *The *Sunshine Boys* (1972), and others. After a span of thirty-four years, he performed again as two zany characters in the Off-Broadway comedy *Power Plays* (1998). Autobiography: *Halfway Through the Door*, 1979.

ARLEN, Harold [né Hyman Arluck] (1905–86), composer. Born in Buffalo, he began his career by writing songs for cabaret productions and by interpolating numbers in Broadway revues. His first success, "Get Happy," came in an otherwise undistinguished show, *9:15 Revue* (1930). Arlen's music was heard in *Earl Carroll Vanities* (1930); *You Said It* (1931); *Life Begins at 8:40* (1934), which offered "Let's Take a Walk Around the Block"; *Hooray for What!* (1937), recalled for "Down with Love"; *Bloomer Girl* (1944); *St. Louis Woman* (1946), whose score included "Come Rain or Come Shine;" *House of Flowers* (1954); *Jamaica* (1957); and *Saratoga* (1959). One of his most famous songs, "I Gotta Right to Sing the Blues," was interpolated in the 1932 edition of the *Vanities*. Arlen's music leaned heavily on commercialized jazz forms, especially blues, and other black musical mannerisms. Biography: *Happy with the Blues*, Edward Jablonski, 1961.

ARLISS, George [né Augustus George Arliss-Andrews] (1868–1946), actor. He was born in London and made his American debut in 1901 opposite Mrs. Patrick *Campbell as Cayley Drummle in *The Second Mrs. Tanqueray*. After playing a season of repertory with her, he was enlisted by David *Belasco to portray the villainous Zakkuri in *The *Darling of the Gods* (1902). Arliss then came under the management of Harrison Grey *Fiske and appeared with Mrs. *Fiske as the Marquis of Steyne in *Becky Sharp* (1904), Raoul Berton in *Leah Kleschna* (1904), Judge Brack in *Hedda Gabler* (1904), Sir Cates-Darby in *The *New York Idea* (1906), and Ulric Brendel in *Rosmersholm* (1907). After playing the title role in *The Devil* (1908) and the absent-minded inventor *Septimus* (1909), Arliss essayed one of his greatest interpretations, the title part in *Disraeli* (1911), a role he played across the country for four years. This was followed by the leading figure in *Paganini* (1916), a revival of *The Professor's Love Story* (1917), and the principal role in *Hamilton* (1918). He toured as a member of the all-star cast of *Out There* (1918) before assuming another of his most famous roles, the malevolent of Rajah in *The Green Goddess* (1921). Alexander *Woollcott wrote of his performance, "With his countenance at once

gentle and diabolic, with his cat-like tread and with his uneasy but sinister hands, he seems to have been roaming our stage all his days in wistful quest of a play about a rajah with . . . an evil heart." After making many films, Arliss returned to Broadway in 1924 to play the dogged eighty-year-old Sylvanus Heythorp in *Old English,* then four years later offered his Shylock on tour and then in New York before retiring. Autobiography: *Up the Years from Bloomsbury*, 1927.

ARMS AND THE GURL. See *Pursuit of Happiness, The.*

ARMSTRONG, Paul (1869–1915), playwright. Born in Kidder, Missouri, he began his writing career as a journalist, and, when he turned to playwriting, he often wrote plays to order, quickly turning out claptrap melodramas created for second-rate touring companies. Some of his plays were written for New York, and several received respectful attention. Significantly, his biggest hits seemed to be either adaptations of good stories or collaborations: *Salomy Jane* (1907), derived from Bret Harte's *Salomy Jane's Kiss;* the comedy *Going Some,* written with Rex Beach, about two imposters at a race; and his most notable work, *Alias Jimmy Valentine* (1910), a tale of a reformed crook based on an O. Henry story. With Wilson *Mizner he wrote two popular dramas, *The Deep Purple* (1911), an early realistic treatment of the underworld, and *The Greyhound* (1912), a tough-fibered play about a transatlantic cardsharp. Among Armstrong's other plays were *The Superstition of Sue* (1904); *The Heir to the Hoorah* (1905); *Via Wireless* (1908), written with Winchell *Smith; *Society and the Bulldog* (1909); *The Escape* (1913); *The Bludgeon* (1914); and *The Heart of a Thief* (1914). Although Armstrong's plays usually had a hard veneer, H. L. *Mencken remembered him as "a very sentimental man [who] often shed tears at his own dinner table over the sufferings of the heroines of his plays."

ARONSON, Boris (1900–80), scenic designer. After studying art and set design in his native Kiev, in Moscow, and in Berlin, he came to New York in 1923 and soon found employment designing sets for the Unser Theatre in the Bronx, for the *Yiddish Art Theatre, and later for the *Civic Repertory Theatre. Aronson soon moved into the commercial theatre, where his work was seen in such shows as *Walk a Little Faster* (1932), *Three Men on a Horse* (1935), *Awake and Sing!* (1935), *The *Gentle People* (1939), *Cabin in the Sky* (1940), *Detective Story* (1949), *I Am a Camera* (1951), *Bus Stop* (1955), A *View from the Bridge* (1955), *The *Diary of Anne Frank* (1955), *Fiddler on the Roof

(1964), *Cabaret (1966), *Company (1970), A *Little Night Music (1973), and *Pacific Overtures (1976). When plays required them, he designed excellent realistic settings, but his forte was highly stylized, often symbolic settings, such as those he conceived for *J. B. (1958) and for such failures as the futuristic Sweet Bye and Bye (1946) and Orpheus Descending (1957). Aronson's stylization, free placement of form, and use of bright colors were heavily influenced by his admiration of Marc Chagall. He was also one of the first to employ projections against neutral backgrounds to effect changes of mood and place. Biography: The Theatre Art of Boris Aronson, Frank *Rich and Lisa Aronson, 1987.

ARONSON, Rudolph (1856–1919), producer and composer. The New York–born entrepreneur conceived and built the *Casino Theatre, which opened in 1882 as the first playhouse designed specifically for Broadway musicals. Initially with John A. *McCaull and later alone, he produced many important turn-of-the-century Continental operettas, giving Americans their first opportunity to hear in English works that were among the reigning hits of their era, some of which have remained popular ever since. He introduced most of Johann *Strauss's best works, including The Queen's Lace Handkerchief (1882), Prince Methusalem (1883), Die Fledermaus (1885), The Gypsy Baron (1886), and Vienna Life (1901). However, his biggest success came with a now-forgotten work, the British musical *Erminie (1886). An accomplished musician, Aronson also composed and orchestrated the scores for several comic operas, notably The Rainmaker of Syria (1893). He eventually lost both the Casino and his producing organization, but to the end remained filled with grand plans, including an "American Palace of Art," a sort of Lincoln or Kennedy Center, a half-century ahead of its time. Autobiography: Theatrical and Musical Memoirs, 1913.

AROUND THE WORLD IN EIGHTY DAYS (1875). In the late summer of 1875 Jules Verne's popular 1873 novel became the source of two competing extravaganzas, which mingled Verne's tale of Phileas Fogg with elaborate settings, trick scenery, lavish ballets, and a variety of musical numbers. The more successful of the two was mounted at the Academy of Music by the *Kiralfy brothers, Bolossy and Imre. It was revived regularly until the mid-1890s and was second in popularity among such musical extravaganzas only to The *Black Crook. In 1946 Orson *Welles mounted his own version, with music by Cole *Porter, and filled his entertainment with magic stunts, circus performers, and such clever scenic bits as a miniature train wreck, and he assumed the role of the villainous Dick Fix. However, the musical was short-lived.

ARRAH NA POGUE; or, The Wicklow Wedding (1865), a play by Dion *Boucicault. [*Niblo's Garden, 68 perf.] Arrah Meelish (Josephine Orton), a simple peasant girl, offers to shelter the fugitive Beamish McCoul (W. E. *Sheridan), when he appears at her cottage. McCoul's presence is discovered by the treacherous informer, Michael Feeney (W. Scallan) who divulges the secret on the eve of Arrah's wedding to Shaun the Post (T. H. Glenney), hinting that more than anti-British sentiments prompted Arrah's actions. Shaun is not deceived, so to save Arrah's life and reputation, Shaun claims that he had urged Arrah to hide the man. In the end Arrah, Shaun, and McCoul all manage to escape official wrath, and Arrah and Shaun are wed. The play was filled with what critics of the day liked to call "sensations," such as Shaun's false confession and his later escape by climbing down a growth of ivy. Although some critics suggested it lacked the heartiness and complexity of similar works, such as The *Colleen Bawn, The *Octoroon, and *Jessie Brown, the public adored the play, and it was revived regularly for the remainder of the century. Boucicault himself, who played Shaun at its London premiere, later frequently assumed the role.

ARSENIC AND OLD LACE (1941), a comedy by Joseph Kesselring. [Fulton Theatre, 1,444 perf.] Abby Brewster (Josephine *Hull) and her sister Martha (Jean *Adair) are two nice, sweet old ladies who murder nice, sweet, lonely old men by offering them elderberry wine laced with arsenic. The sisters' crazy but harmless brother Teddy (John Alexander), who sports a large mustache and a pince-nez, believes he is Teddy Roosevelt and often charges up the flight of stairs as if it were San Juan Hill. Teddy digs graves in the Brewster cellar, burying the sisters' victims whom he believes are yellow fever casualties working on the Panama Canal. Complications set in when their nephew Mortimer (Allyn Joslyn) learns of the sisters' activities; and matters get more farcical when another Brewster nephew, the criminal Jonathan (Boris Karloff) on the lam, and a strange Dr. Einstein (Edgar Stehli) arrive with the body of their latest victim. As next of kin, Mortimer arranges to commit the entire family to a mental institution, but before they leave, the sisters inform Mortimer that he is adopted; he is thrilled and announces to his fiancée that he's a bastard. The play ends with Abby and Martha offering the old gentleman from the mental home a glass of their special elderberry wine. Richard Lockridge of the Sun described the play as "a noisy, preposterous, incoherent joy," adding, "You wouldn't believe that homocidal mania could be such great fun." Legend has it that the play, originally called *Bodies in Our Cellar,* was conceived as a serious thriller and that producers Howard *Lindsay and Russel *Crouse were responsible for turning it into a comedy. A 1986 Broadway revival with familiar television faces managed a healthy run despite mixed notices. **Joseph KESSELRING** (1902–67) was a New York-born teacher, actor, author, and playwright. This was his only success.

ART (1998). Christopher Hampton's translation-adaptation of the Paris and London hit by French playwright Yasmina Reza was deemed slight but entertaining by the press, yet audiences responded to it and its three stars and it ran 600 performances at the Royale *Theatre, winning both the Tony and NYDCC Awards. When Serge (Victor *Garber), a wealthy Parisian doctor, buys an expensive painting that is all white, his friend Marc (Alan *Alda) is shocked that his aesthetically cultured friend could "betray" him like that. Their mutual friend Yvan (Alfred Molina) tries to soothe ruffled feathers, but his own personal problems get in the way. Only after the painting is vandalized and then restored is the fragile three-way friendship able to continue.

ARTEF. Its acronym derived from the Yiddish for Workers' Theater Group, it was founded in 1925 as a dramatic studio under the auspices of *Freiheit,* the Yiddish Communist daily, to produce plays on "a sound social basis." The group flourished through most of the 1930s, mounting both Yiddish classics and modern Yiddish propaganda plays, usually in that formally stylized, almost balletic manner known as agitprop. Few of the actors were professional; most shows were cast from theatrically interested laborers. The group disbanded in 1937 but sputtered back to life at intervals thereafter. Many Broadway critics visited their productions at one time or another, and often reviewed them favorably. Bernard Sobel wrote in the *Daily News* that they displayed "a refinement of inflection, perfect esprit de corps, a joyous bawdiness . . . conscious intellectualization . . . laughter, freshness and sustained emotional elevation."

ARTHUR, Beatrice [neé Frankel] (b. 1926), character actress. A native New Yorker, she was educated at Blackstone College and the Franklin Institute of Science and Arts, and studied acting with Erwin Piscator at the New School for Social Research. Arthur made her professional debut Off Broadway in 1947 and appeared in many classic productions before being noticed in 1954 as the sarcastic Lucy Brown in the legendary revival of *The *Threepenny Opera.* In the 1960s she won further praise for playing the village matchmaker Yente in *Fiddler on the Roof* (1964) and the acerbic actress Vera Charles in *Mame* (1966). The tall, throaty-voiced, sharp-tongued actress became one of America's favorite comediennes because of her television work, then she returned to Broadway after twenty years with her one-woman show *Just Between Friends* (2002).

ARTHUR [Smith], **Joseph** (1848–1906), playwright. One of the most successful turn-of-the-century melodramatists, he was born in Centerville, Indiana, the son of a clergyman, and served as a newspaper reporter and foreign correspondent before turning to the theatre. Despite his wide travels, most of his best plays were set in his native state; but it was neither his settings nor plots that accounted for his sometimes huge successes. Rather, like Dion *Boucicault, he had a special gift for contriving unusual, sensational, and memorable scenes. *The *Still Alarm* (1887) featured a scene in a firehouse in which firemen slide down the pole and prepare the fire engine, horses and all, while in *Blue Jeans* (1890) an unconscious man is placed on a belt moving ever closer to a whirling buzz saw. Among his other plays were a comedy, *A Cold Day When We Get Left* (1885); *The Corncracker* (1893), dealing with family members long separated; *The *Cherry Pickers* (1896), a military melodrama set in India; and *The Salt of the Earth* (1898), in which a country boy rises in politics to win his sweetheart's hand. A shrewd businessman, Arthur died wealthy with no fewer than a dozen touring companies still presenting his plays.

ARTHUR, Julia [née Ida Lewis] (1869–1950), actress. She left her native Canada, where she had participated in amateur theatricals, to spend several seasons playing important Shakespearean roles in Daniel E. Bandmann's touring company. Her first New York appearance was under A. M. *Palmer's aegis as Queen Fortunetta in *The Black Masque* (1891), followed by Lady Windermere in the first American production of *Lady Windermere's Fan* (1892) and the heroine in *Mercedes* (1892). After performing in England with Henry *Irving's Lyceum Company, Arthur became a star when she played the title role in *A Lady of Quality* (1897). But then she temporarily retired, not returning to the stage until 1914 when she gave special performances in Boston and Baltimore. New York applauded her again as the Woman in *The Eternal Magdalene* (1915), followed by the title role in the tragedy *Seremonda* (1917), a member of the all-star cast of *Out There* (1918), Lady Cheveley in *An Ideal Husband* (1921), and Lady Macbeth. After touring in 1924 as *Saint Joan* she retired permanently. A small, dark-haired, large-eyed beauty, Arthur was said to have brought her singular hauteur and dignity to all the roles she played.

ARTISTS AND MODELS, a series of revues mounted by the *Shuberts in 1923, 1924, 1925, 1927, and 1930. Unlike the more lavishly dressed extravagant annual revues of this period, these shows emphasized nude or nearly nude girls and a lower order of comedy, thus mirroring more closely the style of the *Earl Carroll Vanities. A 1943 version credited Lou Walters, the nightclub owner, as producer.

AS THOUSANDS CHEER (1933), a musical revue by Moss *Hart (sketches), Irving Berlin (music, lyrics). [*Music Box Theatre, 400 perf.] This revue was cleverly tied together by the device of pretending that each song and skit was derived from a headline in one imaginary newspaper. Thus, the headlines "Heat Wave Hits New York" and "Unknown Negro Lynched By Frenzied Mob" provided cues for Ethel *Waters's two great numbers, "Heat Wave" and "Supper Time." The latter song was an early attempt to inject serious social comment into a basically lighthearted evening. The first act finale, coming to life from the cover of the paper's rotogravure section, celebrated a turn-of-the-century "Easter Parade," with Marilyn *Miller and Clifton *Webb leading the Fifth Avenue paraders. The sketches poked fun at famous people, such as Miller's impersonation of Barbara Hutton, Waters as Josephine Baker, Helen *Broderick as Aimee Semple McPherson, and Webb as Mahatma Gandhi on a hunger strike and John D. Rockefeller rejecting the gift of Rockefeller Center. *Other notable songs*: How's Chances?; Harlem on My Mind; Lonely Heart; Not for All the Rice in China. Brooks *Atkinson of the *Times* called the revue "a superb panorama of entertainment." Although the Sam *Harris production was often as lavish as the opulent extravaganzas of earlier decades, the spectacle in this case was always secondary to the content, and the show took its place among the new generation of more thoughtful revues. A small-scale Off-Broadway revival in 1998 was well received.

AS YOU LIKE IT, a comedy by William Shakespeare. The bard's sylvan comedy was first offered at the *John St. Theatre in 1786 and later was selected to open the *Park Theatre. Its richly panoplied, highly moral romanticism gave it immense appeal to all the changing approaches and attitudes of the Victorian era, especially so in the last half of the 19th century, when scarcely a season passed without a major presentation. According to William *Winter, many of these mountings, notably in the troubled times of the Civil War and Reconstruction, leaned heavily on the darker, sadder aspects of the work, although *Daly's biographer-brother recalled that in the producer's 1869 offering, "The sing-song of Mrs. Scott-Siddons was like the carol of a bird in the forest of Arden." Twenty years later his restudied version, with Ada *Rehan as Rosalind, discarded "Every tone and every tint of melancholy." Other great 19th-century Rosalinds included Adelaide *Neilson and Julia *Marlowe. With the growing public cynicism that followed World War II, major revivals became less frequent, although the comedy retained its popularity with collegiate and, later, with festival groups. Probably the most famous and successful of later 20th-century Rosalinds was Katharine *Hepburn in an archly traditional *Theatre Guild revival in 1950. Two different all-male versions of *As You Like It* that originated in Great Britain made brief but notable stops in New York City in 1974 and 1994.

ASCAP. See American Society of Composers, Authors, and Publishers.

ASHLEY, Elizabeth [neé Cole] (b. 1939), actress. The angular, intense performer first made her name on Broadway in comedies but later developed into an exceptional dramatic actress. She was born in Ocala, Florida, and attended Louisiana State University before training at the *Neighborhood Playhouse School. Ashley was lauded for her spirited performance as the bouncy college co-ed Mollie in *Take Her, She's Mine* (1961) and then had an even bigger hit as the livewire newlywed Corie in *Barefoot in the Park* (1963). Three of her most memorable performances were in Tennessee *Williams revivals: as the sex-starved Maggie in *Cat on a Hot Tin Roof* (1974), the frowzy Flora Goforth in *The Milk Train Doesn't Stop Here Anymore* (1987), and the calculating Mrs. Venable in *Suddenly Last Summer* (1995). Autobiography: *Actress: Postcards from the Road*, 1978.

ASHMAN, Howard [né Howard Elliott Gershman] (1950–91), librettist, lyricist, and director. Born in Baltimore and educated at Goddard College and Indiana University, Ashman contributed lyrics to several Off-Broadway musicals and revues before teaming up with composer Alan *Menken on *God Bless You, Mr. Rosewater* (1979). The team's *Little Shop of Horrors* (1982) was a long-running hit Off Broadway, but Ashman's *Smile* (1986) with composer Marvin *Hamlisch failed to run. Ashman and Menken scored the animated musical films *The Little Mermaid* (1989), **Beauty and the Beast* (1991), and *Aladdin* (1992) before the librettist-lyricist's death from AIDS. He had a posthumous hit when *Beauty and the Beast* arrived on Broadway in 1994. Ashman, who directed his stage productions, possessed a talent for slangy, lively lyrics and whimsical but solid librettos.

ASIAN-AMERICAN THEATRE AND DRAMA. Plays and theatre companies from Asia were never more than curiosities in America until the second half of the 20th century. Language barriers and the marked dissimilarity of Eastern music to Western modes have, of course, been major obstacles, but the whole approach of Chinese and Japanese theatricals has been counter to the fundamentally realistic styles of Occidental writing and playing. The first major Oriental company to visit America was the Hook Took Tong, an ensemble of 123 artists, which enjoyed a huge success in San Francisco in 1852 and later played in New York and other Eastern cities. However, the novelty soon wore off, and those Chinese players who elected to remain in America were relegated to dingy playhouses in the Chinese quarters of San Francisco. In 1889 the Royal Company of Hong Kong toured major American cities. There were later occasional visits by such troupes as the Chinese acrobats and the Peking Opera. The play *The *Yellow Jacket* (1912) was the only successful American drama to consciously employ Chinese techniques, although some writers have suggested that Thornton **Wilder's *Our Town* (1938) is indebted to Oriental theatrical mannerisms. The Chinese classic *Pi-Pa-Ki* had some success as *Lute Song* (1946). But for the most part, Chinese, Japanese, Indian, and other Asian characters were rarely seen in American plays, and those that were often were mere stereotypes. Just as blackface had been acceptable for generations, so too white actors were usually made up to resemble Asians. This practice was still seen in *The *Teahouse of the August Moon* (1953) and **Flower Drum Song* (1959). Following the opening of Japan to the West, Japanese performers began appearing in American theatres in the late 1860s. They flourished as vaudeville performers, primarily as acrobats, for the next two decades, along with the rage for everything Japanese. However, it was not until after World War II that regular Japanese dramatic companies, such as the Grand Kabuki in 1969, visited America. The exotic nature of these entertainments again prevented their having a major influence on the mainstream of American playwriting or presentation, yet Stephen **Sondheim's *Pacific Overtures* (1973) employed suggestions of Kabuki style.

Asian-American theatre companies have existed since the middle of the 19th century but rarely were widely visible. By 1900 there were professional opera houses in New York and Boston, as well as on the West Coast, but most of these floundered and closed in the Great Depression. It was not until the 1960s that Asian-American theatre started to develop. The **East West Players in Los Angeles was founded in 1965, followed by groups in Seattle, Honolulu, and other centers of Asian immigrants. But these new companies performed in English and were concerned about the Asian-American experience rather than legends from the old world. Yet most of the new plays were firmly rooted in the traditions of the East, often using stylized techniques to tell a very contemporary story. Frank Chin's *The Chickencoop Chinaman*, produced Off Broadway in 1972, is considered the first influential play by an Asian American. The founding of Manhattan's **Pan Asian Repertory Theatre in 1977 was another important development. Henry David **Hwang was the most promising of the Chinese-American writers, and after several successes Off Broadway, he scored with **M. Butterfly* (1988), the first Broadway hit by an Asian-American. Other writers of note include Philip Kan Gotanda, Laurence Yep, R. A. Shimoi, and Ernest Abuba. Asian-American actors, such as Mako, John Lone, Randall Duk Kim, Sab Shimono, B. D. Wong, and Joan Chen, have managed to appear in Western classics and other works where race is not the issue. While most Americans will continue to see Asians in popular attractions like **Miss Saigon* (1991) and *Flower Drum Song*, the presence of Asian-American theatre is continually growing.

ASOLO THEATRE COMPANY (Sarasota, Florida). An 18th-century theatre in Asolo, Italy (which once featured Eleanore **Duse), was purchased by the estate of John Ringling and reassembled in Sarasota in the 1950s. A group of faculty and students from Florida State University (FSU) formed a company in 1960 to perform in the historic structure and the theatre became a fully professional company in 1966. Having outgrown its original home, the troupe moved in 1990 to the new Asolo Center for the Performing Arts, which houses the 500-seat Mertz Theatre and, as of 1994, the 161-seat Cook Theatre. In addition to a full season of classic and modern drama, the group is active in the FSU/Asolo Conservatory for theatre training.

ASSASSINS (1991), a musical play by John **Weidman (book), Stephen **Sondheim (music, lyrics). [*Playwrights Horizons, 25 perf.] Various historic people who have killed or attempted to assassinate U. S. presidents gather in this sometimes surreal, often funny, but chilling concept musical that exposes the dark side of the American dream.

Notable songs: Ballad of Booth; Another National Anthem; Unworthy of Your Love. This bold and uncomfortable musical quickly sold out its limited engagement, but plans to transfer it to Broadway were aborted when the Gulf War and a wave of patriotism discouraged the Off-Broadway company from risking it. *Assassins* has seen many regional productions since, and efforts are still under way to bring it to Broadway.

ASSOCIATION FOR THE PROMOTION AND PROTECTION OF AN INDEPENDENT STAGE IN THE UNITED STATES, THE. Founded either in 1897 or 1898, the organization was established by Mrs. *Fiske, Richard *Mansfield, Helena *Modjeska, James *O'Neill, Francis *Wilson, and other theatrical figures who had been shabbily treated by the growing *Theatrical Syndicate or Trust. Members agreed to try to play only in houses not allied with the Trust, to give fiery curtain speeches and interviews assailing the growing monopoly, and to alert the public in every other way to the menace. The power of the Trust and the cynical defection of Mansfield undermined the group.

ASSOCIATION OF PRODUCING ARTISTS. Popularly known as APA, it was founded by Ellis *Rabb in 1960 and gave its first performances in Bermuda. After serving briefly as the acting company at Princeton's *McCarter Theatre, it moved first to the Fred Miller Theatre in Milwaukee, then to the Folksbiene Playhouse in New York, then later became the resident company at the University of Michigan at Ann Arbor. In 1964 it joined the *Phoenix Theatre at its small *Off-Broadway house, where it won applause for its productions of The *Tavern, Right You Are If You Think You Are, The Lower Depths, and Scapin. Depleted funds forced it to return to Michigan, where its mounting of *You Can't Take It with You was so successful that it was brought to Broadway in 1965. The company spent several seasons at the *Lyceum Theatre in New York, including in its repertory The School for Scandal, Pantagleize, The Cherry Orchard (staged by Eva *Le Gallienne and starring Uta *Hagen), and a rousingly successful 1967 revival of The *Show-Off, with Helen *Hayes. Although a subsequent tour of the George *Kelly play helped fill the company's coffers, internal differences, including the departure of Rosemary *Harris, its finest regular, hurt the troupe, and after several failures it was, for all practical purposes, left in limbo. Several members of the group reunited in 1975 for a superb revival of The *Royal Family.

ASTAIRE, Fred [né Frederick Austerlitz] (1899–1987), dancer and actor. He and his sister

Adele (1898–1981) comprised the preeminent Broadway dance team of the 1920s. They were born in Omaha and achieved recognition in vaudeville before making their Broadway debut in *Over the Top* (1917). There followed appearances in The *Passing Show of 1918, *Apple Blossoms (1919), and The Love Letter (1921). The Astaires became virtual stars in two 1922 shows, For Goodness Sake and The Bunch and Judy, then, after a season in London, earned lasting recognition as the stars of *Lady, Be Good! (1924). Another success, *Funny Face (1927), followed, but Smiles (1930) was a failure. Their last joint success was The *Band Wagon (1931), in which they sang and danced "Hoops" and "I Love Louisa." When the revue closed, Adele retired to marry an English lord, so her brother appeared alone in what proved to be his last Broadway show, *Gay Divorce (1932). The musical gave him the chance to introduce one final great song, "Night and Day." The rest of his career was spent in Hollywood, where his early films with Ginger Rogers at RKO and his later work at Paramount and especially MGM made him one of filmdom's greatest stars. Although neither Fred nor Adele was especially good-looking, they were both slim, agile dancers, whose routines were characterized by a streamlined stylishness and a delightfully impish wit. Writing of their work in Smiles, the Boston Evening Transcript's famous critic, Henry Taylor *Parker, observed, "They are quite unsentimental. Whether they speak, dance or would sing, their touch is light, dry, sophisticated." Until her departure, Adele Astaire was generally considered the better of the two, universally praised not only for her dancing but also for her brilliant gifts as a comedienne. The pair's trademark was a run-around, in which they danced in ever widening arcs until, before their audience realized it, they had danced themselves off stage. Autobiography (Fred): *Steps in Time*, 1959; biography: *Fred Astaire: A Wonderful Life*, B. Adler, 1987.

ASTON, Anthony (*fl.* first half of 18th century), actor and playwright. A vagabond player, he generally is considered to have been the first professional actor to appear on an American stage. In an autobiographical preface to his play The Fool's Opera Aston wrote, "You are to know me, as a Gentleman, Lawyer, Poet, Actor, Soldier, Sailor, Exciseman, Publican; in *England, Scotland, Ireland, New York, East* and *West Jersey, Maryland, Virginia* (on both sides *Chesapeek*), *North* and *South Carolina, South Florida, Bahama's, Jamaica, Hispaniola,* and often a Coaster by all the same." He then adds, "Well, we arriv'd in *Charlestown,* full of Lice, Shame, Poverty, Nakedness and Hunger:—I turn'd *Player* and *Poet,* and wrote one Play on the

Subject of the Country." Aston goes on to tell of visiting New York and "acting, writing, courting, fighting that Winter." No records survive of precisely what roles and plays Aston offered, nor exactly where or when. Most scholars, despite the player's bravado, take him at his word and suggest that he was in America in 1703 and 1704. Biography: *Anthony Aston, Stroller and Adventurer*, Watson Nicholson, 1920.

ASTOR PLACE RIOTS. The most serious disorders ever connected with the American theatre occurred in 1849, although their origins can be traced back to 1826 when their two central figures, the American Edwin *Forrest and the English actor William Charles *Macready, both made debuts in New York. From the beginning both men, but especially the vain, jealous Forrest, perceived themselves as rivals, even though their styles were distinct and each attracted a somewhat different audience. Forrest's thunder and lightning acting appealed principally to the gallery and the pits, while Macready's more severe, formal methods pleased the boxes. When Forrest played London in 1845 he met with a cold reception, which he blamed on Macready. Early in 1846 both men were playing Edinburgh, and Forrest attended a Macready performance, sitting conspicuously in a box and hissing audibly. On Macready's 1849 visit to America, the English actor announced that he would perform *Macbeth* at the Astor Place theatre on May 7. Forrest promptly announced that he would play the same role on the same night at the *Bowery Theatre. Many of Forrest's loyalists attended Macready's performance and created such a ruckus that the evening was a fiasco. Actors were pelted with rotten food, chairs were thrown onstage, and asafoetida thrown from the gallery. Macready wanted to cancel the rest of his New York engagement. A group of prominent citizens, led by Washington *Irving, petitioned him to reconsider, so he agreed to appear again on May 10. While he was performing, a large horde of rabble, led by one E. Z. C. Judson, gathered to attack not only the theatre but also the homes of many of the men who had signed the petition. Judson, who wrote under the name Ned Buntline, was a founder of the Know-Nothing Party and a notorious agitator. When the troublemakers approached the Astor Place theatre, they found it guarded by the police and the militia. Rather than retreat, the mob, armed with stones and clubs, assaulted their better-armed opponents. In the ensuing melee, twenty-two were killed and at least thirty-six more injured, many seriously. Apart from a handful of radicals, most New Yorkers applauded Mayor Woodhull's firm handling of the rioters. Judson was later sentenced to a year's imprisonment for

instigating the incident, but suspicion was widespread at the time and has remained that the real instigator was none other than Forrest. Albeit the whole ugly affair may have begun as a personal rivalry between two men, it quickly involved other issues. America had many Anglophiles, especially among the upper classes, but others still viewed England, thirty-odd years after the War of 1812, with suspicion or enmity. Class distinctions also exacerbated the problem, as did seemingly simple aesthetic disagreements, although these were in no small part interwoven into the class differences. The Astor Place theatre never recovered from the incident, closing three years later. Nor did the Bowery remain a prime house, beginning its descent into a house of blue-collar melodrama just two years later. Many students also date the start of Forrest's decline in popularity and vigor from this time, even if he remained an idol of the gallery gods for some while. The Astor Place Riots were the subject of Richard *Nelson's Broadway drama *Two Shakespearean Actors* (1992).

ATKINSON, [Justin] Brooks (1894–1984), critic. Born in Melrose, Massachusetts, and educated at Harvard, he taught briefly at Dartmouth, then entered the newspaper world as a reporter for the Springfield (Massachusetts) *Daily News*. In 1919 Atkinson joined the Boston *Evening Transcript* as an assistant drama critic but soon moved to the *New York Times*, where he became its drama critic in 1924, a post he held, except for a stint as a war correspondent (1941–46), until 1960. As such he became the best known and most important of New York's reviewers. His writing was gracious and gentlemanly, and his views generally tolerant, except for a strong prejudice against older musicals after the advent of *Oklahoma!* and the "musical play." He also wrote several excellent books on the theatre, including *Broadway Scrapbook* (1947), *Broadway* (1970), and *The Lively Years: 1920–1973* (1974). Typical of his style was the opening of his review of a 1952 revival of *Summer and Smoke:* "Nothing has happened for quite a long time as admirable as the new production at the Circle in the Square—in Sheridan Square, to be precise. Tennessee Williams' *Summer and Smoke* opened there last evening in a sensitive, highly personal performance. When it was put on at the Music Box in 1948 it looked a little detached, perhaps because the production was too intricate or because the theatre was too large." In 1961 the Mansfield Theatre was renamed the *Brooks Atkinson Theatre, the first Broadway house to be named after a theatre critic.

ATLANTIC THEATRE COMPANY (New York). Founded in Burlington, Vermont, by actor William

H. Macy and playwright David *Mamet, the company originated as a summer program with young actors doing new works in a setting away from the hectic city. But the theatre now operates out of two spaces in the Chelsea district of New York, presenting original plays and bold interpretations of old works. Since its beginning, the Atlantic has produced nearly one hundred productions and runs an acting school in conjunction with New York University. Mamet's works have only occasionally been done, though he frequently directs productions.

ATTERIDGE, Harold R. See *Passing Shows, The*.

ATWILL, Lionel (1885–1946), actor. After a long career in his native England, he came to America in 1915 to tour with Lillie *Langtry, staying to produce and star in the mystery play *The Lodger* (1917). Several quick failures followed before he won attention in 1918 playing the leading male roles opposite Alla *Nazimova in Arthur *Hopkins's revivals of *The Wild Duck, Hedda Gabler,* and *A Doll's House.* He also shone as the politician Clive Cooper in *Tiger! Tiger!* (1918), the sadly beset pantomimist *Deburau* (1920), the bittersweet title roles in *The Grand Duke* (1921) and *The Comedian* (1923), and the put-upon inventor Anton Rogatsky in *The Outsider* (1924). In a change of pace the following year Atwill played Caesar opposite the Cleopatra of Helen *Hayes. Thereafter he appeared mostly in failures until he left to spend his last years in films. Atwill was a fine character actor with a curiously quizzical, doleful face and an elegant playing style.

AUBURN, David. See *Proof*.

AUCTIONEER, THE (1901), a play by David *Belasco, Charles *Klein, Lee Arthur. [Bijou Theatre, 105 perf.] Simon Levi (David *Warfield) is a goodhearted, struggling auctioneer on Hester Street who suddenly inherits a small fortune. Only with reluctance does he leave his beloved old haunts, but he understands that his wife and his adopted daughter long to move up in the world. His daughter loves a young, but somewhat naïve stockbroker, who persuades Simon to let him invest Simon's money for him. The stocks tumble and Simon is reduced to peddling toys until the stocks suddenly recover. For Warfield, who had heretofore been known largely as a dialect comedian, the play began his long, profitable association with producer-playwright Belasco and his career as a serious dramatic star. Several critics complained that the evening offered too much Warfield but agreed at the same time that without him the show would have been worthless.

Warfield was able to employ his comic talents to great advantage in the auction and peddling scenes. However, his high moment was the close of the first act in which he took a poignant farewell of his Hester Street home and friends.

AUDIN [or Odin], **Monsieur** (*fl.* late 18th century), scenic designer. Little is known about the personal life of this artist, who, except for Charles *Ciceri, was probably the finest set designer of his day. His most productive years seem to have been spent in Charleston. In his monograph on Ciceri, Edwin Duerr noted of Audin, "He succeeded in bringing to his southern stages some of the most varied and opulent of eighteenth century American theatrical scenes. Elaborate French pantomimes were beautifully colored and costumed; processions were splendidly mounted and arranged; melodramas maneuvered before wild backgrounds . . . all under the supervision of Audin." He was famous for transcribing well-known paintings to the stage, such as Hogarth's drawing of the gate of Calais for a 1793 mounting of *The Surrender of Calais.* In *The Charleston Stage in the XVIII Century*, Eola Willis suggests he may have pioneered in dimming lights to effect scene changes. It is unclear whether the Audin who later worked under Ciceri at the *Park Theatre in 1798 was the father or son.

AUDITORIUM THEATRE (Chicago). Famed architects Adler and Sullivan designed the large theatre on the Loop as part of a complex of offices and a hotel. It opened in 1899 as an opera house and presented musical productions until 1942 when it went bankrupt and was empty for years. A civic campaign to save the Auditorium in 1967 brought the theatre back to life; it was declared a landmark in 1975, and today it houses touring shows.

AUNTIE MAME (1956), a comedy by Jerome *Lawrence, Robert E. *Lee. [*Broadhurst Theatre, 639 perf.] Auntie Mame (Rosalind *Russell), an irrepressible scatterbrain but also a life-affirming optimist, finds she must take under her wing her young orphaned nephew, Patrick Dennis (Jan Handzlik). Mame's often indulgent, freethinking ideas of how to raise a youngster bring her into confrontation with the authorities and sometimes even with her friends. But in the end her guidance proves more than satisfactory. When he grows up to be a stable man, Patrick (Robert Higgins) marries and brings his own son to visit Mame, who promptly hustles the boy off to adventures in Europe. Based on the novel by Patrick Dennis, the play was more a series of entertaining vignettes than a sustained, well-plotted story. Louis *Kronenberger observed, "The adaptors, doubtless wisely, went in for a kind of scene-a-minute technique. Their slapdash method, if wholly uncreative, did manage to make speed a kind of substitute for wit." After Russell left the cast, Bea *Lillie assumed the role, and later played it in London. The comedy was turned into the successful musical *MAME* (1966), which played at the *Winter Garden Theatre for 1,508 performances. Lawrence and Lee adapted their own play and Jerry *Herman provided the tuneful score. Angela Lansbury triumphed as Mame, and it secured her new career in musicals. *Notable songs*: Mame; We Need a Little Christmas; If He Walked Into My Life; Open a New Window. A 1983 Broadway revival with Lansbury failed, but the musical remains popular regionally.

AUTHORS LEAGUE OF AMERICA. See Dramatists Guild.

AWAKE AND SING! (1935), a drama by Clifford *Odets. [*Belasco Theatre, 184 perf.] The Bergers, a lower-middle-class Jewish family in the Bronx, are a miserable lot. The mother, Bessie (Stella *Adler), is shrill and selfish; the father, Myron (Art Smith), a drudging ne'er-do-well; and their unmarried daughter, Hennie (Phoebe Brand), is pregnant with an unwanted child. If there is any hope for redemption, it rests with the Berger son, Ralph (Jules, later John, *Garfield), a bitter but ambitious young man, and his grandfather, Jacob (Morris *Carnovsky), who long ago found his consolation in philosophy. Seeing only one way out for Ralph, Jacob quietly makes him the beneficiary of his $3,000-life insurance policy, then "accidentally" falls from the roof of their tenement. His death allows Hennie to run away with Moe Axelrod (Luther *Adler), a crippled war veteran who offers her financial security. It also liberates Ralph: "Did Jake die for us to fight for nickels? No! 'Awake and sing,' he said . . . I saw he was dead and I was born!" Ralph departs, resolved to become a left-wing agitator. In the uneasy climate of the Great Depression, John Mason *Brown considered the play "a well-balanced, meticulously observed, always interesting and ultimately quite moving drama." A number of critics saw something

Chekhovian in the *Group Theatre presentation (though without Chekhov's gift of understatement). The drama was revived on Broadway in 1939, 1970, 1984, and Off Broadway in 1979, but it never proved as potent as the original.

AXELROD, George. See *Seven Year Itch, The*.

AYERS, Lemuel (1915–55), designer. A New Yorker, he studied at Princeton and the University of Iowa before being chosen by Leonard Sillman to design sets for 1939 revivals of *Journey's End* and *They Knew What They Wanted*. Major recognition came with his costume designs for the Maurice *Evans–Judith *Anderson *Macbeth* (1941). Ayers's settings were subsequently seen in, among others, *Angel Street* (1941); The *Pirate* (1942); *Harriet* (1943); *Oklahoma!* (1943); *Song of Norway* (1944); *Bloomer Girl* (1944); *Cyrano de Bergerac* (1946); *Inside U. S. A.* (1948); *Kiss Me, Kate* (1948) and *Out of This World* (1950), both of which he co-produced; *Kismet* (1953); and The *Pajama Game* (1954). He sometimes designed costumes for these shows as well. Ayers was a master at creating a sense of vast spaciousness within a proscenium frame. His stylized settings for *Oklahoma!* and his richly beautiful settings for *Out of This World* were noteworthy examples of this gift. One critic suggested that despite Cole *Porter's superb score and Charlotte *Greenwood's memorable performance, Ayers's settings were the "real star" of *Out of This World*.

AZENBERG, Emanuel (b. 1934), producer. Born in New York and educated at New York University, Azenberg began presenting Broadway shows, alone or with others, in 1961. Although he frequently works with the *Shubert Organization, he has a reputation for being an outspoken and individual producer. In addition to presenting most of Neil *Simon's plays after 1971, Azenberg's productions include The *Lion in Winter* (1966), *Ain't Supposed to Die a Natural Death* (1971), *Ain't Misbehavin'* (1978), *Children of a Lesser God* (1980), The Real Thing (1984), *Sunday in the Park with George* (1984), *Jerome Robbins' Broadway* (1989), the acclaimed revival of *Joe Egg* in 1985, Side Show (1997), *La Boheme* (2002), and *Movin' Out* (2003).

B

BABES IN ARMS (1937), a musical comedy by Richard *Rodgers (book, music), Lorenz *Hart (book, lyrics). [*Shubert Theatre, 289 perf.] Threatened with assignment to a work farm, the children of traveling vaudevillians band together to mount a musical revue. The show wins critical acclaim but loses money, so the children are sent to the farm. They are rescued when a French aviator on a transatlantic flight makes an emergency landing on their farm and comes to their aid. *Notable songs*: Babes in Arms; I Wish I Were in Love Again; Johnny One Note; The Lady Is a Tramp; My Funny Valentine; Where or When; Way Out West. Hailed by John Mason *Brown as "joyous and delectable," the Dwight Deere *Wiman–produced musical's major claim to fame, apart from its large list of great songs, was the many young talents to which it gave a leg up: Alfred *Drake, Mitzi Green, Ray Heatherton, Wynn Murray, Dan Dailey, and Robert Rounseville. Although professional groups infrequently revive it, schools and summer theatre continue to present the musical with a revised libretto.

BABES IN TOYLAND (1903), a musical extravaganza by Glen *MacDonough (book, lyrics), Victor *Herbert (music). [Majestic Theatre, 192 perf.] When the children Jane (Mabel Barrison) and Alan (William Norris) are shipwrecked through the machinations of their wicked Uncle Barnaby (George W. Denham), they find themselves in Toyland. Barnaby pursues them there, and, while courting Contrary Mary, contrives with the equally wicked Toymaker (Dore Davidson) to do away with them. But all his nefarious plots are foiled with the help of Mary, Jack and Jill, Bo Peep, the Widow Piper and her son Tom Tom, and a host of other Mother Goose figures, as well as by tree spirits, fairies, life-sized dolls, and talking flowers. In the end Barnaby is brought to justice in Toyland's court. *Notable songs*: I Can't Do the Sum; March of the Toys; Toyland. At a time when most musicals had only a few sets, the Fred Hamlin–Julian *Mitchell production (directed and choreographed by Mitchell) was exceptionally lavish. Among the settings were Barnaby's farm, the spectacle of the shipwreck, Mary's garden, the Spider's forest, the floral palace of the Moth Queen, the Toymaker's workshop (filled with giant toys), and the Toyland Palace of Justice. The *Dramatic Mirror* exclaimed of the show, "It will prove a perfect dream of delight to the children, and will recall the happy days of childhood to those who are facing the stern realities of life." Of Herbert's music, Henry Finck wrote in the *Evening Post*, "Every bar is melodious, while some of the incidental and melodramatic music betrays Mr. Herbert's position among the leading American composers." The musical was revived frequently for decades.

BABY MINE (1910), a comedy by Margaret *Mayo. [Daly's Theatre, 287 perf.] Zoie Hardy (Marguerite *Clark) is a compulsive fibber, so when she refuses to acknowledge that she dined in a restaurant with an unidentified man—who, if the truth were known, was actually her husband's best friend, Jimmy Jinks (Walter Jones)—her exasperated husband, Albert (Ernest Glendinning), packs his bag and leaves. Jimmy suggests that the best way to win back Albert would be for Zoie to have a baby—and quickly. He offers to find her one, but ends up bringing three babies home, which totally flusters and confuses Albert. When the real mothers of the tots appear to reclaim them, Albert's anger subsides as he realizes the lengths Zoie will go to show how much she loves him. Welcomed by the *Times* as "one of the funniest farces this town has ever seen," the William A. *Brady–produced comedy was the source of Jerome *Kern's 1918 musical *Rock-a-Bye Baby*.

BACALL, Lauren [née Betty Joan Perske] (b. 1924), actress. Described by Stanley *Green as a "smokey-voiced actress of angular intensity," she was born in New York and studied at the *American Academy of Dramatic Arts before making her New York debut as a walk-on in *Johnny 2 x 4* (1942). That same year she played the ingenue in *Franklin Street*, which folded during its tryout. After nearly twenty years in Hollywood, Bacall returned to New York to play Charlie, the callous philanderer whose punishment is to return to Earth as a woman, in *Goodbye, Charlie* (1959).

Her infrequent stage performances include the dentist's receptionist Stephanie in *Cactus Flower (1965), stage star Margo Channing in *Applause (1970), the high-powered lady newscaster Tess Harding in Woman of the Year (1981), and the retired actress Lotta Bainbridge in Waiting in the Wings (1999). Autobiographies: By Myself, 1978; Now, 1994.

BACON, Frank (1864–1922), actor and playwright. Born in Marysville, California, he spent time as a journalist and photographer before making his stage debut in San Jose, California, in 1890 as Sample Switchell in *Ten Nights in a Barroom. Bacon remained in stock in San Jose for seventeen years, running a small farm to supplement his income, but after the 1906 earthquake he toured for three years as Sam Graham in The *Fortune Hunter. In New York he appeared in Stop, Thief (1912), The Miracle Man (1914), The Cinderella Man (1916), and Barbara (1917), but his crowning moment came when he created the role of the boozy, easygoing spinner of tall tales, Lightnin' Bill Jones, in *Lightnin', a play that he wrote with Winchell *Smith that established a New York long-run record for its time. Bacon played the part more than two thousand times and was touring with it when he died. Many critics saw his Lightnin' Bill as a latter-day Rip Van Winkle and compared him, in both the style and quality of his acting, to Joseph *Jefferson in the earlier play. Bacon acknowledged that his rough-hewn but warm characterization was, in fact, modeled on Jefferson's.

BAGLEY, Ben [Jamin James] (1933–98), producer and director. Coming to New York from his native Vermont while still in his teens, he worked a series of odd jobs before producing The Shoestring Revue (1955), The Littlest Revue (1956), *Shoestring '57, and The Decline and Fall of the Entire World as Seen Through the Eyes of Cole Porter (1965). These revues were among the most consistently witty ever done in New York and gave an important boost to such talents as Chita *Rivera, Beatrice *Arthur, and a superb, sadly short-lived comedienne, Dorothy Greener. Turning to recording with his Painted Smiles label, he released an excellent "Revisited" series, putting on disks the often-neglected songs of major Broadway composers and lyricists.

BAILEY, Pearl [Mae] (1918–90), actress and singer. A native of Newport News, Virginia, the African-American singing comedienne, whose unique style was marked by an informal, broken delivery and sometimes slurred pronunciation, appeared in St. Louis Woman (1946); Arms and the Girl (1950), in which she stopped the show with "There Must Be Somethin' Better Than Love"; Bless You All (1950); and *House of Flowers (1954). Bailey scored her greatest stage success when she headed an all-black company of *Hello, Dolly! in 1967 and in later revivals. Autobiographies: The Raw Pearl, 1968; Talking to Myself, 1971.

BAILIWICK REPERTORY (Chicago). One of the very few major regional theatres dedicated to producing plays and musicals that reflect the diversity of the gay and lesbian community, it was founded in 1982. Under the supervision of David Zak, the company presents new plays and musicals that are experimental in nature but also offers works that are "family friendly."

BAINTER, Fay (1891–1968), actress. After performing as a child actress in stock in her hometown of Los Angeles, she made her New York debut in a musical, The Rose of Panama (1912), appeared in The Bridal Path (1913), and then toured with Mrs. *Fiske in Mrs. *Bumpstead-Leigh (1914). Bainter first called attention to herself in New York as the patriotic Ruth Sherwood in Arms and the Girl (1916) and as Mary Temple, the name given a statue come to life, in The Willow Tree (1917). In 1918 she returned to musicals to play Aline in The Kiss Burglar, then essayed her most famous role, Ming Toy, the spunky young girl who would escape her strict Oriental past, in *East Is West (1918). As one of the most sought-after and busiest actresses of the 1920s, her notable appearances included Elspeth in Victor *Herbert's The Dream Girl (1924), Pauli Arndt in the anti-war play The Enemy (1925), Louise in a revival of The *Two Orphans (1926), Julia Sterrol in Noel *Coward's Fallen Angels (1927), Kate Hardcastle in She Stoops to Conquer (1928), and Mrs. Sullen in The Beaux' Stratagem (1928). In the early 1930s she played important roles in more revivals, among them Kalonika in Lysistrata (1930) and Lady Mary Lasenby in The Admirable Crichton (1931), then essayed Mimi in a road company of The *Gay Divorce (1933). Bainter's last important Broadway assignment was Fran Dodsworth in *Dodsworth (1934). After ten years in Hollywood, she returned to New York as Margaret Brennan in The Next Half Hour (1945), followed by summer stock and touring as Mary Tyrone in *Long Day's Journey into Night. She has been characterized as a "charming, demure" actress whose performances displayed "technical perfection."

BAITZ, Jon Robin (b. 1961), playwright. Although he was born in Los Angeles, Baitz was raised in Brazil and then South Africa where his father was an executive for Carnation Milk. He returned to the States when he was eighteen, finished high school, then started writing and apprenticing at various California theatres. His play *The Film Society*, about a teacher in South Africa faced with a moral dilemma, was first produced in 1987 and was seen in New York the next year. Baitz's other notable works include *The Substance of Fire* (1991), concerning a publisher at odds with his family; *The End of the Day* (1992), about corruption in the medical profession; *Three Hotels* (1993), in which a couple is forced to examine past moral choices; *A Fair Country* (1996), about a diplomat's family living in foreign lands; and *Ten Unknowns* (2002), featuring a famous reclusive artist. Baitz's plays usually have an international setting, concern themselves with global themes, and deal with the individual conscience.

BAKER, Belle [née Bella Becker] (1895–1957), singer. Born on New York's Lower East Side, she first appeared on stage playing a boy in Jacob *Adler's production of *The Homecoming*. Singing in Yiddish productions, Baker came to the attention of vaudeville agents and was soon playing major variety houses. Although she made her Broadway debut in a minor part in *Vera Violetta* (1911), her only important musical comedy appearance was as star of the short-lived *Betsy* (1926), in which she introduced Irving *Berlin's "Blue Skies." The short, dark, plump entertainer with a deep, resonant voice remained primarily a vaudeville star, helping popularize such songs as "My Yiddische Mama," "All of Me," "Put It On, Take It Off, Wrap It Up and Take It Home," and "Cohen Owes Me $97." Baker made one of her last appearances at the *Palace special bill in 1950.

BAKER, Benjamin A. (1818–90), actor, playwright, and manager. Two years after making his stage debut in 1837 in Natchez, Mississippi, where he played small roles opposite Junius Brutus *Booth, he came back to his native New York to join William Mitchell at the Olympic as actor and prompter. On occasion he helped Mitchell write burlesques. His most famous play, which was written for his own benefit performance, was *A *Glance at New York* in 1848. The play was a huge success, establishing a vogue for such local dramas, and Baker quickly churned out sequels, such as *New York As It Is* (1848), *Three Years After* (1849), and *Mose in China* (1850). After several years of running theatres in Washington and San Francisco, he returned to New York in 1856 to manage Edwin *Booth's company. Although he continued to write burlesques and some musical comedy librettos, he spent most of his remaining years as a theatre manager. He was also active as an officer of the Actors' Fund.

BAKER, George Pierce (1866–1935), theatre scholar. Born in Providence, Rhode Island, he graduated from Harvard in 1887. Baker returned to teach there in 1905, sponsoring the *Harvard Dramatic Club when it was founded in 1908 and initiating his soon celebrated *47 Workshop, a laboratory for playwrights whose alumni number among the greatest writers of the first half of the 20th century. In 1925 Baker moved to Yale, where he continued to teach the technique and history of drama, chaired the Department of Drama, and directed the University Theatre. Among his works are *The Development of Shakespeare as a Dramatist* (1907), *Some Unpublished Correspondence of David Garrick* (1907), *Dramatic Technique* (1919), and *Modern American Plays* (1920). Biography: *George Pierce Baker and the American Theatre*, Wisner Payne Kinne, 1954.

BALANCHINE, George [né Gyorgi Melitonovitch Balanchivadze] (1904–83), choreographer. Born in St. Petersburg, he worked with Diaghilev and Colonel de Basil and also choreographed several London revues before settling in New York where he founded the School for American Ballet and organized the New York City Ballet Company. He was probably the greatest of 20th-century choreographers. In his best work, Balanchine moved away from traditional ballet storytelling, and, while retaining the basic dance idioms, attempted to abstract the essence of the music around which he often created his masterpieces. His pioneering work was rarely in evidence in his superb Broadway contributions, which nonetheless displayed what ballet historian Robert Lawrence called a "crispness of phrasing, musicality of movement, and feeling for absolute design." His first Broadway assignment was the *Ziegfeld Follies of 1936*. In the same year he created the first ballet conceived as an integral dramatic part of a musical with "Slaughter on 10th Avenue" in *On Your Toes*. He later choreographed *Babes in Arms* (1937), *I Married an Angel* (1938), The *Boys from Syracuse* (1938), *Keep Off the Grass* (1940), *Louisiana Purchase* (1940), *Cabin in the Sky* (1940), *The Lady Comes Across* (1942), *Rosalinda* (1942), *What's Up* (1943), *Dream with Music* (1944), *Song of Norway* (1944), *Mr. Strauss Goes to Boston* (1945), *The Chocolate Soldier* (1947), *Where's Charley?* (1948), and *Courtin' Time* (1951). Biography: *Balanchine*, Bernard Taper, revised 1983.

BALDERSTON, John. See *Berkeley Square*.

BALDWIN THEATRE (San Francisco). Built on Market Street in 1875 by the celebrated San Francisco gambler and entrepreneur Elias Jackson "Lucky" Baldwin as Baldwin's Academy of Music, it quickly became the principal rival to the

*California Theatre. The older house remained the home of a distinguished resident ensemble, while the Baldwin, designed by Sumner Bugbee, emphasized touring stars and attractions. In 1878 Baldwin built a magnificent hotel, which encompassed the playhouse and occupied the rest of the block. Virtually all the great touring performers of the day appeared in their best-known vehicles at the house. Thomas *Maguire and young Charles *Frohman were among its managers. Both hotel and theatre were destroyed by fire in 1898.

BALL, William [né William Gormaly Ball] (1931–91), director, actor, and manager. Born in Chicago, he studied acting, directing, and design at the Carnegie Institute of Technology. He toured for two years as assistant designer and actor in Margaret *Webster's company, then was associated with such companies as the *Oregon Shakespeare Festival, the Pittsburgh Playhouse, the Antioch Shakespeare Festival, San Diego Shakespeare Festival, *Arena Stage, *Actor's Workshop, *American Shakespeare Festival, the New York City Opera, and the *Circle in the Square, both as a leading actor and as a director. In 1964 Ball founded the *American Conservatory Theatre, and his career was tied almost totally to this organization until his resignation in 1986. A highly respected director who strongly believed in an actor-oriented theatre company, Ball eschewed commercial projects (he turned down *Fiddler on the Roof and other Broadway shows) and spent his career restaging the classics.

BALLARD, Kaye [née Catherine Gloria Balotta] (b. 1926), character actress. The short, squat comic actress and singer, with a loud speaking voice and a Broadway belt, has spent most of her career performing in cabarets and on television but also made several well-remembered stage appearances. She was born in Cleveland and began performing in vaudeville on the RKO Circuit. Ballard made her New York legit debut Off Broadway in 1946 but didn't gain recognition until her sultry, funny Helen in The *Golden Apple (1954). Her other musical performances of note include the magician's sour assistant Rosalie in *Carnival (1961), the would-be writer Ruth Sherwood in the 1963 revival of *Wonderful Town, the famous comic Gertrude Berg in Molly (1973), and the female buccaneer Ruth in The Pirates of Penzance(1981), as well as some revues and one-person shows.

BALLARD, Lucinda [née Goldsborough] (1908–93), costume designer. Born in New Orleans, she studied at the Art Students' League in New York and also in France before her first designs were seen on Broadway with *As You Like It (1937). Ballard's other costume credits include The Three Sisters (1939), *Morning's at Seven (1939), *I Remember Mama (1944), The *Glass Menagerie (1945), *Show Boat (1946), *Annie Get Your Gun (1946), *Happy Birthday (1946), *Another Part of the Forest (1946), Silk Stockings (1955), The *Dark at the Top of the Stairs (1957), *J. B. (1958), and The *Sound of Music (1959). During World War II she created the murals for New York's *Stage Door Canteen. Ballard was the first costume designer to win a *Tony Award and throughout her career her work won numerous awards.

BALLET IN AMERICAN THEATRE. Ballet has been a feature of regular American theatre, as distinguished from a totally separate ballet theatre with great ballet companies, virtually from the start. Indeed, because we could not support whole ballet ensembles, ballet first appeared as an ornament in the ballad operas of the late 18th and early 19th centuries or as divertissements on the extended bills that were common before the Civil War. Occasionally, great ballerinas, such as Fanny Elssler, were able to present entire evenings of dance, but even such celebrated artists as Celine Celeste were required to perform in spoken drama to supplement their dancing. Spectacle ballets, largely decorative and with little narrative connected to any play, became the rage about the time of the Civil War, most notably in The *Black Crook (1866), and remained popular well into the 20th century. Examples of this style remained a staple in the work of Marilyn *Miller in the 1920s, and on a more intimate, artful scale in revues such as the *Greenwich Village Follies. At about the same time, however, some more avant-garde revues began offering examples of more progressive, modern dance, although it was not until the 1930s with the work of George *Balanchine in such shows as *On Your Toes and *I Married an Angel, and the 1940s with Agnes *de Mille's ballets for *Oklahoma! and *Carousel that contemporary ballet began to be woven carefully into the fabric of the modern musical, often telling part of the musical's story in choreographic terms. As a rule these ballets, however excellent, have been too short to offer in regular ballet evenings, albeit several have achieved fame. The most notable is probably "Slaughter on Tenth Avenue" from On Your Toes, which undoubtedly owes its celebrity as much to Richard *Rodgers's fine and well-known music for it as it does to Balanchine's choreography. Another memorable example was Jerome *Robbins's comic gem, the "Mack Sennett Ballet" from *High Button Shoes. Many critics and playgoers would also cite Robbins's "The Small House of Uncle Thomas" from The *King and I, and his dances in *West Side Story that not only advanced the story but were an integral part of the very construction and tempo of the shows. By the

1960s such choreographers as Robbins, Gower *Champion, Bob *Fosse, and Michael *Bennett came to the fore not merely to create dances, but to conceive and direct whole musicals. A good example would be A *Chorus Line, which began as a workshop project with Bennett and became a dance show about dance. To some extent the same could be said about the popular dance musicals *Dancin' (1978), Bring in da Noise, Bring in da Funk (1996), *Fosse (1999), and *Contact (2000).

BALSAM, Martin (1919–96), character actor. He was born in New York and studied at the *Actors Studio, making his Broadway debut in 1941. The gruff-looking, flexible actor made hundreds of films and television appearances but also managed some noteworthy stage performances, such as the Son-in-Law dealing with his father-in-law's autumnal romance in *Middle of the Night (1956), a variety of perplexed characters in *You Know I Can't Hear You When the Water's Running (1967), and the terminally ill patient Joseph Parmigian in Cold Storage (1977).

BALTIMORE, Maryland. Although Baltimore was the scene of occasional theatricals in the early 18th century, it long played second fiddle to nearby Annapolis, which called itself "The Athens of America" and where *Douglass, *Hallam, and the *American Company performed regularly. Thomas *Wall and Adam Lindsay built Baltimore's first important playhouse in 1781 on East Baltimore Street and opened it in January of the following year. In 1794 Thomas *Wignell and Alexander *Reinagle erected the *Holliday Street Theatre, which with several rebuildings remained a major playhouse throughout the 19th century. One of its later managers was John T. Ford, who also built *Ford's Theatre there. In the 20th century the city served as a relatively important touring and tryout town, although by the Great Depression the only surviving active playhouse was Ford's. The theatre was demolished in 1964, and the city had no regular legitimate theatre until the opening of the Morris Mechanic in 1967. Downtown Baltimore, and the riverfront district in particular, was revitalized in the late 1970s and theatregoing has continued to flourish at the Mechanic, the *Center Stage, the Everyman Theatre, the Lyric Opera House, and other venues.

BANCROFT, Anne [née Anna Maria Luisa Italiano] (b. 1931), actress. Born in the Bronx, she studied at both the *American Academy of Dramatic Arts and the *Actors Studio before making her Broadway debut with a Tony Award–winning performance as Gittel Mosca, the Jewish girl who falls in love with a Midwestern lawyer, in *Two for the Seesaw (1958). Of her performance Brooks *Atkinson wrote, "She explodes with gestures that are natural, she modulates the part with vocal inflections that are both funny and authentic, and she creates a gallant character who rings true." Bancroft's other outstanding Broadway role was Annie Sullivan, Helen Keller's devoted teacher, in The *Miracle Worker (1959). Among her subsequent performances of note were wartime marketeer Mother Courage in Mother Courage and Her Children (1963), the sexually charged Prioress in The Devils (1965), scheming Regina in The *Little Foxes (1967), Shakespeare's wife Anne in A Cry of Players (1968), the Israeli political figure Golda (1977), musician Stephanie Abrahams whose career is destroyed by a crippling disease in Duet for One (1981), and Louise Nevelson in the Off-Broadway play Occupant (2002).

BAND WAGON, THE (1931), a revue by George S. *Kaufman (sketches), Howard *Dietz (sketches, lyrics), Arthur *Schwartz (music). [*New Amsterdam Theatre, 260 perf.] The Max *Gordon revue was one of the first to successfully abandon the often heavy-handed opulence of the *Ziegfeld era. Its designer, Albert R. *Johnson, and director, Hassard *Short, made effective use of revolving stages to speed the action, and it was the first show to discard footlights in favor of lighting from the balcony. Among the high points, apart from the great songs, were its opening, where the arriving audience found the curtain up and, onstage, the chorus pretending to be another audience taking its seats and singing "It Better Be Good"; a ballet, "The Beggar Waltz," in which Fred *Astaire played a beggar who dreams he dances with a great ballerina (Tilly Losch); and a skit, "The Pride of the Claghornes," which satirized Southern mores. Other notable songs: Dancing in the Dark; High and Low; I Love Louisa; New Sun in the Sky. Brooks *Atkinson wrote, "Mr. Schwartz's lively melodies, the gay dancing of the Astaires, and the colorful merriment of the background and staging begin a new era in the artistry of the American revue." The stellar cast also included Frank *Morgan, Helen *Broderick, and Adele *Astaire. The show was the last appearance by the Astaires together; after the musical closed, Adele retired to marry an English lord.

BANKER'S DAUGHTER, THE (1878), a play by Bronson *Howard. [*Union Square Theatre, 137 perf.] Lilian Westbrook (Sara Jewett) scoffs at her friend Florence St. Vincent (Maud Harrison), who has announced she will marry a man old enough to be her father. Lilian loves young Harold Routledge (Walden Ramsay), although she is annoyed at his jealousy of her flirtation with Count de

Carojac (M. V. Lingham). However, when her own father is threatened with bankruptcy she throws over Routledge to marry Mr. Strebelow (C. P. *Thorne Jr.), a much older, richer man. Seven years later, Lilian's life now revolves around her young daughter, but she still secretly loves Routledge, and is still seen regularly by both Routledge and the Count. The Count has never forgiven Routledge for being the love of Lilian's life. When the men have an open falling-out, a duel is held in which the Count mortally wounds Routledge. Overcome emotionally, Lilian blurts out to Strebelow that she had never loved him but has been nevertheless a dutiful wife. Blaming himself for not understanding his wife, Strebelow leaves her. More years pass and Lilian comes to realize that she loves Strebelow. Their little daughter's letters, sometimes dictated by Lilian, bring about a reconciliation. The play initially had been done as *Lilian's Last Love* at *Hooley's Theatre in Chicago in 1873. A. R. *Cazauran, producer A. M. *Palmer's "reconstructor," helped rewrite the piece for its New York presentation, discarding its original unhappy conclusion. It was later performed in London as *The Old Love and the New*. Despite its contrived ending, the drama was immensely popular with both critics and playgoers. It was frequently revived, and remained a favorite of stock companies until World War I.

BANKHEAD, Tallulah (1903–68), actress. Born in Huntsville, Alabama, she used her family's influence (her uncle was a U. S. Senator) to land a walk-on part in her first Broadway show, *Squab Farm* (1918). After a brief fling in films, Bankhead replaced others in such plays as *39 East* (1919), *Footloose* (1920), *Danger* (1921), and *Her Temporary Husband* (1922), and originated parts in *Nice People* (1921) and *The Exciters* (1922), but her career seemed stalled so she left for England where, for the next eleven years, she played increasingly important roles. Bankhead returned but found only modest success as the jilted bride Mary Clay in *Forsaking All Others* (1933), the fatally ill Judith Traherne in *Dark Victory* (1934), the sultry Sadie Thompson in a revival of *Rain* (1935), and the cheated-on wife Monica Grey in *Something Gay* (1935). She had better luck as the emotional actress Muriel Flood in George *Kelly's *Reflected Glory* (1936) but was roundly panned as the Queen of the Nile in a revival of *Antony and Cleopatra* (1937). However, her greatest performances soon followed, including Regina Giddens in *The *Little Foxes* (1939), the sibyl-like servant Sabina in *The *Skin of Our Teeth* (1942), and Amanda Prynne in a free-slugging revival of *Private Lives* (1946), a character she played in various venues for four years. Bankhead's later roles were actress

Sophie Wing in *Foolish Notion* (1945), the Queen in *The Eagle Has Two Heads* (1947), the mother determined to legitimatize her children in *Dear Charles* (1954), and the prankish society doyen *Midgie Purvis* (1961). Her last Broadway appearance was as a typical Tennessee *Williams lady in his *The Milk Train Doesn't Stop Here Anymore* (1964). In her last years, when major Broadway success eluded her, she appeared regularly on radio, calling everyone "dahling" in her deep baritone voice and behaving seemingly like a parody of herself. Bankhead's performances occasioned some of the wittiest criticism ever elicited, most famously John Mason *Brown's dismissal: "Tallulah Bankhead barged down the Nile as Cleopatra and sank. As the serpent of the Nile she proves to be no more dangerous than a garter snake." Elliot *Norton, on the other hand, recalled of her Regina in *The Little Foxes*, "A woman driven by Furies, driven and driving . . . cold, calculating and calmly cruel, yet absolutely true and fascinating. . . . Her laughter was a silver ripple on ice, the glint of a glacier. Her wrath . . . was the rumbling of thunder with flashes of lightning." Autobiography: *Tallulah*, 1952.

BARAKA, Amiri [né Everett LeRoi Jones] (b. 1934), playwright. The most radical and influential African-American writer of the 1960s, he first was noticed (under the name of LeRoi Jones) with *Dutchman* (1964), an explosive one-act allegory about a sensuous white woman who teases and taunts a black student on a subway train before killing him. Baraka's other significant drama was *Slave Ship* (1967) where actors and audience experience the Atlantic crossing of a colonial slave-trade vessel. He changed his name and mission in the late 1960s, advocating theatre as a weapon against white supremacy, and his works inspired a generation of African-American writers.

BARBARA FRIETCHIE (1899), a play by Clyde *Fitch. [Criterion Theatre, 83 perf.] Almost all the citizens of Frederick are Confederate sympathizers, so they condemn their neighbor, young Barbara Frietchie (Julia *Marlowe), for accepting the attentions of a Yankee, Capt. Trumbull (J. H. Gilmour). Many had hoped she would marry the boy next door, Jack Negly (Arnold *Daly), but Barbara dismisses him as a coward who won't fight for either side. Her brother Arthur (Lionel Adams), who has been wounded at Gettysburg, returns home and asks Barbara to hide him in the house from Yankee search parties. Trumbull pretends not to see Arthur, and when a search party arrives he sends them away. Though Barbara is loyal to the Confederacy, she loves Trumbull enough to accept his offer of marriage, but the wedding is interrupted by the arrival of Confederate troops. When a Southern sharpshooter attempts to shoot Trumbull, Barbara shoots the Southerner's gun from his hand, then offers him refuge in her house, where Trumbull is also brought in wounded. Negly learns Trumbull is there and would betray him, but Barbara dissuades him. "You have broken my heart," he sobs, to which Barbara replies, "Forgive me—by not breaking mine." For all her ministrations, Trumbull dies just as the victorious Confederates march through town. All the houses display Confederate flags except the Frietchies'; Barbara stands on the porch defiantly brandishing the stars and stripes. Negly goes to shoot her, but Stonewall Jackson, passing by, admires her bravery and orders that anyone molesting her be shot in turn. Nevertheless, Negly does shoot Barbara, and his own father, Col. Negly (W. J. Le Moyne), orders Jackson's command carried out. In his *History of the American Drama*, *Quinn has noted, "Fitch was vigorously criticized for falsification of history, and rather feebly defended himself on the grounds that Barbara Frietchie was ninety-six years old and bedridden when Stonewall Jackson went through Fredericksburg . . . [But] while false to fact and legend, it is true to the spirit of the time, from the social if not from the military point of view." It was also true to the theatrical spirit of the time, which wanted more romance than realism in its war plays. The Charles *Frohman–produced drama was revived successfully several times and was made into the popular operetta **MY MARYLAND** (1926) with music by Sigmund *Romberg and book and lyrics by Dorothy *Donnelly. Evelyn *Herbert was Barbara and the *Shubert production, after a record-breaking forty-week tryout in Philadelphia, played at the Jolson Theatre for 312 performances. *Notable songs*: Silver Moon; Won't You Marry Me?; Your Land and My Land.

BAREFOOT IN THE PARK (1963), a comedy by Neil *Simon. [*Biltmore Theatre, 1,530 perf.] After a glorious six-day honeymoon at the Plaza Hotel, Corie (Elizabeth Ashley) and Paul Bratter (Robert Redford) move into their dilapidated, sixth-floor walk-up where their first visitors are Corie's mother, Mrs. Banks (Mildred *Natwick), and their eccentric gourmet lothario neighbor, Victor Velasco (Kurt Kasznar). Corie unwittingly invites both her mother and Mr. Velasco to dinner, and the foursome end up going to a wild Albanian restaurant. Everyone has a good time except Paul, whom Corie accuses of being so prim and proper that he would prefer to sleep with his tie on. After the couple's first fight, Corie decides she wants a divorce. But when her mother comes in wearing a man's bathrobe after a night with Mr. Velasco, and after Paul has gotten drunk and danced barefoot in the park, Corie realizes she loves Paul and his sane, quiet ways. Henry *Hewes observed that the Saint Subber–produced play "was nothing more than a minor quarrel between two young newlyweds spiced with their amusing responses to the sort of physical discomforts New Yorkers find themselves so illogically putting up with." Yet most other reviewers and the public had no trouble enjoying the refreshing comedy. Director Mike *Nichols had fun with inventing any number of comic entrances after the principals had supposedly climbed many stairs and all of the performances were first rate. Coming after the success of *Come Blow Your Horn*, the play confirmed Neil Simon's mastery of one-liners, although his gift for genuine comic complications was still to be developed.

BARKER, James Nelson (1784–1858), playwright. The son of a prominent Philadelphia family (his father was later to be mayor), Barker's first produced play was *Tears and Smiles* (1807), which contrasted French society airs with American simplicity. His next play, *The Embargo; or, What News?* (1808), provoked riots at Philadelphia's *Chestnut Street Theatre with its support of the Embargo Acts and pro-administration bias. A play with music, *The *Indian Princess; or, La Belle Sauvage* (1808), recounted the legend of Pocahontas with a happy ending. It was thus the first "Indian play" written by an American and produced. Billed as a melodrama, a sign of growing French influence in the American theatre, it was successfully mounted in several cities and became the first American play to be presented in London, where it was offered as *Pocahontas*. Barker's *Marmion; or, The Battle of Flodden Field* (1812) was initially presented as being by an English dramatist "in order to avoid the neglect usually accorded to native playwrights," and his *The Armourer's Escape; or, Three Years at Nootka Sound* (1817) was based on the real-life adventures of John Jewitt, who played himself at its premiere. Barker temporarily set aside playwriting when he was elected mayor of Philadelphia in 1819. However, he returned to the theatre in 1824 with his last and best play, *Superstition; or, The Fanatic Father*, an attack on Puritan excesses. Thereafter, Barker devoted himself to public service, becoming Collector of the Port from 1829 to 1838 and from then until his death Controller of the United States Treasury. Alexander Cowrie has written in *Literary History of the United States*, "Without being fanatically nationalistic, he staunchly did his part in building a native tradition in the drama." Biography: *James Nelson Barker*, Paul H. Musser, 1929.

BARNABEE, Henry Clay (1833–1917), comic actor and singer. Born in Jamaica Plains, Massachusetts, he quit school to work as a dry-goods clerk, but performing in amateur theatricals convinced him his future lay in performing. Barnaby made his professional debut in recital at the Music Hall in Boston in 1865, but his fame as a soloist and as a performer in musical theatre remained largely local until 1879 when he became one of the original members of the *Boston Ideal Opera Company. He stayed with the "Bostonians" for their quarter-century history, serving as their principal comedian. While he was hailed for such interpretations as Sir Joseph Porter in *H. M. S. Pinafore*, Bunthorne in *Patience*, Izzet Pasha in *Fatinitza*, Dulcamara in *The Elixir of Love*, and Lord Allcash in *Fra Diavolo*, his greatest role was the Sheriff of Nottingham in *Robin Hood* (1891), which he created and played for some two thousand times. The horse-faced performer was appreciated for his rare combination of fine bass-baritone singing and humor, one Kansas City critic noting, "At all times he is a gentleman, and nothing in his quiet and Jeffersonian wit is ever vulgar or out of place." Autobiography: *My Wanderings*, 1913.

BARNARD, Charles. See *County Fair, The.*

BARNES, Charlotte. See Barnes, John.

BARNES, Clive [Alexander] (b. 1927), critic. London-born and Oxford-educated, he was a drama and dance critic for several English periodicals before becoming dance critic for the *New York Times* in 1965. Two years later he became the paper's drama critic and for a decade was the most powerful reviewer in New York, often easy to please but sometimes so caught up in new trends that he dismissed many quality shows. In 1977 Barnes switched to the New York *Post* where he yields much less clout but is still read and quoted.

BARNES, John (1761–1841) and his wife, **Mary** (1780?–1864), actors. Coming from England, where she had played at Drury Lane and he at the Haymarket, they made their American debut at the *Park Theatre in 1816, and, for the most part, remained at the playhouse until their retirements. When Mrs. Barnes made her debut there playing Juliet, the *Evening Post* noted, "She *did* and looked Juliet better than we have ever seen it played on this stage, if what we have seen heretofore can be called playing." When John Barnes made his debut as Sir Peter Teazle, the same critic commented, "His person and voice are well calculated for the characters he fills. His judgment was fully displayed, by making Sir Peter what we have long wished to see him, a gentleman." From the start Mrs. Barnes was considered the better, more

versatile performer. Among her roles were Desdemona, Jane Shore, Belvidera, Amy Robsart, Lady Teazle, and Aladdin. Her husband was best at comedy and for the most part confined himself to supporting roles. Mrs. Barnes played only occasionally after 1833, but her husband continued to perform until shortly before his death. Their daughter was **Charlotte** [Mary Sanford] **BARNES** (1818–63) who made her debut at the Park when she was a child then returned to the stage in 1834 as a young adult, playing Angela in *The Castle Spectre*, first at Boston's Tremont Theatre and then in New York. In the following seasons she was applauded for her interpretations of Juliet, Jane Shore, Evadne, Desdemona, and Lady Teazle. After playing in London, Barnes returned to America, married Edmond S. Connor, and acted with him when he managed Philadelphia's *Arch Street Theatre. She translated several French melodramas and wrote several plays based on popular novels or legends. Notable among the last were *Octavia Bragaldi* (1837), a blank-verse tragedy set in Italy; the now-lost melodrama *La Fitte* (1840) about the famous buccaneer; and a version of the Pocahontas legend called *The Forest Princess* (1844).

BARNUM, P. T. See American Museum.

BARNUM'S MUSEUM. See American Museum.

BARR, Richard [né Baer] (1917–89), producer. Born in Washington, D.C., and educated at Princeton, he began his career as an actor with the *Mercury Theatre and later served as a director of plays for New York City's *Center. Subsequently he became active as a producer, usually working in conjunction with one or more other producers. Barr championed young playwrights, such as Edward *Albee, Lanford *Wilson, and Terrence *McNally, as well as presenting the first American productions of works by Samuel *Beckett and Eugene *Ionesco. Among his notable productions were *At Home with Ethel Waters* (1953), Ruth *Draper's 1954 and 1956 solo appearances, *The *Zoo Story* (1960), *The *American Dream* (1961), *Who's Afraid of Virginia Woolf?* (1962), *Tiny Alice* (1964), A *Delicate Balance* (1966), and *The *Boys in the Band* (1968). He served as president of the League of *American Theatre and Producers for twenty-one years.

BARRAS, Charles. See *Black Crook, The.*

BARRATT, Watson (1884–1962), scenic designer. Born in Salt Lake City, he was an illustrator for magazines before turning to design in 1917. The next year he worked with the *Shuberts for the first time and thereafter became virtually their house set designer. Although Barratt was very prolific and remained active until the early 1950s, his heyday was in the 1920s when he created sets for such shows as *The Whirl of New York* (1921), **Blossom Time* (1921), *The *Student Prince* (1924), *Princess Flavia* (1925), and **My Maryland* (1927) as well as for their **Winter Garden revues. He also served with the **St. Louis Municipal Outdoor Opera Company for several years.

BARRETT, George [Horton] (1794–1860), actor. The son of actors in **Dunlap's company at the **Park Theatre, he began performing as a boy in 1798 then years later in repertory he portrayed many of the popular comic figures of the era. One contemporary critic hailed him as "a comedian of the First Class," and established him as a reigning favorite. His most popular representations included Charles Surface, Sir Andrew Aguecheek, Captain Absolute, and Puff. In 1826 he became the principal director at the **Bowery Theatre, where he continued to act, and later served in both capacities at the Tremont in Boston and at Burton's and the Broadway Theatre. Barrett's public posture, as elegant as his acting, soon won him the affectionate nickname "Gentleman George." His wife was the actress **Mrs. BARRETT** [née Anne Jane Henry] (1801–57) who made her debut as a dancer at Boston's **Federal Street Theatre. Her career was marred for a time by a bout with alcoholism, but Fanny **Kemble pronounced her "a faultless piece of mortality in outward loveliness," while Walter **Leman recalled, "She was the petted idol of the Boston public; of rare excellence in her art, it would be hard to say what she played best, she played everything so well."

BARRETT, Lawrence [Patrick] (1838–91), actor. The self-educated son of a poor tailor, he was born in Paterson, New Jersey, but raised in Detroit where he made his debut in 1853 as Murad in *The French Spy*. Three years later he made his New York bow at the Chambers Street Theatre playing Sir Thomas Clifford in *The *Hunchback*. After having performed with Edwin **Booth on several occasions and comanaging San Francisco's **California Theatre, Barrett won fame in New York as the mad poet James Harebell in *The Man o' Airlie* (1871). In 1875 his Cassius earned him additional laurels and he also met with personal success touring during the 1877–78 season in two works by William Dean **Howells, as the mistrusted painter Bartlett in *A Counterfeit Presentment* and the tragic jester in *Yorick's Love*. For many, however, his crowning achievement came in 1883 when he revived **Francesca da Rimini*. William **Winter called the actor's Lanciotto a performance

of "terrible beauty." Much of Barrett's later career was with Booth in several important Shakespearean revivals, including **Julius Caesar, *Othello* (in which the men alternated as hero or villain), and *The *Merchant of Venice*. His last performance, which he was unable to finish, was as de Mauprat opposite Booth's famous Richelieu. The same sense of history that prompted him to revive neglected works may have induced him to become a theatrical historian as well. Among his writings are *Edwin Forrest* (1881) and *Edwin Booth and His Contemporaries* (1886). Most scholars agree with **Odell, who called Barrett "our most farsighted and ambitious, if not our greatest tragedian," citing his willingness to go beyond the standard repertory and the excellent taste of his acting and mountings. "His features," Otis **Skinner recalled, "were attractive; a good nose, wide mobile mouth, deep-set and burning eyes, and a broad and thoughtful forehead. It might have been the face of a monk." Biography: *Lawrence Barrett, A Professional Sketch*, Elwyn A. Barron, 1889.

BARRETT, Mrs. See Barrett, George.

BARRETTS OF WIMPOLE STREET, THE (1931), a British play by Rudolf Besier. [**Empire Theatre, 372 perf.] Dealing with the courtship of Elizabeth Barrett by her fellow poet Robert Browning, it was produced by and starred Katharine **Cornell. Brian Aherne was Browning and Charles **Waldron was Elizabeth's father. It gave Cornell her most famous role. The often acid Dorothy **Parker wrote in *The New Yorker*, that Cornell "is a completely lovely Elizabeth Barrett—far lovelier than the original, I fear. It is little wonder that Miss Cornell is so worshipped; she has that thing we need, and we so seldom have, in our actresses; she has romance . . . she has glamour." After its New York run it was taken first on a twenty-week "short" tour, then on a longer tour during the 1933–34 season, at a time when few shows played anything but major cities. On Christmas night the production was supposed to open in Seattle, but the company's train, delayed by washouts, did not arrive until 11:15. When she was advised that the entire audience was still waiting, Cornell agreed to perform. The final curtain did not come down until nearly four in the morning.

BARRIE, James M[atthew] (1860–1937), playwright. The English dramatist, who hid a barbed wit and slightly mocking view of life beneath often cloyingly sentimental surfaces, was first represented in America by *The Professor's Love Story* (1892) and *Walker, London* (1894). He was long associated with producer Charles **Frohman and actress Maude **Adams, an association that began with *The Little Minister* (1897). His subsequent successes included *Quality Street* (1901), *The Admirable Crichton* (1903) starring William *Gillette, *Peter Pan* (1905), *Alice Sit-by-the-Fire* (1905) with Ethel *Barrymore, *What Every Woman Knows* (1908), *A Kiss for Cinderella* (1916), *Dear Brutus* (1918) with Gillette and Helen *Hayes, and *Mary Rose* (1920). Barrymore toured in vaudeville for many years with his playlet *The Twelve-Pound Look*, while Hayes later appeared in another short play, *The Old Lady Shows Her Medals*. Indeed, Hayes eventually became one of Barrie's leading advocates, appearing in revivals of several of his works, especially *What Every Woman Knows*, her curious blend of saccharine and iron precisely matching his.

BARROW, Julia Bennett (1824?–?), actress. She left the Haymarket company in London to make her American debut in 1851 as Lady Teazle, and she was an instant success, the *Albion* describing her as "a blonde, extremely pretty and prepossessing in her air and manner; her figure is slight, and her movements are easy and graceful. Her voice is rather high pitched." Although Barrow later played a well-received Viola, many of her best roles were in now-forgotten contemporary comedies. She was also adept at more serious impersonations. Indeed, among her last roles before moving to Boston were the principal woman's roles in *Richard III* and *The Marble Heart*, playing opposite John Wilkes *Booth. For many years she ran Boston's *Howard Athenaeum to great acclaim, before apparently returning to England.

BARRY, Philip [Jerome Quinn] (1896–1949), playwright. Born in Rochester, New York, he was the son of a successful Irish immigrant and a mother who was of old Philadelphia Irish-Catholic stock. Young Barry was a frail child with defective eyesight, yet despite his myopia he became an avid reader and a precocious wit, entering Yale in 1914 and plunging eagerly into campus literary activities. During World War I he was rejected for military services but served in the Communications Office of the State Department in London where he became a life-long Anglophile. Returning to Yale after the war, his play *Autonomy* won a prize offered by the school dramatic society, and, over strident family objections, he enrolled in George Pierce *Baker's famed *47 Workshop at Harvard. Barry's play *The Jilts*, in which a businessman attempts an artistic career, won the *Herndon Prize and Richard Herndon himself agreed to produce it in 1923, changing the title to *You and I*. Its success was the first of many on Broadway for Barry. Underlying the charm and razor-sharp wit

of *You and I* was a deep-seated disenchantment with life. This malaise began to seep to the surface in his *In a Garden* (1925), whose dramatist hero sets up his wife for an affair to test a theory. Barry moved even farther away from traditional high comedy with the semifantasy *White Wings* (1926) and the curious Biblical piece *John* (1927), dealing with John the Baptist. Both failed to run, but he had a major hit with *Paris Bound* (1927), a look at infidelity among the rich. Barry's subsequent plays met with varying degrees of success: the mystery *Cock Robin* (1928) written with Elmer *Rice, the civilized drawing room piece, *Holiday* (1928), the fantasy *Hotel Universe* (1930), the domestic drama *Tomorrow and Tomorrow* (1931), and the domestic comedy *The *Animal Kingdom* (1932). Deeply saddened by the death of his baby daughter, Barry took darker turns in his next plays: *The Joyous Season* (1934), a somber story of a nun's attempt to rejuvenate her family spiritually; *Bright Star* (1935), a gloomy tale of misguided ambition and tragic, misdirected love; and *Here Come the Clowns* (1938), an experimental piece concerning a confrontation between an old stagehand and God. Returning to the sort of play the theatre expected of him, Barry enjoyed his greatest success with the high comedy *The *Philadelphia Story* (1939), but the rest of his career was anticlimactic, filled with lesser works, such as the allegory *Liberty Jones* (1941), the Katharine *Hepburn vehicle *Without Love* (1942), the Tallulah *Bankhead vehicle *Foolish Notion* (1945), the adaptation of Jean Pierre Aumont's *My Name Is Aquilon* (1949), and the unfinished *Second Threshold* (1951), which Robert *Sherwood completed with little success. Generally considered our finest creator of high comedy, Barry's strange interplay of wit and despair gives his best works a dramatic tension and meaningfulness unique to our theatre. Biography: *Philip Barry*, Joseph P. Roppolo, 1965.

BARRY, Thomas (1798–1876), director and manager. Coming to America in 1826 from England, where he had performed a highly praised Hotspur to *Macready's Henry IV, Barry made his acting debut at the *Park Theatre, but he later found a major niche as a director, theatre manager, and occasionally as an author of such melodramas as *The Battle of Mexico*. He became the principal stage manager, as directors were then called, at the Park until he took over Boston's Tremont Theatre in 1833, running the latter house until 1839. He then returned to New York to act as manager first at the *Bowery Theatre and later again at the Park. From 1848 to 1851 he ran Boston's National Theatre and subsequently ran the Broadway in New York, the new Boston Theatre, and houses in Cincinnati and Chicago. Walter *Leman recalled his "expressing by a short, spasmodic laugh—something between the grunt which a pugilist would utter if hit below the belt, and the sharp bark of a dog—his opinion of anything not in accord with his taste or judgment."

BARRYMORE, Ethel (1879–1959), actress. Born in Philadelphia, daughter of Maurice *Barrymore and Georgiana Drew *Barrymore, she made her stage debut in 1894 playing opposite her grandmother Mrs. *Drew in *The Rivals*. After performing with her uncle, John *Drew, in *The Bauble Shop* later the same year, she assumed a number of other minor roles before sailing for London to play with William *Gillette in *Secret Service* and to act with Sir Henry *Irving's great company at the Lyceum. Back in America, Charles *Frohman recognized her growing talent and awarded her star billing as Madame Trentoni in *Captain Jinks of the Horse Marines* (1901) and she, indeed, became a star. Barrymore attempted Nora in *A Doll's House* (1905) and Mrs. Grey in *Alice Sit-by-the-Fire* (1905), but most of her assignments were in the polite, well-made importations that Frohman favored. More substantial roles in English works came her way when she played the falsely accused servant Mrs. Jones in *The Silver Box* (1907); the title part in *Lady Frederick* (1908); Zoe Blundell, whose marriage is destroyed by illness in *Mid-Channel* (1910); and Rose in *Trelawny of the Wells*. About this time she began filling in periods between plays with vaudeville tours in which she starred in short or abbreviated dramas, the most famous of which was *Barrie's *The Twelve-Pound Look*. She enjoyed one of her longest runs as the motherly business woman of *Our Mrs. McChesney* (1915), then turned to her own favorite role, Marguerite Gautier in Edward *Sheldon's redaction of *The Lady of the Camellias* (1917). Barrymore scored a major success as the self-destructive Lady Helen Haden in *Déclassée* (1919), only to come a cropper with her interpretation of Juliet (1922). Further revivals saw her play Paula in *The Second Mrs. Tanqueray* (1924), Ophelia, and Portia (1925). In 1926 she created one of her most memorable parts as Maugham's *The Constant Wife*, which she played until she assumed the role of Sister Gracia in *The Kingdom of God* (1928) at the opening of a New York theatre named in her honor. For the next decade success eluded her, albeit she gained some attention playing a 101-year-old grandmother in *Whiteoaks* (1938). Her finest achievement may well have been the compassionate schoolmarm, Miss Moffat, in *The Corn Is Green* (1940). Her last two shows, *Embezzled Heaven* (1944) and *The Joyous Season* (1945), the latter offered only on tour, were failures. John Mason *Brown remembered "the fluttering eyes, the throaty voice, and the imperious beauty, lending her special alchemy to Somerset Maugham's *The Constant Wife*," but many playgoers will recall her most fondly for the famous line she always delivered at the end of her curtain calls: "That's all there is, there isn't any more!" Autobiography: *Memories*, 1955; biography: *The House of Barrymore*, Margot Peters, 1990.

BARRYMORE, Georgiana [Emma] **Drew** (1856–93), actress. The daughter of Mrs. John *Drew, wife of Maurice *Barrymore, and mother of Lionel *Barrymore, Ethel *Barrymore, and John *Barrymore, she made her debut at her mother's *Arch Street Theatre in Philadelphia in 1872 in *The Ladies' Battle*. She continued under her mother's tutelage for several seasons before moving to New York where she first appeared for Augustin *Daly in 1876. There had been some suspicion that her favorable notices in Philadelphia were prompted by critics' affection for Mrs. Drew, but her New York reviews immediately won her recognition as a young actress of great promise. Barrymore's other notable roles, before and after the birth of her three children, include the comic Irish maid Grace in *Divorce, Maria in *The School for Scandal*; Eureka Grubb, the outspoken miner's daughter, in *Nadjezda* (1884); Madge Heskitt, the wronged wife, in *Jack* (1887); Lady Frank Brooks, the other woman, in *On Probation* (1889); Mrs. Hilary, the coquettish widow, in *The *Senator* (1890); Mrs. Rippendale, the impudent adventuress, in *Balloon;* and the title role of Mrs. Wakefield in *The Woman of the World* (these last two plays in an 1890 double bill). Joining Charles *Frohman's Comedians enabled her to play the comically jealous wife in *Mr. Wilkinson's Widows* (1891), the ludicrously sentimental Lucretia Plunkett in *Settled Out of Court* (1892), and Mrs. Briscoe, the neglected wife, in the farce *The Sportsman* (1893). The promising career of the tall, supple actress with large blue eyes was cut short by her early death. The *Journal* said of her, "Her intelligence, naïveté and personal graces, combined with the power of clear musical utterance, took a strong hold on popular appreciation."

BARRYMORE, John [Sidney Blythe] (1882–1942), actor. The younger son of Maurice *Barrymore and Georgiana Drew *Barrymore, he was born in Philadelphia and made his stage debut in Chicago in 1903 as Max in *Magda,* then made his New York debut in the same year as Corley in *Glad of It*. Supporting roles followed in *The *Dictator* (1904), *Yvette* (1904), *Sunday* (1905), *Alice Sit-by-the-Fire* (1905), and *Miss Civilization* (1906). For several seasons he played supporting roles before replacing the leading man in *The Boys of Company B* (1907), following that with the major role of Lord

Meadows in *Toddles* (1908). Later the same year Barrymore turned leading man in musical comedy, playing Mac, the sculptor, in *A Stubborn Cinderella*. For two years he portrayed Nat Duncan, the city slicker determined to win a rich hick, in *The *Fortune Hunter* (1909). A number of failures or modest successes followed, but with his performance as William Falder, the cruelly imprisoned clerk in *Justice* (1916), Barrymore abandoned more superficially theatrical roles and revealed surprising depth. His reputation grew with his *Peter Ibbetson* (1917), a man who attempts to transcend time, and with his Fedor Vasilyevich Protosov in Tolstoy's *Redemption* (1918). A major success, *The Jest* (1919), found him playing the put-upon hero Ginnetto to his brother *Lionel's villainous Neri. In the 1920s he played only three roles, two of which are generally acknowledged as the pinnacles of his career: in 1920 Richard III and in 1923 Hamlet, which established a New York long run for the play at the time. After many years in Hollywood he returned to Broadway briefly in a feeble comedy, *My Dear Children* (1939). Looking back, John Mason *Brown reminisced, "Although I have sat before many Hamlets, some better read and more solidly conceived, John Barrymore, with his slim, proud figure, the lean Russian wolfhound aquilinity of his profile, and the princely beauty of his full face, continues for me to be the embodiment of the Dane . . . though undisciplined, it crackled with the lightning of personality." There seems little disagreement that had he possessed the dedication and determination, he would have been the greatest actor of his generation. After 1925, however, the hedonistic actor dissipated his talents. His antics were satirized in the personage of the gadabout matinee idol Anthony Cavendish in *The *Royal Family* (1927), and decades later the actor was the focal character in a handful of plays, including *Ned and Jack* (1981), *I Hate Hamlet* (1991), *Jack* (1996), and *Barrymore* (1997). Biography: *Damned in Paradise: The Life of John Barrymore*, J. Kobler, 1977.

BARRYMORE, Lionel (1878–1954), actor. The elder son of Maurice *Barrymore and Georgiana Drew *Barrymore, he made his debut in his native Philadelphia in 1893, playing Thomas to the Mrs. Malaprop of his grandmother, Mrs. John *Drew. A year later he appeared with her again when making his New York debut in *The Road to Ruin*. Other early appearances were in *The Bachelor's Baby* (1895), *Mary Pennington, Spinster* (1896), *Squire Kate* (1896), *Cumberland '61* (1897), *Uncle Dick* (1898), and *Honorable John Grigsby* (1898). His colleagues' growing respect for his abilities prompted James A. *Herne to write a small role for him in *Sag Harbor*, but he made his first real hit as Giuseppe,

the organ grinder, in *The Mummy and the Humming Bird* (1902). Barrymore scored as prizefighter Kid in *The *Other Girl* (1903), the title role in *Pantaloon* (1905), the malicious Col. Ibbetson opposite his brother John in *Peter Ibbetson* (1917), and, in what many considered his finest performance, Milt Shanks, a Northerner suspected of Southern sympathies during the Civil War, in *The *Copperhead* (1918). In 1919 he was reunited with John, playing the villain Neri in *The Jest*, then played the cruel judge Mouzon in *The Letter of the Law* (1920), before he floundered as *Macbeth* (1921). His last successes were Achille Cortelon, the radical politician destroyed by his wife, in *The Claw* (1921), and Tito Beppi, a modern-day Pagliacci, in *Laugh, Clown, Laugh!* (1923). When a series of failures followed in 1925, he left Broadway permanently for the West Coast and the movies. John *Corbin wrote of his Neri, "Barrymore illumines it with a touch of genius. Malicious bully though the huge mercenary is, he is yet comprehensibly, deliciously human." While Lionel Barrymore may not have had quite the range or depth of his brother, he was a great actor who scarcely realized his potential. If dissipation kept John Barrymore from the stage, disinclination kept Lionel from it. He preferred the easy money of Hollywood, which allowed him to devote more time to his real loves, painting and music. A crippling illness, which later confined him to a wheelchair, precluded any return to the stage, even had he been so inclined. Autobiography: *We Barrymores*, 1951.

BARRYMORE, Maurice [né Herbert Blythe] (1849–1905), actor. Born in India, he studied law in London and won some fame as an amateur boxer before turning to the stage. After a few London appearances and an American debut in Boston in *Under the Gaslight*, he came to New York where in 1875 he first appeared for Augustin *Daly as Bob Ruggles in *The *Big Bonanza*, replacing John *Drew, whose niece Georgiana *Barrymore he later married. He was an immediate success and in quick succession played Talbot Champeys in *Our Boys*, Laertes and Aumerle opposite Edwin *Booth, Raymond Lessing in *Pique*, and Sir Frederick Blout in *Money*. Moving to *Wallack's, he portrayed, among others, Charles in *London Assurance* and Capt. Molineux in *The *Shaughraun*. In 1882 Barrymore joined Helena *Modjeska as her leading man, acting Orlando, Romeo, Sebastian, Armand, and roles in many now-forgotten contemporary pieces. He moved to A. M. *Palmer's company in 1888, where his parts included Wilding in *Captain Swift* and Captain Davenport in *Alabama*. His greatest role is generally considered to be Rawdon Crawley in *Becky Sharp* (1899), in which he played opposite Mrs. *Fiske. In his last active years, his erratic behavior, stemming from the paresis that ultimately killed him, caused producers to shun him, so he turned to vaudeville. Barrymore also wrote several plays, including *Blood Will Tell* (never produced in America), *Nadjezda* (1884), *The Robber of the Rhine* (1892), and *Roaring Dick & Co.* (1896). He later sued *Sardou, claiming the playwright had stolen the plot of *Nadjezda* for *Tosca,* but failed to prevent *Tosca's* American premiere. A fellow performer once described him as "a tall man, dark and pale, with cool Northern grey eyes. . . . He was lightly built, but of a round-muscled, strong shouldered powerful lightness." The *Evening Sun* observed, "As Rawdon Crawley he was superb. In looks, speech and manner he might have stepped directly out of Thackeray's pages. His performance was a blending of sterling manliness and the gentlest pathos." Biography: *Good Times/Great Times,* James Kotsilibas-Davis, 1977.

BARTER THEATRE (Abingdon, Virginia). In 1932, in the depths of the Great Depression, unemployed actor Robert Porterfield conceived the idea of establishing a theatre where impecunious playgoers could pay for tickets with foodstuffs in lieu of cash. A year later he opened his playhouse in Southwest Virginia. The group has flourished ever since, although most playgoers now pay for their seats in the customary way. However, a children's theatre still encourages youthful audiences to barter for tickets. Over the years the company has operated two theatres in Abingdon, performed at the Fairfax Theatre at George Mason University, and regularly toured the region. The repertory ranges from classics to modern plays. In 1946 the Barter Theatre became the official state theatre of Virginia, the first such honor accorded an acting company, and in 1948 received a special *Tony Award for its contribution to regional theatre. For many years the theatre offered the Barter Theatre of Virginia Award, presented to a notable actor or actress and providing the recipient with a ham, an acre of land in Abingdon, and the right to choose two young performers for the company's intern program. One of the oldest operating theatres in America, the Barter still sets aside performances in which patrons can pay by donations to area food banks.

BARTON, James (1890–1962), character actor. Born in Gloucester, New Jersey, he was carried on stage at the age of two by his actor parents, and made his vaudeville debut at the age of four. For many years he played the Midwest and the South in stock and repertory before making his New York debut in *The *Passing Show of 1919.* Appearances followed in *The Last Waltz* (1921), *The Rose of Stamboul* (1922), *Dew Drop Inn* (1923), *Passing Show*

of 1924, **Artists and Models* (1925), *No Foolin'* (1926), as Skid in a touring company of *Burlesque* (1927), and in *Sweet and Low* (1930). Between stage roles Barton was popular in vaudeville. In 1934 he succeeded Henry *Hull as Jeeter Lester in *Tobacco Road,* a part he played for more than five years. After several failures he distinguished himself as Hickey in *The *Iceman Cometh* (1946). In 1951 Barton returned to musicals to play Ben Rumson in *Paint Your Wagon.* His last Broadway appearance was as Pat in *The Sin of Pat Muldoon* (1957). Gravel-voiced, and with a fighter's punched-in face, he was most famous for his drunk routine, which he managed to insert in practically all his appearances.

BASIC TRAINING OF PAVLO HUMMEL, THE (1971), a play by David *Rabe. [*Public Theatre, 363 perf.] A hand grenade thrown in a Vietnam brothel ends the life of an American soldier, Pavlo Hummel (William Atherton). Flashing back, Pavlo is seen joining the army, eager to be a soldier and a hero. His gaucheries and his patently tall stories make him a butt of ridicule, but he is undeterred. His sergeant, Tower (Joe Fields), represents military establishment, which turns him into a benumbed orderly, while Ardell (Albert Hall), acting as an involved Greek chorus, comforts him and explains the often-baffling world to him. At the end of the play his coffin sits alone on the stage. Hailed by Clive *Barnes of the *Times* as introducing "a new and authentic voice to our theatre," the Joe *Papp production was the first in Rabe's trilogy on the war, the other plays being *Sticks and Bones* and *Streamers.* It employed the cinematic technique of short, quickly changing scenes to portray an unmitigated, often ugly, picture of war. As such it was a far cry from many more romantic earlier war plays. A Broadway revival starring Al *Pacino was a hit in 1977.

BAT, THE (1920), a mystery drama by Mary Roberts *Rinehart, Avery *Hopwood. [*Morosco Theatre, 867 perf.] The elderly spinster Cornelia Van Gorder (Effie *Ellsler) rents the summer home of a banker who reportedly has been killed, but who, it turns out, may have absconded after hiding stolen funds in the house. When a number of people are said to be after the money, Cornelia hires a detective to solve the mystery. But only after she and her guests are beset by sundry frightening occurrences, even murder, is it discovered that the detective is not the man he seems to be. The *Wagenhals and *Kemper–produced thriller was based on Rinehart's story "The Circular Staircase." For many contemporary playgoers, May Vokes's comic performance as the easily terrified maid was the high point of the evening.

When the play closed it was the second-longest-running show in Broadway history. Long popular in stock and amateur theatres, the play was revived in 1953 with Lucile Watson as Cornelia and Zasu Pitts as the maid. Curiously, when Alexander *Woollcott reviewed the original production for the *Tomes*, a production he found "thoroughly interesting," he suggested even then that Watson would have made the ideal Cornelia.

BATEMAN, H[ezekiah] L[inthicum] (1812–75), manager and actor. After making his stage debut in his native Baltimore in 1832, he continued acting for many years. However, when his daughters Kate and Ellen proved to be child prodigies, he gave up acting to take over their management. Thereafter he acted only on rare occasions, usually in support of his daughters or in one of his wife's plays. He himself wrote several plays for Kate, including *Rosa Gregorio; or, the Corsican Vendetta* (1862). His wife was playwright **Mrs. BATEMAN** [née Sidney Frances Cowell] (1823–81), a New Yorker, who also started her career as a performer but was best known for her playwriting. Her finest play was one of her first, *Self* (1856), a study of a girl with cruel, greedy parents. Among her later plays were *Geraldine; or, Love's Victory* (1858), a complicated tragedy of family feuds in the time of Edward I, and *Evangeline* (1860), a play written to allow Kate Bateman to portray the popular figure of Canadian and American legend. Their daughter **Kate BATEMAN** (1842–1917) was born in Baltimore and made her debut in 1846 in Louisville in *Babes in the Woods*. With her sister Ellen she then toured, as a child prodigy, in the leading roles of *Richard III (Kate was Richmond; Ellen, Richard) and other classics as well as in dramas written especially for them. In 1860 she won applause as an ingenue playing the title role of her mother's play *Evangeline*, but it was her performance as Julia in The *Hunchback in 1862 that raised her to star status. The next year she first essayed what became her most famous role, the title part of the Jewess deserted by her Christian lover in *Leah, the Forsaken*, co-produced by her father. Of her portrayal of Leah, the *Albion* wrote, "Its merits are strength, impetuosity and pathos. Its profound defect is its lack of emotional abandon." She also won praise for her Pauline in The *Lady of Lyons* (1866) and for her interpretation as the falsely accused and imprisoned heroine of *Mary Warner* (1869). Meanwhile, H. L. Bateman's production of *La Grande Duchesse de Gérolstein* (1867) began the long rage in America for French *opéra bouffe, and for two more years he continued mounting the operettas. In 1871 he and his wife followed Kate to London, where all three remained for the rest of their lives. Autobiography: (Mrs. Bateman): *Reminiscences*, 1873.

BATES, Blanche (1873–1941), actress. The daughter of a theatre manager and an actress, she was born in Portland, Oregon, and made her debut in San Francisco in 1894 as Mrs. Willoughby in *The Picture*, and then spent several seasons there in T. D. Frawley's stock company. Bates made her New York debut in 1897 as Bianca in The *Taming of the Shrew* with Augustin *Daly's company, later playing such roles as Celia in *As You Like It and Lady Sneerwell in *The School for Scandal*. She first called real attention to herself as Hannah Jacobs in *The Children of the Ghetto* (1899). Coming under David Belasco's management, Bates played briefly as the flirtatious model Cora in *Naughty Anthony* (1900), then won wide acclaim as Cho-Cho-San in *Madame Butterfly*. Other notable performances at the turn of the century include the Foreign Legion camp follower Cigarette in *Under Two Flags* (1910); the forlorn Oriental Yo-San in The *Darling of the Gods*; frontier tavern owner Minnie in The *Girl of the Golden West* (1905); Anna, the wife who destroys the evidence against her embezzling husband, in The *Fighting Hope* (1908); and Roxanna Clayton, who cannot rid herself of a philandering mate, in *Nobody's Widow* (1910). Leaving Belasco's management, Bates appeared in *Diplomacy* (1914), *Getting Together* (1918), and *Medea* (1919), performing in vaudeville between legitimate assignments. Among her late successes were the liberated Nancy Fair in The *Famous Mrs. Fair* (1919); Karen Aldcroft in a play about wife-switching, *The Changelings* (1923); and Maisie Partridge, the domineering mother, in *Mrs. Partridge Presents* (1925). After performing in repertory on the West Coast, Bates temporarily retired, only to return in 1933 to tour as Maud Mockridge, the dinner guest, in *Dangerous Corner*. Her last New York appearance was in 1933 as Lena, a small role in *The Lake*. When she appeared in *The Darling of the Gods*, the *Times* wrote of the "dark, animated" performer: "The acting of Miss Blanche Bates has, all along, shown a sweet wildness of impulse, a freedom of abandonment, a delightful impetuosity of feeling . . . spontaneous, graceful, alert with vigor and free from all restraint of self-consciousness and finical prudery."

BATTLE, Hinton (b. 1956), actor, singer, and dancer. The charismatic African-American performer, who has been singled out for praise each time he appears on Broadway, was born in Neubraecke, Germany, to American parents in the military, and grew up on bases in Florida, Kansas, and Washington, D.C. Battle attended UCLA and trained at the School of American Ballet and the Jones-Hayward School of Ballet before making a sensational New York debut in 1975 as the seemingly spineless Scarecrow in The *Wiz. He was also featured in the revues *Dancin' (1980) and *Sophisticated Ladies (1981) and played the Motown singing star James Thunder Early in *Dreamgirls (1983), the show biz hoofer Uncle Dipsey in The Tap Dance Kid (1983), the passionate GI John trying to save Amerasian kids in *Miss Saigon (1991), and the slippery lawyer Billy Flynn during the long run of *Chicago.

BAY, Howard (1912–86), scenic designer. Born in Centralia, Washington, he studied in a variety of fine schools before first winning public recognition with his set designs for *Federal Theatre productions, including Power and One Third of a Nation. Bay soon became one of Broadway's busiest designers, creating the sets for eleven shows in 1944 alone. Among his designs were The *Little Foxes (1939), The Corn Is Green (1940), The *Patriots (1943), *One Touch of Venus (1943), *Carmen Jones (1943), *Deep Are the Roots (1945), *Up in Central Park (1945), revivals of *Show Boat (1946, 1954, and 1960), *Come Back, Little Sheba (1950), The *Music Man (1957), and *Man of La Mancha (1965). He also directed shows, including As the Girls Go (1949) and There Are Crimes and Crimes (1951). Besides teaching at several universities, he wrote the respected book Stage Design (1975). It is hard to characterize Bay's work, other than remark on its virtually universal excellence. He himself consciously resisted being identified with any particular school. Howard Taubman of the Times praised his work for Man of La Mancha as "sparing in its furniture and props [but] rich in illusion."

BAYES, Nora [née Dora Goldberg?] (1880–1928), singer, songwriter. The earliest history of the famous vaudevillian is clouded by uncertainty about her real name and her birthplace, but it is known that she made her vaudeville debut in Chicago in 1899 and her Broadway stage bow two years later in The Rogers Brothers in Washington. In 1902 she popularized "Down Where the Wurzberger Flows," and her career progressed slowly but steadily thereafter. Major recognition came in 1908 when she left Al Fields, her old partner and manager, to marry and team with **Jack NORWORTH** [né John Knauff] (1879–1959). He was born in Philadelphia and ran away from home to join a minstrel show, later switching to vaudeville. The couple's act had one of the most famous of all vaudeville billings:

NORA BAYES

Assisted and Admired by Jack Norworth.

The twosome appeared in the Ziegfeld Follies of 1908, where they introduced their "Shine On Harvest Moon"; The Jolly Bachelors, in which she introduced "Has Anybody Here Seen Kelly?"; Little

Miss Fix-It (1911), for which she wrote many of the songs; and Roly Poly (1912). Norworth's career waned after 1913 though he still worked in vaudeville and penned song lyrics, most memorably "Take Me Out to the Ball Game." Bayes was featured in Maid in America (1915), The Cohan Revue (1917), Ladies First (1918), Her Family Tree (1920), Snapshots of 1921, and Queen o' Hearts (1922), but it was in vaudeville that she popularized such songs as "Over There," "Just Like a Gypsy," and "Japanese Sandman." Douglas Gilbert has written of the tiny, big-voiced performer, "Nora Bayes was the American Guilbert, mistress of gesture, poise, delivery and facial work. No one could outrival her in dramatizing a song."

BEACH, Lewis. See Goose Hangs High, The.

BEAR AND THE CUB, THE (1655) a play, presumably by an American, which became a cause célèbre in 1665. One Edward Martin accused Cornelius Watkinson, Philip Howard, and William Darby of acting "a play commonly called the Bear and the Cub" in Accomac County, Virginia, on August 27 of that year. The men were ordered to appear in court "in the habiliments which they had acted in" and to repeat their performance. Martin's charge of public wickedness was dismissed and he was ordered to pay court costs. Nothing is known about the play itself, but, for want of more complete early records, Watkinson, Howard, and Darby must be considered the earliest American actors, although they were almost certainly amateurs.

BEATON, Cecil [Walter Hardy] (1904–80), designer. The noted English scenic and costume designer sometimes provided both sets and costumes for Broadway productions, as with Lady Windermere's Fan (1946), The Grass Harp (1952), Quadrille (1954), The Chalk Garden (1955), Saratoga (1959), Tenderloin (1960), and Coco (1969). But he is remembered most for his sumptuous period costumes for *My Fair Lady (1956, 1976, 1981). Beaton was also a noted photographer. Biography: Cecil Beaton, Hugo Vickers, 1980.

BEATTY, John Lee (b. 1948), designer. He was born in Palo Alto, California, and educated at Brown University and Yale where he trained with designer Ming Cho *Lee. After designing many Off-Broadway productions at the *Circle Repertory Company and The *Manhattan Theatre Club, Beatty made his Broadway debut with The Innocents (1976). He is considered one of the finest designers of realism and naturalism in America, usually eschewing musicals and classical pieces and creating detailed and evocative settings for modern American dramas. Among the very prolific

Beatty's outstanding designs are *Talley's Folly (1979), Fools (1981), Alice in Wonderland (1982), Lips Together, Teeth Apart (1991), Redwood Curtain (1993), *Abe Lincoln in Illinois (1993), The *Heiress (1995), The *Last Night of Ballyhoo (1997), The *Little Foxes (1997), *Proof (2000), *Dinner at Eight (2002), and Master Harold . . . and the Boys (2003).

BEAU BRUMMELL (1890), a play in four acts by Clyde *Fitch. [*Madison Square Theatre, 150 perf.] Beau Brummell (Richard *Mansfield), vain, effete, and supercilious, cares only about the pleasures of life. He is totally irresponsible, telling his valet, Mortimer (W. J. Ferguson), to hide his bills where he "would not see them," so that he might "think that they are paid." Only his gambling debts are honored. To replenish his funds, he plans to marry Mariana Vincent (Agnes Miller), daughter of a rich London merchant, unaware that his own nephew Reginald (F. W. Lander) is courting her and has her affections. Brummell's haughtiness extends even to the Prince of Wales (D. H. Harkins), who at first is amused by the man's presumption. But when, on leaving a ball, Brummell snaps at the Prince, "I shall have to order my carriage. Wales, will you ring the bell?," he finally alienates the future king. Realizing the damage he has done to himself, he sends the Prince an expensive gift, only to have it publicly returned. He is further confounded to overhear Mariana and Reginald exchange endearments. Head high, he determines to leave London. Years later we see Brummell, aged, impoverished, and befriended only by his loyal valet, as he sits in his French rooms by the light of a single candle and entertains his old companions, now merely phantoms of his mind, at a regal, if imaginary, supper. The play was Fitch's first major play, although producer and star Mansfield attempted to take credit for it. Fitch replied, "The execution . . . some of the business, and the great bulk of the dialogue is mine. The artistic touch, some of the lines in the comedy, not the most important ones, and the genius that has made it a success are Mr. Mansfield's." Certainly many critics held that it was Mansfield's finest delineation, and he kept it in his repertory until his death. Arnold *Daly later performed it successfully.

BEAUCAIRE (1901), a comedy by Booth *Tarkington, Evelyn Greenleaf *Sutherland. [Herald Square Theatre, 64 perf.] Because his escapades have forced him into hiding, the Duc d'Orleans (Richard *Mansfield) has disguised himself as a French barber, Monsieur Beaucaire, in Bath, England. Yet even his somewhat precarious position cannot restrain the fun-loving nobleman from further ad-venture. When he catches the Duke of Winterset (Joseph Weaver) cheating at cards, he threatens to expose him if the Duke refuses to introduce him into society as a French gentleman. Beaucaire's charm and breeding make him instantly welcome, and he successfully courts Lady Mary Carlisle (Lettice Fairfax). But his newfound friends reject him savagely when they are given to understand he is merely a barber. He returns as the rightful Duc and courteously puts them in their places. This comic attack on society's often-absurd distinctions was based on Tarkington's novelette Monsieur Beaucaire. Star and producer Mansfield, convinced by the failure of his Monsieur de Jadot that Americans were embarrassed by their inability to pronounce "monsieur" correctly, insisted on the shortened title. The success of the production helped the young *Shubert brothers start their first New York theatre on a firm footing and Mansfield kept the play in his repertory until his death. It was later made into a popular operetta by André Messager.

BEAUTY AND THE BEAST (1994), a musical fantasy by Linda Woolverton (book), Alan *Menken (music), Howard *Ashman, Tim *Rice (lyrics). [*Palace Theatre, still running.] The timeless tale of an arrogant prince (Terrence Mann) turned into a beast and saved by the love of a beauty (Susan Egan) had been Broadwayized into a popular 1991 animated film. *Disney recreated this musical version on Broadway with a first-class production filled with some stunning special effects. Notable songs: Beauty and the Beast; Be Our Guest; Belle; Me; Gaston. Because Ashman had died in 1991, Rice teamed up with Menken to write additional songs for the stage score. Several critics dismissed the musical as a theme park show, but audiences continue to enjoy the lavish, tuneful production.

BECK, Martin (1865–1940), theatre owner and manager. Details of his early years are uncertain. He emigrated from Germany while still a young man and soon became manager of a Chicago beer garden, where he induced the owner to build a stage and offer variety acts, and where he earned the nickname "Two Beers Beck." In the 1890s he joined the young *Orpheum circuit, bought into the group, and around 1906 became head of its New York office. In 1913 he opened the *Palace Theatre in New York and quickly made it vaudeville's mecca, although E. F. *Albee soon wrested control of the house from him. Profiting from his experience, he later built the Martin Beck Theatre, the first major legitimate playhouse west of Eighth Avenue and the only legitimate theatre with no mortgage. He also dabbled in producing and was the first man to bring the modern *D'Oyly Carte company to America.

BECKETT, Samuel [Barclay] (1906–90), playwright. The Irish dramatist, whose absurdist, usually actionless, and fundamentally philosophic plays have delighted a coterie of intellectuals and experimental playgoers, is best remembered for his *Waiting for Godot* (1956), which enjoyed a long run on Broadway in large measure because of the performance of Bert *Lahr, a musical comedy clown. However, for the most part Beckett has found success not in mainstream playhouses but *Off Broadway and at more adventuresome regional theatres. Among his best-known works are *Endgame* (1958), *Krapp's Last Tape* (1960), and *Happy Days* (1961). Beckett wrote his plays in French and lived in Paris after 1937. Biography: *Samuel Beckett: The Last Modernist*, Anthony Cronin, 1997.

BECKY SHARP (1899), a play by Langdon *Mitchell. [*Fifth Avenue Theatre, 116 perf.] The adventurous, unprincipled Becky (Mrs. *Fiske) rises from nothing into a life of luxury by secretly marrying Rawdon Crawley (Maurice *Barrymore) while at the same time accepting money from the Marquis of Steyne (Tyrone *Power). When the two men confront each other, Becky seems doomed. But, ever resourceful, she begins to wheedle a new life from the fatuous Joseph Sedley (William F. Owen) and young Sir Pitt Crawley (Robert V. Ferguson). The play, derived from Thackeray's *Vanity Fair*, gave producer-star Mrs. Fiske one of her greatest successes, despite the efforts of the *Theatrical Syndicate to keep it off the boards. She revived it on several occasions over the next twenty years. The *Players produced it in 1929.

BEDFORD, Brian [Anthony] (b. 1935), actor and director. One of the finest classical actors on two continents, the English actor has spent much of his career acting and directing at the Stratford Shakespeare Festival in Canada but has appeared on Broadway sporadically over a forty-year period. Bedford first called attention to himself in America in two importations: *Five Finger Exercise* (1958) and the double bill of *The Private Ear* and *The Public Eye* (1963). Among his memorable performances in the States are the self-righteous General in *The Unknown Soldier and His Wife* (1967), a dry and droll Elyot Chase in *Private Lives* (1969), the absent-minded moral philosopher George in *Jumpers* (1974), British actor William Charles *Macready caught in the *Astor Place Riots in *Two Shakespearean Actors* (1992), and the lordly fop Harcourt Courtley in *London Assurance* (1996). But it was Bedford's classical portrayals that have been particularly cherished, from Molière clowns

to Shakespearean kings. He is a very average-looking actor, but on stage his subtle gestures and crystal-clear voice combine to create magical performances.

BEECHER, Janet [née Meysenburg] (1884–1955), actress. She was born in Jefferson City, Missouri, and was raised in Chicago where her father was German vice-consul. After schooling in Chicago and New York, Beecher made her professional debut in a walk-on role on Broadway in 1903. But she gained attention the next year as the newly wealthy Ida Pipp in *The Education of Mr. Pipp* and played it for two seasons. Among her notable parts were Helen Heyer, who wins her man in a raffle, in *The *Lottery Man* (1909); the uncomplaining wife Helen Arany of a temperamental genius in *The Concert* (1910); the outgoing wife Laura Bartlett in *Fair and Warmer* (1915); Margaret Fairfield, who is caught between an old love and a new one, in *A Bill of Divorcement* (1921); and the widow Mary Colebrook who stands by her illegitimate son in *Courage* (1928). After spending the 1930s in films she scored one final success as Catherine, wife of *The Late George Apley* (1944). Despite playing leading roles on Broadway for more than twenty years, Beecher never achieved star status.

BEGGAR ON HORSEBACK (1924), a play by George S. *Kaufman and Marc *Connelly. [*Broadhurst Theatre, 224 perf.] Neil McRae (Roland *Young) is a talented serious composer who barely makes a living doing hack orchestrations. He is so impractical that his neighbors, Cynthia Mason (Kay Johnson) and Dr. Albert Rice (Richard Barbee), must look after him without seeming to do so, while Gladys Cady (Ann Carpenter), daughter of a rich widget manufacturer from Neil's hometown, is determined to marry Neil. Mr. Cady (George W. Barbier) encourages the match, offering to take Neil into the widget business, and promising that it will even be all right for Neil to compose popular songs on the side, so long as the songs make a million dollars. When Neil takes a sleeping pill Dr. Rice has given him, he dreams of marriage to Gladys, whose wedding bouquet is made of banknotes, and of their home where six butlers announce every caller and where he must fill out requisition forms to obtain a pencil. His new life drives Neil to murder his in-laws. At his trial "Judge" Cady, proclaiming, "This thing of using the imagination has got to stop," sentences Neil to work in an art factory, mass-producing masterpieces. When he wakes from his dream, Neil decides to marry Cynthia instead of Gladys. Producer Winthrop *Ames had given the authors a copy of a German play, *Hans Sonnenstössers Höllenfahrt*, and asked them to adapt it. For all practical purposes, the finished work was a new play, but it fell in with the vogue for *Expressionism. Alexander *Woollcott wrote that it represents "the distaste that can be inspired by the viewpoint, the complacency and the very idiocy of Rotarian America. It is a small and facetious disturbance in the rear of the Church of the Gospel of Success." A lavish 1970 revival at *Lincoln Center, described by John Chapman of the *New York Daily News* as the "most elaborate production I have ever seen at the Vivian Beaumont," was a "gigantic, monstrous curio" that put the struggling company deeper in debt.

BEGLEY, Ed[ward] (1901–70), character actor. Born in Hartford, Connecticut, he ran away from home and school when he was eleven to work in a traveling carnival. Begley later got work as a radio announcer and made his Broadway debut in 1943. He was a large, powerful character actor who specialized in gruff characters, particularly corrupt politicians and businessmen, but he also had a gentle side, as seen in his complex portrayal of the guilty father Joe Keller in *All My Sons* (1947). Begley's other memorable stage role was the belligerent prosecutor Matthew Harrison Brady in *Inherit the Wind* (1955) and the next year he played his rival, the gentle defense attorney Drummond.

BEHMAN, Louis C. See Hyde and Behman.

BEHOLD THE BRIDEGROOM (1927), a play by George *Kelly. [*Cort Theatre, 88 perf.] Spoiled and pampered Antoinette Lyle (Judith *Anderson) returns home from Europe, so bored and lonely that her friends suggest she marry Gehring Fitler (Lester Vail) who long has courted her. But "Tony" rejects him as an alcoholic ne'er-do-well and is not interested in any of her rich beaus until she meets the handsome, reserved businessman Spencer Train (John Marston), "the first man that ever held me cheap." Realizing not only that she is in love but that her life until then has been a waste, Tony is devastated when Spencer does not return her affection. Her father (Thurston *Hall) offers to intercede, but Tony refuses and fatalistically accepts that she is not ready for the "bridegroom" or the singular redemption he might offer. The play, which competed with ten other openings on the busiest first night in Broadway's history, baffled many critics and playgoers with its vague, somewhat mystical ending. Its fine dialogue, honesty, and inexorability make it, nonetheless, as close as Kelly ever came to writing high tragedy.

BEHRMAN, S[amuel] **N**[athaniel] (1893–1973), playwright. Born in Worcester, Massachusetts, he studied at Clark University before enrolling in Professor George P. *Baker's *47 Workshop at Harvard. Behrman worked as book reviewer, play reader, and press agent before he turned to playwriting. His first two efforts, written with others, never reached New York, but he scored with his first solo effort, *The *Second Man* (1927). Behrman found little success with *Love Is Like That* (1927), *Serena Blandish* (1929), *Meteor* (1929), and *Brief Moment* (1931), but he triumphed with what is considered his finest work: *Biography* (1932). Somewhat less successful were *Rain from Heaven* (1934) and *End of Summer* (1936). In 1937 he adapted Jean *Giraudoux's *Amphitryon 38* for the *Lunts, but in the following year came a cropper with *Wine of Choice*. Another high point in Behrman's career was *No Time for Comedy* (1939), but his serious drama *The Talley Method* (1941) did not run. Returning to comedy and to the Lunts, he scored a popular success with *The *Pirate* (1942). A second comic adaptation, from Franz Werfel, won favor as *Jacobowsky and the Colonel* (1944), a saga of a Jewish refugee and an anti-Semitic Polish colonel together fleeing the Nazis. His drama *Dunnigan's Daughter* (1945) and character study *Jane* (1947), based on a Somerset *Maugham story, could not find an audience, while an adaptation of Marcel Achard's *Auprès de Ma Blonde* as *I Know My Love* (1949) ran largely on the appeal of the Lunts. After two attempts that closed out of town, Behrman had a hit when he co-wrote the libretto for *Fanny* (1954) with Joshua *Logan. In 1958 he offered *The Cold Wind and the Warm*, a semi-autobiographical look at Jewish life in his hometown at the turn of the century, and in 1962 wrote *Lord Pengo*, which was loosely based on his biography of the famous art dealer Duveen. Berhman's last play, which he called a "serious comedy," was *But for Whom Charlie* (1964), which depicted the exploitation of a selfless philanthropist. Like those of his closest rival in the field of high comedy, Philip *Barry, Behrman's writings were marked by a distinctive dichotomy. But whereas Barry's best work drew strength from his interweaving of wit and despair, Behrman's sometimes profited and sometimes was hurt by his unique mixture of brilliant, high social comedy and increasingly strong political (leftish) colorings. Joseph Wood *Krutch observed in *Literary History of the United States,* "Faced with the problem of writing comedy in an atmosphere which many are ready to say makes comedy either impossible or impertinent, he thus invented something which might not improperly be called the comedy of illumination." Autobiography: *People in a Diary,* 1972; biography: *S. N. Behrman,* K. Reed, 1975.

BEL GEDDES, Barbara (b. 1922), actress. She was born in New York, the daughter of scenic designer

Norman *Bel Geddes, and made her debut as a walk-on in summer stock in 1940. The next year she came to Broadway as Dottie Coburn, a fledgling actress, in *Out of the Frying Pan*, then toured for the USO as the over-imaginative Judy in *Junior Miss*. After appearing in several failures, Bel Geddes began to earn attention as Cynthia Brown, the daughter who encourages her father to have an affair, in *Little Darling* (1942), followed by her coed-turned-detective Alice, in *Nine Girls* (1943) and Wilhelmina in *Mrs. January and Mr. X* (1944). She first won important recognition as Genevra Langdon, the sympathetic younger daughter, in *Deep Are the Roots* (1945), then scored a major success as the naive actress Patty O'Neill in *The *Moon Is Blue* (1951). Turning again to more serious roles, she portrayed the suicidal Rose Pemberton in *The Living Room* (1954) and Maggie, the unloved wife, in *Cat on a Hot Tin Roof* (1955). Bel Geddes shone as the American chorine Mary in *The Sleeping Prince* (1956) and the lonely Katherine Johnson in *Silent Night, Lonely Night* (1959), but her biggest hit came as the contrary heroine of *Mary, Mary* (1961). Her final roles were the bored housewife-turned-prostitute in *Everything in the Garden* (1967) and the loyal wife Katy Cooper in *Finishing Touches* (1973) before concentrating on television. A strapping blonde, Bel Geddes's performance in *Deep Are the Roots* was praised by Lewis Nichols in the *Times* as having "grace and tenderness and an honesty which breathes life into the part," while Brooks *Atkinson later wrote in the same paper that her acting in *Mary, Mary* had "an agreeably light touch; her quirk of pausing for quick intakes of breath in the midst of phrases, whether a habit or not, seems felicitous."

BEL GEDDES, Norman [né Norman Melancton Geddes] (1893–1958), scenic designer. Born in Adrian, Michigan, he studied at art schools in Cleveland and Chicago before his first designs were seen at Los Angeles's Little Theatre in 1916. Coming to New York under the auspices of Otto Kahn, he created the sets for several Metropolitan Opera productions before turning to Broadway, where his work was seen in, among others, a revival of *Erminie* (1920), *The Truth About Blades* (1921), *The Rivals* (1922), *The School for Scandal* (1923), *Reinhardt's *The Miracle* (1924), *Lady, Be Good!* (1924), *Jeanne d'Arc* (1925), *Ziegfeld Follies of 1925*, *Julius Caesar, The Five O'Clock Girl* (1927), *The Patriot* (1928), *Fifty Million Frenchmen* (1929), *Lysistrata* (1930), *Raymond Massey's *Hamlet* (1931), *Flying Colors* (1932), *Dead End* (1935), *Iron Men* (1936), *The Eternal Road* and *Siege* (1937), *It Happened on Ice* (1940), and *Seven Lively Arts* (1944). Although not an architect, he designed several theatres. Bel Geddes's interests were so broad that he eventually

drifted away from the theatre, but in his earliest days he pioneered in abandoning the proscenium and foresaw the vogue for arena stages. He was an ardent modernist, so his 1920s' musical sets were masterpieces of art deco. However, his most famous theatrical achievements were his settings for *The Miracle, Hamlet*, and *Dead End*. Writing of the first, the *Times*'s John *Corbin observed, "The cathedral into which the Century Theatre has been transformed . . . is indescribably rich in color, unimaginably atmospheric in its lofty, aerial spaces." His *Hamlet* made ingenious use of stairways and rostrums to suggest the various settings. Autobiography: *Miracle in the Evening*, 1960.

BELASCO, David (1853–1931), playwright, producer, and director. He was born in San Francisco to parents of Portuguese-Jewish origin whose name had once been Velasco, and his father had played in London pantomimes. Details about his early years are obscure, but the boy apparently came under the tutelage of a Father McGuire and, even after he ran away from home, Belasco retained an affection for the priest and later claimed his affectation of wearing a clerical collar to be in his honor. It is believed that he made his acting debut in 1864 playing the young Duke of York opposite Charles Kean's Richard III, and at the age of twelve he wrote his first play, *Jim Black; or, The Regulator's Revenge*. By 1873 he was a callboy at the Metropolitan Theatre in San Francisco, but he continued to act as well, performing with John *McCullough, Edwin *Booth, and other leading players. A year later in Virginia City, Nevada, he met Dion *Boucicault, from whom he learned much about acting, directing, and playwriting. Returning to San Francisco, Belasco became an assistant stage manager for Thomas *Maguire and then managed the *Baldwin Theatre for James A. *Herne. Some of his earliest plays, such as *La Belle Russe*, a tale of female treachery, and *The Stranglers of Paris*, which William *Winter called "a repulsive sensation melodrama" and Belasco himself later dismissed as "buncombe," were first mounted at the Baldwin in 1881. The next year he came to New York, where he served as stage manager of the *Madison Square Theatre, later serving in the same capacity for Daniel *Frohman at the *Lyceum. During this time he also wrote a number of plays with Henry C. *de Mille, including, *The *Wife* (1887); *Lord Chumley* (1888), centering on an English eccentric; *The *Charity Ball* (1889); and *Men and Women* (1890). In 1888 Belasco staged Sophocles' *Electra* for the *American Academy of Dramatic Arts in a mounting years ahead of its time in its stark simplicity. Thereafter his luck seemingly ran out until Charles *Frohman asked him to write a play to open the *Empire Theatre. The result was a collaboration with Franklin *Fyles, The *Girl I Left Behind Me (1893), whose love story was set against a background of soldiers and Indians. He firmly established himself as a playwright, producer, and director with the Civil War romance The *Heart of Maryland (1895), followed by the French adaptation Zaza (1899), the slight farce Naughty Anthony (1900), the Japanese tale *Madame Butterfly (1900), the period piece *Du Barry (1901), the touching melodrama The *Auctioneer (1901), the gripping Oriental drama The *Darling of the Gods (1902), the charmer *Sweet Kitty Bellairs (1903), the costume tragedy *Adrea (1905), the frontier romance The *Girl of the Golden West (1905), the Spanish-American melodrama The *Rose of the Rancho (1906), the domestic drama A *Grand Army Man (1907), the supernatural character piece The *Return of Peter Grimm (1911), the tragic revenge play The Son-Daughter (1919), and the French adaptation Kiki (1921). Several of these were cowritten with playwrights John Luther *Long, Charles *Klein, and others. Among the many plays that Belasco produced but in which he had little or no hand in writing were The *Music Master (1904), The *Fighting Hope (1908), The *Easiest Way (1909), The *Woman (1911), The *Boomerang (1915), *Polly with a Past (1917), *Tiger Rose (1917), *Daddies (1918), and *Lulu Belle (1926). In 1901 he leased the Republic Theatre, renaming it the Belasco; but in 1906 he built his own house, calling it the Stuyvesant at first but later gave it his own name.

Belasco was obsessed with realism on stage, in one play re-creating a Child's restaurant in which fresh coffee was brewed and pancakes made. Although many critics felt his determined "arch-realism" of setting masked a lack of artistic seriousness, Walter Prichard *Eaton attempted a balanced assessment when he wrote, "What Mr. Belasco has done has been to write pieces for the play-house, not criticisms of life . . . he has bent his mind to devise them with all possible air of probability and with all possible fidelity of pictorial setting. Especially in the latter respect he has succeeded as no other man of our time has." Many of his better plays, as well as those of fellow authors that he mounted, retain a theatrical effectiveness and might well succeed in an open-minded theatre that does not largely reject its past. Belasco's off-stage life was in some ways as extravagant and carefully staged as his plays. One favorite trick was a temper tantrum in which he would stamp on his own watch, smashing it into uselessness. Close associates knew he kept a stock of cheap, secondhand watches for just such occasions. Biography: The Bishop of Broadway, Craig Timberlake, 1954.

BELASCO THEATRE (New York). Producer-playwright David *Belasco built this up-to-date theatre in 1907 on West 44th Street with a modern stage lighting system to show off his realistic productions. Since he already had another theatre named the Belasco, he called this one the Stuyvesant, but three years later Belasco renamed it after himself when he lost the earlier house. George Keister designed the 1,100-seat theatre that boasted a complex dimmer board, an elevator stage, and a private apartment overhead for Belasco. It opened with A *Grand Army Man, cowritten and directed by the owner, and later featured such famous Belasco productions as The *Return of Peter Grimm (1911), Kiki (1921), *Lulu Belle (1926), and The Governor's Lady (1912) in which he recreated Child's restaurant onstage. The house became an NBC broadcasting studio in 1950 but three years later regained its legitimate status and has been in use as a theatre ever since. In 1991 the Shubert-owned house became the home of Tony *Randall's National Actors Theatre, but other tenants have used it as well.

BELL, BOOK AND CANDLE (1950), a comedy by John *van Druten. [*Ethel Barrymore Theatre, 233 perf.] Gillian Holroyd (Lilli Palmer) is a witch who is certain that through her black arts she can get anything she wants, including the publisher in the neighboring apartment, Shep Henderson (Rex *Harrison). He promptly knocks on her door and falls in love with her and in no time they are set to be married. The happy arrangement is spoiled when Gillian fights with her brother and aunt, who are also witches, and they spill the beans to Shep. To keep Shep she gives up witchery. The play, which the Times described as "completely enchanting . . . a wonderfully suave and impish fancy," gave promise of having a long run, but when Harrison and Miss Palmer left the cast, the producer was unable to find suitable replacements and so closed the show while it was still doing good business. Later, road companies toured successfully with Rosalind *Russell and Dennis Price, and with Joan Bennett and Zachary Scott, starring.

BELL, C.W. See Parlor, Bedroom and Bath.

BELL, Digby [Valentine] (1849–1917), comic actor. Although the Milwaukee-born performer studied in Europe to become a concert singer, he made his mark as a comedian. Long associated with John *McCaull's productions, he first starred in the musical Jupiter (1892). Later he was the leading comedian in Lillian *Russell's company, appearing opposite her in such shows as Princess Nicotine and The *Grand Duchess. Much of Bell's later career was in nonmuscial plays or vaudeville. He was married for a time to Laura Joyce Bell (1854–1904), a popular contralto-character actress on the musical stage.

BELL FOR ADANO, A (1944), a drama by Paul *Osborn. [*Cort Theatre, 296 perf.] Major Victor Joppolo (Fredric *March), an Italian-American, arrives in Adano, Italy, during the war to head the Allied Military Government in that city. He is sympathetic to the needs of the Sicilians, but his commanding officer, who is stationed far away, is not. When the commander orders that carts not be allowed to impede modern traffic in the village, Joppolo ignores the order. His behavior is reported, and he is ordered transferred, but not before he has gotten the villagers one of the things they most want—a new bell to replace one that the Fascists melted down to make arms. Just as he is leaving, the new bell sounds for the first time. "It shakes the whole damned building," Joppolo proudly tells his sergeant. With the war still raging, a realistic treatment of its brutalities was out of the question. In a sense, this play, based on John Hersey's novel, looked back to the romantic war plays of earlier times. Thus while the Leland *Hayward production was unquestionably timely, it was also sentimental and idealistic.

BELLA UNION (San Francisco). Opening on Portsmouth Square as a combination gambling house, saloon, and variety theatre in October 1849, its first attraction was a minstrel show. The tenor of the establishment was set on opening night when one of the performers was shot and killed in an altercation that followed the show, but this very roughness remained part of the house's singular appeal. A San Francisco historian has noted, "What [audiences] wanted from the Bella Union—comfort, liquor, handsome women, entertainment without ornament—they could get nowhere else . . . the free-and-easy atmosphere, the laugh-and-grow-fat attitude, the pungent ribaldry of the Bella Union could be had elsewhere only in duplicate of the original." Gambling was abolished in 1856, and the house became known as a "melodeon," a local term for a vaudeville theatre. Rebuilt after several fires, the original building was demolished in 1868, and the proprietor, Samuel Tetlow, opened a new theatre on its site. It remained active until 1895, when it was converted into a museum. The structure was destroyed in the earthquake and fire of 1906. Among the important performers who began to learn their trade there were Edward *Harrigan and Charlotte *Crabtree.

BELLAMY, Ralph (b. 1904–91), actor. The Chicago-born leading man made his debut in a 1922 production of *The Shepherd of the Hills* on the Chautauqua Circuit and after many seasons in stock first appeared on Broadway in *Town Boy* (1929). A long career followed in films before he returned to New York to create the role of Michael Frame, who helps reeducate a young Nazi, in *Tomorrow the World* (1943). He next scored major successes as presidential candidate Grant Matthews in *State of the Union* (1945) and as the dedicated but harsh Detective McLeod in *Detective Story* (1949). Bellamy's last appearance was generally regarded as his finest: Franklin Roosevelt in *Sunrise at Campobello* (1958). Louis *Kronenberger called Bellamy's Tony Award–winning performance an "extraordinarily effective impersonation of Roosevelt—in his coping with wheelchairs and crutches and braces, in his conversion of the humiliating into the heroic—there was no trace of either virtuosity or tear-jerking vaudevillism; there was a sense of characterization and indeed of character."

BELLE OF NEW YORK, THE (1897), a musical comedy by Hugh *Morton (book, lyrics), Gustave *Kerker (music). [*Casino Theatre, 56 perf.] Violet Gray (Edna *May), a Salvation Army lass, takes it upon herself to reform the spendthrift ways of Harry Brown (Harry Davenport), who has been cast out by his hypocritical, crusading father, Ichabod (Dan *Daly). So grateful is Ichabod that he is prepared to break his son's engagement to another girl, Cora (Ada Dare), and force him to marry Violet. Realizing that Harry and Cora are very much in love, Violet purposely alienates Ichabod by singing a risqué ditty. *Notable songs*: The Purity Brigade; She Is the Belle of New York; They All Follow Me. Although the George *Lederer–produced musical's run in New York was brief, it was taken to London, where it became the first American musical to achieve real success, compiling 674 performances in the West End. It was also mounted with great success on the Continent. While there have been a number of important and profitable European revivals, the musical has never been given a major rehearing in America except for a 1921 rewriting called *The Whirl of New York*.

BELLEW, [Harold] Kyrle (1855–1911), actor. After spending time in the Royal Navy and appearing on English and Australian stages, he came to America in 1885 and made his debut with *Wallack's company as Hubert Hastings in *In His Power*. Bellew continued with the troupe, playing such classic roles as Captain Absolute and parts in popular melodramas of the day, such as Lt. Kingsley in *Harbour Lights* and the title role in an adaptation of *Tom Jones*. In the 1890s he toured as leading man to Mrs. J. *Brown-Potter, a rich woman determined to make her mark as an actress. Again he moved from contemporary parts to classics, such as Antony and Romeo. Bellew retired from the stage and spent several years in Australia, where he is reputed to have made a modest fortune, but returned to America to essay the swashbuckling hero of A *Gentleman of France (1901), Charles Surface in The School for Scandal (1902), and Romeo to Flora Robson's Juliet in 1903. He then had major hits as *Raffles, Chevalier de Vaudrey in an all-star revival of The *Two Orphans (1904), and Richard Voysin in The Thief (1907). A critic in Harper's Weekly wrote of Bellew, "He poses and struts, yet one has to confess that his poses are graceful, and his struttings recall a pleasurable memory of days gone by."

BELLS ARE RINGING (1956), a musical comedy by Betty *Comden, Adolph *Green (book, lyrics), Jule *Styne (music). [*Shubert Theatre, 924 perf.] Ella Peterson (Judy *Holliday), the friendly operator for Susanswerphone, often gets involved with her unseen clients and even falls for the playwright Jeff Moss (Sydney Chaplin). When she finally meets Jeff face-to-face she is not disappointed but complications set in, augmented by bookies using the answering service to take horse-racing bets, which lead the police to Ella and her boss (Jean *Stapleton). Notable songs: The Party's Over; Just in Time; Long Before I Knew You; I'm Going Back. The lighthearted *Theatre Guild production was a tailor-made vehicle for Holliday whose *Tony Award–winning performance was a delight. Faith *Prince was also praised as Ella in the 2001 Broadway revival, though the show had a short run.

BEN-HUR (1899), a melodrama by William *Young. [*Broadway Theatre, 194 perf.] After a prologue recounting the legend of the three wise men, the story centers on Ben-Hur (Edward Morgan), a good-natured Roman Jew who is betrayed into servitude on a galley by his treacherous friend Messala (William S. *Hart). Later freed by a man whose life he saved, Hur is given a good education and eventually leaves for Antioch, where his father's old servant Simonides (Henry Lee) has carefully husbanded the Hur fortune. Learning that his false friend Messala has entered a chariot race, Hur enters his own name as well. Bets carefully placed by Hur and Simonides prompt Messala to stake his whole fortune on the race. Messala attempts to panic Hur's horses, but Hur interlocks his wheels with Messala's, who is thrown and crippled. Hur wins the race. Messala is later murdered, and Hur becomes a devout Christian. Lew Wallace, whose popular novel was the source of the play, had originally refused offers from several producers to dramatize the play. The production that *Klaw and *Erlanger mounted was one of the most extravagant ever seen on Broadway. Besides twenty-two speaking principals, there were eighty in the chorus and more than a hundred supers. The chariot race, using real horses (part of the time on treadmills), was as spectacular as theatrical design of the period could make it. The more serious critics were displeased, Walter Prichard *Eaton dismissing it as "a thing of bombastic rhetoric, inflated scenery, pasteboard piety, and mechanical excitement." The play was presented by innumerable touring companies, some of dubious quality, and was regularly revived successfully in major houses as late as 1916, when films began to offer a superior medium for spectacle and such theatrical mountings came to seem ludicrous by comparison.

BEN-AMI, Jacob [né Shtchirin] (1890–1977), actor. He was born in Minsk, Russia, and acted for Yiddish companies in Odessa, Vilna, and even London before immigrating to America in 1912. Ben-Ami soon joined Maurice *Schwartz's famous theatre at Irving Place, but found his purist ideals clashed with Schwartz's more pragmatic approach. In 1918 he came to the attention of Arthur *Hopkins, who encouraged him to improve his English and perform on Broadway. His first English-speaking role was as Peter Krumback in Samson and Delilah (1920). Thereafter he moved back and forth between American and Yiddish theatres. He played and directed for the *Theatre Guild and supported Eva *Le Gallienne at her *Civic Repertory Theatre (including Trigorin in The Sea Gull and Epihodov in The Cherry Orchard), as well as assuming important roles in other Broadway shows. He established a number of Yiddish theatre groups, dedicated to mountings of Yiddish classics and Yiddish translations of important works in other languages. Called "the knight of the Yiddish intelligentsia," he was praised by Stark *Young as "the most profoundly natural actor we have."

BENCHLEY, Robert [Charles] (1889–1945), writer, actor, and critic. Born in Worcester, Massachusetts, and educated at Harvard, the American humorist was once described by Helen *Hayes as "an enchanting toad of a man." He served as drama critic for Life (1920–29) and The New Yorker (1929–39), where his frequently iconoclastic reviews were leavened with common sense and wit. Examining a new Eugene *O'Neill play, he wrote, "Let us stop all this scowling talk about 'the inevitability of Greek tragedy' and 'O'Neill's masterly grasp of the eternal verities' and let us admit that the reason why we sat for six hours straining to hear each line through the ten-watt acoustics of the Guild Theatre was because Mourning Becomes Electra is filled with good, old-fashioned, spine-curling melodrama." Having to write weekly single-line summaries of each

Broadway show, he once summed up *Abie's Irish Rose,* which he hated, as "Hebrews 13:8." A look at the Bible revealed the reference was to the line "Jesus Christ, the same yesterday, and today, and forever." He also contributed sketches to *The 49ers* (1922) and The *Music Box Revue, 1923–24,* and collaborated with Fred Thompson on the libretto to *Smarty* (1927), which was rewritten without him as *Funny Face.* In the *Music Box Revue* he also performed his famous skit, "The Treasurer's Report." Biography: *Robert Benchley: His Life and Good Times,* Babette Rosmond, 1970.

BENEFITS. These became an American theatrical tradition early on as a means for actors to supplement their often meager salaries. Guest performers were customarily allowed benefits at the end of their visit, while regular members of a troupe had theirs at season's end. They were also offered occasionally to authors and others associated with the theatre. As a rule, the beneficiary was allowed a portion of the gross on a particular night, that portion growing in relation to his or her importance to the company. He or she was also allowed to plan the program. The seats allotted were usually handed over to the beneficiary, who became responsible for selling them. However worthy the practice in theory, it was employed so frequently that it became a nuisance. With the coming of the *Actors' Fund and the growth of unions, benefits were carefully regulated and greatly reduced in number, with the revenues usually accruing to the union or fund. In recent years they have all but disappeared, except for specially organized galas. In postwar theatre the term "benefit" was also applied to the block sale of huge numbers of seats for a particular performance of a show to a charitable group who would then resell the seats for the group's profit. As a result, for a time so many performances of a potential hit were sold out in advance that individual playgoers had difficulty obtaining seats at the box office. The practice has largely disappeared in recent seasons but a few forms arose in the 1980s when the AIDS epidemic struck the theatre so completely. Such organizations as Broadway Cares returned to the old practice of having special performances put aside to benefit AIDS research or hospice care. Some special events, such as the Easter Bonnet Competition, became annual affairs, and the sale of merchandise whose profits were designated for AIDS became a common sight by the 1990s.

BENNETT [Di Figlia], **Michael** (1943–87), choreographer and director. Born in Buffalo, he made his debut as a dancer in *Subways Are for Sleeping* (1961) and, after dancing in several other musicals, he choreographed the short-lived musicals *A*

Joyful Noise (1966) and *Henry, Sweet Henry* (1967). But Bennett's dances for *Promises, Promises* won him widespread recognition and he solidified his reputation with his choreography for *Coco* (1969), *Company* (1970), and *Follies* (1971), co-directing the last with Hal *Prince. He moved closer to totally controlling the conception of his musicals when he served as librettist, director, and choreographer for *Seesaw* (1973) and over the next several years he interviewed dancers and ran workshops to develop his greatest musical triumph, A *Chorus Line (1973). Although his *Ballroom* (1979) failed to run, Bennett had a final hit with *Dreamgirls* (1981) before his premature death. Frank *Rich wrote, "He keeps 'Dreamgirls' in constant motion—in every conceivable direction—to perfect his special brand of cinematic stage effects (montage, dissolve, wipe). . . . Throughout the show, Mr. Bennett uses shadows and klieg lights, background and foreground action, spotlighted figures and eerie silhouettes, to maintain the constant tension." Biography: *One Singular Sensation,* Kevin Kelly, 1990.

BENNETT, Richard (1873–1944), actor. Born in Deacon's Mills, Indiana, he made his debut in Chicago in 1891 as Tombstone Jake in *The Limited Mail,* and then played the role in New York later that year. For the next several seasons he toured in popular plays of the day and spent some time in stock, then in New York he appeared as the rich son Jefferson Ryder in the muckraking *The *Lion and the Mouse* (1905); the social climbing Lennard Willmore in *The Hypocrites* (1906); the first American John Shand, playing opposite Maude *Adams in *What Every Woman Knows* (1908); the ingratiating jewel thief Jack Doogan in *Stop, Thief* (1912); and George Dupont, the man victimized by hereditary venereal disease, in *Damaged Goods* (1913), which he co-produced. A series of failures ensued before Bennett had another long run as Peter Marchmont, who learns the secret of invisibility, in *The *Unknown Purple* (1918), followed by the doomed Robert Mayo in *Beyond the Horizon* (1920); the good brother, Andrew Lane, in *The *Hero* (1921); the tragic clown in *He Who Gets Slapped* (1922); and the barkeep Tony who inherits an English title in *The Dancers* (1923). One of Bennett's most memorable interpretations was Tony, the aging grape-grower, in *They Knew What They Wanted* (1924). His next success came four years later as Jack Jarnegan, the cynical film director, in *Jarnegan.* In 1932 he toured as Cyrano de Bergerac, then made his last Broadway appearance as Judge Gaunt in *Winterset* (1935). His screen actress daughter Joan Bennett described him as "a handsome, virile man with blue-gray eyes, a determined chin, a firm and generous mouth, and a magnificent speaking voice." An intellectual performer, he bore much of the credit for bringing a number of important plays to New York, such as *Beyond the Horizon*. Alexander *Woollcott hailed his Robert Mayo in that play as a performance of "fine eloquence, imagination and finesse." Biography: *The Bennett Playbill*, Joan Bennett and Lois Kibbee, 1970.

BENNETT, Robert Russell (1894–1981), orchestrator. He was born into a musical family and learned harmony, counterpoint, and composition under Carl Busch before migrating to New York from his native Kansas City, Missouri, in 1916 and getting work as a copyist with Schirmer, Inc. His first orchestrations were heard in *Hitchy Koo, 1919*. Among the more than three hundred musicals Bennett orchestrated were *Rose-Marie* (1924), *Show Boat* (1927), *Of Thee I Sing* (1931), *Music in the Air* (1932), *Anything Goes* (1934), *Oklahoma!* (1943), *Annie Get Your Gun* (1946), *Kiss Me, Kate* (1948), *South Pacific* (1949), The *King and I* (1951), *My Fair Lady* (1956), The *Sound of Music* (1959), and *Camelot* (1960). Bennett was the leading orchestrator of his day, and his rich, well-balanced arrangements established the Broadway musical "sound" for the 1940s, 1950s, and much of the 1960s.

BENNETT, Wilda (1894–1967), actress and singer. Born in Winnemucca, Nevada, she made her debut as Conscience in *Everywoman* (1911), but was best known as a leading lady in musicals. Her most noteworthy successes were *The Only Girl* (1914), in which she introduced "When You're Away"; *Apple Blossoms* (1919), in which she sang "You Are Free"; and the 1921 edition of the *Music Box Revue*, in which she introduced "Say It with Music."

BENRIMO, J[oseph] Harry (1874–1942), actor, playwright, and director. A theatrical jack-of-all-trades who often employed only his surname, he made his debut in his native San Francisco in 1892, playing there until 1897, when his performance as Hop Kee, the pipe-bowl vendor, in *The First Born* was seen by David *Belasco, who brought him east to re-create the role in New York. For the next two decades he appeared in important supporting roles in such plays as The *Conquerors* (1898), *Lord and Lady Algy* (1899), *In the Palace of the King* (1900), *Adrea* (1905), The *Girl of the Golden West* (1905), The *Rose of the Rancho* (1906), *Beethoven* (1910), and *Maggie Pepper* (1911). In collaboration with George C. Hazelton Jr., he wrote the enormously popular The *Yellow Jacket* (1912), purportedly based on several classic Chinese dramas, followed by *Taking Chances* (1915), which he and Agnes Morgan translated freely from a Continental comedy. In 1917 he

collaborated with Harrison Rhodes on "a fantasy of Japan," *The Willow Tree*. Early on he proved his skill as a director, staging not only all of his own plays but many others, especially for the *Shuberts.

BERG, Gertrude [Edelstein] (1899–1966), comic actress. A stereotypical plump, homey Jewish mother, the New Yorker adapted her radio character of Molly Goldberg into a starring vehicle, *Me and Molly* (1948). Later she played Mrs. Jacoby, who falls in love with a Japanese businessman, in A *Majority of One* (1959) and Libby Hirsch, who employs psychoanalysis to help her family, in *Dear Me, the Sky Is Falling* (1963).

BERGHOF, Herbert (1909–90), actor, director, and teacher. Born in Vienna, he studied at the Vienna State Academy of Dramatic Art and with Max *Reinhardt, then spent many years performing in Austria and Germany. Berghof first appeared on the New York stage in 1941 and went on to play many roles, most memorably in *Ibsen revivals of the late 1940s and early 1950s. He was also a respected director, staging the Broadway production of *Waiting for Godot* (1956), but he was best known as a leading teacher of acting. He taught at several noted institutions before founding his own studio in 1946, which he ran with his wife, Uta *Hagen.

BERGMAN, Ingrid (1915–82), actress. The wholesome-looking, blonde Swedish leading lady made her New York debut as Julie in a 1940 revival of *Liliom*, and in 1941 she toured in the title role of *Anna Christie*. After a highly successful career in films, Bergman returned to the stage as *Joan of Lorraine* (1946), then portrayed Deborah Harford, the loving mother of a weak son, in Eugene *O'Neill's *More Stately Mansions* (1967). Her last appearances were in revivals, playing Lady Cicely in *Captain Brassbound's Conversion* (1972) and Constance Middleton in *The Constant Wife* (1975).

BERGNER, Elisabeth (1900–86), actress. The famed Viennese-born leading lady came to America as a refugee and first appeared as the unwed mother Gemma Jones in *Escape Me Never* (1935). After some years in London, she returned to New York where she had her biggest success as Sally, whose husband tries to poison her, in The *Two Mrs. Carrolls* (1943). Bergner also successfully directed the comedy *The Overtons* (1945) and the next year was *The Duchess of Malfi*, acting opposite Canada *Lee. Her last American appearance was touring as Mrs. Patrick *Campbell in *Dear Liar* in the early 1960s.

BERKELEY, Busby [né William Berkeley Enos] (1895–1976), director and choreographer. Although best known for the mammoth precision dance routines he created in Warner Brothers films in the 1930s, he was briefly an important figure on Broadway. He came to New York from his native Los Angeles after touring in *The Man Who Came Back* (1917) and made his New York debut as a replacement for dress designer Madame Lucy in the original *Irene* (1919). After several years directing stock in New England and Canada, Berkeley returned to Broadway as choreographer for *Holka Polka* (1925), *The Wild Rose* (1926), *A *Connecticut Yankee* (1927), *The White Eagle* (1927), *Present Arms* (1928), *Earl Carroll Vanities* (1928), *Rainbow* (1928), *Pleasure Bound* (1929), *9:15 Revue* (1930), *International Revue* (1930), *Sweet and Low* (1930), and several others. While his Broadway routines featured the popular precision routines of the day, they were marked as well by an imaginative irreverence that sent dancers scampering over furniture and props. In 1970 Berkeley supervised the successful revival of *No, No, Nanette*.

BERKELEY REPERTORY COMPANY (Berkeley, California). Founded in 1968 by Michael Liebert, who served as artistic director for sixteen years, the company performed in a storefront and placed its emphasis on ensemble acting. As its reputation and audience grew, the company relocated in 1980 to a new facility that includes the 600-seat Roda Theatre and a 400-seat thrust stage. In its recent history (under the direction of Sharon Ott and then Tony Taccone), the Berkeley Rep has concentrated on new works and bold interpretations of the classics. In 1997 it won a *Tony Award for outstanding regional theatre.

BERKELEY SQUARE (1929), a drama in three acts by John L. Balderston. [*Lyceum Theatre, 229 perf.] In 1784 a young American, Peter Standish, comes to London to marry Kate Pettigrew (Valerie Taylor). In 1928 his descendant, also named Peter Standish (Leslie *Howard), has read all of his ancestor's diaries and correspondence and believes he knows the older man so well that he could exchange places with him, which he promptly does. But transported to the 18th century, things do not progress as smoothly for Standish as he had hoped, falling in love with Kate's sister Helen (Margalo *Gillmore). Once back in the 20th century, Peter learns from a tombstone that Helen died shortly after the original Peter resumed his rightful role. He tells his 20th-century sweetheart that he has decided to remain a bachelor, so she leaves as he slowly reads the inscription he has copied from the grave. Heywood *Broun in the *Telegram* called it "easily the finest play now to be seen in New York," while Burns *Mantle in his *Best Plays* observed, "It is neither fantasy nor

straight drama, but an artful combination of the two." Howard and Gilbert Miller produced the drama that was based on Henry James's unfinished *A Sense of the Past*. **John L[loyd] BALDERSTON** (1889–1954), a Philadelphia native who claimed descent from Betsy Ross, went to England as a journalist after failing to graduate from Columbia College. He wrote several successful plays while overseas, including a dramatization of *Dracula* presented in New York in 1927. His *Red Planet* was produced in 1932 and his last years were spent writing horror films in Hollywood.

BERKSHIRE THEATRE FESTIVAL (Stockbridge, Massachusetts). A summer theatre whose reputation for superb revivals is widespread, it started in 1928 as the Three Arts Society, which performed in a Stanford White–designed building in the Berkshire Mountains. The group adopted its present name in 1967 and continues to present classics and new works in its 816-seat Mainstage and its 122-seat Unicorn Theatre. The company claims to be the third-oldest theatre in the nation.

BERLIN, Irving [né Israel Baline] (1888–1989), songwriter. Emigrating from Russia while still a boy, he took a job at sixteen as a singing waiter and began composing songs, publishing his first one, "Marie from Sunny Italy," in 1907. He soon was interpolating songs in Broadway shows and even sang some of his own melodies in the revue *Up and Down Broadway* (1910). The next year he won worldwide recognition with "Alexander's Ragtime Band." His first complete score was for *Watch Your Step* (1914), followed by *Stop! Look! Listen!* (1915), *The Century Girl* (1916), and others. Berlin's all-soldier show *Yip, Yip, Yaphank* (1918) and his score for the *Ziegfeld Follies of 1919* introduced such hits as "Mandy" and "A Pretty Girl Is Like a Melody." In 1921, in partnership with Sam *Harris, he built the Music Box Theatre and initiated his own series of brilliant *Music Box Revues*. Other hits of the 1920s and 1930s include the *Marx Brothers romp, *The *Cocoanuts* (1925), the Great Depression spoof *Face the Music* (1932), and the masterful revue *As Thousands Cheer* (1933), from whose score came "Easter Parade" and "Heat Wave." The political satire *Louisiana Purchase* (1940) was followed by another all-soldier show, *This Is the Army* (1942). In 1946, after the death of Jerome *Kern, Berlin hastily composed the music for what proved to be his biggest hit, *Annie Get Your Gun*. Berlin wrote and co-produced a musical about the arrival of the Statue of Liberty in America, *Miss Liberty* (1949), but the show failed to run. His last two musicals took light-hearted but jaundiced looks at politics: the popular *Call Me Madam* (1950) and the disappointing *Mr. President* (1962), which closed his career on a down note. Berlin was rarely the innovator that his rivals Kern, George *Gershwin, and Richard *Rodgers were, for his music often changed with and took direction from the popular forms of the moment. Some accused him of consciously oversimple writing, both in his melodies and lyrics, but his uncanny melodic ear and his gift for expressing basic feelings succinctly made him probably the most popular composer of his era. Kern said, "Irving Berlin has no place in American music, he is American music." Biography: *As Thousands Cheer: The Life of Irving Berlin*, Laurence Bergreen, 1990.

BERNARD, Barney. See *Potash and Perlmutter*.

BERNARD, John (1756–1828), comic actor. The English low comedian was an established favorite at Covent Garden by the time Thomas *Wignell signed him in 1797 to appear in America. Bernard became a leading artist in Philadelphia and Boston, then in 1810 he became one of the earliest major performers to make an extended tour of all American theatrical cities. He returned to Boston in 1816 and gave his final performance shortly before sailing for England in 1819. Although his repertory included such classic roles as Sir Peter Teazle, Puff, and Gratiano, he was most admired for his playing of comic parts in now-forgotten plays, such as Nipperkin in *The Rival Soldiers* and Sheva in *The Jew*. After his death his *Retrospections of the Stage* was edited by his Boston-born son, **William Bayle BERNARD** (1807–75), who became a well-known London drama critic and playwright. Many of his early works had American settings and enjoyed some popularity in this country as well as in England. These included *Casco Bay* (1832), *The *Kentuckian* (1833), *The Nervous Man* (1833), and a version of *Rip Van Winkle* (1834) for J. H. *Hackett.

BERNARD, Sam [né Barnett] (1863–1927), comic actor. Born in England and brought to America while still a child, Bernard made his first professional appearance in vaudeville in the notorious Five Points section of New York. After touring in vaudeville and in plays, in almost all cases portraying a German or Jewish immigrant, he came to the attention of the dialect comedians Joe *Weber and Lew *Fields who signed him on to the company at their new Music Hall. There the short, stocky, balding performer appeared in the team's celebrated travesties, such as *The Geezer* (1896), *The Glad Hand* (1897), and *Pousse Cafe* (1897). On leaving Weber and Fields, he assumed his first starring role as Hermann Engel, the central figure in *The Marquis of Michigan* (1898). Similar roles followed in *A Dangerous Maid* (1898), *The Man in the Moon* (1899), *The*

Casino Girl (1900), and *The Belle of Bohemia* (1900). Bernard scored a major success as Mr. Hoggenheimer in *The Girl from Kay's* (1903) and reprised the role in *The Rich Mr. Hoggenheimer* (1906). More dialect roles came in such shows as *Nearly a Hero* (1906), *The Girl and the Wizard* (1909), *The Belle of Bond Street* (1914), and *The Century Girl* (1916). In 1918 he portrayed Henry Block in *Friendly Enemies*, a play about anti-German sentiments, then returned to musicals in *As You Were* (1920), *Music Box Revue* (1921) and *Nifties of 1923*. His last appearance was in a modernized version of *The Rich Mr. Hoggenheimer*, presented as *Piggy* (1927).

BERNARD, William Bayle. See Bernard, John.

BERNHARDT, Sarah [née Bernard] (1844–1923), actress. The great French performer had only recently made her front-page departure from the *Comédie-Française and embarked on a career as an independent star when she made her American debut at Booth's Theatre in 1880. Wisely, she chose for her first appearance the role many American critics came to consider her best part, the doomed actress Adrienne Lecouvreur. While she was no beauty, her frizzy red-gold hair, her thin, pale face with its sharp eyes, and her slim, almost frail body were not unattractive. She had a voice variously described as like a "golden bell" and the "silver sound of running water." Her notoriety was such that she had been guaranteed $1,000 per performance plus all traveling expenses, so that when her sellout tour was over, she had earned more than $156,000 for a series of performances that grossed the producer, Henry E. *Abbey, $553,000. Including her first visit and her last, in 1916, she toured America nine times. The most unusual tour was the one that covered the 1905–06 season. Defying the *Theatrical Syndicate, or Trust, whose terms she refused to accept, she was forced to play in tents and oddly assorted makeshift playhouses. Except on rare occasions in later years, she always performed in French. From the start most American critics considered her best in emotional roles and much weaker in truly tragic parts. The *Herald* observed, "In depicting human suffering she seems to absolutely control every organ of her body—her cheek blanches, tears come at her bidding . . . but where her lines call for the grand and imposing effects of concentrated passion . . . Mlle Bernhardt lacked breadth, force and passion." Among her most celebrated vehicles were *Frou-Frou, Phèdre, Ernani, La Dame aux Camélias, Jeanne d'Arc, L'Aiglon*, and *La Tosca*. Autobiography: *Memories of My Life*, 1923.

BERNSTEIN, Aline [née Frankau] (1881–1955), designer. The native New Yorker originally intended to become a portrait painter, but when her interest in costume design surfaced, she worked with Irene and Alice Lewisohn, then designed costumes as well as some sets for the *Neighborhood Playhouse in 1924. Her later costume designs were seen in such notable plays as *Ned McCobb's Daughter (1926), several revivals at the *Civic Repertory Theatre, *Tomorrow and Tomorrow (1931), *Reunion in Vienna (1931), The *Children's Hour (1934), The *Male Animal (1940), *Harriet (1943), and The *Happy Time (1950). In 1937 Bernstein was one of the founders of the *Museum of Costume Art, which was eventually absorbed by the Metropolitan Museum of Art. Helen *Hayes recalled a costume she designed for her *Caesar and Cleopatra (1925) as "hand-dyed blue taffeta appliqués on cloth of gold in the form of little feathers like the wings of ibis. It was a work of art." Thomas Wolfe, with whom she had a prolonged affair, wrote about her as Esther Jack in The Web and the Rock. Biography: Aline, Carole Klein, 1979.

BERNSTEIN, Leonard (1918–90), composer. Born in Lawrence, Massachusetts, and educated at Harvard and the Curtis Institute of Music, he had earned recognition as a symphonic conductor and composer of the ballet "Fancy Free," about three sailors on the town in wartime New York, before adapting that ballet into a musical comedy called *On the Town (1944). In 1950 Bernstein wrote music for *Peter Pan, then scored a major success with *Wonderful Town (1953). His comic operetta *Candide (1956) failed to run, but its score, including the famous overture, has endured triumphantly. *West Side Story (1957) marked a complete change of venue and tone and remains his most-produced work. Because of Bernstein's busy schedule conducting and recording classical music, he did not return to the theatre for twenty years, but suffered a quick failure with 1600 Pennsylvania Avenue (1976). Stanley *Green noted, "Bernstein has shown a certain eclecticism in his work for the theatre that has made it less of an individual expression than highly technical, remarkably effective music with each score sounding almost as if it were the work of a different man." His nontheatrical compositions covered a wide range, including opera and a Mass. Autobiography: Findings, 1982; biography: Leonard Bernstein, Humphrey Burton, 1994.

BERTHA, THE SEWING MACHINE GIRL (1906), a melodrama by Theodore Kremer. [American Theatre, 9 perf.] Bertha Sloane (Edith Browning) and her blind sister Jessie (Leona Francis) come to New York, where Bertha hopes to claim their late father's estate and also earn enough money in a sweatshop to help cure her sister's blind-

ness. Harold Cutting (W. A. Tully), whose father murdered Bertha's father for his money, is determined to thwart the girl, as is Olive Roberts (Rose Tiffany), Harold's fiancée. Together they chloroform Bertha and dump her in a lake. Tom Jennings (W. L. Gibson), who has fallen in love with Bertha, and Mrs. Katzenkopf (Ada St. Alva), the sisters' kind landlady, rescue her. Later Harold and Olive tie Bertha on a belt that is moving into the huge wheels of a machine, and when Tom and Mrs. Katzenkopf again rescue her, the villains frame Bertha for a policeman's murder. But Bertha defends herself in court and wrests a confession from Harold. Several different plays with the same title toured at this time. All were loosely based on a serial that had run in the late 1860s in the New York Weekly. Indeed, a version by Charles Foster, in which the heroine was called Bertha Bascome and in which her agonies, while equally harrowing, were not always the same as in Kremer's dramatization, began touring as early as 1871. **Theodore KREMER** (1871?–1923) was born in Cologne, Germany, and performed in both Europe and Australia before arriving in San Francisco in 1896. Almost immediately he began churning out melodramas for popular-priced theatres. Among his titles were The Slaves of the Orient, The Great Automobile Mystery, Secret Service Sam, and Fallen by the Wayside.

BEST, Edna (1900–74), actress. A British leading lady known for her delicate, gentle characters, she visited Broadway infrequently until the 1950s when she became a U.S. citizen. Best captivated American audiences in her first Broadway play, as the unfaithful wife Pamela in These Charming People (1925), and as Teresa Sanger in The Constant Nymph (1926), but few of her vehicles after were hits, even though her notices were usually complimentary. She particularly shone as the repressed housewife Millie in The Browning Version (1949), the timid but surprising spinster in Jane (1952), and the overbearing actress Madame Alexandra in Mademoiselle Colombe (1954).

BEST LITTLE WHOREHOUSE IN TEXAS, THE (1978), a musical comedy by Larry L. King, Peter Masterson (book), Carol Hall (music, lyrics). [Entermedia Theatre, 1,576 perf.] For decades the Chicken Ranch, where clients could pay in produce, has been a perfectly respectable brothel. Currently operated by Miss Mona Stangley (Carlin Glynn), who keeps her girls strictly in line, it numbers among its friends Sheriff Dodd (Henderson Forsythe) as well as notable politicians and football players. But "Watchdog" Thorpe (Clint Allmon), a self-glorifying regional television preacher, takes aim against the establishment and before long another fine old Texas tradition bites the dust. *Notable songs*: Twenty Fans; Bus from Amarillo; Hard Candy Christmas; Good Old Girl. Based on a real incident, the musical was so well received at its Off-Broadway premiere that it was immediately hustled to Broadway's 46th Street Theatre for a long run. Reasonably good, if raunchy, fun, the show offered a country-and-western-style score and Tommy *Tune's inventive staging. A sequel entitled *The Best Little Whorehouse Goes Public* (1994) retained much of the creative staff of the original but closed quickly.

BEST MAN, THE (1960), a play by Gore *Vidal. [*Morosco Theatre, 520 perf.] The leading contenders in a battle for the presidential nomination are William Russell (Melvyn *Douglas), a gentlemanly liberal of the old school, and Joseph Cantwell (Frank Lovejoy), a calculating, unscrupulous senator. Cantwell obtains a damaging psychiatric analysis once made of Russell and releases it to the press. A feisty ex-president, Arthur Hockstadter (Lee *Tracy), tells Cantwell, "It's not that I mind your being a bastard. . . . It's your being such a stupid bastard, I object to." Hockstadter leaves the Cantwell camp and joins Russell, whom he urges to make public Cantwell's history of homosexuality. Russell refuses, withdraws from the race, and throws his support to a third candidate. A wittily written, shrewdly observed comedy produced by the *Playwrights' Company, it was peopled with figures playgoers recognized as thinly disguised modern political celebrities: Russell was not unlike Adlai Stevenson; Cantwell, Senator Joseph McCarthy; and Hockstadter, Harry Truman. A Broadway revival in 2000 was well received.

BEST PLAYS, THE. A series begun in 1920 by Burns *Mantle, the full title of the first volume was *The Best Plays of 1919–20 and the Year Book of the Drama in America*. Each year a new edition contained extended excerpts from ten selected plays, plus a general review of the season and vital statistics on all of the season's productions, including casts and brief synopses of plots. After Mantle's death the editorship was assumed by such noted critics as John *Chapman, Louis *Kronenberger, Henry *Hewes, and Otis L. *Guernsey Jr. The publication of these volumes, coupled with George *Odell's *Annals of the New York Stage*, meant that a complete record was in print of every major theatrical production mounted in New York City. The two sets are invaluable to both theatre-lovers and scholars. The series began to disintegrate in the 1980s, eventually reducing the synopses of the ten "best" to only award winners. In 2001 the synopses completely disappeared, and the book's usefulness was diminished to only statistics and cast lists.

BEYOND THE HORIZON (1920), a tragedy by Eugene *O'Neill. [*Morosco Theatre, 111 perf.; Pulitzer Prize.] Robert Mayo (Richard *Bennett) has grown up on his family's New England farm dreaming of mysterious, faraway places, unlike his brother, the natural-born farmer Andrew (Edward Arnold). Both Robert and Andrew are in love with Ruth Atkins (Helen MacKellar), and on the day before Robert is to sail away on his Uncle Dick's ship and fulfill his dreams, Ruth persuades him to marry her so Andrew sails in his stead. Three years later, Robert has made a mess of both the farm and his marriage. His only passion is his sickly young daughter Mary (Elfin Finn). His wife and his mother (Mary Jeffery) belittle him and hold Andrew up to him as an example. When Andrew returns, it is clear his experiences have made him hard and unloving. He cruelly tells Ruth, who realizes too late that she really loved him, he had forgotten about her long ago. He goes back to sea, and another five years pass. Mary dies, Ruth grows apathetic, and, with Robert dying of consumption, the farm is in ruins. Andrew returns and Robert asks him to move his bed so that "I can watch the rim of the hills and dream of what is waiting beyond." He urges Andrew to marry Ruth after he dies and save the farm, but Andrew berates Ruth for her behavior and demands that Ruth tell Robert she truly loves him. Ruth at first refuses; but when she finally agrees, it is too late and Robert is dead. "God damn you!" Andrew yells at her. "You never told him!" No major producer wanted to mount the play, but John D. *Williams, pressed by Bennett, finally agreed to give it at a special matinee. The response was so overwhelming that more matinees were offered, and on March 9 the play began a regular run at the Little Theatre. "By that time," Burns *Mantle wrote shortly afterwards, "there were many who were willing to accept this first long play from Eugene O'Neill's pen as representing the closest approach any native author has yet made to the great American play." For many, this stark, unyielding work marks the beginnings of modern American drama. However, one modern critic, Howard Taubman, has noted, "In the light of today's uncompromising freshness of language and unsparing probing of character, it is tame. . . . What impressed people eager for a new voice to lead the American theatre out of its wilderness of mediocrity now strikes us as essentially sentimental . . . a reversion to romanticism." Others would reply that O'Neill's very romanticism coupled with his bleak outlook was a major source of his strength.

BIANCA VISCONTI; *or, The Heart Overtasked* (1837), a tragedy by Nathaniel Parker *Willis. [*Park Theatre, in repertory.] Although their families have long been enemies, Bianca Visconti (Josephine *Clifton) marries Francesco Sforza (J. K. Mason), a 15th-century Duke of Milan. He is a high-minded, ambitious man, but cold and unloving. Nevertheless, Bianca loyally defends his every action. The Viscontis and the other noble houses are jealous of the Duke's power, so plot to assassinate him. Bianca overhears the scheme and arranges to substitute her loving, playful page Giulio (Charles Mestayer). Only after Giulio's death does she learn he was really her brother and the shock drives her insane, so she dies of a broken heart. Awarded one of the many prizes given at the time to encourage native drama, Willis saw the play as a defense of democracy against the forces of aristocracy. However unsympathetic the character of the Duke may seem to modern readers, he was perceived by Willis as an idealist fighting against these forces.

BIG BONANZA, THE (1875), a comedy in four acts by Augustin *Daly. [*Fifth Avenue Theatre, 137 perf.] Lucretia Cawallader (Annie Graham) is a stuffy, domineering wife, annoyed by her husband Jonathan (Charles Fisher) and worried about her daughter of marriageable age, Eugenia (Fanny *Davenport). When she learns that her daughter was escorted from the train station by a shabbily dressed young man, she is horrified. Her distress is interrupted by the arrival of Jonathan's cousin, Professor Agassiz Cawallader (James *Lewis), who argues with her husband about money management. Jonathan gives the Professor $30,000 and bets him that he cannot invest it successfully for a month. The Professor's problems learning the ways of the market are compounded by the arrival of his wife's nephew Bob (John *Drew), a generous, amiable young man fresh from the mines out west. In the end Agassiz's buying and selling come to naught, but he learns to his relief that Jonathan's clerk disobeyed his instructions and he has lost nothing. At the same time, Jonathan and Lucretia discover that Bob was the shabbily dressed young man who helped Eugenia at the station and they agree to let their daughter marry him. Producer-author Daly based his play on Gustav von Moser's German comedy *Ultimo* and its success relieved him of financial difficulties at his new theatre. The play itself succeeded despite largely negative reviews. William *Winter wrote that the piece "has no claim to consideration. The dialogue drivels through four acts of hopeless commonplace in which there is not one spark of wit, not one bright thought, not even a gleam of smartness." Audiences disagreed and the play was so popular that, because of loose copyright laws, several competing versions of von Moser's play were also mounted. Daly's was by far the most successful, and was revived profitably as late as 1899.

BIG RIVER: *The Adventures of Huckleberry Finn* (1985), a musical by William Hauptman (book), Roger Miller (music, lyrics). [*Eugene O'Neill Theatre, 1,005 perf.; Tony Award.] Huck (Daniel H. Jenkins) and a runaway slave, Jim (Ron Richardson), sail the Mississippi on their raft, meeting such figures as the King (Bob *Gunton), the Duke (Rene Auberjonois), and Tom Sawyer (John Short), much as they do in Mark Twain's classic. *Notable songs*: River in the Rain; Waiting for the Light to Shine; Muddy Water; World's Apart. Coming at the end of a season filled with musical disappointments and disasters, the show received a warmer welcome than it might have otherwise. But it drew family audiences and the tuneful show remains popular in stock and in schools. The show returned to Broadway in 2003 in a unique revival that utilized both speaking and deaf actors.

BIKEL, Theodore [Meir] (b. 1924), actor. Born in Vienna and educated locally and in Tel Aviv, Bikel trained at the Royal Academy of Dramatic Art in London then returned to present-day Israel to act. Bikel performed in London before making his Broadway debut in 1955. His most significant New York performances were Joan of Arc's ally Robert de Beaudricourt in *The Lark* (1955), the well-meaning Jewish doctor Jacobson in *The Rope Dancers* (1957), the stern Austrian Captain refuting the Nazis in *The *Sound of Music* (1959), and the aged Holocaust survivor Gabe in *The Gathering* (1999). The internationally acclaimed folk singer also performed in concerts on three continents and played Tevye in road companies of *Fiddler on the Roof*. Autobiography: *Theo*, 2002.

BILLBOARD. The theatrical trade sheet was first published in Cincinnati in 1894. Begun as a monthly, it became a weekly in 1900. With increasing competition from New York–based publications, it soon began to emphasize amateur theatre, carnivals, and circuses. In recent decades its main concern has been the popular music field. For many years, starting in 1920, it published an annual *Billboard Index of the Legitimate Stage*.

BILLINGTON, Ken (b. 1946), lighting designer. He was born in White Plains. New York, and learned his craft at the Lester Polakov Studio and Forum of Stage Design. Billington made his Manhattan design debut doing lights for *Fortune and Men's Eyes* Off Broadway in 1969. Over the years he has won many awards and been represented in New York for such productions as *The Visit* (1973),

The *Skin of Our Teeth (1975), *On the Twentieth Century (1978), *Sweeney Todd (1979), *Fiddler on the Roof (1981), Grind (1985), Meet Me in St. Louis (1985), Lettice and Lovage (1990), Ain't Broadway Grand (1993), Sylvia (1995), *Candide (1997), *Twelfth Night (1998), Waiting in the Wings (1999), and Time and Again (2001).

BILOXI BLUES. See Brighton Beach Memoirs.

BILTMORE THEATRE (New York). This problem-plagued theatre on West 47th Street was nearly lost after years of flops and neglect but in 2003 became the latest restored Broadway house. It was built in 1925 by the speculating Chanin Brothers, but because the Herbert J. *Krapp–designed house had fewer than a thousand seats, it was difficult to book and the brothers lost it during the Great Depression. The *Federal Theatre Project used the theatre for some of its famous "Living Newspaper" productions in the 1930s, and in the 1940s it housed several shows by George *Abbott. The Biltmore became a television studio in 1951, returned to legit status in 1961, then floundered until 1987 when it closed. Years of neglect and vandalism made restoring the small theatre uneconomical, but in 2003 it was restored as part of a new apartment complex and, the auditorium reduced to 650 seats, it reopened as the Broadway home for the nonprofit *Manhattan Theatre Club.

BINGHAM, Amelia [Smiley] (1869–1927), actress and manager. Born in Hicksville, Ohio, and educated at Ohio Wesleyan, she elected a theatrical career despite the vigorous opposition of her deeply religious family. Bingham's earliest appearance was on the West Coast, but she came to New York in 1892 to play in a series of melodramas, including The Struggle of Life, The Power of Gold, and A Man Among Men. Her first important role came opposite Robert *Hilliard in a failure called The Mummy (1896). Thereafter she played for several seasons for Charles *Frohman in such plays as His Excellency the Governor (1899) and Hearts Are Trumps (1900). In late 1900 she determined to become New York's first important actress-manager since Laura Keene. To that end she leased the Bijou Theatre and enjoyed a major success with her first production, The Climbers (1901), in which she played the compassionate Mrs. Sterling. Her subsequent productions were more or less failures, although The Frisky Mrs. Johnson (1903) had a modest run largely because of the publicity that followed her highly vocal battle with the critics who panned it. After that she played in stock until she returned in the unsuccessful The Lilac Room (1907). For several seasons thereafter she

toured successfully in vaudeville, performing "Big Moments from Great Plays." From 1913 through 1916 she played in The New Henrietta, a modernization of Bronson *Howard's 1887 hit. Her last appearance was in a supporting role in The Pearl of Great Price (1926).

BIOGRAPHY (1932), a comedy by S. N. *Behrman. [Guild Theatre, 267 perf.] Marion Froude (Ina *Claire) is a celebrated artist who has had many lovers all over the world but no husbands. One of her earliest loves, Leander Nolan (Jay Fassett), now a successful lawyer and running for Senator, comes to have his portrait painted. At the same time, Richard Kurt (Earle *Larimore), a radical young editor, appears with an offer to publish Marion's autobiography. Although at first she finds Kurt "bumptious and insufferable," she quickly develops a fondness for him and he falls in love with her. When Nolan learns that Marion has agreed to write her life history, he is furious, for he knows it will ruin his chances of election. But the behavior of his prospective father-in-law and his fiancée makes him wonder if he really doesn't still love Marion. Marion recognizes that she would be happy neither with Nolan, who has grown too conservative, nor with Kurt, who is hopelessly hate-filled. She destroys her manuscript and, receiving an offer to paint some Hollywood celebrities, she tells her maid to pack. She will resume her wayfaring, wayward existence. Most critics agreed with Robert Garland of the World-Telegram who noted, "The Theatre Guild has gotten around to a play worthy of the high position it occupies in the history of the modern American theatre . . . adult and provocative . . . an evening of rare playgoing felicity." It remains Behrman's finest work.

BIRCH, Patricia (b. 1930?), choreographer. A native of Scarsdale, New York, she studied with such prominent dancers as Martha Graham and Merce Cunningham before first performing on Broadway in the chorus of Goldilocks (1958). She turned to choreography with *You're a Good Man, Charlie Brown (1967) and her dances were subsequently seen in such shows as *Grease (1972), A *Little Night Music (1973), the 1974 and 1997 revivals of *Candide, *Pacific Overtures (1976), *They're Playing Our Song (1979), and Parade (1998).

BIRD OF PARADISE, THE (1912), a play by Richard Walton *Tully. [Daly's Theatre, 112 perf.] On a languid Hawaiian island, a promising young American scientist, Paul Wilson (Lewis S. Stone), falls in love with a beautiful if superstitious native princess, Luana (Laurette *Taylor). They marry, but the marriage destroys all of Wilson's drive and ambition. Neither an attempt by fellow Americans to foment a revolution that would make Luana queen nor a move back to civilization seems to help. When Mt. Kilauea, long dormant, suddenly begins to rumble, Luana reads it as a sign that the gods are angry with her and demand a human sacrifice. To appease the gods and to give her husband a chance to fulfill his early promise, she throws herself into the crater. Although the play opened in New York to largely favorable notices, the producer Oliver *Morosco's disagreements with several theatre owners cut short its Broadway run. On the road, however, its several companies turned it into one of the biggest moneymakers of its era. In 1930 it was made into an unsuccessful operetta, *Luana*.

BIRD, Robert Montgomery (1806–54), playwright. Born into a well-to-do New Castle, Delaware, family, he lived with relatives when his father died and attended Germantown Academy and then the medical school at the University of Pennsylvania. He had often written poetry, but while at medical school or soon thereafter turned to playwriting. Such works as the farce *News of the Night; or, A Trip to Niagara*, the tragic romance *The Cowled Lover*, the Gothic horror piece *Caridorf; or, The Avenger*, and the comedy of manners *'Twas All for the Best; or, 'Tis a Notion*, and *The City Looking Glass: A Philadelphia Comedy* were strongly influenced by classic writers of the past, but none were produced in his lifetime. In 1830 Bird submitted *Pelopidas; or, The Fall of the Polemarchs* to one of Edwin *Forrest's playwriting contests and the drama about the Theban revolt against the Spartans won first prize but was not produced. The actor was far more receptive to the author's next play, *The *Gladiator* (1831), which was an immediate success and remained one of Forrest's most popular offerings. In 1832 Forrest produced his *Oralloossa*, concerned with the assassination of Pizarro, and two years later mounted his best play, *The *Broker of Bogota*. Bird also revised *Metamora* for the actor, but shortly thereafter had a falling out with him when Forrest refused to pay several thousand dollars due him. Discouraged, he abandoned the theatre and turned to writing novels, one of which, *Nick of the Woods; or, The Jibbenainosay*, was dramatized by Louisa Medina in 1838 and long remained a stage favorite. From 1841 to 1843 he taught at the Philadelphia Medical College and then became editor of the *North American and United States Gazette*. Arthur Hobson *Quinn has written: "Had he lived in a time when the American playwright received fair treatment, it is not easy to put a limit to his possible achievements. For he had a rare sense of dramatic effect, a power to visualize historic scenes and characters, to seize the spirit of the past out of the mass of facts and, in a few lines, to fuse those facts into life." Biography: *The Life and Dramatic Works of Robert Montgomery Bird*, Clement E. Foust, 1919.

BITTER SWEET (1929). Noel *Coward's most popular operetta was presented in America by Florenz *Ziegfeld at the Ziegfeld Theatre in 1929, just short of four months after its London premiere. Its story centered on a great lady whose niece must choose between marrying for love or position. The lady recounts her own similar history to help her niece make the proper selection. British singing actress Evelyn Laye was starred. Although the musical was well received, its short run of 157 performances can be attributed to the onset of the Great Depression. In retrospect the show can be seen as virtually the last in the school of traditional operetta. *Notable songs*: I'll See You Again; If Love Were All; Zigeuner; Alas the Time Is Past.

BLACK CROOK, THE (1866), a melodramatic musical spectacle by Charles M. Barras (book), Thomas Baker and others (music, lyrics). [*Niblo's Garden, 475 perf.] The "Arch Fiend" Zamiel (E. B. Holmes) induces Hertzog (C. H. Morton), the Black Crook, to deliver a human soul into his power once a year on New Year's Eve. Hoping to snare the painter Rudolf (G. C. Boniface), who has been unjustly imprisoned, Hertzog frees him and promises to lead him to a large cache of gold. On his way to the treasure Rudolf saves a dove's life. The dove is really Stalacta (Annie Kemp Bowler), Queen of the Golden Realm. She warns him of his danger, removes him to fairyland, and helps him win Amina (Rose Morton). *Notable songs*: March of the Amazons; You Naughty, Naughty Men; The Broadway, Opera and Bowery Crawl. Allegedly mounted at a cost of $50,000, the musical was the most successful Broadway play up to its time and the first to run for more than a year. Theatrical legend states the production came about when a French ballet troupe, scheduled to perform at the Academy of Music, was deprived of a stage after the theatre burned down. The troupe was hastily combined with a dramatic company about to present Barras's metaphysical melodrama. A 1954 musical, *The Girl in Pink Tights*, retold this fanciful tale. But more recent research by Stanley *Green, Kurt Ganzl, and others, has called this story into question, and it becomes clear that *The Black Crook*'s origins were more a matter of shrewd business arrangements among producers William *Wheatley, Henry Palmer, and Henry C. *Jarrett. No small part of the musical's fame came from its long line of choryphees (chorus girls) in what were euphemistically called pink tights, but were actually flesh colored. Companies quickly sprang up all across the country, and the spectacle was revived regularly throughout the rest of the century. Christopher Morley and Agnes *de Mille staged a popular reconstruction in 1929. Barras (1826–73) was a Philadelphia-born actor-playwright. Most of his works were written-to-order vehicles for contemporary favorites. Clara *Morris paints a vivid picture of him in her autobiography.

BLACKBIRDS. A series of revues, with African-American casts, produced by Lew *Leslie both in London and New York. Of the four American editions, in 1928, 1930, 1933, and 1939, only the first was a success. Its cast included Bill *Robinson, who sang and danced "Doin' the New Low-Down," Adelaide *Hall who performed "Diga Diga Doo," and Aida Ward who introduced "I Can't Give You Anything but Love." The Eubie *Blake standard, "Memories of You," came from the failed 1930 edition, where Minto Cato sang it. The shows, relatively simple in mounting, emphasized song and dance. What little comedy there was represented the stereotypical Negro humor of the era.

BLACKMER, Sidney (1895–1973), actor. Born in Salisbury, North Carolina, he studied law before making his New York acting debut as a Young Man in *The Morris Dance* (1917), then played several other supporting roles prior to becoming the leading man in dozens of plays, though never in a major hit. The tall, dark-haired, classic-featured actor gave highly praised performances as Aaron Winterfield, the mountaineer who inherits a fortune, in *The Mountain Man* (1921); Eugene Thorne, the loyal illegitimate son, in *The Love Child* (1922); Tony Blunt, the explorer, in *Quarantine* (1924); and Janos, the virtuous forester, in *Belasco's Mima* (1928). Following a long career in films, Blackmer came back to Broadway, where once again he was awarded good roles in mediocre plays. His luck changed dramatically in 1950 when he portrayed the failed, alcoholic Doc in *Come Back, Little Sheba* and won a *Tony Award for this performance. His last Broadway appearance was as Paul Cleary, the accused's attorney, in *A Case of Libel* (1963).

BLACKS IN AMERICAN THEATRE. See African Americans in Theatre.

BLAKE, Eubie. See *Shuffle Along*.

BLAKE, William Rufus (1802–63), actor and manager. After playing the Prince of Wales in *Richard III* with a band of strolling players who visited his hometown of Halifax, Nova Scotia, in 1817, he decided to make acting his career. Blake first appeared in New York in 1824 as Frederick in *The Poor Gentleman*. His trim figure and good looks prompted managers to cast him in romantic leads, although early on he exhibited a comic flair. With age and increasing corpulence, he was able to concentrate on comic parts. Among his prime interpretations were Sir Peter Teazle, Mr. Hardcastle, Malvolio, Sampson Legend, and Sir Anthony Absolute, but he also scored heavily in many contemporary, now-forgotten works. Blake was often first comedian in the greatest companies of the time including *Burton's and *Wallack's. A good businessman, he at one time or another managed the *Bowery, Franklin, Olympic, and Broadway theatres, as well as Philadelphia's *Walnut Street Theatre and Boston's Tremont. A contemporary critic wrote of his performance in the long-popular *The Heir at Law* that the actor "is a glorious Lord Duberly—one charm of his acting consists in bringing all the vulgarity of the 'old chandler' out in broad relief, and yet preserving his representation from being coarse—a great stroke of art." Writing in more general terms, Joseph *Jefferson observed, "He was a superior actor. . . . Without seeming to change his face or alter the stolid look from his eyes, Mr. Blake conveyed his meaning with the most perfect effect. He was delicate and minute in his manner, which contrasted oddly with his ponderous form."

BLANEY, Charles E[dward] (1866–1944), playwright. Born in Columbus, Ohio, he began his career as an actor but soon switched to playwriting and became a prolific author of melodramas, tearjerkers, and farce comedies. The titles of some of his plays suggest their nature: *The Curse of Drink, For His Brother's Crime, King of the Opium Ring,* and *More to Be Pitied Than Scorned*. Many of these plays were written for the *Stair and Havlin circuit, while others were created for a chain of theatres (often playhouses fallen on hard times, such as Philadelphia's *Arch Street Theatre), which Blaney ran. The coming of films destroyed his market.

BLEDSOE, Jules (1898–1943), singer and actor. Born in Waco, Texas, the African-American performer appeared on Broadway as the original Abraham McCranie, the rebellious half-breed, in *In Abraham's Bosom* (1926) and also won praise for his performance in the musical *Deep River* (1926). However, he is best remembered as the first Joe in *Show Boat* (1927), in which he introduced "Ol' Man River."

BLESSING, Lee (b. 1949), playwright. He was born in Minneapolis, the son of a salesman, and was educated at Reed College and the University of Iowa. Blessing's work was first produced at the *Actors Theatre of Louisville in 1982 and many of his subsequent scripts would premiere and find success regionally. His most notable plays include *A Walk in the Woods* (1988), dealing with the friendship that develops between an American and a Russian diplomat; *Eleemosynary* (1988), about three generations of independent women; and *Cobb* (2000), which explored the many facets of baseball legend Ty Cobb.

BLINN, Holbrook (1872–1928), actor. Remembered by Ward *Morehouse as "a steadying and inspirational influence . . . an actor of extraordinary finesse and charm," he made his debut in his native San Francisco as a child in an 1878 production of *The *Streets of New York*. Blinn's first New York appearance was as Corporal Ferry in *The New South* (1893). After some years of playing increasingly important roles both in New York and London, he made his mark as Napoleon in *The Duchess of Dantzic* (1903, London; 1905, New York), a musical version of *Sardou's *Madame Sans-Gêne*. His star rose in 1908 when he joined Mrs. *Fiske to play Jim Platt, the jailbird-lover, in *Salvation Nell*, Karsten Bernick to her Lona in *Pillars of Society*, and her leading man in *The Green Cockatoo* and *Hannele* (all in 1910). Blinn's first starring role was the ruthless politician Michael Regan, a corrupt man reformed by a loving wife, in *The *Boss* (1911). When the *Princess Theatre opened in 1913, he was active in promoting its program of experimental plays, acting in and staging many of them. Some of his subsequent successes include Lord Illington opposite Margaret *Anglin in a 1916 revival of *A Woman of No Importance*, Georges Duval in a multistar revival of *The Lady of the Camellias* (1917), Orrin Palmer in the war play *Getting Together* (1918), Louis XIV in *Molière* (1919), Henry Winthrop, an enlightened conservative, in *The Challenge* (1919), Pancho Lopez (read Pancho Villa) in *The Bad Man* (1920), the bandit Don José in *The Dove* (1925), and Sandor Turai in the comedy *The Play's the Thing* (1926).

BLITZSTEIN, Marc (1905–64) composer and lyricist. The Philadelphia-born artist created a furor on Broadway with his propaganda musical *The *Cradle Will Rock* (1937), which was performed despite strenuous efforts to stop it. Blitzstein himself played the piano at the hurriedly moved performance. In 1949 his opera *Regina*, based on *The *Little Foxes*, was performed on Broadway, but his major claim to fame, however, may be his brilliant translation of the Bertolt *Brecht–Kurt *Weill work *The *Threepenny Opera* (1954). *Juno* (1959), Blitzstein's musical rendition of *Juno and the Paycock*, was a quick failure despite praise for its score. Biography: *Mark the Music: The Life and Work of Marc Blitzstein*, Eric A. Gordon, 1990.

BLOCKADE, THE (1775), a play by General John Burgoyne that ridiculed American soldiers, was presented in Boston while the British occupied the city. When the British left, a burlesque called *The Blockheads*, often attributed to Mercy Otis *Warren, was produced as a response in 1776. The burlesque was a dialogue between redcoats and sympathetic refugees after Howe's unsuccessful attempt to take Dorchester Heights.

BLOODGOOD, Clara [neé Stevens] (1870–1907), actress. A young, socially prominent New Yorker, she determined to try her luck on stage and surprised many with her fine acting and purposeful professionalism. Under the aegis of Charles *Frohman she made her debut in *The *Conquerors* (1898), then appeared for him in *Catherine* (1898), *Phroso* (1898), and *Miss Hobbs* (1899). Bloodgood won such good notices as the caustic-tongued Miss Godesby in *The *Climbers* (1901) that author Clyde *Fitch wrote the tormented Jinny Austin in *The *Girl with the Green Eyes* (1902) specifically for her. Another Fitch play for her, *The Coronet of the Duchess* (1904), was a quick failure, but her reputation was reassured when she played Violet Robinson in the first American production of *Man and Superman* (1905). In 1907 she appeared as Becky Warder, the pathological liar, in Fitch's *The Truth*, which opened to unkind notices in New York but was well received on the road. While playing in Baltimore, Bloodgood committed suicide in her hotel room. Fitch thereafter strenuously denied a widely circulated rumor that her suicide had been prompted by his dedicating the published text of *The Truth* to Marie *Tempest who played it in London.

BLOOMER GIRL (1944), a musical comedy by Sig Herzig, Fred Saidy (book), Harold *Arlen (music), E. Y. *Harburg (lyrics). [*Shubert Theatre, 654 perf.] Evelina Applegate (Celeste *Holm), the rebellious daughter of an upstate New York hoopskirt manufacturer, not only refuses to marry the man her father has selected for her but joins her aunt, Dolly Bloomer (Margaret Douglass), in promoting bloomers instead of hoopskirts. Although she is against slavery, she weds Southern slave owner Jeff Calhoun (David Brooks) and convinces her father to manufacture bloomers. *Notable songs*: The Eagle and Me; Evelina; Right as the Rain; It Was Good Enough for Grandma. One of the earliest musicals to follow in the wake of *Oklahoma!*, it featured the look back at a bygone America, and marvelous Agnes *de Mille ballets (especially one in which the women await their men's return from the war), much as the *Rodgers and *Hammerstein operetta had. The musical also included some early but potent commentary, in book and score, about civil rights and feminism.

BLOOMGARDEN, Kermit (1904–76), producer. Born in Brooklyn, he served as a public accountant and general manager to Herman *Shumlin before embarking on his own producing career. His first venture, *Heavenly Express* (1940), was a failure, but his second try, *Deep Are the Roots* (1945), succeeded. Among his important productions were *Another Part of the Forest* (1946), *Command Decision* (1947), *Death of a Salesman* (1949), *The Autumn Garden* (1951), The *Crucible* (1953), The *Diary of Anne Frank* (1955), The *Most Happy Fella* (1956), *Look Homeward, Angel* (1957), The *Music Man* (1957), *Toys in the Attic* (1960), The *Hot l Baltimore* (1973), and *Equus* (1974).

BLOSSOM, Henry [Martyn], **Jr.** (1866–1919), librettist and lyricist. After attending private schools in St. Louis, he rejected college to enter his father's insurance company but soon turned to writing novels, one of which he dramatized successfully as *Checkers* (1903), a horse-racing yarn. Thereafter his work was largely confined to librettos and lyrics for musicals, most often to scores by Victor *Herbert. Among his best were *The Yankee Consul* (1903), *Mlle. Modiste* (1905), The *Red Mill* (1906), *The Only Girl* (1914), *The Princess Pat* (1915), *Eileen* (1917), and *The Velvet Lady* (1919). Although most librettos of the period were loosely structured fripperies, Blossom's work had a colloquial charm and cohesiveness rare at the time, and he proved to be the best librettist Herbert ever had.

BLOSSOM TIME (1921), an operetta by Dorothy *Donnelly (book, lyrics), Sigmund *Romberg (music), based on themes of Franz Schubert. [*Ambassador Theatre, 592 perf.] Kitzi (Frances Halliday), Fritzi (Dorothy Whitmore), and Mitzi Kranz (Olga Cook) are three eligible Viennese young ladies. Franz Schubert (Bertram Peacock) falls in love with Mitzi, and so does Baron Franz Schober (Howard *Marsh). The men's similar initials cause a misunderstanding that prompts Mitzi to favor the Baron. Heartbroken, Schubert dies. *Notable songs*: Serenade; Three Little Maids; Song of Love. The *Shubert-produced operetta was a drastic rewriting of the German operetta *Das Dreimäderlhaus*, which was popular in England as *Lilac Time* and in France as *Chanson d'Amour*. Its tremendous popularity prompted a rash of operettas purporting to be biographical and employing themes by other composers. *Blossom Time* toured incessantly until World War II, often in such shabby mountings that "a road company of *Blossom Time*" became a term of derision.

BLUE JEANS (1890), a play by Joseph *Arthur. [14th Street Theatre, 176 perf.] When Perry Bascom (Robert *Hilliard), a rich young man who is running for Congress in Indiana, marries Sue Eudaly (Judith Berolde), the marriage so infuriates Sue's old suitor, Ben Boone (George *Fawcett), that he runs against Bascom and wins. But Sue turns out to be an adventuress and bigamist, so Bascom divorces her and marries June (Jennie Yeamans), a waif from the county poorhouse. Sue, believing that Bascom cannot prove her first marriage, threatens to bring him to trial as a bigamist. She also tells Boone that Bascom is all that stands in the way of their marrying. Boone lures Bascom and June to a sawmill, where he locks June in a small office and, after knocking out Bascom, places him on a belt that is moving toward a huge, spinning buzz saw. June breaks down the door in time to rescue her husband, who later succeeds in finding Sue's other husband. The scene in which the unconscious hero moves ever closer to the whirling saw was the sensation of the play and became one of the most famous and imitated moments in American melodrama. The play remained a popular favorite for several decades.

BLUE MOUSE, THE (1908), a comedy by Clyde *Fitch. [Lyric Theatre, 232 perf.] Knowing that his boss Mr. Lewellyn (Harry *Conor), the president of the railroad, is an inveterate skirt-chaser, Augustus Rollett (Jameson Lee Finney) persuades a popular cabaret star, Paulette Divine (Mabel Barrison), who is known as "The Blue Mouse," to pretend to be his wife and let his boss have a brief flirtation with her. Augustus banks on this leading to a promotion. What he does not bank on are appearances by Mrs. Lewellyn (Zelda Sears), his own wife (Jane Laurel), and several other friends and relatives, all of whom arrive at inconvenient moments and misconstrue the situation. Fitch freely adapted and Americanized a German play by Alexander Engel and Julius Horst. The comedy was later the source of the 1919 musical *The Little Blue Devil*.

BLYDEN, Larry [né Ivan Lawrence Blieden] (1925–75), character actor. The thin, wiry comic performer was born in Houston, Texas, and was educated at Southern Louisiana Institute and the University of Houston before he went to New York and studied acting with Stella *Adler. Blyden made his Broadway debut in 1949 as a replacement in *Mister Roberts*. He had a strident, insistent voice and specialized in playing comic sidekicks and secondary leads, such as the wisecracking Chinese-American Sammy Fong in *Flower Drum Song* (1958), Bert *Lahr's sidekick Doc in *Foxy* (1964), the Snake and other roles in *The Apple Tree* (1966), Phil *Silvers's sidekick Hysterium in *A Funny Thing Happened on the Way to the Forum* (1972), and the social-climbing Sidney in *Absurd Person Singular* (1974).

BOCK and HARNICK, songwriting team. Jerry [Jerrold Lewis] Bock (b. 1928) was born in New Haven, Connecticut, and began to compose songs for shows in high school and at the University of Wisconsin. After writing for Sid *Caesar and Imogene Coca's television shows and for summer camp revues, Bock collaborated with lyricist Larry Holofcener on several songs for the Broadway revue *Catch a Star* (1955) and Sammy Davis Jr.'s vehicle, *Mr. Wonderful* (1956). Shortly afterwards he teamed up with lyricist Sheldon [Mayer] Harnick (b. 1924), a Chicago native who had written songs while studying at Northwestern and had seen some of his numbers performed in such revues as *New Faces of 1952, Two's Company* (1952), *John Murray Anderson's Almanac* (1953), and *Shoestring Revue* (1955). The twosome's first musical together was the short-lived boxing musical *The Body Beautiful* (1958) but they triumphed with the *Pulitzer Prize–winning *Fiorello!* (1959). This was followed by the period piece *Tenderloin* (1960), the operetta-like *She Loves Me* (1963), and their most popular work, *Fiddler on the Roof* (1964). Their last two projects together were the triptych musical comedy *The Apple Tree* (1966) and the biographical *The Rothschilds* (1970). After the team split, Harnick wrote lyrics for Richard *Rodgers's music for *Rex* (1976) and scored some musicals that were produced regionally. At their best, the Bock and Harnick scores caught the flavor of periods and places in which the musicals were set without ever becoming truly imitative of older styles. Bock's music contains strong melodicism while Harnick's lyrics offer a compassionate, yet often witty, understanding of human longings.

BOGOSIAN, Eric (b. 1953), monologist and playwright. An electric, dark-complexioned actor-writer who brings a sense of danger to all his performances, he is primarily a solo artist, writing and performing in one-person shows that allow him to play a variety of characters, mostly crude and obsessive types. He was born in Woburn, Massachusetts, and educated at the University of Chicago and Oberlin College before cofounding the Woburn Drama Guild and touring in his one-man programs. Bogosian's first solo performance in Manhattan was Off Broadway in 1977, and the most notable of his successive programs were *Fun House* (1983), *Drinking in America* (1986), and *Sex, Drugs, and Rock & Roll* (1990). His multicharacter plays include *Talk Radio* (1987) and *SubUrbia* (1994).

BOKER, George Henry (1823–90), playwright. Born into a comfortable Philadelphia family, he was educated at Princeton and prepared for a career in law, but he elected to travel and write instead. After publishing a volume of poetry, he turned to drama, and his first play, *Calaynos,* a tale of Spanish-Moorish animosities, was published in 1848, produced successfully in London without authorization in 1849, and mounted by James E. *Murdoch in Philadelphia's *Walnut Street Theatre in 1851. Boker's comedy in verse, *The Betrothal* (1850) in which the heroine is saved from an unwanted marriage to a wicked merchant, was played successfully in several cities, and his prose comedy *The World a Mask* (1851) had a brief run at the Walnut. His two most distinguished plays were *Leonor de Guzman* (1853), which told of the tragic rivalry between the heroine and Queen Maria of Castile, and *Francesca da Rimini* (1855), based on the Paolo and Francesca story in Dante's *Inferno.* Boker's last produced play was a melodrama, *The Bankrupt* (1855). His unproduced *Königsmark* was published in 1868 but not until Lawrence Barrett's acclaimed revival of *Francesca da Rimini* in 1882 did Boker again take up playwriting. His last two plays, *Nydia* and *Glaucus,* both derived from *Bulwer-Lytton's *Last Days of Pompeii,* were never produced. He continued to write poetry and served as Minister to Turkey (1871–75) and Minister to Russia (1875–78). One of his modern editors, Richard Moody, has observed, "American audiences of the nineteenth century had an insatiable taste for romantic tragedy, as is clearly demonstrated by the repeated performances of *Hamlet, Othello, Macbeth* and *Lear,* but only George Henry Boker, among the native and foreign dramatists, produced an original romantic tragedy of notable quality for them." Biography: *George Henry Boker: Poet and Patriot,* Edward S. Bradley, 1927.

BOLAND, Mary (1885–1965), comic actress. The Philadelphia-born comedienne made her debut in Detroit in 1901 in *A Social Highwayman,* and over the next several years she toured and played seasons with various stock companies before making her New York debut as Dorothy Nelson in *Strongheart* (1905), a role in which she continued for two years. Boland was at this time a young performer of notable beauty and charm, appearing as Dorothy Osgood in *The Ranger* (1907) and the saucy Lady Rowena Eggington in *When Knights Were Bold* (1907). Under Charles *Frohman's supervision, she became leading lady to John *Drew in *Jack Straw* (1908), *Inconstant George* (1909), *Smith* (1910), *The Perplexed Husband* (1912), *Much Ado About Nothing* (1913), *The Will* (1913), *A Scrap of Paper* (1914), and others. Boland then left Frohman to assume the roles of all the women who wore *My Lady's Dress* (1914), followed by the stepmother, Mrs. Wheeler, in *Clarence* (1919), her first essay as the sort of fluttery grande dame that would become her trademark. Among her major assignments in the 1920s were Paula Ritter, the amateur theatre buff in The *Torch-Bearers (1922); Gertrude Lennos, the inadvertent bigamist, in Meet the Wife (1923); and Susan Martin, whose plans to make her husband jealous backfire, in *Cradle Snatchers (1925). One of her best performances was as the flighty matron Laura Merrick in The Vinegar Tree (1930), and she shone in two musicals, as the nouveau riche Mrs. Meshbesher in Face the Music (1932) and the Queen in *Jubilee (1935). Boland returned from Hollywood to play Mrs. Malaprop in 1942, then again in 1954 as the domineering mother in Lullaby, her last New York appearance.

BOLGER, Ray[mond Wallace] (1904–87), comic actor and dancer. Born in Dorchester, Massachusetts, he made his professional debut in 1922 with a musical comedy stock company in Boston. After several years of touring with similar small troupes and appearing in vaudeville, Bolger first came to Broadway in The Merry World (1926), followed by A Night in Paris (1926), a tour of The *Passing Show of 1926, and Heads Up (1929). His first important assignment was as principal dancer in *George White's Scandals of 1931, then he was billed as one of the stars of Life Begins at 8:40 (1934), in which he introduced "You're a Builder-Upper." A high point of his career was the role of Phil Nolan in *On Your Toes (1936) succeeded by Sapiens in *By Jupiter and, his most fondly remembered performance, Charley Wykeham in *Where's Charley? (1948), with his nightly showstopper, "Once in Love with Amy," which he persuaded audiences to sing along with him; it virtually became his theme song. Bolger's last stage appearances were in short runs: as Professor Fodorski in the collegiate musical All American (1962) and as Phineas Sharp in Come Summer (1969). For all his stage successes, he is unquestionably best remembered as the Scarecrow in the film The Wizard of Oz. The nimble, loose-jointed performer was the best and most loyal "eccentric" dancer of his age. Of his performance as Charley, David *Ewen wrote: "In a ladies' room, in an athletic love scene with a vigorous man, while fussing around with an affected feminine air, Bolger always succeeded in being amusing without stooping to Varsity Show vulgarity or offending good taste."

BOLTON, Guy [Reginald] (1884–1979), playwright. Born in England to American parents, he studied architecture, which he practiced briefly before turning to playwriting. Although Bolton is best remembered as the librettist of innumerable successful musicals, he also has several important straight comedies among his credits. With P. G. *Wodehouse, he scripted *Oh, Boy! (1917), *Leave It to Jane (1917), *Oh, Lady! Lady!! (1918), *Oh, Kay!

(1926), and *Anything Goes. Bolton's other frequent collaborator was writer Fred *Thompson, with whom he wrote *Lady, Be Good! (1924), *Tip-Toes (1925), *Rio Rita (1927), The Five O'Clock Girl (1927), and *Follow the Girls (1944). His other works include *Hit-the-Trail Holliday (1915), written with George *Middleton and George M. *Cohan; *Very Good Eddie (1915), with Philip Bartholomae; *Polly with a Past (1917), with Middleton; *Adam and Eva (1919), with Middleton; *Sally (1920); Polly Preferred (1923); The Ramblers (1926), with Bert *Kalmar and Harry *Ruby; Simple Simon (1930), with Ed *Wynn; and *Girl Crazy (1930), with Jack *McGowan (1934). Bolton's last Broadway show was Anya (1965), a musical version of his previously successful adaptation from the French, Anastasia (1954). His main claim to fame may well be the literate, witty, and cohesive librettos he created for the *Princess Theatre shows between 1915 and 1918. Far advanced for their time, in combination with Wodehouse's brilliant lyrics and *Kern's superior melodies, they helped move an adolescent genre to maturity. Autobiography: Bring on the Girls! The Improbable Story of Our Life in Musical Comedy, with Wodehouse, 1953.

BONIFACE, George C. (1833–1912), actor. After making his theatrical debut in Baltimore in 1851, he first performed in his native New York opposite Charlotte *Cushman during her 1857 repertory season. The following year he appeared in repertory with the *Wallacks at the National Theatre, then in 1859 he briefly co-managed the old *Bowery Theatre, all the while assuming leading roles in now-forgotten plays. Boniface soon switched allegiances to the competing New Bowery Theatre without surrendering his penchant for heroes of contemporary melodrama. One of his most celebrated roles was as Rudolf, the hero of the original The *Black Crook (1866). Trained in a fading school of uninhibited acting, he was on occasion criticized for not bending to the requirements of new techniques of writing and performing. Thus, when he played Pygmalion in Gilbert's Pygmalion and Galatea (1872) the Times remarked, "He mouths in a distressing fashion, the recollection of old-fashioned melodrama, played in an old-fashioned way, seeming to possess his soul to the exclusion of everything else." Nevertheless he was a popular, much sought-after performer, rarely out of work. Among his many appearances were The Twelve Temptations (1870), The *Colleen Bawn (1871), Les Misérables (1871), *Kit, the Arkansas Traveller (1877), The *Streets of New York (1886), Under Cover (1888), *Sam'l of Posen (1894), and The *Climbers (1901). His last appearance was as James Telfer in a 1911 revival of Trelawny of the Wells, a role he had created in the play's American premiere in

1898. His wife, who performed as Mrs. G. C. Boniface, his son George C. Boniface Jr., and his daughter Stella were all well known on the stage.

BONSTELLE, Jessie [neé Laura Justine Bonesteele] (1872–1932), manager and actress. Born in the small town of Greece, New York, she was encouraged by her mother to give public readings and act in amateur productions. Bonstelle's professional debut was as the deserted wife in a touring company of *Bertha, the Sewing Machine Girl.* She later took small parts under Augustin *Daly, then learned theatre management while working for the *Shuberts. After running her own stock companies in Rochester, Syracuse, and Northampton, Massachusetts, she moved to Detroit, where she leased the Garrick Theatre and mounted plays there until 1910. She still sometimes returned to Broadway, in 1910 creating the role of Rhoda in *The *Faith Healer.* Summers she often moved the troupe to Buffalo for a short season. It was here that she helped young Katharine *Cornell, one of the first in a long line of promising performers she encouraged. Others she assisted early in their careers were Ann Harding, Melvyn *Douglas, William Powell, and Frank *Morgan. Bonstelle's ability to pick promising performers earned her the appellation "Maker of Stars." In 1923 she briefly ran the Harlem Opera House in New York, and two years later she took over Detroit's Playhouse, later renaming it the Detroit Civic Theatre. Here she continued to produce plays and encourage young performers. Broadway producers respected her acumen and skill, often asking her to try out new plays for them.

BOOMERANG, THE (1915), a comedy by Winchell *Smith and Victor Mapes. [*Belasco Theatre, 522 perf.] When Budd Woodbridge (Wallace *Eddinger) comes to Dr. Gerald Sumner (Arthur *Byron) for treatment of a baffling ailment, the doctor concludes he is suffering from an acute case of jealousy, brought on by the many flirtations of his sweetheart Grace Tyler (Ruth Shepley). He suggests the cure is for Budd to make Grace jealous. To effect the cure Dr. Sumner assigns his new nurse, Virginia Xelva (Martha Hedman), to flirt publicly with the patient. Suddenly Dr. Sumner suffers the same symptoms. He realizes that he too is jealous because he is in love with Virginia. A sunny, youthful, spirited play, its success was enhanced by the excellent performances of Byron and Hedman, who subtly tilted their playing to the verge of caricature, and by producer David *Belasco's excellent production. **Victor MAPES** (1870–1943) was born in New York, studied at Columbia, and worked in Paris before becoming a stage manager for Daniel *Frohman in 1897. At the same time he assumed the post of drama critic for the *World*, writing under the name Sidney Sharp. Mapes resigned his post as critic when his first American play, *The Flower of Yeddo*, was produced in 1899. More than a dozen of his plays reached Broadway, including *Don Caesar's Return* (1901) and *Captain Barrington* (1903), but he is recalled primarily for *The Boomerang* and two other collaborations: *The New Henrietta* (1913) and *The Hottentot* (1920). During his years as an active playwright he continued to manage theatres in New York and elsewhere.

BOOTH, Agnes [neé Marian Agnes Land Rookes] (1846–1910), actress. Coming from her native Sydney, Australia, she made her first American appearance in San Francisco in 1858 as a child dancer. Using the name Agnes Land, she acted at Maguire's Opera House, then as Mrs. H. A. Perry she made her Broadway debut in 1865 as Florence Trenchard in *Our American Cousin*. When she married Junius Brutus Booth Jr., in 1867, she took the name Mrs. J. B. Booth, later simplified to Agnes Booth. For her performance as the pathologically destructive Diane Bérard in *La Femme de Feu* (1874), the *News* praised her as "the most finished and effective emotional actress at present on the metropolitan stage." In the same season she also essayed Pauline in *The *Lady of Lyons* and Juliet, and in 1877 she offered her lauded Cleopatra. Booth surprised many with her excellent comic skills as the openly selfish Belinda Treherne in *Engaged* (1879) and the rattlebrained Mrs. Chetwyn in *Young Mrs. Winthrop* (1882). Joining A. M. *Palmer in 1885 when his ensemble was at its height, she won distinction as the deceived Mrs. Ralston in *Jim, the Penman* (1886); Mrs. Seabrook, the woman with a secret, in *Captain Swift* (1888); the comic, uninhibited Joan Bryson, otherwise known as *Aunt Jack* (1889); the Marquise D'Alein, who must destroy her own reputation to save her son's marriage, in *Betrothed* (1891); and Audrey in *As You Like It* (1891). After leaving Palmer in 1892, Booth's star began to wane, to some extent because of poorly chosen vehicles but also because her robust acting style was seen as superannuated by the newer naturalistic schools. Her last major appearance was in *L'Arlesienne* in 1897.

BOOTH, Edwin [Thomas] (1833–93), actor and manager. The second son of the elder Junius Brutus *Booth to become an actor, he was born in Belair, Maryland, and made his debut in 1849 at the *Boston Museum playing Tressel to his father's Richard III. Booth made an unobtrusive New York debut in 1850 as Wilford in *The Iron Chest* but later garnered attention when he replaced his ailing father as Richard III. Shortly afterward he left to spend several seasons in California and the South Pacific, during which time his father died. It was on this tour that he mastered virtually all the roles for which he would be famous, notably Hamlet, Cardinal Richelieu, and Sir Giles Overreach. On his return to New York in 1857, he was billed as "the Hope of the living Drama." His season included not only *Hamlet, *Richelieu, and *A New Way to Pay Old Debts*, but also *King Lear, *Romeo and Juliet, The *Lady of Lyons*, and *Othello* (in which he played Iago to Charles *Fisher's Moor), as well as several now-forgotten works. Critics were unawed by his name or billing, the *Tribune* noting, "Mr. Booth is the most unequal actor we remember ever to have seen; and his fine, careful acting in one scene is no guaranty that he will not walk feebly through the next, and let it go by default." By 1862, when he became manager of the Winter Garden, his acting had improved, although many critics still complained about occasional unevenness. Booth mounted many highly praised Shakespearean productions at the house, including a *Julius Caesar* in which he portrayed Brutus, Junius Brutus Booth Jr. played Cassius, and John Wilkes *Booth played Marc Antony. The following night, November 26, 1864, he began a one-hundred-performance run as Hamlet, the longest run the play had ever had until that time. Less than a month after the play closed, Booth went into temporary retirement after learning that his brother had assassinated President Lincoln. He returned to the stage in 1866, and when the Winter Garden was destroyed by fire, he built his own theatre at 23rd Street and Sixth Avenue, opening it in 1869 with *Romeo and Juliet*. His Juliet, Mary McVicker, later became his second wife. Unfortunately, the playhouse sat on the edge of the main theatre district. This, coupled with some poor financial management, forced Booth to declare bankruptcy and lose the theatre in 1873. He then toured the country and from 1880 to 1882 performed successfully in England and Germany. In London he played at Henry *Irving's Lyceum, where he and Irving alternated as Othello and Iago. On his return he formed noteworthy partnerships with Lawrence Barrett, Helena *Modjeska, Madame *Ristori, and Tommaso *Salvini. In 1888 he gave his home on Gramercy Park to the newly organized *Players, though he retained an apartment there until his death. His last appearance was as Hamlet in 1891 at the Academy of Music in Brooklyn.

Booth's personal life was as plagued by tragedy as any of the characters he portrayed. His father and several other close family members died insane; both his first wife, Mary Devlin Booth, and his second died young; his brother's murder of Lincoln gave him his darkest moment; and financial and drinking problems often beset him. Quite possibly the daunting distractions of his private life determined his conservative approach to drama. Unlike Edwin *Forrest, he never sought to promote native plays; unlike Barrett, he never risked reviving obscure or neglected masterpieces. From early on he recognized that he had small ability in comic or in basically romantic plays. Tragedy was his forte, and he remained content with his reasonably large but relatively safe repertory. Booth stood about five feet six inches tall. His black hair, dark complexion, brown eyes, and sad mouth gave him a slightly Latin or Semitic appearance. Of his acting in *Hamlet,* William *Winter wrote, "Surely the stage, at least in our time, has never offered a more impressive and affecting combination than Mr. Booth's *Hamlet* of princely dignity, intellectual stateliness, glowing imagination, fine sensitiveness to all that is most sacred in human life and all that is most thrilling and sublime in the weird atmosphere of 'supernatural soliciting,' which enwraps the highest mood of the man of genius!" A statue of Booth was erected in 1918 in Gramercy Park opposite the Players, making him one of the rare actors so honored, and in 1913 a second New York theatre was named after him. Biography: *Prince of Players,* Eleanor Ruggles, 1953.

BOOTH, John Wilkes (1839–65). actor. The youngest and handsomest son of the elder Junius Brutus *Booth, he was born in Belair, Maryland, and made his debut in Baltimore in 1857 as Richmond in *Richard III*. His New York debut came in 1862 when he assumed the lead in the same play. According to the *Herald*, he created "a veritable sensation.... His face blackened and smeared with blood, he seemed Richard himself; and his combat with Richmond ... was a masterpiece." With the outbreak of the Civil War, he played largely in the South but did cross the lines, ostensibly to act in the North, although quite possibly to transmit secret messages. Among his parts were Hamlet, Marc Antony, and other then-standard romantic and tragic roles. Perhaps out of jealousy of his brother Edwin *Booth, he affected a style much closer to the old school of his father than to the newer, more tempered acting. One Cleveland theatre manager wrote of him that he "has the fire, the dash, the touch of strangeness." How greatly his art would have developed was left unanswered by his death following his assassination of Lincoln. Booth shot Lincoln while the president was watching a performance of *Our American Cousin* from a box at *Ford's Theatre in Washington on April 14, 1865. Jumping from the box, he is said to have shouted, "Sic Semper Tyrannis!" But in his jump he caught his leg and was injured in the fall. Grabbing a horse that had been kept waiting in the alley by the theatre, he eluded pursuers until he was caught on April 26 in a barn on the Richmond and Fredericksburg Railroad. He was shot but refused to leave the barn, and since he was known to be armed, the building was set afire. Only after he was badly burned did he come out. He died shortly thereafter. Biography: *The Man Who Killed Lincoln*, Phillip Van Doren Stern, 1939.

BOOTH, Junius Brutus (1796–1852), actor. Slated for the law in his native England, he elected to become an actor instead and soon rose to play opposite Edmund *Kean, who was seen in many quarters as his rival. In 1821, however, Booth deserted his wife, wed Mary Ann Holmes, a Bow Street flower seller years later, and came to America, where in Richmond he made his debut as Richard III, making his New York debut in the same role the next year. The critic for the *National Advocate* described Booth as "slender, and below middle size; youthful in appearance and rather handsome than otherwise. His countenance is open and expressive; his eye of that peculiar cast which is well adapted to display the workings of a distorted mind; his voice pleasing and capable of great modulation." Among his other famous roles were Hamlet, Sir Giles Overreach, Posthumus, Iago, and Cassius, as well as important parts in such now-neglected plays as *Brutus. Many critics suggested his interpretations were copied from Kean, but nonetheless they recognized his unique abilities and hailed him as the first powerful tragedian of the American stage. Early on he developed a habit of beginning quietly and saving his full force for the final impassioned scenes. At one time he played Oreste in Racine's *Andromaque* in French and claimed to have done Shylock in Hebrew, the last possibly reflecting his Jewish ancestry. As with all actors of his day, he toured regularly. His last performance was in New Orleans, and he died on a Mississippi steamboat while continuing that tour. Because his first wife would not grant him a divorce until 1851, all his children but the first were born out of wedlock. His eldest son by his second marriage, Junius Brutus Booth Jr. (1821–83), made his New York debut as Abder Khan in *Mazeppa* in 1843. Never the fine performer his father or brothers were, he played largely in supporting roles, although he had a moderately successful career as actor-manager, especially in California. He retired early to enter the hotel business. Biography: *Booth Memorials: Passages, Incidents and Anecdotes in the Life of Junius Brutus Booth (the Elder)*, Asia Booth Clarke, 1866.

BOOTH, Shirley [née Thelma Booth Ford] (1898–1992), actress. A native New Yorker, she made her debut with the Poli Stock Company in Hartford in 1919 in *The *Cat and the Canary* and her New York debut as Nan Winchester in *Hell's Bells* (1925). A variety of roles followed before she made her mark as Mabel, a gambler's moll, in *Three Men on a Horse* (1935). Booth won further popularity as Elizabeth Imbrie, the wisecracking photographer, in *The *Philadelphia Story* (1939) and as Ruth Sherwood, the would-be authoress, in *My *Sister Eileen* (1940). Turning to drama, she played Leona Richards, who tries to re-educate a young Nazi, in *Tomorrow the World* (1943), and she earned her first *Tony Award as Grace Woods, the back-talking secretary, in *Goodbye, My Fancy* (1948). Her second Tony came for what many believe her finest performance, the slovenly Lola in *Come Back, Little Sheba* (1950). The versatile, baby-voiced actress was hailed by Brooks *Atkinson, who noted, "She has the shuffle, the maddening garrulity and the rasping voice of the slattern, but withal she imparts to the role the warmth, generosity and valor of a loyal and affectionate woman." After playing the feisty Aunt Cissy in the musical *A *Tree Grows in Brooklyn* (1951), she garnered her third Tony as the lonely Leona Samish in *The *Time of the Cuckoo* (1952). Booth next scored personal success in two minor works, the musical *By the Beautiful Sea* (1954) and a comedy, *The Desk Set* (1955). Her last Broadway appearances were in the short-lived musical *Look to the Lilies* (1970) and that same year in a revival of *Hay Fever*.

BOOTH THEATRES (New York). Two beloved theatres named after Edwin *Booth have flourished in Manhattan. The first Booth Theatre was built in 1869 on 23rd Street to present Shakespeare productions by the renowned actor it was named after. It was a very advanced theatre, designed by the famous New York architect James Renwick Jr., and featured extensive backstage space, room for scene and costume shops, and an early sprinkler system. Booth gave several sparkling performances there and managed the house himself for a few years, then it changed management several times until it was turned into a department store in 1883, which was later demolished. The second and current Booth Theatre on West 45th Street is a small but much-treasured house designed by Henry B. *Herts. It opened in 1913 with its attached sister theatre the Sam S. *Shubert on *Shubert Alley. Producer Winthrop *Ames presented small productions in the elegant, Italian Renaissance style that seated only 785, and over the years the Shubert-owned theatre has become a favorite house for intimate pieces.

BOOTHE [Luce], [Anna] **Clare** (1903–87), playwright. A New Yorker who was briefly a child actress, she turned to playwriting after successfully serving as managing editor of the magazine *Vanity Fair* and writing books. Her first play, *O Pyramids* (1933), never reached Broadway, and her second, *Abide with Me* (1935), a story of a cruel dipsomaniac, was a quick failure. But Boothe won success with *The *Women* (1936), a witty, slashing comedy of female manners. A spoof of Hollywood's celebrated search for a Scarlett O'Hara, *Kiss the Boys Good-bye* (1938), and *Margin for Error* (1939), in which a Jewish policeman is assigned to guard a Nazi diplomat, also won favor. The wife of publisher Henry Luce, she later became active in conservative politics and served a stint as United States ambassador to Italy. Biography: *Rage for Fame*, Sylvia Jukes Morris, 1997.

BORDONI, Irene (1895–1953), singer and actress. The tiny Corsican-born comedienne, who was perceived as a latter-day Anna *Held because of her coyly naughty performing, first appeared in New York in *Broadway to Paris* (1912). Subsequently she played in *Miss Information* (1915) and the 1917 and 1918 editions of *Hitchy Koo*. Bordoni's heyday was in the 1920s, when she was starred by her husband E. Ray *Goetz in *As You Were* (1920); *The French Doll* (1922), in which she sang "Do It Again"; and *Paris* (1928), in which she introduced Cole *Porter's "Let's Do It." In 1938 she played in *Great Lady* and two years later sang Irving *Berlin's "It's a Lovely Day Tomorrow" in *Louisiana Purchase*. Her last major appearances came when she toured as Bloody Mary in *South Pacific* in 1951. Bordoni also appeared in vaudeville and occasionally in nonmusical plays.

BORN YESTERDAY (1946), a comedy by Garson *Kanin. [*Lyceum Theatre, 1,642 perf.] Billie Dawn (Judy *Holliday) is the "dumb-blonde" mistress of the crass but very rich junkman Harry Brock (Paul Douglas) who always lives "at the top of his voice." She is forever embarrassing him with her gaffes, so he hires a handsome young liberal writer, Paul Verrall (Gary Merrill), to tutor her. Brock's reward is to have Billie's eyes opened and to have her turn against him, accusing him of being "not couth." When he orders her to cosign some important papers she refuses, so he slaps her. Billie signs the papers, packs her bags, and heads for the door, quietly asking Harry for just one favor before she leaves. He growlingly wants to know what that favor might be, and she asks softly, "Drop dead?" When Billie later returns to get the rest of her things, she announces that she has turned over to Paul incriminating papers that can send Brock to jail. Since Brock has long since put most of his property in her name, however, she offers a compromise: Paul will not publish the

papers and she will sign back his property to him—but only a bit each year, for as long as he behaves. Like so much Kanin-family writing, the play was a sermon on the virtues of liberalism; but its bright lines, sharp character studies, and superb performances made the Max *Gordon production capital theatre. Holliday's performance was all the more remarkable since she was a relative unknown who had been cast hastily when the original star, Jean Arthur, quit during the tryout. A commendable Broadway revival in 1989 with Madeline Kahn as Billie did disappointing business.

BOSCO, Philip [Michael] (b. 1930), actor. One of Broadway's busiest and most versatile actors, he only became a widely recognized stage star in his later years, but for decades he gave superlative performances in classic and contemporary comedies and dramas. He was born in Jersey City, New Jersey, the son of a carnival operator, and educated at Catholic University of America. The big, burly performer worked as a carnival performer and was a truck driver before becoming a resident actor at Washington's *Arena Stage from 1957 to 1960. He made his Broadway debut as the modern-thinking Heracles in *The Rape of the Belt* (1960), then over the years Bosco would act for all the notable Manhattan theatre companies, including the *New York Shakespeare Festival, *Roundabout Theatre, *Circle in the Square, and *Lincoln Center. Some highlights from his many outstanding performances at these theatres included the understanding father Nat Miller in *Ah, Wilderness!* (1983), recovering alcoholic Doc in *Come Back, Little Sheba* (1984), paranoid Commander Queeg in *The Caine Mutiny Court-Martial* (1983), and principal Shavian parts, such as Undershaft, Boss Mangan, the Waiter (in *You Never Can Tell*), and General Burgoyne. His years of loyalty to live theatre were rewarded when he was starred on Broadway as Saunders, the beleaguered impresario, in *Lend Me a Tenor* (1989). Bosco's later performances of note include the obsessive Harpagon in *The Miser* (1990), Mafioso Mike Francisco in *Breaking Legs* (1991), ham actor George Hay in *Moon Over Buffalo* (1995), Malvolio in *Twelfth Night* (1998), and the Danish physicist Niels Bohr in *Copenhagen* (2000).

BOSS, THE (1911), a play by Edward *Sheldon. [Astor Theatre, 88 perf.] Michael R. Regan (Holbrook *Blinn) is an ex-bartender turned contractor and political boss. By corrupt means he has secured the lucrative grain contracts that are at the heart of the wealth of James Griswold (Henry Weaver). Knowing that Griswold has used funds from his own banks to promote his own companies, Regan threatens to send the man to prison. When Griswold assures Regan that what he did was legal, Regan replies, "Tain't what you do that counts in this world. It's what folks think ye done!" He will spare Griswold (in fact, he will take him on as partner) if Griswold's daughter Emily (Emily *Stevens) will marry him and bring him social position. To save her father, Emily agrees but she tells Regan that she will not be a loving wife: "Everything will stop at the church door." Later Emily's brother Donald (Howard Estabrook) joins up with Archbishop Sullivan (Frank Sheridan), a boyhood friend of Regan's, and the two organize the workers against Regan. They succeed in destroying Regan, who plans to flee to Canada. But when Emily tells him to remain home and take his licking like a man, he realizes that she has come to love him, and he stays. The William A. *Brady production told an exciting story yet, at its best, it was an incisive study of two people and their romance. *Quinn has written, "The attention of the audience is centered upon the relations of 'Regan' and his wife. They are strongly contrasted types and at first glance their union seems impossible. Yet Mr. Sheldon has indicated unobtrusively enough but surely with sufficient definiteness, the inherent attraction which the strength of 'Regan' had for 'Emily Griswold' and the way in which her pity and sympathy finally turned to something deeper." A commendable Off-Broadway revival in 1976 proved that the drama was still potent.

BOSTON (Massachusetts). Although it was long one of the most important American theatrical centers, players found little welcome there in early times when puritanical influences were still strong. Not until 1792, with the opening of the New Exhibition Room (later called the Broad Alley Theatre), did the city have anything resembling a playhouse, and even then the name suggested the subterfuge required. The first major playhouse in the city was the *Federal Street Theatre (1794), which long dominated local theatricals. The Haymarket, erected two years later, was never able to compete successfully and was razed in 1803. The first important opposition came from the Tremont, which opened in 1827 and remained active for a decade and a half. The leading mid-19th-century auditoriums were the *Boston Museum (1841) and the *Howard Athenaeum (1846). In 1879 the *Boston Ideal Opera Company was founded and soon became the nation's leading light-opera ensemble. While it regularly toured the country, Boston remained its base. In the first half of the 20th century, Boston was a major tryout and touring center while supporting such once-famous local organizations as the Jewett Players and Mrs. Lyman

Gale's Toy Theatre. Indeed, theatre flourished, albeit the city was infamous for the harshest theatrical censorship in the land. One reason Boston remained so vital was the excellence of its theatrical criticism as exemplified by the renown of Henry Taylor *Parker and Henry Austin *Clapp. The fine writing of Elliot *Norton of the *Herald-American* and Kevin Kelly of the *Globe* continued this tradition. In addition to the many collegiate theatres in the area, the Huntington Theatre Company, Lyric Stage of Boston, *American Repertory Theatre (in nearby Cambridge), Boston Playwrights' Theatre, and other groups, provide local productions, as well as touring productions at the Charles Playhouse, and the Wilbur and *Colonial Theatres. The annual Elliot Norton Awards have been given to outstanding area theatre productions since 1982.

BOSTON IDEAL OPERA COMPANY. The organization was founded in 1879 by Effie H. Ober specifically to mount an "ideal" production of *H. M. S. Pinafore* for Boston. The production was so successful, establishing a long-run record for the city at the time, that other comic operas were quickly mounted and the troupe became a de facto repertory company. The company soon began touring and eventually covered every important city in the United States and Canada. After an internal dispute the leading performers assumed the management, and the group adopted the simpler name by which it had become popularly known, the Bostonians. Among the members were Henry Clay *Barnabee, Jessie Bartlett *Davis, W. H. MacDonald, Eugene *Cowles, Tom Karl, and other distinguished performers, who were joined for shorter periods by such fine players as Bertha Waltzinger and Camille D'Arville. Their ensemble playing was of such high quality that they were recognized as the foremost group of their kind. The *Montreal Herald* noted, "The Bostonians have been together since the beginning of American lyric opera. It is not strange that they should be its best interpreters." Besides offering lighter operas, such as *Fra Diavolo, Martha,* or *The Elixir of Love,* as well as English and Continental operettas, the company made a determined effort to encourage American works. Their most famous American mounting was *Robin Hood* (1891), but they also produced the earliest works of Victor *Herbert, among them *Prince Ananias* (1894) and *The Serenade* (1897). When one member, Alice *Nielsen, left the company to form her own troupe in 1898, taking with her several other important members, the troupe began to decline and it later disbanded after the 1904–05 season.

BOSTON MUSEUM [and Gallery of Fine Arts], **THE.** Conceived by Moses Kimball, who had purchased the old New England Museum, it was opened in 1841; and its own stock company gave its first performance in 1843, thereafter remaining one of the nation's finest ensembles. Its favorite performers were William *Warren and Mrs. R. H. *Vincent, but at one time or another in its long career many great artists of the era appeared, either as members of the troupe or as guest stars. The subterfuge of housing a theatre in a museum was not uncommon, for it allowed many otherwise puritanical people to enjoy playgoing. The theatre closed in 1893.

BOSTON THEATRE (Boston). One of America's largest and most famous 19th-century playhouses, the Boston Theatre opened in 1854 and seated 3,140 spectators. Dion *Boucicault called it "the finest theatre in the world." Although the house featured its own stock company in the late 1880s, the Boston was better known for the celebrated actors who performed there, from Edwin *Booth to Sarah *Bernhardt. The theatre became a vaudeville house in 1909, and later it was a movie palace before being demolished in 1925.

BOTH YOUR HOUSES (1933), a play by Maxwell *Anderson. [Royale Theatre, 120 perf.; Pulitzer Prize.] After Alan McClean (Sheppard Strudwick) was fired for exposing misappropriations at his school, his muckraking publisher father used the incident as a springboard to elect Alan to Congress. Advised that their freshman colleague is "Serious. Wears mail-order clothes. Reads Thomas Jefferson," the older congressmen on the Appropriations Committee are alarmed. Their fears are quickly justified when Alan denounces the very contractors who supported his election bid and argues against money for a dam in his district. When he fails to defeat a carefully negotiated pork-barrel bill, he does an about-face and offers his own bill, which includes money for every congressman's request, no matter how absurd. To his disgust the bill passes, and he is hailed as a political genius. This preachy, bitter, but powerfully written play, with perceptive portraits of a variety of congressmen, was only a modest hit, and the *Theatre Guild production had already begun its post-Broadway tour when it was awarded the *Pulitzer Prize. It was hastily returned to New York for a short additional run.

BOUCICAULT, Dion[ysius Lardner] (1820?–90), playwright and actor. Named for his parents' friend, Dr. Dionysius Lardner, who may have been his natural father and who was known to have taken a paternal interest in the boy, he left his native Dublin to study in London. He started acting and writing in 1836, making his name in 1841

with his brilliant comedy *London Assurance.* Boucicault made his American acting debut in Boston in 1854 and two months afterward gave his first New York performance as Sir Charles Coldstream in his own play, *Used Up.* He is said to have written at least two hundred plays, many of them during his stays in America from 1853 to 1860 and from 1870 to 1890. Among these plays were The *Poor of New York (1857), adapted from the French and frequently revived as The *Streets of New York; *Jessie Brown; or, The Relief of Lucknow (1858); The *Octoroon (1859); two Charles Dickens adaptations: Dot (1859) and Smike (1859); Jeanie Deans (1860), taken from The Heart of Midlothian; The *Colleen Bawn; or, The Brides of Garryowen (1860); *Arrah Na Pogue (1865); *Rip Van Winkle (1866); the Irish melodramas The O'Dowd (1873) and The *Shaughraun (1874); the Civil War play Belle Lamar (1874); and his last play of any importance, The Jilt, which was mounted in San Francisco in 1885. After the opening of The Poor of New York Boucicault commented, "I can spin out these rough-and-tumble dramas as a hen lays eggs. It's a degrading occupation, but more money has been made out of guano than out of poetry." He also observed, "Sensation is what the public wants and you cannot give them too much of it." "Sensation scenes" were frequent in his works: the rescue from the burning building in The Poor of New York, the blazing ship in The Octoroon, and an underwater rescue in The Colleen Bawn are but three examples. In the long run, his successful struggle to secure passage of a copyright law may have been as important to the development of American drama as his writings. Recalling indignities an author such as Robert Montgomery *Bird suffered at the hands of Edwin *Forrest, he and George Henry *Boker lobbied arduously until the Copyright Law of 1856 was passed. Not only was Boucicault the most successful and popular playwright of his era, he also remained widely admired as an actor, especially in his Irish plays. His personal reputation was seriously hurt late in life when he was involved in a messy divorce case and he spent most of his last years teaching at a drama school established by A. M. *Palmer and serving as that producer's play doctor. William *Winter wrote of his acting that it was "all intellect . . . but he knew the emotions by sight, and he mingled them as a chemist mingles chemicals; generally with success." That his best plays still have theatrical validity was demonstrated when the *Phoenix Theatre revived The Octoroon in 1961. Richard *Watts Jr. wrote in the Post, "Some of its theatrics do seem excessive to us now . . . but, on the whole, it is still a play of sturdy dramatic values and it deserves to be seen far more for its intrinsic merits than for its occasional sins of innocence against modern sophistication." Boucicault's *London Assurance* has remained stage worthy with New York revivals in 1937, 1974, and 1997. His son Aubrey Boucicault (1869–1913) was also a noted actor who made his American debut in 1887 and appeared in many roles associated with his father and also played in numerous musical comedies and in vaudeville. Biography: *Dion Boucicault*, Richard Fawkes, 1979.

BOUGHT AND PAID FOR (1911), a play by George *Broadhurst. [Playhouse, 431 perf.] Although Virginia Blaine (Julia *Dean), a young telephone operator, is uncertain that she really loves millionaire Robert Stafford (Charles *Richman), she accepts his proposal of marriage. At first the marriage seems everything both could want, but Virginia soon learns that Stafford drinks too much and can be demanding when drunk. When she refuses his drunken caresses and locks herself in her room, he breaks down the door and tells her she cannot refuse him since she has been bought and paid for. Virginia announces she will not live with him until he promises to reform, but Stafford honestly replies there is no point in his making a promise he is not sure he can keep. The couple finally come to realize that they are loving and intelligent enough to work out their problems. Several critics saw a similarity between this work and Eugene *Walter's earlier **Paid in Full*, both of which made working-class heroines the central figures of problem plays. For many critics the highlight of the William A. *Brady production was the performance of Frank *Craven as the wiseacre shipping clerk James Gilley, which made him a star.

BOUND EAST FOR CARDIFF. See *S. S. Glencairn*.

BOWERS, Mrs. D. P. [née Elizabeth Crocker] (1830–95), actress. Born in Stamford, Connecticut, she appeared under her maiden name for her debut at the *Park Theatre in 1846 as Amanthis in *The Child of Nature*. The next year she married Bowers, and shortly thereafter they moved to Philadelphia where she and her husband were important members of the *Walnut Street Theatre Company. Among her best-received roles there were Juliet, Camille, Julia in *The *Hunchback*, and Pauline in *The *Lady of Lyons*. After her husband's death in 1857, Bowers played in New York and on tour, then spent several seasons in England. Her star declined somewhat in later years, but she continued to play important supporting roles with major ensembles, most often as strong, regal characters. She was Emilia in the *Booth-*Salvini *Othello* (1886), the Queen in their *Hamlet* (1886), and the Duchess of Berwick in the first American performance of *Lady Windermere's Fan* (1893).

BOWERY THEATRE (New York). Originally planned as the Bull's Head Theatre after a tavern on the site, it was opened in 1826 as the New York Theatre, Bowery. The name never took and it was always known simply as the Bowery Theatre. In its early years the house was the major competition to the *Park Theatre, and was the New York home of Edwin *Forrest. The theatre burned and was rebuilt in 1828. Shortly afterward Thomas *Hamblin took over management, emphasizing new plays, especially increasingly popular melodramas. Shortly before it burned again in 1836, the theatre witnessed the farewell of Thomas Abthorpe *Cooper and the first appearance of Charlotte *Cushman as Lady Macbeth. The rebuilt theatre suffered a third fire in 1838. By the time it was rebuilt in 1839, the theatre district had begun to move away and the area was changing. Ineluctably the house's fare became less lofty. Under a succession of managers, including Edward *Eddy, it gained fame as the home of roaring, all-stops-pulled melodrama and briefly, under George L. *Fox, the home of pantomime. Although from the first the theatre attracted a less-elite audience than the older Park, it was during this period that the playhouse's rambunctious clientele became a theatrical legend. The theatre was the last major auditorium in New York to retain a pit, which survived well into the 1860s. There and in the upper reaches, filthy urchins sold fruit, nuts, and candy. The nutshells, fruit stones, and rinds were often hurled on stage by the disgruntled ruffians who comprised a large segment of the playgoers, and verbal insults accompanied the trash. On happier occasions outspoken encouragement was offered to luckier performers, and they were often expected to depart from the text and drop the character they were portraying to engage in a dialogue with the audience. By 1879 the theatre, which was surrounded by immigrant tenements, was renamed the Thalia and offered plays in German and Yiddish. No attempt was made to rebuild it again when it burned in 1929.

BOWLES, Jane. See *In the Summer House*.

BOY MEETS GIRL (1935), a comedy by Bella and Sam *Spewack. [*Cort Theatre, 669 perf.] Robert Law (Allyn Joslyn) and J. Carlyle Benson (Jerome Cowan) are two rambunctious, practical-joking screenwriters who simply cannot become serious when told they must devise a scenario to save fading cowboy star Larry Toms (Charles McClelland). "Even Wilkes-Barre doesn't want him, and they're still calling for Theda Bara." Learning that a pregnant studio waitress, Susie (Joyce Arling), is about to give birth, Law and Benson obtain power of attorney and set about making the baby Toms's costar. The tot's popularity saves Toms's career, but when a lawyer wrests the power of attorney from the writers, Law and Carlyle attempt to destroy the baby's vogue by hiring a studio extra, Rodney (James MacColl), to claim he is the baby's real father. Susie and Rodney had once met and fallen in love, but she stubbornly plans to run off with Toms until he catches measles from the baby and shows his true dislike for the tot. So Susie ends up with Rodney, who turns out to be a titled Englishman. "An extraordinarily hilarious comedy," as Brooks *Atkinson observed, the play was not only a telling spoof of Hollywood in general, but a particularly adroit send-up of Ben *Hecht and Charles *MacArthur, the real life counterparts of Law and Carlyle. Producer-director George *Abbott kept the "madcap fooling at high speed," filling the stage with a variety of Hollywood moguls, yes-men, players, midgets, and blaring trumpeters.

BOYER, Charles (1899–1978), actor. The romantic French leading man of films came to the theatre only after his movie career had faltered. He made his debut as Hoederer, the vicious Communist leader, in *Red Gloves* (1948), but scored a far greater success as Don Juan in *Shaw's *Don Juan in Hell* (1951). Subsequently, Boyer was the banker Philip Clairin, a mature romantic in *Kind Sir* (1953), the married professor Paul Delville tempted by a Swedish beauty in *The Marriage-Go-Round* (1958), the art dealer in *Lord Pengo* (1962), and the doomed financier Gregor Antonescu in *Man and Boy* (1963).

BOYS FROM SYRACUSE, THE (1938), a musical comedy by George *Abbott (book), Richard *Rodgers (music), Lorenz *Hart (lyrics). [Alvin Theatre, 235 perf.] The twins Antipholus of Ephesus (Ronald Graham) and Antipholus of Syracuse (Eddie Albert), who were separated when young, have taken on twin servants, both named Dromio (Teddy Hart and Jimmy Savo). When the pair from Syracuse come to Ephesus, a comedy of errors ensues that involves the wife Adriana (Muriel Angelus), her sister Luciana (Marcy Wescott), and others in the town. *Notable songs*: This Can't Be Love; Sing for Your Supper; Falling in Love with Love; Dear Old Syracuse; What Can You Do with a Man? Unlike the later *Kiss Me, Kate*, which used much of its Shakespearean source, *The Boys from Syracuse* employed only a single line from *The Comedy of Errors*, which Savo popped out from the wings to alert audiences to. The Abbot produced-directed show was hailed as "the best musical in many a year" by *Time*, and a 1963 Off-Broadway revival ran even longer than the original, though a 2002 version on Broadway was not well received.

BOYS IN THE BAND, THE (1968), a play by Mart Crowley. [Theatre Four, 1,000 perf.] Michael (Kenneth Nelson) is holding a birthday party for his friend Harold (Leonard Frey), and since both men and all their friends are homosexuals no one is surprised when Michael's present to Harold is a fling with a handsome male hustler, Cowboy (Robert La Tourneaux). Drink loosens tongues, and exchanges quickly become bitchy. But the carefully controlled viciousness is shattered by the unwanted arrival of Michael's old school roommate, the heterosexual Alan (Peter White). Realizing the true situation, Alan turns hostile and belligerent, spoiling the evening for Michael. Hurt and a little baffled, Michael tells the last guest, "I don't understand any of it. I never did." The play was one of the earliest of a rash of works centering on homosexuality, and it managed to find acceptance and popularity with a mainstream audience. While gay groups later dismissed the drama as a negative, melodramatic view of homosexual life style, an Off-Off-Broadway revival in 1996 was popular enough to move to Off Broadway for an extended run.

BRADY, Alice (1892–1939) actress. The daughter of producer William A. *Brady, she was born in New York and studied at the Boston Conservatory of Music with the intention of becoming an opera singer but turned to the stage in 1909, making her debut as a minor courtier in Robert *Mantell's mounting of *As You Like It*. Brady was featured in musicals, such as *The Balkan Princess* (1911), and in a 1912 series of *Gilbert and *Sullivan revivals, but she also essayed dramatic roles, such as Meg in *Little Women* (1912), the loyal wife Alice Nelson in *The Family Cupboard* (1913), the sentimental Beulah Randolph in *Things That Count* (1913), and Mary Horton who hides her past in *Sinners* (1915). She then enjoyed long runs as Jennie in *Forever After* (1918), the hostage Mamie in *Zander the Great* (1923), the guilt-ridden Ina Bowman in *Bride of the Lamb* (1926), and blackmailer Laura Sargent in *A Most Immoral Lady* (1928). Brady's last role was generally acknowledged as her best: Lavinia Mannon in *Mourning Becomes Electra* (1931). Brooks *Atkinson wrote, "Miss Brady . . . has one of the longest parts ever written. None of her neurotic dramatics in the past has prepared us for the demonic splendor of her Lavinia. She speaks in an ominous, full voice that only once or twice breaks into the splintery diffusion of artificial climaxes." She enjoyed a successful film career in the 1930s.

BRADY, William A [loysius] (1863–1950), producer. After getting his theatrical start by bluffing his way into a small part in *The White Slave* in his native San Francisco in 1882, Brady turned to producing in 1888. Although he got into trouble for presenting pirated works early in his career, he eventually found favor presenting a series of vehicles for James J. *Corbett and securing the Western rights to *Trilby*, even taking it to Australia. In 1896 he leased the Manhattan Theatre in New York and began to mount plays there, the most successful being *Way Down East* (1898). A year later he married his second wife, actress Grace *George, whose career thereafter was often intermixed with his. In 1911 Brady built the Playhouse, managed such performers as Wilton *Lackaye, Robert *Mantell, and Henry E. *Dixey, and presented notable productions, including *Baby Mine* (1910), *The *Boss* (1911), *Bought and Paid For* (1911), *Bunty Pulls the Strings* (1911), *Sinners* (1915), *The *Man Who Came Back* (1916), *Forever After* (1918), *The Skin Game* (1920), *The Enchanted Cottage* (1923), and *Street Scene* (1929). His daughter was actress Alice *Brady and his son **William A. BRADY Jr.** (1900–35) was also a producer, entering into partnership with Dwight Deere *Wiman and presenting, among others, *Lucky Sam McCarver* (1925), *Little Eyolf* (1926), *The *Two Orphans* (1926), *The *Road to Rome* (1927), *Women Go on Forever* (1927), *The *Little Show* (1929), and *The Second Little Show* (1930). After the partnership was dissolved, he produced *Little Women* (1931) and several failed plays. Autobiography: (William Brady Sr.): *Showman*, 1937.

BRAHAM, David (1838–1905), composer. The London-born musician came to the States while still a relatively young man, and he worked for a time as a violinist with Tony Moore's Minstrels, then became Tony *Pastor's musical director. Braham's heyday came when he doubled as musical director and composer for the shows written by his son-in-law Edward *Harrigan. Among his best-loved melodies were those for "The Babies on Our Block," "Little Widow Dunn," "Maggie Murphy's Home," "The Mulligan Guard," and "Paddy Duffy's Cart." After Harrigan's retirement he continued to compose with less success and to conduct orchestras at various New York playhouses.

BRANDO, Marlon. See *Streetcar Named Desire, A.*

BREAD AND PUPPET THEATRE. An unconventional performing group without a distinct home, company, or financial plan, the group was founded in 1961 in New York by Peter Schumann whose philosophy is that "theatre is like bread, more like a necessity." The troupe uses larger-than-life puppets and avant-garde theatre techniques to explore a theme, usually a controversial topic that elicits vocal reactions from the audience. They prefer to perform for free whenever possible, and often the players hand out bread to the patrons, literally illustrating Schumann's ideas. The company was located at Goddard College in Vermont for four years in the early 1970s, but for most of its existence it has toured nationally and internationally. By the late 1970s the group disbanded, but Schumann reorganized members for special events as late as the 1990s. The home base is now back in Vermont where the Bread and Puppet Museum is located.

BRECHT, [Eugen] **Bertolt** [Friedrich] (1898–1956), playwright and director. The German Marxist playwright and librettist spent time in America as a refugee from Nazism. After he appeared before the House Un-American Activities Committee in 1947, he left for Zurich and moved to East Germany in 1949. There he was given carte blanche and co-founded (and until his death co-directed) the Berliner Ensemble in East Berlin, producing his and other works. American playgoers know Brecht best for his book and lyrics to *The *Threepenny Opera*. The work was one of several musicals he wrote with Kurt *Weill in his Berlin days. Among his other works done with some frequency on American stages, thanks to Eric Bentley's translations and promotion efforts, are *Galileo, The Good Woman of Setzuan, Happy End, The Caucasian Chalk Circle, Arturo Ui*, and *Mother Courage*. Many of these plays exemplified Brecht's concept of epic theatre, which sometimes moved a story beyond the logical or expected unities of time and place, and which regularly imbued it with larger human and political meaning. His "alienation" technique was utilized to get his audiences to think, as opposed to conventional theatre technique, which invited them to become totally emotionally involved. His enormous influence, from plays and critical works alike, is felt in theatre and film to this day.

BREESE, Edmund (1871–1936), actor. Although he never achieved stardom, the Brooklyn-born actor was much sought after for more than forty years. He made his debut in Eureka Springs, Arkansas, in 1895 and later supported James *O'Neill in *The *Count of Monte Cristo* and Robert *Edeson in *Strongheart*. His most famous roles were the Rockefeller-like millionaire John Burkett Ryder in *The *Lion and the Mouse* (1905) and Hiram Draper, who opposes his son's marriage to an English girl, in *So This Is London* (1922). In between he was praised for his devil Dickon in the first New York production of *The *Scarecrow* (1911) and the unhappily married John in *Why Marry?* (1917). He was playing District Attorney Flint in *Night of January 16* (1935) at the time of his death.

BREUER, Lee. See Mabou Mines.

BREWSTER'S MILLIONS (1906), a play by Winchell *Smith and Byron Ongley. [*New Amsterdam Theatre, 163 perf.] Montgomery Brewster (Edward Abeles) is left one million dollars in the will of his grandfather, who died remorseful over neglecting his daughter, Brewster's mother. Monty's joy at his inheritance is at once compounded and confounded when he learns his uncle has also died and left him seven million dollars. But his uncle's will contains a hitch. The uncle hated his father (Monty's grandfather) and demands that Monty spend all of the grandfather's money at once, without revealing why and without giving any money to charity. Monty enlists a group of his friends to help on the spending spree, but complications arise because of the secrecy clause. In this raucous farce, which was based on George Barr McCutcheon's story, Smith introduced a mysterious performer named George *Spelvin, who later reappeared in many of his plays whenever the real identity of a figure had to be kept secret. The name became something of a Smith trademark and is still used today.

BRIAN, Donald (1877–1948), singer and actor. He began singing publicly as a child in his native Newfoundland then, traveling with glee clubs and medicine shows and playing small parts on the road, he came to New York where he made his debut in 1899 as Spangler in *On the Wabash*. After appearing as Tom Schuyler in a touring company of *The Chaperones* and playing parts in *The Supper Club*, *Florodora, and The *Belle of New York, Brian came under George M. *Cohan's aegis, playing Henry Hapgood in *Little Johnny Jones (1904) and Tom Bennett in *Forty-five Minutes from Broadway (1906). His most-famous assignment was as Prince Danilo in the original American production of The *Merry Widow (1907). Brian then was starred as Freddy Smythe in *The Dollar Princess* (1909); the Marquis de Ravaillac in *The Siren* (1911); Jack Fleetwood in *The Marriage Market* (1913); Sandy Blair in *The *Girl from Utah (1914), in which he introduced "They Didn't Believe Me"; the Grand Duke in *Sybil* (1916); André de Courcy in *Her Regiment* (1917); Robert Lambrissac in *The Girl Behind the Gun* (1918); Sonny in *Buddies* (1919); and Bumerli in a 1921 revival of *The Chocolate Soldier*. During the 1920s and early 1930s he also appeared in a number of nonmusical plays, besides heading a road company of *No, No, Nanette. Brian played Danilo again in a 1932 revival of *The Merry Widow* and his last Broadway appearance was as the paternal William Graham, in *Very Warm for May* (1939). Although he was trained as a singer, many critics claimed the wavy-haired, dimpled performer excelled as a dancer. "Light of voice and lighter of feet," the *Herald* said of his Danilo.

BRIAR CLIFF; *or, Scenes of the Revolution* (1826), a play by George P. Morris. [Chatham Garden Theatre, in repertory.] Although Mary Jansen (Mrs. Waring) is a member of a loyalist family, she has fallen in love with Alfred Leslie (Mr. *Duff) who has been fighting for independence and has been captured. Not even General Howe (Mr. Herbert) can change Leslie's sentiments. With the help of a sympathetic Englishman, Eugene Grant (Mr. Stevenson), Mary contrives Leslie's escape. He hides in the cave of Crazy Bet (Mrs. *Duff) and also disguises himself as a preacher. Leslie's rival, the British officer Major Waldron (Mr. Durang), kidnaps Mary and puts her aboard a sloop in Long Island Sound, and when the sloop founders she is rescued by Indians. As the war ends she is reunited with Leslie, but the romance ends tragically when the disgruntled Waldron shoots Mary and she dies holding Leslie's hand. Based on the novel *Whig and Tory*, the play was sometimes spelled *Brier Cliff* and often subtitled *A Picture of Former Times*. The Henry *Wallack production apparently assumed playgoers were familiar with the original, since it is poorly motivated and makes illogical skips of plot. Nevertheless it is filled with colorful characters and interesting dialogue, offering intriguing glimpses of the period. One English soldier exclaims, "America! There's nothing here but mosquitoes, bats, savages, equality, sour crout, 'liberty' and bumble bees." It remained popular for many years, at one time or another being mounted at every New York theatre and in many theatres elsewhere. **George Pope MORRIS** (1802–64), a journalist, novelist, and poet, was editor of the *New York Mirror* when the play was produced. He named his mansion Briarcliff.

BRICE, Fanny [née Borach] (1891–1951), comedienne and singer. The native New Yorker first performed for customers in her parents' saloon, then at thirteen she won an amateur night contest in Brooklyn. In 1909 her performance at a benefit, where she sang Irving *Berlin's "Sadie Salome" with a comic Jewish accent, landed her a part in the burlesque musical comedy *College Girls*. It was while touring with this troupe that she came to the attention of Florenz *Ziegfeld who signed her for his *Follies of 1910*. Brice stopped the show with Berlin's "Goodby, Becky Cohen" and thereafter she was an important performer in the *Ziegfeld Follies* of 1911, 1916, 1917, 1920, 1921, and 1923, as well as in *Honeymoon Express* (1913), the *Music Box Revue 1924–1925, Fioretta* (1929), *Sweet and Low* (1930), and *Billy Rose's Crazy Quilt* (1931). She also appeared in the *Ziegfeld Follies* of 1934 and 1936, which were produced by the *Shuberts after Ziegfeld's death. Although Brice was a great comedienne and introduced such comic songs as

"Second Hand Rose," "I'm an Indian," and "Old Wicked Willage of Wenice," Ziegfeld discovered she could be a moving torch singer as well, and some of her most memorable *Follies'* moments came when she introduced "My Man" and "Rose of Washington Square." She initially played the mischievous brat Baby Snooks (a character she later popularized on radio) in the 1934 *Follies*, having done similar brats earlier. Her personal history, especially her marriage to gangster Nicky Arnstein, served as the basis for the 1964 musical *Funny Girl*. Biography: *Fanny Brice: The Original Funny Girl*, Herbert G. Goldman, 1992.

BRIGADOON (1947), a musical play by Alan Jay *Lerner (book, lyrics), Frederick *Loewe (music). [*Ziegfeld Theatre, 581 perf.] In Scotland, two American hunters, Tommy Albright (David Brooks) and Jess Douglass (George Keane), lose their way and stumble upon a village that seems to belong to another time, and where Charlie Dalrymple (Lee Sullivan) is preparing to marry Jean MacLaren (Virginia Bosler). Tommy falls in love with Jean's sister Fiona (Marion Bell) while Jeff has a comic fling with the man-hungry Meg Brockie (Pamela Britton). Before the wedding, the Americans learn that the village is bewitched, coming back to life for a day only once a century. They flee but Tommy's love for Fiona is so strong that he returns to Scotland where the village miraculously appears just long enough to embrace him. *Notable songs*: The Heather on the Hill; I'll Go Home with Bonnie Jean; Almost Like Being in Love; Come to Me, Bend to Me. Apart from George Jean *Nathan, who savagely attacked the work as unoriginal and dreary (in a personal vendetta, Lerner has stated), most critics were delighted with this sensitive handling of fantasy, although many felt the second act was not as good as the first. All praised the Cheryl *Crawford production, including Agnes *de Mille's ballets, especially the exciting Sword Dance. The musical has remained a favorite in stock and dinner theatres and was revived on Broadway in 1980 with de Mille's original choreography.

BRIGHTON BEACH MEMOIRS (1983), a play in two acts by Neil *Simon. [Alvin Theatre, 1,299 perf.; NYDCC Award.] Eugene Jerome (Matthew *Broderick), an ambitious, somewhat starry-eyed teenager who wants to be a writer, lives with his extended Jewish family in a lower-middle-class home that is filled with tension. His father, Jack (Peter Michael Goetz), works as a cutter in the garment trade, and his long, hard hours have wearied him. His mother, Kate (Elizabeth *Franz), and her sister, Blanche (Joyce Van Patten), have harbored age-old angers that finally explode. But

Eugene also has some assets, such as an ability to see through life's short-range problems and view matters with a cutting wit. Most problems do, in fact, seem to work themselves out for the Jeromes and there is every reason to believe Eugene will realize his ambition. An admittedly autobiographical work, many critics hailed the comedy as a move away from the wisecracking formula plays that Simon had previously offered. He continued the tale with **BILOXI BLUES** (1985), which ran at the Neil *Simon Theatre for 524 performances. Drafted into the army, Eugene (Broderick) resolutely continues to hone his writing skills by keeping a notebook commenting on his fellow draftees and his army life. He also resolves to stay alive and to lose his virginity. He succeeds at both, despite the comic contretemps his notes and his young lusts create. The second play in Simon's semi-autobiographical trilogy won the *Tony Award, though it was slightly less popular than the others, yet it is probably the best written of the three works. **BROADWAY BOUND** (1986) completed the tale, with grown-up Eugene (Jonathan Silverman) and his brother Stanley (Jason Alexander) pushing hard to become writers of comedy for radio. Yet their home life is often unfunny: their father (Philip Sterling) is planning to desert their mother (Linda *Lavin) and their maternal grandfather (John Randolph) has become incontinent and refuses to live with his richer daughter (Phyllis Newman), a move that would go against his Trotskyite beliefs. Eugene is also courting a girl who is engaged to another man. Luckily, Eugene can see humor in all of this, even when things don't turn out in fairy-tale fashion. On the strength of good reviews and Lavin's Tony-winning performance, *Broadway Bound* ran 756 performances in the *Broadhurst Theatre. The trilogy, produced by Emanuel *Azenberg, marked a resurgence in Simon's popularity on Broadway after a long fallow period.

BRISSON, Frederick (1913–84), producer. The Danish-born son of film actor Carl Brisson, he produced, alone or in conjunction with others, such shows as The *Pajama Game (1954), *Damn Yankees (1955), The *Pleasure of His Company (1958), Five Finger Exercise (1959), The Caretaker (1961), Generation (1965), Coco (1969), and Twigs (1971). He was the husband of Rosalind *Russell.

BROADHURST, George [Howells] (1866–1952), playwright and manager. Coming to America from England when he was twenty, he began his theatrical career by running theatres in Milwaukee, Baltimore, and San Francisco. The first play he wrote, *The Speculator* (1896), was a quick failure. Some comedies that followed had better luck, notably

The Wrong Mr. Wright (1897), *What Happened to Jones* (1897), and *Why Smith Left Home* (1899), although, ironically, all were more successful in London than in New York. For the next several seasons Broadhurst tried his hand at dramas, comedies, and musical comedy librettos before writing the hits *The *Man of the Hour* (1906) and **Bought and Paid For* (1911). Other works of note include **Today* (1913), in which a husband discovers his wife in a brothel, and *The *Law of the Land* (1914), about a justifiable homicide. In 1919 the *Shuberts named their newest theatre after him, and he managed it in conjunction with them. Broadhurst produced many of his own plays as well as those of other writers. He was once characterized as a playwright "who had a knack for the sort of melodrama that poses as a serious study of morals."

BROADHURST THEATRE (New York). Named after playwright George H. *Broadhurst, this wide playhouse with plenty of unobstructed views was designed by Herbert J. *Krapp with 1,155 seats and the capability of being used for both plays and musicals. The Broadhurst opened in 1917 with the first American production of Shaw's *Misalliance* starring Maclyn *Arbuckle. Over the years the theatre has been frequently booked, playing to hit dramas, like *Victoria Regina* (1935) and **Amadeus* (1980), and musicals, such as **Hold Everything* (1928) and **Grease* (1972). The Shubert-owned playhouse was declared a landmark in 1987.

BROADWAY. The street running north-south the length of Manhattan Island, it has given its name as a synonym for American theatre or at least for New York theatre. A "Playhouse on Broadway" was shown on a map as early as about 1735. Over the years many important legitimate theatres have, indeed, actually stood on Broadway, the newer ones being built farther north as the city moved upward. Today the theatre district lies largely between Times Square and 53rd Street, with most theatres on Broadway itself film houses, while the legitimate theatres generally are clustered on side streets. When electric lights became prevalent, the area became known as "The Great White Way," another expression that remained popular for decades. Since World War II the expression *Off Broadway has been used to describe many small, often experimental theatres, most of which are situated away from the major playhouses and which some unions have allowed special lower pay scales. And later *Off Off Broadway was devised to denote shoestring operations of an even more experimental nature than Off Broadway.

BROADWAY (1926), a drama by Philip Dunning and George *Abbott. [*Broadhurst Theatre, 603 perf.] At the Paradise Night Club, Steve Crandall (Robert Glecker) kills another gangster. Crandall's girlfriend, "Billie" Moore (Sylvia Field), sees the body being carried out, but Crandall persuades her to claim she has seen nothing, telling her it was a drunken, though important politician. Roy Lane (Lee *Tracy), a hoofer at the club who loves Billie, reveals the truth about the murder. So Billie kills Crandall then goes off with Roy. Percy *Hammond of the *Herald-Tribune* called the Jed *Harris mounting "the most completely acted and perfectly directed show I have seen in thirty years of professional playgoing." A 1987 revival, staged by Abbott, failed to run. **Philip DUNNING** (1891–1968) was born in Meriden, Connecticut, and worked as an actor and stage manager before turning to playwriting. He originally wrote *Broadway* as *A Little White Guy*, then it was produced as *The Roaring Forties*, then as *Bright Lights,* before the play was put into final form by Abbott at Harris's suggestion. Dunning's other plays incude *Lily Turner* (1933), *Page Miss Glory* (1935), and *Remember the Day* (1941). On occasion he also produced shows, most memorably **Twentieth Century* (1934).

BROADWAY BOUND. See *Brighton Beach Memoirs.*

BROADWAY THEATRE (New York). Three New York playhouses have used the name of the celebrated street on which they were situated. The first Broadway Theatre was in lower Manhattan and was modeled after London's Haymarket Theatre, though it was much larger (4,500 seats). It opened in 1836 with the hope of rivaling the popularity of the *Park Theatre, but it failed to do so and was torn down in 1859. The second playhouse named after Broadway was located at 41st Street, the northern edge of the city when it opened in 1888. It was a large musical house designed by J. B. *McElfatrick and was popular until the theatre district moved to the Times Square area. It was briefly a movie house before being torn down in 1929. The current Broadway Theatre opened as a movie house called the Colony in 1924. Eugene DeRosa designed it with 1,765 seats and a plush, spacious feeling to it. Over the years the house has served as both a film and theatre venue, getting its current name in 1930. The Shubert-owned theatre is ideal for large musicals, and during its history it has housed such giants as **This Is the Army* (1942), **Gypsy* (1959), **Les Miserables* (1987), and **Miss Saigon* (1991).

BRODERICK, Helen (1891–1959), comic actress. The Philadelphia-born comedienne, who was the daughter of an actor, made her debut in the chorus of Florenz *Ziegfeld's first *Follies in 1907. For the next decade she developed her caustic, wisecracking style while appearing in a few musicals, but mainly in vaudeville. Broderick began to gain widespread recognition in the 1920s and is best remembered for her appearances in *Oh, Please!* (1926), *Fifty Million Frenchmen* (1929), The *Band Wagon* (1931), and *As Thousands Cheer* (1933). Her last years were spent in films.

BRODERICK, Matthew (b. 1960), actor. The handsome, youthful-looking leading man possesses a vulnerable charm on stage and screen and has already given some cherished performances in New York during his young career. He was born in New York, the son of actor James Broderick, and studied acting with Uta *Hagen. In 1982 he made his professional stage debut Off Broadway as the gay youth David in *Torch Song Trilogy. Broderick was on Broadway the next year receiving applause for his engaging performance as the Brooklyn teenager Eugene in *Brighton Beach Memoirs* (1983). He returned to the same character in the sequel *Biloxi Blues* (1985). Broderick's other Broadway successes include the ambitious corporate climber Finch in the 1995 revival of *How to Succeed in Business Without Really Trying* and the nebbish accountant Leo Bloom in The *Producers* (2001). In the last role, Broderick was described by Ben Brantley in the *New York Times* as "a slumped, adenoidal figure that . . . manages to make hunched introversion into an extroverted style." **James BRODERICK** (1928–1982) was a flexible, all-purpose actor who played both leading men and character types effectively. He was born in Charlestown, New Hampshire, and educated at the University of New Hampshire before making his New York debut in 1953. Broderick was often outstanding in short-run plays, such as *Johnny No-Trump* (1967) and *Wedding Band* (1972), but he was very successful on television.

BROKER OF BOGOTA, THE (1834), a tragedy by Robert Montgomery *Bird. [Bowery Theatre, in repertory.] Because he keeps bad company, Ramon (David Ingersoll) has been disinherited by his father, the honest, respected moneylender Batista Febro (Edwin *Forrest). As a result the Viceroy of New Granada will not allow Ramon to marry his daughter Juana (Mrs. McClure). Ramon is goaded by the profligate Antonio De Cabarero (Henry *Wallack) to rob his father and then claim that Batista himself staged the robbery. Batista is convicted, and, to compound his woes, his daughter Leonor (Mrs. Flynn) elopes with Fernando (H. Jones), the Viceroy's son. "The blows that bruise the body are not much," he wails, "when the heart is crushed." Juana, learning of Ramon's treachery, berates him. Filled with remorse, he commits suicide, and Batista is exonerated but dies of a broken heart. Although the tragedy's blank verse and general construction were Elizabethan, the play was well received and remained in producer-actor Forrest's repertory for most of his career. No doubt Forrest's acting played a large part in its popularity, for the play was rarely revived after his death. Nevertheless, *Quinn wrote, "Certainly in the character of 'Febro,' with his middle-class mind, lifted into tragedy by his passionate love for his children and his betrayal by his oldest and best loved son, Bird drew one of the most living portraits in our dramatic history."

BROOK, THE; or, *A Jolly Day at the Picnic* (1879). This musical farce was first offered to New York in 1879 at the San Francisco Minstrels' Hall. It was presented by the Salsbury Troubadors, whose leader, Nate Salsbury, had earlier written a similar piece called *Patchwork*, which he dropped as unsuitable after touring. The simple plot took a very small handful of performers on a picnic where they entertained with songs, dances, and other turns. The work proved so popular that it gave birth to the whole tradition of *farce-comedy, which in turn led to the development of the American musical comedy. Coming as it did at the end of the same season that saw the premiere of *H. M. S. Pinafore* and the first extended *Harrigan and *Hart vehicle, it marked the 1878–79 season as the real beginning of modern American musical theatre.

BROOK, Peter [Stephen Paul] (b. 1925), director. London born and educated at Oxford, Brook established himself as a major West End director before staging the American musical *House of Flowers* (1954). After directing the *Lunts in their final appearance, The Visit (1958), he subsequently staged The Fighting Cock (1959) and Irma La Douce (1960). For many playgoers the high point of his career has been his work with the Royal Shakespeare Company's production of a play known by its short title as *Marat/Sade* (1965), bringing fluid movement and powerful order to this strange, somewhat loose play about inmates in an insane asylum doing a play about the French Revolution. His direction of The Physicists (1964) and the Royal Shakespeare's A *Midsummer Night's Dream (1971), with its innovative setting of what appeared to be a modern black-and-white gymnasium, were much-discussed sensations. In 1980 his Centre Internationale de Créations Théâtrales was given the *New York Drama Critics Circle Award for its repertory. Among Brook's other controversial productions to play in New York were The Conference of the Birds (1980), La Tragedie de Carmen (1984), The Mahabharata (1987), The Man Who (1995), and revivals of The Cherry Orchard in 1988 and *Hamlet in 2001. Biography: *Peter Brook*, John C. Trewin, 1971.

BROOKLYN ACADEMY OF MUSIC (New York) BAM, as it is usually referred to, was America's first multitheatre arts center. It was built in 1908 on the ashes of a previous theatre and was designed by Henry *Herts with four performance spaces for theatre and concerts. After a checkered history that included concerts and plays by the world's greatest artists, as well as derelict days, the complex was turned into a nonprofit arts center to help revive downtown Brooklyn in the 1980s. Today it houses the 2,000-seat Howard Gillman Opera House, the 1,847-seat Harvey Lichtenstein Theatre, and the 550-seat Lepercq Space, as well as the faded old Majestic Theatre down the street. Under the direction of Lichtenstein, who started running the center in 1967, BAM is an active and prestigious home to visiting groups and, since 1983, the site of the celebrated Next Wave Festival each fall.

BROOKS ATKINSON THEATRE (New York). Opening in 1926 as the *Mansfield Theatre, the wide and practical theatre was built by the enterprising Chanin Brothers on West 47th Street and named after the celebrated actor Richard Mansfield. Herbert J *Krapp designed the 1,000-seat playhouse, which was ideal for nonmusicals. The Mansfield managed to survive the Great Depression years but closed in 1944 and reopened as a television studio in 1950. A decade later it returned to offering legit fare and was renamed after the recently retired journalist Brooks *Atkinson, the first time on record a theatre was named after a critic. Today the playhouse is owned by the *Nederlanders and is steadily booked.

BROOKS, Mel. See *Producers, The*.

BROTHER RAT (1936), a comedy by John Monks Jr. and Fred Finklehoffe. [*Biltmore Theatre, 575 perf.] Although Bing Edwards (Eddie Albert) is his military school's star pitcher, he is not certain that he will win the school's $200 award as its best athlete. He needs the money since he is, against school rules, secretly married. The day before the big game, he learns his wife is pregnant. The news unnerves him and the well-meaning help offered by his friends, Billy (Frank Albertson) and Dan (José *Ferrer), only makes matters worse. He loses the game but discovers he has won $300 as the first father in the class. A typical example of the high school and collegiate comedies that remained popular from the turn of the century until World War II, the play enjoyed producer-director George *Abbott's fast-paced direction and excel-

lent performances by then unknown youngsters. **Fred FINKLEHOFFE** (1910–77), who was born in Springfield, Massachusetts, later produced a number of Broadway shows, including The *Heiress (1947), *Affairs of State* (1950), and *Ankles Aweigh* (1955).

BROUGHAM, John (1810–80), actor, playwright, and manager. Educated at Trinity College in his native Dublin, he spent much of his college career participating in amateur theatricals. He made his professional debut in London in 1830, worked under the celebrated Madame Vestris, and became manager of the Lyceum before sailing to America. Brougham made his American debut at the *Park Theatre in *His Last Legs* (1842), then joined William *Burton and later James *Wallack, acting with both men in important comic roles, such as Sir Lucius O'Trigger, Micawber, Captain Cuttle, and Dazzle. Between 1850 and 1857 he also managed Brougham's Broadway Lyceum and the *Bowery Theatre, but the business side of theatre was not his forte. While acting and managing he nevertheless found time to write no fewer than 126 plays, including burlesques, such as *Pocahontas (1855) and *Much Ado About the Merchant of Venice* (1869); adaptations, such as *Dombey and Son* (1848), a major hit; *Jane Eyre* (1849); and *Vanity Fair* (1849); Gothic melodramas, such as *The Duke's Motto; or, I Am Here* (1863); tear-jerkers, such as *The Dark Hour Before Dawn*; Irish plays, such as *Take Care of Little Charlie* (1858); and social satire, such as The *Game of Love* (1856). After spending the Civil War years in England, he returned in 1865, acting at the Winter Garden and with Augustin *Daly's troupe. When his vogue had faded, he then ventured another unsuccessful attempt at management. His last appearance was in *Boucicault's *Felix O'Reilly* (1879). Brougham was one of the first to bring a bit of the action of his plays into the auditorium. In his popular *Row at the Lyceum* (1851), arriving playgoers found the cast still rehearsing. When the gaslights were lowered, a Quaker in the audience jumped up and began to yell, "My wife! Come off that stage, thou miserable woman!" A fireman wrestled with the upset man, who got away and ran down the aisle. The Quaker was, of course, Brougham. In his heyday he was one of the most popular of American performers, although his fellow actor Joseph *Jefferson regretted that he always "acted a part as though it were a joke." Other commentators, focusing more on his writings, were less critical. In 1890 Laurence *Hutton concluded, "If America has ever had an Aristophanes, John Brougham was his name," while a modern editor, Richard Moody, described him as "a mid-nineteenth-century combination of W. C. Fields and George S. Kaufman."

BROUN, Heywood [Campbell] (1888–1939), critic. Born in Brooklyn and educated at Harvard, he worked as a reporter for several newspapers before becoming drama critic for the *New York World* (1921–28). He was also drama editor for *Vanity Fair* as well as a popular lecturer on theatre. Broun appeared in *Round the Town* (1924) and produced and appeared in *Shoot the Works* (1931), a revue designed to give some employment to out-of-work performers and writers. His criticism was marked by a refreshing directness and wit. Reviewing *Barrymore's *Hamlet* he began, "John Barrymore is far and away the finest Hamlet we have ever seen. He excels all others we have known in grace, fire, wit, and clarity. This final quality should be stressed. Back in high school we remember being asked whether Hamlet was really mad. If we had seen Barrymore it would have been possible for us to tell the teacher, 'Don't be silly.'"

BROWN, Arvin (b. 1940), director and manager. He was born in Los Angeles and studied at Stanford, Harvard, the University of Bristol (England), and at the Yale School of Drama. Brown has directed both classics and new works, as well as the American premieres of foreign plays. He has occasionally worked on Broadway and at the *Circle in the Square, but he is most associated with the *Long Wharf Theatre where he served as artistic director for many years. Broadway has praised his revivals of A *View from the Bridge* (1983), *Joe Egg* (1984), *All My Sons* (1987), *Ah, Wilderness!* (1988), and *Private Lives* (1992), though few were commercial successes. Brown's direction is never flashy or highly conceptual but instead focuses on realism and ensemble acting.

BROWN, Gilmore. See Pasadena Playhouse.

BROWN, Jason Robert. See *Parade*.

BROWN, John Mason (1900–69), critic and author. A native of Louisville, he studied under Professor George P. *Baker at Harvard, then became an associate editor and drama critic of *Theatre Arts Monthly*. Brown left the magazine to become critic of the *Evening Post* in 1929, then moved to the *World-Telegram* in 1939. Following service in World War II, he was appointed drama critic for the *Saturday Review of Literature*. From 1925 to 1931 he was a lecturer at the American Laboratory Theatre, and he conducted courses at Harvard, Yale, Middlebury College, and elsewhere. Among his many books are *The Modern Theatre in Revolt* (1929), *Upstage: The American Theatre in Performance* (1930), *Letters from Greenroom Ghosts* (1934), *The Art of Playgoing* (1936), *Two on*

the Aisle (1939), *Dramatis Personae* (1963), and *The Worlds of Robert E. Sherwood* (1965). His style, often described as courtly or urbane, was suffused with an elegant humor, as in his recollection of his first exposure to theatre: "I have been stage-struck ever since, when eight, I was taken to Macauley's Theatre in Louisville, Kentucky, to see Robert B. Mantell play King Lear, one of the few parts, I realize now, that he was still young enough to act." Biography: *Speak for Yourself, John*, George Stevens, 1974.

BROWN, Lew. See De Sylva, Brown, and Henderson.

BROWN, T[homas] **Allston** (1836–1918), agent and manager, author. Born in Newburyport, Massachusetts, he began his career as an advertising agent for circuses and in 1860 managed Blondin, who was famous for crossing Niagara Gorge on a tightrope. From 1870 on, he ran a theatrical agency in New York (his clients included Dion *Boucicault); in 1859 he founded a theatrical weekly, *The Tatler;* and from 1864 to 1870 was dramatic editor for the *New York *Clipper*. Colonel Brown, as he was often called, remained active as "the oldest theatrical manager in America" until his retirement in 1916. However, he probably will be best remembered as the author of two pioneering studies: *History of the American Stage: 1733-1870* (1870) and *History of the New York Stage: From the First Performance in 1732 to 1901* (1903).

BROWNE, James S. (1791–1869), comic actor. The English comedian made his New York debut as Bob Acres in *The Rivals* (1838) and quickly established himself as "one of the best actors of light and eccentric comedy that ever trod the American stage." He was the first to play Robert Macaire in this country and was long identified with the role. Famous for his high living, he later became mentally unstable and died alone, ill and impoverished.

BROWNE, Maurice. See Little Theatre in America.

BROWNE, Porter Emerson. See *Fool There Was, A*.

BROWNE, Roscoe Lee (b. 1925), actor. The deep-voiced, charismatic African-American actor has worked in all media, acted in classic and modern works, and played traditionally white roles years before it became fashionable. He was born in Woodbury, New Jersey, and educated at Lincoln University, Middlebury College, and Columbia, becoming an international track star as a student athlete. Browne taught French and literature at Lincoln before making his professional acting debut at the *New York Shakespeare Festival in 1956 and his Broadway bow in *Tiger, Tiger, Burning Bright* (1962). Among his many noteworthy performances were the Narrator of *The Ballad of the Sad Cafe* (1963), the native Babu in *Benito Cereno* (1964), the retired teacher Albert mourning his dead son in *Remembrance* (1979), the singing-dancing minister J. D. Montgomery in *My One and Only* (1983), and the elderly sage Holloway in *Two Trains Running* (1992).

BRUSTEIN, Robert [Sanford] (b. 1927), critic, manager, and author. After studying at the High School of Music and Art in his native New York, he attended Amherst, Yale School of Drama, and Columbia. He acted with stock companies and on television before becoming drama critic for the *New Republic* from 1959 to 1968, his criticism winning several awards. During his tenure he also taught drama at Vassar and Columbia. In 1965 Brustein was appointed professor of Drama and English Literature at Yale, where he founded and served as artistic director for the *Yale Repertory Theatre. The troupe quickly became one of the leading collegiate ensembles in America. In 1979 he left Yale for Harvard where he became artistic director of *American Repertory Theatre for twenty years. Among his many books are *The Theatre of Revolt* (1964), *Revolution as Theatre* (1970), *Critical Moments* (1980), *Who Needs Theatre* (1987), *Dumbocracy in America* (1994), and *The Siege of the Arts* (2001).

BRUTUS; or, the Fall of Tarquin (1819), a tragedy by John Howard *Payne. [*Park Theatre, in repertory.] Lucius Junius (James Pritchard), whose noble family has been deposed and murdered by the usurping Tarquins, escapes death by feigning idiocy and becoming the Tarquin court jester. The Tarquin queen, Tullia (Mrs. *Barnes), sneeringly gives him another name, Brutus. But when Sextus, a Tarquin prince, rapes Lucretia (Miss Leesugg), a senator's wife, Brutus drops his disguise to lead the Romans against the usurpers. His son Titus (Edmund *Simpson) sides with the enemy because of his love of Princess Tarquinia, so it falls to his father to sentence him to death, proclaiming, "Justice is satisfied and Rome is free!" Payne compiled the play from seven older works on the subject, including Voltaire's *Brutus, a Tragedy* and English pieces by Nathaniel Lee, William Duncombe, Hugh Downman, and Richard Cumberland. The play was first presented in England with Edmund *Kean in the lead. Producer Edmund *Simpson was apparently unprepared for its American success and had booked other plays to follow quickly. But its success caused it to be brought back regularly in the repertory. Kean

performed it on his American tour, and the play featured importantly in the repertories of Junius Brutus *Booth, Edwin *Booth, and James *Wallack. William *Winter called the play "a series of episodes in Roman history, rather than a single dramatic narrative," but considered it "valuable for its tumultuous action, its splendid pictorial effects and its moments of pathos."

BRYNNER, Yul. See *King and I, The.*

BUCHANAN, Jack (1891–1957), actor, singer, and dancer. The reedy-voiced song-and-dance man, who to many Americans personified the suave, dapper Englishman, made his American debut in *Charlot's Revue* (1924). Subsequently he appeared in only three other musicals: *The Charlot Revue of 1926*, in which he introduced "A Cup of Coffee, a Sandwich and You"; *Wake Up and Dream* (1929); and *Between the Devil* (1937), in which he sang "By Myself." For what proved his final Broadway assignment he deserted the musical theatre to play Daniel Bachelet, the suspicious husband, in Sacha Guitry's comedy *Don't Listen, Ladies* (1948). Biography: *Top Hat and Tails*, M. Marshall. 1978.

BUCKLEY, Betty (b. 1947), actress and singer. She was born in Big Spring, Texas, and educated at Texas Christian College before going to New York and studying acting with Stella *Adler. A Broadway diva who took a long time to become a stage star, Buckley spent a lot of her career replacing others in hit shows, but she did get to originate some important roles on her own: Martha Jefferson in *1776 (1969), the aging glamour cat Grizabella in the American production of *Cats (1982), and the Victorian actress playing the title male lead in The *Mystery of Edwin Drood (1985). Frank *Rich in the *New York Times* described Buckley's performance in *Cats* as "a coursing delivery [that] rattles the rafters . . . in her ratty, prostitute-like furs and mane she is a poignant figure of down-and-out catwomanhood."

BUCKSTONE, J[ohn] B[aldwin] (1802–79), playwright and actor. The Englishman performed in America during the 1840–41 and 1841–42 seasons, but with only middling success. However, many of his plays were long in the standard repertory, especially at more popular, less elite playhouses. These included such works as *A Kiss in the Dark, The Lottery Ticket, Single Life*, and *Weak Points*. Joseph *Ireland has noted, "In America . . . he had contributed to the stage more than one hundred and fifty [plays], scarcely any of which have proved failures, and most of them have had a long career of popularity, and remain among the best approved standard comedies, farces and melo-dramas of the day."

BUFFALO BILL. See Cody, William.

BUFMAN, Zev (b. 1930), producer. A native Israeli, he performed in his homeland and in America before turning producer. Much of his early producing was in California, but he later moved his base to Florida. Bufman has sponsored touring versions of several Broadway plays, and in New York he has co-produced such notable original works as *Your Own Thing* (1968) and *Jimmy Shine* (1968). However, in later years he was best known as co-producer of major revivals, including *Peter Pan* (1979), *Oklahoma!* (1979), *Brigadoon* (1980), *West Side Story* (1980), The *Little Foxes* (1981), *Joseph and the Amazing Technicolor Dreamcoat* (1982), and *Private Lives* (1983).

BULOFF, Joseph (1899–1985), character actor and director. He was born in Wilno, Lithuania, and as a young man joined the Vilna Troupe, which toured across Europe. Buloff immigrated to America in 1928 and acted in Yiddish theatres in Chicago and New York, later founding the New York Art Theatre. He first performed in English in 1936 and gave such fondly remembered performances as peddler Ali Hakim in the original *Oklahoma!* (1943), various colorful Russian characters in *A Chekhov Sketchbook* (1962), and the old furniture dealer Gregory Solomon in the 1979 and 1982 revivals of The *Price*. Buloff spent much of the 1950s and 1960s directing and acting in plays in Israel. Autobiography: *On Stage, Off Stage: Memories of a Lifetime in the Yiddish Theatre*, with Luba Kadison and Irving Genn, 1992.

BULWER-LYTTON, Edward. See Lytton, Edward.

BUNCE, Oliver Bell. See *Love in '76*.

BURGESS, Neil. See Female Impersonators.

BURIED CHILD (1978), a play by Sam *Shepard. [Theatre de Lys, 152 perf.; Pulitzer Prize.] After several years in Los Angeles, Vince (Christopher McCann) returns to the Illinois farm of his grandparents, bringing with him his saxophone, his girl Shelley (Mary McDonnell), and a parcel of fond memories and hopes. He is quickly disillusioned. His grandmother, Hallie (Jacqueline Brooks), preaches morality but spends her evenings on the town with the local priest, Father Dewis (Bill Wiley). His dying, drunken grandfather, Dodge (Richard Hamilton), has murdered an unwanted child and wails, "I'm descended from a long line of corpses and there's not a living soul behind me." Vince must also confront his crazed father, Tilden (Tom Noonan), and brutal, crippled uncle, Bradley (Jay Sanders). The visit leaves Vince to work out a new life in a spiritually bankrupt world. Originally produced by San Francisco's *Magic Theatre, the play was mounted Off Off Broadway before this Off-Broadway engagement began. A slightly revised version of the play arrived on Broadway in 1996 and met with success.

BURK, John Daly. See *Female Patriotism*.

BURKE, [Mary William Ethelbert Appleton] Billie (1885–1970), actress. Born in Washington, D.C., she was raised in England, where her father was a well-known clown. Burke appeared in a number of English musical comedies and with Charles Hawtrey before coming to New York under contract to Charles *Frohman to play the naïve Beatrice Dupré opposite John *Drew in *My Wife* (1907). Successes followed, such as the newlywed Jacqueline in *Love Watches* (1908), the charmingly conniving *Mrs. Dot* (1910), chorine Lily Parradell in The *"Mind-the-Paint" Girl* (1912), Lady Thomasine in *The Amazons* (1913), farmer's wife Norah Marsh in *The Land of Promise* (1914), and the iron-willed heroine *Jerry* (1914). In the same year she married Florenz *Ziegfeld and a year later Frohman died; thereafter she acted for various important producers. She played opposite Henry *Miller in a revival of *A Marriage of Convenience* (1918), then appeared as the heroine in *Caesar's Wife* (1919). Her next two roles were in Booth *Tarkington plays: as the kittenish spinster Isabel in *The Intimate Strangers* (1921) and as the nightclub singer *Rose Briar* (1922). For her husband she did her only American musical, *Annie Dear* (1924), and after his death lent her name as producer to editions of the *Ziegfeld Follies*, although the actual producers were the *Shuberts. Burke's last Broadway appearance was as the widow who is courted by a former president in *Mrs. January and Mr. X* (1944). She later performed in summer stock and in the road company of The *Solid Gold Cadillac*. The dainty redhead with the quivering voice was hailed by John *Corbin of the *Times* as "a comedienne of matchless charm." She is mostly recalled today for her many films. Autobiography: *With a Feather on My Nose*, with Cameron Shipp, 1949.

BURKE, Charles (1822–54), comic actor. Born in Philadelphia, he began his career as a child prodigy (not to be confused with Joseph *Burke), but after a brief retirement returned to the stage as a polished comedian. He was acclaimed for his Rip Van Winkle and his Solon Shingle, the cracker-barrel Yankee in The *People's Lawyer*, as well as for principal parts in many once-popular but now-forgotten comedies. Burke was also a consummate performer in burlesques, many of which he wrote himself. Among such roles were

Iago in a spoof of *Othello* and Clod Meddlenot in *The Lady of the Lions*, a spoof of *The *Lady of Lyons* and its hero Claude Melnotte. During the 1848–49 season he managed the Chatham Theatre. Burke's death at age thirty-two deprived the theatre of one of its most promising and admired artists. His half-brother, the most famous Joseph *Jefferson, insisted Burke's Rip Van Winkle was a masterful interpretation. He wrote, "Burke was subtle, incisive and refined . . . lithe and graceful. His face was plain, but wonderfully expressive. The versatility of this rare actor was remarkable, his pathos being quite as striking as his comedy." Laurence *Hutton observed that in Burke's hands Solon Shingle, until then a stock portrayal, "became the simple-minded, phenomenally shrewd old man from New England, with a soul which soared no higher than the financial value of a bar'l of applesass."

BURKE, Joseph (1818–1902), actor and musician. Master Burke, as he was popularly known, came to America in 1830 as a celebrated child prodigy. Not only did he offer his interpretations of Richard III, Shylock, Sir Giles Overreach, and other celebrated roles, but soloed on the violin and conducted orchestras. As such Joseph *Ireland stated he was "unapproached by any child who has trodden the American stage." In later years he was a distinguished violinist who gave solo concerts and also accompanied such artists as Jenny Lind.

BURLESQUE (1927), a play by George Manker Watters and Arthur *Hopkins. [*Plymouth Theatre, 372 perf.] Bonnie (Barbara Stanwyck) and Skid Johnson (Hal *Skelly) are not only husband and wife but work together in a second-string burlesque company in which Skid is the leading comedian. Bonnie worries about Skid, who is a heavy drinker, takes hurtful pratfalls as part of his act, and has his eye on a cute showgirl who is about to leave for a Broadway musical. To make Skid jealous, Bonnie openly flirts with a rich rancher who has been buying tickets for their show every night. Skid is unconcerned, and when an offer comes for Skid to appear in the same Broadway show as the chorus girl, he takes it. In no time he is having an affair with the showgirl, so Bonnie sues for divorce and agrees to marry the rancher. Just before the divorce becomes final, Skid goes on a binge and loses his job. When a friend offers to produce a musical featuring Bonnie and Skid, the two recognize how much each needs the other. Like *Broadway* the season before, *Burlesque* was written by a new young playwright and revised by an experienced hand. Burns *Mantle saw the play as a "rough drama in the sense that it cross-sections life among the lowly and

uncultured performers of the burlesque theatres, revealing them on good authority as they live and as they are." A 1946 revival by Jean *Dalrymple with Bert *Lahr as Skid and Jean Parker as Bonnie and with Hopkins once again directing ran for over a year.

BURLESQUE IN AMERICA. Traditional burlesque, in the sense of a travesty or satire, came early to America and was well represented both in specific works, such as the 18th-century spoof of *The *Blockade* as *The Blockheads*, and in more extended manifestations, such as the productions mounted in the 1840s by William Mitchell at the Olympic. Notable later 19th-century examples might be John *Brougham's *Pocahontas* and the musicals *Evangeline* and *Adonis*. The modern burlesque, which is perceived as a much lower order of entertainment filled with bump-and-grind strippers and raunchy clowning, began to develop in the last half of the 19th century. Coming on top of the sensation caused by a chorus line of girls in tights in *The *Black Crook* (1866), the arrival in 1868 of Lydia *Thompson and her "British Blondes" in their burlesques started the slow and at first subtle transition. Her burlesques were totally in the older tradition, but the presence of a line of beautiful women in tights added a new and ultimately telling dimension. The decline of minstrelsy, oddly enough, was the next major factor. Michael Leavitt ran an all-girl blackface company called Mme. Rentz's Female Minstrels, and when business waned he changed the nature and name of his troupe, dropping blackface, adding vaudeville turns not unlike the often suggestive comic bits of the time, and emphasizing his line of beautiful girls. Since his leading performer was Mabel Santley, Leavitt called his reconstituted troupe the Rentz-Santley show. Before long another star, May Howard, headed her own companies. The cleaning up of vaudeville by Tony *Pastor and later by *Keith shoved many less-amenable players and producers into the ranks of burlesque and underscored the emerging difference. Many historians suggest that Sam T. Jack, who had worked with Leavitt and who incorporated risqué features of Western honky-tonk entertainments, initiated the more modern show in Chicago. His and other burlesque shows of the turn of the century still assumed much of the form of period musical comedy or revue, to an extent to give the productions a certain legitimacy. During this period the two great circuits were formed. The Empire (or so-called Western) Circuit was first established as a loose confederacy of houses from such cities as Cincinnati, Louisville, Chicago, and Minneapolis in the early 1880s and officially incorporated in

1897. The Columbia (or Eastern) Wheel was established in 1902. Sam A. Scribner, its first president, attempted to de-emphasize the growing bawdy elements, but failed. While suggestive dress and even nudity were not unknown to the legitimate stage, the modern striptease began to come to the fore about the time of World War I and continued to grow in importance until burlesque was finally closed by police order in the 1930s and faded away on its own a decade or two later. The Minskys and their greatest star, Gypsy Rose *Lee, exemplified burlesque at its modern apogee. She was one of the few strippers to move into legitimate theatre and make a mark there, but in its heyday burlesque proved a remarkable training ground for great comedians, among them Fanny *Brice and Bobby *Clark. A few leading clowns, such as Billy "Cheese 'n' Crackers" Hagen, were never able to transplant their art. In 1979 the successful Broadway musical *Sugar Babies, starring Mickey Rooney and Ann Miller, revived much of the old material for a nostalgic look back at the genre's comic aspects. Burlesque was also the subject of two musical plays: the popular *Gypsy (1959) and the dark, short-lived Grind (1985).

BURN THIS (1987), a play by Lanford *Wilson. [*Plymouth Theatre, 437 perf.] Dancer-choreographer Anna (Joan Allen) lives in a trendy Manhattan loft with two gay men, one of whom has recently died in a boating accident. The deceased's brother Pale (John *Malkovich), a fiery yet hypnotic man given to scatological tirades, comes for the funeral and has a tempestuous affair with Anna, separating her from her straightlaced finance (Jonathan Hogan) and alienating her from her remaining roommate (Lou Liberatore). Though more reminiscent of a David *Mamet or David *Rabe drama than Wilson's usual lyrical works, the play was well received (helped by Malkovich's rising popularity) and was revived with success Off Broadway in 2002.

BURNETT, Carol (b. 1933), comedienne. The red-haired, loud-mouthed television comic performed on Broadway before and after her popular career on television. Born in San Antonio, Texas, and raised in Hollywood, California, she trained for an acting career at the local university. After appearing in clubs in New York and in musical revues, Burnett made a sensational Broadway debut as the gawky, funny Princess Winifred in *Once Upon a Mattress (1959). She also played the movie-struck Hope Springfield in the musical Fade Out–Fade In (1964) but did not return to Broadway for thirty years, garnering laudable notices as the harried actress Charlotte Hay in Moon Over Buffalo (1995) and in the revue Putting It Together (1999). Autobi-

ography: One More Time, 1986, which was turned into the play Hollywood Arms (2002).

BURNETT, Frances Hodgson (1849–1924), playwright and novelist. The English-born authoress was often successful at dramatizing her works. Her first success, *Esmeralda (1881), was adapted from her short story and written in collaboration with William *Gillette, but her most-famous work, both as novel and play, was Little Lord Fauntleroy (1888). Both The First Gentleman of Europe (1897), which she wrote with George Fleming, and A Lady of Quality (1897), which she adapted in collaboration with Stephen Townsend, enjoyed modest runs. The Little Princess (1903) was less well received, but Maude *Adams helped The Pretty Sister of Jose (1903) win audiences. Similarly, Eleanor *Robson earned The *Dawn of a Tomorrow (1909) a five-month run. Her last play, Racketty-Packetty House (1912), was written for children and employed films to help tell its tale. Burnett's plays were always sentimental; at worst cloyingly so, at best, the sentimentality was successfully restrained. But some of her novels remain popular, particularly The Secret Garden, which was made into a musical on Broadway with success in 1991.

BURNS, David (1902–71), character actor. A native New Yorker, the pudgy, dour, often snarling comedian made his debut in 1921 and two years later first played in New York. From the early 1930s on he was a sought-after featured performer, who is remembered for playing frustrated and irascible types in such shows as The *Man Who Came to Dinner (1939), Make Mine Manhattan (1948), Out of This World (1950), The *Music Man (1957), A *Funny Thing Happened on the Way to the Forum (1962), and *Hello, Dolly! (1964).

BURNSIDE, R[obert] H[ubber Thorne] (1870–1952), director and librettist. The son of the manager of Glasgow's Gaiety Theatre, he began his career when he was carried on stage as a baby. Moving to London when he was twelve, he served as callboy first to Edward Terry and then for *Gilbert and *Sullivan at London's Savoy Theatre, where he eventually became assistant to Richard Barker. Burnside came to New York in 1894 to work with Lillian *Russell and the following year staged his first musical, the burlesque Thrilby. Between then and 1944, when he staged a revival of *Robin Hood, he directed some sixty other musicals, most notably the gigantic spectacles mounted at the *Hippodrome from 1909 to 1921. Besides serving as director, he wrote the librettos and/or lyrics for many shows, including some Hippodrome productions and the Montgomery and Stone vehicle, *Chin-Chin (1914), as well as Fred *Stone's vehicles after Dave *Montgomery's death: *Jack o' Lantern* (1917), *Tip Top* (1920), and *Stepping Stones* (1923).

BURROWS, Abe [né Abram Solman Borowitz] (1910–85), librettist and director. The native New Yorker turned to the stage after writing for radio and television, striking gold with his first venture: the highly successful *Guys and Dolls* (1950), whose libretto was co-written with Jo Swerling. His later hits were *Can-Can* (1953); *Silk Stockings* (1955), written in collaboration with George S. *Kaufman and Leueen McGrath; *How to Succeed in Business Without Really Trying* (1961); and *Cactus Flower* (1965), a play adapted from the French. Alone or with others he also wrote *Make a Wish* (1951), *Three Wishes for Jamie* (1952), *Say, Darling* (1958), and *First Impressions* (1959). Burrows served as director for many of these plays, as well as for others, and also often acted as play doctor. Autobiography: *Honest Abe*, 1980.

BURTON, Richard [né Jenkins] (1925–84), actor. The Welsh-born performer first came to America to play Richard in *The Lady's Not for Burning* (1950), and thereafter played the Musician in *Legend of Lovers* (1952) and Prince Albert in *Time Remembered* (1957). His best-known stage roles were King Arthur in the musical *Camelot* (1960) and *Hamlet* in a production staged by John *Gielgud in 1964. In 1976 he was a replacement as Dr. Martin Dysart in *Equus*, and in 1981 he toured briefly in a revival of *Camelot*. Burton's last stage role was Elyot Chase, playing opposite his sometime wife Elizabeth Taylor, in a 1983 revival of *Private Lives*. One of the most gifted classical actors of his generation, his theatre career was curtailed by a celebrated film career, though he rarely lived up to his potential in either venue. Biography: *Rich: The Life of Richard Burton*, Melvyn Bragg, 1988.

BURTON, William E[vans] (1804–60), comic actor and manager. The English-born comedian had given up a career in publishing and turned to performing only a few years before coming to America in 1834. Making his debut at Philadelphia's *Arch Street Theatre as Dr. Ollapod in *The Poor Gentleman*, he was immediately recognized for his comic talents. Burton made his first New York appearance in 1837, but maintained Philadelphia as his base for several years, acting and running theatres there. In 1848 in New York he turned Palmo's decaying opera house into Burton's Chambers Street Theatre, where he presented seasons mainly of old comedies, burlesques, and dramatizations of popular novels. His first season included two of his most famous portrayals: Captain Cuttle in *Dombey and Son* and Timothy Toodle in *The *Toodles*. Typical of his range were other hits

of that season, from the burlesque *Lucy Did Sham Amour* to a mounting of Milton's *Comus*. In 1849 Burton offered another celebrated interpretation, that of Aminadab Sleek in *The *Serious Family*. Over the years he also presented several Shakespearean revivals that were deemed among the best of the era. For all his excellences, Burton found himself unable to compete after *Wallack's great ensemble began performing in 1852. He relinquished his theatre at the end of the 1855–56 season, and while he continued to produce and act at other theatres, he never again enjoyed the success of his brief heyday. Joseph *Jefferson recalled, "Burton's features were strong and heavy, and his figure was portly and ungainly." Of his acting Jefferson noted, not unkindly, "Burton colored highly, and laid on the effect with a liberal brush." Biography: *William E. Burton, Actor, Author, Manager*, William Linn Keese, 1885.

BUS STOP (1955), a play by William *Inge. [*Music Box Theatre, 478 perf.] At a small-town Kansas restaurant and bus stop, run by a hardnosed woman called Grace (Elaine *Stritch), a bus discharges its passengers during a blizzard. Among the passengers are a strumpety nightclub "chantoosie," Cherie (Kim *Stanley), and an aggressive, randy cowboy, Bo Decker (Albert Salmi), who is determined to pester Cherie until he gets what he wants. At first Cherie hides from Bo, but the long stopover forces her to change her tack. By the time the bus is ready to move on, Cherie has brought out Bo's tenderness and humility. When he tells her he is virgin enough for the two of them, Cherie responds, "Thass the sweetest, tenderest thing that was ever said to me." They board the bus together, their new-found romance applauded by the oddly assorted travelers who have shared their wait. Another of Inge's treatments of modern sexuality, the play, Louis *Kronenberger noted, had "a rowdy, positive quality that is theatrically very useful to the largely static form, the largely Chekhovian mood of the play; it gives a sense of motion to what is becalmed, and of lustiness to what is basically sentimental." The Robert *Whitehead–Roger L. *Stevens production was particularly applauded for Stanley's performance. A commendable 1996 revival at Circle in the Square that featured Mary-Louise Parker and Billy Crudup as Cherie and Bo failed to run.

BUSCH, Charles (b. 1954), playwright and actor. A native New Yorker who attended the High School of the Performing Arts, he was educated at Northwestern before founding Off Off Broadway's Theatre-in-Limbo, a venue for his own plays and performances as the leading ladies. Busch approached his feminine characters with a touch of camp but mostly with sincerity and dedication. His first success was *Vampire Lesbians of Sodom* (1985), in which he played a pair of vamps at different times in history. Other notable plays/performances include the Gidget-like beach gal Chicklet in *Psycho Beach Party* (1987), the World War II spy Gertrude Garnet in *The Lady in Question* (1989), and the Hollywood star Mary Dale in *Red Scare on Sunset* (1991). Busch's Broadway hit *The *Tale of the Allergist's Wife* (2000) and his book for the musical *Taboo* (2003) were among his few works in which he did not appear.

BUTTER AND EGG MAN, THE (1925), a comedy by George S. *Kaufman. [*Longacre Theatre, 243 perf.] Joe Lehman (Robert Middlemass) and Jack McClure (John A. Butler) are two shoestring Broadway producers with a problem: the gangster backer of their new play has been arrested moments before he could sign the check for the money they needed. Even Joe's wife Fanny (Lucille Webster) thinks so little of the play she refuses to help. In walks Peter Jones (Gregory *Kelly), a yokel from Chillicothe, looking to invest his savings in a play, make a bundle, and return home to buy a hotel. His $20,000 buys forty-nine percent of the piece. When the play opens out of town to dreadful reviews, Lehman and McClure want to close it, but Jones buys out the producers, repairs the play, and opens it in New York where it is a smash hit. However, Jones is confronted with a lawsuit charging the play has been stolen. Without divulging the legal problem, Jones sells the play back to Lehman and McClure for a whopping profit and returns home with his helpful sweetheart to build his hotel. Kaufman's only important solo effort, the play (produced by Crosby Gaige) was praised by Gilbert W. Gabriel of the *Sun* as "the wittiest and liveliest jamboree ever distilled from the atmosphere of Broadway." Malcolm Goldstein, Kaufman's biographer, has noted that the play's underlying theme of a not-too-bright young man spurred to success by a sharper woman had been common to all Kaufman's earlier plays as well. The term "butter and egg man" was originated or popularized by nightclub hostess Texas Guinan to suggest a hick from the sticks.

BUTTERFLIES ARE FREE (1969), a play by Leonard Gershe. [*Booth Theatre, 1,128 perf.] To escape his domineering mother, Don Baker (Keir Dullea) has taken his own apartment in New York. The decision is a brave one, since Don is totally blind. Before long Don is having an affair with his new neighbor, the slightly kooky actress Jill Tanner (Blythe *Danner), but his mother (Eileen *Heckart) will not leave Don alone. She and Jill are soon locked in battle, and for a while it seems that Mrs. Baker will scare Jill into leaving Don. When Jill claims she simply does not want to be tied down to anyone, Don recognizes it as her unwillingness to commit to anyone, calling her "emotionally retarded . . . crippled. I'd rather be blind." Jill stays and Don's mother finally lets him live his own life. A small play with an essentially pathetic theme, it was hailed by Richard *Watts Jr. of the *Post* as "humourous, winning and quietly moving." This was the only successful play by Gershe, who was primarily a screenwriter.

BY JUPITER (1942), a musical comedy by Richard *Rodgers (book, music), Lorenz *Hart (book, lyrics). [*Shubert Theatre, 427 perf.] So long as Queen Hippolyta (Benay Venuta) of Pontus can retain her magic strength-giving girdle, she and her Amazons will rule over their milksop husbands. The Greeks, led by Theseus (Ronald Graham) and Hercules (Ralph Dumke), invade Pontus, hoping to capture the girdle and elevate the hapless consort Sapiens (Ray *Bolger) to the throne. Their swords fail them but their sexual prowess prevails and Theseus is awarded the hand of Hippolyta's sister Antiope (Constance Moore). *Notable songs*: Careless Rhapsody; Everything I've Got; Nobody's Heart. Based on Julian F. Thompson's *The Warrior Husband*, the musical (produced by Dwight Deere *Wiman and Rodgers) was Rodgers and Hart's final collaboration. When it was successfully revived Off Broadway in 1967, *Variety* observed that it "is still a melodious laughrouser."

BYE BYE BIRDIE (1960), a musical comedy by Michael *Stewart (book), Charles *Strouse (music), Lee *Adams (lyrics). [Martin Beck Theatre, 607 perf.; Tony Award.] When the popular rock star Conrad Birdie (Dick Gautier) is about to be drafted, his agent Albert Peterson (Dick Van Dyke), arranges a coup he hopes will keep revenues coming in during Birdie's army stint, allow him to escape from his possessive mother, Mae (Kay Medford), and free him to marry Rosie Grant (Chita *Rivera). Birdie will go to a small American town, and, televised to the nation, sing his latest song to a typical American teenager. The group arrives in Sweet Apple, Ohio, where they have selected Kim McAfee (Susan Watson) as the girl Conrad will sing to, and complications set in with Kim's beau (Michael J. Pollard) and her frustrated father (Paul Lynde). After Conrad takes Kim for a wild night on the town and tries to seduce her, she goes back to her boyfriend just as Albert finally wins Rosie back. *Notable songs*: Put on a Happy Face; A Lot of Livin' to Do; Baby, Talk to Me; Kids. The first musical to pay real attention to the new rock 'n' roll craze, it was suggested by the induction into military service of singing star Elvis Presley. Gower *Champion imaginatively staged the production, and Kenneth Tynan of *The New Yorker* found it "filled with a kind of affectionate freshness that we have seldom encountered." It remains very popular in schools and summer stock, though a 1980 sequel, *Bring Back Birdie*, utilized many of the talents from the original but quickly closed on Broadway.

BYRON, Arthur [William] (1872–1943), actor. The son of performer Oliver Doud Byron, he was born in Brooklyn and made his debut with his father's company in 1889. After playing several seasons under Charles *Frohman's aegis in support of John *Drew, *Byron was playing leading roles, such as the maligned suitor of the heroine in *The Stubbornness of Geraldine* (1902), Maxine *Elliott's vicious suitor in *Her Own Way* (1903), Rev. Gavin Dishart in *The Little Minister* (1904), John Ryder in a touring company of *The *Lion and the Mouse* (1906), and Jerome Le Govain in *Samson* (1908). He was again Elliott's leading man in *The Inferior Sex* (1910), then toured with Maude *Adams as John Shand in *What Every Woman Knows* (1911) and played opposite Mrs. *Fiske in *The High Road* (1912). Byron scored a major success as Dr. Gerald Sumner in *The *Boomerang* (1915) and enjoyed another long run as the Friend to the absurdly jealous Husband in *Tea for Three* (1918). After a lengthy tour and brief New York stand as the aging boulevardier Comte de Larsac in *Transplanting Jean* (1921), he won applause as Dr. John Dillard in *The Ghost Between* (1921). His biggest hit was as Richard Sones, who tames his irresponsible wife in *Spring Cleaning* (1923). In a change of pace he was hailed as Martin Brady, the state's attorney, in *The *Criminal Code* (1929) while another drama, *Five Star Final* (1930), allowed him to play the guilt-ridden editor Randall. In 1936 Byron essayed Polonius to John Gielgud's Hamlet and two years later made his last appearance as the militaristic King Zedekiah in *Jeremiah* (1939).

BYRON, Joseph (1844–1923). photographer. One of the leading photographers of the American stage, he was born in Nottingham, England, and came to this country in 1888. Three years later he began to photograph theatrical productions. Many of the most famous stage pictures of the early 20th century were his. Byron's heirs continued to operate the firm until 1942.

BYRON, Oliver Doud (1842–1920), actor. Born in Frederick, Maryland, he made his first appearance at the *Holliday Street Theatre in Baltimore in 1856, playing with Joseph *Jefferson in *Nicholas Nickleby,* using the name Oliver B. Doud. In 1856 he joined the Richmond (Virginia) Theatre, playing alongside John Wilkes *Booth, then acted with companies in Washington, Pittsburgh, and New Orleans, before becoming a member of *Wallack's celebrated New York ensemble. At one time Byron alternated with Edwin *Booth in the roles of Othello and Iago. Although he claimed to have originated the part of Richard Harre in *East Lynne,* his principal claim to fame was his Joe Ferris in *Across the Continent* (1871), a role he played several thousand times over thirty years. Some critics ridiculed Byron's characterization as being unrealistically virtuous, but *Odell remembered it as "a manly, wholesome, resourceful characterisation that pleased women and men alike." He retired from the stage in 1912 after costly and losing battles with the *Theatrical Syndicate or Trust, to whom he refused to bow. His wife, Kate, and his son, Arthur *Byron, were both popular performers.

C

CABARET (1966), a musical play by Joe Masteroff (book), John *Kander (music), Fred *Ebb (lyrics). [*Broadhurst Theatre, 1,165 perf.; Tony, NYDCC Awards.] At the sleazy Kit Kat Klub the effete Master of Ceremonies (Joel *Grey) bids one and all "Willkommen" to the tumultuous Berlin of the Weimar Republic, where Cliff Bradshaw (Bert Convy), a young American writer, strikes up a series of foredoomed relationships. One is with his landlady, Frau Schneider (Lotte *Lenya), who lives in daydreams of a probably imaginary past and who is courted by a Jewish boarder, Herr Schultz (Jack Gilford). Another is with Ernst Ludwig (Edward Winter), whose main preoccupation is smuggling in funds for the Nazis. However, Cliff becomes closest to Sally Bowles (Jill Haworth), an attractive English girl working as an entertainer in the club. But neither the amoral and hedonistic times nor Sally's unstable charms provide an anchor for the romance, so Cliff elects to leave Germany. A musical redaction of *I Am a Camera, the Hal *Prince–produced-directed musical employed the nightclub as a frame for the action and the club's M.C. as its Elizabethan prologue, Greek chorus, and contemporary colorist. Walter *Kerr noted in the *Times*, "Instead of putting the narrative first . . . it pops the painted clown and gartered girls directly into our faces, making them, in effect, a brilliantly glazed window . . . through which we can perceive the people and the emotional pattern of the plot." The musical was revived successfully on Broadway in 1987 and a 1998 revival ran more than five years. **Joe MASTEROFF** (b. 1919) was born in Philadelphia, educated at Temple University, and began his theatre career as an actor then as assistant to Howard *Lindsay. He made his playwriting debut with *The Warm Peninsula* (1959) and wrote his first libretto for *She Loves Me* (1963). After *Cabaret*, Masteroff scripted the musicals *70, Girls, 70* (1971), and *Six Wives* (1992).

CABIN IN THE SKY (1940), a musical fantasy by Lynn Root (book), Vernon *Duke (music), John *Latouche (lyrics). [Martin Beck Theatre, 156 perf.] When the pious Petunia Jackson (Ethel *Waters) prays to God to spare the life of her troublesome husband, Little Joe (Dooley Wilson), the Good Lord allows Joe six months in which to redeem himself. He even sends the Lord's General (Todd *Duncan) to help, but his move is countered by the appearance of Lucifer Jr. (Rex Ingram). Just as it seems Joe has turned over a new leaf, he has an argument with Petunia and she is accidentally shot. They arrive at the Pearly Gates, where Petunia's loving pleas melt the Lord's heart, so Joe is permitted to enter along with her. *Notable songs*: Cabin in the Sky; Honey in the Honeycomb; Takin' a Chance on Love. One of several adventurous musicals of the 1940–41 season, which included *Pal Joey* and *Lady in the Dark*, the musical's relatively short run was probably attributable to its being perceived as a "Negro" show. But in its willingness to touch on fantasy (always a theatrical bugaboo), its superb *Dunham and *Balanchine dances, and its pervasive sense of restraint and tone, it was several steps ahead of its time. When it was revived in 1964 John McClain of the *Journal-American* observed, "The book by Lynn Root seems to have withstood the ravages of time wonderfully well . . . [*Cabin in the Sky*] is a small classic in our time."

CACTUS FLOWER (1965). An Americanization by Abe *Burrows of Pierre Barillet's and Jean Pierre Gredy's Parisian hit, *Fleur de Cactus*, which told of a philandering bachelor dentist eventually subdued by his strong-willed nurse, it ran for 1,234 performances, the longest run to date of any Continental play on Broadway. Barry *Nelson and Lauren *Bacall were the leads.

CAESAR, Adolph (1934–1986), actor. A powerful African-American character actor whose lined face and gravel voice made him distinctive, Caesar played a variety of classical and contemporary roles in notable regional theatres, but in New York he appeared mostly in new black works, such as *The Sty of the Blind Pig* (1971) and *The Brownsville Raid* (1976). Caesar was born in Harlem and was on the New York stage by 1962. His most famous role was the bigoted Sergeant Waters in A *Soldier's Play* (1981).

CAESAR AND CLEOPATRA. Originally presented at the *New Amsterdam Theatre in 1906 with Johnston *Forbes-Robertson and his wife, Gertrude Elliot, in the leading roles, *Shaw's work was perceived as an interesting, but uneven play made noteworthy by the brilliant scene in which the two principals first meet. The *Theatre Guild used the play to open its new playhouse in 1925, with Lionel *Atwill and Helen *Hayes as the rulers. It was a major success, although such critics as Stark *Young felt both the production and the stars missed the grandeur of Shaw's conception. The best later revival was the production that featured Cedric Hardwicke and Lilli Palmer in 1949. Laurence *Olivier and Vivien Leigh performed the play (in a program alternating with Shakespeare's *Antony and Cleopatra*) in 1951, and the title roles were essayed on Broadway by Rex *Harrison and Elizabeth *Ashley in 1977. The work also served as the basis of a failed musical *Her First Roman* (1968) starring Richard *Kiley and Leslie Uggums.

CAESAR, [Isidor] **Irving** (1895–1996), lyricist. The native New Yorker came to the attention of Al *Jolson when he won a contest for new lyrics to Jolson's World War I tongue twister, "Sister Susie's Sewing Shirts for Soldiers." (The winning lyric was entitled "Brother Benny's Baking Buns for Belgians.") A few seasons later Caesar wrote the lyrics for one of Jolson's most memorable hits, "Swanee," with music by George *Gershwin. After writing several *Greenwich Village Follies*, he created the lyrics to "I Want to Be Happy" and "Tea for Two" to Vincent *Youmans's music for *No, No, Nanette*, as well as "Sometimes I'm Happy" and other songs for Youmans's *Hit the Deck!* (1926). Among his other shows were *No Foolin'* (1926), *Yes, Yes, Yvette* (1927), *Here's Howe* (1928), *Americana* (1928), *Polly* (1929), *Ripples* (1930), *Nina Rosa* (1930), *The Wonder Bar* (1931), *Melody* (1933), and *White Horse Inn* (1936). His last show was *My Dear Public* (1943), for which he served not only as lyricist but also as co-librettist and producer. Caesar's lyrics were bright, often clever and colloquial, but rarely distinguished.

CAESAR, [né Isaac Sidney] **Sid** (b. 1922), comedian. The brash comic, who excelled at aping different accents and types, was born in Yonkers, New York. Although best known for his work on television, especially for *The Show of Shows* (early 1950s), he was starred in two Broadway musicals, *Make Mine Manhattan* (1948) and *Little Me* (1962), in the latter playing all of the heroine's diverse lovers. His return in *Four on a Garden* (1971) and *Sid Caesar and Company* (1989) were both quick failures. The character of TV star Max Prince in Neil *Simon's *Laughter on the 23rd Floor* (1993) was based on Caesar.

CAFÉ LA MAMA. See La MaMa Experimental Theatre Club.

CAFFE CINO. In 1959 the coffeehouse on Cornelia Street in New York's Greenwich Village was turned by its owner Joe Cino into one of the earliest establishments offering avant-garde theatricals. It flourished until Cino's suicide in 1967 and closed shortly thereafter. Lanford *Wilson, Marshall *Mason, and Tom Eyen are artists once closely associated with it and who went on to renown on Broadway or Off Broadway. Ironically, for all its avant-garde reputation, the most famous work to be developed first on its tiny stage was the still frequently revived pastiche musical *Dames at Sea*. Ellen Stewart, duenna of the similar *La MaMa Experimental Theatre Club, has said, "It was Joseph Cino who started Off Off Broadway."

CAGE AUX FOLLES, LA. See *La Cage aux Folles*.

CAHILL, Marie (1870–1933), singer and comedienne. The tiny, plump, feisty performer made her debut in her hometown, Brooklyn, in *Kathleen Mavourneen*, then made her Manhattan debut in 1888 in *C. O. D.* After appearing briefly in *McKenna's Flirtation* and a revival of *A Tin Soldier* in 1889, she left for Europe, where she spent the next several seasons in Paris and London. When Cahill returned, she earned remarkable notices as Lady Patty Larceny, forever seeking the perfect mate, in Victor *Herbert's short-lived *The Gold Bug* (1896), in which she stopped the show singing "When I First Began to Marry, Years Ago." After several other supporting roles, she won widespread attention introducing "Nancy Brown" in *The Wild Rose* (1902). Her most famous song was "Under the Bamboo Tree," which she first sang while playing the title role in *Sally in Our Alley* (1902). Star parts followed in *Nancy Brown* (1903), *It Happened in Nordland* (1904), *Moonshine* (1905), *Marrying Mary* (1906), *The Boys and Betty* (1908), *Judy Forgot* (1910), *The Opera Ball* (1912), and *Ninety in the Shade* (1915). Thereafter her career began to falter, although she remained popular in vaudeville. Her last appearances were in the revue *Merry-Go-Round* (1927) and as the gigolo-seeking Park Avenue matron Mrs. Wentworth in *The New Yorkers* (1930). During her career, the strong-willed actress often won notoriety by insisting on inserting her own interpolations, her battles sometimes costing her important roles.

CAHN, Sammy. See *High Button Shoes*.

CAHN'S GUIDE. Properly known as *Julius Cahn's Official Theatrical Guide*, it was long considered the authoritative source for information required by booking agents and producers who were taking shows on the road. State by state and city by city, it provided details on all playhouses as well as town population figures, newspapers, hotels, and railroads. It was published from 1896 to 1920 when it was merged with the *Gus Hill Theatrical and Motion Picture Guide.*

CAIN'S WAREHOUSE. Opened by John J. Cain in the late 1880s or early 1890s, it specialized in storing theatrical scenery of closed Broadway shows. The scenery was then rented to touring and stock companies. "Going to Cain's" became a euphemism for closing a show. The warehouse itself closed in 1938 when the shrinking road and the decline of stock companies deprived it of its market.

CAIUS MARIUS (1831), a tragedy by Richard Penn *Smith. [*Arch Street Theatre (Philadelphia), in repertory.] The rapid rise to power of the low-born Roman general Caius Marius (Edwin *Forrest) irks the patrician Sylla (Robert C. Maywood) and Metellus (Thomas Archer), both of whom had helped him but now perceive him as a rabble-rouser and an ingrate. A battle for control ensues, couched in terms of a class struggle. At one point, when mobs endanger Sylla, Caius Marius offers him the sanctuary of his home. In the end, however, after Caius has slain Metellus and Sylla's army is at Rome's gates, Caius's beloved and loving slave girl, Martha (Mrs. Sharpe), prevents Caius's humiliating defeat by joining him in drinking a cup of poisoned wine. A subplot details the doomed love of Caius Marius's son, Granius (Mr. Smith), for Metellus's daughter, Metella (Mrs. Rowbotham). Many contemporary critics felt this blank-verse tragedy was Smith's best play, but the public was unresponsive, so after a few additional performances in New York, Boston, and possibly elsewhere, Forrest dropped the piece. It was apparently not revived until 1858, when F. B. *Conway headed the cast at Philadelphia's *Walnut Street Theatre in two performances mounted as a memorial to Smith. The text was lost for nearly a century. Rediscovered, it was published in 1968.

CALDARA, Orme (1875–1925), actor. A virile leading man, he earned fame in such roles as the guilt-ridden Jack Payson in *The *Round-Up* (1907); Richard Gilder, who comes to love the girl who married him for revenge, in *Within the Law* (1912); and Hugh Fullerton, the seducer, in *Common Clay* (1915). Before tuberculosis led to his early retirement and death he played opposite Jane *Cowl in such dramas as *Lilac Time* (1917) and *Smilin' Through* (1919).

CALDWELL, Anne (1867–1936), lyricist and librettist. Born in Boston, she began her career as a singer and briefly turned her hand to composing before deciding to write librettos and lyrics. Caldwell was first represented on Broadway in *Top o' the World* (1907), although songs she composed with her husband James O'Dea had been interpolated into *The Social Whirl* (1906). Growing recognition came when she served as co-librettist for Victor *Herbert's *The Lady of the Slipper* (1912) and as librettist and lyricist for *When Claudia Smiles* (1914). Her work on *Chin-Chin* (1914) so delighted its star, Fred *Stone, that he employed her for all his remaining shows but his last: *Jack o' Lantern* (1917), *Tip Top* (1920), *Stepping Stones* (1923), and *Three Cheers* (1928). Many of Caldwell's other works were written in collaboration with Jerome *Kern: *She's a Good Fellow* (1919), *The Night Boat* (1920), *Hitchy-Koo* (1920), *Good Morning, Dearie* (1921), *The Bunch and Judy* (1922), *The City Chap* (1925), and *Criss Cross* (1926). Her 1926 collaboration with Vincent *Youmans, *Oh, Please!*, left behind "I Know That You Know." Among her other memorable songs were "Wait Till the Cows Come Home," "Ka-lu-a," and "Left All Alone Again Blues."

CALDWELL, James H. (1793–1863), actor and manager. Coming to America from England in 1816, he made his acting debut as Belcour in *The West Indian* first in Charleston then in New York. Although he was an actor of some repute and continued performing until 1843, Caldwell was best known as a builder and manager of theatres in Cincinnati, Mobile, Nashville, and St. Louis. However, he is most remembered for his work in New Orleans, where he managed the St. Philip Street Theatre and the American Theatre, in which he introduced the use of gas lighting. In 1835 he erected the St. Charles Theatre, the city's prime playhouse for many years. In his *Dramatic Life as I Found It*, Noah M. *Ludlow draws a vivid picture of the man.

CALDWELL, Zoë [Ada] (b. 1933), actress and director. The Australian-born leading lady, who was the wife of Robert *Whitehead, acted with the *Royal Shakespeare Company before coming to America, where she has appeared with the *Guthrie Theatre and other regional theatres in a variety of roles. Caldwell's first Broadway appearance was as Sister Jean in *The Devils* (1965), but she is probably best remembered for her portrayal of the title roles in *The Prime of Miss Jean Brodie* (1968) and *Medea* (1982), winning *Tony Awards for both, as she has for Polly, the eccentric gossip columnist, in *Slapstick Tragedy* (1966) and opera diva Maria Callas in *Master Class* (1995). In addition to playing Lillian *Hellman in a one-woman show, *Lillian* (1986), Caldwell has also directed plays, most memorably *Park Your Car in Harvard Yard* (1991). Autobiography: *I Will Be Cleopatra*, 2001.

CALHERN, Louis [né Carl Henry Vogt] (1895–1956), actor. The lanky, suave leading man of screen and stage made his theatrical debut while still a boy with Cecil Spooner's stock company in his native New York. He played stock in St. Louis for two seasons beginning in 1914, then toured with Margaret *Anglin before serving in World War I. The first role Calhern created on Broadway was the minor one of Eugene Poppin in *Roger Bloomer* (1923), which was followed by his portraying Joseph Murdoch in George M. *Cohan's *The Song and Dance Man* (1923). His first major assignment was as the untemptable Jack Race opposite Judith *Anderson in *The Cobra* (1924). Thereafter he suffered a string of failed plays—a string broken only when he assumed the supporting role of Cass Worthing, the hero's rival, in *Brief Moment* (1931). Long runs eluded him until he accepted the role of Father in a touring company of *Life with Father* (1941), and later played the same part in New York. Probably his most-remembered role was the bigoted Colonel Tadeusz in *Jacobowsky and the Colonel* (1944), and he won further laurels as Oliver Wendell Holmes in *The Magnificent Yankee* (1946). Calhern's last important roles were in two disparate revivals: as Sandor Turai in *The Play's the Thing* (1948) and as *King Lear* (1950). A final New York appearance came as the senile Pop in *The Wooden Dish* (1955).

CALIFORNIA THEATRE (San Francisco). William Ralston, the head of San Francisco's Bank of California, was so impressed by the work of two fine performers, John *McCullough and Lawrence *Barrett, that he offered to build a theatre for them. The playhouse opened on Bush Street in 1869 and for many years was home for the finest company away from the East Coast. The house was designed by S. C. Bugbee and Son, and cost $150,000. Under various managements the theatre remained the city's leading playhouse until it was demolished in 1888. Another theatre, using the same name, was erected on the site and continued to flourish until it was destroyed in the 1906 earthquake and fire, but this second house, having to buck increasing competition, never enjoyed the prestige of the first.

CALL ME MADAM (1950), a musical comedy by Howard *Lindsay, Russel *Crouse (book), Irving *Berlin (music, lyrics). [*Imperial Theatre, 644 perf.] Sally Adams (Ethel *Merman) has been appointed ambassadress to Lichtenburg not because of any diplomatic skills, but rather because in Washington she was "The Hostess with the Mostes' on the Ball." At her new post she falls for Prime Minister Constantin (Paul Lukas) while her assistant Kenneth Gibson (Russell Nype) is smitten with Princess Maria (Galina Talva). When the local opposition makes things hot for Constantin, Sally is willing to retreat discreetly until the opposing forces are foiled and both pairs of lovers can continue courting. *Notable songs*: Marrying for Love; You're Just in Love; It's a Lovely Day Today; They Like Ike. The Leland *Hayward–produced musical, which proved to be Berlin's last success, was written as a send-up of the famous Washington hostess Perle Mesta whom President Truman had recently made an ambassador.

CAMELOT (1960), a musical play by Alan Jay *Lerner (book, lyrics), Frederick *Loewe (music). [*Majestic Theatre, 873 perf.] A somewhat reluctant King Arthur (Richard *Burton) awaits the arrival of his bride, Guinevere (Julie *Andrews), an innocent young lady raised on bloody romances, which have prompted her to look forward to a world where "kith will kill their kin for me." Her innocence disappears soon after the marriage when she falls in love with Lancelot (Robert Goulet). Their affair is betrayed by Mordred (Roddy McDowall), and the idyll of Camelot, that "one brief shining moment," is destroyed forever. *Notable songs*: Camelot; If Ever I Would Leave You; Before I Gaze at You Again; How to Handle a Woman. The musical, based on T. H. White's *The Once and Future King*, was beset not only by the serious illnesses of both Lerner and director-producer Moss *Hart during the tryout, but by the unrealistically high expectations in the wake of *My Fair Lady*. An advance sale of more than $3 million allowed *Camelot* to buck disappointed notices and to succeed both on Broadway, on the road, and by amateur groups ever since. The show is also fondly remembered as a nostalgic view of the Kennedy years, it being the president's favorite musical. *Camelot* was revived to more balanced reviews and good business on the road in the 1980–81 season, then taken back to New York with Richard Harris as Arthur, though a revival with Goulet as the King failed in 1993.

CAMILLE [La Dame aux Camélias]. This dramatization of Alexandre Dumas fils's novel was first acted in France in 1852 and brought to America the following year by Jean M. Davenport in her own version, which she called *Camille; or, The Fate of a Coquette*. The story remains well known, largely because of the ongoing popularity of the opera *La Traviata*, which was based on the French original. A courtesan named Marguerite Gautier finds true love with young Armand Duval and prepares to give up her questionable ways. However, Duval's family is scandalized and his father persuades her to sacrifice her love for the sake of Armand's family. She leads Armand to believe she has been unfaithful, but the separation strains Marguerite beyond endurance, and she dies in the arms of the forgiving Armand. The first great American Marguerite was Matilda *Heron, who for many years had no rival in the part. Afterward Clara *Morris was equally popular and the play was one of the triumphs of Sarah *Bernhardt's tours. As late as the early 1930s the work remained a favorite with playgoers, proving one of Eva *Le Gallienne's biggest successes at the *Civic Repertory Theatre. However, a major 1963 revival with Susan Strasberg was a quick failure.

CAMPBELL, Bartley [Thomas] (1843–88), playwright. He began his career as a newspaperman in his hometown of Pittsburgh, later working on Louisville and Cincinnati papers. In 1869 he founded the *Southern Monthly Magazine* in New Orleans, but with the success of his first-produced play, *Through Fire* (1871), he abandoned journalism and determined to support himself solely by his playwriting. Although Campbell is frequently called America's first fully professional dramatist, he often produced and directed plays as well. After writing the social comedy *Peril; or, Love at Long Branch* (1872) for E. L. *Davenport, he helped convert R. M. *Hooley's Chicago theatre (Hooley's Theatre) from minstrelsy into a legitimate playhouse where they staged such plays of his as the melodrama *Fate* (1873), the domestic drama *Risks; or, Insure Your Life* (1873), the Civil War play *The Virginian* (1874), the "military comedy" *On the Rhine* (1875), the Irish rebellion drama *Gran Uaile* (1875), and the comedy *My Foolish Wife* (1877). Not until an 1876 trip to London did Campbell begin to write the type of Western dramas for which he would become famous, most memorably *The Vigilantes; or, the Heart of the Sierras* (1877) and *My Partner* (1879). His other noteworthy plays include the melodrama *The *Galley Slave* (1879), the Russian drama *Siberia* (1882), and *The *White Slave* (1882). A number of other plays that Campbell wrote and produced at the same time failed, with losses outrunning the income from his hits. Unable to handle emotionally the financial problems that followed, he was committed to a mental institution where he died two years later. For a short while, from about 1875 to 1883, Campbell not only was the most successful American playwright but also was hailed by many critics as the best the country had yet produced. Reaction quickly set in, and at his death Andrew C. *Wheeler, writing as Nym Crinkle, noted, "He never quite reached the level of literary greatness, but he overshot the level of generous impulse—if impulse can have a level." Nevertheless, his best plays remain eminently readable, and probably, if given a chance, eminently playable.

CAMPBELL, Mrs. Patrick [née Beatrice Stella Tanner] (1865–1940), actress. The English star famous for her wit and beauty but best recalled for her correspondence with George Bernard *Shaw, made her American debut in 1902 in the title role of *Magda*. On the tour she also offered what then were her two most-celebrated roles, the title parts in *The Second Mrs. Tanqueray* and *The Notorious Mrs. Ebbsmith*. In all she made half a dozen visits to America, including a 1914 visit in which she appeared as Liza Doolittle in *Pygmalion*, a play Shaw had written for her and with which she was long identified. She was, of course, really too old to play the young flower vendor, but that proved only a small drawback. Her last appearance came in 1933. On first seeing her, J. Rankin *Towse wrote, "Her voice is a charming instrument, rich, soft, and musical, with sufficient volume, but no abnormal power or resonance; her eyes, large and dark and deep, often partly veiled, as in Orientals, by drooping lids, lighten finely, in her moments of excitement, and become wonderfully expressive and striking." Biography: *Mrs. Patrick Campbell*, Alan Dent, 1961.

CAN-CAN (1953), a musical comedy by Abe *Burrows (book), Cole *Porter (music, lyrics). [*Shubert Theatre, 892 perf.] A young, straitlaced judge, Aristide Forestier (Peter Cookson), is assigned to investigate stories of scandalous can-can dancing at a Montmartre café. He falls in love both with the dancing and with the café's proprietress, La Mome Pistache (Lilo), helps legalize the dance, and marries the lady. At the same time, one of the dancers, Claudine (Gwen *Verdon), has a duel fought over her by her two suitors. *Notable songs*: Allez-vous-en; Can-Can; C'est Magnifique; I Love Paris; It's All Right with Me. Although the Cy *Feuer and Ernest H. *Martin production opened to indifferent notices and its French star was respectfully received, the real hit of the evening was the superb dancing and comic artistry of Verdon in a merely supporting role. Within a few months much of Porter's score had won recognition, adding to the play's box office appeal. A major revival in 1980 was unsuccessful.

CANDIDA. Arnold *Daly first offered *Shaw's play at a special matinee in 1903 with Dorothy *Donnelly as Candida and himself as Marchbanks. The reception was such that additional matinees were given and then a four-month run followed. Curiously, its good reception was largely the result of word of mouth, since many critics initially ignored the play. Its story of a woman who must choose between a visionary and a practical socialist was less beset by matters of passing topical interest and had more of a genuine love story than virtually any other major Shaw play, and so has retained a loyal following. Of its many revivals, most beloved were those by Katharine *Cornell, who first played the part in 1924 when she gave it its longest run to date, five months. She brilliantly juxtaposed the heroine's frailty and strength, giving a performance Stark *Young found "so delicate and translucent and moving as we rarely see." Richard Bird was her first Marchbanks, but the role was assumed in her later revivals by such eventually more famous actors as Orson *Welles, Burgess *Meredith, and Marlon *Brando. Other New York productions of *Candida* featured Olivia de Havilland in 1952, Celeste *Holm in 1970, Joanne Woodward in 1981, and Mary Steenburgen in 1993.

CANDIDE (1956), a musical satire by Lillian *Hellman (book), Leonard *Bernstein (music), Richard Wilbur, John *Latouche, Dorothy *Parker (lyrics). [Martin Beck Theatre, 73 perf.] Tutored by the incorrigibly optimistic Doctor Pangloss (Max Adrian) who feels we live in "The Best of All Possible Worlds," young Candide (Robert Rounseville) marries Cunegonde (Barbara *Cook) and prepares to enjoy life. Instead, war breaks out and Cunegonde is carried off. At one point she is forced to lead the life of a demimonde while Candide spends years traveling about the world searching for his bride, for success, and for understanding. He discovers Cunegonde and loses her again several times before he takes her back to Westphalia, where they will live a simple life together. *Notable songs*: Glitter and Be Gay; Make Our Garden Grow; I Am Easily Assimilated; What's the Use? Louis *Kronenberger saw this musical rendition of Voltaire's novella as "a medley of the brilliant, the uneven, the exciting, the earthbound, the adventurous and the imperfectly harmonized." Such tempered criticism discouraged all but the most dedicated playgoers. Not until Hal *Prince staged a drastically revised version in 1974 did the operetta win popular acceptance. The revival altered the book and opened up the action, taking it to all parts of the auditorium. Unlike the original, the 1974 production included no instantly recognizable names in the cast. In recent years major opera companies have added the work to their repertories, though a 1997 Broadway revival failed to run. The Overture is the most famous piece from the work, performed by orchestras around he world.

CANTOR, Arthur (1920–2001), producer. Born in Boston and educated at Harvard, he served as a press representative before turning producer. Alone or with others he produced such plays as *The *Tenth Man* (1959), **All the Way Home* (1960), **Gideon* (1961), *A Thousand Clowns* (1962), *In Praise of Love* (1974), **On Golden Pond* (1979), *Pack of Lies* (1985), and *Beau Jest* (1991). During this time he also continued his presswork.

CANTOR, Eddie [né Isidore Itzkowitz] (1892–1964), comedian and singer. The slim, jumpy, pop-eyed performer was born in New York and won an amateur night contest at Miner's Bowery Theatre when he was fourteen. A year later he first performed in professional vaudeville at the Clinton Music Hall, working as a singing waiter when bookings were unavailable. In 1914 he went to England, where he played more vaudeville and made his legitimate debut in *Not Likely*. Returning to America he played a blackface chauffeur in the touring *Canary Cottage* (1916), catching the eye of Florenz *Ziegfeld who signed him to perform in the *Ziegfeld Follies of 1917*. Playing in blackface with an all-too-innocent leer, rolling his eyes, and finishing by prancing off waving a handkerchief, he scored a hit with "That's the Kind of Baby for Me." Further successful appearances followed in the 1918 and 1919 editions of the *Follies* (introducing Irving *Berlin's "You'd Be Surprised" in the latter), *Brevities* (1920), and *Make It Snappy* (1922). In the last revue he introduced his celebrated skit in which he played a mousy tailor whose customer demands a coat with a belt in the back. The "belt" the customer received was not the sort he expected. After a brief stint in the *Follies of 1923*, Cantor returned to book musicals with *Kid Boots* (1923) and **Whoopee* (1928), beginning his successful movie career re-creating the last on the screen. After many years in Hollywood and on national radio, he made his final Broadway appearance in a musical version of **Three Men on a Horse*, called *Banjo Eyes* (1941). Among the many songs with which he was associated were "Dinah," "Makin' Whoopee," "Ida," "If You Knew Susie," and "Margie." Autobiographies: *My Life Is in Your Hands*, 1927; *Take My Life*, 1957.

CAPOTE, Truman. See *House of Flowers*.

CAPTAIN JINKS OF THE HORSE MARINES (1901), a comedy by Clyde *Fitch. [*Garrick Theatre, 168 perf.] When Aurelia Johnson of Trenton, New Jersey, returns to America as a world-famous prima donna, Mme. Trentoni (Ethel *Barrymore), she wins over the newsmen and others at the dock with her beauty, grace, and charm, addressing them gaily as "darlings." She also enchants Captain Robert Carrolton Jinks (H. *Reeves-Smith), who makes a written wager of $1,000 with his friends that he can win her love. He quickly succeeds, and not even the stormy disapproval of his snobbish mother (Mrs. Thomas *Whiffen) can seemingly deter the young couple. But on the eve of her big concert, Mme. Trentoni is shown the wager and she is so distressed that she doubts she can perform that night. However, her American debut is a triumph, made all the sweeter when Jinks convinces her that what began as a cynical bet has blossomed into real affection. Upset by Fitch's strenuous objections, producer Charles *Frohman cast Barrymore with some trepidation, shared by the starlet who found the part "very taxing for so young and inexperienced an actress. There were comedy, pathos and dancing in it. I was more worried about the dancing than about anything else." The tryout was not a success, but New York reviews established the play as a major hit and launched Barrymore's career as a star. In 1925 the comedy was turned into a popular musical comedy, *Captain Jinks*, with a book by Frank *Mandel and Laurence *Schwab, lyrics by B. G. *DeSylva, and music by Lewis E. Gensler and Stephen Jones. Featuring Louise Brown and J. Harold *Murray in the principal roles, it ran five months.

CARIOU, Len[ard] (b. 1939), actor. The Canadian-born leading man had appeared in a wide variety of roles with the Stratford Shakespeare Festival (Ontario), Chichester Festival (England), *Guthrie Theatre, and the *Goodman Theatre before winning widespread recognition in the musical *Applause* (1970). Although he has made several returns to serious drama since then, he is best recalled for his work in two other musicals: the lawyer Frederick in A *Little Night Music* (1973) and the murderer *Sweeney Todd* (1979). Among his other roles were the terminal patient Richard in *Cold Storage* (1977), Stalin in *Master Class* (1986), the Duke in *Measure for Measure* (1989), Supreme Court Justice William O. Douglas in *Mountain* (1990), Viet Nam vet Lou in *The Speed of Darkness* (1991), Hemingway in *Papa* (1996), and Darius in *The Persians* (2003).

CARLE, Richard [né Charles Nicholas Carleton] (1871–1941), comic actor. A native of Somerville, Massachusetts, the gawky, high-voiced comedian made his debut in New York in 1891 playing a minor role in *Niobe*. He won good notices as Worthington, the befuddled butler, in *A Mad Bargain* (1893) and again as Washington Strutt in *The Country Sport* (1893). After essaying the part of Schossi Schmendrik in Zangwill's *Children of the Ghetto* (1899), Carle returned to musicals to play briefly in *The Greek Slave* before appearing in *Mam'selle' Awkins* (1900), for which he provided the libretto. He also wrote several of the songs for *The Rogers Brothers in Central Park*. After appearing in *The Ladies Paradise* (1901), he moved to Chicago where he portrayed Bonaparte Hunter in *The Explorers* (1902), the incompetent magician Malzadoc in *The Storks* (1902), and the dithering Professor Pettibone in *The Tenderfoot* (1903), for which he was also librettist and lyricist. While New York critics assailed his humor as obvious and slightly salacious, Carle retained his popularity there and elsewhere. In 1905 he provided the book and lyrics for *The Mayor of Tokio*, then further successes followed: the flirtatious lawyer in his own adaptation of the London hit, *The Spring Chicken* (1906), the henpecked Leander Lamb in *Mary's Lamb* (1908), the philandering Dr. Petypon in *The Girl from Montmartre* (1912), and the jealous marquis in *The Doll Girl* (1913). When his popularity began to wane, Carle turned to vaudeville, appearing in musicals only intermittently thereafter. His last Broadway assignment was as the mistress-flaunting Dr. Wentworth in *The New Yorkers* (1930).

CARLETON, Henry Guy (1856–1910), playwright. Although best known as a humorist, the sometime inventor, who was born in Fort Union, New Mexico, made his first forays into playwriting with two serious works: the tragedy *Memnon* (1881) and the melodrama *Victor Durand* (1884). *A Gilded Fool* (1892) was written for Nat *Goodwin and proved popular, while for John *Drew he wrote *Butterflies* (1894) and *That Imprudent Young Couple* (1895), a comedy that was quickly dismissed despite a cast that included Maude *Adams, Ethel *Barrymore, and Arthur *Byron. The failure of *Ambition* (1895) was followed by his last play, *Colinette* (1899), an adaptation from the French in which Julia *Marlowe scored a personal success. John *Golden recalled that Carleton insisted on personally reading his plays at first rehearsal despite a grotesque stammer, which led to agonizingly long, wasted hours.

CARMEN JONES (1943), a musical play by Oscar *Hammerstein (book, lyrics), Georges Bizet (music). [*Broadway Theatre, 502 perf.] Carmen Jones (Muriel Smith) works in an old southern cigarette factory that has turned to making parachutes for the duration of the war. When Joe (Luther Saxon), an army corporal, arrests her for creating a ruckus, she seduces him into letting her go. He quickly falls madly in love with her. But when she deserts him for the prizefighter Husky Miller (Glenn Bryant), Joe kills her. *Notable songs*: Beat Out Dat Rhythm on a Drum; Dat's Love; Dere's a Café on de Corner. A modern, American version of *Carmen*, with an African-American cast, the show was turned into a major hit by Hammerstein's ingenious redaction, including his imaginative adaptation of the original lyrics, by producer Billy *Rose's astute publicity, and by wartime prosperity. Even the often bigoted, archconservative Col. Robert R. McCormick of the *Chicago Tribune* hailed it as more pertinent for contemporary audiences than the original opera.

CARMINATI [de Brambilla], **Tullio** (1894–1971), actor and singer. Born in Dalmatia, he is recalled by playgoers primarily for two roles: Count di Ruvo, the charming philanderer who wins the heroine, in *Strictly Dishonorable* (1929), and the writer Bruno Mahler in *Music in the Air* (1932), in which he introduced "The Song Is You."

CARNELIA, Craig (b. 1949), composer and lyricist. A highly esteemed artist who has done high quality work for decades, Carnelia has never seen any of his projects become a hit, so he remains little known outside of theatre circles. He was born in Floral Park on Long Island and dropped out of college to become an actor, playing the boy Matt in The *Fantasticks* for a time Off Broadway in 1969. Carnelia later turned to writing songs and was first produced Off Off Broadway with *Notes: Songs* (1977). His song contributions to *Working* (1978) and his full score for *Is There Life After High School?* (1982) were commended, but both of those Broadway shows failed to run. His work was also heard in *Diamonds* (1984) and *Three Postcards* (1987), and he provided the lyrics for Marvin *Hamlisch's music in *Sweet Smell of Success* (2002) and *Imaginary Friends* (2002).

CARNIVAL (1961), a musical play by Michael *Stewart (book), Bob Merrill (music, lyrics). [*Imperial Theatre, 719 perf.; NYDCC Award.] The orphan Lili (Anna Maria Alberghetti) joins a French carnival and falls for an egotistical magician (James Mitchell), but she is truly loved by the bitter puppeteer (Jerry *Orbach). Yet when he speaks to Lili through his puppets, his true emotions are revealed and she learns to love him back. *Notable songs*: Love Makes the World Go Round; Grand Imperial Cirque de Paris; Always Always You; Mira. David *Merrick produced this enchanting musical tale, based on the 1953 film *Lili*, which was enhanced by Gower *Champion's inventive staging that created a circuslike atmosphere with lights and movement. **Bob MERRILL** [né Henry Lavan] (1921–98), a native of Atlantic City, first found fame as the author of many pop songs on the charts in the 1950s. His early Broadway scores were for *New Girl in Town* (1957) and *Take Me Along* (1959), both based on Eugene *O'Neill plays. Merrill provided lyrics for Jules Styne's music in *Funny Girl* (1964) and *Sugar* (1972). His other scores include *Henry, Sweet Henry* (1967) and cult failures *Breakfast at Tiffany's* (1966) and *Prettybelle* (1971).

CARNOVSKY, Morris (1897–1992), actor. A native of St. Louis, he worked at several stock companies, including that run by Henry *Jewett in Boston, before making his New York debut in *The God of Vengeance* (1922). From 1924 through 1930 he was a member of the *Theatre Guild's acting company, and appeared with it in important supporting roles in such plays as *Marco Millions* (1928), *Uncle Vanya* (1929), *Hotel Universe* (1930), and *Elizabeth the Queen* (1930). After appearing in *Both Your Houses* (1933), Carnovsky joined the *Group Theatre, where he played such memorable roles as the unhappy Dr. Levine in *Men in White* (1933), the self-sacrificing grandfather Jacob in *Awake and Sing!* (1935), the violinist's father Mr. Bonaparte in *Golden Boy* (1937), and dentist Ben Stark in *Rocket to the Moon* (1938). In later years his most distinguished performances came when he played Lear and Shylock with the *American Shakespeare Festival. Elliott *Norton called his 1967 interpretation of the latter role "a heroic performance . . . powerful, rich in understanding, proud to the very end, and infinitely moving." Although he rarely achieved stardom in a career that spanned more than sixty years, he was kept busy regularly and just as regularly was admired for whatever sort of role he tackled, but he excelled as troubled, thoughtful men.

CAROLINA PLAYMAKERS (Chapel Hill, North Carolina). This long-lived company was founded in 1918 at the University of North Carolina at Chapel Hill by Professor Frederick Henry Koch who in 1910 had organized a similar group, the Dakota Playmakers, at the University of North Dakota. North Carolina proved a more fertile field for Koch's ambition to develop a writing and producing company devoted primarily to fostering a drama of native material. The company regularly mounted seasons of new plays, including works by young Thomas Wolfe and Paul *Green. Many of the plays were published in the *Carolina Folk-Plays* series. In time, the group was hailed as "America's Folk Theatre." By the late 1970s it had abandoned its original program and had become a professional repertory company that presented native drama only on rare occasions. Today called the PlayMakers Repertory Company, it continues its association with the university while offering a season of professional performances.

CAROUSEL (1945), a musical play by Oscar *Hammerstein (book, lyrics), Richard *Rodgers (music). [*Majestic Theatre, 890 perf.] Billy Bigelow (John *Raitt), a New England carnival barker, falls in love with Julie Jordan (Jan Clayton) and marries her, but unemployed and bitter, he makes life miserable for both of them. Julie's friend Carrie (Jean Darling), on the other hand, gets married to the ambitious fisherman Mr. Snow (Eric Mattson) and they plan a big family. When Billy discovers that Julie is pregnant, he agrees to join the scowling Jigger Craigin (Murvyn Vye) in a robbery to Earn extra money. The plan misfires and Billy kills himself rather than be caught. Before a heavenly judge, Billy pleads for another chance to return to Earth, to redeem himself and see his grown-up and troubled daughter Louise. But when Louise refuses his gift of a star he has stolen from the sky, he slaps her (as he had once done to her mother), then Billy sadly returns to the afterlife. The widowed Julie and her child are left to continue alone in the world, but find comfort in knowing that they are loved. *Notable songs*: You'll Never Walk Alone; June Is Bustin' Out All Over; If I Loved You; When the Children Are Asleep; What's the Use of Wond'rin'? This lyrical retelling of *Molnar's *Liliom* was hailed by Robert Coleman of the *Mirror* as "the product of taste, imagination and skill. It will bewitch your senses and race your theatrical pulses." Among its notable and venturesome moments in the *Theatre Guild production were its opening ballet-pantomime ("Carousel Waltz"), which was choreographed by Agnes *de Mille, the fully integrated "bench scene" that incorporated "If I Loved You" into the dialogue, and Billy's eight-minute stream-of-consciousness "Soliloquy." Now generally acknowledged to be the finest of the Rodgers and Hammerstein operettas, the musical has been revived regularly, most memorably two productions by *Lincoln Center, one in 1965 and the other in 1994 (which originated in London).

CARPENTER, Edward Childs (1872–1950), playwright. Born in Philadelphia, he became a newspaperman after leaving school and quickly rose to an editorial position. In 1903 he published his first novel and two years later collaborated with John Luther *Long on his first play, *The Dragon Fly*, which was produced in Philadelphia but never reached New York. Over the next three decades, however, more than a dozen of Carpenter's plays did reach New York. The most successful were *The Cinderella Man* (1916), in which a rich young lady falls in love with a starving artist; *The Bachelor Father* (1928), in which a man holds a reunion for all his illegitimate children; and *Whistling in the Dark* (1932), a mystery thriller written with Laurence Gross. Whatever his shortcomings as a dramatist, Carpenter was highly respected for his integrity and was elected as president of both the *Dramatists Guild and the *Society of American Dramatists and Composers.

CARR, Benjamin (1768?–1836), composer. Coming to America in the 1790s from his native England, he was soon established in Philadelphia as a respected composer and music teacher. A good singer and adequate actor, he often performed in the plays for which he provided overtures, songs, and incidental music. Carr's most important contribution to the theatre was his score for one of the best early American operettas, *The Archers* (1796). *Dunlap questioned the theatricality of his writing, noting that his "knowledge of music without the graces of action made him more acceptable to the scientific than to the vulgar auditor." Carr must have come to a similar conclusion, for early on he abandoned the theatre to devote his time to teaching.

CARRÈRE and HASTINGS. The noted architectural firm was founded by John Mervan Carrère (1858–1911) and Thomas Hastings (1860–1920). Besides designing such landmark buildings as the New York Public Library and the Frick mansion, they designed Abbey's (later Knickerbocker) Theatre (1893), the *New (later Century) Theatre (1909), and the Globe (later *Lunt-Fontanne) Theatre (1910). Their work was characterized by classic elegance and spaciousness.

CARROLL, Earl (1892–1948), producer and lyricist. He began his theatrical career as a program seller in his native Pittsburgh. After several years as a seaman, he settled in New York where he took up lyric writing. One of his earliest efforts, "Isle d'Amour," with music by Leo Edwards, was a hit of the *Ziegfeld Follies of 1913. He served as lyricist for *Pretty Mrs. Smith* (1914), *So Long, Letty* (1916), *Canary Cottage* (1916), *The Love Mill* (1918), and *Flora Bella* (1920). Turning his hand to producing, Carroll suffered a number of failures with straight plays before finding success with his revue, *Earl Carroll Vanities of 1923. The show featured scantily clad girls and off-color humor, establishing the pattern for later editions. In 1923 he also produced the hugely successful *White Cargo. Among his other productions were *Laff That Off* (1925), *What Ann Brought Home* (1927), *Fioretta* (1929), *Earl Carroll Sketch Book* (1929 and 1935), and *Murder at the Vanities* (1933). He built two theatres, one in 1922 and the other in 1931, both of which he named for himself. He made headlines in 1926 when he was sent to prison for violating prohibition after allowing one of his showgirls to take a bath in a tub of champagne during a party he threw at his theatre for his principal backer, oilman William R. Edrington. Biography: *The Body Merchant*, Ken Murray, 1976.

CARROLL, Leo G. (1892–1972), character actor. The quiet Englishman who excelled in portraying placid, distinguished types, first came to America in 1924 and appeared in such plays as *The Vortex* (1925), *The Constant Nymph* (1926), and *The Green Bay Tree* (1933). He also brought his skills to classic revivals and modern musicals, but he is best recalled for two later appearances: the wily Detective-Inspector Rough in **Angel Street* (1941) and the title part of the Boston Brahmin in *The *Late George Apley* (1944).

CARROLL, Vinnette. See *Don't Bother Me, I Can't Cope.*

CARTER, Lincoln J. (1865–1926), playwright. A prolific author of blood-and-thunder melodramas, his plays were rarely presented in New York and then usually in minor playhouses. But his best plays remained popular with touring companies and were revived regularly until shortly before World War I. Among his works were *The Fast Mail* (1890), *Tornado* (1894), *The Heart of Chicago* (1898), *Under the Dome* (1898), *Remember the Maine* (1898), *Chattanooga* (1899), *Bedford's Hope* (1906), and *An American Ace* (1918).

CARTER, Mrs. Leslie [née Caroline Louise Dudley] (1862–1937), actress. Born in Lexington, Kentucky, the fiery redhead turned to the stage after being snubbed by society following a sensational divorce case in which she was found guilty of adultery. She persuaded David *Belasco to give her the central role of Kate Graydon in *The Ugly Duckling* (1890), and he agreed, probably as much because of her notoriety as because of her as yet latent acting talents. Nature aptly fitted her for the role, for though she was not beautiful, her slim, willowy figure, piercing green eyes, and expressive face were exceedingly attractive. Carter's acting, however, was criticized as too unrestrained, even if, like Belasco, the critics saw great promise in her. The play was a failure, but Belasco and Charles *Frohman confidently cast her for the title role in Audran's operetta, *Miss Helyett* (1891). Real success came when she played the determined Maryland Calvert in *The *Heart of Maryland* (1895). Her "sizzling" performances as the prostitute Zaza (1899), followed by her courtesan *Du Barry* (1901), added to her popularity. In 1905 she gave what many considered her finest portrayal as the tragic heroine of **Adrea*. William *Winter, who had long been critical of her overplaying, wrote of her Adrea, "No denotement in Mrs. Carter's acting of Du Barry had even remotely indicated such depth of tragical feeling and such power of dramatic expression as she revealed in the scene of the tempest, in pronouncing Kaeso's doom, and, above all,

in the terrible, piteous, tragic self-conflict through which the Woman became the incarnation of Fate and the minister of death." Shortly thereafter she left Belasco after an argument over her second marriage. For many years she toured, primarily in revivals, before winning good notices as Lady Catherine in Somerset *Maugham's *The Circle* (1921), and later she toured as Mother Goddam in *The *Shanghai Gesture*. Carter's last New York appearance was as Mrs. Hardcastle in a 1928 revival of *She Stoops to Conquer*, although she made several appearances on California stages before her retirement.

CARUS, Emma (1879–1927), singer. A chunky, blonde, blue-eyed performer with a big, deep voice, she emigrated from her native Germany while still a youngster. Her mother had sung in opera, but Carus had no interest in the field despite a careful musical training. She made her debut in American vaudeville in 1894 and for the next twenty years alternated between two-a-day and the legitimate stage. After a minor part in *Nell Go-In* (1899), she played important roles in, among others, *The Giddy Throng* (1900), *The Wild Rose* (1902), *The Medal and the Maid* (1904), *Woodland* (1904), **[Ziegfeld] Follies of 1907*, *Up and Down Broadway* (1910), and *The Wife Hunters* (1911). After 1915 she confined her appearances to vaudeville, where she was always more at home. Her ability to sing in Dutch, Scotch, Irish, British, and Negro dialects led to her being billed as "The Human Dialect Cocktail." But she was most famous for her trick of jumping from a contralto to deep baritone voice. Although the famous Chicago critic Amy *Leslie admired her as "the only one of the big-time singers who has a cultivated and genuine voice," a Kansas City critic addressed her penchant for forceful projection by admonishing her publicly, "Remember, you are in an enclosed building and not trying to be heard throughout the whole city, including the stockyards."

CARYLL, Ivan [né Felix Tilkin or Tilken] (1861–1921), composer. After studying music in his native Liège, he moved briefly to Paris and then settled in London where, between 1886 and 1908, he composed a series of popular operettas. Arriving in America in 1910, Caryll's first score in his new home was *Marriage a la Carte* (1911), but he did not achieve major success until *The *Pink Lady* later the same season. His subsequent works were *Oh! Oh! Delphine* (1912), *The Little Cafe* (1913), *The Belle of Bond Street* (1914), **Chin-Chin* (1914), *Papa's Darling* (1914), *Jack o' Lantern* (1917), *The Girl Behind the Gun* (1918), *The Canary* (1918), *Tip Top* (1920), *Kissing Time* (1920), and *The Hotel*

Mouse (1922), the last produced after his death. Best known among his songs are "My Beautiful Lady" and "Wait Till the Cows Come Home."

CASINO THEATRE (New York). The first theatre built in America specifically for the presentation of popular musicals, it opened in 1882 with a performance of Strauss's *The Queen's Lace Handkerchief*. It was the brainchild of Rudolph *Aronson, who originally conceived it as a theatre with restaurants, gambling rooms, and New York's first roof garden playhouse. Designed by Francis Kimball and Thomas Wisebell in the Moorish style then in vogue, it stood at the southeast corner of Broadway and 39th Street. For many of its early years it was home to a distinguished ensemble of singers and comedians, although for its first decade it presented only imports. In 1894, however, it offered the first American revue, *The *Passing Show*. Its summer roof garden was the site of the premiere of *The Origin of the Cake Walk; or, *Clorindy* (1898), the first African-American musical to be offered to a white Broadway audience. The house's beautiful chorus line was so famous that a 1900 musical, called *The Casino Girl*, was based on the imaginary adventures of one of its young ladies. By the turn of the century, the stock company had been disbanded and the Casino, taken over by the young *Shuberts, was booked in the same way as other theatres. Among its hits were *Florodora* (1900), *A Chinese Honeymoon* (1902), *Wildflower* (1923), *The *Vagabond King* (1925), and *The *Desert Song* (1926). It was demolished in 1930.

CASSIDY, Claudia (b. 1900–96), critic. A native of Shawneetown, Illinois, she studied at the University of Illinois before beginning to write on the arts for the *Chicago Journal of Commerce* in 1925. Cassidy moved to the *Chicago Sun* in 1941 and to the *Tribune* a year later, remaining there until her retirement in 1965. By far the most influential critic in the Midwest, she was often condemned for the severity of her judgments but insisted she was merely attempting to battle lowering standards in touring productions. *Variety* noted, "She almost singlehandedly stopped the process of Broadway producers sending third-rate versions of New York hits on the road."

CASSIDY, Jack (1927–76), actor and singer. He was born in Richmond Hill, New York, and was only fifteen years old when he started appearing in the chorus of Broadway shows, finally gaining recognition as the summer camp dancing instructor Chick Miller in *Wish You Were Here* (1952). His other prominent New York performances include the cutthroat Macheath in *The Beggar's Opera* (1957), the ladykiller Kodaly in *She Loves Me* (1963), the Hollywood idol Byron Prong in *Fade Out–Fade In* (1964), and the corrupt Max Mencken in *It's a Bird, It's a Plane, It's Superman* (1966). Cassidy was a dimpled, smiling performer who always brought a satirical leer to his comedy roles.

CASTE (1867). An 1867 British play by W. T. Robertson, it told how an officer, who is a marquise's son, proves by his devotion to the instinctively well-bred daughter of a common drunkard that social class is no barrier to a happy marriage. The production of *Caste* led to one of the American theatre's most-celebrated law cases. Lester *Wallack had expected to premiere the piece in New York as he had earlier Robertson works, but before he could open his season, W. J. *Florence brought out an unauthorized production. Wallack attempted to obtain an injunction, but Florence argued successfully that "in the absence of international copyright" he had done no wrong, since a quirk in the law allowed anyone who could memorize a play to produce it. Florence claimed he had done just that and was upheld. Wallack later had great success with the work, and it was revived with some regularity until World War I. T[homas] W[illiam] **ROBERTSON** (1829–71), an English playwright, whose quiet, restrained examinations of middle-class domesticity were known popularly as "cup and saucer plays," was, as far as most Americans were concerned, caviar to the general public. In New York his best plays were offered by Wallack and were usually produced by the elite organizations in other cities. In addition to *Caste*, Wallack presented *Society* (1866), *Ours* (1866), *School* (1869), and *Progress* (1869).

CASTLE, Vernon [né Blythe] (1887–1918), dancer. Coming to America from his native England, he made his debut in *About Town* (1906), the first of seven Lew *Fields shows in which he danced and often served as Fields's stooge: *The Girl Behind the Counter* (1907), *The Mimic World* (1908), *The Midnight Sons* (1909), *Old Dutch* (1909), *The Summer Widowers* (1910), and *The Hen-Pecks* (1911). After he married Irene Foote (1893–1969), who danced in the chorus of the last two shows, they went to Paris, where they perfected their ballroom technique and became a dancing sensation. On their return they almost single-handedly initiated a rage for ballroom dancing in America, starting what was called "the dancing craze" and introducing or popularizing such dances as the tango, the Maxine, the Castle Walk, and the Turkey Trot. Vernon appeared briefly in *The Lady of the Slipper* (1912), a Victor *Herbert musical Irene had walked out of during rehearsals, but they then danced as a team in *The Sunshine Girl* (1913) and in Irving Berlin's ragtime musical *Watch Your Step* (1914).

The Castles were also applauded for their vaudeville appearances. While Vernon was training pilots for the war, Irene appeared alone in *Miss 1917*. After her husband was killed in a training accident, she retired from performing, although she helped later Broadway shows re-create period dances. Autobiography (Irene): *Castles in the Air*, 1958.

CAT AND THE CANARY, THE (1922), a play by John Willard. [*National Theatre, 349 perf.] At the reading of Ambrose West's will it is discovered that young Annabelle West (Florence *Eldridge) is his sole heir, provided she remain of sound mind. Annabelle and her relatives learn the news at West's eerie castle on the Hudson, minutes before a stormy midnight. Their discomfort is aggravated by the spooky behavior of West's old voodoo-obsessed maid, "Mammy" Pleasant (Blanche Frederici), and by the arrival of Hendricks (Edmund Elton), a guard at a nearby insane asylum who is seeking an escaped homicidal maniac. Shortly, inexplicable screams are heard, a clutching claw appears from behind a sliding panel, and a corpse is seen, only to vanish mysteriously. In the end Annabelle's seemingly Milquetoast suitor, Paul Jones (Henry *Hull), helps catch one of her relatives who, it turns out, was in league with Hendricks. Annabelle retains both her sanity and her inheritance. Called "the prototype of a vast number of let's-scare-the-heroine-to-death chillers," the play was long a favorite of stock and amateur troupes. The San Francisco-born **John Clawson WILLARD** (1885–1942) was an actor and dramatist. This was his only successful play, although half a dozen were produced.

CAT AND THE FIDDLE, THE (1931), a musical play by Otto *Harbach (book, lyrics), Jerome *Kern (music). [Globe Theatre, 395 perf.] In Brussels two young composers meet and fall in love. Unfortunately, their disparate goals soon drive them apart, for Victor Florescu (Georges Metaxa) aims at composing the loftiest music, while Shirley Sheridan (Bettina *Hall) seeks merely to write popular songs. But the ardor of their affections triumphs over their separate ambitions, and by the end their music and hearts are in harmony. *Notable songs*: The Night Was Made for Love; She Didn't Say "Yes"; Try to Forget; I Watch the Love Parade. Although critics came down harshly on the book, with *The New Yorker* noting, "Mr. Harbach has really outdone himself in banality," Kern's lovely score saved the Max *Gordon production. A device he had used timidly before, the extended musical lead-in was employed from beginning to end, and orchestral passages underscored much of the action. The orchestra itself was small (only eighteen pieces) but the musicians were so select that they were listed by name in the program.

CAT ON A HOT TIN ROOF (1955), a play by Tennessee *Williams. [*Morosco Theatre, 694 perf.; Pulitzer Prize, NYDCC Award.] Margaret Pollitt (Barbara *Bel Geddes) is a woman of strong passions and determination. At the moment what she most wants is the love of her detached, alcoholic husband, Brick (Ben *Gazzara), an ex-football star. The family has assembled to celebrate the birthday of its patriarch, "Big Daddy" (Burl Ives), the richest cotton planter in the Mississippi Delta. The gathering exacerbates tensions and animosities, so in a fit of despair Maggie reveals to Brick that she has had an affair with his closest friend, Skipper, even though she knew Skipper was at heart a homosexual. The affair drove Skipper to drink and suicide. Big Daddy also assails Brick, making him see that his alcoholism stems from his refusal to save Skipper because he shared Skipper's homosexual tendencies. Infuriated, Brick reveals that Big Daddy is dying of cancer. Maggie knows that there is no will, and, fearing that Big Daddy might disinherit Brick and her in favor of her brother-in-law and his family, she lies that she is pregnant. Throwing away Brick's liquor, she says, "We can make that lie come true. And then I'll bring you liquor, and we'll get drunk together, here, tonight, in this place that death has come into!" The play (produced by the *Playwrights' Company) was essentially another variation of Williams's favorite themes, Southern decadence and homosexuality. Nevertheless, it was, as Brooks *Atkinson observed, "a stunning drama . . . the work of a mature observer of men and women and a gifted craftsman." Commendable Broadway revivals in 1974, 1990, and 2003 confirmed the drama's theatrical effectiveness.

CATARACT OF THE GANGES, THE (1824). An equestrian melodrama by W. T. Moncrieff, it was presented at the *Park Theatre in 1824, a year after its Drury Lane premiere. The highlight of the complicated plot came when its heroine, Zamine, rode her horse to safety by leaping over the huge waterfall. From the start its spectacle and not its story was its main attraction. The *Mirror* noted, "It is, indeed, a succession of splendid and gorgeous scenes, which beam upon the dazzled eye with almost magical effect . . . the beautiful horses, arrayed in all the trappings of eastern magnificence—the long processions—the chariots . . . the crowds which throng the stage, glittering in such princely apparel—all pass before the mind like a dazzling and glorious dream." The play remained a staple for fifty years, especially in such houses as the *Bowery, which catered to thrill-seeking playgoers.

A major revival succeeded as late as 1873 with John *Brougham and Mrs. John *Wood in the cast.

CATLETT, Walter (1889–1960), character actor. The bespectacled, cigar-chomping comedian who usually played rambunctious "wise guys," was born in San Francisco and spent his earliest theatrical years with West Coast troupes. In the 1910s and 1920s he was notable in many Broadway musicals, especially *Sally* (1920) and *Lady, Be Good!* (1924), in which he introduced the title song. He later performed in many films.

CATS (1982). An English musical first presented in London in 1981, it set many of T. S. *Eliot's poems from *Old Possum's Book of Practical Cats* to music by Andrew Lloyd *Webber. All the characters were cats, and, although there was a slim plot about selecting a cat to ascend to heaven to be reborn, there was no spoken dialogue. Its most popular song was "Memory." The American production opened at the *Winter Garden Theatre and ran for 7,485 performances, a new Broadway record. Trevor *Nunn directed, while Gillian Lynne recreated her highly praised dances.

CAUGHT IN THE RAIN (1906), a farce by William *Collier and Grant Stewart. [*Garrick Theatre, 161 perf.] Publicly, Dick Crawford (Collier), a Colorado mining man, is a grumpy woman-hater. Privately, he is an old softie. Caught in a downpour, he finds himself shoulder to shoulder with a beautiful girl who quickly captures his affections, but she disappears before he can learn her name. About the same time he recklessly promises a friend, Mr. Mason (John Saville), to marry his daughter to help him out of a financial problem. No sooner had he made his promise than he recalls the unknown girl and tries to back out. Even when he discovers that Mr. Mason's daughter, Muriel (Nanette Comstock), and the mysterious beauty are one and the same, his problems are not solved, for Muriel is upset by his fickleness. Of course, all ends happily. Superb staging and playing turned this preposterous farce (produced by Charles *Frohman) into a memorable hit. A 1920 musical, *Pitter Patter*, was based on the play.

CAWTHORN, Joseph (1867–1949), comic actor. Born in New York, he made his debut there as a child performer at Robinson's Music Hall in 1872 and a year later played with Haverly's Minstrels. After several years in England he returned to play in vaudeville and to tour in *Little Nugget* (1883), *A Fool for Luck* (1895), *Excelsior, Jr.* (1896), and *Miss Philadelphia* (1897). Cawthorn's abilities as a dialect comedian first came to New York's attention when he played the leading comic role of Boris in Victor *Herbert's The *Fortune Teller* (1898). With few exceptions, such as his drag performance in the title part of *Mother Goose* (1903), all subsequent roles of the small, round-faced, balding comedian were Dutch dialect parts. Among his notable portrayals were Aufpassen in Herbert's *The Singing Girl* (1899), Siegmund Lump in John Philip *Sousa's The Free Lance* (1906), Baron Hugo Weybach in *The Hoyden* (1907), Louis Von Schloppenhauer in *The Slim Princess* (1911), Schlump in *The Sunshine Girl* (1913), the Mormon Trimpel in *The *Girl from Utah* (1914), Otto Spreckels in *Sybil* (1916), Timothy in *The Canary* (1918), and, his last Broadway appearance, Siegfried Peters in *Sunny* (1925). While playing Dr. Pill in Herbert's *Little Nemo* (1908) in New Haven, Cawthorn was told to stall until a mishap was corrected backstage. The scene called for him to describe imaginary animals he had hunted. One water-dwelling, food-gobbling creature he invented he called a whiffenpoof. Yale students in the audience seized on the name and adopted it when they founded a singing society.

CAYVAN, Georgia (1858–1906), actress. Born in Bath, Maine, this beautiful leading lady spent several years playing in Boston before succeeding Effie *Ellsler as *Hazel Kirke* in New York in 1881. She immediately became a prominent actress, portraying the heroine in such famous comedies or dramas as The *Professor* (1881); The *White Slave* (1882), in which she spoke the once famous lines, "Rags are royal raiment when worn for virtue's sake"; *Siberia* (1883); *May Blossom* (1884); The *Wife* (1887); The *Charity Ball* (1889); and *Squire Kate* (1892). An illness forced a premature retirement and led to her early death.

CAZAURAN, A[ugustus] R. (1820–89), playwright. Born in Bordeaux and educated by Jesuit priests in France and Ireland, he became a reporter for the *New York Herald* shortly after his arrival in America. During the Civil War he was briefly imprisoned as a spy but was released in time to take a post with the *Washington Chronicle*, for which he wrote a once-famous eyewitness account of Lincoln's assassination. A. M. *Palmer hired him as a play reader, and came so to respect his talents that he made him his right-hand man. His ability to speak several languages, combined with his theatrical acumen, helped Cazauran to become the most celebrated adapter and play doctor of his time. Bronson *Howard credited the success of The *Banker's Daughter* (1878) to his revisions. Among his many adaptations were *Miss Multon* (1876), *The Mother's Secret* (1877), *A Celebrated Case* (1878), *Felicia* (1881), *Far From the Madding Crowd* (1882), and *The Fatal Letter* (1884).

CELESTE, Mlle. [née Keppler] (1810–82), dancer and actress. Brought from her native Paris to New York by Charles *Gilfert, she made her debut there in 1827 dancing a *pas seul* on a large bill whose main offering was *The School for Scandal*. She attracted little notice as she performed in small ballets along the Eastern seaboard, but by 1834 Celeste had gained the reputation of being both a fine actress and dancer, and caused a sensation in a double bill of the melodrama *The French Spy* and the ballet *La Bayadère*. Walter *Leman called her "the most profitable star of her day" and said she told him she had cleared more than $100,000 from *The French Spy* alone. In plays such as *The Wizard Skiff, The Wept of Wish-ton Wish,* and *The Spirit Bride* she regularly played two or three different roles in the same night. Celeste simply gave the ruder Bowery audiences what they wanted, prompting the *New York Herald* to accept her "wonderful tragic power amidst peanuts, cigar smoke, and scents of the varied kind. We never saw real pathos and peanuts so mixed up before." She remained in America until 1843, then made two brief returns, in 1851 when she won applause as the Indian Miami in *Green Bushes* and in 1865. By then, age and her refusal to develop fluent English took their toll, so her reception was far more restrained than it had been earlier.

CENSORSHIP IN THE AMERICAN THEATRE. Although the settlement of America coincided with the flourishing of both Jacobean and Restoration playwriting in England, the relatively small number of settlers and their general religious bent precluded the emergence of real theatre during the 17th century and much of the early 18th century. Certainly the New England Puritans, the Dutch in New Amsterdam, and the Quakers in Pennsylvania were all vehemently opposed to theatricals of any sort. Even in the somewhat liberal atmosphere of cavalier Virginia, what may have been the first American play, *The *Bear and the Cub* (1665), was performed at a court hearing after a public performance led to charges of licentiousness. The actors were acquitted, but the trial was the harbinger of nearly three centuries of court battles and other harassment of American theatre by authorities. In the late 18th century many colonies and later many states passed laws banning theatricals. However, by this time a number of cities had grown sufficiently populous that the demand for theatrical entertainments could no longer be ignored. Men such as David *Douglass were politic enough to persuade authorities to permit the erection of playhouses and the production of plays, although even where licenses were granted they were frequently precariously held and just as frequently revoked. Inevitably, as with any prohibition, not only were appetites whetted but also means of circumvention were found. Plays were often advertised as "concerts," "lectures," or "dissertations." No national office equivalent to that of the English Lord Chamberlain was ever established to censor plays in advance. Instead, censorship was left to cities or, occasionally, to states. Actually very few localities ever resorted to advance censorship, the most notorious exception in the late 19th and early 20th century being Boston. But pervasive Victorian concepts of morality conditioned the writing and presentation of many plays, as well as something so seemingly slight as the naming of playhouses. For much of the 19th century, when opera never shared the opprobrium of drama, countless theatres were called opera houses, although they were given over primarily to the presentation of drama and rarely, if ever, offered real operas. Many theatres were also called "halls," and in a few major cities theatres often had additional space devoted to exhibitions and so were called "museums." The most famous of the latter were Barnum's *American Museum and the *Boston Museum. These appellations allowed many publicly prudish people to have the best of both worlds by attending the theatre and retaining their respectability.

Perhaps because most performers, writers, and producers seemed to share the moral consensus, there was little outright censorship in the 19th century. Men such as Augustin *Daly appeared to understand precisely how far they could go in handling what was deemed touchy subject matter. Moreover, most drama critics shared contemporary pruderies and were frequently quick to denounce the slightest overstepping of implicit limitations. Much of the outcry against theatre continued to come from the clergy, who often deplored all theatricals as a matter of principle, and from newspaper editors, who may have agreed with the narrow strictures of the day or who, more likely, were simply seeking to increase circulation with shrill attacks. *The *Black Crook* (1866), with its long line of girls in flesh-colored tights, and Ada Isaacs *Menken's *Mazeppa* (1861), in which she appeared to ride nude on a horse, typified productions that scandalized, while Daly's treatment of divorce in the play of the same name exemplified the use of subject matter that many thought should not be treated. It is to the credit of the better dramatists, producers, and critics of the day that they were able gradually to broaden the scope and depth of American playwriting in the face of the prevalent morality. In the very late 19th century the coming of Ibsenite realism and Shavian farce, both of which, in their disparate ways, touched on many matters previously considered unbroachable, infuriated many conservative critics, playgoers, and lawmakers, so that by the early 20th century the hue and cry for censorship rose to heights unknown before. Throughout the first half of the 20th century, and sometimes later, overt censorship and repression led to frequent and often highly publicized battles between authorities, who were responding to puritanical wailings, and the theatre, which was determined to apply increasingly open standards of honesty and permissibility. One of the most famous cases concerned Clyde *Fitch's *Sapho* (1900), in which a courtesan begs to be seduced and is carried up a flight of stairs to her bedroom in the arms of her latest lover. Goaded by the outcries of clergy and of such yellow journalists as William Randolph Hearst, who wrote, "We expect the police to forbid on the stage what they would forbid in streets and low resorts," New York authorities closed the show and arrested its star, Olga *Nethersole; her leading man; and the manager of the theatre. They were acquitted in court. Among the other distinguished plays of the era to be closed or banned in New York or elsewhere were *Mrs. Warren's Profession, The *Easiest Way,* and *Monna Vanna.* The last was allowed to proceed after Mrs. *Fiske grudgingly capitulated to the demand for revisions, but *The Easiest Way* was not allowed to play Boston and several other cities.

After World War I, when films had lured away the lowest level of playgoers, and when the postwar perception of new freedom and enlightenment prompted playwrights and playgoers to demand a theatre more truly reflective of modern society, the battle intensified. Such fine American plays as *All God's Chillun Got Wings* (1924), *Desire Under the Elms* (1924), The *Firebrand* (1924), *They Knew What They Wanted* (1924), and *What Price Glory?* (1924) were all either forced to make revisions or were closed in New York or elsewhere. So were more patently tawdry but still theatrically interesting works such as Mae *West's *Sex* (1926), The *Shanghai Gesture* (1926), and *Lulu Belle* (1926). In 1927, responding to the agitation for censorship, New York City enacted the Wales padlock law, which not only enabled authorities to arrest the producer and actors in any offensive play, but to deprive the theatre housing the play of its license for one year. The law was not rescinded until 1967. However, the most extreme instances of censorship continued to come from Boston, and to a lesser extent from Chicago, both of which required submission of plays in advance. Thus, many of Eugene *O'Neill's works and, indeed, many of the productions of his producer, the *Theatre Guild, were not allowed to play Boston, so were booked into suburban theatres instead. *Strange Interlude* (1928) was the most

celebrated instance of this exclusion. Almost inevitably the battle between conservative advocates of censorship and liberal proponents of freer speech took on a political coloring in the 1930s. While many of these confrontations remained local, some assumed a national scale because they involved the *Federal Theatre Project (FTP), which had been established and funded by Congress. Thus, the Department of State attempted to censor and finally was able to force the cancellation of the FTP's projected mounting of the anti-Mussolini play *Ethiopia.* Ultimately extremists on both sides prevailed, the FTP by producing plays filled with increasingly left-wing propaganda and the ultra-conservatives in Congress by killing the whole Federal Theatre Project. However, moral considerations still figured heavily in censorship, so it was in this decade that New York's Mayor Fiorello LaGuardia finally succeeded in closing that city's burlesque houses, and Lillian *Hellman's The *Children's Hour* (1934), with its whispered accusation of lesbianism, was banned in Boston and Chicago. Censorship for military reasons became accepted during World War II, although strenuous objections were raised when the military frequently extended its grip and banned plays and performances on moral grounds. Nor were regular plays in regular theatres free from interference. The *Shuberts were threatened with invocation of the Wales law when they mounted a sleazy burlesque-style revue, but, more importantly, another serious study of lesbianism, *Trio* (1944), was closed when its playhouse was faced with loss of its license.

From the 1950s on, serious contretemps gradually faded, especially in New York, and those that did occur usually had a comic touch to them. For example, when *'Tis Pity She's a Whore,* John Ford's three-hundred-year-old classic, was revived in New York, the city refused to allow public billboards to display the last word, and the supposedly liberal *New York Times* refused to accept advertisements unless the word was omitted. Twenty years later there was little objection to the title The *Best Little Whorehouse in Texas,* except when the producer placed advertisements on buses using only the word "whorehouse." In the 1970s, Supreme Court decisions confirmed what had been time-honored practice when it agreed that local authorities were the ones with the right to censor entertainments. However, by this time the road had shrunk to the point where it was all but nonexistent, and censorship was invoked primarily against films and books. Self-appointed vigilantes and clergy, especially Southern fundamentalists and the Roman Catholic Church, still were able to prevent regional productions, but censorship had all but disappeared in New York. Ironically, the abolition of the

Wales padlock law and the virtual disappearance of the slightest theatrical censorship in New York coincided with the explosive freedoms and social turmoil of the 1960s, so that it was significant and not unexpected that the theatre burst forth with the greatest display of obscenity ever seen. Not only did the formerly unspeakable become commonplace, but the most crass nudity and the depiction of everything from bestiality to urination was offered, especially in the Off Broadway theatres, but on Broadway as well. By the early 1980s a reaction had begun to set in. Happily it has not taken the form of a return to public censorship, but rather of a realization on the part of many playwrights, directors, and producers that excesses have been self-defeating and that restraint and suggestion are usually more effective in making a point than careless vulgarity. All the same there were some productions that tested the most liberal of times. Terrence *McNally's *Corpus Christi* (1998), an allegory that depicted Jesus and his disciples as homosexuals, riled enough citizens that death threats and police protection accompanied its opening night Off Broadway. And the *New York Times*, once again justifying its nick name as the "good gray lady," refused to print the titles of *Shopping and Fucking* (1998) and *Fucking A* (2003). But these were isolated incidents and hardly point to a trend. Still the theatre must go on living with the unsettling knowledge that there are those who would, for a number of reasons, still rejoice in the revival of censorship.

CENTER STAGE (Baltimore). Founded in 1963 by a group of ambitious community theatre members, the company's first production was Schnitzler's *La Ronde*, and since then its schedule has included a wide, responsible selection of classics and new plays. When their original facility burned down in 1974, the troupe began performing in the partially renovated Pearlstone Theatre on the campus of Loyola College and High School. The Center Stage expanded significantly under artistic directors Peter Culman and Stan Wojewodski Jr. and is now headed by Irene Lewis. Among the original offerings afterward presented in New York were *Slow Dance on the Killing Ground, The Trial of the Catonsville Nine, G. R. Point, Roza, On the Verge, and Miss Evers' Boys*. In addition to the 541-seat Pearlstone, the company also performs in the smaller, flexible Head Theatre. It is the official State Theatre of Maryland.

CENTRAL CITY OPERA HOUSE (Colorado). This gold-rush wonder in the mountains of Colorado (one of the highest theatre structures in the world) was built in 1876 to provide a place of entertainment for the thousands of miners (and artists) passing through the region. It was designed by Robert S. Roeschlaug, who managed to use the steep slope of the site effectively and even maneuvered a stream below to cool the playhouse in summer. The boomtown of Central City floundered by the end of the nineteenth century and the theatre was briefly used for silent films before closing in 1918. But it was restored as a summer theatre in 1932 and has remained in use to this day.

CENTURY THEATRE (New York). The playhouse on Seventh Avenue at 59th Street had almost as many names as it had tenants. It opened as Jolson's 59th Street Theatre in 1921, and over the next forty years was called the Century, the Shakespeare, the Venice, the Yiddish Art, the Molly *Picon, and the New Century Theatre. Herbert J. *Krapp designed the musical house for the *Shuberts who named it after Al *Jolson, who appeared in the inaugural production of *Bombo* (1921). The show was a hit, but Jolson never performed at the theatre again. Companies ranging from the *Moscow Art Theatre to the *Federal Theatre Project to the *Old Vic were presented here, as well as such illustrious musicals as *The *Student Prince* (1924) and (its longest tenant) *Kiss Me, Kate* (1948). The Century was used as a television studio in the 1950s then in 1962 was demolished to make room for an apartment building.

CHAIKIN, Joseph (1935–2003), director and actor. The Brooklyn-born artist studied at Drake University and with several distinguished acting teachers, including Herbert Berghof, before becoming a member of the *Living Theatre. He left that group to found the Open Theatre in 1963 and for the decade of its existence made it one of the nation's most-admired avant-garde groups. To a large extent its philosophy was that the text was merely a starting point, with actors and director meant to develop freely from there. Yet Chaikin regularly evinced the remarkable ability to bring order out of potential chaos "in that undefined territory where playwright, director, actor, and audience interchange roles, abandon strictly logical texts, and go for soul-broke with improvised sound and unexplained silences." Performances in the loft and other stages the group employed were frequently by invitation only; more regular audiences were allowed in only intermittently. Among the group's mountings were *Viet Rock* and *The Serpent*. Chaikin continued to act and direct elsewhere until he suffered a stroke. He published his ideas of theatre in *The Presence of the Actor* (1972).

CHALFANT, Kathleen. See *Wit*.

CHAMPION, Gower (1920–80), director, choreographer, and dancer. Born in Geneva, Illinois, he became a professional dancer while still in his early teens, and danced in *The Streets of Paris* (1939) and *Count Me In* (1942). Champion's choreography was first seen in *Small Wonder* (1948), but he won much more attention later the same year when he directed and choreographed another revue, *Lend an Ear*. Hits that he afterward both directed and choreographed included **Bye Bye Birdie* (1960), **Carnival* (1961), **Hello, Dolly!* (1964), **I Do! I Do!* (1966), The **Happy Time* (1968), *Sugar* (1972), a revival of **Irene* (1973), and **42nd Street* (1980). His work had great style and wit and often displayed a captivating period charm. Champion's death was announced to a shocked cast at the end of the opening-night performance of *42nd Street*.

CHANDLER, Helen (1906–65), actress. She was born in Charleston, South Carolina, and went to a convent school there before attending the Professional Children's School in New York. Chandler was on Broadway by the age of twelve and played children in such plays as *Penrod* (1918) and **Daddy Long-Legs* (1918) until she matured enough to essay Ophelia in 1925. Although she started making films the next year, Chandler continued to act on stage until 1931. But by the mid-1930s she gave up on Hollywood and returned to Broadway for a few seasons before retiring completely. Her final Broadway appearance was as the deceased passenger Ann in *Outward Bound* (1938).

CHANEY, Stewart (1910–69), designer. Born in Kansas City, Missouri, he studied at Yale under Professor George P. *Baker before embarking on a career as set designer. His work was first seen on Broadway in *Kill That Story* (1934). Among the many other plays for which he designed sets, and sometimes costumes and lighting, were The **Old Maid* (1935), **Having Wonderful Time* (1937), **Life with Father* (1939), The **Voice of the Turtle* (1943), *Jacobowsky and the Colonel* (1944), The **Late George Apley* (1944), and The **Moon Is Blue* (1951). Of his cleverly conceived set for *The Voice of the Turtle* (1943), one of the earliest small-cast plays, Lewis Nichols wrote in the *Times*, "Stewart Chaney has fallen into the spirit of the occasion by constructing a splendid set showing a bedroom, sitting room and kitchen, all apparently of normal size, perfectly appointed. The cast could live there."

CHANFRAU, [Francis S.] Frank (1824–84), actor. Born in a famous New York tenement known as "The Treehouse" or "Old Tree House," and largely self-educated, he left his hometown to work as a ship's carpenter in the West. When he returned to New York, he took up amateur dramatics and shortly thereafter obtained work as a super at the *Bowery Theatre. His imitations of the great star Edwin *Forrest caught the ear of the manager, who gave him small roles. Moving to the Olympic Theatre, he "created a sensation" as Jeremiah Clip in a revival of *The Widow's Victim*, in no small part again because of his mimic abilities. His performance so delighted the theatre's prompter, Benjamin A. *Baker that he wrote Mose, a New York firefighter, in *A Glance at New York* (1848) for Chanfrau's special talents. For nearly twenty years Chanfrau played little except Mose, both in the original play and in numerous sequels. Luckily, when he became too old to perform the youthful, athletic firefighter, two more excellent parts came his way: the clever American *Sam* (1865) and the pioneer Kit Redding in **Kit, the Arkansas Traveller* (1870). The two parts kept him in front of audiences until shortly before his death. Otis *Skinner wrote of him, "Nearly everything about Chanfrau was big: voice, body, limbs, method. He must have been a very handsome man in his younger days." Although some contemporaries described him as smaller than Skinner recalled, they agreed about his good looks, noting in particular his striking dark eyes and dark, curly hair.

CHANNING, Carol [Elaine] (b. 1921), comedienne. The tall, blonde performer, whose voice runs the gamut from babyish squeals to baritone, was born in Seattle and made her debut in the chorus of *No for an Answer* (1941). Later the same year she understudied Eve Arden in *Let's Face It!*, and then after a brief appearance in *Proof Through the Night* (1942), she traveled the nightclub circuit. Channing's fame was assured when she appeared in *Lend an Ear* (1948) where her superb comic talents flourished, most notably as a wildly energetic chorus girl in a spoof of 1920s' musicals. She consolidated her reputation when she essayed the role of Lorelei Lee in the musical **Gentleman Prefer Blondes* (1949). Brooks *Atkinson noted, "She goes through the play like a dazed automaton—husky enough to kick in the teeth of any gentleman on the stage, but mincing coyly in high-heel shoes and looking out on a confused world through big, wide, starry eyes. There has never been anything like this before in human society." In 1954 she succeeded Rosalind Russell in **Wonderful Town*, then appeared in the title role of *The Vamp* (1955) and in an intimate revue designed around her talents, *Show Girl* (1961). Her greatest success was as the pushy Dolly Levi in **Hello, Dolly!* (1964), a role she would return to throughout her life with extensive tours and Broadway returns in 1978 and 1995. She also returned to the character of Lorelei Lee for *Lorelei* (1974), a revised version of *Gentlemen Prefer Blondes*. In 1986 she toured with Mary

*Martin in *Legends*, a play that never reached New York. Autobiography: *Just Lucky I Guess*, 2002.

CHANNING, Stockard [née Susan Stockard] (b. 1944), actress. The New Yorker was educated at Harvard and made her acting debut in Boston in 1966. She came to Broadway in 1971 in the chorus of the musical *Two Gentlemen of Verona*, then after performing for several seasons in California, she replaced the leading lady in *They're Playing Our Song*. By the 1980s Channing was one of the most lauded actresses in New York, giving such memorable performances as the tormented mother Sheila in *Joe Egg* (1985), the flaky Bunny in *The *House of Blue Leaves* (1986), the depressed Susan in *Woman in Mind* (1988), the upper-class Ouisa in *Six Degrees of Separation* (1990), the mastermind Elizabeth in *Hapgood* (1994), the scheming Regina in *The *Little Foxes* (1997), and Queen Eleanor of Aquitaine in *The *Lion in Winter* (1999). *Times* critic Frank *Rich commented that her Ouisa "steadily gained gravity as she journeys flawlessly from the daffy comedy of a fatuous dinner party to the harrowing internal drama of her own rebirth."

CHAPMAN, John [Arthur] (1900–72), critic. Born in Denver, the son of journalists, he studied at the University of Colorado and at Columbia. Chapman began his newspaper career in 1917 on the *Denver Times* and joined the *New York Daily News* in 1920, becoming its drama editor in 1929 and its drama critic in 1943, a post he held until his retirement. He also served as Burns *Mantle's assistant on the *Best Plays* and after Mantle's death edited the series from 1947 to 1952. Thereafter for many years he edited a less-successful series.

CHAPTER TWO (1977), a comedy by Neil *Simon. [*Imperial Theatre, 857 perf.] "Chapter Two in the life of George Schneider" begins when he returns home from a trip abroad, a trip designed to distract him from his grief at the death of his wife. George (Judd Hirsch) is a novelist and is looking for a researcher to help him with his new book. Mistaking her name and number for a suggested helper, he phones a divorced actress, Jennie Malone (Anita Gillette). Their relationship blossoms and before long they are married. Nevertheless, memories of his first wife obsess George, for a time even threatening the marriage. Finally he realizes how much he fears being happy with Jennie and the couple begin to work out their problems together. Another in Simon's long line of observant, witty comedies, the play was said to be semi-autobiographical, written after Simon's remarriage following the death of his own first wife. It was also the second play written subsequent to his move to California, and while the two-apartment set remained throughout the play, the short, quickly moving scenes reflected cinematographic practices. A commentary on theatrical economics was offered when this play with a cast of four was booked into a large musical house.

CHARITY BALL, THE (1889), a play by David *Belasco and Henry C. *de Mille. [*Lyceum Theatre, 200 perf.] John Van Buren (Herbert *Kelcey), the rector of St. Mildred's, has kept his promise to the dying father of blind Phyllis Lee (Grace Henderson) to take her under his protection, unaware that his aggressive brother, Dick (Nelson Wheatcroft), once told the young woman he wanted to marry her and then despoiled her. But Dick is so determined to rise in Wall Street that he has thrown her over and proposed to Ann Cruger (Georgia *Cayvan), whose father is a powerful Wallstreeter. When John learns the truth he confronts Dick and forces him to marry Phyllis. In time John comes to recognize that he loves Ann as much as she has always loved him. The third act, in which John learns about Phyllis and confronts his brother, was considered one of the most powerful scenes in contemporary drama, and was in large measure responsible for the success of the Daniel *Frohman production.

CHARLES THE SECOND; or, *The Merry Monarch* (1824), a comedy by John Howard *Payne and Washington *Irving (uncredited). [*Park Theatre, in repertory.] When his mistress, Lady Clara (Mrs. Clarke), accuses the Earl of Rochester (Mr. Stanley) of being "the chief cause of the king's irregularities," the Earl agrees to help reform Charles II (Edmund *Simpson). He takes the King to a seaman's tavern run by old Captain Copp (Thomas *Hilson). There he deserts the King, leaving him to fend for himself without any money. Copp threatens to have the King arrested, but the King escapes through a window. Realizing the Earl and the lady have had his best interests at heart, the King is forgiving and promises to mend his ways. He pays his debt to Copp and gives him a fine watch as well. Written during Payne's long London sojourn, it was first mounted at Covent Garden in May 1824. Payne based his play on Alexandre Duval's *La Jeunesse de Henri V*, itself taken from earlier works. Much of Payne's original draft was hardly more than a literal translation. The main attraction of the *Simpson–Stephen Price production, Captain Copp, was Irving's invention, as was the comic device of having Copp repeatedly start a risqué song that he was never permitted to finish.

CHARLESTON (South Carolina). One of the earliest important American theatrical centers, it saw its first play when *The Orphan* was presented in 1735. Just over a year later, the *Dock Street Theatre opened to become the city's first regular playhouse. In after years David *Douglass, Thomas *Wall, Dennis *Ryan, the younger *Hallam, and John *Henry all performed in the city. By the end of the century several playhouses were active, and Alexandre Placide was a dominant figure. By the early 19th century the city could boast of its own school of dramatists, including William Ioor, John Blake White, Isaac Harby, and, for a time, Mordecai *Noah. But after the Civil War the city's importance as a theatrical center waned quickly. Today it rarely plays host to major touring companies. However, since 1977 the American branch of the Spoleto festival has been held there annually. It has offered the American premieres of such works as Tennessee *Williams's *Crève-Coeur,* Arthur *Miller's *The American Clock,* and William *Gibson's *Monday After the Miracle.* Eola Willis's *The Charleston Stage in the XVIII Century* (1933) remains the best study of the early years.

CHARLEY'S AUNT (1893). Brandon Thomas's 1892 London hit was offered with great success a year later to Americans. It told how a student, Lord Fancourt Babberley, disguises himself as the aunt of his college roommate Charley in order to fill the need for a chaperone. The real aunt lives in Brazil, "where the nuts come from," and her unwonted appearance naturally leads to complications. Etienne *Girardot created the role of Babberley in America and was identified with it for decades afterward. He also played it in a major 1906 revival. José *Ferrer led a popular 1940 revival. The farce was later turned into the musical *WHERE'S CHARLEY?* (1948) with a libretto by George *Abbott that simplified the plot somewhat by eliminating the character of Babberley and letting Charley (Ray *Bolger) dress up like his own aunt even while he tries to woo the pretty Amy Spettigue (Allyn McLerie). Frank *Loesser wrote the score and Cy *Feuer and Ernest H. *Martin produced the musical, the first Broadway venture for all three men. It ran at the *St. James Theatre for 792 performances. *Notable songs*: Once in Love with Amy; My Darling, My Darling; Make a Miracle; At the Red Rose Cotillion. The musical was Bolger's biggest Broadway hit, highlighted by his showstopping rendition of "Once in Love with Amy," which he regularly persuaded his audience to sing along with him. A revival in 1974 met with little success.

CHARLOT'S REVUE (1924). Compiled largely from the best material that had been offered by André Charlot in his West End revues (it was also known as *Charlot's London Revue*), the musical

marked the American debuts of Jack *Buchanan, Gertrude *Lawrence, and Bea *Lillie. Equally important, its effective intimacy, both in its musical and comic numbers, was a major influence in sounding the death knell for gargantuan extravaganzas of the *Ziegfeld school. A number of earlier American revues, notably *The 49ers,* had embarked on a similar path, but the exceptional finish and widespread success (298 performances) of this English importation give it a special place in the evolution of American revue. *Notable songs*: Limehouse Blues; March with Me; Parisian Pierrot; You Were Meant for Me.

CHASE, Ilka (1905–78), actress and writer. She was born in New York and educated at private schools there and in France. Chase made her Broadway debut in 1924 and was soon cast as friends of the heroine or tough, worldly women. Perhaps her archetypal role was the backbiting Park Avenue wife Sylvia in *The *Women* (1936). She served as the London correspondent to *Vogue* magazine (of which her mother was editor), also wrote plays, a few of which she appeared in, and novels. Autobiographies: *Past Imperfect,* 1945; *Free Admission,*1948.

CHASE, Mary Coyle. See *Harvey.*

CHATTERTON, Ruth (1893–1961), actress. A petite beauty, noted for the "exquisite naturalness" of her acting, she was born in New York City and made her stage debut in Washington, D.C., in 1909. For the next several years she played in stock there, in Milwaukee, and in Worcester, Massachusetts. Her first New York appearance was in a short-lived failure, *The Great Name* (1911) but, coming under the aegis of Henry *Miller, she won her earliest important notices as the daughter who reconciles her mother and father in *The Rainbow* (1912). Chatterton shone as the orphan Judy Abbott in *Daddy Long-Legs* (1914), the disguised Olive Daingerfield in *Come Out of the Kitchen* (1916), the much-wooed Judith Baldwin in *Moonlight and Honeysuckle* (1919), James M. *Barrie's heroine *Mary Rose* (1920), a playwright's mistress Marthe Dellieres in *La Tendresse* (1922), and the switched wife Kay Faber in *The Changelings* (1923). Chatterton then suffered a series of failures in New York, so she spent most of the ensuing years in films, returning to the theatre intermittently though never with a major success. Her last New York appearance was as Irene in a 1951 *City Center revival of *Idiot's Delight.*

CHAYEFSKY, [Sidney] Paddy (1923–81), playwright. The New Yorker attended City College before making a reputation in the early 1950s as a writer of low-key, sentimental, but realistic television dramas, often best remembered for their naturalistic dialogue. His two most memorable Broadway plays were the domestic drama *Middle of the Night* (1956) and The *Tenth Man* (1959), centering on an exorcism in a synagogue. Chayefsky also wrote the Old Testament piece *Gideon* (1961) and the Stalin portrait *The Passion of Joseph D* (1964) before abandoning the theatre to write for films.

CHEATING CHEATERS (1916), a play by Max *Marcin. [Eltinge Theatre, 286 perf.] Nan Carey (Marjorie *Rambeau) enlists a number of suave criminals to pose with her as the rich Brockton family in order to win the friendship of the equally rich Palmer clan and then steal the Palmer jewels. To make her disguise all the more plausible, she even arranges to borrow some very expensive jewels to wear. But just as the Brocktons are not really the Brocktons, so the Palmers are also criminal poseurs who are determined to steal the Brockton jewels. Both groups worry most about a mysterious detective named Ferris, who has sent many of their former colleagues to prison. Ferris turns out to be none other than Nan, who is able to arrest more than half the cast by the final curtain. A. H. *Woods produced the popular show, one of the many skillfully contrived "crook plays" that delighted Broadway in this era.

CHEER, Miss [Margaret] (fl. 2nd half 18th century), actress. Little is known about this performer, who for a brief period of time was a reigning favorite on American stages. She apparently made her debut with *Douglass's company in Charleston in 1764 and later moved with the troupe to Philadelphia and New York. Among the many roles for which she was applauded were her Portia, Ophelia, Juliet, and Cordelia, as well as Belvidera in *Venice Preserved* and Sylvia in *The Recruiting Officer*. She is said to have married Lord Rosehill in Maryland in 1768 and appeared on the stage only infrequently thereafter. However, *Burke's Peerage* gives the name of the Lord's wife as Catherine Cameron, which may have been Miss Cheer's real name. She returned later to England and did not play again in America until 1793, when she returned under the name of Mrs. Long. Her reception was cool and she soon retired permanently.

CHEKHOV, Anton [Pavlovich] (1860–1904), playwright. The great Russian writer of stories and plays did not achieve American recognition until nearly twenty years after his death. The earliest performances of his works in the United States were generally given in Russian by small groups of émigré artists. Among these performers were Alla *Nazimova, who played in *The Seagull* in New York in 1905. A few tentative translations were made available to English-speaking ensembles and allowed such avant-garde companies as the *Washington Square Players to present his one-act *The Bear* in 1915 and *The Seagull* a year later. Almost all of these productions were failures since the plays were perceived as arty, gloomy tragedies instead of as dark comedies about a decaying bourgeoisie. The visits of the *Moscow Art Theatre during the 1922–23 and 1923–24 seasons, and the company's mounting of *The Three Sisters, The Cherry Orchard,* and *Uncle Vanya,* coupled with the virtually simultaneous availability of superior translations, brought about a real appreciation of the works. The *Civic Repertory Theatre offered *The Three Sisters, The Cherry Orchard,* and *The Seagull* between 1926 and 1929. Subsequent noteworthy revivals included the *Lunts in *The Seagull* (1938); Judith *Anderson, Katharine *Cornell, Ruth *Gordon, and Dennis *King in *The Three Sisters* (1942); *Uncle Vanya* by the visiting *Old Vic in 1946; and a series of Off-Broadway revivals under David Ross in the 1950s. Perhaps the most controversial Chekhov production was Andrei *Serban's stark, white-on-white mounting of *The Cherry Orchard* in 1977. *Ivanov,* the playwright's first full-length work, is the most frequently revived of his lesser-known pieces, with productions in 1958, 1966, 1986 (as *Wild Honey*), and 1997. Neil *Simon's *The Good Doctor* (1973) dramatized several Chekhov stories, as did *The Chekhov Sketchbook* (1980).

CHELSEA THEATRE CENTER (New York). One of the most ambitious producing organizations of the later 20th century, the nonprofit theatre was founded by Robert Kalfin in 1965 and performed in churches across New York before settling in at the *Brooklyn Academy of Music in 1968. The company's offerings were eclectic but most had an innovative or experimental flavor. The Chelsea presented revivals (their most famous being the revised *Candide* in 1974 that transferred to Broadway) and produced American premieres of foreign works as well as new native plays. In 1978 the group relocated to Manhattan, but after Kalfin left, the company lost its focus and it folded in 1983.

CHENEY, Sheldon [Warren] (1886–1980), author. Born in Berkeley, California, he studied at the University of California and with Professor George Pierce *Baker at Harvard before founding *Theatre Arts magazine in 1916, where he remained as editor until 1921. Among his books were *The New Movement in the Theatre* (1914), *The Art Theatre*

(1917), *The Open-Air Theatre* (1918), *Stage Decoration* (1927), and *The Theatre—Three Thousand Years of Drama, Acting and Stagecraft* (1929).

CHERRY PICKERS, THE (1896), a play by Joseph *Arthur. [14th Street Theatre, 120 perf.] In the British-Afghan War, John Nazare (William Harcourt), a half-caste, is an officer in the Eleventh Hussars, a regiment popularly known as "The Cherry Pickers." His rival for the hand of the half-caste Nourmallee (Roselle Knott) is his fellow officer, Col. Brough (Ralph Delmore). Brough trumps up a charge to arrest Nazare and ties him to the wall of a fort in range of Afghan bullets. When that fails and the Afghans are about to seize the fort, he turns Nazare over to an Afghan who has vowed to kill him. However, with Nourmallee's help John escapes, and the Afghan kills Brough. Typical of the highly colored melodramas presented by Augustus *Pitou on the road and at this relatively out-of-the-way, low-priced theatre, it nevertheless prompted Edward *Dithmar to note, "*The Cherry Pickers* is an honestly made play, and though we do not look for original and progressive ideas from melodramatists, they are the fellows who now do the most wholesome work for the stage."

CHESTNUT STREET THEATRE (Philadelphia). In 1791 Thomas *Wignell and Alexander *Reinagle convinced a group of Philadelphians to build a theatre to house the company Wignell had formed. Wignell's brother-in-law, John Inigo Richards, obtained the plans of the Theatre Royal in Bath, England, and the new playhouse was erected from these designs. It was built in traditional shape, with three tiers of boxes making a horseshoe around the pits, and was originally painted in pinks and reds. Seating capacity was said to be about two thousand. It opened in 1793 but was immediately shut down by a yellow fever epidemic. The first regular season began in 1794 with a double bill of *The Castle of Andulasia* and *Who's the Dupe?* At first called the New Theatre, it became the city's leading playhouse. In 1816 it was the first American theatre to be lit by gas. Many of the most important American plays of the early 19th century, including virtually all the major works by the Philadelphia school of dramatists, received premieres there. After Wignell retired, the elder William *Warren and William *Wood continued to run the house successfully. However, with the conversion of the *Walnut Street Theatre to legitimate purposes in 1811 and the erection of the *Arch Street Theatre in 1828, the playhouse began to fall on hard times. A small fire in 1820 had forced a temporary closing, and when the theatre burned to the ground in 1856 it was not rebuilt until 1863. Its final production was a stock revival

of *The Second Mrs. Tanqueray* in 1913. Shortly thereafter the theatre was demolished.

CHICAGO (1926), a satirical comedy by Maurine Watkins, produced by Sam H. *Harris. [*Music Box Theatre, 172 perf.] Roxie Hart (Francine *Larrimore) shoots her married lover. With the help of Jake (Charles A. Bickford), a hard-nosed, cynical reporter; Mary Sunshine (Eda Heinemann), a sob-sister newswoman; and, most of all, Billy Flynn (Edward Ellis), Roxie's venal lawyer, her trial is turned into a three-ring circus. The attention the publicity brings turns Roxie's head, and she even lies that she is pregnant to obtain another front-page story. After her acquittal she announces she is going into vaudeville. But her press conference is broken up when the police bring in a new murderess, Machine-Gun-Rosie. Roxie obligingly poses with Rosie for one last photograph. The play was the only success by **Maurine Dallas WATKINS** (1901–69) who was born in Kentucky and later wrote with Leo *Ditrichstein. Watkins worked on a Chicago newspaper for a while, then quit to study with George P. *Baker at Yale, and the first draft of *Chicago* was submitted as a class assignment. The play was turned into the 1975 musical of the same name with Gwen *Verdon as Roxie, Jerry *Orbach as Billy, and Chita *Rivera in the expanded role of fellow murderess Velma Kelly. John *Kander and Fred *Ebb wrote the adaptation and the score and director-choreographer Bob *Fosse turned the sensational tale into a mock vaudeville show with the orchestra onstage and each number announced with sly commentary. *Notable songs*: All That Jazz; Nowadays; Class; The Cell Block Tango; Razzle Dazzle. The Robert *Fryer–James Cresson production ran in the 46th Street Theatre for 898 performances, but a scaled-down revival opened on Broadway in 1996 and is still running.

CHICAGO (Illinois). In his autobiography Joseph *Jefferson speaks of visiting Chicago in 1839 when he was still a young boy and when the city had a population of about two thousand, yet he writes of the city's "new theaters" and recounts his experiences in one. These may have been wooden structures erected by two young actors (Harry Isherwood, brother-in-law to Jefferson's father, and Alexander McKenzie) who had first performed in the dining room of a hotel there two years before. The first major theatre built in Chicago was a wooden structure erected in 1847 by John B. Rice, who later abandoned show business to become one of the city's early mayors. However, Chicago did not become an important theatrical center until after reconstruction following the great 1871 fire. Among the leaders of its revived theatre were David *Henderson and James J. *McVicker. By the late 19th century Henderson was mounting musical spectacles that toured the country successfully, and in the first years of the new century the LaSalle and Princess Theatres were home to musical comedies (often written by Will *Hough, Frank Adams, and Joseph *Howard) that were hugely popular and played the Midwest, if not New York, to great acclaim. Some, such as The *Sultan of Sulu (1902), started the period rage for musical comedies about Americans stranded in exotic lands. Others, such as the long-running The *Time, the Place and the Girl (1907), trafficked in basically home-spun tales. Almost all had sweet, relatively elementary songs closer to contemporary *Tin Pan Alley material than to the best new Broadway music. In the field of nonmusicals, Chicago was less creative. By the 1920s the city was the second most important theatrical center in the country with more than twenty theatres operating simultaneously at its peak. A number of great drama critics, including Burns *Mantle, Percy *Hammond (both of whom later migrated to New York), and Ashton *Stevens helped spark interest. Moreover, Chicago newspapers were leaders in giving women a chance at drama criticism. Amy *Leslie was a noted example, as was Claudia *Cassidy later. Cassidy was famous for her often-harsh notices, written to lament the tackiness of many touring companies. Some historians feel she was excessively and indiscriminately negative, thus playing an unfortunate role in Chicago's decline as a theatrical center, but Glenna Syse, a leading contemporary critic, has suggested the decline was caused by real estate interests who found more profitable use for land occupied by playhouses. Away from the mainstream, Chicago has given rise to a number of noteworthy enterprises, among them the *Goodman Theatre, and many lively "off-Loop" organizations such as the *Steppenwolf Theatre. With the many offerings by the end of the 20th century, Chicago again became a major theatre capital, with full seasons presented by the *Bailiwick Repertory, Chicago Shakespeare Theatre, Pegasus Players, Fourth Wall Productions, Organic Theatre Company, *Victory Gardens Theatre, Chicago Dramatists, Northlight Theatre (in nearby Skokie), and others, as well as several collegiate theatre groups. Touring productions can be seen at the Ford Center for the Performing Arts, the Shubert, Oriental, and new Cadillac Palace Theatres. Since 1968 the Joseph Jefferson Awards have been given to honor local non-Equity productions.

CHILDREN OF A LESSER GOD (1980), a play by Mark Medoff. [Longacre Theatre, 887 perf.; Tony Award.] James Leeds (John Rubinstein) is an instructor at a school for the deaf who tries to teach Sarah Norman (Phyllis Frelich), a janitor who is much older than the other students, as well as difficult and hostile. Sarah refuses to learn to read lips or to try to speak, insisting on only using sign language. After a while James and Sarah fall in love and wed, but the marriage soon falls apart because she fears James pities her and because she is afraid they might have a deaf child. All the pair can tell each other is, "I'll help you if you'll help me." Otis L. *Guernsey Jr. called the play "an outcry for a group which, it insists, speaks more eloquently for itself in signs than hearing people are able to manage with mere words." No small part of Frelich's strength in the role of Sarah came from the fact that she herself was born deaf. **Mark MEDOFF** (b. 1940) was born in Mt. Carmel, Illinois, and was educated at the University of Miami and at Stanford. His earlier plays, When You Comin' Back, Red Ryder? (1973), in which a criminal bully destroys people's illusions, and The Wager (1974), in which a woman is seduced on a bet, were both Off-Broadway successes.

CHILDREN'S HOUR, THE (1934), a drama by Lillian *Hellman. [Maxine Elliott's Theatre, 691 perf.] At the Wright-Dobie School, teacher Karen Wright (Katherine Emery) finds she must punish the young student Mary Tilford (Florence McGee), a habitual liar, by rescinding her privileges. Without meaning to, she also punishes her own associate, Martha Dobie (Anne Revere), when she announces her forthcoming marriage. The vengeful Mary returns home to whisper to her grandmother that Karen and Martha are lesbians. The rumor destroys the school, wrecks Karen's marriage plans, and drives Martha to suicide. When Mrs. Tilford, having learned the truth, comes to apologize, Karen refuses to accept her apologies. The Herman *Shumlin–produced play, based loosely on a 19th-century incident in Scotland, was the sensation of the season. Percy *Hammond wrote in the Herald Tribune that it "will make your eyes start from their sockets as its agitating tale unfolds." The *New York Drama Critics Circle Award was established in no small measure because the *Pulitzer Prize was awarded to another play that year. A 1952 revival was only moderately successful, the whispered accusation, the death off stage, and the general restraint of the work having come to seem tame in comparison to later plays.

CHILDREN'S THEATRE COMPANY, THE (Minneapolis, Minnesota). One of the finest professional companies dedicated to plays for children and families, it began in 1965 as the Moppet Players and developed into its present status and name in 1975. The troupe boasts one of the few theatre facilities designed and operated for young spectators, with wide aisles, stadium-type seating, and optimum sightlines for kids. In addition to a full season of plays, mostly adaptations of classic children's literature from around the world, the company also tours extensively in Minnesota and the upper Midwest. Its production of *A Year with Frog and Toad* arrived on Broadway in 2003, the same year the group won the regional theatre *Tony Award.

CHIN-CHIN (1914), a musical by Anne *Caldwell (book, lyrics), R. H. *Burnside (book), Ivan *Caryll (music), James O'Dea (lyrics). [Globe Theatre, 295 perf.] The evil Abanazar (Charles T. Aldrich) would not only steal the magic golden lamp owned by Aladdin (Douglas Stevenson), he also would help its prospective buyer, the rich American Cornelius Bond (R. E. Graham), stop Aladdin from marrying Bond's daughter, Violet (Helen Falconer). But two canny slaves of the lamp, Chin Hop Hi (Fred *Stone) and Chin Hop Lo (Dave *Montgomery), find magical ways of assuming many wonderful disguises and even of transporting Aladdin to exotic places in order to retain the lamp for him and assist in his winning Violet. *Notable songs*: Goodbye Girls, I'm Through; Ragtime Temple Bells. The Charles *Dillingham show was the biggest musical hit of its season (except for the annual *Hippodrome extravaganza), in large part because of the acrobatic and clean humor of Montgomery and Stone, which invariably mixed knowing wit with childlike fun.

CHODOROV, Edward (1904–88), playwright and director. The New Yorker began his theatre career as an assistant stage manager after attending Brown University. His first play, *Wonder Boy* (1931), about a dentistry student who unwit-tingly becomes a movie star, was a success on the road but failed in New York. Chodorov had better luck with his second play, *Kind Lady* (1935), in which a sinister visitor menaces a kindly matron, but *Cue for Passion* (1940) and *Those Endearing Young Charms* (1943) both failed to run. His other works include *Decision* (1944), a drama about domestic fascism; *Common Ground* (1945), about a U.S.O. troupe captured by the Nazis; and the hit comedy *Oh, Men! Oh, Women!* (1953). Thereafter, luck eluded him, and his last plays all closed out of town. Chodorov usually directed his own works. His brother was playwright **Jerome CHODOROV** (b. 1911), also born in New York, who began his career writing for films. In Hollywood he met Joseph *Fields, with whom he would regularly collaborate. Their first effort, the Hollywood spoof *Schoolhouse on the Lot* (1938), quickly closed, but the team found success with *My Sister Eileen* (1940) and *Junior Miss* (1941). After some failures, the twosome wrote the libretto for the popular musical *Wonderful Town* (1953), based on their *My Sister Eileen*. The other Chodorov-Fields works include *The Girl in Pink Tights* (1954), *Anniversary Waltz* (1954), and *The Ponder Heart* (1956).

CHORPENNING, Charlotte (1873–1955), playwright. One of America's pioneers in children's theatre, Chorpenning wrote plays and laid down guidelines for theatre that used children as spectators and participants. She was long associated with the *Goodman Theatre where she directed many of her scripts and sponsored other writers in the field. Today the American Alliance for Theatre and Education gives the Charlotte Chorpenning Cup to an outstanding children's theatre writer each year.

CHORUS LADY, THE (1906), a play by James *Forbes. [Savoy Theatre, 315 perf.] To help support her family and gain a measure of independence, Patricia O'Brien (Rose *Stahl) has gone into the theatre. When the touring burlesque company in which she is a chorus girl closes, she returns to the Long Island home of her parents, who work for Dan Mallory (Wilfred Lucas) at his stables. For some time Dan has been courting Pat, although at the moment his financial interests are in trouble and he has taken on a partner, Dick Crawford (Francis Byrne). Pat reluctantly agrees to help her irresponsible sister, Nora (Eva Dennison), obtain work in a chorus. Once in New York, however, Nora quickly finds herself in debt. Crawford lends her the money she needs to pay off her debts but also gets her to forge her father's signature on her note and then attempts to blackmail her into having an affair. Pat learns of what has happened and goes to Crawford's apartment to confront him with his treachery. While she is there Dan and Mrs. O'Brien appear. Rather than hurt her sister, Pat makes it appear that she was having an affair with Crawford. Dan is furious until he recognizes the true situation. He buys out Crawford and convinces Pat to leave the theatre to marry him. She agrees, remarking, "Dan, we'll settle down like a couple of Reubens. Us an' the cows." Originally a magazine story by Forbes that was turned into a vaudeville sketch for Stahl, the act was so successful that Forbes developed it into a full-length play for her, and Henry B. *Harris produced it. Walter Prichard *Eaton branded it a "character comedy," which he saw as "a play in which some one or more vivid and entertaining persons are allowed the run of the stage, making the most of their eccentricities and thus always conditioning the story to immediate theatrical demands."

CHORUS LINE, A (1975), a musical by James Kirkwood, Nicholas Dante (book), Marvin *Hamlisch (music), Edward Kleban (lyrics). [*Public Theatre, 6,137 perf.; Pulitzer Prize, Tony, NYDCC Awards.] Zach (Robert LuPone), a director-choreographer, auditions dancers for a chorus line in a forthcoming musical. Not content with collecting photographs and résumés, nor with watching them perform a few sample steps, Zach requests each applicant to tell a little about himself or herself. The subsequent commentaries lead into various issues, some related to dance but most with other kinds of life experiences. With time he eliminates those he cannot use, then the rest unite in a glittering top-hats-and-tails production number. *Notable songs*: One; What I Did for Love; I Hope I Get It; The Music and the Mirror. The celebrated concept musical was the brainchild of its own director and choreographer, Michael *Bennett, who spent months in auditions and workshops recording histories not unlike those employed in the show. Joseph *Papp presented the show Off Broadway but, after the rave notices, moved it to the *Shubert Theatre three months later where it stayed for fifteen years, breaking the Broadway record at the time. Although Walter *Kerr held serious reservations about the "ordinariness" of many of the histories Bennett used, condemning some as too self-pitying and even irrelevant, he admired the show's "lightning-stroke severity" and hailed the total accomplishment as "brilliant."

CHRISTIAN, THE (1898), a play by Hall Caine. [Knickerbocker Theatre, 160 perf.] John Storm (Edward J. Morgan) is a clergyman who proposes marriage to Glory Quayle (Viola *Allen), but she rejects him, preferring to go her own ambitious way. Glory's path takes her farther and farther from the road Storm would have her follow. At one point she sings in music halls; but wherever she goes, John remains watchful, until she eventually joins him in his missionary work in the slums. Based on Caine's novel, it was rejected by all major American and English producers until Elisabeth *Marbury gave the script to Allen, who went to England to help Caine rewrite it. Its success consolidated both her stardom and the position of the year-old producing Liebler and Co.

CHRISTIANS, [Marguerita Maria] Mady (1900–51), actress. The Viennese-born leading lady appeared in German-language productions in New York while still a youngster, then did not return to America until 1931. Although she played such roles as Gertrude to Maurice *Evans's Hamlet in 1938 and Sara Mueller, the exiled woman, in *Watch on the Rhine* (1941), she is recalled primarily as the loving central figure in *I Remember Mama* (1944).

CHRISTIE, Audrey (1912–89), character actress. A flexible, reliable performer in musicals and plays for forty years, Christie was often cast in supporting but scene-stealing roles. She was born and educated in Chicago where she studied dance, eventually appearing in a vaudeville act on the Keith-Orpheum Circuit. Christie played small comic parts on Broadway beginning in 1928 but didn't get noticed until her difficult-to-bed Billie in the comedy *Sailor, Beware!* (1933). Among her notable performances were the crafty divorcée Miriam in The *Women* (1936), the jitterbugging fiancée Anna in *I Married an Angel* (1938), the predatory best friend Olive in The *Voice of the Turtle* (1943), and the producer's bossy wife Frances in *Light Up the Sky* (1948).

CHRISTOFER, Michael. See *Shadow Box, The*.

CICERI, Charles (fl. late 18th century), scenic designer. Called "the first full-fledged scenic artist in America," he was born in Milan and educated in Paris where he learned drawing. Ciceri came to San Domingo as a soldier, but there he purchased his discharge and served as scene painter for the local playhouse. He returned to Europe and worked in Paris, Bordeaux, and at the London Opera House before again coming to America. He was the scene painter at Philadelphia's *Southwark Theatre before moving to New York where his first success was his designs for the operatic spectacle *Tammany; or, The Indian Chief*. Ciceri's scenery was also seen in *Hamlet, Henry VIII, The School for Scandal*, and *Dunlap's *André*, as well as many of the newly popular adaptations of Kotzebue. He was apparently the first scene designer in America to employ the transparent scrims that de Loutherbourg had perfected in England, and he was famous as well for his artificial figure painting and his transformations, such as the one described for *Blue Beard* at the *Park Theatre in 1802: "On Fatima's putting the Diamond Key to the Door, the Pictures all change to scenes of Horror; the Walls of the Apartment are stained with Blood, and the Door, sinking, discovers the internal of the Sepulchre, with its ghastly inhabitants; a moment after, all resumes its former appearance." He returned permanently to Europe sometime before 1807.

CINCINNATI PLAYHOUSE IN THE PARK (Ohio). Founded in 1960 in a Victorian shelter house located in the city's Eden Park, in 1968 the company added the modern Robert Marx Theatre, an unusual thrust stage space that seats 625 patrons. Over the years the group presented the usual mix of classic and modern works but in recent history has consistently presented original plays, many coming from the annual Rosenthal New Play Prize. Harold Scott was artistic director in the 1980s, the first African American to run a major regional theatre. The artistic director since 1992 is Edward Stern.

CIRCLE IN THE SQUARE (New York). The company was founded in 1950 as an offshoot of the Loft Players of Woodstock, New York, under the direction of José *Quintero in association with Theodore *Mann and others. The postwar fascination with arena-style stages had begun, and the company was one of the first to use the new form effectively at their tiny theatre on Sheridan Square. Their opening production was *Dark of the Moon* (1951), but it was the mounting of *Summer and Smoke* (1952) that brought them recognition and established Geraldine *Page as an important actress. Their 1956 revival of *The *Iceman Cometh* caused critics to reevaluate both the drama and Eugene *O'Neill, rekindling an interest in his works. It also gave major impetus to the career of Jason *Robards Jr. A later revival of *Children of Darkness* (1959) helped propel George C. *Scott to stardom. The downtown theatre is often credited for establishing Off Broadway as a potent and influential force in New York theatregoing. When their original premises were demolished in 1960, the company moved to Bleecker Street and continued to present neglected classics, foreign works, and new plays. In 1972 a new theatre, also called Circle in the Square, was built on 50th Street in the same complex as the Uris (now *Gershwin) Theatre. The company retains the downtown space and occasionally presents plays there, but mostly it is rented to others. The uptown theatre is Broadway's only flexible theatre, seating about 650, depending on whether a thrust stage or an arena-style setup is used. The new home allowed the company to present bigger productions than they could downtown (the theatre opened with a revival of O'Neill's trilogy *Mourning Become Electra*), but the economics of being a Broadway house put the nonprofit group in a financial quandary that for decades they have never resolved. Some seasons saw stunning revivals; others saw the house dark much of the time. It is a problematic space, but on occasion astute designers and directors have managed to create a thrilling theatrical environment not possible in a traditional Broadway house.

CIRCLE REPERTORY COMPANY (New York). After several years of informal collaboration and exploratory discussions, the group was founded in 1969 by Tanya Berezin, Marshall W. *Mason, Robert Thirkield, and Lanford *Wilson and was designed to promote the best in American playwriting. Among its many notable productions were Wilson's *The *Hot l Baltimore* (1973), *The *Fifth of July* (1978), *Talley's Folly* (1979), and *Burn This* (1988) as well as Jules *Feiffer's *Knock Knock* (1976), Albert Innaurato's *Gemini* (1977), Sam *Shepard's *Fool for Love* (1983), and William M. Hoffman's *As Is* (1985), one of the first and best plays about the AIDS epidemic. The emphasis at the Circle was always on the playwright, but certain company members, such as Berezin, Judd *Hirsch, Trish Hawkins, Helen Stenborg, Jonathan Hogan, William Hurt, and Jeff *Daniels, became familiar favorites who returned to the small space even after some of them found success on Broadway and elsewhere. The company lost its impetus in the early 1990s and by 1996 decided to close, more from a mutual desire by its creators to move on than for lack of audience interest. For nearly thirty years the Circle was one of Off Broadway's finest venues for promising American playwrights.

CITY, THE (1909), a play by Clyde *Fitch. [Lyric Theatre, 190 perf.] George Rand Jr. (Walter *Hampden), seems to have his world by the tail. He has been nominated to run for governor, is engaged to marry Eleanor Vorhees (Helen Holmes), and has watched his sister, Cicely (Mary *Nash), make an excellent marriage to his private secretary, George Frederick Hancock (Tully Marshall). But matters take an ugly turn when his father (A. H. Stuart) dies after confessing that Hancock is a secret drug addict and his illegitimate son as well. Cicely refuses to divorce Hancock, but when Rand tells him he has married his own sister, Hancock goes berserk, kills her, and attempts suicide. George prevents him from killing himself, even though Hancock has threatened to destroy Rand's career by revealing the family secrets. Rand withdraws from politics and makes a clean breast of his situation. He feared his confession to Eleanor would mean the end of their engagement, but she remains loyal. Fitch and many of his critics considered this his best play, although just how successful he was in contrasting virtuous small-town life with corrupting city life (his expressed purpose) is debatable. The play was the last he wrote and was not mounted (by the *Shuberts) until after his death. The opening night was one of the most sensational in history, with near pandemonium reportedly breaking out after Hancock, learning the truth, screamed at Rand, "You're a God damn liar!" "Damn" had been employed before, but never the complete expletive.

CITY CENTER (New York). The Mecca Temple, built on West 55th Street in 1923 as the home of the Masonic Shriners, was opened in 1943 as an auditorium owned by the city and devoted to presenting opera, ballet, musicals, and plays at popular prices. Many of the productions were return engagements of Broadway hits that had completed their road tours, but with time the theatre began to offer its own mountings, and the practice of producing both musical and nonmusical revivals there was abandoned. It is a large house (nearly 3,000 seats) and not ideal for most theatre productions. But there are two smaller spaces in the building, called Stage I (299 seats) and Stage II (150 seats) that have housed many productions by the *Manhattan Theatre Club. In recent years the large City Center auditorium has been home to the popular *Encores!* Series, which presents staged reading of old and/or neglected musicals.

CITY OF ANGELS (1989), a musical comedy by Larry *Gelbart (book), Cy *Coleman (music), David Zippel (lyrics). [*Virginia Theatre, 878 perf.; Tony, NYDCC Awards.] Novelist Stein (Gregg Edelman) is adapting his detective story into a screenplay for Hollywood producer Buddy Fidler (Rene Auberjonois) but his fictional creation, the hard-boiled Stone (James Naughton), keeps interfering, taking on a life of his own and reminding Stein of his shortcomings as a writer and as a man. *Notable songs*: You're Nothing Without Me; Lost and Found; You Can Always Count on Me. Gelbart's clever spoof of 1940s private eye films balanced two stories (the real-life events in Hollywood and the fictional tale being written) and the ingenious sets and costumes by Robin *Wagner and Florence *Klotz added to the fun by presenting the former world in color and the cinematic one in black and white. The Coleman-Zippel score was distinctive for its Big Band sound and scat-singing quartet called the Angel City Four.

CIULEI, Liviu (b. 1923), director. The Romanian-born artist, the son of an architect, was educated at the Academy of Music and Drama in Bucharest and began an acting career at the Lucia Sturdza Bulandra Theatre, later becoming artistic director for a decade. Ciulei gained international attention when his production of *Danton's Death* was restaged in Berlin in 1966, and by 1975 he was directing in America, serving as the artistic director of the *Guthrie Theatre in the 1980s. His many significant productions include *The Lower Depths* (1977) at the *Arena Stage, *Spring Awakening* (1978) at the *Public Theatre, *The Tempest* (1981) at the Guthrie, and *The Inspector General* (1978) at the *Circle in the Square. Ciulei's productions are known for their bold and surreal images and his eclectic use of different theatrical styles.

CIVIC REPERTORY THEATRE (New York). The company was founded by Eva *Le Gallienne in 1926. Her hope was to reestablish a repertory tradition in America so that actors might develop their art by playing a variety of roles in a single season and that playgoers might be assured of a theatre devoted to presenting the classics and meritorious new plays, which might not be considered commercially viable. To this end Le Gallienne attempted to ensure the sort of large, loyal following that would allow continuity by pricing tickets far below standard charges. The company opened at the old, out-of-the-way 14th Street Theatre in 1926 with a performance of Benavente's *Saturday Night*, followed that season by *The Three Sisters, The Master Builder, John Gabriel Borkman,* and *La Locandiera*. Later offerings included *The Good Hope,* *Peter Pan, *Romeo and Juliet, *Alison's House,* and, its most successful attraction, *Camille*. Although Burgess *Meredith, Alla *Nazimova, and Jacob *Ben-Ami headed the list of distinguished performers who played in support of Le Gallienne, the company was often beset by money problems. Its many and expensive mountings, low admission prices, and the onset of the Great Depression all combined to undermine its finances. When *Actors' Equity refused to allow Sunday performances, the company saw yet another source of revenue denied it and disbanded in 1933. Le Gallienne would later attempt repertory again with the *American Repertory Theatre.

CLAIRE, [Fagan], **Ina** (1892–1985), actress. The svelte, blonde-haired, hazel-eyed beauty with the tipped-up nose and weak chin, who was considered the finest high comedienne of her generation, was born in Washington, D.C., and made her debut in vaudeville as a singing mimic in 1905. Her first New York appearance, in 1909, won attention with her imitation of Harry Lauder. Claire toured in two-a-day for several seasons, before making her musical comedy debut opposite Richard *Carle in *Jumping Jupiter* (1911). After major roles in the musicals *The Quaker Girl* (1911), *The Honeymoon Express* (1913), and the 1915 and 1916 editions of the *Ziegfeld Follies, she made her first appearance in a straight play, *Polly with a Past* (1917), and won such rave notices that she became one of the most sought-after comediennes. Claire consolidated her reputation as chorine Jerry Lamar in The *Gold Diggers (1919), followed by the young bride Monna in *Bluebeard's Eighth Wife* (1921), the divorcee Lucy Warriner in *The Awful Truth* (1922), the neglected wife Denise Sorbier in *Grounds for Divorce* (1923), the thieving heroine in *The Last of Mrs. Cheyney* (1925), and the social-climbing Pearl Grayston in *Our Betters* (1928). After touring in *Reunion in Vienna*, she played one of her best roles: the footloose painter Marion Froude in *Biography* (1932). Claire's last successes were as the flighty Leonie Frothingham in *End of Summer* (1936) and (her final appearance) Lady Elizabeth Mulhammer in T. S. *Eliot's *The Confidential Clerk* (1954). Writing of her last performance, John Mason *Brown observed, "All the farcical joy, all the glitter of high comedy, that Mr. Eliot meant to supply in his script, she supplies in her person. She is a chic Lady Bracknell, a delectable worldling, an irresistible scatterbrain, writing comedy that is unwritten for her by the sparkle of her eyes, the laughter in her voice, and the implications of her expressions. More than a superb comedienne, Miss Claire is the Comic Spirit incarnate."

CLAPP, Henry Austin (1841–1904), critic. Born in Dorchester, Massachusetts, he was educated at Harvard, then taught at the Boston Latin School before becoming drama critic for the *Boston Advertiser*. He remained with the paper for more than twenty years, switching to the *Herald* two years prior to his death. Known as well as a leading Shakespearean scholar and student of dramatic history, Clapp regularly toured the country, lecturing in his field. He also wrote on theatre for many newspapers away from Boston, including such New York dailies as the *Sun*, *Tribune*, and *World*. He is best remembered for his *Reminiscences of a Dramatic Critic* (1902). His style reflected the leisurely, elongated construction of his era, but was marked by genuine erudition, peppery wit, and a determined fairness.

CLARE, Joseph (1846–1917), designer. After serving his apprenticeship at the Theatre Royal, Liverpool, he was brought to America by Lester *Wallack in 1871 and remained at Wallack's until the company was disbanded. During that time he earned a reputation as possibly the finest set designer in America, with his settings admired for their elegance and proper sense of period. Critics of the era rarely devoted much space to commenting on scenery, but, for example, his library setting for *The Man of Honor* (1873) was singled out by one reviewer as "the most exquisitely artistic thing of its kind ever presented in this City."

CLARENCE (1919), a comedy by Booth *Tarkington. [*Hudson Theatre, 300 perf.] Clarence (Alfred *Lunt) is a timid, seemingly bumbling ex-soldier who had been wounded in the war (but during target practice). He is taken in by the Wheelers, a family in desperate disarray. The harried father (John Flood) is almost at his wit's end trying to control his flighty, suspicious wife (Mary *Boland), his wild daughter Cora (Helen *Hayes), and his ne'er-do-well son Bobby (Glenn *Hunter). Clarence succeeds in bringing order out of chaos and wins the hand of the daughter's governess (Elsie Mackay). Only as he is leaving does the family learn he is one of the world's greatest authorities on coleoptera—bugs. Heywood *Broun wrote in the *Tribune*, "*Clarence* is the best light comedy which has been written by an American." The George C. *Tyler production, which deftly caught the optimism and excitement that was to characterize the 1920s, rocketed Lunt into prominence and caused Helen Hayes to be typecast as a flapper for several seasons.

CLARENCE BROWN THEATRE COMPANY (Knoxville, Tennessee). Although it did not become a professional regional theatre with its present name until Ralph Allen and Anthony Quayle organized it in 1972, its history goes back to 1939 when it was called the Loft Theatre and was part of the academic theatre program at the University of Tennessee. Today the company performs in a 576-seat proscenium space, a 100-seat flexible black box theatre, and in the 350-seat Ula Love Doughty Carousel Theatre, one of the nation's first arena-style houses. An early production of *Rip Van Winkle* featuring Quayle went on to play at the *Kennedy Center and the company has sent such shows as *Sugar Babies, Do You Turn Somersaults?*, and *A Meeting by the River* to Broadway.

CLARI, the Maid of Milan (1823), an operetta by John Howard *Payne (book), Henry Rowley Bishop (music). [*Park Theatre, in repertory.] The Duke Vivaldi (Mr. Clarke) lures the rustic maiden Clari (Miss Johnson) to his palace with a promise of marriage, but once there insists "the splendid slavery of rank" prevents his keeping his promise. Not totally unprincipled or unfeeling, the Duke provides Clari with every possible luxury, buying her jewels, Paris gowns, and surrounding her with servants. But Clari can only lament, "Be it ever so humble, there's no place like home." For her entertainment the Duke enlists a troupe of strolling players, and their show tells the story of another maiden enticed by a glamorous suitor. When the father in the play condemns the girl, Clari interrupts to beg his forgiveness. Later she escapes and returns home, where her own father is unforgiving. But the Duke soon appears to announce that the king, impressed by Clari, has consented to their marriage. The play was suggested to Payne by a Parisian ballet, *Clari; or, The Promise of Marriage*. Early advertisements for the

Stephen *Price–Edmund *Simpson production in New York featured the appearance of William Pearman, the famous English singer who had portrayed Jocoso, the Duke's servant, in the original London production. Pearman's singing was praised and the *New York News* called Bishop's whole score "the most beautiful and tender we have ever heard," adding, "The scene at the old home where the flute plays the air of 'Home, Sweet Home' and Clari listens, is one of the prettiest incidents we have ever witnessed on the stage." The work was frequently revived, and "Home, Sweet Home" remains recognized.

CLARK, Barret H[arper] (1890–1953), author. A native of Toronto, he studied at the University of Chicago and in Paris before beginning his theatrical career as an actor and stage manager with Mrs. *Fiske. After teaching at Chautauqua, he was an editor at Samuel *French, Inc., from 1918 to 1936, when he was appointed executive director of the *Dramatists' Play Service. For many years he was a board member of the Drama League of America as well as editor of *Drama Magazine*. Although most of his books, beginning with *The Continental Drama of Today* (1914), dealt with foreign material, Clark wrote one of the earliest studies of Eugene *O'Neill, which was published in 1926. He also edited the multivolumed *World's Best Plays*, as well as the *America's Lost Plays* series.

CLARK and McCULLOUGH, comedy team. [Robert Edwin] Bobby Clark (1888–1960) made his debut in a minor role in *Mrs. Jarley's Waxworks* in his native Springfield, Ohio, in 1902. In 1905 he teamed with Paul McCullough (1883–1936), another Springfield native, with whom he played until McCullough's death thirty-one years later. They performed in *minstrel shows, circuses, and vaudeville, perfecting the basic formula they would employ so successfully in musical comedy and revue. Clark, wearing painted-on glasses and wielding a sawed-off cane and a cigar, portrayed a likable but scoundrelly fellow, while the taller, heftier, mustachioed McCullough was his babyish, whimpering stooge. They first came to playgoers' attention in the 1922 and 1924 editions of the *Music Box Revue*. Thereafter they appeared in *The Ramblers* (1926), *Strike Up the Band* (1930), *Here Goes the Bride* (1931), *Walk a Little Faster* (1932), and *Thumbs Up!* (1934). After McCullough's suicide, Clark appeared alone in *Ziegfeld Follies of 1936*, *The Streets of Paris* (1939), *Star and Garter* (1942), *Mexican Hayride* (1944), *Sweethearts* (1947), and *As the Girls Go* (1948), his last Broadway role. In 1950 he directed *Michael Todd's Peep Show*, and in 1956 toured in *Damn Yankees*. Describing his antics in *Mexican Hayride*, Lewis

Nichols wrote in the *Times*, "Bobby Clark is funny just standing still on a stage, licking ashes from his cigar and with a surprised air looking out over his audience as though he did not expect it might be there."

CLARK, Marguerite (1887–1940), actress. A native of Cincinnati, she made her debut as a chorus girl in Baltimore in 1899 in one of Milton *Aborn's touring musical companies. After understudying and playing small parts in several Broadway musicals, she won attention in *The Wild Rose* (1902), which led to her being cast opposite De Wolf *Hopper in *Mr. Pickwick* (1903). Clark remained with Hopper to be his leading lady in a 1904 revival of *Wang*, *Happyland* (1905), and *The Pied Piper* (1908). A series of short-lived assignments followed before she scored a major success as the pregnant wife Zoie in *Baby Mine* (1910). In 1912 she played opposite John *Barrymore as Hilda in *The Affairs of Anatol*. Her last important assignment was the title role in the fantasy *Prunella* (1913). At the height of her career she left the theatre to become one of its first important stars to have a film career.

CLARK, [Margaret Brownson] Peggy (1915–96), designer. A native of Baltimore she graduated from Smith College, then studied scenic design at Yale. Her first Broadway assignment was creating costumes for *The Girl From Wyoming* (1938). Although she later designed costumes for *Uncle Harry* (1942) and *Dark of the Moon* (1945), she won major recognition for her imaginative lighting design. Among the plays she lit were *Love Life* (1948), *Miss Liberty* (1949), *Gentlemen Prefer Blondes* (1949), *Paint Your Wagon* (1951), *Pal Joey* (1952), *The *Threepenny Opera* (1954), *Peter Pan* (1954), *Plain and Fancy* (1955), *Bye Bye Birdie* (1960), and *Mary, Mary* (1961), as well as many productions of the New York *City Center and the Los Angeles and San Francisco Light Opera Company.

CLARKE, Corson Walton. See *Drunkard, The*.

CLARKE, John Sleeper (1833–99), comic actor. A native of Baltimore, the tiny, elfin-faced comedian made his amateur debut in Belair, Maryland, with his future brother-in-law, Edwin *Booth. His first professional appearance was at the *Howard Athenaeum in Boston in 1851 as Frank Hardy in *Paul Pry*. He then spent several seasons at Philadelphia's *Chestnut Street Theatre before making his New York bow as Diggory in *The Spectre Bridegroom* (1855). Back in Philadelphia, Clarke performed at the *Arch Street Theatre and later took over its management with William *Wheatley. His comic talents were recognized when he returned to New York in 1861 to play Jeremiah Beetle in *Babes in the Wood*, with the *Times* hailing him as "the best eccentric comedian now on the New York stage." His comic repertory, like Booth's tragic one, consisted largely of old favorites. Among his best parts were Dromio, Sam Scudder in *The *Octoroon*, the title role in *Paul Pry*, and Timothy Toodle in *The *Toodles*. The *Tribune* wrote of his interpretation, "His inebriety comes unconsciously out in the unsteadiness of the head, the loppiness of the neck, the thickness of the voice, the spasmodic attempt to conceal the betraying hiccup." In 1864 he became co-manager of the Winter Garden with Booth. However, after his brother-in-law John Wilkes *Booth assassinated Lincoln and Clarke was temporarily jailed with other members of the family, he left for England, where he spent the remainder of his career, returning occasionally for a handful of appearances.

CLASSIC GREEK DRAMA IN AMERICA. American playgoers relatively early were afforded opportunities to see many of the great Greek dramatic stories performed, albeit not in translations directly from the Greek. A version of the Medea legend was on stage in 1800, as was a production of the Oedipus myth by 1834. However, the stories were first really popularized in French versions, such as Legouvé's *Medea*, which *Rachel offered in the original French, Ristori played in Italian, and *Matilda Heron in an English translation. Translations directly from the Greek had to await the rise of academic stages in the very late 19th century and the availability of the efforts of such scholars as Gilbert Murray. Not until the second decade of the 20th century did major classic revivals emerge. Margaret *Anglin was an important figure in the movement, offering her *Antigone* in California in 1910 and her *Electra* and *Medea* in New York in 1918. She had also played in *Hippolytus* and *Iphigenia* in other cities. John *Kellerd was said to have offered the first professional *Oedipus Rex* in New York in 1911. Notable modern offerings have included *Lysistrata* in 1930, the *Old Vic's *Oedipus Rex*, featuring *Olivier, in 1946, and Judith *Anderson in Robinson *Jeffers's translation of *Medea* in 1947. This last was also seen in New York in 1973 with Irene Papas, in 1982 with Zoe *Caldwell, in 1994 with Diana Rigg, and in 2002 with Fiona Shaw. Joe *Papp presented a powerful *Agamemnon* at *Lincoln Center in 1977 that was revived in Central Park, and an all-star *Electra* in 1998 was a popular limited attraction on Broadway. Collegiate theatres remain important as platforms for classic Greek revivals, and on occasion nonprofit theatres will find favor with the genre, such as Andre *Serban's series of unconventional productions at *La MaMa in the 1970s, the *Hartford Stage's nine-play cycle *The Greeks* in 1982, and the *Denver Theatre Center's classics marathon *Tantalus* in 2000.

CLASSIC STAGE THEATRE (New York). Perhaps Manhattan's most adventurous theatre company dedicated to obscure or rarely produced classic plays, it was founded in 1967 by Christopher Martin as a showcase for classic plays presented by students at NYU. At first called the City Stage Company, then the CSC Repertory, Ltd., the company evolved into a notable producer of such difficult pieces as *Faust, Don Juan of Seville,* and other international classics. Under the leadership of new artistic director Brian Kulick, the oft-awarded group continues to produce new translations of world classics in its 180-seat theatre near Union Square.

CLAUDIA (1941), a comedy by Rose *Franken. [*Booth Theatre, 453 perf.] David Naughton (Donald *Cook) is a successful architect living on a colonial farm he has lovingly restored. He is more or less happily married, although he is not certain about this matter since his beautiful wife Claudia (Dorothy McGuire) has never quite grown up. She has a mother-fixation and never seems entirely sure of her sexual appeal. When she impetuously sells the farm to an opera singer and has a brief flirtation with a handsome young Englishman, David is exasperated. Then Claudia learns that her mother (Frances *Starr) is dying and she seems suddenly to mature. "Yes, it's like a miracle," her mother remarks. "It's just as if she were the mother and I were the child." Claudia agrees to return the opera singer's check and to settle down to being a wife. Franken's first play since *Another Language* nine years earlier (and her only other success), the John *Golden–produced comedy was welcomed by Richard *Watts Jr. of the *Herald Tribune* as "the best new American play of the season." *Claudia* was especially popular with women audiences.

CLAXTON, Kate (1848?–1924), actress. Born in Somerville, New Jersey, she made her debut in Chicago in 1869, then played for a time opposite Charlotte *Crabtree. Her first New York appearance came under Augustin *Daly as Jo in *Man and Wife* (1870), then she scored her greatest success as the blind Louise in *The *Two Orphans* (1874). Although Claxton was forever afterward identified with the role, she also gave other memorable performances, such as the guilty Roberte in *Ferreol* (1876). Her career was plagued by her reputation as a tragic jinx, since she was playing Louise when the Brooklyn Theatre caught fire with great loss of life in 1876 and was performing at the time of several other theatre fires. Her grandfather had been on stage at the Richmond Theatre when it burned. To overcome this stigma, as well as to secure roles other than Louise, she attempted to produce plays and manage theatres, but she had little luck and returned to acting *The Two Orphans* wherever she could obtain bookings. Whatever flaws she may have possessed as an actress, according to *Odell, she excelled "in sweetness, in beauty and in an innate refinement of manner."

CLEMENTS, Colin. See *Harriet.*

CLEVELAND PLAY HOUSE (Cleveland, Ohio). Organized in 1915 by journalist Charles S. Brooks, most of the original members were, curiously, painters rather than actors or other theatre people. The group began producing in 1916 under its first director, Raymond O'Neil. With the arrival in 1921 of its second director, Frederic McConnell, the group became professional. Spurred by Brooks and McConnell, the company opened a fine two-theatre complex in 1927: a 500-seat house named for Francis E. Drury, an early fund-raiser, and a 138-seat hall for Brooks. McConnell was succeeded by his associate K. Elmo Lowe whose conservative policies guided the Play House until his retirement in 1969. For a short while after Lowe's retirement, the company seemed disoriented; but it has since found a somewhat more adventuresome, if costly, program under its more recent directors, notably Richard Oberlin. In late 1983 it opened its new theatre complex, designed by Philip Johnson, including the flexible Kenyon C. Bolton Theatre and the intimate Studio 1. With the appointment of Josephine Abady in 1988 the repertory has put more emphasis on new plays, but under present director Peter Hackett the repertory includes traditional revivals, children's plays, and original plays in its Next Stage Festival of New Plays. Among the works the Play House has sent to New York were *It Ain't Nothin' But the Blues, The Smell of the Kill,* and *The Cemetery Club.*

CLIFTON, Josephine (1814?–47), actress. Controversy surrounds the early years of this brawny amazon of a performer. Most historians suggest she was born in New York, although there is some reason to believe she came from Philadelphia and that her real surname may have been Miller. She made her debut at the *Bowery Theatre in 1831, then later that season she appeared as Elvira in *Pizarro* and as Lady Macbeth, then was seen at the *Park Theatre as Bianca in *Fazio.* Clifton was the first American actress of any importance to play major roles in England, where she appeared at Drury Lane in 1835. Returning to America she played opposite the elder J. W. *Wallack in several new plays before embarking on her most celebrated role, the title part in the original *Bianca Visconti* (1837). Much of her career was spent in Philadelphia where she often appeared opposite Edwin *Forrest. Long after her death it was revealed that their relationship was more than professional, and Clifton's name figured prominently in the Forrests' notorious divorce case.

CLIMAX, THE (1909), a play by Edward *Locke. [Weber's Theatre, 240 perf.] Adelina von Hagen (Leona Watson) is studying to become an opera singer, but her fiancé, Dr. John Raymond (William Lewers), fears a stage career will corrupt her, so he hypnotizes her into believing she cannot sing, and, to ensure the spell holds, gives her a medicine to use daily for her throat. One day when she forgets to spray on the medicine her voice comes back and she realizes what Raymond has done. She goes on to continue her lessons and Raymond understands that her dedication and art truly cannot be corrupted. Joseph *Weber produced the Trilby-like, low-budget play, which remained popular for years and was revived with some regularity into the 1930s.

CLIMBERS, THE (1901), a play by Clyde *Fitch. [Bijou Theatre, 163 perf.] Although their greed and pushiness played no small part in killing George Hunter, his wife and younger daughters return from his funeral with only bitterness toward him, for they have discovered he died bankrupt. Only Blanche Sterling (Amelia *Bingham), Hunter's oldest daughter, is genuinely rueful. Paying their formal respects are several women and a social butterfly of a man who, like Mrs. Hunter, have been determined social climbers. Their private comments are brutal, one noting, "Mrs. Hunter went to the most expensive decorator in town and told him, no matter what it cost, to go ahead and do his worst!" Even their actions are thoughtless, with the sharp-tongued Miss Godesby (Clara *Bloodgood) dickering with Mrs. Hunter for gowns she will no longer need. Blanche's problems are exacerbated when she reads her father's papers and learns that her husband (Frank Worthing) indulged in irregular business dealings that could send him to prison. Guilt-ridden and recognizing that his wife has a loyal, loving friend in Edward Warden (Robert *Edeson), Sterling commits suicide. *Quinn has observed, "*The Climbers* is a masterly portrayal of human strength and human weakness. The strong characters are strong just in those qualities of courage, decision and unselfishness which kindle admiration, and the weak ones are tainted by a failing which, directed into a proper channel, might become legitimate ambition . . . their motives always are comprehensible." Bingham produced the play herself and triumphed in the leading role.

CLINCH, C. P. See *Spy, The.*

CLIPPER, THE. Known formally as the *New York Clipper*, it was founded in 1853 as a sporting and theatrical journal. Before it was absorbed by *Variety* in 1924, it had long since minimized sporting and most general theatrical news and had become a trade sheet whose main concern was vaudeville. By the time of its demise it called itself "The Oldest American Theatrical Journal."

CLORINDY; or, *The Origin of the Cake Walk* (1898), a musical afterpiece by Paul Laurence *Dunbar (book, lyrics), Ernest Hogan (music). E. E. *Rice presented the musical program as part of a summer bill on the roof of the *Casino Theatre. Its premiere marked the first occasion on which a show written and performed by African Americans was presented at a major white house. Its most famous song was "Darktown Is Out Tonight."

CLOSE, Glenn (b. 1947), actress. She was born in Greenwich, Connecticut, the daughter of a surgeon who took her with him on his missionary work to Africa. After graduating from the College of William and Mary, Close toured as a folk singer before going to New York and making her legit debut in 1974. She was featured in plays and musicals on and Off Broadway throughout the 1970s, first gaining some attention for her desperate Irene St. Claire, who enlists Sherlock Holmes's help in removing a family curse in *The Crucifer of Blood* (1978). Close also shone as the level-headed wife Charity in *Barnum* and won *Tony Awards for playing the actress-activist Annie in *The Real Thing* (1984), the survivor Paulina from a dictatorial regime in *Death and the Maiden* (1992), and the loony silent screen star Norma Desmond in *Sunset Boulevard* (1994).

CLOTHES (1906), a play by Avery *Hopwood and Channing *Pollock. [Manhattan Theatre, 113 perf.] Olivia Sherwood (Grace *George) likes more expensive clothes than she can afford, so she sets out to marry Richard Burbank (Robert T. Haines) for his money. Before long she has fallen in love with him and thereby winds up with the best of all worlds. Hopwood's first play to be produced (by William A. *Brady and *Wagenhals and *Kemper), it was reworked without his knowledge by Pollock, but he was open-minded enough to recognize the constructive additions the more experienced writer had made.

CLURMAN, Harold [Edgar] (1901–80), director and critic. Born in New York, he began his career at the *Greenwich Village Playhouse, then worked for the *Theatre Guild, acting in small parts and serving as a play reader. In 1931 he was one of the founders of the *Group Theatre, for which he directed *Awake and Sing!* (1935) and *Golden Boy* (1937), among others. After the company was dissolved, his directorial assignments included *The *Member of the Wedding* (1950), *The *Time of the Cuckoo* (1952), *Bus Stop* (1955), *Waltz of the Toreadors* (1957), *A Shot in the Dark* (1961), and *Incident at Vichy* (1964), as well as co-producing *All My Sons* (1947). From 1949 to 1953 Clurman served as drama critic for the *New Republic* and then for many years in the same capacity with the *Nation*. His publications include a history of the Group Theatre titled *The Fervent Years* (1945), *Lies Like Truth: Theatre Essays and Reviews* (1958), *On Directing* (1973), and a loosely structured autobiography, *All People Are Famous* (1974).

COBB, Lee J. [né Leo Jacoby] (1911–76), actor. The native New Yorker began his career in 1929 at the *Pasadena Playhouse and did not make his first Broadway appearance until 1935, when he assumed a minor role in *Crime and Punishment*. That same year he joined the *Group Theatre where his best-remembered roles were Mr. Carp in *Golden Boy* (1937) and the bankrupt Lammanawitz in *The *Gentle People* (1939). After playing important roles in short-lived failures, such as *Thunder Rock* (1939), *The Fifth Column* (1940), and *Clash by Night* (1941), he replaced Alexander Knox as the lead in the comedy *Jason* (1942). Five years in Hollywood followed before Cobb returned to create his most famous role, Willy Loman in *Death of a Salesman* (1949). Brooks *Atkinson wrote in the *Times*, "Mr. Cobb's tragic portrait of the defeated salesman is acting of the first rank. Although it is familiar and folksy in the details, it has something of the grand manner in the big size and deep tone." Cobb's last appearances were in a revival of *Golden Boy* (1952), in *The Emperor's Clothes* (1953), and as *King Lear* (1968). He was described by Cecil *Smith as "a massive man. . . . The face is big, each feature oversize—the large, soft, intelligent eyes; the big nose, jutting chin, wide cheekbones."

COBB, Sylvanus, Jr. (1823–87), author. Reputed to be the first writer to mass-produce popular romances, many of his works serialized in the *New York Ledger* and elsewhere were quickly dramatized by other authors. As plays, his stories proved extremely successful at the *Bowery and other working-class theatres. These adaptations included *The Mystic Bride* (1856), *The Gunmaker of Moscow* (1856), *Orion, the Gold-Beater* (1856),

Karmel, the Scout (1857), *The Oath of Vengeance* (1859), *The Veteran Buccaneer* (1859), *The Hunter Spy of Virginia* (1859), and *The Gipsy Daughter* (1860).

COBURN, Charles [Douville] (1877–1961), actor and manager. Born in Macon, Georgia, he began his career as a program seller at a Savannah theatre and by the age of seventeen was the playhouse's manager. Coburn later performed in stock in Chicago before making his New York debut in 1901 in *Up York State*. After heading a road company of The **Christian* (1904), he and his first wife, Ivah Wills Coburn, formed the Coburn Shakespearean Players in 1906 and toured for several seasons playing virtually the entire Shakespeare canon. His stocky build and slightly pompous style made him an especially notable Falstaff. In 1916 he produced and took a principal role in the Chinese drama *The *Yellow Jacket*, a play he successfully revived on occasion. Coburn's best-known role, however, was probably the bragging Old Bill in *The Better 'Ole* (1918). None of his later appearances was quite as popular, although he won praise as the day-dreaming button-maker David Hungerstolz in *The Bronx Express* (1922) and as widower Samuel Sweetland in *The Farmer's Wife* (1924). In 1925 he played James Telfer in an all-star revival of *Trelawny of the Wells*. Later he accepted major assignments in several revivals mounted by The *Players and in 1934 founded the Mohawk Drama Festival & Institute. Coburn retired from the stage after his wife's death in 1937 and enjoyed a long career in films, but he returned to tour as Falstaff in *The Merry Wives of Windsor* (1946). For several summers shortly before his death he played Grandpa Vanderhof in **You Can't Take It with You* on the straw-hat circuit.

COCKTAIL PARTY, THE (1950). T. S. *Eliot's play, written in an almost conversational blank verse, and dealing with religious faith in the comfortable, modern world, was dismissed as "verbose and elusive" when first produced in New York where many critics could not make head or tail of it. It quickly became the most talked-about and controversial play in many seasons and this, plus a superb cast headed by Alec Guinness, Cathleen *Nesbitt, Irene *Worth, and Robert Flemyng, gave it a year-long run. The *APA revived the work with only small success in 1968.

COCOANUTS, THE (1925), a musical farce by George S. *Kaufman (book), Irving *Berlin (music, lyrics). [*Lyric Theatre, 276 perf.] A vehicle for the *Marx Brothers, this daffy musical produced by Sam H. *Harris was set in Florida where hotelier Henry W. Schlemmer (Groucho Marx) is trying to sell swamp land off as prime real estate. It was a gag-filled, uproarious show that changed each night as the brothers improvised and clowned their way through the thin plot. The only song from Berlin's score to find favor was "Always," yet it was cut before opening. Revivals in regional theatre and in New York in the 1990s have proven that much of the silly show still plays well.

COCONUT GROVE THEATRE (Coconut Grove, Florida). Founded in 1956 in an old 1920s movie palace, the new theatre had a prestigious debut, presenting the American premiere of **Waiting for Godot* with Bert *Lahr and E. G. *Marshall before it went to New York. José *Ferrer was artistic director in the 1980s and the company continued to offer a variety of offerings over the years, sending a few on to Broadway as well. Today, under the leadership of Arnold Mittelman, the group performs in two spaces, the larger Mainstage and the intimate Encore Room Theatre. It also runs an education program called "Artists of Tomorrow" and an in-school touring company.

CODY, William Frederick (1846–1917), actor. Better known as "Buffalo Bill," the Iowan served as a pony-express rider and as a Civil War and Indian scout. A play called *Buffalo Bill*, recounting his exploits, appeared in 1871. To capitalize on his renown, he himself began to act in dramas purporting to recount his adventures, such as *The Scouts of the Prairie*, *The Knight of the Plains*, and *Buffalo Bill at Bay*. Cody toured in these for nearly a decade before founding his *Wild West Show* in 1883. Played in the open air, these entertainments allowed him to re-create vividly the old Indian skirmishes and show off his shooting and riding skills. The *Wild West Show* took on a major attraction when the great sharpshooter Annie *Oakley joined the company in 1885. The show prospered for many years as it toured the entire country, but eventually competition, the need to outspend that competition, and dwindling returns from a public tired of his style of entertainment forced him to merge with his major rival, Pawnee Bill's *Historic Far West and Great Far East Show*, in 1909. But the combined show continued to run up debts and was closed by bankruptcy in 1915.

COE, Richard L[ivingstone] (1916–95), critic. A native New Yorker, he became an assistant drama critic on the *Washington Post* in 1936 and its regular critic in 1946, a position he retained until his retirement in 1981. One of the leading non–New York critics, he was a warm, knowledgeable advocate of all good theatre, and his views were regularly solicited by Broadway producers, even when they did not try out their shows in Washington.

COGHLAN, Charles [Francis] (1842?–99), actor and playwright. The brother of Rose *Coghlan, he was brought from England by Augustin Daly as an addition to his company "where it had sometimes been found weak—in a leading man of distinction and personal charm." He made his debut in *Money* (1876). Although he impressed critics with his Orlando and Charles Surface during the season, he seemed unable to remain with any ensemble for long. By fall 1877 he was at *Palmer's *Union Square Theatre, where he scored major successes as the callous Monjoye in *The Man of Success* and as the doomed soldier Jean Renaud in *A Celebrated Case* (1878). Yet the following fall he had moved to *Wallack's, playing Lovelace in *Clarissa Harlowe* and Charles Surface to his sister's Lady Teazle. Thereafter Coghlan became Lillie *Langtry's leading man in *Enemies* (1886). He toured in the title role of *Jim, the Penman* (1887), then returned to play Antony and Macbeth opposite Langtry in 1889. At the same time he wrote two plays for his sister, *Jocelyn* (1889) and *Lady Barter* (1891), and he was Lord Illingworth in Oscar *Wilde's *A Woman of No Importance* (1894). After a few lean seasons he won applause as Mr. Clarence, a character based on Edmund Kean, in *The Royal Box* (1897). Shortly before his mysterious death, he appeared as a Sidney Carton-like figure in his own play about the French Revolution, *Citizen Pierre*. William *Winter wrote of him, "He had a figure of rare symmetry, a handsome face . . . a voice of wide compass and sympathetic quality, and a natural demeanor of intrinsic superiority."

COGHLAN, Rose (1851–1932), actress. The sister of Charles *Coghlan, the "wide-eyed, velvet-voiced, caressing, fascinating, divinely-smiling" leading lady first came to America in 1871 to play in burlesque with Lydia *Thompson and her British blondes. From 1872 until the company disbanded in 1888, Coghlan appeared with *Wallack's company, playing such classic parts as Lady Gay Spanker, Lady Teazle, and Rosalind, as well as appearing in such plays as *Marriage*, *Diplomacy*, *Clarissa Harlowe*, *A Scrap of Paper*, *The Silver King*, and *Lady Clare*. In 1893 she produced the first American mounting of Oscar *Wilde's *A Woman of No Importance*, playing Mrs. Arbuthnot. Thereafter her star began to fade, and she turned successfully to vaudeville. In 1908 she toured as Kitty Warren in a controversial production of *Shaw's *Mrs. Warren's Profession*, then played opposite John *Drew and Mary *Boland in *Jack Straw*. During the 1909–10 season she was a member of the repertory company at the *New Theatre, offering, among others, her Mrs. Candour, Mistress Page, and Paulina. Coghlan's last major roles were the Duchess of Saurennes in *Our Betters* (1917) and Madame

Rabouin in *Deburau* (1920). *Odell described her as "a ripe and radiant beauty, buxom, blithe and debonair, delightful in high comedy and effective in serious characters or in the high lights of melodrama." Yet while she won the respect of many audiences, she seems rarely to have gained their affection and, by her admission, was never popular away from New York.

COHAN, George M[ichael] (1878–1942), actor, composer, librettist, lyricist, and producer. The first enduring figure of the modern American musical comedy stage, he was born in Providence, Rhode Island, the son of vaudeville performers, with whom he made his theatrical debut. His father, Jerry; his mother, Helen; his sister, Josephine; and he became one of vaudeville's most popular turns, The Four Cohans. Although he appeared briefly in *Daniel Boone* (1888) and toured in the title role of *Peck's Bad Boy* (1890), it was his expansion of a vaudeville skit he had written for his family that marked Cohan's entrance into musical comedy ranks. *The Governor's Son* (1901) and *Running for Office* (1903), another expanded vaudeville sketch, while only modest hits, earned him the reputation as a fast-paced director and as a cocky, jaunty performer. Real success came with *Little Johnny Jones* (1904). Critics dismissed his songs as tinkly Tin Pan Alley ditties and his books as too slangy, chauvinistic, and trite, but he immediately found a public that long remained loyal. In 1906 he had two of his greatest hits, *Forty-five Minutes from Broadway* and *George Washington, Jr.*, in which he starred. Later musicals, many of which he also starred in, included *The Honeymooners* (1907), *The Talk of New York* (1907), *Fifty Miles from Boston* (1908), *The Yankee Prince* (1908), *The American Idea* (1908), *The Man Who Owns Broadway* (1909), *The Little Millionaire* (1911), *Hello, Broadway!* (1914), *The Cohan Revues* (1916 and 1918), *The Voice of McConnell* (1918), *The Royal Vagabond* (1919), *Little Nellie Kelly* (1922), *The Rise of Rosie O'Reilly* (1923), *The Merry Malones* (1927), and *Billie* (1928). Among the still-familiar songs to come from these shows were "Yankee Doodle Boy," "Harrigan," "Give My Regards to Broadway," "You're a Grand Old Flag," and "Nellie Kelly, I Love You." Although *Popularity* (1906) was a failure, Cohan wrote several other nonmusical plays that enjoyed long runs: *Get-Rich-Quick Wallingford* (1910), *Broadway Jones* (1912), *Seven Keys to Baldpate* (1913), *The Miracle Man* (1914), *Hit-the-Trail Holliday* (1915), *The *Tavern* (1920), *Madeleine and the Movies* (1922), *The Song and Dance Man* (1923), *American Born* (1925), *The Home Towners* (1926), *The Baby Cyclone* (1927), *Whispering Friends* (1928), and *Gambling* (1929). His last plays were mostly failures, but Cohan remained a popular performer throughout his long career.

Between 1906 and 1920 he formed a highly successful partnership with Sam *Harris, the duo producing all of Cohan's plays of that period and many other profitable ones as well. They also built the George M. Cohan Theatre. In 1919, as both actor and producer, Cohan attempted to mediate the *Actors' Equity strike, but the union's cold response left him permanently embittered. Following the dissolution of his partnership with Harris, he produced his own plays and those of others. Until late in his career, Cohan appeared solely in his own works, except as an occasional replacement. However, two of his greatest acting successes were in other men's plays. In 1933 he scored a singular triumph as Nat Miller in Eugene *O'Neill's *Ah, Wilderness!, then in 1937 played President Roosevelt in *Rodgers and *Hart's *I'd Rather Be Right. Amy *Leslie drew a picture of the young performer "with big, soulful eyes that speak music and peer cloudily out from under soft blonde hair. His face is pale and swift to mirror sentiment." Walter Prichard *Eaton's condemnation of Cohan for "his lack of good taste and his lack of a real knowledge of the world" typified many critics' dismissal of Cohan's early plays. With time, however, they came to appreciate his excellent technique and acute sense of what audiences wanted. Ironically, critical acceptance grew as Cohan's popularity and sure touch waned. Most of his best shows were among his first, and these fine early plays, for all their simplicity, their apparent naïveté, and their unabashed flag-waving, remain his most appealing and enduring. Perhaps it is doubly ironic, given the still lively popularity of his finest songs, that two of his nonmusical plays, Seven Keys to Baldpate and The Tavern, are the most often revived. Much of the catalog of Cohan songs was featured in the popular Broadway biography musical George M., 1968. Biography: George M. Cohan: The Man Who Owned Broadway, John McCabe, 1973.

COHEN, Alexander H. (1920–2000), producer. The New York-born producer began his career in 1941 with a failure, Ghost for Sale, but later the same year he produced a major success, *Angel Street. Although his record of commercial successes was disappointing, many of his box-office failures were nevertheless meritorious. Among his productions, many of which were importations of London hits, were Louis *Calhern's *King Lear (1950), At the Drop of a Hat (1959), An Evening with Mike Nichols and Elaine May (1960), Beyond the Fringe (1962), The Homecoming (1967), 6 Rms Riv Vu (1972), *Long Day's Journey into Night (1976), A Day in Hollywood/A Night in the Ukraine (1980), Taking Sides (1996), and Waiting in the Wings (1999). For many years he produced the television

coverage for the annual *Tony Awards, and two years before he died Cohen performed a successful one-man show, Star Billing (1998), in which he talked about his decades in the theatre.

COLE, [Robert] Bob (1869–1911), composer and actor. Little is known about the earliest history of this African-American artist, one of the first to make his mark in the theatre. Working first with Billy Johnson, then later with James Weldon *Johnson and Rosamond *Johnson, he wrote music for and often played in such early black shows as A Trip to Coontown (1898), Kings of Koondom (1898), The Shoofly Regiment (1907), and The Red Moon (1909). Because "Negro" shows were still subject to prejudice and never ran long in his day, Cole often found that a more profitable outlet for his talent was interpolating songs into white shows. His most memorable hit was "Under the Bamboo Tree," which Marie *Cahill introduced in Sally in Our Alley (1902).

COLE, Jack (1914–74), choreographer. A native of New Brunswick, New Jersey, he began his career as a dancer in the 1934 failure Caviar. His first choreographic assignment was Something for the Boys (1943), followed by such musicals as *Ziegfeld Follies of 1943, *Kismet (1953), Jamaica (1957), A *Funny Thing Happened on the Way to the Forum (1962), and *Man of La Mancha (1965). Cole's art was noted for its debt to Asian and jazz motifs.

COLEMAN, Cy [né Seymour Kaufman] (b. 1929), composer. A New Yorker who gave concerts as a child prodigy, he later studied at New York's High School of Music and Art and at the New York College of Music. Coleman worked as a nightclub pianist before contributing his first Broadway song to John Murray Anderson's Almanac (1953). His Big Band and jazz-influenced scores have been heard in Wildcat (1960), Little Me (1962), *Sweet Charity (1966), *Seesaw (1973), I Love My Wife (1977), *On the Twentieth Century (1978), Barnum (1980), *City of Angels (1989), Welcome to the Club (1989), The *Will Rogers Follies (1991), and The Life (1997). Coleman has collaborated with a variety of lyricists, including Carolyn *Leigh, Dorothy *Fields, and Betty *Comden and Adolph *Green.

COLLEEN BAWN, THE; or, The Brides of Garryowen (1860), a play by Dion *Boucicault. [Laura Keene's Theatre, 38 perf.] Mrs. Cregan (Mme. *Ponisi) and her son Hardress (H. F. Daly) are impoverished aristocrats who will lose their lands unless Mrs. Cregan marries the corrupt attorney, Corrigan (J. G. Burnett), who holds the mortgage, or Hardress weds rich Anne Chute (Miss Keene). But Anne really loves Kyrle Daly (Charles *Fisher),

Hardress's classmate, and Hardress cannot marry anyone since he is secretly wed to Eily O'Connor (Agnes *Robertson), a poor maiden known as the Colleen Bawn. Anne discovers a letter from Eily to Hardress, which she mistakenly believes was meant for Kyrle, and disclaims any further affection. At the same time Danny Mann (Charles Wheatleigh), Hardress's hunchback servant, is prepared to kill Eily if Hardress will give him a glove as a signal. When Mrs. Cregan innocently gives Danny the glove, he takes Eily to a grotto, where he throws her off a rock. A shot rings out, and Danny falls mortally wounded. The shot was fired by Myles na Coppaleen (Boucicault), a roguish bootlegger who has long loved Eily. Danny's dying words implicate Hardress, and Corrigan comes to arrest him; but Myles appears with Eily, whom he has rescued. Matters are then straightened out, with Anne agreeing to wed Kyrle. "It's a shamrock itself ye have got, sir," Myles tells Hardress, "and like that flower she'll come up every year fresh and green forenent ye." Adapted from Gerald Griffin's novel, *The Collegians*, the play was the first of many by Boucicault on Irish themes to win universal acclaim. When Boucicault took it to London six months after its Laura *Keene production in New York, it ran 278 consecutive nights. *Colleen Bawn* (its title means "the fair-haired girl") remained one of the most popular of 19th-century melodramas.

COLLEGE WIDOW, THE (1904), a comedy by George *Ade. [Garden Theatre, 278 perf.] Jane Witherspoon (Dorothy Tennant), the daughter of the president of Atwater College, is admired for her quick, resourceful mind. Her virtues are called into action when the best football player in the region, Billy Bolton (Frederick Truesdell), threatens to play for Atwater's archrival, Bingham College. Jane sees to it he plays for Atwater and wins his affection in the process. Walter Prichard *Eaton called the play "a genre picture of triumphant skill, executed with exuberant yet loving humor," adding, however, "But Mr. Ade has no power of dramatic development. He cannot penetrate the surface." The comedy was made into the highly successful musical comedy *LEAVE IT TO JANE* (1917) by Guy *Bolton (book), P. G. *Wodehouse (book, lyrics), and Jerome *Kern (music). Edith Hallor and Robert Pitkin played the central couple, and the tuneful show ran 167 performances at the *Longacre Theatre. *Notable songs*: Leave It to Jane; The Siren's Song; Cleopatterer; Just You Watch My Step. A 1958 revival of the musical ran for two years Off Broadway.

COLLEGIATE THEATRE CLUBS. Long before colleges and universities offered academic degrees in theatre, they provided drama productions, usually under the aegis of a club or society. The first such group in America was the Hasty Pudding Club, founded as a social club in 1795 by a group of Harvard undergraduates. They profess to be "the third oldest theatrical organization in the world," outranked only by the *Comédie Française and the Oberammergau Passion Players, but the claim is exaggerated since the club did not enter the theatrical arena for many years. The organization began staging mock trials, called "High Court of Equity." By 1835 these trials were made into theatrical productions by costuming participants, then musical numbers were introduced in 1850. The first more-or-less original Hasty Pudding show, written in 1884 by Lemuel Hayward, was a collegiate burlesque of a then-popular commercial burlesque, *Bombastes Furioso*. Although the club mounted several shows a year, it was generally its spring production on which it lavished special attention and which often toured. Since the time of World War I a separate committee, the Hasty Pudding Theatricals, has overseen the productions. Among performers and writers were such later famous figures as Oliver Wendell Holmes, Franklin Roosevelt, William Randolph Hearst, Henry Cabot Lodge, Owen Wister, Robert *Sherwood, and Alan Jay *Lerner. After Harvard became co-educational, women were allowed to be active behind the scenes, but the casts, including "female" leads and chorus "girls," remained steadfastly male for many years. The shows continue today but with women also on stage. The second-oldest such organization is the Mask and Wig Club, founded at the University of Pennsylvania in 1889. It has produced comic musicals ever since, not allowing women on stage for years after Harvard and others went co-ed. Princeton's Triangle Club was founded in 1888 as the Princeton Dramatic Association. Its first musical was *The Honorable Julius Caesar* (1890), on which Booth *Tarkington collaborated. It adopted its present name in 1893 and since then has specialized in all-student musicals, many of which have toured. It is the only one of such collegiate groups to have produced a song of widespread, lasting popularity. "East of the Sun (and West of the Moon)," with words and music by Brooks Bowman, came from its 1934 production, *Stags at Bay*. Among the group's later-celebrated members were José *Ferrer and Joshua *Logan. The Harvard Dramatic Club was founded in 1908 to encourage playwriting among undergraduates and alumni, producing only their plays until 1917. Its offerings included the premiere of Percy *Mackaye's *The *Scarecrow* in 1909. After World War I it abandoned its original policy, but for many years offered the American premieres of interesting foreign plays. In recent years it has combined with the Radcliffe Dramatic Club and operates much like any other college theatrical organization, albeit it works closely with the *American Repertory Theatre at the Loeb Center. Most other college theatrical clubs fell by the wayside as universities offered degrees in theatre and the theatrical activities became part of an academic program.

COLLIER, William (1866–1944), actor and playwright. A New Yorker with "an inscrutable face and dry voice," he made his stage debut in a juvenile company of *H. M. S. Pinafore* in 1879 after running away from home when his actor parents balked at his following in their footsteps. In 1883 Collier joined Augustin *Daly's ensemble, where for the next five years he played a number of minor roles. He first called attention to himself as John Smith in *The City Director* (1890) and as Judge Willis Hoss in *Hoss and Hoss* (1891), then had major successes as Benjamin Fitzhugh in *The Man from Mexico* (1897) and as the secretly married student Robert Ridgway in *On the Quiet* (1901), before spending a season with *Weber and *Fields. Collier's most famous role was Brook Travers in *The *Dictator* (1904). More fine notices followed his portrayal of Dick Crawford in *Caught in the Rain* (1906), the hypochondriac Dionysius Woodbury in *Never Say Die* (1912), Robert Bennett, sworn to veracity, in *Nothing But the Truth* (1916), Washington Cross, sworn to mendacity, in *Nothing But Lies* (1918), and the fake jockey Sam Harrington in *The Hottentot* (1920). After playing in the *Music Box Revue* and several other musicals, he retired from the stage in 1927. Collier co-wrote some of his vehicles.

COLLINGE, Patricia (1894–1974), actress. The Dublin-born performer appeared briefly in London before coming to America in 1908. Highlights of a career that spanned half a century included Bettina Dean, the stage-struck heroine, in *The *Show Shop* (1914); the title part in *Pollyanna* (1915), a role she played for three years; leading assignments in revivals of *Hedda Gabler* (1926), *The Importance of Being Ernest* (1926), *She Stoops to Conquer* (1928), and *Becky Sharp* (1929); the weakling Birdie in *The *Little Foxes* (1939); and Lavinia Penniman, the heroine's mischievous, secretive aunt, in *The *Heiress* (1947).

COLLINS, John (1811–74), comic actor and singer. The rather sad-faced Irish comedian and tenor was perceived as successor to the late Tyrone *Power when he made his American debut in 1846. His first appearances were in plays and parts long identified with Power, such as McShane in *The Nervous Man* and as Teddy Maloney in *Teddy the Tiler*. Among his other appearances were those in

such standard works as *The Irish Ambassador, The Irish Attorney*, and *Born to Good Luck*. In 1850 Collins played in *The Irish Fortune Hunter*, which John *Brougham wrote for him. He remained in this country until the mid-1850s, then returned occasionally, most notably to create the role of Carrickfergus, the hero's buddy, in the first American production of Brougham's *The Duke's Motto* (1863). His later returns were less successful.

COLONEL SELLERS (1874), a play by George Densmore and Mark Twain (Samuel Clemens). [*Park Theatre, 119 perf.] Col. George Selby (Milnes Levick), although a married man, seduces Laura Hawkins (Gertrude Kellogg). When she learns that he is married she kills him. Hovering not very far in the background is the character of Colonel Sellers (John T. *Raymond), a perennially impoverished dreamer, who is forever concocting schemes to make millions. He sees potential fortune in oddball steamboats, corn speculation, and, if corn speculation fails, cornering the hog market and feeding the hogs corn. The play has a complicated history. It was originally written by Densmore and presented as *The Gilded Age* in San Francisco in April 1874. Clemens brought suit, forced Densmore to waive his royalties, then rewrote the play. When it was presented in New York, its melodramatic main plot was generally dismissed and only Raymond's Sellers was praised. Clemens and Charles Dudley Warner rewrote it as *Colonel Sellers* and Raymond performed Sellers well over a thousand times in his lifetime. Twain and William Dean *Howells later wrote a sequel, *Colonel Sellers as a Scientist*, which Raymond refused to play, considering the lead had been turned into a caricature and the play was itself untheatrical. His judgment was confirmed when the play was finally produced as *The American Claimant; or, Mulberry Sellers Ten Years Later* (1887) and failed.

COLONIAL THEATRE (Boston). A popular playhouse in Boston for more than one hundred years, the 1,650-seat house on Boylston Street is a showcase for decorative arts as it combines Victorian splendor with the glitzy sense of fantasy to be found in the later movie palaces. Clarence Blackall designed the three-level theatre with mirror-lined foyers and extensive ceiling frescos painted by Herman Schadlermundt, and it opened in 1900 with a suitably spectacular production of *Ben-Hur. The Colonial has been a favorite touring house for many decades and continues to feature large-scale musicals in Boston's most ornate setting.

COLORADO SHAKESPEARE FESTIVAL (Boulder, Colorado). Founded in 1958 by Jack Crouch, the summer festival of Shakespearean and other plays has operated on the campus of the University of Colorado, utilizing an outdoor Elizabethan-style theatre and a modern indoor theatre. Over the years the company has completed the entire Shakespeare canon. The longtime artistic director (and lighting designer) is Richard Devin.

COLT, Alvin (b. 1915), designer. He was born in Louisville, Kentucky, and attended Yale School of Drama where he studied with Donald *Oenslager. He has created costumes, and sometimes sets, for such shows as *On the Town (1944), *Guys and Dolls (1950), The *Golden Apple (1954), *Fanny (1954), The Lark (1955), Pipe Dream (1955), Wildcat (1960), Sugar (1972), and Waiting in the Wings (1999), as well as several editions of *Forbidden Broadway. Colt was still active in the theatre in the new century.

COLTON, John B. (1886–1946), playwright. Son of an English diplomat who was serving in Yokohama, Japan, at the time of his birth, he came to America where he found work as drama critic of the Minneapolis Tribune. His first play to reach New York was Drifting (1922), written with D. H. Andrews. It dealt with a woman who is ready to become a prostitute, a variation of a theme that would appear in most of his plays. Colton's hits were *Rain (1922), based on a Somerset *Maugham story and written with Clemence Randolph, and The *Shanghai Gesture (1926). His last plays, Saint Wench (1933) and Nine Pine Street (1933), were failures.

COLVILLE, Samuel (1825–86), producer. After coming from his native Ireland, he began his American career as manager of playhouses in Sacramento, California, and Cincinnati. Shortly after settling in New York he presented *Boucicault's Flying Scud (1867), bringing over George Belmore to re-create the role he had first played in London. The next year, with George Wood, he opened Wood's Museum, and scored an immense success with his importation of Lydia *Thompson and her British blondes in their musical burlesques. Their popularity prompted him to make the musical theatre his main interest and he became one of the pioneering producers in the field. His Colville's Folly Company traveled the country presenting farce-comedies, those primitive precursors of musical comedy. Similarly the Henderson and Colville Opera Company and, more importantly, the Colville Opera Company crossed the country offering early operettas. He also ran the Colville Burlesque Opera Company, which presented travesties of popular operettas and plays. Colville is credited with giving important starts to Julia Mathews and Alice *Oates, two prominent musical performers of the time.

COMDEN and GREEN, songwriting team. Betty Comden (b. 1915) and Adolph Green (1915–2002) were both born in New York and began their professional careers performing in night clubs with Judy *Holliday. As co-librettists and/or co-lyricists their partnership was ultimately to become the longest-lived in Broadway history, beginning with *On the Town (1944). Their subject was almost always their native New York, whose idioms and attitudes they mirrored accurately and affectionately. Other musicals that bore their stamp were Billion Dollar Baby (1945), Two on the Aisle (1951), *Wonderful Town (1953), *Peter Pan (1954), *Bells Are Ringing (1956), Say, Darling (1958), Do Re Mi (1960), Subways Are for Sleeping (1961), Fade Out—Fade In (1964), *Hallelujah, Baby! (1967), *Applause (1970), *On the Twentieth Century (1978), A Doll's Life (1982), Singin' in the Rain (1985), and The *Will Rogers Follies (1991). Both have also been excellent performers, appearing together in On the Town and in a special revue, A Party with Betty Comden and Adolph Green (1958). Among the composers with whom they collaborated were Leonard *Bernstein, Jule *Styne, and Cy Coleman. Autobiography (Comden): Off Stage, 1995.

COME BACK, LITTLE SHEBA (1950), a drama by William *Inge. [*Booth Theatre,190 perf.] Doc (Sidney *Blackmer) is an alcoholic (temporarily on the wagon) who has never finished medical school. His wife, Lola (Shirley *Booth), is a slatternly housewife, forever dreaming of their cute puppy, Little Sheba, who long ago ran away. Doc is concerned about their boarder, Marie (Joan Lorring), a young college girl. He resents her beaux, not quite aware that he is jealous of them. When he realizes the girl will soon marry, he goes on a binge. Home from the hospital, he and Lola settle back into their humdrum existence. Inge's first play opened to sharply divided notices, the main strength of the *Theatre Guild production came from the performances of the two principals, who won virtually every possible award for their acting. The play itself hinted at the layers of repressed sexuality that would become the major preoccupation of Inge's later works.

COME BLOW YOUR HORN (1961), a comedy by Neil *Simon. [*Brooks Atkinson Theatre, 677 perf.] Buddy Baker (Warren Berlinger) appears suddenly at the apartment of his brother Alan (Hal March), having run away from their parents' home on his twenty-first birthday. Like his older brother, Buddy wants the fun and freedom his domineering Jewish parents deny him. Both young men still work for their father (Lou Jacobi) who shows up hot on his son's trail. He is, in his own sarcastic way, understanding: "You work very hard two days a week and you need a five-day weekend. That's normal." The rest of the play is essentially a comic family feud, with the father firing his sons, but ultimately taking them back and accepting Alan's choice of a bride and Buddy's desire to live away from home. While complaining that the comedy was repetitive, Louis *Kronenberger nevertheless felt, "It did squat head and shoulders above its all too recumbent rivals. It managed to keep going, it had some fresh and funny lines, it had some diverting scenes and characters." Simon's first produced play, it began a series of successes that marked him as the most knowing light comedy writer of his generation.

COME OUT OF THE KITCHEN (1916), a comedy by A. E. *Thomas. [Cohan Theatre, 224 perf.] The Daingerfields are an aristocratic Virginia family who have fallen on hard times and so must rent their plantation to a rich Yankee, Burton Crane (Bruce *McRae), whose idea of elegance includes a staff of white servants. When he insists that as part of the arrangement the Daingerfields must become that staff, they are horrified. The younger brother, Charles (Robert *Ames), is particularly indignant but his practical sister, Olivia (Ruth *Chatterton), recognizes they have no choice and wins over the family. They adopt new names and oblige their demanding renter. Since Olivia is as beautiful and charming as she is practical, she eventually wins over Crane, too, thereby keeping the plantation in the family. The play was based on a story by Alice Duer Miller. Producer Henry *Miller lavished special attention on the production, which many critics and playgoers came to consider his best mounting. In 1924 Chatterton starred in a failed musical version called *The Magnolia Lady*.

COMÉDIE FRANÇAISE, LA. See International Theatre Companies Visiting America.

COMIC STRIPS IN AMERICAN THEATRE. Within a few years after their first appearance in American newspapers and swift rise to popularity, comic strips were providing material for American theatrical authors. Perhaps it is significant that almost without exception they were turned not into farces or dramas but into musicals. The first transition to enjoy major success was Victor *Herbert's musical rendition of Winsor McKay's *Little Nemo* (1908). Its success was followed quickly by *The Newlyweds and Their Baby* (1909), based on the cartoons of George McManus. In the 1910s and 1920s, *Mutt and Jeff* provided the basis for a series of slapdash musicals that toured the country with tremendous returns but rarely

ventured into larger, more sophisticated cities. Titles included *Mutt and Jeff, Mutt and Jeff on the Farm*, and *Mutt and Jeff in Mexico*. During the 1914–15 season no fewer than five companies of this last edition were on tour. Another strip to prompt a series of musicals was McManus's *Bringing Up Father*. Again basically a road attraction, all through the 1920s such variations as *Bringing Up Father in Florida* and *Bringing Up Father in Ireland* traveled from small town to smaller town. For several decades thereafter the vogue faded, only to be revived with the success of *Li'l Abner* (1956), based on Al Capp's strip. *Superman* was turned into the highly stylized (but unsuccessful) *It's a Bird . . . It's a Plane . . . It's SUPERMAN* (1966), but two of the most popular musicals of the era were *You're a Good Man, Charlie Brown* (1967), taken from Charles W. Schulz's *Peanuts*, and *Annie* (1977), derived from Harold Gray's *Little Orphan Annie*. *Doonesbury* (1983), based on Garry Trudeau's celebrated cartoon, could not find an audience; neither could *Snoopy* (1982), *Starmites* (1989), and *Annie Warbucks* (1993). Fictitious cartoonists were the central figures in *King of Hearts* (1954), *Rumple* (1957), and *Woman of the Year* (1981).While the best-known characters from the respective strips were generally retained, in virtually all instances fresh stories were created for the librettos. Many of these musicals, as might be expected, had a special appeal to young audiences.

COMMAND DECISION (1947), a play by William Wister Haines. [Fulton Theatre, 409 perf.] There are some who view Brig. Gen. K. C. Dennis (Paul *Kelly) as "a man so drunk with power he thinks he can cover anything he does with other people's blood." Dennis has been sending his bombers far beyond the range of fighter support, and even some of his officers have balked at what they consider his suicide missions. Nor will he bomb installations he has been ordered to attack if he thinks other targets are more important. But Dennis is no coward; he himself tests an untried enemy plane to learn its potential. When he is finally transferred to the Pacific, he reveals to his successor that their predecessor was driven to suicide by the job, and that he himself often contemplated it. Although first published as a novel, the work had originally been written as a play. Many producers rejected it, feeling it followed too closely the war's end to have popular appeal. But Kermit Bloomgarden presented the taut, compelling drama, which was superbly acted, and it won over both critics and playgoers.

COMMON CLAY (1915), a play by Cleves Kinkead. [Republic Theatre, 316 perf.] Ellen Neal

(Jane *Cowl) is housemaid to the Fullerton family and is seduced by the Fullerton son, Hugh (Orme *Caldara). When Hugh quickly abandons her, she sues for support of their child. At the trial she and Judge Samuel Filson (John *Mason) make a horrifying discovery: she is the judge's illegitimate daughter. Ellen runs away to New York where she becomes a famous opera singer. Hugh, having seen the light, comes to reclaim her and their child. In 1914 John Craig of Boston's Castle Square Theatre offered a $500 prize for the best play submitted by a Harvard student. Kinkead (1882–1955), who had come from Louisville to study with Professor *Baker at his *47 Workshop, submitted the script that won first prize. A. H. *Woods produced it, but it was Kinkead's only success. Although immensely popular, the play was perceived even in its own time as contrived, if effective theatre.

COMPANY (1970), a musical play by George Furth (book), Stephen *Sondheim (music, lyrics). [Alvin Theatre, 706 perf.; Tony Award.] An essentially plotless concept musical, it centered on the young bachelor Robert (Dean Jones) and his married friends who, in their efforts to help him, reveal both the flaws and the joys in their marriages. In the end, Robert is not certain that either bachelorhood or marriage is an answer, but he cries out, "Somebody crowd me with love" and assist him to survive "Being Alive." *Notable songs*: Another Hundred People; The Ladies Who Lunch; The Little Things You Do Together; Side by Side by Side; Someone Is Waiting. A brilliantly innovative musical, capped by Sondheim's witty, observant lyrics and producer-director Hal *Prince's fluid staging, as well as Michael *Bennett's excellent dances and Elaine *Stritch's show-stopping delivery of "The Ladies Who Lunch," it was characterized by Clive *Barnes of the *Times* as "a very New York show," filled with the sort of "masochistic fun" that especially delighted its generation of New Yorkers. A *Roundabout Theatre revival in 1995 met with mixed notices.

COMSTOCK, F. Ray (1880–1949), producer. He began his career as an usher in his native Buffalo, then moved to New York where he became assistant treasurer at the Criterion Theatre. His first Broadway production was *Fascinating Flora* (1907), then he mounted *Bandana Land* (1908), one of the earliest "Negro" musicals. Comstock became manager of the *Princess Theatre when it was built to house experimental dramas, and when these failed he initiated a policy of intimate musical comedies that soon became known as the *Princess Theatre musicals: *Nobody Home* (1915), *Very Good Eddie* (1915), *Oh, Boy!* (1917),

and *Oh, Lady! Lady!* (1918). Among his successful nonmusical plays were *Adam and Eva* (1919) and *Polly Preferred* (1923). Comstock also imported a number of major foreign attractions, often in association with Morris *Gest, including *Chu Chin Chow* (1917), *Aphrodite* (1919), *Mecca* (1920), *Chauve-Souris* (1922), and *The Miracle* (1924), as well as the *Moscow Art Theatre and Eleanora *Duse.

CONKLIN, John (b. 1937), designer. The much-in-demand artist often designs both sets and costumes for his productions and usually works in regional theatre, but much of his work has gotten national attention. He was born in Hartford, Connecticut, and was educated at Yale before making his Broadway debut in 1963 with *Tambourines to Glory*. Conklin has designed for all the major regional theatres but is most associated with the *Hartford Stage where he did such memorable productions as *The Mystery Plays* (1984), *Our Country's Good* (1990), and *The *Merchant of Venice* (1993).

CONKLIN, [Margaret Eleanor] Peggy (1912–2003), actress. A native of Dobbs Ferry, New York, she began her career as a chorus girl in 1928 but soon revealed skills as a comedienne and serious actress. Her important assignments included Prudence Kirkland, who loves a Hessian soldier, in *The *Pursuit of Happiness* (1933); Gabby Maple, who wins the affection of the forlorn hero, in *The *Petrified Forest* (1935); Ellen Murray, who has liberal ideas about love, in *Yes, My Darling Daughter* (1937); Mrs. North, half of a husband-and-wife detective team, in *Mr. and Mrs. North* (1941); and Flo Owens, whose family is transformed by the arrival of a vagrant, in *Picnic* (1953).

CONNECTICUT YANKEE, A (1927), a musical comedy by Herbert *Fields (book), Richard *Rodgers (music), Lorenz *Hart (lyrics). [Vanderbilt Theatre, 418 perf.] At a party on the eve of his wedding, Martin (William *Gaxton) flirts with Alice Carter (Constance Carpenter), which so infuriates his bride-to-be, Fay Morgan (Nana Bryant), that she knocks him unconscious with a blow from a champagne bottle. Martin dreams he is in King Arthur's court, where he falls in love with Alisande La Carteloise, who looks just like Alice, but where his wooing and his attempts to modernize the medieval world are thwarted by Merlin (William Norris) and the villainous Morgan Le Fay, the fire-spitting image of Fay Morgan. When he awakes he decides to marry Alice. *Notable songs*: I Feel at Home with You; My Heart Stood Still; On a Desert Island with Thee; Thou Swell. Lew *Fields produced the light-hearted musical rendition of Mark Twain's story, which was praised by Brooks *Atkinson in the *Times* as "a novel amusement in the best of taste." It was successfully revived in 1943, at which time Hart contributed his last Broadway lyric to a riotously black-humored song, "To Keep My Love Alive."

CONNECTION, THE (1959), a play by Jack Gelber. [Living Theatre, 722 perf.] Leach (Warren Finnerty) and his fellow drug addicts sit in his "pad" awaiting the return of Cowboy (Carl Lee) with a fresh supply of narcotics. Cowboy comes in with the innocent Sister Salvation (Barbara Winchester), who has helped him elude the police in the naïve belief that she can redeem the addicts, but she cannot. Presented as a play within a play, with the principal figures stepping slightly out of character to address the playwright, and the playwright addressing the audience, it was hailed by Kenneth Tynan in *The New Yorker* as: "The most exciting new play that Off Broadway has produced since the war." It foreshadowed many of the social problems and Broadway treatment of them that would follow in the 1960s. **Jack GELBER** (1932–2003) was born in Chicago and attended the University of Illinois. Although nearly a dozen of his plays were produced in New York, this was his only success. Gelber also directed many plays Off Broadway and acted on several occasions.

CONNELL, Jane [neé Jane Sperry Bennett] (b. 1925), character actress. A tiny woman with a giant, squeaking voice, Connell was a favorite supporting player on Broadway for more than forty years. She was born in Berkeley, California, and attended the local university before getting experience in stock. She made her New York debut in 1955 and was first noticed as the corrupt Mrs. Peachum in the legendary revival of *The *Threepenny Opera* (1955). Connell's Broadway recognition came in 1966 when she played the introverted governess Miss Gooch in *Mame* (1966), a role she repeated on tour, in stock, in revival, and on film. Her other noteworthy performances include the delightfully insane Gabrielle in *Dear World* (1969), the language-destroying Mrs. Malaprop in *The Rivals* (1974), the aghast Duchess in *Me and My Girl* (1986), the overbearing Mother in *Crazy for You* (1992), and the deaf stage dresser Ethel in *Moon Over Buffalo* (1995).

CONNELLY, Marc[us Cook] (1890–1981), playwright. Born in McKeesport, Pennsylvania, he began writing plays for amateur productions while working as a newspaperman in nearby Pittsburgh. In 1916 he wrote the libretto and lyrics for *The Amber Princess*, but by the time the musical reached New York, others had rewritten the book

and only one of his lyrics survived. After updating the libretto of *Erminie* for a 1921 revival, Connelly joined forces with George S. *Kaufman, and together they wrote *Dulcy* (1921), *To the Ladies* (1922), *Merton of the Movies* (1922), the musical *Helen of Troy, New York* (1923), *The Deep Tangled Wildwood* (1923), *Beggar on Horseback* (1924), the musical *Be Yourself* (1924), and sketches for *The 49ers* (1922). After the two separated, Connelly wrote the fantasy *The *Wisdom Tooth* (1926), and with Herman J. Mankiewicz, the comedy *The Wild Man of Borneo* (1927). Connelly's greatest success was the folklike fantasy *The *Green Pastures* (1930), followed by the popular *The Farmer Takes a Wife* (1934). He directed many plays, most notably *Having Wonderful Time* (1937), and made occasional appearances as an actor when his bald head and avuncular face and voice prompted his casting in folksy parts. Autobiography: *Voices Offstage*, New York, 1968.

CONNOLLY, [Robert] Bobby (1895–1944), choreographer. After dancing in *Hitchy-Koo* (1920) and serving as assistant choreographer for several shows, he devised the dances for *Kitty's Kisses* (1926). Connolly's work was seen in such musicals as *Honeymoon Lane* (1926), *The *Desert Song* (1926), *Good News!* (1927), *Funny Face* (1927), *The *New Moon* (1928), *Follow Thru* (1929), *Flying High* (1930), *Ziegfeld Follies of 1931*, and *Take a Chance* (1932). His last Broadway assignment was *Ziegfeld Follies of 1934*.

CONNOLLY, Walter (1887–1940), character actor. Born in Cincinnati, Ohio, Connolly was educated in his hometown and at the University of Dublin and made his New York debut in 1910 in an outdoor production of *As You Like It*. He joined E. H. *Sothern's company the next year and played supporting roles in Shakespeare productions on the road. The short, chubby Connolly first got noticed as the penny-pinching Rollo in *Applesause* (1925) then went on to portray a wide range of characters, most memorably the hot-blooded Cuban Luis in *The Behavior of Mrs. Crane* (1928), the wily confirmed bachelor Dudley in *Your Uncle Dudley* (1929), the greedy Dr. Haggett in *The Late Christopher Bean* (1932), and the clergyman who loves mystery novels in *The Bishop Misbehaves* (1935).

CONOR, Harry (1856–1931), comic actor. The stocky little comedian was popular in musicals for many years but is largely recalled for a single early success as the hypochondriacal Welland Strong in *A *Trip to Chinatown* (1891), in which he introduced "The Bowery." He occasionally appeared in such nonmusicals as *The *Blue Mouse* (1908).

CONQUERORS, THE (1898), a play by Paul *Potter. [*Empire Theatre, 128 perf.] German invaders have billeted several loutish officers in a French chateau where they brutally smash family heirlooms, invite ladies of dubious repute to a dinner, and generally behave scandalously. Later, when the men are drunk, one of them, Eric von Rodeck (William *Faversham), attempts to seduce Yvonne de Grandpré (Viola *Allen), who is not a demimonde but a noblewoman whose family owns the chateau. She handles herself so skillfully that she shames him and causes him to repent his behavior, whereupon she swoons. Von Rodeck leaves, and a second officer appears, also bent on seducing Yvonne. Learning of his intention, von Rodeck returns and kills him. When Yvonne regains consciousness she believes the second man was killed defending her honor. Von Rodeck eventually manages to convince her of the truth and to win her affection. The most famous scene in the Charles *Frohman production occurred when Yvonne throws the contents of a glass of wine in von Rodeck's face. When *Weber and *Fields mounted a travesty of the show, their heroine threw a pie in the officer's face, probably the first employment of the long popular slapstick device.

CONRAD, Robert. See *Jack Cade*.

CONTACT (2000), a "dance play with music" by Susan *Stroman and John *Weidman. [*Mitzi E. Newhouse Theatre, 1,010 perf.; Tony Award.] Choreographer Stroman conceived and staged this unusual entertainment that Weidman wrote, though there was little dialogue and the music was prerecorded standards. The opener is a danced version of Fragonard's painting "The Swing" in which an aristocrat (Séan Martin Huingston) disguised as a servant woos a lady (Stephanie Michels). The second piece explored the vivid imagination of an abused wife (Karen Ziemba) at an Italian restaurant. The longest section concerned the suicidal Michael (Boyd *Gaines) who is entranced by an elusive Girl in a Yellow Dress (Deborah Yates) whom he meets in a nightclub. Although many critics considered the program unsatisfying as theatre, all applauded its dancing and the attraction was popular enough that Lincoln Center moved it upstairs to the larger *Vivian Beaumont Theatre for a long run.

CONTEMPORARY THEATRE, A (Seattle). Started in 1965 by Gregory Arthur Falls, director of the drama program at the University of Washington, as a summer theatre alternative for the city, the company performed in a 449-seat thrust theatre renovated from a business site. Over the years the company became well known for their commitment to new works, sending several original scripts on to New York. But financial difficulties in late 2002 forced the theatre to announce its closing. At the last moment, funding was found to continue, but the future of the company, under its new artistic director Kurt Beattie, is unstable at best.

CONTESTS AND PRIZES FOR AMERCAN PLAYS. The earliest American theatrical companies, consisting as they did largely of English actors, were satisfied with a repertory of popular English plays. But after independence, with native-born audiences and performers on hand, theatre companies sought to diversify bills and looked to American-made plays, preferably on American themes, both for patriotic and practical reasons. Two great early actors, Edwin *Forrest and James H. *Hackett, actively encouraged potential American dramatists. In 1828, Forrest offered a $500 prize for "the best tragedy, in five acts, of which the hero, or principal character, shall be an aboriginal of this country." The winning script, John Augustus *Stone's *Metamora; or, The Last of the Wampanoags*, proved to be one of Forrest's sturdiest vehicles, and as a result he held eight succeeding contests. Hackett began offering prizes in 1831, and, while he had less luck with some of the winners, did find a popular vehicle in James K. *Paulding's The *Lion of the West*. The relative success of these contests and the publicity they brought the performers prompted many others to offer awards, including G. H. *Hill, Josephine *Clifton, P. T. *Barnum, A. M. *Palmer, Richard *Herndon, and Avery *Hopwood. In the 1890s newspapers adopted the policy, the *Herald* in one instance offering $1,000 for the best new drama by an American on an American theme. These contests may well have been designed to stimulate circulation, but they occurred at the time of a great swell of patriotism that many later historians were to brand as jingoism. In the 20th century such honors as the *Pulitzer Prize, the *New York Drama Critics Circle Awards, and the *Tony Award, are offered to plays already produced and not basically to encourage new playwrights or native drama. But numerous playwriting competitions continue today, offered by schools, foundations, play publishers, and theatre companies.

CONTRAST, THE (1787), a comedy by Royall Tyler. [*John Street Theatre, in repertory.] Mr. Van Rough (Owen *Morris) would have his daughter, Maria (Mrs. Harper), marry the effete anglophile, Dimple (Lewis *Hallam Jr.), although Dimple openly flirts with Letitia (Mrs. Kenna) and Charlotte (Mrs. *Morris). Charlotte's brother, Colonel Manly (John *Henry), who had nobly acquitted himself during the Revolution, loves Maria but is reluctant to press what might be an unacceptable suit. When Dimple's gambling losses cost him his fortune, he is prepared to ditch Maria and marry either Letitia or Charlotte, both of whom he believes are much wealthier. Van Rough recognizes that he is well rid of the man and consents to Maria's wedding Manly. A subplot recounts how Dimple's arrogant servant, Jessamy (Mr. Harper), goads Manly's hickish servant, Jonathan (Thomas *Wignell), into courting the maid, Jenny (Miss Tuke), but she rejects them both. The first comedy written by an American to be presented by a professional American troupe (the *American Company), it was modeled consciously after *The School for Scandal* and written by Tyler in three weeks. It is remembered largely for introducing Jonathan, the classic stage Yankee. Jonathan proudly denies he is a servant, even though he might polish Manly's boots: "I am a true blue son of liberty, for all that. Father said I should come as Colonel Manly's waiter to see the world, and all that; but no man shall master me: my father has as good a farm as the colonel." **Royall TYLER** (1757–1826) was born in Boston, studied law at Harvard, then served in the army before writing *The Contrast*. Tyler's other works included the comic opera *May Day in Town; or, New York in an Uproar* (1781), the comedy *The Georgia Spec; or, Land in the Moon* (1797), and other plays, which have left behind no record of production, including *The Farm House; or, the Female Duellists; The Island of Barrataria; The Origin of the Feast of Purim; or, The Destinies of Haman and Mordecai; Joseph and His Brethren;* and *The Judgment of Solomon*. In after years, he moved to Vermont, where he became that state's Chief Justice from 1807 to 1813 and also taught law at the University of Vermont. Although Tyler was clearly one of the most adept of contemporary gentlemen playwrights—*The Contrast* can still be performed effectively—his importance remains fundamentally historical.

CONWAY, Frederick B[artlett] (1819–74), actor. The son of a famous English actor, he came from his native England in 1850, making his New York debut as Charles Surface, and the following night he offered a much-admired Claude Melnotte in *The *Lady of Lyons*. Two years later he married the Connecticut-born Sarah Crocker (1834–75), who had made her acting debut in Baltimore in 1849 and who, as Mrs. F. B. Conway, thereafter acted regularly with her husband. Although they appeared in many popular contemporary works, the couple was best liked in classic roles. Conway's major parts included Iago, Macbeth, Sir Harcourt Courtly, Sir Peter Teazle, and Malvolio while his wife essayed Emilia, Lady Macbeth,

Lady Gay Spanker, Lady Teazle, and Viola. Conway briefly managed the Metropolitan Theatre in New York, but Mrs. Conway proved a better and more durable manager, assuming leadership of Brooklyn's Park Theatre in 1864. Under her aegis it was Brooklyn's principal playhouse and remained so until she left it to assume management of the new Brooklyn Theatre, which she ran until her death. T. Allston *Brown, after noting briefly that Conway was "a good 'all 'round' actor" and "the best John Mildmay in 'Still Waters Run Deep' ever seen on the American stage," wrote of Mrs. Conway, "She was gifted with an intellect of strong analytic power, sufficient to fit out half a dozen leading ladies. She had a fine, expressive face, a voice full and melodious, a carriage graceful and womanly." Their daughters, Minnie and Lillian, were also popular performers.

CONWAY, Kevin (b. 1942), actor. Conway is a versatile leading man who possesses a seething, belligerent quality that gives his characterizations an edgy persona. A native New Yorker, he trained with Uta *Hagen and at the Dramatic Workshop, acting in regional theatre before making his Manhattan debut in 1969. Conway was first noticed in 1972 as the confused radical college student Mike in *Moonchildren* (1972), then was widely applauded the next year for his raucous mental patient Randle Patrick McMurphy in *One Flew Over the Cuckoo's Nest*. His other notable performances include the antagonistic drifter Teddy in *When You Comin' Back, Red Ryder?* (1973), the itinerant farmhand George in *Of Mice and Men* (1974), the boozing brother Jamie in *Long Day's Journey Into Night* (1976), the self-doubting Victorian doctor Frederick Treves in *The *Elephant Man* (1979), the greedy liquidator Lawrence Garfinkle in *Other People's Money* (1989), and businessman Dan Packard in *Dinner at Eight* (2002).

CONWAY, William A[ugustus] (1789–1828), actor. A handsome but thin-skinned performer, he came to America after his Hamlet was faulted by London critics and made his American debut in the same part in 1824. His reception was such as to convince him to remain in America, and he followed Hamlet with equally well-received interpretations of Coriolanus, Romeo, Petruchio, Jaffier in *Venice Preserved*, and Othello, the last two with Thomas Abthorpe *Cooper. For all the critical praise, Conway was never more than moderately popular. As a result he increasingly had to resort to joint engagements with other prominent actors. T. Allston *Brown observed, "Conway was six feet four inches high, well proportioned, and possessed great muscular power, and a masterly command of his countenance, which seemed to have been formed to express the passions of his soul and to delineate the characters of Shakespeare." He left the stage to devote himself to religion, but later committed suicide by jumping from a ship in Charleston harbor.

COOK, Barbara [Nell] (b. 1927), singer and actress. A native of Atlanta, the doll-faced blonde with an exceptionally beautiful soprano voice made her Broadway debut as the leading lady in *Flahooley* (1951), then toured as Ado Annie in a revival of *Oklahoma!* (1953). Cook scored a major success in *Plain and Fancy* (1955), followed by important assignments as Cunegonde in *Candide* (1956), Julie Jordan in a 1957 revival of *Carousel*, Marian Paroo in The *Music Man* (1957), Anna in a 1961 revival of The *King and I*, Liesel in The *Gay Life* (1961), and Amalia Balash in *She Loves Me* (1963). She also appeared in *Something More!* (1964), *Any Wednesday*, (1965), the 1966 revival of *Show Boat*, *The Grass Harp* (1971), and *Enemies* (1972). In later years, when increasing weight and age eliminated her from leading musical roles, she enjoyed a successful career in nightclubs, and she presented one-woman shows on Broadway in 1987 and 2002.

COOK, Donald (1901–61), comic actor. The slightly foppish, nasal-voiced high comedian was born in Portland, Oregon, and played in vaudeville before turning to the legitimate stage. Among his memorable roles were Jim Hutton, the unfaithful young husband, in *Paris Bound* (1927), the neglected husband Tony Kenyon in *Skylark* (1939), the frustrated husband David Naughton in *Claudia* (1941), Elyot Chase, opposite Tallulah *Bankhead in a 1948 revival of *Private Lives*, the libertine father David Slater in The *Moon Is Blue* (1951), and the egomaniacal cartoonist Larry Larkin in *King of Hearts* (1954). He was co-starring opposite Julie *Harris in the tryout of *A Shot in the Dark* at the time of his death.

COOK, George Cram (1873–1924), manager, playwright, and director. The founder and guiding light of the *Provincetown Players, he was a versatile theatrical figure who not only ran the company but also wrote a number of the plays it mounted, and directed and appeared in many others. Among his plays, some of which were written in collaboration with his wife, Susan *Glaspell, were the satire *Suppressed Desires* (1915), the comedy *Change Your Style* (1915), the antiwar drama *The Athenian Women* (1918), and *The Spring* (1921), dealing with reincarnation. Among the plays Cook directed was the first staging of Eugene *O'Neill's The *Emperor Jones* (1920), while his roles included Yank in the original production of *Bound East for Cardiff* (1916). Bitter at the recognition given O'Neill and what he perceived as neglect of his own work, he left the company to spend his last years in Greece. Biography: *Jig Cook and the Provincetown Players*, Robert Károly Sarlós, 1982.

COOK, Joe [né Joseph Lopez] (1890–1959), comedian. The wide-mouthed, rubeish-looking performer was born in Evansville, Indiana, and played in traveling medicine shows before making his stage debut in vaudeville in 1907 as part of a juggling act that included his brothers. He soon became popular as a single act in which he juggled, brought on ludicrous Rube Goldberg–style inventions, and interspersed this with his zany humor. His most-famous bit was "The Four Hawaiians," in which he started out to imitate four different islanders, digressed to tell how he became a rich man, then exited announcing he is too rich to bother with imitating four Hawaiians. His first Broadway musical was *Hitchy-Koo* (1919), followed by notable appearances in the *Earl Carroll Vanities* in 1923, 1924, and 1925, *Rain or Shine* (1928), *Fine and Dandy* (1930), *Hold Your Horses* (1933), *Off to Buffalo!* (1939), and *It Happens on Ice* (1940).

COOK, Will Marion (1869–1944), composer. Born in Washington, D.C., he studied at Oberlin College and then in Europe with Dvorak and Joachim. Although he hoped to find a place for African-American musical artists in serious music and, indeed, all through his life organized or worked with black choirs and orchestras, he turned to Tin Pan Alley and the Broadway theatre as a source of income. In 1898 he composed the score for the first black musical to play a white theatre, *The Origin of the Cake Walk; or, *Clorindy*. His song from that score, "Darktown Is Out Tonight," was one of the reigning hits of the era. After interpolating fleetingly successful songs in several musicals, Cook wrote the scores for *In Dahomey* (1903), *The Southerners* (1904), *Abyssinia* (1906), and *Bandana Land* (1908). He generally orchestrated and conducted his own scores, and in 1910 he provided Fanny *Brice with the lyric for her first *Ziegfeld Follies* hit, "Lovie Joe."

COOKE, George Frederick (1756–1812), actor. The first great foreign actor to visit America, he was by the time of his visit a dying, emotionally troubled man. Although one of the great London actors of his era, he long had been known for his eccentricity, undependability, and frequent drunkenness. Cooke had a deeply lined face with a huge conspicuous nose and large, dark, soulful eyes, but was often said to lack grace. His debut, which is generally seen as having inaugurated the "star system" in America, came at the *Park Theatre in 1810 as Richard III, considered his best role. *Dunlap recalled, "The high key in which he pitched his voice, and its sharp and rather grating tones, caused a sensation of disappointment in some." Nevertheless, the *Columbian* noted, "Mr. Cooke's style of acting is vivid, original, and impressive." Among the other roles he offered were Macbeth, Shylock, and Sir Giles Overreach. Unfortunately, his drinking marred many of his performances, and he soon dissipated the ardor with which he was first welcomed. Biography: *The Life of George Frederick Cooke*, William Dunlap. 1813.

COOPER, Marilyn (b. 1936), character actress. A busy, dowdy comic, Cooper's performances in musicals over forty years were usually singled out, often for stealing the show. A native New Yorker who was educated at New York University, she made her Broadway debut in 1956 and soon had small but featured roles in two musical classics: as Rosalia in *West Side Story* (1957) and Agnes in *Gypsy* (1959). She continued to find juicy supporting parts for decades, most memorably as the bedraggled housewife Jan Donovan in *Woman of the Year* (1981).

COOPER, Thomas Abthorpe (1776–1849), actor and manager. The son of an English surgeon, he had become a prominent young actor on the London stage when Thomas *Wignell persuaded him to come to America in 1796. He made his debut that year in Baltimore as Macbeth, later playing the same role in Philadelphia, which was his first American home. In 1797 Cooper made his New York debut as Pierre in *Venice Preserved*, followed by his Hamlet, a performance the *Commercial Advertiser* praised as "transcendently excellent." King John, Romeo, and Bland in *André* were other roles he essayed in Philadelphia, but when he fought with Wignell over assignments and salary, he moved to New York where he continued to enlarge his repertory both of classic works and contemporary pieces. He won special applause in the title part of The *Stranger* and in several plays by the newly popular *Kotzebue. After Dunlap went bankrupt, Cooper assumed the management of the *Park Theatre. Although *Ireland noted, "With a handsome face and noble person, a fine mellow voice, unusual dignity of manner and grace of action, and in his declamation most forcible and eloquent, as a tragedian he was without rival," many critics felt he was not totally professional, given as he was to waving and winking at friends in the audience and often failing properly to learn a part and requiring prompting. With time his popularity began to fade, but not before

playing Othello to Edwin *Forrest's Iago and managing the failing Chatham Theatre. His last New York appearance in 1835, at the age of sixty-one, was Antony in *Julius Caesar*. Cooper spent his last years as Inspector of the New York Custom House. Whatever his origins and failings, his acceptance of American citizenship has led to his generally being called the first great American tragedian. Biography: A *Memoir of the Professional Life of Thomas Abthorpe Cooper*, Joseph N. Ireland, 1888.

COPPERHEAD, THE (1918), a play by Augustus *Thomas. [*Shubert Theatre, 120 perf.] Milt Shanks (Lionel *Barrymore) is a reasonably prosperous farmer in southern Illinois at the time of the Civil War. His neighbors are certain that he is a Confederate sympathizer, possibly even a rebel spy. They cannot prove their suspicions, but circumstantial evidence is strong enough to turn even his wife and son against him. All through this Shanks remains silent. Not until decades later, when his behavior in the war is turned against his beloved granddaughter, does he reveal that the secret work he did was for the Northern cause. He has a letter to prove it—from a grateful Abraham Lincoln. Based on a story by Frederick Landis, the play is generally considered Thomas's last important work. Coming as it did during World War I, it was sometimes read as a plea for tolerance of pacifists and even apparent German sympathizers. A large measure of the success of the John D. *Williams production was attributable to Barrymore, considered his finest performance by many.

COQUETTE (1927), a play by George *Abbott and Ann Preston Bridgers. [Maxine Elliot's Theatre, 366 perf.] Norma Besant (Helen *Hayes), the quintessential giddy, flirtatious flapper, loves Michael Jeffrey (Eliot Cabot), a handsome, insolent, and at heart shiftless young man. When Norma's father, Dr. Besant (Charles *Waldron), refuses to consider Michael's request to marry Norma and angrily orders him out of the house, Michael blurts out that he and Norma have slept together, so Dr. Besant's objections no longer matter. The doctor shoots Michael, and, rather than face the physical examination that would almost certainly be demanded at her father's trial, Norma commits suicide. "A fragile and exquisite tragedy, a truly rare and touching evening in the theatre," was John Anderson's assessment in the *Evening Post*. The original idea for the play came from Bridgers, an actress who had worked with Abbott in several plays. Their earliest drafts treated the story as a comedy with a happy ending. Producer Jed *Harris demanded the revised treatment. Ironically, the play was forced to close when Hayes revealed she was pregnant with her "act of God" baby.

CORBETT, James J. (1866–1933), actor. The San Franciscan who won the world heavyweight championship by knocking out John L. Sullivan used his fame to become a stage and vaudeville celebrity for a time. His vehicles included the leads in such works as *Gentleman Jack* (1892) and *Cashel Byron's Profession* (1906), as well as playing the wrestler in *As You Like It* (1899).

CORBIN, John (1870–1959), critic. The Chicagoan was educated at Harvard and Oxford (England), then between 1896 and 1917 served stints as drama critic for *Harper's Weekly*, the New York *Sun*, and the *New York Times*. His views at the time were generally conservative and unexceptional, but he startled many admirers in 1933 when he wrote an article in *Scribner's Magazine* in which he blamed the lowering of standards in the theatre on the influx of Jews.

CORDELIA'S ASPIRATIONS (1883), a play with music by Edward *Harrigan (book, lyrics), David *Braham (music). [Theatre Comique, 176 perf.] When Cordelia Mulligan's jealous brother and sisters arrive in America, they are quick to plant seeds of ambition and discontent in her fertile mind. Before long Cordelia (Annie *Yeamans) has forced her husband, Dan (Harrigan), to leave their happy old home and to move uptown where Dan's easy, comfortable life gives way to Cordelia's starchy pretensions. Cordelia's brother Planxty (H. A. Fisher) overreaches himself when he attempts to trick his sister into signing away her property. Driven to distraction, Cordelia attempts suicide by gulping down a bottle of "Roach Poison" kept by her maid, Rebecca Allup (Tony *Hart) but the poison is simply Rebecca's secret cache of booze. The Mulligans are soon heading back to their old neighborhood. *Notable songs*: Dad's Dinner Pail; Mulligan Guard's March. The Harrigan and Hart production is generally acknowledged as the best in their series of plays dealing with the Mulligan family, Irish immigrants who have settled in the rough-and-tumble Irish ghettos of New York.

CORNELL, Katharine (1893–1974), actress and manager. The daughter of a onetime theatre manager, she was born in Berlin where her father had gone to study medicine, and made her stage debut with the *Washington Square Players in 1916. She afterward continued her apprenticeship in her hometown of Buffalo and in Detroit with Jessie *Bonstelle's stock company before calling attention to herself as the determined flapper Eileen Baxter-Jones in *Nice People* (1921). Further accolades came when she portrayed Sydney Fairfield, the daughter who stands by her mentally disturbed father, in *A Bill of Divorcement* (1921); as the lively Mary Fitton in *Will Shakespeare* (1923); and as the shy, homely Laura Pennington in *The Enchanted Cottage* (1923). Cornell's performance as Candida in 1924 consolidated her reputation, and was followed by two of her most sensational roles: the carnal, doomed Iris March in *The Green Hat* (1925) and Leslie Crosbie, who kills her lover, in *The Letter* (1927). Other successes at that time included Ellen Olenska in *The Age of Innocence* (1928) and Madeline Carey in *Dishonored Lady* (1930). With Guthrie *McClintic, whom she had married in 1921, Cornell embarked on a career as actress-manager, and scored her greatest triumph in her very first offering when she played Elizabeth Barrett in *The *Barretts of Wimpole Street* (1931). "By the crescendo of her playing," Brooks *Atkinson observed, "by the wild sensitivity that lurks behind her ardent gestures and her piercing stares across the footlights she charges the drama with a meaning beyond the facts it records." In 1934 she reprised her Elizabeth Barrett on tour, playing in seventy-seven cities in seven months. Among her subsequent roles were St. Joan in *Shaw's play, the tragic princess Oparre in *Wingless Victory* (1936), the playwright's wife Linda Esterbrook in *No Time for Comedy* (1939), Jennifer Dubedat in a 1941 revival of *The Doctor's Dilemma*, and her Masha in a 1942 revival of *The Three Sisters*. She then spent much of the war years playing Candida and Elizabeth Barrett for soldiers, followed by *Antigone* (1946), Shakespeare's Cleopatra (1947), Constance Middleton in *The Constant Wife* (1951), U. N. delegate Mary Prescott in *The Prescott Proposals* (1953), and the Countess in Christopher *Fry's *The Dark Is Light Enough* (1955). Her last appearance was as Mrs. Patrick *Campbell in *Dear Liar* (1960). Although Cornell seemed tall and regal on stage, she was not quite five feet seven inches, with dark hair, a dark complexion and broad features that were called Oriental and even negroid. With Lynn *Fontanne and Helen *Hayes, she was one of the great actresses of her era, and even though she hated performing, she was far more willing than either of her rivals to extend her range and attempt classics from the entire history of the theatre. Biography: *Leading Lady: The World and Theatre of Katharine Cornell*, Tad *Mosel with Gertrude Macy, 1978.

CORSICAN BROTHERS, THE (1852). A French melodrama in which a brother is prompted to avenge the death of his twin by that twin's ghost, it was first played in America in 1852 and held the stage for more than half a century in various adaptations, including those by Dion *Boucicault and Charles *Fechter. Among the more famous interpreters of Fabian and Louis de Franchi were

Edward *Eddy, J. A. J. *Neafie, Charles Kean, Fechter, F. C. Bangs, and Robert *Mantell.

CORT, John (1859–1929), manager and producer. The son of a Newark, New Jersey, minister, he entered the theatre over his father's objections, beginning as half of a vaudeville comedy team, Cort and Murphy. Before long, however, he abandoned performing to build his first theatre. Cort was so successful at the start that he soon had a major chain of vaudeville houses. When he lost his theatres through overexpansion he started again, this time building legitimate playhouses. As head of the Northwest Theatrical Circuit he dominated the theatre in his area. Later he expanded eastward, and eventually there were Cort Theatres in New York, Boston, and Chicago, as well as in San Francisco and throughout the West. He once claimed that over the years he had owned between two hundred and three hundred playhouses. He was also active as a producer, especially of musicals. Among his hits were Victor *Herbert's The Princess Pat (1915), Flo-Flo (1917), Listen Lester (1918), and *Shuffle Along (1921).

CORT THEATRE (New York). One of Broadway's smaller and most engaging theatres, the *Cort on West 48th Street was designed by Edward B. Corey to hold a thousand spectators comfortably in an auditorium in the style of Louis XVI. It was built by impresario John Cort and opened in 1912 with a resounding hit: *Peg o' My Heart starring Laurette *Taylor. Although it served as a television studio between 1969 and 1972, the playhouse has had a long history presenting nonmusical plays in an intimate setting.

COSTA, David (d. 1873), choreographer. After beginning his dancing career in the early 1840s in his native Italy, he turned to choreography about 1853 and soon was in demand in Rome, Florence, Naples, and other major cities. He came to America in 1866, and his ballets that year for The *Black Crook were credited with a large measure of the musical's phenomenal success. For the next several seasons, Costa was indisputably the leading Broadway choreographer, his dances seen in such musicals as The White Fawn (1868), *Humpty Dumpty (1868), Hiccory Diccory Dock (1869), and The Twelve Temptations (1870). He also served as dance director for the Globe Theatre, an early vaudeville house. Costa's work was totally in the classical romantic tradition, employing huge corps of dancers and using startling scenic effects to heighten its theatricality.

COTTEN, Joseph [Cheshire] (1905–94), actor. The gravelly voiced leading man was born in Peters-burg, Virginia, and had been on Broadway since 1930 before calling attention to himself as a member of the *Mercury Theatre. He later scored a major success as ex-husband C.K. Dexter Haven in The *Philadelphia Story (1939), then spent many years in films. Subsequently he played the misanthropic Linus Larrabee Jr., in *Sabrina Fair (1953), the temperamental conductor Victor Fabian in Once More, with Feeling (1958), and businessman Julian Armstrong in Calculated Risk (1962).

COTTRELLY, Mathilde [née Meyer] (1851–1933), singer and actress. Born in Hamburg, where her father was an opera conductor and several other family members were performers, she made her stage debut at the age of eight, and at sixteen she was singing important roles in contemporary light operas. Cottrelly also appeared in nonmusical plays and performed in circuses with her husband. In 1875, several years after her husband's death, she came to America, and within a few seasons she was a popular player in German-language productions at the Irving Place Theatre as well as in similar theatres around the country. Shortly thereafter she joined McCaull's Comic Opera Company, becoming not only its leading comedienne but also one of its leading directors and costume designers. Her business acumen was such that *McCaull made her his silent partner and generally allowed her to determine the company's budget and handle its finances. In the mid-1890s she abandoned musicals and embarked on a career as a character actress. Her first major role in this field was Mme. Vinard, the heroine's friend, in *Trilby (1895). Because of her accent she was often assigned Jewish parts and played in many of the comedies of the *Potash and Perlmutter series, making her final appearance in Potash and Perlmutter, Detectives (1926). Her most famous characterization was probably Mrs. Isaac Cohen, who can talk of little but her operation, in *Abie's Irish Rose (1922).

COULDOCK, C[harles] **W**[alter] (1815–98), actor. One of the leading character actors of the 19th century, he was born in London and decided on a stage career after watching *Macready perform. His professional debut occurred in 1836, then thirteen years later he came to America where playgoers first saw him in the title role of The *Stranger. After four seasons at Philadelphia's *Walnut Street Theatre, he embarked on a long tour as the old farmer Luke Fielding in The Willow Copse, a role he returned to as late as 1885. Couldock joined Laura *Keene's company in 1858 and later successfully essayed such roles as Iago and Hamlet. However, his most celebrated part was that of Dunstan Kirke, who unjustly banishes his daughter, in

Hazel Kirke (1880). Clara *Morris described the heavy-set, curly-haired actor as looking like "the beau-ideal wealthy farmer" and noted, "The strong point of his acting was in the expression of intense emotion—particularly grief or frenzied rage. He was utterly lacking in dignity, courtliness, or subtlety. He was best as a rustic."

COUNSELLOR-AT-LAW (1931), a play by Elmer *Rice. [*Plymouth Theatre, 397 perf.] George Simon (Paul *Muni) is an aggressive Lower East Sider who has clawed his way just about as far as a Jew could go in the legal profession of his day. With a probable eye to inching a few steps further, he marries a prominent, if cold, socialite. But his career is jeopardized when a bigoted society lawyer discovers that years before Simon had falsified evidence in a case. At the same time his wife runs off to Europe with her lover. Simon would jump from a window, but with the help of his sympathetic secretary, Regina (Anna Kostant), he unearths incriminating material about the society lawyer, presses him into silence, and concludes he can lead a happy life with the loyal Regina. Although some critics felt there was a superfluity of characters, and that many of them verged on caricature, Robert Coleman spoke for the majority when he wrote of the play in the *Daily News*, "It has an inspired fire, a dramatic, compelling surge, a human realism and sufficient comedy relief." The work was successfully revived in 1942.

COUNT JOANNES [né George Jones] (1810–79), actor. One of the more memorable and pathetic eccentrics of 19th-century American theatre, he is generally believed to have been born in London and brought to Boston while still a child, although he sometimes told interviewers that he was born at sea or was the son of a Boston policeman. He made his debut at Boston's *Federal Street Theatre in 1828, then moved to the *Bowery, at the time in its heyday, where he won acclaim as Richard III, Hamlet, and other tragic figures. In later years he played opposite such leading figures as *Forrest and Edwin *Booth, usually to solid acclaim. However, his eccentricities were noticeable almost from the start. Even early on he assumed all applause was for him and so took bows meant for his associates. In 1833 he announced that he had become Count of Sertorii of the Holy Roman Empire of the First Commander of the Imperial Order of Golden Knight and Count Palatine. Thereafter he was never seen in public without his full regalia, and his absurdities led to widespread publicity. In turn this led many playgoers to come to the theatre with the intention of scoffing, only to be impressed by his real skills. With time, however, his eccentricities became more flagrant and

audiences rowdier, forcing him to call the police to keep order. T. Allston *Brown described him as "of medium height, fine figure with an animated countenance, high forehead, expressive dark eyes, resolute chin, and fine, white, even teeth; he wore a heavy moustache, with a fresh and ruddy complexion."

COUNT OF MONTE CRISTO, THE. In this dramatization of Dumas's 1845 novel, a wrongly imprisoned Frenchman learns of a vast buried treasure, escapes from prison, finds the treasure, and comes to Paris to be revenged on those who imprisoned him. J. *Wallack was the first American to play the hero, Edmund Dantès, in 1848, and Edward *Eddy was a popular Dantès of the 1860s. Charles *Fechter made his own version about 1870, and for many years was considered the best interpreter of the Dantès role. However, in 1883 James *O'Neill, who had played in earlier versions, appeared in the Fechter redaction to great acclaim. Two years later he purchased the rights to it, made revisions, and thereafter was generally acknowledged as the greatest of all American Dantès.

COUNTRY GIRL, THE (1950), a play by Clifford *Odets. [*Lyceum Theatre, 235 perf.] Over the objections of his author and producer, Bernie Dodd (Steven Hill), a young director, hires Frank Elgin (Paul *Kelly) to star in a new play. Elgin had long since destroyed a promising career by drinking and blames his problems on his wife, Georgie (Uta *Hagen), whom he insists became a suicidal alcoholic after the death of their daughter. When Elgin goads Georgie into seeking a raise and long-term contract for him from Dodd, the director concludes she is also a meddler and orders her to stay away. But Elgin turns up on opening night too drunk to act and Dodd learns from Georgie that it is Elgin who is the real would-be suicide. Elgin sobers up in time to make a hit at the New York premiere. Although Georgie has grown to admire and even love Dodd, she realizes she must stay with her weakling husband. Praised by Howard Barnes of the *Herald Tribune* as "a fiercely affectionate anecdote about backstage doings," the Dwight Deere *Wiman production revealed Odets at his least sociopolitical. The drama has been revived several times, not always with success.

COUNTY CHAIRMAN, THE (1903), a comedy by George *Ade. [*Wallack's Theatre, 222 perf.] Jim Hackler (Maclyn *Arbuckle), the county chairman, is determined to defeat the shady Judge Rigby (Charles Fisher) in his bid for the prosecuting attorney's office. To that end he nominates his young partner, Tillford Wheeler (Earle Brown), to run against the judge. This creates a dilemma for Tillford, who loves Rigby's daughter, Lucy (Miriam Nesbitt). Hackler has a story that could destroy Rigby if given to the local paper, but the tearful pleas of Lucy and her mother prompt him to tear it up. Yet Tillford wins anyway. Typical of Ade's minor figures was the jingoistic Jefferson Briscoe (Edward Chapman). He has firm and belligerent opinions on the Bering Sea controversy, but when asked where the Bering Sea is, replies, "Don't make no difference where it is. The question is, air we, the greatest and most powerful nation of earth, goin' to set back and be bully-ragged an' hornswoggled by some Jim Crow island that looks, by ginger, like a freckle on the ocean!" Henry W. *Savage produced Ade's first nonmusical play. Arthur Hobson Quinn noted, "As is usual with Ade, the minor characters establish the atmosphere of the town and provide rather obvious comedy. The plot is of no real significance. What carried the play was the character study of Jim Hackler, who represents the politician that dominates his town by his personality . . . and has the saving grace of decency which marks him out from the herd."

COUNTY FAIR, THE (1889), a play by Charles Barnard. [Proctor's 23rd Street Theatre, 105 perf.] Aged Abigail Prue (Neil *Burgess) is in danger of losing her New England farm because she has not enough money to make payments on the mortgage. But she has a horse named Cold Molasses, and when she runs him in a race at the county fair, he wins the $3,000 she needs to buy back the mortgage. This makes everyone happy since Abigail is a nice old lady who has smoothed many a path to the altar for neighboring youngsters. A clean, homey comedy, featuring the era's leading female impersonator, it returned the following two seasons for even longer runs and remained in Burgess's repertory for over a decade. Barnard (1838?–1920), best known for his long association with Scribner's Monthly, was the author of a number of plays, including his collaboration with Henry C. *de Mille, The Main Line (1886).

COURAGE (1928), a comedy by Tom Barry. [Ritz Theatre, 280 perf.] The widowed Mary Colebrook (Janet *Beecher) brings her seven children east from Iowa in the hopes that the rich Massachusetts Colebrooks will help support and educate them. However, Caroline Colebrook (Helen Strickland) resents the fact that one of the children, Bill (Junior Durkin), is illegitimate and succeeds in alienating the other youngsters from their mother and brother. When Bill comes into an unexpected inheritance, Mary and he head back west, where Mary will wed Bill's father. For all the unpleasant

situations in the play, its treatment was essentially sentimental when not comic. It typifies the sort of theatre that could skim the surface of ugliness and still find a large market before the development of sound films, radio soap operas, and television.

COURTENAY, William [Leonard] (1875–1933), actor. Born in Worcester, Massachusetts, he made his stage debut with a traveling company that was playing Portland, Maine, in 1891. After seasons under the aegis of Richard *Mansfield, *Daniel, then Charles *Frohman, Courtenay became leading man to Virginia *Harned, whom he later married, and toured with in Iris, *Camille, and The Light That Lies in a Woman's Eyes. He scored his first major success as Walter Corbin in *Mrs. Leffingwell's Boots (1905), followed by the Duke of Charmerace in Arséne Lupin (1909), Stephen Baird in Ready Money (1912), and Bishop Armstron in *Romance. He began another long run as Stephen Denby in *Under Cover (1914), then turned to a wartime spy melodrama, Under Fire (1915). After playing the tramp in Pals First (1917) and Matt Peasley in Cappy Ricks (1919), a series of less successful plays followed until he enjoyed one final run as the vamped husband Tom Burton in David *Belasco's controversial production of The Harem (1924). His last appearance was as Governor Hazleton in the gangster melodrama The Inside Story (1932). Courtenay was essentially a matinee idol, but one of the handsomest and most durable. Oliver *Morosco felt "he had all the requisites of a star. His voice was perfectly modulated and his poise admirable. He knew how to reach a climax, how to put over comedy, and his intonations and transitions of speech were perfect." Women who came to gape cared little if critics such as Walter Prichard *Eaton considered him "sing-song and artificial," capable only of "playing himself."

COWARD, Noël [Peirce] (1899–1973), actor, playwright, and songwriter. The multitalented Englishman first appeared before American audiences in his own play, The Vortex (1925). He was a small, excessively suave man with a studiously clipped enunciation. Coward returned to America in his revue, This Year of Grace (1928), recalled for "A Room with a View." Subsequently he performed in *Private Lives (1931), Design for Living (1933), Tonight at 8:30 (1936), and Nude with Violin (1957). Among his other plays, in which he did not appear in this country, were Hay Fever (1925), Bitter Sweet (1929), Blithe Spirit (1941), Present Laughter (1946), Sail Away (1961), and, first seen on Broadway decades after his death, Waiting in the Wings (1999). At his peak, he represented to many Americans the ultimate in urbane Englishmen. Coward's life and works were celebrated in two Off-Broadway revues: *Oh, Coward!* (1972) and *If Love Were All* (1999). Autobiographies: *Present Indicative*, 1937; *Future Indefinite*, 1954; biography: *Remembered Laughter: The Life of Noël Coward*, Cole Lesley, 1976.

COWELL, Joe [né Joseph Hawkins Witchett] (1792–1863), actor. Born in Torquay, England, he hastily decided on a theatrical career after fleeing the Royal Navy rather than face a court-martial for striking an officer. Cowell made his acting debut in 1812 and had become a favorite at Drury Lane by the time he first appeared in America at the *Park Theatre in 1821. A small, round-faced, balding man, with large, circular eyes and a long, quizzical mouth, he excelled at comedy but was also adept at scene painting and playhouse managing. He spent several seasons at Philadelphia's *Walnut Street Theatre and was later one of the first actors to gain widespread recognition by touring even the smaller theatrical centers. Throughout his career his most-called-for role was the one in which he had made his American debut, *Crack in the Turnpike Gate*. Autobiography: *Thirty Years Passed Among the Players*, 1844.

COWL, Jane (1884–1950), actress. Born in Boston, she studied at Columbia then began her career under the aegis of David *Belasco, appearing first in his 1903 production of *Sweet Kitty Bellairs* and then in *The *Music Master, The *Rose of the Rancho, A *Grand Army Man, The *Easiest Way*, and *Is Matrimony a Failure?* Leaving Belasco, she became a major star as the wronged, vengeful Mary Turner in *Within the Law* (1912), then scored another success as another wronged woman: Ellen Neal in *Common Clay* (1915). Cowl starred in and co-wrote *Lilac Time* (1917), *Information Please* (1918), and the hugely successful tearjerker *Smilin' Through* (1919). Her classical roles included Juliet, Melisande, and Shakespeare's Cleopatra. Stark *Young observed in the *New Republic*, "Miss Cowl's Juliet is beautiful, first of all, to see. She is a child, a tragic girl, a woman convincing to the eye as few Juliets ever have had the good fortune to be." Her later successes included the mismarried heroine Larita in *Easy Virtue* (1925), the noble beauty Amytis in *The *Road to Rome* (1927), a puppet come to life in *The Jealous Moon* (1928), and the glamorous actress *Jenny* (1929). The failure of her Viola in 1930 signaled a series of disappointments before she again scored as Katherine Markham, the dedicated writer, in *Old Acquaintance* (1940). Her last appearance was in a 1947 revival of *The First Mrs. Fraser*. To the end she remained a slim, dark-haired, dark-eyed beauty, her eyes "so black, so limpid, it was a wonder they didn't dissolve and run down her cheeks."

COWLES, Eugene [Chase] (1860–1948), singer and actor. The Canadian-born basso was raised in Vermont and studied singing while working as a bank clerk in St. Paul. He then joined the *Boston Ideal Opera Company, remaining as their leading bass for several seasons. During his tenure he played Will Scarlet in the original *Robin Hood (1891), introducing "Brown October Ale." After leaving the group Cowles performed in *The *Fortune Teller* (1898), in which he sang "Gypsy Love Song," and later appeared in numerous *Gilbert and *Sullivan revivals.

CRABTREE, Charlotte [Mignon] (1847–1924), actress, singer, and dancer. The petite, redheaded, dark-eyed beauty, best known simply as Lotta, was one of the most successful and beloved of all American entertainers. Although born in New York, she was taken to California at the age of six. There she was befriended by the celebrated Lola *Montez, who taught her to sing and dance. She was soon plying her art in mining camps and small-town variety houses. Her first San Francisco appearance is believed to have been in 1858 in *The Loan of a Lover*. Her rise was relatively rapid, and with each year she added new works to her repertory, playlets that allowed her to exhibit the singing and dancing at which she excelled. Crabtree made her New York debut in 1864 in two of these playlets, *The Mysterious Chamber* and *Jenny Lind*. The critic for the *Herald* described her as "a very extended and most versatile talent. She plays the banjo with great spirit, and dances a breakdown in such style as to cause the star of the champion in that line to pale. Added to which Miss Lotta possesses a quick and ready repartee, which she launches at her audience with infinite grace." Her other New York appearances included *The Pet of the Petticoats* (1867), *Family Jars* (1867), and *Little Nell and the Marchioness* (1867). Among her other famous vehicles, in which she toured incessantly, were *Hearts Ease, or, What's Money Without; Musette, or, Little Bright Eyes; The Firefly, or, The Friend of the Flag*; and *Zip, or, Point Lynde Light*. All of these had basically melodramatic parts into which she interpolated her happy musical numbers. Retaining her youthful looks and vigor, she continued performing in these plays until her retirement in 1891. When she died, Crabtree left a $4 million estate. Biography: *The Triumphs and Trials of Lotta Crabtree*, David Dempsey with Raymond P. Baldwin, 1968.

CRADLE SNATCHERS (1925), a comedy by Russell Medcraft and Norma Mitchell. [*Music Box Theatre, 485 perf.] Having caught her own husband lunching with an attractive flapper, Kitty Ladd (Margaret Dale) has no trouble convincing her friends Susan Martin (Mary *Boland) and Ethel Drake (Edna May Oliver) that their husbands' sporting weekends are not what they're made out to be. They invite three attractive college boys to a party of their own where the champagne flows freely and before long all six are tipsy and not a little disorderly. Of course, the husbands walk in at this very moment. An uproar ensues, but in the end the boys go off to seek younger women and the married couples are pleasantly, if not irrevocably, chastened. The Sam H. *Harris and Hassard *Short–produced comedy was hailed by Walter *Winchell in the *Graphic* as "unquestionably the funniest play in town." Many critics gave their brightest adjectives to the performance of Humphrey Bogart as one of the college boys. **Russell Graham MEDCRAFT** (1897?–1962) was an actor, director, and playwright. This was his only major play. However, his partner, Norma Mitchell (d. 1967), an actress and playwright, enjoyed a second hit when she collaborated with her husband, Wilbur Daniel Steele, on *Post Road* (1934), a comedy melodrama about a kidnapping. *Cradle Snatchers* was made into the successful musical *LET'S FACE IT!* (1941) with book by Herbert and Dorothy *Fields, and music and lyrics by Cole *Porter. Its cast included Danny *Kaye, Eve Arden, Mary Jane Watson, Benny Baker, Vivian Vance, and Nanette *Fabray. *Notable songs*: Farming; Let's Not Talk About Love; Ace in the Hole. The musical opened at the *Imperial Theatre and ran for 547 performances.

CRADLE WILL ROCK, THE (1938), a musical drama by Marc *Blitzstein (book, music, lyrics). [Windsor Theatre, 108 perf.] Steeltown is run by the rich, greedy Mr. Mister (Will Geer) who dominates not merely the town's industry but its press, its church, and its social organization. Larry Foreman (Howard *da Silva) organizes the workers into a union and fights for the cause of the little man. *Notable songs*: The Cradle Will Rock; Nickle Under the Foot. This leftist view of the world through red-colored glasses has a curious history. Dropped as a WPA project in Washington, its 1937 New York premiere was stopped by an injunction. Led by *Mercury Theatre producer John *Houseman and director Orson *Welles, the cast and audience trekked twenty blocks to another, vacant, theatre where the players, to circumvent the injunction, performed from seats in the theatre. Because the musicians' union refused to cooperate, Blitzstein played the score from an onstage piano. After a series of special matinees, the musical was allowed to begin a regular run at the tiny Windsor. In the climate of the time its radical position won some support, but a 1947 revival was dismissed as an "angry, theatrical prank" and

quickly folded. Later Off-Broadway revivals have sometimes received better press yet have failed to find a large audience.

CRAIG'S WIFE (1925), a drama by George *Kelly. [*Morosco Theatre, 360 perf.; Pulitzer Prize.] Harriet Craig (Chrystal *Herne) is a woman obsessed with her home and her possessions. She will not even allow her husband to smoke in the house, lest he stain or mar something. Luckily Walter Craig (Charles Trowbridge) is blind to her faults; but his maiden aunt, Miss Austen (Anne Sutherland), is anything but blind, and she warns Harriet her obsession will cost her all her friends and her family as well: "other people will not go on being made miserable indefinitely for the sake of your ridiculous idolatry of house furnishings." Matters are brought to a head not by a piece of furniture but by the suicide of a neighbor. Walter would call the police to offer help, since he visited the man's home shortly before the suicide. Harriet, however, will not permit her name to be brought in, even indirectly. In a fury Walter breaks one of Harriet's favorite knickknacks, then sits down to enjoy a cigarette. Both Walter and his aunt leave, taking the housekeeper with them. Alexander *Woollcott wrote in the *World*, "*Craig's Wife* is a thorough, unsmiling, patiently detailed and profoundly interesting dramatic portrait of a woman whom every playgoer will recognize with something of a start and yet whose prototype has never before appeared in any book or play that has passed my way." Its only major revival, in 1947, was unsuccessful.

CRANE, William H[enry] (1845–1928), actor. A native of Leicester, Massachusetts, he made his debut in 1863 as the Notary in *The Daughter of the Regiment* in Harriet Holman's touring company, with which he remained for eight seasons. He then played low comedian roles with the Alice Oates Light Opera. In 1874 Crane created the role of Le Blanc, another Notary, in the original *Evangeline*. Three years later he was first teamed with **Stuart ROBSON** [né Henry Robson Stuart] (1836–1903). Robson was born in Annapolis and made his acting debut in Baltimore in 1852. The comic actor performed with Laura *Keene's company in New York, with Mrs. *Drew at the *Arch Street Theatre in Philadelphia, and with William *Warren in Boston before his celebrated partnership with Crane that would survive until 1889. Their initial success was as the quarreling neighbors in *Our Boarding House* (1877), followed by *The Comedy of Errors* (1878, revived 1885), *Our Bachelors* (1878), *Sharps and Flats* (1880), *Twelfth Night* (1881), *My Mother-in-Law* (1884), and their biggest success, *The *Henrietta* (1887). After the team split, Crane continued to act until 1917. Among his most notable later roles were the manipulative, but sympathetic Hannibal Rivers in *The *Senator* (1890), the seemingly innocent W. Farragut Gurney in *For Money* (1892), and the likable horse-trader *David Harum* (1900). Robson continued to appear in some of his old roles, as well as in such vehicles as *The Meddler* (1898) and *The Gadfly* (1899). In the latter he was praised for his "wooden countenance, his staccato utterance, and his long familiar squeak." In an age when many a clergyman regularly railed at theatre people, Robson took pleasure in maintaining a scrapbook filled with published accounts of erring ministers. Autobiography (Crane): *Footprints and Echoes*, 1927.

CRAVEN, Frank (1875–1945), actor and playwright. Born in Boston, he was the son of actors and made his first stage appearance with them as a child in *The Silver King* in 1887. Although Craven made his New York debut in *Artie* (1908), he did not create a stir until he appeared as the parasitic brother-in-law Jimmy Gilley in *Bought and Paid For* (1911). He followed this by playing the newlywed Albert Bennett in his own play *Too Many Cooks* (1914). Lesser successes came in *Under Fire* (1915), and *Seven Chances* (1916) before he enjoyed a long run as the reluctant flyer Robert Street in the musical *Going Up!* (1917). His own fine comedy, *The *First Year* (1920), afforded him the chance to play another young husband, Thomas Tucker. For several years thereafter Craven seemingly had little luck, having only a modest run as the golf-addicted writer Vernon Chase in his own play *The Nineteenth Hole* (1927). He found himself in bigger hits as the good Samaritan Robert Grant in *That's Gratitude* (1930) and as the crime reporter Kirk in *Riddle Me This* (1932), which he also directed. In the same season he also directed the comedy hit *Whistling in the Dark*. Virtually his last major assignment was one of his finest, the Stage Manager in *Our Town* (1938). His final appearance was as the former president in *Mrs. January and Mr. X* (1944).

CRAWFORD, Cheryl (1902–86), producer. Born in Akron, Ohio, she started her theatrical career by staging plays while a student at Smith College. She later worked for the *Theatre Guild before helping to found the *Group Theatre in 1931 where she directed *The House of Connelly* (1931) and several other plays. Crawford's first successful independent production after leaving the Group Theatre was a 1942 revival of *Porgy and Bess*. Among her later productions were *One Touch of Venus* (1943), *The *Tempest* (1944), *Brigadoon* (1947), *The *Rose Tattoo* (1951), *Paint Your Wagon* (1951), *Oh, Men! Oh, Women!* (1953), and *Sweet Bird of Youth* (1959).

While working as an independent producer she was also a founder of the short-lived *American Repertory Theatre, a founder of the *Actors Studio, and Joint-General Director of the *ANTA play series. Autobiography: *One Naked Individual*, 1977.

CRAZY FOR YOU. See *Girl Crazy*.

CREWS, Laura Hope (1880–1942), actress. She began her career as a child performer in her native San Francisco where she played for many years in stock before coming to New York in 1901. Crews started to attract notice when she appeared as Rosie Leadbetter in *Merely Mary Ann* (1903) and as Evelyn Kenyon in *Brown of Harvard* (1906). For the next several seasons she was a prominent member of Henry *Miller's company, then she played Beatrice in *Much Ado About Nothing*, (1913) and the daydreaming Louise Marshall in *The Phantom Rival* (1914). Walter Prichard Eaton said of her performance, "She has, to a degree possessed by almost no other player of her age on our stage, the technical command of her trade . . . [she] plays Louise, the wife, with a skill, a variety, a force and a charm that delight the soul." Although she regularly earned such praise and remained a sought-after performer, Crews never quite became a star of the first rank. Among her later roles were Mistress Page in a 1916 Boston revival of *The Merry Wives of Windsor;* Mrs. Deane in *Peter Ibbetson* (1917); Olivia Marden, who may have entered a bigamous marriage inadvertently, in *Mr. Pim Passes By* (1921); Dora Faber in the comedy *The Changelings* (1923); Judith Bliss in *Hay Fever* (1925); the possessive mother Mrs. Phelps in *The *Silver Cord* (1926); Amalia in *Right You Are If You Think You Are* (1927); and the flighty Aunt Min in *Her Master's Voice* (1933). Her last Broadway appearance was in *Save Me the Waltz* in 1938, although in 1941 she headed a road company of *Arsenic and Old Lace*.

CRIMES OF THE HEART (1981), a play by Beth Henley. [*John Golden Theatre, 535 perf.; Pulitzer Prize, NYDCC Award.] The story depicts a day in the life of three unhappy Mississippi sisters. Babe (Mia Dillon) is out on bail after shooting her husband because she "didn't like his looks." Meg (Mary Beth Hurt) is a failed singer who has spent more time in psychiatric wards than in performing. Spinsterish Lenny (Lizbeth Mackay) is unloved and frustrated. The sisters are not alone in their troubles; their family history is dismal, including a mother who hung herself and her cat. They are helped by Babe's lawyer, Barnette Lloyd (Peter MacNicol) but must rely on their strong family loyalty to see them through. Another in the sort of Chekovian-style plays that have long been popular and which Max Beerbohm once classified as "adramatic," it nevertheless was written with great warmth and wit. The tragicomedy originated at the *Actors Theatre of Louisville, was presented Off Broadway by the *Manhattan Theatre Club, and then reopened on Broadway. Frank *Rich wrote in the *Times*, "Be grateful that we have a new writer from hurricane country who gives her characters room to spin and spin and spin." **Beth HENLEY** (b. 1952) was born in Jackson, Mississippi, and attended Southern Methodist University and the University of Illinois. Her other plays, including *The Wake of Jamie Foster* (1982), *The Miss Firecracker Contest* (1984), *The Lucky Spot* (1986), *Abundance* (1990), and *Impossible Marriage* (1998), have been less successful.

CRIMINAL CODE, THE (1929), a melodrama by Martin *Flavin. [National Theatre, 174 perf.] Robert Graham (Russell Hardie), an amiable brokerage clerk, is sent to prison by the state's attorney, Martin Brady (Arthur *Byron), for a murder that Graham insists was self-defense. " 'An eye for an eye,' That's the basis and foundation of our criminal code," Brady tells the young man, although the attorney is not without sympathy for the man's plight. Six years later, Graham has remained a model prisoner, although his spirit is broken. Brady's daughter, Mary (Anita Kerry), works at the prison and has taken a liking to Graham and prevailed on her father to seek his parole. But when another prisoner is killed, Graham, accepting the fact that there is a code among criminals, refuses to testify. Mary, her father, and the prison officials beg and cajole, but Graham will not budge. Moved, they proceed with the parole, which is granted. But one cruel prison officer, Gleason (Leo Curley), beats Graham, who kills him in reprisal. There is nothing now that anyone can do for Graham. "It's just the way things break sometimes," a stunned Brady tells his daughter. Quite possibly the best of all American prison dramas, William *Harris Jr.'s production was hailed by Burns *Mantle as "a thoughtful study, not only of our methods of prison conduct and corrective punishments, but also of the normal reactions, of both prisoners and keepers, to the law, to the system, and to their respective codes." **Martin [Archer] FLAVIN** (1883–1967) was born in San Francisco, raised in Chicago where he attended the University of Chicago, and spent several years as a businessman before seriously turning his hand to playwriting. Two of his one-act dramas were produced on Broadway in 1921 and his first full-length play to reach New York was *Children of the Moon* (1923). During the 1929–30 season, three of Flavin's plays reached New York and all three won substantial critical

endorsement: *The Criminal Code, Broken Dishes*, and *Cross Roads*. Few of his later works were popular, so Flavin turned to writing novels and was successful.

CROMWELL, John (1887–1979), actor, director, and producer. A native of Toledo, Ohio, his theatre career spanned nearly three-quarters of a century. After making his debut in 1907 with the R. C. Herz stock company in Cleveland, Cromwell toured for three years before coming to New York in 1910 to appear in *Baby Mine*. He next spent several seasons as director and actor with William A. *Brady, then embarked on his own. Among the many plays he directed were *The *Man Who Came Back* (1916), *At 9:45* (1919), *The Law Breaker* (1922), *The *Silver Cord* (1926), and *Yankee Point* (1942). He produced such works as *Oh, Mama!* (1925) and *Lucky Sam McCarve* (1925), appearing as the title character Sam in the latter. Cromwell's other performances of note include Babe Callahan in the Chicago company of *Ned McCobb's Daughter* (1926), Captain McQuigg in *The *Racket* (1927), John Gray in *Point of No Return* (1951), Linus Larrabee in *Sabrina Fair* (1953), and Oscar Nelson in *Mary, Mary* (1961). In his later years he directed at the *Cleveland Play House and acted at both the *Guthrie Theatre and the *Long Wharf Theatre. He was also active as a director of films.

CRONYN, Hume (1911–2003), actor and director. A small man with a long face and prominent mouth and teeth, he was born in London, Ontario. After performing in Canada and in stock in Washington, D.C., he took additional training at the *American Academy of Dramatic Arts and elsewhere, then joined the *Barter Theatre as performer and director. Early Broadway appearances were in *Hipper's Holiday* (1934), *Boy Meets Girl* (1936), *Room Service* (1937), *High Tor* (1937), and *The Three Sisters* (1939). In 1950 Cronyn directed *Hilda Crane*, which starred his wife, Jessica *Tandy, and thereafter appeared with her as Michael in the two-character *The *Fourposter* (1951), and as the devil Dr. Brightlee in *Madam, Will You Walk* (1953). He created the role of Jimmy Luton, the fussy art teacher, in *Big Fish, Little Fish* (1961) before spending a few seasons with his wife at the *Guthrie Theatre in Minneapolis and playing classical roles. His Polonius in the Richard *Burton *Hamlet* (1964) won him a *Tony Award. Among Cronyn's many other memorable productions with Tandy were *A *Delicate Balance* (1966), *Noel Coward in Two Keys* (1974), *The *Gin Game* (1977), *Foxfire* (1982), and *The Petition* (1986).

CROSMAN, Henrietta [Foster] (1861–1944), actress. A native of Wheeling, West Virginia, she made her first appearance on the stage in 1883 as Lily in The *White Slave. She was an attractive, if slightly pouty-faced actress, who rose rapidly in ever more important roles as she moved from one major management to another. By the turn of the century she had performed for Augustin *Daly, both *Daniel and Charles *Frohman, and A. M. *Palmer. However, it was not until she approached middle age that she achieved stardom in the role of Nell Gwynne in *Mistress Nell (1900), a performance that was generally acknowledged as one of the sensations of the season. In 1902 she enjoyed praise and a long run as Rosalind in *As You Like It, then the next year she was acclaimed as the wily Irish heroine of *Sweet Kitty Bellairs. Thereafter she toured successfully in such plays as All-of-a-Sudden Peggy, The Christian Pilgrim, Anti-Matrimony, and The Real Thing, although their New York stands were short. For many years she alternated between vaudeville and the legitimate theatre, then in her last active years she played prominent roles in several all-star revivals, including The School for Scandal, The *Two Orphans, Trelawny of the Wells, The Merry Wives of Windsor, and The Beaux Stratagem. Her final New York appearance was in Thunder in the Air (1929), although she continued to act until shortly before her death. In Sixty Years of Theatre, J. Rankin *Towse suggested, "Henrietta Crosman is an actress who is entitled to more general critical and popular appreciation than she has obtained. She is an exceedingly bright and capable performer, of considerable range and much technical expertness. . . . Her Nell Gwynn . . . will long be remembered for its variety, its animation, its delightful deviltry, and its general fascination."

CROTHERS, Rachel (1878–1958), playwright. Born in Bloomington, Illinois, she had dabbled at playwriting before she entered the State Normal School of Illinois. After studying acting at the Stanhope-Wheatcroft School and performing professionally for several seasons, Crothers abandoned acting when her first play, Nora (1903), was produced. Her first successful work was The *Three of Us (1906), a story of a spunky sister who protects her brothers' interests in a Nevada mine. Several subsequent plays had short runs before she had better luck with A Man's World (1910), Young Wisdom (1914), Old Lady 31 (1916), A *Little Journey (1918), and 39 East (1919). Crothers then hit her stride with a series of plays that explored the roles men and women played in contemporary society: *He and She (1920), *Nice People (1921), *Mary the Third (1923), *Expressing Willie (1924), A Lady's Virtue (1925), Venus (1927), *Let Us Be Gay (1929), As Husbands Go (1931), and *When Ladies Meet (1932). Her last play was *Susan and God (1937), describing the problems that ensue when a rich matron discovers religion. During World War I Crothers founded *Stage Women's War Relief. She was a consummate craftsman, who, as Howard Taubman noted, "used the stage to articulate the case for woman's freedom. When the battle was won, she did not shrink from poking fun at the liberated woman's pretensions."

CROUSE, Russel. See Lindsay and Crouse.

CROWLEY, Mart. See Boys in the Band, The.

CRUCIBLE, THE (1953), a play by Arthur *Miller. [Martin Beck Theatre, 197 perf.; Tony Award.] Abigail Williams (Madeleine Sherwood), the promiscuous niece of the Reverend Samuel Parris (Fred Stewart), is employed by John Proctor (Arthur Kennedy) until Proctor's wife, Elizabeth (Beatrice *Straight), fires her. In revenge she accuses Elizabeth of being a witch. In the highly charged climate of 1692 Salem, her charges are given ample credence. Proctor comes to his wife's defense, but in the process admits to adultery with Abigail. Hoping to save his own life, he signs a confession, but soon recants and is sentenced to death by Deputy-Governor Danforth (Walter *Hampden), thereby finding redemption for himself. The Kermit *Bloomgarden production boasted a strong cast under the direction of Jed *Harris. Appearing at the height of the McCarthy era, the play was perceived as a thinly veiled indictment of McCarthy and his followers. Time felt the work demonstrated "more fieriness of purpose than vision. . . . The material seems not there for the sake of the play, but the play for the sake of the material." Yet the passage of time suggests that the drama, for all its preachiness, may have more universal and permanent validity than any other of Miller's works. Aside from hundreds of productions in regional and academic theatres, there have been noteworthy New York revivals in 1958, 1964, 1972, and 1991.

CRUZ, Nilo. See Anna in the Tropics.

CRYER, Gretchen. See I'm Getting My Act Together . . .

CULLUM, John (b. 1930), actor and singer. The Knoxville native studied at the University of Tennessee before understudying Richard *Burton in *Camelot and playing Laertes to Burton's *Hamlet (1964). The full-voiced, blond-haired leading man replaced the principal players in several musicals before finding acclaim in the central role of pacifist farmer Charlie Anderson in *Shenandoah (1975). Among his many noteworthy performances were the psychiatrist Mark Bruckner in On a Clear Day

You Can See Forever (1965), flamboyant producer Oscar Jaffe in the musical *On the Twentieth Century* (1978), Victor in the 1983 Burton-Taylor revival of *Private Lives,* the tennis buff Gus in *Doubles* (1985), a 50-year-old Tom Sawyer in *The Boys in Autumn* (1986), the tormented Joe Keller in *All My Sons* (1997), and the monopolist Caldwell B. Caldwell in *Urinetown* (2001).

CUMBERLAND, John (1880–?), comic actor. The Canadian-born performer began his career in 1900 playing opposite Sol Smith *Russell. He was a short, balding man with a round face and puzzled mien whose brief heyday came when he played the central male roles in a number of slam-bang sex farces: *Twin Beds* (1914), *Fair and Warmer* (1915), *Parlor, Bedroom and Bath* (1917), *Up in Mabel's Room* (1919), and *Ladies' Night* (1920). Cumberland's career faltered when the vogue for this sort of farce waned, and he dropped out of the public eye.

CUMMINGS, Constance [neé Halveerstadt] (b. 1910), actress. Cummings is a classy leading lady often mistaken for an English actress since she spent much of her time in London. She was born in Seattle and by the age of sixteen was in stock productions, later appearing in the chorus of Broadway musicals and finding recognition as the secretary-turned-actress Linda in *Accent on Youth* (1934). While some gratifying Broadway engagements followed, it was in England that Cummings came into her own, playing classic roles at the *Old Vic and, later, the *National Theatre. Perhaps her most memorable New York performances came near the end of her career: the stroke victim Emily Stilson in *Wings* (1978) and the demanding Mrs. St. Maugham in *The Chalk Garden* (1982).

CURRAN, Homer F. (1885–1952), producer. Called at his death the "dean of West Coast theatrical producers," he was born in Springfield, Missouri, and attended Stanford University, where he developed an interest in theatre. He later purchased the Cort Theatre in San Francisco, but sold it after he built the Curran Theatre in 1922. When the Great Depression discouraged New York producers from taking their plays to California, Curran, in association with Fred Butler and Edward Belasco, brother of David *Belasco, regularly bought the rights for new (and older) plays and mounted them for Western tours. As a result he is generally credited with retaining interest in live theatre on the West Coast. In 1939 he founded the San Francisco Light Opera Company, later combining it with Edwin *Lester's Los Angeles Light Opera Company. Curran collaborated on the writing of *Song of Norway* (1944) and *Magdalena* (1948),

which his and Lester's joint company produced. He also brought to New York his highly successful 1946 revival of *Lady Windermere's Fan.*

CUSHING, Catherine Chisholm (1874–1952), playwright. Born in Mt. Perry, Ohio, she scored a modest success with her first comedy, *The Real Thing* (1911). After writing *Widow by Proxy* (1913) for May *Irwin, she enjoyed a smash hit with *Kitty Mackay* (1913), the story of a Scottish girl who falls in love with her half-brother. Also successful were *Jerry* (1914), a vehicle for Billie *Burke, and her adaptation of Eleanor Porter's novel *Pollyanna* (1916). While many of Cushing's subsequent plays never reached New York, she had better luck as a librettist and lyricist. Her musical credits include *Glorianna* (1918), *Lassie* (1920), *Marjolaine* (1922), and *Topsy and Eva* (1923), a musical version of *Uncle Tom's Cabin* that was written for the *Duncan Sisters and was one of the most profitable musicals of the decade.

CUSHMAN, Charlotte [Saunders] (1816–76), actress. A relatively tall, burly, homely woman, she is generally acknowledged as the first great tragedienne of the American stage. Born in Boston and descended from several old, distinguished New England families, she is believed to have been self-educated. Cushman had intended to become an opera singer, but when her singing voice gave out she turned to acting, making her debut in New York in 1835 as Lady Macbeth, a role afterward considered among her finest. She caused a stir in 1837 when she essayed Romeo, thus displaying early on a penchant for men's roles that persisted almost until the end of her career. That same year she first performed the role much of her public most admired her for, Meg Merrilies in the popular dramatization of *Guy Mannering.* Mary *Anderson recalled, "When, in the moonlight of the scene, she dashed from her tent on to the stage, covered with the gray, shadowy garments of the gypsy sibyl, her appearance was ghost-like and startling in the extreme. In her mad rushes on and off stage she was like a cyclone.... When Dick Hatterick's fatal bullet entered her body, and she came staggering down the stage, her terrible shriek, so wild and piercing, so full of agony and yet of the triumph she had given her life to gain, told the whole story of her love and her revenge." In the fall of 1837 she became a member of the *Park Theatre Company, where her roles included Goneril, Emilia, and Volumnia to Edwin *Forrest's Coriolanus. She first played another of her famous roles, Nancy Sykes in *Oliver Twist,* in 1839. "The horror of her death scene was unmatched," *Odell recorded years later. In 1841 she was the first American Lady Gay

Spanker. After briefly managing Philadelphia's *Walnut Street Theatre, Cushman performed with *Macready in 1844. He saw in her a fine but imperfect actress, so advised her to improve her art in London, where she spent the next several years. When she returned to America in 1852 she had added one more of her celebrated interpretations, Katherine in Shakespeare's *Henry VIII*, and another of her controversial portrayals of men: Claude Melnotte in The *Lady of Lyons*. She continued to play actively until 1857, when she announced her "farewell" tour, the first of several of these during her career, bringing her a share of unnecessary ridicule. Her repertory was extensive, including Beatrice, Rosalind, Bianca, and Pauline (in *The Lady of Lyons*) as well as important roles in contemporary plays. She also continued to play men's parts, eventually adding Hamlet and Cardinal Wolsey to her list. Her last New York appearance was as Lady Macbeth in 1874. During her final years age and ill health plagued her, so she often abandoned traditional acting in favor of readings. Although there was little dissent about the greatness of her acting, especially in serious and tragic roles, some controversy exists about her personality. Most published recollections are highly favorable, recalling her consideration and charity, but several associates remember her peculiarly masculine hardness and her occasional slugging of performers who annoyed her. In 1907 a club was established in Philadelphia as a hostel for traveling actresses and gathering place for theatrical aficionados. Named in her honor, it houses a collection of her personal memorabilia. Biography: *Bright Particular Star*, Joseph Leach, 1970.

CYRANO DE BERGERAC. This tale of a huge-nosed, comic-tragic poseur, who is so homely he must woo by proxy, remains one of the great French romantic plays of the late 19th century. *Rostand's work was first presented in New York by Richard *Mansfield in 1898 and by Augustin *Daly in Philadelphia with a cast headed by Charles J. *Richman, Ada *Rehan, and Mrs. *Gilbert. Within a month of its opening, *Weber and *Fields presented their famous spoof, *Cyranose de Bric-a-Brac*, while in 1899 Victor *Herbert's failed musical version was produced with Francis *Wilson as its star. Walter *Hampden revived the play in 1923 and returned to it at intervals. In 1946 José *Ferrer led a successful revival. Two other musical versions, in 1973 and 1993, both failed, although Christopher *Plummer was highly praised in the former. The *Royal Shakespeare Company's revival, with Derek Jacobi, earned rave notices in 1984, while Frank *Langella had one of his rare disappointments when he essayed Cyrano in 1997.

D

DA COSTA, Morton [né Tecosky] (1914–89), director and actor. Born in Philadelphia, he was educated at Temple University and served as president of the Templers, later teaching at Temple's School of the Theatre. Da Costa worked with Clare Tree *Major's Children's Theatre and in 1937 co-founded the Civic Repertory Theatre in Dayton, Ohio. He made his New York debut as an actor, playing the Broadcast Official in The *Skin of Our Teeth (1942). Among his other roles were Osric in Maurice *Evans's *Hamlet (1945) and Henry Straker in *Man and Superman (1949). His first New York directorial assignments were at the New York *City Center, where he staged The Alchemist (1948), She Stoops to Conquer (1949), Captain Brassbound's Conversion (1950), *Dream Girl (1951), and The Wild Duck (1951). His Broadway credits included *Plain and Fancy (1955), *No Time for Sergeants (1955), *Auntie Mame (1956), The *Music Man (1957), Saratoga (1959), Maggie Flynn (1968), and a revival of The *Women (1973). Although Da Costa was one of the finest directors of his era, no singular characteristic of style differentiates him from his leading competitors.

DA SILVA, Howard [né Herbert Silverblatt] (1909–86), character actor. The deep-voiced, bulky Da Silva, who could play heavies as well as twinkling teddy bears, was also a respected director, producer, and playwright but will always be most remembered for his sterling performances in musicals. He was born in Cleveland, the son of a tailor and a suffragette. He grew up in the Bronx, then the family moved to Pittsburgh, where Da Silva worked in a steel mill to pay for his education at Carnegie Tech. He made his New York debut in 1929 with the *Civic Repertory Theatre and got his first significant role as the everyman-like Larry Foreman in the legendary agitprop musical The *Cradle Will Rock (1937), then solidified his reputation as the lonely but dangerous farmhand Jud in the original *Oklahoma! (1943). Other notable New York performances include a dandy Volpone (1957), the prosecutor Horn in Compulsion (1957), the corrupt politician Ben Marino in *Fiorello! (1958), the jingle-laden Archbishop in The Unknown Soldier and His Wife (1967), and the sly old Benjamin Franklin in *1776 (1969).

DADDIES (1918), a comedy by John L. Hobble. [*Belasco Theatre, 340 perf.] Several confirmed bachelors, who insist "marriage was made for women" and who dread the thought of raising children, nevertheless are talked into adopting war orphans. Their experiences vary, with one of them finding himself saddled with triplets, and several, on coming to care for the tots, agreeing to wed the mothers when they are found. But one bachelor, the writer Robert Aubrey (Bruce *McRae), is disconcerted to discover that his orphan is not a tot but a seventeen-year-old beauty, Ruth Atkins (Jeanne *Eagels). She not only persuades him to turn his writing skills toward helping the orphans' cause but wins his love in the process. During the war, David *Belasco produced a number of successful comedies such as this, a departure from his more serious earlier productions. But his sense of production values remained steadfast. George *Abbott, who in only his second Broadway acting experience was cast as the bachelor with the triplets, recalled that in the first act soda siphons sometimes drowned out actors' laugh lines. When the actors complained to Belasco he replied, "I'd rather lose three laughs than lose the atmosphere created by that sound."

DADDY LONG-LEGS (1914), a comedy by Jean Webster. [Gaiety Theatre, 264 perf.] The selfish superintendent of the John Grier Home for Orphans has refused to allow Judy Abbott (Ruth *Chatterton) to be adopted, telling prospective parents that the girl is incorrigibly selfish; but she really wants to keep her on as a drudge and to help raise the younger children. One day in front of all the trustees Judy rebels, arguing, "I can make my own way in the world. Just give me a chance." One fortyish trustee, Jervis Pendleton (Charles *Waldron), is so impressed that he quietly insists the girl be sent to college at his expense. At first Judy does not know who her benefactor is. She has seen him only briefly, when the lights of his limousine cast his elongated shadow on the ground, so she calls him Daddy Long-Legs. In time they meet, with Judy still unaware of his role in her life, and fall in love. The romance grows, and only after Judy at first rejects his proposal of marriage does Jervis reveal his full identity. The warmly written comedy was one of the major hits of its day and made Chatterton a star. Actor-producer Henry *Miller, sensing this beforehand, decided not to play the role of Pendleton lest he steal the limelight. **Jean WEBSTER** [Mrs. Glen Ford McKinney] (1876–1916) was born in Fredonia, New York, and was known primarily as a novelist. She adapted this, her only successful play, from one of her own books.

DAILEY, Peter F. (1868–1908), comic actor. The hefty but nimble farceur, famous for his humorous ad-libs, made his debut as a child dancer at the Globe Theatre in his native New York in 1876. Following a brief stint with a circus, he became one of "The American Four," a popular vaudeville act for many years. In 1884 he joined the *Howard Athenaeum company in Boston and remained there for three seasons. He earned New York's praise by virtually stealing *A Straight Tip* (1891) from its star, James T. *Powers, with his performance as Jack Postand Poole, a race track habitué. So pleased was author J. J. *McNally that he wrote two starring vehicles for Dailey: *A Country Sport* (1893) and *The Night Clerk* (1895). Dailey joined Weber and *Fields in 1897 and was a favorite in their celebrated burlesques. He left that troupe to star as Rudolf Roastemsum in *Hodge, Podge, and Co.* (1900), then scored a major success as Benton Scoops, whose excursion-boat party is hijacked to South America, in *The Press Agent* (1905). His last appearances were for his old associates, first in Fields's revue *About Town* (1906), then in Weber's *The Merry Widow Burlesque* (1908). Weber and Fields's biographer, Felix Isman, eulogized Dailey as: "Inimitable Peter! Born comedian, the quickest-witted man that ever used grease paint; splendid voice; an acrobat and agile dancer despite his two hundred and fifty pounds; no performance ever the same; needing neither lines nor business, but only to be given the stage."

DAISY MAYME (1926), a comedy by George *Kelly. [Playhouse, 112 perf.] Cliff Mettinger (Carlton Brickert) is a forty-three-year-old real estate broker and a bachelor who has long been the principal support of his married sisters. When one of his sisters dies, he takes her daughter May (Madge Evans) to Atlantic City to recover from her bereavement. To the dismay of Mettinger's surviving sisters, Olly Kipax (Josephine *Hull) and Laura Fenner (Alma Kruger), he returns not only with May but with Daisy Mayme Plunkett (Jessie Busley), an outgoing, slightly uncouth spinster. A horrified Laura is certain she knows Daisy Mayme's type: the sort of woman who "has no more home . . . than a tomcat" and who will "hang

around fashionable hotels, with their ear to the ground." The sisters set aside their animosities in an attempt to cool their brother's ardor for his new-found friend. Although she shrewdly fights back, they succeed in convincing Daisy that Cliff wants her solely as a companion for May. But Cliff proves he is fond of Daisy for herself. She agrees to marry him, purring, "I'll sit here in the lady's chair. I've always wanted to be a lady." "When Daisy finally carries the fray," Brooks *Atkinson noted, "the audience is accordingly unable to rejoice over the triumph of virtue. For Mr. Kelly has carefully indicted every character in the play." So unrelentingly observant a comedy commanded at best a modest audience, and only the healthy theatrical economics of the 1920s allowed the play to become a commercial success. It remains, however, a valid, if biting, portrait of aspects of American society, as illustrated by a 2003 revival Off Broadway.

DALE, Alan [né Alfred J. Cohen] (1861–1928), critic. Born in Birmingham, England, he first became a New York drama critic for the *Evening World* in 1887. Later he moved to the *Journal* and then to the *American,* where his often vitriolic notices helped sell papers and so won the backing of William Randolph Hearst. They did, however, alienate producers and theatre owners, who often tried to ban him from theatres. Whereas the *Dramatic Mirror* once noted, "When he takes pen in hand the playhouses throughout the land tremble upon their foundations and the faces of actors burn white with fear," *Who's Who in the Theatre* observed, "His criticisms probably carried more weight than any others in New York," but his precise position on the theatre was often unclear. Dale was Jerome *Kern's earliest and for many years only advocate. But he could also dismiss a lesser *Shaw play, *John Bull's Other Island,* as "a thick, glutinous, and imponderable four-act tract." He also wrote several books on theatre.

DALE, Jim [né James Smith] (b. 1935), actor. The lithe, lanky actor, who at one time studied ballet, was born in England, where he made his debut in 1951. Stints at the *National Theatre and the Young Vic followed before he first appeared in America in the Young Vic mountings of The *Taming of the Shrew* and *Scapino* in 1974, winning him wide recognition in the latter. Dale's memorable performances include the title role in the musical *Barnum* (1980), the troubled father Bri in a 1985 revival of *Joe Egg,* a long-term replacement as Bill in *Me and My Girl* (1987), and a variety of male and female characters in *Travels with My Aunt* (1995) and *Candide* (1997).

DALLAS THEATRE CENTER. The DTC, as it is popularly called, was founded in 1959 by Baylor

University professor Paul Baker and a group under the leadership of Robert D. Stecker Sr. and Beatrice Handel to offer the best in professional theatre for Dallas, Texas. Plays are presented in the only public playhouses designed by Frank Lloyd Wright, the 516-seat Kalita Humphreys Theatre, the 56-seat Down Center Stage, and smaller Lab Theatre spaces. The company also uses the Arts District Theatre, laid out by scenic designer Eugene *Lee, which allows for easy rearranging of seating and stage plans. Under the leadership of Adrian *Hall in 1983, the group became a professional company with a repertory consisting of both classics and new works, most memorably the premiere of Preston Jones's A Texas Trilogy. The company continues a regular children's program. For a time the DTC offered graduate school studies in conjunction with Trinity University in San Antonio.

DALRYMPLE, Jean (1910–98), producer. Although she became best known for her work with the New York *City Center, Dalrymple, who was born in Morristown, New Jersey, began her professional career writing vaudeville sketches. For a time she worked with John *Golden, then established her own office as publicist and manager in 1937. In the late 1940s she produced several shows on Broadway, most notably a revival of *Burlesque (1946) and Red Gloves (1948). She had been associated with the City Center since its inception, but not until she was named to its board of directors did she start to mount productions there, including a series of plays with José *Ferrer (*Cyrano de Bergerac, The *Shrike, *Richard III, and *Charley's Aunt), *King Lear, and *Mister Roberts. From 1957 to 1968, Dalrymple was general director of the *City Center Light Opera Company, mounting forty-seven revivals of thirty different musicals, the most frequently staged of which were *Brigadoon and *South Pacific. She also wrote several books on theatre and the autobiographical September Child (1963) and From the Last Row (1975).

DALY, [Peter Christopher] Arnold (1875–1927), actor and producer. Born in Brooklyn, he began his theatrical career as an office boy for Charles *Frohman. Daly's first acting assignment was a small role opposite Fanny Rice in The Jolly Squire (1892). After touring for several seasons, he made his New York debut as Chambers in Pudd'nhead Wilson (1895). Among his important early roles were the rejected Jack Negly in *Barbara Frietchie (1899), the drunken, brutal husband in Hearts Aflame (1902), and the hero's Irish servant in Major André (1903). Daly's family back in Ireland had connections to George Bernard *Shaw and Shaw's family, so Daly and Winchell *Smith secured the

rights for the first American production of *Candida, with Daly as Marchbanks. He became Shaw's strongest advocate in America and in 1904 organized, with *Liebler and Company, an ensemble devoted to presenting Shaw, in several instances giving the first New York or American mountings of plays such as You Never Can Tell, The Man of Destiny, How He Lied to Her Husband, John Bull's Other Island, and Mrs. Warren's Profession. The performance of the last play led to Daly's arrest for presenting an immoral work, but he was acquitted in court. Constant harassment from authorities continued, however, and this, coupled with the continuing disdain from moralistic critics, led him to abandon his hope for "a theatre of ideas." His last years were spent largely in standard commercial vehicles, most notably creating the role of the Vagabond in George M. *Cohan's The *Tavern (1920). A somewhat stocky man with a large round head, Daly was considered a good, if occasionally erratic and temperamental, actor. He possessed "an Irish voice of lilting cadence and great variety of tone." Biography: Arnold Daly, Berthold H. Goldsmith, 1927.

DALY, [John] Augustin (1838–99), producer, director, and playwright. The multi-talented man of the theatre came from very nontheatrical origins. His father was a sea captain and his mother was a soldier's daughter. Daly's first exposure to the theatre was in Norfolk, Virginia, where his widowed mother had moved from their North Carolina home. After seeing James E. *Murdoch play in Rookwood, he began to organize amateur theatricals. When the family's move to New York placed him closer to the theatrical mainstream, he took work at the Sunday Courier, soon becoming its drama critic. In 1862 he turned to playwriting, dramatizing S. H. von Mosenthal's Deborah as *Leah, the Forsaken. First produced at the *Boston Museum and brought to New York in January 1863, the play was an immediate hit. Several subsequent efforts were less successful, but in 1867 he wrote a largely original work, *Under the Gaslight, which enjoyed widespread acclaim. Its sensational effects of an approaching railroad train and a man tied to the tracks in its path were widely copied. Two years later he leased the *Fifth Avenue Theatre. His intention was to assemble the finest company and offer seasons mixing the best new works with revivals of the classics, although one of Daly's few faults was his insistence on rewriting even the most famous plays. "The old playwrights must have turned in their graves at his ruthlessness," Otis *Skinner observed. In a remarkable departure from accepted practice, he broke with the tradition of having each performer play only those roles in his or her "line." Daly expected his artists to be able to switch from comic roles to serious ones and from heroes to villains. He annoyed some players by assigning them minor roles after they had played major ones. However, his plans succeeded famously, and within a short time his company was the only serious rival to *Wallack's. Daly's tiny playhouse became known as the "parlor home of comedy." One of his few disappointments was the reaction to most of the new American plays he offered. "American press writers," he noted, "are proud of everything American except other American writers."

When the Fifth Avenue Theatre burned in 1873, he quickly restored another old theatre, continuing until he temporarily retired in 1877. Among the plays he offered during this first period were *London Assurance, *Twelfth Night, *As You Like It, *Frou-Frou, Fernande, *Saratoga, *Divorce, Article 47, The Fast Family, The School for Scandal, The *Big Bonanza, Our Boys, and *Pique. His company included Mrs. *Gilbert, James *Lewis, William *Davidge, Charles *Fisher, and several young ladies whose careers he promoted: Agnes *Ethel, Fanny *Morant, Fanny *Davenport, and Clara *Morris. During this time Daly attempted to operate other New York theatres, including the Grand Opera House, where he presented opéra bouffe and some musical spectacles. These proved burdensome and unpopular and were soon dropped. In 1879 he restored yet another old playhouse, renaming it after himself, and initiated what George *Odell called "one of the most distinguished theatres in the history of the American stage." Many of his former actors returned to his fold, including Mrs. Gilbert, Lewis, Davidge, Fisher, and the rising John *Drew. For his leading lady, Daly enlisted Ada *Rehan, who would become his finest and most beloved performer. Operettas and musical comedies were included in the repertory and, later, several London musical imports. The list of major hits this second company offered included *Needles and Pins, Boys and Girls, *7-20-8, The Country Girl, Red Letter Nights, She Would and She Would Not, A Night Off, The Magistrate, The *Taming of the Shrew, Dandy Dick, The *Railroad of Love, A *Midsummer Night's Dream, The *Lottery of Love, The *Last Word, and Tennyson's The Foresters. Daly had sent out road companies of his earlier hit plays, but this second company he took as an ensemble not only across country, but on one visit to Germany, three visits to France, and numerous visits to England.

As playwright, Daly claimed credit for approximately one hundred plays, although virtually all his works were adapted from foreign pieces. Most of his sources were German or French, though he was not above rewriting Shakespeare and the 18th-century English playwrights. Indeed, his modern editor, Catherine Sturtevant, suggests that so few of his plays are without known sources that it is not unreasonable to suppose we are merely ignorant of the models for his so-called original plays. No source has been found for what many consider his finest work, *Horizon (1871), a story set in the Wild West that recounted the adventures of a girl adopted by a villainous type after her father's murder. The hit plays Divorce (1871) and Pique (1875) were exceedingly free adaptations of novels. Modern research has revealed that many of the plays he took credit for were written largely by his brother Joseph. William *Winter summed up Daly by noting, "He made the Theatre important, and he kept it worthy of the sympathy and support of the most refined taste and the best intellect of his time." Biography: The Life of Augustin Daly, Joseph Francis Daly, 1917.

DALY, Charles Patrick (1816–99), author. The distinguished New York jurist, a devoted lover of theatre, often gave legal counsel free or at cost to needy actors and producers. He collected a notable theatrical library and was the author of First Theatre in America: When Was the Drama First Introduced in America? (1896), a pioneering work.

DALY, Dan (1858–1904), comic actor. The lanky performer began as a circus and variety acrobat "who seems to be boneless one moment and in the next stands on his head with his feet in the air, and in that position plays the castanets." However, he soon discovered his true métier was pure comedy. Harry B. *Smith recalled his "rueful countenance" and "guttural bass voice." His first legitimate appearance in The City Directory (1891) was followed by increasingly important roles in A Society Fad (1892), The Golden Wedding (1893), About Town (1894), The Twentieth Century Girl (1895), The Merry World (1895), The Merry Countess (1895), The Lady Slavey (1896), The Whirl of the Town (1897), The *Belle of New York (1897), The Rounders (1899), The Cadet Girl (1900), The Girl from Up There (1901), The New Yorkers (1901), and John Henry (1903).

DAMN YANKEES (1955), a musical comedy by George *Abbott, Douglass Wallop (book), Richard *Alder (music), Jerry *Ross (lyrics). [46th Street Theatre, 1,019 perf.; Tony Award.] For years the New York Yankees have won the pennant, while the forlorn Washington Senators remain in the cellar. A Senators fan, middle-aged Joe Boyd (Robert Shafer), blurts out that he would sell his soul to have his team in first place. Obligingly, the devil in the person of Mr. Applegate (Ray Walston) appears and transforms the aging Joe into young

Joe Hardy (Stephen Douglass). As "Shoeless Joe from Hannibal, Mo." he sparks the team into surging ahead to the top. When something inside the new Joe yearns for the wife he left behind, Applegate sends the sultry Lola (Gwen *Verdon) to seduce him. But Joe cannot forget his wife and, with Lola's help, he reneges on his agreement with the devil and returns home. *Notable songs*: Heart; Near to You; Whatever Lola Wants; Two Lost Souls. Although the 1905 baseball musical *The Umpire* had enjoyed a long run in Chicago, this production by Hal *Prince, Frederick *Brisson, and others was the first successful New York musical dealing with the national pastime. The work was based on Wallop's popular novel *The Year the Yankees Lost the Pennant*. A Broadway revival in 1994 with Victor *Garber as Applegate and Bebe Neuwirth as Lola was very popular.

DANCE A LITTLE CLOSER. See *Idiot's Delight*.

DANCIN' (1978), a choreographic revue featuring original dance pieces by Bob *Fosse. [*Broadhurst Theatre, 1,774 perf.] Using such diverse composers as Johann Sebastian Bach, George M. *Cohan, Neil Diamond, and John Philip *Sousa for its music, Fosse devised a variety of "dance for dance's sake" numbers. The Shubert production enjoyed an exceptionally long run not only because of its fine dancing but because it became a prime attraction for foreigners, who found it offered no language problems. Some numbers were later repeated in the Livent-produced revue *Fosse* (1999) which ran for 1,100 performances at the same theatre, winning the *Tony Award. Ann Reinking and others re-created several of the late Fosse's numbers from various Broadway shows and movies.

DANCING MOTHERS (1924), a play by Edgar *Selwyn and Edmund Goulding. [*Booth Theatre, 311 perf.] Ethel Westcourt (Mary Young) is not sympathetic when a friend is expelled from their club for unseemly behavior, but she is concerned when priggish young Kenneth Cobb (Michael Dawn), a suitor to her daughter Kittens (Helen *Hayes), informs her that Kittens spends time in the rooms of Gerald Naughton (John Halliday), a notorious man-about-town. The ultimate shock for Ethel comes when she learns her husband, Hugh (Henry Stephenson), is actively philandering. Her reaction is to teach her free-thinking friend, daughter, and husband a lesson by outdoing them in socially unacceptable wildness. "Times have changed," she announces. "I have become a woman of today. I have become a dancing mother." She even competes with Kittens for Naughton's attentions. Throwing over her straitlaced ways

gives her so much pleasure that she throws over her family, too. She heads for Europe, leaving her husband and daughter to console each other. Although the Selwyn-produced show received largely lukewarm notices, it caught the public's fancy with its accurate, if overdramatic, view of the new flapper morality. Many commentators felt that the startling ending was the key to the play's success.

DANIELE, Graciela (b. 1939), choreographer and director. The Argentine-born Daniele began her New York career in 1963 in the dancing chorus of Broadway musicals, but in the 1980s she established her reputation as a choreographer when she staged musical numbers for the New York Shakespeare Festival's *The *Pirates of Penzance* (1981) and *The *Mystery of Edwin Drood* (1985). Other Manhattan choreography credits include *Zorbá* (1983), *The Rink* (1984), *The Goodbye Girl* (1993), and *Ragtime* (1997). By the 1990s Daniele was directing as well, helming such musicals as *Once on This Island* (1990), *Chronicle of a Death Foretold* (1995), *A New Brain* (1998), *Annie Get Your Gun* (1999), and *Marie Christine* (1999).

DANIELS, Frank [Albert] (1860–1935), comic actor and singer. Although born in Dayton, Ohio, the genial, bantam, imp-faced Daniels grew up in Boston, where he attended business school before studying singing at the New England Conservatory of Music. He made his professional stage debut as the Sheriff in *The Chimes of Normandy* in 1879, then served a second apprenticeship with several light opera companies. Daniels first won major recognition in New York as Old Sport, the boxing fan drugstore clerk, in *A Rag Baby* (1884). Other successes included the transformed father in *Little Puck* (1888), the loyal (if comic) lighthouse man Shrimps in *Princess Bonnie* (1895), and the title role in Victor *Herbert's *The Wizard of the Nile* (1895). His success in the latter musical was so pronounced that Herbert immediately wrote two more vehicles especially for him: *The Idol's Eye* (1897) and *The Ameer* (1899). *Miss Simplicity* (1902), *The Office Boy* (1903), and *Sergeant Bruce* (1905) all depended on his antics for their popularity. Among his later credits were the tailor-made vehicle *The Tattooed Man* (1907) by Herbert, *The Belle of Brittany* (1909), and a touring company of *The *Pink Lady* (1911). He retired after performing in Joe *Weber and Lew *Fields's last double bill, *Roly Poly* and *Without the Law* (1912). A broad comedian, Daniels was famous for his vividly expressive eyebrows, which were often put to best use in his equally celebrated curtain speeches. Describing one of these, a critic noted, "He rambled about in a mock effort at forensic eloquence that brought tears to the eyes of a good many people out front."

DANIELS, Jeff (b. 1955), actor. The genial, innocent-looking leading man of films and television often returns to the theatre, both in New York and at the Purple Rose Theatre, which he founded in his hometown of Chelsea, Michigan. Daniels was educated at Central Michigan University and trained at the *Circle Repertory Theatre, where he first started performing in 1976. Among his stage roles of interest were the quiet gardener Jed Jenkins in *5th of July (1978), the scholar Tom researching the memoirs of a secretive old woman in *The Golden Age* (1984), the young Alan facing up to his estranged father in *Lemon Sky* (1985), and the Vietnam vet Lyman living in a California forest in *Redwood Curtain* (1993).

DANIELS, William (b. 1927), character actor. The loud, strident supporting player was born in Brooklyn, educated at Northwestern, and trained with Lee *Strasberg at the *Actors Studio before making his New York debut in 1943 as one of the sons in *Life with Father. Daniels was involved with important productions in the late 1950s and early 1960s, such as a replacement for the bitter Jimmy Porter in *Look Back in Anger (1958) and originating the role of Peter in the first American production of The *Zoo Story (1960). He also shone as the narrow-minded social worker Albert in *A Thousand Clowns* (1962), the over-practical fiancé Warren in *On a Clear Day You Can See Forever* (1965), and most memorably as the quarrelsome delegate John Adams in *1776 (1969).

DANITES, THE; or, The Heart of the Sierras (1877), a play by Joaquin Miller. [*Broadway Theatre, 30 perf.] When a band of Danites, members of a Mormon secret society, attempt to murder the Williams family, two youngsters escape. One is Nancy Williams (Kitty Blanchard), who, fearing the Mormons will continue to pursue her, disguises herself as a boy and takes the name Billy Piper and seeks refuge in a mining camp. There a comely young schoolteacher, Huldah Brown (Lillie Eldridge), falls in love with the supposed young man. Huldah is courted by Alexander "Sandy" McGee (McKee *Rankin), and when Billy refuses to return her affection she agrees to marry Sandy. Learning Billy's true identity, Huldah takes her into her confidence and carelessly invites her into the privacy of her rooms. Sandy misconstrues these actions and becomes ragingly jealous. Several Danites appear at the camp, having searched out Nancy, and try to incite the mob into lynching the presumed boy. Luckily, Sandy discovers that Billy is a girl, dissuades the mob, and turns its ire

against the Mormons. The work was first contrived in London with the help of an unidentified English actor and was based on two stories by Miller. The play version, called *The First Families of the Sierras* in London, was revised by a Philadelphia actor, Alexander Fitzgerald, as a vehicle for Rankin and his wife, Kitty Blanchard. Although it was not the first play about Western life, the success of *The Danites* initiated a vogue for such plays. It remains of interest as well because of its cruel depiction of Mormons. For half a century the Mormon was portrayed either as a villain or as a somewhat unsavory comic. So long as this view had popular currency, the play remained well received. It was regularly revived, and Rankin himself played in it for many years. **Joaquin MILLER** (1841?–1913), whose real first name was Cincinnatus, was well known as a writer of Western stories. *The Danites* was his first play and the only one to achieve prolonged success. Miller's other work of interest was the pioneer tale *Forty-Nine* (1881).

DANNER, Blythe (b. 1943), actress. The slim, agile leading lady with a pleasingly husky voice was born in Philadelphia and educated at Bard College before making her New York debut Off Broadway in 1966. After some noteworthy supporting roles, she was acclaimed for her kooky, lovable Jill Tanner in *Butterflies Are Free* (1969). The film actress often returned to the theatre, both in New York and at the *Williamstown Theatre Festival. Among her memorable performances were Viola in *Twelfth Night* (1972), Londoner Emma involved in a romantic triangle in *Betrayal* (1980), socialite Tracy Lord in The *Philadelphia Story* (1980), a frantic but moving Blanche Du Bois in A *Streetcar Named Desire* (1988), the wife Kate whose marriage seems threatened by a dog in *Sylvia* (1995), and the cynical Phyllis Stone in *Follies* (2001).

DARK AT THE TOP OF THE STAIRS, THE (1957), a play by William *Inge. [*Music Box Theatre, 468 perf.] The Floods are a lower-middle-class family living in a small Oklahoma town in the 1920s. Rubin Flood (Pat *Hingle) is a harness salesman at a time when automobiles are killing the demand for his product. His wife, Cora (Teresa Wright), is the daughter of a schoolteacher and has married somewhat below her station. They have two children, teenager Reenie (Judith Robinson) and ten-year-old Sonny (Charles Saari). The Floods' humdrum life is shaken by three events: Cora's sister, Lottie (Eileen *Heckart), comes for dinner and confesses her marriage is sexless; Reenie's date at a dance, a young Jewish boy, commits suicide after he is humiliated by an anti-Semite; and

Rubin announces that the harness company is going out of business. The incidents contrive to bring about a certain understanding and compassion and, with them, the small hope of a somewhat happier life. Reviewing the Saint Subber–Elia *Kazan production, Louis *Kronenberger felt that "Inge's most definite quality—his feeling for human loneliness—became too insistent," yet most critics and playgoers applauded the semi-autobiographical drama, which was a revision of a 1947 work, *Farther off from Heaven*.

DARLING OF THE GODS, THE (1902), a play by David *Belasco, John Luther *Long. [*Belasco Theatre, 182 perf.] Prince Saigon of Tosan (Charles Walcot) has invited the outlawed Prince Kara (Robert T. Haines) to a banquet because Kara saved Saigon's daughter, Princess Yo-San (Blanche *Bates), from death and respected her innocence. Yo-San is betrothed to the effete Tonda-Tanji (Albert Bruning), but she does not love him and hopes to discourage him by insisting that before their wedding he must kill a dangerous outlaw. Her wish falls in with the plans of the sinister war minister, Zakkuri (George *Arliss), who is determined to kill Kara. He has planted assassins around Saigon's house, but Kara eludes them. When he and Yo-San meet again, Yo-San falls in love with him and hides him from Zakkuri's men. For forty days she lives secretly with the outlaw. Kara eventually decides he must join his band; he leaves and is captured by Zakkuri's men. Zakkuri refuses to kill Kara at once, hoping Kara will lead him to more outlaws, but Kara declines. When Yo-San visits Zakkuri to plead for Kara's life, he attempts to turn her into his courtesan. She rebuffs him, but he does succeed in having her reveal the whereabouts of Kara's band. Zakkuri releases Kara, who joins his men, but they are immediately attacked, and Kara is mortally wounded. Yo-San appears to confess her love, the two of them agreeing they will meet a thousand years hence in the First White Heaven. After Kara dies, Yo-San commits suicide. A thousand years pass and the lovers do meet, and arm in arm prepare to ascend to the next celestial level. Following the success of their *Madame Butterfly*, producer Belasco suggested to Long that they write a full-length drama with a Japanese setting. Even in its day the play was judged contrived and its dialogue ("How is your honorable health? Do you happily eat well?") preposterous. Fine acting and sumptuous settings were its main attraction for many, although here, too, not all critics were totally pleased. One wrote that the "stage scenes, however gorgeous, never rise to the altitude of high art, but they give a very real delight to the vast multitudes who considerately forbear to wear out the steps of the Metropolitan Museum with their sole leather." Nevertheless, the same critic noted the ten settings were "a triumph of richly artistic light and movement and color."

DAVENPORT, [Benjamin] **Butler** (1871–1958), actor, playwright, and manager. A versatile but mildly eccentric figure, the New York–born Davenport began his career playing walk-ons and serving as understudy in Augustin *Daly's company. He later played small parts opposite Richard *Mansfield, John *Drew, Eleanora *Duse, and Sarah *Bernhardt, and worked with David *Belasco. In 1910 the *Shuberts produced his play, *Keeping Up Appearances*, centering on a family dominated by a cruel father. The play failed, and Davenport decided to strike out on his own. He opened several little theatres at which he produced, directed, and starred in his own plays. To encourage patronage he charged no admission, merely passing the hat after each performance. Bearing titles such as *The Importance of Coming and Going, The Depths of Purity,* and *The Comforts of Ignorance,* they attracted small audiences. Only his 1916 revival of *Keeping Up Appearances* enjoyed an appreciable run, and that one was apparently somewhat forced. His Davenport Free Theatre continued to offer his own plays and those of others in intermittent seasons as late as 1944.

DAVENPORT, E[dward] L[oomis] (1815–77), actor. The son of a Boston innkeeper, Davenport made his debut in Providence, Rhode Island, in 1837, billed simply as Mr. E. Dee and playing opposite Junius Brutus *Booth in *A New Way to Pay Old Debts*. His first New York appearance was as Frederick Fitzallen in *He's Not A-Miss*, in a company led by Mrs. Henry Hunt (the future Mrs. John *Drew). Davenport later demonstrated the range of his repertory by first playing Othello to F. B. *Conway's Iago, followed by Hamlet, Claude Melnotte, Sir Giles Overreach, and William (in *Black-Eyed Susan*), as well as creating the part of Lanciotto in *Boker's *Francesca da Rimini*. His performances regularly won critical acclaim, but for some reason he was never able to earn the affection of playgoers. His fellow actors, however, admired his talents, and at one time or another he was welcomed into all the major ensembles of his day: *Burton's, *Wallack's, and *Daly's. Much of the time he toured in a company headed by himself and his wife, the former Fanny [Elizabeth] Vining (1829–91), highlighted by his Brutus to Lawrence Barrett's *Cassius in a celebrated mounting of *Julius Caesar* (1875) and Edgar to Barrett's Lear (1876), his final New York appearance. His farewell was as Dan'l Druce in Washington in 1877. Attempting to explain Davenport's lack of popularity with the public, George *Odell suggested, "Perhaps his versatility, his finish, his lack of sensational clap-trap, militated against him with a people that admired the physical vigour of Forrest and the electrical effects of the elder Booth." Whatever his failings, he fathered a large theatrical family. Four of his children attained some distinction in the theatre, most notably Fanny *Davenport. His younger daughter, May Davenport (1856–1927), was an important member of the companies at the *Chestnut Street Theatre in Philadelphia, *Daly's, and the *Boston Museum. His son Edgar L[ongfellow] (1862–1918) played at both the Chestnut and the *Walnut Street in Philadelphia, toured as leading man with Kate *Claxton and McKee *Rankin, and was long a major actor at the Boston Museum. A younger son, Harry [George Bryant] (1866–1949), first gained fame as Sir Joseph Porter in the celebrated 1879 children's company of *H. M. S. Pinafore and later became a popular leading man in both straight plays and musical comedies, creating the leading man's role of Harry Brown in The *Belle of New York (1897). He was one of the earliest important performers to leave the stage for a career in silent films, though he continued to return to theatre as late as 1935. Biography: Edward Loomis Davenport, Edwin Francis, 1901.

DAVENPORT, Fanny [Lily Gypsy] (1850–98), actress and producer. To many observers this celebrated performer's career was precisely the opposite of that of her father, E. L. *Davenport. She was adored by her public but accorded a grudging respect by fellow professionals. Born in London during her American parents' English visit, she made her stage debut shortly after their return when she played one of the children in a Boston mounting of *Metamora. In 1862 she played New York for the first time, performing Charles II to her father's Ruy Gomez in Faint Heart Never Won Fair Lady. Augustin *Daly thought she had great promise and enlisted her in his first major ensemble. "What Daly saw in her," his brother recalled, "besides her dazzling beauty, splendid presence, and blooming health were confidence and self-possession." Among her most popular roles at Daly's were Lady Gay Spanker, Maria in *Twelfth Night, Lu Ten Eyck in *Divorce, Lady Teazle, and Eugenia in The *Big Bonanza. She also won applause for masking her beauty as the haggish Ruth Tredgett in Charity and, most of all, for her portrayal of the tormented mother Mabel Renfrew in *Pique. Davenport toured successfully in the last-mentioned role, and it apparently played a large part in her decision to assume dramatic roles instead of comic ones. After leaving Daly, four major roles occupied the remainder of her career: the determined heroine in Fedora (1883), the tragic

heroine of La Tosca (1888), Cleopatra (1890), and the vengeful duchess in Gismonda (1894). All four plays were by *Sardou, had been created by *Bernhardt in Paris, and were produced by Davenport herself, thus markedly increasing her profits. The not entirely flattering assessment of her associates was recorded by Otis *Skinner in his autobiography: "Miss Davenport was a handsome woman, her business sense keen and her industry untiring. To these qualities rather than her acting, she owed the late success in which she accumulated a fortune in her productions."

DAVID HARUM (1900), a play by R. and M. W. Hitchcock (and Edward E. *Rose, uncredited). [*Garrick Theatre, 148 perf.] In the small upstate New York town of Homeville, David Harum (William H. *Crane) is known as a shrewd banker, an even shrewder horsetrader, and a kindly philosopher. He gives the all-too-lordly Deacon Perkins (Homer Granville) a costly lesson in horses, pays a long-standing "debt" to patient Widow Cullum (Eloise Frances Clark), and sees to it that his young assistant, John Lenox (George S. Probert), wins the hand of comely Mary Blake (Katherine Florence). Charles *Frohman produced the folksy, sentimental piece, based on Edward Noyes Westcott's best-seller, and Crane toured in it for four seasons, while secondary companies crisscrossed the country for over a decade.

DAVIDGE, William [Pleater] (1814–88), comic actor. Long popular as a principal comedian, the English-born performer made his professional debut in 1836 and his first American appearance in 1850 when he played Sir Peter Teazle. Davidge acted at the *Broadway, *Bowery, and Winter Garden Theatres for several seasons, in addition to supporting Frederick and Mrs. *Conway in Brooklyn. Later he acted with *Daly's first ensemble throughout its entire existence, and afterward for *Palmer at the *Madison Square. "Rare old Bill," as he was popularly known, was awarded a special testimonial on the occasion of his fiftieth year on the stage and continued acting almost until the time of his death. Generally regarded as an actor of the old formal school, his assignments ranged from classic roles such as Bottom and Sir Toby Belch to important comic parts in newer, ephemeral works. Autobiography: Footlight Flashes, 1866.

DAVIDSON, Gordon (b. 1933), director and manager. He was born in Brooklyn, the son of a theatre professor at Brooklyn College, and studied electrical engineering at Cornell and theatre at Case Western University. Davidson was a protégé of John *Houseman and directed for his Theatre

Group at UCLA, later becoming artistic director of the company. In 1967 it became known as the Center Theatre Group and took over Los Angeles's *Mark Taper Forum, eventually becoming one of the nation's outstanding regional theatres under Davidson's leadership. Among his productions to transfer to New York are *In the Matter of J. Robert Oppenheimer* (1969), *The Trial of the Catonsville Nine* (1971), *The *Shadow Box* (1977), *Zoot Suit* (1979), and **Children of a Lesser God* (1980). Davidson is known as a playwright's director, working closely with writers on new scripts and helping develop new ways to tell a story.

DAVIS, Jessie Bartlett (1861–1905), singer and actress. Born on a farm near Morris, Illinois, the contralto studied voice in Chicago, where she made her debut in 1879 in **H. M. S. Pinafore*. Bartlett then spent several years with various opera companies before joining the new *Boston Ideal Opera Company and remaining with this troupe for virtually its entire history. Her most famous role was the trouser part of Alan-a-Dale in **Robin Hood* (1891), in which she introduced "Oh, Promise Me." She later was briefly popular in vaudeville and also appeared in several other Broadway musicals.

DAVIS, Ossie [né Raiford Chatman Davis] (b. 1917), actor, director, and playwright. The multi-talented African American was born in Cogdell, Georgia, the son of a railroad engineer, and educated at Howard University before going to New York to be a writer. Instead he was drawn to the theatre and made his Broadway acting debut in 1946. Davis found fame years later as the author of the comedy **Purlie Victorious* (1961), and he played the ambitious, unconventional preacher Purlie Judson opposite his wife, actress Ruby *Dee. Davis continued to write and direct and also appeared in many plays on and Off Broadway, including *Jamaica* (1957), *A *Raisin in the Sun* (1960), *The Zulu and the Zayda* (1965), and **I'm Not Rappaport* (1986).

DAVIS, Owen (1874–1956), playwright. Born in Portland, Maine, the Harvard-educated Davis proved unsuccessful at blank-verse tragedy, so, to support his family, he began churning out cheap melodramas for popular touring companies. Finishing them at the rate of one every second or third week, he wrote over two hundred, with titles such as *Edna, the Pretty Typewriter; Nellie, the Beautiful Cloak Model; Driven from Home;* and *Convict 999.* In his autobiography Davis called them "practically motion pictures," observing, "One of the first tricks I learned was that my plays must be written for an audience who, owing to huge, uncarpeted, noisy theaters, couldn't always hear the words

and who, a large percentage of them having only recently landed in America, couldn't have understood them in any case. I therefore wrote for the eye rather than the ear." When dialogue was necessary he filled it with "noble sentiments so dear to audiences of that class." Davis was first represented on Broadway with the *Hippodrome musical spectacle *The Battle of Port Arthur* (1908), and his first regular play to reach New York was *Making Good* (1912). It was a quick failure, but he scored commercial successes with *The Family Cupboard* (1913), **Sinners* (1915), **Forever After* (1918), and *Opportunity* (1920). To many playgoers' surprise, Davis then wrote two highly praised dramas: *The Detour* (1921) and **Icebound* (1923), the latter winning a *Pulitzer Prize. Although several of his other plays, such as *The *Nervous Wreck* (1923) and *Mr. and Mrs. North* (1941), were commercially profitable, they did not fulfill the promise he briefly displayed. Many of his later works were dramatizations of other writers' stories. Autobiographies: *I'd Like to Do It Again*, 1931; *My First Fifty Years in the Theatre*, 1950.

DAVIS, Richard Harding. See *Dictator, The.*

DAVY CROCKETT; or, Be Sure You're Right, Then Go Ahead (1873), a play by Frank *Murdoch. [Wood's Museum, 12 perf.] Davy Crockett (Frank *Mayo) returns to his forest home carrying a buck he has shot and bearing the news that his childhood sweetheart, Little Nell, has come back from a long stay abroad. Little Nell now calls herself by her proper name, Eleanor Vaughn (Rosa Rand), and she brings with her, her guardian Major Hector Royston (T. W. Keene), and her fiancé, Neil Crampton (Harry Stewart). The travelers are headed for the estate of Neil's uncle, Oscar Crampton (J. J. Wallace). Davy is quick to sense something is wrong. He decides to run ahead of the party and offer them the shelter of his hunting hut, since it has started to snow. The decision proves wise, for Neil has been hurt and his blood has attracted wolves. Davy singlehandedly keeps the wolves at bay, while Eleanor reads him Scott's poem of Lochinvar. When the party finally reaches old Crampton's estate, the uncle is revealed as a villain who is blackmailing Royston with forged papers and forcing his nephew to marry. Davy, like young Lochinvar, arrives to rescue his sweetheart. He takes her home and marries her, then destroys the uncle's papers. Although the play is usually set down among the major works dealing with frontier life, it is actually little more than a drawing room melodrama unfolding in the wilderness. Despite Crockett's first appearance with a deer over his shoulder, his later fending off of wolves, and dialogue such as, "Yes, this is my crib. This is where I come and bank when I'm out on a long stretch arter [sic] game," the play could have been set elsewhere with little change. Still, the contrast of the rough and the polished, the openhearted and the venal, was underscored by the setting. *Davy Crockett* was first produced in Rochester, New York, in 1872 and was received coolly. However, Mayo had faith in the piece and kept rewriting it. Even its initial New York reception was reserved, but the public took to it, so Mayo was able to play it for the rest of his life, including a performance two days before his death.

DAWN [Tout], **Hazel** (1891–1988), singer and actress. The "dewy-eyed blonde" was born in Ogden City, Utah, studied violin and singing in Europe, and made her theatrical debut in London. Her first American assignment was her most memorable: the demimondaine Claudine in *The *Pink Lady* (1911), in which she introduced "My Beautiful Lady," both singing it and playing it on the violin. Dawn was featured in the musicals *The Little Cafe* (1913), *The Debutante* (1914), and *The Century Girl* (1916), then displayed her farceur talents as Mabel Essington in *Up in Mabel's Room* (1919), Gertie Darling in *Getting Gertie's Garter* (1921), and the temperamental actress Gloria Graham in *The Demi-Virgin* (1921). After touring in the *Ziegfeld Follies of 1923*, Dawn appeared in three more revues, *Nifties of 1923*, *Keep Kool* (1924), and *Great Temptations* (1926), before making her last appearance in *Wonder Boy* (1931).

DAWN OF A TOMORROW, THE (1909), a play by Frances Hodgson *Burnett. [*Lyceum Theatre, 152 perf.] When Sir Oliver Holt (Fuller Mellish) concludes he is terminally ill, he takes a pistol and wanders the streets of London to get up enough nerve to kill himself. But when he meets a poor young girl, Glad (Eleanor *Robson), who enthusiastically believes that good works can overcome despair and pain, she lifts his spirits. Glad's ruffian boyfriend, Dandy (Henry *Stanford), is accused of a crime he did not commit and promises Glad that if he is exonerated he will behave thereafter. But the only man who can provide Dandy with a real alibi is Holt's ne'er-do-well son (Aubrey *Boucicault). Prodded by Glad, the young man tells the police the real story, and the four walk away confident that their futures are bright. The *Liebler and Co. offering was inspired by the growing popularity of Mary Baker Eddy's Christian Science movement.

DAY, Edith (1896–1971), actress and singer. The beautiful, round-faced, dark-haired performer, who was born in Minneapolis, Minnesota, made her stage debut in 1915. By 1917 she was the leading

lady of *Going Up!*, then scored a huge success in the title role of *Irene* (1919), in which she introduced "Alice Blue Gown." Day enjoyed further acclaim in *Orange Blossoms* (1922), in which she sang "A Kiss in the Dark," and in *Wildflower* (1923), introducing "Bambalina." For many years thereafter she was one of London's leading musical stars, earning the title of Queen of Drury Lane.

DAY, Edmund. See *Round Up, The*.

DAYS WITHOUT END (1934), a modern miracle play by Eugene O'Neill. [*Henry Miller Theatre, 57 perf.] John Loving is two men simultaneously: John (Earle *Larimore), his generous, idealistic half, and Loving (Stanley Ridges), his baser self. Embittered at life, he has abandoned religion and made a god of love. But he has not been faithful even to his new deity. Loving decides to write a book about his experiences and tells his story to a priest (Robert *Loraine) and his wife, Elsa (Selena Royle). The shock of hearing her husband's history makes Elsa deathly ill. Mortified, John prostrates himself before the cross and re-embraces Catholicism; John's reaffirmation kills Loving and saves his wife. Although highly praised by the Catholic press, most other American critics treated the *Theatre Guild production harshly, seeing it largely as a failed literary exercise rather than a vital drama. Curiously, the play was accorded a better reception the following year when it opened in London. The play's American failure may have played some part in the withdrawal of O'Neill, heretofore prolific, from the stage. He did not return to Broadway until twelve years later with The *Iceman Cometh, though he continued to write.

DAZEY, C. T. See *In Old Kentucky*.

DAZIAN'S THEATRICAL EMPORIUM. Founded in 1842 by a Bavarian immigrant, Wolf Dazian, as a supplier of fancy and dry goods, it quickly became the leading supplier of materials and, most importantly, costumes to the theatrical trade. In short order the house was costumer to leading producers, including the celebrated costumes for The *Black Crook. After Wolf's death his son, Henry, took charge, but he abandoned the practice of providing finished costumes in 1919, preferring to sell bulk goods to other costume houses.

DE ANGELIS, [Thomas] **Jefferson** (1859–1933), comic actor. The San Francisco–born comedian made his debut shortly before his eleventh birthday at a Baltimore vaudeville house. In the early 1880s he toured the world at the head of his own dramatic company but soon recognized that his forte was acrobatic clowning. From 1887 to 1889 he was a principal comedian with John *McCaull and then served in the same capacity from 1891 to 1895 at the *Casino Theatre. De Angelis co-starred in the first major American revue, The *Passing Show (1894), and with many of the leading prima donnas of his day, including Lillian *Russell, in shows such as The Tzigane (1895), Fleur-de-Lis (1895), The Wedding Day (1897), The Jolly Musketeer (1899), and Fantana (1905). He continued to play in musicals but gradually varied his assignments with roles in non-musicals, such as his memorable portrayal of theatrical producer Oscar Wolfe in The *Royal Family (1927). His last appearance was in Apron Strings (1930). Autobiography: A Vagabond Trouper, with Alvin E. Harlow, 1931.

DE BAR, Ben[edict] (1812?–77), actor and manager. A pioneering theatre figure, he was born in London to parents of French background and settled in New Orleans in 1834. A year later he made his acting debut at that city's St. Charles Theatre as Sir Benjamin Backbite in The School for Scandal. At the time, De Bar was slim and handsome enough (with attractive blue eyes and a round, boyish face) to assume roles such as Mazeppa, albeit from the start he excelled as a comedian. Two years later he joined J. W. *Wallack's company at the National in New York. Although he subsequently played several seasons in New York, he preferred what was then known as "the Western circuit"—the cities along or near the Mississippi. He eventually bought out theatre interests in New Orleans and St. Louis and thereafter commuted by riverboat between the two cities, running playhouses and acting. In his later years De Bar grew quite corpulent, so Falstaff became his most celebrated role.

DE CORDOBA, Pedro (1881–1950), actor. A tall, brooding performer, de Cordoba played a wide variety of roles on stage between 1903 and 1934 and later aristocratic Latins in the movies. He was born in New York to Cuban-French parents and learned his acting skills first in stock companies and then as a member of E. H. *Sothern's classics company. De Cordoba later graduated to leading roles, such as Orlando in *As You Like It (1914 and 1918) and Sir Lancelot in Lancelot and Elaine (1921), but he was more frequently seen in meaty supporting parts, such as the conniving Cassius in *Julius Caesar (1914, 1927, and 1931) and the cocky Maj. Sergius in Arms and the Man (1925).

DE GRESAC, Fred. See Gresac, Fred de.

DE KOVEN, [Henry Louis] Reginald (1859–1920), composer. The composer of *Robin Hood (1891), the first enduring American operetta, De Koven was

for a very brief time the most respected and promising melodist of the American theatre. Born in Middletown, Connecticut, and educated in England, he then pursued his musical studies in Germany and France. De Koven's initial score was for The Begum (1887), but it was not until Robin Hood won instant acclaim, along with its great songs, "Oh, Promise Me" and "Brown October Ale," that De Koven earned national fame and fortune. His later scores included The Knickerbockers (1892), The Algerian (1893), The Fencing Master (1893), Rob Roy (1894), The Tzigane (1895), The Mandarin (1896), The Highwayman (1897), Papa's Wife (1899), The Little Duchess (1901), Maid Marian (1902), The Jersey Lily (1903), Happyland (1905), The Student King (1906), The Golden Butterfly (1908), The Wedding Trip (1911), and Her Little Highness (1913). The arrival on the scene of Victor *Herbert and other fresh talents revealed that De Koven's archly conservative musical compositions often were derivative and repetitive. It appears doubtful that any of his works, except possibly Robin Hood, will survive. Biography: A Musician and His Wife, Anna De Koven, 1926.

DE LIAGRE, Alfred, Jr. (1904–87), producer and director. Born in Passaic, New Jersey, De Liagre was a Yale graduate who entered the theatre in 1930, working at the Woodstock Playhouse and serving as stage manager for a New York revival of *Twelfth Night. With Richard *Aldrich he produced Three Cornered Moon (1933) and several other plays, the most successful of which was Petticoat Fever (1935). In 1937 De Liagre began producing on his own. His best-known productions, many of which he directed, included *Yes, My Darling Daughter (1937), Mr. and Mrs. North (1941), The *Voice of the Turtle (1943), The Madwoman of Chaillot (1948), Second Threshold (1951), The Deep Blue Sea (1952), the *Phoenix Theatre production of The *Golden Apple (1954), *Janus (1955), *J. B. (1958), and Photo Finish (1963). With Roger *Stevens he produced the long-running thriller *Deathtrap (1978).

DE MILLE, Agnes [George] (1905–93), choreographer. The New York–born daughter of William C. *de Mille, she was graduated with honors from the University of California and then studied dancing in London with Theodore Koslov, Marie Rambert, Anthony Tudor, and others. In 1928 she appeared as a dancer in the Grand Street Follies and a year later created the choreography for a much discussed revival of The *Black Crook in Hoboken. The next several seasons were spent dancing and choreographing in London before she returned to New York to develop the dances for Hooray for What! (1937) and Swingin' the Dream (1939). Major success and popular renown came to her with her ballets for *Oklahoma! (1943), her dances changing the nature of Broadway choreography. Heretofore there had been little ballet except for a few notable examples by George *Balanchine and in some progressive revues. More than any other choreographer, de Mille popularized modern ballet styles in the theatre and made ballets dramatic, often allowing them to develop the story. Her subsequent choreography was seen in *One Touch of Venus (1943), *Bloomer Girl (1944), *Carousel (1945), *Brigadoon (1947), *Allegro (1947), *Gentlemen Prefer Blondes (1949), Paint Your Wagon (1951), The Girl in Pink Tights (1954), Goldilocks (1958), Juno (1959), Kwamina (1961), and *110 in the Shade (1963). De Mille also created traditional ballets for various dance companies and served as director-choreographer for *Allegro (1947), Out of This World (1950), and Come Summer (1969). She has written several books about both her life and her art, including Dance to the Piper (1952), And Promenade Home (1957), and Speak to Me; Dance with Me (1973).

DE MILLE, Henry C[hurchill] (1855?–93), playwright. De Mille came to New York from his North Carolina home with the intention of studying for the clergy, but his exposure to the theatre changed his plans. After graduating from Columbia, he joined the faculty of the Columbia College Grammar School, where he helped write school plays. His work came to the attention of the *Frohmans at the *Madison Square Theatre, and he was hired as a play reader. De Mille's first play to be produced professionally was John Delmer's Daughters; or, Duty (1883) a story of overreaching social climbers. It failed to run but his railroad melodrama, The Main Line; or, Rawson's Y, written with Charles *Barnard, was an immediate hit and was played around the country for many years. With playwright-producer David *Belasco he wrote four very successful plays: The *Wife (1887), Lord Chumley (1888), The *Charity Ball (1889), and *Men and Women (1890). Departing from Belasco, de Mille adapted Ludwig Fulda's Das verlorene Paradies as The *Lost Paradise (1891), an early serious look at labor-management problems that was highly praised. His modern editor, Robert Hamilton Ball, has noted, "The factor which determined the nature of these plays was the stock company. For that purpose they were admirably suited. They gave great and enduring pleasure to a large number of people. Moreover, Henry de Mille would have gone much farther, had he not died before he was forty years old." De Mille was the father of Cecil B. and William C. *de Mille, and the grandfather of Agnes *de Mille. His wife, Beatrice, was a well-known playwrights' agent. Biography: The De Milles: An American Family, Anne Edwards, 1988.

DE MILLE, William C[hurchill] (1878–1955), playwright. The son of Henry C. *de Mille and father of Agnes *de Mille, he was born in Washington, North Carolina, and studied at Columbia University, then at the *American Academy of Dramatic Arts. De Mille enjoyed a modest success with his first produced play, the Indian drama Strongheart (1905). After co-writing the short-lived comedy The Genius (1906) with his brother Cecil, he and Margaret Turnbull penned the well-received comedy about West Point cadets, Classmates (1907), then on his own scored a hit with the Civil War drama The *Warrens of Virginia (1907). De Mille's biggest success came with the political drama The *Woman (1911). After striking out with two plays written with his brother, The Royal Mounted (1908) and After Five (1913), the two siblings went west, where they spent the rest of their careers in films.

DE SHIELDS, Andre (b. 1946), actor and singer. He was born in Baltimore and educated at the University of Wisconsin and New York University before getting work as a backup singer for Bette Midler. After appearing in the Chicago company of *Hair, De Shields made his New York debut Off Broadway in 1973 and found success two years later with the title role of The *Wiz (1975). He found himself in another major hit in 1978 with *Ain't Misbehavin' (1978), and he would reprise both roles for several years. After two decades in short-runs, De Shields made an impressive comeback as the elderly would-be stripper Horse Simmons in The Full Monty (2000). The electric African-American actor-singer has a unique singing style that employs scat and gospel, and it has been used effectively in some of his mesmerizing characterizations.

DE SYLVA, BROWN, and HENDERSON, songwriting team. [George Gard] B. G. De Sylva (1895–1950), known popularly as "Buddy," was born in New York and raised in Los Angeles. While attending the University of Southern California, he performed with a small ukulele combo and wrote some of their songs. One of these songs, " 'N' Everything," caught the ear of Al *Jolson, who used it in Sinbad (1918). Afterward De Sylva collaborated on several other songs that became Jolson standards: "Avalon," "April Showers," and "California, Here I Come." In 1919 he wrote the lyrics to George *Gershwin's first score for La, La Lucille and in 1922 and 1924 the words to Gershwin's melodies for *George White's Scandals, including the hit songs "I'll Build a Stairway to Paradise" and "Somebody Loves Me." De Sylva also created the lyrics for Jerome *Kern's "Look for the Silver Lining" and Victor *Herbert's "A Kiss in the Dark." In 1925 he joined with Lew *Brown and Ray *Henderson, and for the next five years the team of De Sylva, Brown, and Henderson was the most successful in the musical theatre, their shows deemed the quintessential musical comedies and revues of the era. Ray[mond] [né Brost] Henderson (1896–1970) was the composer of the team. Born and raised in Chicago, he studied at the Chicago Conservatory of Music, then played piano in local dance bands before moving to New York, where he served as song-plugger and arranger. In 1922 his publisher introduced him to lyricist Lew Brown and together they wrote "Georgette," a hit song in the *Greenwich Village Follies of 1922*. Lew [né Louis Brownstein] Brown (1893–1958), the Russian-born lyricist and occasional librettist, came to America at the age of five. His first important collaborator was Albert Von Tilzer, for whom he wrote the lyrics to "I'm the Lonesomest Gal in Town" and "I May Be Gone for a Long, Long Time," the latter introduced in *Hitchy-Koo, 1917*. The songs by the trio of De Sylva, Brown, and Henderson were characterized by jazz-inspired rhythms and simple, upbeat lyrics. The shows, all hits, included *George White's Scandals of 1925, 1926,* and *1928* (introducing "Birth of the Blues," "Black Bottom," and "Lucky Day"), *Good News!* (1927), *Manhattan Mary* (1927), *Hold Everything* (1928), *Follow Thru* (1929), and *Flying High* (1930). After the team split, Henderson and Brown wrote *George White's Scandals of 1931, Hot-Cha!* (1932), and *Strike Me Pink* (1933). Henderson had little luck on his own, but Brown found some success with *Calling All Stars* (1934) and *Yokel Boy* (1939) with other composers. De Sylva had the most fruitful career, producing and/or co-writing such shows as *Take a Chance* (1932), *Du Barry Was a Lady* (1939), *Louisiana Purchase* (1940), and *Panama Hattie* (1940). One historian has described the work of De Sylva, Brown, and Henderson as possessing a "distinctive vernacular touch—lowdown in rhythm, piquant in love."

DE WALDEN, T. B. See *Kit, the Arkansas Traveller.*

DEAD END (1935), a drama by Sidney *Kingsley. [*Belasco Theatre, 684 perf.] On a New York street dead-ending at the river, a crippled, failed young architect, Gimpty (Theodore Newton), sits sketching and observing the occupants of the new luxury apartments on one side of the street and of the tenements on the other. Among those he observes are Tommy (Billy Halop), who exercises a precarious hold on his gang of youthful ruffians. Tommy's well-meaning, loving sister, Drina (Elspeth Eric), desperately tries to keep him on the straight and narrow, but Tommy leads his gang in stealing the watch of a rich boy who lives in the swank apartment house, and when the boy's father attempts to recover the watch, Tommy stabs him. At the

same time, Babyface Martin (Joseph Downing), once a gang member on the same street and now a major racketeer and murderer, returns on a secret visit to his mother (Marjorie Main), only to find she will have nothing to do with him. He is killed by the police, while Tommy is hauled off to jail. Gimpty is left to comfort Drina and to continue his sketching. One highlight of the evening was producer Norman *Bel Geddes's magnificent setting depicting the new high-rise and the tenements. The front of the stage was a pier, and the orchestra pit represented the river, into which characters occasionally jumped. Reviewers took note of the fact that the play was housed at the Belasco, where in earlier years David *Belasco himself had offered his own famous realistic settings. *Dead End* was hailed as a compassionate, forthright study of New York low-life, although most critics were offended at what, for the time, was its shocking language.

DEAN, Julia (1830–68), actress. Born in Pleasant Valley, New York, the daughter and granddaughter of performers, she made her professional debut in Louisville in 1845 as Lady Ellen in *Lady of the Lake* and her New York bow at the *Bowery Theatre in 1846 as Julia in *The *Hunchback*. The *Herald* hailed her as "a child of nature," while Laurence *Hutton later recalled, "We have never seen her equal. Her light, graceful figure and beautiful face won her the sympathy and interest in the first act that her genius and fire enabled her to maintain until the fall of the curtain." Dean followed her success with equally acclaimed performances in *The *Lady of Lyons, The *Stranger, *Pizarro,* and *Romeo and Juliet*. For several seasons she continued to tour and expand her repertory. She briefly performed as Julia Dean Hayne after her marriage, then retired, returning to the stage when she divorced Hayne for non-support. But Dean's career was cut short when she died in childbirth after her second marriage. Perhaps because of her early sudden death, the blue-eyed, golden-haired beauty was long remembered with a special fondness.

DEAN, Julia (1880–1952), actress. A beautiful blonde with warm, vivid eyes, she was born in St. Paul, Minnesota, but raised in Salt Lake City, where she made her first stage appearances with a local stock company. After playing briefly with Joseph *Jefferson, James *O'Neill, and in vaudeville, she made her New York debut in *The Altar of Friendship* (1902). Small roles followed in *Merely Mary Ann* (1903) and *The Serio-Comic Governess* (1904) before she won attention as Anna Gray, who destroys evidence that might incriminate her lover, in *The Little Gray Lady* (1906) and as the carefree Polly Hope in

The *Round Up (1907), then toured as Emma Brooks in *Paid in Full (1908). Dean's performance as the desperate Christiane in The Lily (1909) earned her further recognition, and after playing the part for two seasons she was acclaimed for her poor telephone operator Virginia Blaine in *Bought and Paid For (1911) and her murderess Mrs. Harding in The *Law of the Land (1914). None of her later performances found success, including her last New York appearance opposite George *Arliss in Poldekin (1920). Dean was praised as an actress of "absolute naturalness and much varied emotional expressiveness."

DEAR RUTH (1944), a comedy by Norman *Krasna. [*Henry Miller Theatre, 683 perf.] Miriam Wilkins (Lenore Lonergan) is almost sweet sixteen and determined to do her share for the war effort. She writes over sixty letters to a lonely American soldier overseas, signing them all with the name of her elder sister, Ruth (Virginia Gilmore), and enclosing Ruth's picture. Home on leave, the soldier, Lt. William Seawright (John Dall), appears at the Wilkins home without warning, on the very day that Ruth has accepted a proposal of marriage from Albert Kummer (Bartlett Robinson). Although Bill has only two days to spare, it is time enough for Ruth to fall in love with him and ditch Albert. Ruth's father (Howard Smith), a judge, performs a hasty wedding ceremony, and the newlyweds rush off to a quick honeymoon. They are no sooner gone than the doorbell rings. It is a young sailor looking for Ruth. Miriam has obviously been doing more than her share. Welcomed by Howard Barnes of the Herald Tribune as "slight but eminently satisfying," the play typified the vogue for preposterous but joyous comedies that went out several years later when television flooded the market with situation comedies.

DEAREST ENEMY (1925), a musical comedy by Herbert *Fields (book), Richard *Rodgers (music), Lorenz *Hart (lyrics). [Knickerbocker Theatre, 286 perf.] When the British General Howe (Harold Crane) stops at the home of New Yorker Mrs. Robert Murray (Flavia Arcaro) for some rest and refreshment, the good lady contrives to delay him and his associates until the American troops of General Putnam (Percy Woodley) have time to escape and join Washington (H. E. Eldridge) at Harlem Heights. The delay allows Mrs. Murray's niece, Betsy Burke (Helen *Ford), to fall in love with British Captain Sir John Copeland (Charles *Purcell). The romance seems to fall apart when Copeland believes Betsy has signaled the Americans, but after the war he reconsiders and returns to consummate the courtship. Notable songs: Bye and Bye; Here in My Arms; I Beg Your Pardon.

Hailed by Arthur *Hornblow in *Theatre as "something very akin to a genuine comic opera," the musical was Rodgers and Hart's first book show following their success with *Garrick Gaieties. It united the pair with Herbert Fields, thus creating a new team that for several seasons gave promise of rivaling the great *Princess Theatre trio of *Bolton-*Wodehouse-*Kern.

DEATH OF A SALESMAN (1949), a play by Arthur *Miller. [*Morosco Theatre, 742 perf.; Pulitzer Prize, Tony, NYDCC Awards.] Willy Loman (Lee J. *Cobb) is a salesman who has seen better days, or at least lets himself believe he was once more appreciated by his employers. His life has been devoted to his work, his wife, Linda (Mildred *Dunnock), and his sons, Happy (Cameron Mitchell) and Biff (Arthur *Kennedy). His boys are the apple of his eye, so he cannot see that they will probably never amount to much and that Biff has never gotten over his disgust at finding his father in a hotel room with a woman. At sixty-three Willy loses his job then kills himself in an automobile crash, hoping his $20,000 insurance policy will resolve financial problems and give his boys another chance. At his funeral a neighbor characterizes Willy as "a man way out there in the blue, riding on a smile and a shoeshine. And when they start not smiling back—that's an earthquake." The long-suffering Linda, informing her dead husband that the mortgage has finally been paid, can only sob, "We're free and clear. We're free." John Mason *Brown noted the "play is the most poignant statement of man as he must face himself to have come out of our theatre," but added, "Mr. Miller's play is a tragedy modern and personal, not classic and heroic. Its central figure is a little man sentenced to discover his smallness rather than a big man undone by his greatness." The Kermit *Bloomgarden production boasted a superb cast, directed by Elia *Kazan, and a landmark setting by Jo *Mielziner that allowed one to view the Loman household through its skeletal structure and see the world encroaching on the home. The oft-revived drama has seen some outstanding Willy Lomans, including New York versions with George C. *Scott in 1975, Dustin *Hoffman in 1984, and Brian Dennehy in 1999.

DEATH OF GENERAL MONTGOMERY, THE (1777), a blank-verse tragedy by H. H. Brackenridge. Written as an exercise for his students at the Somerset Academy in Maryland, the play described Montgomery's ill-fated attack on Quebec, but all the real action took place offstage and was merely recounted. Nevertheless, it was perceived as a serious attempt at historical reporting

and is credited with bolstering patriotic sentiments at a low point in the Revolution.

DEATHTRAP (1978), a thriller by Ira *Levin.
[*Music Box Theatre, 1,809 perf.] Sidney Bruhl
(John *Wood), a mystery writer suffering a dry
spell, tells his wife, Myra (Marian *Seldes), that he
intends to steal the play a young writer, Clifford
Anderson (Victor *Garber), has sent him and then
kill the young man. To his wife's horror he apparently carries out his plan, burying the young man
in their garden. When Clifford later seemingly
returns from the dead, it proves too much for
Myra, and she dies of a heart attack. That was Sidney's intention from the start, for Sidney has
homosexual leanings and would set up a new life
with Clifford, whose murder was a hoax. But in a
falling out, Sidney mortally wounds Clifford, who
has just enough life in him before he dies to kill
Sidney. John Beaufort of the Christian Science Moni-
tor wrote, "Mr. Levin has a fiendishly clever way of
mixing chills and laughter, clues and climaxes. . . .
He can twist a plot until it almost cries out for
mercy." If many playgoers felt the evening was
sometimes more claptrap than deathtrap, the
play's small cast and low budget allowed the
Alfred De *Liagre, Jr.–Roger L. *Stevens production to become the longest-running mystery in
New York history.

DÉCLASSÉE (1919), a drama by Zoë *Akins.
[*Empire Theatre, 257 perf.] When Sir Bruce
Haden (Harry Plimmer) catches one of his guests,
Edward Thayer (Vernon Steel), cheating at cards,
Haden's wife, Lady Helen (Ethel *Barrymore),
comes to the defense of Edward, her paramour.
She is not one to avoid a fight since she is the last
of the "Mad Varvicks," who for five hundred
years have been dying for causes in which they
believe. Indeed, she has married a bit below her
station, since Sir Bruce is a new knight, a butcher
lately elevated by the king. But after Lady Helen
catches Thayer cheating again, she threatens to
expose him, although he counters by vowing to
reveal letters she has written to him. Undeterred,
she exposes him and thus ruins her own reputation. Moving to New York, she befriends a rich
Jew, Rudolf Solomon (Claude King), and she lives
by selling her jewelry. Solomon proposes marriage and Helen accepts, though she confesses
that she still loves Thayer. Thayer suddenly
reappears, so Solomon offers to release Helen
from her promise. Misunderstanding Solomon's
change of heart, Helen rushes out into the night,
where she is struck down by a taxi. Only as she
is dying and sees Thayer does she understand
Solomon's action. Although critics were impressed
with the sensitivity and acuity with which the

Missouri-born Akins depicted English high
society, it was generally agreed that the strength
of the evening came from Barrymore's acting.
Dorothy *Parker, so often venomously critical,
wrote that she had never seen "any other performance so perfect."

DEE, Ruby [neé Ruby Ann Wallace] (b. 1923),
actress. The small, vibrant African-American leading lady managed to play interesting and powerful women in her career, rarely in servant or other
typical black roles. She was born in Cleveland, the
daughter of a train porter and a schoolteacher,
and grew up in Harlem. Dee was educated
at Hunter College before joining the American
Negro Theatre in 1941, making her Broadway
debut two years later as a native woman in the
drama South Pacific. She gained attention in 1946
when she took over the title character in *Anna
Lucasta and went on to such memorable performances as the struggling wife Ruth in A *Raisin in
the Sun (1959), the funny, naive Lutiebelle in *Purlie
Victorious (1961), the itinerant South African Lena
in Boesman and Lena (1970), the South Carolina
working girl Julia caught up in an interracial love
affair in Wedding Band (1972), and her well-
received memoir program, My One Good Nerve
(1998). Dee is married to actor-director-playwright
Ossie *Davis, and she also has written several
plays herself. Autobiography: With Ossie & Ruby:
In This Life Together, with Davis, 1998.

DEEP ARE THE ROOTS (1945), a play by Arnaud
d'Usseau and James Gow. [Fulton Theatre, 477
perf.] Brett Charles (Gordon Heath) grew up in
the home of Senator Langdon (Charles *Waldron),
where his mother was a servant. Though Brett
was black, he was allowed to play with the senator's daughters, Genevra (Barbara *Bel Geddes)
and Alice (Carol Goodner). Now Brett has
returned home from the war with several decorations and with ideas about his place in life that
disturb the conservative Southern senator. When
Brett enters the public library through the front
door, the town begins to gossip and turn against
him, and when he is accused of stealing a watch,
he is arrested. But Brett has the support of
Genevra and Alice. Genevra, in fact, is fond
enough of him and optimistic enough about the
future to suggest that he marry her. But the realist
Brett dismisses the idea, still grateful for the girls'
support. "We're on the same side," he tells Alice.
An effectively written propaganda play, its suggestion of miscegenation offended some conservative playgoers, but its essentially reasonable
stand on racial tolerance found a welcome in the
liberal climate of the period. The George Heller–
Kermit *Bloomgarden production typified the

hopeful outlook for the future expressed frequently in early postwar dramas.

DEFORMED, THE; or, Woman's Trial (1830), a play by Robert Penn *Smith. [*Chestnut Street Theatre (Philadelphia), 4 perf.] Adorni (Mr. Maywood) is so physically deformed he cannot understand why his wife, Eugenia (Mrs. Rowbotham), loves him. He prevails on his friend Claudio (Mr. Forbes) to test her fidelity, then turns on Claudio and has him condemned to death. At the last minute he recognizes how blindly jealous he has been, so he prepares to take Claudio's place at the execution. But the Duke of Florence (Mr. *Wemyss) pardons Adorni. The United States Gazette began its notice by welcoming a serious new drama into a season given over to musical spectacles and frivolous comedies, a perennial critical cry. It continued, "The character of the Deformed is entirely new, and we believe unique in the whole range of the drama. . . . There are so many bold traits in this character, such as entitle Mr. Smith to a distinguished rank as a dramatic observer." The play is an early example of the intermittent fascination that American playwrights have had for freaks and disabled people, a fascination still evident in plays such as The *Elephant Man, The *Miracle Worker, and *Children of a Lesser God. The play was revived as late as 1839.

DELAWARE THEATRE COMPANY (Wilmington). Begun in 1978 in a former firehouse in the city's downtown, the company quickly grew and moved into its modern facility on the riverfront in 1985, where it continues to present an eclectic season of revivals and occasional new works. The group has some ambitious outreach programs, such as the Delaware Young Playwrights Festival, theatre classes for adults, a summer theatre camp, and programs for at-risk urban teens and for mentally challenged and hearing-impaired audiences.

DELICATE BALANCE, A (1966), a play by Edward *Albee. [*Martin Beck Theatre, 132 perf.; Pulitzer Prize.] Sitting in their comfortable library after dinner, Agnes (Jessica *Tandy) confides to her husband that she sometimes worries about losing her mind. But her husband, Tobias (Hume *Cronyn), assures her he knows no saner woman. In short order the couple are visited by Agnes's younger sister (Rosemary Murphy), a bitter, malicious alcoholic; by the couple's much married daughter (Marian *Seldes); and by Tobias's best friend (Henderson *Forsythe) and his wife (Carmen Mathews), both of whom are frightened by something they cannot identify. The visits force Agnes and Tobias to reevaluate all their relationships and to recognize that they must maintain a delicate balance between sanity and madness. A curiously elusive play filled with stilted dialogue ("I apologize that my nature is such to bring out in you the full force of your brutality"), it was often more satisfying as an intellectual exercise than as a dramatic theatre piece. But an acclaimed *Lincoln Center–produced revival in 1996, directed by Gerald *Gutierrez and featuring Rosemary *Harris, George Grizzard, and Elaine *Stritch, revealed the play to be very funny and inexplicably moving.

DELL, Gabriel [né Gabriel Del Vecchio] (1919–88), character actor. He was born in Brooklyn and was on Broadway in 1932 as a boy in the *Theatre Guild production of The Good Earth. He played one of the street youths in *Dead End (1935), then went to Hollywood with other members of the gang where they were billed as the Dead End Kids in a series of films. Dell returned to New York as an adult and studied acting with Lee *Strasberg before starting a second career as a supporting player, usually in comic parts. His most notable leading role was the title Greenwich Village artist in The Sign in Sidney Brustein's Window (1964).

DENHAM, Reginald (1894–1983), director, playwright, and actor. The multi-talented Englishman first came to American playgoers' attention with his direction of Rope's End (1929) and Josef Suss (1930). He settled in America in 1940 and thereafter directed such plays as Ladies in Retirement (1940), which he wrote; Guest in the House (1942); The *Two Mrs. Carrolls (1943); Dial M for Murder (1952); *Sherlock Holmes (1953); The Bad Seed (1954); and Hostile Witness (1966). Denham's forte seemed to be plays with an element of mystery to increase dramatic suspense. With his wife, Mary Orr, he wrote several plays as well as a book of reminiscences, Footlights and Feathers (1966).

D'ENNERY, Adolphe-Philippe (1811–99), playwright. Alone or with collaborators, this French dramatist was one of the most successful authors of melodrama, many of which were huge hits when adapted for the American stage. The most notable of these triumphs were The *Two Orphans (1874) and A Celebrated Case (1878). Other works included: Cartouche, The Highwayman of Paris (1864), Michael Strogoff (1880), and The Creole (1881).

DENNIS, [Sandra Dale] Sandy (1937–92), actress. Born in Hastings, Nebraska, she first called attention to herself as Sandra, the compassionate social worker, in A Thousand Clowns (1962), then played Ellen Gordon, the kooky mistress in *Any Wednesday (1964). Dennis excelled at playing slightly odd characters who were either pathetic, as in Come Back to the 5 & Dime, Jimmy Dean, Jimmy Dean

(1982), or bizarrely comic, as in *Absurd Person Singular* (1974). Between Broadway assignments she assumed many leading roles at major regional theatres, in touring productions, and in films.

DENVER CENTER THEATRE COMPANY. The largest regional theatre between Chicago and the West Coast, it was founded in 1972 by Donald R. Seawell. By 1979 it had grown enough to move into the large Helen Bonfils Theatre complex, housing the 700-seat Stage Theatre, the 427-seat Space Theatre, the 250-seat Ricketson Theatre, and the 200-seat Source Theatre. Under the direction of Edward Payson Call, the group filled its many venues with revivals and modern works, as well as an annual new-play festival and a training conservatory. The Colorado company won the 1998 *Tony Award for outstanding regional theatre.

DEROSA, Eugene. An architect who alone or as part of the firm of Derosa and Pereira designed such Broadway theatres as the Apollo, Coliseum, Colony (now the *Broadway), Gallo, Klaw, Times Square, and Vanderbilt.

DERWENT, Clarence (1884–1959), actor. Born in England, he made his first New York appearance as Stephen Undershaft in *Major Barbara* in 1915 and for the next thirty-one years played important supporting roles in a wide variety of works, including *The Letter of the Law* (1920), *Love for Love* (1925), *The Woman of Bronze* (1927), *The *Three Musketeers* (1928), *Serena Blandish* (1929), *Topaze* (1930), *The Late Christopher Bean* (1932), *Kind Lady* (1940), *The Doctor's Dilemma* (1941), *The *Pirate* (1942), and *Rebecca* (1945). His last appearance was as the President in *The Madwoman of Chaillot* (1948). Derwent served two terms as president of the *Actors' Equity and for many years was president of the *American National Theatre and Academy (ANTA). In 1945 he established the annual Clarence Derwent Awards to be given for the best performances in supporting roles in both London and New York. Autobiography: *The Derwent Story*, 1953.

DESERT SONG, THE (1926), an operetta by Otto *Harbach, Oscar *Hammerstein II (book, lyrics), Frank *Mandel (book), Sigmund *Romberg (music). [*Casino Theatre, 465 perf.] In the mountains of Morocco, the French are fighting the rebellious Riffs, who are led by a mysterious figure known as the Red Shadow. Pierre Birabeau (Robert *Halliday), the son of the French commander, loves one of the beautiful women at the encampment, Margot Bonvalet (Vivienne *Segal), but she has little time for the shy, seemingly backward young man. Matters come to a head when the Red Shadow kidnaps Margot. The French bribe a Riff dancing girl into betraying the leader, but he escapes, leaving behind only a red cloak. All that the French discover is Pierre wandering aimlessly in the desert. The French and the Riffs reach an accommodation. Margot, however, is forlorn, since she has fallen in love with her romantic captor. She looks on Pierre with new eyes when he reveals he was the leader. *Notable songs*: The Desert Song; One Alone; The Riff Song; Romance. Suggested by the real-life exploits of a contemporary Berber chieftain named Abd-el-Krim, the exotic backgrounds and Romberg's lush score made this one of the biggest and best-loved hits of the era, albeit Richard *Watts Jr. observed in the *Herald Tribune*, "The lyrics gave indication that W. S. Gilbert had lived and died in vain." Perennially revived for decades, it is still produced by opera companies.

DESIRE UNDER THE ELMS (1924), a drama by Eugene *O'Neill. [Greenwich Village Theatre, 208 perf.] Ephraim Cabot (Walter *Huston), unsparing and miserly, works the New England farm he inherited from his second wife with the help of his three sons. The youngest, Eben (Charles Ellis), blames his father for his mother's death, insisting he killed her with overwork. Eben's older half-brothers, Simeon (Allen Nagle) and Peter (Perry Ivins), long for a better life in California. When the seventy-five-year-old Ephraim appears with his third wife, an ambitious young widow, Abbie Putnam (Mary Morris), the older boys sell their shares to Eben and head for the gold fields. Abbie seduces Eben, and when their child is born, Ephraim, believing the child his, makes the baby his heir. Eben denounces Abbie, but she has come to love him. To prove her love, she kills the baby. Eben calls the police, but recognizing that he, in turn, has come to love Abbie, claims he assisted in the killing. Ephraim prepares to tend the farm alone as the young couple are taken away. Stark *Young saw the work's similarity to *Beyond the Horizon* but judged it "better written throughout; it has as much tragic gloom and irony, but a more mature conception and a more imaginative austerity." When the play was moved uptown it was not particularly successful until the police attempted to close it. The notoriety helped the play achieve an acceptable run. An *ANTA revival in 1952 met with a modest run but a *Circle in the Square production in 1963, featuring George C. *Scott, Colleen *Dewhurst, and Rip *Torn, was very successful.

DETECTIVE STORY (1949), a melodrama by Sidney *Kingsley. [*Hudson Theatre, 581 perf.] Detective McLeod (Ralph *Bellamy) of the 21st Precinct, New York, is a fanatically committed policeman whose ideas of justice and law are in some ways as warped as those of the hoodlums with whom he deals. McLeod believes that suspects are guilty until proven innocent, and even when they are acquitted in the courts insists, "There's a higher court," and, by implication, that he is it. He is not above brutally treating suspects such as Dr. Kurt Schneider (Harry Worth), a suspected abortionist. But when he learns that his wife, Mary (Meg Mundy), once had an abortion and that Schneider performed it, his world collapses. He walks into a suspect's gun, and the man shoots him dead. Although the main story was well written and its principal figures perceptively drawn, much of the strength of the Howard *Lindsay–Russel *Crouse production came in its vignettes of minor figures: burglars, shoplifters, shady lawyers, and policemen. Burns *Mantle, who had been a police reporter early in his career, observed that the "melodrama possesses so much naturalism and realism, and performs so easily, that a careless onlooker might use a film term and call it a documentary."

DEVIL AND DANIEL WEBSTER, THE (1939), a musical folk play by Stephen Vincent Benét (text) and Douglas Moore (music). [Martin Beck Theatre, 6 perf.] Jabez Stone (John Gurney), a New Hampshire farmer who has sold his soul to the devil in return for a decade of prosperity, is confronted on his wedding day by Mr. Scratch (George Rasely), demanding payment. Jabez prevails on his neighbor Daniel Webster (Lansing Hatfield) to defend him before a jury of the devil's selection. Webster's eloquence carries the moment, and Jabez is acquitted. Despite its brief New York run, the work, which was based on Benét's own short story, remained a favorite of small dramatic and musical groups for many years.

DEVIL'S DISCIPLE, THE (1897). George Bernard *Shaw's only important work set in America and dealing with events during the Revolutionary War, the play was his second to receive a professional mounting, when *Mansfield offered it with himself as Dick Dudgeon. William *Winter called his performance "picturesque, sympathetic, and effective." The production ran for seven weeks, a run far exceeded when the *Theatre Guild revived it in 1923. With Basil *Sydney as Dick and Roland *Young in the brilliant cameo part of General Burgoyne, the production was hailed by the *Times* as "one of the few great comedy hits of the season" and ran six months. A superb 1950 revival starred Maurice *Evans as Dick but was stolen by Dennis *King as the General. Brooks *Atkinson called his performance "humorously insufferable," adding, "The sardonicism rolls off his lips with wonderful grace and condescension." The comedy was revived in 1988 at the *Circle in the Square.

DEWHURST, Colleen (1926–91), actress. Born in Montreal, she studied at the *American Academy of Dramatic Arts and with Harold *Clurman before making her debut as a neighbor in a 1952 revival of *Desire under the Elms*. Much of her early work was Off Broadway, including her highly praised performance of the ostentatiously ladylike Laetitia in *Children of Darkness* (1958) at the *Circle in the Square. On Broadway she received *Tony Awards for her devout wife Mary Follet in *All the Way Home* (1960) and as Josie in a 1973 revival of A *Moon for the Misbegotten*. In the latter she was described by Clive *Barnes in the *Times* as a "virgin earth-mother, with common sense shining through her eyes like stars, and love clinging to her big red hands." Dewhurst's other memorable roles include Cleopatra in *Antony and Cleopatra* (1963), Sara in *More Stately Mansions* (1967), Shen Te in *The Good Woman of Setzuan* (1970), Christine Mannon in *Mourning Becomes Electra* (1972), Martha in *Who's Afraid of Virginia Woolf?* (1976), Olga in *You Can't Take It with You* (1983), Carlotta Monterey O'Neill in *My Gene* (1987), Essie in *Ah, Wilderness!* (1988), and Mary Tyrone in *Long Day's Journey into Night* (1988).

DIAMOND LIL (1928), a play by Mae *West. [*Royale Theatre, 171 perf.] Lil (West) is the mistress of Gus Jordon (J. Merrill Holmes), who runs a Bowery saloon and dance joint known as Suicide Hall and who traffics in white slavery on the side. Gus is not especially loyal to Lil, but then when he is not around Lil is delighted to entertain any number of men friends. She even falls for Captain Cummings (Curtis Cooksey), a Salvation Army evangelist. When Cummings breaks up the white slave trade and discloses that he is really a police officer, Lil is not too shocked. She has grown tired of Gus and, well, just might even reform. Although more straitlaced critics assailed the show as "lurid," more liberal reviewers took a line not unlike that of Charles Brackett in *The New Yorker*, who wrote, "Pure trash, or rather impure trash though it is, I wouldn't miss *Diamond Lil* if I were you." A nearly year-long run in London during the 1947–48 season prompted a New York revival in 1949. By then the play was perceived as harmless hokum, but with West again as star it ran 181 performances and might have run longer had she not broken her ankle.

DIARY OF ANNE FRANK, THE (1955), a play by Frances Goodrich, Albert Hackett. [*Cort Theatre, 717 perf.; Pulitzer Prize, Tony, NYDCC Awards.] Shortly after the war Otto Frank (Joseph *Schildkraut) returns with his former stenographer, Miep Gies (Gloria Jones), to the attic where Mr. Kraler (Clinton Sundberg) had hidden the Frank family and some other Jews from the Gestapo. There Frank discovers the diary kept by his thirteen-year-old daughter Anne (Susan Strasberg). His thoughts fly back to the months they spent there, often in silence lest they give away their whereabouts; to happy moments such as a Chanukah celebration and to bitter ones such as catching a fellow Jew stealing their food. The announcement of Allied landings brings hope of a quick release, but shortly before the liberation their hiding place is betrayed. Anne and the others are sent to the gas chambers. Only Mr. Frank manages to escape. Now he reads the last line in the diary. "In spite of everything," Anne writes, "I still believe people are really good at heart." "She puts me to shame," the still bitter Frank acknowledges. The play was based on the real Anne Frank's diary (published in English as *Anne Frank: The Diary of a Young Girl*), which had become a worldwide best-seller after the war. The Kermit *Bloomgarden production was widely praised, Richard *Watts Jr. of the *New York Post* noting, "By wisely shunning any trace of theatricality or emotional excess, the playwrights have made the only-too-true story deeply moving in its unadorned veracity." It was successfully produced in almost every major theatre center, with noteworthy New York revivals in 1978 and 1997. New Yorker **Albert HACKETT** (1900–95) and his wife, **Francis GOODRICH** (1891–1984), a native of Belleville, New Jersey, began their careers as performers. Their first two plays were the moderately successful comedies *Up Pops the Devil* (1930) and *Bridal Wise* (1932). After a long, successful career as film writers they returned to Broadway with the short-lived *The Great Big Doorstep* (1942).

DICTATOR, THE (1904), a farce by Richard Harding Davis. [Criterion Theatre, 64 perf.] Believing he has fatally struck a cab driver in a fight over a fare, Brooks Travers (William *Collier) and his valet (Edward *Abeles) take the first boat for Porto Banyos, where revolutions are weekly events. The latest revolution was engineered by none other than the American Consul (George Nash) with the aid of General Santos Campos (Robert McWade Jr.). But the Consul's reign as dictator is short, for the General organizes another coup and makes himself dictator. Fearing for his life, the Consul assigns Travers both his position and a battle-ax widow (Louise Allen) who has been pursuing him. Travers must choose between returning to America and going to jail, or fighting not only the General but the harridan señora. He elects to fight. To give his men backbone, he ups their pay from twenty-eight cents a day to thirty, then announces the next revolution will take place at 11 o'clock. But the General proves a determined opponent

until Travers gets his cocktail-swilling telegraph operator (John *Barrymore) to send a message asking that Admiral Dewey come to his aid with the *Olympia*. Just as the opposition capitulates, Travers learns that the cab driver was not seriously hurt. He decides to take the next ship back, preferring obnoxious taxi men to Latin instability. The comic piece, produced by Charles *Frohman, toured successfully for several seasons and was frequently revived by little theatre groups. A musical version was presented in 1920 as *The Girl from Home*. **Richard Harding DAVIS** (1864–1916), a native of Philadelphia, was best known as a war correspondent and short-story writer, but he wrote several successful plays, and his stories provided others with material for dramatization. Davis's other hit comedy was *The Galloper* (1906), in which the hero poses as a famed war correspondent. Plays based on his stories include Robert *Hilliard's *The Littlest Girl* (1895) and later Augustus *Thomas's *Soldiers of Fortune* (1902). His brother was the noted critic Charles Belmont Davis (1866?–1926). Biography: *Richard Harding Davis: His Day*, Fairfax Downey, 1933.

DIETZ and SCHWARTZ, songwriting team. Howard Dietz (1896–1983), one of Broadway's most urbane lyricists and librettists, was born in New York and was a classmate of Oscar *Hammerstein and Lorenz *Hart at Columbia University. While in college his witty verses began to appear in newspapers, notably in Franklin P. Adams's famous "Conning Tower." Broadway first heard his rhymes when he wrote a lyric for "Alibi Baby" in *Poppy* (1923). He soon came to the attention of Jerome *Kern, who asked him to create the lyrics for *Dear Sir* (1924). During this time he also began a successful career as publicist for the MGM film company. In the late 1920s Dietz started to collaborate with composer Arthur Schwartz (1900–84). Born in Brooklyn, Schwartz studied piano and music over his lawyer-father's strenuous objections. He wrote songs for vaudeville performers and occasional numbers for revues before joining with Dietz to create the songs for the leading revues of the day: *The *Little Show* (1929), *The Second Little Show* (1930), *Three's a Crowd* (1930), *The *Band Wagon* (1931), and *Flying Colors* (1932). Dietz wrote sketches for many of these revues and served as director for the latter. While the team's book musicals *Revenge with Music* (1934) and *Between the Devil* (1937) were not as successful, they still boasted fine scores. After reteaming for the popular revues *At Home Abroad* (1935) and *Inside USA* (1948), the twosome attempted book shows again with *The Gay Life* (1961) and *Jennie* (1963), but again the songs outshone the rest of the material. In 1944 Dietz collaborated with Vernon

Duke on songs for the short-lived musicals *Jackpot* and *Sadie Thompson*, writing the libretto for the latter. Schwartz collaborated with Ira *Gershwin on the disappointing *Park Avenue* (1946), but with lyricist Dorothy *Fields came up with exceptional songs for *Stars in Your Eyes* (1939), *A *Tree Grows in Brooklyn* (1951), and *By the Beautiful Sea* (1954). Dietz sometimes rivaled Lorenz *Hart with his pungent lyrics, while Schwartz was one of the most underrated of Broadway's great composers, his music ranging from moody ballads to sprightly rhythm numbers. Curiously, each man's book shows were commercial failures and only their revues made money. Autobiography (Dietz): *Dancing in the Dark*, 1974.

DIGGES, Dudley (1879–1947), character actor. The Dublin-born performer had distinguished himself with the Irish National Players before embarking for America in 1904. Among his early appearances were roles in *The Rising of the Moon* (1908) opposite Mrs. *Fiske, *The Spitfire* (1910), and *The *Squaw Man* (1911). After playing opposite George *Arliss in *Disraeli* (1911), Digges served as Arliss's stage manager for seven years. In 1919 he joined the newly formed *Theatre Guild and quickly established himself as one of its finest character actors, remaining with the Guild for eleven years and giving nearly 3,000 performances under its aegis. The avuncular, gravel-voiced actor's notable assignments included the cowardly, selfish Henry Clegg in *Jane Clegg* (1920); Boss Mangan in *Heartbreak House* (1920); the villainous Sparrow in *Liliom* (1921); the foredoomed Mr. Zero in *The *Adding Machine* (1923); the heavenly examiner Rev. Thompson in *Outward Bound* (1924); the helpful Critic in *The Guardsman* (1924); Feodor in *The Brothers Karamazov* (1927); the wise Chu-Yin in *Marco Millions* (1928); industrialist Andrew Undershaft in *Major Barbara* (1928); and the atheistic Ramsey Fife in *Dynamo* (1929). He also directed a number of Guild productions, including *Candida* (1925), *Pygmalion* (1927), *Love Is Like That* (1927), and *The Doctor's Dilemma* (1927). Digges scored as Gramps, who defies death's messenger, in *On Borrowed Time* (1938), then appeared as the rich Uncle Stanley in *George Washington Slept Here* (1942), and as Mr. Burgess in *Candida* (1942). His last appearance was as Harry Hope, owner of the seedy bar, in *The *Iceman Cometh* (1946). Of this performance Brooks *Atkinson commented, "To anyone who loves acting, Dudley Digges' performance as the tottering and irascible saloon proprietor is worth particular cherishing. Although the old man is half dead, Mr. Digges' command of the actor's art is brilliantly alive; it overflows with comic and philosophic expression."

DILLINGHAM, Charles [Bancroft] (1868–1934), producer. Born in Hartford, Connecticut, the son of an Episcopal clergyman, Dillingham rejected college in favor of becoming a journalist and served on newspapers in Hartford, Washington, D.C., and Chicago before moving to the *New York Evening Sun*. A stint as that paper's drama critic convinced him his future lay in the theatre. In 1896 he wrote and produced a play called *Ten P.M.*, a failure that nonetheless brought him to the attention of Charles *Frohman, who hired him as a press agent and production assistant. In 1898 he became Julia *Marlowe's manager and began to produce actively. In the next thirty years Dillingham produced over two hundred plays, including the non-musicals *Man and Superman* (1905), *A Bill of Divorcement* (1921), *Bulldog Drummond* (1921), and *The Last of Mrs. Cheyney* (1925). However, he was most celebrated for his musical productions, which in lavishness and taste were considered second only to Florenz *Ziegfeld's. Among his many successes were *Mlle. Modiste* (1905), *The *Red Mill* (1906), *Chin-Chin* (1914), *Watch Your Step* (1914), *Jack o'Lantern* (1917), *Apple Blossoms* (1919), *Tip Top* (1920), *Good Morning, Dearie* (1921), *Stepping Stones* (1923), *Sunny* (1925), and *Criss Cross* (1926). In 1910 he built the Globe (now *Lunt-Fontanne) Theatre, and from 1915 to 1922 ran the mammoth *Hippodrome. Dillingham was famous for his gentlemanly conduct and his dapper appearance; his derby became a trademark. So respected was he that when he went bankrupt in the Depression his friends regularly took up collections to support him and even mounted a show, giving him credit as producer.

DINEHART, Alan. See *Separate Rooms*.

DINING ROOM, THE (1982), a play by A. R. Gurney. [*Playwrights Horizons, 583 perf.] In a series of scenes that take place in a series of dining rooms from the 1940s to the present, characters from different families come and go, each adding a piece of the mosaic of social life of the vanishing upper classes. The entertaining commentary on the WASP culture was more than just a string of sketches and was generally applauded by the press as "clear-eyed, touching, and buoyantly funny." The play opened in Playwrights Horizons' small downstairs space but was soon moved to the larger theatre upstairs, where it was very popular, followed by hundreds of productions across the country.

DINNER AT EIGHT (1932), a play by George S. *Kaufman and Edna *Ferber. [*Music Box, 232 perf.] The guests invited to the dinner party of Millicent Jordan (Ann Andrews) have all seemed to reach turning points in their lives. Larry Renault

(Conway Tearle), a broke, alcoholic, fading matinee idol, loses his last chance for a comeback, so commits suicide. His young mistress, Paula Jordan (Marguerite Churchill), is the daughter of Oliver Jordan (Malcolm Duncan), who is seriously ill and whose shaky shipping interests are in danger of being taken over by the greedy upstart Dan Packard (Paul Harvey). Packard's sluttish wife, Kitty (Judith Wood), a former hatcheck girl, is in love with Dr. Wayne Talbot (Austin Fairman), but Talbot has tired of her and prefers to return to his wife, Lucy (Olive Wyndham). The long-retired star, Carlotta Vance (Constance Collier), once Jordan's mistress, has sold her stock in his company, unaware that his interests are beleaguered. Even Millicent's servants are touchy and quick to blow up. Then the cook announces that part of the dinner has been spoiled. Nevertheless, tired of waiting for Renault and unaware of his suicide, the guests and their hostess head for the dining room to make the best of it. Praised by the *Herald Tribune* as "one of the best of the shrewdly literate Broadway dramas," the Sam *Harris production broke theatre records in its early weeks. But its large cast, expensive production, and effects of the Depression, then at its nadir, prevented the play from spanning the summer. A 1966 Broadway revival with an all-star cast somehow missed capturing the original's glitter, and a 2002 revival by *Lincoln Center was praised for its high style but criticized for its uneven acting.

DINNER WITH FRIENDS (1999), a play by Donald Margulies. [Variety Arts Theatre, 654 perf., Pulitzer Prize.] Suburban couple Gabe (Matthew Arkin) and Karen (Lisa Emery) are international food writers who once introduced friend Beth (Julie White) to Tom (Kevin Kilner), the latter two marrying and all four bonding in a cozy friendship. But when Tom leaves Beth for another woman and declares how unhappy he was all those years, Gabe and Karen find that their trust has been shattered and are left to question the validity of their own happiness. Described by the press as "wry and keenly observed," the four-character drama managed to look at a familiar subject with fresh eyes. **Donald MARGULIES** (b. 1954) was born in Brooklyn, the son of a salesman, and was educated at SUNY Purchase. He was first noticed with his Off-Broadway plays *Found a Peanut* (1984) and *The Loman Family Picnic* (1989) but received recognition with *Sight Unseen* (1992), an insightful drama set in the contemporary art world. Margulies's other works include *What's Wrong with This Picture?* (1994) and *Collected Stories* (1998).

DIPLOMACY (1878). The Victorien *Sardou drama was first offered in America by Lester *Wallack in

an adaptation by Saville and Bolton Rowe. Its story centers on Dora, a poor girl who is married to Julian Beauclere after he had spurned the Countess Zicka. The countess steals an important document and implicates Dora in the theft. The play, which proved one of Wallack's greatest successes, featured H. J. *Montague as Julian, Maude *Granger as Dora, and Rose *Coghlan as the Countess. It remained a favorite for fifty years, its last important revival coming in an all-star production in 1928 with a cast that included Margaret *Anglin, Jacob *Ben-Ami, Charles *Coburn, William *Faversham, Helen *Gahagan, Rollo *Peters, and Tyrone *Power.

DISNEY THEATRICAL PRODUCTIONS. Started in 1993 as part of the Buena Vista Theatrical Group, the company has made quite an impact on New York theatre in a short time, as well as finding success across the country and internationally. The goal of the program, headed by Thomas Schumacker, is to develop and produce live theatre. Its first production, *Beauty and the Beast* (1994), was not warmly greeted by the critics, theatre community, or the *Tony Awards but was immediately popular with audiences in New York and later on tour. In 1997 Disney restored the *New Amsterdam Theatre as a home for its future Broadway productions, thereby aiding the redevelopment of 42nd Street and leading the way for other important restorations on the block. After a limited run of the concert *King David*, the *New Amsterdam once again became a legit house with Disney's The *Lion King* (1997), this time winning critical and popular approval. With its home base occupied by that hit musical, Disney opened its next offering, *Aida* (2000), at the Palace Theatre, again creating an audience favorite even though critical reaction was mixed. All three musicals continue to run on Broadway and are touring extensively, marking a very impressive track record for the young company. Disney's stage version of *The Hunchback of Notre Dame* premiered in Germany in 1999 as *Der Glöckner Von Notre Dame* and also found success. Plans to bring it to America are under way, as are many other projects.

DITHMAR, Edward A[ugustus] (1854–1917), critic. The son of a newspaper composing-room foreman, he was born in New York and began his own newspaper career as a reporter for the *Evening Post* in 1871. Six years later he moved to the *Times*, where he remained for the rest of his life. He became the paper's principal drama critic in 1884 and held the post until 1901. Dithmar's approach was what he himself called "Impressionistic," judging a play by his immediate reaction to it and not by academic canons of correctness or by primarily puritanical moralistic considerations. He also wrote such works as *Memories of Daly's Theatre* (1897) and *John Drew* (1900).

DITRICHSTEIN, Leo [James] (1865–1928), actor. Son of a count and grandson of a famous Austrian novelist, the heavy-set, gruffly handsome, round-faced actor apprenticed in Berlin before coming to America in 1890. His first appearances were in German plays at the Amberg Theatre. After learning sufficient English, he toured in *Mr. Wilkinson's Widows* before making his New York debut under Charles *Frohman's aegis in *The Other Man* (1893). He first caught Broadway's eye as Zou Zou in *Trilby* (1895), then enhanced his reputation as the comic Otto Whisky in *A Stag Party* (1895) and the mad scientist Achille Rabon in *Under the Polar Star* (1896). Ditrichstein was George Tesman in the first New York mounting of *Hedda Gabler* (1898), then later gave such notable performances as the explosive Colonel Larivette in *Before and After* (1905), the cynical Bernard in *The Lily* (1909), the philandering pianist Gabor Arany in *The Concert* (1910), Jacques Dupont in *The Temperamental Journey* (1913), Sascha Taticheff in *Molnar's *The Phantom Rival* (1914), the seducer Jean Paurel in *The *Great Lover* (1915), the title role in *The King* (1917), and Napoleon's adversary Armand in *The Purple Mask* (1920). His last appearance was in *The Business Widow* (1923). Even in cameo parts, such as Bernard in *The Lily*, Ditrichstein won critical respect. One reviewer observed, "In a brief role confined to the first act [he], with perfect art, also delivered a little gem of characterization—the figure of a middle-aged cynic, a role expressed with complete naturalness and splendid touches of acrid humor." Alone or with collaborators, he wrote or adapted many plays, often appearing in them or directing them. He retired while still at the height of his fame and returned to Europe.

DIVORCE (1871), a play by Augustin *Daly. [*Fifth Avenue Theatre, 200 perf.] The day of the marriage of convenience of her daughter, Lu Ten Eyck (Fanny *Davenport), to the much older De Wolf De Witt (William *Davidge), Mrs. Ten Eyck (Fanny *Morant) learns that Alfred Adrianse (D. H. Harkins) has returned from a long trip abroad. Alfred had left New York when Mrs. Ten Eyck cut short his courtship of her other daughter, Fanny (Clara *Morris), insisting Fanny was too young. Now that Fanny is older, Mrs. Ten Eyck's objections fade, so Alfred and Fanny are married along with Lu and De Wolf. Both marriages, however, quickly fall apart. Alfred becomes unjustly suspicious of Fanny, especially of her actually innocent relations with Captain Lynde (Louis *James), while Lu finds her aged mate dismayingly complacent.

Fanny and Alfred's problems are more serious, and Fanny leaves, taking their young son with her. Alfred kidnaps the boy, and Fanny follows them to Florida to reclaim the child. Alfred and Lu are brought to their senses in time for a happy ending. Producer-author Daly took his characters and incidents from Anthony Trollope's novel, *He Knew He Was Right,* but rearranged matters with a free hand, moving the setting to America, adding a subplot, and contriving reconciliations at the close. The *Herald* commented, "The subject . . . is a real live one, and certainly its treatment evinces rare delicacy and skill and a thorough knowledge of society of the present day." The play was the reigning hit of the day, at one point playing simultaneously in New York, Boston, Philadelphia, Buffalo, and St. Louis. Its Manhattan run was said to have been a record for a comedy at the time. It was also the first play performed in Chicago after the fire. Later critics looked less kindly on the play, but it was revived successfully in Philadelphia as late as 1892.

DIVORÇONS (1882). This play by Victorien *Sardou deals with a foolish young wife, Cyprienne, who feels she must divorce her husband, des Prunelles, and marry a handsome ne'er-do-well. Her husband's kindness and generosity bring her to her senses. The work was first offered in an English version in 1882 with an undistinguished cast, but quickly became a major success and was revived regularly as late as World War I.

DIX, Beulah Marie. See *Road to Yesterday, The*.

DIXEY, Henry E. (1859–1943), actor. After making his debut at the age of ten at the *Howard Athenaeum in his native Boston playing Peanuts in *Under the Gaslight*, he trained with the pantomimist James S. Maffitt, then made his first New York "appearance" as one-half of the heifer in E. E. *Rice's *Evangeline* (1874). Subsequently, Dixey appeared in numerous other musicals before creating the role for which he was afterward famous, the statue brought to life as *Adonis* (1884), the first show in Broadway history to run more than five hundred performances. He played the part for several seasons and later returned to tour with it occasionally. Unlike most comedians, Dixey was an exceptionally handsome man, who later sought roles that allowed him to display his figure in tight-fitting period costumes. Unfortunately, the rest of his career was anticlimactic. Two major musicals written especially for him, *The Seven Ages* (1889) and *Rip* (1890), both failed. Thereafter, he alternated between musicals and straight plays, usually comedies, but never again savored the acclaim he had won in *Adonis*. One of his better later roles was the absurdly troublesome Peter Swallow opposite Mrs. *Fiske in *Mrs. Bumpstead-Leigh (1911).

DIXON, George Washington (1808?–61), singer and dancer. One of the earliest blackface entertainers, he was briefly popular in the late 1820s and early 1830s and claimed to have written and introduced the once well-known "Old Zip Coon." He later abandoned the stage to edit a notoriously scurrilous newspaper and died in poverty in New Orleans.

DO I HEAR A WALTZ? See *Time of the Cuckoo, The.*

DOCK STREET THEATRE (Charleston, South Carolina). An announcement in the *South Carolina Gazette* in 1736 read: "On Thursday, February 12, will be opened the New Theatre in Dock Street in which will be perform'd 'The Recruiting Officer'." The house became known as the Dock Street Theatre for the two years it was in operation. It closed in 1738 and burned in the great Charleston fire of 1740. Two more playhouses were built on or near its site, one in 1754 and a second in 1766, then a hotel was built in its place. In 1937, using funds and people from the Works Progress Administration, a replica of the original 1736 interior (with seating for 563 spectators in pewlike seating) was constructed inside the crumbling hotel. Owned by the city, the restored theatre opened, as its ancestor had, with a production of *The Recruiting Officer.* The Dock Street Theatre (which is actually located on Church Street, the name having changed in 1809) was an outgrowth of the *little theatre movement.

DOCTOR OF ALCANTARA, THE (1866), an opéra bouffe by Benjamin Edward *Woolf (book), Julius Eichberg (music). [French Theatre, 12 perf.] Two young lovers, Carlos and Isabella, are ordered by their fathers, Doctor Paracelsus and Señor Balthazar, to marry mates they have never seen. No one realizes that the mates selected are none other than the lovers themselves. Carlos's adventures in the difficult courtship include hiding in a basket, which is thrown in the river with Carlos inside, and being mistaken for dead after drinking a sleeping potion. The comic opera had its first performances in Boston, where its authors were based, in 1862. For several years it was regularly included in the repertory of numerous traveling opera companies and was presented in most major cities. Of negligible value, it represents the style and drift of operetta in America before the coming of *Offenbach and *Gilbert and *Sullivan.

DODGE, D. Frank, designer. One of the busiest turn-of-the-century set designers, he specialized in colorful settings for musicals as exemplified by his work for *De Koven's *Rob Roy* (1894), the Lillian *Russell vehicle *An American Beauty* (1896), and the long-running importation *A Chinese Honeymoon* (1902). His work for non-musicals ranged from spectacular settings for *Ben-Hur* (1899) to realism in *Salvation Nell* (1908) and *Mrs. Bumpstead-Leigh* (1911).

DODSWORTH (1934), a play by Sidney *Howard. [*Shubert Theatre, 317 perf.] A rich, retired automobile manufacturer, Samuel Dodsworth (Walter *Huston), decides to take his wife, Fran (Fay *Bainter), on a grand tour of Europe. To his chagrin, however, Fran is more interested in indiscreet affairs with other men than in Europe's treasures. On the eastward sailing Dodsworth has met Edith Cortright (Nan Sunderland), a woman Fran's age but more mature. When the time comes to sail back, Dodsworth decides to remain in Europe with Edith. Fran, alone on the ship, can only exclaim dazedly, "He's gone ashore. He's gone ashore." This dramatization of Sinclair Lewis's novel was one of the most successful transfers from book to stage of the era, helped immensely by Huston's and Bainter's luminous performances and producer Max *Gordon's skillful production. Burns *Mantle noted, "It combined the homeliness of subject and the vigorous honesty of the best plays of the year."

DOG DRAMAS. In the 1840s Barkham Cony and Edwin Blanchard introduced plays at the *Bowery Theatre in which trained dogs took a significant part in the action: holding villains at bay, rescuing the heroine, or uncovering evidence that exonerates the hero. With titles such as *The Planter and His Dogs* and *The Dogs of the Wreck,* the plays soon became popular features at the theatre. When Cony and Blanchard separated at the end of the decade, Cony, with his young son Eugene and their dog Yankee, continued to appear at the Bowery in a number of specially written vehicles, among them *The Cross of Death; or, The Dog Witness* and *The Butcher's Dog of Ghent.* At the same time Blanchard, with his dogs Hector and Bruin, moved to the National Theatre, where they starred in *The Watch Dogs, The Fisherman and His Dogs,* and similar pieces. All through the 1850s and 1860s, dog dramas continued to be popular, especially in the less elite playhouses. Cony soon disappeared from the scene, but Blanchard found a new rival in Fanny *Herring, who, with her dogs Lafayette and Thunder, performed in *The Rag Woman and Her Dogs* and other such plays. By the early 1870s the vogue for the genre had largely exhausted itself, while trained dogs found new opportunities on the rapidly multiplying vaudeville stages.

DOLLY SISTERS, singing-dancing team. Jennie Dolly [née Janszieka Deutsch] (1892–1941) and Rosie Dolly [née Roszika Deutsch] (1892–1970), two small, dark-complexioned, almond-eyed beauties, were the most successful sister act of their day, their four-week run at the *Palace being the longest such stand for any sister act at that theatre. Born in Hungary, but raised on New York's Lower East Side, they were headliners in vaudeville before they were chosen to sing and dance in the *Ziegfeld Follies of 1911. Other major appearances included A Winsom Widow (1912), the national tour of Oh, Look! (1918), and *Greenwich Village Follies of 1924. Rosie appeared alone in The Whirl of New York (1914), after Jennie temporarily broke up the act to team with her husband, Harry Fox.

DONAHUE, Jack (1892–1930), dancer. A native of Charlestown, Massachusetts, the supple, eccentric hoofer had begun making a name for himself in vaudeville before his Broadway debut in 1919 in Angel Face. His best-known appearances came when he played opposite Marilyn *Miller in *Sunny (1925) and in Rosalie (1928) and starred in Sons o'Guns (1929), for which he was co-librettist.

DONALDSON, Walter. See Whoopee.

DONALDSON AWARDS. Established in 1944 in honor of the founder of *Billboard, W. H. Donaldson (1864–1925), they were offered in numerous categories, including best new play, best new musical, best performances, best debuts, and best costumes and set designs. They were discontinued in 1955 when it was recognized that they were redundant and overshadowed by more prestigious honors.

DONNELLY, Donal (b. 1931), actor. A slender, forever-youthful looking Irishman, Donnelly spent most of his career in America, excelling in Irish types but playing a wide variety of characters over the years. He was born in Bradford, England, to Irish parents and was educated in Dublin, where he later trained at the Gate Theatre. Donnelly made his London debut in 1959 and first came to America to play the alter ego of the Irish lad Gar in Philadelphia, Here I Come! (1966). Among his memorable New York performances, several of which were as replacements, were the victim-turned-victor Milo Tindle in *Sleuth (1971), the Cockney agent Teddy in Faith Healer (1979), the witty George Bernard Shaw in both the one-man program My Astonishing Self (1983) and in the two-character Dear Liar (1999), a diabolical Dr. Watson in Sherlock's Last Case (1987), the senile priest Jack in Dancing at Lughnasa (1991), and the town gossip Johnnypateenmike in The Cripple of Inishmaan (1998).

DONNELLY, Dorothy [Agnes] (1880–1928), lyricist, librettist, and actress. Daughter of the manager and lessee of New York's Grand Opera House, she made her acting debut in the stock company run by her brother, Henry V. Donnelly, at the Murray Hill Theatre. She came to critics' and playgoers' attention in 1903 when she played the title roles in Yeats's Kathleen ni Houlihan and *Shaw's *Candida in their first American performances. The next year Donnelly was the first American to play the Lady in Shaw's The Man of Destiny. Her most celebrated performance was in the title role of Madame X (1910), and she continued to act for another decade. In 1916 she was co-librettist for Flora Bella and two years later for Fancy Free. The success of her book and lyrics for Sigmund *Romberg's adaptations of Schubert's melodies in *Blossom Time (1921) prompted her to abandon performing. Further success came with her libretto for Poppy (1923), but her biggest hit was The *Student Prince (1924), for which she wrote the lyrics to such popular Romberg songs as "Deep in My Heart, Dear," "The Drinking Song," "Golden Days," and "Serenade." Donnelly's other collaborations with Romberg were My Maryland (1927) and My Princess (1927).

DON'T BOTHER ME, I CAN'T COPE (1972), a musical revue by Micki Grant (music, lyrics). [Playhouse Theatre, 1,065 perf.] Vinnette Carroll, the artistic director of Off Broadway's Urban Arts Corps Theatre, devised and directed this sly look at contemporary life and the pressures of modern living as viewed by African Americans, and it was so popular in her little theatre that the revue transferred to Broadway for a long run. The songs by Micki Grant and the dances by George Faison ranged from rock and gospel to calypso and blues and used both humor and anger in covering a variety of issues. Notable songs: Don't Bother Me, I Can't Cope; Fighting for Pharaoh; Thank Heaven for You. **Micki GRANT** was born in Chicago and educated at the University of Illinois, Roosevelt University, and De Paul University. She started performing in New York in 1962 and eight years later formed a partnership with Carroll and presented a series of musical revues at the Urban Arts Corps. Grant contributed to several scores in the 1970s, including Your Arms Too Short to Box with God (1976), Working (1978), Eubie (1978), and It's So Nice to Be Civilized (1979). **Vinnette CARROLL** (1922–2002) was one of the earliest African-American women to run her own theatre company. She trained with Erwin Piscator, Lee *Strasberg, and Stella *Adler before beginning her acting and directing career, then turned to teaching and later founding the Ghetto Arts Program in Manhattan. After running the Urban Arts Corp, Carroll ran a repertory company in Florida.

DOOLEY, [Rachel Rice] **Ray** (1891–1984), actress. Daughter of a circus clown who gave her her earliest training, Dooley was born in Scotland but grew up in Philadelphia. While still a child she made her vaudeville debut at that city's Keith's Theatre and she eventually played the *Palace. Her Broadway debut was in *Words and Music* (1917), followed by appearances in the 1919, 1920, and 1921 *Ziegfeld Follies, The Bunch and Judy* (1922), *Nifties of 1923, Ziegfeld Follies of 1925, No Foolin'* (1926), *Sidewalks of New York* (1927), *Earl Carroll Vanities of 1928,* and *Thumbs Up!* (1934). Dooley specialized in playing young spoiled brats, often named Gertie. Typical of her antics was a skit in *No Foolin'*, in which she taunted a train conductor, refusing to give him her ticket and leading him a merry chase over seats and passengers alike.

D'OYLY CARTE OPERA COMPANY. See International Theatre Companies Visiting America.

DORO, Marie [Kathryn] [née Stuart] (1882–1956), actress. Born in Duncannon, Pennsylvania, the lithe, delicately beautiful actress made her acting debut in St. Paul in 1901 and first appeared in New York in *The Billionaire* (1903). She next played in *The Girl from Kay's* (1903), before essaying Lady Millicent in James Barrie's *Little Mary* (1904). Doro's first starring part was in the title role of the waif in *Friquet* (1905), but she did not have a major success until her ingenious heroine Carlotta in *The Morals of Marcus* (1907). One critic noted, "She has a persuasive little personality, with eerie beauty as an asset. And she is charming in comedy and genuinely touching in emotion." Most of her later successes were in London, but she did delight her American public as Oliver Twist (1912) and in the title role of *Patience* (1912). Doro's last appearance was as the wronged wife whose revenge is to dabble in prostitution in *Lilies of the Field* (1921).

DOUGHGIRLS, THE (1942), a comedy by Joseph *Fields. [*Lyceum Theatre, 671 perf.] Just as Edna (Virginia Field) is about to be evicted from her hotel suite in overcrowded wartime Washington, D.C., she discovers the woman who is taking the rooms is her old friend Vivian (Arleen Whelan), so she forces Vivian to let her remain. Before long another old friend, Nan (Doris Nolan), joins the group, all of whom are unmarried and have taken lovers. The quarters are further crowded when a Russian sniper, Natalia Chodorov (Arlene *Francis), is imposed on them. Natalia, who has shot 397 Nazis, is a vigorous, forceful woman who, for exercise, takes short hikes to Baltimore and back. All sorts of complications ensue. A wife of one of the lovers suddenly appears; a marriage is put off when divorce papers turn out to be a report from the Wordsworth Chemical Laboratory; and an admiral, a general, and even a group of Marines briefly make their home in the suite. In the end all the difficulties are resolved, in no small part by the aid of Natalia. Although some cries were raised that the Max *Gordon–produced comedy was immoral, most playgoers and critics agreed with Lewis Nichols of the *Times*, who hailed this "mad salute to wartime Washington" as "very funny indeed."

DOUGLAS (1758). John Home's only successful tragedy tells of Lady Randolph, who, after the death of her husband and disappearance of her son, has married Lord Randolph. When he goes off to war, he is rescued from certain death by the brave Young Norval, who has been raised by a shepherd, Old Norval. The young man, of course, turns out to be Lady Randolph's long-lost son and assumes his rightful name of Douglas. But Lord Randolph's mind is poisoned against Douglas by the crafty Glenalvon. Douglas is murdered, Lady Randolph throws herself from a cliff, and Lord Randolph (recognizing the wrong he has abetted) goes off, hoping to die in battle. The play apparently was first produced in America in 1758, two years after its London premiere, although the original cast-list has not survived. It was revived shortly afterward in Philadelphia with the young Lewis *Hallam as Young Norval, David *Douglass as Lord Randolph, and Mrs. Douglass (the elder Hallam's widow) as Lady Randolph. The play remained popular for about one hundred years, and the role of Young Norval became a popular debutant role for such performers as John Howard *Payne.

DOUGLAS, Melvyn [né Melvyn Edouard Hesselberg] (1901–81), actor and director. The suave leading man, who developed into a fine character actor, was born in Macon, Georgia, and made his stage debut in Chicago. He next spent several seasons with Jessie *Bonstelle before briefly operating his own company in Madison, Wisconsin. Douglas first appeared in New York as the gambler Ace Wilfong in *A Free Soul* (1928). His acting in plays landed him a Hollywood contract, but he returned to Broadway in 1934 to play the philandering husband Sheridan Warren in *No More Ladies* and to win acclaim for his direction of *O'Casey's *Within the Gates*. His next appearances were in failures, and Douglas returned to Hollywood until he re-emerged after World War II as co-producer of the ex-soldier revue *Call Me Mister* (1946). His post-war performances of note include newspaperman Tommy Thurston in *Two Blind Mice* (1949), the callous nightclub owner Wally Williams in *The Bird Cage* (1950), the middle-aged bachelor-father Steve Whitney in *Glad Tidings* (1951), and the staid banker-father Howard Carol in the frivolous farce, *Time Out for Ginger* (1952). Douglas played this part for three seasons, before replacing Paul *Muni in 1956 as the Clarence Darrow-like Henry Drummond in a retelling of the Scopes evolution trial, *Inherit the Wind*. Following several failures, he won a *Tony Award for his portrayal of William Russell, the idealistic presidential candidate, in *The *Best Man* (1960). His last Broadway appearance was as a retired chicken farmer encroached on by suburbanites, the title role in *Spofford* (1967).

DOUGLASS, David (d. 1786), manager and actor. The Englishman began his theatrical career when, at the last minute, he was selected to supervise a new company to play in Jamaica. By coincidence, a company led by Lewis *Hallam Sr. was also playing on the island, so the troupes merged, Hallam died, and Douglass married Mrs. *Hallam. The company came to New York in 1758, where it built a new playhouse, and soon was traveling up and down the coast playing in Philadelphia, Annapolis, Newport, and elsewhere. Douglass was not a distinguished actor (by consensus the best member of the troupe was Lewis *Hallam Jr.), but he was a tactful politician and forceful businessman. His diplomacy was required because wherever he went he encountered puritanical opposition to the theatre, which he was able to overcome for a while. His business acumen helped him to arrange the construction of proper playhouses in the cities where his company played, including the *Southwark in Philadelphia, the *John Street in New York, and the *Dock Street Theatre in Charleston. Douglass's company adopted the name The *American Company as early as 1763. Under his aegis colonists were offered a large repertory of classics and new London successes, as well as the first professional mounting of a play by an American author, *The Prince of Parthia* (1767). He also brought to America such popular performers as Miss *Cheer and John *Henry. With the onset of the Revolution he returned to Jamaica, where he became a government official and died leaving an estate of £25,000.

DOWLING, Eddie [né Joseph Nelson Goucher] (1894–1976), actor, director, producer, and playwright. Born in Woonsocket, Rhode Island, he made his acting debut in nearby Providence in 1909 in *Quo Vadis?* After spending some time in England, Dowling returned to America to join the *Ziegfeld Follies of 1918 on tour. His first New York appearance was as a policeman in Victor *Herbert's *The Velvet Lady* (1919), after which he performed as a song and dance man in the 1919 and 1920 editions of the *Ziegfeld Follies*. He co-wrote and starred in *Sally, Irene and Mary* (1922) for three seasons, co-authored another starring vehicle for himself, the successful *Honeymoon Lane* (1926), then repeated the same chores for *Sidewalks of New York* (1927) with his wife, Ray *Dooley. For several seasons the couple toured in vaudeville, then made a final musical appearance (except to replace a star in later years) in *Thumbs Up!* (1934), which he also produced. Thereafter, his career took an unusual turn for a performer until then identified with the most frivolous musicals. He was acclaimed for his work in a number of distinguished straight plays, although his triumphs were interspersed with several dismaying dry spells. In 1938 he produced and appeared in Philip *Barry's curious religious fantasy *Here Come the Clowns*, then directed and played in *The *Time of Your Life*. Another major success was Tennessee *Williams's *The *Glass Menagerie* (1945), which he directed and co-produced and in which he created the role of Tom. In 1946 Dowling directed *The *Iceman Cometh*. John Mason *Brown wrote of his direction, "His groupings are fluid; his modulations of pace admirable; and his eye for the pictorial unflagging. He never fails to heighten and interpret the meanness of life, so that they cease to be photography and emerge as art." He won further praise when he directed and acted in a bill of one-act plays, the best of which was *Hope Is the Thing with Feathers* (1948). Except for his stint as James *Barton's replacement in *Paint Your Wagon* (1952), all his subsequent endeavors were short-lived.

DRAKE, Alfred [né Alfredo Capurro] (1914–92), actor and singer. A "Broadway old-timer" is reputed to have said, "Nobody looks at a woman like Alfred Drake. It turns out he looks at everything like that. It's a good look." Whatever the reason for his particular magnetism, the darkly handsome Drake was the finest leading man of the 1940s and 1950s, combining a superb baritone voice with exceptional acting and comic skills. He studied singing in his native New York, then made his debut in the chorus of several 1935 *Gilbert and Sullivan revivals and *White Horse Inn* (1936). After playing increasingly important roles in *Babes in Arms* (1937), *The Two Bouquets* (1938), *One for the Money* (1939), *The Straw Hat Revue* (1939), and *Two for the Show* (1940), Drake won widespread recognition when he created the role of Curly in *Oklahoma!* (1943). He was applauded for his performances in *Sing Out, Sweet Land* (1944), *The Beggar's Holiday* (1946), *The *Cradle Will Rock* (1947), and *Joy to the World* (1948), before starring as the shrew-taming Fred Graham in **Kiss Me, Kate* (1948). After a brief appearance as the egotistical David Petri in *The Gambler* (1952), he scored again as the wily Hajj in **Kismet* (1953), then played Othello and Benedick for the *American Shakespeare Festival. Drake later garnered excellent notices in three failures, *Kean* (1961), *Lorenzo* (1963), and *Gigi* (1973). Drake helped adapt several Italian plays, including *The Gambler*, and directed a number of shows.

DRAKE [Bryant], **Samuel** (1768–1854), actor and manager. Drake, born in Barnstable, England, is believed to have been a strolling player before coming with his family to America in 1810. He made his debut that year at Boston's *Federal Theatre, remaining there until he was appointed manager for John *Bernard at the latter's theatre in Albany in 1813. When his wife died in 1814, he packed up his family and embarked on a pilgrimage along the Ohio, Allegheny, and Mississippi Rivers. In many of the cities along the way, his was the first professional company ever to offer theatrical performances. Young Noah *Ludlow, who was a member of his troupe for a time, has painted a vivid picture of their vicissitudes in *Dramatic Life as I Found It*. Ludlow also noted that "Drake was quite successful the first ten or twelve years." Thereafter, however, his age and increasing competition made touring less profitable for him. He had made prudent investments and retired to a farm in Kentucky. Among Drake's most notable roles were Lear, Julius Caesar, and Shylock. Although he elected to spend a good part of his career in backwaters, his contemporaries were virtually unanimous in suggesting that he was a fine enough actor to have become a major star had he chosen to remain in the important theatrical centers.

DRAMA CRITICISM IN AMERICA. All too little is known about early American drama critics. Newspapers of the 18th and even early 19th century were published as much for the convenience of classified advertisers as they were for the dissemination of other news, so there was little room for theatrical reviews, and these were often written to please advertisers. Most criticism was unsigned or at best given a fictitious byline. Eola Willis, in her history of the 18th-century Charleston stage, records what she claims was "the first dramatic criticism given of an American performance," but the unsigned excerpt she quotes from the *Charleston Gazette* of May 28, 1737, simply acknowledges that a performance of *The Recruiting Officer* had taken place and was well attended and passes no judgment on either the play or the mounting. It was typical of many later notices. Not until the early years of the 19th century did a few critics such as Stephen Cullen Carpenter of the *Charleston Courier*, J. W. S. Hows of the *New York Albion*, or, more importantly, Washington *Irving begin to make names for themselves with what today would be perceived as proper criticism. Yet even here, they and others frequently published initially under pseudonyms (although cognoscenti undoubtedly were aware of the real authorship), and their work was often first given major recognition when republished in contemporary theatrical magazines or in book form. Indeed, much of the more interesting criticism of the period came not in newspapers but in the usually short-lived theatrical journals that sprang up in larger theatrical centers. As a rule newspapers remained largely uninterested or blatantly partisan in favor of (or against) certain theatres or performers. Not until after the Civil War and the emergence of William *Winter did American theatrical criticism come of age. His lead was followed by the appearance of such noted writers as T. Allston *Brown, Henry Austin *Clapp, E. A. *Dithmar, William Dean *Howells, James *Huneker, Laurence *Hutton, J. R. *Towse, and A. C. *Wheeler. Many, though not all, of these early critics were archly conservative, relating dramatic merit to moral standards and observance of traditional forms. The arrival on the scene of *Ibsen and realism sharply divided critics into essentially an older, unyielding school and a newer, more open one. The controversy probably played a significant role in rushing American dramatic criticism into final maturity by broadening the scope of interest and knowledge required of critics, sharpening their reasoning and writing faculties, and attracting new readers. At about the same time, the flowering of American newspapers and the concurrent rivalries caused papers to seek better critics, thereby improving standards everywhere. Only Clapp, among the critics just named, was not based in New York, but the simultaneous proliferation of both theatres and newspapers led to the rise of any number of fine critics away from New York. As a rule, these men rarely achieved national celebrity, but they were known and respected in the trade. Cincinnati's Montgomery *Phister is a typical example.

The list of great 20th-century drama critics might include Brooks *Atkinson, Robert *Benchley, John Mason *Brown, Claudia *Cassidy, Percy *Hammond, Walter *Kerr, George Jean *Nathan, Dorothy *Parker, Henry Taylor *Parker, Ashton *Stevens, Alexander *Woollcott, and Stark *Young. Many of these critics departed from the Brahmin-like aloofness and impersonal approach of their predecessors, giving their writings a fresh vigor and feistiness. However, not all newspapers maintained a totally impartial approach, and as late as the 1920s there were papers that refused to review plays if not advertised, and, in the same spirit, some papers bent over backwards to be kind to advertisers. In more recent years several problems have arisen. The marked shrinkage of theatrical production, especially on Broadway and in major road houses, has given critics fewer chances to hone their art. Moreover, in many cities newspaper competition has disappeared and the surviving paper has often viewed what is left of local theatre with indifference, even to occasionally appointing men or women with no real theatrical background as critics. The result has been a drastic falling off of the quality of dramatic criticism in several major cities, sometimes marked not only by ineptitude and ignorance but coupled with a monopolistic arrogance as well. Of course, some newspapers and national magazines have retained high standards. Television has attempted to take up some of the slack, but the brevity of the reviews and television's insistence on attractive, lively, and personable reviewers rather than knowledgeable ones does not bode well for the future. By the 1960s and the demise of several New York papers, the *New York Times* became the most powerful voice in theatre criticism; in consequence, the *Times* critic yielded more weight than any reviewer in the past. Walter *Kerr was the best of the *Times* staff and, sensing the disproportionate clout he had, resigned from daily reviewing and concentrated on weekend features. Clive *Barnes, a British journalist whose background was in dance criticism, was the most influential critic of the 1960s, his opinion alone determining the fate of many shows. In the 1980s the *Times's* Frank *Rich dominated the theatre scene to the point that if Rich disliked a play in London, producers would not bother to bring it to New York. Since Rich left in 1993, the paper has seen a series of reviewers who have failed to carry the same amount of influence. Ben Brantley, for example, is much feared and remains an influential force, but many shows that he disapproved of have been supported by other critics and the public and have gone on to long runs. Although a few critics have been accorded biographies or other studies, the whole field of American dramatic criticism remains ripe for scholarship.

DRAMA DESK, THE. Founded in 1949 and chartered as a non-profit corporation in 1974, this association of writers on the theatre holds monthly luncheons in New York at which prominent theatre people are invited to talk and to discuss modern problems with the members. To the public at large, they are most known for their annual Drama Desk Awards given to productions and artists both on and Off Broadway.

DRAMATIC MIRROR. Founded in 1879 as the *New York Mirror* but soon changed to the *New York Dramatic Mirror*, the theatrical trade paper was popularly known by its shorter name. Under the editorship of Harrison Grey *Fiske, it was for many years the leading American theatrical trade journal, offering not only a wealth of important professional information but gossipy items for non-professionals as well. Fiske often turned the paper into a crusading sheet, as in his successful attempt to establish the *Actors' Fund and in his far less successful effort to fight the *Theatrical Syndicate, or Trust's monopolistic practices. Fiske retired in 1911, and under less imaginative editors the paper's popularity declined. By the time it suspended publication in 1922, *Variety* had long since supplanted it.

DRAMATISTS PLAY SERVICE, INC. Disgruntled with the contracts offered playwrights for amateur rights, in 1936 Sidney *Howard, then president of the *Dramatists Guild, encouraged the establishment of this new group. Many leading authors of the period, including Howard *Lindsay, George S. *Kaufman, and others, quickly joined in support. Today the company is the principal rival to *Samuel French, Inc. Although it does offer the work of some leading English dramatists, its emphasis has been on American writers. For many it is now the exclusive agent for amateur rights. It also encourages young American authors. The Dramatists Guild remains a major partner in the company.

DRAMATIC REVIEW FOR 1868, THE (1869), a burlesque afterpiece by John *Brougham. [*Brougham's Fifth Avenue Theatre, 28 perf.] This afterpiece opened with an allegory featuring Manhatta and Brooklyna, "the oldest of Manhatta's family, and a remarkably forward young lady . . . holding but ferry little intercourse with her Ma, and that she means to abridge." Other characters in the opening were New Jersia, North Rivero (a fluent individual), East Rivero, and Public Opinion. Succeeding skits travestied opéra bouffe as "Bouffe à la Mode," G. L. *Fox and Humpty Dumpty as "The Fox's Nest," as well as new theatres and straight plays. A number of songs included one making fun of the velocipede craze. The Brougham production is significant only as a curiosity, a precursor to the revues that first took hold of New York in 1894 with *The *Passing Show.*

DRAMATISTS GUILD, INC. The most success-ful and enduring of organizations designed to protect the rights of dramatists, it was not the first. In 1878 Steele *MacKaye and Clay M. *Greene had established the American Dramatic Authors' Soci-ety "to secure protection for their work," but the group was short-lived and was followed in 1891 by the American Dramatists Club, which was later known as the *Society of American Drama-tists and Composers and which was headed by Bronson *Howard. This group quickly enlisted thirty-three leading playwrights but made little headway and remained for a time largely a social organization. In 1911 the Authors League of America was founded and included playwrights among its members. A subcommittee was formed in 1914 to work "towards the standardization of a dramatic contract," although initial attempts proved fruitless. Following the successful 1919 strike of *Actors' Equity, Channing *Pollock sug-gested the League form "an autonomous commit-tee" to work exclusively for dramatists' rights. Out of this came the Dramatists Guild. Matters were brought to a head in 1925 when it was dis-covered that Fox Films had contracts with seven important producers, which granted Fox uncon-tested film rights in return for backing plays. In March 1926 the committee met with producers, and on April 27 the first contract was signed. The Guild became an independent corporation in 1946 and has continued to serve as guardian of drama-tists' welfare, guaranteeing, among other matters, minimum royalties, mediation in disputes between authors and management, and competi-tive bidding for film and other rights. The Guild publishes newsletters, a quarterly magazine called *The Dramatist*, and an annual *Resource Directory*. Less visible to the public than the actors or musi-cians union, the Guild nevertheless has had some controversial bouts with producers and even directors.

DRAMATISTS' THEATRE, INC. Founded in 1923 to present the works of its members and other play-wrights, the group may be seen as an unsuccessful predecessor to the *Playwrights' Company. Found-ing members were Edward Childs *Carpenter, Owen *Davis, James *Forbes, Cosmo *Hamilton, and Arthur *Richman, but their first offering, *The *Goose Hangs High* (1924), was by an outsider, Lewis Beach. Subsequent productions included *Cock o' the Roost* (1924), *Young Blood* (1925), and *Scotch Mist* (1926)—the last two by Forbes—but when none of these presentations was as well received as the first, the organization was disbanded.

DRAPER, Ruth (1884–1956), actress. The most famous of all American monologuists, she made her debut as a maid in *A Lady's Name* (1916) but shortly thereafter decided that her gifts for mim-icry were best disclosed when she was alone on a bare stage with little more than a scarf and a hat for props. She began to write her own mono-logues, offering them professionally first in Lon-don in 1920 and in New York the following year. Some of her monologues dealt with a single char-acter, others with a succession of people. Draper frequently departed from her own script, impro-vising as the moment suggested. Her characters ranged from the most lordly to the most beggarly and on some occasions, as in her depiction of a French wife saying good-bye to her husband who is leaving to join the Free French in the war, were done entirely in a foreign language. But her unique gift of expression made every line intelli-gible. She won applause throughout the world and was offering her show in New York, in her early seventies, when she died in her sleep after a performance. Biography: *The Art of Ruth Draper*, Morton D. Zabel, 1960.

DREAM GIRL (1945), a comedy by Elmer *Rice. [Coronet Theatre, 348 perf.] Georgina Allerton (Betty Field), who writes unpublishable novels and runs a small bookshop, wakes up to confront the likelihood of another awful day. To escape from her mundane existence, she daydreams. The moment she flicks on the radio and hears the voice of a broadcasting psychiatrist, she imagines she is on the air with him, pouring out her prob-lems. All through the day, a word here, a gesture there, send her into fantasy land. Her life changes only when she meets a young man, Clark Redfield (Wendell Corey), who reviews books he doesn't read and hopes to be a sportswriter. They fall in love and will probably marry, "as long," Clark insists, "as you run your dreams, instead of letting them run you." She promises to try, because this newfound reality seems "some wonderful dream." The Playwrights' Company produced the show, one of Elmer Rice's few ventures into light com-edy. Its principal part required the heroine (played by Rice's wife) to be on stage all but two minutes of the performance. A musical version, *Skyscraper* (1965), starred Julie *Harris as Georgina and featured a score by James Van Heusen (music) and Sammy *Cahn (lyrics). It met with mixed notices and ran 248 performances in the *Lunt-Fontanne Theatre.

DREAMGIRLS (1981), a musical by Tom Eyen (book, lyrics), Henry Krieger (music). [*Imperial Theatre, 1,522 perf.] The Dreams are an African-American singing group who have emerged from the ghetto to scale the heights of success in the 1960s. However, just as they appear to reach the pinnacle, their manager, Curtis Taylor Jr. (Ben Harney), decides to dump one of the trio, Effie (Jennifer Holliday). Although he is her lover as well as her manager, Curtis has decided that the overweight Effie lacks the class to push the group to the top and keep it there. Besides, he has a new girl. But Effie goes on to achieve a personal success alone. *Notable songs*: And I Am Telling You I Am Not Going; When I First Saw You; I Am Changing. The real talent behind this show's success was co-producer-director-choreographer Michael *Bennett, who took a solid, although by now traditional, book about sordid backstage manipulations and a score that effectively re-created the black musical styles of the 1960s and turned it all into a dazzling piece of entertainment. Added strengths were the superb performances of Holliday and a physical production that Elliot *Norton of the *Boston Herald American* described as "a vivid moving pageant of lights in perpendicular towers and horizontal bridges, lights visible and invisible, that move about the stage to frame the actors and keep the action moving."

DRESSER, Louise [née Kerlin] (1882–1965), singer. The blue-eyed, blonde performer was best known as a vaudevillian and identified with one song, "My Gal Sal." She was the daughter of a railroad engineer who had once stopped some rowdies from badgering a fat newsboy on the train. That newsboy became the celebrated composer Paul Dresser, and it was he who, in grateful memory of her father, gave the singer her stage name and wrote "My Gal Sal" for her. She also performed it in many Broadway shows, including *About Town* (1906), *The Girl Behind the Counter* (1907), *A Matinee Idol* (1910), *Broadway to Paris* (1912), *Potash and Perlmutter* (1913), and *Rock-a-Bye Baby* (1918).

DRESSLER, Marie [née Leila Marie Koerber] (1869–1934), actress. Famous as a hefty, bulldog-faced comic harridan, she was born in Coburg, Canada, and made her debut as Cigarette, the camp follower, in *Under Two Flags*, but soon switched to musicals. Her first New York appearance was in *The Robber of the Rhine* (1892), followed by appearances in *Princess Nicotine* (1893), *Giroflé-Girofla* (1894), *Madeleine* (1895), *A Stage Party* (1895), *The Lady Slavey* (1896), *Hotel Topsy-Turvy* (1898), *The Man in the Moon* (1899), *Miss Prinnt* (1900), *The King's Carnival* (1901), *The Hall of Fame* (1902), *King Highball* (1902), *Higgledy Piggledy* (1904), *Twiddle Twaddle* (1906), and *The Boy and the Girl* (1909). In 1910 Dressler created her most famous Broadway role, Tillie, the drudge who dreams of richer worlds, in *Tillie's Nightmare*, and introduced "Heaven Will Protect the Working

Girl." After *Roly Poly* (1912), she played largely in revues: *Marie Dressler's All-Star Gambols* (1913), *The Century Girl* (1916), *The *Passing Show of 1921*, and in a book show that many critics felt to be a revue, *The Dancing Girl* (1923). Dressler was long popular in vaudeville but received more universal recognition in films. Autobiographies: *The Life Story of an Ugly Duckling*, 1924; *My Own Story*, 1934. Biography: *Marie Dressler: The Unlikeliest Star*, Betty Lee, 1997.

DREW, John (1827–62), actor and manager. He came as a ten-year-old with his parents from his native Dublin to New York, where his father assumed the post of treasurer at *Niblo's Garden. Not until after going to sea and running a dry-goods store in Ireland did he settle into the family profession, finding success in New York as Dr. O'Toole in *The Irish Tutor* at the *Bowery Theatre. Thereafter, most of his best-received roles were his Irish characters. In 1850 he joined the company at the Albany Museum, where he met and married Louisa Lane. Two years later he and Mrs. John *Drew joined the ensemble at Philadelphia's *Chestnut Street Theatre, and in 1853 they became co-managers of the *Arch Street Theatre with William *Wheatley. An attempt by Drew to run the National Theatre in Washington quickly failed, so he returned to touring, both in America and in Ireland and England. When Mrs. Drew took over sole management of the Arch Street in 1861, he appeared under her aegis, playing not only his famous Irish parts but Meddle in *London Assurance*, William in *Black-Eyed Susan*, and Sir Lucius O'Trigger in *The Rivals*, as well as Sir Andrew Aguecheek and Dromio. He died as a result of injuries sustained in a fall.

DREW, John (1853–1927), actor. Like his namesake father, his familiarity with theatre made him decide to look elsewhere for work, but a brief stint as a clock salesman for a department store in his native Philadelphia proved so boring that he reluctantly agreed to go on stage. Drew made his debut at his mother's *Arch Street Theatre in 1873 and continued to act there for two seasons, until Augustin *Daly spotted him and invited him to New York. His New York bow was as the seemingly impecunious suitor Bob Ruggles in *The *Big Bonanza* (1875). He remained with Daly for many years, earning particular renown as a high comedian after the producer formed his second company in 1879. Among his great successes with the ensemble was his Petruchio. Of his performance one critic wrote, "His acting was consistently vigorous, and his speech, as usual, flawless." But it was as a polished gentleman—a roué, a blasé prince, or an avuncular guardian—in the era's drawing room comedies that he was best known. When Drew moved from Daly to Charles *Frohman, the striking-looking actor, with the large, heavy-lidded eyes and a drooping black moustache, continued in similar parts, mostly in works now long-forgotten. In 1908 he played the title role in Somerset *Maugham's *Jack Straw*, prompting the *Times* to exclaim, "John Drew at fifty, reveling like a boy, full of the spirit of juvenile lightheartedness, is an agreeable sight to see." Among his last appearances were Maugham's *The Circle* (1921), *The School for Scandal* (1923), and *Trelawny of the Wells* (1925 and 1927). He was the uncle of Lionel *Barrymore, Ethel *Barrymore, and John *Barrymore. Autobiography: *My Years on the Stage*, 1922.

DREW, Mrs. John [née Louisa Lane] (1820–97), actress and manager. Born in Lambeth Parish, London, she was the daughter of performers who traced their theatrical heritage to Elizabethan times. After her father's death she was brought to America by her mother and made her American debut in 1827 playing the Duke of York to Junius Brutus *Booth's Richard III at Philadelphia's *Walnut Street Theatre. Shortly thereafter she played Albert to Edwin *Forrest's William Tell in Baltimore, then won critical acclaim in her New York debut at the *Bowery Theatre as Little Pickle in *The Spoiled Child*. She continued to act for the next seventy years, her most celebrated role being Mrs. Malaprop in *The Rivals*, in which she often toured with Joseph *Jefferson as Bob Acres. T. Allston *Brown called her "the most wonderfully versatile actress on the American stage." But her principal claim to fame was her stint as manager of Philadelphia's *Arch Street Theatre, which she ran with an iron hand from 1861 to 1892 and which, under her rule, was generally considered to offer the finest company and finest productions outside of New York. She presented a repertory of classics interspersed with many of the most popular new plays of her era. A small, somewhat wispy woman with large eyes, which she passed on to her Barrymore heirs, her appearance belied her inner strengths. She was married at least three times, always to actors: Henry Hunt, whom she divorced, George Moosop, and John *Drew. Under her stern tutelage her son John *Drew and her daughter Georgiana Drew *Barrymore began their own careers, and she was responsible for much of the upbringing of Georgiana's children: Lionel *Barrymore, Ethel *Barrymore, and John *Barrymore. Autobiography: *Autobiographical Sketch of Mrs. John Drew*, 1899.

DRIVING MISS DAISY (1987), a play by Alfred *Uhry. [*Playwrights Horizons, 1,195 perf.; Pulitzer Prize.] Daisy Werthan (Dana Ivey) is an aging Jewish matron in post–World War II Atlanta. Because she cannot safely drive herself any longer, her son (Ray Gill) hires Hoke (Morgan *Freeman), a mature African-American man, to drive her around and to look after her as unobtrusively as possible. At first the relationship is prickly, but with time the twosome (both of whom having experienced forms of religious and racial prejudice) develops a rewarding friendship. A small, warm, but fundamentally lightweight play, its winning of the Pulitzer Prize attested again to the paucity of serious and meritorious writing either on Broadway or off. Wisely, this production remained Off Broadway for its entire run. The economical two-hander has been produced frequently in regional and community theatres.

DROOD. See *Mystery of Edwin Drood, The*.

DRUNKARD, THE; or, *The Fallen Saved* (1844), a play by W. H. Smith. The villainous Lawyer Cribbs has long held a grudge against the Middleton family, even though he has served as their attorney. When young Edward Middleton's father dies, Cribbs attempts to persuade Edward to dispossess a poor mother and daughter who are Middleton's tenants. Instead, Edward falls in love with the daughter, Mary, and marries her. But Edward has a weakness: drink. Cribbs insidiously encourages Edward's weakness, until Edward, ashamed and seemingly impoverished, flees to the degradation of New York's Five Points district. Cribbs follows him there and attempts to turn him into a forger, but Edward's better nature prevails. Edward's foster-brother William and a rich philanthropist, Arden Rencelaw, seek him out, rehabilitate him, and reunite him with his wife and young daughter. Cribbs is forced to reveal that he has hidden Edward's grandfather's will and that Edward is really still a wealthy man. The melodrama was first presented, as part of a temperance crusade, in Boston in 1844, and within a year it had been played there a hundred times, including performances at the Tremont Temple and at the *Boston Museum. The play was offered by a temperance group in New York in 1844 but failed to cause a stir. However, in 1850 it was revived by several New York theatres, most notably at *Barnum's American Museum, where its run of one hundred consecutive performances set a long-run record for the time. A revival in 1933 in a small Los Angeles theatre was played for laughs but ran twenty years, chalking up an American record of 7,510 performances; only the musical *The *Fantasticks* has run longer in this country. **Corson Walton CLARKE** (1814–67), who played Edward at Barnum's, was ever afterward identified with the role and was known popularly as "Drunkard Clarke." Born in Elizabethtown, New Jersey, he made his debut in 1838 under the elder James *Wallack. After playing several seasons with Wallack and elsewhere, he moved to *Barnum's American Museum. W[illiam] H[enry] [Sedley] SMITH (1806–72), the son of a British army officer, was born in Wales and came to America to perform at the *Walnut Street Theatre in Philadelphia in 1827, making his debut as the sponging Jeremy Diddler in *Raising the Wind*. He also played in New York and Boston before joining the Boston Museum in 1843 as actor and stage manager. In later years Smith managed the *California Theatre for *Barrett and *McCullough as Barnum's director of amusements.

DU BARRY (1901), a play by David *Belasco. [Criterion Theatre, 165 perf.] Jeanette Vaubernier (Mrs. Leslie *Carter) is a sweet Parisian milliner who promises to meet a young soldier, Cosse-Brissac (Hamilton Revelle), but instead is lured into a gambling house by Comte Du Barry (Campbell Gollan). There she becomes the plaything of French society and is married to Du Barry's brother to give her a certain respectability. She continues to love Cosse-Brissac, although their meetings bring them little but pain. In the end, like her royal associates, she is caught up in the revolution and sent to the guillotine. Although William *Winter bemoaned the fact that the play contained "a plenitude of needless talk," his dissent was in the minority. Shortly after the drama opened, a sensational, headline-grabbing lawsuit disclosed that producer-author Belasco had taken most of the play from *La Du Barry*, a work by a French poet-dramatist Jean Richepin.

DU BARRY WAS A LADY (1939), a musical comedy by B. G. *De Sylva, Herbert *Fields (book), Cole *Porter (music, lyrics). [46th Street Theatre, 408 perf.] Louis Blore (Bert *Lahr) is a nightclub washroom attendant. He loves the floor show's star, May Daley (Ethel *Merman), who has eyes only for a reporter, Alex Barton (Ronald Graham). Louis attempts to give Alex a mickey, but accidentally drinks it himself. Unconscious, he dreams that he is Louis XV and that May is Madame Du Barry. When he awakes he realizes the futility of his quest, so resumes scrubbing basins. *Notable songs*: Do I Love You?; Friendship; Katie Went to Haiti; Well, Did You Evah? Although the De Sylva–produced musical had a rather flimsy premise, the brashness and brassiness of the Porter songs and its superb stars turned the offering into a hit.

DU BOIS, Raoul Pene (1914?–85), designer. A New York–born designer, famous for his colorful, often gaudy costumes and sets, his work was first seen on Broadway when he created costumes for the *Ziegfeld Follies of 1934*. He later designed costumes for such shows as *Jumbo* (1935), *Ziegfeld Follies of 1936, Hooray for What!* (1937), *Leave It to Me!* (1938), *Carmen Jones* (1943), *The *Music Man* (1957), and *Gypsy* (1959). Du Bois created both costumes and sets for, among others, *Du Barry Was a Lady* (1939), *Panama Hattie* (1940), *Call Me Madam* (1950), *Wonderful Town* (1953), *No, No, Nanette* (1971), and *Irene* (1973).

DUFF, James C. (1854–1928), producer. Best known for first bringing *H. M. S. Pinafore* to New York, Duff offered the American or New York premieres of many other *Gilbert and *Sullivan, Strauss, and Von Suppe operettas as well as French *opéra bouffe. His J. C. Duff Opera Company was an important touring ensemble in the 1880s and 1890s, bringing comic opera to many large and small theatrical centers. Harry B. *Smith called him the "most able and artistic producer of operetta" in this early period. He remained active, although on a reduced scale, all through his life, his last production being a revival of *The Beggar's Opera* a few months before his death. Duff was the son of **John A. DUFF** (1820–89), who was born in Ireland but came to America as a young man. After successfully operating restaurants in Albany and New York, he took over the Olympic Theatre in 1866 and later operated the Broadway and Standard Theatres. He was the father-in-law of Augustin *Daly, with whom he worked closely for many years.

DUFF, John (1787–1831), actor. The Dublin-born leading man left a successful stage career in his homeland to try his luck in America. He made his debut in Boston in 1810, but Philadelphia first saw him and his "stupendous" range when he acted Macbeth and the Three Singles (Pertinax Single, Peregrine Single, and Percival Single) in *Three and the Deuce* (1812). Two years later Duff made his New York debut playing Octavian and the Three Singles. Among his most famous parts were the title roles in the tragedy *Richard III* and the melodrama *The *Stranger*, and Jeremy Diddler, the impecunious sponger, in the farce *Raising the Wind*. He frequently performed with his wife, **Mrs. John DUFF** [née Mary Ann or Marianna Dyke] (1794–1857). She made her debut in her native Dublin as a dancer but soon showed ability as an actress. Marrying fellow performer John *Duff and coming to the States with him, she made her American debut in Boston in 1810 as Juliet, remaining there for two years before following her husband to Philadelphia, where she initially appeared in 1812 and where she remained five years. Her New York bow was Hermione in *The Distressed Mother* (1823) opposite the Orestes of Junius Brutus *Booth. She soon came to eclipse her husband in esteem and popularity and is generally looked back upon as one of the first great artists of our stage. Among her major roles were Ophelia, Jane Shore, Belvidera, Portia, and Lady Macbeth. According to William *Winter, who never saw her, "Mrs. Duff seems to have been lovely more than beautiful; strong in affectionate, melting charms of womanhood rather than in resolute, commanding, brilliant intellect. . . . She had dark, brilliant eyes, and she had a voice that ranged from the clarion call of frantic passion to the softest accents of maternal love." The elder Booth, writing from closer experience, called her simply "the greatest actress in the world." Biography: *Mrs. Duff*, Joseph N. Ireland, 1882.

DUFF, John A. See Duff, James C.

DUFF, Mrs. John. See Duff, John.

DUFF, Mary (1811?–52), actress. The daughter of John *Duff and Mrs. *Duff, she made her debut as Ernestine in *The Somnambulist* in 1831 at Philadelphia's *Arch Street Theatre. Her first New York appearance followed shortly thereafter, but she performed largely on Arch Street until she married A. A. *Addams in 1835. Joseph N. *Ireland recalled, "On her first appearance she was radiant in youthful loveliness . . . her spirits so exuberant, that even in her novitiate her best friends feared that 'overacting' would be the rock on which her bark would split—an apprehension all too truthfully fulfilled." The marriage was short-lived, as was her second to Joseph Gilbert. Meanwhile, she began to tour the eastern seaboard, but also played extended engagements in the western states, whose baleful influences New York critics blamed for her increasingly broad style. Among her more popular roles were Kate Hardcastle, Lady Teazle, and Lady Macbeth, along with such now forgotten parts as Donna Hypolita in *The Phantom Bride* and Genevra in *The Dragon Knight*. After her marriage to J. G. Porter she sometimes performed as Mrs. Porter, but playbills usually included the reminder that she had been Mary Duff. She died while still at the height of her popularity.

DUKAKIS, Olympia (b. 1931), actress and manager. The dry, subtle character actress has spent much of her career in regional theatre, particularly at the Whole Theatre Company in New Jersey, which she ran, but she has managed to give several potent performances in New York as well. She was born in Lowell, Massachusetts, the daughter of Greek immigrants, and educated at Boston University. Dukakis appeared in Boston theatres (she co-founded the Charles Street Theatre) before making her Manhattan debut in 1960, playing many roles at the *New York Shakespeare Festival and other Off-Broadway venues. But she would find fame first on television and then in the movies, coming back to Broadway as a star in *The Marriage of Bette and Boo* (1985), *Social Security* (1986), and *Rose* (2000). Autobiography: *Ask Me Again Tomorrow*, 2003.

DUKE, Vernon [né Vladimir Dukelsky] (1903–69), composer. Russian-born and classically trained, he wrote scores for London musicals before coming to New York in the early 1930. Duke's first American score, for *Walk a Little Faster* (1932), included "April in Paris." In 1934 he interpolated "Autumn in New York" in *Thumbs Up!*, and created melodies for the *Ziegfeld Follies. *Cabin in the Sky* (1940) is generally acknowledged to be his best score, offering "Taking a Chance on Love" and the title song. Eddie *Cantor introduced "We're Having a Baby" in Duke's score for *Banjo Eyes* (1941), but thereafter all his efforts, both in Manhattan and London, failed to please playgoers: *The Lady Comes Across* (1942), *Jackpot* (1944), *Sadie Thompson* (1944), *Two's Company* (1952), and *The Littlest Revue* (1956). Autobiography: *Passport to Paris*, 1955.

DULCY (1921), a comedy by George S. *Kaufman and Marc *Connelly. [Frazee Theatre, 246 perf.] Dulcinea Smith (Lynn *Fontanne) is an ambitious but feather-brained young lady given to spouting bromides and getting her husband, Gordon (John Westley), into jams whenever she attempts to help him out. Since Gordon is about to merge his business with that of C. Rogers Forbes (Wallis Clark), Dulcy invites the Forbeses and their daughter Angela (Norma Lee) for a weekend. She also invites the scenario writer Vincent Leach (Howard *Lindsay), who is in love with Angela; her brother, Bill (Gregory *Kelly); and a rich young man she has met at a party, Schuyler Van Dyck (Gilbert Douglas). She manages to irritate Mr. Forbes by encouraging Angela and Vincent to elope and by having Schuyler offer to support Gordon in a venture in opposition to Mr. Forbes. But Blair Patterson (George Allison) arrives, announcing that Schuyler is actually simply a harmless madman who thinks he is rich. Luckily for Dulcy, Forbes sees Patterson, who is an attorney for the real Van Dycks, and offers Gordon an even better deal than he did at first. And then it is discovered that Angela eloped not with Vincent, but with Bill. Though things have turned out well, Dulcy promises never again to meddle. After all, "A burnt child dreads the fire. Once bitten—" Heywood *Broun wrote in the *Tribune*, "*Dulcy* is an ingenious trick play and the patter which introduces the legerdemain is even better than the stunts." The George C. *Tyler and H. H. *Frazee production not only established the reputations of Kaufman and Connelly but made a star of Fontanne.

DUMMY, THE (1914), a comedy by Harvey J. O'Higgins and Harriet *Ford. [*Hudson Theatre, 200 perf.] Young Barney Cook (Ernest *Truex) may still be in knickers, but he has earned a reputation as a brilliant boy detective. So when little Beryl Meredith (Joyce Fair) is kidnapped, he poses as a dimwitted youngster to catch the kidnappers and free the child. Based on O'Higgins's popular Detective Barney stories, the play successfully blended elements of the then voguish "crook play" with comedy. Joyce Fair was later better known as Clare *Boothe [Luce].

DUNBAR, Paul Laurence (1872–1906), librettist, lyricist, and author. Most famous as an early African-American poet and novelist, he was also an important figure in the development of black musical theatre. In 1898 he wrote the libretto and lyrics for the first major black musical to play a first-class white house, *Clorindy; or, The Origin of the Cake Walk*, although the entertainment was not a full-length show and the house was the *Casino's summer roof garden. But Dunbar also served as lyricist for *In Dahomey* (1903), the first full-length black musical to play a standard Broadway theatre. He also wrote lyrics for several songs that were interpolated into other musicals.

DUNCAN, Augustin (1873–1954), actor and director. After making his debut in 1893 in his native San Francisco, he toured for seven years before first appearing in New York in 1900 as Jamy opposite the Henry V of Richard *Mansfield. Duncan continued to play opposite such celebrated figures as William *Gillette and Charles *Coburn in increasingly important roles both in New York and London. In 1919 he was a charter member of the *Theatre Guild, and his performance in the title role of John Ferguson as well as his direction of the play helped give the new company its first success. After he separated from the Guild over artistic differences, Duncan both directed and acted in such productions as *The Cradle Song* (1921), *The Detour* (1921), *The First Man* (1922), *Hell-Bent for Heaven* (1924), and *Juno and the Paycock* (1926). He also directed plays in which he did not appear, such as *Kempy* (1922). In the late 1920s his eyesight began to fail and by the early 1930s Duncan was blind. Nevertheless, he continued to perform, playing John of Gaunt and

the Ghost in Maurice *Evans's productions of *Richard II* (1937) and *Hamlet* (1938) and making his last appearance as the Father in *Lute Song* (1946). He was the brother of the famed dancer Isadora Duncan.

DUNCAN, Rosetta and Vivian. See *Topsy and Eva*.

DUNCAN, [Robert] Todd (1903–98), singer and actor. The African-American performer was born in Danville, Kentucky. His Broadway appearances were rare but always memorable. Duncan was the original Porgy in *Porgy and Bess* (1935) and later appeared as the Lawd's General in *Cabin in the Sky* (1940) and the minister Stephen Kumalo in *Lost in the Stars* (1949).

DUNHAM, Katherine (b. 1910), dancer and choreographer. The Chicago-born African-American performer appeared in *Cabin in the Sky* (1940) and in *Carib Song* (1945), but she is best remembered by playgoers for dance-revues she created and starred in, which featured black dancing from around the world: *Tropical Revue* (1943), *Bal Negre* (1946), and a titleless 1950 offering.

DUNLAP, William (1766–1839), manager and playwright. The earliest enduring figure of the American theatre, he was born in Perth Amboy, New Jersey, and although he apparently had little formal education, he read Shakespeare as a youth. His attraction to the theatre was consolidated during the Revolutionary War when he watched British soldiers perform in New York, where the family had moved. Although he sailed for England in 1784 to study painting with Benjamin West, the London theatres proved an irresistible lure. Watching the latest plays and classics performed by Mrs. Siddons, Charles Kemble, and the other leading performers of the day established standards which he strove to maintain throughout his career. Dunlap returned to America in 1787, where, inspired by Royall Tyler's The *Contrast, he wrote *The Modest Soldier; or, Love in New York* for the *American Company. The play was rejected, but his comedy The *Father; or, American Shandyism* (1789) was successfully produced. He continued to write for the company and in 1796 was made one of its partners, along with John *Hodgkinson and Lewis *Hallam. When Hallam withdrew from the partnership in 1797, Dunlap and Hodgkinson continued and together opened the *Park Theatre in 1798. Two of his most successful plays appeared in 1798: the Revolutionary War drama *André and The *Stranger*, based on a von *Kotzebue work. Dunlap's translation initiated Kotzebue's American vogue, and he translated at least ten more of his plays. In addition to running the Park alone (after Hodgkinson's retirement), he also leased the Haymarket in Boston and worked closely with the *Chestnut Street Theatre in Philadelphia.

Under his aegis the Park presented a repertory of modern and traditional works and offered English performers opportunities of appearing in America. He was forced to relinquish his management in 1805, when he declared bankruptcy, but a year later he returned to serve as assistant to the new manager, Thomas Abthorpe *Cooper. Even after he retired, Dunlap continued to write plays (some sixty or seventy in all, mostly adaptations from the French or German) and in 1832 published his monumental *History of the American Theatre*. He also attempted to publish his plays, but only one volume was issued before his death. During his theatrical career, Dunlap endeavored, with only limited success, to overcome the snobbish preference for things British. Although he welcomed the best artists and works from overseas, he actively encouraged American actors and playwrights. He was also aware of the conflict in the theatre between commercialism and art and tried, without success, to get the government to subsidize playhouses. A highly puritanical man, he frequently eliminated what he deemed offensive passages in works he translated, and he fought futilely against the accepted practice of allowing a special section in theatres set aside for ladies of questionable virtue. Arthur Hobson *Quinn concluded a long chapter devoted to Dunlap by noting, "[he] had the soul of an artist and the intrepidity of the pioneer, and his place in our dramatic literature will remain secure." Autobiography: *Diary of William Dunlap*, 1930.

DUNNING, Philip. See *Broadway*.

DUNNOCK, Mildred [Dorothy] (1901–91), actress. Born in Baltimore, she made her debut in *Life Begins* (1932) and later appeared in such plays as *The Corn Is Green* (1940) and *Another Part of the Forest* (1946). For years one of the most respected supporting actresses in American theatre despite her mousy looks and plaintive voice, Dunnock is best remembered for three roles: the long-suffering, loving wife Linda in *Death of a Salesman* (1949); the weak, boozy Mrs. Constable in *In the Summer House* (1953); and the vacuous, subjugated wife Big Mama in *Cat on a Hot Tin Roof* (1955).

DUPREE, Minnie (1875?–1947), actress. Born in La Crosse, Wisconsin, the gamin-faced performer made her debut in 1887 in a touring company of the *The Unknown*. The following year she appeared in a small role in New York in *Held by the Enemy*, but her talents were immediately recognized, and for the next dozen years Dupree was awarded important supporting roles in an unending series of plays. Her first leading role was the hapless heroine Mary Andrews in *Women and Wine* (1900), followed by the piquant Clara in *The *Climbers* (1901); the good-hearted Rose in *A Rose o' Plymouth-town* (1902); the waitress who loves but loses her student prince in *Heidelberg* (1902); Helen Stanton, the daughter loyal to her long-lost father, in *The *Music Master* (1904); and both Elspeth and Lady Elizabeth Tyrrell in *The *Road to Yesterday* (1906). After portraying the unhappily married Kate Grayson in *The Real Thing* (1911), she spent several years touring vaudeville in short plays. Most of Dupree's later appearances were in failures, the notable exceptions being the patient wife Matilda in *The *Old Soak* (1922), the sullen stepmother Mrs. Burns in *The *Shame Woman* (1923), and the newly dead Mrs. Midget in a touring company of *Outward Bound* (1924). In 1941 she was a replacement in the role of Martha Brewster in *Arsenic and Old Lace*. Dupree's final appearance was as the grandmother in *Land's End* (1946).

DURANG, Christopher [Ferdinand] (b. 1949), playwright and actor. Born in Montclair, New Jersey, the son of an architect and a secretary, Durang was educated at Harvard and Yale, his first scripts produced when he was a student at the latter. His New York playwriting debut was the one-act *Titanic* (1976) Off Broadway, where all of his subsequent plays would be seen. Durang is known for his broad and irreverent satire with an intellectual bent, and his plays often target church, family, and other bastions of conservatism. His first major success was *Sister Mary Ignatius Explains It All for You* (1981), followed by such notable works as *Beyond Therapy* (1981), *Baby with the Bath Water* (1983), *The Marriage of Bette and Boo* (1985), *Betty's Summer Vacation* (1999), and several popular one-acts. He has appeared in his own works and in plays and musicals by others. Autobiography: *Christopher Durang Explains It All for You*, 1983.

DURANG, John (1768–1822), dancer, acrobat, puppeteer, and actor. He was born in Lancaster, Pennsylvania, but grew up in York, where he attended the German school attached to Christ Lutheran Church, and in Philadelphia. It was in the latter city that he was first exposed to theatricals, and he made his debut there at the *Southwark Theatre in 1785 as a dancer, having been hired by Lewis *Hallam Jr. Although Philadelphia remained his base, Durang performed up and down the northeastern coast and made an extended tour of

Canada. He worked under all the great managers of his day, including William *Dunlap, John Bill *Ricketts, Thomas *Wignell, and Alexander *Reinagle. He appeared in numerous pantomimes, often taking the role of Scaramouche, entertained between acts, and sometimes accepted small dramatic parts—a necessity in an era of quick-changing repertory. For a time Durang was so popular that he was often the only performer mentioned in the cramped newspaper advertisements of his day. In his later years he wrote and illustrated a memoir, which was not published until a century and a half after his death. Durang had five children, all of whom spent some time on the stage. Autobiography: *The Memoir of John Durang*, 1966.

DURANTE, [James Francis] Jimmy (1893–1980), comedian. Famed for his prominent nose which he called his "schnozzola," his raspy voice, his fractured English, and his stiff-kneed strut, the comic began his career in 1910 as a honky-tonk pianist at Diamond Tony's Saloon in Coney Island. Sometime between 1919 and 1923 he formed a trio with Lou Clayton and Eddie Jackson. Their "nut" act won instant popularity, and they were invited to play Loew's State in 1926. A year later they played the *Palace. From the start Durante was the center of attraction, so when the team appeared in *Show Girl* (1929) and *The New Yorkers* (1930) he was assigned important roles while his partners played bit parts. The act was disbanded in 1931, although it was frequently reunited for special appearances. Durante then appeared in *Strike Me Pink* (1933), *Jumbo* (1935), *Red, Hot and Blue!* (1936), *Stars in Your Eyes* (1939), and *Keep Off the Grass* (1940). At a time when much humor was increasingly biting, his humor remained sunny and he himself the butt of his sharpest digs: "There are a million good lookin' guys, but I'm a novelty." In a typical rough and tumble antic, he sang "Wood" in *The New Yorkers* while cluttering the stage with every conceivable wooden object. Another favorite routine was his wild dismantling of a piano. In later years he was popular in nightclubs and films, as well as on radio and television.

DURNING, Charles (b. 1923), character actor. The beefy performer was born in Highland Falls, New York, and left home as a teenager to earn his living as a boxer, construction worker, bartender, cab driver, and even a ballroom dance instructor. After serving in the army during the Korean War, Durning used the GI Bill to study at Columbia and New York University, afterwards going into acting. He made his New York debut in 1955 but started to arouse interest in the 1960s for the clown characters he played in Shakespeare works in Central Park. Durning's big break came in 1972 as the ineffectual mayor George in *That Championship Season*, opening up his movie career and allowing him to play major roles for the rest of his career. Among his memorable stage performances were the Irish laborer Eugene Hartigan in *The Au Pair Man* (1973), the vulgar Big Daddy in *Cat on a Hot Tin Roof* (1990), the irascible card player Martin Weller in *The *Gin Game* (1997), the narrow-minded William Matthew Brady in *Inherit the Wind* (1996), and the agitating ex-President Arthur Hockstader in *The *Best Man* (2000).

DUSE, Eleonora (1858–1924), actress. The greatest Italian player of her age, she made her American debut in 1893 as Marguerite Gautier in *La Dame aux Camélias*. This tour was followed by several more over the next eleven years; then, after a nineteen-year hiatus, she made a farewell tour in 1923, during which she died in Pittsburgh. Duse was a small, darkish, lithe woman with sad eyes, who was credited by many with furthering the movement toward realistic acting. She is said to have eschewed the heavy makeup common at the time and, despite occasional marked moments of fidgetiness, to have usually seemed to underplay and to have been most eloquent in repose. Among her notable vehicles were *Magda, Ghosts, Rosmersholm, The Lady from the Sea*, and three by her lover D'Annunzio: *La Gioconda, Francesca da Rimini*, and *La Citta Morta*. Biography: *Eleonora Duse*, Arthur Symons, 1926.

DYNAMO (1929), a play by Eugene *O'Neill. [Martin Beck Theatre, 50 perf.] The Reverend Light (George Gaul), a devout but somewhat arrogant Christian, and Ramsay Fife (Dudley *Digges), an atheist, are unfriendly neighbors. When the minister's son, Reuben (Glenn *Anders), falls in love with Fife's daughter, the teasing Ada (Claudette Colbert), father and son have a falling out. Reuben denounces religion and goes in search of truth. He returns years later, having made science his god, but when he is seduced by Ada he kills her and then electrocutes himself by throwing himself on the dynamo. Although Brooks *Atkinson observed, "Writing on the most essential theme of modern life, Mr. O'Neill has strength and breadth, and a lashing poetry," the play, which O'Neill planned as the first of a trilogy, failed to run. For some critics Lee *Simonson's brilliant second-act setting, showing the interior of a hydro-electric plant, was the most memorable feature of the *Theatre Guild production.

E

EAGELS, Jeanne (1894–1929), actress. For a brief time one of the most exciting and promising actresses of the American theatre, the slender, intense blonde beauty had her career cut down at its height by her erratic personal behavior and a reputed drug addiction. Born in Kansas City, Missouri, she made her debut at the age of seven as Puck in *A *Midsummer Night's Dream*. Eagels first appeared in New York in 1911 when she took a small part in the musical *Jumping Jupiter*. Minor roles followed in *The Mind-the-Paint Girl* (1912) and *Outcast* (1916) before she first garnered critical attention playing opposite George *Arliss in *Paganini, The Professor's Love Story, Disraeli,* and *Hamilton*. In his autobiography, Arliss echoed the praises of contemporary critics, extolling her as an "amazingly clever" performer "with unerring judgment and artistry." She later scored as war orphan Ruth Atkins in *Daddies* (1918), store mannequin Mary Furlong in *A Young Man's Fancy* (1919), and seductress Sadie Thompson in *Rain* (1922), a role with which she was identified thereafter. The *Times*'s John *Corbin described her as acting "with an emotional power as fiery and unbridled in effect as it is artistically restrained." Eagels played the part for over four years before essaying the role of Simone, a rich lady who falls in love with a man she had hired to masquerade as her paramour, in *Her Cardboard Lover* (1927). Biography: *The Rain Girl*, Edward Doherty, 1930.

EAMES, Clare (1896–1930), actress. Born in Hartford, Connecticut, and raised in Cleveland, the petite, aristocratic leading lady, who was a niece of soprano Emma Eames, studied in Paris and at the *American Academy of Dramatic Arts before making her debut in 1918 in a triple bill that included Eugene *O'Neill's *Ile*. She won critical attention when she played the title role in John Drinkwater's *Mary Stuart* (1921). Alexander *Woollcott observed, "Miss Eames brings much to the part—the keen wit, the entire comprehension, the royal quality. It is only as Mary, the arch fascinator, that she is a little lacking." Although other critics also lamented the absence of a certain fire or glamour, she kept busy for the remainder of her short career before her early death. Among her notable roles were Miss Tiffany in *Fashion*, Lady Macbeth opposite James K. *Hackett, and *Hedda Gabler*. Eames also played important parts in two plays by her husband, Sidney *Howard: the amoral socialite Carlotta Ashe in *Lucky Sam McCarver* (1925) and informer Carrie Callahan in *Ned McCobb's Daughter* (1926).

EARL CARROLL VANITIES. A series of revues produced by Earl *Carroll annually from 1923 through 1932 (except for 1927 and 1929) and again in 1940, they were celebrated and sometimes attacked for their emphasis on nude girls and salacious humor. Joe *Cook, W. C. *Fields, and Sophie *Tucker were among the many stars who appeared in the shows, which left behind few memorable melodies.

EARL OF PAWTUCKET, THE (1903), a comedy by Augustus *Thomas. [*Madison Square Theatre, 191 perf.] To escape a summons from the House of Lords and to see how well he can survive without his title, Lord Cardington (Lawrence D'Orsay) sails to America and adopts the name of an old American friend, Putnam, who lives in England. Once landed, he falls in love with Harriet Fordyce, unaware that she was once Mrs. Putnam. The Lord's mysterious disappearance leads to the belief that the real Putnam, with whom he was last seen publicly, may have murdered him. So the fake Putnam finds himself pursued by the police as well as by lawyers seeking alimony payments due from his namesake. Written as a vehicle for D'Orsay, the play was rejected by Charles *Frohman on the grounds that the actor could not sustain so large a role. He was proved wrong when Kirke *La Shelle produced the comedy and it became a huge success.

EASIEST WAY, THE (1909), a play by Eugene *Walter. [Belasco-Stuyvesant Theatre, 157 perf.] Laura Murdock (Frances *Starr) is a mediocre actress who has been unable to make a living by acting, so has allowed herself to be kept in style by Willard Brockton (Joseph Kilgour). While appearing in Denver, however, she meets and falls in love with a young newspaper man, John Madison

(Edward H. Robins). John's romantic view of women clashes with both Brockton's cynical one and Laura's situation. When Brockton learns of Laura's feelings, he makes her write to John and test him by revealing the truth. Laura reluctantly writes the letter, but after Brockton leaves, she burns it. Eventually, John earns a small fortune and prepares to marry Laura, until he learns of her past life and deserts her. Laura is left to take "the easiest way" out by remaining a kept woman. She tells her maid to get her best dress ready. "I'm going to Rector's to make a hit," she announces, "and to hell with the rest." Burns *Mantle appraised the play as "the first bold denial of the happy ending in modern [American] drama, the first deliberate attempt to prove that a play could be emotionally appealing because of its essential truth and the validity of its performance." Certainly the ending, its famous curtain line, and Starr's performance were the talk of the season. Producer David *Belasco is reported originally to have wanted to rewrite the ending, allowing John and Laura to wed, but Walter obstinately refused. He felt that other contemporary plays, such as *Leah Kleschna, had been irreparably damaged artistically by contrived happy endings.

EAST IS WEST (1918), a comedy by Samuel *Shipman and John B. Hymer. [Astor Theatre, 680 perf.] Although she was given a proper Chinese upbringing, Ming Toy (Fay *Bainter) is something of a hoyden. Brought to San Francisco's Chinatown, she falls in love with a handsome young American, Billy Benson (Forrest Winant). Two obstacles stand in the way of their marrying: both laws and sentiment argue against an interracial marriage, and a cynical Chinese man-about-town, Charlie Yang (George Nash), has purchased Ming Toy and by Chinese custom is thereby entitled to her. Matters turn out satisfactorily when it is learned that Ming Toy was adopted while still a baby and is Spanish by birth. Although the play itself was dismissed by most critics as absurd hokum, the gorgeous settings of Livingston *Platt and Bainter's droll performance turned the William *Harris Jr. production into one of the greatest hits of its era.

EAST LYNNE (1863), a play by Clifton W. Tayleure. [*Winter Garden Theatre, approx. 20 perf.] Lady Isabel Mount Severn (Lucille *Western) marries her childhood sweetheart, Archibald Carlyle (A. H. Davenport), but after several years of happiness she is led by Sir Francis Levison (Lawrence *Barrett) to believe that Archibald is unfaithful. She elopes with Sir Francis, who later refuses to keep his promise of marriage. Carlyle remarries and the years pass. Ill and dying, Isabel returns to Carlyle's home, East Lynne, to see her children and to beg her husband's forgiveness. She comes disguised as a Madam Vine, but Archibald, who quickly recognizes her, does forgive her as she dies. Western paid Tayleure $100 to adapt Mrs. Henry Wood's popular Victorian novel of the same name. It served her as a vehicle for many years and was also popular with other actresses. It became such a favorite of touring and stock companies that "Next week, *East Lynne*" was soon a well-known, if slighting, expression to indicate the seemingly inevitable nature of their repertories. From the start, however, the play was never as well received by critics as it was by the public, the *Albion* dismissing its first presentation as "sickly nonsense." **Clifton W. TAYLEURE** (1831–87) began his career as an actor who specialized in playing old men. Much of his earliest career seems to have been spent at Baltimore's *Holliday Street Theatre, where he continued to serve as the house's dramatist after his retirement from performing in 1856. By the late 1860s he managed several important Broadway theatres, including the Olympic and the Grand Opera House. Tayleure's other (and mostly undistinguished) melodramas included *Horseshoe Robinson (1856), A Woman's Wrongs (1874), Rube; or, The Wall Street Undertow (1875), and Parted (1876).

EAST WEST PLAYERS (Los Angeles). The nation's first Asian-American regional theatre company, it was started in 1965 by five Asian-American artists who wished to improve the conditions for other actors, writers, and directors who were stereotyped in mainstream American theatre. At first the troupe presented world classics with Asian actors, but in the 1970s, under the leadership of artistic director–actor Mako, the company started to emphasize new works written by Asian Americans. The plays of David Henry *Hwang and others helped bring the group recognition. In 1998 the company moved from its 99-seat black box to a 240-seat facility named the David Henry Hwang Theatre, located in the Union Center of the Arts in Los Angeles's "Little Tokyo" district.

EATON, Charles Henry (1813–43), actor. The son of a prosperous Boston merchant, he made his debut in his hometown in 1833 in the title role of The *Stranger. Although he remained primarily a Boston actor, he toured all the leading theatrical centers, winning praise for his interpretations of Richard III, Hamlet, William Tell, and other popular figures. A fatal fall in Pittsburgh cut short a career of growing acclaim and promise.

EATON, Mary (1902–48), actress, dancer, and singer. A native of Norfolk, Virginia, the petite blonde began performing professionally while still a child and made her New York debut as Tyltyl in *The Blue Bird* (1915). She was spotted by Florenz *Ziegfeld, who groomed her as a successor to Marilyn *Miller, and she appeared for him in the 1920, 1921, and 1923 editions of the *Ziegfeld Follies* and as Eddie *Cantor's leading lady in *Kid Boots* (1923). However, her biggest and last success came only after she left the producer to star in *The Five O'Clock Girl* (1927), in which she introduced "Thinking of You."

EATON, Walter Prichard (1878–1957), critic and author. Born in Malden, Massachusetts, he graduated from Harvard and accepted a position as assistant drama critic on the *Tribune* before becoming principal drama critic for the *Sun* and *American Magazine*. He wrote numerous books on theatre, including *The American Stage of To-Day* (1908), *At the New Theatre and Others* (1910), *Plays and Players* (1916), *The Actor's Heritage* (1924), and *The Theatre Guild: The First Ten Years* (1929). In 1933 he accepted the post of Associate Professor of Playwriting at Yale. Although he consistently argued for a progressive, serious drama, Eaton's views were fundamentally conservative, and he welcomed much that now would be unpalatable. His sharp observations and pleasant style made his criticisms eminently readable.

EAVES-BROOKS. The principal costume maker and renter for theatre, opera, and television, the company was formed in 1981 by a merger of the two leading manufacturers. Brooks was the older of the two, having been founded in 1861; Charles Eaves formed his company in 1864. At the turn of the century the Geoly family took over Eaves and headed the merged company. The costume house went through unstable management changes in the 1980s and early 1990s. Today it is called Dodgers Costumes.

EBB, Fred. See Kander and Ebb.

ECKART, William [Joseph] (1920–2000) and **Jean** [née Levy] (1921–93), designers. A successful husband and wife team, he was born in New Iberia, Louisiana, and studied architecture at Tulane and stage design at Yale; she was born in Chicago and also studied stage design at Yale. Beginning with *Glad Tidings* (1951), they created sets for such productions as *Oh, Men! Oh, Women!* (1953), *The *Golden Apple* (1954), *Damn Yankees* (1955), *Li'l Abner* (1956), *Take Her, She's Mine* (1961), and *Mame* (1966). They often designed lighting for their sets and occasionally, the costumes. In later years they moved to Texas, thereafter designing primarily for regional playhouses across the country and teaching.

ECONOMICS OF THE AMERICAN THEATRE. The American theatre has moved from humble beginnings through decades of great strength and huge financial returns only to lapse, in the last decades of the 20th century, into a curious situation. Now rewards for occasional success are enormous, but on balance production and consequent employment have dwindled and most theatrical enterprises are economically precarious. The earliest years left behind little solid statistical evidence, but it may be safely assumed that the lots of performers and other professionals were uncertain and hard up for steady income. Not until the late 18th century had American cities grown populous enough and Americans themselves sufficiently prosperous to allow larger centers to support permanent ensembles. Even so, the record is unclear about how well the average professional lived. A few early luminaries were apparently able to save comfortable sums for retirement, and John *Henry, sometimes called America's first matinee idol, led a flamboyant, expensive life, even maintaining a private coach. He realized a then significant $10,000 when he sold his interest in the *American Company but seemingly never saved much and was in relatively poor financial condition when he drowned. Nor were theatrical impresarios or playwrights in better shape, as witnessed by the problems of William *Dunlap and others. Costs of production, however, must have been comparatively small, since individual sets and costumes were rarely provided. Actors were expected to supply their own costumes, and most theatres kept a handful of basic sets—a domestic interior, a castle, a woods, a garden—which saw service in whatever play was being performed. Some of the figures relating to New York's *Park Theatre are enlightening. Opened in 1798, it had been projected to cost just over $42,000, a considerable sum at the time, but actually cost an exceptional $130,000. Top seats were 75¢, soon raised to $1, and the cheapest tickets were either 12¢ or 25¢. Because of the house's large capacity, a performance could gross over $1,200. Ironically, this figure remained about the standard for capacity houses for over a century, since the higher ticket prices that came into being at the time of the Civil War were coupled with the development of more intimate theatres. The entire ensemble's salaries came to a mere $480 per week, with *Hodgkinson receiving top reimbursement at $20 per week, plus $5 per week for wardrobe and $30 for his managerial concerns. When all other expenses were included (among them $150 for orchestra, $109 for lighting, and $68 for printing), the weekly nut was $1,200. In theory, the theatre could have been extremely profitable, especially since it was the city's only playhouse for many years, but extant records reveal many nights and longer stretches of dismal business.

The coming of stars in the early 1800s proved both a source of additional revenue and a drain on those revenues, as most stars' contracts called for them to receive a sizable portion of the gross. Yet even the *Kembles rarely filled the Park, and on nights when they did not perform grosses averaged only $150. With the coming of competition, both in New York and elsewhere, theatres encountered new problems, often having to lower prices to attract trade. For a time during the lean years of the early 1840s, 75¢ was generally the top ticket price. At the same time, actors' salaries began to creep up, albeit slowly. Until the panic of 1857, the 1850s were comparatively prosperous times for theatres, and tickets again went to a $1 top. A few exceptional attractions demanded more, but *Rachel is believed to have encountered stiff opposition when she charged a $3 top and a $1 minimum. (Three decades later her compatriot, Sarah *Bernhardt, dared ask only a $2 top.) At the same time, actors' salaries again rose. For the 1857–58 season at Wallack's, Lester *Wallack received a weekly $100 as both actor and director. William Rufus *Blake was listed as earning $80, and the emerging Mrs. *Hoey $55. It should be noted that contracts for all leading performers allowed them one or more benefit nights, at which they were entitled to a substantial share of the gross. Lesser players at the house were paid about $25 and shared no benefits. The leading scene designer received a salary on a par with lesser actors. By 1861, with the coming of wartime prosperity, salaries had risen still further. Prosperity and rising costs allowed Edwin *Booth and his brothers to charge a then record $5 top when they appeared together in their 1864 special production of *Julius Caesar; and two years later, in 1866, Wallack led the way to a standard $1.50 top, a figure which was to prevail at first-class houses for the rest of the century. While most plays continued to be mounted for a few thousand dollars, with the coming of elaborate musicals new record figures followed one another rapidly. The *Black Crook (1866) is said to have cost $50,000, and subsequent spectacles advertised yet larger, if somewhat suspect, figures. In 1869 the Times listed the previous year's grosses for leading Broadway houses. In all of 1868 *Niblo's Garden, the home of spectacle, was reported taking in $359,879, while the elite Wallack's, given over to non-musical attractions, grossed $263,319. The typical comic opera of the 1890s is believed to have cost between $10,000 and $25,000 to produce. Moreover, the basically healthy economic climate of the time allowed most shows to recoup their costs after four weeks at capacity business. De Wolf

*Hopper claimed that many of the era's musicals ran at a loss in smaller New York theatres, so that they could claim long Broadway stands and retrieve their investments at larger touring houses. His statement cannot be corroborated precisely, but as late as the 1920s many shows that failed in New York went on tour and closed with a profit. At the end of 1911, Adolph *Klauber reported in the Times that in the first half of the 1911–12 season, from August 8 to December 31, sixty-four plays of all variety had opened on Broadway and thirty of them had already recouped their costs. However, the road began to change noticeably in the early years of the 20th century, when films arrived to lure less affluent and less educated playgoers away from live theatre. Cheap touring companies such as the *Ten-Twent'-Thirt' groups, which presented lurid melodramas, treacly comedy, and old operettas at prices between 10¢ and 30¢, quickly disappeared.

Real changes started to affect theatrical economics about the time of World War I. Wartime inflation was coupled with the rise of unions, most notably *Actors' Equity. The justice of union demands for rehearsal pay, overtime pay, better working conditions, and higher salaries cannot be gainsaid but nonetheless played a major role in the marked escalation of costs and therefore of ticket prices. Top prices, which had remained at $1.50 or at best $2 since the Civil War, rose during World War I to $3.50. By 1919, while plays could still be mounted for under $10,000, musical production costs had soared. The *Ziegfeld Follies of the era cost about $200,000 apiece, admittedly an exceptional figure. *Irene (1919), a more typical example, cost $40,000. By 1927 Good News!, again typical, cost $75,000 and charged a $6 top. Some musicals went as high as $8. Nonetheless, both Irene and Good News!, along with many other successes of the era, returned their investments in four weeks. The economic pinch began to be felt during the Depression, when the theatre found itself competing with radio's and Hollywood's glittering rewards and confronting union militancy. Although ticket prices plummeted ($3 and $4 became standard tops again), the costs of productions did not necessarily fall proportionately. Shows began to take longer and longer to pay off. These discouraging developments led to fewer mountings, and in the late 1930s the number of major productions dropped below one hundred for the first time in the century and never again passed the mark. World War II brought a measure of prosperity, and the theatre seemed reasonably healthy for the next decade, albeit the number of plays continued to fall and the percentage of shows to repay their investment decreased. For example, *Variety reported that for the 1955–56 season only about a dozen of some fifty commercial productions showed a profit. A one-set, small-cast comedy such as *Fallen Angels* could run nearly three hundred performances and a musical such as *Mr. Wonderful* run almost a year without closing in the black. The rampant inflation that was precipitated by the Vietnam War and the international oil cartel threw theatrical economics into turmoil. By the early 1980s simple plays cost hundreds of thousands of dollars to mount and musicals were budgeted at a million or more. *Cats* (1982) was reputed to have cost $5 million. Top ticket prices skyrocketed to $55, actually not excessive in view of inflation and the rise of other prices, but dissuading to many casual theatregoers kept at home by "free" television. Producers, too, had to be dissuaded since a $55 top for a musical costing $5 million could not possibly promise the prompt payoff that a $6 top could for a $75,000 production. No small part of the problem derived from the absurdity of union demands. Union bonds alone, which had to be figured into initial costs, were in the hundreds of thousands of dollars. Nor were union demands conducive to reasonable weekly running costs. Actors' Equity, for example, negotiated contracts in which a performer's minimum salary per week was $850 (1990) at the same time that the Bureau of Labor Statistics reported the average American's weekly salary at $399. Ever more questionable were such practices as the musicians' union frequently requiring producers to pay musicians who were not used. Many smaller theatres, especially on the road, became uneconomical, and producers, who now demanded huge guarantees from playhouses instead of simply a percentage of the gross, sought out grotesquely large old film-houses and convention halls as auditoriums for their attractions. At the end of the 1980–81 season, *Variety* recorded that only three of the forty-odd productions were commercial successes, although one or two others were expected to prove profitable eventually.

The picture has not improved appreciably in subsequent seasons. The pattern in the late 1980s and beyond was one of feast or famine. A musical costing $8 million to open may have had to run six years to break even, but the financial rewards were staggering, especially taking into account tours and international companies. On the other hand, a modest $5 million musical that only ran eighteen months would end up losing millions. Plays were in an even more precarious position since few ran longer than a year. The result was that two and three-character plays or one-person programs were the only entries making a profit in a reasonably short period of time. Manhattan non-profit theatre groups, such as the *Roundabout Theatre and the *Public Theatre, have sometimes found success by opening a show in their Off-Broadway space and then, only after winning rave reviews and strong popular demand, moving the piece to a Broadway house. A hit like *A *Chorus Line* kept the Public solvent for years; but that same organization has seen millions of dollars lost when, say, a popular Central Park production was moved to Broadway, where it floundered and increased its financial loss while trying to find an audience. Ticket prices by the end of the 20th century had reached $100 for a musical, though most kept their top ticket around $95. Considering inflation, this top price was no greater than what Broadway was asking in the 1920s. The difference was in the lower-price tickets. Theatres that used to offer seven or eight different prices for the same show, based on location and performance day, were now priced with only three or possibly four choices, none qualifying as "cheap seats," though the poor location was the same as in the past. This has resulted in the loss of younger audience members attending the theatre on a regular basis. A popular favorite like *Rent* or *Hairspray* has a strong appeal for young patrons, but attendance is in the form of a special event, not a matter of routine theatregoing. Despite all the youths seen at many New York musicals, the average age of the Broadway audience climbs higher and higher. Particularly for non-musical plays, this does not bode well for the future.

ED SULLIVAN THEATRE (New York). One of Manhattan's theatres to experience a name change every time it changed management, the musical house on Broadway and 53rd Street opened in 1927 as Hammerstein's Theatre, a tribute to the late impresario Oscar *Hammerstein by its owner Arthur *Hammerstein. When the family lost it in the crash of 1929, it was sold and two years later was named the Manhattan Theatre. Billy *Rose renamed it after himself when he bought it in 1934 and turned it into a theatre restaurant, but it switched to the Manhattan Music Hall when Rose lost it. By 1936 it was a CBS radio studio and, later, a popular television studio, known to all of America from the *Ed Sullivan Show*, which was broadcast live every Sunday night. In 1967 the space was named the Ed Sullivan Theatre, which it is still called, and is now known as the home of David Letterman's television program.

EDDINGER, Wallace (1881–1929), actor. He was born in Albany, New York, and made his debut as a child actor in 1888. He continued to play children's roles for the next five years, notably as Cedric in *Little Lord Fauntleroy*. Returning to the stage as an adult in 1902 as a replacement in

Soldiers of Fortune, Eddinger quickly made playgoers note his polished skills both as a comic and serious actor, as well as the boyish, down-home attractiveness he was never to lose. Prominent supporting roles followed in *The Optimist* (1906), **Caught in the Rain* (1907), and *Classmates* (1907). His versatility was further demonstrated when he essayed the weakling Howard Jeffries in *The *Third Degree* (1909), the flying author Robert Street in *The Aviator* (1910), art collector Travers Gladwin in **Officer 666* (1912), and novelist William Magee in **Seven Keys to Baldpate* (1913). Eddinger's other hits included the jealous Budd Woodbridge in *The *Boomerang* (1915), the groom-to-be Reginald Carter in *Wedding Bells* (1919), and the overimaginative Ambrose in *Captain Applejack* (1921). His last successes were as the Novelist in *The Haunted House* (1924) and diarist Samuel Pepys in *And So to Bed* (1927).

EDDY, Edward (1822–75), actor. Long the leading star at the popular-priced *Bowery Theatre, the manly, handsome, stentorian-voiced performer was born in Troy, New York, and first appeared in public at a New York recital in 1839. He then toured for several seasons before making his New York debut in 1846 as Othello at the New Greenwich Theatre. In the same season Eddy offered his Claude Melnotte in *The *Lady of Lyons*, Clifford in *The *Hunchbuck*, and the title part in *The *Stranger*, all of which were to be favorite interpretations in his later Bowery years, which began with his Richelieu in 1851. Highlights at the Bowery include Edmond Dantes in *The Count of Monte Cristo* and his Richard III. His emotive, scene-chewing style of acting led to his being called "robustious Eddy." Throughout these years he continued to essay a wide range of parts, even participating in the *dog dramas that were briefly the rage, but, whether he wore out his welcome or playgoers became more sophisticated, he eventually lost popularity. He later drifted among a number of lesser theatres before leaving to set up a theatrical troupe in the West Indies, where he died in poverty.

EDESON, Robert (1868–1931), actor. The sternly handsome leading man, the son of an actor, was born in New Orleans and made his stage debut in Brooklyn in 1887, playing two small parts in *Fascination*. He performed at the *Boston Museum until he was spotted by Charles *Frohman, who cast him as Harry Winters in *Incog* (1892). Edeson remained with Frohman for several seasons, his most notable assignment being Rev. Gavin Dishart opposite Maude *Adams in *The Little Minister* (1897). In 1901 he was applauded for his portrayal of the faithful Edward Warden in *The*

*Climbers, followed by such successes as the mining engineer Clay in *Soldiers of Fortune* (1902), the Indian Soangataha in *Strongheart* (1905), and the cruel, cynical cadet Duncan Irving in *Classmates* (1907). Thereafter, he moved from play to play with little success, often accepting supporting roles. At the same time, Edeson became one of the earliest important theatrical figures to move into films. His last Broadway appearance was in 1922 as the Vagrant in *The World We Live In* (aka *The Insect Comedy*).

EDOUIN, [William Frederick] **Willie** [né Boyer] (1846–1908), comic actor. Although he spent little more than a decade on American stages, he became an especially popular comedian and was one of the progenitors of American musical comedy. The son of an English dance instructor, he and his five brothers and sisters made their debuts in children's shows in London and Brighton. Coming to America in 1869, Edouin first appeared under Laurence *Barrett and John *McCullough at San Francisco's *California Theatre. He won quick celebrity there with his travesties of popular plays and local figures. His initial New York appearance was in 1870, playing Narcissus Fitzfrizzle in *The Dancing Barber*, then he joined Dan Bryant to perform Murphy in *Handy Andy*. In 1871 he was enlisted in Miss Thompson's troupe as its principle male comedian. Edouin remained with her for six years, appearing in *Blue Beard, Lurline, Robin Hood, Mephisto and the Fourscore*, and *Robinson Crusoe*. His make-up, clowning, and acrobatics as Friday in the last-mentioned play earned him special praise. At this time, a genre of elementary, prototypical musical comedies called farce-comedy began to take hold. Edouin performed briefly in 1877 with an early *farce-comedy troupe, *Colville's Folly Company, then switched to an even more famous band, E. E. *Rice's Surprise Party, where he appeared in such pieces as *Babes in the Woods, The Lost Children*, and *Horrors*. In 1880 he organized his own troupe, Willie Edouin's Sparks, collaborating on one of the most successful of farce-comedies, *Dreams*, and taking several of the principal roles in it as well. He left for England in 1884, returning only occasionally, most memorably to play Tweedlepunch in **Florodora* (1900).

EDWARDS, Gus [né Simon] (1879–1945), producer and songwriter. Born in Germany, he was brought to America while still a child and soon was employing his boy soprano voice to help support his family. In his late teens he organized the first of many similar vaudeville acts consisting entirely of promising youngsters. His eye for young talent was so impressive that he was nicknamed "The

Star Maker." Among the many future stars to whom he gave starts in his acts were Eddie *Cantor, George *Jessel, Georgie Price, Walter *Winchell, and the Duncan sisters. While assembling acts, he also began to write songs. Still popular are his "In My Merry Oldsmobile," "By the Light of the Silvery Moon," and "School Days." On Broadway his scores or songs were heard in *When We Were Forty-one* (1905), *Hip! Hip! Hooray!* (1907), *School Days* (1908), *The Merry-Go-Round* (1908), and the *Ziegfeld Follies of 1910*.

EDWARDS, Julian (1855–1910), composer. The Englishman studied in Edinburgh and London before accepting a post as conductor of the Carl Rosa Opera Company. James C. *Duff brought him to New York and produced his first show to reach Broadway, *Jupiter* (1892). Between that premiere and his death eighteen years later he wrote the scores for seventeen New York musicals. Among the best received or more interesting were *King René's Daughter* (1893), *Madeleine* (1895), *The Goddess of Truth* (1896), *The Wedding Day* (1897), *The Jolly Musketeer* (1898), *Princess Chic* (1900), *Dolly Varden* (1902), *When Johnny Comes Marching Home* (1902), *Love's Lottery* (1904), and *The Girl and the Wizard* (1909). Although none of his music remains popular, he was highly respected in his own time, and his work was sufficiently admired to lure such stars as Lillian *Russell, Jefferson *De Angelis, Della *Fox, Christie *MacDonald, and Lulu *Glaser.

EFFECT OF GAMMA RAYS ON MAN-IN-THE-MOON MARIGOLDS, THE (1970), a play by Paul Zindel. [Mercer-O'Casey Theatre, 819 perf.; Pulitzer Prize, NYDCC Award.] Beatrice (Sada Thompson) is a slatternly, widowed housewife who takes her hatred of the world out on her two children, Ruth (Amy Levitt) and Matilda or Tillie (Pamela Payton-Wright). She badgers them and often keeps them out of school to help with housework, which never gets properly done anyway. The extroverted Ruth is an epileptic and has little love or respect for her mother. The younger Tillie escapes her nightmarish daily life by making scientific experiments in school, studying the effects of cobalt-60 on marigolds. Only her laboratory work sustains her, and when she wins a science competition she begins to see a brighter future. The play was originally written for television, and was later staged at Houston's *Alley Theatre and the *Cleveland Play House before being presented Off Broadway. Jerry Talmer of the *New York Post* wrote, "I don't know of a better play of its genre since *The Glass Menagerie*. It is stronger and funnier and tougher than I can report." In 1971 the play became only the second Off-Broadway

production to receive the *Pulitzer Prize. Because of its strong female cast of characters, the drama was frequently done in theatres across the country. **Paul ZINDEL** (1936–2003), a native of Staten Island, had been a high school science teacher and a novelist, many of his juvenile books read in schools. Zindel's other plays include *And Miss Reardon Drinks a Little* (1971), *The Secret Affair of Mildred Wild* (1972), and *Ladies at the Alamo* (1977).

EIGHTH OF JANUARY, THE (1829), a play by Robert Penn *Smith. [*Chestnut Street Theatre (Philadelphia), in repertory.] The War of 1812 has divided the Bull family. John Bull (William *Warren), its aging patriarch, remains loyal to England, although he refuses to take an active part in the battle. His son Charles (Mr. Southwell) is a loyal American and willing to lay down his life for his country and for General Jackson (Mr. Rowbotham). Jackson fights the battle of New Orleans on January 8, unaware a peace treaty has been signed. A lovable Cockney, Billy Bowbell (the first Joseph *Jefferson), wanders in and out of the play. One of the few plays written about the war, it was inferior as drama to the best play about the conflict, *The *Triumph at Plattsburg*. Indeed, the *United States Gazette* complained of its "peculiarly undramatic nature." Actually, however, it was hastily written to celebrate Jackson's 1828 election. For all its faults, the *Gazette* welcomed it as "uncommonly interesting," especially in that it "displays effectually more variety of humor than the generality of pieces in which national peculiarities are harped upon."

EISENHAUER, Peggy. See Fisher, Jules.

EL CAPITAN (1896), a comic opera by Charles *Klein (book), John Philip *Sousa (music, lyrics), Tom Frost (lyrics). [*Broadway Theatre, 112 perf.] Don Medigua (De Wolf *Hopper), the viceroy of Peru, captures the rebel El Capitan, executes him, and assumes his place in disguise. The rebels capture Medigua's servant, Pozzo (Klein), mistaking him for his master, and news of the viceroy's apparent capture prompts his wife (Alice Hosmer) and daughter (Bertha Waltzinger) to go in search of him. Meanwhile, as El Capitan, Medigua flirts with Estrelda (Edna Wallace Hopper), a former viceroy's daughter. When the Spanish army arrives, Medigua leads the rebels in circles until they are too tired to fight. The revolution is put down, but Medigua has some explaining to do to his wife about his flirtation. *Notable songs*: El Capitan's Song; Sweetheart, I'm Waiting; A Typical Tune of Zanzibar. Sousa's great score and Hopper's superb clowning were in large measure responsible for the success of the original production. "El Capitan's Song," later known as "El Capitan March," was the most famous melody to come from a Sousa operetta. In his autobiography Sousa insisted that Klein's libretto was the finest ever written for a comic opera. While that assessment is open to dispute, the book proved durable enough when the work was revived in the 1970s by the *Goodspeed Opera House.

ELDRIDGE, Florence [née Florence McKechnie] (1901–88), actress. The Brooklyn-born leading lady made her professional debut in the chorus of a 1918 musical but first won major attention when she portrayed the terrified heroine Annabelle West in The *Cat and the Canary (1922) and the Step-daughter in Six Characters in Search of an Author (1922). In 1927 she married Fredric *March and subsequently played opposite him in many shows, most notably The *Skin of Our Teeth (1942), *Years Ago (1946), and *Long Day's Journey into Night (1956).

ELEPHANT MAN, THE (1979), a play by Bernard Pomerance. [*Booth Theatre, 916 perf.; Tony, NYDCC Awards.] In Victorian London, Dr. Frederick Treves (Kevin *Conway) discovers the misshapen, seemingly retarded John Merrick (Philip Anglim) in a freak show and rescues him in order to study his peculiar deformity. But Merrick turns out to be unusually bright and articulate, becomes the toast of high society, then commits suicide because his ugly exterior and isolated interior are too much to bear. Pomerance, an American living and writing in England, based the play on actual events but told his tale in a detached Brechtian manner. The ANTA production opened Off Off Broadway at St. Peter's Church and was so well received that it transferred to Broadway with significant success. A 2002 Broadway revival failed, though the acting by Billy Crudup and Kate Burton was roundly commended

ELIOT, T[homas] S[tearns] (1888–1965), playwright and poet. The expatriate American, who spent most of his creative career in England as a British subject, is remembered by American playgoers largely for three plays: *Murder in the Cathedral (1936), The *Cocktail Party (1950), and The Confidential Clerk (1954). None of the three was received in America with unequivocal acclaim. The merits of the poet's unique dramatic blank verse were open to serious question, the writing seen as verbose and elusive, and the plotting perceived as frequently too shaky. Nevertheless, all three works found reasonably large audiences and have been revived occasionally. Indirectly, Eliot may have been far more important to modern theatre in several ways. In his position as an arbiter of taste he was instrumental in promoting a reconsideration of long-neglected Jacobean

playwrights. His *Sweeney Agonistes: Fragments of an Aristophanic Melodrama* is recognized as a precursor of the now popular style and approach of such later writers as Samuel *Beckett, Harold *Pinter, and Sam *Shepard. Lastly, his tremendous prestige made him a leading voice in the rebellion, however unsuccessful, against the reigning school of Ibsenite realism. His *Old Possum's Book of Practical Cats* provided some of the lyrics for the 1982 musical *Cats.

ELITCH'S GARDEN THEATRE (Denver). America's longest-operating summer playhouse, in operation from 1890 until 1994, it was founded by John Elitch, a former actor, and his wife, Mary, who had come to Denver in 1882 and purchased a sixteen-acre plot where they eventually built a wooden, octagonal theatre. Elitch died before the theatre opened, so Mrs. Elitch assumed its management. The house was used at first for vaudeville, but in 1897 a stock company was organized. In the 1950s a modern stagehouse was added. For many years regular plays touring summer circuits were booked, but this was discontinued after 1987. Concert and special attractions were then the mainstay. The theatre was equally famous for the gardens that surrounded it, including a large greenhouse where Colorado carnations were grown. The gardens were later enlarged to thirty-two acres. Among its early attractions was a cart, pulled by an ostrich, in which rides were offered. In 1932 Caroline Lawrence Dier wrote its history in *The Lady of the Gardens*.

ELIZABETH THE QUEEN (1930), a drama by Maxwell *Anderson. [Guild Theatre, 147 perf.] The aging Queen Elizabeth (Lynn *Fontanne) has fallen in love with her young, handsome courtier Robert Devereaux (Alfred *Lunt), the Earl of Essex. While he is away on an Irish campaign, Sir Walter Raleigh (Percy Waram) and Lord Cecil (Arthur Hughes) conspire to make the Queen doubt not merely his love but his loyalty as well. To test Essex, the Queen orders him to disband his army. He does, after which Elizabeth has him arrested and sentenced to death. She calls him to her, hoping he will plead for mercy and forgiveness, thereby allowing their romance to resume. But the proud, stubborn Essex refuses and is sent to his death. Alone, Elizabeth laments that she is old and only Essex's love could have given her a breath of youth. Brooks *Atkinson hailed the *Theatre Guild production of the blank-verse tragedy as "magnificent drama. It is a searching portrayal of character, freely imaginative in its use of history, clearly thought out and conveyed in dialogue of notable beauty." The play was revived successfully in 1961 with Eva *Le Gallienne and in 1966 with Judith

*Anderson, and a well-received mounting by Washington's *Folger Theatre in 2003 demonstrated that the script's potency has not waned.

ELIZABETHAN AND JACOBEAN PLAYS [Other Than Shakespeare] **IN AMERICA.** Although some non-Shakespearean Tudor and Stuart plays were performed by the earliest professional ensembles, these productions were few and far between, a situation that persisted all through the 19th century. There was, however, one notable exception, Massinger's *A New Way to Pay Old Debts*, which seems to have first been staged during the 1794–95 season in Philadelphia and soon became one of the leading vehicles for early American tragedians. The meaty role of the villainous Sir Giles Overreach afforded Junius Brutus *Booth and Edwin *Booth, as well as many other less distinguished actors, a chance for a tour de force. The play held the stage with marked regularity as late as 1886, when the younger Booth offered his last revival of the work. The rise of academic playhouses in the late 19th and early 20th century may have whetted interest in many of these long-neglected plays, and the 20th century did see some notable revivals, although they were highly infrequent and never fully in the theatrical mainstream. A few of the more noteworthy revivals have been the *Theatre Guild's 1928 staging of *Volpone*; Orson *Welles's *Dr. Faustus* (1937) and *The Shoemaker's Holiday* (1938); Elisabeth *Bergner's 1946 mounting of *The Duchess of Malfi*; the *Phoenix Theatre's 1950 production of *The White Devil*; and Anthony Quayle as *Tamburlaine the Great* (1956).

ELLIOTT, Maxine [née Jessie Dermot] (1868–1940), actress. The daughter of a New England sea captain, she had no specific affection for the stage but took up acting solely as a means of support and quit when she had made her fortune, although much of her wealth actually derived from gifts and financial advice from her well-placed admirers. While most recognized that her dramatic abilities were limited, Elliott's beauty and charm, coupled for a time with a careful selection of vehicles, made her a favorite for some twenty years. Her biographer-niece pictured her as having "brilliant black hair, ivory skin, enormous eyes . . . described as 'midnight eyes,' and features of even proportion." After assuming her stage name at the suggestion of Dion *Boucicault, she made her debut in New York in 1890 in *The Middleman*, then toured with its star, E. S. *Willard, in a repertory of plays for two years. She briefly joined the company of Augustin *Daly, but his policy of frequently changing plays and assigning his actors both major and minor roles displeased the ambitious actress, so she left and married actor Nat

*Goodwin, whom she co-starred with in *An American Citizen* (1897), *The Rivals* (1897), *Nathan Hale* (1899), *The Cowboy and the Lady* (1899), *When We Were Twenty-one* (1900), and *The *Merchant of Venice* (1900). After divorcing Goodwin she shone as Georgiana in the Spanish-American War play *Her Own Way* (1903). Elliott's last success was as American Jo Sheldon wooed by a prince in *Her Great Match* (1905). In 1908 she opened her own theatre in New York, but all her productions there failed, so she retired in 1911, returning briefly as Cordelia in *Trimmed in Scarlet* (1920). Of her work in this last play Alexander *Woollcott repeated what had been often said, "Besides her lustrous beauty, she has dignity, a pleasing and thoroughly mastered voice, taste, humor and intelligence." She passed her remaining years in France and England. Biography: *My Aunt Maxine*, Diana Forbes-Robertson, 1964.

ELLISTON, Grace [née Rutter] (1881–1950), actress. The beautiful leading lady was born in Memphis, Tennessee, and made her New York debut in a series of Frank *Daniels musicals. Although she later appeared opposite George *Arliss, Richard *Bennett, Henry *Miller, and other prominent leading men, her most famous role was Shirley Rossmore, the fighting heroine of *The *Lion and the Mouse* (1905).

ELLSLER, Effie (1855?–1942), actress. Born in Cleveland, where her parents were popular actors and her father ran the leading playhouse, she made her debut while still a child and for many years played supporting and ingenue roles, acting with Edwin *Booth, Lawrence *Barrett, John *McCullough, and other celebrities during their Cleveland visits. Ellsler came to New York in 1880, making a sensation in her very first part, the title role of *Hazel Kirke*. She won ecstatic notices for her forceful yet natural portrayal of the character, which she played for three years. Thereafter, however, her choices of starring parts were ill-advised. She appeared in numerous unsuccessful claptrap melodramas: *Courage* (1883), *Storm Beaten* (1883), *Woman Against Woman* (1886), *The Keepsake* (1888), and *Judge Not* (1888). For most of the 1890s she toured in road companies, and in 1900 headed the tour of *Barbara Frietchie*. Three years later she was Jessica to Maxine *Elliott's Portia in *The *Merchant of Venice*. Minor roles in a number of plays followed before Ellsler scored one last hit as Cornelia Van Gorder, who rents a summer home and finds herself in the middle of a murder, in *The *Bat* (1920).

ELTINGE, Julian (né William Julian Dalton] (1883–1941), actor and female impersonator. He was born in Newtonville, Massachusetts, and made his debut in Boston at the age of ten, playing a little girl. His appearance was so well received that he continued to develop his art and made his New York debut in 1904 in E. E. *Rice's production of *Mr. Wix of Wickham*. The musical was a failure, but he quickly began to make a name for himself in vaudeville. Unlike most earlier female impersonators, who had emphasized the comic, often grotesquely exaggerated, side of their trade, Eltinge portrayed beautiful young women, carefully and tastefully imitating their make-up, dress, and mannerisms. His comedy came from the situations his women found themselves in and only incidentally from the fact that he was a man in drag. In 1908 and 1909 he toured with the Cohan and Harris Minstrels, then in 1911 returned to Broadway to portray Hal Blake, who is forced to disguise himself as a Mrs. Monte to pursue his courtship of his sweetheart, in *The Fascinating Widow*. Producer A. H. *Woods made so much money from this production that when he built a new theatre a year later he named it in Eltinge's honor. He appeared in two more musicals, *The Crinoline Girl* (1914) and *Cousin Lucy* (1915), and continued to star in vaudeville throughout the 1920s. Thereafter, his vogue faded, and his few attempts to revive it were poorly received.

EMENS, Homer [Farnham] (1862–1930), designer. One of the distinguished set painters of his era, he was born in Volney, New York, and started his career as an apprentice to Philip *Goatcher at the *Madison Square Theatre. He spent several years at the *Chestnut Street Theatre in Philadelphia before returning to New York. In keeping with the practice of his day, he frequently designed only one or two of the several settings used in a play, generally creating the outdoor scenes, which were considered his forte. His setting for the fourth act of *Gismonda* (1894), showing a starlit vista just before dawn, was called by one critic "probably the most beautiful ever put on stage" for its "simplicity, grandeur, hint of splendid architecture, [and] poetic reflection." Among Emens's other design credits were *Blue Jeans* (1890), *Mavourneen* (1891), *Alabama* (1891), *Babes in Toyland* (1903), *Twelfth Night* (1904), *Mlle. Modiste* (1905), The *Red Mill* (1906), and *Kismet* (1911).

EMERSON, John (1874–1956), actor, director, and playwright. After preparing for the ministry at Oberlin, Heidelberg, and the University of Chicago, the native of Sandusky, Ohio, decided to enter the theatre and made his acting debut in 1904 in *Tit for Tat*. He continued to act for several seasons, including a tour with Mrs. Fiske, before turning his hand to directing. He successively served the *Shuberts, Charles *Frohman, and A. H.

*Woods, staging such diverse pieces as Clyde *Fitch's The *City (1909) and the Julian *Eltinge musical, *The Crinoline Girl* (1914). He served as president of *Actors' Equity during its 1919 strike. In the 1920s he wrote several plays with his wife, Anita *Loos, including *The Whole Town's Talking* (1923) and a 1926 dramatization of Loos's *Gentlemen Prefer Blondes*.

EMERY, Gilbert. See *Hero, The*.

EMERY, Miss [also known as Mrs. Burroughs] (d. 1832), actress. A fine tragedienne whose ghastly death gave her greater notice than any of her performances, she had become a favorite at the Surrey Theatre in her native London before *Wemyss brought her to America. She made her American debut in 1827 at Philadelphia's *Chestnut Street Theatre as Belvidera in *Venice Preserved* and also won acclaim there and in New York for her Portia, Bianca in *Fazio*, and other popular heroines of the era. For reasons now lost she was suddenly denied parts and finally sank to prostitution in the notorious Five Points slum, where she was discovered dying after a bloody brawl. T. Allston *Brown adds the unusual note that she was "the largest woman ever seen on the American stage."

EMMET, J[oseph] **K**[lein] (1841–91), actor and singer. Born in St. Louis, he was apprenticed to a sign painter who also painted sets for local playhouses. Working on these gave him a taste for the stage and before long he was performing his own song and dance act. A stint in minstrelsy, including an engagement with Dan Bryant, was followed by several seasons in variety, where he perfected a "Dutch" act, wearing a green blouse and cap and wooden shoes and singing in broken English. In 1870 the wide-eyed actor with curly black hair first appeared as Fritz, the young man seeking his long-lost sister, in *Fritz, Our Cousin German*. Singing "Emmet's Lullaby," the role made him a star and provided a vehicle for the rest of his life. He also appeared in a number of similar pieces such as *Carl, the Fiddler* (1871), *Max, the Merry Swiss Boy* (1873), and *Fritz in Ireland* (1879). His skill with such instruments as the guitar, the violin, and the harmonica and his fine Irish tenor voice and supple dancing combined with his winning personality to assure him steady occupation in what were essentially the flimsiest of plays. He died, apparently of paresis, while still at the height of his popularity.

EMPEROR JONES, THE (1920), a play by Eugene *O'Neill. [*Neighborhood Playhouse, 204 perf.] The African-American Pullman porter, Brutus Jones (Charles S. *Gilpin), escapes from the prison he has been sent to as the result of a fight in a crap game and flees to a West Indies island. There he establishes himself as emperor, running an abusive, corrupt dictatorial regime. A white Cockney trader, Smithers (Jasper Deeter), warns him that the incessant drum beating signifies an imminent revolt, but Jones is cocky and assures Smithers only a silver bullet can kill him. The revolt forces him to flee and hide in the forest where eventually the troops of Lem (Charles Ellis), a native chief, find him and kill him with a silver bullet that Lem has had specially made. Looking at the body, Smithers remarks, "Where's yer 'igh an' mighty airs now, yer bloomin' Majesty? Silver bullets! Gawd blimey, but yer died in the 'eight of style, any'ow." Based loosely on an incident in Haitian history, the play was originally called The Silver Bullet. George Jean *Nathan thought it a compelling drama "touched by a visionary ecstasy." The *Provincetown Players production was an early attempt by O'Neill at expressionism, albeit framed in two realistic scenes, with innovative settings designed by Robert Edmond *Jones that viewed the Caribbean jungle through Jones's nightmarish point of view. This stylized scenery and a persistent beating of drums in the background accentuated the theme of modern man destroyed by a belligerent civilization. This play has been revived on several occasions, was a standard in the repertory of the *Hedgerow Theatre, and remained popular with little theatre and college groups for decades.

EMPIRE THEATRE (New York). For many years the oldest and most prestigious playhouse in New York, it was built by Al *Hayman and Charles *Frohman and stood directly across Broadway from the Metropolitan Opera House, one door away from 40th Street. The architect was J. B. *McElfatrick, and while his design was undistinguished it was nonetheless attractive. A long lobby, in later seasons hung with portraits of noted stars, led to a rococo auditorium decorated in rich reds and gold. The theatre opened in 1893 with The *Girl I Left Behind Me and for the next twenty-two years, until Frohman's death, served as his flagship. The producer was insistent that the theatre's first attraction be an American play on an American theme, but his penchant for English and French successes meant that its early bills were primarily importations. Thus, the house witnessed the American premieres of numerous works by Pinero, Henry Arthur *Jones, *Barrie, and *Maugham. *Peter Pan (1905) opened there, as did Captain Brassbound's Conversion (1907). The house was also the home of Frohman's most celebrated stars, such as Maude *Adams, Ethel *Barrymore, and John *Drew. After Frohman's death the theatre continued to offer the greatest stars, often in fine plays: Barrymore in *Déclassée (1919); Katharine *Cornell in several plays, including her most famous vehicle, The *Barretts of Wimpole Street (1930); Judith *Anderson; Ruth *Chatterton; Jane *Cowl; Julie *Harris; Doris *Keane; Helen *Menken; Alfred *Lunt and Lynn *Fontanne; and Ethel *Waters. The Empire was also home to America's longest-running play, *Life with Father (1939). For all its fame the theatre was threatened with the loss of its license in 1926 when it housed a controversial play about lesbianism, The Captive. Authorities closed the play but never otherwise penalized the theatre. Its last play was The *Time of the Cuckoo (1952), starring Shirley *Booth. The building was demolished in 1953.

END OF SUMMER (1936), a comedy by S. N. *Behrman. [Guild Theatre, 152 perf.] Leonie Frothingham (Ina *Claire) is a rich woman of old stock, as her mother, Mrs. Wyler (Mildred *Natwick), is only too happy to point out. However, Leonie's concern is not her mother but her daughter Paula (Doris Dudley), who is courted by two men. The older of the suitors is Dr. Kenneth Rice (Osgood *Perkins), who is obviously something of a fortune hunter but promises to maintain Paula in her comfortable world. The other suitor is Will Dexter (Shepperd Strudwick), a young radical who promises only revolution and a new social order. When Paula decides in Will's favor, Leonie acquiesces, accepting the likelihood that the brilliant summer of her own life is about to fade. She even agrees to back a radical magazine that Will's friend, Dennis McCarthy (Van Heflin), hopes to publish. Although Brooks *Atkinson suggested that Behrman's play was "one of those tolerant, witty, gently probing essays in modern thinking," he concluded, "you scarcely know which side he is taking." Yet the *Theatre Guild production, perhaps more clearly than any other Behrman comedy, suggested that the playwright was all in favor of a more open, even-handed society, provided it subscribed to some of the elegances and graces of the old order.

ENGEL, Lehman (1910–82), composer, conductor, and author. He was born in Mississippi and studied at the University of Cincinnati, the Juilliard School of Music, and with Roger Sessions before writing incidental music for a 1934 production of Within the Gates. Engel later composed background music for several other shows as well as creating the score for A Hero Is Born (1937). He was better known, however, as a conductor. Beginning with The *Cradle Will Rock (1937), he conducted the orchestras for such musicals as Call Me Mister (1946), *Wonderful Town (1953), *Fanny (1954), *Li'l Abner (1956), Jamaica (1957), *Take Me Along (1959),

Do Re Mi (1960), and *I Can Get It for You Wholesale* (1962). But he was also a serious student of musical theatre, teaching both at the American Musical and Dramatic Theatre Academy and at New York University. Among his books are *Musical Shows: Planning and Producing* (1957), *The American Musical Theatre* (1967), *Words with Music* (1972), and an autobiography, *This Bright Day* (1974).

ENGLANDER, Ludwig (1859–1914), composer. Born in Vienna, where he received his earliest musical training, he moved briefly to Paris and there worked for a time with Jacques *Offenbach. On coming to America he took a post as conductor for the Thalia Theatre, a playhouse catering to German immigrants, where his first musical score, *Der Prinz Gemahl* (*The Prince Consort*), was heard. He later moved to the *Casino Theatre, where he was musical director but in short order provided a score for The *Passing Show* (1894), the first American revue. Englander left the Casino to write independently and during the next fourteen years scored nearly thirty Broadway musicals, among them *The Casino Girl* (1900), *The Strollers* (1901), *The Wild Rose* (1902), *Sally in Our Alley* (1902), *The Office Boy* (1903), *The Rich Mr. Hoggenheimer* (1906), and *Miss Innocence* (1908). After a long hiatus he wrote one final show, *Madam Moselle* (1914), shortly before his death. Englander regularly did his own orchestrations and frequently conducted his own and scores by others. For all his prolificacy, he produced no songs of lasting fame. His lack of melodic inspiration was recognized even in his own day (critics described his work as "tinkly"), and many of his musicals had interpolations that proved far more popular and enduring than his contributions.

ENGLISH MUSICALS [other than Gilbert and Sullivan] **IN AMERICA.** It is not generally recognized that, while American musicals have won worldwide fame for their daring and excellence, English musicals have time and again been the real pioneers. American lyric works have simply moved forward from the impetus provided by West End examples. In addition to *Gilbert and Sullivan, many of their contemporaries such as Cellier and Solomon enjoyed some popularity with American audiences, and *Erminie's success was exceptional. But it was the Savoyard comic operas that served as exemplars to American writers of the period and that opened all American stages to song and dance entertainments. When the vogue for comic opera faded, the Gaiety Theatre musical comedies that George Edwardes had instituted in London came across the Atlantic, beginning in 1894 with *A Gaiety Girl*, to speed the development of the new genre. Of course, America had also been evolving its own

musical comedy tradition, but the sophistication and elegance of the Gaiety musicals set new standards and propelled the advance. Although it was not a Gaiety musical, *Florodora* (1900) proved the most popular importation of the period. In the 1920s the popularity of *Charlot's Revue* similarly promoted the cause of the intimate revue and signaled the end of the gargantuan extravaganza of the *Ziegfeld school. A handful of later English musicals were noteworthy successes, such as *Bitter Sweet, The Boy Friend, *Oliver!*, and *Stop the World—I Want to Get Off*. However, these were looked upon as almost sui generis and had little real influence on the development of American musicals. Since then such Andrew Lloyd *Webber musicals as *Evita, *Cats, and The *Phantom of the Opera* have enjoyed remarkable successes, but their influence on mainstream American lyric theatre remains to be seen. *Me and My Girl* was an unusual case of a British musical not finding success on Broadway until decades after it premiered in London.

ENGLISH RESTORATION AND 18TH-CENTURY PLAYS IN AMERICA. Although the earliest Restoration (1660–1700) plays were about eighty years old when professional theatre emerged in America and while the last of these works were approaching the half-century mark, they remained among the most popular and frequently revived pieces on the London stage, and so constituted a substantial part of the repertory of the first actors to play in America. Dryden, Otway, Congreve, Vanbrugh, and Farquhar appeared regularly in the lists of playwrights offered by Walter *Murray and Edmund *Kean, by Robert *Upton, and by the elder Lewis *Hallam. At the same time such later authors as Cibber, Garrick, Rowe, and Lillo began to make numerous appearances. From the start Otway's *Venice Preserved* and Farquhar's *The Beaux' Stratagem*, possibly along with his *The Recruiting Officer*, were the most popular of the Restoration works. Indeed, throughout the first half of the 19th century *Venice Preserved* remained far and away the most revived work from this era. The roles of Jaffier and Pierre were favored parts of such early American tragedians as Edwin *Forrest and the two great *Booths. Congreve's *Love for Love* came early to American stages, and while revivals were not numerous, the play did return at intervals, always respected and admired. Curiously, the first professional American staging of his equally great *The Way of the World* seems not to have taken place until 1924. Rowe's *The Tragedy of Jane Shore* and eventually Gay's *The Beggar's Opera* were the most often produced of the earlier 18th-century pieces. Later, Home's *Douglas* became for a long time one of the most familiar of all the period's plays.

During the last years of the century, by which time professional theatre was permanently established in America, five then-new plays won huge audiences: Farquhar's *The Belle's Stratagem*, Goldsmith's *She Stoops to Conquer*, and *Sheridan's *Pizarro, The Rivals,* and *The School for Scandal*; the last-mentioned was the most regularly seen. In the 20th century, mountings of the 18th-century and, on the rarest of occasions, of Restoration plays became very infrequent and were largely special events. The *Players offered several highly acclaimed all-star revivals in the 1920s, and, to cite one later example, Cyril *Ritchard headed a superb revival of *The Relapse* in 1950. Visiting English ensembles have generally provided the best presentations, such as John *Gielgud's *Love for Love* in 1947. To a small extent regional and collegiate theatres have helped fill the void.

ENNERY, A. P. See D'Ennery, Adolphe-Philippe.

ENTER MADAME (1920), a comedy by Gilda Varesi and Dolly Byrne. [*Garrick Theatre, 350 perf.] Gerald Fitzgerald (Norman Trevor) has been married for more than twenty years to the great prima donna Lisa Della Robbia (Varesi) but has tired of following her all over the world in the wake of her sycophantic entourage. When one newspaper calls him Gerald Della Robbia and another nominates him as "President of the Only Her Husband's Club," he decides enough is enough. When Gerald meets a sedate widow, Flora Preston (Jane Meredith), and falls in love with her, Lisa agrees to a divorce, although she still loves him. After the divorce comes through, Lisa invites Gerald and Flora to dinner. Turning on the charm, she persuades him to leave Flora and marry her again. Heywood *Broun noted of the Brock *Pemberton production, "Here is an excellent light comedy. . . . The story is slight, but it is briskly told." The play was revived for a successful road tour in 1930 with Helen *Menken as the prima donna. Actress, playwright **Gilda VARESI** was the daughter of the celebrated opera star Elena Varesi and acknowledged that much of the play derived from memories of her own childhood with her mother.

EPSTEIN, Alvin (b. 1925), actor, director, and manager. He was born in New York and, after attending the High School of Music and Art, studied dance with Martha Graham, mime with Etienne Decroux, and acting with Sanford *Meisner. He made his professional New York acting debut Off Broadway in 1946, then traveled and performed across Europe and in the Middle East. Epstein made his Broadway debut in a Marcel Marceau mime program in 1956, the same year he played the Fool to Orson

*Welles's *King Lear* and originated the role of the unintelligible Lucky in the first American production of *Waiting for Godot* (1956). His acting career also included the disillusioned Clov in the absurdist *Endgame* (1958), the tormented Father in *Six Characters in Search of an Author* (1988), and the dying title professor in *Tuesdays with Morrie* (2002). Epstein co-founded the *Berkshire Theatre Festival and ran the *Yale Repertory Theatre and the *Guthrie Theatre in the 1970s.

EQUITY LIBRARY THEATRE (New York). Founded in 1943 by Sam Jaffe, representing *Actors' Equity, and George *Freedley, at the time curator of the New York Public Library Theatre Collection (ELT, as it is often referred to), was designed to provide a showcase for young actors, directors, and technicians and to create an audience from among those who could not afford commercial theatre. A non-profit organization, it originally presented its plays at libraries and charged no admission but asked instead for a contribution to help sustain it. Beginning in 1949 it operated its own theatre, first at the Lenox Hill Playhouse and later at other auditoriums. Actors whose careers were helped by early appearances with the organization include James Earl *Jones, Richard *Kiley, and Jason *Robards. Financial problems forced its closing during the 1989–90 season.

EQUITY PLAYERS (New York). An acting and producing ensemble formed in 1922 by members of *Actors' Equity, its goal was the presentation of superior new plays and classical revivals. Although most of its mountings won critical praise, they proved unappealing to a majority of playgoers. One notable exception was a 1922 production of Jesse Lynch *Williams's *Why Not?* After some reorganization the name was changed to the Actors' Theatre. Under this banner during the 1924–25 season it offered distinguished revivals of *Candida and *The Wild Duck*. In 1927 the group was absorbed by Kenneth *MacGowan's company in Greenwich Village.

EQUUS (1974). Peter *Shaffer's 1973 London success, centering on a psychiatrist and his young male patient who is obsessed with horses, was produced by Kermit *Bloomgarden and others at the Plymouth Theatre for a run of 1,209 performances. Anthony Hopkins was the original doctor and Peter Firth, the boy. Several other notable actors, including Anthony *Perkins and Richard *Burton, later assumed the role of the psychiatrist.

ERLANGER, A[braham] L[incoln] (1860–1930), producer and manager. As a young boy in his native Cleveland, he sold opera glasses at the

Academy of Music and was later appointed treasurer of the Euclid Avenue Opera House. Erlanger soon developed a cynical business philosophy and, to go with it, an unwieldy collection of Napoleonic memorabilia. The blocky, balding, bull-faced man directed and produced contemporary melodramas, eventually going into partnership with a lawyer, Marc *Klaw. The pair came east and bought out the Taylor Theatrical Exchange, changing its name to the Klaw and Erlanger Exchange. Among the celebrated performers they represented were Effie *Ellsler, Joseph *Jefferson, and Fanny *Davenport. Theatrical bookings of the day were loosely organized and often chaotic, so in 1895 the pair met quietly with producers Charles *Frohman, Al *Hayman, William *Harris Sr., Samuel F. *Nixon-Nirdlinger, and Fred *Zimmerman to attempt to bring some order to the system, and in the following year the group established what became known as the *Theatrical Syndicate or Trust, with Erlanger in effective control. Within a short time the Syndicate controlled several hundred theatres across the country and denied theatres to performers and producers who refused to meet its often unreasonable demands. Such distinguished players as Mrs. *Fiske and Sarah *Bernhardt were reduced to performing in tents and lesser theatres but won huge audiences and widespread admiration for their defiance. In 1907 the Syndicate seemingly attempted to take over vaudeville as well, but in a short while sold out to *Keith for well over a million dollars, suggesting to many that the move was merely a gigantic blackmail attempt against Keith. Erlanger's stranglehold would eventually be diminished by the *Shuberts and the coming of films. Although most theatre figures looked on him as a vicious, callous, arrogant man, Erlanger had a number of loyal admirers, such as George M. *Cohan and, until he fought with them late in their careers, Florenz *Ziegfeld and Charles *Dillingham. He bankrolled most of their productions, including the first *Follies. Beginning with The Great Metropolis (1889), he produced hundreds of plays in New York and silently underwrote many others. Although he took public credit, usually as co-producer, for such plays as *Rebecca of Sunnybrook Farm (1910), *Kismet (1911), Pollyanna (1916), The *Famous Mrs. Fair (1919), and *To the Ladies (1922), he was better known as producer or co-producer of such musicals as *Forty-five Minutes from Broadway (1906), The *Pink Lady (1911), The Count of Luxembourg (1912), Two Little Girls in Blue (1921), and Honeymoon Lane (1926).

ERMINIE (1886). An English musical with libretto by Harry Paulton and music by Edward Jacobowski, it opened at the *Casino Theatre less than a year after its English premiere and enjoyed the longest run (571 performances) of any musical during that playhouse's early heyday. Audiences especially admired the clowning of Francis *Wilson as the comic vagabond Cadeaux and the song "Lullaby (Dear Mother, in Dreams I See Her)." Though the work was long held in affection and esteem and was successfully revived as late as 1921, it had little real importance in the development of the American musical theatre.

ERROL, Leon (1881–1951), comic actor and director. The balding, sour-faced comedian, famous for his rubber-legged drunk scenes, was born in Australia and originally planned a medical career. To earn money for tuition, he played in vaudeville, where he was so successful that he abandoned his medical ambitions. Errol performed in Shakespearean repertory, with a circus, and in comic opera before Florenz *Ziegfeld discovered him and enrolled him in the *Ziegfeld Follies of 1911, where he scored a huge success. Ziegfeld then cast him in A Winsome Widow (1912); the 1912, 1913, 1914, and 1915 editions of the Follies; and The Century Girl (1916). After appearing in the 1917 and 1918 editions of Hitchy-Koo, Errol returned to the Ziegfeld fold to play Connie, the impoverished nobleman who befriends the heroine-waif in *Sally (1920). Later appearances were in Louie the 14th (1925), Yours Truly (1927), and Fioretta (1929). Describing his antics in this last musical, one critic wrote, "For these many years Mr. Errol has never stood quietly on his feet. In Fioretta he slides down pairs of stairs, handicapped by a metal breast-plate and a basket of fruit, falls into a canal, bends, sags, and teeters all evening." He occasionally wrote his own sketches and served as director or co-director for the 1914 and 1915 Follies, The Century Girl, Words and Music (1917), and The Blue Kitten (1922). In later years Errol was famous for his film shorts in which he often portrayed a henpecked husband.

ERTÉ [né Romain de Tirtoff] (1892–1990), designer. The internationally acclaimed fashion and stage designer was born in St. Petersburg, Russia, and studied painting in his native country and in Paris. He started his career in theatrical scenic and costume design in 1914, and by the 1920s he was working in America for Florenz *Ziegfeld and George *White. Erté's costumes for several editions of the *George White's Scandals were particularly famous.

ESMERALDA (1881), a play by Francis Hodgson *Burnett, William *Gillette. [*Madison Square Theatre, 350 perf.] Esmeralda Rogers (Annie *Russell), a winsome North Carolina farm girl, falls in love with her rugged, good-natured neighbor, Dave Hardy (Eben *Plympton), but her ambitious mother, Lydia Ann (Kate Denin Wilson), objects. As always, her acquiescent father, Elbert (Leslie Allen), accepts his wife's ultimatums. When some gold is found on what the Rogerses believe is their property, the newly rich Lydia Ann rushes Esmeralda off to Paris, where she hopes to marry her daughter to the Marquis de Montessin (Davenport Bebus). The facetious but kindly Mr. Estabrook (Thomas Whiffen), sensing Esmeralda's unhappiness, manages to delay the wedding until it is learned that the gold is really on Dave Hardy's land. Mrs. Rogers looks on Hardy with new eyes, returns home, and allows Esmeralda to marry Dave. Called a "sweet, harmless play" by George *Odell, the dramatization of Burnett's novelette was criticized by some contemporary critics, who suggested that the play really ended in the second act, when Esmeralda marries Hardy. The rest of the story described their early married life. Audiences had no time for such quibbles, so the play enjoyed one of the longest runs of its era and afforded both Russell and other actresses a popular vehicle for the next twenty years.

ETHAN FROME (1936), a play by Owen *Davis and Donald Davis. [National Theatre, 120 perf.] When Mattie Silver (Ruth *Gordon) comes to live with her cousin, Zenobia Frome (Pauline *Lord), and Zenobia's husband, Ethan (Raymond *Massey), Ethan and Mattie fall in love. Zenobia orders Mattie from the house. On the way to the station, Ethan and Mattie attempt suicide but are instead crippled for life, leaving the slatternly, bitter Zenobia to care for them. This dramatization of Edith Wharton's short novel was enhanced by producer Max *Gordon's production featuring Jo *Mielziner's superb settings, Guthrie *McClintic's brilliant staging, but most of all by the luminous performances of its three stars.

ETHEL, Agnes (1853–1903), actress. Briefly one of the most popular and promising of American performers, she trained with Matilda *Heron and made her debut in New York in 1868, playing Heron's most famous role, Camille. Ethel's performance caught the attention of Augustin *Daly, who enlisted her as a member of his first *Fifth Avenue Theatre ensemble. She portrayed Rosie Farquhere in the opening attraction, *Play* (1869). "What the audience saw," Daly's biographer wrote, "was a slender figure, candid eyes, flowing auburn hair, an oval face, and regular features always lit up by an expression of childish appeal." She scored her biggest success at Daly's as the spoiled child bride Gilberte in *Frou-Frou* (1870). Her success led her to refuse several roles, so Daly thereafter rarely cast her but lent her to his father-in-law, James C. *Duff, to play Med, the

gun-toting "Wild Flower of the Plains," in *Horizon* (1871), which furthered her popularity. Ethel then moved to the rival *Union Square Theatre, winning applause in the title role of *Agnes* (1872). However, her rejection of subsequent parts led to her dismissal, and she retired when she married in 1873.

ETHEL BARRYMORE THEATRE (New York). The *Shuberts built and named the theatre after the famous actress in order to entice her to sign with them, and it worked. She appeared in the inaugural production, the religious drama *Kingdom of God*, in 1928, the end of the building spree on Broadway that stopped with the Depression. Herbert J. *Krapp designed the 1,000-seat playhouse on West 47th Street with an unusual terracotta grillwork screen on the facade. Suited for plays and small musicals, the Barrymore has also seen many of the theatre's greatest female stars on its stage, from Lynn *Fontanne and Katharine *Cornell to Jessica *Tandy and Katharine *Hepburn. The Shubert-owned theatre was designated a landmark in 1987.

ETTING, Ruth (1907–78), singer. Born in David City, Nevada, the blonde torch singer, whose personal life often mirrored the sad songs she sang, was best known as a nightclub performer but appeared in several Broadway shows. She introduced "Shaking the Blues Away" in *Ziegfeld Follies of 1927*, "Love Me or Leave Me" in *Whoopee* (1928), "Get Happy" in *9:15 Revue* (1930), and "Ten Cents a Dance" in *Simple Simon* (1930). She also revived "Shine on Harvest Moon" in *Ziegfeld Follies of 1931*.

EUGENE O'NEILL MEMORIAL THEATRE CENTER (Waterford, Connecticut). Founded in 1963 by George C. White, the center is housed in an old home that had been slated for demolition until White and his associates intervened. White felt the American theatre at the time was in dire need of revitalization, so he established his "forum of ideas," whose principal aim was "to provide channels for communication between artists of the highest caliber." To this end, regular summer seminars were instituted, which have served to encourage new playwrights, technicians, and critics. The *National Playwrights Conference, National Critics Institute, National Theatre Institute (for college students), National Musical Theatre Conference, and the *National Theatre of the Deaf have all been developed under its aegis. The Center also operates the O'Neill Library and Museum at Monte Cristo Cottage, the former home of James *O'Neill and Eugene *O'Neill at nearby New London.

EUGENE O'NEILL THEATRE (New York). The Georgian-style playhouse on West 49th Street opened in 1925 as the Mansfield Theatre, named after the actor Richard *Mansfield, and housed a series of flops until 1934 when it struck pay dirt with the long-running *Tobacco Road. Designed by Herbert J. Krapp with 1,200 seats and a substantial backstage area, the playhouse has successfully presented both plays and musicals over the decades. It was renamed the Coronet Theatre in 1945, but when producer Lester Osterman bought it in 1959 he named it after playwright *O'Neill, who had died six years before. In the late 1960s and 1970s playwright Neil *Simon owned the O'Neill and presented a handful of his new plays there. But he sold it to *Jujamcyn Theatres in 1982 and the company still owns it.

EVANGELINE; or, The Belle of Acadia (1874), a musical burlesque by J. Cheever *Goodwin (book, lyrics), E. E. *Rice (music). [*Niblo's Garden, 16 perf.] When her people are expelled by the British from their Acadian village, Evangeline (Ione Burke) and her lover Gabriel (Connie Thompson) are separated. Evangeline wanders the world, from the wilds of Africa to the wilder West, before she is reunited with her fiancé. Freely adapted from Longfellow's poem, the burlesque included such characters as a dancing heifer, an amorous whale, and the Lone Fisherman, who is forever looking for the sea with his telescope but who never utters a word. The burlesque began the careers of both Goodwin and Rice, later giving an important leg up to such later famous performers as Henry E. *Dixey and Francis *Wilson (both of whom played half of the heifer) and William H. *Crane. Originally a Boston production, this most popular and enduring of American musical burlesques was played incessantly for the remainder of the century, although it produced no songs of note.

EVANS, Maurice (1901–89), actor and producer. The Englishman came to America in 1935 after establishing himself on the London stage, including a stint with the Old Vic. His first appearance was as Romeo to Katharine *Cornell's Juliet, followed by the Dauphin to her Saint Joan and Napoleon in *St. Helena* (1936). Major recognition came when he mounted his interpretation of *Richard II* (1937). Brooks *Atkinson called his a "glowing performance," one of "infinite subtlety and burning emotion," although some dissenters suggested his interpretations were more intellectual than deeply felt. Additional accolades appeared in the wake of his full-length *Hamlet* (1938) and his portrayal of Sir John Falstaff in *Henry IV, Part I* (1939). By this time recognized as the finest and most loyal proponent of Shakespeare on the New York stage, Evans continued his series of highly praised performances with his cockney Malvolio opposite Helen *Hayes's Viola in 1940 and his Macbeth to Judith *Anderson's Lady Macbeth the following year. During World War II he entertained troops with a cut-down version of *Hamlet,* which he later successfully mounted on Broadway in 1945. Evans next scored as John Tanner in *Man and Superman* (1947), then played in a double bill of *The Browning Version* and *Harlequinade* (1949) before returning to Shaw to play Dick Dudgeon in *The *Devil's Disciple* (1950). In 1952 he began a long run as Tony Wendice, who bungles his attempt at a perfect crime, in *Dial M for Murder.* After appearances as King Magnus in *Shaw's *The Apple Cart* (1956) and Captain Shotover in *Heartbreak House* (1957), his luck at picking hits ran out when he essayed the crusading Rev. Brock in the musical *Tenderloin* (1960). In 1962 he toured with Helen Hayes in *Shakespeare Revisited: A Program for Two Players.* Besides being the producer of most of his own productions, he was co-producer of two Broadway hits: *The *Teahouse of the August Moon* (1953) and *No Time for Sergeants* (1955). In later years he appeared on television and in occasional films. Autobiography: *All This—and Evans Too!,* 1987.

EVE OF ST. MARK, THE (1942), a drama by Maxwell *Anderson. [*Cort Theatre, 305 perf.] Shortly before America enters World War II, Private Quizz West (William Prince) returns home on leave to his family's farm in upstate New York and announces to his mother, Nell (Aline McMahon), and father, Deck (Matt Crowley), that he has fallen in love with a neighbor girl, Janet Feller (Mary Rolfe). Back at camp he remains loyal when his buddies take him to a local honky-tonk, while Janet, too, is faithful at home. After the war comes, Quizz is sent to the Philippines. The lovers correspond, but Quizz comes to her even more vividly in her dreams. Before long, news arrives that Quizz has been killed. Janet and Quizz's family accept his death stoically. When his younger brothers enlist, the father tells them, "Make a new world, boys." Hailed by Howard Barnes of the *Herald Tribune* as "a war drama of emotional tension, humor and poetic splendor," the play was a far cry from Anderson's less romantic, less sentimental *What Price Glory?,* the most celebrated American play about World War I. The *Playwrights Company production was one of the few plays dealing with World War II that succeeded at the time.

EVELYN [Morris], Judith (1913–67), actress. The darkish, somewhat stern-looking performer was born in Seneca, South Dakota, and made her acting debut when she was fifteen. She is recalled primarily for two notable performances: as Mrs. Manningham, whose husband tries to drive her insane, in *Angel Street (1941), and Ann Downs, the vicious wife, in The *Shrike (1952).

EVITA (1979). The musical about the factual Eva Peron, from her humble beginnings to her marriage to the Argentine dictator Juan Peron to her early death, was a London hit before opening at the *Broadway Theatre for a run of 1,567 performances, becoming the longest-running foreign musical yet seen on Broadway. The sung-through musical by Andrew Lloyd *Webber (music) and Tim *Rice (lyrics) featured Patti *LuPone in the title role, making her a Broadway star. Hal *Prince staged the Robert Stigwood production, using Brechtian techniques, film footage, and expressionistic imagery to tell the often cynical political story. Notable songs: Don't Cry for Me, Argentina; On This Night of a Thousand Stars; Another Suitcase in Another Hall; High Flying Adored.

EWELL, Tom [né S. Yewell Tompkins] (1909–94), actor. A native of Owensboro, Kentucky, the quizzical-faced comedian made his Broadway debut in 1934 and enjoyed a stage career that spanned nearly fifty years. He is best known as Richard Sherman, the summer bachelor who falls in love with his upstairs neighbor, in The *Seven Year Itch (1952). Ewell's other Broadway credits include *Stage Door (1935), *John Loves Mary (1947), The Tunnel of Love (1957), A Thurber Carnival (1960), and *Waiting for Godot (1971).

EWEN, David (1907–85), author. Brought to the United States from his native Austria at the age of three, he studied briefly at the City College of New York and at Columbia. In 1943 he wrote The Story of George Gershwin, a biography of the composer designed for young readers. He later published similar biographies of Irving *Berlin, Jerome *Kern, Cole *Porter, and Richard *Rodgers, as well as a general history of American musical theatre. For adults he wrote biographies of *Gershwin, Kern, and Rodgers and a survey of composers in the American theatre. His best-known work is The Complete Book of the American Musical Theatre (1950), which was drastically revised and updated in 1970. Although some later scholars have criticized his work as frequently careless, his books remain readable and useful, and his importance as a pioneer in books on modern American musicals and their composers cannot be gainsaid.

EXCESS BAGGAGE (1927), a comedy by John *McGowan. [Ritz Theatre, 216 perf.] Eddie Kane (Eric Dressler) and Elsa McCoy (Miriam Hopkins) are a small-time vaudeville act. Eddie juggles while the attractive Elsa merely stands by to assist, being, she claims, only excess baggage. Hoping for a more important career, Elsa tries out for a film and is soon a star. Eddie quits performing and lives off Elsa until shame drives him back to the stage. His single act seems about to fail, but Elsa, sitting in the audience, runs to join him and saves the day. The play appeared to many critics a more superficial, comic version of *Burlesque, which had opened earlier in the same season. The play itself was one of eleven openings on December 26, the busiest night in Broadway history. It was the only one to enjoy a huge commercial success, although *Behold the Bridegroom, another opening that night, received far more critical acclaim and attention.

EXPERIENCE (1914), a play by George V. *Hobart. [*Booth Theatre, 255 perf.] Youth (William Elliott), goaded by an insidious but faint-hearted Ambition, leaves his happy garden and sets out on the Road of Life. His journeys take him to the Street of Vacillation, the Primrose Path, the Corridors of Chance, and the Street of Disillusion. His fortunes fail, and he moves from one frustrating, unhappy adventure to the next. When he is about to take up with Crime (Frank McCormack), the voices of his past call to him, and he stumbles home. There, with the help of Love (Miriam Collins), he finds a better life. Originally presented as a one-act play at the Lambs, it was expanded by the author and produced by Elliott on Broadway, becoming one of the few out-and-out morality plays to find commercial success.

EXPERIMENTAL THEATRE, THE (New York). Conceived in 1940 and incorporated under the aegis of *ANTA as a nonprofit organization in 1941, with Antoinette *Perry as president, it began to offer plays in early 1947 at the *Princess Theatre. During the 1947–48 season it moved to Maxine Elliott's Theatre, where it presented well-received productions of Galileo (1947), Skipper Next to God (1948), Hope Is the Thing with Feathers (1948), and Ballet Ballads (1948). Several notable actors, including Charles *Laughton and John *Garfield, appeared in these productions, performing for token salaries, and several of the plays moved on to extended runs. The group was assailed early on for its emphasis on foreign playwrights and so changed its program. But even a change of program and praiseworthy productions could not cut the mounting deficits that eventually caused abandonment of its plans.

EXPRESSING WILLIE (1924), a comedy by Rachel *Crothers. [48th Street Theatre, 293 perf.] Willie Smith (Richard Sterling), scion of a toothpaste magnate, builds a luxurious Italianate mansion on Long Island and is soon surrounded by hosts of sycophantic spongers and social climbers. Notable among them is Frances Sylvester (Merle Maddern), a pushy but talentless actress who is determined to marry Willie for his money. Willie's observant mother, Mrs. Smith (Louise Closser *Hale), sets about to save him from Frances's clutches by inviting Minnie Whitcomb (Crystal *Herne), his music teacher and friend, to help bring Willie to his senses. Minnie's artistry and reasonableness put the pretentious actress to shame, and soon Willie is made to recognize where his affections (and money) belong. John *Corbin wrote in the *Times*, "The sallies of [Miss Crothers's] wit took the audience by storm. . . . The varied group of her characters was so subtly and saliently limned that half a dozen actors, long loved and honored, seemed lifted above themselves as by the touch of genius." At a time of conspicuous nouveau-riche consumption, the play treated lightly the same theme F. Scott Fitzgerald would approach more seriously the next year in *The Great Gatsby*. Yet the real center of interest was not Willie or his predicaments but, as in all of Crothers's best plays, the relationships and interaction of her principal women.

EXPRESSIONISM IN AMERICAN THEATRE. Although evident in the latter plays of August *Strindberg and a few other late 19th-century playwrights, the movement—which found advocates in almost all the arts—was not given formal theatrical definition until shortly before World War I and then primarily in Germany. It did not affect American drama and production until after the war. Most immediately it was a reaction to neo-romanticism and impressionism, but mainly it sought to move behind the facade of naturalism and to unmask inner emotions and hidden realities. For a time Eugene *O'Neill was its major American exponent, employing it with great skill in such works as The *Emperor Jones* (1920) with its irresistibly pulsating drums, the total indifference of the rich shoppers to the hero's rough jostling of them in The *Hairy Ape* (1922), and the symbolic masks of The *Great God Brown* (1926), all audible or visible manifestations of the points the playwright was driving home in his texts. Perhaps the most famous and completely successful expressionistic American play is Elmer *Rice's The *Adding Machine* (1923), in which huge numbers whirled around the bookkeeper-hero who was dwarfed by a gigantic adding machine. Another famous play was the work of two unlikely figures, George S. *Kaufman and Marc *Connelly, who set their *Beggar on Horseback* (1924) in a fantastic dream world. Also popular were European playwrights such as Ernst Toller and Karel Capek,

especially the latter's 1922 offerings: *R. U. R.* and *The World We Live In* (*The Insect Comedy*). By the late 1920s the movement's vogue had waned, although its characteristics remained to be seen in the distorted dialogue, the flattened figures, and surrealistic settings and props of later post-expressionistic theatre. Broadway entries as different as *Lenny* (1971), *Evita* (1979), *Nine* (1982), *Angels in America* (1993), *Kiss of the Spider Woman* (1993), *Jackie* (1997), and The *Lion King* (1997) all used expressionistic techniques.

EYES OF YOUTH (1917), a "comedy-drama" by Charles Guernon, Max *Marcin. [Maxine Elliott's Theatre, 414 perf.] Worried about her future, Gina Ashling (Marjorie *Rambeau) consults a yogi, who gazes into his ball and tells her he can see several paths, one of which he may not reveal. The first path makes Gina a schoolteacher, dismissed for incompetence and deserted by her caddish lover; the second turns her into a prima donna in an amoral world. Another road takes her into a disastrous marriage, a divorce court on trumped-up charges of infidelity, and finally into prostitution. In the end, Gina elects to take the one course the yogi cannot reveal. Considered, in theatrical parlance of the time, a "trick melodrama," the A. H. *Woods-*Shuberts production was one of the runaway successes of its day, both in New York and on the road. Because the play was listed as a comedy-drama, playgoers could assume the implied correctness of the path Gina took, all the while enjoying the sensationalism of the episodes depicted.

EYTINGE, Rose (1835–1911), actress. Born in Philadelphia and raised there and in Brooklyn, the "black-eyed, black-haired Jewess," as Daniel *Frohman described her, made her debut in 1852 in Syracuse, New York, as Melanie in *The Old Guard*. Ten seasons in stock followed before she became an understudy to Laura *Keene and made an unscheduled New York debut in 1863, playing Nellie O'Donaghue in *Bantry Bay*, when Keene was indisposed. Coming to Edwin *Booth's attention, she played opposite him in *The Fool's Revenge* (*Le Roi s'amuse*), *The Marble Heart*, and *Richelieu* and impressed the Manhattan critics. Eytinge won more laudatory notices when she appeared with J. W. *Wallack and E. L. *Davenport in 1865 as Hortense de Piermont in *The Iron Mask*, as Mrs. Sternhold in *Still Waters Run Deep*, Florence in *Our American Cousin*, and Kate Peyton in *Griffith Gaunt*, prompting the *Times* critic in 1866 to write, "We have long considered Miss Eytinge the leading actress of the American stage." With Wallack's ensemble she portrayed, among others, Nancy Sykes in *Oliver Twist*, Lady Gay Spanker, Beatrice, and other leading roles in many long-forgotten but once-popular contemporary plays. Eytinge left the group temporarily to perform in *Under the Gaslight (1867), creating the role of Laura Courtlandt, who saves a benefactor from death under the wheels of a speeding train. After several seasons abroad she returned to play the French wife Gabrielle in The Geneva Cross (1873), the unsatisfied wife Armande in *Led Astray (1873), and the outcast Marianne in The *Two Orphans (1874). To many her greatest performance was the title role of Rose Michel (1875). According to the Herald, her performance "attained to the exalted pitch of perfect truth, in delineation of horror and agony, and it swept to this apex with the spontaneity of perfect ease." Unfortunately, the hyper-temperamental actress's battles with management and with talkers in her audience, notorious since early in her career, apparently became uncontrollable. Engagements with Mrs. John *Drew in Philadelphia and at the *California Theatre in San Francisco were both abruptly terminated. Thereafter, she toured for many years with her own company, mostly in her old successes, and appeared in New York only on occasion. Her last appearance was in the short role of the hero's mother in The Bishop's Carriage (1907). Autobiography: The Memories of Rose Eytinge, 1905.

F

FABRAY, Nanette [née Ruby Bernadette Nanette Theresa Fabares] (b. 1922), actress and singer. The bubbly, snub-nosed redhead made her debut at the age of three in vaudeville in Los Angeles, not far from her native San Diego, and afterwards toured as Baby Nanette. Later she won scholarships to the Max Reinhardt School of the Theatre and appeared in its productions of *The Miracle, Six Characters in Search of an Author,* and *Servant with Two Masters.* Broadway first saw her in *Meet the People* (1940), then in **Let's Face It!* (1941), **By Jupiter* (1943), *My Dear Public* (1943), and *Jackpot* (1944). After replacing Celeste **Holm as the lead in **Bloomer Girl* (1945), she was awarded the role of Sara Longstreet in **High Button Shoes* (1947), introducing "Papa, Won't You Dance with Me?" and "I Still Get Jealous." Fabray's subsequent credits include the perennial wife Sara Cooper in *Love Life* (1948), the American girl Jo Kirkland who loves a Hessian soldier in *Arms and the Girl* (1950), the orphan Jeanette in *Make a Wish* (1951), and First Lady Nell Henderson in *Mr. President* (1962). Her later New York performances were sporadic but memorable, as in *No Hard Feelings* (1973) and *Bermuda Avenue Triangle* (1997).

FAIR AND WARMER (1915), a farce by Avery **Hopwood. [Eltinge Theatre, 377 perf.] Billy Bartlett (John **Cumberland) is content to be a stay-at-home, although his wife, Laura (Janet **Beecher), would prefer a steady diet of fun on the town. By contrast, Billy's friend Jack Wheeler (Ralph **Morgan) is forever making excuses to get away from his homebody wife, Blanche (Madge **Kennedy). So when Laura also makes excuses and joins Jack for a night out, Billy and Blanche decide to spend a quiet evening together. They sit around and chat and drink—and before long get drunk and innocently cozy. The gadabout spouses return in time to misconstrue everything. Tempers flare, followed by explanations and a return to normal. Comparing the play with similar contemporary farces, the *Times* concluded it was "twice as well written and about four and half times as amusing." The public agreed, so the **Selwyns's production became one of the longer-running hits of its day.

FAIRBANKS, Douglas [né Ulman] (1883–1939), actor. The handsome, flamboyant actor, whose acrobatic antics were as celebrated offstage as on, was born in Denver and made his stage debut in Richmond, Virginia, in 1900 as Florio in *The Duke's Jester.* His New York debut occurred two years later in *Her Lord and Master.* After playing "now familiar, breezy, attractive" young men in New York and on the road, major success came as senatorial secretary "Bud" Haines in A **Gentleman from Mississippi* (1908). He toured with the play for several seasons before portraying the impoverished Philosopher Jack in *The Lights o' London* (1911), and then amateur crook Robert Pitt in *A Gentleman of Leisure* (1911). For a time Fairbanks turned his attention to vaudeville but found another legit success as the swashbuckling Anthony Hamilton Hawthorne in *Hawthorne of the U.S.A.* (1912) and again as Wall Streeter Bertie in *The New Henrietta* (1913). His last role was the wealthy suitor Jerome Belden in *The **Show Shop* (1914). The rest of Fairbanks's career was spent in films, in which he was long a leading romantic, swashbuckling figure.

FAITH HEALER, THE (1910), a play by William Vaughn **Moody. [Savoy Theatre, 13 perf.] Ulrich Michaelis (Henry Miller), a faith healer in the Middle West, comes to the farm of the skeptical Matthew Beeler (Harold Russell) and makes Beeler's wife, Mary (Mable Bert), walk for the first time in many years. Mary urges Ulrich to go out in the world and heal others, but he is reluctant to leave the area since he loves Mary's niece Rhoda Williams (Jessie **Bonstelle). Ulrich's ministrations are opposed by the local physician Dr. Littlefield (Theodore Friebus) and by the Reverend John Culpepper (Edward See), who suspects the occult. When Rhoda admits to Ulrich that Littlefield has been her lover, Ulrich's self-confidence wanes, and with it his faith-healing abilities. On Easter morning he determines to fight back and to love Rhoda despite her history. As his gifts return he tells Rhoda, "You needed what the whole world needs—healing, healing, and as I rose to meet that need, the power that I had lost poured back into my soul." Producer Henry **Miller, who had so successfully presented and starred in *The **Great Divide,* mounted the play out of a sense of obligation to the dying Moody, knowing it would almost certainly fail. Contemporary critics dismissed the work as closet drama, but *Quinn called it "the most significant of Moody's dramas because the theme is the largest and the treatment most secure . . . it had a deeper imaginative quality than *The Great Divide*."

FALK, Benjamin J[oseph] (1853–1925), photographer. Born in New York, he began his photographic career shortly after graduating from City College. Until his time theatrical photographs consisted almost entirely of formally posed portraits of stars and other prominent figures. In 1883, after a performance of *A Russian Honeymoon*, he and producer Daniel *Frohman assembled the cast on the stage of the *Madison Square Theatre and had them pose for a photograph of the closing tableau of Act II. This was the first full-stage scene ever photographed. Later in his career Falk took similar pictures of scenes from other plays, but unlike several photographers who followed in his pioneering efforts, he never devoted himself primarily to theatrical photography.

FALL, Leo (1873–1925), composer. Known in Europe as a creator of *Viennese operetta, he is significant in America for the success of his early work, *The Dollar Princess* (1909). Among Fall's other works performed here were *The Siren* (1911), *The Doll Girl* (1913), *The Rose of Stamboul* (1922), and *Madame Pompadour* (1924).

FALL OF BRITISH TYRANNY, THE; *or, American Liberty Triumphant* (1776), a political satire ("tragicomedy") by John Leacock. Lord North and Governor Hutchinson, called Lord Catspaw and Judas in the play, conspire to convince the English cabinet that the American rebels can be readily defeated. They are opposed by Camden, Wilkes, Burke, and Pitt (called Lord Justice, Lord Patriot, Bold Irishman, and Lord Wisdom respectively). The battle of Lexington and the war in Virginia are depicted, after which Generals Gage, Howe, and Burgoyne (called here Lord Boston, Elbow Room, and Mr. Caper) blame each other for the early debacles. A final scene shows Washington and his men at camp. The work, which was published but has no record of production, was probably the earliest American chronicle play and the first to portray Washington on stage. This sprawling prose piece was designed to stimulate patriotism among the colonists. **John** (or, in some sources, Joseph) **LEACOCK** (1729–1802) was a goldsmith and silversmith and later a farmer. A well-known Philadelphian, he was a member, possibly a founder, of the Patriotic Society of the Sons of St. Tammany and was also an acceptable poet.

FALLS, Robert [Arthur] (b. 1954), director and manager. One of the most respected artists on the Chicago theatre scene, Falls was born in Springfield, Illinois, and educated at the University of Illinois at Urbana-Champaign. He was artistic director of the Wisdom Bridge Theatre in the late 1970s and took over management of the *Goodman Theatre in 1986, directing dozens of plays, usually American classics. Falls's productions that played in New York include *Standing on My Knees* (1982), The *Rose Tattoo* (1995), The *Night of the Iguana* (1996), The *Young Man from Atlanta* (1997), *Death of a Salesman* (1999), *Aida* (2000), and *Long Day's Journey into Night* (2003).

FALSETTOLAND. See *Falsettos*.

FALSETTOS (1992), a musical play by William Finn (book, music, lyrics), James *Lapine (book). [*John Golden Theatre, 486 perf.] Three Off-Broadway musicals by Finn were revised and combined to make this Broadway sung-through musical. *In Trousers* (1979) introduced Marvin (Michael *Rupert), a neurotic married man who falls in love with the handsome but demanding Whizzer (Stephen Bogardus). In *March of the Falsettos* (1981), Marvin's wife, Trina (Barbara Walsh), seeks help from his psychiatrist, Mendel (Chip Zien), and ends up marrying him, much to Marvin's disapproval and the confusion of their son, Jason (Jonathan Kaplan). The saga concludes with *Falsettoland* (1990), in which Whizzer is dying of AIDS and Jason's Bar Mitzvah is held in Whizzer's hospital room. *Notable songs*: I'm Breaking Down; Four Jews in a Room Bitching; I Never Wanted to Love You; What Would I Do? The frantic, contemporary musical avoided camp and easy cliches and found a mainstream audience who responded to its humor, warmth, and honesty. **William FINN** (b. 1952) was born in Boston and educated at Williams College, where he first started writing offbeat musicals. In addition to the three Marvin plays, he has written *Dangerous Games* (1989), *Romance in Hard Times* (1989), and *A New Brain* (1998), an autobiographical musical about a songwriter finding a new perspective on life after undergoing an operation on a brain tumor.

FAMOUS MRS. FAIR, THE (1919), a play by James *Forbes. [*Henry Miller Theatre, 343 perf.] Nancy Fair (Blanche *Bates), having served as an ambulance driver in World War I and earned a Croix de Guerre for her bravery, returns after the armistice to find a lucrative contract for a lecture series awaiting her. Being an ardent feminist, Nancy would accept the offer, but she gradually realizes that in her absence her family has drifted away from her. Her husband (Henry *Miller) has been paying too much attention to a neighboring widow; her daughter, Sylvia (Margalo *Gillmore), has become rebellious and has taken up with an ambitious, loose-moraled young man; and her son, Alan (Jack Devereaux), seems all at sea and loves a stenographer. Matters come to a head when Sylvia tries to elope, and Mrs. Fair is brought to her senses. She decides to devote her time to her family and forget her feminist inclinations. Hailed by Burns *Mantle as "the most timely of the post-bellum dramas and easily the most entertaining," the A. L. *Erlanger production opened to largely ecstatic notices. Although now something of a period piece, it remains interesting for its rueful observations on feminism, the incipient flapper rage, and upper-middle-class social mores of its day.

FANCHON, THE CRICKET (1862), a play by Charlotte Birch-Pfeiffer. [Laura Keene's Theatre, 24 perf.] Fanchon (Maggie *Mitchell) is a sharp-tongued, wild, and somewhat mysterious young country girl whose mother long ago deserted her and who has been raised by her grandmother, Old Fadet (Mrs. A. Hind), a reputed witch. Because she is poor and they fear she too may be a witch, Fanchon is shunned by the villagers, including the relatively well-to-do bourgeois Barbeauds. Even when she helps the Barbeaud son Landry (J. W. Collier) locate his missing twin brother, Didier (A. H. Davenport), Landry is reluctant to seem grateful. But with time Landry discovers Fanchon's basic common sense and goodness and proposes to her, only to discover she will not marry him because his parents, especially the haughty, strict Father Barbeaud (J. H. *Stoddart), are dead set against her. However, she has come to love Landry, so she sets about winning over his stern parent and soon succeeds. Landry then learns that while his bride-to-be may have magic powers, she will be a rich lady when Old Fadet dies. The play was one of several dramatizations of George Sand's *La Petite Fadette*. Mitchell, who served as her own producer, apparently used the Birch-Pfeiffer version, which she altered to suit her special talents. Her "Shadow Dance" and the scene in which she wins over the older Barbeaud were among the most famous theatrical moments of the era. Mitchell returned to this play for over twenty seasons. *Odell has written, "As Jefferson's Rip Van Winkle, Kate Claxton's Louise in *The Two Orphans*, and Mrs. G. C. Howard's *Topsy*, Maggie Mitchell's *Fanchon the Cricket* was for years and years a household word in America."

FANNY (1954), a musical play by S. N. *Behrman, Joshua *Logan (book), Harold *Rome (music, lyrics). [*Majestic Theatre, 888 perf.] César (Ezio *Pinza), owner of a small Marseilles café, hopes his son Marius (William Tabbert) will marry their young neighbor Fanny (Florence Henderson) and take over the business. Instead, Marius runs off to sea, leaving Fanny pregnant but unwed. Frightened, she marries a benevolent old sail maker, Panisse (Walter *Slezak). Years pass and Marius returns, hoping to marry Fanny. But César, not wanting his friend Panisse to be hurt, chases Marius away. On his deathbed, Panisse urges Fanny to marry Marius after all, so that Fanny and Marius's young son can have a proper home. *Notable songs*: Fanny; Love Is a Very Light Thing; Restless Heart; Welcome Home. Based on Marcel Pagnol's film trilogy, *Marius, Fanny*, and *César*, this Joshua Logan–David *Merrick production was a major hit in a season of superior musicals, thanks largely to Rome's fine score and the performances of Pinza and Slezak.

FANTASTICKS, THE (1960), a musical by Tom *Jones (book, lyrics), Harvey *Schmidt (music). [Sullivan Street Playhouse, 17,162 perf.] The fathers of the Boy called Matt (Kenneth Nelson) and the Girl called Luisa (Rita Gardner) build a wall between their homes, not because of any real animosity but on the assumption that the best way to kindle a romance is to appear to oppose it. They even hire El Gallo (Jerry *Orbach) to stage a mock abduction so that Matt can rescue Luisa and seem a hero. The youngsters discover their parents' ploy, fall out, and go their separate ways. Eventually, however, they return to each other, disillusioned but more mature. *Notable songs*: Try to Remember; Soon It's Gonna Rain; They Were You; Much More; I Can See It. The musicalization of Edmond Rostand's *Les Romanesques* opened to indifferent notices at the 150-seat theatre and seemed in danger of closing, but producer Lore Noto and a small band of loyalists helped publicize it, and the little Off-Broadway musical went on to run for forty-three years, the longest-running show in New York theatre history. *The Fantasticks* has not only been popular with schools and community playhouses, but it was one of the first American musicals to be produced around the world.

FARCE-COMEDY. This genre of prototypical musical comedies was first introduced with *Patchwork* (1875), a piece by Nate Salsbury (1846–1902), with which he toured with some small success for several years. However, it was the popularity of Salsbury's sequel, *The *Brook* (1879), which established the vogue for the type and led to a rash of imitators. These pieces could hardly be said to have a plot. Rather, they placed four or five performers in a situation—in the case of *The Brook*, a picnic—and let them offer songs, dances, and other turns all tied together with the simplest dialogue. The tremendous and sudden rage for farce-comedy inevitably led writers and producers to expand them, enlarging the once tiny casts and complicating the originally elementary story lines. Some early successes of the type include *Our Goblins* (1880), *Dreams; or, Fun in a Photographic Gallery* (1880), and *Greenroom Fun* (1882). The names of early farce-comedy troupes were entertainments in themselves, running to Salsbury's Troubadours, Rice's Surprise Party, and Edouin's Sparks. Within a decade these plays had ineluctably evolved into full-fledged musical comedy. The term persisted well into the 1890s, when many of Charles *Hoyt's plays were offered as farce-comedies.

FARNUM, Dustin (1874–1929), actor. The popular matinee idol was born in Hampton Beach, New Hampshire, and took part in amateur theatricals in Maine before turning professional in 1897. Although he appeared briefly in New York in *A War Correspondent* (1898), *A Romance of Athlone* (1899), and *Marcelle* (1900), his first years were occupied largely with touring and playing in stock. Farnum won major recognition as Lieutenant Denton in *Arizona* (1901), playing the role for several seasons, then scored an even greater success as the rugged but chivalrous cowboy The *Virginian* (1904). Farnum also shone as the fighting Captain Esmond in *The Ranger* (1907), the reformed train robber Rev. Prince in *The Rector's Garden* (1908), gambler Eugene Kirby in *Cameo Kirby* (1909), and the Yankee Lt. Colonel Morrison in *The Littlest Rebel* (1911). One unidentified critic wrote of him, "There is no more ingratiating and charming personality on our stage . . . and in roles of the romantic hero type there is no other man who acts half as well." After appearing in a 1913 revival of *Arizona,* he devoted the rest of his career to films, frequently in cowboy roles. Although his brother, **William FARNUM** (1876–1953) was never quite as popular on stage as Dustin, he too became a celebrated matinee idol. He was born in Boston and made his debut in 1890 in Richmond, Virginia, as Lucius in *Julius Caesar.* A decade of touring, with occasional New York engagements, passed before he won attention when he replaced Edward Morgan in the title role of *Ben-Hur* in 1900. His notable roles include Prince Mohammed in *The Prince of India* (1906), the tragic Capt. Severi in *The White Sister* (1909), and the title role in a revival of *Ingomar.* The two brothers performed together in *The Littlest Rebel* (1911) and *Arizona* (1913). Although William also turned to films, he made occasional New York appearances, most notably as Banquo in a 1928 revival of *Macbeth.* His last appearance was as Inspector Bill Regan in *Headquarters* (1929).

FARREN RIOTS. A benefit for the English comedian George F. Farren, who had served for several seasons as a performer and stage manager at the *Bowery Theatre, was announced for July 9, 1834. Edwin *Forrest, who was about to sail for Europe, was slated to perform *Metamora* at the benefit. In his diary for the next day Philip Hone recorded what happened initially.

Our city last evening was the scene of disgraceful riots. The first was at the Bowery Theatre. An actor by the name of Farren, whose benefit it was, had made himself obnoxious by some ill-natured reflections upon the country, which called down the vengeance of the mob, who seemed determined to deserve the bad name which he had given them. An hour after the performance commenced, the mob broke open the doors, took possession of every part of the house, committed every species of outrage, hissed and pelted poor Hamblin [Thomas S. *Hamblin, manager of the Bowery], not regarding the talisman which he relied upon, the American flag, which he waved over his head. This they disregarded, because the hand which held it was that of an Englishman, and they would listen to nobody but "American Forrest."

Later the mob moved on to sack the house of an abolitionist. The riots presaged the more destructive *Astor Place Riots, although no one has suggested that Forrest had a hand in the Farren affair as he did in the later one.

FASHION; or, Life in New York (1845), a comedy by Anna Cora *Mowatt. [*Park Theatre, 20 perf.] The upstart Mrs. Tiffany (Mrs. Barry) is determined to make her way in the world. To this end she hires a large staff and teaches herself French, dropping "jenny-says-quois" and "ee-lights" everywhere she goes. She rejects all her daughter's suitors, insisting instead that Serphina (Miss K. Horn) marry the Count di Jolimaitre (Mr. Crisp). A thorn in Mrs. Tiffany's side is brusque but honest Adam Trueman (Mr. Chippendale), a fine specimen of Yankee integrity. Trueman is an old friend of Mr. Tiffany (Thomas *Barry), a not entirely honest businessman, who is being blackmailed by one of his daughter's suitors, Snobson (Mr. Fisher). Trueman's long-lost granddaughter helps expose the Count as merely an old French chef whose real name is Gustave Treadmill. With this brought out into the open, Trueman is able to persuade Tiffany to send his wife and daughter to the country to learn simple values and to rid him of Snobson. Edgar Allan *Poe, then a drama critic with the *Broadway Journal,* observed, "Compared with the generality of modern dramas, it is a good play— compared with most American dramas it is a very good one." The play's run was an American record for its day, and it has been revived regularly ever since, most recently Off Broadway in 2003. One notable revival, produced by Kenneth *MacGowan,

Robert Edmond *Jones, and Eugene *O'Neill at the *Provincetown Playhouse in 1924, chalked up 235 performances.

FATHER, THE; *or, American Shandyism* (1789), a comedy by William *Dunlap. [*John Street Theatre, in repertory.] Mr. Racket (Lewis *Hallam Jr.) is a carefree young merchant whose fun-loving ways have not always included Mrs. Racket (Mrs. Owen *Morris). As a result, she has been flirting with Ranter [in some versions, Rusport] (Mr. Biddle), who is masquerading as a British officer, though he is really the servant of Captain Haller (Mr. Harper). Ranter is not as interested in Mrs. Racket as he is in her sister, Caroline (Mrs. Henry), whom he wants to marry for her money. Ranter's plans are frustrated by the arrival of Haller and his long-lost father, Colonel Duncan [in some versions, Colonel Campbell] (John *Henry). Interwoven throughout the action is a charlatan-doctor, Tattle [in some versions, Quiescent] (Thomas *Wignell). While the *Gazette of the United States* recorded that "sentiment, wit and comique humor are happily blended" and that "this Comedy bids fair to be a favorite entertainment," Dunlap himself concluded, "Its merits have never entitled it to a revival." Yet the comedy played occasionally in the early 19th century under the title of *The Father of an Only Child*. The "Shandyism" of the subtitle refers to Sterne's popular novel *Tristram Shandy*.

FAVERSHAM, William (1868–1940), actor, director, and producer. Born and trained in London, he made his New York debut as Dick in *Pen and Ink* (1887), which was a quick failure, so he found himself stranded in America. But Faversham's boyish, curly-haired good looks and his patent dramatic abilities caught Daniel *Frohman's attention, and he quickly won acceptance in Frohman's productions and later playing opposite Mrs. *Fiske. In 1893 he signed with Charles *Frohman and for the next eight years assumed a variety of parts for him, including Algernon in the first American production of *The Importance of Being Earnest* (1895), Romeo to Maude *Adams's Juliet, as well as leading roles in *Under the Red Robe, The *Conquerors, Phroso*, and *Lord and Lady Algy*. Subsequent performances of note included the dissolute yet noble Don Caesar de Bazan in *A Royal Rival* (1901), the exiled Englishman Capt. James Wynngate in *The *Squaw Man* (1905), the title role in the tragedy *Herod* (1909), and the demigod who becomes a human prince in *The Faun* (1911), producing and staging the last two. Two high points in his career followed when he staged *Julius Caesar* (1912) and *Othello* (1914), playing Marc Antony and Iago. Walter Prichard *Eaton wrote of the latter, "Where his 'Othello' differs from tradition is chiefly in Mr. Faversham's

own interpretation of Iago, and the consequent hue that gives to the entire play. It is a novel, refreshing, stimulating impersonation, and it gives the drama a new vitality, a new holding power. . . . The keynote of his Iago is humor." Faversham scored another hit when he played the Bishop of Chelsea in *Shaw's *Getting Married* (1916), which he produced and directed. Thereafter, his career faltered, and much of it was spent in revivals of earlier successes. His final Broadway appearances were as the exiled King George in *Her Friend, the King* (1929) and in some 1931 Shakespearean revivals. The public last saw him when he toured as Jeeter Lester in *Tobacco Road* in 1934.

FAWCETT, George (1860–1939), actor and manager. The Virginia-born artist, who made his professional debut in 1886, was best known for the company he headed from 1900 to 1905 in conjunction with his wife, Percy Haswell (1871–1945), at Albaugh's Lyceum Theatre in Baltimore. The ensemble was nationally respected for its fine productions of a wide variety of classic and modern plays, but the day for such quality stock troupes had passed, and Fawcett was unable to sustain it. He remained a highly admired character actor on Broadway until the early 1930s and appeared in numerous films.

FAY, [Francis Anthony] Frank (1897–1961), actor. The "handsome, saturnine and brilliantly redheaded" monologuist was born in San Francisco and made his stage debut as the child in *Quo Vadis?* (1901). His early career ran a theatrical gamut, from playing a teddy bear in the original *Babes in Toyland* (1903) to walking on as one of the crowd in Sir Henry *Irving's The *Merchant of Venice* (1903). For a while he was part of the vaudeville team of Dyer and Fay, with Johnny Dyer, but by 1918 critics and playgoers were taking note of him as a lone storyteller. His soft-spoken, daffy yarns told of such quirky people as the little boy who would not get off the wagon and the family who saved scraps of string. During this same period, from 1918 to 1933, he also appeared in a number of Broadway musicals, generally failures. Then his career languished for about a decade until he scored his most memorable success when he returned to Broadway to play Elwood P. Dowd, the boozer whose best friend is an invisible rabbit, in *Harvey* (1944). Autobiography: *How to Be Poor*, 1935.

FECHTER, Charles [Albert] (1824–79), actor. Born in London, the son of a French father of German lineage and a Flemish mother of Italian lineage, the short, hulky, bull-necked actor was acclaimed for many years in romantic melodrama, in both Paris and London, before coming to America in

1869. After a brief tour, Fechter opened at *Niblo's Garden in 1870, offering his Ruy Blas in *The Duke's Motto* and Hamlet. He immediately became the center of controversy. Laurence *Hutton wrote, "The acting of no man, native or foreign, in the whole history of the American stage has been the subject of so much or of such varied criticism as his. There was no medium whatever concerning him in public opinion. Those who were his admirers were wildly enthusiastic in his praise; those who did not like him did not like him at all." William *Winter detested his Hamlet, noting, "His speaking of it was much marred by a sing-song cadence, and his delivery of English blank verse, accordingly, was abominable." Conversely, Henry Austin *Clapp praised his interpretation for its "outward and visible charm, its vitality, directness, and fervid sincerity." In later engagements he appeared as Claude Melnotte in *The *Lady of Lyons*, as Monte Cristo, and as Obenreizer in *No Thoroughfare*. His Monte Cristo was performed from a dramatization he himself had prepared in collaboration with Arthur LeClercq, which James *O'Neill was later to employ with even greater success. Fechter continued to perform for several seasons, making his last appearances in 1877. By that time his waning health, coupled with a reputation for arrogance that verged on madness, had lost him his audiences. He died in poverty on his farm in Quakertown, Pennsylvania. Biography: *Charles Albert Fechter*, J. R. Osgood, 1882.

FEDER, Abe (1909–97), lighting designer. A native of Milwaukee, he studied at the Carnegie Institute of Technology before providing the lighting for *Trick for Trick* in 1932. Subsequently he designed the lighting for dozens of plays and musicals, including the original *My Fair Lady* (1956). He created the basic lighting arrangements for many new theatres, including Washington's *Kennedy Center, and taught workshops in several universities.

FEDERAL STREET THEATRE (Boston). Sometimes called the Boston Theatre, it was the first auditorium built in the city specifically for theatrical presentations. The theatre was erected from designs by the famous architect Charles Bulfinch and opened in 1794. A handsome brick structure with an arcaded front, it seated approximately one thousand people and was said by John *Bernard to display "a taste and completeness that was worthy of London." The theatre burned to the four walls in 1798 but was promptly rebuilt. Although it was sometimes plagued by mismanagement, it retained a virtual monopoly on Boston theatricals for nearly thirty years and continued to house drama after the arrival of competition from other houses. In the early 1870s it was converted into a business establishment but was totally destroyed by another fire shortly thereafter.

FEDERAL THEATRE PROJECT. Established under the Works Progress Administration (WPA) in 1935 by an act of Congress, it was designed to offer work to theatrical professionals idled by the Depression. A second aim, according to President Roosevelt's assistant Harry Hopkins was to provide "free, adult, uncensored theatre." Hallie *Flanagan, director of the Vassar Experimental Theatre, was named national director. For a time it succeeded in both its aims. At its height it employed 10,000 people, most of whom had been on relief rolls. In New York alone in 1936, some 5,385 professionals were at work, and during its just over three years of life no fewer than 12 million people attended performances in the city. Numerous companies sprang up across the country, officially directed from Washington but in reality semiautonomous, and these also provided hard-pressed playgoers with a wide variety of inexpensive and often very good theatre. Productions ranged from imaginative revivals of old classics through new plays, children's plays, African-American productions, plays in foreign languages, marionette shows, and evenings of dance. Elmer *Rice was placed in charge of the New York branch. One of his most noteworthy, albeit controversial, innovations was the Living Newspaper, plays which were essentially theatrical documentaries. The very first offering was to be *Ethiopia*, which dealt with Mussolini's attack on that country and employed excerpts from his speeches and Roosevelt's response. The State Department, fearful of offending the dictator, ignored Hopkins's promise and attempted to censor the play, which prompted Rice's resignation. The play never opened. The most successful of the Living Newspapers was Arthur Arent's *One Third of a Nation* (1938), which took its title from Roosevelt's claim that one-third of the country was ill-housed, ill-clad, and ill-nourished. Orson *Welles and John *Houseman also encountered censorship problems from bureaucrats and subservient or frightened unions when they attempted to mount the virulently left-wing musical *The *Cradle Will Rock* (1938), but they successfully defied their opposition. Numerous African-American theatre projects flourished in Harlem and elsewhere, as did specifically Catholic and Jewish mountings. Two particularly successful offerings were *The Swing Mikado*, a black jazzed version of the *Gilbert and Sullivan operetta, and a "voodoo" *Macbeth* set on a Caribbean island. Other high points in the Project's short life were Sinclair Lewis's political drama *It Can't Happen Here* (1926), which opened simultaneously in twenty-three cities, Paul Green's long-running outdoor history pageant *The Lost Colony*

(1937), and the American premiere of T. S. *Eliot's *Murder in the Cathedral (1936). Among the other artists whose careers were launched by the Project were Joseph *Cotten, Howard *Bay, Will Geer, Mary *Chase, Marc *Blitzstein, Arlene *Francis, Canada *Lee, John Huston, Virgil Thomson, and Helen *Tamiris. However, because many of the productions were perceived as and, indeed, often were blatantly left-wing propaganda pieces, opposition to the project grew, especially among conservatives. In 1939, after heated debate, Congress abolished the project. A detailed, highly readable account of the Federal Theatre Project can be found in Flanagan's Arena (1940).

FEIFFER, Jules. See Little Murders.

FEMALE IMPERSONATION. Never as popular on American stages as in England, where there is a long tradition of pantomimes that featured comic crones and other women played by men, female impersonation nevertheless has enjoyed times of popularity in our theatre. One of the most famous impersonators of the 19th century was [Patrick] **Francis LEON** [né Glassey] (b. 1844), who worked largely in the minstrel tradition. Born in New York and noted as a boy soprano, his company, Leon's Minstrels with Edwin Kelly, quickly became famous for its "Africanized opéra bouffe," spoofs of such contemporary comic operas as The *Grand Duchess or La Belle Hélène as "The Grand Dutch S" and "La Belle L. N.," with Leon in the prima donna parts. The *Clipper observed that his clowning was never offensive. "He does it with such dignity, modesty, and refinement that it is truly art." Leon wore only the finest, most expensive costumes and excellent imitation jewelry. He was also an accomplished dancer in ballet as well as in the clogs and other standard routines of the time. Kelly and Leon disbanded their company in 1869. Leon continued to be a star attraction, often billed as "The Only Leon," in minstrel groups, vaudeville, and in the loosely contrived musical comedies of the day well into the 1890s. The century's other famed impersonator was **Neil BURGESS** (1846–1910), a Bostonian who made his stage debut in variety with Spalding's Bell Ringers in 1865 and his New York debut as a solo artist in 1872 at Tony *Pastor's, where he was billed as an "Ethiopian Comedian." His first New York appearance as a female impersonator was in a *Harrigan and *Hart folio at their Theatre Comique in 1877 as "The Coming Woman." Two years later he earned widespread fame in the title role of *Widow Bedott, a role he played for the rest of his career. Two other great parts of his were Tryphena "Betsy" Puffy in Vim; or, A Visit to Puffy Farm (1882) and Aunt Abby Prue in The *County Fair (1889). In 1891

he portrayed Lady Teazle in the first *Lambs' Gambol. The greatest 20th-century impersonator was Julian *Eltinge, who brought the art to a refinement unequaled before or since. A major rival was Bert Savoy, who was far more outrageous and grotesque in his characterizations. In more recent times T. C. Jones offered superb satires of famous ladies, but his promising career was cut short by his early death. Female impersonation became more evident in the 1970s, but it was often associated with gay transvestite plays or camp comedy. Two artists who rose above this often amateurish exhibitionism were actor-playwrights Charles *Ludlam and Charles *Busch, both refining the comic and camp aspects of impersonation into a fine art. Also recently popular are Australian comic Barry Humphries, whose impersonation of Dame Edna Everedge in the one-person show Dame Edna: The Royal Tour (1999) was a hit on Broadway and the road, and Harvey *Fierstein, who shone as the drag queen Arnold in his *Torch Song Trilogy (1982) and as the Baltimore housewife Edna Turnblad in *Hairspray (2002).

FEMALE PATRIOTISM; or, The Death of Joan d'Arc (1798), a blank-verse tragedy by John Daly *Burk. [*Park Theatre, in repertory.] The young maiden is so determined to lift France from tyranny that she is willing to sacrifice her home, her love, and her life. Many Frenchmen see her as a divine manifestation, but she disabuses them saying, "I am no more of heaven than yourselves," acting as an advocate of reason and republicanism. Condemned to death and abandoned by the king and her former friends, she writes to her beloved Chastel, predicting not only the French Revolution but an alliance of England and France in the cause of democracy. Although the play was a failure, because—according to *Dunlap—of a slipshod performance, scholars generally consider this Burk's best play. **John Daly BURK** (1775?–1808) was forced to flee Ireland after he was expelled from Dublin's Trinity College for his free-thinking religious and political stands. Coming to Boston, he wrote his first play, Bunker-Hill; or, The Death of General Warren (1797), which was presented at the Haymarket Theatre. Although Warren was ostensibly the central figure, his role consisted of little but bombastic speeches in praise of America and against the British. The real interests were the staged battle scenes and the love story in which an American girl goes mad after her redcoat lover chooses duty above romance and is killed. Dismissed by critics as "a deplorable play," it was widely popular with audiences for its often fiery theatricality and was revived regularly. Arrested for sedition, he was forced to flee to Virginia and there wrote his last surviving play, the Gothic revenge tragedy *Bethlem Gabor, Lord of Transylvania; or, The Man-Hating Palatine* (1807). Four other plays are generally attributed to him: *The Death of General Montgomery in Storming the City of Quebec, The Fortunes of Nigel, The Innkeeper of Abbeville,* and *Which Do You Like Best, the Poor Man or the Lord?* The contentious Burk was killed by a Frenchman in a duel.

FEMINIST THEATRE. Because there have been women actors, managers, and playwrights since the colonial days, the goal of feminist theatre has not been about women in the theatre as much as the role of women in society. Female directors, scenic designers, and composers have not been common until the last decades of the 20th century, yet the voice of women has been heard on stage for over one hundred years. The concept of "plays by women and about women" is not new, but it remains central to the feminist movement. In the late 1960s the women's movement in America gained momentum. The establishment of the National Organization for Women (NOW) and its efforts in the 1970s to pass an Equal Rights Amendment solidified the movement. It was at this time that feminist theatre groups were born, such as It's Alright to Be a Woman Theatre, Omaha Magic Theatre, Women's Experimental Theatre, Spiderwoman Theatre, and At the Foot of the Mountain Theatre. But much of the movement to dramatize women's issues came from outspoken individuals such as Megan Terry, Maria Irene *Fornes, Terry and Jo Ann Schmidman, and Sondra Segal. Some of their works utilized agitprop theatre techniques from the past to raise political and social consciousness, while others employed the avant-garde style of the Open Theatre and the *Living Theatre. Feminist theatre was often confused with lesbian theatre because many of the issues were the same, as seen in the potent productions by the Split Britches troupe. While the feminist movement in theatre continues, the most gifted women seem to have been assimilated into mainstream theatre. Playwrights such as Beth *Henley, Marsha *Norman, Paula *Vogel, and Wendy *Wasserstein may be labeled as feminist playwrights because they write about the roles of women in America but, more accurately, they are simply superior dramatists.

FENCES (1987), a play by August *Wilson. [46th St. Theatre, 526 perf.; Pulitzer Prize, Tony, NYDCC Awards.] Troy Maxson (James Earl *Jones), once a promising baseball player in the Negro leagues, is stuck in the 1950s driving a garbage truck in Philadelphia. He is bitter because even his athletic abilities have not allowed him to rise in a white world. Troy builds a fence around his house—not only to keep the white world at a distance but also to keep away Death, with whom he insists he has wrestled and won. When his high-school-age son Cory (Courtney B. Vance) shows possibilities as a football star and is wooed by college scholarships, Troy belittles the offers and blocks Cory's chances for success. Troy's resilient wife, Rose (Mary *Alice), who is raising Troy's illegitimate baby after his mistress dies in childbirth, tries to comfort Cory. Only after Troy is dead and Cory returns home from the Marines can the two of them begin to reconcile their feelings for the strict, tormented Troy. Lloyd *Richards directed the engrossing drama that allowed Jones and Alice to give towering performances; all three won *Tony Awards.

FENNELL, James (1766–1816), actor. The Englishman was slated for the law but, over family objections, went on the stage, making his debut in Edinburgh and appearing at Covent Garden before he came to America at Thomas *Wignell's behest in 1794. Fennell's New York debut was as Zanga in *The Revenge* (1797). When he played Jaffier in *Venice Preserved* at the *Park Theatre in 1799, the *Commercial Advertiser* remarked, "Few things can excel the performance of the excellent Fennell. The power of expression by countenance and gesture he possesses in an eminent degree." Whether it was this independence, the fecklessness he displayed in his autobiography, or the pressure of his outside business interests (which were ultimately to bankrupt him), he slowly fell from popularity and was forced to accept occasional small assignments. He made several comebacks, with varying success. But in his last performances as Othello (always considered his best role), Richard III, and Macbeth, he was criticized for his ungainly stance, his rigid expression, and unexciting voice. Exceedingly tall for his day, Fennell stood over six feet. Autobiography: *An Apology for the Life of James Fennell*, 1814.

FERBER, Edna (1887–1968), playwright. Born in Kalamazoo, Michigan, the celebrated novelist wrote for the stage, although most of her better plays were collaborations. In 1915, working with George V. *Hobart, she gave Ethel *Barrymore one of the actress's favorite roles as *Our Mrs. Chesney.* Following an unsuccessful solo effort, *The Eldest,* and a collaboration with Newman Levy, *$1200 a Year* (both in 1920), Ferber joined with George S. *Kaufman to write the plays for which she is best remembered: *Minick* (1924), The *Royal Family (1927), *Dinner at Eight* (1932), and *Stage Door (1936). Less well received were two other collaborations with Kaufman: *The Land Is Bright* (1941) and *Bravo!* (1948). Two of her novels were made into musicals, *Show Boat* (1927) and *Saratoga* (1959), the latter from *Saratoga Trunk.* Biography: *Ferber,* Julie Goldsmith Gilbert, 1978.

FERGUSON, Elsie (1885–1961), actress. An exquisite beauty, the native New Yorker made her debut in the chorus of *The *Belle of New York* (1901), then graduated to small parts in both musicals and straight plays before calling prominent attention to herself as the unlucky Jen Galbraith in *Pierre of the Plains* (1908) and as the tenement waif Jenny in *The Battle* (1908). Ferguson became a star as Anna Victoria in *Such a Little Queen* (1909), followed by such successful assignments as *Caste* (1910), *Dolly Madison* (1911), and *Rosedale* (1913). She next portrayed Inez de Pierrefond in *The Strange Woman* (1913), girl of the streets Miriam in *Outcast* (1914), the spy *Margaret Schiller* (1916), and Portia to Sir Herbert *Tree's Shylock* (1916). Turning to light comedy, she pleased audiences as the unfettered patrician suffragette *Shirley Kaye* (1916). For the next several seasons Ferguson devoted herself to films, returning in 1920 to play Carlotta Peel in *Sacred and Profane Love* and the old grand dame Madam Leland in *The Varying Shore* (1921). Critics had long extolled her gorgeous looks and charm but felt her acting abilities were limited, so when *The Moonflower* (1924), *The Grand Duchess and the Waiter* (1925), *The House of Women* (1927), and *Scarlet Pages* (1929) all failed, she retired from the stage, returning only for a last appearance in 1943 as the mysterious Crystal Grainger in *Outrageous Fortune*.

FERRER, José [Vicente] (1912–92), actor and director. Born in Puerto Rico but educated in New York and at Princeton, the rather well-built, heavy-featured, rich-voiced performer made his professional debut in 1934 in a series of melodramas performed on a show boat cruising Long Island Sound. Broadway first saw him as a policeman in *A Slight Case of Murder* (1935), then he won critical attention in the roles of the gadfly Lippincott in *Spring Dance* (1936) and the meddling cadet Dan Crawford in *Brother Rat* (1936). Important supporting assignments followed as Jesse James associate Billy Gashade in *Missouri Legend* (1938), the white St. Julien in the black drama *Mamba's Daughters* (1939), and the poet Victor d'Alcala in *Key Largo* (1939). Ferrer triumphed as Lord Fancourt Babberley in a revival of *Charley's Aunt* (1940) and subsequently starred in two more highly praised revivals, playing Iago to Paul Robeson's Othello in 1943 and the title role in *Cyrano de Bergerac* (1946). "His Cyrano," Brooks *Atkinson noted, "has sardonic wit, a strutting style, a bombastic manner of speech and withal a shyness and modesty." In 1948 Ferrer was appointed general director of the New York City Theatre Company at the *City Center, producing and appearing in *Volpone, Angel Street*, a bill of *Chekhov one-act plays, *The Alchemist*, *S. S. Glencairn*, and *The Insect Comedy*. Other memorable performances of the period include Oliver Erwenter in *The Silver Whistle* (1949), frantic producer Oscar Jaffe in a revival of *Twentieth Century* (1950), and mental patient Jim Downs in *The *Shrike* (1952), a play he also produced and directed. In 1953 he revived the work at the City Center, also playing in revivals of *Charley's Aunt* and *Richard III*, and as the Prince Regent in *The Girl Who Came to Supper* (1963). Thereafter, he appeared largely as replacements for original stars or in productions outside New York. He also directed and occasionally produced plays, including *Strange Fruit* (1945); *Stalag 17* (1951); *The *Fourposter* (1951); *The Chase* (1952); *My Three Angels* (1953); *Oh, Captain!* (1958), for which he was also co-librettist; and *The Andersonville Trial* (1959).

FEUER and MARTIN, producers. Cy Feuer (b. 1911) and Ernest Martin [né Markowitz] (1919–93) were, for a time, the most successful presenters of musicals on Broadway. Beginning with *Where's Charley?* (1948), they produced *Guys and Dolls* (1950), *Can-Can* (1953), *The Boy Friend* (1954), *Silk Stockings* (1955); *Whoop-up* (1958), *How to Succeed in Business without Really Trying* (1961), *Little Me* (1962), *Skyscraper* (1965), *Walking Happy* (1966), and the play *The Goodbye People* (1968). Feuer also directed *Little Me, Skyscraper,* and *Walking Happy.* In 1975 they became co-managers of the Los Angeles and San Francisco Light Opera Association. Feuer was born in New York, Martin in Pittsburgh. Autobiography (Feuer): *I Got the Show Right Here*, with Jed Feuer, Ken Gross, 2003.

FEUILLET, Octave. See *Led Astray.*

FIDDLER ON THE ROOF (1964), a musical play by Joseph *Stein (book), Jerry *Bock (music), Sheldon *Harnick (lyrics). [*Imperial Theatre, 3,242 perf.; Tony Award, NYDCC Award.] Tevye (Zero *Mostel) is a pious dairyman living in the impoverished Jewish shtetl of Anatevka. He and his wife Golde (Maria Karnilova) hire the matchmaker Yente (Beatrice *Arthur) to find husbands for their five daughters. But the three eldest daughters break with tradition and marry for love, one even eloping with a Christian. A pogrom and threats of increasing anti-Semitism finally force Tevye and his neighbors to leave Anatevka and seek homes in other countries. *Notable songs*: If I Were a Rich Man; Matchmaker, Matchmaker; Sunrise, Sunset; To Life. Based on Sholom Aleichem's *Tevye's Daughters,* this warm, melodic, sentimental musical was a surprise hit, establishing a long-run record that held for a decade. Among the highlights of the Hal *Prince production were Mostel's engaging performance, Boris *Aronson's Chagall-like settings, and the inspired choreography and direction by Jerome

*Robbins. The musical has been seen around the world and regularly revived in every venue from Broadway to churches.

FIELD, Betty (1918–73), actress. A native New Yorker, she studied acting at the *American Academy of Dramatic Arts and worked in stock and in London before her Broadway debut in 1934 as a newspaper reporter in *Miss Page Glory*. Field appeared in a series of comedy hits in the 1930s but found richer characters in the 1940s, most memorably the imaginative Georgina in *Dream Girl* (1945), written for Field by her then-husband Elmer *Rice. Other notable Broadway performances were as Nora, the mystical Irish maid, in *If I Were You* (1938); the pert co-ed Barbara in *What a Life* (1938); the amorous dipsomaniac Mildred Tynan in *The Ladies of the Corridor* (1953); the troubled society woman Deborah in A *Touch of the Poet* (1958); and the worried, secretive Mrs. Evans in the 1963 revival of *Strange Interlude*. Field's final Broadway appearance before her premature death was as the Nurse in Edward *Albee's drama *All Over* (1971).

FIELD, Joseph M. (1810–56), actor, manager, and playwright. Born to English parents in Dublin and distantly related to the Elizabethan playwright Nathaniel Field, he was brought to America at the age of two and made his acting debut at Boston's Tremont Theatre in 1827. By 1830 he had performed in all the major American theatre centers and had written a popular afterpiece, *Down South; or, A Militia Training*. Although Field excelled at comedy roles such as Jeremy Diddler in *Raising the Wind*, Sir Benjamin Backbite in *The School for Scandal*, and Flutter in *The Belle's Stratagem*, he was not unsuccessful in essaying Sir Giles Overreach, Romeo, Othello, Jaffier, Claude Melnotte, and other tragic and melodramatic parts. In 1835 Noah *Ludlow brought him west, where he began to figure as an important playwright and performer, especially in St. Louis. Indeed, Ludlow's editor speaks of Field as "the first Western playwright who in any sense could wear that label, and a Western actor who almost made the grade into the rarefied air of stardom." During this period he also played New York, Philadelphia, Mobile, and New Orleans, temporarily abandoning the stage in 1841 to become the *New Orleans Picayune*'s foreign correspondent. Field returned to America in 1842 to become William Mitchell's right-hand man at the Olympic. While continuing to act and write in later years, he also managed a theatre in Mobile and Field's Varieties Theatre in St. Louis. Among his many plays are *Victoria; or, The Lion and the Kiss* (1839), *Tourists in America* (1840), *Oregon, or, The Disputed Territory* (1846), and *Family Ties; or, The Will of Uncle Josh* (1846).

FIELD, Ron[ald] (1934–89), choreographer. The native New Yorker worked as a child performer and later as a dancer in the chorus of some 1950s Broadway musicals before getting noticed for his choreography in the popular Off-Broadway revival of *Anything Goes* in 1962. His dances were seen in *Cabaret* (1966), *Zorbá* (1968), *Applause* (1970), *On the Town* (1971), *King of Hearts* (1978), and *Rags* (1987), as well as for theatres across America and in London.

FIELDS, Dorothy (1905–74), lyricist and librettist. Daughter of Lew *Fields and sister of Herbert *Fields and Joseph *Fields, she was born in Allenhurst, New Jersey, and became in her own right a major lyricist whose work was distinguished by a sophistication coupled with a down-to-earth humor that frequently gave refreshing slants to clichés. Fields's lyrics were heard in *Blackbirds of 1928*, in which she put words to Jimmy *McHugh's "I Can't Give You Anything But Love" and "Diga Diga Doo"; *Hello, Daddy* (1928); *International Revue* (1930), teaming again with McHugh for "Exactly Like You" and "On the Sunny Side of the Street"; *Stars in Your Eyes* (1939); *Up in Central Park* (1945); *Arms and the Girl* (1950); A *Tree Grows in Brooklyn* (1951); *By the Beautiful Sea* (1954); *Redhead* (1959); *Sweet Charity* (1966), collaborating with Cy *Coleman to write "Big Spender" and "If My Friends Could See Me Now"; and *Seesaw* (1973). With her brother Herbert she also wrote the librettos for *Let's Face It!* (1941), *Something for the Boys* (1943), *Mexican Hayride* (1944), *Up in Central Park* (1945), *Annie Get Your Gun* (1946), *By the Beautiful Sea* (1954), and *Redhead* (1959). Biography: *On the Sunny Side of the Street*, Deborah Grace Winer, 1997.

FIELDS, Herbert (1897–1958), librettist. Son of Lew *Fields and brother of Dorothy *Fields and Joseph *Fields, he was born in New York and educated at Columbia before turning his hand to librettos. His earliest work, done with Richard *Rodgers and Lorenz *Hart, was considered to be among the most advanced and sophisticated of its day. His works included *Dearest Enemy* (1925), *The Girl Friend* (1926), *Peggy Ann* (1926), *Hit the Deck!* (1927), A *Connecticut Yankee* (1927), *Present Arms* (1928), *Chee-Chee* (1928), *Hello, Daddy* (1928), *Fifty Million Frenchmen* (1929), *The New Yorkers* (1930), *America's Sweetheart* (1931), *Pardon My English* (1933), *Du Barry Was a Lady* (1939), and *Panama Hattie* (1940). After 1941, all his works were collaborations with his sister: *Let's Face It!* (1941), *Something for the Boys* (1943), *Mexican Hayride* (1944), *Up in Central Park* (1945), *Annie Get Your Gun* (1946), *Arms and the Girl* (1950), *By the Beautiful Sea* (1954), and *Redhead* (1959).

FIELDS, Joseph [Albert] (1895–1966), playwright. Son of Lew *Fields and brother of Dorothy *Fields and Herbert *Fields, he was born in New York and attended New York University with the intention of becoming a lawyer. While in the navy during World War I, he wrote sketches for shows and appeared in them, and then decided to make the theatre his career. Fields contributed sketches to some revues and afterward spent some time in Hollywood before collaborating with Jerome *Chodorov on a spoof of film life, *Schoolhouse on the Lot* (1938). The team next wrote two major hits, *My Sister Eileen* (1940) and *Junior Miss* (1941). He also succeeded with a solo venture, the wartime comedy The *Doughgirls* (1942). He collaborated again with Chodorov on *The French Touch* (1945); *Wonderful Town* (1953), a musical version of *My Sister Eileen*; *The Girl in Pink Tights* (1954); *Anniversary Waltz* (1954); and *The Ponder Heart* (1956). With Anita *Loos he scripted the musical version of *Gentlemen Prefer Blondes* (1949) and with Peter De Vries on *The Tunnel of Love* (1957). His last work was his collaboration with Oscar *Hammerstein on the libretto of *Flower Drum Song* (1958). Fields also occasionally served as a director.

FIELDS, Lew [né Lewis Maurice Shanfield] (1867–1941), actor and producer. One of the most successful and popular of American theatrical figures, he was born to immigrant parents on New York's Lower East Side. Joining an amateur vaudeville act, he first met **Joseph** [Morris] **WEBER** (1867–1942), a native New Yorker who grew up a few blocks from Fields's home. Within a few years the pair was touring in vaudeville with their comic "Dutch" turn. The routine, in a German or Yiddish accent, frequently consisted of Fields suggesting some course of action to Weber, of Weber's bungling the matter, and of a wild-eyed Fields then pummeling or choking Weber. Within a few years they were touring the country in vaudeville houses and even circuses, and by 1887 they had a complete company. Their "Dutch" act emphasized the fact that they were modern comedians, for dialect comics had come to replace the grotesque comedians who had been the rage. But Weber and Fields always had a respect for tradition, so their act was performed in the grotesque costumes and make-up just then beginning to lose favor. Fields, the taller, slimmer of the pair, wore an undersized derby hat, oversized checkered suit, and a hayseed beard. Weber dressed in similar fashion but exaggerated his shorter, stockier build with excessive padding. Sometime during this period they reputedly developed one of the most famous of all American jokes, with Weber delivering the punch line, "Dat vas no lady. Dat vas my wife." The team

was so successful that in 1896 they took over the tiny Broadway Music Hall, renaming it Weber and Fields' Music Hall, and presented double bills which consisted of a short musical comedy and a burlesque of a current Broadway success. The musicals had such names as *Hurly Burly* (1898), *Helter Skelter* (1899), *Fiddle-Dee-Dee* (1900), *Hoity Toity* (1901), *Twirly Whirly* (1902), and *Whoop-Dee-Doo* (1903). The burlesques made a mockery of both the story of the play, often of its scenery and costumes, and almost always of its title. For example, in 1896 *The Geisha* became *The Geezer*, while in 1898 *Cyrano de Bergerac* was distorted into *Cyra-nose de Bric-a-brac*. The satires proved so popular that managements supposedly offered Weber and Fields bribes to spoof their plays, and the entertainments as a whole were in such demand that the partners were able to auction off opening night seats at outlandish prices. The popularity of the entertainments was enhanced by the striking productions squeezed onto the small stage, the gorgeous chorus line—the most famous before *Ziegfeld's—and a host of great supporting performers, including Lillian *Russell, Fay *Templeton, Bessie Clayton, Sam *Bernard, Peter *Dailey, David *Warfield, and De Wolf *Hopper. The Music Hall immediately became one of Broadway's most popular attractions and continued so until the pair split up in 1903. For a time Weber by himself attempted to continue the policy at the theatre, but some of the magic was gone and he soon abandoned the attempt. He produced several regular musicals and plays, the most successful of which was The *Climax* (1909). The team was reunited briefly in 1912, after which Weber continued to produce, including such shows as *The Only Girl* (1914), *Eileen* (1917), *Honeydew* (1920), and *Caste* (1927). Fields, on the other hand, had a very successful career as a producer, often starring in his own productions. His first offerings were *It Happened in Nordland* (1904), *About Town* (1906), and *The Girl behind the Counter* (1907), followed by twelve musicals in four years, many of them distinguished by their elaborate productions, exceptional for Broadway at the time. Fields's career slowly waned, catching fire again only in the late 1920s, when he successfully produced a series of musicals written by his son Herbert *Fields with Richard *Rodgers, and Lorenz *Hart: *The Girl Friend* (1926), *Peggy Ann* (1926), A *Connecticut Yankee* (1927), and *Present Arms* (1928). He also co-produced *Hit the Deck!* (1927) with Vincent *Youmans. His last Broadway production was *The Vanderbilt Revue* (1930). Although Fields was hardly an innovator and in interviews disclosed his commercial philosophy as pragmatic, at his peaks he gave the public what it wanted and expected, but with a special panache and style.

Biographies: *Weber and Fields,* Felix Isman, 1924; *From the Bowery to Broadway: Lew Fields and the Roots of American Popular Theatre,* Armon Fields and L. Marc, 1993.

FIELDS, W. C. [né William Claude Dukenfield] (1879–1946), comedian. Born in Philadelphia, the great comic began his career in 1897 as a tramp juggler, an act he continued to develop and perform worldwide until 1914. For a time in 1905 he incorporated the routine into *McIntyre and Heath's The Ham Tree.* He played briefly in *Watch Your Step* (1914) before being signed by Florenz *Ziegfeld, for whom he appeared in six editions of the Follies between 1915 and 1921, missing only the 1919 production. It was during these seasons that he largely abandoned his juggling to perfect the misanthropic character he is remembered for. A portly man with grayish blond hair, a bulbous nose, vulpine eyes, and a voice described as reedy or croaky, he clowned deadpan, with a bored, slightly haughty air. His characters were amoral and contemptuous of suckers, children, animals, teetotalers (he was a notorious drinker), and sentimentalists. Fields appeared in *George White's Scandals of 1922,* starred as Eustace McGargle in *Poppy* (1923), performed in the 1925 *Follies* and the *Earl Carroll Vanities of 1928,* and starred as Q. Q. Quayle in *Ballyhoo* (1930) before beginning his celebrated film and radio career. Between shows he continued to be a popular attraction in vaudeville. In the 1930s he made several immensely popular films and later appeared regularly on radio. Biography: *W. C. Fields,* James Curtis, 2003.

FIERSTEIN, Harvey. See *Torch Song Trilogy.*

FIFTH AVENUE THEATRE (New York). The name was given to two different playhouses, neither of which was on Fifth Avenue and both of which were for a time connected with Augustin *Daly. The first was built on 24th Street in 1862 as an adjunct to the once-famous Fifth Avenue Hotel and stood at the rear of the hostelry. Conceived as a stock exchange, it was not turned to theatrical uses until 1865, when it was occupied by George Christy's Minstrels. In 1867 it began booking other sorts of light entertainment but closed soon after when a playgoer was murdered in a brawl. James Fisk then bought the house, redecorated it, and leased it to John *Brougham, who failed miserably, so Daly took it over later in 1869 and housed his first great company there until the building was destroyed by fire in 1873. *Frou-Frou,* *Saratoga,* *Horizon,* and *Divorce* were among Daly's notable hits at the theatre. It lay in ruins for several years until shortly before Steele MacKaye obtained control. Since by that time

Daly had opened his new Fifth Avenue Theatre, *MacKaye called his auditorium the *Madison Square Theatre. Meanwhile, Daly had immediately set about remodeling Gilsey's Apollo Hall on 28th Street, just west of Broadway. The New Fifth Avenue Theatre's beginnings were inauspicious, for while Daly had retained most of his ensemble intact, he could not at first find plays to please critics and playgoers. Moreover, the 1873 financial panic was hurting all theatrical trade. Daly was close to bankruptcy when his 1875 production of The *Big Bonanza saved the day. After Daly went into temporary retirement in 1878 the theatre came under the management of others. The world premiere of The *Pirates of Penzance was offered there in 1879 and Mary *Anderson and Helena *Modjeska both made their New York debuts on its stage. The house underwent several name changes, burned in 1891, was rebuilt and served as a vaudeville, film, and cheap burlesque theatre before being torn down in 1938.

FIFTH COLUMN, THE (1940), a drama by Ernest Hemingway and Benjamin Glazer. [Alvin Theatre, 87 perf.] Newspaperman Philip Rawlings (Franchot *Tone) works with the Loyalist counterespionage forces during the Spanish Civil War along with his even more rabidly anti-Nazi friend Max (Lee J. *Cobb). During a bombardment, Rawlings despairs of victory, gets drunk, and attacks a woman in a neighboring hotel room. Later, sober and remorseful, he takes the girl to Paris and marries her. But the situation in Spain is deteriorating, so when Max urges Rawlings to return to help, he does. Hemingway wrote the play while under fire in Spain but had trouble getting it produced. He finally allowed Glazer to write revisions, which made the play acceptable to the *Theatre Guild, which produced it. Many critics felt the love interest was extraneous and diverted the story from its hard look at the war. A brilliant performance by Tone and a supporting performance by Lenore *Ulric as a Spanish trollop, along with Lee *Strasberg's direction and Howard *Bay's superb settings, were unstintingly hailed. Nevertheless, the play found only a small audience and but for the Guild's advance subscription sales might have had an even shorter run.

FIFTH OF JULY. See *Talley's Folly.*

FIFTH SEASON, THE (1953), a comedy by Sylvia Regan. [*Cort Theatre, 645 perf.] Max Pincus (Menasha *Skulnik) and Johnny Goodwin (Richard *Whorf) run a faltering garment company which is in trouble to some extent because of the traditional ups and downs of the industry, but also because Johnny spends too much time away philandering.

So most of the company's woes fall on the already woeful Max. Luckily, Max is lovable and good enough to help matters to a happy ending. This slim, cliché-ridden comedy succeeded handsomely on the strength of the tiny, doleful Skulnik's clowning.

FIFTY MILLION FRENCHMEN (1929), a musical comedy by Herbert *Fields (book), Cole *Porter (music, lyrics). [Lyric Theatre, 257 perf.] In Paris, the rich American Peter Forbes (William *Gaxton) bets a friend $25,000 that he can win American tourist Looloo Carroll (Genevieve *Tobin) without disclosing how wealthy he is. He takes a job as a Parisian guide and wins Looloo away from the titled Russian, whom her snobbish parents hope she will marry. *Notable songs*: Find Me a Primitive Man; You Do Something to Me; You've Got That Thing; You Don't Know Paree. The E. Ray *Goetz production had such lavish sets that they had to be cut down before they would fit into the theatre, but the musical's biggest problem was the onset of the Depression, which shortened what might have been a longer run. All the same, it was the first of Porter's many hit shows.

FIGHTING HOPE, THE (1908), a play by William J. *Hurlbut. [Stuyvesant Theatre, 231 perf.] When Robert Granger (Howell Hansel) is sent to prison for stealing huge sums from his employer, his wife, Anna (Blanche *Bates), assumes an alias and goes to work for his old boss, Burton Temple (Charles *Richman), convinced that Temple is the real thief and that she can find the evidence to exonerate her husband. What she does find is proof of her husband's guilt, and this proof she promptly destroys. Temple catches her but, since he has begun to fall in love with her, is forgiving. When Granger appears, saying he is paroled, he discerns the affection that Temple has developed for Anna and questions her motives in going to work for him. Then it is discovered that Granger has not been paroled, but has escaped from prison and plans to run off with another woman with the fortune he has hidden away. But the police close in, killing Granger as he flees, and Temple and Anna are free to pursue their budding romance. Although the merits of the melodrama sharply divided the critics, David *Belasco's fine mounting and Bates's popularity gave the work a long run.

FINIAN'S RAINBOW (1947), a musical fantasy by E. Y. *Harburg (book, lyrics), Fred Saidy (book), Burton *Lane (music). [46th Street Theatre, 725 perf.] Finian McLonergan (Albert Sharpe) and his daughter, Sharon (Ella Logan), come to America from Ireland lugging a crock of gold, which Finian hopes to plant at Fort Knox and watch grow. They are pursued by the former owner of the gold, the mischievous leprechaun Og (David *Wayne), who is slowly turning into a human. Stopping at Rainbow Valley, Missitucky, Sharon falls in love with labor organizer Will Mahoney (Donald Richards) and encounters the racist Senator Billboard Rawkins (Robert Pitkin), who whines, "My whole family's hated immigrants ever since we came to this country." Through the magic power of the crock, Rawkins is turned black and made to see the penalties of his attitudes before being restored to his former self. Sharon gets Will, Og falls for a human female, and Finian continues his wandering, hoping that "we meet in Glocca Morra some fine day." *Notable songs*: How Are Things in Glocca Morra?; If This Isn't Love; Look to the Rainbow; Old Devil Moon; When I'm Not Near the Girl I Love; Something Sort of Grandish. The creative and daring musical, which twitted reactionaries, was so sunny, so witty, and so melodic that it delighted almost everyone. Billboard Rawkins, for example, spoofed Mississippi's notorious Senator Bilbo and Congressman Rankin. Because much of the humor was topical, revivals have been infrequent, though the Lane-Harburg score remains one of Broadway's best.

FINKLEHOFFE, Fred. See *Brother Rat*.

FINN, Henry James (1785–1840), actor. Born in Cape Breton, he was educated at Princeton for the law as a career but turned to the theatre when he became an assistant prop boy at the *Park Theatre, possibly playing minor roles there in 1804. After performing at London's Haymarket Theatre, Finn debuted in New York as Shylock in 1818, then spent several seasons in Charleston. Although he played such characters as Hamlet, The Stranger, and Othello back in New York, he began to gravitate toward comic roles, by 1824 playing Sir Andrew Aguecheek, Paul Pry, Sir Peter Teazle, and Bob Logic. The *New York Mirror* noted, "Mr. Finn's style of playing is broadly ludicrous. His delineations are sketched with a strong and masterly hand, and are generally correct, though sometimes rough likenesses." He scored a major success as Sergeant Welcome Sobersides in his own play *Montgomery; or, The Falls of Montmorency* (1825). He may also have been the author of *The Indian Wife* (1830), which made Sobersides a major character. Later, he wrote a farce about President Jackson's battle with the United States Bank called *Removing the Deposits* (1835). Finn died in a ship fire while traveling between New York and Boston.

FINN, William. See *Falsettos*.

FIORELLO! (1959), a musical by Jerome *Weidman, George *Abbott (book), Jerry *Bock (music), Sheldon *Harnick (lyrics). [*Broadhurst Theatre, 795 perf.; Pulitzer Prize, Tony, NYDCC Awards.] When Fiorello La Guardia (Tom Bosley) is told by his loyal secretary, Marie (Patricia Wilson), and her friend Dora (Pat Stanley) that a labor organizer, Thea (Ellen Hanley), has been arrested on trumped-up charges, he rushes to Thea's defense and berates the corrupt policeman, Floyd (Mark Dawson), who arrested her. Later, he runs for mayor with the grudging approval of the Republican ward leader, Ben Marino (Howard *da Silva). Meanwhile, Floyd rises in Tammany ranks and befriends Dora, who drifts away from her old crowd. La Guardia marries Thea, who dies during his second campaign and then fires Marie so he can propose to her. But his romances never stop his battles against injustice. *Notable songs*: Little Tin Box; Politics and Poker; Till Tomorrow; When Did I Fall in Love? Characterized by Walter *Kerr of the *Herald Tribune* as "a song-and-dance jamboree with a curious streak of honest journalism and a strong strain of rugged sobriety about it," the Robert *Griffith–Hal *Prince production was made especially memorable by Bosley's affectionate portrayal of the mayor. Always a New York kind of show, the musical was quickly forgotten and is revived less than perhaps any other triple award winner.

FIREBRAND, THE (1924), a comedy by Edwin Justus Mayer. [*Morosco Theatre, 287 perf.] Benvenuto Cellini (Joseph *Schildkraut) has purchased his beautiful model Angela (Florence Mason) from her haggish mother for forty ducats. His plans to romance her, however, are frustrated by the arrival in his workshop of the flighty Duke of Florence (Frank *Morgan), who is instantly captivated by Angela and takes her to his palace. Cellini is in no position to argue since the sight of Angela has prompted the Duke to pardon Cellini for a murder he has committed. Moreover, Cellini has been having an affair with the Duchess (Nana Bryant). Later, Cellini attempts to steal Angela away from the Duke but once again his plans are thwarted, so he must content himself with continuing to see the Duchess. Based loosely on an incident in Cellini's autobiography, the play was perceived as "racy" entertainment at a time when such plays were felt to demonstrate a new freedom and maturity on the stage. **Edwin Justus MAYER** (1896–1960), a New York native, was a newspaper reporter for many years and briefly an actor before writing this play. His drama *Children of Darkness* (1930) initially failed, but a 1958 revival by the *Circle in the Square was a major success and forced a reevaluation of the play. Mayer was long active as a screen-

writer. A musical version of *The Firebrand* titled *The Firebrand of Florence*, with songs by Ira *Gershwin and Kurt *Weill, failed in 1945.

FIREFLY, THE (1912), a "comedy opera" by Otto *Harbach (book, lyrics), Rudolf *Friml (music). [Lyric Theatre, 120 perf.] To flee from her drunken guardian, the young street urchin Nina Corelli (Emma *Trentini) disguises herself as a boy and boards a yacht headed for Bermuda. On board are Jack Travers (Craig Campbell) and his bitchy fiancée, Geraldine Van Dare (Audrey Maple). Nina falls in love with Jack but cannot disclose her real identity. However, when she is mistaken for a sought pickpocket she is forced to reveal that she is a girl. A kindly musician, who has heard her sing, sends her to Europe to be educated. Nina returns as a celebrated prima donna and marries Jack. *Notable songs*: Giannina Mia; Love Is Like a Firefly; Sympathy. The Arthur *Hammerstein-produced operetta was originally to have had a score by Victor *Herbert, but after a series of rows with Trentini, Herbert asked to be released from his contract. The score was Friml's first and won him immediate recognition.

FIRES IN AMERICAN THEATRE. Until the early 20th century, when stringent laws and safer building materials were developed, the threat of fire was omnipresent in American theatres. The first major fire recorded in an American playhouse occurred at the *Federal Street Theatre in Boston in 1798. Between then and 1903, over one hundred serious fires destroyed and heavily damaged theatres, although most occurred when no performance was on and lives were not lost. No fewer than five New York theatres (*Barnum's, "444" Broadway, the Academy of Music, the New Bowery, and the Winter Garden) burned in the period from July 1865 to March 1867. Walter *Leman noted that in these years fires were so frequent that theatrical people felt the average life of an auditorium was only fifteen years. The three worst catastrophes were the burning of the Richmond (Virginia) Theatre, during the playing of an afterpiece, *Raymond and Agnes; or; The Bleeding Nun,* in 1811 when 71 people perished; the destruction of the Brooklyn Theatre during a performance of *The *Two Orphans* in 1876 with the loss of 197 lives; and the fire at the newly opened, supposedly fireproof Iroquois Theatre in Chicago during a performance of the musical *Mr. Bluebeard* in 1903, which claimed over 600 lives.

FIRST YEAR, THE (1920), a comedy by Frank *Craven. [Little Theatre, 725 perf.] Grace Livingston (Roberta Arnold) of Rochester, Illinois, has been proposed to by young, ambitious Dick Loring

(Lyster Chambers). She has also been courted by shy Tommy Tucker (Craven), who is not nearly as handsome as Dick and will probably spend all his life as a Rochester real estate agent. Grace's Uncle Myron (Tim Murphy) finally goads Tommy into proposing, and Grace accepts. But their married life is not all bliss. Tommy thinks their problems are merely the dark before the dawn, but Grace suggests they've "had a long arctic night." Just as a dinner party starts to fall to pieces, Tommy blames Loring, who has returned on a visit, for breaking up a big deal he had in the works. In a snit, Grace runs home to Mother, where she learns that Tommy's deal has, in fact, gone through and he is rich. But Tommy appears as Loring is talking to Grace and a melee ensues, with Grace, attempting to stop Dick from hurting Tommy, inadvertently knocking out her husband with a vase meant for Dick's head. Tommy misconstrues her behavior and it takes all of Uncle Myron's persuasive abilities, plus the announcement that Grace is pregnant, to reunite the couple. Welcomed by Burns *Mantle, who called it "one of those true, homely little comedies which are a blend of character, keenly observed, and the human comedy situation, overlaid with a suggestion of farce," the John *Golden production was the biggest hit of the season. At the time of its closing it was the third-longest-run show in Broadway history.

FISHER, Charles (1816–91), actor. The Englishman had already made a name for himself at London's Princess Theatre when William *Burton enlisted him for his American company. He made his debut as Ferment in *The School of Reform* in 1852, then won acclaim the following year as the art fancier Triplet in *Masks and Faces*. Fisher remained with Burton for several seasons before moving to Laura *Keene's company. In 1855 he created the role of the treacherous jester Pepe in *Francesca da Rimini*. He joined *Wallack's ensemble in 1861 and for many years was one of the group's principal supporting players, assuming such roles as Joseph Surface and important parts in newer plays, including Matthew Leigh in *Rosedale* (1863). During one summer hiatus he created the role of the villainous Colonel Crafton in *Fritz, Our Cousin German*. In 1872 Fisher switched to Augustin *Daly's troupe, in which he remained for the rest of his life. As at Wallack's, he played important roles in many of the new plays Daly mounted as well as interpreting such classic roles as Falstaff and Sir Peter Teazle. Daly's biographer characterized his style as "more French than English," suggesting his forte for light, elegant impersonations, and although he never became a star he remained one of the most respected American performers for nearly forty years.

FISHER, Clara [later known as Clara Fisher Maeder or Mrs. James G. Maeder] (1811–98), actress. Born in London, where her father was a well-known librarian and auctioneer, she was a child prodigy who began to perform at the age of six, playing in such standard favorites as *Little Pickle* and *Richard III,* and at sixteen made her American debut at the *Park Theatre in 1827. *The Albion* wrote of her performance as Albina Mandeville in *The Will*, "Miss Fisher succeeded most admirably. . . . In her hoydenish airs, there was nothing vulgar; in her passion, nothing indelicate; in her gentility, nothing affected." During the following seasons she was immensely popular, displaying a remarkable range as Ophelia, Lady Teazle, and Clari (in the operetta of the same name). In 1834 she married James G. Maeder, a well-known conductor and musical coach, then retired from the stage shortly after the birth of their son. When Fisher attempted a comeback in the 1880s, she met with only small success. According to *Ireland, "Her person, below middle height, and just reaching but not exceeding a delicate plumpness, was exquisitely formed . . . her expression arch and intelligent . . . her fine hair closely cut on the back of the head, while on her brow she wore the then fashionable rolls, or puffs, a style that was immediately adopted by all fashionable ladies under twenty-five." Autobiography: *Autobiography of Clara Fisher Maeder*, 1897.

FISHER, Jules (b. 1937), lighting designer. Born in Norristown, Pennsylvania, he was educated at Pennsylvania State University and Carnegie Institute of Technology. Since arriving in New York in 1959, Fisher has become the preeminent lighting designer of his era with dozens of Manhattan credits in shows as diverse as *Anyone Can Whistle* (1964), *Black Comedy* (1967), *Hair* (1968), *Home* (1970), *Lenny* (1971), *No No Nanette* (1971), *Pippin* (1973), *Ulysses in Nighttown* (1974), *Frankenstein* (1982), *La Cage aux Folles* (1985), *Grand Hotel* (1989), *Jelly's Last Jam* (1992), and *Angels in America* (1993). In the 1990s he began working with **Peggy EISENHAUER** (b. 1962), a native New Yorker who trained at Carnegie Mellon and designed lights for concerts and dance musicals. Fisher and Eisenhower have collaborated on such productions as *Victor/Victoria* (1995), *Bring in da Noise, Bring in da Funk* (1997), *Jane Eyre* (2000), *The Wild Party* (2000), and *Gypsy* (2003). Fisher has also produced some of the shows he designed, such as *Dancin'* (1978) and *Rock 'n Roll! The First 5,000 Years* (1983).

FISKE, Harrison Grey (1861–1942), critic, producer, and playwright. The New York–born son of a wealthy hotel owner, he became drama critic for the *Jersey City Argus* while still in his teens but quit after he discovered the paper was in debt to his father and had hired him as a courtesy. After a brief time at New York University, he left when his father bought him a one-third interest in the *Dramatic Mirror* in 1880 and he was made editor. In 1890 Fiske married Minnie Maddern, who had already developed a reputation as a promising actress and who thereupon changed her professional name to Mrs. *Fiske. As editor, Fiske had been a crusader from the start. His 1880 editorials were instrumental in establishing the *Actors' Fund of America. When stories about the practices of the newly formed *Theatrical Syndicate, or Trust, began to gain currency, Fiske printed them without editorial comment. But after the members of the Trust threatened to destroy his paper if he mentioned it again, he initiated a mammoth crusade against the monopoly. The result was that his wife was barred from playing in Trust houses. Fiske was forced to lease theatres and produce plays to keep his wife on the boards. He also wrote several plays, including *Hester Crewe* (1893), *The District Attorney* (1895), *Marie Deloche* (1896), and *The Privateer* (1897). He withdrew from the *Dramatic Mirror* in 1911 but continued to produce plays, both for his wife and others. Ironically, one of his biggest hits was *Kismet* (1911), produced in association with his old adversaries from the Trust: *Frohman, *Klaw, and *Erlanger.

FISKE, Mrs. Minnie Maddern [née Mary or Marie Augusta Davey] (1865–1932), actress and playwright. Born in New Orleans, she was the daughter of the manager of the St. Charles Theatre and of Lizzie Maddern, an actress, who first carried "Little Minnie Maddern" on stage at the age of three. She made her New York debut in *A Sheep in Wolf's Clothing* (1870), then a month later created the role of Little Fritz in the long-popular *Fritz, Our Cousin German*. In 1871 she played opposite Laura *Keene as Willie Leigh in *Hunted Down,* and later created the part of Little Alice in the premiere of another play destined for years of popularity, *Kit, The Arkansas Traveller*. Although her role was relatively small, the *Herald* singled her out for praise, hailing her as "a wonder" and suggesting her talents surpassed "that [of] some of the mature artists who surround her." After touring for a decade as Little Eva in *Uncle Tom's Cabin,* Prince Arthur in *King John,* and other youthful parts, Maddern returned to New York, where she shone as Chip in *Fogg's Ferry* (1882) and Mercy in *Caprice* (1884). Daniel *Frohman awarded her stardom when she played Stella in *In Spite of All* (1885). In 1890, several years after a brief, unsuccessful marriage to Legrand White, she married Harrison Grey *Fiske and announced her retirement. For the

moment she satisfied her theatrical yearnings by writing plays: *Countess Roudine, The Rose, The Eyes of the Heart, A Light from St. Agnes,* and *Fontenelle,* which met with varying degrees of success. By 1893 the lure of the footlights proved irresistible, and she returned to the stage as Mrs. Fiske in *Hester Crewe,* followed by Nora in *A Doll's House* (1894), which earned her recognition as a serious actress. Her *Tess of the D'Urbervilles* (1897) was one of her biggest triumphs, but it coincided with the Fiskes' problems with the *Theatrical Syndicate, or Trust. Like Sarah *Bernhardt, the Fiskes were barred from performing in Syndicate houses so were forced to play undesirable theatres and even in tents. Neither the Fiskes nor their followers were discouraged, and she triumphed as *Becky Sharp (1899), *Hedda Gabler* (1903), *Leah Kleschna* (1904), Mrs. Karslake in The *New York Idea* (1906), Rebecca West in *Rosmersholm* (1907), *Salvation Nell* (1908), Lona Hessel in *Pillars of Society* (1910), and *Mrs. Bumpstead-Leigh* (1911). Many of these were at the Manhattan Theatre, which the Fiskes owned. But the costs of maintaining the house were too much, and the Fiskes eventually lost it. For a number of years Mrs. Fiske appeared in a series of relatively weak plays, which only her acting and her loyal admirers kept afloat. During World War I she was a member of an all-star cast for *Out There.* Not until the end of her career, when she appeared in several superb revivals, did she again know the acclaim that had been hers earlier: Mrs. Malaprop in *The Rivals* (1925), Mrs. Alving in *Ghosts* (1927), and Mistress Page in *The Merry Wives of Windsor* (1928). Her last New York appearance was as Mrs. Tyler in *It's a Grand Life* (1930). Ill health and age forced her to withdraw from a pre-Broadway tour of *Against the Wind.*

Short and red-headed, Mrs. Fiske was one of the greatest American actresses. Ward *Morehouse has written, "Mrs. Fiske never had beauty, but she had magnetism. She had with all of her nervous, jerky manner, subtlety and finesse, and she was as much at ease in light-handed drawing-room comedy as she was in the problem plays of Ibsen." Many critics saw her style as heavily influenced by *Duse's underplaying. She herself called it "natural, true acting." She once created a furor by delivering an important speech to George *Arliss with her back to the audience, and elsewhere awed playgoers by holding their attention for ten minutes without moving and without speaking as she cradled her drunken lover's head in her lap in *Salvation Nell.* Yet she was also sometimes too subservient to the demands of less thoughtful playgoers. She forced C. M. S. *McLellan to write an extra act for *Leah Kleschna,* giving the play a contrived happy ending instead of his original, ambiguous one. Much of the criticism leveled at her during her career is suspect, possibly written by critics susceptible to the Trust's bribes. In a curious way, Franklin P. Adams's droll verse best sums up most playgoers' reactions:

Somewords she runstogetherso, Some others are distinctly stated.
 Somecometoofast and s o m e t o o s l o w And some are syncopated,
 And yet no voice—I am sincere—Exists that I prefer to hear.

FITCH, [William] Clyde (1865–1909), playwright. He was born in Elmira, New York, the son of a Union army officer and a Maryland belle. Fitch's "sissy" manners made him a loner at school, but the same effeminacy won him major women's roles in the dramatic club at Amherst College. Arriving in New York to seek a career as an architect and interior decorator, he wrote a number of stories and short plays, which were afterwards successfully performed at the *Boston Museum. He also made a number of important theatrical friends, including the *Times* critic Edward A. *Dithmar, who, along with William *Winter, urged him to write *Beau Brumell* (1890) for the celebrated actor Richard *Mansfield. The play was an immediate hit and launched Fitch's career. During the next nineteen years he wrote nearly sixty plays, thirty-three of them original, and the remainder translations of foreign plays or adaptations of novels. Among his more important works were *Nathan Hale* (1898), *The Moth and the Flame* (1898), *The Cowboy and the Lady* (1899), *Barbara Frietchie* (1899), *The *Climbers* (1901), *Captain Jinks of the Horse Marines* (1901), *The *Girl with the Green Eyes* (1902), *The Truth* (1907), and *The *City* (1909). Fitch is considered the finest American playwright at the turn of the 20th century. His range and variety are startling, as is his prolificacy. Some works are domestic melodramas, others social critiques, still others historical romances. Quite probably his most glaring fault by modern standards was his contrived happy endings. Thus, the jealous woman in *The Girl with the Green Eyes* is thwarted in her suicide attempt, and the lying girl in *The Truth* is ultimately brought to her senses. These conclusions were not the result of haste on Fitch's part, but of his need to please contemporary audiences and thereby provide him with the income required for his notoriously luxurious way of life. Arthur Hobson *Quinn has pointed to Fitch's three salient virtues as "the ability to visualize any place or period in terms of its social values, the power to incarnate virtues and vices in characters who are essentially dramatic, and the gift of writing clever dialogue." Walter Prichard *Eaton added to this list Fitch's dramatized observations of small details such as the thumping of

steampipes in one play and the sound of an object falling down an airshaft in another. He concluded, "If we took Fitch's worlds and correctly illustrated them, they would give to future generations a better idea of American life from 1890 to 1910 than newspapers or historical records." Certainly Fitch's best plays, whatever their flaws, remain gripping reading and are probably exceptionally playable even today. Biography: *Clyde Fitch and His Letters*, Montrose J. Moses and Virginia Gerson, 1924.

FIT-UP. A name given in the 18th and 19th centuries to small bands of actors, often composed largely of members of a single family, who traveled with plays to backwater villages. They customarily performed in makeshift theatres, using barns, store porches, or any other available site. A number of celebrated American performers, such as John *Durang and G. L. *Fox, were at one time members of such companies.

FITZGERALD, Geraldine (b. 1914), actress and director. The Irish performer with a musical voice and a keen sense of character appeared in some two dozen New York productions in between her movie career and work in theatres on two continents. She was born in Dublin, the daughter of an attorney, was educated at the Dublin Art School, and first acted professionally at the Gate Theatre in her hometown. Fitzgerald made her Broadway debut as the innocent Ellie Dunn opposite Orson *Welles in the *Mercury Theatre production of *Heartbreak House* in 1938. Among her memorable New York performances were the determined artist's wife Jennifer Dubedat in *The Doctor's Dilemma* (1955), Goneril to Welles's *King Lear* (1956), the haunted Mary Tyrone in *Long Day's Journey into Night* (1971), the motherly Essie Miller in *Ah, Wilderness!* (1975), the senile Felicity hanging onto life in *The *Shadow Box* (1977), and Nora, the put-upon wife of a braggart, in *A *Touch of the Poet* (1977). Fitzgerald is also a respected director, and later in life she became popular as a singer of Irish folk songs in concert.

FIVE STAR FINAL (1930), a melodrama by Louis Weitzenkorn. [*Cort Theatre, 175 perf.] Caring only about circulation, the callous newspaper owner Bernard Hinchcliffe (Berton Churchill) orders his editor, Randall (Arthur *Byron), to revive the sordid, long-buried story of Nancy Vorhees (Merle Maddern), who had been acquitted of the charge of shooting her lover. Nancy is now married to Michael Townsend (Malcolm Duncan) and is preparing for the wedding of her daughter Jenny (Frances Fuller). When a reporter visits her, she gives him a picture of Jenny, thinking it is for the marriage notices. Learning the truth, Nancy begs

Randall to kill the story, but he insists it is still news. The story is published on Jenny's wedding day, and Nancy and Michael commit suicide. Jenny comes to the newspaper office to kill Randall but, learning that Randall has quit in revulsion, walks away. Richard Lockridge of the *Sun* observed that the A. H. *Woods–produced play displayed such "scathing contempt for tabloid journalism and its supporters that in the end only a few charred bones remain to mark the place." The *Theatre Guild had produced a similar play the night before, Claire and Paul Sifton's *Midnight*, which some critics thought had more literary value. But the dramatic effectiveness of Weitzenkorn's play succeeded, while *Midnight* failed. **Louis WEITZENKORN** (1893–1943) was born in Wilkes-Barre, Pennsylvania, and later studied at Columbia. He was primarily a newspaperman but wrote several plays, of which this alone was successful.

FLAHERTY, Stephen. See Ahrens and Flaherty.

FLANAGAN, Hallie [née Ferguson] (1890–1969), author, educator, and producer. Born in Redfield, South Dakota, she studied at Grinnell College, then spent time as an assistant to Professor George Pierce *Baker at his *47 Workshop before returning briefly to teach at the Grinnell Experimental Theatre. In 1925 she was appointed professor of drama and director of experimental theatre at Vassar. Flanagan took a leave of absence between 1935 and 1939 to serve as the head of the *Federal Theatre Project. Afterwards she returned to Vassar, retiring in 1952. Besides writing numerous articles for leading magazines and journals, she was the author of *Shifting Scenes of the Modern European Theatre* (1928), *Arena, the Story of the Federal Theatre* (1940), and *Dynamo, the Story of the Vassar Theatre* (1943).

FLASH OF LIGHTNING, A (1868), a play by Augustin *Daly [*Broadway Theatre, 52 perf.] Garry Fallon (J. H. Jack) is a greedy, ambitious man who rules his family with an iron hand. He has made his wife totally subservient and devoted all his attentions to advancing his haughty daughter, Rose (Kitty Blanchard), neglecting his other daughter, Bessie (Blanche Grey). Shortly after Rose's beau, Chauncey (McKee *Rankin), has presented her with some gold jewelry, Bessie's former suitor Jack Ryver (J. K. Mortimer) visits Bessie and steals the jewelry. The family blames Bessie, who runs away and takes refuge on a steamboat, which catches fire. Luckily, Chauncey and Ryver have followed her and rescue Bessie at the last minute. Ryver also manages to make the family believe that the electricity from a flash of

lightning moved the jewelry, which he has quietly replaced. Daly derived the basic plot from Victorien *Sardou's *Le Perle noire*, adding the burning ship to provide the requisite thrill required by contemporary "sensation drama." Coming on top of his successes with *Leah, the Forsaken and *Under the Gaslight*, the play not only consolidated Daly's reputation but helped give him the wherewithal to consider founding a permanent company.

FLAVIN, Martin. See *Criminal Code, The.*

FLETCHER, Bramwell (1904–88), actor. A blond, distinguished-looking leading man equally comfortable in melodramas and *Shaw comedies, Fletcher was born in Bradford, England, and worked as an insurance company clerk before going on the stage in 1927. He first came to New York two years later and settled in the States, where he alternated between Broadway and Hollywood. Fletcher's most-remembered performances were in plays by Shaw, including the artist Louis Dubedat in *The Doctor's Dilemma* (1941), Mr. Burgess opposite Olivia de Havilland's *Candida* (1952), his one-man Off-Broadway program *The Bernard Shaw Story* (1965), and as Rex *Harrison's replacement in *My Fair Lady* for over a hundred performances.

FLORENCE, W[illiam] **J**[ames or Jermyn] [né Bernard Conlin] (1831–91), actor and producer. Born in Albany, New York, where he showed dramatic ability early and became an important member of the local Murdoch Dramatic Association, he made his professional debut in Richmond, Virginia, in 1849, playing Tobias in *The *Stranger*, and his New York bow in 1850 as Hallagan in *Home.* His Irish good looks and charm coupled with his "frank, ingenuous" acting style kept him playing preponderantly Irish parts for the next dozen years, often in conjunction with his wife, the former Malvina Pray (1831–1906). They also appeared successfully in a number of burlesques. Florence scored a major success as the first American Bob Brierly in *The *Ticket-of-Leave Man* (1863), then produced the first American presentation of *Caste* (1867), taking for himself the part of George D'Alroy. His other noteworthy credits include the tricky villain Obenreizer in the American premiere of *No Thoroughfare* (1868), the garrulous Hon. Bardwell Slote in *The *Mighty Dollar* (1875), Sir Lucius O'Trigger in *The Rivals* (1890), and Zekiel Homespun in *The Heir-at-Law* (1890). William *Winter recalled, "The secret of his success lay in his profound feeling, guided by good taste and perfect self-control. He was an actor of humanity, and he diffused an irresistible charm of truth and gentleness."

FLORIDA STUDIO THEATRE (Sarasota). A small but noteworthy theatre dedicated to new works, it was founded in 1973 by Jon Spelman with the idea of presenting small-cast plays and musicals in an intimate setting. The company's main stage seats only 167 and its cabaret space is even smaller and more flexible. New works are encouraged by the group's Florida Playwrights Festival and its award of residencies for promising playwrights.

FLORODORA (1900). An 1899 English musical comedy with book by Owen Hall, lyrics by E. Byrd Jones and Paul Rubens, and music by Leslie Stuart, it told the story of an attempt to cheat a beautiful young heiress out of her rights to a famous perfume. Its New York premiere, with a somewhat revised book by Frank *Pixley, opened at the *Casino Theatre and ran for 505 performances, longer than the London run, an unheard-of phenomenon. No small part of the show's popularity stemmed from the fame of its sextette (actually a double sextette of six men and six women) who sang "Tell Me Pretty Maiden," the first major song hit from a Broadway show not sung by the principals. Legend has it that the six original women of the sextette (Daisy Greene, Marjorie Relyea, Vaughn Texsmith, Margaret Walker, Agnes Wayburn, and Marie L. Wilson) all married millionaires. The musical was revived on frequent occasions, including a very successful production during the 1919–20 season.

FLOWER DRUM SONG (1958), a musical comedy by Joseph *Fields (book), Oscar *Hammerstein (book, lyrics), Richard *Rodgers (music). [*St. James Theatre, 600 perf.] In the Chinatown section of San Francisco, nightclub owner Sammy Fong (Larry *Blyden) loves the sassy, all-American Linda Low (Pat Suzuki), but he is betrothed to his "picture bride" Mei Li (Miyoshi Umeki), who has just arrived from China with her father. The Chinese-American youth Wang Ta (Ed Kenney) falls for Mei Li, and Sammy manipulates matters so that two weddings take place. *Notable songs*: You Are Beautiful; I Enjoy Being a Girl; Love, Look Away; A Hundred Million Miracles. The only Rodgers and Hammerstein work clearly in the musical comedy genre, the tale (based on a book by C. Y. Lee) took a lighthearted look at East-West differences and the generation gap in Asian-American families. A 2002 revival, which originated at the *Mark Taper Forum and transferred to Broadway, used a much-changed libretto by David Henry *Hwang that kept the story in the early 1960s but updated some of the sentiments of the musical, dropped and added characters, and even satirized Chinese clichés.

FLOYD COLLINS (1996), a musical play by Tina Landau (book), Adam Guettel (music, lyrics). [*Playwrights Horizons, 25 perf.] In the winter of 1925, Kentucky farmer Floyd Collins (Christopher Innvar) is exploring a cave on the family property when he gets trapped 150 feet below the surface. The efforts to rescue him make national news, and the site soon turns into a media circus as journalists and thousands of curious onlookers arrive. By the time the rescuers reach Collins, he has died of exposure, and the circus disbands. *Notable songs*: The Ballad of Floyd Collins; The Call; The Riddle Song. Based on a true event, the musical eschewed conventional storytelling, using dreams, flashbacks, and other theatrical techniques to explore the mindset of Floyd and his family. The score was an eclectic mix of country, ragtime, atonal, and avant garde music and was greeted enthusiastically by the press and the company's subscribers during its limited run. **Adam GUETTEL** (b. 1964), composer and lyricist. He was born in New York, the son of composer Mary *Rodgers and the grandson of Richard *Rodgers. He performed as a boy, singing with the Met in the children's chorus, then was educated at Yale and began writing experimental pieces in a new, innovative form quite unlike that of his illustrious grandfather. Guettel first attracted attention with *Floyd Collins* and was also praised for *Saturn Returns* (1998) and *The Light in the Piazza* (2003).

FLYING HIGH (1930), a musical comedy by John *McGowan (book), B. G. *De Sylva, Lew *Brown (book, lyrics), Ray *Henderson (music). [Apollo Theatre, 347 perf.] While the flashy aviator Tod Addison (Oscar *Shaw) pursues a courtship of Eileen Cassidy (Grace Brinkley) that began when he parachuted onto her apartment balcony, his dithering mechanic "Rusty" Krause (Bert *Lahr) attempts to escape the advances of hefty, lovelorn Pansy Sparks (Kate Smith). Her dogged pursuit prompts "Rusty" to steal Tod's plane. Only when he is airborne does he remember that he has no idea of how to land the plane. Without meaning to, he breaks records for sustained flight. *Notable songs*: Red Hot Chicago; Thank Your Father; I'll Know Him. This final De Sylva, Brown, and Henderson musical, produced and directed by George *White, was a success largely because of Lahr's comic antics.

FOLGER SHAKESPEARE MEMORIAL LIBRARY (Washington, D.C.). The library was founded in 1930 and opened in 1932, with monies and a collection of Shakespeareana bequeathed it by Henry Clay Folger (1857–1930). While a student at Amherst, Folger, who became chairman of the board of Standard Oil of New York, was inspired by Ralph Waldo Emerson to begin his lifelong acquisitions. The collection includes seventy-nine First Folios and is equaled only by collections in the British Museum and the Bodleian Library at Oxford. The Library has been administered by Amherst under the direction of Dr. Joseph Quincy Adams, Louis B. Wright, and other respected scholars. In 1970, its director at that time, O. B. Hardison Jr. joined with Richmond Crinkley to found the Folger Theatre Group and to mount numerous Shakespearean revivals as well as modern plays in the Elizabethan-style theatre housed within the Library. In 1985 the theatre end became a separate entity, incorporated as the *Shakespeare Theatre at the Folger. But that group, under the direction of Michael Kahn, left to occupy another space (dropping "at the Folger" from its name), and the Folger Globe replica is now used for touring groups and special events.

FOLKSBIENE (New York). Yiddish for "People's Stage," it was called by theatre historian Nahma Sandrow "one of the most illustrious of Yiddish amateur groups." It has certainly been the most durable, being formed in 1915 by a merger of several older companies, including the Progressive Dramatic Club and the Hebrew Dramatic League. From the start it was closely allied with left-wing and labor organizations and still operates under the auspices of the Arbeiter Ring (Workmen's Club). No season since its founding has gone by without its offering at least one presentation, and usually more. It performs generally serious plays, mostly by Yiddish writers, but has often turned to Eugene *O'Neill, Upton Sinclair, and important European playwrights as well. The group frequently hires distinguished professional directors and, because its actors are amateurs, performs only on weekends.

FOLLIES (1971), a musical play by James *Goldman (music), Stephen *Sondheim (music, lyrics). [*Winter Garden Theatre, 522 perf.; NYDCC Award.] With the Weismann Theatre under demolition, many of the aging performers who had played in the various editions of Weismann's *Follies* gather for a last, bittersweet reunion. As they talk about what has happened to them since their earlier successes and as they recall those bygone days, "memory figures" of their younger selves help jolt the recollections. By the dawn, they go their separate ways, some enlightened, others scarred. *Notable songs*: I'm Still Here; Losing My Mind; Too Many Mornings; Broadway Baby; Could I Leave You; Who's That Woman? Director-producer Hal *Prince provided one of the most lavish Broadway productions of the era, and the expensive show could not turn a profit. Yet it remains a beloved cult favorite, in no small part because of its rich score that includes acerbic contemporary songs as well as pastiche numbers of past styles. Revivals have been inconsistent, including a Broadway mounting in 2001.

FOLLOW THE GIRLS (1944), a musical comedy by Guy *Bolton, Eddie Davis, Fred *Thompson (book), Dan Shapiro, Milton Pascal, Phil Charig (music, lyrics). [*Century Theatre, 882 perf.] When burlesque queen Bubbles La Marr (Gertrude Niesen) takes over a servicemen's canteen as her contribution to the war effort, her 4-F suitor, Goofy Gale (Jackie Gleason), is forced to disguise himself as a Wave to gain entrance. *Notable songs*: I Wanna Get Married; Today Will Be Yesterday, Tomorrow; Follow the Girls. This loosely structured "girlie" show, whose thin plot served for little more than to frame its many vaudeville turns and skimpily clad chorus girls, was of a type often called "glorified burlesque." It was particularly popular with servicemen in town on leave. The show was Bolton's last successful effort as a collaborator on musical comedy books, although it was a marked comedown in quality from his work of two or three decades earlier.

FOLLOW THRU (1929), a musical comedy by Laurence *Schwab (book), B. G. *De Sylva, Lew *Brown (book, lyrics), Ray *Henderson (music). [46th Street Theatre, 403 perf.] Lora Moore (Irene Delroy) and Ruth Van Horn (Madeline Cameron) are rivals both for their country club's golf championship and for handsome Jerry Downs (John Barker). At the same time, brash Angie Howard (Zelma *O'Neal) attempts to catch Jack Martin (Jack *Haley). Angie has no rivals, but the shy, oddball Jack proves remarkably elusive. In the end, however, Lora and Angie win their men, and Lora also gets her loving cup. *Notable songs*: Button Up Your Overcoat; My Lucky Star; You Wouldn't Fool Me, Would You? Called in its programs "a musical slice of country club life" (a small indication of its punning humor), the Schwab–Frank *Mandel show expressed the zesty, sometimes frenetic hedonism of the 1920s in melody and comedy. Gilbert Gabriel wrote in the *Sun* that it seemed "dedicated to the task of making youth flame and love shout out, with crisp, crazy, lusty, ankle-loosing, hip-seizing songs, and lyrics that give this whole razzing, jazzing society circus its cue to get gay."

FONDA, Henry [Jaynes] (1905–82), actor. The lanky, slightly twangy-voiced leading man was born in Grand Island, Nebraska, and raised in Omaha, where he first appeared on stage in 1925 as Ricky in *You and I* with the Omaha Community Playhouse. After performing with various stock groups for several years, he made his Broadway debut as a walk-on in *The Game of Love and Death* (1929). Shortly thereafter, he joined the *University Players and remained with them until 1932. Fonda next appeared on Broadway in *I Love You Wednesday* (1932), *Forsaking All Others* (1933), and *New Faces* (1934), before winning acclaim as canal man Dan Harrow in *The Farmer Takes a Wife* (1934). Apart from a brief run in *Blow Ye Winds* (1937), he devoted himself to films until he returned to play *Mister Roberts* (1948). John Mason *Brown wrote of his performance, "He is to the full the unheroic hero; the shy, modest, everyday young man whose decencies and hidden strength have somehow made a leader of him. His is a quiet performance . . . Its power is its understatement, its reticence, its utter and communicated honesty." Thereafter, Fonda became one of the few major stars to shuttle regularly between Hollywood and Broadway. Among his memorable stage performances were businessman Charles Gray in *Point of No Return* (1951); the reluctant prosecuting attorney Lt. Greenwald in *The Caine Mutiny Court-Martial* (1954); staid Irish lawyer Jerry Ryan in *Two for the Seesaw* (1958); John, who finds an evening of love in a New England inn, in *Silent Night, Lonely Night* (1959); the drama critic Parker Ballantine in *Critic's Choice* (1960); the conservative executive Jim Bolton in *Generation* (1965); the one-man show *Clarence Darrow* (1974); and liberal Supreme Court Justice Daniel Snow in *First Monday in October* (1978). Autobiography: *Fonda: My Story*, with Howard Teichman, 1981; biography: *Henry Fonda: His Life and Work*, Norm Goldstein, 1982.

FONTANNE, Lynn [née Lillie Louise Fontanne] (1887–1983), actress. One of the great ladies of the American stage, the willowy, dark-haired, sharp-eyed actress with the throaty contralto voice and regal bearing was born in England, where she studied with Ellen *Terry before making her debut in 1905 in *Cinderella*. She came to America in 1910, appearing in *Mr. Preedy and the Countess* but shortly returned home and did not settle here permanently until 1916. Thereupon she appeared in a rapid succession of plays, including *A Young Man's Fancy* (1916), in which she met her future husband, Alfred *Lunt. Fontanne enjoyed an early major hit as the pushy, cliché-ridden wife in *Dulcy* (1921). Her first important joint appearance with her husband was as the Actress in *The Guardsman* (1924), after which she appeared, often with him, in such *Theatre Guild productions as *Arms and the Man* (1925), *The Goat Song* (1926), *Pygmalion* (1926), and *The Brothers Karamazov* (1927). Two outstanding productions with Lunt in 1927 were *The *Second Man* and *The Doctor's Dilemma*. After creating the role of Nina Leeds in *Strange Interlude* (1928), the couple permanently reunited and gave many superior performances, including *Caprice* (1928), *Meteor* (1929), *Elizabeth the Queen* (1930), *Reunion in Vienna* (1931), *Design for Living* (1933), *The Taming of the Shrew* (1936), *Idiot's Delight* (1936), *Amphitryon 38* (1937), *There Shall Be No Night* (1940), and *The *Pirate* (1942). By the 1940s there was an obvious decline in the quality of the pieces the couple had to work with, so it was largely their acting that kept their plays running: *O Mistress Mine* (1946), *I Know My Love* (1949), *Quadrille* (1954), and *The Great Sebastians* (1956). The Lunts found a powerful vehicle for their farewell performances, *The Visit* (1958), with Fontanne playing the millionairess Claire Zachanassian and Lunt as her faithless lover. The play was mounted at the old Globe Theatre, renamed in their honor the *Lunt-Fontanne. Always the more restrained, controlled performer of the team, Fontanne was early on characterized by Brooks *Atkinson as an actress with "glamour, poise and subtlety." Theresa *Helburn, who worked with her for years, called her "a brilliant and beautiful tiger" and suggested that both she and Lunt always retained something of the characters they first made famous. In her case that meant she ever afterwards displayed a touch of Dulcy's inherent cruelty in all her roles. Biography: *The Fabulous Lunts*, Jared Brown, 1986.

FOOL, THE (1922), a melodrama by Channing *Pollock. [Times Square Theatre, 360 perf.] Parishioners at New York's Church of the Nativity are disturbed by their new assistant rector, Daniel Gilchrist (James Kirkwood), who has condemned the fancy Christmas decorations. He has also read contributors to the church a lecture on the rich man entering heaven, and spoken of "ill gotten gains." As if that were not enough, he has welcomed poor worshipers into the upper-class church and has even given his own overcoat to an impoverished Jew who was shivering in the cold. The rector, Rev. Wadham (Arthur Eliot), has warned Gilchrist that he courts trouble. "What would happen if anybody really tried to live like Christ?" Gilchrist asks. Wadham replies it cannot be done. Gilchrist is dismissed and takes his private ministry to striking workers and opens a mission, only to be beaten by hoodlums. Although he helps the crippled woman Mary (Sara Sothern) walk again and saves a marriage, he continues to be assailed as a "nut." Only the woman whose paralysis he cured retains faith in him. Pollock was turned down by virtually every important producer, until he persuaded Arch *Selwyn to back the play. When it opened to generally unfavorable notices, Selwyn was ready to close it, but Pollock, who owned 25 percent of the work, would not let him. Pollock began a primitive publicity campaign, writing letters, making speeches, and printing advertisements with favorable remarks from the few notables who had liked the play. The publicity turned business around. According to Pollock, "Before the end of the season, seven companies were touring... reaching audiences of not less than 85,000 people each week, or close to five million theatregoers in a single season."

FOOL FOR LOVE (1983), a play by Sam *Shepard. [Circle Repertory Theatre, 1,000 perf.] May (Kathy Whitton Baker) and Eddie (Ed Harris), both lowlifes, are half-brother and half-sister who long have had a love-hate relationship. At a cheap motel, with their hopelessly besotted or senile father (Will Marchetti) sitting nearby, they once again rage through their gamut of emotions, until Eddie finally walks out. The production originated at San Francisco's *Magic Theatre and was brought to New York, where commendable notices and its small cast helped earn it a long run. It remains popular in regional and college theatres.

FOOL THERE WAS, A (1909), a play by Porter Emerson Browne. [Liberty Theatre, 93 perf.] There are two kinds of love, says the Woman (Katherine Kaelred): one like white roses, wan and bloodless, and the other like red roses, warm and vital. When the Husband (Robert *Hilliard) sails on an important diplomatic mission, he sees the Woman, throws his wife's pale bouquet overboard, and before long is in the Woman's clutches. She destroys his career and his marriage and drives him to drink. Realizing the damage that she has wrought, he attempts to strangle her. The struggle proves too much, and he falls dead. The Woman laughingly scatters red rose petals over his body. This unrelenting, if obvious, melodrama was even more popular on the road and was eventually made into a famous silent film. **Porter Emerson BROWNE** (1879–1934), a native of Beverly, Massachusetts, worked as a journalist and novelist before turning playwright. He enjoyed success with this play and *The Spendthrift* (1910), but it was followed by several failures: *Waste* (1910), *Chains* (1912), *Wild Oats* (1914), *A Girl of Today* (1915), *Rich Man, Poor Man* (1915), and *Don't Shoot* (1915). Browne scored a final success with *The Bad Man* (1920).

FOOTE, Horton. See *Young Man from Atlanta, The*.

FORBES, James (1871–1938), playwright and director. Born in Canada, he moved to America to seek a career, first trying his hand as an actor, a press agent, and a drama critic for the *Pittsburgh Dispatch* and later for the *New York World*. Forbes found playwriting most congenial, so he began by writing vaudeville sketches. One of these was turned into his first produced full-length play, the very popular *The *Chorus Lady* (1906). Also successful were *The *Traveling Salesman* (1908), *The Commuters* (1910), and *The *Show Shop* (1914). When styles of playwriting began to change with the coming of World War I, Forbes attempted to change with them. His best play was the family drama *The *Famous Mrs. Fair* (1919), followed by the less successful *Endless Chain* (1922), *Young Blood* (1925), *Precious* (1929), and *Matrimony PFD* (1936). Forbes was one of the founders of the *Dramatists' Theatre. Admired in his own day for his pungent dialogue, he was also respected as a director. He staged all of his own plays along with several by other playwrights.

FORBES-ROBERTSON, Johnston (1853–1937), actor. The handsome, if ascetic, slightly craggy-featured English leading man made his American debut in 1885, playing Orlando opposite Mary *Anderson. On his numerous subsequent visits he offered many of his most admired Shakespearean interpretations, including Shylock and Hamlet. Comparing his Dane with that of another English artist, Sir Henry *Irving, Walter Tallmadge Arndt observed in *Current Literature*, "Irving's is artistic artificiality, while Mr. Robertson's is artistic naturalness." However, for most American playgoers his greatest role was the divine figure called the Passer-by in *The Passing of the Third Floor Back* (1909). Adolph *Klauber wrote of his performance in this play, "There is something so illusive in the appeal of Mr. Forbes-Robertson's acting as almost to baffle complete description. It has been termed an aloofness or a certain spiritual-like quality." After formally retiring from the London stage in 1913, he spent three seasons touring America. Autobiography: *A Player Under Three Reigns*, 1925.

FORBIDDEN BROADWAY (1982). A very small-scale revue that spoofed Broadway shows and Broadway stars, it was first presented at Palsson's, a supper club in 1982, and for over twenty years the revue moved from location to location, changing its title (one version was called *2001: A Spoof Odyssey*), and updating its satire as the seasons went by. While most of the music was borrowed from shows being kidded, the lyrical spoofs were by Gerard Alessandrini. A parallel program called *Forbidden Hollywood* was attempted in the early 1990s, but it failed to catch on.

FORD CENTER FOR THE PERFORMING ARTS, THE (New York). One of Broadway's oldest and also newest theatres is actually two *42nd Street playhouses, the Lyric and the Apollo, that were combined into one and opened in 1998 as part of the 42nd Street Redevelopment. The Lyric

Theatre was built by the *Shuberts in 1903 as a musical house, and its design by Victor Hugo Koehler featured a Renaissance-style atrium and lobby, entrances on both 42nd and 43rd Streets, and an elegant auditorium with eighteen ornate boxes. During the Depression it reverted to a movie house, then was refurbished in 1979 but closed in 1992. The Apollo was built as a vaudeville house and opened in 1910 as the Bryant Theatre. The *Selwyn brothers bought the playhouse in 1920 and turned it into a legit venue for musicals, renaming it the Apollo. They found some success until the Depression forced the Apollo to become a movie theatre and then a burlesque house. In 1979 a remodeled Apollo opened as a legit venue once again, but an entrance was built on 43rd Street because patrons feared the seamy 42nd Street of the 1970s. It managed to find a few tenants before folding in 1983 and becoming a grind movie house once again. While the Ford Center (so named because of a considerable contribution by the Ford Motor Company) is a new 1,839-seat theatre, it retains elements from both the Apollo and the Lyric, including the atrium, details from the boxes and proscenium, and the beautiful stone facade. The first tenant of the new theatre was *Ragtime (1998), a large and impressive show that was fitting for the new-old playhouse.

FORD, Harriet (1863–1949), playwright. A native of Seymour, Connecticut, she studied acting at the *American Academy of Dramatic Arts and performed for several seasons before turning to playwriting. Nearly two dozen of her works, almost all either adaptations of novels or collaborations, were given major productions, among them, *A *Gentleman of France* (1901), *The Fourth Estate* (1909), *A Little Brother of the Rich* (1909), *The Argyle Case* (1912), and *The *Dummy* (1914).

FORD, Helen [Isabel] [née Barnett] (1894–1982), actress and singer. The petite, vivacious singer, who was one of the more popular musical comedy queens of the 1920s, was born in Troy, New York, and made her debut there as a child performer. Although she had played New York earlier, she first came to critics' attention as the French nurse Toinette Fontaine in *Always You* (1920), followed by appearances in *The Sweetheart Shop* (1920) and *For Goodness Sake* (1922). Ford had one of her biggest hits as businesswoman Mary Thompson in *The Gingham Girl* (1922), then began a long relationship with Richard *Rodgers, Lorenz *Hart, and Herbert *Fields, playing American colonist Betsy Burke in their *Dearest Enemy* (1925), the daydreaming *Peggy Ann* (1926), and the Chinese wife Chee-Chee in *Chee-Chee* (1928). Between engagements she toured in vaudeville, then later played Adele in a 1933

version of *Fledermaus*, called *Champagne Sec*. Her last appearance in a major musical was in *Great Lady* (1938), although she performed in several non-musicals before retiring.

FORD, Hugh (1868–1952), director. After beginning his career as an actor, he served several seasons in stock, both as a player and a director, before coming to the attention of George C. *Tyler. For many years thereafter he was the leading director for *Liebler and Co. Tyler came to consider him "the greatest director alive," and Owen *Davis recalled that he "had probably the longest unbroken string of successes of any contemporary director." While these may have been exaggerations, his list of credits included *Salomy Jane* (1907), *The *Man from Home* (1908), *The Melting Pot* (1909), *The *Dawn of a Tomorrow* (1909), *Alias Jimmy Valentine* (1910), *The Deep Purple* (1911), *The *Garden of Allah* (1911), *Potash and Perlmutter* (1913), *The Yellow Ticket* (1914), and *Merton of the Movies* (1922). He was also famous as a director of silent films.

FORD, John T[hompson] (1829–94), manager. Descended from an old Maryland family, he was born in Baltimore, which remained his base throughout his career as a builder and manager of theatres. As a young man he worked in a family tobacco factory but left the company in 1850 to become business manager and press agent for a concert ensemble. In 1854 he assumed management of Baltimore's famed *Holliday Street Theatre, which he ran for the next twenty-five years. He quickly took over the running of numerous other theatres in the South and eventually built many playhouses, including *Ford's Theatre in Washington, where Lincoln was assassinated and which remains an active legitimate theatre today; Ford's Theatre in Baltimore, which remained the city's principal playhouse until the 1960s; and the Academy of Music in Philadelphia, which is still the main concert hall there. He was generally acknowledged as one of the most honest and important theatrical figures of his day.

FORD, Nancy. See *I'm Getting My Act Together*.

FORD [Weaver], **Paul** (1901–76), character actor. The beloved performer with a drolly grim long face was born in Baltimore and made his debut in summer stock in 1920 as Sir Lucius O'Trigger. His first Broadway appearance was as Sgt. Carey in *Decision* (1944). Although he was a fine dramatic actor, he is remembered largely for his comic portraits, notably the befuddled Colonel Purdy in *Teahouse of the August Moon* (1953), a variety of characters in *A Thurber Carnival* (1960), and Harry Lambert, the middle-aged husband who suddenly finds he is to become a father, in *Never Too Late* (1962).

FORD'S THEATRE (Washington, D.C.). In 1861 John T. *Ford converted the empty First Baptist Church into a playhouse, and it was a profitable venture until it burned down a year later. Ford then built a new brick theatre holding 1,700 patrons, which he opened in 1863 as Ford's New Theatre. Once again the theatre flourished until President Lincoln was shot there on April 14, 1865, while watching a performance of *Our American Cousin*. The War Department prevented Ford from reopening the auditorium and purchased it from him and his brothers. The building was gutted and converted into an office building and storage facility, but its jinx continued. Part of the building collapsed in the 1890s, killing twenty-two government employees. Between 1965 and early 1968 the building was restored to its original appearance but with a seating capacity of only 741. In January 1968 it reopened as a playhouse and is used for touring groups and special events. The basement of the structure houses a museum about the history of the famous theatre.

FOREIGNER, THE (1984), a comedy by Larry Shue [Astor Place Theatre, 686 perf.] British proofreader Charlie Baker (Anthony Heald) seeks refuge from the world in a rural Georgia fishing lodge where the proprietor and patrons think he is a foreigner who doesn't understand English. Consequently, Charlie becomes privy to secret plots to swindle the innocent and even gets involved with the Ku Klux Klan before he puts matters right. The contrived but enjoyable play met with mostly favorable notices and was very popular Off Broadway and in theatres across the country. **Larry SHUE** (1946–85) was a character actor who wrote three plays before his premature death. He was born in New Orleans, the son of a college president, and educated at Illinois Wesleyan before pursuing an acting-writing career in regional theatre. His other plays are *The Nerd* (1987), telling of an oddball whose visit upsets his former army buddy, and *Wenceslas Square* (1988), in which an American professor of Czech Studies returns to Prague after a regime change.

FOREMAN, Richard (b. 1937), director and playwright. The controversial director, who stages his original works like an artist placing objects in a three-dimensional canvas, was born on Staten Island and educated at Brown University and Yale. In 1968 he founded the Ontological-Hysteric Theatre in Manhattan, where most of his works have been presented over the years. Because of their unique nature, Foreman's theatre pieces are created for a select audience, offered on a limited basis, then disappear. He has had few traditional hits, but many memorable productions such as *Total Recall* (1970), *Dr. Selavy's Magic Theatre* (1972), *The *Threepenny Opera* (1976), *Penguin Touquet* (1981), *Egyptology* (1983), and *Woyzek* (1990).

FOREST ROSE, THE; *or, American Farmers* (1825), a play by Samuel *Woodworth (book), John Davies (music). [Chatham Garden Theatre, in repertory.] Although William (Arthur Keene), a decent country lad, loves Harriet (Mrs. Burke), Harriet and her friend Lydia (Mrs. Henry Wallack), two New Jersey farm girls, or "forest roses," long to escape their bucolic life for the excitement of the city. Lydia is loved by the rich Blandford (Mr. Howard), but the romance must be kept secret in order not to offend Blandford's snobbish father. Blandford's English-born friend Bellamy (Edward N. Thayer) courts Harriet, whom he promises Blandford he will love for a whole month. Later he persuades the seemingly naive Yankee Jonathan Ploughboy (Alexander Simpson) to help him kidnap Harriet. But Jonathan is not as gullible as he appears. A servant girl is substituted, Harriet marries William, and Lydia weds Blandford. *Notable songs*: Here in Scenes of Sweet Seclusion; When Bashful Lubin Sought My Hand; The Morn Awakes; The Heart Sustained by Hope Alone; Is There a Light? Often called a "pastoral opera," the play was one of the first, and for many years the most popular, American rural dramas. Woodworth apparently based his Jonathan Ploughboy on the Jonathan in Royall *Tyler's The *Contrast, but it was Ploughboy who kindled the real vogue for such Yankee characters. Virtually all the great 19th-century Yankee specialists and other fine comedians (G. H. *Hill, Dan *Marble, Henry *Placide, and Joshua *Silsbee) frequently played the part.

FOREVER AFTER (1918), a play by Owen *Davis. [Central Theatre, 312 perf.] A grievously wounded soldier, Ted (Conrad Nagel), recounts the tale of his unfulfilled romance to his buddy. Before the war he had loved the wealthy Jennie (Alice *Brady), but her ambitious, snobbish mother had forced her to break off the affair. Now Ted is taken to a field hospital where Jennie serves as a Red Cross nurse, and their tearful reunion and her obvious love give him the strength to survive. Davis recalled this mawkishly romantic play as "one of the best money-makers I have ever had," at the same time recognizing that along with such other works as *Sinners* and *At 9:45* it marked a major turning point in his career, representing "one step up" from the cheap melodramas of his earlier years. William A. *Brady produced the popular attraction.

FORNES, Maria Irene (b. 1930), playwright. One of Off Broadway's most familiar and durable writers, the Cuban-born Fornes is known for her surreal plays that use humor and movielike visuals to present her ideas on worldwide angst and feminism. She was first noticed for her avant-garde play *Tango Palace* (1964) and the offbeat musical *Promenade* (1965). Fornes's most notable plays include *Fefu and Her Friends* (1977), about a group of women expressing their thoughts in different rooms of a New England house; *Mud* (1983), concerning a love triangle among a pig farmer, his illiterate wife, and an older, educated admirer; and *The Conduct of Life* (1985), in which a Latin American lieutenant uses military strategies in dealing with his wife and mistress. She often directs her own works and those by others as well.

FORREST, Edwin (1806–72), actor. Generally acknowledged as the first grand tragedian of the American stage, Forrest was born in Philadelphia to the impoverished, runaway son of a Scottish squire and the daughter of middle-class German immigrants. His theatrical debut came about by accident in 1817 when the manager of the *Southwark Theatre, noting his attractiveness, asked him to substitute for an ailing actress in the small role of the odalisque Rosina in *Rudolph; or, The Robber of Calabria*. The experience thrilled him, and though he had little formal education he studied elocution and organized a Thespian Club. His real debut was as Norval in *Douglas* at the *Walnut Street Theatre in 1820. He then spent the next several seasons touring what was called the Western circuit (western Pennsylvania, Ohio, and Kentucky) before performing in New Orleans. During this time he first performed many of the roles for which he would become famous, including Damon in *Damon and Pythias*, Jaffier in *Venice Preserved*, Tell in *William Tell*, and the Indian chief in *She Would Be a Soldier*. His New York debut was as Othello in 1826 at the *Park Theatre, and he repeated his performance at the *Bowery Theatre. Both playhouses were to figure importantly in his career. What critics and playgoers saw was a dark-haired, sardonically handsome man of noticeably muscular build (he always favored roles that allowed him to display his arms and legs) who stood five feet ten inches tall and had a deep, stentorian voice, which he sometimes employed with a crude vigor. Implicit in his appearance and acting were the seeds of class differences that would beset his career. From the start Forrest's appeal was to the mass of playgoers, the more genteel members of the audience often balking at what they perceived as his sometimes vulgar display of physique and his unlettered readings. In 1828 he offered prizes for new American plays, preferably on American themes. First prize went to John Augustus *Stone for *Metamora*, which was soon one of Forrest's most popular vehicles. Other winners included Richard Penn *Smith's *Caius Marius*; three plays by Robert Montgomery *Bird: *The *Gladiator*, *Oralloossa*, and The *Broker of Bogota*; and Robert T. Conrad's *Jack Cade*. The well-intentioned contest also added to the actor's increasingly questionable personal reputation, for he was accused of not paying money owed to several of the playwrights. Forrest then added a number of major roles to his repertory, including the title parts of *King Lear, *Hamlet, *Macbeth, and *Virginius*. His career may be said to have peaked in the late 1840s, after which two incidents further tarnished his reputation. In 1849 his rivalry with the English actor William *Macready came to a head in the bloody *Astor Place Riots, in which Forrest almost certainly had a hand. In 1851 he and his wife were divorced after each had noisily (and probably accurately) accused the other of infidelity. Thereafter, his popularity began to wane, although he still retained a large and vocal following, especially in the upper reaches of theatres. But increasing age, a sameness in repertory, as well as new faces and newer styles of performing also militated against the actor. Loss of favor embittered Forrest, but he continued to play until shortly before his death. William *Winter called Forrest a "vast animal, bewildered by a grain of genius," who was personally an "utterly selfish" man. But while he was reluctant to "canonize" Forrest, Winter concluded, "As an actor Forrest, at his best, was remarkable for iron repose, perfect precision of method, immense physical force, capacity for leonine banter, fiery ferocity and occasional felicity of elocution." Biography: *Edwin Forrest: First Star of the American Stage*, Richard Moody, 1960.

FORREST, George. See Wright, Robert.

FORREST, Sam (1870–1944), director. Born in Richmond, Virginia, he made his debut as an actor but soon turned to directing. His first Broadway assignment was staging *Springtime* (1909), then he caught the attention of George M. *Cohan and Sam *Harris, for whom he co-directed his first major hit, *Get-Rich-Quick Wallingford* (1910). Over the next thirty years he staged approximately one hundred plays, mainly for Cohan and Harris. Among his notable successes were *Officer 666* (1912), *Seven Keys to Baldpate* (1913), *On Trial* (1914), The *Great Lover* (1915), A *Tailor Made Man* (1917), *Three Faces East* (1918), *Six-Cylinder Love* (1921), The *Hero* (1921), *Icebound* (1923), *Cradle Snatchers* (1925), and *Baby Cyclone* (1927). His final assignment was Cohan's *The Return of the Vagabond* (1940).

FORSYTHE, Henderson (b. 1917), actor. He was born in Macon, Missouri, and educated at Culver-Stockton College and the University of Iowa before beginning his acting career in stock in 1940. A durable stage actor with a wide range, Forsythe appeared in dozens of regional theatre productions before making his Broadway debut in 1957 and then worked in New York another twenty years before he received wide recognition as Sheriff Dodd in *The *Best Little Whorehouse in Texas* (1978). He often played featured or supporting characters, replaced stars in leading parts, and essayed leads in modern classics Off Broadway.

FORTUNE HUNTER, THE (1909), a comedy by Winchell *Smith. [Gaiety Theatre, 345 perf.] Spoiled as a youth by a rich father who eventually died penniless, Nat Duncan (John *Barrymore) is at a loss to provide himself with champagne and lobster. His friend Henry Kellogg (Hale Hamilton) suggests the best way is to marry a rich girl and that the best place to find one is a small town. The two friends bet on the outcome, then Nat selects a particular village and picks as his objective the banker's daughter, Josie Lockwood (Edna Bruna). Taking a job as a drug store clerk, Nat finds himself falling in love instead with the druggist's daughter, Betty Graham (Mary Ryan). He decides Betty means more to him than champagne and lobster. This fresh, wholesome comedy, produced by George M. *Cohan and Sam *Harris, gave a major boost to Barrymore's career. A musical version called *The City Chap* (1925) failed to run.

FORTUNE TELLER, THE (1898), a comic opera by Harry B. *Smith (book, lyrics), Victor *Herbert (music). [*Wallack's Theatre, 40 perf.] Irma (Alice *Nielsen), an heiress studying ballet in Budapest, is in love with the handsome hussar, Ladislas (Frank Rushworth), but is being pressed to marry Count Berezowski (Joseph *Herbert). She is able to discourage the Count by having the fiery gypsy fortune teller Musette (also Nielsen) take her place for a while. This creates problems for Musette and her gypsy lover Sandor (Eugene *Cowles), but matters are eventually resolved happily. *Notable songs*: Always Do as People Say You Should; Gypsy Love Song; Only in the Play; Romany Life. Written as a vehicle for Nielsen, the musical had a short Broadway run mainly because it had been booked for an entire season on the road before it opened. The score was Herbert's finest up to that time and established him as the leading American composer of operetta. Revivals were frequent until the early 1930s.

FORTY-FIVE MINUTES FROM BROADWAY (1906), a play with music by George M. *Cohan. [*New Amsterdam Theatre, 90 perf.] When Tom Bennett (Donald *Brian) learns he is the sole heir of his uncle, who died in New Rochelle apparently without leaving a will, he announces he will marry the actress Flora Dora Dean (Lois Ewell). The townsfolk had hoped the uncle would leave his money to his loyal maid Mary (Fay *Templeton). Dan Cronin (James H. Manning) had courted Mary in hopes of getting his hands on the money. Tom's wise-guy secretary, Kid Burns (Victor *Moore), falls in love with Mary and finds the will, which in fact leaves the estate to her. But Mary fears Kid might also be a fortune hunter. Realizing this, Kid tears up the will, and Mary agrees to marry him. Cronin is exposed as a crook and Flora Dora and her mother as little more than accomplices. Tom is left with the money but no sweetheart. *Notable songs*: Forty-five Minutes from Broadway; Mary's a Grand Old Name; So Long, Mary; I Want to Be a Popular Millionaire. Not truly a musical comedy (there were only five songs with none in the second act), the play remains one of Cohan's best and is still revived on occasion. The *Klaw and *Erlanger production helped establish Moore as a star comic, and he reprised the role of Kid in Cohan's sequel *The Talk of New York* (1907).

42ND STREET (1980), a musical comedy by Michael *Stewart, Mark Bramble (book), Harry Warren (music), Al Dubin (lyrics). [*Winter Garden Theatre, 3,486 perf.; Tony Award.] Julian March (Jerry *Orbach), the harassed, sardonic director of a new musical, is having no end of trouble with his impossibly difficult leading lady, Dorothy Brock (Tammy *Grimes). When Dorothy breaks her ankle he pushes young, aspiring Peggy Sawyer (Wanda Richert) into the lead and she becomes a star overnight. *Notable songs*: About a Quarter to Nine; 42nd Street; Lullaby of Broadway; Shuffle Off to Buffalo; You're Getting to Be a Habit with Me. Reversing the usual trend, this lavish David *Merrick production was the first hit show to be made from a movie musical. The plot came from the landmark 1933 film with Warren-Dubin songs from other movie musicals added to fill out the score. To a public satiated with socially significant musicals, its harmless story, melodic songs, and colorful sets and costumes proved a tonic, although its biggest attraction was unquestionably the huge, happy tap routines devised by director-choreographer Gower *Champion, who died the day of the opening. A 2001 Broadway revival was less elaborate but popular all the same.

42ND STREET REDEVELOPMENT. The center of the American theatre during the 1920s was the block of 42nd Street between Eighth Avenue and

Broadway, where several legit houses were located. But during the Depression most were switched over to movie houses, the elaborate interiors covered up, and the boxes torn out. Burlesque houses proliferated until Mayor LaGuardia stepped in; but by outlawing burlesque, some theatres became grind movie houses (the pornography theatres of the 1940s), and 42nd Street began a long period of decline. It reached a low point by the late 1960s with only blue movies in each house, and the street itself was the recognized capital for drugs, hustlers, pickpockets, and prostitutes. The opening of the new Port Authority Bus Terminal at Eighth Avenue and 42nd Street added vagrants and homeless to the thoroughfare. Plans to redevelop the area began in the 1980s. Sponsored by Mayor Koch's administration, a Times Square Redevelopment Plan and a 42nd Street Redevelopment Plan were outlined. But the organizations were thwarted by corrupt officials (several of the top individuals were indicted), and the whole project, which existed only on paper, was highly criticized. It was not until the mid-1990s that hopes to save 42nd Street were raised by the *Disney company's interest in restoring the *New Amsterdam Theatre, once the home of *Ziegfeld's spectacles of the 1910s and 1920s. With advantageous tax breaks and help from the city, Disney made the old theatre the scene of Broadway's hottest ticket, The *Lion King (1997). The Ford company followed suit, and soon after the New Amsterdam opened, the new *Ford Center for the Performing Arts (created from the old Apollo and Lyric theatres) joined, followed by the New Victory, the *American Airlines Theatre, and others. Other restored houses became cinema centers, and such tourist attractions as restaurants, nightclubs, and a wax museum made the old stretch of 42nd Street a safe and successful entertainment thoroughfare once again. Some have complained about the mall-like feeling of the street today, others admitting that they miss the seedy aspects of the past. But the redevelopment of 42nd Street has been one of the city's most interesting success stories.

47 WORKSHOP (Cambridge, Massachusetts). An outgrowth of Professor George Pierce *Baker's course at Harvard in playwriting (the course was listed as English 47), it offered his students a chance to produce their plays, although without academic credit. The course had been started in 1905 and the workshop in 1913. Among the many aspiring playwrights who profited from the workshop were George *Abbott, Philip *Barry, S. N. *Behrman, Sidney *Howard, and Eugene *O'Neill. Other later important theatrical figures also enrolled, including critic John Mason *Brown, executive Theresa

*Helburn, and designer Donald *Oenslager. The course and the workshop are generally acknowledged to have been among the most significant academic contributions to the creative commercial stage.

FOSSE. See *Dancin'*.

FOSSE, [Robert Louis] **Bob** (1927–87), choreographer and director. Born in Chicago, he began dancing professionally at the age of fourteen and later appeared in the choruses of several Broadway musicals before choreographing The *Pajama Game (1954). Fosse was immediately recognized as a fresh, imaginative talent, whose style leaned heavily on clever, angular groupings and showed a marked debt to urban street dancing. He later did the dances for, among others, *Damn Yankees (1955), *New Girl in Town (1957), *How to Succeed in Business without Really Trying (1961), and Little Me (1962). Fosse served as both director and choreographer for *Redhead (1959), *Sweet Charity (1966), *Pippin (1972), *Chicago (1977), *Dancin' (1978), and Big Deal (1986). He sometimes returned to performing, as when he played the title role in a 1963 *City Center revival of *Pal Joey. The dance musical Fosse (1999) was a compilation of his work re-created by others after his death. Biography: All His Jazz: The Life and Death of Bob Fosse, Martin Gottfried, 1990.

FOSTER, Frances [neé Frances Helen Brown] (1924–97), actress. Foster was a versatile African-American performer who was also a founding member of the *Negro Ensemble Company, where she gave some of her finest performances. She was born in Yonkers, New York, and trained with the *American Theatre Wing before making her Manhattan debut in 1955. Three years later Foster was on Broadway replacing actresses in supporting roles while she played major ones Off Broadway. She was most effective as sassy, outspoken types, frail victims, and wise grandmothers. Among her many notable performances were the Barbados slave Tituba in The *Crucible (1958), the crusty grandmother in The *River Niger (1973), the reflective Gremmar in The First Breeze of Summer (1975), and the Harlem derelict Henrietta (1985).

FOSTER, Gloria (b. 1936), actress. A revered African-American performer, Foster more often than not played classical roles that were rarely performed by blacks in her day. She was born in Chicago, educated at Illinois State University, and trained at the *Goodman Theatre, eventually performing major roles there. Foster made her New York debut Off Broadway in 1963 and was soon playing Medea, Yerma, Madame Ranevskaya, and other classical heroines. She eventually acted in classic revivals that were cast with African Americans, bringing new nuances to her portrayals of Clytemnestra in *Agamemnon* (1977), Volumnia in *Coriolanus* (1979), *Mother Courage* (1980), and Mary Tyrone in *Long Day's Journey into Night* (1981). Foster's most cherished contemporary role was the aged but spry Sadie Delaney in *Having Our Say* (1995).

FOURPOSTER, THE (1951), a play by Jan de Hartog. [*Ethel Barrymore Theatre, 632 perf.; Tony Award.] The warm comedy-drama follows the marriage of Michael (Hume *Cronyn) and Agnes (Jessica *Tandy) from their wedding night in 1890 to the day in 1925 when they move out of the house and leave their four-poster bed behind. Some critics carped about the two-character script's sentimentality, but audiences made the *Playwrights' Company production the longest-running play of the season. A musical version titled *I DO! I DO!* opened at the 46th Street Theatre in 1966, and with Broadway favorites Mary *Martin and Robert *Preston playing Agnes and Michael, the show ran 560 performances. Tom *Jones and Harvey *Schmidt wrote the felicitous score. *Notable songs*: My Cup Runneth Over; Nobody's Perfect; I Love My Wife; What Is a Woman?

FOX, Della [May] (1871–1913), singer and actress. Born in St. Louis, the round-faced, snub-nosed, tiny blonde beauty made her acting debut in the chorus of one of the numerous all-children-cast versions of *H. M. S. Pinafore* in 1879. She spent many seasons with the Bennett and Moulton Opera Company before being cast as the soubrette Blanche opposite De Wolf *Hopper in *Castles in the Air* (1890), then enjoyed her greatest success in the trouser role of the Siamese prince Mataya, again opposite Hopper, in *Wang* (1891). After a final appearance as Hopper's leading lady in *Panjandrum* (1893), she received star billing in the musicals *The Little Trooper* (1894) and *Fleur-de-Lis* (1895). In 1897 Fox co-starred with Lillian *Russell and Jefferson *De Angelis in *The Wedding Day*. She was appearing in *The Little Host* (1899) when illness forced her to retire temporarily. On her return she played mostly vaudeville engagements, although she also performed in *The Rogers Brothers in Central Park* (1900), *The West Point Cadet* (1904), and, shortly before her death, in one play revival, *Rosedale* (1913). Many critics professed to be baffled by her popularity, seeing her as possessing little real talent and attributing her popularity simply to "magnetism." Nevertheless, for about a decade she remained one of the principal attractions of our musical theatre.

FOX, Frederick (1910–91), designer. Born in New York and educated at Yale and the National Academy of Design, he spent an apprenticeship at the Ivoryton, Connecticut, summer theatre before creating the Broadway sets for *Farewell Summer* (1937). Between then and the mid-1960s he created the sets, and occasionally the lighting, for nearly one hundred shows, including *Johnny Belinda* (1940), *Junior Miss* (1941), The *Doughgirls* (1942), The *Two Mrs. Carrolls* (1943), *Anna Lucasta* (1944), *Dear Ruth* (1944), *Make Mine Manhattan* (1948), *Light Up the Sky* (1948), and The *Seven Year Itch* (1952).

FOX, G[eorge Washington] L[afayette] (1825–77), actor and manager. The greatest American exponent of classical pantomime and often called the first "star" of the American musical theatre, he was born in Boston into a family of "actors of a mediocre kind such as used to delight rural New England audiences but rarely appeared before city theatre-goers." He did play Boston, however, at the age of seven, appearing in *The Hunter of the Alps* but did not make his New York debut until 1850, when he joined the company of the National Theatre, using the name Lafayette Fox. He remained there for several seasons, playing a large variety of roles and is generally credited with persuading the company to mount *Uncle Tom's Cabin*, the theatre's greatest success. He later moved to the *Bowery Theatre, where as manager he regularly inserted pantomimes into the bill. His greatest success came, after he moved to the Olympic Theatre, as *Humpty Dumpty* (1868), which he wrote, possibly in collaboration with his brother Charles, and which established a long-run record for the day. This was followed by other pantomimes and burlesques: *Hiccory Diccory Dock* (1869), *Hamlet* (1870), *Macbeth* (1870), and *Wee Willie Winkie* (1870). Afterwards, he continued to play for several seasons in various versions of *Humpty Dumpty* until increasingly erratic behavior (he once ran into the auditorium and attacked members of the audience without provocation) forced his removal from the stage. He died a short time later, apparently of paresis. Fox was a small, lean man with sharp darting eyes and pointed features that reflected his name. At the height of his popularity he was the highest-paid entertainer in America, with a yearly income that exceeded $20,000.

FOY, Eddie [né Edwin Fitzgerald] (1856–1928), comic actor. Described by Stanley *Green as a "Puckish comic with pointed nose and wide V-shaped mouth, noted for his slurred way of speaking and his acrobatic dancing," he began his career in vaudeville in 1869 and later toured Western mining towns with a minstrel troupe before settling in Chicago, where he clowned in such musicals as *The Crystal Slipper* (1888), *Bluebeard, Jr.* (1890), *Sinbad the Sailor* (1891), *Ali Baba* (1892), and *Little Robinson Crusoe* (1893). In 1894 Foy toured in *Off the Earth*, then played in *Hotel Topsy Turvey* (1898), *An Arabian Girl and Forty Thieves* (1899), *The Strollers* (1901), and *The Wild Rose* (1902). By 1903 he was a popular star when he appeared as Sister Anne in *Mr. Bluebeard,* one of the high points in the show being his routine with a stubborn bustle that determined to go its own way. But the humor turned to tragedy when he was performing the show at Chicago's Iroquois Theatre at the matinee at which the worst fire in American theatre history occurred. More starring roles followed in *Piff! Paff!! Pouf!!!* (1904), *The Earl and the Girl* (1905), *The Orchid* (1907), *Mr. Hamlet of Broadway* (1908), *Up and Down Broadway* (1910), and *Over the River* (1912). Between engagements he regularly played in vaudeville and in 1910 first brought his children into the act. Eddie Foy and the Seven Little Foys rapidly became one of the most popular two-a-day turns, so after 1912 Foy abandoned musical comedy. After World War I, as the children grew older, the act was disbanded, and Foy toured alone. Autobiography: *Clowning through Life*, with Alvin F. Harlow, 1928.

FOY, Eddie, Jr. [né Edwin Fitzgerald Jr.] (1905–83), comic actor. The son of the famous older comedian was born in New Rochelle, New York, and while still a child made his debut in his father's famous vaudeville act, Eddie Foy and the Seven Little Foys. Among his early Broadway appearances were *Show Girl* (1929), *Ripples* (1930), *Smiles* (1930), *The *Cat & the Fiddle* (1931), and *At Home Abroad* (1935). However, he is best recalled for his starring roles in a 1945 revival of *The *Red Mill* and in *The *Pajama Game* (1954), as well as for playing the comic lead in the tour of *High Button Shoes*. His last New York appearance was in *Donnybrook* (1961).

FRANCESCA DA RIMINI (1855), a tragedy by George H. *Boker. [*Broadway Theatre, 8 perf.] In hopes of putting an end to the long feud between Guelfs and Ghibellines, Lanciotto (E. L. *Davenport) of Rimini is engaged to Francesca (Elizabeth *Ponisi) of Ravenna. Lanciotto is a spindly hunchback whose brother Paolo (Mr. Lanergan) has often had to defend him from cruel jibes. The brothers love each other, so Lanciotto asks Paolo to go to Ravenna to bring back the bride. Paolo and Francesca fall in love, but at first both attempt to constrain themselves. The sight of Lanciotto, however, drives Francesca into the handsome Paolo's arms. When the vicious jester, Pepe (Charles *Fisher), reports the rendezvous to Lanciotto, Lanciotto kills him. In a jealous fury he rushes to find Paolo and Francesca in an embrace.

He kills them, too, then stabs himself. Derived from an incident in Dante, the drama was only moderately successful at first. Fine revivals by Lawrence *Barrett in 1882 and Otis *Skinner in 1901 led to a further appreciation of its merits. Boker's modern biographer, Professor Sculley Bradley, has written in *Literary History of the United States*, "In Francesca da Rimini . . . Boker found his masterpiece. Of seven plays on this theme in four languages, his is the only one to conceive the pathos of the deformed husband, Lanciotto, without sacrificing the enduring appeal of the young lovers, Paolo and Francesca, and to recognize that callous society, not fate, was the agent of the tragedy. . . . With this play, romantic tragedy in America achieved the dignity of art."

FRANCIS, Arlene [neé Arlene Kazanjian] (1908–2001), actress. She was born in Boston and was playing supporting roles on Broadway by 1935, most notably in productions of Orson *Welles's *Mercury Theatre. Francis gained recognition in 1942 for her Russian sniper Natalia in the comedy *The *Doughgirls*, followed by noteworthy performances as the married "Nifty" Overton who set out to have a fling in *The Overtons* (1945), Dolly Fabian rekindling an old romance in *Once More with Feeling* (1958), and the outspoken Carlotta Vance in the 1966 revival of *Dinner at Eight*. But Francis's fame rested on her many television appearances in game shows, talk programs, and original dramas.

FRANKEN, Rose. See *Another Language*.

FRANKIE AND JOHNNY IN THE CLAIRE DE LUNE (1987), a play by Terrence *McNally. [*City Center, 533 perf.] Frumpy waitress Frankie (Kathy Bates) and pudgy short-order cook Johnny (Kenneth Welsh) work in the same Manhattan restaurant and, after knowing each other a few weeks, go on a first date, which ends with their lovemaking in her apartment. During the post-coital evening that follows, Frankie's bruised and disappointing life is revealed as she resists and finally succumbs to Johnny's wish for more than a one-night stand. The two-character piece, presented by the *Manhattan Theatre Club, was greeted by the press as a "romantic, ribald comedy" and a "richly warm, humorous, clear-eyed" play. It was revived with success on Broadway in 2002 with television stars Edie Falco and Stanley Tucci.

FRANZ, Elizabeth (b. 1941), actress. Born in Akron, Ohio, Franz studied at the *American Academy of Dramatic Arts before making her Off-Broadway debut in 1965. Although she was featured both on and Off Broadway, Franz was not lauded until her smiling, deadly nun in *Sister Mary Ignatius Explains It All for You* (1981), followed by such estimable performances as the Brooklyn mother Kate in *Brighton Beach Memoirs* (1983) and *Broadway Bound* (1987), the reticent widow Ida in *The Cemetery Club* (1990), the concerned Irish aunt Kate in *The Cripple of Inishmaan* (1998), the steadfast wife Linda in *Death of a Salesman* (1999), and the quarreling spinster Ari in *Morning's at Seven* (2002).

FRAZEE, H[arry] H[erbert] (1880–1929), producer. Beginning his career in his hometown of Peoria, Illinois, at the age of sixteen as a theatre usher, he quickly rose to be treasurer of the theatre and soon became an advance man for traveling shows. In 1902 Frazee produced his first play, *Uncle Josh Perkins*, which toured successfully but never reached New York. His later productions included *Madame Sherry* (1910), *Ready Money* (1912), A *Pair of Sixes* (1914), *A Full House* (1915), *Nothing But the Truth* (1916), *Dulcy* (1921), and *No, No, Nanette* (1925), his biggest success. Frazee was also a major figure in the sports world, and it was as owner of the Boston Red Sox that he sold Babe Ruth to the New York Yankees.

FREEDLEY, George [Reynolds] (1904–67), author. Born in Richmond, Virginia, he attended Yale, where he enrolled in Professor George P. *Baker's Workshop, then began his career as an actor and technical director with the *Theatre Guild. In 1931 he joined the New York Public Library and shortly thereafter established its theatre collection, becoming its first curator in 1938. Freedley also served as secretary to the *New York Drama Critics Circle and, for a time, as drama critic of the *Morning Telegraph*. He lectured and wrote books and articles on the theatre, including many entries for *The Oxford Companion to the Theatre*.

FREEDLEY, Vinton (1891–1969), producer. Born in Philadelphia and educated at Harvard and the University of Pennsylvania, he began his theatrical career as an actor, appearing in such diverse entertainments as the musical comedy *For Goodness' Sake* (1922) and the expressionist drama *The World We Live In* (1922). In 1923 he joined forces with Alex A. *Aarons, and for the next ten years the team produced some of Broadway's most interesting musicals, including *Lady, Be Good!* (1924), *Tip-Toes* (1925), *Oh, Kay!* (1926), *Funny Face* (1927), *Hold Everything!* (1928), and *Girl Crazy* (1930). The men also built the Alvin Theatre, deriving its name from the first syllables of theirs. With the coming of the Depression they lost the theatre and dissolved their partnership. Freedley continued to produce alone, his more successful or memorable offerings being

Anything Goes (1934), *Red, Hot and Blue!* (1936), *Leave It to Me!* (1938), *Cabin in the Sky* (1940), and *Let's Face It!* (1941). At various times he also served as president of the *Actors' Fund of America, the *American National Theatre and Academy, and the Episcopal Actors' Guild and held important positions with the *American Theatre Wing and the Council of Living Theatre.

FREEMAN, Max (d. 1912), actor, playwright, and director. Beginning his theatrical career in his native Germany, he made his American debut at New York's German-language Germania Theatre in 1873. After spending some time at the *California Theatre in San Francisco and touring with the Emily *Melville Light Opera Company, Freeman first appeared in New York in an English-speaking role in *Divorçons* (1882), playing the small part of Joseph. By that time his English was sufficiently fluent to allow him to adapt plays and direct, all the while continuing to act. He was lauded in a variety of plays, from the melodrama *Siberia* (1883) and the comedy *The *Rajah* (1883) to later comedies such as *Over Night* (1911). Similarly, his adaptations ranged from the opéra bouffe *Orpheus and Eurydice* (1893) to the melodrama *Claudius Nero* (1890). For many years Freeman was Rudolph *Aronson's director at the *Casino Theatre, staging, among many others, the 1890 revival for Lillian *Russell of *The *Grand Duchess* and Reginald *De Koven's *The Fencing Master* (1892). After leaving the Casino he continued to direct until shortly before his death, working primarily with musicals.

FREEMAN, Morgan (b. 1937), actor. The commanding yet gentle African-American leading man has given some distinguished stage performances in Manhattan before and after he found fame in the movies. He was born in Memphis, Tennessee, and after serving in the Air Force took classes at Los Angeles City College. Freeman made his New York debut in 1967 in the Pearl *Bailey version of *Hello, Dolly!* and went on to play a variety of characters, such as the alcoholic ex-gang member Zeke in *The Mighty Gents* (1978), the ragged prospector Winston in *White Pelicans* (1978), a regal *Coriolanus* (1979), the quiet but influential chauffeur Hoke in *Driving Miss Daisy* (1987), and a raucous Petruchio in *The *Taming of the Shrew* (1990).

FRENCH, Arthur (b. 1942?), actor. The deep-voiced, gentlemanly African-American performer, who speaks with refined clarity and authority, has been appearing regularly on and Off Broadway for forty years. A native New Yorker who was educated at Brooklyn College, French made his Manhattan debut in 1962 and was an original cast member of the legendary black comedy *Day of Absence* in 1965. Over the decades he has played leading and supporting roles in new works about African Americans, such as *A *Soldier's Play* (1982) and **Joe Turner's Come & Gone* (1996), and in the classics, such as his Kreon in **Medea* (2002) and his **King Lear* (2002).

FRENCH, Samuel. See Samuel French, Inc.

FRESH, THE AMERICAN (1881), a play by A. C. *Gunter. [*Park Theatre, 63 perf.] Ferdinand Nervy Fresh (J. T. *Raymond) is a brash, somewhat uncouth but likable Yankee. His attempts to corner the market on Wall Street and other grandiose schemes have failed, but he has always found simple, practical ways of extricating himself from the trouble and of rationalizing his failures. Fresh's wanderlust takes him to Egypt, where he falls in love with a harem beauty, Erema Almi (Laura Don). Despite the machinations of the Egyptians, he manages to marry the girl, remove her from the harem, and escape the dire revenge the locals plan for the couple. Written by Gunter at Raymond's request, this loosely contrived farce provided the actor with a major hit for two years, and he returned to it occasionally later in his career. Next to Colonel Sellers, it was considered his best role. Harry B. *Smith recalled a different origin for the play, stating that it was first mounted at *McVicker's Theatre in Chicago as a serious piece but that the audience laughed so much at its patent absurdities that Don, McVicker's leading lady, persuaded the producer to play it as comedy.

FRIARS. See Theatrical Clubs.

FRIEDMAN, Bruce Jay. See *Scuba Duba*.

FRIENDLY ENEMIES (1918), a comedy drama by Samuel *Shipman and Aaron *Hoffman. [*Hudson Theatre, 440 perf.] Henry Block (Sam *Bernard) and Karl Pfeifer (Louis *Mann) are German-born Americans who have been lifelong friends. When World War I breaks out in Europe, however, their friendship is sorely tested, for Block is totally American in his outlook, while Pfeifer retains strong loyalties toward the fatherland. To Pfeifer's horror, his son William (Richard Barbee) leaves college and enlists in the American army. Pfeifer's wife, Marie (Mathilde *Cottrelly), is caught in the verbal crossfire. When William is lost in a troop-ship sinking, Block proves a loyal and compassionate friend. Their animosities are put aside, and the men agree to work towards peace in the world. At a time of raging hatred, this plea for tolerance of divergent views in war became the biggest hit of its season.

John Corbin wrote in the *Times*, "As dramatic literature the play may, perhaps, not win any high rank. . . . But it has the rarer virtues of broaching a new, vital, and timely subject . . . in a spirit that is wholesome and invigorating. Among the many plays touching upon our part in the war it stands quite alone."

FRIGANZA, Trixie [née Delia O'Callahan] (1870–1955), comedienne. Born in Grenola, Kansas, the large, bouncy performer made her stage debut in 1889 in *The Pearl of Pekin*. Thereafter, she appeared in numerous musicals, including *The Orchid* (1907), *The *Passing Show of 1912*, and *Canary Cottage* (1917), but won her greatest celebrity as a vaudeville comedienne. Hers was a jolly, clean act in which she had fun kidding her own figure, describing herself as "a perfect forty-six." She added to her girth by coming on stage wearing several costumes, one under the other, and in effect doing a chaste striptease as she discarded each outer garment in turn. She was often billed as "Broadway's Favorite Champagne Girl."

FRIML, [Charles] Rudolf (1879–1972), composer. Born in Bohemia into a poor but musical family, he displayed remarkable abilities so early that his neighbors took up a collection to send him to the Prague Conservatory. While there, he eventually won a scholarship and studied with Antonin Dvorák. After graduating he began to compose but, in order to support himself, accepted a position as violinist Jan Kubelik's accompanist. Friml made two trips to America with Kubelik, on the second journey electing to remain permanently. Here he continued to give concerts and write light compositions. His chance came when Victor *Herbert refused to create a second score for Emma *Trentini after fighting with her over *Naughty Marietta. Friml's score for the Trentini vehicle, *The *Firefly* (1912), established Friml immediately in the front rank of composers, and he followed it with *High Jinks* (1913) and **Katinka* (1915). Several subsequent operettas were less successful, so Friml tried his hand at musical comedies. Some of these enjoyed profitable runs but left behind nothing memorable. In 1924 he returned to operetta and wrote his greatest success, **Rose-Marie*, the most popular operetta of the 1920s. Two operetta hits followed: *The *Vagabond King* (1925) and *The *Three Musketeers* (1928). Friml's principal competitor during the 1920s was Sigmund *Romberg. Although Friml's music was generally perceived to have more melodic originality and fervor, it was Romberg who proved more pliable when musical tastes changed in the 1930s. Friml wrote only two short-lived operettas at the time, *Luana* (1930) and *Music Hath Charms* (1934), then retired.

FRINGS, Ketti. See *Look Homeward, Angel*.

FRITZ, OUR COUSIN GERMAN (1870), a play by Charles *Gayler. [*Wallack's Theatre, 63 perf.] Fritz (J. K. *Emmet) arrives in America to seek both his long-lost sister and money his father left with the girl. On shipboard he has fallen in love with another immigrant, Katarina (Georgia Langley), but his courtship is cut short temporarily when the villainous Colonel Crafton (Charles *Fisher) kidnaps Katarina. Fritz rescues her and later finds his sister has been adopted by Crafton. Fritz's singing of an old family lullaby brings about recognition and reunion. Fritz and Katarina marry, and before long they have a child. But they have not heard the last of Crafton. He now kidnaps Little Fritz (Minnie Maddern, later Mrs. *Fiske), so Fritz must once more come to the rescue. This time he kills Crafton. *Notable songs*: Emmet's Lullaby (added some years later); Oh, Schneider, How You Vas?; Valking Dat Broadway Down. Written expressly for Emmet's manifold talents, it provided a vehicle for him for the rest of his life. Sequels telling basically the same story included *Carl, the Fiddler* (1871) and *Max, the Merry Swiss Boy* (1873), but these were less successful, as were attempts by his son and others to assume the role of Fritz after Emmet's death.

FROHMAN, Charles (1860–1915), producer. The youngest of three brothers who made names for themselves in the theatrical arena, he was born in Sandusky, Ohio, the son of an itinerant peddler. At the age of twelve he came to New York and took work first with the *Tribune* and later with the *Daily Graphic*. But having long loved theatre, Frohman took an evening job selling tickets at Hooley's Theatre in Brooklyn. By 1877 he was serving as advance agent for traveling shows, including Haverly's Minstrels. Steele *MacKaye invited Charles and his brothers, Gustave and Daniel *Frohman, to help manage the *Madison Square Theatre, and in sending out complete duplicate road companies of the theatre's hits they are credited with inaugurating a policy that was to change the nature of provincial theatre. In 1888 he was an agent for Bronson *Howard, whose play *Shenandoah* had been mounted with only small success at the *Boston Museum. Frohman, nevertheless, saw possibilities in it and remounted and produced it the following year in New York, where it was an immediate success and launched Frohman's producing career. In 1890 he took over Proctor's Theatre and organized a stock company there and later moved it to the *Empire Theatre, which he built with Al *Hayman in 1893. Two years later Frohman met secretly with Hayman, Abe *Erlanger, Mark *Klaw, and several other men to organize what became known as the *Theatrical Syndicate, or Trust. Ostensibly the group's aim was to bring order out of chaos in cross-country bookings, but it soon controlled all the important theatres in the country and demanded exorbitant fees from producers and performers. Failure to meet its demands often meant a show could not play in a major city. Frohman's precise role in the organization has remained a matter of dispute. His supporters have claimed that he was the idealist in the group, looking the other way at its shady practices because he felt more benefits than harm came from its methods. Others have seen him as manipulating as Erlanger and company. Most likely the truth lies somewhere in between. But the certainty of comfortable bookings allowed him to work with ease, develop a roster of great stars, and present a steady stream of popular plays. Among the many stars who played for years under Frohman's auspices were John *Drew, Ethel *Barrymore, Maude *Adams, and Billie *Burke. He was particularly adept at taking relatively unknown actresses and, with his careful nurturing, make them stellar attractions. Detractors have suggested that, as a result of his emphasis on stars, Frohman cared little about the value of his plays, ignoring promising American playwrights and preferring to buy up wholesale the rights to tested European works. Yet he was responsible for the American premieres of many works by such significant and durable playwrights as Oscar *Wilde, Sir James *Barrie, Arthur Wing Pinero, Somerset *Maugham, and Georges Feydeau. Nor did he totally neglect the best American talent, producing several of Clyde *Fitch's plays. Moreover, he promoted an international respect for rising American playwrights by presenting their works abroad even when he had not produced the original New York mountings. Frohman was at the height of his career when he died in the sinking of the *Lusitania*. He has been described as a "little, round, slant-eyed Buddha." Biography: *Charles Frohman: Manager and Man*, Isaac F. Marcosson and Daniel Frohman, 1916.

FROHMAN, Daniel (1851–1940), producer. Like his younger brother, Charles *Frohman, he was born in Sandusky, Ohio, and came to New York, where he served in various capacities on several newspapers, including the *Tribune*, the *Standard*, and the *Daily Graphic*, before becoming an advance man for the Georgia Minstrels from 1874 to 1879. With Charles and his other brother, Gustave, he then helped manage Steele *MacKaye's *Madison Square Theatre, also assisting in sending out road companies of the theatre's hits. In 1885 he took over the old *Lyceum Theatre and opened it with *In Spite of All*. Employing an excellent stock company that he developed there, Frohman quickly mounted such successes as *The Highest Bidder* (1887), *The *Wife* (1887), *Lord Chumley* (1888), and *The *Charity Ball* (1889). The performances of E. H. *Sothern in two of these helped start that actor on his career as a major figure. An important later success was *The *Prisoner of Zenda* (1895). He also produced several plays by Henry Arthur *Jones and Arthur Wing Pinero, offering the American premieres of such plays as *The Case of Rebellious Susan* (1894) and *Trelawny of the Wells* (1898). For a time in 1899, after Daly's death, he managed Daly's Theatre. After the Lyceum was demolished in 1902, he built a new (and current) Lyceum a year later. With time he gradually abandoned producing but remained active in theatrical affairs. From 1904 until his death he served as president of the *Actors' Fund of America. He found time as well to write several books, including two volumes of reminiscences, *Memories of a Manager* (1911) and *Daniel Frohman Presents* (1935), and a collection of essays on theatrical history, *Encore* (1937). Unlike his squat, clean-shaven brother Charles, he was a wiry, balding man with a closely cropped beard and moustache.

FRONT PAGE, THE (1928), a play by Ben *Hecht and Charles *MacArthur. [Times Square Theatre, 276 perf.] To his fellow newsmen hanging around the press room of Chicago's Criminal Court Building awaiting a murderer's execution, Hildy Johnson (Lee *Tracy) announces that he is quitting the *Herald Examiner,* getting married, and heading for New York. His plans are temporarily stymied when the murderer, Earl Williams (George Leach), escapes, and Hildy phones in a scoop to his paper. Williams suddenly appears in the press room, and Hildy and a prostitute, Molly Malloy (Dorothy Stickney), hide him in a folding desk. Hildy's dapper, devilish editor Walter Burns (Osgood *Perkins) appears, prepared to take over. Amid the mayhem that ensues it is discovered that the governor has pardoned Williams. Telling Hildy of his gratitude for the scoop, Burns presents him with a watch, apologizing for the fact that the watch has his own name engraved in it. Hildy and his fiancée head off to catch the train. But Burns really has had no intention of allowing Hildy to go. He sends a wire to the chief of police in La Porte, Indiana, telling him to arrest Hildy: "The son of a bitch stole my watch!" Alison Smith of the *World* rejoiced, " 'The Front Page,' with its rowdy virility, its swift percussion of incident, its streaks of Gargantuan derision, is as breath-taking an event as ever dropped . . . on Broadway." The play, produced by Jed *Harris, while not the first to be set in a press room, remains an exemplar of its kind and has enjoyed numerous revivals, the most notable American one in 1969

with Bert Convy as Hildy and Robert Ryan as Walter Burns. A 1986 revival at *Lincoln Center received mixed notices. It has been made into at least three films. In 2003 John *Guare rewrote the comedy as *His Girl Friday,* based on the 1940 film of the same title, and it premiered in London.

FROU-FROU (1870). Meilhac and Halévy's French play was adapted for American audiences by Augustin *Daly and first presented by him in 1870. The story tells of an irresponsible young wife who invites her staid sister to live with her and her family so that she herself can flit about the town. She loses everyone's affection and returns home to repent and to die. Agnes *Ethel was the original heroine Gilberte. The play was revived regularly until the early years of the 20th century and was one of *Bernhardt's most popular vehicles on her American tour.

FRY, Christopher [né Harris] (b. 1907), playwright. The English dramatist's attempt to restore blank-verse drama to the stage caused a flurry of interest in the 1950s. However, what success his works had in this country could be largely attributed to the allure of the stars who appeared in his plays: *The Lady's Not for Burning* (1950) with John *Gielgud and Pamela Brown; *A Sleep of Prisoners* (1951), performed in a small church without stars; *Venus Observed* (1952) with Rex *Harrison and Lilli Palmer; and *The Dark Is Light Enough* (1955) with Katharine *Cornell and Tyrone *Power. He has also provided excellent translations of two French plays: *Ring Round the Moon* (1950) and *Tiger at the Gates* (1955).

FRYER, Robert (1920–2000), producer. A native of Washington, D.C., who studied at Western Reserve University, he produced, alone or with others, such shows as *A *Tree Grows in Brooklyn* (1951), *Wonderful Town* (1953), *Auntie Mame* (1956), *Sweet Charity* (1966), *Mame* (1966), *Chicago* (1975), *California Suite* (1976), *Sweeney Todd* (1979), *Noises Off* (1983), and *Benefactors* (1985).

FUGARD, Athol (b. 1932), playwright. He was born in Middleburg, South Africa, the son of an Afrikaner mother and a father of Irish-Huguenot descent, and educated at the University of Capetown before writing plays in 1959. Fugard's first work to be produced in America was *Nongogo* (1978) at the *Manhattan Theatre Club. His other plays to be seen in New York include *The Blood Knot* (1964), *Boesman and Lena* (1970), *The Island/Sizwe Banzi Is Dead* (1974), *A Lesson from Aloes* (1980), *Master Harold . . . and the Boys* (1982), *The Road to Mecca* (1988), and *Valley Song* (1995). Most of Fugard's plays concern apartheid and how it affects both the white and black citizens of his native country, and he is known for his poetic, philosophical tone rather than angry socialistic stance.

FULLER, Charles. See *Soldiers Play, A.*

FULLER, Loie (1863–1928), actress. Born in Fullersburg, Illinois, she demonstrated her precociousness by giving temperance lectures while still a small child. From the lecture stage to the legitimate stage was a simple move, which she made still in her teens, playing in a variety of touring companies. Fuller's New York debut was in *Humbug* (1886), and thereafter she acted with Nat *Goodwin in *Little Jack Sheppard* (1886), *Turned Up* (1886), *The Skating Rink* (1887), and *The Gentlemanly Savage* (1887). Her performances won her commendatory notices, especially in the trouser title role of Sheppard. She next played Aladdin in *Arabian Nights* (1887) and Ustane in a musical dramatization of Rider Haggard's *She* (1887). While in England, she devised the skirt or serpentine dance that made her famous; in it she performed with the voluminous drapery twirling and shedding prismatic hues in the calcium light. Fuller first offered the dance in America in *Quack, M. D.* (1891) and later in *Uncle Celestin* (1892) and in *A *Trip to Chinatown* (1892). Although she appeared briefly in several other Broadway entertainments, she spent most of her remaining career in dance recitals. Autobiographies: *Fifteen Years of My Life*, 1908; *Fifteen Years of a Dancer's Life*, 1913.

FUNNY FACE (1927), a musical comedy by Fred *Thompson, Paul Gerard Smith (book), George *Gershwin (music), Ira *Gershwin (lyrics). [Alvin Theatre, 250 perf.] When the straitlaced guardian Jimmie Reeves (Fred *Astaire) refuses to allow Frankie (Adele *Astaire) to have her jewels, she arranges with her friend Peter Thurston (Allen *Kearns) to steal them. Two comic burglars, Herbert (Victor *Moore) and Dugsie (William Kent), are also after the jewels but they have a falling out, although Herbert is unable to shoot Dugsie since he has forgotten to get a shooting license. So everything ends happily, with Frankie keeping both her jewels and her man. *Notable songs*: The Babbitt and the Bromide; Funny Face; He Loves and She Loves; 'S Wonderful. Originally, the Alex A. *Aarons and Vinton *Freedley production was titled *Smarty* with a libretto by Thompson and Robert Benchley. But *Benchley bowed out when the show was drastically rewritten and renamed. Applauded by Brooks *Atkinson as "uncommonly rollicking entertainment," the musical was blessed with a rare melange of melody, comedy, and superb danc-

ing. It was in this show that Fred Astaire first danced in evening clothes and a top hat. Some of the songs (but little else) remained when a revival of the show opened at the *St. James Theatre in 1983 as *MY ONE AND ONLY* and ran a profitable 767 performances. Peter *Stone and Timothy Meyer were credited with the book that concerned a barnstorming aviator (Tommy *Tune) who romances a swimming star (Twiggy), the two of them getting mixed up with a bootlegger-turned-minister (Roscoe Lee *Browne), some Russian spies, and a tap dancing philosopher (Charles "Honi" Coles). A few Gershwin songs from other musicals were used to fill out the score, and Tune's ingenious direction and dancing turned the slight piece into a stylish art deco entertainment.

FUNNY GIRL (1964), a musical comedy by Isobel Lennart (book), Jule *Styne (music), Bob *Merrill (lyrics). [*Winter Garden Theatre, 1,348 perf.] Sitting in her *Follies* dressing room, Fanny Brice (Barbra Streisand) reminisces about her career. Her thoughts wander back to the days when she was a gawky, stage-struck young girl, to her first failure at Keeney's Music Hall, and her eventual success there. That success brings two men into her life, the great Broadway producer Florenz *Ziegfeld, who sets about making her a star, and an attractive gambler, Nicky Arnstein (Sydney Chaplin), whom she marries. Her career flourishes, although her marriage is destroyed by Arnstein's gambling and prison sentence. *Notable songs*: Don't Rain on My Parade; People; You Are Woman; His Is the Only Music That Makes Me Dance. Despite some glaring faults in the script and its lack of historical accuracy, the show was made into an electric entertainment by its young star, Streisand. Ted Kalem of *Time* welcomed her as "the theatre's new girl for all seasons" and described her as "an anthology of the awkward graces, all knees and elbows, or else a boneless wonder, a seal doing a balancing act." **Barbra STREISAND** [née Barbara] (b. 1942) was a New Yorker who had garnered attention earlier in an Off-Broadway revue, *Another Evening with Harry Stoones* (1961), and as the comic secretary Miss Marmelstein in *I Can Get It for You Wholesale* (1962). *Funny Girl* was her last Broadway appearance before she went on to become a major film and recording star.

FUNNY THING HAPPENED ON THE WAY TO THE FORUM, A (1962), a musical comedy by Burt *Shevelove, Larry *Gelbart (book), Stephen *Sondheim (music, lyrics). [Alvin Theatre, 967 perf.; Tony Award.] The Roman slave Pseudolus (Zero *Mostel) attempts to earn his freedom by procuring the sexy, but brainless, courtesan Philia (Preshy

Marker) for his young master, Hero (Brian Davies). Hero's own father, Senex (David *Burns), also has his eye on the girl, but the dashing Miles Gloriosus (Ronald Holgate) apparently has first claim, as he has purchased her from brothel owner Lycus (John Carradine). Pseudolus spreads the word that Philia has contracted the plague and died, and the mock funeral degenerates into a wild chase. When Miles learns that Philia is his sister, he gives her to Hero and Pseudolus is set free at last. *Notable songs*: Comedy Tonight; Free; Lovely; Everybody Ought to Have a Maid. Based very loosely on material in *Plautus,* the Hal *Prince–produced musical was described by Howard Taubman of the *Times* as "noisy, coarse, blue and obvious like the putty on a burlesque comedian." Other fine clowns in the cast included Jack *Gilford as the hysterical Hysterium and Raymond Walburn as the doddering Erronius. The show was the first for which Sondheim composed both lyrics and music, demonstrating from the start that, whatever his gift for melody, it was as a lyricist that he excelled. Broadway revivals in 1973 with Phil *Silvers and 1992 with Nathan *Lane as Pseudolus were both popular, and the musical remains a favorite in amateur theatres across the country.

FURNESS, Horace Howard (1833–1912), scholar. Born in Philadelphia, the son of a Unitarian minister, he attended Harvard and was admitted to the bar but devoted most of his life to the study of Shakespeare and the preparation of various editions of his works. Beginning with *Romeo and Juliet*, he edited fifteen plays, while his wife, Helen Kate Furness, compiled *A Concordance to the Poems of Shakespeare*. After his death, his son, Horace Jr. and other scholars attended to editions of the remaining plays.

FURST, William [Wallace] (1852–1917), composer and conductor. Born in Baltimore, Furst was for many years conductor of the orchestra and composer of background music at the Tivoli *Opera House in San Francisco. New York first heard his incidental music in a dramatization of Rider Haggard's *She* (1887). He moved permanently to New York in 1893 to become conductor for the orchestra at the new *Empire Theatre. For the remainder of his career he was busy conducting theatre orchestras and creating background material for such successes as *The *Conquerors* (1898), *The *Christian* (1898), *A Royal Family* (1900), and a 1916 revival of *The *Yellow Jacket*. If theatre orchestras were then commonplace for even non-musical plays, so, unfortunately, was the writing of comic operas by conductors for star-centered musicals. Furst composed the scores for Thomas *Seabrooke's *The Isle of Champagne* (1892), Lillian *Russell's *Princess Nicotine* (1893), Della Fox's *The Little Trooper* (1894), and *Fox's and Joseph *De Angelis's *Fleur-de-Lis* (1895). This practice led the *Dramatic Mirror* to complain, "It is time that orchestral leaders of the [Gustave] Kerker and Furst order should cease to figure as operatic composers." The situation was not remedied until Victor *Herbert and his later great successors appeared on the scene, by which time there was also increasingly little demand for incidental music. A dedicated amateur horticulturist, Furst died as the result of a fall sustained from tripping over a flowerpot.

FYLES, Franklin. See *Girl I Left Behind Me, The*.

G

GABEL, Martin (1912–86), character actor and producer. Born in Philadelphia and educated at Lehigh University and the *American Academy of Dramatic Arts, Gabel made his professional debut on Broadway at the age of twenty-one and was busily employed thereafter. As a member of Orson *Welles's *Mercury Theatre, he played the conspirator Cassius in the modern dress *Julius Caesar* (1937), the title revolutionary in *Danton's Death* (1938), and other roles that brought him notice. He played both comic roles and sinister characters for decades in films and on Broadway, where he also directed productions and even produced a few, most notably the long-run champ *Life with Father* (1939). But he became most famous for his many appearances on television quiz shows.

GAHAGAN, Helen [Mary] (1900–80), actress. Although best known for her later political career, Gahagan was a highly respected actress in the 1920s and early 1930s. Born in Boonton, New Jersey, and educated at Barnard College, she made her initial New York appearances in *Shoot!* (1922) and *Manhattan* (1922). Her first important assignment was as Anne Baldwin in *Dreams for Sale* (1922), followed by the avaricious secretary Paula in *Fashions for Men* (1922), flapper Jean Trowbridge in *Chains* (1923), and the title role in a 1924 revival of *Leah Kleschna*. After several failures, she scored as the schoolmaster's wife Laura Simmons in *Young Woodley* (1925), then played Rose and Countess Zicka in revivals of *Trelawny of the Wells* (1927) and *Diplomacy* (1928). Gahagan returned from a tour of Europe, where she sang in opera, to play the Prima *Donna in *Tonight or Never* (1930). Her leading man was Melvyn *Douglas, whom she married. The remainder of her theatre career was undistinguished, and her last appearance was at the *City Center as Lucy Chase Wayne in a 1952 revival of *First Lady*, but this was long after she had become famous for her espousal of liberal causes and her career as congresswoman had been destroyed by Richard M. Nixon.

GAIGE, Crosby [né Roscoe Conkling Gaige] (1882–1949), producer. Born in Skunk Hollow,

New York, and educated at Columbia, he served a brief stint on the *New York Times* before joining the famous theatrical agent Elisabeth *Marbury. Soon thereafter he became a partner with Edgar *Selwyn and Arch *Selwyn, producing with them such celebrated hits as *Within the Law* (1912) and *Why Marry?* (1917). After severing his connections with the firm, he produced on his own, among others, The *Butter & Egg Man* (1925), *The Enemy* (1925), *The Shannons of Broadway* (1927), *Little Accident* (1928), and *Accent on Youth* (1934). He occasionally directed plays and also served as vice president of the Managers Protective Association. Respected as a gourmet, he wrote several books on cooking as well as an autobiography, *Footlights and Highlights*, in 1948.

GAINES, Boyd (b. 1953), actor and singer. The boyish-looking, very physical leading man of plays and musicals has attracted attention even in minor roles. He was born in Atlanta, Georgia, and educated at Juilliard, making his Manhattan debut in 1978. Gaines' notable performances include the gay doctor Peter Petrone battling the AIDS epidemic in The *Heidi Chronicles* (1989), the maddeningly passive writer Keith in *The Extra Man* (1992), the lovesick Hungarian clerk Georg in *She Loves Me* (1993), the Manhattan bachelor Robert in *Company* (1995), and the suicidal executive Michael Wiley in *Contact* (1999).

GALATI, Frank. See *Grapes of Wrath, The*.

GALE, Zona. See *Miss Lulu Bett*.

GALLAGHER and SHEAN, comedy team. Edward Gallagher (1873?–1929) and Al Shean (1868–1949) were one of the greatest and most popular of vaudeville teams, although their career together was surprisingly short. The American-born Gallagher was relatively tall, slim, and bespectacled and sported a minimoustache, while the German-born Shean, whose real surname was Schonberg, was stockier and clean-shaven. Gallagher was a superb straight man who had spent much of his early career in partnership with Joe Barrett, generally performing comic military sketches. Shean began his career in vaudeville in 1890 as a member of the Manhattan Comedy Four. This group disbanded in 1900, after which Shean teamed with Charles L. Warren for several seasons. Gallagher and Shean joined ranks in 1910, appearing in vaudeville and in the 1912 Broadway musical *The Rose Maid*, before splitting for reasons never divulged. Both then played single turns in vaudeville, while Shean also appeared in such Broadway musicals as *The Princess Pat* (1915) and *Flo Flo* (1917). They were reunited in 1920 through the good offices of Minnie Marx, Shean's sister and mother of the *Marx brothers. Because their new act initially was called "Mr. Gallagher and Mr. Shean in Egypt," Gallagher thereafter wore a straw hat and Shean a fez. Sometime during the next year they first sang the song that helped make them famous, "Mister Gallagher and Mr. Shean," with its celebrated tagline, "Positively, Mr. Gallagher—Absolutely, Mr. Shean." The team at first claimed authorship of the song but later became entangled in litigation over it. Although Gallagher then claimed Ernest Ball assisted in the composition, the real author was apparently Bryan Foy, son of Eddie *Foy. The song was reprised when the pair appeared in the *Ziegfeld Follies of 1922*. They later continued in vaudeville and performed in the *Greenwich Village Follies of 1924*. In 1925 the team split for good. Gallagher briefly developed another vaudeville act before suffering a nervous breakdown and dying shortly thereafter. Shean continued in vaudeville, Broadway shows, and films for many years.

GALLAGHER, Helen (b. 1926), actress and singer. The energetic Gallagher never quite achieved stardom on Broadway but replaced stars in major musicals and played leads in revivals in New York and across the country. She was born in Brooklyn and studied dance at the American Ballet School before appearing in the chorus of several Broadway musicals in the 1940s. Gallagher starred as the supposedly dying *Pal Joey* (1951), then went on to give such applauded performances as the wisecracking Gladys in *Hazel Flagg* (1953), the street-smart Nicky in *Sweet Charity* (1966), the married flirt Lucille in *No No Nanette* (1971), and her uncanny impersonation of Tallulah Bankhead in two one-woman programs.

GALLAGHER, Peter (b. 1955), actor and singer. The dark, handsome leading man has mostly played sleazy phonies on screen but likable guys on stage. He was born in Armonk, New York, and started acting in Boston while attending Tufts University. Gallagher studied with Robert *Lewis at the *Actors Studio and made his Broadway debut in 1977 as a replacement for the leading role

in *Grease*. He first attracted attention as the romantic composer Otto in the short-lived musical *A Doll's House* (1982), followed by such notable performances as the Welsh youth Morgan Evans yearning for education in *The Corn Is Green* (1983); the sickly, poetic Edmund Tyrone in *Long Day's Journey into Night* (1986); the swank gambler Sky Masterson in *Guys and Dolls* (1992); and the frustrated director Lloyd Dallas in *Noises Off* (2001).

GALLEY SLAVE, THE (1879), a play by Bartley *Campbell. [Haverly's Theatre, 101 perf.] Cicely Blaine (Maude *Granger), an American girl in Europe, loves Sidney Norcott (Frank Evans) but is led to believe he has been unfaithful by the treacherous Baron Le Bois (J. J. Sullivan), who himself has wed and deserted a girl named Francesca (Emily *Rigl). When Sidney is caught visiting Cicely he pretends to be a thief rather than compromise her position, and so he is sent to prison where he meets Francesca. Cicely has learned of Sidney's whereabouts and goes to talk with him in prison. When the Baron follows her, he is confronted by Francesca and the truth is exposed, leaving Cicely and Sidney free to wed. Originally presented at Philadelphia's *Chestnut Street Theatre with a different cast except for Rigl, the play remained popular for a quarter of a century, although there is some reason to question whether it could have compiled 101 performances in a two-and-a-half-month New York run, as its advertisements and some historians have claimed.

GALLO, Paul (b. 1953), lighting designer. After studying theatre at Ithaca College and Yale, he designed lights for various regional and Off-Broadway theatres before making his Broadway debut in 1980. Since then Gallo has been one of New York's busiest designers, with dozens of credits including *The *Little Foxes* (1981), *The *Mystery of Edwin Drood* (1985), *The *House of Blue Leaves* (1986), *The *Front Page* (1987), *City of Angels* (1989), *Crazy for You* (1992), *Big* (1996), *Titanic* (1997), *On the Town* (1999), *The *Man Who Came to Dinner* (2000), *The Rocky Horror Show* (2000), and *42nd Street* (2001).

GALSWORTHY, John (1867–1933), playwright. The English novelist and dramatist was much admired for his serious examination of the inequities of contemporary life. His critical look at the British legal system, *The Silver Box* (1907), was highly praised but failed to run despite the fine acting of its star, Ethel *Barrymore. Nor did the labor troubles drama *Strife* (1909) fare any better. But Galsworthy's grim picture of prison life in *Justice* (1916) appeared at the same time that a young

Eugene *O'Neill and other American playwrights were beginning to move drama away from 19th-century artificiality, and the play was instantly recognized by more venturesome playgoers and critics as another important breakaway from fading traditions. The work's popularity was enhanced by the brilliant performance of John *Barrymore, whose stardom was then assured. Among his subsequent successes were *The Skin Game* (1920), *Loyalties* (1922), and *Escape* (1927).

GAME OF LOVE, THE (1855), a play by John *Brougham. [*Wallack's Theatre, 23 perf.] After Alice Devereux (Mrs. John *Hoey) is jilted by her betrothed, she decides to marry the first man who comes her way: the well-educated but poor Paul Weldon (Lester *Wallack). Because Alice is wealthy, Paul readily agrees, only to find that the marriage contract makes him little more than a servant. It takes all of Councillor Foxglove's (Henry *Placide) thoughtful diplomacy to make Alice and Paul realize they love each other and settle into a happy marriage. The play exemplifies the ephemeral material that producer J. W. *Wallack so skillfully mounted, along with revivals of great classics, and which helped establish his playhouse and ensemble as the greatest of its day.

GANNON, Mary (1829–68), comedienne. Born in New York, she made her debut as a child actress and dancer but shortly evolved into a brilliant comic, whose career was cut short by her early death. It is believed that Gannon made her debut around 1832, and by 1840 she was assuming all seven roles in *The Actress of All Works*, which prompted the *Spirit of the Times* to call the youngster "the genius of the dance." She spent successful seasons at the *Bowery and at William Mitchell's Olympic. "She was in those days," T. Allston *Brown recalled, "a beauty, fresh and plump, with a foot that Titania might have envied, eyes that sparkled . . . a sweet ever ready laugh, and a vivacious nature." Gannon never lost her vivacity, but her plumpness increased until before long she had a marked double chin. In 1855 she joined Lester *Wallack's company, in which she remained until her death, playing such roles as Betty in *The Clandestine Marriage*, Jenny in *The Provoked Husband*, Atalanta Cruiser in *How She Loves Him*, and Mary Netley in *Ours*. Joseph *Ireland, writing shortly before her death, declared that Gannon "is now universally acknowledged to be the best general comic actress in the city."

GARBER, Victor (b. 1949), actor. The baby-face leading man graduated from good-looking juvenile roles to sinister or stuffy characters, appear-

ing in many hits along the way. He was born in London, Canada, and acted in various regional theatres before making an impressive New York debut as the cursed son Osvald in *Ghosts* (1973). Appearing in both musicals and plays, Garber has been lauded for such performances as the mystery writer's doomed lover Clifford in *Deathtrap* (1978), the innocent sailor Anthony Hope in *Sweeney Todd* (1979), a variety of wacky caricatures in *Little Me* (1982), the obtuse leading man Garry Lejune in a provincial theatre company in *Noises Off* (1983), the would-be opera singer Max in *Lend Me a Tenor* (1989), a mesmerizing John Wilkes Booth in *Assassins* (1991), the rugged American actor Edwin *Forrest in *Two Shakespearean Actors* (1992), the gleeful devil Applegate in *Damn Yankees* (1994), the snob literary critic Benedict Nightingale in *Arcadia* (1995), and the Parisian art collector Serge in *Art* (1998).

GARDEN OF ALLAH, THE (1911), a play by Robert Hichens and Mary *Anderson. [Century Theatre, 241 perf.] At first the beautiful Domini (Mary *Mannering) sees little to admire in the boorish stranger, Boris Androvsky (Lewis Waller), who seems far more out of place than even she in the warm, romantic, and exotic desert lands. But with time she falls in love and marries him. Only then does she discover he is a runaway monk. He eventually returns to his monastery, and she is left to raise their child alone. Anderson was lured out of retirement by George *Tyler to assist the English author Hichens (1864–1950) in dramatizing his novel. *Liebler and Co. produced his tale of Christian love set against the lush backgrounds of Islam and gave it one of the most elaborate and gorgeous spectacles ever mounted on Broadway. It was a type of play and production Hollywood was soon to usurp.

GARDENIA, Vincent [né Vincente Scognamiglio] (1922–92), character actor. Gardenia was a jowly comic player who excelled in ethnic types, particularly hassled husbands, fathers, and businessmen. He was born in Naples, Italy, but grew up in New York, where he studied acting at the Italian Theatre, making his professional Manhattan debut in 1955. He played minor roles in dramas until the late 1960s, when he established himself as an adept comic actor. Among Gardenia's most-remembered performances were the frantic father Carol Newquist in *Little Murders* (1969), the overcautious brother Harry Edison in *The *Prisoner of Second Avenue* (1971), the Job-like manufacturer Joe Benjamin in *God's Favorite* (1974), the widower Alfred Rossi in an autumnal romance in *Ballroom* (1978), and the Italian-restaurant owner Lou Graziano in *Breaking Legs* (1991).

GARDNER, Herb (1934–2003), playwright. The Brooklyn native was educated at New York's High School of the Performing Arts, Carnegie Tech, and Antioch College before working in television commercials and children's programming, giving him the inspiration for his first Broadway script, *A Thousand Clowns* (1962). Although *The Goodbye People* (1968), *Thieves* (1974), and the musical *One Night Stand* (1980) did not enjoy long runs, his comedy-drama *I'm Not Rappaport* (1985) was very popular, and praise was forthcoming for his nostalgic play, *Conversations with My Father* (1992). Gardner's characters tend to be colorful, unconventional, and outspoken.

GARFIELD, John [né Jules Garfinkel] (1913–52), actor. The handsome if pug-faced performer was born in New York, where he was an amateur boxer and then later studied at the Heckscher Foundation and Maria Ouspenskaya drama schools. He made his debut in 1930 playing small parts with the *Civic Repertory Theatre but called attention to himself only after he joined the *Group Theatre. Among his notable roles there was the ambitious but embittered son Ralph Berger in *Awake and Sing!* (1935). After failing to win the title role in *Golden Boy* (1937), Garfield left the company, then showed a gift for comedy as the amorous law student Chick Kessler in *Having Wonderful Time* (1937). After playing the legendary hobo Overland Kid in *Heavenly Express* (1940), he spent several years in films before returning to portray the Dutch sea captain Joris Kuiper in *Skipper Next to God* (1948) and Hollywood star Charlie Castle in *The Big Knife* (1949). In 1951 he essayed *Peer Gynt* and the following year gave his last performance, somewhat ironically, as prizefighter Joe Bonaparte, the title role in a revival of *Golden Boy*. Garfield was a likable, realistic actor, best in parts requiring a streak of toughness. Biography: *Body and Soul: The Story of John Garfield*, Larry Swindell, 1975.

GARRETT, Betty (b. 1919), actress and singer. Born in St. Joseph, Missouri, the daughter of a traveling salesman, Garrett won a scholarship to the *Neighborhood Playhouse School in Manhattan, where she studied acting, singing, and dancing. She made her Broadway debut in 1938 as a member of the crowd in the *Mercury Theatre production of *Danton's Death*, then was cast in several revues, getting the most attention for singing "South America, Take It Away" in *Call Me Mister* (1946). Whenever she returned to Broadway, Garrett usually found herself in short-lived vehicles, though she shone in her one-woman Off-Broadway program *No Dogs or Actors Allowed* (1990) and as the veteran hoofer Hattie in the 2001 revival of *Follies*. Autobiography: *Betty Garrett and Other Songs*, with Ron Rapoport, 2002.

GARRICK GAIETIES, THE, a series of revues produced by the *Theatre Guild in 1925, 1926, and 1930. The 1925 edition was originally mounted only for two Sunday performances in an effort to raise funds for tapestries for the new Guild Theatre. However, it was so well received that the revue was soon brought back for a regular run. Richard *Rodgers and Lorenz *Hart wrote the songs for the first two editions, including "Manhattan" and "Mountain Greenery," as well as a short jazz opera, "The Joy Spreader," and a spoof of operetta, "The Rose of Arizona."

GARRICK THEATRE (New York). Built as the Harrigan Theatre in 1890 by Edward *Harrigan after he had split up with partner Tony *Hart, the romanesque-style house on West 35th Street was designed by Francis H. Kimball and featured an intricate facade. Richard *Mansfield bought the theatre in 1895 and, wishing to save money, renamed it the Garrick so that the sign needed only minimal letter changes. Charles *Frohman owned the theatre until his death in 1915, and then it fell into derelict condition until millionaire Otto Kahn saved it and refurbished it in 1917. The house was later the first home for the *Theatre Guild, but when that group built their own theatre, the Garrick was reduced to a burlesque house and was razed in 1932 after a fire.

GASSNER, John [Waldhorn] (1903–67), critic and scholar. Born in Hungary, he was brought to America while still a youngster and was educated at Columbia. He served as a drama critic, a professor, and an adviser to several important theatrical organizations but was best known to the public for his numerous anthologies of plays and such books as *The Theatre in Our Times* (1954), *Form and Idea in Modern Theatre* (1956), and *Theatre at the Crossroads* (1960).

GATES and MORANGE, scenic designers. The firm of designers and builders was founded in 1894 by Frank and Richard Gates and Edward A. Morange. Their first contract was painting a curtain with one of the landscapes popular on drops of that era. Soon thereafter, their sets for a touring musical, *Off the Earth* (1895), and the Broadway play *Kismet* (1895) won them widespread praise and numerous subsequent assignments. The firm remained active for forty years. Among their most noteworthy settings were the orchard scene in *Leah Kleschna* (1904) and the London Bridge set for a 1912 production of *Oliver Twist*. Their designs for *Pomander Walk* (1910) are said to have inspired a New York City development of the same name and similar appearance.

GATES, William F. (d. 1843), actor. He is one of the many theatrical meteors who briefly shone brightly and then burned out. Gates's early history is unknown. It was generally believed that he was born in America and began his career in the circus. Gates made his New York debut at the Chatham Theatre as Orson in *Valentine and Orson* (1828), but it was during his thirteen seasons at the *Bowery Theatre, commencing in 1830 and ending just before his death, that he won his real fame. Although he sometimes essayed serious roles, his forte was low comedy. He excelled as Trinculo and the First Gravedigger but was best known for his acting in contemporary, long-discarded comedies such as *The Cannibals*, *Blue Laws*, and *Loan of a Lover*. Gates had a round, wide-eyed, youthful face, with an impish quality appropriate for his sort of roles, and a broad, unpolished style. T. Allston *Brown stated simply that "he became, as low comedian, the greatest favorite ever seen."

GAUNT, Percy (1852–96), composer. The Philadelphian was best known as musical director for Charles *Hoyt, whom he joined in 1883. He composed the scores for several of Hoyt's farce-comedies, most notably *A *Trip to Chinatown* (1891), which included "The Bowery," "Push Dem Clouds Away" (played at his funeral by an organ-grinder), and "Reuben and Cynthia," this last adapted from an older song. Many felt his early death deprived the musical theatre of a promising melodist.

GAXTON, William [né Arturo Antonio Gaxiola] (1893–1963), comic actor and singer. The distinguished-looking comedian, whose pushy, frenetic style somewhat belied his appearance, was born in San Francisco and educated at military school and the University of California. He entered vaudeville at the age of fifteen and was soon doing a popular single turn. Gaxton made his Broadway musical debut in the *Music Box Revue* (1922), then rose to leading man status as Martin in *A *Connecticut Yankee* (1927) and as Peter Forbes in *Fifty Million Frenchmen* (1930). He scored his biggest hit when he first teamed with Victor *Moore to play President Wintergreen in *Of Thee I Sing* (1931). His manly, brash style proved a superb counterpart to Moore's wispy timidity, so they were paired again in a sequel, *Let 'Em Eat Cake* (1933), and in *Anything Goes* (1934), *Leave It to Me!* (1938), *Louisiana Purchase* (1940), *Hollywood Pinafore* (1945), and *Nellie Bly* (1946).

GAY AND LESBIAN THEATRE IN AMERICA. Decades before homosexual characters were seen

in American plays on a regular basis, there were isolated incidents when a gay or lesbian appeared in the plot, always a curiosity, often as a freak. Works such as *The Captive* (1926), *The Drag* (1927), *The Pleasure Man* (1928), *The Green Bay Tree* (1933), *The *Children's Hour* (1934), *Trio* (1944), and others dealt with homosexuality, though often in a sensational manner. The first play to go beyond such stereotypes was Robert *Anderson's *Tea and Sympathy* (1953). The central character was not gay but was suspected all the same and the drama approached the subject of homophobia in an honest (if gingerly) fashion. Homosexuality entered into the mainstream through works by Edward *Albee, William *Inge, Tennessee *Williams, and others, but again the subject was secondary. Only in adventurous Off-Off-Broadway one-acts by Megan Terry, Sam *Shepard, Robert Patrick, Al Carmines, Charles *Ludlam, and other young, radical playwrights of the 1960s and 1970s were gay and lesbian characters central to the plot. It was Mart Crowley's *The *Boys in the Band* (1968) that brought the gay play to the forefront, finding success with mainstream audiences. While its self-hating, confessional presentation of homosexuality offended some, *Boys in the Band* was the first honest work about gay lifestyle that most Americans experienced. It was followed by many lesser, sensational works, many using the new freedom of the times to shock and titillate rather than explore any truths. Yet there were also outstanding exceptions, such as *Kennedy's Children* (1973), *Gemini* (1977), *Fifth of July* (1978), and *Bent* (1978). By the 1980s several notable works arrived and proved that a gay or lesbian work could be judged and enjoyed simply as a new play. *Last Summer at Bluefish Cove* (1980), *Torch Song Trilogy* (1983), and *The Lisbon Traviata* (1985) were among the decade's finest examples, as well as the musicals *La Cage aux Folles* (1983) and *March of the Falsettos* (1981). Many of the plays written in the late 1980s and 1990s concerned the AIDS epidemic, and while several were preachy and bitter without being enlightening, there were such fine works as *As Is* (1985), *The Normal Heart* (1985), *The Destiny of Me* (1992), *Angels in America* (1993), *Love! Valour! Compassion!* (1994), and the musicals *Falsettoland* (1990) and *Rent* (1996). But by the 1990s it was possible to have a gay or lesbian play that was not about AIDS, such as *Six Degrees of Separation* (1990), *The Food Chain* (1995), *As Bees in Honey Drown* (1997), *A New Brain* (1998), *Stop Kiss* (1998), *The Laramie Project* (2000), *A Man of No Importance* (2002), and *Take Me Out* (2003). Perhaps the American theatre has come to the point where the designation of being a "gay play" is no longer necessary.

GAY DIVORCE (1932), a musical comedy by Dwight Taylor (book), Cole *Porter (music, lyrics).

[*Ethel Barrymore Theatre, 248 perf.] To give her husband grounds for divorce, Mimi Pratt (Clare Luce) arranges to be caught with the paid corespondent Tonetti (Erik Rhodes). But Guy (Fred *Astaire), who has fallen in love with Mimi, manages to get himself confused with the corespondent and uses the confusion to pursue his courtship. *Notable songs*: Night and Day; After You, Who?; Mister and Missus Fitch. In Astaire's only Broadway appearance without his sister, both he and the show were greeted with a certain indifference at first. However, the popularity of "Night and Day" and Astaire's superb performance, his last on Broadway, turned the Dwight Deere *Wiman and Tom Weatherly production into a hit. Hollywood codes forced the film version to be called *The Gay Divorcée*.

GAYLER, Charles (1820–92), playwright. One of the most prolific dramatists of the second half of the 19th century, as well as a sometime actor and novelist, he is said to have written well over one hundred plays, covering a range from minstrel skits through farce, comedy, spectacle, melodrama, and tragedy. Many of his plays were written to order for some of the most popular and respected performers of the era, and though a number of his works held the stage for years, none is probably performable today. Among his more notable vehicles were *Taking the Chances* (1856), *The Love of a Prince* (1857), *There's Many a Slip'Twixt the Cup and the Lip* (1859), *The Magic Marriage* (1861), *The Connie Soogah; or, The Jolly Peddler* (1863), and *Atonement; or, The Child Stealer* (1866). His most durable success was the J. K. *Emmet vehicle *Fritz, Our Cousin German* (1870). Writing swiftly, Gayler had *Bull Run; or, the Sacking of Fairfax Courthouse* (1861) on stage less than a month after the battle and *Hatteras Inlet; or, Our Naval Victories* (1861) ready three months after the incidents described in the play. By the 1880s the New York–born writer's style was no longer in vogue, although plays such as *Jacqueline, Lord Tatters: The Bohemian*, and *Lights and Shadows* found audiences at lesser houses and on the road.

GAZZARA, [Biagio Anthony] **Ben** (b. 1930), actor. The small, darkly handsome New Yorker studied at City College, Erwin Piscator's Dramatic Workshop, and the *Actors Studio before making his debut in summer stock in 1952. He won immediate recognition when he portrayed the vicious Jocko de Paris in *End as a Man* (1953), then portrayed the guilt-ridden Brick in *Cat on a Hot Tin Roof* (1955). He also shone as the drug-addicted Johnny Pope in A *Hatful of Rain* (1955), the doctor Edmund Darrell in *Strange Interlude* (1963), salesman "Erie" Smith in *Hughie* (1974),

college professor George in *Who's Afraid of Virginia Woolf?* (1976), and the Aussie war vet Eric Dawson in *Shimada* (1992).

GEAR, Luella [Gardner Van Nort] (1899–1980), actress. The New Yorker made her debut in the 1917 musical *Love o' Mike* and over the next decade used her often acid, knowing style of comedy to win increasingly important roles in such comedies and musicals as *The *Gold Diggers* (1919), *Poppy* (1923), and *Queen High* (1926). Gear enjoyed major assignments in *Gay Divorce* (1932), *Life Begins at 8:40* (1934), and *On Your Toes* (1936). In later years her best role was the bitter worldling Julia McKinlock in *Sabrina Fair* (1953).

GEFFEN PLAYHOUSE (Los Angeles). During its young history this theatre company has attracted famous actors and playwrights and has produced some works of national interest. Founded in 1995 by Gil Cates and Lou Moore and named after producer David Geffen, the company presents classic and modern works in an old Masonic club that was home to the former Westwood Playhouse. A second performance space is currently being designed for a 2004 opening. The group is affiliated with the University of California at Los Angeles. Neil *Simon's latest work, then titled *Rose and Walsh*, premiered there in 2003. The company performed its 2003–2004 season at the nearby Brentwood Theatre while its own facility was renovated.

GELBART, Larry (b. 1928), librettist and playwright. He was born in Chicago and as a teenager began writing for radio, later contributing sketches for television and screenplays for Hollywood. Gelbart's first Broadway credit was the libretto for the short-lived musical *The Conquering Hero* (1961), followed by his first stage success as co-writer of A *Funny Thing Happened on the Way to the Forum* (1962). Gelbart's other musical hit was *City of Angels* (1989). Among his non-musical plays are *Sly Fox* (1976), an Americanized version of *Volpone*, and *Mastergate* (1989), a satire of a congressional hearing. Autobiography: *Laughing Matters*, 1998.

GELBER, Jack. See *Connection, The*.

GEMINI (1977), a comedy by Albert Innaurato. [Circle Theatre, 1,778 perf.] Francis Geminiani (Robert Picardo) returns to his South Philadelphia Italian family on a college break from Harvard to celebrate his twenty-first birthday. He is visited by two WASP college friends, Randy (Reed Birney) and his sister Judith (Carol Potter). She is supposedly Francis's girlfriend, but Fran, uncertain of his own sexual proclivities, finds he is attracted more to Randy. The chaos that results is complicated by Francis's loud, pushy family, the sluttish neighbor Bunny Weinberger (Jessica James), and her fat son Herschel (Jonathan Hadary), who is attracted to Randy as well. The play trafficked in such contemporary concerns as homosexuality and neuroses, and it took a fresh and funny slant and placed its action in a setting, South Philadelphia, usually ignored by New York–centered playwrights. The *Circle Repertory Theatre production was quickly transferred to Broadway for a long run. *Gemini* was successfully revived Off Broadway by the *Second Stage in 1999. **Albert INNAURATO** (b. 1948) is a Philadelphia-born playwright who first called attention to himself with his one-act play, *The Transfiguration of Benno Blimpie* (1977), the study of an unloved man who becomes a compulsive eater. Later plays, none running very long, include *Ulysses in Traction* (1977), *Passione* (1980), *Coming of Age in Soho* (1985), and *Gus and Al* (1989).

GENNARO, Peter (1924–2000), choreographer. Born in Metairie, Louisiana, he made his debut as dancer with the San Carlo Opera Company and later danced in the chorus of numerous Broadway musicals before creating the choreography for *Seventh Heaven* (1955). Later choreographic assignments included *West Side Story* (1957), on which he worked with Jerome *Robbins; *Fiorello!* (1959); *The Unsinkable Molly Brown* (1960); *Mr. President* (1962); *Bajour* (1964); *Jimmy* (1969); *Irene* (1973); *Annie* (1977); and *Carmelina* (1979). He also served for many years as choreographer at the Radio City Music Hall.

GENTLE PEOPLE, THE (1939), a play by Irwin *Shaw. [*Belasco Theatre, 141 perf.] Jonah Goodman (Sam Jaffe) and Philip Anagnos (Roman Bohnen) are gentle souls who would like nothing better than to fish off of the pier near their home. But their simple, idyllic life is threatened by a racketeer, Harold Goff (Franchot *Tone), who demands protection money. Goff would also have Jonah's daughter, Stella (Sylvia Sydney), and when he learns the men have saved money to buy a small fishing boat, he would have that, too. So the men take Goff out in the boat, kill him, and throw him overboard but not before retrieving the money and additional sums from his wallet. Shaw called his work a "Brooklyn fable," adding, "justice triumphs and the meek prove victorious over arrogant and violent men. The author does not pretend this is the case in real life." Seen by some as an antifascist allegory, the *Group Theatre production was dismissed by Brooks *Atkinson as "pleasant, discursive

writing" that had "the disadvantage of seeming a little uneventful."

GENTLEMAN FROM MISSISSIPPI, A (1908), a play by Harrison Rhodes and Thomas A. *Wise. [Bijou Theatre, 407 perf.] William H. Langdon (Wise), the new senator from Mississippi, is a quiet, honest gentleman and proud of his state. When the brash young reporter "Bud" Haines (Douglas *Fairbanks) announces he is from New York, Langdon replies he knows it as "the Vicksburg of the North." The men strike up a friendship, and Haines is appointed Langdon's private secretary. Some corrupt senators hope to push through a bill establishing a naval base in Mississippi and have secretly been buying up land. They have even involved the senator's daughter, Hope (Lola May). But Langdon and Haines thwart the plan, and Haines wins Hope. Described by one critic as "full of bright lines, tender sentiment, and genuine local color," this straightforward, wholesome if simplistic play, produced by William A. *Brady and Joseph R. *Grismer, was one of the major hits of its day.

GENTLEMAN OF FRANCE, A (1901), a play by Harriet *Ford. [*Wallack's Theatre, 120 perf.] Gaston de Marsac (Kyrle *Bellew) loves Mlle. de la Vire (Eleanor *Robson), but he will not have her if the villainous M. de Bruhl (John Blair) succeeds in his machinations. Not until de Marsac kills de Bruhl and several of his cohorts (with Mlle. de la Vire assisting by conking another over the head) can he safely claim her. This swashbuckler, presented by *Liebler and Co., was taken from Stanley Weyman's novel. Although *Harper's Weekly* joined others in complaining that the somewhat effeminate Bellew was miscast, it concluded the play was "better worth seeing than most dramatizations of historical novels that have been recently produced."

GENTLEMEN PREFER BLONDES (1926), a comedy by Anita *Loos and John *Emerson. [Times Square Theatre, 199 perf.] Lorelei Lee (June *Walker), a gold-digging blonde from Little Rock, Arkansas, has all her expenses paid by a rich button manufacturer, Gus Eisman (Arthur S. Ross). He even sends Lorelei and her friend Dorothy (Edna Hibbard) to Europe, where Lorelei wangles a tiara from an English lord and dates dashing young Henry Spofford (Frank *Morgan). When she learns that Spofford may be richer than Eisman, she plans to dump Eisman. By that time, however, Dorothy has claimed Spofford. Based on Loos's famous novel, the Edgar *Selwyn production capitalized on the book and the current Roaring Twenties setting. The story became a popular musical of the same title in 1949 with a book by Loos and Joseph *Fields, lyrics by Leo Robin, and music by Jule *Styne. The Herman *Levin and Oliver *Smith production ran at the *Ziegfeld Theatre for 740 performances and made Carol *Channing, who played Lorelei, a Broadway star. Yvonne Adair was Dorothy, Jack McCauley was Gus, and Eric Brotherson was Spofford. *Notable songs*: A Little Girl from Little Rock; Bye Bye Baby; Diamonds Are a Girl's Best Friend. The musical has been successfully revived both in its original version and in a revised version with Channing called *Lorelei* (1974).

GEORGE, Grace (1879–1961), actress. The fair-haired, blue-eyed beauty was born in New York and educated at a convent, later studying at the *American Academy of Dramatic Arts before making her debut as a schoolgirl in *The New Boy* (1894). Her first important role was the inn-keeper's daughter Juliette in *The Turtle* (1898). George quickly mastered a style that her husband, producer William A. *Brady, would later describe as "the fast-building, vivacious, chin up and tongue-sparkling sort of thing, with wit and tears mingled." She demonstrated these skills in over fifty subsequent plays. Among her notable roles were Peg Woffington in *Pretty Peggy* (1903); Louise in an all-star revival of The *Two Orphans* (1904); the flighty Lady Kitty in *The Marriage of William Ashe* (1905); Cyprienne in a revival of *Divorçons* (1907); the sly Marion Stanton in *A Woman's Way* (1909); Lady Teazle in *The School for Scandal* (1909); Lady Cicely in *Captain Brassbound's Conversion* (1916); the socialite Anne De Rhonde in *The Merry Wives of Gotham* (1924); Janet Fraser, who is courted by her former husband, in *The First Mrs. Fraser* (1929); the gentle spinster Mary Herries in *Kind Lady* (1935); and school mistress Mother Hildebrand in *The Velvet Glove* (1949). George's last appearance was as Mrs. Culver opposite Katharine *Cornell in a revival of *The Constant Wife* (1951). She also adapted several plays, some of which she acted in.

GEORGE WASHINGTON SLEPT HERE (1940), a comedy by George S. *Kaufman and Moss *Hart. [*Lyceum Theatre, 173 perf.] When Newton Fuller (Ernest *Truex) shows his wife, Annabelle (Jean Dixon), a decrepit country home in which George Washington reputedly slept, Annabelle can only remark, "Martha wasn't a very good house-keeper." But when Newton surprises his wife with the news that he has bought the place, she becomes angry enough to "spit from here to Mount Vernon." The Fullers' problems have only begun. The old well, for example, has long since run dry. Even after the house is virtually in order,

their family's problems have hardly ended. Their daughter, Madge (Peggy French), is going around with a married actor in a local summer stock company, and they are visited by the demanding, difficult, but rich Uncle Stanley (Dudley *Digges), who suddenly seems all the more irritating when he announces he is broke. Worse, the Fullers learn it was not Washington who slept there, but Benedict Arnold. However, when the property is about to be foreclosed, Uncle Stanley slyly comes to the rescue. The last of the Kaufman-Hart collaborations, the Sam H. *Harris production was awaited with such exalted expectations that disappointment was almost inevitable. Malcolm Goldstein, Kaufman's biographer, condemned the comedy: "The play proceeds with intermittent merriment, but without a display of true wit. The characterization is slight and the twists of plot improbable, excessive, and dull." Nevertheless, the play has enjoyed occasional successful summer stock revivals.

GEORGE WHITE'S SCANDALS. This series of revues, produced by *White from 1919 through 1926, and then in 1928, 1929, 1931, 1935, and 1939, were given to elaborate show numbers much like the *Ziegfeld Follies*, but were less ornate and cumbersome. Their comedy tended to be far more topical and, because White had been a dancer, the productions were fast-paced and featured better dancing and music than similar revues. Most of the scores were written either by George *Gershwin or by *De Sylva, Brown, and Henderson. Memorable songs from these shows included "I'll Build a Stairway to Paradise," "Somebody Loves Me," "Black Bottom," "Birth of the Blues," "Lucky Day," and "Life Is Just a Bowl of Cherries."

GERMON, Effie (1843?–1914), actress. The daughter of performers and great-granddaughter of the first Joseph *Jefferson, she was born in Augusta, Georgia, and raised in Baltimore. After making her debut with a Philadelphia stock company in 1857, Germon joined Laura *Keene's New York ensemble in 1858, appearing first as Kate Rocket in *Old Heads and Young Hearts* and a short time later creating the role of Augusta in the first American performance of *Our American Cousin* (1858). In 1865 she played Ophelia to Edwin *Booth's Hamlet, then spent several seasons with John *Brougham. She joined Lester *Wallack's company in 1868, essaying as her first assignment the East Indian heiress Naomi Tighe in *School*. Her "rollicking" performances quickly won the doll-faced actress the position formerly held in the troupe by the late Mary *Gannon, and she remained with the company for seventeen years. After the company disbanded she continued to play important roles such as Audrey to Helena *Modjeska's Rosalind in *As You Like It* (1886) and the comic servant in *Little Lord Fauntleroy* (1888). Much of her later career was spent touring, notably as Aunt Polly in *David Harum*.

GERRY SOCIETY. Formally known as the New York Society for the Prevention of Cruelty to Children, it was founded by Elbridge T. Gerry, Henry Bergh, John D. Wright, and others in 1875. Gerry, a banker, lawyer, and grandson of a signer of the Declaration of Independence, was by far the most prominent of the figures, so that the writings of many late 19th-century theatrical figures simply called the group by his name. For the most part the group successfully attacked abuses by inconsiderate producers and selfish stage mothers but occasionally went too far in its zeal. One memorable instance occurred when Francis *Wilson, charmed by two African-American waifs he saw dancing in the streets, gave them a number in his latest musical. The Gerry Society went to court to forbid the children's performing, thus depriving the needy youngsters of paychecks and a chance to improve their talents, as well as denying audiences a harmless entertainment. Gerry himself wrote, "I am a friend of the stage, but I am a better friend of the children." Although most of the abuses disappeared with the coming of child labor laws and the rise of unions, theatrical producers must still get the Society's approval for children to perform, and the group still monitors the treatment of child actors and sees that they have proper schooling.

GERSHWIN, George [né Jacob Gershvin] (1898–1937), composer. One of the greatest and most original of Broadway songwriters, he was born in Brooklyn to a poor immigrant family. Young George's love of music came early on and was helped by his friendship with his classmate, violinist Max Rosen. When the Gershwins purchased a piano for his older brother, Ira *Gershwin, it was George, then twelve, who monopolized it. At fourteen he began lessons with a key figure in his musical life, Charles Hambitzer, a composer and pianist of broad, advanced musical tastes. From Hambitzer, Gershwin received a thorough classical training, but he was also aware of the native musical upheaval around him (particularly the work of Jerome *Kern). Gershwin achieved recognition after Al *Jolson sang "Swanee" in *Sinbad* in 1919. That same year he composed his first score, for *La La Lucille*. From 1920 to 1924 he created scores for *George White's Scandals*, including such hit songs as "I'll Build a Stairway to Paradise" (1922) and "Somebody Loves Me" (1924). From late 1924 on he worked almost exclusively with Ira. Their first hit was *Lady, Be Good!* (1924), a show that marked a turning point in American musical comedy; its jazz-based melodies, harmonies, and rhythms set a new standard and allowed musical comedy to be clearly distinguished from operetta, which retained allegiances to European mannerisms. Gershwin's melodic lines tended to be angular and aggressive, as exemplified by the show's "Fascinating Rhythm" and title song but could on occasion be soft, sentimental, almost wailing, as in "So Am I," suggesting that his Jewish background as well as black sources influenced his composition. A succession of hits and near misses followed: *Tell Me More!* (1925), *Tip-Toes* (1925), *Song of the Flame* (1925), *Oh, Kay!* (1926), *Funny Face* (1927), *Rosalie* (1928), *Treasure Girl* (1928), *Show Girl* (1929), *Strike Up the Band* (1930), *Girl Crazy* (1930), *Of Thee I Sing* (1931), *Pardon My English* (1933), and *Let 'Em Eat Cake* (1933). From early in his career Gershwin had been interested in more serious composition, writing numerous concert pieces that remain popular today. Even his political musicals can be seen as a step away from traditional material. In 1935 he attempted a folk opera, *Porgy and Bess*. The initial reception was mixed and public response lukewarm, but the musical's popularity has grown with time and may well prove his most durable work. Decades after his death Gershwin had two Broadway hits (based on earlier shows): *My One and Only* (1983) and *Crazy for You* (1992), and his music was featured in *George Gershwin Alone* (2001). Biography: *Gershwin: A Biography*, Edward Jablonsky, 1987.

GERSHWIN, Ira [né Israel Gershvin] (1896–1983), lyricist. Born in New York and the older brother of George *Gershwin, he was a bookish, introspective youth. When he first decided to write lyrics professionally he did it under a pseudonym derived from the first names of another brother and a sister, Arthur Francis. It was as Francis that he created lyrics for Vincent *Youmans's *Two Little Girls in Blue* (1921). During the 1920s he occasionally wrote with composers other than his brother; his work with his brother is listed in the entry for George Gershwin immediately above. He also wrote lyrics for *Americana* (1926), *Life Begins at 8:40* (1934), and the 1936 edition of the *Ziegfeld Follies*. After his brother's death he wrote the innovative *Lady in the Dark* (1941) with Kurt Weill, but his last two shows were failures: *The Firebrand of Florence* (1945), written with *Weill; and *Park Avenue* (1946), written with Arthur *Schwartz. He did live to see another Gershwin hit on Broadway: *My One and Only* (1983). Ira Gershwin was often in his brother's shadow and only later was he recognized as one of the best American lyricists, with superior work that was cheery, colloquial, and marked with a unique, slangy shorthand.

GERSHWIN THEATRE (New York). Broadway's first full-size theatre in forty-one years, the Uris Theatre (as it was called when it opened in 1972), was designed by Ralph *Alswang as the district's largest house (1,900 seats) with more backstage and lobby space than any other. What it lacked in aesthetics it certainly had in conveniences, such as escalators, spacious rest rooms, and long open bars and lobby space. The Uris was part of a building complex that housed offices, the newly built *Circle in the Square Theatre, and a Theatre Hall of Fame. The Nederlander-owned theatre was renamed after George and Ira *Gershwin in 1983, which was somewhat appropriate since most of the playhouse's tenants have been large musicals such as *Sweeney Todd* (1979) and *Show Boat* (1994).

GEST, Morris (1881–1942), producer. Born in Russia, he came to America as a child and was educated in the Boston public schools. Gest made his debut as a producer there in 1903 but soon moved to New York, where in 1905 he went into partnership with F. Ray *Comstock. Many of their successes were large spectacles such as *The Wanderer* (1917) or light comedies such as *Polly Preferred* (1923), but they were best known as importers of such attractions as the English musical *Chu Chin Chow* (1917), the Russian revue *Chauve Souris* (1922), the *Moscow Art Theatre (1923), Eleonora *Duse (1923), and Max *Reinhardt's production of *The Miracle.* (1924). After the partnership dissolved in the late 1920s, Gest continued to produce until shortly before his death, but his later record was undistinguished.

GET-RICH-QUICK WALLINGFORD (1910), a comedy by George M. *Cohan. [Gaiety Theatre, 424 perf.] J. Rufus Wallingford (Hale Hamilton) and his crony Horace "Blackie" Daws (Edward Ellis) are consummate con men. They move from town to town setting up promising businesses, selling stock in the companies by telling the local "boobs" that "There's millions in it!," then disappearing before the bubble bursts. A favorite Wallingford trick is to walk into a hotel when he first arrives and, as he signs the register, beg the clerk not to sell his autograph. But when Wallingford comes to Battlesburg to set up a plant for the manufacture of covered carpet tacks that will match any carpet, his plans go awry. The company succeeds, and Battlesburg prospers. Wallingford looks to become richer than he ever dreamed and even wins the hand of Fannie Jasper

(Frances Ring), who believed in him. Based on George Randolph Chester's short stories in the *Saturday Evening Post*, the play was Sam H. *Harris and Cohan's first successful work without music. Cohan's fast-paced co-direction (with Sam *Forrest) glossed over myriad improbabilities, while the colorful minor figures that filled the play led the Boston *Evening Transcript* to note that his characters were "Americans, keenly observed, shrewdly put to speaking [for] themselves in their own idiom."

GETTING GERTIE'S GARTER (1921), a farce by Wilson Collison and Avery *Hopwood. [Republic Theatre, 120 perf.] When Gertie (Hazel *Dawn) was dating Ken Waldrick (Donald MacDonald), he gave her a diamond-studded garter with his picture in it. But that was a year ago. Now Gertie is married to Teddy Darling, while Ken has married a girl named Pattie, so it seems time to return the garter before the spouses learn of it. Quietly returning the garter, however, proves easier said than done. It turns out to involve all sorts of misunderstandings, including a curious romp in a haystack. Because many of the figures involved with the show had been involved with the earlier *Up in Mabel's Room*, comparisons were obvious and not altogether flattering. Percy *Hammond of the *Herald Tribune* judged it "duller," adding, "There is no more interest in a garter as a naughty thing than there is in a virgin's wimple." The public disagreed. Not only was the original A. H. *Woods production and its road companies highly profitable, but for many years the play remained popular with stock companies and on summer circuits.

GETTING OUT (1978), a play by Marsha *Norman. [Marymount Manhattan Theatre, 22 perf.] When Arlene Holsclaw (Susan Kingsley) is released from prison, she is determined to lead a decent life but remains haunted by her younger, more vicious self, Arlie (Pamela Reed). Settling into the dingy room that she expects to call home, Arlene is visited by her mother (Madeleine Thornton-Sherwood), who dredges up old memories; by Carl (Leo Burmester), a pimp who was her lover and who would have her return to prostitution; and by Bennie (Barry Corbin), her former jailer, who tries to seduce her. With the help of an understanding neighbor, Ruby (Joan Pape), she begins to realize that she can handle herself properly and even live with the vestiges of Arlie that still cry within her. A sordid, foulmouthed, yet compassionate and moving play, the work was first mounted in 1977 by the *Actors Theater of Louisville and later won the *American Theatre Critics Association award as the season's outstanding play. After its original New York engagement by the *Phoenix Theatre, it reopened at the Theatre de Lys and ran for an additional 237 performances.

GEVA, Tamara [née Tamara or Sheversheieva Gevergeva] (1907–97), dancer. The Russian-born ballerina, who was once the wife of George *Balanchine, made her American debut in *Chauve Souris* in 1927 and subsequently appeared in such musicals as *Three's a Crowd* (1930) and *Flying Colors* (1932), as well as several nonmusical plays. However, she is best remembered as one of the original stars of *On Your Toes* (1936), in which she danced to "Slaughter on Tenth Avenue" with Ray *Bolger.

GEVA THEATRE (Rochester, New York). Named after the Genessee Valley in which the city is located, this regional theatre was founded in 1972 by William and Cynthia Mason Selden. Productions were mounted in the basement space of a Rochester Business Institute building until a new home was found in 1985: a 500-seat modified thrust stage located in the former Naval Armory downtown. The group also presents new and/or small plays in the 180-seat Next Stage space. The repertory is an eclectic variety of classics, musicals, and modern works.

GIBBS, [Oliver] Wolcott (1902–58), critic. A descendant of Oliver Wolcott, signer of the Declaration of Independence, he was born in New York and attended the Hill School but not college. He held such odd jobs as architect's apprentice and railroad conductor before joining *The New Yorker,* for which he became drama critic when Robert *Benchley retired in 1939 and held the post until his death. Gibbs could be acerbic, as when he wrote of *Saroyan's *My Heart's in the Highlands,* "This collision between the most completely undisciplined talent in American letters and the actors of the Group Theatre bored me utterly to distraction." But he could also be warm and open, as when he confessed to a "feeling of rising excitement" while watching *Abe Lincoln in Illinois, concluding, "I suppose it was just the surprise and gratitude and somehow sorrow of seeing a very great man exactly as he must have been." He was one of those rare critics who successfully worked both sides of the footlights, writing the well-received comedy *Season in the Sun* (1950).

GIBSON, William (b. 1914), playwright. A native New Yorker who studied at City College, Gibson had his earliest dramas produced at regional theatres. His first play to reach Broadway was the successful two-hander *Two for the Seesaw* (1958), followed by the popular The *Miracle Worker* (1959) about Helen Keller and her tutor, Annie Sullivan.

Gibson later collaborated on the book of the musical *Golden Boy* (1964) and then rewrote *A Cry of Players* (1968), an earlier play dealing with Shakespeare's decision to become a playwright. His *Golda* (1977) dealt with the Israeli political leader Golda Meir. He returned to the Keller-Sullivan relationship in the sequel *Monday after the Miracle* (1982) and rewrote the Meir work as a one-woman program called *Golda's Balcony* (2003). A number of his other plays have been produced by regional stages.

GIDEON (1961), a play by Paddy *Chayefsky. [*Plymouth Theatre, 236 perf.] God comes to earth as an Angel (Fredric *March) and exhorts the young farmer Gideon (Douglas Campbell) to lead his people against the Midianites. At first Gideon is disbelieving, but when the Angel performs miracles and even gives Gideon the very plan that wins the battle, he accepts that the Angel is indeed Yahweh or Jehovah. But later Gideon refuses God's order to slay the elders of Succoth. His head has been swelled by praise, and so he comes to attribute his success not to God but to "historico-economic, socio-psychological forces." The Angel can only rue that for all Man's belief in God, Man believes first and foremost in himself. Hailed by Howard Taubman of the *Times* as "a graceful conceit tinged with innocent wonder and wise laughter," the play demonstrated Chayefsky's increasing preoccupation with mystical and metaphysical concerns.

GIELGUD, [Arthur] John (1904–2000), actor and director. A grandnephew of Ellen *Terry, the slightly arch, musical-voiced actor first appeared in New York in 1928 as the Grand Duke Alexander in *The Patriot*. However, he did not win major American recognition until his 1936 *Hamlet. The consensus was that his interpretation was intelligent and exquisitely recited but lacking in a certain passionate power. In 1947 he scored major successes when he starred in his revivals of *The Importance of Being Earnest* and *Love for Love*. Later that same year he played Jason to Judith *Anderson's Medea, which he directed, and also appeared as Raskolnikoff in *Crime and Punishment*. He returned to America for such memorable performances as Thomas Mendip in *The Lady's Not for Burning* (1950), his solo performance of Shakespeare called *Ages of Man* (1958), Benedick in *Much Ado about Nothing* (1959), Joseph Surface in *The School for Scandal* (1963), Brother Julian in *Tiny Alice* (1964), mental patient Harry in *Home* (1970), and the failed writer Spooner in *No Man's Land* (1976). Gielgud directed some of these, as well as the New York productions of *Five Finger Exercise* (1959), *Big Fish, Little Fish* (1961), Richard

*Burton's *Hamlet* (1964), *Ivanov* (1966), *Private Lives* (1975), and *The Constant Wife* (1975). Autobiography: *An Actor and His Time*, 1997.

GILBERT and SULLIVAN, operetta creators. Librettist-lyricist William Schwenck Gilbert (1836–1911) and composer Arthur Seymour Sullivan (1842–1900) were first represented in America in 1875 by a failed production of their *Trial by Jury*. However, their *H.M.S. Pinafore* became one of the biggest successes in the history of the American theatre after its premiere during the 1878–79 season. So many companies were hurriedly put on the stage that contemporaries spoke of "a Pinafore craze." More importantly (as detailed in the entry for the show), it opened all American stages to musical entertainments and served as a model for American musicals that shortly followed. All of their subsequent offerings received immediate American productions, the most successful being *The *Pirates of Penzance* (1879), *Patience* (1881), and *The *Mikado* (1885). By the turn of the century the vogue for these Savoyard gems waned, but there were many amateur groups dedicated to producing the works and also several mammoth all-star revivals. Winthrop *Ames's highly praised revivals in the 1920s once again whetted interest, as did visits of the *D'Oyly Carte in the 1930s and revivals by Tyrone *Guthrie. Sensing that the tradition of pure D'Oyly Carte no longer appealed to most Americans, Joseph *Papp brought out a defiantly unconventional *The Pirates of Penzance* in 1981, a production that enjoyed far and away the longest run ever accorded a Gilbert and Sullivan work in America.

GILBERT, Mrs. [George Henry] [neé Ann Hartley] (1821–1904), comic actress. No beauty (she had an angular, pinched face and heavy-lidded protruding eyes), she was for many decades one of the most skillful and beloved American comediennes. She was born in England and trained as a ballet dancer in London. In 1846 she married George Henry Gilbert, an actor and dancer, and together they toured England and Ireland before coming to America, where they performed in Milwaukee, Chicago, Cleveland, Cincinnati, Louisville, and finally New York. During these seasons Mrs. Gilbert developed her acting skills, dancing less and less. She performed opposite many of the era's stars, playing Lady Macbeth to Edwin *Booth's Macbeth and Osric to his Hamlet. Gilbert made her New York debut as Baroness Freitenhorsen in *Finesse* (1864) with Mrs. John Wood's company but first earned major plaudits as the Marquise de St. Maur in the American premiere of *Caste* (1867). Two years later she joined Augustin *Daly's company and, with very short breaks,

remained with it through its thirty-year history. She acted comic old women in approximately 150 different plays for Daly, ranging from Shakespeare and Sheridan to such important new plays as *Saratoga* (1870) and *Pique* (1875) to many long-discarded contemporary pieces. During the last years of Daly's heyday she was, with Ada *Rehan, John *Drew, and James *Lewis, the core of his great comic productions. Her last appearance was as "Granny" Thompson in *Granny* (1904). One critic said of her at this time, "The older and broader school never had anything richer and truer in its sphere, and the new school of naturalism cannot show anything of finer and firmer veracity." She died while touring as Granny. Autobiography: *The Stage Reminiscences of Mrs. Gilbert*, 1904.

GILBERT, John [né Gibbs] (1810–89), actor. One of the finest actors of his day, most distinguished in comic parts such as Sir Anthony Absolute and Sir Peter Teazle, he was born in Boston, where his next-door neighbor and childhood friend was Charlotte *Cushman. Gilbert made his stage debut at the local Tremont Theatre as Jaffier in *Venice Preserved* (1828). Shortly thereafter, he left to work in Mississippi River towns before making his New York bow as Sir Edmund Mortimer in *The Iron Chest* (1839). Although Gilbert continued for several years to play in tragedy and melodrama, he turned increasingly to comic parts. His somewhat portly build and round, sober-miened face led him to prefer roles as older men. He performed at the *Park Theatre until it burned down, then served unsuccessfully as manager of the *Chestnut Street Theatre in Philadelphia. In 1862 he joined Lester *Wallack's company, making his first appearance there as Sir Peter. He remained with Wallack until the company disbanded in 1888, serving not only as a principal comedian but as stage manager as well. He also assumed serious roles such as Miles McKenna in *Rosedale* (1863). He died while touring with Joseph *Jefferson in *The Rivals*. Gilbert was an archly conservative actor of the old school. He was considered a cold, haughty person but respected as a conscientious and skilled artist. He prided himself as well on his learning and had amassed a fine library before his death.

***GILDED AGE, THE.** See *Colonel Sellers*.

GILDER, Rosamund (1891?–1986), critic. The daughter of writer and editor Richard Watson Gilder, she was born in Marion, Massachusetts, and was for many years the drama critic and editor of *Theatre Arts Monthly*. Besides serving as secretary of the National Theatre Conference, director of the Playwrights' Bureau of the *Federal

Theatre Project, and a secretary of the *American National Theatre and Academy, she wrote numerous books on the theatre, including: *Enter the Actress* (1931), *A Theatre Library* (1932), *Theatre Collections in Libraries and Museums* (1936) with George *Freedley, and *John Gielgud's Hamlet* (1937).

GILFORD, Jack [né Jacob Gellman] (1907–90), character actor. Gilford was a small, withered-looking comedian who rarely played a leading role but was a familiar favorite in vaudeville, on stage, screen, and television. He was born in New York, the son of a divorced mother who supported her family as a bootlegger, and began his show business career as a stand-up comic in clubs, then went on to vaudeville and eventually started appearing in New York legit revues in 1940. He toured with the USO during World War II, then started winning interesting supporting roles on Broadway, such as the dentist Mr. Dussel in *The *Diary of Anne Frank* (1955) and the mute King Sextimus in *Once upon a Mattress* (1959). Gilford's other fondly remembered performances were the worried slave Hysterium in *A *Funny Thing Happened on the Way to the Forum* (1962), the Jewish fruit merchant Herr Schultz in *Cabaret* (1966), the mousy Erwin Trowbridge in *Three Men on a Horse* (1969), the happy-go-lucky Jimmy Smith in *No No Nanette* (1971), and the miserly old Jethro Crouch in *Sly Fox* (1976).

GILLETTE, William (1855–1937), actor and playwright. The lean, haughtily handsome stage star with vivid blue eyes and an aquiline nose was born in Hartford, Connecticut, the son of a United States senator. He studied at Yale, Harvard, and the Massachusetts Fine Arts Institute and made his professional debut as Guzman in *Faint Heart Ne'er Won Fair Lady* (1875) in Boston. Gillette performed numerous supporting roles at the *Boston Museum before making his New York bow as the Prosecuting Attorney in *The *Gilded Age* (1877). In 1881 he appeared in the title role of his own play, *The *Professor,* then toured in *Young Mrs. Winthrop* and played briefly in his own *Digby's Secretary* (1884). Three major successes followed: as the comic newspaperman Thomas Beene in his own Civil War drama, *Held by the Enemy* (1886); the perennial liar Augustus Billings in *Too Much Johnson* (1894); and the Northern spy Captain Thorne in *Secret Service* (1896). Gillette's greatest success came in the title role of *Sherlock Holmes* (1899), which he adapted from Conan Doyle's famous stories. One critic wrote that the actor, famous for his "scarce gesture and staccato sentence," "looks the part and carries it in his accustomed nonchalant and pictorially effective way." He scored again in the title role of *Barrie's *The Admirable*

Crichton (1903), then spent most of his later career reviving his earlier successes. Yet he shone as millionaire Henry Wilton in *A Successful Calamity* (1917) and as Mr. Dearth in Barrie's fantasy *Dear Brutus* (1918). Of this last performance John *Corbin wrote in the *Times* that Gillette "has never been more humanly gracious and delicately real," while Helen *Hayes, who was in the play, recalled his "silken quality," his "felicitous combination of grain and polish" and added, "I was never again to see such timing as this man had." Among the many other plays that Gillette wrote were such adaptations as *Esmeralda* (1881) with F. H. *Burnett, *She* (1887), *All the Comforts of Home* (1890), *Mr. Wilkinson's Widows* (1891), and *Settled out of Court* (1892). Biography: *Sherlock Holmes and Much More*, Doris E. Cook, 1970.

GILLMORE, Margalo (1897–1986), actress. A member of an old acting family, she was born in London but while still a child was brought to America, where she studied at the *American Academy of Dramatic Arts, then made her professional debut in *The Scrap of Paper* (1917). Gillmore was first widely noticed as the rebellious daughter Sylvia in *The *Famous Mrs. Fair* (1919), followed by the tubercular patient Eileen Carmody in Eugene *O'Neill's *The Straw* (1921). Her first appearance with the *Theatre Guild, with which she was long associated, was as the bareback rider Consuelo in *He Who Gets Slapped* (1922). Although she never became a star, she was much admired for her beauty and fine talent. Among her later roles were Ann, one of the newly dead, in *Outward Bound* (1924); Venice Pollen in *The Green Hat* (1925); Hester in *The *Silver Cord* (1926); Monica Gray in *The *Second Man* (1927); Kukachin in *Marco Millions* (1928); Helen Pettigrew in *Berkeley Square* (1929); George Washington's first love, Mary Philipse, in *Valley Forge* (1934); Mary Haines, who wins back her husband from a bitchy rival, in *The *Women* (1936); Amanda Smith in *No Time for Comedy* (1939); and Mrs. Darling in the musical version of *Peter Pan* (1954). Autobiography: *Four Flights Up*, 1964.

GILPIN, Charles S[idney] (1878–1930), actor. The African-American performer was born in Richmond, Virginia, and spent some time apprenticing to a printer before taking to the stage in 1903. He toured for many years with black companies and in 1916 became director of the *Lafayette Theatre in Harlem, the first African-American stock company in the city. His fine performance on Broadway as clergyman William Curtis in *Abraham Lincoln* (1919) prompted Eugene *O'Neill to cast him as Brutus Jones in *The *Emperor Jones* (1920). Although Gilpin's performance was praised, problems soon emerged. An arrogance born of sudden fame, coupled with an increasing drinking problem, made him difficult to work with. He was not signed for the London production, his role going to Paul *Robeson, whom many considered even better in the part. Gilpin rarely worked after The Emperor Jones. He appeared in a 1926 revival but never again performed professionally. Moss *Hart, who took the role of Smithers in the 1926 revival, wrote of Gilpin, "He had an inner violence and a maniacal power that engulfed the audience." Hart concluded, "Gilpin was the greatest actor of his race."

GILROY, Frank D. See Subject Was Roses, The.

GIN GAME, THE (1977), a play by D. L. Coburn. [*John Golden Theatre, 517 perf.; Pulitzer Prize.] At a home for the aged, the cantankerous, somewhat unstable Weller Martin (Hume *Cronyn) invites Fonsia Dorsey (Jessica *Tandy) to play gin rummy with him. As the couple play, they reveal their personal histories. But Fonsia's persistent winning provokes Weller's ire, and when he explodes in a profane rage, the games are apparently over. To many the Shubert production exemplified the peculiar state of American playwriting of its day. Soaring costs made two-character plays commonplace, and this was the first to win a *Pulitzer Prize. Almost by necessity these plays had minimal plots and action, consisting instead simply of dialogue. Yet when this play toured, it was often performed in large auditoriums, and the Cronyns sometimes resorted to amplification. A 1997 revival with Julie *Harris and Charles *Durning was successful.

GINGOLD, Hermione [Ferdinanda] (1897–1987), comic actress. The frowsy-miened comedienne, who combined a certain hauteur with a streak of raffishness, was born in London and was long a favorite on West End stages before making her American debut in John Murray Anderson's Almanac (1953). She later starred in several Broadway and West Coast productions and occasionally replaced other stars in shows, most notably in *Oh, Dad, Poor Dad. However, her most memorable Broadway role was the grande dame Mme. Armfeldt in A *Little Night Music (1973).

GIRARDOT, Etienne (1856–1939), actor. One of many performers remembered for a single role, the London-born actor captivated Broadway when he made his New York debut as Lord Fancourt Babberley, who helps his college roommate by dressing as an old lady and pretending he is *Charley's Aunt (1893). He later played in several revivals of the farce. Although Girardot continued

to appear regularly for the next forty years, often in important supporting roles, he never again equaled his early success. Among his other roles was Valentine, opposite Mrs. *Fiske, in *Leah Kleschna (1904). His last assignment was as the religious zealot Matthew Clark in *Twentieth Century (1932).

GIRAUDOUX, [Hippolyte] Jean (1882–1944), playwright. Thanks to a number of fine productions, Giraudoux has been the most successful of the modern French playwrights in the American theatre. He met varying measures of popularity with four works: Amphitryon 38 (1937), The Madwoman of Chaillot (1948), Ondine (1954), and Tiger at the Gates (1955). His best works were felicitously witty mixtures of fantasy and realism.

GIRL AND THE JUDGE, THE (1901), a play by Clyde *Fitch. [*Lyceum Theatre, 125 perf.] When Judge Chartris (Orrin Johnson) grants the Stantons a separation, he allows their daughter, Winifred (Annie *Russell) to choose which parent she will live with. Winifred elects to live with her mother, for she knows the real reason for the separation: Mrs. Stanton (Mrs. McKee Rankin) is a kleptomaniac, and Winifred hopes to cure her. The judge has fallen in love with Winifred and proposes, but when his mother, old Mrs. Chartris (Mrs. *Gilbert), comes to visit, Mrs. Stanton promptly steals the lady's jewels. Winifred forces her mother to confess, and Mr. Stanton returns and agrees to accompany his wife to a special home. Fitch took the story from a real incident told to him by an Ohio judge. The Charles *Frohman production was the last to be seen at the old Lyceum.

GIRL CRAZY (1930), a musical comedy by Guy *Bolton, John *McGowan (book), George *Gershwin (music), Ira *Gershwin (lyrics). [Alvin Theatre, 272 perf.] To keep him from nightclubs, gambling casinos, and women, Mr. Churchill sends his son Danny (Allen *Kearns) to Custerville, Arizona, to run a dude ranch. Danny hires New York taxi driver Gieber Goldfarb (Willie *Howard) for the journey, and soon after their arrival Danny has transformed the ranch into a club with gambling rooms and bevies of girls. But he falls in love with Molly Gray (Ginger Rogers) and woos and wins her with the help of Kate Fothergill (Ethel *Merman), daughter of the local saloonkeeper. Notable songs: Bidin' My Time; But Not for Me; Embraceable You; I Got Rhythm; Sam and Delilah; Boy! What Love Has Done to Me! The Alex A. *Aarons and Vinton *Freedley production was the last traditional musical comedy by the Gershwins before they attempted their political satires. Merman made a sensational debut singing "I Got Rhythm" and "Sam and Delilah," and it made her a star. In 1992 a revised version of the musical titled *CRAZY FOR YOU* opened at the *Shubert Theatre and ran 1,622 performances, winning the *Tony Award. Ken Ludwig wrote the new libretto that worked in some Gershwin standards from other plays and films, and Harry Groener and Jodi Benson were featured as the primary couple, though Susan *Stroman's exuberant choreography was the show's real star.

GIRL FROM UTAH, THE (1913), an English musical by James T. Tanner (book), Paul A. Rubens, Sidney Jones (music), Percy Greenbank, and Adrian Ross (lyrics), it told of an American girl who is pursued to England by a Mormon but who is saved from a bigamous marriage by a handsome musical comedy star. Charles *Frohman presented the American version at the Knickerbocker Theatre in 1914, with Julia *Sanderson, Joseph *Cawthorn, and Donald *Brian in the leading roles. What made this production so important in American musical theatre history were its Jerome *Kern interpolations, in particular "They Didn't Believe Me." This song singlehandedly established the ascendancy of the modern 4/4 ballad over the older waltz and set the pattern for musical comedy love songs for the next half century or more.

GIRL I LEFT BEHIND ME, THE (1893), an "American Drama" by David *Belasco and Franklin *Fyles. [*Empire Theatre, 208 perf.] When American soldiers disrupt a Blackfoot Indian religious ceremony, the Native Americans, led by Jack Ladru or Scar Brow (Theodore Roberts), plan their revenge. Their hope is to cut off communication between Fort Assinaboine and Post Kennion, both in Blackfoot territory in Montana, then attack the post, which is named after General Kennion (Frank Mordaunt). The general's daughter Kate (Sydney Armstrong) loves one of the post's officers, Lt. Edgar Hawkesworth (William *Morris), but his rival for Kate's hand, Lt. Morton Parlow (Nelson Wheatcroft), spreads stories of Hawkesworth's cowardice. Only when Hawkesworth rides through the hostile Indian forces to call for relief are matters set right. Seeing Kate and Hawkesworth embrace, the General comments, "This looks like—union forever." According to Belasco, producer Charles *Frohman commissioned the play in order to open the Empire Theatre with an American work on a native theme. The drama's modern editors, Glenn Hughes and George Savage, remarked, "The keynote of the play was suspense, and it was suspense par excellence that Belasco's maturing art achieved in its production." The play was revived

regularly for a decade after its premiere. **Franklin FYLES** (1847?–1911) was born in Troy, New York, where he began his career as a newspaperman, then served as drama critic for the *New York Sun* for twenty-five years. This was his first playwriting effort, but his subsequent works were generally not so well received, though some were popular: *The Governor of Kentucky* (1896), *Cumberland '61* (1897), *A Ward of France* (1897), and *Kit Carson* (1901). He was also the author of *The Theatre and Its People* (1900).

GIRL OF THE GOLDEN WEST, THE (1905), a play by David *Belasco. [*Belasco Theatre, 224 perf.] Minnie Falconer (Blanche *Bates) may be the owner of the Polka Saloon in a California mining camp called Cloudy Mountain, but she is also the town's respected schoolmarm, and she is courted by the gentlemanly but dangerous sheriff Jack Rance (Frank Keenan). While the town seeks a bandit named Ramerrez, she falls in love with a handsome young man named Dick Johnson (Robert *Hilliard), who she soon discovers is none other than the hunted bandit. When Johnson is shot by Rance, Minnie hides Johnson in her loft, but his whereabouts are revealed to Rance by blood dripping from the ceiling. She agrees to play a game of poker with Rance, Johnson's fate to be determined by the winner. She cheats to win, pulling a pair of aces from her petticoat after distracting the sheriff. However, the miners would still hang Johnson, and only Minnie's pleas spare him. Reluctantly she agrees to leave her beloved golden hills, and she and Johnson ride off to find a new life. Responding to criticism about the mechanics of his plot, especially the dripping blood, Belasco wrote, "I know the period of Forty-nine as I know my alphabet, and there are things in my *The Girl of the Golden West* truer than many of the incidents [in the stories by] Bret Harte." However, Belasco's biographer, Craig Timberlake, has suggested the many debts the dramatist owed Harte, among them a heroine who ran a Polka Saloon. Typical of producer-director's Belasco's striking theatrical effects was his opening, in which a vertically moving panorama took audiences from Minnie's cabin high in the hills down a path to the front of the saloon. The rest of the stage was then lit to reveal the first act set. The play was made into a popular opera by Puccini in 1910.

GIRL WITH THE GREEN EYES, THE (1902), a play by Clyde *Fitch. [Savoy Theatre, 108 perf.] A streak of pathological jealousy besets the Tillmans. Geoffrey Tillman (John W. Albaugh Jr.), having married a housemaid while drunk, enters into a secret bigamous marriage with Ruth Chester

(Lucille Flaven), lest a rival wed her. Geoffrey tells his brother-in-law, John Austin (Robert Drouet), of his first marriage, but John learns the horrifying truth when Ruth reveals she, too, has married him. Ruth breaks down while telling John the news, and John's wife, Jinny (Clara *Bloodgood), who is also Geoffrey's sister, enters in time to misconstrue the scene. Her jealousy is boundless and destroys her marriage, John refusing to betray the dark secret he has learned. Jinny is driven to attempt suicide, but John arrives to rescue her. What to many critics was a play moving compellingly toward tragedy was marred by the contrived happy ending that Fitch felt obligated to attach in order to please producer Charles *Frohman and to assure popular acceptance. Some other critics felt the play was weakened by an absence of any genuine motive for John Austin's persistent silence.

GISH, Dorothy. See Gish, Lillian.

GISH, Lillian (1893–1993), actress. Born in Springfield, Ohio, she made her debut at a small theatre in Rising Sun, Ohio, in 1902, in the melodrama *In Convict Stripes*. She continued in children's roles for many years, once acting with Sarah *Bernhardt and later under David *Belasco. Gish left the stage to become one of the first important silent film stars and did not return to Broadway until 1930, when she appeared as Helena in *Uncle Vanya*. Two years later she played Marguerite Gautier in *Camille*. Among her subsequent assignments were Ophelia to John Gielgud's *Hamlet* (1936), Martha Minch in The *Star Wagon* (1937), as replacement for the leads in such important plays as The *Old Maid* and *Life with Father*, and several other highly praised performances in a number of failures. Her sister, **Dorothy GISH** (1898–1968), had a similar career of early stage parts and later success in films before returning to New York in 1928 as the mate-swapping Fay Hilary in *Young Love*. Later appearances included the spinster sister Aaronetta Gibbs in *Morning's at Seven* (1939) and Chief Justice Holmes's wife, Fanny, in The Magnificent Yankee (1946). Like Lillian, she was one of many actresses to serve a stint as Vinnie, the mother in *Life with Father*. Autobiography (Lillian): *Dorothy and Lillian Gish*, 1973. Biography: *Lillian Gish: Her Legend, Her Life*, Charles Affron, 2002.

GLADIATOR, THE (1831), a tragedy by Robert Montgomery *Bird. [*Park Theatre, in repertory.] To free his wife, Senona (Mrs. Sharpe), and young son (Julia Turnbull), the captive Spartacus (Edwin *Forrest) agrees to fight in a Roman gladiatorial contest. But when his opponent turns out to be his brother, Phasarius (Thomas *Barry), and the Romans insist they fight to the death, the brothers decide to rebel. But Phasarius's impetuosity, aggravated by his obsession with the praetor's niece Julia (Mrs. Wallack), undermines their plans. With his brother, wife, and son all dead, Spartacus fights on until he, too, is slain. One of Forrest's most successful roles (he played it more than one thousand times), the actor never fully paid Bird for the work, but at the same time he refused to allow Bird or his heirs to publish it. After Forrest's death, it was revived by John McCullough and others until the end of the century.

GLANCE AT NEW YORK, A (1848), a "local drama" by Benjamin A. *Baker. [Olympic Theatre, approx. 75 perf.] When George Parsells (G. Clark), a "greenhorn" from the country, comes to New York to visit his cousin Harry Gordon (G. J. Arnold), they embark on a tour of the city, often encountering the most unsavory con men. They also disguise themselves as women to enter a "ladies' bowling saloon." Helping them out of their scrapes, and once or twice unwittingly getting them into trouble, is a handsome, rugged fireman, Mose (Frank *Chanfrau), one of the "B'hoys." The William Mitchell production was one of the earliest, and certainly the most successful, of American plays using the tour-of-the-city theme taken from Pierce Egan's *Tom and Jerry; or, Life in London*. It was performed in city after city, with the title and setting changed to reflect local pride and points of interest, and made frequent use of contemporary slang, until then a rarity in plays. The show boosted the career of Chanfrau, who played in numerous other sequels written around the character of Mose. *A Glance at New York* was revived Off Broadway in a mixed-media production in 2003.

GLASER, Lulu (1874–1958), actress and singer. Born in Allegheny City, Pennsylvania, she came to Broadway with no previous professional experience and was placed in the chorus of *The Lion Tamer* (1891), where she was assigned to understudy the prima donna. In one of those rare instances when a popular theatrical motif becomes reality, she was catapulted to stardom when the leading lady was taken ill. The show's principal male comedian, Francis *Wilson, wrote, "She was graceful in form and action and had wonderfully luminous eyes," though he diplomatically neglected to mention that critics were divided about her singing ability. For the next twenty years she was a reigning favorite, appearing in revivals of *The Merry Monarch* (1892) and *Erminie* (1893) and in *The Devil's Deputy* (1894), *The Chieftain* (1895), *Half a King* (1896), *The Little Corporal* (1898), *Cyrano* de Bergerac (1899), *Sweet Anne Page* (1900), *The Prima Donna* (1901), *The Madcap Princess* (1904), *Miss Dolly Dollars* (1905), *Lola from Berlin* (1907), *The Merry Widow Burlesque* (1908), *Mlle. Mischief* (1908), and *The Girl and the Kaiser* (1910), but her greatest success was as *Dolly Varden* (1902). Glaser also performed in several nonmusical plays and was long popular in vaudeville.

GLASPELL, Susan (1882–1948), playwright. Born in Davenport, Iowa, the playwright and novelist studied at Drake University and the University of Chicago. With her husband, George Cram *Cook, she was a founder and director of the *Provincetown Players. Alone or with Cook, she wrote several one-act plays for the troupe, including the spoof *Suppressed Desires* (1914), the domestic dramas *Trifles* (1916) and *Close the Book* (1917), the feminist play *A Woman's Honor* (1918), and the comedy *Tickless Time* (1918). Glaspell's full-length works include *Bernice* (1919), *The Inheritors* (1921), *The Verge* (1921), and *Alison's House* (1930), which won the *Pulitzer Prize. With her second husband, Norman Matson, she wrote *The Comic Artist*, which succeeded in Europe in the late 1920s but failed when brought to America in 1933. Her plays often reflected the most advanced intellectual thinking of her time and recorded her frequently telling observations, although many of them seemed more like literary exercises than theatrically knowing and effective dramas.

GLASS MENAGERIE, THE (1945), a drama by Tennessee *Williams. [Playhouse, 561 perf.; NYDCC Award.] Looking back, Tom Wingfield (Eddie *Dowling) recalls his life in a shoddy St. Louis tenement during the Depression with his mother, Amanda (Laurette *Taylor), who lives in dreams of a probably imaginary past, and his crippled sister, Laura (Julie *Haydon), who seems to live only for a collection of glass animals. At Amanda's insistence, Tom invites his friend Jim (Anthony Ross) from the warehouse where he works to the Wingfield apartment for dinner. It turns out Jim went to high school with Laura, who has long been quietly in love with his memory, and the two hit it off quite well until Jim mentions that he is engaged to be married. After Jim has gone, Amanda scolds Tom, who runs off to join the merchant marine. Called "a memory play" by Williams, and "a mood-memory play" by some later writers, it was hailed by Ward *Morehouse of the *Sun* as "fragile and poignant . . . a vivid, eerie and curiously enchanting play." The success of the *Dowling and Louis J. Singer production placed Williams in the front ranks of contemporary dramatists, and Taylor's performance was considered one of the memorable acting gems

of the time. Pauline *Lord headed the road company, and the play has remained a favorite in regional and educational theatres. New York revivals have been less successful; a 1983 revival with Jessica *Tandy and a 1994 production with Julie *Harris were rare failures for the two gifted actresses.

GLASS, Montague [Marsden] (1877–1934), playwright. The English-born dramatist and short story writer was brought to America while very young and began his career by contributing to various magazines. All his successful plays were collaborations, and many of them were based on his stories about a pair of comic Jewish business partners: *Potash and Perlmutter* (1913), written with Charles *Klein; *Abe and Mawruss* (1915), written with Roi Cooper *Megrue; and four with Jules Eckert *Goodman: *Business before Pleasure* (1917), *His Honor Abe Potash* (1919), *Partners Again* (1922), and *Potash and Perlmutter, Detectives* (1926). Although several of his other plays received favorable notices, they had short runs.

GLEASON, [Herbert John] **Jackie** (1916–87), comic actor. The burly, aggressive Brooklyn-born comedian is best known to Americans for his popular television series. He first appeared on Broadway in *Keep Off the Grass* (1940) but is recalled primarily for his clowning in *Follow the Girls* (1944), *Along Fifth Avenue* (1949), and *Take Me Along* (1959).

GLEASON, James (1886–1959), actor and playwright. Born in New York into an old family of troupers, he was carried on stage at the age of two, then performed around the country with numerous touring and stock companies. Gleason returned to New York in 1914 to appear in *Pretty Mrs. Smith*, then soon graduated to such important roles as the pretend millionaire Nathaniel Alden in *Like a King* (1921) and the disillusioned playwright James Leland in *The Deep Tangled Wildwood* (1923) before scoring a major success as the tough-talking fight manager "Hap" Hurley in *Is Zat So?* (1925), which he wrote with Richard Taber. Later that same season he collaborated with George *Abbott to write another hit, *The Fall Guy* (1925). With his wife, Lucille Webster, he wrote the successful comedy *The Shannons of Broadway* (1927), and he also produced several plays. With the coming of sound films, Gleason moved to Hollywood, where he was long typecast in tough guy roles.

GLEASON, Joanna [neé Johanna Hall] (b. 1950), actress and singer. A classy leading lady of musicals and plays, Gleason specializes in intelligent if slightly affected women. She was born in Toronto, the daughter of a television producer and an actress, and educated at Occidental College and University of California at Los Angeles. Gleason made an auspicious Broadway debut as the New Jersey housewife Monica caught up in the sexual revolution in *I Love My Wife* (1977) and was also lauded as the snooty Pam in the 1985 revival of *Joe Egg*. Her other New York roles include the drugged leading lady Virginia Noyes in *It's Only a Play* (1986), the Baker's Wife hoping for a child in *Into the Woods* (1987), the estranged daughter Artie in *Eleemosynary* (1989), and the Park Avenue sleuth Nora Charles in the short-lived musical *Nick & Nora* (1991).

GLENGARRY GLEN ROSS (1984), a play by David *Mamet. [Golden Theatre, 378 perf.; Pulitzer Prize.] In three separate scenes at a Chinese restaurant Shelly Levene (Robert Prosky), a failing real estate salesman, pleads with his boss, John Williamson (J. T. Walsh), for a better list of prospects; Dave Moss (James Tolkan) tries to inveigle George Aaronow (Mike Nussbaum) into robbing the real estate office to obtain the same lists; and the high-flying Richard Roma (Joe Mantegna) hustles James Lingk (Lane Smith), an unsuspecting prospect. However, when the real estate office is burglarized it turns out that Levene, not Aaronow, is the culprit. Moss quits, Aaronow reluctantly continues in a job he hates, and the foul-mouthed Roma continues to bull his way from sale to sale. This "drama-cum-comedy," as Bernard Weiner of the *San Francisco Chronicle* branded it, was an unflinching, powerful play doing for the cynical, hard-nosed real estate world of the 1980s what *The Front Page* did for the newspaper world of the 1920s.

GLENVILLE, Peter (1913–96), director. London-born, he was active in England as an actor, producer, and director but is known in America primarily for staging such shows as *The Browning Version* (1949), *The Innocents* (1950), *Separate Tables* (1956), his own translation of *Hotel Paradiso* (1957), *Take Me Along* (1959), *Becket* (1960), and *A Patriot for Me* (1969).

GOAT, THE; or Who Is Sylvia? (2002), a play by Edward *Albee. [*John Golden Theatre, 309 perf.; Tony, NYDCC Awards.] When architect Martin (Bill Pullman) announces to his friend Ross (Stephen Rowe) that he is in love with a goat, Ross tells Martin's wife, Stevie (Mercedes Ruehl), and repercussions set in that threaten his marriage and career. But Albee's play is not about bestiality as much as the dark corners in any relationship, and the script was surprisingly comic as well as moving. Some

enthusiastic notices encouraged the Off-Broadway production to transfer to the John Golden, where it ran nearly a year, though still not breaking even.

GOATCHER, Philip W. (1852–1931), designer. The son of a London scene painter, he served his apprenticeship under his father, then worked in Australia before coming to America in 1875. After several seasons at the *Park Theatre, he became the principal set designer at *Wallack's. Among his many notable achievements were the settings for the William H. *Crane–Stuart *Robson *The Comedy of Errors* (1878), such Wallack productions as *The Silver King* (1883) and *Hoodman Blind* (1885), the musical *The Lady or the Tiger?* (1888), and Arnold *Daly's 1889 revival of *As You Like It*. Of his work for *Hoodman Blind*, the *Times* noted, "The views of English rural scenery by Mr. Philip Goatcher are full of mellow beauty: A moonlit grove, with a rustic stile and winding pathway, is notable for excellent perspective; the Thames Embankment scene, showing the Egyptian Column, the semicircle of lights, and the 'dark, flowing' river called forth a storm of cheers when displayed." After losing a divorce case in 1890, he returned to England, then moved to Australia, where he remained an important scene painter until just before World War I.

GODFREY, Thomas. See *Prince of Parthia, The*.

GODSPELL (1971), a musical by John-Michael Tebelak (book), Stephen *Schwartz (music, lyrics). [Cherry Lane Theatre, 2,124 perf.] John the Baptist interrupts a meeting of the great men of history, from Socrates to Buckminster Fuller, to announce the coming of Jesus (Stephen Nathan), who arrives sporting a red nose, a heart painted on his forehead, and a Superman shirt. His history, following the Gospel according to St. Matthew, is then told by means of circus and commedia dell' arte tricks, a parody of TV quiz shows, cartoon voices, and similar theatrics. *Notable songs*: Day by Day, We Beseech Thee; Light of the World; All for the Best. Although no one found the treatment of the gospel sacrilegious, many critics objected to a persistent tone of cuteness. For the most part, playgoers apparently disagreed, for not only did the musical enjoy a long run Off Broadway but it was revived on Broadway at the Broadhurst Theatre in 1976 and ran an additional 527 performances, and the musical continues to be a favorite in theatres (and churches) across the country. It also marked the first professional production for composer-lyricist Schwartz.

GOETZ, E. Ray (1886–1954), producer and lyricist. Born in Buffalo, New York, he began to write lyrics and sometimes melodies for Broadway shows in 1910, when he set words to A. Baldwin *Sloan's score for *The Prince of Bohemia*. He remained active until better songwriters emerged about the time of World War I. Thereafter, he confined himself largely to producing, mounting several musicals for his wife, Irene *Bordoni: *As You Were* (1920), *The French Doll* (1922), and *Paris* (1928), as well as several of Cole *Porter's earliest musicals, such as *Fifty Million Frenchmen* (1929) and *The New Yorkers* (1930).

GOETZ, Ruth and Augustus. See *Heiress, The.*

GOLD DIGGERS, THE (1919), a comedy by Avery *Hopwood. [*Lyceum Theatre, 720 perf.] When rich, proper Stephen Lee (Bruce *McRae) learns that his nephew, Wally Saunders (Austen Harrison), would marry a chorus girl, Violet Dayne (Beverly West), he is duly alarmed. He decides to talk to Jerry Lamar (Ina *Claire), a worldlywise showgirl he has known and who, he learns, has taken Violet under her wing. Jerry assures Stephen that Violet is an exception to the rule that all chorus girls are out to marry rich men solely for their money, a rule exemplified by Mable Monroe (Jobyna Howland), Trixie Andrews (Lilyan Tashman), Eleanor Montgomery (Luella *Gear), and Gypsy Montrose (Gladys Feldman). But while she is reassuring Stephen, she is also plying him with whiskey. When he is drunk he proposes, and she accepts. Because she is in love with him, she soon confesses he trickery, but since Stephen loves her in return, he is forgiving. Although Arthur *Hornblow of *Theatre Magazine* typified the many negative critical reactions when he dismissed the play as a "trivial hodge-podge of chorus girl slang, bedroom suggestiveness and false sentiment," the David *Belasco production was the second longest-running show in Broadway history when it closed, and it gave popular currency to the expression "gold digger." The play later was the basis of several successful Hollywood musicals.

GOLDEN APPLE, THE (1954), a musical comedy by John *Latouche (book, lyrics), Jerome Moross (music). [*Phoenix Theatre, 173 perf.; NYDCC Award.] Angel's Roost, Washington, is a small turn-of-the-century American village where little happens until the traveling salesman Paris (Jonathan Lucas) arrives in a balloon and so beguiles Helen (Kaye *Ballard), the wife of Sheriff Menelaus (Dean Michener), that she elopes with him to Rhododendron. Ulysses (Stephen Douglass) and his neighbors pursue the pair, while the town's mayor, Hector (Jack *Whiting), throws road blocks in the pursuers' path. After Ulysses outclasses Paris in a boxing match, the Angel's Roost

soldiers begin their detour-laden journey home, where Ulysses finds his wife, Penelope (Priscilla Gillette), waiting for him. *Notable songs*: Doomed, Doomed, Doomed; Lazy Afternoon; It's the Going Home Together; Windflowers. This brilliant recreation of *The Iliad* and *The Odyssey* in terms of 1900 America garnered general critical approbation but failed to find a large public. While there was virtually no dialogue, Latouche's adroit, witty lyrics and Moross's charming music were at once contemporary yet period in flavor. Thus, in the song "Scylla and Charybdis" the returning soldiers were beguiled by two shady financial manipulators to a melody and words reminiscent of *Gallagher and Shean. The show has enjoyed several revivals but has yet to be given a major Broadway mounting and find the success it deserves.

GOLDEN BOY (1937), a drama by Clifford *Odets. [*Belasco Theatre, 250 perf.] Although Joe Bonaparte (Luther *Adler) knows his father (Morris *Carnovsky) wants him to become a violinist, Joe feels the best way out of the slums is with his fists, as a professional fighter. He enjoys some early victories, but when he breaks his hand, doubts about his choice seem resolved. "Hallelujah!! It's the beginning of the world!" he exclaims. But that world quickly turns sour when his girl, Laura (Frances Farmer), seems to desert him and when he kills a man in the ring. Laura returns to console Joe, and the two drive off, only to be killed in a car crash. One of Odets's least political early plays, "its pungent, flashy story" was marred, according to Brooks *Atkinson of the *Times*, by "an unwillingness to be simple in style." For all its faults the *Group Theatre's production proved popular, and it has been revived frequently, most notably in 1952 with John *Garfield. The drama was given a racial retelling in the 1964 musical version of the same title in which Italian Joe Bonaparte became African-American Joe Wellington (Sammy Davis Jr.) who strives to get out of the black ghetto and make good through his boxing talents. Odets worked on the libretto, but when he died William *Gibson completed it. Charles *Strouse (music) and Lee *Adams (lyrics) wrote the commendable score, which was atypical of the team with its moody ballads and sly take on racial stereotypes. Hillard Elkins produced *Golden Boy* at the *Majestic Theatre, and Davis's popularity helped it run 569 performances. *Notable songs*: I Want to Be with You; Night Song; Golden Boy; While the City Sleeps.

GOLDEN, John (1874–1955), producer and lyricist. Born in New York, his first theatrical job was as a super at *Niblo's Garden. He later entered New York University, intending to study law, but while there he produced a college play and abandoned the notion of becoming a lawyer. Golden served briefly as actor-manager for a touring company, then turned his hand to lyric writing. His major successes as a lyricist included "Goodbye Girls, I'm Through" (from the 1914 musical *Chin-Chin*) and "Poor Butterfly" (from *The Big Show*, a 1916 *Hippodrome extravaganza). Royalties from these songs allowed him to produce his first play, *Turn to the Right* (1916). Among his many later productions were *Lightnin'* (1918), *Three Wise Fools* (1918), *The *First Year* (1920), *Seventh Heaven* (1922), *The *Wisdom Tooth* (1926), *Let Us Be Gay* (1929), *That's Gratitude* (1930), *As Husbands Go* (1931), *Susan and God* (1937), *Skylark* (1939), and *Claudia* (1941). Some measure of his acute judgment of contemporary public taste can be gauged by the fact that, at the time of *Seventh Heaven*'s closing, Golden was on record as the producer of three of the five longest-running shows in Broadway history. For the most part his plays avoided material that might offend many playgoers. He wrote in his autobiography, "I think *Mrs. Warren's Profession* is a great play, but personally I prefer *Turn to the Right*. Given equal literary value, I should infinitely prefer a wholesome play." In 1926 he built the *John Golden Theatre but lost it in the Depression. He later purchased the more centrally located Masque Theatre and renamed it for himself. Autobiography: *Stage-Struck John Golden*, with Viola Brothers Shore, 1930.

GOLDFADEN, Avrom (1840–1908), producer and playwright. Often called the "Father of Yiddish Theatre," he is generally acknowledged to have been the first to put it on a professional basis and to have written its earliest plays, which remained part of the repertory as long as Yiddish theatre flourished. Goldfaden was born in Russia and spent most of his life in Europe. Coming to America in 1887, he made several attempts to produce Yiddish drama in New York and other American cities. When he failed he returned home. His last play, *Ben-Ami (Son of My People)*, was produced in New York shortly before his death. Among his plays long popular with Yiddish-speaking audiences in America were *Koldunye (The Witch)*, *Bar Kochba (The Last Days of Jerusalem)*, and his masterpiece, *Shulamis*.

GOLDMAN, James. See *Lion in Winter, The*.

GOOD GRACIOUS ANNABELLE (1916), a play by Clare *Kummer. [Republic Theatre, 111 perf.] The group of young women who have gathered at the posh St. Swithen Hotel are nice, but they are all broke. So when one of them, a pert lady named Annabelle Leigh (Lola Fisher), suggests they sign on as servants at the Wimbledon mansion on Long Island, they agree. Annabelle was married to a strange mining man when she was sixteen, but she ran away. He has continued to support her, although she regularly lives beyond her means. The new servants find the mansion has been rented in Wimbledon's absence by a handsome, rich miner, John Rawson (Walter *Hampden). When Wimbledon returns unexpectedly, he and Rawson prove to be rivals, at first only in business but soon for Annabelle. Rawson wins, turning out to be not merely a decent man but Annabelle's old husband as well. Kummer had originally approached producer Arthur *Hopkins, hoping to have her script turned into a musical, but he liked the piece as written. Alexander *Woollcott described the farce as belonging to "the leisure class," adding, "It is idle with a lorgnette and orange pekoe idleness. At times it is a little vague within, but it is always vogue without." The play might have run longer but for the depression that hit Broadway immediately before the country's entry into World War I. Ironically, when the show was finally turned into a musical, called *Annie Dear* (1924) with Florenz *Ziegfeld as producer, it failed.

GOOD NEWS! (1927), a musical comedy by Laurence Schwab (book), B. G. *De Sylva (book, lyrics), Ray *Henderson (music), Lew *Brown (lyrics). [46th Street Theatre, 557 perf.] Tom Marlowe (John Price Jones), the star of football-mad Tait College's team, may not be able to play if he fails his astronomy exam. Connie Lane (Mary Lawlor) agrees to tutor Tom, since she loves him even though she suspects he really loves another girl. Tom passes, Tait wins, and Connie gets Tom. *Notable songs*: The Best Things in Life Are Free; Good News; Just Imagine; Lucky in Love; Varsity Drag. This melodic, roistering musical has often been called the quintessential musical of the 1920s. Walter *Winchell welcomed the Schwab–Frank *Mandel show as "flip, fast, furious, free and flamingly festive." A botched 1974 revival lasted only two weeks in New York, but it has been successfully revived in regional and summer theatres.

GOODBYE AGAIN (1932), a comedy by Allan Scott and George Haight. [Masque Theatre, 212 perf.] Years before Kenneth Bixby (Osgood *Perkins) had become a famous author, he had a brief affair with a fatuous, wispy young lady named Julia (Katherine Squire). Now that he is successful and lecturing around the country, Julia suddenly appears at his hotel room, anxious to rekindle the old flame. By this time, however, Julia is Mrs. Wilson, and Mr. Wilson (Leslie Adams) soon appears on the scene to further complicate Kenneth's life. Luckily Kenneth's loyal, loving secretary, Anne Rogers (Sally Bates), is also on the scene, and she finally helps Kenneth explain away everything. Consequently, Kenneth begins to look at Anne in a new light. Writing in *Judge,* George Jean *Nathan praised the work as "a humorously observant fable . . . told with a saucy eye to authentic character."

GOODBYE, MY FANCY (1948), a comedy by Fay Kanin. [*Morosco Theatre, 446 perf.] Agatha Reid (Madeleine Carroll), a famous liberal author and congresswoman, returns to her alma mater to accept an honorary degree. She had been expelled years before, covering up for her then fiancé James Merrill (Conrad Nagel), who is now the president of the college. He is also a widower and a stuffy, confirmed arch-conservative. Nevertheless he falls in love again with Agatha, who is repelled by his politics. After threatening to reveal the truth about her expulsion if he doesn't allow his daughter to pursue her own liberal ways, she heads off with a charming magazine photographer. An amusing if slightly preachy play, its success was enhanced by the popularity of former film star Carroll. Kanin was an actress and screen writer as well as the sister-in-law of Garson *Kanin.

GOODMAN, Jules Eckert (1876–1962), playwright. Born in Gervais, Oregon, and educated at Harvard and Columbia, he spent some time as a journalist, including a stint on the *Dramatic Mirror,* before turning his hand to playwriting. Most of his plays were adaptations or collaborations, but he enjoyed a few small successes with original, solo efforts. His first long run was *Mother* (1910), followed by such successes as *The Silent Voice* (1914), *Treasure Island* (1915), and *The *Man Who Came Back* (1916). Several of his most popular works were collaborations with Montague *Glass on the Potash and Perlmutter series: **Business before Pleasure* (1917), *His Honor Abe Potash* (1919), *Partners Again* (1922), and *Potash and Perlmutter, Detectives* (1926). Two other moderately popular plays were *Chains* (1923) and *Many Mansions* (1937), written with his son Eckert.

GOODMAN, Philip (1885–1940), producer. The self-educated, Philadelphia-born entrepreneur used some of his profits from his garment district enterprises to become a successful producer for a while. His lightweight hits were *The *Old Soak* (1922), *Poppy* (1923), *The Ramblers* (1926), and *The Five O'Clock Girl* (1927). Curiously, his few attempts at trying something a little out of the ordinary all failed: Jerome *Kern's *Dear Sir* (1924), Marc *Connelly's *The Wild Man of Borneo* (1927), and Vincent *Youmans's *Rainbow* (1928). Goodman also wrote

a book of childhood reminiscences, *Franklin Street* (1942).

GOODMAN THEATRE (Chicago). Founded in 1925 with a memorial gift from the family of Kenneth Sawyer Goodman, who had been active in little theatre movements and had written some plays before being killed in World War I, the 683-seat theatre was designed by Howard Van Doren Shaw and built alongside the Art Institute of Chicago on Lake Shore Drive, where city ordinances relating to height forced it to be placed underground. The house opened in 1925 with the first American performance of *Galsworthy's *The Forest,* and its resident company continued to mount original plays and classics until it was forced to disband temporarily in 1930 because of the Depression. It served as a drama school before it was reactivated in 1969. Under the direction of Gregory *Mosher and then Robert *Falls, the company became nationally known for premiering such works as *Glengarry Glen Ross* and *Hurlyburly* and presenting sterling revivals, some of which transferred to Broadway with success, such as the 1999 mounting of *Death of a Salesman.* It has continued to mount a responsible repertory in both the original auditorium and its smaller, more experimental Stage 2. The school was dissociated from the organization in 1978 and was moved to DePaul University, and today the Goodman operates independently from the Art Institute. Most recently it has become a favorite tryout theatre for New York–bound productions, such as *Hollywood Arms* (2002) and *Bounce* (2003). In 1992 the Goodman won the regional theatre *Tony Award.

GOODRICH, Francis. See *Diary of Anne Frank, The.*

GOODSPEED OPERA HOUSE (East Haddam, Connecticut). Built in 1876 by William H. Goodspeed to contain a local 400-seat playhouse and offices for his mercantile endeavors, the Victorian Gothic wooden structure closed as a theatre in 1920. In 1959, shortly before it was slated to be demolished, conservationists organized the Goodspeed Opera House Foundation to restore and reactivate the auditorium, and it reopened in 1963. Since then the company has presented old and new musicals each season, usually with imagination and taste shown in the selection of offerings. Among the new musicals first tried out at the theatre are *Man of La Mancha, *Shenandoah, Something's Afoot, Harrigan 'n' Hart,* and *Annie.* Similarly, a sense of theatrical history has been manifest in the choice of revivals, which have ranged as far back as *Sousa's *El Capitan.* Sometimes these mountings have included substantial revisions of text and interpolation of songs not written for the shows in question, and some stagings have leaned towards a snickering style called "camp." In the 1980s a second theatre, a two-hundred-seat space named for Norma Terris, a musical star of the 1920s and early 1930s, was opened for more intimate productions. Under the direction of Michael P. Price for most of its modern existence, the Goodspeed has sent a dozen musicals to Broadway. Also located nearby is the group's valuable library-archives on the American musical theatre. The Goodspeed received special *Tony Awards in 1980 and 1995.

GOODWIN, J. Cheever (1850–1912), librettist and lyricist. The first American to enjoy a long, successful career writing musical librettos, Goodwin was born in Boston and graduated from Harvard. He spent a short time in support of E. A. *Sothern before joining forces with E. E. *Rice to write *Evangeline (1874), the musical burlesque that was to remain a favorite for the rest of the century. He continued to act and also translated French *opéra bouffe until *H. M. S. Pinafore (1879) began the modern rage for musicals, allowing him to work virtually full time at creating books and lyrics for musical shows. Among his more popular efforts were The Merry Monarch (1890); *Wang (1891); Dr. Syntax (1894); Fleur-De-Lis (1895); Lost, Strayed or Stolen (1896); and An Arabian Girl and Forty Thieves (1899). Noting that Goodwin had sold his rights in the hugely profitable Wang for a mere fifty dollars a week, De Wolf *Hopper in his autobiography said that the librettist never fully realized his abilities because of a lack of business acumen and a certain personal irresponsibility. "Had he possessed a rudder," Hopper observed, "Goodwin might have become the American Gilbert. Gilbert himself never excelled Goodwin's 'The Man with an Elephant on His Hands' song in Wang." Towards the end of his career Goodwin worked solely as a lyricist. He also wrote several nonmusical plays and was active in politics.

GOODWIN, Nat[haniel Carl] (1857–1919), actor. The comedian, who was as famous in his own day for his offstage roistering as for his performances, was born in Boston and educated at the Little Blue Academy in Farmington, Maine. His acting in school productions came to the attention of several famous performers, though later it was Stuart *Robson who gave him his professional start when he persuaded John B. *Stetson to cast Goodwin as a shoeblack in Law in New York (1874) at Boston's *Howard Atheneum. After appearing as a mimic at Tony *Pastor's, Goodwin played for several seasons in E. E. *Rice's musicals and then organized his own farce-comedy troupe, the Froliques. He performed in many written-to-order pieces such as The Skating Rink (1885), Little Jack Sheppard

(1886), Turned Up (1886), and Lend Me Five Shillings (1887), then scored a major hit as Chauncey Short in A Gilded Fool (1892). A year later he essayed a more serious role, the sheriff Jim Rayburn in *In Mizzoura. Augustus *Thomas, who wrote the play, recalled; "In person he [was] under the average height, and, then, was slight, graceful, and with a face capable of conveying the subtlest shades of feeling. The forehead was ample; the eyes were large and blue, clear and steady. The nose was mildly Roman; the hair was the colour of new hay. His voice was rich and modulated." Among his subsequent later successes were the title role in Nathan Hale (1899) and as Richard Carewe in When We Were Twenty-one (1900), both opposite his wife, Maxine *Elliott. Goodwin's final success came shortly before his death: the monogamist-at-heart Uncle Everett in *Why Marry? (1917). In his early career Goodwin espoused the broad, grotesque low comedy so popular at the time, but as styles changed so did he. In his later roles he was praised for his warmth and polished restraint. Although he longed throughout his career to play Shakespeare, his attempts at Bottom, the First Gravedigger, and Shylock were failures. Autobiography: Nat Goodwin's Book, 1914.

GOOSE HANGS HIGH, THE (1924), a play by Lewis Beach. [Bijou Theatre, 186 perf.] Bernard Ingals (Norman Trevor) and his wife have scraped and sacrificed so that their three children could have a better life. Bernard, in fact, gave up dreams of being a horticulturist, taking a political desk job instead. The children—Hugh (John Marston), Bradley (Eric Dressler), and Lois (Miriam Doyle)— seem indifferent to their parents' sacrifices, living expensively while chattering on about the benefits of socialism. Suddenly Bernard loses his job, and the children are forced to go to work. To everyone's surprise, they do so with gusto and skill. They even persuade their snobbish grandmother (Mrs. Thomas *Whiffen) to set their father up in the horticultural business. Although many critics questioned the facile happy ending, the *Dramatists' Theatre, Inc., offering suggested that there was another, deeper, and more responsible side to the era's high-living flappers. **Lewis BEACH** was born in Saginaw, Michigan, and educated at Harvard. His one-act play The Clod (1916) was produced by the *Washington Square Players. Later full-length works included A Square Peg (1923) and Merry Andrew (1929).

GORDIN, Jacob [Michailovitch] (1853–1909), playwright. Born in Russia, the son of a well-to-do merchant, he was given a good education but soon came into conflict with growing Russian anti-Semitism, so he immigrated to America in 1891

to help found a socialistic farming commune. When it failed Gordin began to write plays to support his large family. His first play, *Siberia* (1891), was a success, followed by his most popular Yiddish theatre offerings *The Jewish King Lear* (1892); *Mirele Efros* (1898); *God, Man and Devil* (1900); and *The Kreutzer Sonata* (1902). In all he wrote at least thirty-five plays, and possibly many more, since he often employed pen names. Gordin eschewed the particularly Jewish stories, especially the sentimental and comic ones that had been the mainstay of Yiddish theatres. He wanted to depict Jewish life in terms of larger and more universal themes. He also rebelled against the freewheeling ways of contemporary Yiddish actors, insisting they follow his dialogue precisely and wear clothes proper to the time and characters of his plays. His seriousness of purpose is generally said to have initiated the Golden Age of Yiddish-American theatre.

GORDON, Max [né Mechel Salpeter] (1892–1978), producer. The native New Yorker started his career as a press agent for *Hyde and *Behman, later becoming a vaudeville agent. For a time he was associated with Sam H. *Harris before embarking on his own. In the 1930s and during much of the 1940s he was one of Broadway's most successful producers. His offerings included *Three's a Crowd* (1930), The *Band Wagon (1931), The *Cat and the Fiddle (1931), Flying Colors (1932), Design for Living (1933), *Her Master's Voice (1933), *Roberta (1933), *Dodsworth (1934), The Great Waltz (1934), The Farmer Takes a Wife (1934), *Jubilee (1935), *Ethan Frome (1936), The *Women (1936), *My Sister Eileen (1940), *Junior Miss (1941), The *Doughgirls (1942), The *Late George Apley (1944), *Born Yesterday (1945), and The *Solid Gold Cadillac (1953). A small, professorial-looking man, Gordon was known for his mercurial behavior, once perching himself on a window ledge and threatening to jump if money was not forthcoming for a new production. Nevertheless, George S. *Kaufman characterized him as "the comparable Max Gordon." Autobiography: *Max Gordon Presents*, with Lewis Funke, 1963.

GORDON [Jones], **Ruth** (1896–1985), actress and playwright. Born in Wollaston, Massachusetts, she was determined to become an actress after watching Hazel *Dawn in The *Pink Lady. To this end she studied at the *American Academy of Dramatic Arts before making her stage debut as Nibs opposite Maude *Adams in a 1915 revival of *Peter Pan. One of her first important assignments was as Lola Pratt in *Seventeen (1918), after which she played Cora Wheeler in the road company of *Clarence (1920). Subsequent important roles included Bobby in *Saturday's Children (1927); the

guileless *Serena Blandish* (1929); the tragic Mattie Silver in *Ethan Frome (1936); Mrs. Pinchwife in a revival of *The Country Wife* (1936); Nora in *A Doll's House* (1937); Natasha in *The Three Sisters* (1942); writer Paula Wharton in her own comedy, *Over 21 (1944); and Dolly Levi in The *Matchmaker (1955). Brooks *Atkinson, writing of the tiny, gravel-voiced actress's performance as Dolly, suggested she gave "her most extravagant performance—sweeping wide, growling, leering, cutting through her scenes with sharp gestures." Gordon also wrote a successful, semiautobiographical play about a stagestruck young girl, *Years Ago (1946). Her last New York appearances were as the actress Zina in *Dreyfus in Rehearsal* (1974) and the title role in *Mrs. Warren's Profession* (1976). One of the last old-school performers to demand footlights whenever she appeared, she was married to the promising young actor Gregory *Kelly and, after his death, to playwright Garson *Kanin. Autobiography: *Myself Among Others*, 1971.

GORDONE, Charles. See *No Place to Be Somebody*.

GORELIK, Mordecai (1899–1990), designer. One of the American theatre's most influential designers, Gorelik was also a respected scholar and author whose ideas about theatrical design inspired many later artists. He was born in Shchedrin, Russia, and as a young boy immigrated to America, where he studied at the Pratt Institute and with Robert Edmond *Jones and others. He designed for the *Neighborhood Playhouse and the *Group Theatre and was represented on Broadway by *Processional* (1925), *Men in White (1933), *All My Sons (1947), A *Hatful of Rain (1957), and others. Gorelik was a strong advocate of Bertolt *Brecht's ideas and used a form of selective realism in much of his work.

GOTTFRIED, Martin (b. 1933), critic and author. The native New Yorker was educated at Columbia and began writing theatre reviews for the *Village Voice* in the early 1960s. He later wrote for *Women's Wear Daily* and the *New York Post*, where he was considered an opinionated, hard-to-please, but insightful critic. Much of his later career has been spent writing books about the theatre and stage biographies.

GRAIN, F. P., and P., Jr. (fl. first half of the nineteenth century), scenic designers. They first appeared on the New York scene about 1823, when they were advertised as having gained fame in Charleston, Savannah, and Richmond. Among their early work in Manhattan were settings for Henry Barrière's production of *The Lady of the Lake* (1826) and *The Battle of Algiers* (1829). Later they were important designers for the *Bowery Theatre and *Niblo's Garden. The Grains also created sets for the Floating Theatre in 1845, shortly before their names disappeared from advertisements. However, the mere fact that their names appeared in numerous advertisements attested to their fame, and one critic called them "among the best artists in the country."

GRAND ARMY MAN, A (1907), a play by David *Belasco, Pauline Phelps, and Marion Short. [Stuyvesant Theatre, 149 perf.] Wes Bigelow (David *Warfield), a Civil War veteran, has adopted and raised Robert (William Elliot), the son of a comrade killed in the war. Unfortunately, Robert gets into bad company, lends one worthless friend funds he has been given in trust, and is sent to jail when that friend squanders the money. Matters are eventually set right, and Robert returns to marry Hallie (Antoinette *Perry), the daughter of the judge who imprisoned him. Although this was the least successful of the Belasco-Warfield vehicles, it nonetheless enjoyed a reasonable success thanks to the theatrical brilliance of the two men.

GRAND DUCHESS, THE (La Grande Duchesse de Gérolstein). This Offenbach operetta was first presented in America in 1867 with Lucille Tostée in the title role. It tells of a duchess who hopes to win the love of a common soldier by promoting him but finds he remains loyal to his simple sweetheart. Its great aria, "Voici le sabre de mon père," became one of the most popular melodies of its day. The show began the decades-long vogue for French *opéra bouffe in this country and was regularly revived. One of the most successful of American duchesses was Lillian *Russell. When it was first performed in English a short time after its American premiere, which had been in French, some playgoers and critics took offense at what they deemed its salaciousness, but by the 20th century the work seemed harmless enough. The piece is usually revived by opera companies today.

GRAND HOTEL (1930) a play by Vicki Baum, translated by W. A. Drake. [National Theatre, 444 perf.] Over the course of three days at Berlin's finest hostelry, the lives of various characters overlap with romantic and tragic results. A jaded ballerina (Eugenie Leontovich) has a doomed affair with a penniless count (Henry Hull), a businessman (Siegfried Rumann) sees his career destroyed, a dying accountant (Sam Jaffe) ends his tired life in splendor, and a stenographer (Hortense Alden) starts her climb to fame. Based on Baum's novel that had been successfully dramatized in Berlin,

the melodrama was an early hit for producer Herman *Shumlin. After a celebrated film version and sporadic revivals, the tale returned as a musical in 1989. Luther Davis adapted the script, and half of the score was by Maury *Yeston, the other half by Robert *Wright and George *Forrest. Notable songs: Love Can't Happen; We'll Take a Glass Together; Bonjour Amour; Who Couldn't Dance with You? The commendable cast included David Carroll (count), Liliane Montevecchi (ballerina), Timothy Jerome (businessman), Michael Jeter (accountant), and Jane Krakowski (stenographer), but the true star of the production was director-choreographer Tommy *Tune, who inventively staged the piece like an endless dance of death that often turned the melodrama into refined theatrics. The musical was well received and ran at the Martin Beck Theatre for 1,018 performances.

GRANGER, Maude [neé Anna Brainerd Follen] (1851?–1928), actress. Something of a curiosity, she began her career as a celebrated beauty and ended it as a fine character actress. In between she was occasionally a star, but her stardom was precarious and intermittent. George *Odell wrote, "Miss Granger was in her youth one of the most beautiful and most photographed of actresses. Every college man, every sentimental girl, every collector had numerous pictures of her." She made her New York debut in 1873 in Without a Heart and quickly rose to such important assignments as Clare Dart in The *Mighty Dollar (1875) and millionairess Olivia Schuyler in Fifth Avenue (1877). That same year she was leading lady to John *McCullough in revivals of Virginius, The *Gladiator, *Richelieu, and *Othello and was judged a good enough actress to appear with Lester *Wallack's company as Dora in *Diplomacy (1878) and with Augustin *Daly to play the humiliated, doomed Gervaise in L'Assommoir (1879). Granger next appeared in two Bartley *Campbell plays, as Mary Brandon in *My Partner (1879) and as Cicely Blaine in The *Galley Slave (1879), followed by the adventuress Antonia in Two Nights in Rome (1880). Apparently her early promise was not being fully realized, for by this time her acting ability was coming under question, one critic suggesting, "a few gestures, postures, facial expressions, and verbal tones—these are her effects and these she repeats to a tiresome extent." After playing in a series of revivals of popular contemporary plays opposite James *O'Neill, her star quickly began to fade. For some years she played either important roles in lesser touring companies or supporting roles in major productions. With time, however, Granger appears to have carefully honed her limited abilities, and she won plaudits for her final appearances as the heroine's mother Mrs. Livingston in The *First Year (1920) and as the selfish, domineering Grandma Spenser in *Pigs* (1924).

GRANT, Micki. See *Don't Bother Me, I Can't Cope.*

GRAPES OF WRATH, THE (1990), a stage adaptation of John *Steinbeck's novel by Frank Galati. [*Cort Theatre, 188 perf.; Tony Award.] Originating at Chicago's *Steppenwolf Theatre, this earthy and captivating version staged by Galati was perfectly suited to the gritty kind of acting at which the company excelled. Lois Smith was the indomitable Ma Joad, Gary Sinise was her ex-con son Tom, and Terry Kinney was the preacher Casey, the conscience of the epic tale about destitute "Okies" who seek a new life in California. Presented simply on a planked stage with the Joads's overflowing truck as the visual focal point, the play allowed the story to speak for itself without gimmicks or artistic flourishes. Despite favorable notices, the Manhattan run was disappointingly short. **Frank GALATI** (b. 1943) is a respected director and successful writer. He was born in Highland Park, Illinois, and educated at Northwestern before embarking on a teaching career. But soon he was directing for Chicago theatres, including the *Goodman and the Steppenwolf. He has adapted literary works for the stage and screen and staged the New York productions of *The *Glass Menagerie* (1994) with Julie *Harris, *Ragtime* (1998), and *Seussical* (2000).

GRAU, Maurice (1849–1907), manager. Although best known for his successful tenure as head of the Metropolitan Opera, he was also important in the growth of popular musical theatre in America. Born in Brünn, Austria, and brought to this country at the age of five, Grau studied at Columbia and embarked on a law career. But he abandoned his legal position to help his uncle, Jacob Grau, then manager of the French Theatre in New York. His first solo venture was to bring to America the great French star of opéra bouffe, Marie Aimée. The success of her performances helped consolidate the vogue for *opéra bouffe in particular and musical theatre in general. Grau later persuaded Jacques *Offenbach to make an American tour and sponsored the great Italian actor *Salvini. At various times he was occupied with the management of several New York legitimate theatres.

GRAY, Spalding (b. 1941), actor and monologist. The intense, experimental performer is mostly known for his autobiographical monologue programs covering everything from movie making to writer's block to fatherhood. He was born in Providence, Rhode Island, and educated at Emerson College before making his New York debut in 1968. Seven years later he co-founded the alternative theatre company the *Wooster Group, where he wrote avant-garde theatre pieces with Elizabeth *LeCompte. Gray began doing his one-man shows in 1979 and eventually was widely known because of *Swimming to Cambodia* (1986), *Monster in a Box* (1990), *Gray's Anatomy* (1993), and other works. He occasionally performed in traditional plays as well, most notably as the Stage Manager in *Our Town* (1988) and the liberal candidate William Russell in *The *Best Man* (2000).

GREASE (1972), a musical comedy by Jim Jacobs, Warren Casey (book, lyrics, music). [Eden Theatre, 3,388 perf.] Innocent, sweet Sandy Dumbrowski (Carole Demas) transfers from Immaculata to Rydell High, where she promptly wins the affection of Danny Zuko (Barry Bostwick), a member of the "Burger Palace Boys," a toughtalking but harmless gang of youngsters who are known as greasers because of their slicked-down hair. When Danny refuses to conform to her canons of behavior, she dons tight jeans, changes to a bouffant hairdo, and stoops to conquer. At the same time she gives her rival, Betty Rizzo (Adrienne Barbeau), her comeuppance. *Notable songs*: Greased Lightnin'; Look at Me, I'm Sandra Dee; Summer Nights; Freddy, My Love; Beauty School Dropout. After expressing the bewilderment of so many that this totally undistinguished musical, whose songs reverted to the rock and roll styles of the late 1950s, could become (for a time) the longest-running show in Broadway history, musical theatre historian Stanley *Green attempted to explain its success by concluding, "But obviously the musical hit a nerve. Though the air was primarily one of parody, *Grease* let us see with unerring authenticity and total lack of sentimentality the way kids actually looked and acted and felt during those . . . days that we look back on as somehow being both placid and plastic." The musical moved from Off Broadway to the *Broadhurst and then *Royale Theatres for its long run. A 1994 Broadway revival was also very popular, and the musical continues to be a favorite in schools.

GREAT DIVIDE, THE (1906), a play by William Vaughn *Moody. [*Princess Theatre, 238 perf.] Although of old New England stock, Ruth Jordan (Margaret *Anglin) has come to Arizona to get away from the stifling, effete East and to help her brother's Western venture. She rejects a proposal of marriage from a New England doctor who seems too bloodless to her. Left alone in the Jordan cabin, she finds herself confronting three rough-hewn men, who would apparently attack her. She pleads to the most decent looking, Stephen Ghent (Miller), to help her. He buys off the others but then demands that Ruth come and live with him as his wife. She does and, although Ghent proves both an honorable man and a successful entrepreneur, drawing strength and goodness from his wife, Ruth cannot bring herself to love him. She remains haunted by her puritanical upbringing, yet she returns to New England, only to have Ghent follow her. There he reveals he has helped save her brother's enterprise. At first Ruth remains reluctant to return, but at last she sees she must. She tells Ghent that she lived "the only way I knew—the only way my fathers knew—by wretchedness, by self-torture, by trying blindly to pierce your careless heart with pain." Now she begs him to teach her how to live. Basing his play on an actual incident that did not end happily, Moody was inspired to develop the story as a classic battle between the tight puritanical mind and the free spirit of the West. The play was first performed at Anglin's urgings in Chicago as *The Sabine Woman*, then slightly rewritten for the Henry *Miller production in New York. Walter Prichard *Eaton noted shortly after its premiere, "No other American play has ever gone so deep, has ever seized hold of so powerful an idea; and no other American play has ever wrought an idea into a dramatic story with such dignity and grace of language, such poetry of image and emotion."

GREAT GOD BROWN, THE (1926), a play by Eugene *O'Neill. [Greenwich Village Theatre, 271 perf.] William A. Brown (William *Harrigan) and Dion Anthony (Robert Keith) are the sons of business partners and will soon take over the business. Both men love Margaret (Eleanor Wesselhoeft), but she chooses Dion, although it is not the real Dion she elects, not the tortured, sensitive, and artistic Dion but rather the Dion of the mocking, cynical mask. Indeed, when Dion briefly removes his mask in a moment of ecstatic passion, Margaret is revolted. Dion retires from the business partnership, fails in his attempt to become a painter, returns as Brown's employee, but soon withers and dies. Taking Dion's mask, Brown also takes his place as Margaret's husband, until the deception is revealed. By that time the real, inner Brown has languished. When Brown is accused of murdering his true self, only the prostitute, Cybel (Anne Shoemaker), who wears no mask, comforts him. Years after both men's deaths, Margaret looks back and swears eternal love to Dion, or at least to Dion's mask. "From passages of winged poetry he shifts quickly to mordant irony," Brooks *Atkinson noted of O'Neill's writing, continuing, "from the abstract he passes to the concrete without missing a beat." Although many playgoers were baffled by the expressionistic work, in which the actors often spoke from behind masks, enough

were intrigued to give the production a surprising commercial success. The play is reputed to have been O'Neill's own favorite among his works. A 1959 revival was unsuccessful, but a New Phoenix Repertory Company production in 1972 was generally commended.

GREAT LAKES THEATRE FESTIVAL (Cleveland, Ohio). Begun in 1962 as the Great Lakes Shakespeare Festival, the group was founded by Dorothy Teare, who persuaded a homeless Shakespeare troupe, which had formed a decade earlier at Antioch College in southern Ohio, to take residence in the Lakewood Civic Auditorium. Over the years the company, under the supervision of artistic directors Vincent Dowling, Gerald Freedman, and James Bundy, expanded the group's repertory and gave it a more encompassing name. Currently performing in the Ohio Theatre in Playhouse Square, the company is headed by Charlie Fee.

GREAT LOVER, THE (1915), a play by Leo *Ditrichstein and Frederic and Fanny *Hatton. [*Longacre Theatre, 245 perf.] Jean Paurel (Ditrichstein) is the world's greatest bass-baritone, the highest paid, most glamorous star of New York's Gotham Opera Company. His most famous part is Don Giovanni, a role he is notorious for playing offstage as well as on. But at the height of his career his great voice fails, and he must stand in the wings listening to a new star challenge his supremacy. As his career fades away so do the women who were once only too willing to be his conquests. Jean sits alone in despair when the phone rings. The caller is a lady for whom he never could find time but with whom he now eagerly agrees to meet. Written entirely as a vehicle for one star, the George M. *Cohan and Sam H. *Harris production created a furor because the settings were designed to look precisely like rooms at the Metropolitan Opera House and the hero's name was so similar to that of the Met's great Don, Victor Maurel. Walter Prichard *Eaton, despite some reservations, granted it "was about as sure fire as anything can be in the theatre."

GREAT WHITE HOPE, THE (1968), a play by Howard Sackler. [Alvin Theatre, 556 perf.; Pulitzer Prize, Tony, NYDCC Awards.] To the dismay of racists, Jack Jefferson (James Earl *Jones), a black prizefighter, rises to the top of his profession and becomes the heavyweight champion. But even some people who would not consider themselves racists bristle at Jefferson's arrogant, impolitic behavior. He flaunts his wealth and, worse, flaunts his white girl friend, Ellie (Jane *Alexander). Arrested by the authorities for breaking racial laws, the pressures finally drive Ellie to suicide. To the joy of many, Jack is toppled by a white fighter, but not before he has first pounded his opponent to a pulp. Based on the career of Jack Johnson, this gripping, magnificently mounted blank-verse drama was initially presented at Washington's *Arena Stage before producer Herman *Levin brought it to Broadway, one of the first such transfers from regional theatre. **Howard SACKLER** (1929–82) was born in New York and educated at Brooklyn College, served as a record director, screenwriter, and poet, as well as author of several plays mounted in regional theatres, before he was represented on Broadway by this play. His subsequent plays, such as *Goodbye, Fidel* (1980), were shortlived.

GREEN, Abel (1900–73), journalist and author. Born in New York and educated at New York University, he began his career as a cub reporter for *Variety* in 1919. He remained with the publication for the rest of his life, first organizing its European news service and establishing its Paris office, briefly directing its Hollywood office, and then becoming editor in 1933. He continued the policy of Sime *Silverman of attempting full, impartial coverage of all forms of entertainment. Among his books are *Inside Stuff on Popular Songs* (1927), *Show Biz, From Vaude to Video* (1951), and *The Spice of Variety* (1952).

GREEN, Adolph. See Comden, Betty.

GREEN BOOK, THE. A periodical first published in 1909 as *The Green Book Album*, it called itself "The Magazine of the Passing Show." In 1912 the title was changed to *The Green Book Magazine*. The publication featured "novelized" versions of current plays as well as biographical, critical, and other essays, but rarely attempted first-night coverage. It also regularly offered pages of superb, rare photographs, all too often neglected by modern theatrical historians. Publication ceased in 1921.

GREEN PASTURES, THE (1930), a fable play by Marc *Connelly. [Mansfield Theatre, 640 perf.; Pulitzer Prize.] In a small "Negro" church in the South, Mr. Deshee (Charles H. Moore) sets out to teach his children the Bible. He begins with a pre-Creation fish fry, which is interrupted when the angel Gabriel (Wesley Hill) arrives and announces, "Gangway! Gangway for de Lawd God Jehovah!" The Lawd God (Richard B. *Harrison) enters, dressed in a Prince Albert coat, black trousers, and congress gaiters. The story then proceeds through the legends of Adam and Eve, Cain and Abel, Noah, Moses, and other Old Testament figures and continues up to the crucifixion of Jesus. Based on Roark Bradford's stories, the play was praised by Heywood *Broun in the *Telegram* as "more stirring than anything I have seen in the theatre" and by Robert Littell in the *World* as "simply and briefly one of the finest things that the theatre of our generation has seen . . . it will move you to tears and make you gasp with the simple beauty of the Old Testament pageantry." Theatre historian William Torbert Leonard has called Gabriel's announcement "one of the greatest entrance cues ever written for the stage." A revival in 1954 failed to run.

GREEN, Paul [Eliot] (1894–1981), playwright. Born in Lillington, North Carolina, and educated at the University of North Carolina and at Cornell, he wrote numerous one-act plays before one of them, *The No 'Count Boy* (1925), made New York aware of his skills. The following year his first full-length play, *In Abraham's Bosom*, won the *Pulitzer Prize. His other noteworthy plays include *The Field God* (1927), *The House of Connelly* (1931), *Roll, Sweet Chariot* (1934), the musical *Johnny Johnson* (1936), and *Native Son* (1941). Much of Green's early work was looked on as folk plays, stories of the most downtrodden people, often written with explicit or implicit left-wing attitudes. In 1937 he wrote the first of his outdoor historical pageants, *The Lost Colony*, which has been presented on Roanoke Island, North Carolina, regularly ever since, except for the years of World War II. Similar pageants followed, including *The Common Glory* (for Williamsburg, Virginia) and *Faith of Our Fathers* (for Washington, D.C.). Green also taught drama at the University of North Carolina and elsewhere. Biography: *Paul Green*, Vincent B. Kenny, 1971.

GREEN, Stanley (1923–90), scholar and author. Born in New York and educated at Union College and the University of Nebraska, Green became a leading modern authority of our musical theatre. His works included *The World of Musical Comedy* (1960, and later revised editions); *The Rodgers and Hammerstein Story* (1963); *Ring Bells! Sing Songs!* (1971), a detailed examination of the musical theatre of the 1930s; *Encyclopedia of the Musical Theatre* (1976); *The Great Clowns of Broadway* (1984); and *Broadway Musicals* (1985). These books were characterized by an accuracy all too rare in popular show business histories, sound judgment, and an especially felicitous writing style.

GREENBERG, Richard. See *Take Me Out*.

GREENE, Clay M[eredith] (1850–1933), playwright. Born in San Francisco and educated at Santa Clara College and the University of California, Greene had established himself as a successful

San Francisco stock broker and businessman before turning his attention to playwriting and occasional acting. His first success was *M'liss (1878), followed by about eighty plays (many written with others), including Sharps and Flats (1880), Chispa (1882), The New South (1892), and Under the Polar Star (1896). At the same time, he wrote librettos for such musicals as Bluebeard, Jr. (1890), The Maid of Plymouth (1894), The Little Trooper (1894), and In Gay Paree (1899). Greene also mounted his own version of the Passion Play in California. He typifies the many creative theatrical figures, long popular and successful, who have left nothing enduring behind.

GREENWICH VILLAGE FOLLIES, THE. The series of revues was originally presented in a small Greenwich Village theatre but later moved to larger playhouses uptown. Editions were offered from 1919 through 1925 and again in 1928. The brainchild of John Murray *Anderson, they were considered the principal rival to the *Ziegfeld Follies in elegance and taste, and Ziegfeld early on tried to prevent the revues from using the word "Follies" in the titles. The shows were also admired for their fine comedy, including excellent female impersonators, and their imaginative ballets. Famous songs from these productions included Ted *Lewis's "When My Baby Smiles at Me," "Three O'Clock in the Morning," and Cole *Porter's "I'm in Love Again."

GREENWOOD, [Frances] Charlotte (1893–1978), comic actress and dancer. The tall, thin comedienne, with blonde hair and large blue eyes, was most celebrated for her long-legged, flat-footed kicking. Born in Philadelphia, where her mother ran a theatrical boardinghouse, she made her debut as an eccentric dancer in The White Cat (1905). After appearances in vaudeville and several more Broadway musicals, including two editions of The *Passing Show, she won critical acclaim for her performance as Letitia Proudfoot, a supporting role in Pretty Mrs. Smith (1914). The show was a failure, but its producer, Oliver *Morosco, ordered a musical written around the character of Letty. For nearly a decade she toured in such "Letty" shows as Long, Lanky Letty (1915); So Long, Letty (1916); Linger Longer, Letty (1919); Let 'Er Go, Letty (1921); and Letty Pepper (1922). Only three of them played New York, where they were quickly dismissed as too unsophisticated, but in other cities and smaller towns Greenwood built a special following that long remembered her with affection. Afterwards she appeared in several revues: *Music Box Revue (1922), The Ritz Revue (1924), and Rufus LeMaire's Affairs (1927). In the 1930s, when not in films, she appeared in several

California and London productions, including a final "Letty" show, Leaning on Letty (1935). She toured for two years as Mama in the road company of *I Remember Mama (1947 to 1949), then made a final appearance in New York when she portrayed Juno in the musical Out of This World (1950). Autobiography: Never Too Tall, 1947.

GREENWOOD, Jane (b. 1934), costume designer. Born in Liverpool, England, and educated at London's Central School of Arts and Crafts, she designed at the Oxford Playhouse before moving to Canada to assist Tanya Moiseiwitsch at the Stratford Festival. Greenwood made her New York debut with Ballad of a Sad Cafe (1963), followed by such memorable productions as The Prime of Miss Jean Brodie (1968), A *Moon for the Misbegotten (1973 and 2000), A Texas Trilogy (1976), *Medea (1982), Heartbreak House (1983), The *Iceman Cometh (1985), The Circle (1989), I Hate Hamlet (1991), The *Heiress (1995), Scarlet Pimpernel (1997), *James Joyce's The Dead (1999), Old Money (2000), and A Man of No Importance (2002). She has also designed costumes for film, television, and opera and taught at Yale.

GREET, [Philip] Ben (1857–1936), actor and manager. The noted English actor, director, and producer spent twelve seasons in America, from 1902 to 1914. Although he mounted a few original plays, he was best known for his Shakespearean revivals and for his production of Everyman. His troupe toured the country and served as a training ground for many young actors.

GRESAC, Fred[erique Rosine] de (1866–1943), playwright. The French wife of the famed opera singer Victor Maurel and a celebrated journalist in France, she was also a successful playwright and librettist. Among her better-known librettos were The Enchantress (1911) and *Sweethearts (1913), both written with Harry B. *Smith; The Purple Road (1913) with William Cary Duncan; Flo-Flo (1917); and Orange Blossoms (1922), which was based on her play La Passerelle.

GRESHAM, Herbert (1852–1921), actor and director. The lean, handsome English-born leading man made his New York debut in 1883 as Gabriel Gadforth in The Frolics of a Day, then won excellent notices the following year when he created the role of the comically villainous Marquis de Baccarat in *Adonis, remaining with the musical for several seasons. In 1891 he joined Augustin *Daly's famous company, and with that ensemble he created the roles of Little John in the American premiere of Tennyson's The Foresters (1892) and Sir John Garnett in The Great Ruby (1899). In between he appeared as Flutter in *The Belle's Strat-agem*, Meddle in *London Assurance*, and Dandy Dinmont in *Meg Merrilies*, as well as in such Shakespearean parts as Malvolio, Speed, Touch-stone, Stephano, and Gratiano. On occasion Gresham left the group to act for Daly in some of the English musicals the producer was importing. After Daly's death he became a director for *Klaw and *Erlanger, and their associates, staging such diverse offerings as *The Rogers Brothers in Paris* (1904), *The Ham Tree* (1905), *The Prince of India* (1906), the 1907 and 1908 editions of the *Ziegfeld Follies*, *The *Round Up* (1907), and *The Trail of the Lonesome Pine* (1912).

GREVILLE [first name and dates unknown], actor. He is said to have been a student at Prince-ton who abandoned his studies to join David *Douglass's company at the *John Street Theatre in 1767. This would make him probably the first native American to become a professional, since all known earlier performers appear to have been English-born. Greville played only minor roles, such as Marcellus in *Hamlet* and Escalus in *Romeo and Juliet*, and after a single season seems to have retired or moved elsewhere, where no record has been found.

GREY, Joel [né Katz] (b. 1932), actor. The pint-sized son of comedian Mickey Katz was born in Cleveland and made his professional debut with his father while still a youngster. Although he headed road companies or served as Broadway replacements for leads, he did not gain major attention until he appeared as the Master of Cere-monies in the musical *Cabaret* (1966). Walter *Kerr, writing about *Cabaret* in the *Times*, described how he "burst from the darkness like a tracer bullet . . . Mr. Grey is cheerful, charming, soulless and con-spiratorially wicked." His other Broadway suc-cess was impersonating George M. *Cohan in the musical *George M!* (1968). Grey returned to both roles in stock for many seasons. His other perfor-mances of note include the Dauphin of France in *Goodtime Charley* (1975), movie director Stony McBride in *Marco Polo Sings a Solo* (1977), Jewish refugee S. L. Jacobowsky in *The Grand Tour* (1977), chump Amos Hart in *Chicago* (1996), and the Wiz-ard of Oz in *Wicked* (2003).

GRIFFES, Ethel [neé Wood] (1878–1975), character actress. A durable player on the British and Ameri-can stage for over sixty years, the small, angular Griffes was ideal in matronly roles. She was born in Sheffield, England, and was on the stage by the age of four, touring in *East Lynne* and other plays. Griffes appeared in most of the major classic plays in England and was a seasoned performer by the

time she made her Broadway debut in 1924. Some of her memorable New York performances include the aristocratic Mrs. Higgins in *Pygmalion* (1927), the querulous Mrs. White suffocating her son's romance in *The Druid Circle* (1947), the domineer-ing matriarch Mrs. Hallam in *The Hallams* (1948), the sly Parisian Countess in *Miss Liberty* (1949), the crusty grandmother Mrs. Ellis in *The Autumn Gar-den* (1951), and the grande dame veteran actress Fanny Cavendish in the 1951 revival of *The *Royal Family*.

GRIFFITH, Robert E. (1907–61), producer. Born in Methuen, Massachusetts, he co-produced a series of musical hits with Hal *Prince: *The *Pajama Game* (1954), *Damn Yankees* (1955), *New Girl in Town* (1957), *West Side Story* (1957), and *Fiorello!* (1959). But his last two productions with Prince, *Tenderloin* (1960) and a nonmusical play, *Call on Kurpin* (1961), failed to run.

GRIMES, Tammy (b. 1934), actress. The petite blonde, with a voice that has been compared to a buzz saw, was born in Lynn, Massachusetts, and studied at the *Neighborhood Playhouse School of Theatre before making her professional debut by replacing Kim *Stanley as Cherie in *Bus Stop* (1955). She later appeared in *The Littlest Revue* (1956) before starring in the title role of *The Unsinkable Molly Brown* (1960). Long runs also followed as the prostitute Cyrenne in *Rattle of a Simple Man* (1963), the blithe spirit Elvira in *High Spirits* (1964), Amanda Prynne in *Private Lives* (1969), Elmire in *Tartuffe* (1977), Russian aristocrat Natalya in *A Month in the Country* (1979), and Broadway diva Dorothy Brock in *42nd Street* (1980).

GRISMER, Joseph R[hode] (1849–1922), play-wright and actor. Born in Albany, New York, he made his debut as an actor about 1870, later rising to leading man at the Grand Opera House in Cincinnati and at several major theatres in San Francisco. He managed to make many roles believable, although his stubby appearance was decidedly against him. As he reached middle age, however, Grismer gradually abandoned acting in favor of writing, directing, and producing. His first effort in this line was the Civil War drama *The New South* (1892), which he wrote in collaboration with Clay M. *Greene. Later plays, all adaptations or collaborations, included *A Gay Deceiver* (1898) and *The Manicure* (1899). His greatest success came when he rewrote a play by Lottie Blair Parker called *Annie Laurie*, changing its title to *Way Down East* and producing it with William A. *Brady in 1898. Brady later recalled Grismer as "the finest play-doctor who ever made a spavined manuscript jump through hoops." They enjoyed other successes with *As Ye Sow* (1905), *The *Man of the Hour* (1906), and *A *Gentleman from Mississippi* (1908).

GRIZZARD, George (b. 1928), actor. The boyish-looking actor, who specialized in wimpy or seemingly wimpy characters, was born in Roanoke Rapids, North Carolina. As a teen he acted in summer stock, then joined the *Arena Stage in 1952. Grizzard played important roles on Broadway in *The Desperate Hours* (1955), *The Happiest Millionaire* (1956), and *Big Fish, Little Fish* (1962) but really called attention to himself as Nick, the puzzled young professor, in **Who's Afraid of Virginia Woolf?* (1962). He portrayed a variety of leading characters in two evenings of one-acters, **You Know I Can't Hear You When the Water's Running* (1967) and *California Suite* (1976). Between Broadway appearances he worked with major Off-Broadway and regional companies. Grizzard's later appearances include John Tanner in **Man and Superman* (1978), college professor Henry Harper in *Another Antigone* (1988), and the questioning Tobias in *A *Delicate Balance* (1996).

GROODY, Louise (1897–1961), actress and singer. One of the brightest musical comedy stars of the 1920s, the vivacious, dimpled performer was born in Waco, Texas, and began her career in cabarets, then was first on Broadway as a dancer in *Around the Map* (1915). After playing important supporting roles in *Toot-Toot!* (1918), *Fiddlers Three* (1918), and *The Night Boat* (1920), she was awarded the part of the heroine Rose-Marie in *Good Morning, Dearie* (1921). Groody scored her biggest success as the spirited Nanette in **No, No, Nanette* (1925). Her last major appearance was as the persistent Loulou in **Hit the Deck!* (1927). She later played in vaudeville and in several nonmusical failures.

GROS, ERNEST M. (fl. 1890–1920), designer. Born in Paris, he came to America originally to paint the huge, realistic panoramas that were in fashion in the 1880s and 1890s. His mastery of realism quickly made him one of the most sought-after set designers, especially by advocates of this style such as David *Belasco. Among the dozens of Broadway shows displaying his work were **El Capitan* (1896), **Sherlock Holmes* (1899), **Ben-Hur* (1899), *The *Darling of the Gods* (1902), *The *Music Master* (1904), **Adrea* (1905), **Peter Pan* (1905), *The *Girl of the Golden West* (1905), **Salvation Nell* (1908), *The *Easiest Way* (1909), *The *Bird of Paradise* (1912), *The *Gold Diggers* (1919), and *Kiki* (1921). One of his most memorable scenes was a rocky pass in North Africa in which the heroine rides through a sand storm in **Under Two Flags* (1901). The ride,

not unlike one in *Mazeppa*, took the heroine and her horse virtually up into the flies.

GROSSMITH, Lawrence (1877–1944), actor. The English leading man, a member of a once famous theatrical family, often played America, taking major roles in such musicals as *About Town* (1906), **Nobody Home* (1915), *Flora Bella* (1916), *Love o' Mike* (1917), and *The *Cat and the Fiddle* (1931), as well as in such plays as *Too Many Husbands* (1919) and *Call It a Day* (1936).

GROUP, THE (1775), a play by Mercy Otis *Warren. A group of men who, for a variety of reasons and with varied shades of enthusiasm, have embraced the loyalist cause, gather to discuss the growing movement towards rebellion in the colonies. They implore Sylla (read General Gage) to take action, but Sylla is torn between his sense of duty and a compassion for the plight of the colonials. Described by Arthur *Quinn as more conversation than play, the text was widely circulated among anti-British factions. No record of performance survives, although the title page states "As lately acted."

GROUP THEATRE, THE (New York). After about a year of discussions, the Group Theatre was founded in 1931 by Harold *Clurman, Cheryl *Crawford, and Lee *Strasberg. An early announcement described the company as "an organization of actors and directors formed with the ultimate aim of creating a permanent acting company to maintain regular New York seasons." All three founders had been associated in one capacity or another with the *Theatre Guild, and their breakaway was to a large extent a protest over the Guild's essentially apolitical policies. The founders, especially Strasberg and Clurman, were committed leftists and felt the theatre should provide a stage for more sharply oriented political plays. In retrospect, the rupture was seen to mark the beginning of the Guild's decline. The new company's first effort was *The House of Connelly* (1931), followed by such notable productions as **Men in White* (1933), **Awake and Sing!* (1935), **Waiting for Lefty* (1935), **Johnny Johnson* (1936), **Golden Boy* (1937), **Rocket to the Moon* (1938), *The *Gentle People* (1939), and **My Heart's in the Highlands* (1939). The Group Theatre ceased production in 1940 and disbanded. Although most of the playwrights whose works were mounted had already established their reputations, the company was the first to present Clifford *Odets and Marc *Blitzstein to playgoers. The many theatrical figures whose careers were boosted by the company included Luther *Adler, Stella *Adler, John *Garfield, Elia *Kazan, and Franchot *Tone, who provided much of the financial backing in the early seasons. A detailed history of the company was written by Clurman in *The Fervent Years* (1945).

GROVER, Leonard. See *Our Boarding House*.

GUARE, John (b. 1938), playwright. Nephew of a Hollywood casting director, he was born in New York and studied at the Yale School of Drama. He won an *Obie Award for his one-act play, *Muzeeka* (1968), but his first major success was *The *House of Blue Leaves* (1971). Subsequent full-length plays have included *Rich and Famous* (1976), *Marco Polo Sings a Solo* (1977), *Landscape of the Body* (1977), *Bosoms and Neglect* (1979), and *Lydie Breeze* (1982). Not until *Six Degrees of Separation* (1990) did he enjoy another major hit. Guare's later works include *Four Baboons Adoring the Sun* (1992), *Lake Hollywood* (1999), and *Chaucer in Rome* (2001); he also scripted the librettos for *Two Gentlemen of Verona* (1971) and *Sweet Smell of Success* (2002). Guare's work is difficult to categorize, mixing absurdist touches with a quirky kind of satire that relies on inflated language.

GUERNSEY, Otis L[ove], Jr. (1918–2001), critic. Born in New York and educated at Yale, he served as a drama critic for the *Herald Tribune* and *Show*, as a lecturer on theatre, and as the editor of the *Dramatists Guild Quarterly*. However, he is best known as the editor of the *Best Plays* series, supervising thirty-six volumes between 1964 and 2000 (the longest stint in the history of the series).

GUETTEL, Adam. See *Floyd Collins*.

GUNTER, A[rchibald] C[lavering] (1847–1907), playwright. The English-born author was raised in California and studied at the University of California. While working as a chemical and civil engineer he wrote his first play, *Found a True Vein* (1872), dealing with life in a mining camp. Its success prompted him to come east, where he scored a success with a crude but powerful drama, *Two Nights in Rome* (1880). Gunter's later plays included *Fresh, the American* (1881), *A Dime Novel* (1883), Richard *Mansfield's popular vehicle *Prince Karl* (1886), and two successful adaptations of novels, *Mr. Barnes of New York* (1888) and *Mr. Potter of Texas* (1891). His two dozen produced plays were generally perceived as lacking in real merit, but theatrically effective. He also wrote thirty-nine novels.

GUNTON, Bob (b. 1945), actor and singer. The flexible, all-purpose leading man was born in Santa Monica, California, and educated at St. Peter's College and the University of California before serving as a sergeant in Vietnam, where he was decorated. Gunton made his New York debut Off Broadway in 1971 and was on Broadway six years later when a Brooklyn production of *Happy End* transferred to Manhattan. His most successful performances have been in hit musicals: the Argentine dictator Juan Peron in *Evita* (1979), the phony King in *Big River* (1985), and the psychotic barber *Sweeney Todd* (1989).

GURNEY, A[lbert] R[amsdell], Jr. (b. 1930), playwright. A native of Buffalo, New York, he studied at Williams College and at Yale and for years supplemented his writing income by teaching at the Massachusetts Institute of Technology (MIT). His plays reveal him as the logical heir to Philip *Barry and S. N. *Behrman, time and again presenting an amused look at rich WASP American society, in which mothers doggedly try to squelch their daughters' intellectual aspirations, and shallowness and lovelessness are kept from chaos by a studied observance of polite form. Among his more noted plays have been *Scenes from American Life* (1971), *The *Dining Room* (1982), *The Middle Ages* (1982), and *The Perfect Party* (1986). All these were mounted Off Broadway and at regional theatres. Gurney's first play to reach Broadway was *Sweet Sue* (1987), but he had better luck Off Broadway with subsequent works such as *The Cocktail Hour* (1988), *Love Letters* (1989), *Later Life* (1993), *Sylvia* (1995), *Overtime* (1996), *Labor Day* (1998), *Far East* (1999), *Ancestral Voices* (1999), and *O Jerusalem* (2003).

GUSSOW, Mel (b. 1933), critic. One of the few major theatre reviewers to concentrate on Off and Off Off Broadway, Gussow is considered a reasonable voice in writing about offbeat and unusual theatre productions. The native New Yorker was educated at Middlebury College and Columbia and began writing criticism for *Newsweek* in 1959. Since the late 1960s, Gussow has reviewed theatre for the *New York Times*. He has also written some books of criticism and biographies.

GUTHRIE THEATRE (Minneapolis, Minnesota). The theatre was established by Oliver Rea, Peter Zeisler, and Tyrone *Guthrie. The idea was to form a permanent repertory company away from the commercialism of New York theatre. The three men put an open ad in the *New York Times* inviting cities to indicate if they were interested in Guthrie's concept. Seven urban centers responded positively, and it was decided to place the theatre in the Minneapolis/St. Paul area after the Walker Art Center offered the trio a $400,000 grant and land on which to build a playhouse. Guthrie and his designer, Tanya Moiseiwitsch, worked out details for the famous auditorium seating 1,437 people in a 200-degree arc around an asymmetrical thrust stage. The theatre opened in 1963 with a performance of *Hamlet. Among Guthrie's personal successes there were his mountings of *The Three Sisters, Henry V, Volpone,* and *Richard III.* After Guthrie's death the season was expanded, the company went on occasional tours, and a smaller theatre opened for the presentation of experimental plays. Other noteworthy artistic directors over the years have included Douglas Campbell, Michael Langham, Alvin *Epstein, Liviu *Ciulei, and Garland Wright. Currently under the leadership of Joe Dowling, the Guthrie remains one of the nation's most respected regional theatre companies with a wide range of activities. It received a *Tony Award for its activities in 1982.

GUTHRIE, Tyrone (1900–71), director and manager. The distinguished English director, long associated with the Old Vic, first came to America to direct *Call It a Day* (1936), later returning to stage a 1946 revival of *He Who Gets Slapped.* Thereafter, he moved back and forth between continents, offering New York his stagings of *The *Matchmaker* (1955), *Tamburlaine the Great* (1956), *Candide* (1956), *The Makropoulos Secret* (1957), *The *Tenth Man* (1959), *Gideon* (1961), and *Dinner at Eight* (1966). He was largely responsible for the creation of the Shakespearean Festival Theatre in Stratford, Ontario, in 1953 and the *Guthrie Theatre and Guthrie Theatre Foundation in Minneapolis in 1963. Guthrie was at his best in bringing to life Elizabethan, especially Shakespearean, plays, but he displayed his fine sense of pacing, tension, and understanding in productions of many modern works. He also wrote a number of books, including *Theatre Prospect* (1932), *A New Theatre* (1964), and *In Various Directions* (1965). Autobiography: *A Life in the Theatre,* 1959.

GUTIERREZ, Gerald (b. 1952), director. The son of a police detective and a flamenco dancer, the Brooklyn-born Gutierrez was educated at the State University of New York (SUNY) Stony Brook and Juilliard before making his Manhattan directorial debut with *A Life in the Theatre* (1977). Although he staged many productions for *Playwrights Horizons, the *Acting Company, and other Off-Broadway companies, Gutierrez was not widely recognized until his Tony Award–winning direction of the 1995 Broadway revival of *The *Heiress.* His other major credits include *Isn't It Romantic* (1983), *A *Delicate Balance* (1996), and *Dinner at Eight* (2002). While he has also directed musicals, Gutierrez excels at detailed realism and intimate character dramas.

GUYS AND DOLLS (1950), a musical comedy by Jo Swerling, Abe *Burrows (book), Frank *Loesser (music, lyrics). [46th Street Theatre, 1,200 perf.; Tony, NYDCC Awards.] Nathan Detroit (Sam *Levene), who runs the oldest established permanent floating crap game in New York, needs to find a place to gamble, a special problem since high rollers, including the biggest plunger of all, Sky Masterson (Robert *Alda), are in town and ready to play. When Sky boasts that he can have any woman he wants, Nathan sees his chance. He wagers that Sky cannot win any woman Nathan points to and Sky takes the bet. At that moment, Sister Sarah (Isabel Bigley) of the Save-a-Soul Mission comes marching by, and Nathan points to her. Sky lures her to Havana, but in the end Sarah converts him to her ways. When he wins big at dice he forces all the losers to attend a revival meeting at the mission. Sky wins Sarah's heart and Nathan agrees to wed Adelaide (Vivian Blaine), a nightclub singer with whom he has had a fourteen-year engagement. *Notable songs*: Guys and Dolls; Adelaide's Lament; A Bushel and a Peck; If I Were a Bell; I'll Know; I've Never Been in Love Before; Sit Down, You're Rockin' the Boat. Based on Damon Runyon's short stories and billed as "a musical fable of Broadway," the Cy *Feuer and E. *Martin entertainment created its own special, raffish world, with people sporting such colorful monikers as Nicely-Nicely Johnson and Harry the Horse. Howard Barnes of the *Herald Tribune* noted that "the work uses music and dancing as embellishments to the libretto, rather than making the latter a loose clothesline for assorted capers," while John Chapman in selecting his *Best Plays* thought its cohesiveness and brilliance made it better than any straight play of the season. The show has enjoyed regular revivals, including a highly praised mounting by Great Britain's *National Theatre in 1982 and popular Broadway revivals in 1976 and 1992. [Alfred] **Damon RUNYON** (1884–1946), born in Manhattan, Kansas, was long admired for his columns depicting colorful Broadway life for the Hearst papers and for his short stories of the same demimonde. In 1935 he collaborated with Howard *Lindsay on the gangster play *A Slight Case of Murder,* and his colorful Manhattan characters showed up in several movies as well as in *Guys and Dolls.* Biography: *Damon Runyon: A Life,* Jimmy Breslin, 1992.

GYPSY (1959), a musical play by Arthur *Laurents (book), Jule *Styne (music), Stephen *Sondheim (lyrics). [*Broadway Theatre, 702 perf.] Rose (Ethel *Merman), a pushy stage mother, is determined to make a star of her daughter "Baby June," so she makes candy salesman Herbie (Jack

Klugman) the manager for her kiddie act and they try to make it in vaudeville. But as June (Lane Bradbury) grows up she develops a mind of her own and runs away, so Rose centers her drive on her other daughter, Louise (Sandra Church). Louise flops in vaudeville but manages to become the great burlesque queen, Gypsy Rose *Lee. Rich and famous, Louise thinks she no longer needs Rose, who is left uncertain whether all the ambition and sacrifice were worth the effort. *Notable songs*: Everything's Coming Up Roses; Rose's Turn; Let Me Entertain You; Small World; Together; You'll Never Get Away from Me. Based on Gypsy Rose Lee's autobiography, the David *Merrick and Leland *Hayward musical inspired Styne's finest score and Merman's greatest performance. The show was revived on Broadway in 1973 with Angela *Lansbury as Rose, in 1989 with Tyne Daly, and in 2003 with Bernadette *Peters.

H

H.M.S. PINAFORE; or, The Lass That Loved a Sailor (1878). A landmark *Gilbert and Sullivan comic opera, it tells of a young lady who is pursued by the head of the English navy but who loves an ordinary tar. Her loyalty is rewarded when it is discovered that the sailor is really entitled to be a captain. *Notable songs*: I'm Called Little Buttercup; Never Mind the Why and Wherefore; We Sail the Ocean Blue; When I Was a Lad. The operetta's American premiere was in Boston in 1878, opening in New York two months later. Within weeks the so-called *"Pinafore* craze" swept the nation. In Manhattan alone three companies performed at the same time, when New York had only a dozen first-class theatres. By season's end twelve theatres had offered a version on one occasion or another. *Pinafore*'s popularity can be attributed to its literate, witty libretto and captivating melodies, as well as the fact that it was such a clean show that ministers, who had heretofore railed against the theatre, encouraged their flocks to attend. The real beginnings of the popular American musical theatre can be traced to this work's unprecedented success. Prior to *Pinafore*'s appearance, only a few of what could be called musicals were presented each season. Immediately thereafter and for almost the next hundred years Broadway never again saw fewer than fifteen or twenty musicals a year. The earliest great American musicals were openly modeled on this and other Gilbert and Sullivan works. *H.M.S. Pinafore* has been revived regularly ever since, making it arguably the most produced musical in the English language.

HACKETT, Albert. See *Diary of Anne Frank, The.*

HACKETT, J[ames] H[enry] (1800–71), actor and manager. Born in New York, he studied law and went into business before making his acting debut at the *Park Theater in 1826 as Justice Woodcock in *Love in a Village.* Not until he essayed Dromio of Ephesus later that year did he win widespread fame. Hackett would become probably the finest Shakespearean comedian of his day, but to most playgoers he was a favorite because of his Yankee characterizations. Examples of the latter include Solomon Swop in his own adaptation, *Jonathan in England* (1928), Rip Van Winkle, and the unlettered Kentucky congressman Colonel Nimrod Wildfire in *The *Lion of the West.* This last character proved so popular that Hackett reprised the character in *The Kentuckian* (1833). His finest Shakespearean creation was Falstaff, which prompted William *Winter to write, "He interpreted a mind that was merry, but one in which merriment was strongly tinctured with scorn. It cared nothing about virtue, except that some persons trade on that attribute; and it knew nothing about sweetness, except that it is a property of sugar and a good thing in sack." Later in his career Hackett attempted Lear and Hamlet, but these were unsuccessful, so most of his long theatrical life was passed playing roles he popularized early on. Hackett also managed theatres, including the *Bowery, the Chatham, the National, and the Astor Place Opera House, this last at the time of the *Astor Place Riots. Considered something of a Shakespearean scholar as well, he was instrumental in New York's erecting a statue of Shakespeare in Central Park. His first wife, Catherine Leesugg (1797–1848), was a popular singer and actress.

HACKETT, James K[eteltas] (1869–1926), actor. The Canadian-born son of J. H. *Hackett, like his father he studied law before electing to become an actor. He made his debut early in 1892 and later the same year joined Augustin *Daly's ensemble, in which his assignments ranged from Master Wilford in *The *Hunchback* to Jacques in *As You Like It.* From 1895 to 1899 he worked with Daniel *Frohman at the *Lyceum, playing in a series of romantic comedies and dramas. His most famous role there was the one with which he was afterwards always identified, Rudolf in *The *Prisoner of Zenda.* Hackett was a tall, slim, dark-haired, handsome man but a relatively wooden actor whose career was largely confined to similar, if less memorable roles. Typical of his later characterizations were the swashbuckling Basil Jennico in *The *Pride of Jennico* (1900) and the righteous Jack Frobisher in *The Walls of Jericho* (1905). Late in his career he attempted a number of Shakespearean revivals, which met with only modest success, and his last

Broadway appearance was in 1924 as Macbeth. For a short time, Hackett also ran the theatre originally built as the Lew Fields', renaming it for himself during his tenure.

HAGEN, Uta (b. 1919), actress and teacher. Born in Germany but educated in America, she studied at England's Royal Academy of Dramatic Arts before making her Broadway debut as Nina in *The Seagull* (1938). After winning praise for her Desdemona opposite Paul *Robeson's Othello in 1943, her career faltered for several seasons until she replaced Jessica *Tandy as Blanche Du Bois in *A *Streetcar Named Desire* in 1948, then played the loyal wife Georgie in The *Country Girl* (1950) and *Shaw's *Saint Joan* (1951). Hagen's performance as Joan, which displayed the high intelligence she brought to all her work, was admired for its common sense, down-to-earth qualities. In 1962 she created the role of Martha, the unhappily married woman, in *Who's Afraid of Virginia Woolf?* In the 1980s she starred in several Shavian revivals Off Broadway, then gave two outstanding performances in the 1990s: the psychologist *Mrs. Klein* (1995) and the author Ruth in *Collected Stories* (1998). Hagen taught acting for many years at the Manhattan school started by her husband, Herbert *Berghof, and wrote some notable books on acting technique.

HAGGIN, [James] Ben Ali [Jr.] (1882?–1951), designer. Playgoers recalled Haggin for the sumptuous tableaux, or "living pictures," often revealing draped beauties, that he created for the *Ziegfeld Follies* and for *Ziegfeld's cabaret shows, the *Midnight Frolics*. Revue historian Robert Baral has said of Haggin's tableaux, "He incorporated drama and historical sweep, making groupings look like old masters." The New York–born son of the famous horseman, James B. A. Haggin, and grandson of James B. Haggin, owner of the Anaconda copper mine, the young Haggin studied art in Munich and returned home to become a celebrated society portrait painter. He also staged numerous lavish pageants and balls.

HAIR (1967), a rock musical by Gerome Ragni, James Rado (book, lyrics), Galt MacDermott (music). [*Public Theatre, 1,836 perf.] Claude (Walker Daniels) is a somewhat bewildered, long-haired hippie rebel. Although he was born and raised in Brooklyn, he gives his birthplace as Manchester, England, and hangs out with his friend Berger (Ragni) and Berger's girl, Sheila (Jill O'Hara). His own girl, Jeannie (Sally Eaton), is pregnant with another man's child. Around their lives swirl problems of racial inequality, drugs, homosexuality, and poverty, but most of all the Vietnam War. For a time Claude considers burning his draft card but finally enters the army, is sent to Vietnam, and killed. His friends mourn his senseless death. *Notable songs*: Aquarius; Let the Sunshine In; Frank Mills; Easy to Be Hard; Good Morning, Starshine. Filled with antiestablishment protest, profanity, and seediness, the musical nevertheless caught the spirit of the decade and was one of the earliest to adapt rock music successfully for the popular theatre. After a short run Off Broadway at the *Public Theatre, the musical was revised, recast, and restaged (including a much publicized nude scene) and moved to Broadway, where publicity and the vogue of its popular songs assured it a long run.

HAIRSPRAY (2002), a musical comedy by Mark O'Donnell, Thomas *Meehan (book), Marc Shaiman (music, lyrics), Scott Wittman (lyrics). [*Neil Simon Theatre, still running; NYDCC, Tony Awards.] Hefty teenager Tracy Turnblad (Marissa Jaret Winokur) lives in Baltimore in 1962 and dreams of appearing on the Corny Collins dance show on local television. When the program sponsors an open contest for Miss Teenage Hairspray, Tracy enters and, with the reluctant help of her mother, the overabundant Edna (Harvey *Fierstein), protests the exclusion of "Negroes" from the competition. Tracy ends up winning the crown and striking a blow for desegregation. *Notable songs*: Good Morning, Baltimore; Welcome to the 60's; Mama, I'm a Big Girl Now; You Can't Stop the Beat. Based on the 1988 cult film, this cartoonish fable captured the musical sound of the era, and a strong cast, under the direction of Jack *O'Brien, turned the cliché-ridden tale into a joyous celebration.

HAIRY APE, THE (1922), a play by Eugene *O'Neill. [Provincetown Theatre, 120 perf.] Richard "Yank" Smith (Louis *Wolheim) is an ape-like coal stoker on a luxury liner. Mildred Douglas (Mary Blair), do-gooder daughter of the line's president, visits the boiler room and faints at the sight of the brutish man. Her behavior causes Yank to question his worth and his place in society. He leaves the ship to stroll up Fifth Avenue, where his boorish behavior lands him in jail. Cell mates urge him to join the "Wobblies," but the union refuses him. Confused and upset, he heads for a zoo. After asking a gorilla, "Where do I fit in?" he attempts to release the animal. But the beast, like everyone else, misunderstands him, and kills him. One of O'Neill's most popular early plays, the innovative *Provincetown Players production was welcomed by Alexander *Woollcott as "a bitter, brutal, wildly fantastic play of nightmare hue and nightmare distortion." It has enjoyed occasional revivals, including a dynamic mounting by the *Wooster Group in 1997.

HAJOS, Mitzi [Magdalena] (1891–1970), singer and dancer. Born in Budapest, where she began to perform professionally while still a young child, she came to America in 1909 and played cabarets and vaudeville before appearing in the 1911 *La Belle Paree*. After performing in *Her Little Highness* (1913), the petite singer and dancer became a star when she assumed the title role in the operetta *Sari* (1914). Soon afterwards she changed her billing simply to Mitzi and starred in *Pom-Pom* (1916), *Head over Heels* (1918), *Lady Billy* (1920), *The Magic Ring* (1923), and *Naughty Riquette* (1926). In later years she accepted supporting roles in numerous nonmusical plays.

HALE, George (1902–56), choreographer. He began his career as a tap dancer, performing in *The Rise of Rosie O'Reilly* (1923) and other musicals before creating the choreography for *Heads Up!* (1929), *Strike Up the Band* (1930), *Girl Crazy* (1930), *The New Yorkers* (1930), *Earl Carroll Vanities of 1931*, *Of Thee I Sing* (1931), *Pardon My English* (1933), and *Red, Hot and Blue!* (1936). His work was generally considered lively but unexceptional. Hale later co-produced some musicals, including *Hold On to Your Hats* (1940).

HALE, Louise Closser (1872–1933), actress. Born in Chicago, she studied at the *American Academy of Dramatic Arts before making her debut in Detroit in 1894 in *In Old Kentucky*. After touring with William H. *Crane and in *Arizona*, she made her first New York appearance as Prossy in Arnold Daly's production of *Candida* (1903). Later important appearances included the Fairy Berylune in Maeterlinck's *The Blue Bird* (1910), Mrs. Atkins in *Beyond the Horizon* (1920), the cantankerous Mrs. Bett in *Miss Lulu Bett* (1920), Ase in *Peer Gynt* (1923), and the understanding mother Mrs. Smith in *Expressing Willie* (1924). Hale also wrote several novels dealing with theatre life.

HALEY, [John] Jack (1902–79), comic actor. Born in Boston, the wide-eyed, eager comedian made his professional debut in vaudeville in the early 1920s when he teamed with Charlie Crafts as Crafts and Haley. His first Broadway appearances were in two revues, *Round the Town* (1924) and *Gay Paree* (1925 and 1926 editions). Haley scored heavily as the shy chain-store heir Jack Martin in *Follow Thru* (1929), then starred as the wealthy Steve Potter mixed up in radical politics in *Free for All* (1931) and as the shady Duke Stanley in *Take a Chance* (1932). After a long sojourn in Hollywood (he played the Tin Man in *The Wizard of Oz*), Haley

appeared in *Higher and Higher* (1940) and *Show Time* (1942), then returned for one final appearance, playing opposite Beatrice *Lillie in the revue *Inside U.S.A.* (1949).

HALL, Adelaide [Louise] (1895–1993), singer. The short, hefty African-American performer, who was celebrated for her sizzling renditions of popular songs, was born in Brooklyn and first appeared before a New York audience in the chorus of *Shuffle Along* (1921). She performed in night clubs, in vaudeville, including star turns at the *Palace, and in several other all-black Broadway musicals but was best known for her appearance in *Blackbirds of 1928*, in which she introduced "Diga Diga Doo," "I Can't Give You Anything But Love," and "I Must Have That Man." Her last important assignment was as Grandma Obeah in the musical *Jamaica* (1957).

HALL, Adrian (b. 1928), director and manager. A native of Van, Texas, he studied at Texas State Teachers' College, the *Pasadena Playhouse, and with Lee *Strasberg. After staging plays Off Broadway and at regional theatres he helped found in 1964 the *Trinity Square Repertory Company in Providence. In 1983 he assumed double duty by also taking over the directorship of the *Dallas Theatre Center. Hall's choice of plays and his mountings have often been controversial, using space in unconventional ways and employing cross-gender and cross-racial casting. He now works independently with various major regional troupes. Among his notable New York productions are *Orpheus Descending* (1959), *The Grass Harp* (1966), *Wilson in the Promised Land* (1970), *The Hothouse* (1982), *As You Like It* (1992), *Two Gentlemen of Verona* (1994), *On the Waterfront* (1995), and *King Lear* (1996).

HALL, Bettina (1906–97), actress and singer. A native of North Easton, Massachusetts, she won major notices when she appeared in a series of *Gilbert and Sullivan revivals beginning in 1926. Later she played leading roles in *The *Cat and the Fiddle* (1931) and *Anything Goes* (1934). Her older sister, **Natalie** (1904–94), who was born in Providence, Rhode Island, was also a prominent musical comedy performer, starring in *Through the Years* (1932) and *Music in the Air* (1932).

HALL, Juanita [neé Juanita Long] (1901–68), character actress. The beloved African-American performer, who also passed for Asian in less discriminating times, was born in Keyport, New Jersey, and trained at Juilliard before singing with the Johnson Hall Choir, making her New York legit debut in 1934. The short, squat singer is most remembered for her enchanting portrayal of the wartime marketeer Bloody Mary in *South Pacific (1949), but she also gave splendid performances in other musicals and plays, particularly as the Caribbean brothel proprietor Madame Tango in House of Flowers (1954) and the crafty Chinese-American aunt Madam Liang in *Flower Drum Song (1958).

HALL, Pauline [née Pauline Fredericka Schmidgall] (1860–1919), singer. One of the most popular turn-of-the-century prima donnas, she began her career as a dancer in her native Cincinnati in 1875. Shortly thereafter she joined the Alice Oates Opera Company, leaving it to spend time touring in straight plays with Mary *Anderson. By 1880 she was working for E. E. *Rice, who cast her in several of his musical productions, giving her, among others, the trouser role of the hero Gabriel in a revival that year of *Evangeline. Her shapely figure allowed her to take men's parts, as she did most notably in the title role of Ixion (1885). However, her greatest success came when she played the title role in the first American production of *Erminie (1886). In 1892 she portrayed the hero Earl Trevelyan in a comic opera written especially for her, Puritania. In all, she played in over two dozen Broadway operettas. Her last appearance came just before her death, when she created the role of the impoverished old prima donna in The *Gold Diggers (1919).

HALL, Peter [Reginald Frederick] (b. 1939), director and manager. One of Great Britain's leading theatre artists, Hall has sent many of his London and Stratford productions, both classics and new works, to America over the past four decades. He was born in Bury St. Edmunds, England, and educated at Cambridge, where he started directing. He has served as artistic director of the Royal Shakespeare Company and the Royal National Theatre and has directed for other companies across the English-speaking world. Among Hall's many credits in the States are The Rope Dancers (1957), The Homecoming (1965), No Man's Land (1975), *Amadeus (1979), Orpheus Descending (1988), The *Merchant of Venice (1989), and An Ideal Husband (1996).

HALL, Thurston (1882–1958), actor. The rather heavyset, mannishly handsome performer was born in Boston and made his professional debut in 1901. New York first saw him as the courting editor Bob in *Mrs. Wiggs of the Cabbage Patch (1904). After some years touring he returned to New York to take the romantic leads in such musicals as The Only Girl (1914) and Have a Heart (1917). When Hall turned to character parts in nonmusicals, he

scored notable successes as Sam McGinnis in Civilian Clothes (1919) and Robert Lyle in *Behold the Bridegroom (1927). His last years were spent as a featured performer in films.

HALLAM, Lewis (1714–56), actor and manager. His father, Adam, and brother, William, were both actors at London's Covent Garden. William later became a manager, and though he failed, he was left with enough theatrical properties and supporters to organize a company of actors for the American colonies. To this end, he appointed Lewis as head of the troupe, and the company set sail in 1752 for Virginia, where he quickly obtained the governor's permission to act and set about refurbishing the primitive auditorium he found. The company's first bill offered The *Merchant of Venice and The Anatomist. Then Hallam moved the troupe to New York, where he had to battle formidable antitheatrical sentiment as well as rebuild another inadequate playhouse. Puritanical opposition plus the limited audiences in what were still relatively small cities forced Hallam to keep on the move. So after his New York stand he traveled with his players to Philadelphia and then to Charleston. In all of these cities he attempted to offer as broad and extended a repertory as possible, ranging from Shakespeare through the Restoration and contemporary dramatists. Some time in late 1754 or early 1755, he took the company to Jamaica, in the West Indies, where he died.

HALLAM, Lewis, Jr. (1740–1808), actor and manager. He came to America with his parents in 1752 and gave his first performance in Williamsburg in The *Merchant of Venice. He continued to act small parts with the troupe until it left for Jamaica. In 1758 he returned with a new company organized by his mother and stepfather, David *Douglass, the ensemble that soon was known as the *American Company. By this time his art had matured, and Hallam was the company's leading man. He was thin, of medium height, and not unattractive despite a noticeable cast in one eye. To him fell the honor of being the earliest known American Hamlet and of playing Arsaces, the hero of the first professionally produced American play, The *Prince of Parthia (1767). He essayed Romeo to his mother's Juliet, and ranged from Young Norval to central figures in contemporary comedies. After spending the Revolutionary War years in the West Indies, he returned in 1784 to reopen the *Southwark Theatre in Philadelphia and the *John Street Theatre in New York. With John *Henry he revitalized the American Company, working with John *Hodgkinson and William *Dunlap after Henry's withdrawal. Although he was approaching fifty, Hallam continued to play the same leading parts he had assumed twenty years before, for he was as good a performer as was active at the time, and he frequently staged imaginative, responsible, and applauded productions. For example, he restored *Hamlet's Grave Diggers' scene, which traditionally had been shortened or eliminated, and attempted some semblance of correct costuming. With the opening of the *Park Theatre he withdrew from management but continued to act almost until his death. Seemingly improvident, he is said to have died in poverty. Looking back, John *Durang recalled Hallam as "a sterling actor, but an inactive manager. His style of acting was of the old school. He was celebrated in all the gentlemanly dashing profligateness of young men, in epilogues, correct in Harlequin, and performed them with ease and spirit to a great age."

HALLAM, Mrs. Lewis (d. 1773), actress. Already established as an actress of some small importance in London, she came with her husband to America in 1752. *Ireland described her as "a woman of great beauty and elegance, still in the prime of life and enabled to play the youthful heroines of tragedy and comedy with due effect. Far superior to any actress who had preceded her, she retained for many years all the kind feelings of the public, who regarded her with an admiration reaching almost to idolatry." Her most popular roles included Desdemona, Juliet, Cordelia, Portia, Jane Shore, and the leading ladies of some contemporary comedies. After Lewis Hallam Sr.'s death, she married David *Douglass, then retired in 1769. Although *Odell points to a Mrs. David Douglass performing in 1774, most historians agree she died in 1773.

HALLELUJAH, BABY! (1967), a musical play by Arthur *Laurents (book), Betty *Comden, Adolph *Green (music, lyrics). [Martin Beck Theatre, 293 perf.; Tony Award.] Sixty years of African-American culture were surveyed in this episodic musical chronicle in which ghetto dweller Georgina (Leslie Uggams) moves through the decades without hardly getting older, ending up in the Civil Rights movement of the 1960s. *Notable songs*: My Own Morning; Now's the Time; Feet Do Yo' Stuff. Wavering between earnest social commentary and brassy Broadway entertainment, the show received mixed notices, but there were plenty of compliments for Uggams's Tony Award-winning performance.

HALLIDAY, John (1880–1947), actor. Although born in Brooklyn, he was raised in England where he studied to become an engineer. He returned to America in order to work for Western mining interests, but soon decided to join Nat *Goodwin, who was touring the region. His first New York appearance was as the Earl of Brancaster in *The Whip* (1912). Halliday quickly rose to become a leading man, playing such roles as the troubled sculptor Lenard Hunt in *The Woman of Bronze* (1920), the despairing George Conway in *East of Suez* (1922), the caddish man-about-town Gerald Naughton in *Dancing Mothers* (1924), the magician Chartrand the Great in *The Spider* (1927), the murderer Maurice in *Jealousy* (1928), and the impoverished Prince Mikail in *Tovarich* (1936).

HALLIDAY, Robert (1891–1975), actor and singer. The Scottish-born baritone came to America in 1913 and appeared in vaudeville before touring with several Broadway musicals. His New York debut was in the chorus of *The Rose Girl* (1921), after which he was assigned increasingly important roles in *Dew Drop Inn* (1923), *Paradise Alley* (1924), *Topsy and Eva* (1924), *Holka Polka* (1925), and *Tip-Toes* (1925). Halliday rose to leading man when he took the part of "The Red Shadow" in The *Desert Song* (1926), followed by Robert Misson in The *New Moon* (1928). His subsequent musical appearances were in *Princess Charming* (1930), *Music Hath Charms* (1934), *White Horse Inn* (1936), and *Three Wishes for Jamie* (1952).

HAMBLIN, Thomas S[owerby] (1800–53), manager and actor. Born in London, he had performed in the English provinces, at Sadler's Wells, and at Drury Lane and had risen to some prominence as an actor before coming to America in 1825. He made his debut at the *Park Theatre as Hamlet, immediately becoming embroiled in controversy. Some critics suggested his interpretation surpassed Thomas Abthorpe *Cooper's, while others thought he was vastly overrated. Hamblin continued to act for several years, although increasingly troubled by asthma. In 1830 he found a more congenial theatrical niche when he took over the *Bowery Theatre, which he ran, with only minor interruptions, for the next twenty years. These seasons are looked on as the heyday of the house, becoming a principal rival to the Park. As competition increased with the opening of several fine new playhouses, Hamblin gradually moved the theatre towards melodrama, and in his last years it became New York's main home for blood-and-thunder pieces. He was a tough-fibered man, undaunted by three fires that destroyed the theatre during his tenure, and even ignored critics' complaints and falling attendance whenever he persisted in returning to the stage. In 1848 he assumed management of his former opposition, the Park, only to have this house, too, destroyed by fire later the same year. For all his vicissitudes, he is said to have retired with a sizable fortune.

HAMLET. Shakespeare's most famous play was first offered to Americans in Garrick's version at a theatre in Philadelphia's Society Hill in 1759, with the younger Lewis *Hallam Jr. in the title role, and remains the most frequently produced of all Shakespeare's works. At one time or another every great American classical tragedian assumed the role. In his *Curiosities of the American Stage*, Laurence *Hutton devoted an extended chapter to comparing all the major interpreters up to his time. Besides Hallam, his list includes such notables as John *Hodgkinson, Thomas Abthorpe *Cooper, James *Fennell, John Howard *Payne, George Frederick *Cooke, Edmund *Kean, Junius Brutus *Booth, James William *Wallack, John Jay *Adams, William *Macready, Charles *Kemble, Edwin *Forrest, Charles *Kean, Edward *Eddy, George *Vandenhoff, Edward L. *Davenport, Lawrence *Barrett, James *Murdoch, Charles *Fechter, Daniel Bandmann, and Tommaso *Salvini. Hutton attempted brief descriptions and comparisons of their performances. Noting that both Forrest and Edwin *Booth offered interpretations in 1860, he concluded that "the contrast between the powerful robustious figure, deep chest tones, and somewhat ponderous action of the elder actor, and the lithe, poetic, romantic, melancholy rendition of the younger was very marked," and added, "In many minds Booth is Hamlet, and Hamlet is Booth." All these 19th-century artists performed in mountings that today would be perceived as top-heavy with scenery and very slow-moving. In 1912 a relatively minor star, John E. *Kellerd, established a then long-run record of 102 performances. Noted 20th-century Hamlets have included John *Barrymore, Leslie *Howard, John *Gielgud, and Richard *Burton. As a rule these actors played in versions that included substantial cuts in text and limited, more suggestive scenery, and allowed the strength and depth of their interpretations to carry the evening. Only Maurice *Evans offered anything approaching a totally uncut version, but his often singsong delivery was seen by some critics as standing in the way of a completely satisfying study. Recent notable Hamlets in New York include Sam *Waterston, Kevin *Kline, Stephen Lang, Ralph Fiennes, and Alex Jennings.

HAMLISCH, Marvin (b. 1944), composer. A New Yorker who won a scholarship to Juilliard when he was only seven and who studied music at Queens College, he became a well-known composer of screen background music before writing the scores for two exceptionally long-run Broadway musicals: A *Chorus Line* (1975) and *They're Playing Our Song* (1979). Hamlisch's other scores were often commendable but, for various reasons,

failed to run: *Smile* (1986), *The Goodbye Girl* (1993), and *Sweet Smell of Success* (2002). Autobiography: *The Way I Was*, 1992.

HAMMERSTEIN, Arthur (1872–1955), producer. The son of the first Oscar *Hammerstein, he began his theatrical career as his father's assistant and became a producer when his father, leaving the theatre to resume his work as an opera impresario, handed over the flourishing *Naughty Marietta* to him. Among his own noteworthy mountings were The *Firefly* (1912), *High Jinks* (1913), *Katinka* (1915), *Wildflower* (1923), *Rose-Marie* (1924), *Song of the Flame* (1925), and *Sweet Adeline* (1929). In 1927 he built the Hammerstein Theatre, which he lost shortly thereafter in the Depression.

HAMMERSTEIN, Oscar (1847–1919), manager. Born in Berlin, he ran away from home in 1863 and immigrated to America. Unable to employ his musical training, he accepted work with a cigar manufacturer. His alert, inventive mind quickly saw ways to mechanize many of the laborious operations, and his patents soon made him wealthy. Hammerstein then wrote several one-act musicals for New York's Germania Theatre, and his success prompted him to become manager of the Stadt Theatre. In 1889 he built his first theatre, the Harlem Opera House but soon lost it because of his reckless management. Much of his history would be a sad repetition of this building and then losing of playhouses, including the Columbus Theatre, the Manhattan, the Olympia, and the Republic. For a time his most successful venture was the Victoria, which briefly served as New York's leading vaudeville theatre. Attractions were booked by his son William, who found a special success with such freak acts as the Cherry Sisters. Oscar also wrote a number of musicals, which he produced, including *Santa Maria* (1896), *In Greater New York* (1897), and *War Bubbles* (1898). However, his most successful Broadway production was Victor *Herbert's *Naughty Marietta* (1910). But for his obsession with opera, which caused several of his Broadway enterprises to fail, he might have been a more important figure in popular musical theatre. Biography: *Oscar Hammerstein I*, Vincent Sheean, 1956.

HAMMERSTEIN, Oscar [Greeley Clendennning], II (1895–1960), librettist and lyricist. The grandson of the first Oscar *Hammerstein and the nephew of Arthur *Hammerstein, he was educated at Columbia, where he wrote lyrics for collegiate musicals, and began his professional career as stage manager for his uncle's production of *Sometime* (1918). After attempting a serious drama, which quickly failed, Hammerstein wrote the book and lyrics for

Always You (1920) and in that same year came under the tutelage of Otto *Harbach. Together they wrote libretto and lyrics for such shows as *Wildflower* (1923), *Rose-Marie* (1924), *Sunny* (1925), *Song of the Flame* (1925), and *The *Desert Song* (1926). Many critics consider Hammerstein's masterpiece to be *Show Boat* (1927), which he wrote with composer Jerome *Kern. The show was the first successful modern musical play with an American theme and employing American idioms. Another success was a more traditional operetta, *The *New Moon* (1928), for which he created the book and lyrics to Sigmund *Romberg's melodies. He returned to Kern to create *Sweet Adeline* (1929) and *Music in the Air* (1932). But much of the 1930s were barren years for Hammerstein, although one failure written with Kern, *Very Warm for May* (1939), produced the classic "All the Things You Are." His greatest and best-known successes came when he joined Richard Rodgers in 1943. Between then and 1959 they wrote nine shows, five of which were among the most towering triumphs of the American musical theatre: *Oklahoma!* (1943), *Carousel* (1945), *South Pacific* (1949), *The *King and I* (1951), and *The *Sound of Music* (1959). Hammerstein's other collaborations with Rodgers were *Allegro* (1947), *Me and Juliet* (1953), *Pipe Dream* (1955), and *Flower Drum Song* (1958). At the time he resumed his collaboration with Rodgers, he also wrote on his own a modern version of *Carmen*, told in terms of contemporary black America and called *Carmen Jones* (1943). With Rodgers he also entered into a successful career as producer, mounting not only all their shows from *South Pacific* on but also such other hits as *I Remember Mama* (1944), *Annie Get Your Gun* (1946), *Happy Birthday* (1946), and *John Loves Mary* (1947). In his early career Hammerstein also directed such works as *Show Boat*, *The New Moon*, and *Music in the Air*. Although critics sometimes complained about his excessive sentimentality and preachiness, Hammerstein's best lyrics displayed a colloquial freshness and a recourse to genuinely poetic imagery rare in popular musical theatre. As a librettist he was respected for his sharp dialogue and superb ability to trim a cumbersome script. Biography: *Getting to Know Him*, Hugh Fordin, 1977.

HAMMOND, Percy (1873–1936), critic. Born in Cadiz, Ohio, where he fell in love with the theatre at the age of thirteen after witnessing a tent show, Hammond began his newspaper career with small Ohio papers, eventually joining the *Chicago Evening Post*, where he became its drama critic. In 1908 he moved to the *Chicago Tribune*, then in 1921 became critic for the *New York Tribune* (later *Herald Tribune*), a position he held until his death. His

criticism was sharp, and his style a curious, identifiable mixture of hominess and Latinate phrases. He opened one notice, "Well, as Grandfather would say, draw up your chair and let's talk about the *Follies of 1917*." Later, reviewing Alexander *Woollcott's acting debut, he wrote, "Observation of his billowy amplitudes suggests that the world might be a safer globe on which to live were the abdomens of its inhabitants more convex and less concave." His best writings were anthologized in *But—Is It Art?* and *This Atom in the Audience*. After his death Franklin P. Adams and other writers published *Percy Hammond: A Symposium in Tribute* (1936).

HAMPDEN [Dougherty], **Walter** (1879–1955), actor. Although born in Brooklyn and educated at the Brooklyn Polytechnic Institute and at Harvard, he served his theatrical apprenticeship with F. R. Benson's company in England, learning a wide range of Shakespearean parts. His American debut came in 1907 when he played opposite Alla *Nazimova as Comte Silvio in *The Comtesse Coquette*, Halvard Solness in *The Master Builder*, and Dr. Rank in *A Doll's House*. Success then followed in more commercial ventures, notably as Manson, the reincarnation of Jesus, in *The *Servant in the House* (1908); as gubernatorial hopeful George Rand Jr. in *The *City* (1909); and as miner John Rawson in *Good Gracious Annabelle* (1916). In the 1920s Hampden starred in a number of Shakespearean revivals, offering his Marc Antony, Hamlet, Romeo, Macbeth, Shylock, and Othello, but had even greater success with two 19th-century classics, *Cyrano de Bergerac* and *Richelieu*, two roles he continued to revive for many years. He was an important member of the *American Repertory Theatre in the mid-1940s, playing Cardinal Wolsey in *Henry VIII* and Charles Venable in *What Every Woman Knows*. His last Broadway appearance was as the bigoted Deputy-Governor Danforth in *The *Crucible* (1953). A tall, slim, handsome man, he was an advocate of the older, romantic school of acting and fortunate that in his prime years an audience still existed for his style of play and performance.

HANSBERRY, Lorraine. See *Raisin in the Sun, A*.

HAPGOOD, Norman (1868–1937), critic. Although best known as editor of *Collier's* when it was a leading muckraking magazine and later of *Harper's Weekly* and *Hearst's International*, the Chicago-born, Harvard-educated author was also a distinguished drama-critic and writer on theatre. He served as critic for the *New York Commercial Advertiser* and the *Bookman*. His works included *The Stage in America* (1901), *Why Janet Should Read*

Shakespeare (1929), and his autobiography, *The Changing Years* (1930).

HAPPY BIRTHDAY (1946), a comedy by Anita *Loos. [*Broadhurst Theatre, 564 perf.] Addie Bemis (Helen *Hayes), a mousy librarian, has fallen so in love with the young bank clerk Paul (Louis Jean Heydt) that she follows him to the Jersey Mecca Cocktail Bar and there has her first drinks: some Scotch and a few Pink Ladies, which she has been told is a "tart's" drink. The alcohol sends her spinning but also liberates her from her inhibitions. These gone, she wins Paul away from a jezebel, Myrtle (Jacqueline Page). Written as a vehicle for Hayes, it was her brilliant performance that lured playgoers to the *Rodgers and *Hammerstein production.

HAPPY TIME, THE (1950), a comedy by Samuel *Taylor. [*Plymouth Theatre, 614 perf.] Bibi (Johnny Stewart) is the adolescent son of a Scottish Maman (Leora Dana) and a French-Canadian Papa (Claude Dauphin). Maman worries that Bibi will be corrupted by Papa's heavy-drinking brothers. But as Bibi embarks on his first puppy-love affair, all seems secure. Based on Robert Fontaine's autobiographical novel, the affectionate play was produced by *Rodgers and *Hammerstein and was popular with audiences seeking a gentle, domestic comedy. It was turned into a musical of the same title in 1968 with a greatly altered book by N. Richard Nash. The central character was now a young uncle of Bibi's named Jacques (Robert Goulet), an international photographer who returns to the small town and inspires the boy to live life to the fullest. The fine score by John *Kander (music) and Fred *Ebb (lyrics), filled with soft ballads and modest comic songs, was atypical of the team. The David *Merrick production was directed and choreographed by Gower *Champion and ran 286 performances at the *Broadway Theatre. *Notable songs*: The Happy Time; I Don't Remember You; The Life of the Party; A Certain Girl; Seeing Things.

HARBACH, Otto [né Hauerbach] (1873–1963), librettist and lyricist. Born in Salt Lake City to Danish immigrant parents, he taught English and public speaking after graduating from Knox College, then came to New York in 1901 to work towards a doctorate at Columbia. But he abandoned his studies and took up journalism before he began to collaborate with composer Karl *Hoschna in 1902. Their first success was *Three Twins* (1908), a huge success whose hit song was "Cuddle Up a Little Closer, Lovey Mine." Thereafter, he collaborated with Hoschna on five more musicals, most memorably *Madame Sherry* (1910). Following Hoschna's

death, Harbach worked with Rudolf *Friml on The *Firefly* (1912), *High Jinks* (1913), and *Katinka* (1915). With Louis *Hirsch he wrote *Going Up!* (1917) and *Mary* (1920). In 1923 he joined forces with his young protégé Oscar *Hammerstein, Vincent *Youmans, and Herbert *Stothart to write *Wildflower*, then in 1924 worked with Hammerstein, Stothart, and Friml to create the biggest musical success of the 1920s, the operetta *Rose-Marie*. Harbach's next effort was the greatest musical comedy hit of the era, *No, No, Nanette* (1925), although the lyrics for that show's most popular songs were by Irving *Caesar. In that same year he worked with Jerome *Kern and Hammerstein on *Sunny* and with Hammerstein, Stothart, and George *Gershwin on *Song of the Flame*. With Hammerstein and Sigmund *Romberg he created The *Desert Song* (1926). His last successful collaborations were with Kern: The *Cat and the Fiddle* (1931) and *Roberta* (1933). In all, he helped write over thirty musicals. Harbach's work was sometimes assailed as heavy-handed and humorless but at best was fresh and even poetic. He was also one of the first librettists who attempted to integrate song and story, something his pupil Hammerstein would later accomplish with others.

HARBURG, E[dgar] Y. [né Isidore Hochberg] (1898–1981), lyricist and librettist. Familiarly known as "Yip," he was born in New York and educated at City College. He turned to lyric writing after his appliance business failed in the Depression. His first efforts were heard on Broadway in *Earl Carroll's Sketch Book* (1929), with music by Jay Gorney. With Gorney he wrote his first big hit, "Brother, Can You Spare a Dime?" Included in the 1932 edition of *Americana*, it soon became a Depression theme song. That same year *Walk a Little Faster* produced "April in Paris," with music by Vernon *Duke. With composer Harold *Arlen, Harburg provided songs for *Life Begins at 8:40* (1934), *Hooray for What!* (1937), and *Bloomer Girl* (1944). In 1947 he served as lyricist and co-librettist for *Finian's Rainbow*, with music by Burton *Lane. Later shows were *Flahooley* (1951), *Jamaica* (1957), *The Happiest Girl in the World* (1961), and *Darling of the Day* (1968). Probably the most politically committed of major Broadway lyricists and certainly the most patently leftist, his lively, impish wit usually made his most controversial rhymes palatable. Biography: *Who Put the Rainbow in The Wizard of Oz? Yip Harburg, Lyricist*, Harold Meyerson and Ernie Harburg, 1993.

HARE, David (b. 1947), playwright. The British author of many sociopolitical plays, Hare was produced in New York perhaps more than any other English playwright during the last three decades of the 20th century. In the 1998–1999 season alone, he had three new productions in Manhattan, each of them a hit. Hare was born in St. Leonard's and educated at Lansing College and Cambridge. His first play to be produced in the States was *Slag* (1971), followed by *Plenty* (1982), *A Map of the World* (1985), *The Secret Rapture* (1989), *Racing Demon* (1995), *Skylight* (1996), *The Judas Kiss* (1998), *The Blue Room* (1998), *Via Dolorosa* (1999), and *Amy's View* (1999).

HARKRIDER, John (fl. 1910–1940), costume designer. The Texas-born artist began his career as an actor in films, playing opposite such silent favorites as Mary Pickford and Theda Bara. He later turned to costume designing and created costumes for virtually all of *Ziegfeld's final productions, including *Rio Rita* (1927), *Ziegfeld Follies of 1927*, *Show Boat* (1927), *Rosalie* (1928); *The *Three Musketeers* (1928), *Whoopee* (1928), *Show Girl* (1929), *Simple Simon* (1930), *Smiles* (1930), and the 1931 edition of the *Follies*. Harkrider also designed the costumes for *Music in the Air* (1932) and *Let's Face It!* (1941). However, most of his later years were spent either as a designer for films or in various personal entrepreneurial endeavors.

HARNED [Hickes], **Virginia** (1868–1946), actress. Born in Boston but raised in England, she returned to America to make her stage debut in *Our Boarding House*. After touring for several seasons she made her first Broadway appearance in 1890 in *A Long Lane*. Later that same year she was enlisted by Daniel *Frohman for his *Lyceum Theatre company, playing opposite E. H. *Sothern, whom she eventually married. Harned scored a popular success as the libertine Drusilla Ives in *The Dancing Girl* (1891), then consolidated her reputation when she played Fanny Haddon in *Captain Lettarblair* (1892). Perhaps her most memorable assignment came when she created the title role of *Trilby* (1895). Other noteworthy performances included Julie de Varion in *An Enemy to the King* (1896); the improvident, doomed *Iris* (1902); and the Shakespearean Actress in *The Light That Lies in a Woman's Eyes* (1903). Her repertory included several classic parts, including Ophelia, which she played to Sothern's Hamlet, as well as Pauline in *The *Lady of Lyons* and *Camille*. She continued to perform in both new plays and revivals until her retirement in 1918. One writer described her as a mature actress with "sex, vitality, dignity and beauty."

HARNICK, Sheldon. See Bock, Jerry.

HARRIET (1943), a play by Florence Ryerson and Colin Clements. [*Henry Miller Theatre, 377 perf.]

When Harriet Beecher (Helen *Hayes) marries Professor Calvin Stowe (Rhys Williams), she is not fully aware that she has done so partly to escape her overbearing family. Her writing, too, begins as a way of removing herself from family pontifications. At first, the Beechers are not altogether pleased, but then Harriet's novel, *Uncle Tom's Cabin*, makes her famous and wealthy. Soon what started as an escape becomes a crusade, and she even supports her son when he goes off to the war that President Lincoln has suggested she helped precipitate. Producer Gilbert *Miller persuaded the somewhat reluctant Hayes to play Harriet, and although the drama was leisurely and loose-jointed, it proved successful because of her artistry. **Florence RYERSON** [Willard] (1892– 1965), who was born in Glendale, California, and **Colin CLEMENTS** (1895–1948) a native of Omaha, were a husband and wife team, both having studied with Professor George Pierce *Baker at his *47 Workshop. Their only other success was *Strange Bedfellows* (1948), a comedy focusing on the suffragette movement.

HARRIGAN, Edward (1844–1911), actor, producer, librettist, and lyricist. Born in New York, where he originally apprenticed in the shipbuilding trade, he ran away from home and sailed to San Francisco. Although he had appeared briefly as a youngster with Campbell's Minstrels, Harrigan made his real debut in the burgeoning West Coast variety theatres, such as the *Bella Union. After being teamed up with different comics, he met with **Tony HART** [né Anthony J. Cannon] (1855–91). Born into a poor Irish family in Worcester, Massachusetts, Hart apparently was the shortest member of the household and thus the butt of much unpleasant humor. His response was often so abusive that he was sent to reform school. He soon ran away, coming to New York, where he sang and danced for pennies in saloons, then performed with a circus and several minstrel troupes. While appearing with one in Chicago he met Harrigan. The fatherly or avuncular-looking Harrigan, with his dry wit, and the almost femininely beautiful Hart, with his more rambunctious style, proved perfect foils. They quickly became one of vaudeville's most popular attractions. Harrigan wrote the sketches as well as the lyrics for their songs, which Harrigan's father-in-law, David *Braham, set to music. Soon Harrigan began writing extended playlets, and these proved so popular that he eventually started expanding some. The pair took over the Theatre Comique, where at first the entertainments consisted of an olio followed by one of the playlets, but in time the latter continued to be so popular that Harrigan turned them into full-length musicals. One of the earliest was *The Mulligan Guards*, a spoof of contemporary paramilitary groups that involved the adventures of Dan Mulligan, his wife, and son. Harrigan used the Mulligan family in many of his best works, including *The *Mulligan Guards' Ball* (1879), *The Mulligan Guards' Surprise* (1880), *The Mulligans' Silver Wedding* (1880), and *Cordelia's Aspirations* (1883). Harrigan usually was Dan Mulligan while Hart played either the Mulligan son Tommy or the family's rambunctious black maid Rebecca; the latter was his most famous role. Harrigan peopled his plays largely with immigrant classes and spoofed not only the Irish but also the "Negroes," Italians, Germans, and Jews. Among his other successes at this time were *The Major* (1881), *Squatter Sovereignty* (1882), and *McSorley's Inflation* (1882). Harrigan and Hart broke up following mutually recriminatory accusations after their theatre burned. Hart's subsequent roles included the desperate Isaac Roost in *A Toy Pistol* (1886) and the befuddled moonshiner Upton O. Dodge opposite Lillian *Russell in *The Maid and the Moonshiner* (1886). His behavior, however, was becoming increasingly erratic and he was committed to a home, where he died of paresis. After the team separated, Harrigan's skills began to wane, although he enjoyed one final important success with *Reilly and the Four Hundred* (1890), with which he opened the new theatre he had built and named after himself. His last new work was *The Woolen Stocking* (1893). In later years he leased the theatre and acted intermittently in a few plays by other men. Harrigan's songs were among the most popular of his era. Hits such as "The Mulligan Guard March," "The Babies on Our Block," and "Maggie Murphy's Home" had widespread and long-lasting vogues. His works presented working-class life in relatively realistic, if comic, terms. The characters he created were richly developed and three-dimensional, and their virtues and flaws were depicted consistently from one work to the next. At first Harrigan's works appealed only to regular theatregoers and were especially popular with newsboys and similar gallery gods of the time. Eventually, however, they attracted the notice and respect of leading critics and of writers such as William Dean *Howells, whose praise gave the pieces a new cachet. Harrigan has been called both the Dickens and the Hogarth of 19th-century American theatre, while Hart was considered one of the finest and most popular performers of his era. Biography: *Ned Harrigan: From Corlear's Hook to Herald Square*, Richard Moody, 1980.

HARRIGAN, William (1894–1966), actor. Harrigan was a reliable, general, all-purpose actor on stage and screen who never became a star but remained a familiar face for decades. He was the son of the innovative Edward *Harrigan and made his New York debut as a child in his father's 1898 musical *Reilly and the Four Hundred*. He grew up touring with the family and even performed in Australia and London. By 1920 he was playing adult characters on Broadway, and he continued to play supporting roles or solid leading men for the next thirty-five years. Perhaps his most notable role was the dictatorial Captain Morton in *Mister Roberts* (1956).

HARRIS, Barbara (b. 1935), actress. The baby-faced, grainy-voiced Harris has had a limited stage career, but she is never less than fascinating to watch. She was born in Evanston, Illinois, and studied at the *Goodman Theatre School and the University of Chicago before joining the improvisational group Second City. Harris was first noticed in 1962 as the perky prostitute Rosalie in *Oh Dad, Poor Dad . . .* and the next year was applauded for her saucy Yvette in *Mother Courage and Her Children*. Her most unforgettable performances were in two Broadway musicals: as the kooky psychic Daisy Gamble in *On a Clear Day You Can See Forever* (1965) and three sparkling heroines in *The Apple Tree* (1966).

HARRIS, Elmer. See *Johnny Belinda*.

HARRIS, Henry B. (1866–1912), producer. The "pudgy, friendly, aggressive" son of William *Harris Sr. and brother of William *Harris Jr., he was born in St. Louis and raised in Boston. After assisting his father's theatrical enterprises he embarked on his own producing career with *Soldiers of Fortune* (1901). Subsequent productions included *Strongheart* (1905), *The *Lion and the Mouse* (1905), *The *Chorus Lady* (1906), *The Struggle Everlasting* (1907), *The *Traveling Salesman* (1908), and *The *Third Degree* (1909). In 1911 he built the Folies Bergere dinner theatre in conjunction with Jesse Lasky, a house which they converted into the Fulton Theatre shortly before Harris died in the sinking of the *Titanic*.

HARRIS, Jed [né Jacob Horowitz] (1899–1979), producer and director. The abrasive but brilliant theatre artist, who once described himself as "an adventurer with a passion for the theatre and an indifference to show business," was born in Vienna, brought to America while still very young, and was educated at Yale. After a brief stint in journalism, including time with the New York *Clipper*, Harris found modest success with *Love 'Em and Leave 'Em* (1926) and *Spread Eagle* (1927), then produced a series of hits that were not merely fine theatre but eminently "show business": *Broadway*

(1926), *Coquette (1927), The *Royal Family (1927), and The *Front Page (1928). Although he quickly earned a reputation as the "wonder boy" of Broadway, his eccentric behavior antagonized many. Once he called several of his associates to his apartment to discuss revisions for a play. When they arrived they found him lounging, totally naked, and he remained so throughout the discussions. As one of the men was leaving (some accounts say it was George S. *Kaufman, others, Charles *MacArthur) he said to Harris, "Jed, your fly is open." Harris gained national notoriety when he sued Helen *Hayes, who was leaving Coquette to have a baby. He argued that an actress should not be pregnant when accepting a role or become pregnant while playing a part. Hayes countered that a baby was an "act of God." The brouhaha resulted in "act of God" clauses being inserted in subsequent contracts to protect actresses. In the 1930s Harris began directing his productions, including interesting revivals of Uncle Vanya and The Inspector General and a mounting of the controversial The Green Bay Tree (1933). For the most part, however, his earlier success eluded him until he produced and directed *Our Town (1938). Thereafter, only his productions of a slight comedy, Dark Eyes (1943), and the drama The *Heiress (1947) were commercial successes, although some of his mountings, such as the thriller The Traitor (1949), received good notices. In 1953 he directed The *Crucible. Autobiography: A Dance on the High Wire, 1979.

HARRIS, [Julia Ann] Julie (b. 1925), actress. Born in Grosse Pointe, Michigan, and educated at the *Yale School of Drama, the somewhat elfin actress made her Broadway debut in It's a Gift (1945). After a series of failures she won high praise for her performance as the lonely tomboy Frankie Addams in The *Member of the Wedding (1950). Further laurels came when she starred as the drifting, amoral Sally Bowles in *I Am a Camera (1951). Brooks *Atkinson wrote of her performance, "She plays with a virtuosity and an honesty that are altogether stunning, and . . . has the quick-silver and the genius we all long to discover on the stage." Among her other memorable performances were the ambitious actress Mademoiselle Colombe (1954), a gamin Joan of Arc in The Lark (1955), daydreaming Georgina in the musical *Skyscraper (1965), middle-aged divorcée Ann Stanley in Forty Carats (1968), the emotionally disturbed teacher Anna in And Miss Reardon Drinks a Little (1971), Mary Todd Lincoln in The Last of Mrs. Lincoln (1972), the dying wife Lydia Crutwell in In Praise of Love (1974), and poet Emily Dickinson in the one-person program The Belle of Amherst (1976). Only a few of these scripts were of much value, and Harris would struggle throughout her long career to find vehicles that were worthwhile. In her later years she replaced others and led touring productions of *On Golden Pond, *Driving Miss Daisy, and The *Gin Game (1997).

HARRIS, Rosemary [Ann] (b. 1930), actress. The beautiful, stately English-born actress, who has artfully combined elegance and warmth, made her American debut in The Climate of Eden (1952) and returned to New York as a member of the *Old Vic to play Shakespeare's Cressida in 1956. Among her subsequent American appearances were several important roles with the *Association of Producing Artists, including Alice in *You Can't Take It with You and Lady Teazle. Her many memorable performances included Eleanor of Aquitaine in The *Lion in Winter (1966), hassled actress Julie Cavendish in The *Royal Family (1975), flamboyant Hesione Hushabye in Heartbreak House (1983), the worried wife Barbara Jackson in Pack of Lies (1985), dizzy West End star Judith Bliss in Hay Fever (1985), the guilty Mrs. Birling in An Inspector Calls (1994), the questioning wife Agnes in A *Delicate Balance (1996), and the retired actress May Davenport in Waiting in the Wings (1999). Harris has also appeared in leading roles with numerous important American regional theatres.

HARRIS, Sam H[enry] (1872–1941), producer. Born on New York's Lower East Side, Harris had been a newsboy, cough drop salesman, and steam laundry operator before becoming manager of prizefighter Terry McGovern. Between bouts McGovern had been appearing in a touring burlesque show, The Gay Morning Glories. Harris purchased an interest in the affair, and found himself in show business. He next formed the company of *Sullivan, Harris, and Woods, with P. H. "Paddy" Sullivan and A. H. *Woods, sending popular melodramas such as The Bowery After Dark on tour. In 1904 he met George M. *Cohan and the two became friends and organized a partnership. Among their many productions were *Little Johnny Jones (1904), The Talk of New York (1907), The *Fortune Hunter (1909), The Man Who Owns Broadway (1909), *Get-Rich-Quick Wallingford (1910), *Seven Keys to Baldpate (1913), The *House of Glass (1915), *Hit-the-Trail Holliday (1915), The *Great Lover (1915), A *Tailor Made Man (1917), Going Up! (1917), *Three Faces East (1918), and The Royal Vagabond (1919). When the partnership was dissolved in 1920, Harris embarked on a career as solo producer. His productions included the *Music Box Revues, *Six-Cylinder Love (1921), *Rain (1922), *Icebound (1923), The *Jazz Singer (1925), *Cradle Snatchers (1925), The *Cocoanuts (1925), *Chicago (1926), Animal Crackers (1928), *June Moon (1929), *Once in a Lifetime (1930), *Of Thee I Sing (1931), *Dinner at Eight (1932), *As Thousands Cheer (1933), *Merrily We

Roll Along (1934), **Room Service* (1935), **Stage Door* (1936), **You Can't Take It with You* (1936), **Of Mice and Men* (1937), *The *Man Who Came to Dinner* (1939), **George Washington Slept Here* (1940), and **Lady in the Dark* (1941). Besides the *Music Box, he also managed the Harris Theatres in New York and Chicago. Obviously a shrewd judge of plays, Harris was equally admired for his integrity and courtesy.

HARRIS, William, Sr. (1844–1916), manager. Born in Prussia and brought to America at the age of six, he was removed from school after only three months and put to work at his father's clothing store. He later took employment as a cigar stripper before becoming a minstrel in 1867. After several seasons he moved from minstrelsy to vaudeville, then in the 1880s took over the management of Boston's *Howard Athenaeum. His success was so marked that he soon began acquiring other playhouses. In 1895 he joined *Klaw, *Erlanger, Charles *Frohman, and others in forming the *Theatrical Syndicate, or Trust. At the time of his death he controlled no fewer than six New York theatres and at least as many in other cities. Harris also worked closely with Klaw, Erlanger, and Frohman in producing plays. His sons, Henry B. *Harris and William *Harris Jr. were both well-known producers.

HARRIS, William, Jr. (1884–1946), producer and director. Son of William *Harris and brother of Henry B. *Harris, he was born in Boston but raised in New York, where he studied at Columbia. After working briefly under his father, he tried his hand unsuccessfully as a lyricist and librettist, then turned to producing. In collaboration with others, but mostly alone, he produced such hits as *The *Yellow Jacket* (1912), **Twin Beds* (1914), *The *Thirteenth Chair* (1916), **East Is West* (1918), *Abraham Lincoln* (1919), *The Bad Man* (1920), *In Love with Love* (1923), *Outward Bound* (1924), *The *Criminal Code* (1929), and *The Greeks Had a Word for It* (1930). Late in his career Harris often directed his own productions. Described as "tall, lank and frequently caustic," he retired in 1939.

HARRISON, Bertram (1877–1955), director. Although he began his career as an actor, eventually playing important supporting roles with Henry *Miller, he found even greater success when he turned to directing. Harrison staged a wide range of plays, but seemed to have best luck with fast-paced farces. Among his noteworthy productions were *Little Women* (1912); **Parlor, Bedroom and Bath* (1917); **Up in Mabel's Room* (1919); **Ladies' Night* (1920); **Getting Gertie's Garter* (1921); *Partners Again* (1922); *Lawful Larceny* (1922); *The Kiss in the Taxi* (1925); and *Swing Your Lady!* (1936).

HARRISON, [Reginald Carey] **Rex** (1908–90), actor. The slim, suave, slightly reptilian English-born leading man made his first American appearance as the witty friend Tubbs Barrow in *Sweet Aloes* (1936). The play was a failure, and Harrison did not return to the New York stage until after he had become a celebrated film star. He then starred as Henry VIII in **Anne of the Thousand Days* (1948), publisher Shepherd Henderson in **Bell, Book and Candle* (1950), the philandering Duke Hereward in *Venus Observed* (1952), and the evil spirit called the Man in *The Love of Four Colonels* (1953). But his greatest success came when he created the role of Henry Higgins in **My Fair Lady* (1956). Walter *Kerr wrote of his performance, "Mr. Harrison's slouch was a rhythmic slouch. His voice was a showman's voice—twangy, biting, confident beyond questioning. . . . But most of all Mr. Harrison was still an actor, believing every cranky, snappish, exhilarating syllable of the Alan Jay Lerner lyric he was rattling off, and a fourteen-carat character simply crashed its way onto the stage." He played the role for several years and revived it afterwards. Subsequent performances of note include the General in *The Fighting Cock* (1959), the crazed *Emperor Henry IV* (1973), the indifferent husband Sebastian Crutwell in *In Praise of Love* (1974), the aged lover Hawkins in *The Kingfisher* (1979), Captain Shotover in *Heartbreak House* (1983), Lord Gresham in *Aren't We All?* (1985), and Lord Porteous in *The Circle* (1989). Autobiography: *Rex*, 1974. Biography: *The Incomparable Rex: The Last of the High Comedians*, Patrick Garland, 1998.

HARRISON, Richard B[erry] (1864–1935), actor. Harrison is one of many actors remembered for a single role. It was his interpretation of De Lawd in *The *Green Pastures* (1930) which made that play so mesmerizing. He played the part nearly two thousand times before his death. Marc *Connelly recalled him thus: "Topping his six-foot height was a head of leonine gray hair. Below it, we saw a face that had managed to weather sixty-five years of struggle and disheartenment. . . . He spoke with a voice like a cello's." Harrison was the son of slaves who had escaped to Canada via the Underground Railroad. Moving later to Detroit, he studied elocution and then offered Shakespearean and other recitals on the L. E. Behymer and Chautauqua circuits. *The Green Pastures* marked his only professional appearance in a play.

HARRY BURNHAM (1851), a play by James Pilgrim. [National Theatre, 18 perf.] Harry Burnham (Harry *Watkins) rouses his fellow Yale students against the British. He joins the Revolutionary army, is wounded and captured, but escapes. At the Battle of Trenton he replaces the British flag with an American one and is hailed as a hero. Typical of the melodramatic patriotic spectacles that appeared in the wake of the Mexican-American war, the story was dramatized from a novel then being serialized in a newspaper and featured George Washington as an important character. **James PILGRIM** (1825–77) was a minor English-born actor but a prolific playwright, dashing off numerous once-popular plays, many of which dealt with Irish themes or Irish heroes and heroines. Among his other works were *Ireland and America* (1851), *Robert Emmet* (1853), *Irish Assurance and Yankee Modesty* (1853), and *Katy O'Shiel* (1857).

HART, Lorenz [Milton] (1895–1943), lyricist. Born in New York, he was educated at Columbia, where he wrote lyrics for college shows. Hart left college to accept a job as translator for the Messrs. *Shubert, then Broadway first heard his lyrics when Lew *Fields interpolated "Any Old Place with You" in *A Lonely Romeo* (1919). Working with composer Richard *Rodgers, the team had songs heard in *Poor Little Ritz Girl* (1920) but did not find recognition until the 1925 and 1926 editions of the *Garrick Gaieties*, introducing such hits as "Manhattan" and "Mountain Greenery." Subsequent successes included *Dearest Enemy* (1925), *The Girl Friend* (1926), *Peggy-Ann* (1926), A *Connecticut Yankee* (1927), *Present Arms* (1928), *Spring Is Here* (1929), and *Simple Simon* (1930). After a stint in Hollywood, Rodgers and Hart returned to New York to create a series of even more memorable shows: *Jumbo* (1935), *On Your Toes* (1936), *Babes in Arms* (1937), *I'd Rather Be Right* (1937), *I Married an Angel* (1938), The *Boys from Syracuse* (1938), *Too Many Girls* (1939), *Higher and Higher* (1940), *Pal Joey* (1940), and *By Jupiter* (1942). Hart also collaborated on the books for *On Your Toes*, *Babes in Arms*, and *I Married an Angel*. He was a master at polysyllabic and internal rhymes and at innovative lyric forms. His work was pervaded with his essentially misanthropic view of the world. Although personal problems, especially alcoholism, beset his later years, Hart's gifts never waned. His lyric for "To Keep My Love Alive," which was added to the 1943 revival of *A Connecticut Yankee* just before his death, was the equal in wit and style to anything he had written earlier. Biography: *Lorenz Hart: A Poet on Broadway*, Frederick Nolan, 1994.

HART, Moss (1904–61), playwright and director. Born in New York, he received his earliest theatrical training as assistant to producer Augustus *Pitou. Hart's first two plays failed, but success came when he collaborated with George S. *Kaufman on the Hollywood spoof *Once in a Lifetime* (1930). The team of Kaufman and Hart would write some of the most popular or interesting plays of the day, including *Merrily We Roll Along* (1934), *You Can't Take It with You* (1936), *The Fabulous Invalid* (1938), *The American Way* (1939), The *Man Who Came to Dinner* (1939), and *George Washington Slept Here* (1940), as well as the libretto for the musical *I'd Rather Be Right* (1937). With others or alone, Hart wrote the books or sketches for the musicals *Face the Music* (1932), *As Thousands Cheer* (1933), *The Great Waltz* (1934), *Jubilee* (1935), *Sing Out the News* (1938), and *Lady in the Dark* (1941). His solo nonmusical efforts include *Winged Victory* (1943), *Christopher Blake* (1946), *Light Up the Sky* (1948), and *The Climate of Eden* (1952). Because so many of Hart's earlier works were collaborations, it is difficult to assess his precise contribution to them, but his solo efforts revealed a gift for superior, literate dialogue and probing characterization, this last quality probably reflecting his interest in human psychology following his own much-publicized psychoanalysis. Besides directing many of his own shows, he also staged such hits as *Junior Miss* (1941), *Dear Ruth* (1944), *My Fair Lady* (1956), and *Camelot* (1960). Autobiography: *Act One*, 1959. Biography: *Dazzler: The Life and Times of Moss Hart*, Steven Bach, 2001.

HART, Tony. See Harrigan, Edward.

HART, William S. (1870–1946), actor. Although most famous as an early screen cowboy, this rugged actor had an interesting stage career. A native of Newburgh, New York, he made his debut in Daniel Bandmann's company in 1889, then played leads opposite such distinguished actresses as *Modjeska and Julia *Arthur, offering his Armand Duval, Benedick, Macbeth, Ingomar, Romeo, and Orlando. He was the original Messala in *Ben-Hur* (1899) and between 1907 and 1910 headed a touring company of The *Virginian*.

HARTFORD STAGE. Founded by Jacques Cartier in 1963, the Connecticut company performed in a former supermarket until it moved into its modern facility, the 489-seat John W. Huntington Theatre, designed by Robert Venturi. Under the leadership of Cartier and then Paul Wiedner, the group presented a traditional repertory of offerings. But under Mark *Lamos in the 1980s and 1990s, the theatre became more adventurous, presenting original works and epic productions of classics, such as the cycle program *The Greeks* (1982). Among the Hartford productions to transfer to New York were *Marvin's Room*, *Our Country's Good*, *Tiny Alice*, *The Carpetbagger's Children*, *Tea at Five*, and *Enchanted April*. The theatre won the Tony Award in 1989. Michael Wilson was named artistic director in 1998.

HARVARD DRAMATIC CLUB. See Collegiate Theatre Clubs.

HARVEY (1944), a comedy by Mary Chase. [48th Street Theatre, 1,775 perf.; Pulitzer Prize.] Flibbertigibbet Veta Louise Simmons (Josephine *Hull) and her haughty, homely spinster daughter, Myrtle Mae (Jane Van Duser), are exasperated with Veta's boozy but mild-mannered brother, Elwood P. Dowd (Frank *Fay), who has befriended Harvey, an invisible rabbit who stands over six feet tall. When Elwood introduces Harvey to the socially prominent Mrs. Chauvenet (Frederica Going), Myrtle Mae is furious and insists Uncle Elwood be sent to a "booby hatch" called Chumley's Rest. When Veta visits the home, she is mistaken for a prospective patient and confusion reigns until matters are cleared up and Elwood is admitted. But at the last minute Veta realizes that she prefers Elwood as the harmless, benign man he has always been rather than as an unhappy resident at Chumley's, so Elwood returns home, taking Harvey with him. Originally called *The Pooka* (a Celtic term describing a fairy spirit in animal form), Brock *Pemberton produced the play against the advice of his fellow professionals and after all his initial choices for Elwood turned him down. His casting of Fay, a recovering alcoholic who had fallen on hard times, was a desperate inspiration. John *Chapman of the *Daily News* called the comedy "the most delightful, droll, endearing, funny and touching piece of stage whimsy I ever saw." It has been revived regularly in theatres across the country and in New York, where James Stewart and Helen *Hayes starred in a popular 1970 production. A musical version called *Say Hello to Harvey*, starring Donald O'Connor and Patricia Routledge, closed on the road in 1981. **Mary Coyle CHASE** (1907–81) was born in West Denver, Colorado, and had a long career there as a journalist before writing her first play for the *Federal Theatre Project and a second for Broadway, both of them failures. After the success of *Harvey* she wrote *The Next Half Hour* (1945), *Mrs. McThing* (1952), *Bernadine* (1952), and *Midgie Purvis* (1961).

HARWOOD, John Edmund (1771–1809), comic actor. Although Harwood was indisputably among the ranking comedians of his time, there is some question whether he was American-born or English-born. His entire stage career was spent in America, where he made his professional debut in 1794 at Philadelphia's *Southwark Theatre under *Wignell's auspices as Gradus in the comic afterpiece *Who's the Dupe?* Later in the same season he played such roles as Sir Fretful Plagiary in *The Critic* and Stephano in *The Tempest*. Harwood also played for Wignell in Annapolis and New York before temporarily retiring from the stage to go into the bookselling business. Returning to acting when the venture failed, he was hired by *Dunlap for the *Park Theatre in 1803, where he enjoyed a huge success as Dennis Brulgruddery in *John Bull; or, An Englishman's Fireside*. Growing increasingly corpulent, he soon established himself as the finest Falstaff America had yet seen. While much of Harwood's reputation was established in low comedy roles, in his last years he was often acclaimed for his high comedy parts. He died at the height of his popularity.

HASTINGS, Thomas. See Carrère and Hastings.

HASTY PUDDING CLUB. See Collegiate Theatrical Clubs.

HATFUL OF RAIN, A (1955), a drama by Michael V. Gazzo. [*Lyceum Theatre, 398 perf.] Johnny Pope (Ben *Gazzara), who had picked up a drug habit in the hospital and had overcome it, suffers a relapse. He hides his problem from his wife, Celia (Shelley Winters), and his father, John Sr. (Frank Silvera). Celia suspects his sometimes peculiar behavior means there is another woman; his father is also alienated by his actions. Only his brother, Polo (Anthony Franciosa), understands him and supplies the money he needs. Johnny finally confesses to his wife, and they agree to work through the hell of withdrawal. One of the earliest plays after World War II to deal openly with a growing problem, it was faulted by many critics for failing to explore many aspects of the personal relationships it brought up, such as the interaction of father and son, but was nevertheless seen as a powerful piece of theatre.

HATTON, Fanny Locke (1870?–1939), **and Frederic H.** (1879–1946), playwrights. A husband and wife team who worked together on the drama desks of several Chicago newspapers before turning to playwriting, they found success with their first produced play, *Years of Discretion* (1912), a story of a New England widow who has a fling in New York. Subsequent hits included *The *Great Lover* (1915), *Upstairs and Down* (1916), and *Lombardi, Ltd.* (1917). One critic described this last work as "just another of those Hatton plays, in which familiar characters bounce along through an even more familiar stage love story, to the accompaniment of a patter of racy and spicy lines attuned to the mood of the all too familiar Broadway audience." While the Hattons were regularly represented on Broadway until the early 1930s, all of their later efforts failed. Their last plays were not originals but adaptations. Frederic Hatton was born in Peru, Illinois, and studied chemistry at the University of Wisconsin and at Princeton. Fanny Locke Hatton was a Chicago native.

HAVING WONDERFUL TIME (1937), a comedy by Arthur Kober. [*Lyceum Theatre, 372 perf.] Having quarreled with an older man whom she had been dating, Teddy Stern (Katherine Locke), a Bronx stenographer, comes to Camp Kare-Free in the Berkshires for a vacation. She is quickly courted by a young lawyer, Chick Kessler (John *Garfield, still billed as Jules Garfield), who is working as a waiter to meet expenses. Chick's eagerness puts off Teddy, but when she is next courted by an unscrupulous Lothario, Pinkie Aaronson (Sheldon Leonard), she comes to appreciate Chick's sincerity. This comic view of Jewish camp life was turned into an even more successful musical, **WISH YOU WERE HERE** (1952), with a book by Kober and Joshua *Logan and a score by Harold *Rome. Patricia Marand was Teddy; Jack Cassidy, Chick; and Paul Valentine, Pinky. *Notable songs*: Wish You Were Here; Flattery; Where Did the Night Go? The tuneful musical comedy, which got a lot of publicity because of its practical swimming pool on the Imperial Theatre stage, ran for 598 performances. **Arthur KOBER** (1900–75) was born in Austria. These were his only successful plays.

HAVOC, June [neé Ellen Evangeline Hovick] (b.1916), actress and playwright. Havoc was in show business for over eighty years, acting in as well as writing and directing plays. She was born in Seattle and was put onto the vaudeville stage at the age of two by her stage mother. With her sister, Gypsy Rose *Lee, she performed on the Orpheum Circuit and was a headliner before vaudeville waned. Havoc made her Broadway debut in 1936, and her featured role in *Pal Joey* (1940) led to a Hollywood contract. Film stardom eluded the blue-eyed blonde so she returned to Broadway, where she found work for the next twenty years. Havoc was still acting Off Broadway in 1995. She is the author of some plays, most notably *Marathon '33* (1963). Her early years were dramatized in the musical *Gypsy. Autobiographies: *Early Havoc*, 1960; *More Havoc*, 1980.

HAYDON, Julie [née Donella Lightfoot Donaldson] (1910–94), actress. The shyly beautiful daughter of a publisher and editor and his musician wife, she was born in Oak Park, Illinois, but raised in California. Haydon's stage debut was as a maid in a 1929 West Coast revival of *Mrs. Bumpstead-Leigh*, and she first appeared in New York in *Bright Star* (1935). She is best remembered for three later per-

formances: Brigid, the maid caught in the feud between a canon and a schoolmaster, in *Shadow and Substance* (1938); Kitty Duval, the streetwalker who dreams of a better world, in *The *Time of Your Life* (1939); and Laura, the crippled girl who lives for her collection of glass figurines, in *The *Glass Menagerie* (1945). In 1955 she married the much-older critic George Jean *Nathan and after his death toured in a program of readings from his work.

HAYES [Brown], **Helen** (1900–93), actress. The daughter of a small-time actress and a traveling salesman, she was born in Washington, D.C., and made her stage debut there at the age of five with a local stock company. She soon came to the attention of Lew *Fields, who cast her as Little Mimi in *Old Dutch* (1909), her Broadway debut. After appearing in several more of his musicals she moved on to such teenage roles as *Pollyanna* (1917), Margaret Schofield in *Penrod* (1918), and Margaret in *Dear Brutus* (1918). In the early 1920s Hayes won recognition and seemed for a short while type-cast as a flapper, including the parts of Cora Wheeler in *Clarence* (1919), Elsie Beebe in *To the Ladies* (1922), and Catherine Westcourt in *Dancing Mothers* (1924). After playing Cleopatra in *Caesar and Cleopatra* (1925) she appeared for the first time in what became her favorite part: Maggie Wylie in *What Every Woman Knows*. This role of a seemingly mousy, unassertive woman who bends everyone to her will succinctly caught the dichotomy that characterized much of Hayes's later acting, a curious and unique combination of apparent softness, even cuteness, with a hard, iron resolve. Following memorable portrayals of the doomed flapper Norma Besant in *Coquette* (1927) and Mary Stuart in *Mary of Scotland* (1933), Hayes essayed what is probably her most famous part, the title role in *Victoria Regina* (1935). She portrayed the Queen from her young, innocent years into aged widowhood. Robert Garland of the *World-Telegram* hailed her performance as one of "consummate skill and comprehension." Subsequent performances of note included Viola in *Twelfth Night* (1940); the determined actress Madeleine Guest in *Candle in the Wind* (1941); author Harriet Beecher Stowe in *Harriet* (1943); the tipsy librarian Addie Bemis in *Happy Birthday* (1946); Southern aristocrat Lucy Andree Ransdell in *The Wisteria Trees* (1950); Mrs. Howard V. Larue II, whose son is spirited away by a wicked witch, in *Mrs. McThing* (1952); the Duchess of Pont-au-Bronc in *Time Remembered* (1957); and the loyal wife Nora Melody in *A *Touch of the Poet* (1958). For the rest of her career, playing in both America and Europe, she appeared largely in revivals. The most memorable of these was her sweetly calculating Mrs. Fisher in *The *Show-Off* (1967) and the flustered Veta Louise Simmons in

*Harvey (1970). In her heyday Hayes ranked with Katharine *Cornell and Lynn *Fontanne as one of the theatre's great ladies. She lived to see two Broadway theatres named after her. Autobiography: *My Life in Three Acts*, 1990.

HAYMAN, Al (1847–1917), manager. Born in Wheeling, West Virginia, he apparently began his theatrical career as manager of a touring company of The *Black Crook in 1871 that covered not only the Southern states but Mexico and Central America as well. Hayman managed the magician Harry Keller and ran M. B. Leavitt's Australian interests before he met Charles *Frohman, and the two teamed up to present the hit *Shenandoah and build the *Empire Theatre in 1893. With Marc *Klaw, A. L. *Erlanger, and others they then formed the *Theatrical Syndicate, or Trust, ostensibly to bring order out of chaotic booking practices but in reality to exert monopolistic powers over the theatres of their day. Hayman served from 1901 to 1904 as president of the *Actors' Fund and was the largest personal contributor in the drive to erect a home for retired actors, which was opened during his tenure. Hayman's decision to leave artistic matters to Frohman and to allow Frohman lone public credit for productions mounted largely with Hayman's money meant that to playgoers he was little more than a shadowy figure. His fiscal acumen, however, was such that he left an estate of $1,692,815, while his more visible partner, Frohman, left behind a mere $451. **Alf[red] HAYMAN** (1865–1921), the younger brother of Al *Hayman with whom he is sometimes confused, was also born in Wheeling and tried his hand in sales before his brother induced him to become treasurer of the *Baldwin Theatre in San Francisco. By the mid-1890s he was right-hand man to Charles *Frohman, and after Frohman's death he continued as head of Frohman's production company. Under the Frohman name he produced such shows as *Dear Brutus* (1918), *Déclassée* (1919), and *Mary Rose* (1920).

HAYWARD, Leland (1902–71), producer. Born in Nebraska City, Nebraska, and educated at Princeton, he spent some years working in films before becoming a talent agent. In 1944 he produced A *Bell for Adano and for the next two decades was one of New York's most successful producers. Among his other hits, produced alone or in collaboration, were *State of the Union* (1945), *Mister Roberts* (1948), *Anne of the Thousand Days* (1948), *South Pacific* (1949), *Call Me Madam* (1950), *Point of No Return* (1951), *Wish You Were Here* (1952), *Gypsy* (1959), and The *Sound of Music* (1959).

HAZEL KIRKE (1880), a play by Steele *MacKaye. [*Madison Square Theatre, 486 perf.] Hazel Kirke (Effie *Ellsler) is disowned by her father, Dunstan Kirke (C. W. *Couldock), when she marries Arthur Carrington (Eben *Plympton) instead of the man of his choice. Carrington's mother, Emily Carrington (Mrs. Cecil Rush), is equally unhappy about the marriage, since Carrington is also Lord Travers and his mother feels he has married below his station. When she leads Hazel to believe the marriage is illegal, the newlywed rushes off and attempts suicide by drowning but becomes frightened and screams for help. Her father, who has gone blind by this time, hears her but can do nothing. Fortunately, Arthur appears and rescues her. Although it received a divided press, the MacKaye production was an immediate hit and enjoyed the longest run up to its day of any nonmusical play. It could be seen as a typical late-19th-century melodrama, but it was distinguished from them, as *Quinn has noted, by "the quiet natural dialogue and the absence of the usual stage villain." It was also among the very first plays to send out road companies, five of them touring while the original production remained in New York.

HAZELTON, George. See *Mistress Nell*.

HE AND SHE (1920), a play by Rachel *Crothers. [Little Theatre, 28 perf.] Ann Herford (Crothers) and her husband, Tom (Cyril Keightley), are architects whose seventeen years of happy marriage seem threatened when each submits a separate entry to a contest for a frieze design. Ann wins the $100,000 prize but soon comes to recognize that she has won it at the cost of probably losing her husband and of neglecting her daughter, Millicent (Faire Binney). She declines the prize, prepares to spend time with Millicent in Europe, and knows that she has lost neither the money nor Tom, since he was second and will now be the winner. The play had an interesting history. Originally produced as The Herfords (1911), it failed, and Crothers blamed the failure on miscasting. However, she was not able to find another producer until she persuaded the Messrs. *Shubert to produce it with her. Even then she was unable to find an actress to play Ann so took the part herself. The play was hailed by almost every major critic, who looked on it as a fine study of the plight of the modern, emancipated woman. Yet the play did not find an audience, although (or because) an equally fine play on the same theme, The *Famous Mrs. Fair, had succeeded earlier in the season. He and She has received some revivals, most recently in 1980 with Laurie Kennedy as Ann.

HEARN, George (b. 1934), actor and singer. The full-voiced baritone was born in St. Louis and educated at Southwestern University before making his

New York debut in 1963 in Shakespeare productions in Central Park. He was first noticed on Broadway ten years later as the rugby player Trevor in *The Changing Room* (1973). Although he was praised for his refugee Kurt Muller in *Watch on the Rhine* (1980), the Jewish father Otto Frank in *The *Diary of Anne Frank* (1997), and other dramatic roles, Hearn's most treasured performances have been in musicals, in particular the crazed barber *Sweeney Todd* (1980), the insecure homosexual Albin in *La Cage Aux Folles* (1983), the former movie director Max Von Mayerling in *Sunset Boulevard* (1994), and the jaded Husband in *Putting It Together* (1999).

HEART OF MARYLAND, THE (1895), a melodrama by David *Belasco. [Herald Square Theatre, 229 perf.] The Civil War has split apart Maryland families. Colonel Alan Kendrick (Maurice *Barrymore) fights for the North, while his father, General Hugh Kendrick (Frank Mordaunt), is a Confederate. Similarly, Alan's sweetheart, Maryland Calvert (Mrs. Leslie *Carter), remains loyal to the South and so has broken their engagement, while her brother, Lloyd (Edward J. Morgan), spies for the Federal troops. When Alan sneaks through the lines to see Maryland, he is captured by Colonel Fulton Thorpe (John E. *Kellerd), a former Northern officer whom Alan once court-martialed and who now fights with the Confederate troops. Seeking revenge, Thorpe arranges to have Alan shot as a spy. Maryland comes to plead for Alan's life, only to have Thorpe attempt to seduce her. She grabs Thorpe's bayonet and stabs him with it, giving Alan time to escape. The wounded Thorpe orders the local church bell rung to announce a prisoner's escape, but Maryland climbs into the belfry and, shouting "The bell shall not ring!," grabs the clapper and swings with it to prevent the bell from sounding. Later Alan returns with Federal troops and besieges Thorpe. He also intercepts letters from General Robert E. Lee in which Lee reveals he has learned that Thorpe is an untrustworthy double agent. Thorpe is imprisoned, and Alan and Maryland are reunited. Written as a vehicle for Carter and suggested by the poem "Curfew Shall Not Ring Tonight!," it was this play that firmly established Belasco's reputation as author, producer, and director. Many critics felt the story was unduly complicated and cliché-ridden, but the fine production and, most of all, the famous scene with Maryland swinging on the clapper made the play a huge success. It toured for three consecutive seasons and was occasionally revived.

HEATH, Thomas. See McIntyre and Heath.

HECHT, Ben (1894–1964), playwright. Born in New York and raised in Wisconsin, Hecht made unsuccessful attempts at becoming an acrobat and a violinist before finding a niche as a flamboyant Chicago newspaperman. Besides his newspaper writing, novels, and other literary works, he wrote numerous plays, most memorably with **Charles MacARTHUR** (1895–1956), a native of Scranton, Pennsylvania, the son of a clergyman and a respected, if antic, figure in Chicago journalism, working for the Hearst papers. Broadway first knew MacArthur when he collaborated with Edward *Sheldon on *Lulu Belle* (1926), followed by a thinly veiled exposé of evangelist Aimee Semple McPherson called *Salvation* (1928), written with Sidney *Howard. That same year, he teamed up with Hecht to write a marvelous comedy about the jungle-like world of reporting, *The *Front Page*. The twosome also wrote the show business comedy *Twentieth Century* (1932), the book for the musical *Jumbo* (1935), *Ladies and Gentlemen* (1939), and *Swan Song* (1946). On his own MacArthur wrote a failed political satire, *Johnny on a Spot* (1942), while Hecht wrote or co-wrote *The Egotist* (1922), *The Stork* (1925), *The Great Magoo* (1932), *To Quito and Back* (1937), *A Flag Is Born* (1946), and the libretto for *Hazel Flagg* (1953). Autobiography (Hecht): *A Child of the Century*, 1954. Biography: *Charlie: The Improbable Life and Times of Charles MacArthur*, Ben Hecht, 1957.

HECKART, [Anna] Eileen (1919–2001), actress. A native of Columbus, Ohio, she made her New York debut in 1943 and soon rose to important supporting roles in such plays as *Picnic* (1953), *The Bad Seed* (1954), *A *View from the Bridge* (1955), and *The *Dark at the Top of the Stairs* (1957). Heckart achieved stardom in a failed comedy, *Everybody Loves Opal* (1961), then went on to play a variety of roles in *You Know I Can't Hear You When the Water's Running* (1967) and the possessive mother Mrs. Baker in *Butterflies Are Free* (1969). Later she was more active in regional theatre and television but did appear in the New York productions of *Ladies at the Alamo* (1977), *Eleemosynary* (1989), *The Cemetery Club* (1990), *Northeast Local* (1995), and *The Waverly Gallery* (2000).

HEDGEROW THEATRE (Moylan, Pennsylvania). Although it was founded as a professional summer theatre in 1923 by Jasper Deeter, the theatre, housed in a converted 1840 grist mill near Philadelphia, had seen performances as early as 1904. The company, which usually consisted of about thirty actors, performed in traditional repertory style, giving different plays nightly during a season that generally ran from early spring until late fall. In winter months they would offer occasional performances and sometimes would tour. The repertory eventually consisted of over two hundred plays, with *Chekhov, *Ibsen, *Shaw, and *O'Neill as special favorites. Along with the classics the troupe revived many rarities and gave the world premieres of such plays as *Rancour* (1928), *The Cherokee Night* (1932), *Winesburg, Ohio* (1934), and *In the Summer House* (1951) and the American premiere of Brecht's *The Caucasian Chalk Circle*. A school was established by the troupe, offering a three-year course in all aspects of theatre, and in 1963 formed the Studio Players. After the repertory policy was abandoned in 1956, shows were mounted for brief runs. The theatre's interior was destroyed by fire in 1985 but was later restored through the efforts of generous donors. Today, under the direction of Penelope Reed, productions are again mounted in the 144-seat proscenium theatre. The nearby Hedgerow House is a hall for artists and technicians in residency.

HEGGIE, O. P. (1879–1936), character actor. Born in Australia, he spent many years on his native and London stages before coming to America in 1907 with Ellen *Terry to appear as Alexander Oldworthy in *Nance Oldfield* and as Osman in *Captain Brassbound's Conversion*. He later returned to settle in New York and to become the first Australian Androcles in *Androcles and the Lion* (1915) in America. Subsequent memorable roles included the solicitor's clerk Robert Cokeson in *Justice* (1916), the phony poet Oliver Blayds in *The Truth about Blayds* (1922), Old Man Minick in *Minick* (1924), and numerous revivals of classics ranging from Shylock in *The *Merchant of Venice* to Diggory in *She Stoops to Conquer*. His last Broadway assignment was as William Owen in *The Green Bay Tree* (1933). Although never a star of the first magnitude, Heggie was almost always praised for his singularly warm, knowing interpretations.

HEIDI CHRONICLES, THE (1989), a play by Wendy *Wasserstein. [*Plymouth Theatre, 621 perf.; Pulitzer Prize, Tony, NYDCC Awards.] Heidi Holland (Joan Allen) lectures on women artists and is active in the women's movement, but she herself is not the happiest of women. A series of scenes chronicling her life, from schoolgirl to mature woman, reveals that Heidi is unfulfilled and unhappy. The would-be politician (Peter Friedman) she loves goes off to marry someone else, and her only other male friend is a homosexual doctor (Boyd *Gaines) who is more dedicated to fighting AIDS than to listening to her problems. Finally, she adopts a baby. Yet the doctor is probably right when he warns she will continue "looking back at your life and regretting your choices." The *Shuberts and others produced the knowing comedy-drama, which benefited from a strong cast under the direction of Daniel *Sullivan.

HEIRESS, THE (1947), a play by Ruth and Augustus Goetz. [*Biltmore Theatre, 410 perf.] Dominated by her unloving father, Dr. Austin Sloper (Basil *Rathbone), Catherine Sloper (Wendy Hiller) is receptive to the courtship of Morris Townsend (Peter Cookson). But Townsend is a fortune-hunter, so when he learns Catherine will be disinherited if they wed, he jilts her. After Dr. Sloper's death, Catherine gets her revenge by allowing Townsend to seek her hand again and then spurning him. Based on Henry James's *Washington Square*, the play was rejected by several important producers who insisted on a happy ending. The Goetzes finally acquiesced, but the production failed out of town. Recast and revived with the ending the authors had initially written, it succeeded. Robert Coleman of the *Daily Mirror* called it "a bitter, relentless, absorbing character study." A Broadway revival with Jane *Alexander and Richard *Kiley failed to interest audiences or critics in 1976, but a beautifully staged and acted version with Cherry *Jones and Philip *Bosco in 1995 was a critical and popular hit. **Ruth GOETZ** [née *Goodman] (1912–2001), the daughter of producer Philip *Goodman, and her husband, **Augustus GOETZ** (1901–57), were also the authors of the dramas *One Man Show* (1945), *The Immoralist* (1954), and *The Hidden River* (1957).

HEISTER, George (b. 1822?), designer. Probably the most important scenic artist in New York in the 1850s, he seems to have been a native New Yorker. His name first appears in credits in 1840 when he designed sets for *Gamblers of the Mississippi* at the Franklin and later that year became a scenic artist at the *Bowery. When the new *Broadway Theatre opened in 1847, he was its principal designer, and it was during the next decade at this house that he did his best-known work. Among the productions he designed were *Faustus* (1851), *The Vision of the Sun* (1851), *The *Cataract of the Ganges* (1853), and *A *Midsummer Night's Dream* (1854). In one of his effects in *The Vision of the Sun*, after a character is thrown into a lake, "The waters become agitated and rise, and in their progress to the whole height of the Stage, they assume various tints, till a most Brilliant Palace rises out of the Water!" During the 1860s Heister designed sets for Philadelphia theatres. Although his celebrity waned in later years, he remained busy, designing such works as *Le Roi Carotte* (1872), *A Midsummer Night's Dream* (1873), *Antony and Cleopatra* (1877) at *Niblo's Garden, the *Kiralfys' touring production of *Around the World in Eighty Days* (1878), and James William *Wallack's mounting of *Wolfert's Roost* (1879).

HELBURN, Theresa (1887–1959), producer. Born in New York, she became interested in professional theatre while studying at Bryn Mawr. After continuing her studies at Radcliffe, the Sorbonne, and with Professor George Pierce *Baker, she tried her hand briefly at acting and also served as drama critic for *The Nation*. Helburn then joined the *Theatre Guild and soon became its executive director, a post she held for the rest of her career. Her associate, Lawrence *Langner, described her as "a wild-looking . . . woman with a high forehead," but added, "she possessed the faculty of conscientiously carrying out the decisions of the Board, yet at the same time holding to her own opinions . . . her nerves were like whipcord and her power like steel." Autobiography: *A Wayward Quest*, 1960.

HELD, Anna (1873–1918), singer and actress. The tiny, slightly plump, coquettish entertainer, with reddish-brown hair and large, expressive brown eyes was born in Paris of Polish-French parentage. Her early years were impoverished, and when her father died young, her mother took her to London, where she appeared in the chorus of some musicals. In 1895 Florenz *Ziegfeld, who later married her, saw Held perform and brought her to America. Playgoers first saw her in an 1896 revival of *A *Parlor Match*. The "veiled naughtiness of her songs" coupled with her sly, teasing delivery won her instant fame. She appeared in *La Poupee* (1897), *Papa's Wife* (1899), *The Little Duchess* (1901), *Mam'selle Napoleon* (1903), *Higgledy Piggledy* (1904), *The Parisian Model* (1906), and *Miss Innocence* (1908). After her separation from Ziegfeld she devoted most of her time to vaudeville, but she returned to musical comedy for a final time in *Follow Me* (1916). Among the songs associated with her were "Won't You Come and Play with Me?," "I Just Can't Make My Eyes Behave," and "It's Delightful to Be Married."

HELD BY THE ENEMY (1886), a play by William *Gillette. [*Madison Square Theatre, 70 perf.] When Federal troops capture a Confederate city, Brigade Surgeon Fielding (Melbourne McDowell) falls in love with a Southern belle, Rachel (in some texts and programs, Eunice) McCreery (Kathryn Kidder), although she is engaged to Lieutenant Gordon Hayne (John E. *Kellerd). Hayne comes through the lines to spy for the Confederacy and is captured, and Fielding serves as the judge in his court-martial. Hayne escapes and is shot, playing dead to allow Rachel and her family to carry him to safety. When Fielding recognizes the ploy, Rachel agrees to marry him if he will allow Hayne to escape. Later Hayne returns and forces Fielding to release Rachel from her promise. Although the play now seems merely an effective melodrama, it was long looked upon as the first meritorious

drama about the Civil War. It held the stage for nearly a decade.

HELEN HAYES THEATRES (New York). The famous actress has had her name attached to two Broadway theatres, which seems only right for one of the American theatre's most beloved stars. The first was a structure on West 46th Street that opened in 1911 as a restaurant-theatre called the Folies-Bergère, but the plan to copy the famous Paris attraction quickly failed, so it was remodeled into a legit theatre called the Fulton a few months later. The Henry *Herts- and Tallant-designed playhouse had only 1,000 seats and featured a pastel-colored interior that was deemed one of the loveliest on Broadway. Although it switched to films a few times during the Depression, the Fulton was a favorite venue for plays, and it was renamed after Helen *Hayes in 1955. Despite many protests, the old theatre was torn down in 1982 to make way for the Marriott Marquis Hotel, which included a new, larger theatre for musicals. The developers offered to name the new venue after Hayes, but she politely declined the offer. Instead the Little Theatre on West 44th Street was renamed after her in 1983, and it remains the Helen Hayes Theatre today. The Little was built by Winthrop *Ames in 1912 as a small space (299 seats) in the colonial style for new and innovative plays. The venture failed and a balcony was added in 1916 to make it a more traditional Broadway house. With twice as much seating, the Little found tenants until it became a lecture hall in 1931 and a television studio in 1959. It returned as a legit house in 1963 and was renamed the Winthrop Ames Theatre for two years. Today the intimate little space is ideal for small or one-person shows and has been frequently booked.

HELL-BENT FOR HEAVEN (1924), a play by Hatcher Hughes. [Klaw Theatre, 122 perf.; Pulitzer Prize.] The courtship of Sid Hunt (George *Abbott) and Jude Lowry (Margaret Borough) promises to end their mountain families' long feud. But Rufe Prior (John F. Hamilton), who has refused to fight in the recent World War and who has become a religious fanatic, rekindles the hatred so that he can win Jude away from Sid. He nearly succeeds in destroying both the courtship and family reconciliation, until he is exposed and cravenly flees. A controversial play from the start, condemned by some for its excessive melodramatics and by others for what they deemed was its irreverence, the Marc *Klaw–produced drama won the *Pulitzer and immediately became embroiled in further controversy. The play jury had actually selected George *Kelly's The *Show-Off but was overruled by a higher committee. One jurist resigned and another issued a letter of protest. **Hatcher HUGHES** (1883–1945) was born in Polkville, North Carolina, and educated at the University of North Carolina and at Columbia, where he later taught drama for many years. His first play, *Wake Up, Jonathan*, written with Elmer *Rice, reached Broadway in 1921. After *Hell-Bent for Heaven* (1923), his works included the backwoods comedy *Ruint* (1925), the domestic comedy *Honeymoon* (1927), the social drama *It's a Grand Life* (1930), and the battle of the sexes play *The Lord Blesses the Bishop* (1934).

HELLMAN, Lillian (1905–84), playwright. The New Orleans–born writer studied at New York University and Columbia, then took employment as a manuscript reader for Herman *Shumlin and book reviewer before Shumlin produced her first play, the controversial *The *Children's Hour* (1934), about two school teachers falsely accused of lesbianism. Hellman's labor drama, *Days to Come* (1936), was a quick failure, but her third play, *The *Little Foxes* (1939), was a huge hit and is generally acknowledged to be her finest work. With the coming of World War II Hellman turned to current affairs, writing two timely (and popular) dramas, *Watch on the Rhine* (1941) and *The Searching Wind* (1944). *Another Part of the Forest* (1946) was a prequel to *The Little Foxes* and her *Montserrat* (1949) an adaptation of Emmanuel Robles's French drama about hostages who gave their lives to protect Simon Bolívar. Perhaps Hellman's most subtle, even Chekhovian, work was *The Autumn Garden* (1951), about some idlers at a summer resort who are forced to face the reality of their failures. Her translation of Jean Anouilh's version of the Joan of Arc story *The Lark* (1955) was a success, but her libretto for *Candide* (1956) was not. Hellman's final theatre efforts were the popular *Toys in the Attic* (1960) and the short-lived *My Mother, My Father and Me* (1963). Her best writing has been characterized by a superb sense of theatre, taut construction, and acute personal observation of human behavior, often coupled with an attempt to probe major moral and political issues. Often a political activist, Hellman also wrote three controversial memoirs: *An Unfinished Woman* (1969), *Pentimento* (1973), and *Scoundrel Time* (1976). Biography: *Lillian Hellman: The Image, The Woman*, William Wright, 1986.

HELLO, DOLLY! (1964), a musical comedy by Michael *Stewart (book), Jerry *Herman (music, lyrics). [*St. James Theatre, 2,844 perf.; Tony, NYDCC Awards.] Matchmaker Dolly Levi (Carol *Channing) will jump in wherever there is a quick buck to be made. As she puts it, "I meddle." Her meddling becomes self-serving when she sets about to find a mate for Yonkers businessman Horace Vandergelder (David *Burns). She suggests two possible candidates, the milliner Irene Molloy (Eileen Brennan) and the wealthy Ernestina Money (Mary Jo Catlett), but all along she plans to grab Horace for herself. After a day of adventure in New York involving Vandergelder's clerks Barnaby (Jerry Dodge) and Cornelius (Charles Nelson Reilly) and his niece (Alice Playten), all complications lead to romance and marriage. *Notable songs*: Hello, Dolly!; Before the Parade Passes By; It Only Takes a Moment; Put On Your Sunday Clothes; So Long, Dearie. Based on *The *Matchmaker*, the musical almost certainly would have enjoyed a reasonable run on the strength of Miss Channing's clowning and Gower *Champion's stylish staging alone. The popularity of the title song and a succession of star Dollys (including Ginger Rogers, Betty Grable, Pearl *Bailey, and Ethel *Merman) immeasurably enhanced the musical's success, helping the David *Merrick production become (temporarily) the longest-running musical in Broadway history. The show was revived on Broadway with Channing in 1978 and 1995.

HELLZAPOPPIN (1938), a comic revue by Ole *Olsen, Chic Johnson (sketches), Sammy Fain (music), Charles Tobias (lyrics), others. [46th Street Theatre, 1,404 perf.] This was a zany revue in which men carried ladders through rows of seated playgoers, a woman stopped the show on occasion to look for her missing spouse, a man peddled a plant that grew larger with each appearance, a magician offered tricks that would not work, and dozens of pistol shots rang out from all corners of the theatre. The Olsen and Johnson production opened to divided, if largely favorable reviews, but owed much of its success to persistent plugging by Walter *Winchell, at the time probably the most influential Broadway columnist.

HENDERSON, David (1853–1908), producer. Born in Scotland, where he was orphaned at the age of twelve, he apprenticed himself in the newspaper trade, then came to America at the age of eighteen to work on papers from New York to California before settling in Chicago. There he began to take an active role in theatricals, building the Chicago Opera House in 1887 and producing a series of musicals that enjoyed long runs and toured the country: *The Arabian Nights*; *The Crystal Slipper*; *Bluebeard, Jr.*; *Sinbad the Sailor*; and *Ali Baba*. Henderson also worked closely with John *McCaull, mounting many midwestern versions of comic operas and managing several theatres in Chicago as well as in Denver, Kansas City, Pittsburgh, and New York. He was often credited with reestablishing Chicago as a major theatre center after the great fire and of initiating the city's heyday as a producing center second only to New York, a heyday that lasted until World War I.

HENDERSON, Ray. See De Sylva, Brown, and Henderson.

HENLEY, Beth. See *Crimes of the Heart*.

HENRIETTA, THE (1887), a play by Bronson *Howard. [*Union Square Theatre, 158 perf.] Gruff but kindly Nicholas Van Alstyne (William H. *Crane) has made a fortune in a bullish stock market, but his unscrupulous son Nicholas Jr. (Charles Kent) attempts to make his own fortune by creating a bear market and destroying his father. He even steals some of his father's securities to serve his own ends. Young Nicholas's faithlessness extends to his loving wife, Rose (Sibyl Johnstone), but his philandering is kept from her by Nicholas's younger brother Bertie, "the Lamb" (Stuart *Robson), who burns incriminating evidence. Just as Nicholas manages to create a panic, his father learns of his treachery and confronts him. Young Nicholas dies of a heart attack, while Bertie gives his father all his savings to help revitalize the market and save the family wealth. The loyal Rose at first refuses to believe any charges against her husband but is finally made to see the truth and marries a man who has long loved her. One of the most memorable entertainments of its era, its initial run was cut short when the Union Square Theatre burned. But the play continued to be revived regularly until the early 1900s, and an updated version was offered in 1913 as *The New Henrietta*. The subplot of Rose's and Nicholas's affairs was derived from Thackeray's *Vanity Fair*.

HENRY IV. Shakespeare's historical drama was first performed in New York with David *Douglass as Falstaff, though only Part I was traditionally played until about 1820, and even then Part II was mounted only intermittently. James H. *Hackett was by far the most famous American interpreter of Falstaff. Curiously, after Hackett's retirement the two plays virtually disappeared from the boards. Almost no major revivals were mounted in the last decades of the 19th century or the early years of the 20th century. The only interesting production of this period came in 1896 when Julia *Marlowe assumed the role of Prince Hal. The major Falstaff after Hackett's day was Ben *De Bar, but he rarely played in New York, preferring to tour. In more modern times Maurice *Evans played Falstaff in a 1939 revival, and the *Old Vic presented a brilliant mounting in 1946 with Ralph *Richardson as Falstaff and *Olivier as Hotspur and Justice Shallow. Recent New York Falstaffs of note include Kenneth

McMillan in 1981, Donald Moffat in 1987, and Louis *Zorich in 1991. A star-studded production of the history play, directed by Jack *O'Brien, was presented at *Lincoln Center in 2003. Of course, collegiate and festival stages have presented the play with some regularity.

HENRY, John (1738–94), actor. Sometimes called the first matinee idol in America, although matinees were not given in his day, he was born in Ireland and had appeared both in Dublin and at London's Drury Lane before sailing to America, making his debut under David *Douglass at the *John Street Theatre in 1767 as Aimwell in *The Beaux' Stratagem*. Although a handsome and apparently accomplished actor, he seems to have been somewhat weak in his personal determination, so for a long while he was assigned relatively minor roles. After the Revolution he joined the younger *Hallam in the management of the *American Company and is thought to have been responsible for the production of William *Dunlap's first play and was also the first professional performer to play Sir Peter Teazle in America, which he played with his "incurable Irish brogue." In 1792 he encouraged John *Hodgkinson to come to America, but Hodgkinson quickly turned against him, not only assuming his roles but forcing him to sell his interest in the American Company for $10,000. His attempts to regain his stature failed, and he drowned while sailing to New England, where he may have hoped to start another company. His personal life was flamboyant and led to much unfavorable gossip. He was the only actor of his time to maintain a private coach; Henry claimed he suffered from gout, although this seems highly unlikely, and the carriage was therefore a necessity. And scandal grew largely out of his romances with the Storer sisters. He married the eldest, had an affair with her younger sister, who bore him a child, then later married the youngest of the sisters, who went insane at the time of his death.

HENRY MILLER THEATRE (New York). Actor-manager Henry *Miller built this medium-sized theatre on West 43rd Street to house plays that he produced, and it soon became a favorite venue for both American and British classics. Harry Creighton Ingalls and Paul R. Allen designed the Georgian-style playhouse that seated only 700 but still had a balcony because Miller, remembering his days as a youth who was unable to afford anything but cheap balcony seats, insisted that his theatre have one. The playhouse opened in 1918 and stayed in the family for decades, Miller's son Gilbert continuing in his father's footsteps. The theatre ceased to present legit productions in 1966, was turned into a movie house and soon reverted to a porno palace. In 1978 it became a disco club named Xenon, then a dance hall called Shout! While still in this nightclub configuration, the Henry Miller returned to legit status with the 1998 revival of *Cabaret. When that popular production transferred to Studio 54, the playhouse was restored into a more traditional theatre arrangement with 635 seats and hosted another musical hit, *Urinetown (2001).

HEPBURN, Katharine [Houghton] (1907–2003), actress. A lithe, horsey beauty with a haughty voice, she enjoyed a long, distinguished career as much by dint of glamour and dedication as by acting abilities. She was born in Hartford, Connecticut, educated at Bryn Mawr, and made her acting debut in 1928 with the Edwin Knopf Stock Company in Baltimore in The Czarina. Under the stage name of Katherine Burns she made her New York bow in Night Hostess. Recognition came when she portrayed the determined Amazon Antiope in The Warrior's Husband (1932), but a certain ignominy followed when she attempted the part of Stella Surrege in The Lake (1933). It was of this performance that Dorothy *Parker complained Hepburn's gamut of emotions ranged from "A to B." Although she subsequently toured in the title role of Jane Eyre in 1937, she did not return to Broadway until after she had become a celebrated film star. Her vehicle was The *Philadelphia Story (1939), written expressly for her by Philip *Barry. The play was a tremendous success, but another Barry play, Without Love (1942), failed. She did not again play Broadway until she essayed Shakespeare's Rosalind in 1950. Moving from Shakespeare to *Shaw, Hepburn was the Lady in The Millionairess (1952). In 1957 and 1960 she appeared at the *American Shakespeare Festival as Portia, Beatrice, Viola, and Cleopatra. Three later appearances were in lightweight vehicles that ran largely on the strength of her attraction: the famous designer Chanel in the musical Coco (1969), the slightly eccentric Mrs. Basil in A Matter of Gravity (1976), and the old curmudgeon Margaret Mary Elderdice in West Side Waltz (1981). Autobiography: Me, 1991. Biographies: Katharine Hepburn, Barbara Leaming, 1995; Kate Remembered, A. Scott Berg, 2003.

HER MASTER'S VOICE (1933), a comedy by Clare *Kummer. [*Plymouth Theatre, 224 perf.] Ned Farrar (Roland *Young), a would-be singer and ineffectual businessman, has just lost another job. This creates problems for him with his affectionate but rattled wife, Queena (Frances Fuller,) and his battle-axe mother-in-law, Mrs. Martin (Elizabeth Patterson). However, they are nothing like the problems that arrive with Queena's regal Aunt Min (Laura Hope *Crews), who has disapproved of Queena's marriage from afar and never met Ned, and who now mistakes him for a servant. When Aunt Min seemingly breaks up the marriage, Ned accepts her offer to indeed be her new servant. She calls him George, and after he sneaks into her bed, believing Queena is there, she likes him even more. Of course, nothing happens that night. Eventually Ned becomes a radio crooner. Mrs. Martin runs off with Ned's sponsor; Aunt Min is made to understand the situation; and Ned and Queena go home together. Based on a Kummer vaudeville sketch, the play was written for her son-in-law, Young, and Max *Gordon produced it. Burns *Mantle saw the comedy as "written with many graceful twists of dialogue and many revealing bits of character observation." A 1964 Off-Broadway revival was unsuccessful.

HER OWN WAY (1903), a play by Clyde *Fitch. [*Garrick Theatre, 107 perf.] Believing that Georgiana Carley (Maxine *Elliott) prefers Sam Coast (Arthur *Byron) to him, Richard Coleman (Charles Cherry) quietly sails for the Philippines. Actually, Georgiana does not love Sam, who hopes to destroy her family's fortune in order to force her to marry him. When he nearly succeeds at the same time that Richard is reported to have died, Georgiana's future looks bleak. But Richard returns in time to rectify everything. Produced by Charles Dillingham and written expressly for Elliott, who rejected all of the author's suggested titles, leaving him to call it what he did out of exasperation, it was judged by many critics to be Fitch's finest comedy up to that time as well as Elliott's best performance.

HERBERT, Evelyn [née Hostetter] (1898–1975), singer and actress. Although she was generally acknowledged as the finest singer in Broadway musicals of her era, her theatre career was brief and remembered for two parts. Born in Philadelphia, she was taken to New York while still in her teens to study with Caruso, who prevailed on the Chicago Opera to hire her. She sang important roles there and in New York before developing voice problems. Retrained, she took a job in a touring company of Honeydew, then made her Broadway debut in Stepping Stones (1923). Herbert soon graduated to leading roles in The Love Song (1925), Princess Flavia (1925), and in the revue The Merry World (1926). In 1926 she also created the role of Barbara Frietchie in *My Maryland, followed by another success, Marianne in The *New Moon (1928). Thereafter, the vogue for full-throated operettas waned, so her final appearances were in two short-run musicals, Princess Charming (1930) and Melody (1933), as well as in a 1934 revival of Bitter Sweet.

HERBERT, F[rederick] Hugh (1898?–1958), playwright. Born in Vienna, but raised in England, he studied at London's Royal School of Mines with the intention of becoming an engineer. However, wounded in World War I, he elected to take a position in the advertising office of a London department store before coming to America to write for films. His first stage play, *Quiet Please* (1940), written with Hans Kraly, satirized Hollywood morals and had a short run, but his first solo effort, the comedy *Kiss and Tell* (1943), was a hit. Herbert's subsequent works included *For Keeps* (1944), *For Love or Money* (1947), the book for the musical *Out of This World* (1950), and his biggest hit, *The *Moon Is Blue* (1951). A subsequent comedy, *A Girl Can Tell* (1953), failed, as did his adaptation of an Italian play, *The Best House in Naples* (1956).

HERBERT, Joseph (1867–1923), playwright and actor. Born in Liverpool, he came to America while still a young man and embarked on a career as an actor, making his first appearances with John *McCaull's comic opera company. When Augustin *Daly began importing English musicals, Herbert appeared in many of them and quietly helped revise them for American audiences. At the same time he wrote the successful burlesque *Thrilby* (1895). Herbert later moved to *Weber and *Fields, writing some of their celebrated burlesques, notably *The Geezer* (1896), and occasionally performing in them. For the rest of his career he continued both to write and act and sometimes direct. Alone or with partners, he wrote such musicals as the American version of *A Waltz Dream* (1908), *The Honeymoon Express* (1913), *The Beauty Shop* (1914), and *Honeydew* (1920). Herbert also appeared in such shows as *The *Fortune Teller* (1898), *It Happened in Nordland* (1904), and *Deburau* (1920).

HERBERT, Victor (1859–1924), composer. The first great American creator of operetta, he was born in Dublin and studied music in Germany Afterwards he played cello in several major German orchestras. While there he met and married the prima donna Therese Foerster, and it was her signing to sing with the Metropolitan Opera that brought Herbert to New York, where he was a cellist with the Met. Shortly thereafter, Herbert accepted the post of director of the 22nd New York National Guard Band, and he started composing for the stage. Although the Bostonians mounted his *Prince Ananias* in 1894 and kept it in its repertory for several seasons, Herbert received little recognition until *The Wizard of the Nile* (1895) gave him his first success. *The Gold Bug* (1896), *The Serenade* (1897), and *The Idol's Eye* (1897) followed. His first great, enduring achievement was *The *Fortune Teller* (1898), succeeded by *Cyrano de Bergerac* (1899), *The Singing Girl* (1899), *The Ameer* (1899), and *The Viceroy* (1900). He then briefly abandoned the stage to become conductor of the Pittsburgh Symphony, returning in 1903 with one of his best-loved scores, *Babes in Toyland*. Also well received were *It Happened in Nordland* (1904), *Mlle. Modiste* (1905), *The *Red Mill* (1906), and *Naughty Marietta* (1910), generally acknowledged to be his masterpiece. Herbert's later works include *The Enchantress* (1911), *Sweethearts* (1913), *The Only Girl* (1914), and *The Princess Pat* (1915). Herbert was to write just one more great score, for the Irish-flavored *Eileen* (1917). His final operettas were *The Velvet Lady* (1919) and the posthumously produced *The Dream Girl* (1924). In all he composed scores for over forty musicals, including *Babette* (1903), *Miss Dolly Dollars* (1905), *Wonderland* (1905), *The Tattooed Man* (1907), *Little Nemo* (1908), *The Prima Donna* (1908), *Old Dutch* (1909), *The Duchess* (1911), *The Madcap Duchess* (1913), *The Débutante* (1914), *The Century Girl* (1916), *Miss* (1917), *Her Regiment* (1917), *My Golden Girl* (1920), and *The Girl in the Spotlight* (1920). Although Herbert in his lifetime made distinctions between what he considered his musical comedies and his operettas, his richly lyrical music today is perceived as almost wholly operetta-ish. He sometimes claimed that he was writing in an American idiom, and his contemporaries often agreed with him, but, again, today his influences are seen largely as French and Middle European. He moved from thumping marches to lilting waltzes to sentimental ballads with grace and ease. Whatever his sources, he raised the artistic level of American theatrical music and for many years did so virtually alone. Herbert was also one of the organizers of the *American Society of Composers, Authors & Publishers (ASCAP), which he was moved to found after hearing his music played in restaurants without his receiving any remuneration. Biography: *Victor Herbert: A Life in Music*, Edward Waters, 1955.

HERMAN, [Gerald] Jerry (b. 1932), composer and lyricist. Born in New York and raised in Jersey City, he had no formal musical education, although his mother taught piano and voice. At Miami University, he wrote a musical revue that was later reproduced Off Broadway. Several more Off-Broadway revues followed before Herman got his first Broadway assignment, the Israeli-set musical *Milk and Honey* (1961). He next scored the mammoth hits *Hello, Dolly!* (1964) and *Mame* (1966), followed by the more experimental (but initially unpopular) musicals *Dear World* (1969), *Mack and Mabel* (1974), and *The Grand Tour* (1979). In 1983 Herman retrieved his fortunes with *La Cage aux

Folles. There were also two retrospective revues of his songs: *Jerry's Girls* (1985) and *Jerry Herman on Broadway* (2001). While he has been criticized for the lack of innovative twists and richness in his scores, Herman's best songs are light, lively, and quickly hummable and often boast sprightly, engaging lyrics. Autobiography: *Showtune: A Memoir*, with Marilyn Stasio, 1996.

HERNDON, Richard G[ilbert] (1873?–1958), manager. He was born in Paris and educated at private schools before producing his first play in 1914. But it failed to reach New York, so Herndon began importing celebrated foreign performers and companies, including Théâtre du Vieux Colombier and Théâtre Parisien, as well as several famous ballet troupes. With his profits from these tours, he returned to more traditional, commercial theatre with offerings that ranged from the commonplace to the daring. Taking over two of Broadway's most intimate playhouses, the Belmont and the Klaw, Herndon produced Elliot *Nugent's first play, the popular *Kempy* (1922). The next year, working with Professor George Pierce *Baker of Harvard, he offered a prize for a new play. The result was Philip *Barry's first New York production, *You and I* (1923). Among Herndon's other successes were *Hurricane* (1923), *The Patsy* (1925), *Americana* (1926), *Sinner* (1927), and *The Unexpected Husband* (1931). His more noteworthy failures included Maxwell *Anderson's *Gypsy* (1929).

HERNE, [Katherine] **Chrystal** (1883–1950), actress. The daughter of James A. *Herne, she was born in Dorchester, Massachusetts, and made her earliest appearances in plays of her father, beginning in 1899. As a mature actress, she was best as regal, if sometimes haughty or cold, women. Among her more memorable roles were the forgiving wife Mrs. Clayton in *As a Man Thinks* (1911), Lady Grayston in the original American production of *Maugham's *Our Betters* (1917), music teacher Minnie Whitcomb in *Expressing Willie* (1924), and the houseproud Mrs. Craig in *Craig's Wife* (1925).

HERNE, James A. [né Ahearn] (1839–1901), playwright and actor. The son of a poor Irish immigrant who had adopted the rigorous philosophy of the Dutch Reformed Church, he was taken out of school in his native Cohoes, New York, at the age of thirteen and put to work in a brush factory. Although his father forbade his attending theatricals, when he was fourteen he saw Edwin *Forrest perform. That spurred him to pursue a career. However, it was not until he was twenty that he joined a traveling troupe performing the *dog dramas then popular. Herne performed in upstate

New York, Washington, Baltimore, Philadelphia, Montreal, and then to New York before serving a stint as manager of Manhattan's Grand Opera House. He next managed several theatres in California, where he met David *Belasco and married Katharine Corcoran. Herne had already begun to adapt novels for the stage, but it was with Belasco that he wrote his first important play, *Hearts of Oak* (1880). The play was unusual for its day, offering neither a clear hero nor a clear villain. After quarreling with Belasco, Herne wrote an unsuccessful patriotic drama, *The Minute Men of 1774–75* (1886). The movement toward naturalistic writing, which Herne had manifested in *Hearts of Oak*, was seen more clearly in his next play, *Drifting Apart* (1888), which brought him to the attention of such important literary figures as Hamlin Garland and William Dean *Howells. Along with his actress wife, both men encouraged him as he worked on his next play, *Margaret Fleming* (1891), the first important American play to demonstrate a significant debt to *Ibsen. That connection was held against it by many contemporary playgoers; even Mrs. Herne's fine acting of the title role could not ensure its acceptance. However, Herne's next play, *Shore Acres* (1893), enjoyed widespread success with the author in the leading role. His last works were *The Reverend Griffith Davenport* (1899) and *Sag Harbor* (1900), in which Herne assumed the role of an aging guardian angel, Captain Dan Marble. Herne was more of an enlightened, progressive writer than a great one. Even if his plays had revealed greater literary or artistic merits, it seems doubtful that they would have been more successful, for he paid the price for being in the avant-garde: forced runs, small profits, and often downright commercial failure. As a result, even when his reputation as a playwright was established, to make ends meet he was often required to act in or direct other men's works. However, his principal celebrity comes from his effectively introducing Ibsen's theories into American drama. His daughter was actress Chrystal *Herne. Biography: *James A. Herne: The American Ibsen*, John Perry, 1978.

HERO, THE (1921), a play by Gilbert Emery. [Belmont Theatre, 80 perf.] Andrew Lane (Richard *Bennett), an insurance salesman, has struggled during the war years to support his wife, his son, his widowed mother, and a Belgian refugee the Lanes had taken in. On the other hand, Andrew's brother, Oswald (Robert *Ames), has been fighting overseas and comes home a wounded, much-decorated hero. Before the war, Oswald had been something of a blackguard, so the family hopes his experiences have changed him. But they have not. He is no sooner home than he seduces the refugee and steals church funds. But as Oswald is running off, he stops to rescue some boys from a fire and is burned to death. Andrew can only conclude that Oswald was a hero after all. Originally presented the preceding season for four special matinees, producer Sam H. *Harris gave it a regular booking on the strength of its excellent notices. The new reviews were also enthusiastic, but playgoers apparently found the drama discomfiting. It remains one of the best plays to come out of World War I. The New York–born, Amherst-educated **Gilbert EMERY** [né Gilbert Emery Bensley Pottle] (1875–1945), was an actor, playwright, and short-story writer. His longest-run success was *Tarnish* (1923), and his social comedy *Love in a Mist* (1926), written with Amelie *Rives, was his only other work to achieve a modest run.

HERON, Matilda [Agnes] (1830–77), actress. Born in Ireland and brought to America while still quite young, she studied with Peter *Richings before making her professional debut at Philadelphia's *Walnut Street Theatre in 1851 as Bianca in *Fazio*. Her intelligent reading and fine acting won her instant plaudits, although Heron was not an especially attractive woman. Even by the standards of the time her figure was "ample," while her facial features were heavy. Nevertheless she followed her Bianca with equally praised interpretations of Juliet, Lady Macbeth, Ophelia, Parthenia in *Ingomar, Pauline in The *Lady of Lyons, and Julia in The *Hunchback. Her New York debut was at the *Bowery Theatre in 1852 as Lady Macbeth, following a year of performing in California and a trip to Paris in 1855, where she saw a performance of *La Dame aux Camélias* and made her own English version of it, which she first offered in 1857. Other adaptations had been on American stages since 1853, but it was Heron's performance that was considered definitive by American critics and playgoers for as long as she lived. The *Tribune* wrote: "She exuded the electricity of genius . . . there was about her a halo of individuality—a brilliancy of vitality—which convinced everyone present able to distinguish gauds from glories, that the palpitating actuality of perceptive genius was before them." Shortly thereafter, she offered her version of Legouve's *Medea and was also admired for her Nancy in *Oliver Twist*. Heron continued to perform these and other roles until illness forced her premature retirement. Her daughter, Hélène Stoepel, known professionally as Bijou Heron (1862–1937), was also a popular actress.

HERRING, Fanny (1832–1906), actress. The daughter of popular performers, the tiny, dark-haired, hoydenish performer was born in London and came to America four years later. As a teenager she moved from theatre to theatre, and it was not until she performed at the *Bowery Theatre in the late 1850s that she found her niche. There Herring soon became the darling of the gallery gods, offering them everything from her Ophelia and Juliet to leading roles in such now forgotten pieces as *The Female Detective* and *The Dumb Girl of Genoa*. However, her forte was trouser roles, and she won the loudest cheers for characterizations on the order of Mose in A *Glance at New York* and the title parts of *Jack Sheppard* and *Sinbad the Sailor*. By the early 1870s her popularity at the Bowery began to wane, so she often took herself to important vaudeville houses. Herring continued to perform, still frequently playing youthful street urchins, well into the 1890s, when she was billed at once comically and pathetically as "The Bernhardt of the West Side."

HERRMANN, Edward (b. 1943), actor. The tall, distinguished-looking leading man resembles Franklin D. Roosevelt and he has portrayed him on several occasions. Herrmann was born in Washington, D.C., and educated at Bucknell University and the London Academy of Music and Dramatic Art before making his Manhattan debut in 1971. Among his many notable performances were the slow-witted Aston in *The Caretaker* (1974), the jovial minister's son Frank Gardner in *Mrs. Warren's Profession* (1976), the writer-journalist Macauley Connor in The *Philadelphia Story* (1980), the poet T. S. *Eliot in *Tom and Viv* (1985), the controlling psychiatrist Dr. Block in *Psychopathia Sexualis* (1997), and the jilted barrister husband William in *The Deep Blue Sea* (1998).

HERTS, Henry B[eaumont] (1871–1933), architect. A native New Yorker, he was graduated from Columbia in 1893, then spent seven years in Europe studying architecture at Paris's Beaux Arts and the universities of Rome and Heidelberg. Between 1900 and the outbreak of World War I Herts designed over thirty theatres and is credited with perfecting the principles of cantilevered arch construction that eliminated the need for pillars to support balconies. Among his New York playhouses were the *Booth, the Fulton (later Helen *Hayes), the Gaiety, the Liberty, the *Lyceum, the *New Amsterdam, and the *Shubert, as well as the *Brooklyn Academy of Music.

HEWES, Henry (b. 1917), critic. He was born in Boston and educated at Harvard, Carnegie Tech, and Columbia before he started doing theatre reviews for the *New York Times* in 1948. But much of Hewes's career was spent at the *Saturday Review*, where he worked for over forty years, gaining a reputation for writing direct and pointed reviews.

He served as editor of the *Best Plays* in the 1960s and edited other theatre books as well. In 1999 the *American Theatre Wing changed the name of its recognition in design to the Henry Hewes Awards.

HEWLETT, James (fl. early 19th century), actor. Possibly the first professional African-American actor in America, he seems to have been a performer of modest merit, although his opportunities were few and his career was beset by prejudice, particularly at the hands of vociferous white hooligans. In 1821 he attempted *Richard III with an all-black cast. He later may have played either Othello or Iago with the same company. Both productions were interspersed with lighthearted songs and dances. In 1823 Hewlett assumed the title role in The Drama of King Shotaway, based on a West Indies insurrection and conceivably the first black play in American history. Thereafter, he seems to have confined his appearances to recitals devoted largely to imitations of famous white actors. An 1826 advertisement called him "the most astonishing phenomena of the age: a young man, who, notwithstanding the thousand obstacles which the circumstance of complexion must have thrown in his way of improvement, has, by the mere dint of natural genius and self-strengthened assiduity, risen to a successful competition with some of the first actors of the day." He was later billed as "Shakespeare's proud Representative." After a farewell benefit in 1831 he disappears from the records.

HEYWARD, Dubose. See *Porgy*.

HIELGE [sometimes spelled Heilge], **George** (fl. mid 19th century), designer. Called "a native artist" when he painted both scenery and murals for the Franklin Theatre in 1837, he soon moved to Philadelphia and became a major scene painter for the *Walnut Street Theatre and *Arch Street Theatres, where he met manager William E. *Burton. The two men developed a mutual respect, and he became Burton's set designer for the rest of that great actor-manager's career. Among the many productions that Hielge designed were *Burton's famous revivals of The *Merry Wives of Windsor (1853) and A *Midsummer Night's Dream (1854). After Burton's retirement Hielge served as P. T. *Barnum's chief set designer, then he disappears from the records about 1865. During his career Hielge was also famous for panoramas and landscape paintings.

HIGGINS, David K. (1858?–1936), playwright and actor. The Chicago native wrote numerous melodramas and rustic comedies at the turn of the century. Most of these plays had only short New York runs, frequently in secondary houses, but toured in smaller towns for many years. His best work was probably *At Piney Ridge* (1897). Among his other works were *Our Rich Cousin* (1886), written with his brother Milton; *The Plunger* (1890); *The Vendetta* (1891); *Kidnapped* (1892); *The Turn of the Tide* (1896); *A Union Soldier* (1898); *Up York State* (1901); and *His Last Dollar* (1904). Higgins often performed in his own plays, and after the market for his writings was destroyed by the rise of silent films he continued to act in other men's works.

HIGH BUTTON SHOES (1947), a musical comedy by Stephen Longstreet (book), Jule *Styne (music), Sammy Cahn (lyrics). [New Century Theatre, 727 perf.] Con artist Harrison Floy (Phil *Silvers) arrives in New Brunswick, New Jersey, in 1917 and hoodwinks Mr. and Mrs. Longstreet (Jack McCauley and Nanette *Fabray) out of some money from the sale of their property. The chase to catch Floy brings everyone to Atlantic City before the charlatan loses all his winnings on a football game. *Notable songs*: Papa, Won't You Dance with Me?; I Still Get Jealous; There's Nothing Like a Model T. The merry show was based on Longstreet's autobiography but much of the libretto was rewritten by director George *Abbott, who staged the musical in his typical rapid style. A highlight of the evening was the Tony Award–winning choreography by Jerome *Robbins, in particular his farcical "Keystone Kops" ballet set on the beach at Atlantic City. **Sammy CAHN** (1913–93) was one of Hollywood's most successful lyricists, but this was his only Broadway hit. The native New Yorker also wrote lyrics for the stage musicals *Skyscraper (1965) and Look to the Lilies (1970).

HIGH TOR (1937), a fantasy by Maxwell *Anderson. [Martin Beck Theatre, 171 perf.; NYDCC Award.] Van Van Dorn (Burgess *Meredith) is disgusted with civilization. Having fought with his sweetheart, Judith (Mab Maynard), he flees to a hill that he owns, overlooking the Hudson. There, with an Indian (Harry Irvine), he spends an eventful night. The pair encounters bank robbers, land developers determined to buy Van Dorn's hill, and the ghosts of old sailors. Come morning, the ghosts vanish, the robbers are apprehended, and a profitable deal is consummated with the developers. Van Dorn is even reconciled with Judith. Although he may appear to have sold out to the forces of progress, he has not totally capitulated, for the Indian assures him, "Nothing is made by men, but makes, in the end, good ruins." Guthrie *McClintic produced the blank-verse fantasy, which was one of Anderson's best, if lightest, plays.

HILL, Arthur [Edward Spence] (b. 1922), actor. A low-keyed, solid Canadian performer, he had appeared in several London productions before making his Broadway debut in The *Matchmaker (1955). He is best recalled for four roles: Ben Gant, the hero's frail brother, in *Look Homeward, Angel (1957); Jay Follet, the doomed father, in *All the Way Home (1960); George, the husband in an unhappy marriage, in *Who's Afraid of Virginia Woolf? (1962); and the weakling son Simon Harford in More Stately Mansions (1967).

HILL, G[eorge] **H**[andel] (1809–49), character actor. Best known as "Yankee" Hill, he was born in Boston, the son and brother of celebrated musicians, and his early career was given over to acting in minor roles and to offering recitals based on New England character sketches. With the rise in popularity of similar figures in American comedy, Hill quickly found stardom as the best Yankee interpreter of his day. Among his famous roles were Jonathan Ploughboy, Major Enoch Wheeler, Nathan Tucker, Jedediah Homebred, Hiram Dodge, and Solomon Swop. The Knickerbocker Magazine in 1838 noted, "In the exhibition of the quiet, dry humor peculiar to the Yankee, par excellence, he stands unrivaled. His acting is nature itself." An elongated, naively cheerful face enhanced his attraction. Hill's personal behavior appears to have been quirky, and he retired from the stage on several occasions for various reasons, only to soon return, and continued to act until his death. Autobiography: Scenes from the Life of an Actor, 1853 (reissued 1969).

HILLIARD, Robert C. (1857–1927), actor. Considered "the handsomest, as well as one of the best leading men" of his era, he was born in New York and made his stage debut in Brooklyn in 1886 in False Shame, appearing on Broadway in A Daughter of Ireland later that same year. Hilliard then succeeded Maurice *Barrymore as leading man to Lillie *Langtry. In 1891 he played Johann Tonnessen in The Pillars of Society, one of the earliest American productions of Ibsen's play. Although he was a star for many years, most of the plays in which he acted were popular but ephemeral works. His best-known roles were the bandit Dick Johnson in The *Girl of the Golden West (1905), the doomed John Schuyler in A *Fool There Was (1909), and the cool-headed detective Asche Kayton in The Argyle Case (1912). Between plays, Hilliard was equally popular on the vaudeville stage, where he appeared in numerous playlets.

HILSON, Thomas [né Hill] (1784–1834), actor. Born in England into a family careful of its respectability, he dutifully changed his name when he embarked on a theatrical career and made his American debut in 1811 at the *Park Theatre, playing Walter in The Children of the Wood. His success was immediate, and he soon earned a reputation in comedy parts such as Falstaff, Figaro, Sir Peter Teazle, Touchstone, and Tony Lumpkin. But his range was remarkable, and Hilson seems to have been equally skilled in playing the passionate figures of the romantic plays of the time, as well as tragic role. He offered a fine Richard III, while Thomas Abthorpe *Cooper considered him the best contemporary Iago. Mrs. Hilson, the former Ellen Augusta Johnson (1801–37), was a well-thought-of actress.

HINES, Gregory. See Jelly's Last Jam.

HINGLE, [Martin] Pat[terson] (b. 1924), actor. A native of Denver, Colorado, he made his debut in End as a Man (1953) and, after playing Gooper in *Cat on a Hot Tin Roof (1955), scored major successes as the troubled harness salesman Rubin Flood in The *Dark at the Top of the Stairs (1957) and as the Job-like title figure in *J. B. (1958). Subsequently he played Macbeth and Hector at the *American Shakespeare Festival, then appeared as Sam in a 1963 revival of *Strange Interlude. His only other long run has been as Victor Franz, the failed brother, in The *Price (1968), but Hingle also shone in Child's Play (1970), The Lady from the Sea (1976), A Life (1980), and as Ben Franklin in the 1997 revival of *1776.

HIPPODROME THEATRE (New York). The largest theatre of its day, it had a seating capacity of 5,200 and room for nearly 800 standees, with a stage 110 feet deep and over 200 feet long. The theatre, which stood on Sixth Avenue between 43rd and 44th Streets and which was the only major legitimate theatre ever built that far east of Broadway, opened in 1905 with the musical spectacle A Society Circus and for the next seventeen years offered similar spectacles annually, generally giving two performances a day. In its heyday the theatre was the most successful in New York, and its productions often chalked up the longest runs of their seasons. Besides choruses that reputedly numbered over five hundred the Hippodrome was famous for its horses, which dove into the huge tank in front of the stage. The productions all featured exceedingly lavish scenery. Between the runs of the major spectacles the house offered vaudeville. But with the growing competition from spectacular films and an increasing sophistication that put an end to the spectacle's attraction, the house was used solely for vaudeville. It later converted to films, but shortly before it was demolished in 1939 it returned to the legitimate fold to house *Jumbo (1935).

HIRSCH, Judd (b. 1935), character actor. The popular performer, with a "street face" that allows him to play everymen of different ethnic types, was born in the Bronx and studied engineering at City College before training as an actor at the *American Academy of Dramatic Arts and with various acting coaches. Hirsch worked in stock before making his Broadway debut in 1966, eventually getting noticed as the switchboard operator Bill in The *Hot l Baltimore (1973) at the *Circle Repertory Company, a group with whom he would often perform. He had become a familiar face in television by the time he starred as the widower-writer George Schneider in *Chapter Two (1977), followed by such successes as the Jewish accountant Matt Friedman in *Talley's Folly (1979), the feisty senior citizen Nat in *I'm Not Rappaport (1985 and 2002), and the crusty old bar owner Eddie in Conversations with My Father (1992). Mel *Gussow in the New York Times described Hirsch's performance as Matt Friedman the "quintessential portrait of an outsider . . . part bookkeeper, part clown."

HIRSCH, Louis A[chille] (1881–1924), composer. Born in New York, he began his career as a staff composer for the *Shuberts. After contributing songs for The Golden Widow (1909) and The Girl and the Wizard (1909), his first full score was heard in He Came from Milwaukee (1910). Hirsch wrote melodies for *Winter Garden revues and much of the music for the *Ziegfeld Follies (1915), including the hit song "Hello, Frisco." In all he wrote the principal scores for eighteen Broadway musicals, best remembered of which are Going Up! (1917) and *Mary (1920). Many of his contemporaries felt that Hirsch's early death deprived the American musical of a composer who had not yet reached his inventive zenith.

HIRSCHFELD, Al[bert] (1903–2003), artist. The St. Louis native began working for the New York Times as a caricaturist specializing in theatrical figures in 1925 and continued chronicling in sketches every season until the day he died seventy-seven years later. After 1945 he hid his daughter Nina's name in many of his cartoons, indicating the number of Ninas alongside his signature. Hirschfeld also illustrated a number of books with similarly witty, observant line drawings. A Broadway theatre was named after him the year he died.

HIRSCHFELD THEATRE (New York). The Byzantine-style playhouse on West 45th Street was built in 1924 as the Martin Beck Theatre, named for its owner and operator. G. Albert Lansburgh designed the thirteen-hundred-seat theatre with distinctive features such as a grand promenade, wrought iron details, and stained glass. Although the playhouse is located a block west from the other district theatres, it has always been a favorite venue for both plays and musicals. The Beck family continued to own the house until it was bought in 1966 by *Jujamcyn Theatres. In 2003 it was renamed after caricaturist Al *Hirschfeld on his one hundredth birthday; sadly, he had died only a few months before.

HISPANIC-AMERICAN THEATRE. Spanish-speaking theatre in North America has existed as early as the late 1500s, predating the first English theatre companies in the East coast colonies. Modern-day Mexico was particularly active in the theatre, and by the 1800s professional touring groups were performing throughout the American Southwest. Later, Spanish-language plays were common in American cities with large Hispanic populations, though these were often amateur community theatres that played in particular neighborhoods. The 1920s was a fertile time for Hispanic theatre in America, with both plays and musical revues (called zarzueles) gaining popularity in larger cities. But activity dwindled during the Depression and the war years. By the last decades of the 20th century, theatre companies were formed that were bilingual and started to reach wider audiences. Many feel the new movement began with Luis Valdez and his El Teatro Campesino in 1965. Valdez is a playwright-manager whose works, such as Zoot Suit (1978) and I Don't Have to Show You No Stinking Badges (1986), have found audiences outside the Hispanic community. By the 1970s Hispanic theatre in the United States was found in three forms: Chicano theatre, Cuban-American theatre, and Puerto Rican theatre, often called Nuyorican. The first has produced political and social dramas by such playwrights as Valdez, Jorge Huerta, Milcha Sanchez-Scott, and Estela Portillo and such companies as Teatro de la Gente, Teatro de la Esperanza, and others, organized under the National Aztlán Theatre. Cuban-American theatre is largely found in Florida and maintains traditions and techniques from its island home, including the Cuban "blackface" farces. Maria Irene *Fornes is the most prominent playwright of this form of Hispanic theatre; other notable writers include Iván Acosta, Nilo *Cruz, Manuel Martín, Mario Peña, Dolores Prida, and Omar Torres. As the name implies, Nuyorican refers to theatre about the Puerto Rican culture in New York City. The productions tend to be bilingual and are centered on neighborhoods, as seen in the work of the

*Puerto Rican Traveling Company. Miguel Piñero, whose powerful drama *Short Eyes* (1974) was a mainstream hit, was the most known Puerto Rican playwright, but others emerged from such groups as the Nuyorican Poets' Café: Juan Shamsul Alam, Edward Gallardo, Federico Fraguada, Richard Irizarry, Yvette Ramírez, and Candido Tirado. Hispanic theatre is not limited exclusively to these three categories; the *Public Theatre, *Repertorio Español, and other groups present a wide range of bilingual theatre. There are also noteworthy playwrights, such as Josefina López, Eduardo Machado, Carlos Morton, and José Rivera, who cannot be easily categorized. In truth, Hispanic-American theatre is as diverse and complex as the many Spanish-speaking groups in North America.

HIT THE DECK! (1927), a musical comedy by Herbert *Fields (book), Vincent *Youmans (music), Leo Robin, Clifford Grey (lyrics). [*Belasco Theatre, 352 perf.] Loulou (Louise *Groody) runs a coffee house on the docks at Newport but is prepared to give it all up to follow a sailor, "Bilge" Smith (Charles King). When Bilge ships out, Loulou follows him around the world. She finally persuades him to marry her, only to have him change his mind when he learns she is an heiress. But Bilge changes his mind again after Loulou agrees to assign her inheritance to their children. *Notable songs*: Hallelujah; Sometimes I'm Happy; Why, Oh Why? Based on Hubert Osborne's 1922 play, *Shore Leave*, the musical had the longest Broadway run of any original Youmans show. It was welcomed by Percy *Hammond of the *Herald Tribune* as "a clean, pretty, bright and happy show."

HIT-THE-TRAIL HOLLIDAY (1915), a farce by George M. *Cohan. [Astor Theatre, 336 perf.] Billy Holliday (Fred Niblo), a celebrated New York barman, comes to a small New England town to help open a new hotel. But when he has a falling-out with the local liquor magnate, he turns prohibitionist. Billy campaigns so vigorously that he puts the local bars and breweries out of business and even wins the hand of Edith Holden (Katherine La Salle), the minister's daughter. Many saw this play as a spoof of Billy Sunday, the leading evangelist of the day, and no doubt Cohan intended a comparison. But the original story was based on a bookmaker named Peter De Lacey, whose business was shut down after racing-track interests forced his patrons to bet at the tracks and who then successfully crusaded against the immorality of the tracks, closing them down.

HITCHCOCK, Raymond (1865–1929), comic actor and producer. Described by Stanley *Green as "a lanky, raspy-voiced comic with sharp features and straw-colored hair that he brushed across his forehead," he was born in Auburn, New York, and came to the theatre after some unhappy years in other trades. From 1890 on he began to call attention to himself in musicals such as *The Brigands* and *The Golden Wedding*. His performance in *King Dodo* (1901) made him a star, and he subsequently played principal roles in *The Yankee Consul* (1904), *Easy Dawson* (1905), *The Galloper* (1906), *The Student King* (1906), *The Yankee Tourist* (1907), *The Man Who Owns Broadway* (1909), *The Red Widow* (1911), and *The Beauty Shop* (1914). Beginning in 1917 Hitchcock produced and starred in a series of revues called *Hitchy-Koo*. In 1921 he appeared in the *Ziegfeld Follies*. When another revue, Raymond Hitchcock's *Pinwheel*, failed in 1922, he took to the road as Clem Hawley in The *Old Soak. Thereafter, his fortunes began to wane. His last Broadway appearance was as Boniface in *The Beaux' Stratagem* (1928). At his best, Hitchcock had a casual, homespun humor not unlike that of the later Will *Rogers.

HOBART, [Philpot] **George V**[ear] (1867–1926), librettist and lyricist. One of the most prolific writers of vaudeville sketches and plays of his day, he was born at Cape Breton, Nova Scotia, and spent time as a journalist in New York prior to writing for the stage. Alone or with collaborators he wrote such musicals as *Broadway to Tokio* (1900), *The Wild Rose* (1902), *The Boys and Betty* (1908), and *Buddies* (1919) and sketches for the *Ziegfeld Follies, Hitchy-Koo*, and the *Greenwich Village Follies. Hobart's most successful plays were the Lillian *Russell vehicle *Wildfire* (1908), written with George *Broadhurst; the morality play *Experience (1914); and the Ethel *Barrymore vehicle *Our Mrs. McChesney* (1915), written with Edna *Ferber. He also directed many of his own works. While clearly a knowing theatrical craftsman, Hobart left nothing of importance behind.

HODGE, William T[homas] (1874–1932), actor and playwright. Born in Albion, New York, he is said to have formed his own amateur repertory company while still a boy. In his teens he turned professional but did not make his New York debut until 1898 in *The Heart of Chicago*. Hodge won recognition as the gabby bumpkin Freeman Whitemarsh in *Sag Harbor (1900), followed by the disillusioned husband Mr. Stubbins in *Mrs. Wiggs of the Cabbage Patch* (1904). But he did not become a star until his shrewd but kindly Daniel Vorhees in The *Man from Home (1907), a role he played for five years. Thereafter, he made a career of appearing in similar roles in similar plays, all of them written by himself: Jim Whitman in *The Road to Happiness* (1915), Dr. Pendergrass in *A Cure for*

Curables (1918), John Weatherbee in *The Guest of Honor* (1920), Tom Griswold in *For All of Us* (1923), Eugene Thomas in *Straight through the Door* (1928), and others. His plays usually enjoyed only modest runs in New York, where they were perceived as superannuated hokum, but continued to have long, profitable road tours. Hodge was a rather attractive man with a slightly gaunt face and sharp features.

HODGKINSON, John [né Meadowcroft] (1767–1805), actor and manager. Son of a British farmer turned publican, he enlisted in a troupe playing in Bristol and Bath, then in 1791 wrote to Lewis *Hallam Jr. and John *Henry, requesting a position in their company. Hodgkinson made his American debut at Philadelphia's *Southwark Theatre in 1792 as Belcour in *The West Indian*. William *Dunlap described him as "five feet ten inches in height, but even at the period we speak of, at the age of twenty-six, he was too fleshy to appear tall, and in a few years became corpulent. . . . His face was round, his nose broad and not prominent, his eyes gray, and of unequal sizes, but with large pupils and dark eyelashes." Among his early roles, both in Philadelphia and in New York, were Macheath, Macbeth, Marc Antony, Bob Acres, and Jaffier. He later distinguished himself in the title role of *André and as Rolla in Dunlap's version of *Pizarro*. His looks and fine acting won him rapid public approval, but behind the scenes he was apparently a ruthless, ambitious, and quarrelsome man, squeezing first Henry then Hallam out of their positions. However, Hodgkinson was a skilled manager, and his partnership with Hallam at the *John Street Theatre resulted in several excellent seasons. He played in other cities and continued to act in New York, until he died in a yellow fever epidemic. For all his flaws, he was probably the finest actor American audiences had seen up to his time.

HOEY, Mrs. John [née Josephine Shaw] (1824?–96), actress. A slightly mousy but still attractive performer with a style that many critics insisted was too stilted and artificial, she was nevertheless a reigning favorite for several seasons under the *Wallacks. Born in Liverpool, she came to America with her musician father and made her debut at the Museum in Baltimore in 1839. She appeared briefly with William E. *Burton in New York before her second marriage to a rich shipping magnate, then retired from the stage. But James *Wallack Sr. persuaded her to return in 1854. Evidently, he and a large segment of the public disagreed with the critics who rejected Hoey. T. Allston *Brown recollected: "Her peculiar forte lay in rendering that class of characters in which the manners of the modern lady of fashion were

required." Brown claimed her Beatrice was "a portrayal which for delicacy, sensibility, and grace, never, perhaps, had its equal." Hoey's gift for playing ladies of fashion was enhanced by her reputation as an extravagantly rich and beautiful dresser. In 1865 she quarreled with Wallack and retired permanently.

HOEY, William F. (1855–97), actor. Alone or with partners he was for many years a popular vaudeville performer. However, his greatest fame came when he joined with his brother-in-law, Charles E. Evans, in A *Parlor Match* (1885). Hoey played a bibulous, bearded tramp, Old Hoss, and was regularly afterwards known as "Old Hoss" Hoey. He continued in the part with only intermittent interruptions almost until his death. Among his other legitimate appearances were *The Flams* (1894) and *The Globe Trotter* (1895).

HOFFMAN, Aaron (1880–1924), playwright. The St. Louis native, who began creating vaudeville skits and monologues while still a student at the University of Chicago, became fully professional when he wrote such turn-of-the-century touring shows as *Bankers and Brokers* and the libretto for *The Belle of Avenue A*. Hoffman came to New York's attention when he collaborated on the libretto of *The Rogers Brothers in Panama* (1907). His best-known plays were the World War I drama *Friendly Enemies* (1918), written with Samuel *Shipman; *Nothing But Lies* (1918); *Welcome Stranger* (1920), about small-town anti-Semitism; and the family drama *Give and Take* (1923).

HOFFMAN, Dustin (b. 1937), actor. A native of Los Angeles, he studied acting at the *Pasadena Playhouse and with Lee *Strasberg, among others, before winning fine notices Off-Broadway in the mid-1960s and on Broadway in *Jimmy Shine* (1968), then engaging in a long, highly successful film career. But Hoffman returned to Broadway with an original interpretation of Willy Loman in *Death of a Salesman* (1984) and as Shylock in *The *Merchant of Venice* (1989), which he had originally played in London.

HOGAN'S GOAT (1965), a play by William Alfred. [St. Clement's Church, 607 perf.] Matt Stanton (Ralph Waite) determines to take on the incumbent, Edward Quinn (Tom Ahearne), in a contest for the mayoralty of Brooklyn in 1890. But Stanton is consumed by ambition and subordinates everything to his attempt to rise to power. He finally alienates his wife, Kathleen (Faye Dunaway), and when she dies in a fall down the stairs as she goes to leave him, her death destroys his overreaching hopes. Otis L. *Guernsey Jr. called this blank-verse drama "the very best play of 1965–66," adding, "its examination of a human being's drive to emerge from the ruck in defiance of all rules and risks is extremely pertinent to our modern population-swelling, status-seeking, amoral society." The drama was a surprise hit for the *American Place Theatre.

HOLBROOK, [Harold Rowe Jr.] **Hal** (b. 1925), actor. A native of Cleveland, he made his professional debut in 1942 and later assumed leading roles in such important Broadway offerings as the 1964 revival of *Marco Millions*; *After the Fall* (1964), in which he alternated with Jason *Robards; and *I Never Sang for My Father* (1968). But Holbrook is recalled primarily for his superb one-man show, *Mark Twain Tonight!*, which he first performed in 1955 and afterwards toured with for many seasons, returning for a Manhattan reprise as late as 1977. His later New York productions include *The *Country Girl* (1984), as *King Lear* (1990), and in *An American Daughter* (1997).

HOLD EVERYTHING! (1928), a musical comedy by B. G. *De Sylva (book, lyrics), John *McGowan (book), Ray *Henderson (music), Lew *Brown (lyrics). [*Broadhurst Theatre, 413 perf.] "Sonny Jim" (Jack *Whiting) is a welterweight contender. When he agrees to fight in a charity bout, his trainer suggests he pull his punches rather than risk problems, but his sweetheart, Sue Burke (Ona Munson), tells him to fight as if it meant the title. Jim is uncertain whether to follow his trainer's or his sweetheart's advice until his opponent slaps Sue. Then he quickly wins both the bout and Sue. *Notable songs*: Don't Hold Everything; To Know You Is to Love You; Too Good to Be True; You're the Cream in My Coffee. Prizefights had become big in this sports-mad era, and earlier in the same season several straight plays had centered on boxing. So this Alex A. *Aarons and Vinton *Freedley musical production was well timed. For many critics and playgoers, the highlight of the evening was the clowning of Bert *Lahr as the punch-drunk fighter Gink Schiner, his antics in this show making him a star.

HOLGATE, Ron (b. 1937), actor and singer. The rich-voiced baritone was born in Aberdeen, South Dakota, and educated at Northwestern before studying for an opera career at the New England Conservatory and the Music Academy of the West. Holgate made his opera debut in Boston in 1958 but soon switched to the theatre, making his Broadway bow three years later. He first aroused interest as the pompous Roman officer Miles Gloriosus in the original *A *Funny Thing Happened on the Way to the Forum* (1962), followed by such delightful performances as the boastful delegate Richard Henry Lee in *1776* (1969), the bigoted Polish colonel Stjerbinsky in *The Grand Tour* (1979), and the Italian opera star Tito Merelli in *Lend Me a Tenor* (1989).

HOLIDAY (1928), a play by Philip *Barry. [*Plymouth Theatre, 230 perf.] Having made a small fortune while still a young man, Johnny Case (Ben Smith) decides to use his wealth to live a carefree, easy life. As he tells his prospective sister-in-law, Linda Seton (Hope Williams), "I just want to save part of my life for myself. There's a catch, though. It's got to be part of the young part." He can work again later, if need be. This philosophy sits well with Linda, but not with Johnny's fiancée, Julia Seton (Dorothy Tree), nor with her father. So when Johnny goes off to put his ideas into action, it is Linda, not Julia, who follows him. While critics saw this play as everything from an intellectual defense of the hedonism of the 1920s to an Edith Whartonish satire on society, Barry's modern editor, Brendan Gill, viewed it as "an embodiment of Barry's continued preoccupation with the relations between outsiders and insiders," noting that at the time of this Arthur *Hopkins production, Barry was a newly rich young man, watching with fascination from outside the curious games of society insiders. The comedy was turned into the short-lived Broadway musical *Happy New Year* (1980) using Cole *Porter songs.

HOLLAND, George (1791–1870), comic actor. The son of a London tradesman, he himself spent several years in trade before electing to make a career of acting. Holland was already an experienced comedian when he came to America in 1827 and won over *Bowery Theatre playgoers as Jerry, the man who assumes several disguises, in *A Day after the Fair*. After some time he performed in the South, where he became a regional favorite, particularly in New Orleans where Sol *Smith recalled "he enjoyed a popularity never perhaps equaled by any other actor in that city." Holland was back in New York in the 1840s, and by 1853 he was a member of William E. *Burton's celebrated company, joining James *Wallack's ensemble two years later. Except for a brief stint with Christy's Minstrels in 1857 he remained a principal comedian with Wallack until 1869, when he briefly joined Augustin *Daly. T. Allston *Brown observed, "He was unlike any other actor I ever saw . . . an opportunity of tumbling over a chair, upsetting a table or burning his nose with a candle, was worth to him more than all the finest sentences of wit and sentiment. In the overstrained, unnatural and exaggerated style of farce . . . [he] was in many respects unequaled." Yet it was not his art but an incident after his death for which he is best remembered. His son and the actor Joseph *Jefferson went to arrange his burial, only to be told by the Reverend Lorenzo Sabine that his church did not welcome actors but that there was "a little church around the corner where they do that sort of thing." Holland's funeral thus gave a special cachet to New York's Church of the Transfiguration in American theatrical history. Biography: *Holland Memorial: Sketch of the Life of George Holland, the Veteran Comedian, with Dramatic Reminiscences*, William B. Maclay, 1871.

HOLLAND, John Joseph (1776?–1820), scenic designer and architect. The English-born artist was reputedly a pupil of Marinelli in London before being brought to America by *Wignell to serve at Philadelphia's *Chestnut Street Theatre. He later moved to New York, where he was largely responsible for the 1807 redesigning of the *Park Theatre, at which he served for several seasons as principal scenic artist. In 1813 he left (temporarily) to become one of the leaders of the rebellious, short-lived *Theatrical Commonwealth. The Gothic settings he created for the Park's 1809 mounting of *De Montfort* are sometimes said to be the first American attempt at historical accuracy in scenery. William *Dunlap suggested he was a slow, deliberate worker who insisted "an Artist was not bound to work by the hour like a mechanick," whereas Joseph *Ireland recalled, "He was an artist of great taste, and as a scenic and decorative painter, surpassed all who had been known before him in this country."

HOLLIDAY, Judy [née Judith Tuvim] (1922–65), actress. A New York-born, baby-voiced blonde, she began her theatrical career as a telephone operator with the *Mercury Theatre. She performed with a nightclub act, "The Revuers," which also included Betty *Comden and Adolph *Green, before appearing in films and then making her Broadway debut as Alice in *Kiss Them for Me* (1945). Holliday is remembered primarily for two roles: Billy Dawn, the dumb mistress of a crass junk dealer, in *Born Yesterday* (1946), and Ella Peterson, who finds love while running a telephone answering service, in the musical *Bells Are Ringing* (1956). Her last appearance was as Sally Hopwinder, a Peace Corps volunteer, in the musical *Hot Spot* (1963). Biography: *Judy Holliday*, Will Holtzman, 1982.

HOLLIDAY STREET THEATRE (Baltimore). Built by Thomas *Wignell and Alexander *Reinagle in 1794, it was a wooden structure and stood on Holliday Street near Peale's Museum and directly across from the site of Baltimore's future city hall. Although it was officially the New Theatre, it soon became known as the Holliday. Later managers

included William *Warren and William B. *Wood. After playing there John Howard *Payne noted, "The attraction was the acting, not the scenery, of which the less said the better, nor the comfort experienced by the audience, since the seats were long, uncushioned benches without backs." In 1813 it was replaced by a brick structure called the Baltimore Theatre, but again called the Holliday by Baltimoreans. "The Star Spangled Banner" received its first public performance there in 1819. The playhouse burned in 1873 and was rebuilt with a similar facade by John T. *Ford, finally officially called the Holliday Street Theatre. Management was later assumed by John W. Albaugh. Long known as Baltimore's "Old Drury," it remained an important playhouse until shortly before its demolition in 1917.

HOLM, Celeste (b. 1919), actress. The versatile, bright-eyed blonde, a native New Yorker, made her professional debut in 1936 and later that year understudied Ophelia in Leslie *Howard's *Hamlet*. However, her greatest fame came when she created the role of the irrepressible Ado Annie in *Oklahoma!* (1943). Holm next starred in *Bloomer Girl* (1944) but thereafter never seemed to be able to find major roles worthy of her. She did briefly replace Gertrude *Lawrence in The *King and I* and later led a touring company of *Mame*. Her other New York credits include *Candida* (1970), *Habeas Corpus* (1975), the one-woman program *Paris Was Yesterday* (1979), *I Hate Hamlet* (1991), and *Don Juan in Hell* (2000).

HOLM, Hanya [née Johanna Eckert] (1893–1992), choreographer. A German-born dancer who worked with Max *Reinhardt before immigrating to America, she performed alone or with an ensemble prior to choreographing "The Eccentricities of Davy Crockett" in the Broadway production of *Ballet Ballads* (1948). Later assignments included *Kiss Me, Kate* (1948), *Out of This World* (1950), The *Golden Apple* (1954), *My Fair Lady* (1956), *Camelot* (1960), and *Anya* (1965). Her work was eclectic, ranging from lively, witty routines to elegant dances. Biography: *Hanya Holm: The Biography of an Artist*, Walter Sorrell, 1969.

HOLM, John Cecil. See *Three Men on a Horse*.

HOLMAN, Libby [née Elizabeth Holtzman] (1906–71), singer and actress. One of the most celebrated torch singers of the 1920s and early 1930s, the dark-haired beauty was born in Cincinnati and made her professional debut in a 1924 touring company of the nonmusical play The *Fool*. Holman first appeared on Broadway in the *Garrick Gaieties* (1925), then was in other revues and played the sultry Lotta in *Rainbow* (1928) before she scored heavily in The *Little Show (1929), in which she sang "Moanin' Low." She introduced "Body and Soul" and "Something to Remember You By" in Three's a Crowd (1930) and "You and the Night and the Music" in Revenge with Music (1934). Later appearances were in You Never Know (1938) and in a one-woman show Blues, Ballads and Sin Songs (1954). Besides occasional performances in plays in summer stock, she frequently sang in cabarets.

HOLMES, Rupert. See Mystery of Edwin Drood, The.

HOLTZ, Lou (1898–1980), comedian. Yiddish-dialect comic, famed for his zany version of "O Sole Mio" with which he often ended his vaudeville act, he was born in San Francisco and made his vaudeville debut in 1914. A year later he made his Broadway debut in A World of Pleasure. Thereafter, he moved back and forth between two-a-day and the legitimate stage. Holtz was featured in such musicals as the 1919, 1920, and 1921 editions of *George White's Scandals, The Dancing Girl (1923), Tell Me More (1925), Manhattan Mary (1927), You Said It (1931), Calling All Stars (1934), Priorities of 1942, and Star Time (1944). Popular mainly in cities with large Jewish communities, his highly ethnic humor was sometimes assailed for exceeding the boundaries of good taste.

HONOLULU THEATRE FOR YOUTH. Hawaii's only professional nonprofit theatre, it was founded in 1955 by Nancy Corbett, who was the creative drama director for the city's Department of Parks and Recreation. While the company presents plays for children ranging from elementary school to high school in its main stage space, much of the group's work is done in schools. Shakespeare, myths, fairy tales, and literary classics are adapted and presented for children in imaginative productions that seek to overcome racial and economic barriers.

HOOKER, [William] Brian (1880–1946), playwright and lyricist. A professor of English at both Yale and Columbia, his renowned translation of *Cyrano de Bergerac was used by Walter *Hampden, José *Ferrer, and others. Hampden also used his version of Ruy Blas (1933). Hooker also served as lyricist and librettist for several musicals, most memorably The *Vagabond King (1925).

HOOKS, Robert. See Negro Ensemble Company.

HOOLEY'S THEATRE (Chicago). A popular venue during the last decades of the 19th century, the theatre was built in 1871 by former minstrel Richard M. Hooley as Hooley's Opera House.

"Uncle Dick" had to rebuild the house nine months later after it was destroyed in the infamous Chicago fire, and the new 1,400-seat house became home to his stock company. Hooley's was later renamed Power's New Theatre when Harry J. Powers took over in 1893.

HOPE, [Leslie Townes] Bob (1903–2003), comic actor. Born in England but raised in Cleveland, he made his professional debut in vaudeville and his Broadway debut in the chorus of The Ramblers (1926). He subsequently appeared in Sidewalks of New York (1927), Ups-a-Daisy (1928), Smiles (1930), and Ballyhoo of 1932. By 1932 he had become a headliner at the *Palace Theatre, where Max *Gordon caught his act, which consisted largely of brash one-liners, and cast him for the part of Huckleberry Haines in *Roberta (1933). He played similar wise-cracking roles in Say When (1934), The *Ziegfeld Follies of 1936, and Red, Hot and Blue! (1936), then abandoned the theatre for films, radio, and television, becoming one of the most successful comedians of the time, especially remembered for his extended tours of army camps during various wars.

HOPKINS, Arthur [Melancthon] (1878–1950), producer and director. One of the most distinguished of Broadway producers, he was born in Cleveland and spent time as a newspaper reporter (he was the first to uncover background material on Leon Czolgocz, President McKinley's assassin) before becoming a vaudeville press agent, with Irene and Vernon *Castle as his most famous clients. Hopkins's first production, Steve (1912), failed to run, but The Poor Little Rich Girl (1913) brought him his initial success. Later hits (solo or with others) included *On Trial (1914); *Good Gracious Annabelle (1916); A Successful Calamity (1917); The Jest (1919); *Anna Christie (1921); The *Hairy Ape (1922); The *Old Soak (1922); *What Price Glory? (1924); *Burlesque (1927), which he co-authored; *Paris Bound (1927); *Machinal (1928); *Holiday (1928); The *Petrified Forest (1935); and The Magnificent Yankee (1946). He was also responsible for bringing John *Barrymore to the stage in *Richard III (1920) and *Hamlet (1922), as well as for Lionel *Barrymore's Macbeth in 1921 and Ethel *Barrymore's Juliet in 1922. As a rule, Hopkins directed all his own productions and wrote the modern-day version of Hamlet called Conquest (1933). In conjunction with the *Shuberts, he built the *Plymouth Theatre in New York. Hopkins also wrote two books: How's Your Second Act? (1931) and an autobiography, To a Lonely Boy (1937). In the latter he expressed a philosophy of producing in which "the final test of producers . . . is the amount of new talent they have brought into the theater. It was the joy of old producers like Belasco and Tyler to develop new talent. That was the high adventure of the theater." John Mason *Brown remembered him as "that amazing, moon-faced little cherub . . . looking like a small town banker and thinking like an artist."

HOPPER, De Wolf [William D'Wolf Hopper] (1858–1935), comic actor. Descendant of a family that traced its ancestry back to colonial America, he was born in New York and raised in expectation of following in his father's footsteps as a lawyer. Instead he used his inheritance to form his own short-lived theatrical company, then studied voice with the hopes of an opera career. However, when John *McCaull cast him as a singing comedian in *Désirée* in 1884, his success was so pronounced that he realized immediately he had found his life's work. Among his major early musicals were *The Black Hussar* (1885), *The Beggar Student* (1885), *The Begum* (1887), *The Lady or the Tiger* (1888), and *Castles in the Air* (1890), his first starring vehicle. A major success was his conniving regent, the title role of *Wang* (1891), followed by the less successful *Panjandrum* (1893) and *Dr. Syntax* (1894). In 1896 Hopper first played the role with which he is most identified, the wily viceroy of Peru Don Medigua in John Philip *Sousa's *El Capitan*. In subsequent seasons he appeared in *The Charlatan* (1898), *Fiddle-Dee-Dee* (1900), *Hoity Toity* (1901), *Mr. Pickwick* (1903), *Happyland* (1905), *The Pied Piper* (1908), *A Matinee Idol* (1910), a series of *Gilbert and Sullivan revivals, *Lieber Augustin* (1913), *Hop o' My Thumb* (1913), *The *Passing Show of 1917*, *Everything* (1918), a revival of *Erminie* (1921), *Snapshots of 1921,* and *Some Party* (1922). He also played Falstaff, as well as David in *The Rivals*. By this time his popularity had waned with Broadway audiences, but he found a welcome touring in revivals of *El Capitan*, *The Chocolate Soldier*, and a road company of *The *Student Prince* (1927). An exceedingly tall, thin man with a deep basso voice, he made famous the poem "Casey at the Bat" early in his career, and thereafter recited it either in his shows or as part of his curtain calls. He was notorious for having been married six times. One of his wives was **Edna Wallace HOPPER,** (1864?–1959), an exceptionally tiny (said to be well under five feet) singer and comedienne who was born in San Francisco and made her New York debut in 1891. She was a rising member of Charles *Frohman's stock company when she married Hopper and turned to the musical stage. She played major roles in such shows as *El Capitan* (1896) and *Florodora* (1900). In later years she remained popular in vaudeville, in which she traded on her deceptively youthful appearance. Autobiography (De Wolf): *Once a Clown, Always a Clown,* with Wesley Winan Stout, 1927.

HOPWOOD, [James] **Avery** (1882–1928), playwright. One of the most successful dramatists of his day, he was born in Cleveland, and educated at the University of Michigan. Like many other contemporary playwrights he spent time as a newspaperman before seeing his first play, *Clothes* (1906), produced. Hopwood never laid claim to serious artistic pretensions, wanting only to be a successful, respected commercial craftsman. He worked alone or with collaborators (often with Mary Roberts Rinehart) and frequently wrote to order. More often than not his plays were looked upon as risqué, although only once did the police suggest he had overstepped the line of decency. His most successful works were *Seven Days* (1909), *Nobody's Widow* (1910), *Fair and Warmer* (1915), The *Gold Diggers* (1919), *The Girl in the Limousine* (1919), *Ladies' Night* (1920), *Spanish Love* (1920), The *Bat* (1920), *Getting Gertie's Garter* (1921), *The Demi-Virgin* (1921), *Why Men Leave Home* (1922), *Little Miss Bluebeard* (1923), *The Best People* (1924), *The Harem* (1924), and *Naughty Cinderella* (1925). Brooks *Atkinson wrote, "The mechanical formula for play-writing that made the value of American drama negligible was perfect for Hopwood, and he developed it with the skill and polish of an ingenious workman." A tall, thin man with blue eyes and blond hair, he was known for his exceedingly grave expression. That demeanor apparently masked serious private problems, for Hopwood eventually became a heavy drinker and may have committed suicide by drowning himself in the Mediterranean. He left his alma mater a large bequest to be made the basis of an annual playwriting award. Biography: *Avery Hopwood: His Life and Plays,* Jack F. Sharrar, 1989.

HORIZON (1871), a play by Augustin *Daly. [Olympic Theatre, 65 perf.] Alleyn Van Dorp (Hart Conway), a recent West Point graduate, is dispatched to the Far West on his first commission. He employs his spare time seeking the lost daughter and husband of his foster mother. He soon learns that Med (Agnes *Ethel), whom the Indians call "the White Flower of the Plains," and her drunkard father, Wolf (J. B. *Studley), are the very persons he seeks. After Wolf is murdered, the notorious criminal John Loder (J. K. Mortimer), who is known as "Panther Loder" or "the White Panther," takes Med under his protection. He loves her and treats her well, but she is kidnapped by the Indian chief, Wannamucka (Charles Wheatleigh). Van Dorp rescues her, and Loder kills Wannamucka. For all his cruelty and dishonesty, Loder cares enough about Med to recognize she will fare better with Van Dorp, so he relinquishes her to the soldier. Critics praised the play for its reasonably accurate picture of the contemporary West and for its willingness to see virtue in villains and faults in heroes and heroines. One of Daly's great rivals, A. M. *Palmer, later said not only was it Daly's best play but the finest American play he had ever seen. Despite critical and professional admiration for the work, the public's acceptance of the John A. *Duff offering was minimal.

HORNBLOW, Arthur (1865–1942), playwright and critic. The English-born writer and editor studied literature and painting in Paris before moving to America in 1889. He became a member of the staff of the *Dramatic Mirror*, supplementing his salary by serving as a play reader for A. M. *Palmer. From 1901 to 1926 he was the editor and principal dramatic critic for *Theatre Magazine*. During this period he novelized several successful Broadway plays as well as wrote several plays of his own. He also wrote his two-volume *A History of the Theatre in America, from Its Beginnings to the Present Time* (1919).

HOROVITZ, Israel. See *Indian Wants the Bronx, The*.

HORSESHOE ROBINSON (1856), a play by Clifton W. *Tayleure. [*Holliday Street Theatre (Baltimore), in repertory.] The roughhewn woodsman and Indian fighter Galbraith "Horseshoe" Robinson (William Ellis) is helping his friend Major Arthur Butler (George C. *Boniface) sneak through redcoat lines during the Revolution. Not only does Butler want to reach friendly forces, but he wants to visit the Lindsay home. Although Mr. Lindsay (J. H. Jack) is a loyalist, his daughter Mildred (Mrs. I. B. Phillips) is a rebel supporter who has secretly married Butler. At one point Butler and Robinson are surrounded, but Robinson escapes and uses all his wiles to enlist further aid to free Butler, now under sentence of death. His ruses include making himself and one associate appear to outnumber the British force. Based on John P. Kennedy's historical romance, *Horseshoe Robinson: A Tale of the Tory Ascendency*, it was originally adapted (probably by Charles Dance) in 1836 as a vehicle for the elder James *Hackett, who played the role for several seasons. Whether Tayleure made his own version or simply revamped Dance's is unknown, for Tayleure's alone survives. It is a lively piece, filled with colorful characters. In one form or another, the play remained popular, especially at lower-class houses, well beyond the Civil War.

HOSCHNA, Karl (1877–1911), composer. Born in Kushchwarda, Bohemia, he graduated with honors from the Vienna Conservatory and accepted a post as oboist in the Austrian army band. Hoschna came to America in 1896 and found work with Victor *Herbert. According to rumor, he developed a fear that oboe playing would affect his mind, so he left Herbert to work as a copyist at a music publisher. While there he composed three operettas that were produced but folded before reaching New York. His luck changed when he wrote the score for the popular *Three Twins* (1908) with lyricist Otto *Harbach. *Bright Eyes* and *Madame Sherry* opened in 1910, the latter his biggest hit and the source of the still recognized "Every Little Movement." In the following year *Jumping Jupiter*, *Dr. Deluxe*, *The Girl of My Dreams*, and *The Fascinating Widow* all reached Broadway, while his *The Wall Street Girl* (1912) was mounted posthumously. Hoschna was a fine melodist, his work characterized by great charm. His death at thirty-four left unanswered how he would have developed.

HOT CORN: LIFE SCENES IN NEW YORK ILLUSTRATED. Solon Robinson's collection of loosely interconnected stories depicting the drink-doomed habitués of Five Points, a notorious Manhattan slum, was first published in mid-1853 in the *New York Tribune*, then a year later was expanded into a hardcover best-seller. Dramatizations, according to George *Odell, soon "swept the stages with a blast second only to that of *Uncle Tom's Cabin*." New York saw no fewer than three popular versions during the 1853–54 season: *Little Katy; or, The Hot Corn Girl* by C. W. *Taylor; *Hot Corn; or, Little Katy* at Barnum's *American Museum; and *The Hot Corn Girl* at the *Bowery Theatre. The versions varied greatly, often changing characters' names and, apparently, sometimes adding original materials. The colorful characters in the pieces were the missionary Rev. Mr. Pease; the supposedly reformed Wild Maggie and her father; the seamstress Athalia Lovetree, who marries a drunkard; the tragic youth Madalina, whose death spares her the life of prostitution her ragpicker mother would force her into; and Little Katy, a tot selling peanuts in winter and hot corn in summer, who dies after her drunken mother beats her for falling asleep and allowing a thief to steal her nightly quota of corn.

HOT L BALTIMORE, THE (1973), a play by Lanford *Wilson. [*Circle in the Square, 1,166 perf.; NYDCC Award.] The Hotel Baltimore, once fashionable but now home to prostitutes, petty thieves, drifters, and indigents, has become seedy. The "e" in "hotel" in its sign has gone out, but no one has bothered to replace it since the building is about to be torn down. Little happens in the Chekhovian character piece: people reminisce about their past, the prostitutes come and go with their trade, one tenant robs another, and a young man comes seeking his grandfather who may or may not have lived there. Originally produced Off Off Broadway by the *Circle Repertory Company, the compassionate ensemble piece was remounted by producers Kermit *Bloomgarden and Roger Ailes for a long run. The play marked the first major success for playwright Wilson, director Marshall W. *Mason, and actor Judd *Hirsch, who played the night clerk Bill.

HOTEL UNIVERSE (1930), a play by Philip *Barry. [Martin Beck Theatre, 81 perf.] Ann Field (Katherine Alexander) has invited a variety of guests to her Riviera estate, including her old beau Pat Farley (Glenn *Anders); the actress Lily Malone (Ruth *Gordon); publisher Tom Ames (Franchot *Tone) and his wife, Hope (Phyllis Povah); the rich Jew Norman Rose (Earle *Larimore); Alice Kendall (Ruthelma Stevens), who is in love with Norman; and Ann's strange old father, Stephen (Morris *Carnovsky). The guests have all found their promising beginnings somehow thwarted. Moreover, they have been unnerved by odd stories about the house and by the suicide of a young friend. Stephen's probing questions and incisive remarks force them to examine their past and exorcise the demons that have bedeviled them. They leave filled with new hope, but unaware that Stephen has quietly died while sitting in his chair. Although the *Theatre Guild offering baffled most critics and was rejected by playgoers, it remains one of Barry's more interesting excursions away from his high comedy forte, yet is filled with his typically witty lines and trenchant observations.

HOUGH, Will M. See Adams, Hough and Howard.

HOUSE OF BLUE LEAVES, THE (1971), a play by John *Guare. [Truck and Warehouse Theatre, 337 perf.; NYDCC Award.] News of the Pope's impending visit to New York in 1965 seems to unhinge the zany Shaughnessy family. The father, Artie (Harold Gould), is a zookeeper who dreams of becoming a Hollywood songwriter and writes lyrics such as "Where is the devil in Evelyn?" The mother, Bananas (Katherine Helmond), is flakier still, sometimes confusing Brillo pads and hamburgers. Their son, Ronnie (William Atherton), has gone AWOL in hopes of blowing up the Pope. Even Artie's mistress, Bunny (Anne Meara), is kooky, living her life through *Modern Screen* magazine. Ronnie's plans backfire, and he is blown up by his own bomb. Bunny runs off with a Hollywood producer whom Artie had hoped would help him. Artie's reaction to all this is to throw his crazy wife out the window, then compose another inane ditty. Guare's first success, the play was a superb black comedy that was frequently produced across the country. It was revived by *Lincoln Center to great acclaim in 1986 with John Mahoney, Stockard *Channing, and Swoozie Kurtz in the cast.

HOUSE OF FLOWERS (1954), a musical by Truman Capote (book, lyrics), Harold *Arlen (music). [Alvin Theatre,165 perf.] During a West Indies trade war between two brothel keepers, Madame Tango (Juanita *Hall) and Madame Fleur (Pearl *Bailey), the latter sells one of her girls, Ottilie (Diahann Carroll), to a rich man. But Ottilie prefers young, handsome Royal (Rawn Spearman) and, despite Madame Fleur's machinations, she gets her way. *Notable songs*: House of Flowers; A Sleeping Bee; Two Ladies in de Shade of de Banana Tree; I Never Has Seen Snow. The show had a superb Arlen score and an exceptionally beautiful production featuring Oliver Messel's pastel settings and costumes, but it could not overcome indifferent notices and unusually strong competition. Although it became one of those failures that developed a cult following, an Off-Broadway revival in 1968 quickly failed. **Truman CAPOTE** [né Truman Streckfus Persons] (1924–84), a New Orleans native better known as a novelist, also wrote the play *The Grass Harp* (1952). Several of his other works were adapted for the stage by other writers, albeit unsuccessfully.

HOUSE OF GLASS, THE (1915), a play by Max *Marcin. [Chandler Theatre, 245 perf.] Margaret Case (Mary Ryan) is sent to prison for a crime she did not commit. After she is paroled she hides her prison record from the man she eventually marries, Harvey Lake (Frederick Burt). However, Lake believes one of his employees is stealing, and when he calls in a detective to get the evidence, he learns the truth about his wife. A kindly state governor helps reconcile the couple. Because of similarities in the early part of its story, many critics compared the play with *Within the Law and found the new work somewhat inferior but still agreed it was gripping theatre. Co-producer George M. *Cohan is said to have helped Marcin whip the play into shape. A sign of the healthy theatrical economics of the time was the fact that while this was Marcin's first play, the very next show to open on Broadway (the next night) was another Marcin play.

HOUSEMAN, John [né Jacques Haussmann] (1902–88), director, actor, and producer. Romanian-born and English-educated, he first came to playgoers' attention when he directed *Four Saints in Three Acts* (1934). Houseman consolidated his reputation that same year by directing a revival of

The Lady from the Sea and *Valley Forge* and then producing Archibald *MacLeish's *Panic* (1935). The following year he staged Leslie *Howard's *Hamlet*. He was a producer for the *Federal Theatre Project, then in 1937 he founded the *Mercury Theatre with Orson *Welles. Designed largely to offer "plays of the past—preferably those which seem to have emotion or factual bearing on contemporary life," the company in its all too short existence mounted several notable productions, the most remarkable being its modern-dress version of *Julius Caesar*. After the troupe disbanded, Houseman directed *The *Devil and Daniel Webster* (1939) and Philip *Barry's *Liberty Jones* (1941) and co-produced *Native Son* (1941). He did not work again in the theatre until after World War II, directing *Lute Song* (1946), Louis *Calhern's *King Lear* (1950), and the *Phoenix Theatre's *Coriolanus* (1954). From 1956 to 1959 he was artistic director for the *American Shakespeare Festival, then held a similar position until 1964 with the Theatre Group of the University of California. He next headed the drama division of Juilliard and after 1972 staged several productions of the *Acting Company, which he headed. In his last years Houseman became well known as a film and TV actor. Autobiographies: *Run-Through*, 1972; *Front and Center*, 1979; *Final Dress*, 1983.

HOW I LEARNED TO DRIVE (1997), a play by Paula Vogel. [Century Theatre, 400 perf.; Pulitzer Prize, NYDCC Award.] Li'l Bit (Mary-Louise Parker) narrates the memory play, using sarcasm and jokes while revealing the long-term sexual abuse she endured from her Uncle Peck (David Morse). While he teaches her to drive, Li'l Bit sees her uncle as a man of the world; he views her as a retreat from his alcoholism and despair. By the end of the narrative it is learned that Uncle Peck's sexual fumbling with his niece began when she was only eleven years old. Encouraging notices, controversial subject matter, and strong word of mouth enabled the Vineyard Theatre to move the play from Off Off Broadway to Off Broadway, where it ran a year. **Paula VOGEL** (b. 1951) was born in Washington, D C., and educated at Catholic University and Cornell. She was noticed in New York with her first produced play, *The Baltimore Waltz* (1992), an allegory about the AIDS epidemic. Her other works include *And Baby Makes Seven* (1993), *Desdemona—A Play about a Handkerchief* (1993), *The Mineola Twins* (1999), and *The Long Christmas Ride Home*, 2003.

HOW TO SUCCEED IN BUSINESS WITHOUT REALLY TRYING (1961), a musical comedy by Abe *Burrows, Jack Weinstock, Willie Gilbert (book), Frank *Loesser (music, lyrics). [46th Street Theatre, 1,417 perf.; Pulitzer Prize, Tony, NYDCC Awards.] Although J. Pierpont Finch (Robert *Morse) is only a window washer, he is determined that nothing will stop his rise to the top of the business world. Reading from his "How To" book, he proceeds to step over every obstacle (and fellow employees) at World Wide Wickets, including the boss's ambitious nephew, Bud Frump (Charles Nelson *Reilly), until all that stands in the way is the boss himself, J. B. Biggley (Rudy Vallee). Even when one of Finch's promotional gimmicks backfires, he manages to come out on top, even marrying the secretary Rosemary (Bonnie Scott), who loves him. *Notable songs*: I Believe in You; Coffee Break; Grand Old Ivy; Brotherhood of Man; The Company Way. Based on Shepherd Mead's satiric guide of the same name, the *Feuer and *Martin musical was praised by Walter *Kerr in the *Herald Tribune* as "a sassy, gay and exhilarating evening." It was Loesser's last show; and it made Morse a Broadway star. The highly satirical, unsentimental musical was marked by its cleverly iconoclastic placement of songs; even the show's hit love song, "I Believe in You," was sung by the egomaniacal hero as he admired himself in a men's room mirror. A Broadway revival starring Matthew *Broderick in 1995 was very popular.

HOWARD ATHENAEUM (Boston). Built in 1843 as a church by the Millerite sect, its congregation abandoned the site following disappointment with the minister's promise that the end of the world would occur in 1844. It was converted to a theatre in 1846, and for several decades thereafter it vied with the *Boston Museum as that city's leading playhouse. While the Museum relied largely on its great stock company, the Howard became the home of leading touring actors. Edwin *Booth, Charlotte *Cushman, and other stellar performers played there regularly. In the early 1870s, faced with increasing competition, the theatre became a vaudeville house and in 1920 turned to bump-and-grind burlesque. The city refused to renew its license in 1953, so the auditorium was dark for many years. In 1960 the Howard National Theatre and Museum Committee was formed to raise $1,500,000 to refurbish "Boston's most celebrated theatre" and restore it to the legitimate fold. However, before the committee could realize its ambition the building burned to the ground in 1961.

HOWARD, Bronson [Crocker] (1842–1908), playwright. Often called "the dean of the American drama," he is generally considered the first American dramatist to earn a living entirely by playwriting. He came from old American stock, and his father, a successful merchant, served as mayor of Detroit, where Howard was born. Forced to leave Yale because of eye problems, Howard served as drama critic with the *Detroit Free Press* as he wrote *Fantine* (1864), a play based on incidents in Hugo's *Les Misérables*. He then moved to New York, accepting positions with the *Tribune* and then the *Post*. In 1870 Augustin *Daly produced his *Saratoga*, a huge success that later played profitably in England and Germany. Howard, however, was uncertain whether its popularity was a fluke, so he continued for several more years in the newspaper field. At the same time he wrote the comedy of manners *Diamonds* (1872), the drama *Moorcroft* (1874), and the romance *The *Banker's Daughter* (1878), which remained popular for many years and convinced Howard to abandon newspaper work. Several lesser plays followed before he wrote the social plays *Young Mrs. Winthrop* (1882) and *One of Our Girls* (1885). His last popular works were the comedy-drama *The *Henrietta* (1887) and the Civil War play *Shenandoah* (1889). Arthur *Quinn has written, "It is just because Howard so well illustrated . . . the development of American play-writing during the period of his creative achievement from 1870 to 1906, that his work becomes of such significance." Howard fought to have American themes made more welcome on stage and to secure the position of the American playwright. To the latter end, in 1891 he organized the American Dramatists Club, which evolved into the *Society of American Dramatists and Composers. Although he left no personal autobiography and no full-fledged biography of him has been written, his *The Autobiography of a Play* (1914) gives a detailed, fascinating history of *The Banker's Daughter* and provides numerous insights into his character.

HOWARD, Cordelia (1848–1941), actress. A niece of G. L. *Fox, the tiny, dark-haired charmer was only four and a half years old when she first played Little Eva in *Uncle Tom's Cabin*, a role she performed or regularly returned to for several years. One writer noted, "The name of Little Cordelia has become synonymous with that of Little Eva." She withdrew from the stage while still in her teens.

HOWARD, Eugene. See Howard, Willie.

HOWARD, Joe. See Adams, Hough, and Howard.

HOWARD, Ken (b. 1944), actor and singer. The tall, blond, athletic leading man of musicals and plays was born in El Centro, California, and educated at Amherst College and Yale before working in stock. Howard was on Broadway in 1968 in minor roles in *Promises, Promises*, then gained

notice the next year as a reticent, homesick Thomas Jefferson in *1776*. His other notable New York performances include the gym teacher Paul Reese in a haunted boys' school in *Child's Play* (1970); the lawyer Jerry Ryan in love with a kooky New York dancer in *Seesaw* (1973); the befuddled, dense Tom in *The Norman Conquests* (1975); several presidents in the ill-fated *1600 Pennsylvania Avenue* (1976); and yet another president, Warren G. Harding, in *Camping with Henry and Tom* (1995).

HOWARD [Stainer], **Leslie** (1893–1943), actor. The suave, slender, handsome English-born leading man first appeared before New York audiences as Sir Calverton Shipley in *Just Suppose* (1920). Thereafter, he played in New York more than in England. Best recalled among his many roles were the suicide victim Henry in the fantasy *Outward Bound* (1924), the loyal Napier Harpenden in *The Green Hat* (1925), the hired lover André Sallicel in *Her Cardboard Lover* (1927), the prisoner Matt Denant in *Escape* (1927), the time-traveling Peter Standish in *Berkeley Square* (1929), the prince's valet Joseph who impersonates his master in *Candle Light* (1929), publisher Tom Collier in *The *Animal Kingdom* (1932), and the disillusioned idealist Alan Squier in *The *Petrified Forest* (1935). His last Broadway appearance was in 1936 as Hamlet. Howard also enjoyed a successful career in films before his death in a plane downed during World War II. John Mason *Brown recalled him as "a player supreme as a water-colorist but without strength for oils. Of a negative he made a positive; of diffidence, an act of caring. No one could write of him . . . without falling back on the word 'charm,' which he had in such easy abundance that he could turn nighttime theatregoers into matinee audiences." Biography: *A Quite Remarkable Father*, Leslie Ruth Howard, 1959.

HOWARD, Sidney [Coe] (1891–1939), playwright. Born to pioneer stock in Oakland, California, he studied at the University of California and with Professor George Pierce *Baker in his *47 Workshop at Harvard. Howard then worked on magazines and newspapers before his first play, the romantic verse drama *Swords* (1921), reached New York. His first success was *They Knew What They Wanted* (1924), followed by *Lucky Sam McCarver* (1925), *Ned McCobb's Daughter* (1926), and *The *Silver Cord* (1926). Howard endured a series of failures before finding success again with *The Late Christopher Bean* (1932), *Alien Corn* (1933), and his 1934 dramatization of Sinclair Lewis's *Dodsworth*. In 1938 he joined in founding the *Playwrights' Company. For the rest of his career Howard's new plays met with divided notices and poor box office response. Ironically, after he died in an accident on his farm, two of his works found better receptions: the adaptation of an old Chinese classic, *Lute Song* (1946), written with Will Irwin; and the fantasy *Madam, Will You Walk* (1953), a play that had closed on the road in 1939 but was superbly revived by the *Phoenix Theatre. Theatre historian Glenn Hughes observed, "Howard's work was always vigorous and biting, but frequently repellent. At times, too, it lacked form and compactness. He was a headstrong writer, and his enthusiasms were apt to carry him beyond the bounds of dramatic propriety." But his best work also showed a compassionate, tolerant understanding of human foibles and a zest for life.

HOWARD, Willie [né Wilhelm Levkowitz] (1886?–1949), comedian. Born in Germany, he grew up on New York's Lower East Side and made his debut in vaudeville in 1897 as a boy soprano. He later appeared with Anna *Held in *The Little Duchess* (1901). In 1903 the tiny, tousle-haired, impish-faced Willie joined his taller, heavy-set, dapper brother **Eugene HOWARD** [né Isidore] (1880–1965), who had made his debut in the chorus of *The Belle of New York* (1897) in a vaudeville act called "The Messenger Boy and the Thespian." At about the same time, Willie began his well-liked imitations of other popular performers. The brothers remained in vaudeville for ten years. Two of their most famous turns were "French Taught in a Hurry," in which Willie played a language teacher whose French was more Yiddish and broken English than Gallic, and a spoof of the quartet from *Rigoletto*, in which Willie was a singer who could not keep his eyes off the prima donna's huge bust. In 1912 they joined the first *Passing Show, remaining with later editions and in other *Shubert revues until 1922. They then returned to vaudeville until appearing in *George White's Scandals of 1926 and several later editions. They also appeared in *Ballyhoo of 1932*, the *Ziegfeld Follies of 1934*, and *The Show Is On* (1937). Willie played without Eugene in *Sky High* (1925) and *Girl Crazy* (1930) and, after Eugene's retirement in 1940, in *Crazy with the Heat* (1941), *My Dear Public* (1943), and a 1948 revival of *Sally.

HOWE, Tina. See *Pride's Crossing*.

HOWELL, Alfred (1809–62), costume designer. An Englishman who came to America as an actor and spent most of his career in Boston, he gained widespread fame as a costumer at a time when most actors had to provide their own clothes and when the idea of a costume designer was virtually unheard of.

HOWELLS, William Dean (1837–1920), playwright. Although this distinguished man of letters was best known as a novelist, editor, essayist, and critic, he also figured prominently in the development of the American theatre. His first play was *Samson* (1874), a translation of D'Aste's *Sansone* written for the actor Charles Pope; it held the stage intermittently for twenty-five years. Lawrence *Barrett was responsible for the presentation of Howells's two best-known dramas: the romance *A Counterfeit Presentment* (1877) and the blank-verse tragedy *Yorick's Love* (1878). One of his more interesting efforts was his collaboration with Mark Twain on *Colonel Sellers as a Scientist* (1887). In all, Howells wrote about three dozen plays, many of them one-acters and most centered on Back Bay Boston characters. Their dialogue is infinitely superior to most stage dialogue of the time, and their scenes would appear to make for good theatre. Yet many of them were never produced, and those that were often had small success. They were collected by Walter J. Meserve in 1960 and published by New York University Press. Biography: *William Dean Howells: A Critical Study*, Delmar G. Cooke, 1922.

HOYT, Charles H[ale] (1860–1900), playwright. The only child of a railway mail clerk who also served one term as a state legislator, Hoyt was born in Concord, New Hampshire. He briefly attended Boston Latin School, tried studying law, and served on a Western cattle ranch before accepting work with the *Boston Post*. Within a few months he was awarded a humorous column called "All Sorts," and in its paragraphs can be found the prototypes of many of his later characters. He made friends with the theatre magnate William *Harris Sr., and when Harris suddenly found himself with an empty week at the *Howard Athenaeum in 1881, Hoyt quickly threw together a farce, *Gifford's Luck*. The play was a hit but a second effort, *Cazalia* (1882), failed; both plays have been lost. Hoyt's revisions of Willie *Edouin's farce-comedy *Dreams* turned the piece into a success, so the following year Edouin persuaded Hoyt to write a new play, *A Bunch of Keys* (1883), and the comedy was an immediate success, regularly performed as late as 1900. His subsequent plays included *A Rag Baby* (1884), *A *Parlor Match* (1884), *A Hole in the Ground* (1887), *A Brass Monkey* (1888), *A Midnight Bell* (1889), *A Texas Steer* (1890), and his most important work, *A *Trip to Chinatown* (1891). Among Hoyt's later works were *A Temperance Town* (1893), *A Milk White Flag* (1894), *A Runaway Colt* (1895), *A Black Sheep* (1896), *A Contented Woman* (1897), *A Stranger in New York* (1897), and *A Day and a Night in New York* (1898). By this time Hoyt was displaying symptoms of mental instability. When his next play,

A Dog in a Manger (1899), opened in Washington to a severe drubbing and immediately closed, the failure apparently proved too much. His mind snapped and he was committed to an insane asylum. He was soon released but died a few months later. With Hoyt, *farce-comedy reached its peak. Indeed, even more than the works of Edward *Harrigan, with whom he was often compared and whom his contemporaries suggested he had succeeded, most of his plays can be seen as primitive musical comedies. Their loosely structured plots allowed the insertion of numerous songs. However, where Harrigan was interested mainly in what today would be viewed as New York ethnic types, Hoyt built his plays around more established, acclimated American figures. Both men wrote essentially sunny, wholesome works of questionable literary merit, especially in Hoyt's case, but eminently theatrical. Biography: *The Life and Work of Charles H. Hoyt*, Douglas L. Hunt, 1945.

HOYT, Henry E. (1834–1906), scenic designer. The early history of this New Hampshire-born artist is uncertain. However, in the 1880s and 1890s he was probably the most respected set designer in the profession. In keeping with the practice of the day, he frequently created only one or two of the settings for a particular production, but his reputation was such that he sometimes was asked to devise all the scenes of important mountings. Hoyt's work regularly graced the *Casino Theatre musicals when that playhouse was new and in its prime, and he also executed major assignments for Augustin *Daly. His 1888 designs for *Daly's *A *Midsummer Night's Dream* were described as "severely Greek in pillars and vistas for the palace of Theseus, and soft and dreamy for the wood of perplexity." Hoyt also conceived Daly's decor for *As You Like It* (1889), *The Foresters* (1891), and *Twelfth Night* (1893). Among his other designs were those for Fanny *Davenport's 1890 production of *Cleopatra*, Lillian *Russell's 1891 vehicle *Apollo*, and the first American mounting (in a legitimate theatre, not an opera house) of *Cavalleria Rusticana* in 1891.

HUBBELL, Raymond (1879–1954), composer. A prolific songwriter who left behind only one enduring song, Hubbell was born in Urbana, Ohio, and grew up in Chicago. There he studied music and led a dance orchestra before taking a position as staff composer with Charles K. Harris's company. His songs were soon being sung in vaudeville and interpolated into Chicago musicals. Hubbell's first full score was offered to Chicago as *Chow Chow* and later brought to New York as *The Runaways* (1903). One of his biggest successes was *Fantana* (1905). Thereafter, he composed the music for many of Lew *Fields's musical productions; for the 1911, 1912, 1913, 1914, and 1917 editions of the *Ziegfeld Follies*; and for six of the extravaganzas at the *Hippodrome. It was for a 1916 production, *The Big Show*, in the last venue that he composed his best-remembered song, "Poor Butterfly." By 1922 the appearance of numerous superior talents and changes in style had lessened the demand for his services. In all Hubbell composed the scores for over thirty musicals, most of them highly successful in their day.

HUDSON THEATRE (New York). One of Manhattan's many theatres stuck in limbo, this classically styled Beaux-Arts playhouse on West 44th Street is infrequently used as a theatre venue, but its exterior has been designated a landmark so it is protected until better days come along. J. B. *McElfatrick designed the 1,000-seat theatre with such lovely details as marble columns and a glass ceiling with intricate metalwork. The Hudson was built by producer Henry B. *Harris in 1903, but he died on the *Titanic* nine years later, and the playhouse suffered from years of shaky management. It was a CBS radio studio for a time in the 1930s and an NBC television studio in the 1950s, other times serving as a movie house, burlesque theatre, porn palace, and disco. A partial restoration was done on the interior in the 1980s, but the Hudson has yet to return to being a full-fledged Broadway house.

HUFFMAN, J[esse] C. (1869–1935), director. The son of a Civil War general, he was born in Bowling Green, Ohio, and began to act professionally at sixteen. Huffman abandoned performing to become director of a Pittsburgh stock company before Richard *Mansfield brought him to New York. In 1911 he became general dramatic director for the *Shuberts and staged many hit plays, such as *Whispering Wires* (1922), but was best known for his work in musicals, such as the various editions of *Passing Show, Sinbad* (1918), *Blossom Time* (1921), *The *Student Prince* (1924), *Countess Maritza* (1926), and *My Maryland* (1927). Huffman is credited with staging more than two hundred Broadway shows.

HUGHES, Barnard (b. 1915), character actor. The durable and beloved performer, on the New York stage for over sixty years, often was cast in colorful supporting roles, but by the 1970s he was considered a Broadway star. He was born in Bedford Hills, New York, and educated at Manhattan College, making his professional debut Off Broadway in 1934. Hughes was usually cast in roles older than himself, so he was playing fathers, doctors, military officers, and other mature characters from the start. Among his dozens of delightful performances were the Keystone Kop–like Dogberry in

Much Ado about Nothing (1972), various Russian characters in *The Good Doctor* (1973), a twinkling Falstaff in *The *Merry Wives of Windsor* (1974), the crusty father who will not depart even after death in *Da* (1978), the Irish rural schoolteacher Hugh in *Translations* (1981), the desolate bartender Harry Hope in *The *Iceman Cometh* (1985), the mysterious Old Man in *Prelude to a Kiss* (1990), and the octogenarian suitor Osgood Meeker in *Waiting in the Wings* (1999).

HUGHES, Hatcher. See *Hell-Bent for Heaven*.

HUGHES, Langston. See *Mulatto*.

HULL, Henry (1890–1977), actor. Like his brother Shelley *Hull, this handsome leading man was born in Louisville, Kentucky. He made his name largely in weakling roles such as the degenerate Henry Potter in *The *Man Who Came Back* (1916), the seemingly diffident suitor Paul Jones in *The *Cat and the Canary* (1922), the barber George Randall in *Lulu Belle* (1926), and the black sheep Baron von Gaigern in *Grand Hotel* (1930). Hull also won success as the shy hero Richard Winslow in *The Youngest* (1924). In later years he served as the replacement to the original lead in *Springtime for Henry*, then created the part of the shiftless sharecropper Jeeter Lester in *Tobacco Road* (1933). Thereafter, he rarely enjoyed success and eventually accepted supporting roles.

HULL, Josephine [née Mary Josephine Sherwood] (1886–1957), actress. Born in Newtonville, Massachusetts, and educated at Radcliffe, she studied for the stage with the popular 19th-century actress Kate Reingolds. Her earliest experience was with stock troupes, Boston's Castle Square Theatre Company among them, and in a few Broadway failures. She retired when she married Shelley *Hull in 1910 and did not return to the stage until after his death. In the 1920s she began to attract notice in plays such as *Neighbors* (1923), *Fata Morgana* (1924), *Craig's Wife* (1925), and *Daisy Mayme* (1926) but did not win widespread acclaim until she portrayed the daffy unproduced playwright Penny Sycamore in *You Can't Take It with You* (1936). Hull consolidated her reputation as a comic character actress when she created the role of the sweet murderess Abby Brewster in *Arsenic and Old Lace* (1941), followed by two other major successes: the flustered Veta Louise Simmons in *Harvey* (1944) and the naive stockholder Mrs. Laura Partridge in *The *Solid Gold Cadillac* (1953). A tiny, heavy-set woman with huge brown eyes (and, early on, brown hair), Hull excelled at dithering but lovable old ladies. Biography: *Dear Josephine*, William G. B. Carson, 1963.

HULL, Shelley (1883–1919), actor. Born in Louisville, Kentucky, where his father was drama critic of the *Courier-Journal*, he first came to New York's attention playing the small part of Captain de Crespigny in *The Crossing* (1906). For several seasons he moved from play to play, unable to find a suitable success, until he was cast as leading man to Billie *Burke in *The Mind-the-Paint Girl* (1912). Hull continued to play opposite her in *The Amazons* (1913), *The Land of Promise* (1913), and *Jerry* (1914). She remembered him as "a graceful actor, lithe and handsome, one of the first to play with the light and natural touch." He scored a major hit as the impoverished poet Anthony Quintard in *The Cinderella Man* (1916), followed by the young scientist Ernest in *Why Marry?* (1917), Petruchio to Laurette *Taylor's Kate in 1918, and the dual roles of cousins Arthur Ford and Captain Hartzmann in *Under Orders* (1918). Many critics considered this last Hull's finest moment, but his early death cut short his promising career.

HUMMEL, Abraham Henry (1850–1926), attorney. The son of a Jewish peddler, he was born in Boston and raised in New York, where at age thirteen he became office boy to the famed lawyer William F. Howe. He so impressed Howe that the attorney had the young man admitted to the bar six years later. As Howe and Hummel, they became "the cleverest, most picturesque, most sought-after, most highly remunerated criminal lawyers in the country." Hummel was a small man with a large, bald head who always dressed in black. He was also a bon vivant, counting many celebrated performers and other theatrical figures among his friends. These friendships led to his handling major, often highly publicized cases for Maurice *Barrymore, Edwin *Booth, Abe *Erlanger, Henry *Irving, Lillie *Langtry, and Lester *Wallack and becoming the most renowned theatrical attorney of his era. Unfortunately, his ethics were not the highest, and he was disbarred in 1905.

HUMPHREYS, David. See *Yankey in England, The*.

HUMPHREYS, Joseph [né Murphy] (1861–1904), actor and director. Born in Boston, he served as a clerk in a dry-goods store and then worked for several circuses before becoming a character actor and director for the *Kiralfy brothers. In 1889 Charles *Frohman placed him in charge of casting all Frohman productions, except for their stars, and also made him his house director. Humphreys staged many of Frohman's early successes, such as *The Masqueraders* (1894), *Under the Red Robe* (1896), *The Little Minister* (1897), *The Liars* (1898), and *Quality Street* (1901). His briskness and firmness antagonized many performers, but Frohman admired his work and kept him at his post until Frohman's death.

HUMPTY DUMPTY (1868), a musical pantomime. [Olympic Theatre, 483 perf.] The musical recounted the adventures of Humpty Dumpty (George L. *Fox), Goody Two Shoes (Emily *Rigl), Dan Tucker (G. K. Fox), and One Two Button My Shoe (F. Lacy) as they visit not only the sights of New York, such as City Hall, a famous candy store, and the Olympic Theatre itself, but such marvelous places as the Farm of Plenty, an Enchanted Garden, and the Retreat of the Silver Sprites. Their cavortings at an end, they are transformed, in classic pantomime fashion, into Clown, Columbine, Pantaloon, and Harlequin. The longest-running musical up to its day, it marked the apogee both of G. L. Fox's career and of traditional pantomime in America. Its authorship was by various hands, including A. Oakey Hall, once mayor of New York, and G. L. Fox himself. Music was attributed to one A. Reiff Jr. In the pattern of the time, the musical was regularly revised to prompt return visits.

HUNCHBACK, THE (1832). Sheridan *Knowles's romantic drama was written for Fanny *Kemble and first acted by her in 1832 in London. The story centers on a country girl, Julia, who comes to London, where her eyes are seemingly blinded by the allures of high society. She would throw over her faithful, good-natured lover and marry a much richer man, but luckily she sees the error of her ways, repents, and is happily reunited with the right man. The first New York performance, also in 1832, offered Mrs. Sharpe as Julia. The drama remained extremely popular for the rest of the century. In 1870 the *Times* referred to it as "the play that has stirred the hearts of lovers more than, with one exception, any other in the modern repertory" and called Julia "the most difficult serious part written for a heroine in the last fifty years." Among the great interpreters of the role on American stages were Kemble, Charlotte *Cushman, Clara *Morris, Mary *Anderson, Julia *Marlowe, and Viola *Allen. Opinions on the play changed with the coming of the new century, and in 1902 the same *Times* dismissed the work by branding it "as absurd and false a play as ever took the manner of Shakespeare in vain."

HUNEKER, James Gibbons (1859?–1921), critic. Born in Philadelphia of Irish-Hungarian parentage, he became a music critic before he was hired as a theatre reviewer for the *New York Sun* in 1902. Huneker immediately took up the cudgels for *Ibsen and *Shaw, two playwrights who were confusing and infuriating the more traditional critics. He wrote of Ibsen, "In his bones he is a moralist, in practice an artist." Although he later was to have reservations about Shaw, he wrote the introduction to a 1906 edition of Shaw's collected criticisms and called him "jester to the cosmos and the most serious man on the planet." He also warred against the prudery that infused so much contemporary dramatic criticism. In 1912 he left the *Sun* to write for the *New York Times* but eventually returned to the former. Brooks *Atkinson called him "the best critic Broadway ever had." Among his books, which ranged broadly and knowingly among all the arts, was *Iconoclasts: A Book of Dramatists*.

HUNTER, Glenn (1893?–1945), actor. Born in Highland Mills, New York, the boyish-looking actor made his first professional appearances with the *Washington Square Players in 1916. After replacing the original performers as Willie Baxter in *Seventeen* (1918) and as Robert Williams in *Penrod* (1918), he scored as the infatuated Bobby Wheeler in *Clarence* (1919). Hunter's biggest success came as Merton Gill, the grocery clerk who almost accidentally becomes a film star, in *Merton of the Movies* (1922), but he won equal praise when he portrayed the title role of the sensitive schoolboy in *Young Woodley* (1925). Although he continued to perform regularly thereafter, none of his subsequent work was in successful plays. Best received of his later roles was his robustly boorish Tony Lumpkin in an all-star 1929 revival of *She Stoops to Conquer*.

HUNTER, Kim [neé Janet Cole] (1922–2002), actress. The pretty yet strong-featured leading lady was born in Detroit and trained for an acting career at the *Actors Studio. Hunter made an auspicious Broadway bow as Stella in the original *A *Streetcar Named Desire* (1947). Although she was blacklisted in the 1950s, the film actress found work in the classics in regional theatres, on Broadway, and years later in many television programs. Her last Broadway appearance was in the 1996 revival of *An Ideal Husband,* and she continued to act on the stage into 2001.

HUNTER, Richard (dates unknown). Sometime between May 1699 and May 1702 a Richard Hunter petitioned the acting governor of New York, John Nanfan, that "having been at great charge and expense in providing persons and necessary's in order to the acting of Play's in this City," he be allowed to stage performances. Whether Hunter was an actor or merely a producer and whether he actually staged any performances is unknown. If he did, he antedated Anthony *Aston.

HUNTER, Robert. See *Androboros*.

HUROK, Sol (1888–1974), producer. The Russian-born impresario, best known for his work in the fields of music and ballet, frequently brought over major foreign theatrical companies to America, including the Habimah Players in 1926, the Moscow Art Players in 1935, and, after World War II, Compagnie Madeleine Renaud-Jean Louis Barrault, Théâtre Nationale Populaire, *Comédie Française, the *D'Oyly Carte Opera Company, the Bristol Old Vic, and many others. Hurok also occasionally arranged tours for such American artists as Margaret *Webster and Eva *Le Gallienne. Autobiography: *Impresario*, with Ruth Goode, 1946.

HUSTON, Walter [né Houghston] (1884–1950), actor. The gruff-voiced, Canadian-born actor made his debut in Toronto in 1902, then first appeared in New York in *In Convict Stripes* (1905). From 1909 to 1924 he toured in vaudeville in an act that never quite reached the top, but when Huston returned to Broadway he made a pronounced impression as the unyielding old farmer Ephraim Cabot in *Desire under the Elms* (1924). Subsequent roles included Ponce de Leon in *The Fountain* (1925), the sadistic black ruler Flint in *Kongo* (1926), the glib pitchman Nifty Miller in *The Barker* (1927), and the brainless baseball pitcher Elmer Kane in *Elmer the Great* (1928). Huston spent time in films before returning to New York in 1934 to play the title role of the unhappy retired businessman in *Dodsworth*. In 1937 he offered his Othello, then turned to the musical theatre to portray Pieter Stuyvesant in *Knickerbocker Holiday* (1938), introducing "September Song." The remainder of Huston's stage career offered little of note. His final appearance was as Sam Stover, an old farmer in love with a young girl, in *Apple of His Eye* (1946).

HUTTON, Joseph (1787–1828), playwright and actor. Born in Philadelphia, where he served as a schoolmaster for several years, he turned to the stage to become both an actor and a dramatist. Hutton seems to have been a restless person, spending much of his career traveling up and down the coast. His plays ranged widely: a broad comedy, *The School for Prodigals* (1808); a Gothic melodrama, *The Orphan of Prague* (1808); a musical afterpiece, *The Wounded Hussar; or, The Rightful Heir* (1809); and a social satire, *Fashionable Follies*, written about 1810 and revised later. In after years he is said to have abandoned the stage to take up farming and possibly newspaper work in the South, but much of his history is uncertain.

HUTTON, Laurence (1843–1904), critic and editor. Born in New York and educated at Princeton, he served as drama critic for the *New York Evening Mail* in the 1870s, then became literary editor of *Harper's Magazine*. He held the post until 1898, frequently contributing reviews and essays on the theatre. Hutton was one of the first to revive interest in books on American theatrical history and to have his criticisms collected in hardcover editions. Among his books, which have been described as "chatty, impressionistic," were *Curiosities of the American Stage* (1891) and the five-volume *American Actor* series (1881–82). He was an organizer of the Authors' Club and of the International Copyright League.

HWANG, David Henry (b. 1957), playwright. America's preeminent Asian-American playwright was born in Los Angeles, the son of Chinese immigrants, and attended Stanford and Yale before settling in New York, where his early work *FOB* (1980), about a shy "fresh off the boat" Chinese man, was produced at the *Public Theatre. Hwang was applauded for his plays *The Dance and the Railroad* (1981) and *Family Devotions* (1981), which were also seen there, but found wider recognition with the Broadway hit *M. Butterfly* (1988). His other credits include the drama *Golden Child* (1996), about a Chinese businessman trying to embrace Western ways; co-author of the libretto for *Aida* (2000); the new libretto for *Flower Drum Song* (2002); and music theatre pieces with composer Philip Glass such as *1000 Airplanes on the Roof, The Voyage,* and *The Sound of a Voice*. Hwang's plays are usually about the Chinese-American experience, often viewed with humor, pathos, and a sense of awe at ancient rituals.

HYMAN, Earle (b. 1926), actor. The African-American leading man, who has played dozens of classical roles in theatres on two continents, has performed the role of Othello more than anyone on record, with hundreds of performances in four countries over a span of twenty-five years. He was born in Rocky Mount, North Carolina, and grew up in Brooklyn, later studying acting at the *American Theatre Wing and the *Actors Studio. Hyman appeared in some Off-Broadway productions by the American Negro Theatre before gaining attention as Rudolf, who is in love with the streetwalker *Anna Lucasta* (1944). He also was lauded for the title role of the amiable young African *Mister Johnson* (1956), who accidentally murders a man; the confused Vladimir in *Waiting for Godot* (1957); the useless aristocrat Gaev in an all-black revival of *The Cherry Orchard* (1972); the deathlike specter Oscar in *The Lady from Dubuque* (1980); and several other classical roles in addition to his Othello.

HYTNER, Nicholas (b. 1956), director. The British director-manager, who has staged a very eclectic body of work in America, was born in Manchester and educated at Cambridge. Hytner's productions seen in America include *Miss Saigon* (1991), *The Madness of George III* (1993), *Carousel* (1994), *Twelfth Night* (1998), and *Sweet Smell of Success* (2002). In 2003 he was named director of the *Royal National Theatre in London.

I

I AM A CAMERA (1951), a play by John van *Druten. *[Empire Theatre, 262 perf.; NYDCC Award.] Sitting in his room in Fräulein Schneider's flat in Berlin, the young writer Christopher Isherwood (William Prince) records his impressions of the city. Although Berlin is disturbed by ominous Nazi rioting, Isherwood notes, "I am a camera, with its shutter open, quite passive." Some of his carefully nurtured passivity disappears when he is introduced to Sally Bowles (Julie *Harris), an attractive, flamboyant singer at a local night club, and they strike up an immediate friendship. Neither Sally's insistence that Isherwood never ask about her past nor her becoming pregnant by another man seriously affects their relationship. What does come between them is the growing political turmoil. Isherwood elects to leave Berlin, but Sally, as apolitical as she is amoral, chooses to remain. Based on Isherwood's autobiographical *Berlin Stories*, the play was perceived by many critics as a loosely strung together but theatrically effective series of scenes. To most playgoers its main attraction was Harris's incandescent performance. The play served as the basis for the 1966 musical *Cabaret*.

I DO! I DO! See *Fourposter, The*.

I MARRIED AN ANGEL (1938), a musical comedy by Richard *Rodgers (book, music), Lorenz *Hart (book, lyrics). [*Shubert Theatre, 338 perf.] Willie Palaffi (Dennis *King), a banker and ladies' man, breaks off his engagement to Anna (Audrey *Christie) and swears he will marry only an angel. When a real angel (Vera Zorina) promptly flies into his life, he marries her. But her angelic honesty causes no end of problems for him until his sister, Countess Palaffi (Vivienne *Segal), teaches the angel the ways of a cynical world. The Countess also bribes cab drivers to delay Willie's creditors until a way is found to save her brother's bank. *Notable songs*: I Married an Angel; Spring Is Here; At the Roxy Music Hall; A Twinkle in Your Eye. Basing it on a Hungarian play, Rodgers and Hart had originally worked on it with Moss *Hart as a musical film. The film was scrapped, so the work was rewritten for the stage. In the *Journal-American*, John Anderson characterized the Dwight Deere *Wiman production as "a winged wonder-work from the musical heavens of Rodgers and Hart."

I REMEMBER MAMA (1944), a comedy by John *van Druten. [*Music Box Theatre, 714 perf.] The writer Katrin (Joan Tetzel) reads from her memoirs of growing up in turn-of-the-century San Francisco, recalling how her Mama (Mady *Christians) was forever putting away pennies in a home "bank-account" for a rainy day. She also remembers cantankerous Uncle Chris (Oscar Homolka), who promises to leave his money to the family, and her mother defending Aunt Trina (Adrienne Gessner) when other aunts objected to Trina's marriage. Uncle Chris finally dies, and the family discovers that through the years he had given his money away to help crippled children. Moreover, Mama is forced to confess that there is no bank account. She had lied because "It is not good for little ones to be afraid." So, though Mama urges Katrin to write about all the other members of the family, Katrin concludes, "First and foremost, I remember Mama." Based on Kathryn Forbes's *Mama's Bank Account*, the Richard *Rodgers and Oscar *Hammerstein production appeared during the height of World War II and was welcomed by Burns *Mantle as "a pleasantly undisturbing evening in the theatre." The play was turned into a long-running television series but failed when made into a Broadway musical in 1979 starring Liv Ullmann as Mama. Thomas *Meehan wrote the book, Martin Charnin the lyrics, and Rodgers the music; it was his last Broadway show.

IBSEN, Henrik [Johan] (1828–1906), playwright. Probably no foreign dramas caused debate so prolonged and impassioned as did the emergence of Ibsen's Norwegian plays in the American theatre. What was the first American production of Ibsen is uncertain, but Scandinavian performers did offer the world premiere of *Ghosts* to Chicago and other midwestern cities in 1882, and that same year the play later known as *A Doll's House* was offered in English as *The Child Bride*, albeit given a happy ending. The same play, with a similar happy ending, was presented by Helena *Modjeska as *Thora* in 1883. However, it fell to an 1889 production of *A Doll's House*, faithfully translated and given its correct name, to spread Ibsen's fame and precipitate the controversy. To the leading anti-Ibsenite, William *Winter, Ibsenism was seen as "rank, deadly pessimism . . . a disease, injurious alike to the Stage and to the Public—in as far as it affects them at all—and therefore an evil to be deprecated." Aligned against Winter and his allies were such other leading figures as Walter Prichard *Eaton, William Dean *Howells, and James *Huneker. The pro-Ibsen cause was taken up by such distinguished performers as Mrs. *Fiske, Alla *Nazimova, and Richard *Mansfield. Their appearances in Ibsen plays gained the writer such widespread acceptance that by 1908 Eaton could write, "Ibsen is one of the most popular playwrights in America today." Mrs. Fiske had done *A Doll's House* (1894), *Hedda Gabler* (1903), and *Rosmersholm* (1907). Late in her career she would star in *Ghosts* (1927). Nazimova did *Hedda Gabler* (1906), *A Doll's House* (1907), *The Master Builder* (1907), and *Little Eyolf* (1910). In 1906 Mansfield offered *Peer Gynt*. Blanche *Bates and Nance *O'Neill offered their Heddas about the same time and Ethel *Barrymore her Nora. For a while interest in and enthusiasm for Ibsen dwindled, but Eleanora *Duse's performance in *The Lady from the Sea* sparked a revival, as did the *Theatre Guild's production of *Peer Gynt* with Joseph *Schildkraut. Eva *Le Gallienne and Walter *Hampden both became advocates and appeared in several major revivals. Le Gallienne was the more doggedly loyal of the two. Beginning in 1925, when she portrayed Hilda Wangel in *The Master Builder*, she appeared in or staged numerous mountings, including several of *Hedda Gabler* (1928, 1934, 1948), *John Gabriel Borkman* (1926, 1946), and *Rosmersholm* (1935). She also played Mrs. Alving in *Ghosts* (1948). Hampden's most notable offering was *An Enemy of the People* (1928, 1937). A somewhat lesser performer, Blanche *Yurka, headed revivals of *The Wild Duck* (1925, 1928), *Hedda Gabler*, and *The Lady from the Sea* (1929).

In the 1930s and 1940s a reaction set in, prompted by the perception that the problems Ibsen dealt with were no longer those of immediate concern to contemporary American society. Probably the most interesting production of this period was Thornton *Wilder's adaptation of *A Doll's House* (1937), which Jed *Harris presented with Ruth *Gordon and Paul Lukas. Ibsen's appeal waxed again in the 1950s, which saw Arthur *Miller's version of *An Enemy of the People* (1950), Lee *Strasberg's staging of *Peer Gynt* (1951), and the *Phoenix Theatre's productions of *The Master Builder* (1955) and *Peer Gynt* (1960). In the 1960s David Ross offered a much admired cycle of Ibsen plays Off Broadway. More recently there have been fewer major mountings, though some outstanding performances in Ibsen plays were seen. Claire Bloom essayed both Nora and Hedda with success in 1971, Susannah York played the latter in 1981, and Liv Ullmann shone as Nora and Mrs. Alving in 1982. That same year there was a short-lived musical on Broadway called *A Doll's Life* that attempted to show Nora's life after she walked out. Stacy *Keach made a fascinating *Peer Gynt* in the Central Park production in 1969, while Stephen Elliott and Philip *Bosco were praised as the Stockmann brothers in a *Lincoln Center production of *An Enemy of the People* in 1971. Beatrice *Straight was Mrs. Alving in a long-running *Ghosts* in 1973 with a young Victor *Garber commended as Osvald, and Vanessa Redgrave was the star attraction in *The Lady from the Sea* in 1976. E. G. *Marshall was quietly impressive as *John Gabriel Borkman* in 1980, but Janet McTeer's Nora in 1997 was a whirling dervish in a performance one either loved or loathed. The most recent Broadway Hedda was Kate Burton in 2001. The influence of Ibsen's sociological realism was immediately felt in American playwriting. James A. *Herne was the first to openly acknowledge his debt, but his work was overshadowed in later decades by the plays of such writers as Eugene *O'Neill and Arthur Miller, both of whom looked to Ibsen as an exemplar.

ICEBOUND (1923), a play by Owen *Davis. [Sam H. Harris Theatre, 170 perf.; Pulitzer Prize.] At the old homestead near Veazie, Maine, the Jordan clan greedily and impatiently awaits Mother Jordan's death like, as she told Judge Bradford (Willard Robertson), "carrion crows around a sick cow in a pasture, watchin' till the last twitch of life is out of me before they pounce." When she dies, her family is furious to learn that she has left her entire estate to a distant cousin, Jane Crosby (Phyllis Povah), who with the help of a loyal hired hand, Hannah (Edna May Oliver), faithfully tended Mother Jordan during her last days. The sole exception to the family chagrin is the black sheep son, Ben (Robert *Ames). With time Jane reforms Ben, falls in love with him, and agrees to marry him. Hannah sends them on their way, happy that marriage will further assure Ben's reformation. In *Theatre*, Arthur *Hornblow wrote, "The breath of life sweeps through this pack of New England jackals and exposes them roundly, honestly and effectively." The Sam H. *Harris production marked a conscious move away from claptrap melodrama for Davis.

ICEMAN COMETH, THE (1946), a play by Eugene *O'Neill. [Martin Beck Theatre, 136 perf.] At Harry Hope's seedy bar, a group of down-and-out, besotted regulars live on their booze and their dreams. Besides Harry (Dudley *Digges), a former Tammany ward heeler, the regulars include Harvard-trained lawyer Willie Oban (E. G. *Marshall), Boer War general Piet Wetjoen (Frank Tweddell), old newsman James Cameron (Russell Collins), one-time anarchist Larry Slade (Carl Benton Reid), and a young, frightened drifter, Dan Paritt (Paul Crabtree). Into their midst comes hardware salesman Theodore Hickman (James *Barton), more familiarly known as "Hickey." He tells the barflies he is out for a toot, since his wife is "with the iceman," and he would make the drinkers rid themselves of "the damned guilt that makes you lie to yourselves you're something you're not, and the remorse that nags at you and makes you hide behind lousy pipe dreams about tomorrow." One probable effect of Hickey's insistence is to goad Slade into convincing Paritt to commit suicide. But all Hickey's talk goes for naught when he confesses that he has murdered his wife and that the "iceman" is Death. After the police take away Hickey, the men return to their whiskey and their illusions, without which they cannot live. This four-hour-long play, based on O'Neill's 1917 short story, "Tomorrow," and marking his return to the theatre after an absence of twelve years, was welcomed by most critics, albeit with reservations. Howard Barnes of the *Herald Tribune* wrote the *Theatre Guild mounting was "mystical and mystifying . . . the stuff of a great and moving tragedy gleams through scene after scene of the drama, but it has not been properly refined." A superior 1956 revival at the *Circle in the Square won the work renewed respect and made José *Quintero, who staged it, and Jason *Robards Jr., who played Hickey, names to be reckoned with. A highly praised 1985 revival, again with Robards, failed to run, but a 1999 British revival featuring American Kevin *Spacey as Hickey was a sellout during its limited run on Broadway.

I'D RATHER BE RIGHT (1937), a musical comedy by George S. *Kaufman, Moss *Hart (book), Richard *Rodgers (music), Lorenz *Hart (lyrics). [Alvin Theatre, 290 perf.] Peggy Jones (Joy Hodges) and Phil Barker (Austin Marshall) would like to marry but cannot until Phil receives a raise in pay contingent on President Roosevelt's balancing the budget. Falling asleep in Central Park, Phil dreams that he and Peggy meet Roosevelt (George M. *Cohan), who summons his cabinet and even goes to battle with the Supreme Court to help the youngsters. Seemingly stymied, Roosevelt suggests the couple marry anyway, and when

Phil awakes from his dream that is precisely what he and Peggy decide to do. *Notable songs*: Have You Met Miss Jones?; Off the Record; I'd Rather Be Right. Apparently the first important American play to employ a living president as the leading figure, the Sam H. *Harris production was Cohan's only appearance in a musical that he did not write himself and was also his last song-and-dance role. Cohan's ingratiating performance (despite his much publicized hatred of Roosevelt) turned this affectionate satire of the New Deal into a hit.

IDIOT'S DELIGHT (1936), a comedy by Robert E. *Sherwood. [Shubert Theatre, 299 perf.; Pulitzer Prize.] The Hotel Monte Gabrielle had been an Austrian sanatorium until the area was ceded to Italy after World War I. Now, with another war looming, a handful of guests, caught by border closings, sit languidly in the hotel's cocktail lounge, unsure just when the war will begin and how sides will be drawn. As one guest remarks, "The map of Europe supplies us with a wide choice of opponents. I suppose, in due time, our government will announce its selection—and we shall know just whom we are to shoot at." Into their midst comes the mediocre American song-and-dance man Harry Van (Alfred *Lunt) and his bevy of girls, returning from a Balkan tour. Among the guests, Harry spots a supposed Russian countess, Irene (Lynn *Fontanne), who is traveling with a rich munitions manufacturer, and recognizes her as a former trouper with whom he once had a brief fling in Omaha. As the war clouds darken, they gingerly resume their old affair. The other guests leave, but Harry stays behind to convince Irene to flee with him and create a new mind-reading act. They share a bottle of champagne and sing "Onward, Christian Soldiers" as bombs begin to fall. Brooks *Atkinson observed of this strongly pacifist and ardently antifascist comedy presented by the *Theatre Guild, "Mr. Sherwood has spoken passionately about a grave subject and settled down to writing a gusty show." The comedy became the musical *DANCE A LITTLE CLOSER* (1983), which librettist-producer Alan Jay *Lerner updated to the eve of World War III, with Len *Cariou and Liz Robertson as the central couple. The show closed on opening night, leaving only a superior score by Charles *Strouse (music) and Lerner (lyrics) and marking the sad end of Lerner's long and illustrious career. *Notable songs*: Dance a Little Closer; Another Life; There's Always One You Can't Forget.

IF I WERE KING (1901), a play by Justin Huntly McCarthy. [Garden Theatre, 56 perf.] To the humble Tavern of the Fir Cone, where the vagabond poet François Villon (E. H. *Sothern) recites poetry and sneers at his weak king, come none other than a disguised Louis IX (George W. Wilson) and Lady Katherine de Vaucelles (Cecilia *Loftus). At once impressed and irked, the King discloses himself and gives Villon a week in which to make good his boasts of making a better monarch, after which he will die. During Villon's royal week he defeats the Burgundians. Louis would still hang him until the suicide of the loyal camp follower, Huguette (Suzanne Sheldon), and Katherine's announcement that she will marry the poet, dissuade the King. This most famous play by the renowned Irish politician and writer was offered in America by producer Daniel *Frohman before it was presented in London. The play consolidated Sothern's stardom and was revived regularly until World War I. In 1925 it became the source of the operetta *THE VAGABOND KING* by Brian *Hooker (book, lyrics), W. H. Post, Russell Janney (book), and Rudolf *Friml (music). Janney presented the musicalization at the *Casino Theatre for 511 performances, followed by decades of revivals in summer theatres. Dennis *King was Villon, Carolyn Thomson was Katherine, and Jane Carroll was Huguette. *Notable songs*: Only a Rose; Huguette Waltz; Some Day; Song of the Vagabonds.

ILLINGTON, Margaret [née Maude Ellen Light] (1881–1934), actress. This "lovely, stately, talented" leading lady, as her first husband, Daniel *Frohman, described her, was born in Bloomington, Illinois, and studied at Illinois Wesleyan and then at a Chicago dramatic school. Her first professional appearance was made under Frohman in The *Pride of Jennico* (1900). In 1903 she scored a major success as the Japanese girl Yuki in *A Japanese Nightingale*, followed by Henrietta in an all-star revival of The *Two Orphans*. One of Illington's most memorable assignments was as the wife falsely accused of having an affair with a young man in *Mrs. Leffingwell's Boots* (1905). After playing Shirley Rossmore in a road company of The *Lion and the Mouse* and the unhappy second wife Nina Jesson in *His House in Order* (1906), she gave what many admirers consider her finest performance: the guilty Marie Louise Voysin in *The Thief* (1907). As often happens she found it hard to find an equally effective successor to this play and did not have another major success until she played the poor wife Maggie Shultz in *Kindling* (1911). This was her last significant new role, although she later took leading parts in several road companies before retiring in 1919.

I'M GETTING MY ACT TOGETHER AND TAKING IT ON THE ROAD (1978), a musical play by Gretchen Cryer (book, lyrics), Nancy Ford (music). [*Public Theatre, 1,165 perf.] The thirty-nine-year-old singer Heather (Cryer) auditions her new act for her manager (Joe Fabiani), hoping to convince

him that she should present a more honest portrayal of herself instead of the glossy, fanciful one he insists is more lucrative. Between the numbers she performs with a small band and some backup singers, Heather and Joe argue, commiserate, and compromise on their feeling about women, aging, and role playing. *Notable songs*: Old Friend; Strong Woman Number; Natural High; Dear Tom. The intimate little musical was often described as a feminist piece, but its context was far more outreaching. It was so popular at the Public that after six months producer Joe *Papp moved it to the *Circle in the Square downtown, where it ran for over three years. **Gretchen CRYER** [neé Kiger] (b. 1935) was born in rural Indiana and was educated at De Pauw University, where she met **Nancy FORD** (b. 1935), a composer who was born in Kalamazoo, Michigan. As the New York theatre's first notable female songwriting team, their Off-Broadway musicals, such as *Now Is the Time for All Good Men* (1967) and *The Last Sweet Days of Isaac* (1970), were noticed and commended for their interest in rock music, antiwar sentiments, and exploration of human relationships. Cryer and Ford's *Shelter* (1973) had a short run on Broadway before they found success with *I'm Getting My Act Together*.

I'M NOT RAPPAPORT (1985), a play by Herb *Gardner. [*Booth Theatre, 890 perf.; Tony Award.] Two very old men, Nat (Judd *Hirsch), a Jew who constantly makes up stories about his imaginary pasts, and Midge (Cleavon Little), an African American who has little time for Nat's lies but nowhere else to go, regularly occupy adjacent benches in Central Park. Callous or interfering people or even vicious muggers sometimes interrupt their conversations, which seem destined to go on until one of the men dies. A slight, ingratiating play, it exemplified a vogue for light pieces pitting a somewhat eccentric Jew against a more down-to-earth black, as did the later *Driving Miss Daisy*. A 2002 Broadway revival with Hirsch reprising his Nat was short-lived.

IMPERIAL THEATRE (New York). The 1,400-seat musical house on West 45th Street has had only fifty-seven tenants in its eighty-year history and rarely has it been empty, testifying to the number of hits that have played here. The playhouse was designed by Herbert J. *Krapp with entrances on both 45th and 46th Streets and they have both been needed to handle the crowds for *Rose-Marie* (1924), *Annie Get Your Gun* (1946), *Fiddler on the Roof* (1964), *Pippin* (1972), *Les Misérables* (transferred in 1990), and other smash musicals. The *Shuberts built the Imperial and had success with it even during the Depression. It remains a Shubert house.

IMPOSSIBLE YEARS, THE (1965), a comedy by Bob Fisher and Arthur Marx. [Playhouse, 670 perf.] Dr. Jack Kingsley (Alan King) is a famous psychiatrist who sets about writing an all-knowing book on how to raise teenagers. What he does not reckon with are his own teenaged daughters, the slightly kooky, freewheeling Linda (Jane Eliot) and the precocious, impertinent Abbey (Neva Small). They run in and out of the Kingsley household with an odd assortment of friends and associates. Mrs. Kingsley (Janet Ward) tries to keep order and prevent Jack from losing his mind, but when Linda announces she left her virginity on a beach, Mrs. Kingsley becomes so rattled that she bids "three novirgins" at her weekly bridge game. A slick but well-written comedy, it far outran most of the season's superior offerings. Many critics credited nightclub comedian King for much of the comedy's success. The authors Fisher and Marx, the son of *Groucho Marx, were film and television writers.

IN ABRAHAM'S BOSOM (1926), a play by Paul *Green. [Provincetown Theatre, 277 perf.; Pulitzer Prize.] Near the Turpentine Woods of eastern North Carolina, Abraham McCranie (Jules *Bledsoe) has grown up, the troubled son of white Colonel McCranie (L. Rufus Hill) and a black woman. He is determined to "rise him up wid eddication" and to become the savior "to lead 'em up out'n ignorance." But his all-white half-brother, the Colonel's vicious son Lonnie (H. Ben Smith), is just as determined to thwart him, to close the school he would open for African Americans, and to keep him in his place. Only Goldie McAllister (Rose *McClendon) offers him love. As the years pass Lonnie's tormenting becomes too much and in a rage Abraham kills him. He in turn is shot dead by other local white men. The *Provincetown Players production was hailed by the *Herald Tribune* as "so well-written and so well-played that even near-Southerners who applaud Dixie the loudest may be urged to sympathy." Nevertheless, the play struggled to find an audience and had closed when it won the Pulitzer. It was quickly reopened.

IN DAHOMEY (1903), a musical comedy by J. A. Shipp (book), Will Marion *Cook (music), Paul Laurence *Dunbar (lyrics). [New York Theatre, 53 perf.] When Rareback Pinkerton (George Walker) is sent to Florida by the "Negro" Get-the-Coin Syndicate to bamboozle a rich old man, he discovers that his bumptious companion, Shylock Homestead (Bert *Williams), is an even richer man. So he proceeds to bamboozle Shylock and uses the money to live a sporting life both in Florida and Africa until Shylock suddenly sees through him. While *The Origin of the Cake Walk; or, *Clor-

indy (1898) was the first all-black-written, black-performed show to play before major white audiences, it was a relatively short afterpiece and was performed on a summer roof garden. *In Dahomey* thus became the first African-American musical to play a regular New York legitimate theatre. Despite generally favorable reviews and many raves for Williams, large segments of traditional white playgoers refused to attend the Jules Hurtig and Harry Seamon production. In London, where such prejudices were not so widespread, the musical ran seven months.

IN MIZZOURA (1893), a play by Augustus *Thomas. [*Fifth Avenue Theatre, 64 perf.] Sheriff Jim Radburn (Nat *Goodwin) of Bowling Green, Missouri, is a kindly, middle-aged man who never shoots to kill and will even stop to make a cast for a wounded dog. Having something of a private income, he has paid for the education of young Kate Vernon (Mabel Amber), his neighbors' daughter, whom he has grown to love. But Kate returns from school with newfound airs and has little time for Jim, instead falling for a dashing young man, Robert Travers (Emmett Corrigan). However, Travers turns out to be a train robber, and when he shoots a man, Radburn gives him a pony with which to escape rather than see Kate's feelings hurt. The village would turn against the sheriff, until they recognize the good-heartedness behind his action. Even Kate begins to love Radburn, but he has come to realize they must go their separate ways. When Mrs. Vernon (Jean Clara Walters) suggests that Kate is "comin' to her senses" and that Radburn need only talk to her to win her hand, he replies laconically, "Some other time." Written as a vehicle for producer-actor Goodwin, this comedy of rural manners remained popular for many years. Its compassion, acute observation, and theatrical effectiveness make it one of Thomas's best plays, all too neglected.

IN OLD KENTUCKY (1893), a play by Charles T. Dazey. [Academy of Music, 160 perf.] Madge Brierly (Bettina Gerard) is a girl who longs to escape from the ages-old feuding and fanaticism of her fellow Kentucky mountain folk. When she meets handsome, young, and rich Frank Layson (William Courtleigh), she sees her chance. She is a skilled horsewoman, so when Layson enters his prize runner in the Ashland Oaks Derby, Madge rides it. Overcoming treachery and the opposition of his snobbish friends, who would cut any woman in jockey's clothes, she wins both the race and Layson. One of the most popular of all late-19th-century melodramas, the play remained a favorite for several decades. Arthur *Quinn records that it "was performed for twenty-seven consecutive seasons in New York or on the road." C[harles] T[urner] **DAZEY** (1855–1938), who was born in Lima, Illinois, attended the College of Arts in Lexington, Kentucky, and Harvard. Most of his plays were period melodramas designed for popular-priced touring companies, although nearly a dozen of his works reached New York, from *Elsa* (1882) to *The *Stranger* (1911). But his fame rests solely on *In Old Kentucky*, based on his observations of the Kentucky life he knew while at school there.

IN THE PALACE OF THE KING (1900), a play by Lorimer Stoddard. [Republic Theatre, 138 perf.] To be near her beloved hero, Don John (Robert T. Haines), the spunky Dona Maria Dolores (Viola *Allen) disguises herself as a blind woman at the court of Philip II (Eben *Plympton). She witnesses an attempted murder for which Don John is framed by her treacherous rival and wins his acquittal by defending him before the King. One of the many dramatizations of floridly romantic novels that were popular at the time, this *Liebler and Co. offering was based on F. Marion Crawford's best-seller. Stoddard was an actor and dramatist, probably best remembered for his adaptation of *Tess of the D'Urbervilles* (1897) for Mrs. *Fiske.

IN THE SUMMER HOUSE (1953), a play by Jane Bowles. [Playhouse, 55 perf.] Gertrude Eastman-Cuevas (Judith *Anderson) is a viciously domineering mother who would keep her daughter, Molly (Elizabeth Ross), firmly under her thumb. By contrast, the boozy, weak Mrs. Constable (Mildred *Dunnock) has long since been deserted by her family. When Molly finally finds the strength to leave her harridan mother, Gertrude finds herself helpless, while Mrs. Constable continues to take solace in her drink. Originally presented at the *Hedgerow Theatre, the play was brought to Broadway by Oliver *Smith and the *Playwrights' Company. Although it was written with great insight and style, it remained too demanding and dramatically ineffectual to recruit large audiences. A high point was Gertrude's ten-minute monologue, which opened the play. The play was revived with some interest at *Lincoln Center in 1993. **Jane Auer BOWLES** (1917–73), the wife of composer and author Paul Bowles, was best known for her novels and short stories. This was her first and only important play.

IN THE ZONE. See *S.S. Glencairn*.

INDIAN PRINCESS, THE; or, La Belle Sauvage (1808), an "operatic melo-drama" by James Nelson *Barker, John Bray (music). [*Chestnut Street Theatre (Philadelphia), in repertory.] The English land in Virginia to establish a settlement at Jamestown.

Some of the men sing of their sweethearts back home, but one lovesick traveler attacks the wife of another settler. Captain Smith (Mr. Rutherford) leads an expedition into the hinterlands, where he is captured by the Indians. Lieutenant Rolfe (William *Wood) and his comrades set out to find their leader and, when he comes to the Indian encampment, Pocahontas (Mrs. Wilmot) falls in love with Rolfe, to the fury of the Indian Prince Miami (Mr. Mills). When the Englishmen return to their settlement, Miami plans an attack, but Pocahontas alerts the settlers. Originally conceived simply as a blank-verse drama by Barker, the music helped make the piece a huge success. The love scene in Act III between Pocahontas and Rolfe was especially well done. When the play was offered in New York two months after its Philadelphia premiere, the *Evening Post* called it "in point of dramatic composition, one of the most chaste and elegant plays ever written in the United States." It was the first American play to be done in London, where it was performed at the Drury Lane in 1820 under the title *Pocahontas; or, The Indian Princess*.

INDIAN WANTS THE BRONX, THE (1968), a one-act play by Israel Horovitz. [Astor Place Theatre, 204 perf.] At a quiet Manhattan bus stop at night, two punks (Al *Pacino and Matthew Cowles) tease and then, just for kicks, beat up a Hindu man (John Cazale) unable to speak English. The explosive little drama (presented with Horovitz's one-acter *It's Called the Sugar Plum*) introduced Pacino to the public and marked the beginning of Horovitz's long career. **Israel [Arthur] HOROVITZ** (b. 1939) was born in Wakefield, Massachusetts, and educated at Harvard. He has written over fifty produced plays, most finding more success outside of New York. Among his notable works are *Morning* (1968), about a black family who wake one day to find they are now white; *Line* (1971), concerning various characters jockeying for power as they wait in line; *Park Your Car in Harvard Yard* (1991), in which a grumpy retired music teacher is faced with a former student; and *My Old Lady* (2002), in which an American inherits a Paris apartment inhabited by a stubborn old woman.

INDIANA REPERTORY THEATRE (Indianapolis). Founded in 1972 by Benjamin Mordecai, Edward Stern, and Gregory Poggi, the company occupied the Atheneum Theatre and presented an extensive season of classic and modern plays. In 1980, artistic director Tom Haas helped revitalize the group when they moved into the restored Indiana Theatre, a complex with a 610-seat modified proscenium theatre and a 314-seat thrust stage. After Haas's death in 1991, leadership was taken over by Libby Appel and then Janet Allen.

INDIANS IN AMERICAN DRAMA. See Native Americans in Drama.

INGE, William (1913–73), playwright. A writer who wrote knowingly of lonely, sexually obsessed but otherwise normal Midwesterners, he was born in Independence, Kansas, and educated at the University of Kansas. Inge was employed as a schoolteacher and as an actor before accepting the post of drama critic for the *St. Louis Star-Times* in 1943, but he left the paper when his first play, *Farther Off from Heaven* (1947), was presented by Margo *Jones at her Dallas theatre. It never reached New York, but his second play, *Come Back, Little Sheba* (1950) was an immediate success on Broadway. This was followed by three more successes: *Picnic* (1953), *Bus Stop* (1955), and The *Dark at the Top of the Stairs* (1957), the last a rewriting of his earlier *Farther Off from Heaven*. Thereafter, Inge's plays were failures, the critics sensing a certain limited sameness of outlook and subject as well as a falling away of theatricality in *A Loss of Roses* (1959), *Glory in the Flower* (1959), *Natural Affection* (1963), *Where's Daddy?* (1966), and *The Last Pad* (1970). His death was a suicide. Biography: *A Life of William Inge: The Strains of Triumph*, R. Voss, 1989.

INGOMAR (1851). This romantic drama, adapted by Maria Lovell from a German play by Friedrich Halm, premiered simultaneously at the *Broadway and the *Bowery Theatres The story tells of a sweet, comely maiden, Parthenia, who wins over Ingomar, the leader of the invading Allemanni barbarians—a beauty-and-the-beast legend set in classic times. The play was famous for its celebrated couplet, "Two souls with but a single thought,/Two hearts that beat as one," which closed the second act. Mme. *Ponisi and Frederick B. *Conway were the leads in the Broadway's production, Amelia Parker and Edward *Eddy at the Bowery. The play was revived regularly as late as 1909. Among its famous interpreters were Mary *Anderson and Julia *Marlowe. Also, *Salvini was a controversial Ingomar.

INHERIT THE WIND (1955), a play by Jerome *Lawrence and Robert E. *Lee [National Theatre, 806 perf.] When Bertram Cates (Karl Light) is brought to trial for violating his state's law against teaching Darwinian evolution, the great liberal, flamboyant lawyer Henry Drummond (Paul *Muni) leads his defense. Heading the prosecution is the equally flamboyant orator and politician Matthew Harrison Brady (Ed *Begley). The appearance of these men brings the press en masse, led by the famed curmudgeon from Baltimore, E. K. Hornbeck (Tony *Randall). The trial quickly becomes a circus, in which Drummond devastates Brady. But when it is over, with Cates found guilty and given a token fine, and with Brady dead, Drummond surprises Hornbeck by coming to the defense of Brady and the Bible. "You never pushed a noun against a verb except to blow something up," he says, insisting every man has the right to be wrong and that Brady's fault was that "he was looking for God too high up and far away." Closely following the events of the 1925 Scopes "Monkey" Trial in Tennessee, the authors made little attempt to hide the fact that Drummond was Clarence Darrow; Brady, William Jennings Bryan; and Hornbeck, H. L. Mencken. Writing in the *Daily News*, John *Chapman hailed the Herman *Shumlin–Margo *Jones production as "one of the most exciting dramas of the last decade." A Broadway revival in 1996 with George C. *Scott and Charles *Durning as Drummond and Brady was very popular but closed prematurely because of Scott's health. It was his last Broadway appearance.

INNAURATO, Albert. See *Gemini*.

INTERNATIONAL THEATRE COMPANIES VISITING AMERICA. Before the *Hallams and the first American theatrical troupe, all theatre in the colonies consisted of visiting companies from abroad. But beginning in the late 19th century renowned theatres from Europe came to the States (sometimes as part of international tours) and found both money and fame. Leading the way was the D'Oyly Carte Opera Company and its *Gilbert and Sullivan productions. Its founder, Richard D'Oyly Carte, and some members of the company first appeared in America in 1879 to offer *H.M.S. Pinafore* and the world premiere of The *Pirates of Penzance*. However, American performers were also enlisted in these casts, and American musicians were employed. This remained the practice, for all its original Gilbert and Sullivan mountings in this country. The company as a whole did not appear in America until 1934, after Winthrop *Ames revived what had been a flagging interest in the Savoyard comic operas. Between then and its dissolution, the ensemble made numerous American visits. At first the tours were immensely successful and popular, and offered such great performers as Martyn Green, Derek Oldham, and Darrell Fancourt. However, in its last seasons its members and productions seemed tired and trapped in tradition, and the final tours were not commercial successes. Dublin's Abbey Theatre, founded by Miss E. F. Horniman in 1903, initially played in America in 1911 and offered new works by Lady Gregory, William Butler Yeats, and John Millington Synge. *The Playboy of the Western World* by Synge precipitated riots by hooligans offended at some of the depictions of Irish life. In New York, vegetables (including, of course, potatoes) and asafetida balls were hurled at the stage; in Philadelphia, the company and the rioters were arrested. The turmoil continued when the troupe appeared on a second visit in 1913. Both the plays and the acting received a mixed reception. When the Irish Players of the Abbey Theatre (as it was officially called) returned for several visits in the 1930s, the plays were no longer unfamiliar, and many of them had become accepted as modern classics. By then the ensemble playing was much admired, featuring performers such as Arthur Sinclair, Sara Allgood, and Barry Fitzgerald.

La Comédie Française, the world's oldest ongoing acting ensemble, founded in 1680, waited 275 years before making its initial American visit in 1955. Some critics were dismayed by the relatively safe, conservative repertory it presented, which consisted of Molière's Le Bourgeois gentilhomme, Marivaux's Arlequin poli par l'amour and his Le Jeu de l'amour et du hasard, Beaumarchais's Le Barbier de Seville, and Musset's Un Caprice. Yet, as Louis *Kronenberger noted, the works were "done with not only every last nuance of phrasing and diction, but with a ballet lightness and wit." On later visits in the 1960s and 1970s the troupe ranged more broadly, offering such classics as Corneille's Le Cid, Montherlant's La Reine Morte, and Feydeau's La Puce a l'oreille. These subsequent visits have also offered several more Molière plays, but none by Racine. Among the notable performers who have appeared with the company have been Louis Seigner, Jacques Charon, and Robert Hirsch.

The Moscow Art Theatre, founded in 1898 by K. *Stanislavsky and Nemirovich-Danchenko, first visited America during the 1922–23 season and created an excitement rarely paralleled in American theatre annals. Its repertory consisted of Tolstoy's Tsar Fyodor Ivanovitch, Gorky's The Lower Depths, Chekhov's The Cherry Orchard and The Three Sisters, and Turgenieff's The Lady from the Provinces, coupled with excerpts from Dostoevski's The Brothers Karamazoff. Additional plays, including Uncle Vanya, were offered the next season. The troupe's remarkable ensemble playing, according to one critic, raised "spiritual realism" to new heights of perfection. Its example also gave rise to another in the many recurrent movements to establish a permanent repertory company in America and played no small part in the early impetus behind the founding of the *Civic Repertory Theatre. Perhaps more importantly and enduringly, these tours gave most American playgoers their first exposure to the works of *Chekhov. The company again visited America in 1965, offering The Cherry Orchard, The Three Sisters, a dramatization of Gogol's Dead Souls, and a piece of political propaganda, Kremlin Chimes.

The troupe was still admired for its realism and fine ensemble playing, but political considerations tempered the response.

The Old Vic, England's finest and most historic acting company until it was superseded in 1963 by the National Theatre, paid a highly praised visit to New York in 1946. Its repertory was *Henry IV, Parts I and II; Uncle Vanya; Oedipus; and The Critic. The company included Laurence *Olivier, who offered his memorable Oedipus, Hotspur, and Justice Shallow; Ralph *Richardson, praised for his Falstaff; Joyce Redman; and Margaret *Leighton. Many critics felt that the company at the time was at its artistic height and that the ensemble playing had not been matched by any troupe since the visit of the Moscow Art Theatre more than two decades before. In 1956 and 1958 the company returned to offer two series of Shakespearean revivals (*Richard II, *Romeo and Juliet, *Macbeth, and Troilus and Cressida in 1956; *Twelfth Night, *Hamlet, and Henry V in 1958) and in its final visit in 1962 presented *Shaw's *Saint Joan along with two more Shakespearean offerings. Although the roster of performers on these last visits included several distinguished performers, such as Rosemary *Harris, Barbara Jefford, John Neville, and Jeremy Brett, the consensus was that the acting lacked the glittering finish and intensity seen in 1946.

The Royal Shakespeare Company, an outgrowth of the Shakespearean theatre at Stratford-on-Avon in England, expanded its repertory to include non-Shakespearean classics and modern plays when it opened a branch theatre in London. It has since come to be considered by many critics as the finest contemporary English acting ensemble. Although it has occasionally offered American playgoers examples of its Shakespearean productions since the mid-1960s, its most successful offerings here have been non-Shakespearean works. The most notable have been Marat/Sade (1965); a gymnastic, almost psychedelic A *Midsummer Night's Dream (1971); *Sherlock Holmes (1974); and The *Life and Adventures of Nicholas Nickleby (1981). These large-cast productions were striking for the skillful fluidity and dramatic effectiveness with which numbers of people were moved, and testified to the excellence of such modern British directors as Peter *Brook and Trevor *Nunn. Among the rising performers seen in these mountings were Glenda Jackson, Patrick Magee, Ian Richardson, Ben Kingsley, and John *Wood. Other RSC productions were mounted in the 1980s and 1990s, though not necessarily with their London casts. Great Britain's other famous subsidized theatre company, the National Theatre of Great Britain, opened in London in 1963 as the successor to the *Old Vic. Today called the Royal National, it has rarely brought a full production to America, but many

National hits, such as *Rosencrantz and Guildenstern Are Dead* (1967), *The National Health* (1974), *No Man's Land* (1976), *Bedroom Farce* (1979), **Amadeus* (1980), *Plenty* (1983), and *Wild Honey* (1986), have been produced on Broadway, sometimes with players and the directors from the original English productions. The National's offshoot, the Young Vic, presented a diverse repertory of three plays in 1974 and has appeared again since then. Finally, some of the great Eastern theatre troupes have also visited the States on occasion, most memorably Kabuki and Bunraku companies from Japan and the Peking Opera from China.

INTO THE WOODS (1987), a musical play by James *Lapine (book), *Stephen Sondheim (music, lyrics). [Martin Beck Theatre, 764 perf.; NYDCC Award.] A handful of familiar fairy tales and an original one were combined, all of the characters and events overlapping in the same forest. The first act followed the traditional storylines, but the second half went beyond the happy endings to explore the consequences of the characters' actions. *Notable songs*: Children Will Listen; No One Is Alone; Agony; Giants in the Sky. Critics were divided on how effective the script was but praised the score and applauded the superior cast that included Bernadette *Peters, Joanna *Gleason, Chip Zien, Robert Westenberg, and Tom *Aldredge. Audience reaction was not so mixed, and the musical (produced by Rocco and Heidi *Landesman and others) became one of Sondheim's longest runs and most-produced works across the country. A beautifully staged Broadway revival in 2002 was highly commended but failed to show a profit.

IONESCO, Eugene (1912–94), playwright. The French-Romanian playwright, an exponent of the Theatre of the Absurd, has been a favorite of Off-Broadway companies and collegiate and regional theatres since the early 1950s. Among his better-known works are *The Lesson* (1956), *The Chairs* (1958), and *The Bald Soprano* (1958). His only major commercial successes on Broadway were *Rhinoceros* (1961), although the remarkable performance of Zero *Mostel was as much responsible for its popularity as was the excellence of the play, and a superb London production of *The Chairs* in 1998, which was a sellout during its limited engagement.

IRELAND, Joseph N[orton] (1817–98), author. One of the major early historians of the American theatre, he entered his father's business after graduating from high school in his native New York. Leaving the company in 1855 and retiring to Bridgeport, Connecticut, Ireland devoted the rest of his long life to studying and writing about the

stage. His major work was *Records of the New York Stage from 1750–1860* (2 vols., 1866–67). Although the work may be faulted for some factual errors, most of which George *Odell later corrected in his own *Annals*, Ireland was an excellent historian who filled the book with numerous useful biographical sketches and other background information. He also wrote two biographies: *Mrs. Duff*, 1882 and *A Memoir of the Professional Life of Thomas Abthorpe Cooper*, 1888.

IRENE (1919), a musical comedy by James *Montgomery (book), Harry *Tierney (music), Joe *McCarthy (lyrics). [Vanderbilt Theatre, 670 perf.] Irene O'Dare (Edith *Day), "a little bit of salt and sweetness," is a poor shopgirl who is sent on an errand to the Marshalls' Long Island estate. There Donald Marshall (Walter Regan) falls in love with her and helps her land a job at a couturier's shop run by a man known as Madam Lucy (Bobby Watson). At first both families oppose the match. Mrs. O'Dare (Dorothy Walters) is suspicious of the rich, and Donald's family feels he would be marrying beneath him. But when Irene sings and dances while she models at a party held by the J. P. Bowdens, she wins everyone's heart—and a wedding ring from Donald. *Notable songs*: Alice Blue Gown; Irene; The Last Part of Ev'ry Party; Castle of Dreams. This charming, intimate musical is generally credited with initiating the vogue for Cinderella librettos, a trend which dominated Broadway for several years. From the time of its closing, until *Pins and Needles* surpassed it in 1939, *Irene* remained the longest-running musical in Broadway history. A 1973 revival, which took many liberties with the original text and score, starred Debbie Reynolds and enjoyed a long run.

IRISH IN AMERICAN THEATRE AND DRAMA. Early Irish immigrants, speaking English as they did, found a relatively easy acceptance in colonial society, especially since there were not too many of them and they represented a better educated class than their countrymen who later left their homeland during the potato famine of the 1840s. English plays about Irishmen, while not all that numerous, generally treated their figures without prejudice, and such plays as *The Irish Widow* (1773) and *The True-Born Irishman* (1787) retained a certain popularity for many decades. The first Tyrone *Power, the great Irish comedian who made his American debut in 1833, started the rage for Irish themes on American stages, impersonating Irish gentlemen of "debonair manners and some sense of the impetuosity for which his countrymen were remarkable." When Power was drowned in the sinking of the *President* in 1841, his place was taken by such diverse actors as John *Broughham and John

*Collins. Their appearances coincided with the beginnings of mass Irish immigration to America, with the Irish settling primarily in the great cities that were also the theatrical centers of the time. In the 1850s dozens of plays with Irishmen as central figures and with Ireland itself often the scene held the stage, their titles ranging from *The Irish Ambassador* through *The Irish Fortune Hunter* and *The Irish Know Nothing* to *The Irish Yankee*, as well as *Ireland and America* and *Ireland as It Is*. The character of the sophisticated Irish gentlemen, popularized by Power, gave way to the working-class Irishmen, raucous, bibulous, and sly, if not very bright. The increasing immigration also brought on increasing anti-Catholic and specifically anti-Irish prejudices, making many of the Irish-centered plays unfashionable for certain groups and confining the works to cheaper playhouses. But the cream of the Irish artists and Irish plays still found widespread audiences.

By the post–Civil War period the Irish had infiltrated and influenced the American theatre beyond all proportion to their numbers in society. Three figures represent the broad-ranging development of Irish talent: playwright, director, and producer Augustin *Daly, who represented the pinnacle of theatrical excellence and achievement in his era; the Dublin-born actor, playwright, and director Dion *Boucicault, whose works ranged from sensation-filled melodramas with American settings, such as *The *Octoroon*, to his more rustic but still sensation-crammed plays of Irish life, such as *The *Shaughraun;* and Edward *Harrigan, who lovingly if amusingly depicted the lives and struggles of immigrants (Irish mostly, but others as well) in New York. Harrigan was a product of the early vaudeville stages, and as such he rubbed elbows with a long list of great Irish entertainers both in variety and in minstrelsy: his partner, Tony *Hart; Dan Bryant; Hughey Dougherty; Dan Emmett; and others. In the field of the American musical, the Irish were also preeminent at the time. Victor *Herbert was unquestionably the first truly great composer of American operetta, while George M. *Cohan could be called the father of American musical comedy. His exuberant, patriotic, brash shows have been seen by some as the essence of the working-class Irish contribution to the contemporary stage. The romantic plays with music that featured Chauncey *Olcott appeared during roughly these same years and appealed hugely to working-class Irish audiences. The roster of other notable Irish-Americans of the 19th-century stage ranged from Lawrence *Barrett to Annie *Yeamans and included not only actors but writers, producers, directors, and designers, among them the *Drews, James A. *Herne, John *McCullough, J. B. *McElfatrick, John J. *McNally, James H. *McVicker, and

James *O'Neill. In the years just before World War I the Irish hegemony, at least in the musical theatre and in the business end of the theatre, was challenged and largely routed by Jews. But at the same time several Irish-American playwrights emerged who may, in the long run, be seen as the most significant Irish contributors yet to the American stage: Eugene *O'Neill, Philip *Barry, and George *Kelly, as well as lesser Irish playwrights such as James *Gleason. One curious phenomenon in the early 1920s was in the musical theatre, when during the so-called Cinderella Era musical comedies essentially had the same story: a poor Irish girl, often a secretary, winning the hand of a rich man, usually the boss's son. By World War II the Irish no longer loomed as large as they had in the preceding century, and although there was no shortage of talented artists of Irish descent, few plays addressed the issue of Irish heritage. Perhaps the group had become so assimilated into the culture that they no longer demanded to be heard, unlike the African Americans, Asian Americans, and others still fighting for acceptance in the land they had lived in for so long.

IRVING, George S. [né Shelasky] (b. 1922), character actor. A comic who specializes in foreign types, Irving appeared in Broadway musicals and revues for twenty-five years before he became a familiar favorite in supporting roles. He was born in Springfield, Massachusetts, and studied voice for an opera career. But after appearing in operettas in stock, he made his Broadway debut in the chorus of *Oklahoma! (1943) and was usually seen in musicals thereafter. Irving's most impressive nonmusical role was a frantic president in *An Evening with Richard Nixon and . . .* (1972).

IRVING, Henry [né John Henry Brodribb] (1838–1905), actor and manager. The renowned Englishman, who was long the subject of both adulation and savage criticism, was credited with making acting a respectable profession in his homeland and with ridding English playgoers of Puritan obsessions. He was the first actor to be knighted. Irving made six visits to America between 1883 and 1903, most in the company of Ellen *Terry. For his American debut he selected one of his most celebrated roles, the guilt-ridden Mathias in *The Bells*. Among his other American offerings were his Shylock, Hamlet, Macbeth, Doricort in *The Belle's Stratagem*, Dubosc in *The Lyons Mail*, Benedick, and Richelieu. Neither good-looking nor well built and with a peculiar style of delivery, he divided American critics much as he did English reviewers. Despite critical complaints, his tours were among the most financially profitable of his era, and he was often able to charge twice the going rate for tickets. Biography: *Henry Irving, the Actor and His World*, Laurence Irving, 1951.

IRVING, Washington (1783–1859), author and critic. If this great early American writer is best remembered for his biographies, histories, and romantic short stories, he was also an important, if largely indirectly so, figure in the American theatre of his day. Among his first published pieces were "The Letters of Jonathan Oldstyle, Gent.," which were serialized in 1802–03 in the *New York Morning Chronicle* and also published separately and which offered his personal views of contemporary plays and performers. Further observations on the theatre, usually satirical and not nearly as important, appeared in *Salmagundi*, which he wrote in 1807–08 with his brother, William, and J. K. *Paulding. Both in America and in Europe, where he spent some time, Irving made many important theatrical friends, including John Howard *Payne, with whom he collaborated on half a dozen plays, the most important of which were *Charles the Second; or, The Merry Monarch* (1824) and *Richelieu, A Domestic Tragedy* (1826). The former enjoyed widespread popularity but the failure of the latter and other works prompted Irving to write to Payne, "I am sorry to say I cannot afford to write any more for the theatre. . . . The experiment has satisfied me that I should never at any time be compensated for my trouble." In the long run, it was other men's adaptations of his stories, especially *Rip Van Winkle*, that made him an enduring figure in our theatre.

IRWIN, Bill (b. 1950), actor and mime. Broadway's favorite (and practically only) mime during the late 20th century, Irwin has embraced many areas of entertainment in his unusual career, having also been a dancer, a clown, a street performer, an actor, a choreographer, and a teacher. He was born in Santa Monica, California, and educated at Oberlin College, the University of California at Los Angeles, the California Institute of the Arts, and the Ringling Brothers and Barnum and Bailey's Clown College. Irwin taught dance and mime before going to New York in 1980 and first presenting his innovative wordless performance pieces, most memorably *The Regard of Flight* and *The Clown Bagatelles* (1982 and 1987), *Largely New York* (1989), and *Fool Moon* (1995). He eventually performed some of them on Broadway to great acclaim and played roles in traditional plays as well, most notably as the slave Lucky in a star-studded production of *Waiting for Godot* in 1988.

IRWIN, May [née Ada May Campbell] (1862–1938), singer and comedienne. In 1899, when she was at the height of her fame, Lewis C. *Strang, a popular writer on theatrical themes, observed, "May Irwin is a personality rather than an artist, an entertainer more than an actress. Her career has vacillated between the variety stage and the legitimate, until at last she has become identified with that hybrid species of the theatrical amusement called farce comedy. Miss Irwin is a famous fun-maker; of jolly rotund figure, and with a face that reflects the gaiety of nations, she is the personification of humor and careless mirth, a female Falstaff." The Canadian-born blue-eyed blonde made her professional debut with her sister, Flora, at a Buffalo vaudeville house in 1875. By the early 1880s she was a popular attraction at Tony *Pastor's, appearing both in his olios and his versions of *Gilbert and Sullivan favorites. Irwin left Pastor in 1883 to assume important supporting roles in Augustin *Daly's great ensemble, four years later returning to vaudeville, then appearing in those prototypical musicals that were called *farce-comedies at the time. Stardom came in 1895 when she appeared in *The Widow Jones* and introduced "The Bully Song," putting her in the forefront of what then were termed "coon shouters." Subsequent hits, all of a similar nature, included *Courted into Court* (1896); *The Swell Miss Fitzwell* (1897); *Kate Kip, Buyer* (1898); *Sister Mary* (1899); *Mudge Smith, Attorney* (1900); and *Mrs. Black Is Back* (1904). Thereafter, she alternated between vaudeville and musical plays, although her vogue had begun to wane. Her last Broadway assignment was in *The 49ers* (1922), then she retired after making an appearance in a 1925 "Old Timers' Week" at the *Palace.

IS ZAT SO? (1925), a comedy by James *Gleason and Richard Taber. [39th Street Theatre, 634 perf.] Boxer Chick Cowan (Robert Armstrong) and his manager Hap Hurley (Gleason) are down on their luck when they meet rich, young Clinton Blackburn (Sidney Riggs). Clinton is determined to prove his brother-in-law, Robert Parker (John C. King), is a crook and to sock it to him in more ways than one. To this end, he takes on Chick and Hap as his sparring partner and trainer, and introduces them into his household as butler and footman. When Chick is accidentally knocked out in a fight, his somewhat befuddled mind becomes clear, and it is he who provides the evidence Clinton needs to unmask Parker. This "rough and ready comedy" competed successfully with another Gleason farce of the same season, *The Fall Guy*, and far outran it, though most critics thought *The Fall Guy* the better work.

ISAACS, Edith J[uliet] **R**[ich] (1878–1956), critic and author. Born in Milwaukee and educated at Downer College, she served as drama critic for

Ainslee's Magazine in 1913. In 1918 she became editor of *Theatre Arts magazine and retained that post until 1946. Under her aegis the magazine was the leading intellectual theatrical periodical of the era. Isaacs also edited Theatre: Essays on the Arts of the Theatre (1927) and Plays of American Life and Fantasy (1929) and wrote The Negro in the American Theatre (1947).

ISHERWOOD, Henry (1803–85), designer. The son of famous New York confectioners, he was hired by the *Park Theatre in 1817 as a super and apprentice scene painter. Although he continued to act until the mid-1850s, it was his work as a scene painter for which he was most admired. By the mid-1840s he was designing important sets for productions at *Niblo's Garden and elsewhere. In 1857 Isherwood was signed by James *Wallack Jr. to be the principal scene painter for his great company. His salary was $25 a week, actually not a bad salary when Lester *Wallack, then the company's leading man, received $100. Isherwood remained with the Wallacks until his retirement in 1875. He designed everything from Shakespeare to contemporary comedies. One of his last assignments was to create the sets for Wallack's very successful production of The *Shaughraun (1874).

IT PAYS TO ADVERTISE (1914), a farce by Roi Cooper *Megrue and Walter Hackett. [Cohan Theatre, 399 perf.] Cyrus Martin (John W. Cope) so dominates the soap business that one of his associates remarks, "If he were to go busted, the whole country would go dirty." But Martin is dismayed at the refusal of his playboy son Rodney (Grant *Mitchell) to settle down to work. So is Rodney's fiancée, Mary Grayson (Ruth Shepley). Irked by their disapproval, Rodney joins with Ambrose Peale (Will Deming) to found a rival soap company. He invents a soap that costs three cents a bar to make and which, with proper advertising, they plan to sell for a dollar a bar. They call their soap "#13" and launch a huge publicity campaign announcing "Number Thirteen Soap Is Unlucky for Dirt." The demand for the new soap overwhelms the men, for they have exhausted their funds in advertising and have no money left to manufacture the product, so the elder Martin buys them out. But Rodney has caught the fever and, as soon as he marries Mary, promises to settle down to business. The Times praised the *Cohan and *Harris offering for having "something more than the gayety of the average farce" and for humor rich in "genuineness and substance."

IT'S A WISE CHILD (1929), a comedy by Laurence E. Johnson. [*Belasco Theatre, 378 perf.] Although she is engaged to the prosperous middle-aged banker G. A. Appleby (Harlan Briggs), Joyce Stanton (Mildred McCoy) meets and falls in love with a younger man, Roger Baldwin (Humphrey Bogart). To break her engagement, she announces darkly that she is pregnant, an idea which she gets on learning the condition of one of the Stantons' serving girls. But her plan backfires when she loses both Appleby and Baldwin. However, the family's young attorney, James Stevens (Minor Watson), is so taken with Joyce that he proposes marriage. "It's a wise child in the theatre who can write so comic a play," Brooks *Atkinson noted in his review of the David *Belasco production. Its popularity allowed the comedy to override the onset of the Depression. **Laurence E. JOHNSON** (1872–1933) was a minor playwright who wrote half a dozen plays that were produced on Broadway between 1925 and 1933. This was his only success.

IVEY, Dana (b. 1942), actress. She was born in Atlanta, Georgia, and educated at Rollins College and the London Academy of Music and Dramatic Art. Ivey spent many years in regional theatre before making her New York debut in 1981. She was first noticed giving proficient supporting performances in such Off-Broadway plays as Quartermaine's Terms (1983) and Baby with the Bathwater (1983), then on Broadway in Heartbreak House (1983) and *Sunday in the Park with George (1984). Ivey originated the role of the stubborn Southern senior citizen Daisy in *Driving Miss Daisy (1987) and also shone as the spy Helen Kroger in Pack of Lies (1985), the secretive refugee Evelyn in Kindertransport (1994), and the Atlanta matriarch Boo Levy in The *Last Night of Ballyhoo (1997).

IVEY, Judith (b. 1951), actress. A versatile leading lady capable of portraying high-class dames as well as kooky lower-class broads, Ivey was born in El Paso, Texas, the daughter of a college president and a teacher, and was educated at Illinois State before acting at the *Goodman Theatre and other regional theatres. She appeared in some Off-Broadway productions before finding success as the crass but honest Cockney Josie in Steaming (1982). Ivey was also lauded for her hardened stripper Bonnie in Hurlyburly (1984); the uptight second wife Ruth in Blithe Spirit (1987); Kathleen, the Irish housekeeper with a grudge in Park Your Car in Harvard Yard (1991); the estranged mother Patrice in A Fair Country (1996); the ex-chorine Sally who still carries a torch in *Follies (2001); and the grieving mother Madeline in The Women of Lockerbie (2003).

J

J. B. (1958), a play by Archibald MacLeish. [ANTA Theatre, 364 perf.; *Pulitzer Prize.] J. B. (Pat *Hingle) is a successful businessman who seems to have everything in life. Walking through the great traveling circus that is the world, he comes to the attention of Mr. Zuss (Raymond *Massey), a downtrodden balloon seller, and Nickles (Christopher *Plummer), a sardonic popcorn vendor. After Nickles puts on the Satanmask and Zuss the Godmask, they confront J. B. One by one his blessings are taken away—his wealth lost, his children killed, his body diseased, his wife deserting him. But J. B. refuses to condemn God, so his wounds are healed. He concludes, "What suffers, loves." The American poet **Archibald MACLEISH** (1892–1982), a native of Glencoe, Illinois, studied at Yale and at Harvard Law School. He wrote several other verse dramas, such as *Panic* (1935) and *The Music Crept by Me upon the Waters* (1953), but *J. B.* was his only commercial success. Louis *Kronenberger noted, "Judged as a theatre piece, *J. B.*—at least in the first half—had a striking theatricality. . . . Judged as philosophic drama, though an effort of a sort and size unusual in today's American theatre, *J. B.* was not altogether satisfying." For all its flaws, the Alfred *de Liagre Jr.—produced play, suggested by the Book of Job, was a noteworthy success.

JACK CADE (1835), a play by Robert T. *Conrad. [*Walnut Street Theatre (Philadelphia), in repertory.] The villainous Lord Say (Mr. Connor), who typifies the arbitrary power of the nobles, cruelly oppresses his people. He has long since killed Jack Cade's father and exiled Jack (Mr. Ingersoll), who now returns to take his revenge. Jack succeeds in capturing London, forcing the king to flee, and fatally stabbing Lord Say, but the evil lord finds enough strength before he dies to dig his poisoned dagger into Jack. As Jack is dying, his wife, Mariamne, appears, crazed by an attack on her by Lord Clifford (Mr. Porter), whom she has murdered in self-defense. She dies moments before her husband, whose last words are, "The bondman is avenged, my country free!" Conrad based his story on the Kentish rebellion of 1450, emphasizing the social rather than the political aspects of the revolt.

The play was only a modest success until Edwin *Forrest assumed the leading role in 1841 and kept it in his repertory until his death. Afterward John *McCullough assumed the part on several occasions, and it was revived with some regularity as late as 1887. **Robert T[aylor] CONRAD** (1810–58), the son of a famous early American publisher, was himself a publisher and journalist as well as a lawyer, jurist, and mayor of his native Philadelphia. His tragedy *Conrad of Naples* was mounted at Philadelphia's *Arch Street Theatre in 1832 with James E. *Murdoch in the title role. In addition to *Jack Cade*, Conrad is also believed to be the author of a romantic tragedy, *The Heretic*, which was not produced until several years after his death.

JACKSON, Anne (b. 1926), actress. Born in Allegheny, Pennsylvania, she made her professional debut in 1944 but called attention to herself when she played the peevish wife Mildred in *Oh, Men! Oh, Women!* (1953) and the Daughter who opposes her father's remarriage in *Middle of the Night* (1956). Many of her subsequent appearances have been with her husband, Eli *Wallach, in such plays as *Rhinoceros* (1961), *The Typists* and *The Tiger* (1963), *Luv* (1964), *The Waltz of the Toreadors* (1973), *The *Diary of Anne Frank* (1978), *Twice Around the Park* (1982), *Cafe Crown* (1988), *The Flowering Peach* (1994), and *Down the Garden Paths* (2000). Among her credits without her husband are *The Madwoman of Chaillot* (1985), a replacement for Grandma Curtis in *Lost in Yonkers* (1992), and *Mr. Peters' Connections* (1998).

JACOBI, Lou (b. 1913), character actor. The strongly ethnic comic was often cast as the grumpy Jewish father but sometimes got to break away from typecasting and surprise audiences with a serious portrayal. He was born in Toronto where he first started acting as a youth. After appearing on the London stage in the early 1950s, Jacobi made an impressive Broadway debut in 1955 as the Jew-in-hiding Mr. Van Daan in *The *Diary of Anne Frank* (1955). His noteworthy performances include the synagogue worshiper Schlissel in *The *Tenth Man* (1959); the manufacturer of plastic fruit, Mr. Baker, in *Come Blow Your Horn* (1961); the Samuel

Goldwynish movie producer Lionel Z. Governor in *Fade Out—Fade In* (1964); the American-Jewish caterer Walter Hollander caught behind the Iron Curtain in *Don't Drink the Water* (1966); and two different Jews in *Unlikely Heroes* (1971).

JACOBS, Bernard B. See Shuberts.

JAMES, Henry [Jr.] (1843–1916), author. The famous expatriate novelist was also a passionate playgoer and harbored serious ambitions for a place in the theatre. He dramatized his own novel, *Daisy Miller* (1883), as well as writing such plays as *Guy Domville* (1895) and *The High Bid* (1908), but none was commercially viable. James also wrote numerous essays on the theatre, many of them collected after his death and published as *The Scenic Art* (1949). Ironically, several of his novels provided the bases for popular plays long after his death. The most notable were *Berkeley Square (1929), suggested by his unfinished A Sense of the Past; The *Heiress (1947), derived from Washington Square; and The Innocents (1950), whose source was The Turn of the Screw.

JAMES JOYCE'S THE DEAD (1999), a musical play by Richard Nelson (book, lyrics), Shaun Davey (music, lyrics). [*Playwrights Horizons, 112 perf.; NYDCC Award.] At the Dublin home of the Misses Morkans (Sally Ann Howes, Marni Nixon, and Emily Skinner), the annual Christmas party brings together relatives, friends, some students, and even an opera celebrity (John Kelly) for conversation and singing. But, as in Joyce's novella, memories are evoked and relationships are altered during the course of the evening. The lovely, subdued piece was successful enough Off Broadway that Playwrights Horizons transferred it to the *Belasco Theatre where it failed to find a mainstream audience. **Richard NELSON** (b. 1950) was born in Chicago and educated at Hamilton College before working as a literary manager for various theatres. Nelson's plays were first produced regionally, and in 1978 he made his Manhattan debut with *Conjuring an Event* at the *American Place Theatre. His writing credits include the revised book for the musical *Chess* (1988); *Some Americans Abroad* (1990), concerning educators from the States touring the English theatre circuit; *Two Shakespearean Actors* (1992), illustrating events leading up to the *Astor Place Riots; *New England* (1995), a look at discontented Brits living in America; and *Goodnight Children Everywhere* (1999), about an English youth returning home after spending the war years in Canada. Nelson's career is unusual in that many of his works are about Englishmen and are usually produced first in London where he is more popular than in the States.

JAMES, Louis (1842–1910), actor. A much respected leading man who never quite attained the highest order of public acceptance, he was born in Tremont, Illinois, and made his debut with a Louisville stock company in 1863. He left to join Mrs. John *Drew at Philadelphia's *Arch Street Theatre, then in 1872 became a member of Augustin *Daly's famous ensemble. In 1886 James branched out on his own, producing and starring in a series of Shakespearean revivals, beginning with *Othello (1886), *Hamlet (1888), and *Much Ado About Nothing (1888), and continuing through *Henry VIII* and *The Comedy of Errors* during the 1907–08 season. The productions were generally admired by critics, but found more welcome on the road than in New York.

JANAUSCHEK, [Francesca Romana Magdalena] **Fanny** (1830–1904), actress. The tempestuous Czech performer had become a reigning favorite on European stages before she made her American debut in 1867. Her opening play was *Medea*, which she performed in German with a company she had brought with her from the Continent. The selection invited comparison with Adelaide *Ristori, who had only recently triumphed in the part, and comparisons were not totally favorable to the newcomer. Nevertheless, she soon developed a loyal following. In 1870 Janauschek decided to learn English, and thereafter most of her career was spent in America. Among her best roles were Lady Macbeth and the title parts in *Deborah* and *Mary Stuart*. Otis *Skinner, who played opposite her when he was a young man, recalled her as "a short, rather stockily built woman. . . . Her eyes were of hazel-gray, large and weary-lidded, but when they suddenly opened, it was the unmasking of a battery." She died nearly blind and impoverished and was to be buried in an indigent's grave until her fellow actors took up a collection for a proper funeral.

JANIE (1942), a comedy by Josephine Bentham and Herschel Williams. [*Henry Miller Theatre, 642 perf.] When seventeen-year-old Janie Colburn (Gwen Anderson) meets Pvt. Dick Lawrence (Herbert Evers), the son of her mother's old friend, she instantly forgets her high school beau, Scooper Nolan (Frank Amy). And when her parents and their friends go out for the night, Janie has Dick invite all his army buddies to a hastily got-up party at the Colburn house. The older Colburns return to find the house overrun. Dick must go off to war, so Janie realizes she will have to make up with Scooper. Almost every critic compared this play unfavorably with the earlier *Junior Miss. Both comedies exemplified the recourse playwrights had to youngsters and old folks as principals when so many draft-age men and women had joined the war effort. Although business was slow at first, good word-of-mouth and wartime prosperity turned the Brock *Pemberton production into a hit.

JANIS, Elsie [née Bierbower] (1889–1956), singer. Best known as the "Sweetheart of the A. E. F.," for her entertaining of troops during World War I, the slim, hoydenish performer was born in Columbus, Ohio, and, driven by her infamous stage mother, made her debut in her hometown as a boy in *The *Charity Ball* in 1897. She quickly rose to popularity in vaudeville as "Little Elsie," then turned to Broadway in 1906 in *The Vanderbilt Cup*, later appearing in *The Hoyden* (1907), *The Fair Co-ed* (1909), *The Slim Princess* (1910), and *The Lady of the Slipper* (1912). But two-a-day remained her main stamping grounds, where her singing and imitations won the loudest applause. *The *Dramatic Mirror* wrote of her, "You caught a splendid semblance of the divine fire—enough to truly thrill you," while Sime *Silverman called her "the most natural person in vaudeville." She continued to perform throughout the twenties, but retired after the death of her mother in 1932. Autobiography: *So Far, So Good!*, 1932.

JANSEN, Marie [née Hattie Johnson] (1857–1914), singer. The Boston-born singing comedienne joined Colonel *McCaull's company in 1883, then appeared in principal roles at the *Casino. However, she is best recalled as leading lady to Francis *Wilson in such shows as *The Oolah* (1889) and *The Merry Monarch* (1890).

JANUS (1955), a comedy by Carolyn Green. [*Plymouth Theatre, 251 perf.] Every summer Jessica (Margaret *Sullavan) and Denny (Claude Dauphin) go off to an apartment in Washington Square, where they write novels under the pen name Janus. Jessica and Denny are married, but not to each other. Even their spouses don't know where they go and what they do. But this particular summer their idyll is interrupted successively by their aggressive agent (Mary Finney), Jessica's husband (Robert *Preston), and the tax man (Richard Emhardt). It is some time before matters are cleared up and they can return to their writing. A delightful escapist comedy of what even in 1955 was becoming an old school, the Alfred *de Liagre Jr. production did good business to no small extent because of its fine performers.

JARRETT, Henry C. (1828–1903), manager. He began his career as an actor in amateur theatricals in his native Baltimore, then in 1851 he purchased the Baltimore Museum and four years later assumed the management of Washington's *National Theatre. In 1861 Jarrett added the new *Brooklyn Academy of Music to his roster of theatres and in 1864 the Boston Theatre. He brought the "Parisienne Ballet Troupe" to New York for an engagement, but the ballerinas ended up being in *The *Black Crook* (1866), a milestone in the history of the American musical theatre. At the same time Jarrett took over management of *Niblo's Garden, then in 1874 he joined A. M. *Palmer to take over the *Booth Theatre, and to produce plays, including a highly successful revival of *Uncle Tom's Cabin*. He retired to England in the mid-1880s.

JAZZ SINGER, THE (1925), a comedy-drama by Samson *Raphaelson. [Fulton Theatre, 303 perf.] Jackie Rabinowitz (George *Jessel) fights with his cantor father (Howard Lang), who objects to his obsession with jazz music and his neglect of his religion. Running away from home, he takes the name of Jack Robin and quickly rises as a popular singer. His big break comes when he lands a major role in a new Broadway revue, but on the eve of its premiere he learns his father is dying. Jackie rushes to his father, who persuades him to return to the synagogue and follow in the older man's footsteps. Although this tearjerker was one of the major hits of its season—called by one paper "a shrewd and well-planned excursion into the theatre"—it is best remembered as the source of Al *Jolson's famous early "talkie" of the same name. From the start critics felt the story was based on Jolson's career, but Raphaelson is said always to have denied this.

JEFFERS, Robinson. See *Tower Beyond Tragedy, The*.

JEFFERSON, Joseph (1774–1832), comic actor. Although best remembered as the grandfather of the famous Joseph *Jefferson, he was one of the most accomplished and beloved comedians of his own day. He was born in Plymouth, England, and given his earliest tutelage by his father, Thomas Jefferson, a minor actor at Drury Lane. *Hodgkinson brought him to America in 1795, and he made his American debut appearing in Boston, playing La Gloire in *The Surrender of Calais*. His New York debut was at the *John Street Theatre as Squire Richard in *The Provoked Husband* in February 1796. He was a small, slender man, with a Grecian nose and blue eyes "full of laughter." After an argument with Hodgkinson, he left for Philadelphia in 1803. There, with his brother-in-law, the first William *Warren, he became the mainstay of the *Chestnut Street Theatre. His best roles were in then-popular, if now-forgotten, light comedies, such as Farmer Ashfield in *Speed the Plough*, Jeremy Diddler in *Raising the Wind*, and Jacob Gawky in *The Chapter

of Accidents. He left Philadelphia during the theatrical depression of 1830, attempting to find work
in the hinterlands. But by then his age had begun
to tell on him, and he was unsuccessful. His son
Joseph Jr. (1804–42) was an actor and scene painter
of only modest repute.

JEFFERSON, Joseph (1829–1905), comic actor and
manager. Beyond question the most popular and
respected American comedian of the 19th century,
he was the scion of an old theatrical family. His
father was attempting, unsuccessfully, to manage
a theatre in Philadelphia when the future actor
was born there. The youngster did not wait long
before making his debut at the age of four, performing alongside of and mimicking the celebrated singer of "Jim Crow," T. D. *Rice. He had
little schooling, and when he was thirteen, he
toured with his actress mother in theatrical backwaters. Within a few years Jefferson was playing
important roles in support of the great actors of the
day, including Junius Brutus *Booth and Edwin
*Forrest. In 1853 he became stage manager of the
Baltimore Museum and a year later was hired by
John T. *Ford to manage a theatre in Richmond,
Virginia. The turning point in his career came in
1857 when Laura *Keene hired him as a member of
her company. Under her aegis he scored notable
successes as Dr. Pangloss in *The Heir-at-Law* and as
Asa Trenchard in *Our American Cousin*. Moving to
the Winter Garden, he consolidated his reputation
when he played Caleb Plummer in *Dot* and Salem
Scudder in *The *Octoroon*. In 1859 he produced his
own version of *Rip Van Winkle*, but it was unsuccessful. After performing a revised version of the
play in London, Jefferson reprised his Rip Van
Winkle in New York in 1866, and the performance
brought him fame and fortune; for many years he
played little else. The *Times* noted, "In *Rip Van
Winkle* he evinces all his abilities and sounds the
gamut of all quiet and natural emotions. He is no
doubt the best comedian America has yet produced, and probably unsurpassed in England, that
nidus of comedians . . . the smile excited by his
scarecrow figure actually forces more quickly the
tear we bestow on his misery." In 1880 he produced his version of *The Rivals*, playing Bob Acres
to the Mrs. Malaprop of Mrs. John *Drew. While
some critics condemned his rewriting of Sheridan,
his performance was universally hailed and added
one final great portrait to his theatrical canon. He
made his last appearance, as Caleb Plummer, in
1904, ending a stage career of seventy-one years.
Jefferson was a man of slightly more than average
height, with a noticeably smallish head and long
brown hair. Even as a relatively young man his
quizzical face was wizened. He had a prominent
nose and chin and described himself as presenting

"a classical contour, neither Greek nor Roman, but
of the pure Nut-cracker type." His beguiling *Autobiography of Joseph Jefferson* (1890) is filled with
superb pictures of the theatre of his day and
remains one of the landmarks in American theatrical writing.

JEKYLL AND HYDE (1997), a musical thriller
by Leslie Bricusse (book, lyrics), Frank Wildhorn
(music). [*Plymouth Theatre, 1,543 perf.] Ambitious scientist Dr. Jekyll (Robert Cuccioli) experiments with the chemical properties of evil,
turning himself into the crazed Mr. Hyde who
murders innocent victims, including the prostitute (Linda Eder) who is beloved by Jekyll. *Notable
songs*: This Is the Moment; A New Life; Someone
Like You. Because the score had already been
recorded and released, selling more than two hundred thousand CDs, the negative reviews did not
dampen business, and the musical soon developed a cult following. **Frank WILDHORN** (b.
1958) is a pop songwriter whose first Broadway
credit was providing the music for additional
songs for *Victor/Victoria* (1995). His other theatre
scores are *The Scarlet Pimpernel* (1997) and *The
Civil War* (1999).

JELLY'S LAST JAM (1992), a musical play by
George C. *Wolfe (book), Jelly Roll Morton,
Luther Henderson (music), Susan Birkenhead
(lyrics). [*Virginia Theatre, 569 perf.] Composer
Jelly Roll Morton (Gregory Hines) has died
and faces the Chimney Man (Keith David), the
"concierge" of the light-skinned African American's soul. In a series of flashbacks, the young
Jelly (Savion Glover) picks up the sounds of New
Orleans and grows up to invent jazz, though he
often denies his black heritage, and his relationships with others are far from noble. *Notable songs*:
That's How You Jazz; Jelly's Jam; Lovin' Is a Low-
down Blues. A dark musical biography where the
hero is an unlikable man with a tortured soul,
Jelly's Last Jam was given a highly stylized production by director Wolfe, and the performances
were riveting; both Hines and Tonya Pinkins,
as Morton's lover, won Tonys. **Gregory HINES**
(1946–2003), a native New Yorker and the son of
entertainer Maurice Hines, was on stage as a boy,
becoming part of the Hines Kids act in the 1950s
and then in the 1960s danced with his father and
brother Maurice Jr. as Hines, Hines, and Dad. Hines
made his Broadway debut in 1954 as a child dancer
in *The Girl in Pink Tights*, then returned decades
later in the revues *Eubie* (1978) and *Sophisticated
Ladies* (1981). He also played the Harlem version of
Scrooge in the short-lived *Comin' Uptown* (1979).
Hines was considered one of the best tap dancers
ever to grace the stage.

JENKINS, George (b. 1908?), designer. Born in Baltimore and educated at the University of Pennsylvania, he worked under Jo *Mielziner from 1937 to 1941. In 1943 he designed the sets and lighting for *Early to Bed,* and for the next twenty years was in steady demand. Among his design credits are *Mexican Hayride* (1944), *I Remember Mama* (1944), *Dark of the Moon* (1945), *Lost in the Stars* (1949), *Bell, Book and Candle* (1950), *Two for the Seesaw* (1958), *The *Miracle Worker* (1959), *A Thousand Clowns* (1962), *Generation* (1965), and *Sly Fox* (1976).

JEROME ROBBINS'S BROADWAY (1989), a musical revue featuring numbers from Broadway shows that Jerome *Robbins had choreographed. [*Imperial Theatre, 633 perf.; *Tony Award.] Memorable production numbers from nine Robbins-staged musicals were re-created with accuracy and skill under the watchful eye of the master choreographer himself. The large cast of sixty-two singer-dancers featured Jason Alexander (Tony Award), Faith *Prince, Charlotte d'Amboise, Scott Wise (Tony), Debbie Shapiro (Tony), and Robert LaFosse in scenes from *On the Town* (1944), *High Button Shoes* (1947), *The *King and I* (1951), *Peter Pan* (1954), *West Side Story* (1957), *Fiddler on the Roof* (1964), and others. Because of the expensive overhead, the show failed to realize a profit after running nearly two years.

JEROME, William. See Schwartz, Jean.

JESSEL, George [Albert] (1898–1981), comic actor and producer. Born into a poor Jewish family in the Bronx, he took to the stage in 1907 to help support his sick father. Jessell formed a vaudeville act with Jack Wiener, who became a Hollywood agent, and Walter *Winchell, the renowned columnist. Later Winchell and Jessel joined Gus *Edwards's famous schoolchildren act, performing alongside Georgie Price and Eddie *Cantor, and by 1920 Jessel was producing his own miniature revues for vaudeville. About the same time he first did his most celebrated turn, his monologue that pretended to be a phone call to his demanding mother. In it he swore he knew nothing about the money missing from the cupboard, he hadn't eaten a piece of the cake she had baked for a charity affair, and no, that was not his cigar butt, since he didn't smoke. Jessel appeared on Broadway in the *Shubert Gaieties of 1919, The *Passing Show of 1923, Sweet and Low* (1930), and *High Kickers* (1941). He co-produced the latter as well as several other shows. On occasion Jessel also appeared in straight plays, most notably as Jackie Rabinowitz in *The *Jazz Singer* (1925). His last years were spent as a Hollywood producer and as a celebrated after-dinner speaker. Autobiography: *So Help Me,* 1943.

JESSIE BROWN; or, The Relief of Lucknow (1858), a drama by Dion *Boucicault. [*Wallack's Theatre, 42 perf.] Led by the treacherous Nena Sahib (Boucicault), the Sepoy Rebellion has succeeded in trapping a garrison of European troops at Lucknow. As the days move on, the situation seems more and more hopeless. The women and children, even the soldiers (though they are reluctant to admit it), have begun to despair as it appears that surrender is their only recourse. As fear grows, a young Scottish girl, Jessie Brown (Agnes *Robertson), slowly raises her head and listens. She tells her neighbors she can hear the Campbell's pibroch. At first they are disbelieving, but in time the sound of the bagpipes grows louder, and before long kilted Highlanders have broken through to rescue the besieged. So fresh was the memory of these events that, according to popular theatre legend, no actor would assume the role of Nena Sahib for fear of being hissed off stage, so Boucicault was forced to play the role himself. Pronounced a "capital drama" by William *Winter, the play held the boards for over twenty years.

JESSOP, George H. (1851?–1915), playwright. Born in Ireland, he was educated at Trinity College and used his small inheritance to come to America in 1873. His first play, *A Gentleman from Nevada* (1880), about an uncouth American, was accused of plagiarism and bad writing by the critics, but was popular with the public. His next work, *Sam'l of Posen* (1881), centered on a Jewish peddler. For several years afterward he collaborated with William Gill on a series of similar comedies with melodramatic overtones: *In Paradise* (1883), *Facts; or, His Little Hatchet* [later called *Our Governor*] (1883), *Stolen Money* (1884), *Mam'zelle* (1884), and *A Bottle of Ink* (1885). Subsequent works (alone or with others) included the romantic Irish comedy *Myles Aroon* (1889), the melodramatic comedy *A Gold Mine* (1889), the melodrama *The Great Metropolis* (1889), the comedy *On Probation* (1889), the crime drama *The Power of the Press* (1891), and Irish romances *Mavourneen* (1891) and *The Irish Artist* (1894).

JESUS CHRIST SUPERSTAR (1971). This "rock opera" by Andrew Lloyd *Webber (music) and Tim *Rice (lyrics) began as a hit song, then was a concept album, followed by concert versions in major cities, then finally a London stage musical. By the time the rock version of the last seven days in the life of Christ opened at the *Mark Hellinger Theatre, it was fairly familiar to audiences. Director Tom O'Horgan gave the Robert Stigwood production a campy, anachronistic, and sometimes outrageous staging, and the public vetoed the mostly negative reviews, keeping it on the boards for 720 performances. *Notable songs*: Jesus Christ Superstar; I Don't Know How to Love Him; Heaven on Their Minds; Everything's Alright. Broadway revivals in 1977, 1995, and 2000 all failed to run, but the rock musical continues to be popular in amateur theatre.

JEWETT, Henry (1861–1930), actor and manager. The Australian-born performer came to America in 1891 and shortly was leading man to Julia *Marlowe, Fanny *Davenport, and other noted actresses. He also played second leads opposite Richard *Mansfield. At the turn of the century he moved to Boston where he established the Henry Jewett Players (also known as the Repertory Theatre), a company that soon gained national recognition for the excellence of its repertory and acting. One observer described him as "a robust and powerful fellow, with the chest and muscles of an athlete" and noted "sincerity was the chief characteristic of his work."

JEWISH REPERTORY THEATRE (New York). Committed to presenting new and old plays relating to the Jewish experience, the company was founded in 1974 by Ran Avni and has been housed in various Manhattan locations over the years. The JRT productions are performed in English, though the scope of the repertory is broad enough to include works about Jews around the world. Classic and forgotten American plays are regularly revived, and sometimes foreign classics are presented with a Jewish interpretation. Lately the company has been known for giving staged readings of forgotten or failed American musicals that deal with Jews.

JEWS IN AMERICAN THEATRE AND DRAMA. Jewish immigration to America began in the mid-17th century and small enclaves developed in Rhode Island, New Amsterdam, and several other more tolerant settlements. Because their numbers and influence were so small, there appears to have been little overt or organized anti-Semitism. Moreover, they appear to have served largely as tradesmen and to have taken no part in the beginnings of American theatre. Thus scarcely any significance can be attached to the fact that The *Merchant of Venice* was one of the first professionally mounted plays in the colonies, the initial American offering by the elder *Hallam's company in 1752. Some suggestion that there existed a widespread willingness to view Jews sympathetically can be assumed from the success that attended the American premiere of Richard Cumberland's *The Jew* (1795) less than a year after its English premiere. In his humane portrayal of Sheva, Cumberland publicly acknowledged that he was attempting to discard deroga-

tory stereotypes and present Jews "according to the new doctrine of human perfectibility . . . and the universal sentiment of tolerance associated with the era of the French Revolution." On the other hand, the earliest-known depiction of a Jew in American drama was in Susanna Haswell Rowson's *Slaves of [in?] Algiers* (1794) in which the villain describes himself "as a forger and a crook, as one who cheated the Gentiles because Moses so commanded." In the early 19th century the older stereotype was perpetuated in such foreign works as the comic *The Jew and the Doctor* (1808), which held American stages for decades. One curious piece was Henry E. Milner's once-famous *The Jew of Lubeck* (1819), in which a disgraced aristocrat disguises himself as a Jew. At the same time actors such as Edmund *Kean attempted more compassionate portrayals of such stereotypical figures as Shylock and Marlowe's Barabas. Yet while Jewish men continued to be presented as sly, callous, mercenary, and pushy, a new figure began to appear: the tragically beset, but rather beautiful and noble Jewish woman. Rebecca in Scott's novel *Ivanhoe* and *Rachel in the *Scribe-Halevy opera, *La Juive*, gave widespread currency to the figure. *The Hebrew* (1823) was a successful dramatization of the former, while *The Jewess* (1835), taken from the latter and frequently mounted without the music, remained a favorite for many years. Sol *Smith's and Noah *Ludlow's version tacked on a happy ending to ensure its acceptance with less sophisticated audiences.

The most important Jewish playwrights of the era studiously avoided plays with Jewish themes or even Jewish characters, perhaps out of fear of rejection, but more likely because they felt no need for advocacy. For the most part such characters as the venal Solomon Isaac of *London Assurance* (1841), the sleazy Melter Moss in *The *Ticket-of-Leave Man* (1863), as well as Fagin in numerous versions of *Oliver Twist* continued to typify the stage Jew. Augustin *Daly's earliest success came when he took another play dealing with the figure of the noble Jewess, S. H. von Mosenthal's *Deborah*, and transformed it into *Leah, the Forsaken* (1863). The idea of the tragic Jewish beauty may have played a small part in public approval in this country of the great French actress Rachel. Indeed, it is interesting that many of the earliest reigning Jewish stars were to be women, such as Rose *Eytinge and Sarah *Bernhardt, all of whom excelled at tragic parts. For the most part, during the last half of the century the stage picture of the Jew changed little, although many intellectuals attempted minor rebellions. One of the most interesting was the leading character of *Sam'l of Posen* (1861), a character written to order for the Jewish actor M. B. Curtis by the Irish-American George H. *Jessop. Curtis aside, few Jewish actors of the era attained so much as secondary rank. But even if the legitimate theatre was seemingly closed to Jews, except the infrequent leading lady, the vaudeville stage began offering outlets. On the other side of the footlights, Jews were becoming increasingly important as theatregoers. Looking back in her memoirs, Clara *Morris recalled "Hebrew citizens [as] enthusiastic and most generous patrons of the theatre," adding, "better judges of matters theatrical it would be hard to find." Behind the scenes a similar state of affairs began to emerge. The late 19th century saw no American-Jewish playwrights of any significance, but American playgoers welcomed plays by European Jews. Among the most popular were Adolphe-Philippe *D'Ennery and Arthur Wing *Pinero. At the same time, the business side of the theatre started to attract a growing number of Jews. Jonas Phillip's brother, H. B. Phillips, for example, was the manager of *Ford's Theatre until it was closed by the assassination of Lincoln. Jews soon entered the producing field either directly or as backers, but, more importantly, they increasingly took over the ownership and running of theatres. The *Frohmans, playwright David *Belasco, and Oscar *Hammerstein are prominent examples. The extent to which they rapidly took over virtual control of the American theatre became public with the formation in 1895 of the Theatrical Syndicate or *Trust. This group, which sought to monopolize major bookings, consisted almost entirely of Jews, headed by A. L. *Erlanger. Their success exacerbated some anti-Semitic tensions, largely because it gave to many a specific complaint and target, but their monopoly was broken after little more than a decade by other Jews, the *Shubert brothers. To this day the business end of the American theatre remains largely Jewish-dominated.

Early in the 20th century Jewish creative talent and Jewish performers came ever more into the forefront. Nowhere was this more evident than in the musical theatre, where one has only to think of such composers as Jerome *Kern, Irving *Berlin, Sigmund *Romberg, George *Gershwin, Richard *Rodgers, Arthur *Schwartz, and Harold *Arlen. Joe *Weber, Lew *Fields and his children, Ira *Gershwin, and Lorenz *Hart were but a few of the other talented Jews to play important creative roles. Lew Fields was also a comedian of first rank. Fields, his partner Weber, and others such as Sam *Bernard gained fame initially as "Dutch" comedians, a term employed to suggest they used a German or, usually, Yiddish dialect. If many other early Jewish stars flourished as comedians or comic singers (Al *Jolson, Eddie *Cantor, and Fanny *Brice are notable examples), some Jewish performers distinguished themselves in more serious endeavors. Many of these came out of the Yiddish theatre, which had sprung up in the 1880s with the onrush of Russian-Jewish immigrants and which served as a platform for such famous players as Jacob *Adler, Bertha *Kalish, and Maurice *Schwartz. The treatment of Jews on stage began to change noticeably in the 1920s. Two totally different plays were pivotal to the change. One was a superficial, somewhat outlandish American comedy, *Welcome Stranger (1920), which was one of the earliest American theatre pieces to deal directly with native anti-Jewish sentiment. The other was John *Galsworthy's perceptive and understanding examination of English anti-Semitism, Loyalties (1922), which nonetheless owed much of its success to the fact that it was perceived first and foremost as a rattling good thriller. The series that began with *Potash and Perlmutter (1913), and the long-running *Abie's Irish Rose (1922), although they trafficked almost entirely in comic stereotypes, helped move Jews into a social mainstream. Nevertheless, for many years Jews were depicted in American plays as people a bit apart socially, albeit not unlike others by nature. Such Jewish writers as Aaron *Hoffman and Montague *Glass wrote many of these plays. Jewish writers of more serious purport, such as Elmer *Rice and S. N. *Behrman, also began to appear during this time, as did such a uniquely talented figure as George S. *Kaufman. But the real explosion of Jewish writing talent on Broadway occurred with the Great Depression. Historian Ellen Schiff has called Clifford *Odets's *Awake and Sing! (1933) "the earliest quintessentially Jewish play outside the Yiddish theatre," and it certainly signaled a movement away from the more universal or at least largely nonsectarian interests of even Rice, Behrman, or Kaufman toward interest in a specifically Jewish experience. The theatre of protest and rebellion that sprang up so violently in the 1930s seemed a particularly fertile field for Jewish playwrights and has remained so, long after the initial reasons for protest have receded into history. Thus, Arthur *Miller, one of the two major American dramatists to emerge in the 1940s, wrote almost totally in this tradition, deriving much of his inspiration from Jewish life and Jewish concerns, even when he couched in non-Jewish terms his stories such as *Death of a Salesman (1949), which could be seen to examine the futility and emptiness of much lower-middle-class Jewish commercial life, or The *Crucible (1953), which responds to the perennial Jewish story of unjust persecution. In a sense Miller might be said to be the ultimate Jewish-American playwright, in whose works Jewish problems are American problems while American dilemmas encompass Jewish dilemmas. A writer such as

Paddy *Chayefsky, on the other hand, remained more redolently Jewish and injected a distinctly Talmudic mysticism into some of his stories. In more recent seasons the voguish thrust of plays with preeminent Jewish characters, has been to show them interacting with blacks, as in *I'm Not Rappaport (1985) and *Driving Miss Daisy (1987). Other important Jewish names, to cite but a few, include Leonard *Bernstein, Betty *Comden and Adolph *Green, Joseph *Papp, Jerome *Robbins, Stephen *Sondheim, Neil *Simon, and Jule *Styne, as well as such performers as John *Garfield and Eli *Wallach. Some recent playwrights have focused their writing on the Jewish experience, such as Wendy *Wasserstein in The Sisters Rosensweig (1992) and Tony *Kushner in *Angels in America (1993). The musical theatre continues to feature Jewish songwriters who also explore contemporary Jewishness, particularly William *Finn in this three Marvin musicals.

Not everyone has seen the large—disproportionately large in relation to their percentage of the population—contributions of American Jews to American theatre as beneficial. Writing in May 1933 in Scribner's Magazine, John *Corbin, who had served as drama critic for the Times off and on from 1902 to 1933, complained of the "acrid intelligence of our new Jewry." Regardless of how one editorializes, the Jews, so often excluded from mainstream establishments and thus able to observe those establishments with the fresh, if sometimes bitter eyes of the outsider, have long advocated change of one sort or another. Given the opportunity they have helped expand the horizons of the American stage, often thereby giving it both new depth and new breadth. This same advocacy of progress may at times have driven them to promote objectionable excesses in the name of intellectual freedom, but it has also resulted in such great forces for good as the early *Theatre Guild, in its heyday the most exciting and responsible producer in American history. Only the Irish, among American minorities, can claim an influence on the American theatre equal to the Jewish loyalty and influence.

JIM, THE PENMAN (1886). Sir Charles Young's drama, about an attractive forger who is eventually unmasked by a wife he had deceived, was presented by A. M. *Palmer at the *Madison Square Theatre in 1886, within months of its London premiere, and became what *Odell called "one of the greatest triumphs in the history of the New York stage." Frederic Robinson was the first American Jim Ralston, but Charles *Coghlan was among the later actors who scored successes in the part. The play was revived regularly for thirty years.

JITNEY (2000), a play by August *Wilson. [Second Stage, 311 perf., NYDCC Award.] A group of African-American gypsy-cab drivers hang out in the decaying garage of the taxi company run by Becker (Paul Butler) in Pittsburgh in 1977, each one bringing his or her troubles and jealousies to work each day. But Becker is more concerned about seeing his son Booster (Carl Lumbly), who is getting out of prison after serving a twenty-year sentence. Also the news that the whole city block is to be demolished for urban renewal hangs over the heads of all the characters. Written in 1979 before he found fame, Wilson's play (substantially revised by the author) was hailed for its vivid characterizations and incisive ensemble acting under the direction of Marion McClinton.

JOE TURNER'S COME AND GONE (1988), a play by August *Wilson. [*Ethel Barrymore Theatre, 105 perf.; NYDCC Award.] At a boardinghouse in Pittsburgh in 1911, the intense African-American Herald Loomis (Delroy Lindo) appears with his young daughter, claiming that he has escaped from the Mississippi bounty hunter Joe Turner and is seeking his wife who ran off ten years ago. After paying a dollar to a white "people finder," Loomis is reunited with his wife (Angela Bassett) who has become a religious fanatic. To wash himself "in the blood of the Lord" and free himself from Joe Turner, Loomis slashes his chest open with a knife, then leaves his daughter with her mother. Perhaps the most engrossing aspect of the play, which was described by Newsday as "filled with strangeness and wonders of the unpredictable," was the various boardinghouse residents who were written and acted vibrantly. The drama was revived Off Broadway in 1996.

JOHN, Elton. See Aida.

JOHN F. KENNEDY CENTER. see Kennedy Center for the Performing Arts.

JOHN GOLDEN THEATRE (New York). A Broadway house that feels like an Off-Broadway theatre, this 800-seat playhouse on West 45th Street has been home to many famous one-person shows and two-character plays. It was designed by Herbert J. *Krapp in the Spanish style and was built by the Chanin brothers in 1927 as the Theatre Masque, a venue for small, experimental productions. But such programs rarely made money and the Chanins lost the theatre in the Great Depression to the *Shuberts, who leased it to producer John *Golden and renamed it after him in 1937. Over the years the theatre has housed several Pulitzer Prize plays and solo star turns. It is still owned by the Shuberts.

JOHN LOVES MARY (1947), a comedy by Norman *Krasna. [*Booth Theatre, 423 perf.] John (William Prince) returns home from the war with an English bride, but she is not his sweetheart; rather, she is the fiancée of a buddy who saved his life in battle. Since the girl is English, marrying her was the only way to get her into the country promptly. John's real love is Mary (Nina Foch), and her parents insist they marry at once. Obviously, John cannot until he divorces his English bride. Rather than simply tell the true story, John piles lie on lie, each one further complicating matters. Mary's father is a Senator, so the lies have far-reaching but ultimately harmless effects. Several critics suggested that the play was a return to the seemingly moribund tradition of "farce-comedy," while Ward *Morehouse of the *Sun* concluded it was a play "definitely of the manufactured variety, and one for which there would be no second and third acts if the simple truth has been told in the first."

JOHN STREET THEATRE (New York). The first permanent playhouse in New York, it was erected at the behest of David *Douglass and opened in 1767, remaining the town's principal and, usually, only theatre for thirty-one years, until it was demolished after the erection of the *Park Theatre. *Dunlap says that it was modeled after Philadelphia's *Southwark Theatre and that "it was principally of wood; an unsightly object, painted red." He adds that the stage was as large as that of London's Haymarket Theatre. The house was opened with *The Beaux Stratagem* and was naturally given over primarily to plays imported from England. Nevertheless, it was here that two historically important American plays had their premieres: Royall *Tyler's *The *Contrast* (1787) and Dunlap's *The *Father; or, American Shandyism* (1789). During the Revolutionary War the playhouse was known as the Theatre Royal but reverted to its original name after the end of hostilities. It then housed the *American Company, first under Lewis *Hallam and John *Henry, and later under John *Hodgkinson.

JOHNNY BELINDA (1940), a drama by Elmer Harris. [*Belasco Theatre, 321 perf.] Belinda McDonald (Helen Craig) is a deaf mute held in contempt by her harsh father and her insensitive neighbors. When Dr. Jack Davidson (Horace McNally) arrives in her Prince Edward Island village, he takes an instant liking to her, so sets about to teach her sign language. He slowly falls in love with her, even though she is pregnant with the child of a village ruffian, Locky McCormick (Willard Parker). After the child is born, McCormick attempts to take it from her so Belinda kills him. Davidson defends her at the trial; and when she is acquitted, Belinda agrees to marry the doctor. Most critics found the

play overwrought and even offensive, John Mason *Brown of the *Post* branding it "barely passable" and Richard *Watts Jr. in the *Herald Tribune* dismissing it as "just trash." Yet the play quickly found a loyal public. **Elmer Blaney HARRIS** (1878–1966) was a Chicago-born playwright whose first produced play was *Sham* (1909). Apart from *Johnny Belinda,* his major successes were his collaboration with Oliver *Morosco on the libretto for *So Long Letty* (1916) and his comedy *Young Sinners* (1929).

JOHNNY JOHNSON (1936), a play with music by Paul *Green (book, lyrics), Kurt *Weill (music). [44th Street Theatre, 68 perf.] While Johnny Johnson (Russell Collins) is a quiet, dedicated pacifist, he eventually finds himself fighting in World War I, where he is wounded. As an act of protest, he sprays the Allied High Command with laughing gas. The act lands him in a mental institution, where he and his fellow inmates pretend they are great statesmen and establish a League of World Republics. When he is released, Johnny returns home to peddle nonmartial toys in his war-happy village. *Notable songs*: Johnny's Song; Song of the Guns; Democracy March. Called by Stanley *Green a "daring fusion of music and satiric fantasy," the *Group Theatre production mirrored the widespread pacifist feelings of the 1930s. Weill's first American musical, it was a failure but enjoyed frequent revivals away from Broadway and remained a regular attraction in Iron Curtain countries.

JOHNSON, Albert [Richard] (1910–67), scenic designer. He was born in La Crosse, Wisconsin, and began his theatrical career painting scenery for the Farmingdale Opera House on Long Island. After studying briefly with Norman *Bel Geddes, Johnson was hired at the age of nineteen to create the sets of *The *Criminal Code* (1929). His designs were praised for their realism, but he insisted he had not gone near a jail and that he would not work "from real life." Johnson is credited with perfecting the use of revolving stages, which he employed to stunning effect in *The *Band Wagon* (1931). His designs were also seen in *Three's a Crowd* (1930), *Face the Music* (1932), **As Thousands Cheer* (1933), *Let 'Em Eat Cake* (1933), **Ziegfeld Follies of 1934, Life Begins at 8:40* (1934), *The Great Waltz* (1934), **Jumbo* (1935), **Leave It to Me!* (1938), *The *Skin of Our Teeth* (1942), and the 1956 revival of *Show Boat.*

JOHNSON, J[ohn] **Rosamond** (1873–1954), and **James Weldon JOHNSON** (1871–1938), songwriting team. The brothers, born in Jacksonville, Florida, and educated at Atlanta University and Columbia, were pioneers scoring African-American musicals. At the turn of the century, working with Bob *Cole, they began interpolating what were then called "coon songs" into Broadway musicals. Best remembered of their lyrics was that for "Under the Bamboo Tree," although they were not given proper credit on the published sheet music. Attempting to get away from this stereotype, they later wrote several highly thought of, if commercially disappointing, musicals, including *The Shoo-Fly Regiment* (1907) and *The Red Moon* (1909). Music publisher Edward B. Marks later recalled, "The Johnson brothers were emphatically new Negro. Their father was a minister—and they combined a clerical dignity, university culture, and an enormous amount of talent.... They wrote songs sometimes romantic, sometimes whimsical, but they eschewed the squalor and squabbles, the razors, wenches and chickens of the first ragtime." James left the theatre to pursue a career as a diplomat, poet, and essayist. J. Rosamond remained in the theatre and continued to provide music for all-black shows into the 1930s. Because these shows rarely had long runs, he was also forced to serve as musical director for his own and other shows and to act in others' musicals, including, *Porgy and Bess* (1935), *Mamba's Daughters* (1939), and *Cabin in the Sky* (1940).

JOHNSON, Laurence E. See *It's a Wise Child*.

JOLSON, Al [né Asa Yoelson] (1886–1950), singer and actor. Born in Srednike in what is now Lithuania, he was brought to America when still a youngster and settled in Washington, D.C., where his father was a cantor. In 1897 he ran away from home to join Rich and Hoppe's Big Company of Fun Makers, then worked in a circus and later as a super in the Washington tryout of *Children of the Ghetto* (1899), until his father forced him to return home. Within a few months he was back onstage, in vaudeville. For the next eleven years Jolson moved back and forth between two-a-day, burlesque, and minstrelsy. He signed with the *Shuberts in 1911 and appeared in *La Belle Paree* when it opened the Shuberts' new flagship, the *Winter Garden. He performed in blackface, with an exuberance and warmth that quickly made him the most popular box-office attraction in New York. As one critic was later to write, "He sang with his old-time knee-slapping, breast-beating, eye-rolling ardor, sang with a faith that moved mountains and audiences." Major assignments followed in *Vera Violetta* (1911), *The Whirl of Society* (1912), *The Honeymoon Express* (1913), *Dancing Around* (1914), *Robinson Crusoe, Jr.* (1916), *Sinbad* (1918), *Bombo* (1921), and *Big Boy* (1925). Among the many songs Jolson introduced in these shows, and with which he was afterward identified, were "April Show-

ers," "Avalon," "California, Here I Come," "My Mammy," and "Rockabye Your Baby with a Dixie Melody." In many of his early vehicles he reputedly often dismissed the cast and spent much of the evening singing to audiences from directly in front of the footlights or on ramps leading out into the house. His most famous pose was down on one knee, arms outstretched. By 1925 his popularity had begun to slip slightly, so he went to Hollywood, where he starred in the first "talkie," *The *Jazz Singer*, and for a few years was a major film star. He returned to Broadway only twice, in *The Wonder Bar* (1931) and *Hold on to Your Hats* (1940), which he co-produced. In neither show did he play the blackface clown that made him famous. No longer a star of stage or screen, Jolson still remained a popular recording artist until he died. Biography: *Jolson: The Legend Comes to Life*, Herbert G. Goldman, 1988.

JONES and SCHMIDT, songwriting team. Librettist-lyricist Tom Jones (b. 1928) was born in Littlefield, Texas, the son of a turkey farmer, and attended the University of Texas where he majored in theatre and met composer Harvey [Lester] Schmidt (b. 1929), an art student from Dallas. The two collaborated on student shows and, after Jones served in the army, reteamed to write songs for Off-Broadway revues. Their one-act musical version of *Les Romanesques* became The *Fantasticks (1960), the longest-running American musical on record. The team's Broadway shows are *110 in the Shade* (1963), *I Do! I Do!* (1966), and *Celebration* (1969). In the 1970s, Jones and Schmidt returned to Off Broadway where they presented a series of small, experimental works at the Portofino Theatre Workshop, most memorably *Philemon* (1975). Other works have been seen regionally, and in 1997 the duo appeared in a popular Off-Broadway retrospective revue called *The Show Goes On*.

JONES, Cherry (b. 1956), actress. One of the brightest new acting talents to come out of the last decade of the 20th century, Jones is a striking leading lady with a wide smile that camouflages complex and fascinating characters. She was born in Paris, Tennessee, and was educated at Carnegie Mellon University before getting experience in regional theatre. Although praised for some of her early Off-Broadway efforts, she gained wide attention with her 1991 Broadway debut as the condemned prisoner-actress Liz in *Our Country's Good* (1991) and gave a luminous portrayal of the reclusive Catherine Sloper in The *Heiress* (1995). Jones's other exceptional performances include the spinster artist Hannah Jelkes in The *Night of the Iguana* (1996), the champion swimmer Mabel seen at different ages in *Pride's Crossing* (1997), a small but hardened Josie Hogan in *A *Moon for the Misbegotten* (2000), the idealistic *Major Barbara* (2001), and the bitchy writer Mary McCarthy in *Imaginary Friends* (2002). Clive *Barnes in the *New York Post* described Jones's Catherine Sloper as "radiant in hope, tragic in despair, chilling in conviction, [she] resonates with passions that seem all the more vibrant for being suppressed."

JONES, George. See Count Joannes.

JONES, Henry Arthur (1851–1929), playwright. Along with *Pinero and *Shaw, a leading English dramatist of his day, he was an advocate of the tautly constructed problem play. Jones made his reputation in America as in England with his collaboration with Henry Herman, *The Silver King* (1883). On his own he later wrote such notable successes as *The Middleman* (1890), *The Dancing Girl* (1891), *The Bauble Shop* (1894), *The Masqueraders* (1894), *The Case of Rebellious Susan* (1894), *The Rogue's Comedy* (1896), *The Liars* (1898), and *Mrs. Dane's Defense* (1900). Although Jones's gift for comic aphorisms was inferior to *Wilde's and his characters rarely as fascinating as Pinero's, his best works remain interesting period pieces.

JONES, James Earl (b. 1931), actor. The Mississippi-born African American studied at the University of Michigan and with Lee *Strasberg before making his Broadway debut in *Sunrise at Campobello (1958). He began to call himself to playgoers' attention when he essayed a number of roles for the *New York Shakespeare Festival, including Caliban, MacDuff, and Othello. His performance as Jack Jefferson, the despised black boxer, in *The *Great White Hope* (1968), won him wide recognition. Clive *Barnes in the *Times* wrote, "Jones pounded into the role, spitting and shouting . . . he roared with pain and when he even chuckled it seemed like thunder." However, important roles for black actors continued to be hard to come by, so for many seasons he performed *Off Broadway, usually with the same New York Shakespeare Festival. In 1973 he played Hickey in *The *Iceman Cometh*, King Lear, and *Paul Robeson*, and the following year was Lenny in *Of Mice and Men. Jones won further laurels in 1982 when he played Othello on Broadway to Christopher *Plummer's Iago, then served as a replacement in *Master Harold and the Boys*. One of his greatest triumphs was as the ex-baseball player Troy in *Fences (1987). The popular film actor is celebrated for his deep, rich bass voice and strong physical presence.

JONES, Joseph Stevens (1809–77), playwright, actor, and manager. The "indefatigable Dr. Jones" was one of the most prolific of American drama-tists. Estimates of his output range from a low of 60 plays to a high of more than 150. He was born in Boston, and after making his acting debut in 1827 in Providence as Crack in *The Turnpike Gate*, returned to Boston where, for the next ten years, he acted regularly at one or another Boston playhouse. His first successful play, *The Liberty Tree; or, Boston Boys in '76*, was premiered in 1832, with the author in the part of "Yankee" Bill Ball. The next year his *The Green Mountain Boy* gave G. H. *Hill one of his most famous roles, the outspoken servant Jedediah Homebred. In 1839 Jones assumed management of the Tremont Theatre and at the same time wrote one of his popular trial dramas, *The *People's Lawyer* (later better known as *Solon Shingle*). But Jones also wrote many romantic melodramas "of a wild and strenuous type," such as *The Usurper; or, Americans in Tripoli* (1835?), *The Surgeon of Paris; or, The Massacre of the Huguenots* (1838), and *The Carpenter of Rouen; or, The Massacre of St. Bartholomew* (1840). Jones's letters suggest he was bitter about the chances of making a proper living in the theatre. When the Tremont was forced to close in 1843, he withdrew from the profession, returning only on occasion. His withdrawal was assisted by Harvard's making him a Doctor of Medicine that same year. Thereafter he practiced medicine and lectured on anatomy and physiology. On one of his rare returns in 1852 he wrote the successful *The *Silver Spoon*. Jones's last play was *Paul Revere and the Sons of Liberty* (1875).

JONES, LeRoi. See Baraka, Amiri.

JONES, Margo (1913–55), manager and director. Born in Livingston, Texas, she attended Texas State College for Women then worked at the *Pasadena Playhouse and other community theatres, until she was hired to be assistant director of the *Federal Theatre Project in Houston. Jones remained in Houston, producing plays for that city's recreation department and first employed the arena-style stage so long identified with her. In 1944 Jones applied to the Rockefeller Foundation for a grant to open an arena theatre for professional repertory in Dallas, resulting in an auditorium that opened in 1947 as Theatre '47, a name that was updated yearly. Among the plays first presented at her house were William *Inge's *Farther Off from Heaven* (later rewritten as *The *Dark at the Top of the Stairs*), *Summer and Smoke, and *Inherit the Wind. Even more important than the new talents she encouraged was her theatre's influence in spreading the vogue for arena-style staging, her ideas expressed in her 1951 book *Theatre-in-the-Round*. Her theatre closed in 1959, four years after her all-too-early death. Jones was also a respected director who staged plays in New York, most memorably her co-direction of the original The *Glass Menagerie (1945) and of Ingrid Bergman in Joan of Lorraine (1946). In 1961 Jerome *Lawrence and Robert E. *Lee established the Margo Jones Award, given each year "to the producing manager of an American or Canadian theatre whose policy of presenting new dramatic works continues most faithfully in the tradition of Margo Jones." Biography: Margo: The Life and Theatre of Margo Jones, Helen Sheehy, 1989.

JONES, Robert Edmond (1887–1954), designer. One of the most influential figures in 20th-century American theatre, the New Hampshire–born designer, producer, director, and lecturer was educated at Harvard. He began designing sets in 1911, but it was his work for The Man Who Married a Dumb Wife (1915) that is said to have "sounded the note that began the American revolution in stage scenery." Jones rebelled against the various forms of realism that dominated set design at the time, in particular the meticulously painted flats in general use or the careful reconstructions of David *Belasco. "The artist," he was later to write, "should omit details, the prose of nature, and give only the spirit and the splendor." Not all his sets were so strikingly poetic, but after his death John Mason *Brown was to remember "The Renaissance glories of his backgrounds for The Jest; the ominous outline of the Tower of London which dominated his Richard III; the great arch at the top of the long flight of steps in John Barrymore's Hamlet; the brooding austerity of his New England farm house in Desire Under the Elms; the background of mirrors, as bright as Congreve's wit, in Love for Love . . . the bold bursts of Chinese Red in Lute Song; or the George Bellows-like depths and shadows of his barroom for The Iceman Cometh." In 1925 he joined forces with Kenneth *MacGowan and Eugene *O'Neill to produce O'Neill's and other fine plays at the Greenwich Village Playhouse. Among the productions he directed were *Gilbert and *Sullivan's Patience (1924), and O'Neill's The Fountain (1925) and The *Great God Brown (1926). Most critics felt his direction was less innovative than his design work. With MacGowan he wrote Continental Stagecraft (1922). Biography: The Theatre of Robert Edmond Jones, Ralph Rendelton, ed., 1959.

JONES, Tom. See Jones and Schmidt.

JUBA. See Lane, William Henry.

JUBILEE (1935), a musical comedy by Moss *Hart (book), Cole *Porter (music, lyrics). [*Imperial Theatre, 169 perf.] As the anniversary of the coronation approaches, the King (Melville Cooper) and the Queen (Mary *Boland) admit they have become jaded with their luxurious but constrained life. Prince James (Charles Walter) and Princess Diana (Margaret Adams) agree. When a royal nephew leads an insurrection, the royal family rushes into seclusion and emerges incognito. The Queen flirts with a movie star, the Princess has a brief romance with a writer, the Prince takes a celebrated dancer out for a night on the town, and the King is happy to remain home, playing his beloved parlor games. Inevitably they are recognized, so when the insurrection dies aborning, the royal family returns to its comfortable, restricted world. Notable songs: Begin the Beguine; Just One of Those Things; Why Shouldn't I?; A Picture of Me Without You. The musical, suggested by the Silver Jubilee of the English royal family, was written while Hart and Porter were on a world cruise together. Sam H. *Harris and Max *Gordon presented the show on Broadway, and the critics, as they so often did on first hearing, insisted Porter's score was not up to snuff. Time proved them wrong.

JUDAH, Mrs. [née Marietta Starfield] (1812?–83), actress. Hailed as "San Francisco's Favorite Actress" and eventually as the "Grand Old Woman of the Western Stage," she was born in New York State and was married at an early age to actor Emmanuel Judah. They traveled together throughout the South until Judah was drowned in a shipwreck while sailing between Florida and Cuba in 1839. She made her New York debut a year later, then in 1851 she remarried (but continued to perform as Mrs. Judah) and relocated to San Francisco at the behest of Thomas *Maguire. The small, stocky, square-faced, and stern-visaged actress remained an important artist there for a quarter century. She was praised for a wide range of interpretations from shrews in contemporary comedies to Lady Macbeth, but her most famous role was the Nurse in Romeo and Juliet, which she first performed in 1855 and beside which, according to reliable critics, many a celebrated Juliet paled. Although Judah retired in 1878, she continued to play at benefits and similar special occasions until just before her death.

JUDAH, Samuel B[enjamin] **H**[elbert] (1804–76), playwright. Shortly after graduating from college in his native New York he wrote his first play, The Mountain Torrent (1820), followed by the revenge melodrama, The Rose of Arragon (1822). After the premiere of his historical comedy, A Tale of Lexington (1922), he devoted the rest of his life to practicing law. Although most scholars condemn Judah's writing as absurdly stilted and his dramatic scenes as minimal, the plays were not unpopular in their day.

JUJAMCYN THEATRES. Founded in 1956 by Virginia and James Binger, and named for their children Judy, James, and Cynthia, the organization became a major force on Broadway in the last quarter of the 20th century. Jujamcyn operates the Al *Hirschfeld, Eugene *O'Neill, *St. James, *Virginia, and *Walter Kerr Theatres. It actively encourages productions and has selected so intelligently that its record of housing hits is outstanding. Rocco *Landesman, the company's president, is credited with much of this success.

JULIA, Raul (1940–94), actor. Julia was a robust, masculine leading man in musicals and plays who exuded a sensuous, dangerous quality even in his comic roles. He was born in San Juan, Puerto Rico, and educated at the University of Puerto Rico before studying acting in New York. Julia made his Manhattan debut in 1964 in a Spanish-language production Off Broadway, then two years later he toured the city boroughs with the *New York Shakespeare's Festival's mobile unit, the beginning of his long and fruitful association with that organization. He first found wide recognition as Proteus in the Central Park musical version of *Two Gentlemen of Verona (1971), a role he recreated on Broadway. Julia's other significant performances include a devastating Edmund to James Earl *Jones's *King Lear (1973); a daffy, smirking Charley Wickham in *Where's Charley? (1974); a dangerously cold Mack the Knife in The *Threepenny Opera (1977); a rich, fulsome *Othello (1979); the womanizing film director Guido Contini in *Nine (1982); and the double role of Cervantes and Don Quixote in *Man of La Mancha (1992).

JULIUS CAESAR. By far the most popular of Shakespeare's Roman histories, the work is believed to have been first performed in America in Charleston, South Carolina, in 1774. Most of the great 19th-century tragedians appeared in it. Thomas Abthorpe *Cooper long held a virtual monopoly on the role of Antony, although late in his career he was forced to portray Cassius while ceding the role of Antony to Edwin *Forrest, who did not make a particular success of it. For decades the drama was a standby at the *Bowery Theatre. The work also holds the dubious distinction of being the last play in which John Wilkes *Booth appeared in New York, when he acted Antony in 1864 to Edwin *Booth's Brutus and Junius Brutus *Booth Jr.'s Cassius. The most memorable modern production was Orson *Welles's modern-dress version for the *Mercury Theatre, staged in 1937 with antifascist slanting. It remains popular with collegiate and festival theatres, though it has rarely been seen in New York since the Welles production.

JUMBO (1935), a musical comedy by Ben *Hecht, Charles *MacArthur (book), Richard *Rodgers (music), Lorenz *Hart (lyrics). [*Hippodrome, 233 perf.] Two feuding circus magnates, Matthew Mulligan (W. J. McCarthy) and John A. Considine (Arthur Sinclair), are dismayed to learn that their children, Matt Jr. (Donald Novis) and Mickey Considine (Gloria Grafton), have fallen in love. Considine's drinking and his imminent bankruptcy compound his problems. The money difficulties are solved when his unorthodox press agent, Claudius B. Bowers (Jimmy *Durante), burns down Considine's house, allowing him to collect the insurance. And when the youngsters bring about a reconciliation between the two older men, Considine promises to put the bottle on the shelf. *Notable songs*: Little Girl Blue; The Most Beautiful Girl in the World; My Romance. The Billy *Rose show marked Rodgers and Hart's return from a four-year stay in Hollywood. It was also the last legitimate production to play the famed Hippodrome, which Rose reconstructed to make it resemble a circus arena. Gilbert Gabriel of the *American* found the entertainment "chockful of so many thrills, musical, scenic, gymnastic and humanitarian, it deserves an endowment as an institution."

JUNE MOON (1929), a comedy by Ring *Lardner and George S. *Kaufman. [*Broadhurst Theatre, 273 perf.] Fred M. Stevens (Norman Foster) gives up his job as a shipping clerk in Schenectady to try his luck as a Tin Pan Alley lyricist. He hits it big when Paul Sears (Frank Otto), who has been living off the meager royalties of his song hit "Paprika," puts music to Fred's lyric for "June Moon." Success goes to Fred's head, and he abandons his old sweetheart, Edna Baker (Linda Watkins), in favor of the beautiful, but vicious and rapacious Eileen (Lee Patrick), Paul's sister-in-law. But just as Fred is about to leave for Europe with Eileen, his eyes are opened up by the caustic pianist, Maxie (Harry Rosenthal). Fred asks Maxie if the steamship line would mind his changing wives. Maxie assures him there will be no problem, "If you don't do it in midstream." Robert Littell of the *World* called the Sam H. *Harris–produced comedy "a lively show that gave Tin Pan Alley . . . a rich and merciless kidding." Lardner later described the writing of the play in his "Second-Act Curtain." A successful Off-Broadway revival in 1998 proved the comedy's stageworthiness.

JUNIOR MISS (1941), a comedy by Jerome *Chodorov and Joseph *Fields. [*Lyceum Theatre, 710 perf.] Thirteen-year-old Judy Graves (Patricia Peardon) has seen too many movies and believed them all. Being an overimaginative child, she convinces herself that her father (Phillip Ober) is having an affair with his boss's daughter, Ellen (Francesca Bruning), and that her Uncle Willis (Alexander Kirkland) is a reformed criminal. To set matters right, she and her friend, Fuffy Adams (Lenore Lonergan), determine to mate Willis with Ellen. None of this sits well with Ellen's father, J. B. Curtis (Matt Briggs), for with every move, Judy and Fuffy seem to make matters worse. Things return to normal only when Judy finds herself about to have her first date. She is now a young lady, a junior miss, with her own problems to work on. Greeted by Brooks *Atkinson as "a harumscarum antic and a darlin' play," the Max *Gordon production was one of the first shows, at a time when the draft was taking many men and women were employed in the war effort, to use younger female talents as principals and older performers in support. The comedy was based on short stories by Sally Benson, which had appeared in *The New Yorker*.

K

KAHN, Madeline (1942–99), actress and singer. The bold, offbeat comedienne had dozens of different voices, all of them funny. She was born in Boston and educated at Hofstra University to teach speech therapy while she also prepared for an opera career. Kahn made her New York debut in 1965 and appeared in several Off-Broadway revues where she honed her comic talents. She got to show off her operatic skills in the musicals *Two by Two* (1970) and *On the Twentieth Century* (1978), but Kahn's finest performances were in comedy-dramas, such as her not-so-dumb blonde Billie Dawn in *Born Yesterday* (1989) and her outspoken radio hostess Gorgeous in *The *Sisters Rosensweig* (1992).

KALISH [also transliterated Kalisch or Kalich], **Bertha** (1874–1939), actress. Born in Galicia, when it was part of the Austro-Hungarian Empire, she studied at the Lemberg Conservatory and appeared in Yiddish productions before moving to Romania to become a leading lady in the Bucharest National Theatre. Anti-Semitic prejudices prompted her to sail for New York where she soon began to demonstrate her skill as a tragedienne and comedienne, appearing in Yiddish versions of *A Doll's House, Fedora, Madame Sans-Gêne,* and other contemporary plays. Her performance in *The Kreutzer Sonata* (1902) brought many major Manhattan critics to the Lower East Side to witness and praise her abilities. It was her greatest role, and after she perfected her English she played it on Broadway in 1906. Among Kalish's other English-speaking assignments were *Fedora* (1905), *Monna Vanna* (1905), *Sappho and Phaon* (1907), *Marta of the Lowlands* (1908), *The Unbroken Road* (1909), and *The Witch* (1910). After she played in *The Riddle: Woman* (1918), failing eyesight forced her to act less frequently, though she did make occasional appearances as late as 1924, when she revived *The Kreutzer Sonata* in 1926, when she portrayed the title role in *Magda,* and finally in 1935 when she revived *Sappho.* Kalish was described as "a woman of classic beauty with a magnificent voice."

KALMAN, Emmerich (1882–1953), composer. The Hungarian-born creator of *Viennese operettas found Americans cool to his first imported work, *The Gay Hussars* (1909). However, his lovely collection of waltzes for *Sari* (1914) turned the tide. His up-and-down career in America included *Miss Springtime* (1916), *Her Soldier Boy* (1916), *The Riviera Girl* (1917), *The Yankee Princess* (1922), *Countess Maritza* (1926), *The Circus Princess* (1927), *Golden Dawn* (1927), and *Marinka* (1945). Yet despite his failures (and while *Lehar's The *Merry Widow* was a far bigger hit than any of his works) on the whole Kalman was probably the most successful of all 20th-century Viennese composers on American stages.

KALMAR and RUBY, songwriting team. Lyricist-librettist Bert Kalmar (1884–1947) began his career as a child magician in tent shows and later appeared in vaudeville. In 1923 he teamed with New York–born composer Harry Ruby [né Rubinstein] (1895–1974), who began his career as a vaudeville pianist. The team created the songs for *Helen of Troy, New York* (1923), followed by such hits as *The Ramblers* (1926), *The Five O'Clock Girl* (1927), *Good Boy* (1928), and the *Marx Brothers vehicle *Animal Crackers* (1928). After a brief Hollywood career in the 1930s, they were last represented on Broadway by *High Kickers* (1941). Among the many memorable Kalmar and Ruby songs are "All Alone Monday," "Thinking of You," "I Wanna Be Loved by You," and "Hooray for Captain Spaulding."

KANDER and EBB, songwriting team. Composer John [Harold] Kander (b. 1927) was born in Kansas City, Missouri, then studied at Oberlin College and Columbia prior to spending nine years in journeyman work at summer theatres and as an orchestrator. His first score was heard in *A Family Affair* (1962). That same year he was introduced to Fred Ebb (b. 1932), the New York–born lyricist and librettist who was educated at Columbia and first contributed lyrics to Broadway in the revue *From A to Z* (1960). Their debut as a team was with *Flora, the Red Menace* (1965) and a year later they enjoyed their first hit, *Cabaret* (1966). Subsequent musicals were *The *Happy Time* (1968); *Zorbá* (1968); *70, Girls, 70*

353

(1971); *Chicago (1975); The Act (1977); Woman of the Year (1981); The Rink (1984); *Kiss of the Spider Woman (1993), and Steel Pier (1997). The two Kander and Ebb shows that followed failed to make it to New York, but the team had simultaneous hits on Broadway for several years in the late 1990s–early 2000s when both Chicago and Cabaret revivals enjoyed long runs. Stanley *Green has written, "If, like their creators, [their] songs have escaped individual acclaim, they have nevertheless performed the demanding function of heightening the emotion and strengthening the texture of the varied dramatic works for which they were created." Autobiography (both): Colored Lights, 2003.

KANE, Helen [née Schroeder] (1904–66), singer and comedienne. Celebrated as the "Boop-Boop-a-Doop" Girl, the petite, moon-faced, baby-voiced New Yorker was one of the meteoric stars of the late 1920s. She appeared on Broadway in A Night in Spain (1927) and Good Boy (1928), introducing "I Wanna Be Loved by You" in the latter. For a brief time she was a headliner in vaudeville and appeared in early talkies. Her last Broadway role was in Shady Lady (1933).

KANE, Whitford (1881–1956), character actor. The flexible and reliable performer was born in Larne, Ireland, the son of a doctor, and studied at the Royal Academical Institution in Belfast where he first started acting. After touring Ireland, Kane made his London debut in 1910 and his Broadway bow two years later, remaining in America for most of his subsequent career of forty years. Kane could play comic bumpkins, such as Will Mossop in Hobson's Choice (1915), as well as tragic characters, like Judas Iscariot in Dust of the Road (1915). As he aged he created vivid characterizations in important supporting roles and late in life he was very effective as elderly Shakespearean characters. Autobiography: Are We All Met?, 1931.

KANIN, Garson (1912–99), playwright and director. The Rochester, New York, native began his career as an actor, playing a small part in Little Ol' Boy (1933). For several years he served as assistant director to George *Abbott before accepting directorial chores for Hitch Your Wagon (1937). After serving in World War II he achieved success both as director and playwright with his *Born Yesterday (1946), then later that same year he directed *Years Ago, a play by his wife, Ruth *Gordon. Kanin later wrote and directed three interesting but unsuccessful plays: The Smile of the World (1949), The Rat Race (1949), and The Live Wire (1950). Subsequent directorial assignments included The *Diary of Anne Frank (1955), A Hole in the Head (1957), and the musicals Do Re Mi (1960) and

*Funny Girl (1964). He was also active in television and films, sometimes working in collaboration with his wife.

KAPP, Jack (1901–49), record producer. The Chicago-born record company executive was president of Decca Records from 1934 until his death. It was in this capacity that he produced the original cast recording of *Oklahoma! in 1943. The album was so successful that it sparked a parade of similar recordings of other shows. Oddly, the English had been producing original cast recordings since the turn of the century, but Americans had not. One quirky result was that the only large-scale cast recordings of American shows before 1943 were recordings made with their London casts.

KARNILOVA, Maria [neé Maria Karnilovich Dovgolenko] (1920–2001), character actress. A sharp-voiced, lively performer mostly in musicals, she worked her way up to star billing by the peak of her Broadway career. She was born in Hartford, Connecticut, and trained for a career in ballet at the Metropolitan Opera School where she performed as a child. She was a featured dancer in several Broadway musicals before she was cast in the colorful role of stripper Tessie Tura in *Gypsy (1959). From that point on Karnilova played character parts, sometimes in the leading role. Her most notable performances were the Russian mother Golde in *Fiddler on the Roof (1964), the faded courtesan Hortense in Zorbá (1968), and the Parisian guardian Inez in Gigi (1973).

KASZNAR, Kurt [né Serwischer] (1913–79), character actor. Kasznar was a colorful comic performer with a deep, growly voice that never lost its Austrian flavor. He was born in Vienna and educated at Minerva University in Zurich before training for the stage with Max Reinhardt. Kasznar first came to America in 1937 as part of *Reinhardt's international tour. He stayed in New York where he wrote, produced, and acted in plays in the 1940s, then became a favorite supporting player in the 1950s and 1960s with such memorable performances as the crusty Uncle Louis in The *Happy Time (1950), the guilt-ridden Father in Six Characters in Search of an Author (1955), the pompous Pozzo in the first American production of *Waiting for Godot (1956), the Austrian impresario Max Detweiler in The *Sound of Music (1959), and the eccentric neighbor Victor Velasco in *Barefoot in the Park (1963).

KATINKA (1915), an operetta by Otto *Harbach (book, lyrics), Rudolf *Friml (music). [44th Street Theatre, 220 perf.] Katinka (May Naudain) loves Ivan Dimitri (Samuel Ash), so when she is forced to marry Boris Strogoff (Count Lorrie Grimaldi), she runs away and hides in a harem. But matters are resolved when it is learned that Boris is already married to another woman. *Notable songs*: Allah's Holiday; Rackety Coo; 'Tis the End. Although this Arthur *Hammerstein–produced operetta competed for attention with the far more American and contemporary *Very Good Eddie* and *Stop! Look! Listen!*, which opened the same week, it held its own for public esteem.

KAUFMAN, George S[imon] (1889–1961), playwright and director. He was born in Pittsburgh and served on the staffs of newspapers in Washington, D.C., and New York before joining with Marc *Connelly to write his first successful play, the comedy *Dulcy* (1921). The collaboration continued for three more years and resulted in seven additional offerings, most memorably *To the Ladies* (1922), *Merton of the Movies* (1922), and *Beggar on Horseback* (1924). Throughout his career, Kaufman was known as the "Great Collaborator" because all of his works (with the exception of the 1925 solo effort The *Butter and Egg Man*) were written with others. With Edna *Ferber, he penned *Minick* (1924), The *Royal Family* (1927), *Dinner at Eight* (1932), and *Stage Door* (1936). With Morrie *Ryskind he wrote the musical librettos for *Animal Crackers* (1928), *Strike Up the Band* (1930), *Of Thee I Sing* (1931), and *Let 'Em Eat Cake* (1933). But it was with Moss *Hart that Kaufman wrote his most interesting (and often successful) shows: *Once in a Lifetime* (1930), *Merrily We Roll Along* (1934), *You Can't Take It with You* (1936), *I'd Rather Be Right* (1937), The *Man Who Came to Dinner* (1939), *George Washington Slept Here* (1940), and others. Other works with other collaborators included The *Cocoanuts* (1925), *June Moon* (1929), The *Band Wagon* (1931), The *Late George Apley* (1944), The *Solid Gold Cadillac* (1953), and *Silk Stockings* (1955). Kaufman was also a much-sought-after director. Besides staging many of his own plays, he directed such hits as The *Front Page* (1928), *My Sister Eileen* (1940), and *Guys and Dolls* (1950). To the public, Kaufman was a master of the barbed riposte, but his professional associates also admired his ability as a play doctor and his impeccable sense of timing. Biography: *George S. Kaufman: His Life, His Theatre*, Malcolm Goldstein, 1979.

KAUFMAN, Stanley (b. 1916), drama critic and author. The erudite reviewer of both film and stage was known for his analytical commentary that usually considered theatre in relationship to the other arts and the social-political situation. A native New Yorker, Kaufman was educated at NYU and first gained recognition for his criticism in the *New Republic*. He later wrote for the *New York Times* and the *Saturday Review*, as well as writing several books on drama. Autobiography: *Albums of Early Life*, 1980.

KAUSER, Alice (1872–1945), agent. Born in Budapest, where her father was the American consul, she received most of her schooling on the Continent. Her mother was the celebrated opera singer Berta Gester, who introduced her to many theatrical figures. These connections served her handsomely when she became a play broker in the late 1890s. Klauser helped get several *Sardou plays produced here and was one of the first to take up cudgels for *Ibsen. She also fought to achieve recognition for such American clients as Edward *Sheldon and Langdon *Mitchell, proving instrumental in the production of such plays as *Salvation Nell* and The *New York Idea*. Among her other clients were Channing *Pollock and Edward Childs *Carpenter.

KAY, Hershy (1919–81), orchestrator and composer. Although better known as a composer of light concert pieces and of the music for such modern ballets as *Stars and Stripes*, the Philadelphia native was also an important orchestrator of Broadway musicals. He was a classmate of Leonard *Bernstein at the Curtis Institute of Music, and his first major Broadway assignment was Bernstein's *On the Town* (1944). Kay's notably breezy arrangements were later heard in such shows as The *Golden Apple* (1954), *Candide* (1956), *Milk and Honey* (1961), A *Chorus Line* (1975), *On the Twentieth Century* (1977), and *Evita* (1980).

KAYE, Danny [né David Daniel Kominsky] (1913–87), comic actor. The slim, supple, Brooklyn-born comedian worked in vaudeville and at summer camps before making his Broadway debut in *The Straw Hat Revue* (1939). He called attention to himself as the effeminate Russell Paxton in *Lady in the Dark* (1941), in which he sang the tongue-twisting "Tschaikowsky." After appearing in *Let's Face It!* (1941), he left for Hollywood and, except for appearances in vaudeville at the *Palace and at the *Ziegfeld, did not return to New York until he starred in the musical *Two by Two* (1970), in which he clowned as the Biblical Noah. Biography: *Nobody's Fool: The Lives of Danny Kaye*, Martin Gottfried, 1994.

KAYE, Judy (b. 1948), actress and singer. The short, dark-haired, powerful-voiced performer was born in Phoenix, Arizona, and educated at UCLA and Arizona State before working in stock. Kaye made her Broadway debut in 1977 as a replacement for the role of Rizzo in *Grease then became famous the next year when she moved from a minor role to the leading lady in *On the Twentieth Century when Madeleine *Kahn suddenly left the musical. Her other notable Broadway appearances include the temperamental opera diva Carlotta in The *Phantom of the Opera (1987), the feisty labor organizer Babe Williams in The *Pajama Game (1989), the anarchist Emma Goldman in *Ragtime (1998), and the former pop singer Rosie in *Mamma Mia (2002).

KAYE, Stubby [né Bernard Kotzin] (1918–97), character actor. A native New Yorker who went into show business after winning a talent contest on the radio, Kaye was a short, rotund comic mostly remembered for originating two delightful musical comedy roles: bookie Nicely-Nicely Johnson in *Guys and Dolls (1950) and the spirited Marryin' Sam in *Li'l Abner (1956). His final Broadway performance was as the seedy burlesque comic Gus in the dark musical Grind (1985).

KAZAN, Elia (1909–2003), director and actor. Born in Istanbul but raised in America, he attended Williams College and did graduate work at Yale before joining the *Group Theatre as an apprentice. He appeared with the company as an actor in such plays as *Men in White (1933), *Waiting for Lefty (1935), *Johnny Johnson (1936), *Golden Boy (1937), and The *Gentle People (1939). Kazan's first major directorial assignment was Casey Jones (1938), but it was his freshly imaginative staging of The *Skin of Our Teeth (1942) that gave his career its major boost. Among his subsequent successes (some of which he co-produced) were *Harriet (1943), *One Touch of Venus (1943), *Deep Are the Roots (1945), *All My Sons (1947), A *Streetcar Named Desire (1947), *Death of a Salesman (1949), *Tea and Sympathy (1953), *Cat on a Hot Tin Roof (1955), The *Dark at the Top of the Stairs (1957), *J. B. (1958), *Sweet Bird of Youth (1959), and *After the Fall (1964). He staged this last play when he assumed the co-directorship (with Robert *Whitehead) of the Repertory Theatre of *Lincoln Center, but his tenure was not a success, so he withdrew from the theatre in general. Kazan was also a founding member of the *Actors Studio. As his list of credits suggests, he was the most important American director of the late 1940s and the 1950s, bringing a vitality and poetic intensity to virtually all his efforts. John Mason *Brown observed of his work on Streetcar, "He succeeds in combining stylization with realism. He is able to capture to the full the inner no less than the outer action of the text. He knows when to jab a climax, when to rely on mood, when to focus the attention pitilessly on the principals, or when to establish . . . the tenement atmosphere."

KEACH, Stacy (b. 1941), actor. The masculine, tough-faced leading man exudes an oddly delicate yet crude persona in performance that makes him ideal for antiheroes. He was born in Savannah, Georgia, the son of a drama coach and film producer, and as a child underwent four operations on his face, leaving him with his unusual look. Keach was educated at the University of California at Berkeley and at Yale before studying at the Royal Academy of Dramatic Art in London. He worked in various Shakespeare festivals before making his Manhattan debut in 1964 in a Central Park production of *Hamlet. Keach first gained attention in the Off-Broadway spoof Macbird! (1967) and soon was playing leading roles in *New York Shakespeare Festival classics. His other significant performances include Buffalo Bill in Indians (1969), alcoholic Jamie Tyrone in *Long Day's Journey Into Night (1971), and a variety of potent backwoods characters in The *Kentucky Cycle (1993).

KEAN, Charles. See Kean, Edmund.

KEAN, Edmund (1787?–1833), actor. The first great English performer to visit America while still at the height of his powers, he made his debut at the Anthony Street Theatre in 1820 as Richard III, the most popular Shakespearean role of his era. The Evening Post remarked, "We saw the most complete actor . . . that ever appeared on our boards," continuing, "Mr. Kean appears to be beneath the middle size . . . his features are good and his eye particularly expressive and commanding; his voice, in which he is most deficient, is, however, in its lower tones, sonorous, and he has the power of throwing it out so as to be heard at the extremity of the house." He followed his Richard with Othello, Shylock, Brutus (in *Payne's tragedy), Hamlet, Sir Giles Overreach, King Lear, and Macbeth. Kean performed for a percentage of the gross and for many nights received £125, far and away the highest figure yet paid to a performer in America. However, his tour ran into problems when he refused to appear before an uncrowded house in Boston later in the season. The brouhaha that ensued prompted him to leave the country. After he returned in 1825 less temperate journals revived the controversy, and when he attempted to appear again as Richard at the *Park Theatre a riot broke out. He soon mollified playgoers and acted across the country for the rest of the season and part of the next, but he never again revisited America. Biography: Edmund Kean: The Story of an Actor, W. J. Macqueen-Pope, 1960. His son **Charles** [John] **KEAN** (1811–68) had only begun his career as an actor when he made his American debut at the *Park Theatre in 1830 as Richard III, then continued by offering many of the same parts associated with his father. He later returned to America three times and, with his wife Ellen

*Tree, presented a repertory of standard classic favorites interspersed with such once popular contemporary works as *The *Hunchback* and *The Iron Chest*. James E. *Murdoch recalled, "Charles Kean was an imitator of his father's style of acting. But to the method which made the elder Kean famous the son added a grace and finish that gave repose and beauty to what would otherwise have been a mere copy. . . . Of all our tragedians of the analytic and passionate order, approaching the mechanical in execution, Charles Kean may be said to have been the most finished, and yet the most earnest." Biography: *The Life and Theatrical Times of Charles Kean*, John W. Cole, 1859.

KEAN, Thomas (fl. mid-18th century), actor and manager. Little is known about him, save that in 1749, with his partner Walter *Murray, he staged some Shakespearean and Restoration revivals as well as contemporary plays in Philadelphia, and a year later appeared in a similar repertory with what may have been the same troupe in New York. Among the plays were *The Beggar's Opera*, *Richard III*, *Cato*, and *Love for Love*. Kean's New York stay was marred by conflicts with authorities and apparently by religious opposition, by atrocious weather, and by accusations that he oversold his houses. Although this overselling may have been either accidental or a reflection of a certain lack of ethics, it also suggests that a definite demand for theatricals existed at the time. After New York, he headed a company of players in Virginia, then disappears from the record.

KEANE, Doris (1881–1945), actress. One of many performers remembered for a single role, this piquant beauty was born in Michigan and educated largely in Europe. She apparently also spent some time at the *American Academy of Dramatic Arts and with the school associated with the *Empire Theatre. Keane's first professional assignment was a small role in *Whitewashing Julia* (1903). She then rose rapidly to such leading roles as the neglected wife Joan Thornton in Clyde *Fitch's *The Happy Marriage* (1909), the loyal wife Bess Marks in *The Lights o' London* (1911), and the vulgar music-hall performer Mimi in the *The Affairs of Anatol* (1912). In 1913 she first appeared as Margherita Cavallini, the great opera star who forsakes her young clergyman lover rather than ruin his career, in Edward *Sheldon's *Romance*. Walter Prichard *Eaton wrote of her in this part, "Miss Keane . . . has dark, magnetic eyes, a curious mouth that is extremely mobile and can suggest either impish glee or profound sorrow very easily . . . and a general attractiveness of face and figure which arrests our attention. Having arrested our attention, we soon realize other features of her

personality, notably her humor, not without its capacity for a sarcastic edge, her sensitiveness to impressions, her alert mind. We sense her as rather an unusual person." She played Cavallini uninterruptedly in America and Europe for the next five years and returned to the role in regular revivals until the late 1920s. Although Keane afterward appeared as the heroine in several other plays, among them a 1919 revival of *Romeo and Juliet* and Eugene *O'Neill's failed *Welded* (1924), her only other success was as Catherine the Great in *Czarina* (1922), a European play especially revised for her by Sheldon.

KEARNS, Allen (1893–1956), actor and singer. A native of Ontario, he began his career as a chorus boy in musicals and with a vaudeville act. By the 1920s he was in demand as a leading man, appearing in such musicals as *Mercenary Mary* (1925), *Tip-Toes* (1925), *Funny Face* (1927), *Here's Howe* (1928), and *Girl Crazy* (1930). Kearns got to introduce such song favorites as "That Certain Feeling," " 'S Wonderful," and "Embraceable You."

KEENE, Laura (1826?–73), actress and manager. Her early history is obscure, even her birth year given as anywhere from 1820 to 1836, although her daughters insisted their mother was forty-seven at her death. Her real surname is given as Foss, Moss, or Lee. Similarly, the year and place of her professional debut are uncertain, though it is known she did at one time act with Madame Vestris. Keene came to America in 1852 and first appeared before New York audiences as Albina Mandeville in J. W. *Wallack's mounting of *The Will*, remaining with the company to become a popular favorite before leaving to assume management of a Baltimore theatre. When this failed she toured California and Australia before returning to New York in 1855 to open her own playhouse and quickly become Wallack's only serious rival. Although Keene staged some highly praised Shakespearean mountings, her company was best known for its contemporary works. Among her successes were *Camille*, *Jane Eyre*, and *Our American Cousin*. It was in these productions that Joseph *Jefferson and E. A. *Sothern rose to prominence. Her mounting of *Our American Cousin* established a long-run record at "a first class house," although *Uncle Tom's Cabin* and *The *Drunkard* had run longer at more popular theatres. The onset of the Civil War presented financial problems for her, which she met initially by offering elaborate musical spectacles. When these finally palled, she abandoned her theatre and took to the road. She was playing *Our American Cousin* at *Ford's Theatre in Washington when Lincoln was assassinated there. While she had no part in the assassination, her career never recovered from her association with the incident. Although a somewhat puffy-faced, heavy-featured woman, she was, Jefferson noted, "esteemed a great beauty in her youth; even afterwards her rich and luxuriant auburn hair, clear complexion and deep chestnut eyes, full of expression, were greatly praised; but to me it was her style and carriage that commanded admiration, and it was this quality that won her audience. She had, too, the rare power of varying her manner, assuming the rustic walk of a milkmaid or the dignified grace of a queen." Biography: *The Life of Laura Keene*, John Creahan, 1897.

KEENE, Thomas Wallace [né Eagelson or Eagleson] (1840–98), actor. A huge, florid performer long more popular in small towns than in New York or other major theatre centers, he spent his early career in such playhouses as the *Bowery, when it was turning to melodrama, and Wood's, under Edward *Eddy. There he learned the emotive, scene-chewing style of acting he was never fully to abandon. Although Keene played in support of such great actors as J. H. *Hackett and Edwin *Booth, he seems to have profited little from them. His *Richard III* was much admired in the backwaters, but his repertory consisted largely of tried-and-true melodramas, such as *Across the Continent*, *Drink (L'Assommoir)*, *The French Spy*, and *Ten Nights in a Barroom*.

KEISTER, George, (fl. 1900–25), architect. His New York houses include the Astor, *Belasco, Earl Carroll, George M. Cohan's, and Selwyn theatres.

KEITH, B[enjamin] F[ranklin] (1846–1914), manager. Born in Hillsboro, New Hampshire, he left his family farm to join a circus but by the early 1880s had moved into the realm of theatre management, taking over the Gaiety Musée in Boston in 1885. Keith claimed that a dream convinced him of the value of continuous vaudeville, which he initiated at the theatre. His policy's success was immediate, and he soon owned a series of theatres east of the Mississippi. At the turn of the century he enlarged his chain by merging with F. F. *Proctor, at the same time forming the *United Booking Office to control the hiring and firing of performers. At its height his organization controlled well over a hundred theatres, many of them named after him.

KELCEY, Herbert [né Lamb] (1856–1917), actor. The eldest son of a well-to-do English country family, he was intended for the army, but elected to become an actor instead and changed his name to avoid hurting his family. After two years on English stages, he came to America, where he made his debut with *Wallack's company in 1882. Kelcey subsequently acted with the *Madison Square Theatre company, then in 1887 became the leading man in Daniel *Frohman's *Lyceum Theatre ensemble, remaining there nine seasons. He left in 1896 to replace Maurice *Barrymore as Alan Kendrick in *The *Heart of Maryland*. The round-faced, heavy-lidded, but handsome actor became a star with his appearance as the dissipated Edward Fletcher in *The Moth and the Flame* (1898), followed by des Grieux in *Manon Lescaut* (1901), Richard Milbank in *The Daughters of Men* (1906), and William De Burgh Cockane in *Shaw's *Widowers' Houses* (1907). Whether because of age or because he failed to enlist the support of sufficient New York playgoers, much of his remaining career was spent performing major roles in touring companies of Broadway successes.

KELLERD, John E. (1863–1929), actor. The English leading man first came to America in 1883 to appear at the *Boston Museum, and subsequently played important roles in such New York productions as *Held by the Enemy* (1886), *Shenandoah* (1889), and *The *Heart of Maryland* (1895). Kellerd pioneered in presenting classical Greek drama professionally, but his place in American theatrical history came when he performed *Hamlet in New York for 102 consecutive showings in 1912, thus surpassing Edwin *Booth's old record.

KELLOGG, Marjorie Bradley (b. 1946), scenic designer. She was born in Cambridge, Massachusetts, and educated at Vassar College before serving as an assistant to Ming Cho *Lee. Kellogg specializes in unconventional spaces (she designed many sets for the *Circle in the Square) and using selective realism to create evocative locales. Her New York credits include *Death of a Salesman* (1976), *The *Best Little Whorehouse in Texas* (1978), *Da* (1979), *American Buffalo* (1983), *A Month of Sundays* (1987), and *Everybody's Ruby* (1999).

KELLY, George [Edward] (1887–1974), playwright. The Philadelphia-born dramatist entered the theatre when he was twenty-one, playing juvenile roles, then drifted into vaudeville where he performed in his own sketches. Kelly's first successful play was the satire *The *Torch-Bearers* (1922), followed by three popular works: the comedy *The *Show-Off* (1924), the penetrating character study *Craig's Wife* (1925), and the romantic *Daisy Mayme* (1926). After writing sketches for the revue *A la Carte* (1927), he produced a series of plays that could not find an audience: *Behold the Bridegroom* (1927), *Maggie the Magnificent* (1929), *Philip Goes Forth* (1931), *Reflected Glory* (1936), *The Deep Mrs. Sykes* (1945), and *The Fatal Weakness*

(1946). At his best Kelly was a superb technician, trenchant observer, and satirist of human folly. But a certain coldness and misanthropy eventually made his later plays unpalatable to most critics and theatregoers. His older brother **Walter C. KELLY** (1873– 1939) was a pudgy vaudeville comic who was famous for his hilarious courtroom sketch. Their other brother was John B. Kelly, the Olympic sculler, and they were uncles of Princess Grace of Monaco.

KELLY, Gregory (1891?–1927), actor. The boyish-looking performer from New York, whose promising career was cut short by his early death, performed in stock with his wife, Ruth *Gordon, then won rave notices as Willie Baxter, the puppy-lovelorn hero in *Seventeen (1918) and as Peter Jones, the yokel looking to strike it rich on Broadway, in The *Butter and Egg Man (1925).

KELLY, Paul (1899–1956), actor. Born in Brooklyn, the lean, sternly handsome leading man made his debut in 1907 in A *Grand Army Man, then spent time in stock before returning to Broadway as George Cooper in *Seventeen (1918) and Robert Williams in Penrod (1918). Kelly won praise for his performance as the jazzed-up husband John Allen in Up the Ladder (1922), then enjoyed long runs as crime solver Barry McGill in Whispering Wires (1922) and as the rejected lover Harry in Chains (1923). None of his subsequent roles in the 1920s and early 1930s were in successful plays, so he left for Hollywood in 1933. He is best remembered for two roles he played after he returned from films: the agonized Brigadier General K. C. Dennis in *Command Decision (1947) and the alcoholic actor Frank Elgin trying for a comeback in The *Country Girl (1950).

KEMBLE, Charles (1775–1854), actor. A member of a distinguished theatrical family in England, he paid only one two-year visit to America and that relatively late in his career. He made his debut in 1832 at the *Park Theatre as Hamlet and was warmly greeted, but was even more eagerly applauded for such later roles as Charles Surface and Benedick. Indeed, *Wemyss afterward looked back on him as "the best representative of high comedy belonging to the British stage." He was a rather boyishly handsome, curly-headed man, whose career in England had been overshadowed by those of his brother, John Philip, and sister, Mrs. Siddons, and whose American appearances were often distracted by adulation accorded his beautiful daughter, **Fanny** [Frances Anne] **KEMBLE** (1809–93). The great beauty came to America with her father and made her debut at the Park Theatre as Bianca in Fazio. She continued

by demonstrating her skill as Juliet, Portia, Belvidera, and as other classic heroines of the period's standard repertory. One of her most famous roles was Julia in The *Hunchback, a part she had created in England. She retired from the stage in 1834 following her marriage to Pierce Butler, later U. S. Senator from South Carolina. Out of this marriage came her diary of Southern life. After her divorce some years later she largely confined herself to offering formal readings, before returning permanently to England in 1868. Perhaps because she acted here so briefly and retired at the height of her powers, she was remembered with a special affection. T. Allston *Brown recalled, "She was full of the true, heavenly fire, with every other requisite of physical and intellectual endowment, but her representations were mere dash sketches, though with here and there a touch of the most masterly and overwhelming power." While she set a high standard for actresses, Charles Kemble was considered a model of an English gentleman and set an example for future American players. Biographies: Charles Kemble, Man of the Theatre, Jane Williamson, 1970; Fanny Kemble, J. H. Furnas, 1982.

KEMPER, Collin. See Wagenhals, Lincoln.

KEMPY (1922), a comedy by J. C. and Elliott Nugent. [Belmont Theatre, 212 perf.] James Kemp (Elliott *Nugent), who is known as "Kempy," is a somewhat naïve and pliable plumber who dreams of becoming an architect. Coming to fix a leaky pipe in the house of his fiancée, Ruth Bence (Ruth Nugent), he is confronted by Ruth's sister Katherine (Lotus Robb), who has just had a nasty fight with her boyfriend, "Duke" Merrill (Grant *Mitchell), and decides to get even by bamboozling Kempy into marrying her. But that night she makes him sleep alone on the living room couch. The next morning more sober thoughts win the day, so Duke, who is a lawyer, arranges to pair everyone happily. Written with an uncredited assist from Howard *Lindsay, the Richard G. *Herndon production was the comedy sleeper of the season and helped establish Elliott, whose family had heretofore been largely associated with vaudeville, as an important figure in the legitimate theatre.

KENDAL, Mr. and Mrs., acting team. Kendal [né William Hunter Grimston] (1843–1917) and his wife [née Margaret (Madge) Robertson] (1848–1935), one of the finest English acting couples, made their American debut in 1889 under Daniel *Frohman's aegis in *Sardou's A Scrap of Paper. The *Dramatic Mirror noted of Mrs. Kendal, "Her art is as fine as old point lace, and yet it is laid upon a temperament so genuinely sympathetic and so pliant and transitional that there is no sign of effort, no direct exhibition of method in anything she does"; while the *Times* called her husband's performance "deliberate, careful, good-humored, and unquestionably effective." Their repertory consisted entirely of contemporary plays. The Kendals made several highly successful visits to America over the next several seasons, although they ultimately antagonized more prudish players and critics, led by William *Winter, when they gave the first American mounting of the then shocking *Pinero play, *The Second Mrs. Tanqueray*, in 1893. Biography: *The Kendals*, T. Edgar Pemberton, 1900.

KENNEDY, [John] Arthur (1914–90), actor. A native of Worcester, Massachusetts, the light-haired, slightly boyish-looking leading man, who always conveyed an impression of intense dedication, made his debut in Maurice *Evans's 1937 revival of *King Richard II*. He won major recognition as the surviving son Chris Keller in *All My Sons* (1947), followed by such memorable performances as the troubled son Biff in *Death of a Salesman* (1949); John Proctor, who is caught up in the Salem witch hunts, in The *Crucible (1953); judge advocate Col. William Edwards in *Time Limit!* (1956); the hot-tempered father Patrick Flannigan in *The Loud Red Patrick* (1956); the successful brother Walter Franz in The *Price (1968); and the menacing Man in *Veronica's Room* (1973).

KENNEDY CENTER FOR THE PERFORMING ARTS (Washington, D.C.). In 1958 President Eisenhower signed P. L. 85-874, which provided land and authorized a private fund campaign to establish the National Cultural Center in Washington. Shortly thereafter Edward Durell Stone was selected to be the architect. Following the assassination of President Kennedy and just before the groundbreaking, President Johnson changed the center's name to the John F. Kennedy Center for the Performing Arts, making it the only Washington monument to the late president. The Center, housed in a single, imposing building, contains three major auditoriums: the 2,318-seat Opera House, the 1,142-seat Eisenhower Theatre, and a 2,750-seat Concert Hall. There are also three small houses, including the 512-seat Terrace Theatre and a 120-seat Theater Lab. The Opera House has been home to some large touring musicals, while the Terrace and Theater Lab have offered experimental productions. However, the principal legitimate activity has been in the Eisenhower. Under the chairmanship of Roger L. *Stevens, the theatre has offered a series of distinguished new plays and revivals, several of which, such as the 1983

production of *You Can't Take It with You*, have gone on to Broadway. While the theatre component of the Kennedy Center is mostly concerned with national and international touring groups, it has co-produced some Broadway musicals, such as *Titanic (1997) and the 2000 revival of The *Music Man, with the understanding that the productions play at the Center before or after the Broadway run. The most ambitious theatre project at the Kennedy Center in recent years was the summer-long festival of Stephen *Sondheim musicals in 2002, with a similar festival of Tennessee Williams works planned for 2004. These original productions at the Center point to a more active role in theatre producing in the future.

KENNEDY, Charles Rann. See *Servant in the House, The*.

KENNEDY, Madge (1892–1987), comic actress. The Chicago-born comedienne became a professional in 1910, then went on to give notable performances as Blanche Hawkins, who is pursued by a drunken tenor, in *Twin Beds (1914); Blanche Wheeler, the determinedly stay-at-home wife, in *Fair and Warmer (1915); the title role in the musical *Poppy* (1925); and Mary Hutton, who learns to live with infidelity, in *Paris Bound (1927).

KENTUCKIAN, THE. See *Lion of the West, The*.

KENTUCKY CYCLE, THE (1993), a play in two parts by Robert Schenkkan. [*Royale Theatre, 34 perf.; *Pulitzer Prize.] In this sprawling epic that filled two full-length plays, three families (two white and one black) who inhabit a section of Eastern Kentucky are traced from 1775 to 1975, the sins of the ancestors coming back to haunt later generations. The plays also served as a history of the whole nation as everything from tribal Indian skirmishes, the opening of the West, the Civil War, coal miners' strike and the emerging labor movement, the recession, and the government's "war on poverty" served as the background for the extended tale. The drama was seen in Seattle, Los Angeles, and Washington, and was awarded the Pulitzer before its Broadway production (co-produced by the *Kennedy Center, the *Mark Taper Forum, and others), which boasted a large cast, led by Stacy *Keach, playing multiple roles. But mixed notices and an expensive production shortened the run to a month.

KERKER, Gustave [Adolph] (1857–1923), composer. Born in Germany, where he began studying cello at the age of seven, he continued his musical studies when his family moved to Louisville in 1867. Kerker started his professional career playing in pit orchestras at local theatres and soon rose to the post of conductor. His 1879 operetta, *Cadets*, toured the South, coming to the attention of E. E. *Rice, who offered the composer-conductor a chance to work with him. Shortly after moving to New York, he became the principal conductor at the *Casino Theatre. Although he interpolated his songs into other men's scores, notably in Lecocq's *The Pearl of Pekin*, his first complete score was not heard in New York until the production of *Castles in the Air* (1890). Over the next two decades he provided the music for more than twenty shows, most importantly the international hit *The *Belle of New York* (1897), as well as *An American Beauty* (1896), *The Girl from Up There* (1901), *Winsome Winnie* (1903), *The Tourists* (1906), and *Fascinating Flora* (1907). His work was musicianly and highly popular in its day, but none of it has proved memorable.

KERN, Jerome [David] (1885–1945), composer. Born in New York, the son of a German-born immigrant who became a moderately successful merchandiser and an American-born mother of Bohemian descent who had once contemplated a career as a professional pianist, he moved with his family to Newark when he was ten and started music lessons with his mother. While still in high school, Kern composed music for a class show as well as for a production by the Newark Yacht Club. His success prompted him to quit high school after his junior year and enroll instead at the New York College of Music, where his teachers included Paolo Gallico, Alexander Lambert, and Austin Pierce. He employed what was then the accepted method of breaking into Broadway: interpolating songs into other men's scores. Playgoers first heard Kern melodies when Lew *Fields inserted two numbers into a 1903 importation, *An English Daisy*. A year later, when E. E. *Rice allowed Kern to write half the score for another importation, *Mr. Wix of Wickham*, recognition began to come Kern's way. His first big hit, "How'd You Like to Spoon with Me?," was interpolated into *The Earl and the Girl* (1905), then for the next decade the young composer shuttled back and forth between New York and London where he picked up an abiding love for Gaiety musical comedy and met his future wife, Eva Leale. Among the shows with inserted Kern melodies during these years were *The Doll Girl*, *The Dairymaids*, *Fascinating Flora*, *Fluffy Ruffles*, and *The Girl from Montmartre*. He soon developed a unique musical idiom, a distinct amalgam of his German and Bohemian heritage, turn-of-the-century English musical theatre styles, and identifiable American mannerisms. An especially important influence was "the dancing craze," a rage for ballroom dancing that exploded across America shortly before

World War I. It was in answer to this demand for new dance songs that Kern finally found his first real style and achieved lasting recognition. In 1914 Charles *Frohman brought the London hit *The *Girl from Utah* to New York and added some Kern songs, most memorably "They Didn't Believe Me," which changed the course of American musical comedy writing. This great, enduring composition established the ballad as the most basic style of popular song in place of the heretofore-reigning waltz. Within a year Kern had joined forces with Guy *Bolton and the pair began to write intimate musical comedies for the tiny *Princess Theatre. The first, *Nobody Home* (1915), was a modest hit, but *Very Good Eddie* (1915) was a huge success. When P. G. *Wodehouse joined the team, adding his incomparable lyrics, the shows hit full stride with *Oh, Boy!* (1917), *Oh, Lady! Lady!!* (1918), *Have a Heart!* (1917) and *Leave It to Jane* (1917). These musical comedies, with their sensible books about believable people, their literate and witty lyrics and their enchanting melodies (songs that were well integrated into the story) became exemplars of their kind. In the next decade most of Kern's scores were far more blatantly commercial enterprises: the Marilyn *Miller vehicles *Sally* (1920) and *Sunny* (1925), the Fred *Stone vehicles *Stepping Stones* (1923) and *Criss Cross* (1926), and the ambitious but short-lived *Dear Sir* (1924). Three years later he and librettist-lyricist Oscar *Hammerstein created the first successful, totally American operetta, *Show Boat*. Its masterful score, engaging epic story, and ability to tie the two together made for what most consider the first "musical play." The success of the pair's next work, *Sweet Adeline* (1929), was dampened by the onset of the Great Depression. In the early 1930s Kern attempted still another style of operetta writing, interweaving Middle-European and American mannerisms. *The *Cat and the Fiddle* (1931), written with Otto *Harbach, and *Music in the Air* (1932), written with Hammerstein, both enjoyed long runs. A weak Harbach libretto nearly scuttled *Roberta* (1933), but Kern's luminous score, in particular "Smoke Gets in Your Eyes," saved the day. For the rest of the decade he worked in Hollywood, returning only in 1939 for the unsuccessful *Very Warm for May*, which left behind the enduring Kern-Hammerstein classic "All the Things You Are." Kern was preparing to write the score for the musical that became *Annie Get Your Gun* when he died in 1945.

Kern's remarkable melodic gifts and his crucial pioneering—popularizing the ballad, modernizing musical comedy, and creating the modern American operetta or musical play—have won him general recognition as the father of the American musical theatre as we know it today.

Harold *Arlen, George *Gershwin, Cole *Porter, Richard *Rodgers, Arthur *Schwartz, and Vincent *Youmans all at one time or another acknowledged that he had served as their idol and model. For all his experimentation, however, Kern could be a difficult, obstinate associate. He almost never would write a melody to a lyric, and once he did create a melody he refused to change a note of it. As a result, even when his lyricist was a master such as Wodehouse or Hammerstein, there were occasional clashes of words and music. Witness, for example, the verse to "Make Believe." Kern's full scores, other than those already mentioned, were *The Red Petticoat* (1912), *Oh, I Say!* (1913), *Miss Information* (1915), *Love o' Mike* (1917), *Toot-Toot!* (1918), *Head Over Heels* (1918), *Rock-a-Bye Baby* (1919), *She's a Good Fellow* (1919), *The Night Boat* (1920), *Hitchy-Koo* (1920), *Good Morning Dearie* (1921), *Sitting Pretty* (1924), *The City Chap* (1925), *Lucky* (1927), and *Gentleman Unafraid* (1938), done in St. Louis but never brought to New York. Biography: *Jerome Kern: His Life and Music*, Gerald Bordman, 1980.

KERR, [Bridget] **Jean** [née Collins] (1923–2003), playwright. The popular dramatist was born in Scranton, Pennsylvania, and educated at Marywood College and Catholic University. Her first play to reach New York was *Jenny Kissed Me* (1948), then with her husband, Walter *Kerr, she wrote sketches for the revue *Touch and Go* (1949), with Eleanor Brooke the comedy *King of Hearts* (1954), and with her husband the musical *Goldilocks* (1958). Kerr's biggest hit was the comedy *Mary, Mary* (1961), followed by *Poor Richard* (1964), *Finishing Touches* (1973), and *Lunch Hour* (1980). Her work is marked by a biting wit and shrewd personal observation.

KERR, Walter [Francis] (1913–96), critic and playwright. He was born in Evanston, Illinois, and educated at De Pauw and Northwestern Universities, then from 1938 to 1945 he taught speech and drama at Catholic University in Washington. Kerr wrote librettos and/or sketches for the musicals *Count Me In* (1942), *Sing Out, Sweet Land!* (1944), and *Touch and Go* (1949), directing the last two as well. In 1950 he became drama critic for *Commonweal* and the next year for the *Herald Tribune*. It was during his tenure on this paper that he staged his wife Jean *Kerr's comedy, *King of Hearts* (1954), and with her wrote the book for the musical *Goldilocks* (1958), which he directed. With the demise of the *Herald Tribune* in 1966, he became drama critic for the *Times*, but soon confined himself to Sunday critiques. Among his books are *How Not to Write a Play* (1955), *Pieces at Eight* (1957), *The Decline of Pleasure* (1962), *Theatre in*

Spite of Itself (1963), and *Journey to the Center of the Theatre* (1979). Kerr's writings, known for their insight, readability, and intuitive sense of quality, earned him a *Pulitzer Prize, and in 1990 Broadway's Ritz Theatre was renamed after him.

KESSELRING, Joseph. See *Arsenic and Old Lace*.

KESSLER, David (1859?–1920), actor and manager. The Yiddish theatre artist was born in Russia but spent most of his career on New York's Lower East Side. A tall, broad man, with a markedly peasant neck, he seemed to have the highest artistic principles and instinct even though he apparently had little or no formal education. While Kessler performed in highly praised productions of such works as Sudermann's *Heimat* [*Magda*] and Jacob *Gordin's *God, Man and Devil*, he was forced by his public to appear mostly in plays that he considered trash. He ran several theatres, and it was his move to a new playhouse on Second Avenue that is often credited with moving the American-Yiddish theatre's center there from the Bowery. When Kessler appeared on Broadway in *The Spell* (1907), one critic, citing his "emotional gymnastics and physical contortions," branded him an actor of "the old German school."

KESTER, Paul. See *When Knighthood Was in Flower*.

KEY LARGO (1939), a drama by Maxwell *Anderson. [*Ethel Barrymore Theatre, 105 perf.] Concluding his side has lost the Spanish Civil War, King McCloud (Paul *Muni) urges his men to join him in deserting, but they refuse and die fighting. Back in America, King is beset by guilt. He attempts to expiate his feelings by visiting the families of his fallen comrades, including the D'Alcalas who run a small hotel in Key Largo and are being menaced by gangsters. At first King would wave away the problem, but concluding his life is now worthless he kills one gangster and is himself killed. His death spares two innocents' being framed for the killings that a gangster has committed. Although the *Playwrights' Company offering was dismissed by some critics as a well-intentioned tract, poorly developed, it reflected the deep concern of many theatrical figures over the events and implications of the war.

KICK IN (1914), a play by Willard *Mack. [*Longacre Theatre, 188 perf.] Chick Hewes (John *Barrymore) is an ex-convict who is determined to go straight. But when a former cellmate is shot during a robbery, Chick and his wife, Molly (Jane Grey), offer to hide him. The cellmate dies, but not before a valuable necklace he has stolen disappears.

Although Chick and Molly dump the body in the river, they are still arrested in the case. When Molly's drug-addicted brother, Charles Cary (Forrest Winant), learns his pregnant sister may go to prison, he confesses that he took the necklace. By rights, Chick and Molly should still be held for harboring a criminal, but a compassionate police commissioner decides to give them another chance. The A. H. *Woods production was hailed by one critic as "engrossing from beginning to end." Chick was one of Barrymore's best interpretations and led directly to his being cast in more serious, artful works.

KIDD, Michael [né Milton Greenwald] (b. 1919), choreographer and director. Born in New York, he left City College, where he was studying chemical engineering, to become a pupil at a ballet school. He performed with the Eugene Loring Dance Players and the Ballet Theatre before choreographing *Finian's Rainbow* (1947). His dances were later seen in such musicals as *Love Life* (1948), *Guys and Dolls* (1950), *Can-Can* (1953), *Li'l Abner* (1956), *Destry Rides Again* (1959), *Wildcat* (1960), *Subways Are for Sleeping* (1961), *Skyscraper* (1965), *The Rothschilds* (1970), and *The Goodbye Girl* (1993), some of which he also directed. Kidd's choreography, which was also seen in a handful of movie musicals, was characterized by ingenious groupings and a raffish liveliness.

KIDDER, Edward E. (1846–1927), playwright. Born in Charleston, Massachusetts, but raised in New York, he was an actor's manager (working with Charlotte *Crabtree, John T. *Raymond, and others) before turning playwright. Between 1883, when he wrote *Three of a Kind* for Nate Salsbury and Nellie McHenry, and 1905, when he created *Easy Dawson* for Raymond *Hitchcock, he was the author of some twenty or thirty Broadway and touring plays, most of them vehicles for important stars. His biggest success was *A Poor Relation* (1889), written for Sol Smith *Russell and centering on a likable, inventive hobo.

KILEY, Richard [Paul] (1922–99), actor and singer. A native Chicagoan, he played in summer stock before assuming the role of Stanley Kowalski in a road company of *A *Streetcar Named Desire* in 1950. New Yorkers first saw him as Joey Percival in a 1953 revival of Shaw's *Misalliance*, then as the Caliph in *Kismet* (1953). Kiley would comfortably shift from dramas to musicals throughout his stage career, giving such memorable performances as the suspicious Major Harry Cargill in *Time Limit!* (1956), the sleuthing Tom Baxter in *Redhead* (1959), the young senator Brig Anderson in *Advise and Consent* (1960), novelist David Jordan in *No

Strings (1962), the dual roles of Cervantes and Don Quixote in *Man of La Mancha* (1965), various characters in *The Incomparable Max* (1971), the stuffy businessman Ronald Brewster-Wright in *Absurd Person Singular* (1974), and Joe Keller in *All My Sons* (1987).

KILNER, Thomas (1777–1862), actor and manager. An Englishman who made his American debut at the *Park Theatre in 1818, his fame rests on his career as manager of Boston's *Federal Street Theatre, where he not only provided fine productions but distinguished himself in such "old men" roles as Sir Anthony Absolute and Polonius. He retired in the early 1830s.

KIM, Willa (b. 1930?), costume designer. After studying at Los Angeles's Chouinard Institute of Art, she assisted theatre designer Raoul Pene *Du Bois for several years before designing in regional theatres. Kim was first noticed for her work in alternative New York productions, such as *Promenade* (1969), *Operation Sidewinder* (1970), and *The Screens* (1971), but eventually was in demand for big Broadway musicals. Among her many notable productions are *Dancin'* (1979), *Sophisticated Ladies* (1981), *Song and Dance* (1985), *The *Will Rogers Follies* (1991), *Grease* (1994), and *Victor/Victoria* (1995). She is also a much sought after designer for dance companies and operas.

KING AND I, THE (1951), a musical play by Oscar *Hammerstein (book, lyrics), Richard *Rodgers (music). [*St. James Theatre, 1,246 perf.; *Tony Award.] When the English tutor Anna Leonowens (Gertrude *Lawrence) arrives with her young son in Siam to teach the children of the King (Yul Brynner), she finds the monarch something of a despot, but she is drawn to his many children (through many wives) and puts up with him to a point. But when the King goes to punish two young lovers who seek to elope, Anna can take no more and prepares to leave Siam. Only when the King is on his deathbed does he confess he has begun to see the wisdom of her more civilized ways, and he dies as his teenage son begins to rule Siam with a more modern approach. *Notable songs*: Hello, Young Lovers; We Kiss in a Shadow; Getting to Know You; I Whistle a Happy Tune; Something Wonderful; Shall We Dance? Based on Margaret Landon's novel, *Anna and the King of Siam*, it portrayed, as Richard *Watts Jr. wrote in his *Post* review, "an East of frank and unashamed romance seen through the eyes of . . . theatrical artists of rare taste and power." Although for many Lawrence's luminous performance was a high point of the show, after her death during the run Brynner's acting was thrown in the spotlight and he usually headed its many major revivals. Other notable Annas in New York include Constance Towers, Patricia Morrison, Angela *Lansbury, Donna Murphy, and Faith *Prince. **Yul BRYNNER** (1911?–85) gave varying birthplaces and birth dates throughout his life, but it is believed he was born on Sakhalin Island and his real name was Taidje Khano. The bald, muscular actor had made Broadway appearances, including a 1941 revival of *Twelfth Night* and *Lute Song* (1946), before this role catapulted him into the limelight. His subsequent career was largely in films, including the movie version of *The King and I*, except when he toured in several revivals of the musical, ultimately performing his part more than four thousand times. He also starred in a failed musical, *Home Sweet Homer* (1976). Biography: *Yul: The Man Who Would Be King*, Rock Brynner (his son), 1989.

KING, Dennis [né Pratt] (1897–1971), actor and singer. While best remembered as the leading man of many 1920s operettas, the handsome, English-born King was a versatile performer who enjoyed a long and varied career. His earliest professional assignment was as a callboy with the Birmingham Repertory Theatre. He rose rapidly in the company to stage manager and finally actor. He came to America in 1921 to play the Marquis de Trois Fleurs in *Clair de Lune*, but first called prominent attention to himself when he essayed Mercutio to Jane *Cowl's Juliet in 1923 and became a star the following year when he took the role of Jim Kenyon in *Rose-Marie*. This was followed by two more popular roles in Rudolf *Friml operettas, François Villon in The *Vagabond King* (1925) and D'Artagnan in The *Three Musketeers* (1928). Among his other notable performances were as *Peter Ibbetson* (1931), Ravenal in a 1932 revival of *Show Boat*, the sex-hungry telegraph operator Dascom Dinsmore in *Petticoat Fever* (1934), Dr. Rank in *A Doll's House* (1937), Willie Palaffi in *I Married an Angel* (1938), Vershinin in *The Three Sisters* (1942), the fence-straddling diplomat Alexander Hazen in *The Searching Wind* (1944), General Burgoyne in *The Devil's Disciple* (1950), Captain Vere in *Billy Budd* (1951), Bruno Mahler in *Music in the Air* (1951), and the boozy Judge Sullivan in *Lunatics and Lovers* (1954). His last success was as the writer's alter ego Sam Elderly in *Photo Finish* (1963), and his last appearance was as the homosexual Baron von Epp in *A Patriot for Me* (1969).

KING LEAR. Shakespeare's tragedy was first mounted in New York in 1754 and soon became a popular vehicle for all the great American tragedians. Junius Brutus *Booth, himself a little mad, was a noteworthy interpreter as was Edwin *Forrest. It was also a favorite role of Edwin *Booth, though critics divided on the merits of his performance, which, especially in early years, seemed to have been copied from his father's. Modern revivals, including those featuring Louis *Calhern, Orson *Welles, Paul *Scofield, James Earl *Jones, Hal *Holbrook, and F. Murray *Abraham, have found surprisingly little favor at the box office.

KING, Walter Woolf [né Woolf] (1895–1984), actor and singer. A popular leading man in operetta in the 1920s, he was born in San Francisco and began his career in vaudeville. Under the name Walter Woolf, he made notable appearances in the musicals *The Last Waltz* (1921), *The Lady in Ermine* (1922), *The Dream Girl* (1924), *Countess Maritza* (1926), and *The Red Robe* (1928). In the 1930s he went to Hollywood (where he was billed as Walter Woolf King) and played both in singing and nonsinging roles. King returned to the stage for *Melody* (1933) and *May Wine* (1935), then spent his later years as a screen character actor.

KINGSLEY, Sidney [né Kirschner] (1906–95), playwright and director. He was born in Philadelphia and studied at Cornell where he wrote one-act plays for the University's drama club. His first play to reach Broadway was *Men in White* (1933), the *Pulitzer Prize–winning drama about the medical profession that the *Group Theatre presented with success. Kingsley was a slow, careful writer, so it took two years to write *Dead End* (1935), which was also a hit. He also directed the play, as he did all his subsequent offerings. After disappointing runs for *Ten Million Ghosts* (1936), *The World We Make* (1939), and The *Patriots* (1943), he scored a success with the police drama *Detective Story* (1949), followed by *Darkness at Noon* (1951), *Lunatics and Lovers* (1954), and *Night Life* (1962). Kingsley's best works were hard-hitting dramas with a moral and social point of view.

KIRALFY, Bolossy (1848?–1932) and **Imre** (1849?–1919), producers. The Hungarian-born dancers and acrobats who, with their sister Haniola made their American debut in George L. *Fox's production of *Hiccory Diccory Dock* (1869), performed in numerous spectacles at *Niblo's Garden before turning producers there with *The Deluge* (1874). It was said to have been the first production to employ a primitive form of electricity for its lighting; although some historians suggest it was their later production of *Enchantment* (1879) that can actually claim this distinction. Certainly for about fifteen years they were New York's principal purveyors of spectacle, including *Azurine* (1877), *Excelsior* (1883), *Sieba and the Seven Ravens* (1884), and *The Water*

Queen (1889). During that time they sent out lavish touring companies of two popular extravaganzas, *The *Black Crook* and **Around the World*, both of which made seasonal visits to New York. In later years they assisted with the staging of Barnum and Bailey's circus and in mounting spectacles in arenas and elsewhere. Their last years were spent in England. Autobiography: *Bolossy Kiralfy, Creator of Great Musical Spectacles*, Barbara M. Barker, ed., 1988.

KIRBY, J. Hudson (1810–48), actor. The idol of the cheap theatres of his day, he was born in London and came to America apparently in 1837, making his debut at Philadelphia's *Walnut Street Theatre. He first appeared in New York at Wallack's National Theatre in 1838 when he played Antonio to J. M. *Wallack's Shylock. Kirby might have made a career in better roles, but he chose to star in the tawdry, overwrought melodramas of the time. He was particularly adept at handling a noisy audience, his voice ringing out above the din. Kirby's scene-chewing technique gave rise to the expression "Wake me up when Kirby dies."

KIRKLAND, Jack. See *Tobacco Road*.

KISMET (1911), a play in three acts by Edward *Knoblauch. [Knickerbocker Theatre, 184 perf.] The wily Baghdad beggar and poet Hajj (Otis *Skinner) is arrested on a minor infraction by the Wazir Mansur (Hamilton Revelle) who agrees to release him if he will kill the Caliph Abdullah (Fred Eric). Hajj's attempt fails and he is thrown in jail alongside his old enemy Sheik Jawan (Sheridan Block) whom he kills before escaping in the Sheik's clothing. Learning his daughter Marsinah (Rita Jolivet) has become a concubine in the Wazir's harem, he drowns the Wazir and frees Marsinah. The Caliph, who has disguised himself as a gardener to court Marsinah, now marries her. By law he must banish Hajj, which he does, but he looks the other way when Hajj simply returns to his old haunts to beg and write poetry again. Initially rejected by all the major Broadway producers, it was presented in New York by Charles *Frohman, *Klaw, and *Erlanger only after its successful London premiere. The role of Hajj was generally considered Skinner's most popular. In 1953 a musical version with a book by Charles Lederer and Luther Davis, lyrics by Robert Wright and George Forrest, and music based on Aleksandr Borodin themes, ran 583 performances at the *Ziegfeld Theatre with Alfred *Drake as Hajj and Richard *Kiley as the Caliph. *Notable songs*: And This Is My Beloved; Baubles, Bangles and Beads; Stranger in Paradise; Night of My Nights. It has been revived several times, including an all-

black version in 1978 called *Timbuktu*. **Edward KNOBLAUCH** [later Anglicized to Knoblock] (1874–1945) was born in New York and educated at Harvard, but spent most of his professional career in England where he became a British subject in 1916. He began his career as an actor but soon switched to playwriting. While *Kismet* was his biggest hit, Knoblauch also found success with *The Faun* (1911) and *Marie-Odile* (1915). Autobiography: *Round the Room*, 1939.

KISS AND TELL (1943), a comedy by F. Hugh *Herbert. [*Biltmore Theatre, 957 perf.] The Archers and the Pringles have been feuding, especially since they caught their teenage daughters, Corliss Archer (Joan Caulfield) and Mildred Pringle (Judith Parrish), selling kisses for charity. So when Lt. Lenny Archer (Richard Widmark) elopes with Mildred, he swears Corliss to secrecy. Mildred, it turns out, is soon pregnant, but Mrs. Pringle sees only Corliss leaving the obstetrician's office. Since she is sworn not to reveal the truth, Corliss says she is pregnant. That means she will have to marry her dim-witted boyfriend, Dexter Franklin (Robert White), whose limited vocabulary consists largely of "Holy Cow." Matters are properly resolved after Lenny becomes a war hero and reveals his marriage. Welcomed by John Anderson of the *Journal-American* as "a fresh, funny and completely beguiling comedy," the George *Abbott production was another of the many successful plays of the war that relied heavily on young performers.

KISS ME, KATE (1948), a musical comedy by Sam and Bella *Spewack (book), Cole *Porter (music, lyrics). [New Century Theatre, 1,077 perf.; Tony Award.] The stars of the new musical version of *The Taming of the Shrew*, currently trying out in Baltimore, are the egomaniac Fred Graham (Alfred *Drake) and the temperamental Lilli Vanessi (Patricia Morison), who were once married to each other but are now divorced and still bickering with each other. Lilli receives a bouquet from Fred, leading her to believe he still loves her, but when she learns the flowers are meant for the flirty Lois Lane (Lisa Kirk), she determines to be revenged by walking out on the show. Fred's problems are compounded when another member of the company, Bill Calhoun (Harold Lang), signs Fred's name to a gambling debt. Opening night is peppered by warfare between Fred and Lilli, and by the demands by two comic hoods for payment of the IOU. Fred convinces the hoods that they must force Lilli to perform in order to get their money, which they do until their boss is wiped out and the IOU becomes invalid. Just as Shakespeare's Kate and Petruchio come to terms on stage, so do Fred and Lilli make up backstage.

Notable songs: Wunderbar; So in Love; Always True to You in My Fashion; Brush Up Your Shakespeare; Too Darn Hot; Why Can't You Behave? Called by Brooks *Atkinson "a blissfully enjoyable musical show," the work is generally acknowledged as Porter's masterpiece. Not only did he employ Shakespearean lines and whole passages with wit and taste, but his songs actually seemed to come out of and be a part of the libretto, both in the *Shrew* scenes and in the backstage story, a rare thing for the cavalier composer. The Saint Subber–Lemuel *Ayers production was an immediate hit and the musical has been revived in all venues ever since, most recently a 1999 production that was popular on Broadway and the West End.

KISS OF THE SPIDER WOMAN (1993), a musical play by Terrence *McNally (book), John *Kander (music), Fred *Ebb (lyrics). [*Broadhurst Theatre, 906 perf.; Tony, NYDCC Awards.] In a South American prison, cellmates Molina (Brent Carver), a gay window dresser sentenced for corrupting the morals of a youth, and Valentin (Anthony Crivello), a revolutionary, move from being cold strangers to close friends and even lovers under the harsh conditions they suffer together. Molina deals with the situation by fantasizing about the screen goddess Aurora (Chita *Rivera) who is also the symbol of death. When Molina is freed in the hopes of leading the police to Valentin's comrades, the plan misfires and Molina is executed. *Notable songs*: Where You Are; Anything for Him; You Could Never Shame Me; Gimme Love. Although the Manuel Puig novel and 1984 film made for an unlikely subject for a musical, the Hal Prince–directed show was both gripping and entertaining. The Livent-produced musical had tried out at SUNY Purchase and was rewritten in Toronto and London before arriving on Broadway where it was a critical and popular success.

KISS THE BOYS GOODBYE (1938), a comedy by Clare *Boothe. [*Henry Miller Theatre, 286 perf.] Into Hollywood's frantic search for an actress to play Velvet O'Toole in the filming of a novel about the Civil War, *Kiss the Boys Goodbye*, comes Georgia belle Cindy Lou Bethany (Helen Claire). Whether she is the "half Hepburn, half Bette Davis, half Myrna Loy" that one figure says is required is moot. To a collection of show-wise characters assembled in Westport, Connecticut, she is merely a bore. Furious at the other guests' behavior toward her, Cindy Lou punches one and shoots at another. In the end she decides she prefers marriage to a career. Despite critical reservations that the comedy was mechanical and contrived, the Brock *Pemberton offering was a big

success and quickly sent out a road company. Although most critics and playgoers saw it as a spoof of Hollywood's search for an actress to play Scarlett O'Hara, Boothe muddied the waters by insisting in her preface to the published version that it was really an attack on fascism (Southern fascism in particular).

KISSEL, Howard (b. 1942), critic and author. He was born in Milwaukee and studied comparative literature at Columbia and journalism at Northwestern before writing for various papers and journals. Kissel's reviews in *Women's Wear Daily* in the 1970s and 1980s were highly respected and in 1986 he took over as the theatre critic for the New York *Daily News*. He is known as a direct, unflowery writer and a keen observer of theatre. Kissel has also written a lively biography of David *Merrick.

KIT, THE ARKANSAS TRAVELLER (1871), a play by T. B. De Walden and Edward Spencer. [*Niblo's Garden, 40 perf.] Young Arkansas farmer Kit Redding (Frank *Chanfrau) and his wife, Mary (Rose Evans), live happily with their young daughter Alice (Minnie Maddern [*Fiske]) until Mary's former suitor, the crooked gambler Manuel Bond (George C. *Boniface), abducts both mother and child. Years later, Kit has become a wealthy, but disconsolate merchant, who continually searches for his wife and child when he is not in his cups. He finally encounters Manuel, who now calls himself Hastings, and a grown Alice (played by Evans) on a Mississippi River steamboat. Mary has died, so it is up to Kit to convince Alice that she is his daughter. At the same time, Hastings sets fire to the boat, hoping in the confusion to rob it. The passengers are shipwrecked on a small island, where Kit kills Hastings and reclaims Alice. The play had toured the country for over a year before coming to New York. It was well received, the *Times* noting it offered "realistic pictures of every-day life in the West—reasonably realistic, be it understood—[and] exciting situations" as well as "representative types from distant places." It became Chanfrau's principal vehicle for the rest of his life. After his death it continued to be played by others well into the 1890s. **T. B. DE WALDEN** [né Thomas Blades] (1811–73) was a London-born actor, playwright, and manager, who made his American debut in 1844. He was Chanfrau's business manager for many years. His last play, written for Edward *Eddy, was *The Life and Death of Natty Bumppo*.

KITTREDGE, George Lyman (1860–1941), author. The distinguished American scholar taught Shakespeare and early English literature at

Harvard. His writings, such as his 1916 *Shakespeare* and his monographs, were often referred to by producers and actors planning Shakespearean revivals.

KITTY MACKAY (1914), a comedy by Catherine Chisholm *Cushing. [Comedy Theatre, 278 perf.] Kitty McNab (Molly McIntyre), a foundling, has been lovingly raised in Scottish backwaters by the religious Sandy McNab (Ernest Stallard) and his wife. Suddenly, the family who abandoned Kitty calls to bring her back to London. There, as Kitty Mackay, she falls in love with Lt. David Graham (Eugene O'Brien). But when they learn Kitty is Graham's half sister, the marriage is called off and Kitty returns to Scotland. Graham follows her with the news that as a baby she was switched for his real half sister, who had died. Since they are not blood relatives, they can wed. This sentimental comedy was highly praised by critics for its warmheartedness and humor and was one of the major hits of its day. But a musical version called *Lassie* (1920) failed to run.

KIVIETTE (fl. 1930s) [née Yetta Kiviat], designer. Said to have been born on Staten Island, she attended the Women's School of Applied Design and worked closely for a time with Charles *Le Maire. Her costume designs began to attract attention in the late 1920s when she worked on such musicals as *Here's Howe!* (1928), but her heyday was the 1930s. Her clothes were seen in, among others, *Girl Crazy* (1930), *Three's a Crowd* (1930), *The *Band Wagon* (1931), *The *Cat and the Fiddle* (1931), *Face the Music* (1932), *Take a Chance* (1932), *Walk a Little Faster* (1932), *Let 'Em Eat Cake* (1933), *Roberta* (1933), *Ziegfeld Follies of 1934*, *Life Begins at 8:40* (1934), and *Between the Devil* (1937). Thereafter Kiviette worked less frequently on Broadway, one of her last important assignments being *Light Up the Sky* (1948). The fashion show in *Roberta* may have represented the high point in her career, the streamlined simplicity and elegance of its gowns exemplifying her best work.

KLAUBER, Adolph (1879–1933), producer and critic. Born in Louisville and educated at the University of Virginia, he began his career on the staffs of the *Commercial Advertiser* and the *Tribune*. In 1906 he was appointed drama critic of the *New York Times*, a post he held until 1918, but left the paper when he became a producer and scored a modest hit with his first solo offering, *Nighty-Night* (1919). In 1920 Klauber was the uncredited co-producer of two Eugene *O'Neill plays, *The *Emperor Jones* and *Diff'rent*. His 1922 production of *The Charlatan* was well received, but had only a mediocre run. With the *Selwyns and his wife,

Jane *Cowl, he produced many of her starring vehicles, such as *Lilac Time* (1917), *Smilin' Through* (1919), *Pelleas and Melisande* (1923), and *Antony and Cleopatra* (1924), although he remained a silent partner in these enterprises.

KLAW, Marc (1858–1936), manager. Although he was born in Paducah, Kentucky, his widowed mother moved the family to Louisville when he was five, and it was there that he received his degree in law and began to practice. In 1881 he was employed by Gustave and Daniel *Frohman to act against pirated productions of *Hazel Kirke*. His work was so successful that he soon came to the attention of Abe *Erlanger and in 1888 the pair bought out the Taylor Theatrical Exchange, renaming it the Klaw and Erlanger Exchange. By 1895 they were the second-largest agency in the country, representing such notables as Joseph *Jefferson and Fanny *Davenport, and controlled most of the principal Southern theatres. That same year they met secretly with Charles *Frohman, Al *Hyman, William *Harris Sr., and others to organize what became known as the Theatrical Syndicate or *Trust. The organization's monopoly was not broken until the arrival of the *Shuberts a decade later and remained a powerful force until it was quietly dissolved in 1916. During those years Klaw and Erlanger also produced numerous shows, including many George *Arliss vehicles and Otis *Skinner's *Kismet* (1911), as well as such musicals as *Forty-five Minutes from Broadway* (1906) and *The *Pink Lady* (1911). Unlike his crass partner, Klaw was gentlemanly in appearance and demeanor. Their personal differences apparently led to an irrevocable rupture in 1919. A year later Klaw formed his own production company and in 1921 built the Klaw Theatre. Most notable among his solo ventures was *Hell-Bent for Heaven* (1924).

KLEIN, Charles (1867–1915), playwright. Coming to America from his native London at the age of fifteen, he began his career as an actor in juvenile roles. Klein's first writing success was the libretto for *El Capitan* (1896). Over the next nineteen years he wrote several dozen comedies, melodramas, and musical librettos, most notably *Heartsease* (1897), *The *Auctioneer* (1901), *The *Music Master* (1904), *The *Lion and the Mouse* (1905), and *The *Third Degree* (1909). Although his best works are now perceived as too sentimental or as contrived melodrama, they were widely praised and highly popular in their time. Klein also served as Charles *Frohman's play reader and the two died when the *Lusitania* was sunk. His brother Manuel (1876-1919) was the conductor who also composed scores for extravaganzas at the *Hippodrome for a decade.

KLINE, Kevin (b. 1947), actor. The lanky, very physical performer was born in St. Louis and studied at Indiana University and at Juilliard. Much of his earliest work was done in a variety of roles with the *New York Shakespeare Festival and the *Acting Company. Kline first won praise as the pompous fiancé Bruce Granit in the musical *On the Twentieth Century* (1978) and as the unsettled writer Paul in *Loose Ends* (1979). He later undertook such classical roles as Richard III, Hamlet, Henry V, Benedict, Ivanov, Bluntschli, the Duke in *Measure for Measure,* and Trigorin in *The Seagull,* as well as the flamboyant Pirate King in *The Pirates of Penzance* (1980). Regardless of his great success in films, Kline has returned regularly to the theatre.

KLOTZ, Florence (b. 1920?), designer. The work of this New York–born costume designer has been seen in such shows as *Take Her, She's Mine* (1961), *Never Too Late* (1962), *The Owl and the Pussycat* (1964), *Follies* (1971), *A *Little Night Music* (1973), *Pacific Overtures* (1976), *On the Twentieth Century* (1978), *The *Little Foxes* (1981), *Jerry's Girls* (1985), *Kiss of the Spider Woman* (1993), and *Show Boat* (1994).

KNICKERBOCKER HOLIDAY (1938), a musical comedy by Maxwell *Anderson (book, lyrics), Kurt *Weill (music). [*Ethel Barrymore Theatre, 168 perf.] As he writes his history of New York, Washington Irving (Ray Middleton) seems to wander back into the 17th century just as New Amsterdam is awaiting the arrival of Pieter Stuyvesant (Walter *Huston). The town council seeks to divert the new governor from its corruption and ineptitude by staging a hanging, and they select a rebellious young man, Brom Brock (Richard *Kollmar), who brashly has asked to marry Tina Tienhoven (Jeanne Madden), daughter of one councillor. Stuyvesant pardons Brock but refuses to allow him to marry Tina because Stuyvesant himself decides to marry her. This prompts Brock to rouse the citizens against the governor, who senses the way the political winds are blowing and backs down. His decision is aided by Irving's warning him he must think of his place in history. *Notable songs*: September Song; It Never Was You; How Can You Tell an American? Many critics considered Anderson's libretto preachy and cumbersome but the *Playwrights' Company production found an audience because of Huston's memorable performance, especially his singing of "September Song."

KNOBLAUCH, Edward. See *Kismet.*

KNOWLES, [James] **Sheridan** (1784–1862), actor and playwright. The Irish performer failed to impress Americans when he arrived in 1834, but that in no way diminished the opinion of many of his contemporaries that he was the greatest dramatist of his day. Such plays as *William Tell* and *The Wife* were in the American repertory for many years, but it was another pair of dramas that capped his reputation: *Virginius* (1820) and *The *Hunchback* (1832), both of which held the stage for the rest of the century and served as vehicles for many of the greatest American actors and actresses.

KOBER, Arthur. See *Having Wonderful Time.*

KOLLMAR, Richard (1910–71), actor and producer. A native of Ridgewood, New Jersey, who studied at Yale with Professor George Pierce *Baker, he played prominent roles in such musicals as *Knickerbocker Holiday* (1938) and *Too Many Girls* (1939) before turning producer. Alone or with others, he presented *By Jupiter* (1942), *Early to Bed* (1943), *Are You with It?* (1945), and *Plain and Fancy* (1955).

KOPIT, Arthur [Lee] (b. 1937), playwright. A native New Yorker, his first plays were produced while he was a student at Harvard, including his dark farce *Oh Dad, Poor Dad, Mamma's Hung You in the Closet and I'm Feelin' So Sad* (1962) which was presented at the university and in London before being produced Off Broadway and then on Broadway. Kopit's subsequent works of note include *Indians* (1969), *Wings* (1979), *Nine* (1982), *End of the World* (1984), *Road to Nirvana* (1990), and *Y2K* (1999). He also wrote numerous other plays, which were mounted regionally with success but not seen in New York, such as the musical *Phantom* (1991).

KOTZEBUE, August Friedrich Ferdinand Von (1761–1819), playwright. Hailed briefly by some of his contemporaries as the German Shakespeare, he burst upon the American scene in *Dunlap's translation of his *Menschenhass und Reue,* here called *The *Stranger.* The play's tremendous success not only saved Dunlap's faltering fortunes at the new *Park Theatre but also initiated the vogue of theatrical romanticism. The play retained its popularity for decades, as did his *Pizarro.* Before Dunlap's retirement in 1805, more than a dozen of Kotzebue's plays were premiered in New York and elsewhere, their increasing sensationalism precipitating the deluge of melodrama, much as *The Stranger* helped open the gates to romanticism. The American titles were *Lover's Vows, False Shame, The Wild Goose Chase, The Force of Calumny* and *The Virgin of the Sun.*

KRAPP, Herbert J. (1887–1973), architect. The most productive of all American theatre designers, he was born in New York and studied at the Cooper Union Institute. At the height of his career, Krapp was the principal designer of playhouses for the *Shuberts as well as for other theatre owners. In New York alone he drew up the plans for the Alvin (now the *Neil Simon) the *Ambassador, the Bijou, the *Biltmore, the Central, the *Century, the *Ethel Barrymore, the Forrest (now the *Eugene O'Neill), the 49th Street Theatre, the 46th Street Theatre (now the *Richard Rodgers), Hammerstein's, the *Imperial, the *Majestic, the Mansfield (now the *Brooks Atkinson), the Masque (now the *John Golden), the *Morosco, the *Plymouth, the Ritz (now the *Walter Kerr), the *Royale, and the Waldorf.

KRASNA, Norman (1909–84), playwright. Born in Corona, New York, he studied at Columbia and at St. John's Law School before becoming a dramatic critic for the *World* and then the *Evening Graphic*. After seeing two of his plays on Broadway, *Louder, Please* (1931) and *Small Miracle* (1934), Krasna went to Hollywood, returning for *The Man with Blond Hair* (1941) before finally finding success with the wartime comedy *Dear Ruth* (1944). Thereafter all of Krasna's best work was of a similar order: *John Loves Mary* (1947), *Time for Elizabeth* (1948), *Kind Sir* (1953), *Who Was That Lady I Saw You With?* (1958), *Sunday in New York* (1961), and *Love in E Flat* (1967). His final Broadway entry was the short-lived melodrama *We Interrupt This Program* (1975).

KREMER, Theodore. See *Bertha, the Sewing Machine Girl.*

KRONENBERGER, Louis (1904–80), critic. Born in Cincinnati and educated at the University there, he served as drama critic for *Time* (1936–61), for *PM* (1940–48), and briefly for *Town and Country*. At the same time he taught drama at numerous universities, including Columbia and Harvard, but most importantly at Brandeis, where he remained for many years. For Broadway he adapted *Anouilh's *Mademoiselle Colombe* (1954). Kronenberger was also the author of many books, and from 1952 to 1961 edited the *Best Plays* series. His writing featured a rapier wit and a unique sense of stylistic balance, which reflected his admiration of the elegances of the 18th century. Autobiography: *No Whippings, No Gold Watches*, 1970.

KRUGER, Otto (1885–1974), actor. One of Broadway's most popular leading men in the 1920s, he was born in Toledo and educated at the University of Michigan and Columbia. He first appeared before the public in 1900 in *Quo Vadis?* More than a decade in stock and touring companies followed before he made his New York debut as Jack Bowling in *The Natural Law* (1915). Among his best-remembered roles were the reformer Adam Smith in *Adam and Eva* (1919), the tubercular patient Stephen Murray in Eugene *O'Neill's *Straw* (1921), the reformed crook Lee Randall in *Alias Jimmy Valentine* (1921), the conceited but incompetent salesman Leonard Beebe in *To the Ladies* (1922), the title role in *Will Shakespeare* (1923), the hypochondriac Henry Williams in *The *Nervous Wreck* (1923), and the John Barrymore-like actor Anthony Cavendish in *The *Royal Family* (1927). After many years in films, Kruger returned to Broadway in the 1940s without ever finding a successful play.

KRUTCH, Joseph Wood (1893–1970), critic. Born in Knoxville, he earned degrees at the University of Tennessee and Columbia, where he taught for many years. From 1924 to 1952 he was also drama critic for *The Nation*. Among his many works on theatre are *The American Drama Since 1918* (1939), and *'Modernism' in Modern Drama* (1953). Krutch's interest was not so much in the presentation and immediacy of plays as in their value as enduring literature.

KUMMER, Clare [Rodman] [née Beecher] (1873?–1958), playwright. She began her career as a songwriter, but enjoyed a huge success with her first produced play, *Good Gracious Annabelle* (1916), followed by the hit William *Gillette vehicle, *A Successful Calamity* (1917). Although over a dozen more of her plays were produced on Broadway, her only other important successes were two vehicles written for her son-in-law, Roland *Young: *Rollo's Wild Oat* (1920) and *Her Master's Voice* (1933).

KUSHNER, Tony. See *Angels in America.*

L

LA CAGE AUX FOLLES (1983), a musical comedy by Harvey *Fierstein (book), Jerry *Herman (music, lyrics). [*Palace Theatre, 1,761 perf.; Tony Award.] Georges (Gene Barry), a nightclub operator, and Albin (George Hearn), a female impersonator, have long been lovers, although Georges once had a heterosexual affair that left him with a son (John Weiner). The now-grown son wants to marry the daughter of a political figure (Jay Garner) who is a crusader against homosexuals, so when the two families meet, Albin puts on his dress and is introduced as the mother of the groom. *Notable songs*: I Am What I Am; Song on the Sand; The Best of Times. Despite a potentially difficult and offensive theme, the musical's essential lightheartedness and melodiousness, coupled with a glitzy production, made it a success.

LA JOLLA PLAYHOUSE (San Diego, California). Founded by film actors Gregory Peck, Dorothy McGuire, and Mel Ferrer in 1947 to encourage live theatre on the West Coast, the company was active for only a few seasons before floundering and existing only on paper for many years. The group was revived and revitalized in 1983 by Des McAnuff who was artistic director for a decade and brought the company prestige and a *Tony Award in 1993. While the nonprofit theatre, in residence at the University of California at San Diego, has a diverse repertory, it is most known for the musical productions it has sent to Broadway: *Big River (1985), The *Who's Tommy (1993), *How to Succeed in Business Without Really Trying (1995), and *Thoroughly Modern Millie (2002). The playhouse also has a teaching institute and encourages new works.

LA MAMA EXPERIMENTAL THEATRE CLUB (New York). Founded in Greenwich Village in 1962 by Ellen Stewart, the group is the city's oldest, most durable, and least compromising experimental theatre. The performance space originally was a combination boutique and theatre, but in 1970 moved to its current location on East 4th Street where in its three theatres it has presented hundreds of events ranging from theatre to poetry readings, dance, and *performance art. In addition to its own productions, Café La MaMa (as it is more popularly known) has sponsored avant-garde companies from around the world, such as Jerzy Grotowski's Polish Lab Theatre, and produced early works by Sam *Shepard, Lanford *Wilson, Harold *Pinter, Andrei *Serban, Megan Terry, Rochelle Owens, and many others. The group also tours extensively. **Ellen STEWART** (b. 1920?) was born in Alexandria, Louisiana, of Cajun ancestry, came to New York in the 1950s, and worked as an elevator operator and clothing designer before opening her boutique that turned into a theatre.

LA SHELLE, Kirke (1862–1905), manager. Born in Wyoming, Illinois, he left school to work in newspapers, eventually rising to managing editor of several Chicago dailies. He became the business manager for E. S. *Willard, then a partner to George *Lederer, and then business manager of the *Bostonians. La Shelle embarked on an independent producing career by presenting the comic opera *The Wizard of the Nile* (1895), followed by *The Idol's Eye* (1897), *The Ameer* (1899), and *Miss Simplicity* (1902). Among the successful plays he produced were *Arizona (1900), The *Earl of Pawtucket (1903), and his collaborative dramatization with Owen Wister of that author's The *Virginian (1904).

LaCHIUSA, Michael John (b. 1962), composer, lyricist, and librettist. Born in Chautauqua, New York, LaChiusa briefly attended junior college in Boston before going to New York where he started writing musicals, first getting noticed for his *First Ladies Suite* (1993). His musical adaptation of Schnitzler's *La Ronde* called *Hello Again* (1993) was a success Off Broadway, but his Broadway efforts *Marie Christine* (1999) and *The Wild Party* (2000) were more admired than popular. LaChiusa's other works include *The Petrified Prince* (1994) and *Little Fish* (2003). The multitalented composer-writer tackles difficult and demanding projects and is highly regarded in the theatre community.

LACKAYE, Wilton (1862–1932), actor. Born in Loudon County, Virginia, and educated at Georgetown University, he was barely out of college when he made his debut as Lucentio opposite Lawrence

*Barrett in an 1883 revival of *Francesca da Rimini*. Afterward he played important roles in support of Fanny *Davenport and other stars. Among his most significant early assignments were the revolutionary Gouroc in *Paul Kauvar* (1887) and the thieving twin brother Robert in *Allan Dare* (1887). Lackaye was seen in *Featherbrain* (1889), *Shenandoah* (1889), *Money Mad* (1890), *The Power of the Press* (1891), and *Aristocracy* (1892) before playing his most famous role, the villainous Svengali in *Trilby* (1895). In 1898 he was Sir Lucius O'Trigger in Joseph *Jefferson's revival of *The Rivals*, then played leading roles in, among others, *The Children of the Ghetto* (1899), *Don Caesar's Return* (1901), *Colorado* (1901), *A Modern Magdalen* (1902), and *The Frisky Mrs. Johnson* (1903). In 1904 he produced and starred in a much-praised version of *The Pillars of Society*. He continued to appear both in new plays and revivals, especially of *Trilby*, until shortly before his death. Lackaye had a pleasant, round face, with large eyes, and for many years sported a prominent handlebar moustache.

LADDER, THE (1926), a play by J. Frank Davis. [Mansfield Theatre, 794 perf.] Margaret Newell (Antoinette *Perry) has proposals from two men, the charming, but vacillating Roger Crane (Vernon Steele) and the ruthless Stephen Pennock (Hugh Buckler), who has ruined Roger in business. Thinking back, Margaret realizes that the men's proposals are nothing new. In the 14th century, when Stephen was the Earl of Orleton, he murdered Roger to win her. Under other names Stephen did similar dastardly acts in the 17th and 19th centuries. So Margaret throws her lot with Roger again, come what may. Ridiculed by most critics, the Brock *Pemberton offering nevertheless was the fourth-longest-running show in Broadway history when it closed. It was able to run so long because a millionaire oil man, Edgar B. Davis, who believed in reincarnation as much as the author, underwrote the play for its entire stand and even admitted the public free when playgoers would not buy tickets. The play never made a profit, and Davis is reputed to have spent between a half million and a million dollars on it.

LADIES' NIGHT [often called *Ladies' Night in a Turkish Bath*] (1920), a farce by Avery *Hopwood and Charlton Andrews. [Eltinge Theatre, 375 perf.] Because Jimmy Walters (John *Cumberland) is so shy and prudish, his friends decide to take him to an artists' ball, a sort of pseudo-pagan ritual where he will see lots of bare flesh. Unfortunately, the police raid the party, so Jimmy flees through a window into the building next door, which houses a Turkish bath. It so happens it is a special night at the bath catering only to ladies, so it takes Jimmy

two acts to calm down and explain his actions. A brainless but funny farce, the A. H. *Woods production was one of the major hits of its day and was long popular in summer stock. It was revived Off Broadway in 1961.

LADY, BE GOOD! (1924), a musical comedy by Guy *Bolton, Fred *Thompson (book), George *Gershwin (music), Ira *Gershwin (lyrics). [Liberty Theatre, 330 perf.] After Dick Trevor (Fred *Astaire) rebuffs Josephine Vanderwater (Jayne Auburn), she evicts him and his sister Susie (Adele *Astaire) from an apartment building she owns. By coincidence both the Trevors and Josephine have the same lawyer, "Watty" Watkins (Walter *Catlett), so he sets about righting matters. Since Watkins himself is in a jam, his fee to the moneyless Trevors is to demand that Susie pose as a Mexican wife in order to collect money from a divorce case. In the end, Susie marries Jack Robinson (Alan Edwards), and Dick ditches Josephine permanently for Shirley Vernon (Kathlene Martyn). *Notable songs*: Fascinating Rhythm; Oh, Lady Be Good!; So Am I. This was one of the most important of American musicals, for its Gershwin score established the ascendancy of native, jazz-based lyricism in American musical comedy and helped promote a clear distinction between musical comedy and operetta. The first collaboration of George and Ira Gershwin to reach Broadway, the Alex A. *Aarons and Vinton *Freedley production brought them instant fame as a team. It also consolidated the growing reputation of the Astaires.

LADY IN THE DARK (1941), a musical comedy by Moss *Hart (book), Kurt *Weill (music), Ira *Gershwin (lyrics). [Alvin Theatre, 467 perf.] Although Liza Elliott (Gertrude *Lawrence) is a successful fashion magazine editor, privately she is an unhappy woman. She tells her analyst that while her dreams are filled with familiar figures, they act in unfamiliar ways. Most prominent in her dreams are Kendall Nesbitt (Bert Lytell), her lover and the man who has helped her to the top of her profession; Charley Johnson (MacDonald Carey), her crusty advertising manager; Russell Paxton (Danny *Kaye), the magazine's effeminate photographer; and Randy Curtis (Victor Mature), a handsome but stupid movie star. By recounting her dreams, Liza comes to realize that her father's disdain for her when she was a child has warped her relations with men, yet she finds a soul mate in Charley. *Notable songs*: My Ship; The Saga of Jenny; Tschaikowsky; This Is New. Prompted by Hart's interest in psychoanalysis, the script was innovative in that all but one of the musical numbers were presented as part of Liza's essentially surrealistic dream sequences. The Sam H.

*Harris production was one of Larwence's greatest triumphs and it made a star of Kaye.

LADY OF LYONS, THE (1838). This romantic drama by *Bulwer-Lytton centers on Pauline Deschapelles, who is tricked by her rejected suitor, the Marquis Beauséant, into marrying Claude Melnotte, her gardener's son. Beauséant had persuaded Melnotte to pose as a foreign prince, but when, after the marriage, Melnotte takes Pauline to the home of his widowed mother, she learns the truth. The remorseful Melnotte joins the army and the marriage is annulled. Beauséant induces Pauline to marry him to save her father from bankruptcy. However, Melnotte returns from the wars as a hero and Pauline realizes that she truly loves him. The original American cast at New York's *Park Theatre in 1838 included Mrs. Richardson as Pauline, Edwin *Forrest as Melnotte, and Peter *Richings as Beauséant. No less than Charlotte *Cushman was the Widow Melnotte. The work remained one of the most popular of all plays for the rest of the century. The list of important performers who acted in the play would include virtually every major serious actor and actress of the period.

LAFAYETTE THEATRE (New York). Along with the vaudeville house *Apollo, the Lafayette was the most famous theatre in Harlem. Built in 1912, at a time when New York's major African-American district was moving from San Juan Hill to the area, it gained widespread celebrity when it offered the hugely successful *Darktown Follies* (1913). The emphasis on musicals was abandoned when Anita Bush moved her stock company to the theatre in 1915. The company soon became known as the Lafayette Players and helped "Negro" performers, such as Charles *Gilpin, gain recognition. Its repertory ranged from Shakespeare to new plays of contemporary black life. The Players disbanded in 1932, and later in the 1930s it became the Harlem center for the *Federal Theatre Project under whose aegis it offered highly praised mountings of such works as *Run, Little Chillun!*, *Stevedore*, *Macbeth*, and *The Swing Mikado*. Thereafter the house fell on hard times and for a while was used as a church, and part of the upstairs housed a company called the New Lafayette Theatre. The structure burned in 1968, soon after an attempt had been made to restore it to live theatre. The theatre was sometimes called "The House Beautiful." A large tree, reputedly an elm, which stood in front of it, was considered a talisman by struggling African-American performers, who felt that touching it would bring them luck and so named it the "Tree of Hope."

LAHR, Bert [né Irving Lahrheim] (1895–1967), comic actor. The rubber-faced, caterwauling comedian, famous for his "gnong-gnong" and "Some fun, eh kid?," began his career in vaudeville and burlesque. His first Broadway assignment was in *Delmar's Revels* (1927), but it was his clowning as the punch-drunk Gink Schiner in *Hold Everything!* (1928) that made him a star. Appearances followed in *Flying High* (1930), *Hot-Cha!* (1932), *George White's Music Hall Varieties* (1932), *Life Begins at 8:40* (1934), *George White's Scandals of 1935*, *The Show Is On* (1936), *Du Barry Was a Lady* (1939), and *Seven Lively Arts* (1944). In 1946 he was praised for his performance as Skid in a revival of *Burlesque*, then, after appearing in *Two on the Aisle* (1951), he won further laurels for his portrayal of Estragon in *Waiting for Godot* (1956), a role he claimed he never understood. Lahr's later performances included Boniface in the farce *Hotel Paradiso* (1957), the revue *The Boys Against the Girls* (1959), a number of quick-change roles in *The Beauty Part* (1962), and, his last Broadway appearance, the sly miser *Foxy* (1964). His son is critic and author **John LAHR** (b. 1941) who was born in Los Angeles and educated at Yale and Oxford University. After working as a dramaturg for some regional theatres, he started writing reviews in *Evergreen Review*, the *Village Voice*, and later *The New Yorker*. Among his many books is a biography of his father, *Notes on a Cowardly Lion*, 1969.

LAMB, Thomas (1871–1942), architect. Born in Dundee, Scotland, he came to America while still a youth and studied architecture at the Cooper Union Institute. Although he is best remembered for his Adamesque movie palaces and for designing the second Madison Square Garden, he also was the designer of numerous legitimate theatres. His New York playhouses were the Eltinge, the Harris, the *Mark Hellinger, and, with Joseph *Urban, the *Ziegfeld.

LAMBS, THE. See Theatrical Clubs.

LAMOS, Mark (b. 1946), director, manager, and actor. He was born and raised in Chicago and educated at Northwestern with intentions of becoming a concert violinist. Long associated with the Hartford Stage where he has served as artistic director since 1980, Lamos is an actor-turned-director who is known for his daring theatrical concepts in staging classic works, often changing time periods and locations but still remaining faithful to the text. Among his many outstanding productions in regional theatre are *Undiscovered Country* (1981), *Twelfth Night* (1985), *Peer Gynt* (1990), *The *Merchant of Venice* (1993), and the nine-play cycle *The Greeks* (1982). Lamos's Hartford Stage production of *Our Country's Good* transferred to Broadway in 1991 with high critical approval.

LANDER, Mrs. [née Jean Margaret Davenport] (1829–1903), actress. The daughter of English performers, she made her American debut in 1838 as a child prodigy. When she returned to New York in 1849, both she and her art had matured. She won applause for her interpretation of the heroines in such popular plays as *Romeo and Juliet*, *The *Hunchback*, *The *Lady of Lyons*, and *Ingomar*. In 1853 she was the first actress to portray Adrienne Lecouvreur and Camille in English to American audiences. She retired briefly after her marriage in 1860 to Frederick Lander, but resumed her career after he was killed in the Civil War. Among her later parts were the title role in Legouvé's *Medea*, Colombe in *Colombe's Birthday*, Peg Woffington in *Masks and Faces*, and Hester Prynne in *The Scarlet Letter*. A small, attractive woman, she was, according to William *Winter, "remarkable for thoroughness of impersonation, complete command of the essential implements of histrionic art, a fine intellect, a lovely feminine temperament, peculiar clarity and sweetness of elocution, and the controlling faculty of taste."

LANDESMAN, Rocco (b. 1947), producer. A student and then a teacher at Yale, Landesman was a stock trader and racehorse owner before embarking on theatrical producing with the Broadway hit *Big River* (1985). Landesman subsequently presented such varied shows as *Into the Woods* (1987), *City of Angels* (1989), *Moon Over Buffalo* (1995), *The *Piano Lesson* (1990), and *The *Producers* (2001). He is president of *Jujamcyn and has supervised dozens of productions in the corporation's theatres.

LANDESMAN-ETTINGER, Heidi (b. 1951), designer. The innovative scenic (and sometime costume) designer studied at Occidental College and Yale and is known for her poetic depictions of locale that defy realism but still evoke a sense of place vividly. After working in regional theatre, Landesman was first noticed in New York for her landscaped setting for A *Midsummer Night's Dream* (1982) in Central Park. Her bold design for *Painting Churches* (1983) Off Broadway led to her award-winning sets for *Big River* (1985) in which she depicted the Mississippi River through a series of gleaming wooden planks. Her other Broadway success was the dollhouse-like settings for *The *Secret Garden* (1991). Landesman's other notable designs include *The Red Shoes* (1993), *Moon Over Buffalo* (1995), *Smokey Joe's Cafe* (1995), *The Triumph of Love* (1997), *The *Sound of Music* (1998), and *Tom Sawyer* (2001). She co-produced some of these with her then-husband Rocco *Landesman but since separating uses the name Landesman-Ettinger.

LANE, Burton [né Levy] (1912–96), composer. The New York native began his professional career by writing the music for songs that were interpolated into the revues *Three's a Crowd* (1930) and *The Third Little Show* (1931). He then wrote the score for *Earl Carroll's Vanities of 1931*, after which he spent a decade in Hollywood. Lane returned to provide songs for *Hold On to Your Hats* (1940) and *Laughing Room Only* (1944) but wrote his best score for *Finian's Rainbow* (1947). He also provided commendable music for the less-successful musicals *On a Clear Day You Can See Forever* (1965) and *Carmelina* (1979).

LANE, Nathan [né Joseph Lane] (b. 1956), character actor. The pudgy comic who has the qualities and talents of the great Broadway clowns, has appeared in Shakespeare and serious new plays but is most beloved for his comedies and musical farces. He was born in Jersey City, New Jersey, and worked as a telemarketer, pollster, and stand-up comic before acting in stock and dinner theatres. Lane was on the New York stage by 1978 and was first noticed four years later as the wild playwright Roland Maule in *Present Laughter* (1982). He became a major stage star when he played comic gambler Nathan Detroit in the 1992 revival of *Guys and Dolls,* and his other musical triumphs were the conniving slave Pseudolus in A *Funny Thing Happened on the Way to the Forum* (1996) and the shyster theatrical producer Max Bialystock in *The *Producers* (2001). Lane's nonmusical roles include the opera-loving Mendy in *The Lisbon Traviata* (1989), the vacationing Sam in *Lips Together, Teeth Apart* (1991), the gay costume designer Buzz in *Love! Valour! Compassion!* (1994), the complex television star Max Prince in *Laughter on the 23rd Floor* (1993), and the curmudgeonly Sheridan Whiteside in *The *Man Who Came to Dinner* (2000). Ben Brantley in the *New York Times* described Lane as "droll and exhibitionistic" as Max Bialystock, "with a clarinet speaking voice that segues naturally into song."

LANE, William Henry (1825?–52), dancer. An African American, probably born in New York, he first attracted attention in the early 1840s with his superb jigs and other dances at a hall in the notorious Five Points district where he performed as Juba or Master Juba. He was considered for a time the major rival to Master John *Diamond, the young white dancer, and is said to have bested him in several challenge dances. Lane performed in 1846 with White's Serenaders, a minstrel band, but in 1848 left for England, where he died.

LANG, Harold (1923–71), actor, singer, and dancer. The athletic song-and-dance man was born in Daly City, California, and began dancing for the American Ballet Theatre before being cast as a featured dancer on Broadway in *Mr. Strauss Goes to Boston* (1945). Lang was first applauded for his careless, breezy Bill Calhoun in *Kiss Me, Kate* (1948) and received more plaudits for his amoral Joey in the popular 1951 revival of *Pal Joey*. His subsequent Broadway appearances were less successful, and in his later years Lang became a dance coach.

LANGELLA, Frank (b. 1940), actor. The dark, youthful-looking leading man, whose versatility has allowed him to shine in both classic and contemporary plays, has been a durable and favorite actor on the New York stage for forty years. He was born in Bayonne, New Jersey, and studied theatre at Syracuse University before appearing in stock productions. Langella made his New York debut in 1963 and started to get noticed as a member of the *Lincoln Center Theatre Company, particularly as the young Will Shakespeare in *A Cry of Players* (1968). Among his many memorable performances were the personified lizard Leslie in *Seascape* (1975), the honorable title hero in *The Prince of Homburg* (1976), a young and sensuous Dracula (1977), the guilt-ridden lawyer Quentin in *After the Fall* (1984), an egotistical Sherlock Holmes in *Sherlock's Last Case* (1987), the tormented Captain in *The Father* (1996), and the Russian fop Tropatchov in *Fortune's Fool* (2002). Langella frequently returned to regional theatre, in particular the *Williamstown Theatre Festival.

LANGNER, Lawrence (1890–1962), producer. Born in Wales, he drifted into theatrical work in London before immigrating to America. In 1914 he was one of the founders of the *Washington Square Players, and after that troupe disbanded he was an organizer of the *Theatre Guild, which he was to run with Theresa *Helburn for all of its greatest years, supervising more than two hundred productions. Langer also built the Westport (Connecticut) Country Playhouse and was founder and president of the *American Shakespeare Festival in Stratford (Connecticut). Alone or with his wife, Armina Marshall, he wrote several plays, the most notable of which was The *Pursuit of Happiness* (1933). Autobiography: *The Magic Curtain*, 1951.

LANGTRY, Lillie (sometimes spelled Lily) [née Emilie Charlotte Le Breton] (1853–1929), actress. The daughter of a minister on the island of Jersey, she married into London society and became one of the first Englishwomen from high society to embark on a stage career. Known popularly as "The Jersey Lily," she was a great beauty who was not always careful of the proprieties of the time (one of her extended affairs was with Edward, Prince of Wales) but her glamour and the hints of scandal helped make her a celebrity. Langtry made her American debut in 1882 as Hester Grazebrook in *An Unequal Match*. Although she attempted such classic roles as Rosalind and Lady Macbeth, she was at her best in contemporary pieces. She made a number of American visits and was best received in such plays as *Gossip* (1895) and the controversial *The Degenerates* (1900). Surprisingly, given his customarily strict moral attitudes, William *Winter was one of her admirers. He praised "her well proportioned, lissome figure, shapely and finely poised head, long, oval face, pure white complexion, large gray eyes," adding that her acting "put detraction to silence and won and held a large measure of public sympathy and critical respect." Biography: *Because I Loved Him: The Life and Loves of Lillie Langtry*, Noel B. Gerson, 1971.

LANSBURY, Angela [Brigid] (b. 1925), actress. The versatile London-born performer came to Broadway after a long career in films. Her first New York role was the high-strung wife Marcelle in the farce *Hotel Paradiso* (1957), followed by the independent mother Helen in *A Taste of Honey* (1960), the corrupt but lovable mayor Cora Hoover Hoople in *Anyone Can Whistle* (1964), the unconventional *Mame* (1966), the pleasantly demented Aurelia in *Dear World* (1969), and the domineering Rose in *Gypsy* (1974). But her greatest stage performance was probably the delightfully vicious Mrs. Lovett in *Sweeney Todd* (1979). Richard Eder, describing her Lovett in the *Times*, noted "her face is a comic face; her eyes revolve three times to announce the arrival of an idea; but there is a blue sadness blinking behind them." Biography: *Balancing Act: The Authorized Biography of Angela Lansbury*, Martin *Gottfried, 1999.

LAPINE, James (b. 1949), playwright and director. A native of Mansfield, Ohio, he studied design at the California Institute of the Arts and apprenticed at the Yale School of Drama. But he turned to writing and directing, first calling attention to his abilities with his play *Table Settings* (1980), then earned wide acclaim for his staging of the Off-Broadway musicals *March of the Falsettos* (1981) and *Falsettoland* (1990). Lapine is most known for the musicals with Stephen *Sondheim that he wrote and directed: *Sunday in the Park with George* (1984), *Into the Woods* (1987), and *Passion* (1994). His other directing credits include A *Midsummer Night's Dream* (1982) and *A Winter's Tale* (1989) for the *New York Shakespeare Festival, and on Broadway The *Diary of Anne Frank* (1997), *Golden Child* (1998), *Dirty Blonde* (2000), and *Amour* (2002).

LARDNER, Ring[gold Wilmer] (1885–1933), playwright. The famed humorist and short-story writer was best known to playgoers as George S. *Kaufman's collaborator on *June Moon* (1929), a spoof of Tin Pan Alley. A year earlier he had been the author of a play about baseball, *Elmer the Great*. He also contributed sketches and lyrics to several musicals, among them some editions of the *Ziegfeld Follies*, *The 49ers* (1922), and *Smiles* (1930).

LARIMORE, Earle (1899–1947), actor. He was born in Portland, Oregon, where he began acting while still a child, then made his New York debut in 1925. Larimore's early performances showed great promise: the ruthless husband George in *Ned McCobb's Daughter* (1926), the cowed son Robert in The *Silver Cord* (1926), the determined suitor Alistin Lowe in The *Second Man* (1927), the weak husband Sam Evans in *Strange Interlude* (1928), the rich Jew Norman Rose in *Hotel Universe* (1930), the Orestes-like son Orin Mannon in *Mourning Becomes Electra* (1931), the radical editor Richard Kurt in *Biography* (1932), and John, the better half of the hero's split personality, in *Days Without End* (1934). Following this impressive series his career inexplicably faltered. His last appearance on Broadway was in 1935, after which he gradually faded into obscurity until his premature death.

LARRIMORE, Francine [née Fanya Levovksy] (1898–1975), actress. Niece of the great Yiddish actor, Jacob *Adler, the blue-eyed beauty with reddish-gold hair was born in France but came to America while still very young and made her debut as a child in 1910 in A *Fool There Was*. Her first major success came as the baby-talking, homebody Blanche Wheeler in *Fair and Warmer* (1916) in Chicago. Among Larrimore's later successes were the hired "other woman" Nita Leslie in *Parlor, Bedroom and Bath* (1917), the brazen flapper Theodora Gloucester in *Nice People* (1921), the publicity-seeking murderess Roxie Hart in *Chicago* (1926), the divorcée Kitty Brown in *Let Us Be Gay* (1929), and the nightclub singer Abbey Fane who marries into society in *Brief Moment* (1931).

LARSON, Jonathan. See *Rent*.

LAST MILE, THE (1930), a drama by John Wexley. [Sam H. Harris Theatre, 285 perf.] The prisoners on death row at Keystone State Penitentiary help Richard Walters (James Bell) sit out his last moments. Two weeks later it is Eddie Werner's turn to die. But as a guard comes to give Eddie (George Leach) his final meal, the other prisoners, led by the hardened, ruthless John Mears (Spencer Tracy), seize the guard and kill him. A bloody mutiny has begun, which for a time appears to be succeeding. However, the odds against the prisoners ultimately prove irresistible. Realizing the futility of his uprising, Mears walks out to surrender and is gunned down. Noting that it had been many years since a play caused so much excitement in theatrical circles, Burns *Mantle found the Herman *Shumlin production "a tragedy so tense, so stripped of theatrical artificialities, and emotionally so moving that even calloused reviewers of plays were frank to admit its disturbing and unsettling effect upon their nerves." The first act was derived largely from a short play written by an inmate, Robert Blake, who had been executed shortly afterward. He claimed his dialogue was mostly verbatim transcriptions of actual conversations. The New York–born **John WEXLEY** (1907–85) was a nephew of Maurice *Schwartz and was also an actor. He wrote numerous one-act plays as well as two other full-length plays that were presented in New York: the labor drama *Steel* (1931) and *They Shall Not Die* (1934), a dramatization of the Scottsboro case. **Spencer TRACY** (1900–67), a native of Milwaukee, had appeared in a number of Broadway plays during the 1920s, but only achieved major attention with this performance. His distinguished film career began when he re-created this role on screen. Except for starring in the short-lived Robert *Sherwood drama *The Rugged Path* (1945), the remainder of his career was in films.

LAST NIGHT OF BALLYHOO, THE (1997), a play by Alfred *Uhry. [*Helen Hayes Theatre, 557 perf.; Tony Award.] In Atlanta in December of 1939, *Gone with the Wind* is about to premiere and news of Hitler invading Poland is all over town, but the only important event for local Jews is Ballyhoo, a festival and formal dance at the exclusive Standard Club. German Jew Beulah "Boo" Levy (Dana Ivey) is desperate for her plain daughter Lala (Jessica Hecht) to get a date for the dance, especially since Lala's attractive cousin Sunny (Arija Bareikis) from Wellesley College is going with a New Yorker named Joe Farkas (Paul Rudd). But it turns out Joe is an Eastern European Jew from Brooklyn, and when he encounters snobbery and prejudice at the club, he walks out. Sunny and Joe work out their difficulties and Lala ends up marrying a well-connected Jew nicknamed Peachy. A "well-crafted, audience pleasing play," it benefited by a first-class cast (particularly *Ivey) skillfully directed by Ron Lagomarsino. The play had originated at the *Alliance Theatre in Atlanta.

LAST OF THE RED HOT LOVERS, THE (1969), a comedy by Neil *Simon. [*Eugene O'Neill Theatre, 706 perf.] Barney Cashman (James Coco), the owner of a fish restaurant, is middle-aged, overweight, married, and anxious to have one last fling.

Knowing that his mother's apartment is empty on certain days, three times he lures a totally different type of woman there and attempts to seduce her. He bungles every attempt. In desperation he asks up the only other woman he can think of: his wife, Thelma. But apparently even she is not too eager to accept his invitation. One of Simon's many gag-filled yet probing comedies, it was assessed by Richard *Watts Jr. of the New York *Post* as "delightfully hilarious and witty, as well as filled with the wisdom about human nature characteristic of all his work."

LAST WORD, THE (1890), a comedy by Augustin *Daly. [Daly's Theatre, 101 perf.] When Faith Rutherwell (Isabel Irving) announces she will marry Boris Bagoleff (Sidney Herbert) instead of the Baron Stuyve (Sidney Bowkett), whom her father (George Clarke) has selected for her, she is forced to leave her father's house. The Baroness Vera Boraneff (Ada *Rehan), a beautiful and rich "Witch from the Neva," whose laugh is "a full yard of velvet sunshine," and who is also Boris's sister, takes Faith under her wing. Faith's brother, Harry (John *Drew), a conscientious but bookish physician, comes to Vera's house to demand that Faith change her mind. But Vera not only proves to Harry that the Baron is treacherous and her brother worthwhile, she makes Harry realize that he loves her. Together they make the elder Rutherwell see things their way. Based on Shoenthan's *Das letzte Wort*, the play was one of Daly's last major successes in modern comedy.

LATE GEORGE APLEY, THE (1944), a comedy by John P. Marquand and George S. *Kaufman. [*Lyceum Theatre, 385 perf.] George Apley (Leo G. *Carroll) is a Harvard-educated Boston Brahmin who has lived a happy, if stolidly conventional life. But his contentment is jolted when his daughter Eleanor (Joan Chandler) falls in love with a Greenwich Village bohemian who is, horror of horrors, a Yale graduate. At the same time, George's son, John (David McKay), announces he will marry the daughter of a rich manufacturer from Worcester. Eleanor has the gumption to marry, but John goes off to Europe after his fiancée's father also objects to John's marriage plans. Twelve years later George is dead and John has become a stuffy Brahmin, thereby continuing the family tradition. Although some critics found the play formless, little more than a series of amusing, loosely related incidents, Robert Garland of the *Journal-American* hailed the Max *Gordon production as "an evening of sheer delight, wise, witty and enchantingly satirical." Carroll's performance captured Brahmin stuffiness to a T, but never lost the audience's interest or affection. The comedy was based on Marquand's *Pulitzer Prize–winning novel of the same name.

LATEINER, Joseph (1853–1935), playwright. For many years this European-born author of Yiddish plays and operettas was one of the most prolific and popular figures in American-Jewish theatricals, although, as historian Nahma Sandrow has written, his name is now "synonymous with vulgar baked goods of uncertain freshness." Lateiner wrote more than eighty plays, including *Ezra; or, The Eternal Jew*, *Mishke and Moshke; or, Europeans in America*, and *The Jewish Heart*.

LATHAM, Frederick G. (1853?–1943), producer and director. The Englishman had a long, successful theatre career in London before coming to America in 1897 to work with Maurice Grau. Shortly thereafter he managed the American tours of Sarah *Bernhardt and *Coquelin. For many years Latham was an important director of musicals, including *Mlle. Modiste* (1905), *The *Red Mill* (1906), *The *Firefly* (1912), *The Only Girl* (1914), *The Princess Pat* (1915), *Eileen* (1917), *Apple Blossoms* (1919), and *The Night Boat* (1920).

LATOUCHE, John [Treville] (1917–56), lyricist and librettist. The brilliant writer, whose early death deprived the musical theatre of a major talent, was born in Richmond, Virginia, and contributed his first lyrics to *From Vienna* (1939). He called attention to his art with his work in *Cabin in the Sky* (1940). Subsequent collaborations included *Banjo Eyes* (1941), *Beggar's Holiday* (1946), and *Ballet Ballads* (1948). Latouche's finest achievement was his libretto for *The *Golden Apple* (1954), a recounting of the *Iliad* and the *Odyssey* in terms of turn-of-the-century America. Since there was no spoken dialogue, his lyrics in effect comprised the complete libretto. His last lyrics were heard in *The Vamp* (1955) and in *Candide* (1956). Latouche's work was celebrated in the Off-Broadway revue *Taking a Chance on Love* (2000).

LAUGHTON, Charles (1899–1962), actor and director. The heavyset, wry-faced Englishman first appeared in America in two thrillers, *Payment Deferred* (1931) and *The Fatal Alibi* (1932). He did not return to the stage until after a long, distinguished film career, appearing in his own adaptation of *Galileo* (1947) then playing the Devil in *Don Juan in Hell* (1951), also directing the production. He next adapted and directed *John Brown's Body* (1953) and staged *The Caine Mutiny Court-Martial* (1954). Laughton's last appearance was as Undershaft in a 1956 revival of *Major Barbara*, which he staged. Biographies: *Charles Laughton and I*, Elsa Lanchester (his wife), 1939;

Charles Laughton: A Difficult Actor, Simon Callow, 1987.

LAURENTS, Arthur (b. 1918), playwright and director. He was born in Brooklyn and educated at Cornell before his first play, *Home of the Brave* (1945), was praised by many critics, but failed commercially. His only play to find major success was one of his lightest, *The *Time of the Cuckoo* (1952). Laurents found more favor as a librettist, especially with *West Side Story* (1957) and *Gypsy* (1959). His other librettos were *Anyone Can Whistle* (1964), **Do I Hear a Waltz?* (1965), **Hallelujah, Baby!* (1967), and *Nick and Nora* (1991). He directed most of these, as well as *I Can Get It for You Wholesale* (1962), **La Cage aux Folles* (1983), and several revivals of *Gypsy*. Autobiography: *Original Story By: A Memoir of Broadway and Hollywood*, 2001.

LAVIN, Linda (b. 1937), actress. She was born in Portland, Maine, and educated at William and Mary College before going to New York and getting cast in Off-Broadway productions, most notably as a variety of kooky characters in *The Mad Show* (1966). Lavin was first noticed on Broadway in 1966 as the seductive Sydney singing "You've Got Possibilities" in *It's a Bird, It's a Plane, It's Superman,* followed by more plaudits for her cold, hilarious Elaine in *The *Last of the Red Hot Lovers* (1969). During the late 1970s and early 1980s she was busy with television work that made her a familiar face across America, so she received star billing (and rave reviews) when she returned to the New York stage with her tender performance as the Jewish mother Kate in *Broadway Bound* (1986). Subsequent roles of note include two very different New Yorkers in *Death Defying Acts* (1995), the outspoken Mrs. Van Daan in *The *Diary of Anne Frank* (1997), the depressed Marjorie trying to hold on to her sanity in *The *Tale of the Allergist's Wife* (2000), and the indomitable grandmother Nanny in *Hollywood Arms* (2002). John *Lahr in *The New Yorker* described Lavin as "Nancy Walker's natural heir" and her Marjorie as "small but not demure . . . even when she shuffles about the stage in her black slippers, she walks like a guardsman on parade."

LAW OF THE LAND, THE (1914), a play by George *Broadhurst. [48th Street Theatre, 221 perf.] Mrs. Harding (Julia *Dean) puts up with her savagely sadistic husband (Charles Lane) for the sake of her young son, Bennie (Master Macomber), but when Harding slashes at Bennie with a bullwhip, Mrs. Harding grabs a gun and shoots. The understanding family doctor is willing to declare the death accidental, Mrs. Harding's friends are prepared to tamper with the evidence to exonerate her, and her most ardent admirer, Geoffrey Morton (Milton Sills), stands ready to claim he shot Harding. For a time Mrs. Harding seems willing to let Morton take the blame, only finally to blurt out a confession. However, the kindly Inspector Cochrane (George *Fawcett), seeing the whip marks on the young boy, writes a report that assures no jury would convict the woman. While not as successful as Broadhurst's earlier and not dissimilar *Bought and Paid For*, the play was sufficiently taut and thrilling to find a wide audience.

LAWRENCE and LEE, playwriting team. Jerome Lawrence (b. 1915), a native of Cleveland and a graduate of Ohio State University, collaborated on all his major works with Robert E. Lee (1918–94), a native of Elyria, Ohio, who was educated at Ohio Wesleyan and Drake. They wrote the books for such musicals as *Look, Ma, I'm Dancin'!* (1948) and *Mame* (1966), the latter taken from their popular play, **Auntie Mame* (1956), which in turn had been based on a best-selling novel. The team's plays include *The Incomparable Max* (1971) and *First Monday in October* (1978), but their most notable drama was **Inherit the Wind* (1955), a retelling of the 1925 Scopes "Monkey" trial. Another work, *The Night Thoreau Spent in Jail*, was popular regionally but never played in New York.

LAWRENCE, Gertrude [née Gertrud Alexandra Dagmar Lawrence Klasen] (1898–1952), actress. Although she could not dance well and sometimes sang off-key, this graceful, haughty beauty was one of the great stars of the musical stage, as well as of nonmusical comedy. She was born in London, where she had begun to make an important name for herself in revues before coming to America with **Charlot's Revue* (1924). After appearing in a 1926 version of the same show, Lawrence was starred in **Oh, Kay!* (1926), followed by leading roles in *Treasure Girl* (1928), *Candle-Light* (1929), and *The International Revue* (1930). Lawrence then scored a major success as Amanda Prynne, playing opposite Noel *Coward, with whom she was long and closely associated, in his **Private Lives* (1931). She returned to New York in 1936 to again play opposite Coward in his *Tonight at 8:30*, a bill of one-act plays. Successes followed as Susan Trexel in **Susan and God* (1937), and as the neglected wife Lydia Kenyon in *Skylark* (1939). Lawrence returned to musicals to play editor Liza Elliott in **Lady in the Dark* (1941). After the war she appeared as Eliza Doolittle in a revival of **Pygmalion* (1945). Her last appearance on stage was perhaps her most beloved: as the English teacher Anna Leonowens in *The *King and I* (1951). Bio: *Gertrude Lawrence*, Sheridan Morley, 1981.

LAWSON, John Howard (1894–1977), playwright. He was born in Manhattan and educated at Williams College where he began writing plays, several of them produced outside of New York. His first play to reach Broadway was the expressionistic satire *Roger Bloomer* (1923), and his extreme left-wing bent was even more pronounced in the labor drama *Processional* (1925). Lawson continued, although with less success, to write similarly controversial pieces, most memorably the *Group Theatre mounting of his *Marching Song* (1937). Ironically, he left the theatre for more lucrative film writing, remaining an important screenwriter until he was blacklisted in the McCarthy era. Lawson was also the author of *Theory and Technique of Playwriting* (1936).

LAYTON, Joe [né Joseph Lichtman] (1931–94), choreographer and director. The Brooklyn-born dancer made his debut in the chorus of *Oklahoma!* in 1947 and danced in several other shows before choreographing a 1959 Off-Broadway revival of *On the Town*. He subsequently created the dances for *Once Upon a Mattress* (1959), The *Sound of Music* (1959), *Greenwillow* (1960), *Tenderloin* (1960), and *Sail Away* (1961). In 1962 he handled both the choreography and direction of *No Strings*, doing double duty also for *The Girl Who Came to Supper* (1963), *Drat! The Cat!* (1965), *Sherry!* (1967), *George M!* (1968), *Dear World* (1969), *Two by Two* (1970), *Platinum* (1978), and *Barnum* (1980).

LE GALLIENNE, Eva (1899–1991), actress, manager, and director. Daughter of the famous novelist and poet Richard Le Gallienne, she was born in London and trained at the Royal Academy of Dramatic Arts, acting briefly in England before making her American debut as Rose in *Mrs. Boltay's Daughters* (1915). Le Gallienne scored her first major success as Julie who loves the ne'er-do-well hero in *Liliom* (1921), and consolidated her newfound fame when she played Princess Alexandra in a second *Molnar play, *The Swan* (1923). In the 1925–26 season she mounted her own productions of *The Master Builder* and *John Gabriel Borkman*, playing Hilda Wangel and Ella Rentheim, and later the same year established her *Civic Repertory Theatre in an attempt to offer low-priced productions of classics. She directed and appeared in many of its productions over the next six years, playing, among others, Masha in *The Three Sisters*, Viola in *Twelfth Night*, Sister Joanna in *The Cradle Song*, Elsa in *Alison's House*, the White Queen in *Alice in Wonderland*, and the title roles of *Hedda Gabler* and *Peter Pan*. In 1942 she won applause as the spiteful sister Lettie in *Uncle Harry*. With Cheryl *Crawford and Margaret *Webster she made another attempt at forming a permanent ensemble in 1946, calling it the *American Repertory Company, but its life was short. Many of Le Gallienne's subsequent appearances were in short-lived failures, but years later she scored a major success as the theatrical dowager Fanny Cavendish in a 1975 revival of The *Royal Family*. Her last appearances were in *To Grandmother's House We Go* (1981) and *Alice in Wonderland* (1982). A small woman, with a tiny, tight-featured face, her acting struck many as too studiously mannered, but she brought an exceptional intelligence and dedication to all her work. Autobiographies: *At 33*, 1934; *With a Quiet Heart*, 1953; biography: *Eva Le Gallienne*, Helen Sheehy, 1996.

LEACOCK, J. See *Fall of British Tyranny, The*.

LEAGUE OF AMERICAN THEATRES AND PRODUCERS. Founded in 1930 as the League of New York Theatres, its purpose was "to protect the general public, patrons of the theatre, owners of theatrical entertainments, operators of theatres and reputable theatre ticket brokers against the evils of speculation in theatre tickets." Since its founding it has significantly enlarged its scope, most notably in the field of labor relations. It now regularly negotiates with all major theatre unions as well as with the *Dramatists Guild. In 1973 the name was broadened to include theatres and producers outside of New York.

LEAGUE OF HISTORIC AMERICAN THEATRES. A nonprofit association founded in 1977 by Michael P. Price of the *Goodspeed Opera House and Gene Chesley, professor of theatre design at the University of California, its purpose is to promote the preservation and use of historic auditoriums. The League defines a historic theatre as one built before 1940, which 1) is an architecturally significant structure deemed worthy of preservation; 2) has played an important role in the history of the American stage; or 3) can be used as a performing-arts facility. More than forty important historic theatres are members.

LEAGUE OF RESIDENT THEATRES. Founded in 1965 by Peter Zeisler of the *Guthrie Theatre, Thomas C. Fichandler of the *Arena Stage, and Morris Kaplan, an attorney, its purpose was to serve as a trade organization for resident professional theatres. It regularly negotiates contracts with pertinent theatrical unions. More than sixty nonprofit theatres across the country are members of LORT (as it is usually called), each one ranked as either A, B, C, or D (depending on budgets, size of audience, number of seats, and so on) to determine equitable salaries and royalty payments.

Some consider the LORT network America's national theatre.

LEAH KLESCHNA (1904), a drama by C. M. S. *McLellan. [Manhattan Theatre, 131 perf.] Leah Kleschna (Minnie Maddern *Fiske) has long admired a man who saved her during a shipwreck, but she does not know his name. Her admiration would seem to be one of Leah's few commendable qualities, for she is a thief who steals at her father's behest. When her father sends her to steal jewels from the home of Paul Sylvaine (John *Mason), Sylvaine catches her in the act, and she recognizes him as the man who saved her life. A certain rapport is instantly kindled between the two, but while they are talking, Raoul Berton (George *Arliss), the dissolute brother of Sylvaine's fiancée, enters and himself steals the jewels Sylvaine had meant for his betrothed. Sylvaine's refusal to blame Leah for the theft, which is what Raoul hopes will happen, and his reluctance to implicate the real thief, alienate Sylvaine's fiancée. So in the end, it is Sylvaine and Leah who marry. McLellan's original ending, when the play was called *Into the Great White Light*, was equivocal, leaving Leah's future open to conjecture. But producers *Harrison and Mrs. Fiske, bowing to the era's theatrical requirements, insisted he add a fifth act in which Sylvaine marries the heroine. It was revived in 1924 as the author had first written it, but by that time styles of dramaturgy had changed and the work was perceived merely as a dated "crook play."

LEAH, THE FORSAKEN (1863), a play by Augustin *Daly. [*Niblo's Garden, 35 perf.] Against the laws of 17th-century Germany, the Jewess Leah (Kate *Bateman) loves a young Christian farmer, Rudolf (Edwin *Adams). Their liaison is discovered by an apostate Jew, Nathan (J. W. *Wallack Jr.), who betrays them to the authorities. The Jews are threatened with expulsion from the village, and Rudolf is led to believe that Leah has deserted him in return for a payment of silver. In despair, Rudolf marries a local Christian girl, Madelena (Mrs. Frank Chanfrau). Some time thereafter the Jews, who have kept their part of the bargain in dissuading Leah, are nevertheless ordered to leave. Just before their departure, word arrives that the laws against the Jews have been abrogated. But by that time Madelena has had a child, and Leah's heart has been broken. Rudolf learns of Nathan's treachery and of Leah's loyalty and he begs her forgiveness just as Leah dies. The play, loosely adapted by Daly from S. H. von Mosenthal's German drama, *Deborah*, gave the author his first success and started him on his distinguished career. It also gave Kate Bateman the role with which she was thereafter identified.

LEAN, Cecil (1878–1935), singer and dancer. The Canadian-born performer first came into prominence when he played opposite Frank *Daniels in *Miss Simplicity* (1902). Settling in Chicago, he quickly became a star in that city's musical comedies, often sharing star billing with his first wife, Florence Holbrook. Lean's important assignments included *The Isle of Bong Bong*; *The Yankee Regent*; *The *Umpire*; *The *Time, the Place and the Girl*; *The Honeymoon Trail*; and *The Girl at the Helm*. He continued to appear both in musical comedies and vaudeville with his second wife, Cleo Mayfield [née Cleonte Empy], throughout the teens and 1920s. Together they played in such shows as *Look Who's Here!*, *The Blushing Bride*, and a touring company of *No, No, Nanette*. Like many performers of the day, Lean and his wives were always more popular on the road than in New York.

LEAVE IT TO JANE. See *College Widow, The.*

LEAVE IT TO ME! (1938), a musical comedy by Bella and Sam *Spewack, Cole *Porter (music, lyrics). [*Imperial Theatre, 291 perf.] Mrs. Goodhue (Sophie *Tucker) has contributed so generously to Roosevelt's campaign coffers that the president makes her husband, "Stinky" (Victor *Moore), ambassador to Russia. There his undiplomatic behavior, like kicking a Nazi and shooting a counterrevolutionary, is brushed aside. But when Stinky proposes a plan for world peace, he is declared persona non grata. His problems are often compounded by a brash newspaperman, Buckley Thomas (William *Gaxton), who is courting a girl named Colette (Tamara). *Notable songs*: Get Out of Town; Most Gentlemen Don't Like Love; My Heart Belongs to Daddy. Typical of the highly topical musical comedies of the period, the Vincent *Freedley musical made a star of Mary *Martin, who sang "My Heart Belongs to Daddy" as a genteel striptease. When the show went on tour the following season, the Stalin-Hitler pact had been signed, so some of the characters and topical references were eliminated or changed. The musical was based on the Spewacks' 1932 comedy, *Clear All Wires*.

LEBLANG'S TICKET OFFICE (New York). In its heyday situated in the basement of Gray's Drug Store on Broadway between 42nd and 43rd Streets, it was founded by Hungarian immigrant Joe Leblang, who started in business with a small tobacco shop on 30th Street. At the time it was customary to give free passes to shopkeepers who displayed theatrical advertisements in their windows. Not only did Leblang sell his own passes, he collected them from other shopkeepers and sold them at cut-rate prices. He was so successful that before long theatres were sending him unsold seats several hours prior to curtain time. During the 1920s he is said to have sold as many as three thousand seats a night both to knowledgeable playgoers and less-aware passers-by lured into his office by pitchmen barking the virtues of the various plays. Leblang died in 1931, but his widow and associate ran the agency until shortly after World War II, when the marked drop in the number of theatres seemed to make the operation unprofitable. The same concept would reappear decades later with the *TKTS Booth.

LE COMPTE, Elizabeth. See Wooster Group.

LED ASTRAY (1873), a drama by Dion *Boucicault. [*Union Square Theatre, 161 perf.] Armande (Rose *Eytinge) marries widower Count Rudolphe Chandoce (C. R. *Thorne Jr.) but he proves an indifferent and faithless husband, soon enmeshed in an affair with the calculating Suzanne O'Hara (Elizabeth Weathersby). Although Armande loves both the Count and his daughter, Mathilde (Kate *Claxton), she is eventually driven into an affair of her own with the poet George de Lesparre (McKee *Rankin). When the Count learns of their relationship, he challenges George to a duel, but he purposely shoots to miss and then promises Armande he will be faithful thereafter. Based loosely on Octave Feuillet's *La Tentation*, the play was described by the *Times* critic as "told with cleverness and a thorough knowledge of dramatic effect; its personages are not so conventional as to be absolutely commonplace; and the language assigned to them is generally appropriate and often impressive." It soon became, as *Odell noted, "one of the most famous dramas of its decade in America." The French novelist and playwright **Octave FEUILLET** (1821–90), who wrote sentimental romances and highly charged melodramas, was frequently adapted to American tastes. Not only were his plays translated but his novels dramatized as well. In addition to *Led Astray*, three of his other works enjoyed relatively long careers on American stages: *The Sphinx* (1874), *The Romance of a Poor Young Man* (1874), and the play that gave Richard *Mansfield his earliest fame, *A Parisian Romance* (1883).

LEDERER, George W. (1861–1938), producer and director. He was born in Wilkes-Barre, Pennsylvania, and began his professional career as an actor in an 1873 production of *The Naiad Queen*. In his teens he began to write vaudeville sketches and also served a stint on the drama desk of the *New York Journal*. After collaborating with Sydney *Rosenfeld in sending out a tour of *Florizel*, he took over the *Casino Theatre with Thomas Canary in 1893, though it quickly became clear that Lederer was the dominant partner. During the decade in which he ran the theatre, he produced numerous highly successful musicals, including the first important American revue, *The *Passing Show* (1894), and the first American musical to achieve major international success, *The *Belle of New York* (1897). Lederer directed many of these productions as well. In his later years he joined with H. H. *Frazee to produce such hits as *Madame Sherry* (1910) and *Angel Face* (1919). His last years were spent as general manager for Sam H. *Harris.

LEE, Canada [né Leonard Canegata] (1907–52), actor. The New York–born African American made his first professional appearance in *Meek Mose* (1928), but did not gain attention until he played Blacksnake in a *Civic Repertory Theatre revival of *Stevedore* (1934). Much of his work for the rest of the decade was with all-black troupes, but Lee came into real prominence when he played the unintentional murderer Bigger Thomas in *Native Son* (1941). He won additional laurels for his Caliban in a 1945 revival of *The Tempest,* and in 1946 he played Daniel de Bosola in white-face, opposite Elisabeth *Bergner, in a revival of *The Duchess of Malfi*. Lee's last appearance was as George, whose treachery defeats an uprising, in *Set My People Free* (1948).

LEE, Eugene (b. 1939), scenic designer. Long associated with the *Trinity Repertory Theatre and the *Dallas Theatre Center, Lee received wider recognition when he designed striking environmental settings for *Slave Ship* (1970) and *Candide* (1974) in New York. Among his many memorable productions were *Sweeney Todd* (1979), the Central Park productions of *As You Like It* (1992) and *The Two Gentlemen of Verona* (1994), *Show Boat* (1994), *On the Waterfront* (1995), *Ragtime* (1998), *Seussical* (2000), and *Wicked* (2003). Much of his work in the 1970s was done in collaboration with his former wife Franne [neé Newman] Lee (b. 1941), who designed the costumes for his productions.

LEE, Gypsy Rose [née Rose Louise Hovick] (1913–70), actress and playwright. Although she was probably the most famous of all American "stripteasers," Lee was also successful in the legitimate theatre. Under the guidance of her pushy stage mother, she began her career in a children's act in vaudeville; but when variety began to fade, she moved into burlesque, quickly becoming one of its greatest stars, her restraint and elegance separating her from the vulgar, sexually suggestive run-of-the-mill strippers. Lee also played small roles in such musicals as *Hot-Cha!* (1932), *Strike Me Pink* (1933), and the **Ziegfeld Follies of 1936* and acted briefly in the comedy *I Must Love Someone* (1939). Her most important Broadway assignment was as co-star to Bobby *Clark in *Star and Garter* (1942). Lee wrote the semiautobiographical comedy *The Naked Genius* (1943), as well as several novels. Her 1957 autobiography, *Gypsy*, provided the basis for the 1959 musical of the same name.

LEE, Ming Cho (b. 1930), designer. The most influential American scenic designer during the last four decades of the 20th century, Lee was born in Shanghai and studied art at Occidental College and UCLA. He was an assistant to Jo *Mielziner for several years, but Lee developed a style of stage design that was more skeletal and minimalist than the poetic realism of past designers, using nontraditional materials and daring textures. Much of Lee's work has been in regional theatres and for opera, yet he designed many productions for the *Public Theatre and bold, structural sets for the *Delacorte Theatre in Central Park. He rarely did musicals, and only a few of his sets have been seen on Broadway, though he was roundly applauded for his startling re-creation of a mountain for *K2* (1983). Since the 1980s Lee has devoted much of his time to teaching student designers at Yale.

LEE, Robert E. See Lawrence and Lee.

LEE, [Samuel] Sammy [né Levy] (1890–1968), choreographer. A New York native, he began his career as a dancer in *The *Firefly* (1912) and other pre–World War I musicals, but he soon developed into one of the leading choreographers of the 1920s. His fast-paced routines enlivened such shows as *Mary Jane McKane* (1923), **Lady, Be Good!* (1924), **No, No, Nanette* (1925), *The *Cocoanuts* (1925), **Tip-Toes* (1925), **Queen High* (1926), *The Ramblers* (1926), **Oh, Kay!* (1926), **Rio Rita* (1927), **Ziegfeld Follies of 1927*, and **Show Boat* (1927).

LEFT BANK, THE (1931), a play by Elmer *Rice. [Little Theatre, 242 perf.] For several years John Shelby (Horace Braham) and his wife, Claire (Katherine Alexander), have been living in France and enjoying what John insists is "the most civilized country that there is in the world today." He adds, "No civilized man can live decently in America." But Claire has begun to miss the American way of life with which she grew up. Arriving at the same Left Bank hotel at which they are housed is an American couple. Waldo Lynde (Donald MacDonald) clearly is educated but remains totally Yankee in his interests. His wife, Susie (Merle

Maddern), is more of a restless, free spirit. Before long John and Susie have gone off to tour the Midi together, so Claire elects to take her young son and return with Waldo to the States. Brooks *Atkinson considered the play "the shrewdest contribution to the literature of the American émigré in Paris" and suggested it represented "the modern American theatre at its best." Perhaps because expatriates no longer loom large in our artistic culture, the play has become one of Rice's most neglected.

LEFTWICH, Alexander (1884–1947), director. The Philadelphia native began his career as a teenage actor in Baltimore. After spending some years in stock, he worked as assistant to Jesse Lasky and Cecil B. De Mille when both men were still active on Broadway. After grooming acts for B. F. *Keith, Leftwich became a director for Daniel *Frohman in 1915 and then for the *Shuberts in 1924, directing for the latter such shows as *Big Boy* (1925). He is best remembered for the musicals he staged after leaving the Shuberts, including **Hit the Deck!* (1927), *A *Connecticut Yankee* (1927), *Rain or Shine* (1928), *Present Arms* (1928), *Spring Is Here* (1929), **Strike Up the Band* (1930), and **Girl Crazy* (1930). In later years he was director of the *Federal Theatre Project in California.

LEGAL WRECK, A (1888), a play by William *Gillette. [*Madison Square Theatre, 102 perf.] Olive Grey (Nina Boucicault) is the adopted daughter of an eccentric old New England sea captain, Edward Swift (Alfred Hudson), and is courted by both Swift's ruffian son Ed (George *Fawcett) and suave Henry D. Leverett (Boyd Putnam). The men fight over the girl, after which a young attorney, Richard Merriam (Sidney Drew), leads each man to believe he has murdered the other. But there is some method in Merriam's cavalier humor, since he knows who Olive's real mother and sister are. He hopes to effect a match for himself by reuniting them. This light summer entertainment was later turned into a novel by Gillette, one of the earliest examples of a practice that for many years was popular both in the theatre and in films.

LEHAR, Franz (1870–1948), composer. The Hungarian artist who was the most famous exponent of 20th-century operetta is best known worldwide for his masterpiece, *The *Merry Widow* (1907). Of his other works only two were successful in America, *Gypsy Love* (1911) and *The Count of Luxembourg* (1912), although their popularity by no means matched that of the earlier hit. Several of his operettas were produced later, only to fail, while a number of his greatest works have never been given major professional mountings in New York. As a composer Lehar moved away from the more florid, quasi operatic style of 19th-century *Viennese operetta.

LEIBER, Fritz (1883–1949), actor and director. After making his stage debut in 1902 with a stock company in his native Chicago, he joined the Ben Greet Players, learning the basic Shakespearean repertory with them and first appearing before New York audiences in 1905 as Macduff in their *Macbeth. He later spent many seasons as a principal supporting player to Robert *Mantell, often alternating with Mantell in the roles of Othello and Iago. Leiber then organized his own Shakespearean company. John *Corbin of the *Times* said of his Hamlet, "His lean, trim figure and poetic masque are well suited to the role. In enunciation he at times lacks purity, and his voice has no great variety or range, but his reading is for the most part cultivated and intelligent." From 1929 to 1932 he directed and appeared with the Chicago Civic Shakespeare Company, then toured with a reorganized Shakespeare ensemble in the mid-1930s. He said to have played more than a hundred different Shakespearean parts.

LEIGH, Carolyn. See *Peter Pan*.

LEIGHT, Warren. See *Side Man*.

LEIGHTON, Margaret (1922–76), actress. The slender English leading lady first came to America with the *Old Vic in 1946, but did not receive major attention until she essayed two disparate roles in Terence *Rattigan's double bill, *Separate Tables* (1956). After playing Beatrice to John *Gielgud's Benedick in 1959, she won praise for her gentle spinster Hannah Jelkes in The *Night of the Iguana* (1961). Subsequently Leighton was seen as the starchy Englishwoman Pamela Pew-Pickett in *Tchin-Tchin* (1962), in two roles in Tennessee *Williams's double bill, *Slapstick Tragedy* (1966), and as Regina in a 1967 revival of The *Little Foxes*.

LEMAIRE, Charles (1897–1985), costume designer. Born in Chicago, but raised in Salt Lake City, he tried his luck as a song-and-dance man before turning to costume design. Although he had no formal design training, Florenz *Ziegfeld quickly recognized his talent and allowed him to create some dresses for the 1919 editions of the *Midnight Frolics* and the *Follies. Between then and his work for the 1939 edition of *George White's Scandals he designed costumes for numerous extravaganzas of Ziegfeld, *White, and Earl *Carroll as well as for such shows as *Wildflower* (1923), *Poppy* (1923), *Rose-Marie* (1924), The *Cocoanuts* (1925), The *New Moon* (1928), *Strike Up the Band* (1930), *Flying High

(1930), *Fine and Dandy* (1930), *Of Thee I Sing* (1931), and *Take a Chance* (1932). Among the most memorable of his imaginative, colorful conceptions were the costumes simulating totem poles worn by the forty chorus girls in *Rose-Marie* for the "Totem Tom Tom" number.

LEMAN, Walter M. (b. 1810), actor and playwright. He was born in Boston and spent most of his career there, in Philadelphia, and in San Francisco playing important supporting roles, but he is remembered solely for his autobiographical *Memories of an Old Actor* (1886). Although the work is largely a catalogue of the names with whom he worked, it does offer some unusual and telling glimpses into the theatre of his day.

LEMMON, Jack (1925–2001), actor. The much-lauded film star, equally adept in both comedies and dramas, worked in the New York theatre as a struggling actor then returned years later as a star. He was born in Boston and educated at prep school and at Harvard before joining the Navy, making his Manhattan stage bow in 1953 and his film debut the next year. Lemmon gave superb stage performances as the charming PR man Scotty Templeton in *Tribute* (1978) and the family patriarch James Tyrone in A *Long Day's Journey Into Night* (1986).

LEND ME A TENOR (1989), a farce by Ken Ludwig. [*Royale Theatre, 481 perf.] World-renowned opera tenor Tito Merelli (Ron *Holgate) has agreed to perform *Otello* for the Cleveland Grand Opera as their 1934 season gala opening, but when he accidentally takes too many tranquilizers before the performance and passes out cold, the high-strung general manager Saunders (Philip *Bosco) and his assistant Max (Victor *Garber) try to keep it quiet and set off a string of shenanigans that include Max donning blackface and playing the Moor in his place. Jerry *Zaks directed the old-fashioned, door-slamming farce with precision, and the play was a hit on Broadway and in theatres across the country. Although it was an American work, the comedy was originally presented in London and Paris before Martin Starger and the Really Useful Theatre Company produced it in New York. **Ken LUDWIG** (b. 1950) was born in York, Pennsylvania, and educated at Haverford College, Cambridge, and Harvard for a law career. His first scripts were produced Off Off Broadway in the early 1980s and he had his first success with *Lend Me a Tenor*. Ludwig also wrote the comedies *Moon over Buffalo* (1995) and *Shakespeare in Hollywood* (2003), and the librettos for the Broadway musicals *Crazy for You* (1992) and *Tom Sawyer* (2001).

LENIHAN, Winifred (1898–1964), actress. A New Yorker, she studied at the *American Academy of Dramatic Arts before making her debut in 1918. Although she portrayed the would-be eloper Anne in *The Dover Road* (1921), Anne Hathaway in *Will Shakespeare* (1923), and the resourceful Mary Todd in *White Wings* (1926), she is recalled mostly as Joan of Arc in the original American production of *Saint Joan* (1923).

LeNOIRE, Rosetta [neé Rosetta Olive Burton] (1911–2002), actress and manager. LeNoire was an untiring African-American actress-singer who also ran the Off-Broadway AMAS Repertory Theatre for many years. A native New Yorker who was educated at Hunter College, she worked as a secretary while she trained at the *American Theatre Wing School. LeNoire made her professional debut in 1936 as one of the witches in Orson *Welles's legendary all-black production of *Macbeth* and she later shone as Stella in *Anna Lucasta* (1944). Much of her long New York stage career would be in supporting roles in such varied works as *Finian's Rainbow* (1955), *Blues for Mister Charlie* (1964), *Lost in the Stars* (1972), The *Sunshine Boys* (1975), and *You Can't Take It With You* (1983).

LENYA, Lotte [née Karoline Blamauer] (1900–81), actress and singer. Best known as the wife of composer Kurt *Weill and as Jenny in the 1954 revival of his *Threepenny Opera*, she was born in Vienna and was a popular cabaret and musical star in Berlin before the advent of the Nazis forced her to flee Germany. Lenya appeared in several of her husband's works in Germany, including creating the role of Jenny in 1928. Her first American appearance was in *The Eternal Road* (1937), followed by *Candle in the Wind* (1941), Weill's *The Firebrand of Florence* (1945), and *Barefoot in Athens* (1951). She later appeared in *Brecht on Brecht* (1962), and as Freulein Schneider in *Cabaret* (1966). Her "steel-file voice" made her the definitive interpreter of her husband's songs.

LEON, Francis. See Female Impersonation.

LEONARD, Robert Sean (b. 1969), actor. The handsome leading man, who has quickly become one of Broadway's most accomplished actors, is equally adept at the classics as with new works. He was born in Westwood, New Jersey, and was in summer stock at the age of twelve, essaying Shakespearean roles by the time he was fifteen. Leonard studied at Fordham University and made his New York debut in 1985, first getting noticed on Broadway as the British youth Christopher in *Breaking the Code* (1987). Among his notable performances were a passionate Eugene

Marchbanks in *Candida* (1993), the Irish alter ego "Private Gar" in *Philadelphia, Here I Come!* (1994), the math scholar Valentine Coverly in *Arcadia* (1995), the romantically inclined dentist Valentine in *You Never Can Tell* (1998), the young poet-scholar A. E. Housman in *The Invention of Love* (2002), the Vietnam vet Ken Talley in *Fifth of July* (2003), and the would-be poet Edmund in *Long Day's Journey Into Night* (2003).

LEONOR DE GUZMAN (1853), a tragedy by George H. *Boker. [*Walnut Street Theatre (Philadelphia), 6 perf.] When Leonor (Julia *Dean), who has been the real power behind the Spanish throne, learns that King Alfonso XII has been killed in battle, she determines to retain her influence. But the courtiers quickly desert her and flock to the new king, Don Pedro (Mr. Perry), and his mother, Queen Maria (Mrs. Duffield). Both are strongly influenced by Don Juan Albuquerque (Mr. Adams), who, as prime minister, is determined to assure a peaceful transfer of the royal reins. But Leonor's persistent machinations finally prompt Maria to stab her to death. Arthur *Quinn has observed that "The most marked advance in *Leonor de Guzman* lies in the character drawing." He calls attention to how well Boker evokes sympathy for Leonor while at the same time painting a three-dimensional portrait of an even more interesting figure, Maria. The blank-verse drama was less successful when it was later presented in New York than it was at its Philadelphia premiere.

LERNER and LOEWE, songwriting team. Lyricist and librettist Alan Jay Lerner (1918–86) was born into a wealthy New York family and educated at selective private schools and at Harvard, where he collaborated on two *Hasty Pudding musicals. He worked as a radio script writer before he teamed up with the German-born composer Frederick Loewe (1901–88), the son of a popular leading man in operetta. Loewe studied with such notable figures as Ferruccio Busoni and Eugène d'Albert before coming to America in 1924. For a decade he could not make a living with his music, so took numerous odd, unrelated jobs. Some of his songs were interpolated into *Petticoat Fever* and *The Illustrators' Show*, then his full score was heard in the short-lived *Great Lady* (1938). The new team of Lerner and Loewe scored the unsuccessful Broadway musicals *What's Up* (1943) and *The Day Before Spring* (1945) before finding success with the Scottish-set musical *Brigadoon* (1947). The gold-rush musical *Paint Your Wagon* (1951) enjoyed a modest run, but their masterpiece, *My Fair Lady* (1956), broke all records and remains a triumph of the Broadway stage. The final Lerner and Loewe collaboration was *Camelot* (1960), though the team did supply a few new songs for the 1973 Broadway version of their hit film musical *Gigi*. Lerner wrote the innovative but failed musical *Love Life* (1948) with music by Kurt *Weill, then years later, after Loewe's retirement, he wrote two musicals with Burton *Lane, *On a Clear Day You Can See Forever* (1965) and *Carmelina* (1979). Other Lerner credits without Loewe include *Coco* (1969), *1600 Pennsylvania Avenue* (1976), and *Dance a Little Closer* (1983). While Lerner's librettos offered excellent dialogue, they sometimes betrayed an inability at proper construction and a lack of theatrical tension. On the other hand, as a writer of elegantly literate and witty lyrics, Lerner had no peer among his contemporaries. Loewe was a traditionalist whose music followed long-established patterns, but it was marked by his uncommon gift for fresh melody and his ability to capture the essence of a far-off time or place. Autobiography (Lerner): *The Street Where I Live*, 1978; biographies: *Inventing Champagne: The Worlds of Lerner and Loewe*, Gene Lees, 1990; *Alan Jay Lerner*, Edward Jablonski, 1996.

LES MISÉRABLES (1987). The musical play by Alain Boublil (book, lyrics), Claude-Michel Schönberg (book, music), and Herbert Kretzmer (English lyrics) turned Victor Hugo's novel into a sung-through pop operetta. It was originally released as a recording, then given a Paris production before British producer Cameron *Mackintosh ordered a revised and expanded script, which he mounted first in London and then in New York at the *Broadway Theatre. Always more popular with audiences than critics, the impressive production supplanted *La Plume de Ma Tante* as the longest running Continental musical in Broadway history and continued on to chalk up a run of 6,680 performances. *Notable songs*: I Dreamed a Dream; On My Own; Bring Him Home; Empty Chairs at Empty Tables.

LESLIE, Amy (1860–1939), critic. Born in West Burlington, Iowa, she made a small reputation for herself as a prima donna in operetta during the 1880s and early 1890s, performing under the name Lillie West. She then retired from the stage to become drama critic for the *Chicago Daily News*, a position she held for forty years. Leslie was the first woman to have such a prestigious assignment. Her criticisms leaned over backward to be kind to even the most woebegone entertainments, and as a result she was sometimes accused of "puffing," writing favorable notices to help at the box office. She nonetheless won the respect of her fellow reviewers and of the theatrical profession as well.

LESLIE, Elsie [née Lyde] (1881–1966), actress. Daughter of a prosperous New Yorker, she made her debut in 1885 and two years later became the darling of playgoers when she played Editha, the tot who can more than hold her own as she encounters *Editha's Burglar*. Successes followed in the title roles of *Little Lord Fauntleroy* (1888) and *The Prince and the Pauper* (1890), after which she temporarily retired. When Leslie returned eight years later, she was not able to recapture her early appeal.

LESLIE, Lew [né Lewis Lessinsky] (1886–1963), producer. Born in Orangeburg, New York, he began his career as a performer in vaudeville and later became manager of the famous New York nightclub Café de Paris. While there he recognized the growing popularity of African-American entertainers and so produced the *Plantation Revue* (1922) for Broadway. With the exception of his *International Revue* (1930), all of Leslie's subsequent productions were ethnic musicals: *Dixie to Broadway* (1924), *Rhapsody in Black* (1931), and a series of *Blackbirds* revues, with editions in 1928, 1930, 1933, and 1939.

LESTER, Edwin (1895–1990), producer. Probably the last important West Coast theatrical giant, he was born in Providence, Rhode Island, and settled in California, where he spent many years as an executive for a music company, then became an artists' representative; then in 1935 he organized the Los Angeles Light Opera Festival. Lester and Homer *Curran founded the more permanent San Francisco Light Opera Association in 1937, then the next year established the companion Los Angeles Light Opera Association. Lester headed both groups until his retirement in 1976. Under his aegis the companies mounted yearly series of splendid revivals of past musicals, interspersed with new productions. Among these original mountings were *Song of Norway* (1944), *Magdalena* (1948), *Kismet* (1953), and *Peter Pan* (1954), all of which traveled to Broadway.

LET US BE GAY (1929), a comedy by Rachel *Crothers. [*Little Theatre, 363 perf.] When Kitty Brown (Francine *Larrimore) and her husband Bob (Warren William) quarrel, he stalks out of the house vowing never to return. Three years later, old Mrs. Boucicault (Charlotte Granville) is worried about her young granddaughter, Deirdre Lessing (Rita Vale), who has seemed too receptive to the advances of a divorced man. So Mrs. Boucicault invites Kitty to a weekend house party, hoping to distract the suitor. Of course the divorced man is Bob, and by the time the guests are ready to leave, he and Kitty have kissed and made up.

The John *Golden production was one of the most successful of Rachel Crothers's frothy but observant high comedies, and it remained a favorite in summer stock and little theatres for many years.

LET'S FACE IT! See *Cradle Snatchers*.

LEVENE, Sam[uel] [né Levine] (1905–80), actor. The sour-faced comedian, who spoke with the pronounced accent of his native New York, studied at the *American Academy of Dramatic Arts before making his professional debut in *Wall Street* (1927). Major recognition came eight years later when he played the racing addict Patsy in *Three Men on a Horse* (1935). Successes followed in a series of noteworthy performances: the shoe-string producer Gordon Miller in *Room Service* (1937), the Jewish policeman Officer Finkelstein in *Margin for Error* (1939), the aggressive, foul-mouthed producer Sidney Black in *Light Up the Sky* (1948), and gambler Nathan Detroit in *Guys and Dolls* (1950). Levene then portrayed stereo-typical New York Jewish types in such plays as *Fair Game* (1957), *Make a Million* (1958), *Paris Is Out!* (1970), and *Horowitz and Mrs. Washington* (1980), all of which owed what runs they achieved to his clowning. More interesting interpretations were his Boss Mangan in *Heartbreak House* (1959) and veteran producer Oscar Wolfe in a 1975 revival of *The *Royal Family*.

LEVIN, Herman (1907–90), producer. The Philadelphia-born lawyer turned to the stage in 1949 with the musical revue *Call Me Mister* and the Sartre drama *No Exit*. In 1949 he produced the popular musical version of *Gentlemen Prefer Blondes*, but his greatest success came when he presented *My Fair Lady* (1956). The *Great White Hope* (1968) was his only subsequent hit.

LEVIN, Ira (b. 1929), playwright. A New Yorker who studied at New York University, he scored a huge hit with his first work to reach Broadway, his adaptation of the novel *No Time for Sergeants* (1955). Although Levin has written for Broadway with some regularity, his only other successes have been the comedy *Critic's Choice* (1960) and the thriller *Deathtrap* (1978). Among his other plays are *Veronica's Room* (1973), *Break a Leg* (1979), and *Cantorial* (1989). Levin has also enjoyed success as a novelist.

LEWIS, Ada (1875–1925), actress. Discovered performing in her native San Francisco by Edward *Harrigan, she virtually stole the show when he brought her East to play a rough girl of the streets in his *Reilly and the 400* (1890). For the next decade or so, Lewis played similar characters, then aged into the imperious grande dame. Her numerous appearances included *The Widow Jones* (1905), *Fascinating Flora* (1907), *Very Good Eddie* (1915), *The Night Boat* (1920), and *Good Morning, Dearie* (1921).

LEWIS, James (1838–96), comic actor. The slim, short comedian with blue pop eyes and reddish-blond hair was born in Troy, New York, and began his theatrical apprenticeship touring while still in his early teens. He came to New York in 1866, quickly making a name for himself in Mrs. John *Wood's burlesques at the Olympic Theatre and in similar pieces at Lina Edwin's Theatre. When Augustin *Daly began assembling his soon-famous ensemble in 1869, Lewis was one of his first choices. Within a brief time he became the company's leading farceur and remained with the group until his early death. Along with John *Drew, Mrs. *Gilbert, and Ada *Rehan he was considered a mainstay of the organization. Most of his assignments were in now-forgotten comedies, but he was also applauded for such roles as Captain Lynde in *Divorce (1873), Bob Sackett in *Saratoga (1874), Tony Lumpkin in She Stoops to Conquer (1874), Professor Cawallader in The *Big Bonanza (1875), Sammy Dymple in *Pique (1875), Sir Benjamin Backbite in The School for Scandal (1876), Bottom in A *Midsummer Night's Dream (1888), Touchstone in *As You Like It (1891), and Sir Toby Belch in *Twelfth Night (1893). William *Winter recalled, "Lewis was an artist. He caused effects in acting not by grimace, posturing and extravagance, but by getting inside of characters and permitting his droll humor to permeate them."

LEWIS, Mrs. Henry [née Bertha (?) Harvey] (d. 1855), actress. The native Londoner was reputed to have been a great favorite in England before coming with her husband to New York in 1835. Although she was said to have been an attractive, graceful woman and a skilled dancer, her principal fame derived from interpretation of men's parts, such as Richard III and Othello. Lewis spent all of her American career traveling with her specialties from city to city, never establishing the firm base that many more ordinary performers were able to achieve. Her husband, from whom she was divorced in 1849, began his career in pantomime and later spent much of his career in Pittsburgh, where he won respect as a director and delineator of old men.

LEWIS, Robert (1909–94), director. The New Yorker studied at City College and at Juilliard before turning to acting. In 1938 he directed the road company of *Golden Boy* and thereafter was known primarily for his staging. Among his later efforts were *Saroyan's *My Heart's in the Highlands (1939), *Brigadoon (1947), The *Happy Time (1950), An Enemy of the People (1950), The *Teahouse of the August Moon (1953), Witness for the Prosecution (1954), Jamaica (1957), and On a Clear Day You Can See Forever (1965). Lewis co-founded the *Actors Studio, taught at leading schools, and directed for major regional playhouses. Autobiography: Slings and Arrows, 1984.

LEWIS, Ted [né Theodore Leopold Friedman] (1891–1971), singer. Born in Circleville, Ohio, where he made his professional debut singing in a nickelodeon, he established the Ted Lewis Nut Band, playing what at the time was called "jazz." By 1919 he was a headliner in vaudeville and in nightclubs. Lewis also performed on Broadway in such revues as Ziegfeld's Midnight Frolics (1919), several editions of *Greenwich Village Follies, and *Artists and Models of 1927. He would appear with his battered top hat and his clarinet and ask with a mocking sentimentality, "Is ev'rybody happy?" Performing in his cheerily forlorn style he made famous such songs as "When My Baby Smiles at Me" and "Me and My Shadow."

LIBERTY THEATRES. Huge, temporary wooden auditoriums, they were erected during World War I largely to entertain troops at military camps. Touring companies of Broadway shows or hastily assembled vaudeville bills would perform in them for soldiers who had paid to see the entertainments with coupons from Smileage Books, which sold for nominal amounts and which were usually bought by the public and then donated to the troops.

LIE OF THE MIND, A (1985), a play by Sam *Shepard. [Promenade Theatre, 185 perf.; NYDCC Award.] Jake (Harvey Keitel) believes he has beaten his wife Beth to death and so runs away. Beth (Amanda Plummer) is not dead, but she has suffered brain damage and is returned to her oddball family. Jake's brother, Frankie (Aidan Quinn), visits them, hoping to bring about a reconciliation or at least an understanding while Jake returns to his home and his flighty mother (Geraldine *Page). In the end Jake and Beth are left to work out for themselves their probably bleak futures. Although the play took four hours to perform, it was usually gripping, especially in the fine production accorded it. However, viewed from a distance it could be seen as a modern-day *Tobacco Road, crossed with strong influences of The *Glass Menagerie school of drama.

LIEBERSON, Goddard (1911–77), record producer. Born in England but raised in America where he studied at the University of Washington and the Eastman School of Music, he later became president of Columbia Records. In this capacity Lieberson produced numerous original cast recordings of Broadway musicals, following in the pioneering footsteps of Decca's Jack *Kapp. But he moved one important step further, re-creating, often with Lehman *Engel, virtually complete versions of the scores of Broadway shows that predated the era of contemporary recordings. His re-creation of *Pal Joey is generally credited with prompting the highly successful 1952 revival of that musical.

LIEBLER and Co. See Liebler, Theodore.

LIEBLER, Theodore (1852–1941), producer. Born in New York, shortly after his father was forced to flee Germany for partaking in an insurrection, he began working as a commercial artist, and before long he had a modestly successful lithograph firm in Park Place. When his establishment was destroyed by fire, George *Tyler persuaded him to join forces to produce The Royal Box (1897). The play was a success, inaugurating the long career of Liebler and Company. Among its memorable productions were The *Christian (1898), The Children of the Ghetto (1899), *Sag Harbor (1900), *In the Palace of the King (1900), A *Gentleman of France (1901), *Raffles (1903), *Mrs. Wiggs of the Cabbage Patch (1904), The *Squaw Man (1905), *Salomy Jane (1907), The *Man from Home (1908), *Alias Jimmy Valentine (1910), Pomander Walk (1910), Disraeli (1911), and The *Garden of Allah (1911). Liebler was also responsible for bringing to America such celebrated foreign artists as Mrs. Patrick *Campbell, *Duse, and *Rejane. His importation of the Irish Players of the *Abbey Theatre in 1911 precipitated a riot when many Irishmen objected to the sentiments in their production of The Playboy of the Western World. After a series of expensive failures during World War I, the company was dissolved and Liebler retired.

LIFE AND ADVENTURES OF NICHOLAS NICKLEBY, THE (1981). No play of the decade had a more expensive ticket ($100 for the two full-length parts), received higher critical praise, and aroused such excitement in New York than this ingenious London stage version of Charles Dickens's novel. The nine-and-a-half-hour production by the *Royal Shakespeare Company employed forty-two actors to portray 138 speaking roles in telling the tale of poverty-stricken schoolmaster Nicholas (Roger Rees) and his fight for survival and righteousness during the Industrial Revolution. David Edgar wrote the adaptation and Trevor *Nunn and John Caird co-directed the sprawling tale of passion, humor, pathos, villainy, and adventure that won the

*Tony and *NYDCC Awards. The limited ninety-eight-performance run at the *Plymouth Theatre was sold out once the rave reviews were forthcoming; scalpers were reportedly getting $2,000 a ticket for the much-sought-after attraction. It was revived by the RSC on Broadway in 1986 but was only mildly successful the second time around.

LIFE WITH FATHER (1939), a comedy by Howard *Lindsay and Russel *Crouse. [*Empire Theatre, 3,224 perf.] Clarence Day (Lindsay) is certain he dominates his Madison Avenue brownstone and his family, which includes four young sons and his wife, Vinnie (Dorothy Stickney). He constantly complains to Vinnie about her housekeeping, and his blustering tantrums have cost the Days many a maid. But when the Rev. Dr. Lloyd (Richard Sterling) pays a visit, Day accidentally reveals that he has never been baptized. Father Clarence argues, "They can't keep me out of heaven on a technicality," but Vinnie is determined that the oversight must be rectified. Clarence, however, is adamant until in a weak moment, when he believes Vinnie may be dying, he agrees. Vinnie holds him to his promise, so he goes off to church bellowing, "I'm going to be baptized, damn it!" The comedy, based on Clarence Day Jr.'s *New Yorker* recollections, remains the longest running nonmusical play in Broadway history. Arriving as war broke out in Europe and while America was still feeling the effects of the Great Depression, its affectionate portrait of 19th-century home life evoked a past of simple values. A sequel, *Life with Mother* (1948), had only a modest run despite generally warm notices.

LIGHT UP THE SKY (1948), a comedy by Moss *Hart. [*Royale Theatre, 216 perf.] Just before the opening of a new play in Boston, the leading figures involved in the show assemble in the Ritz-Carlton suite of the leading lady, Irene Livingston (Virginia Field). The others include the coarse-mouthed producer Sidney Black (Sam *Levene); his brassy wife, Frances (Audrey *Christie); the swishy, lugubrious director Carleton Fitzgerald (Glenn *Anders); and the young playwright Peter Sloan (Barry *Nelson). They are gushily sweet and loving to each other until they return from the first performance, which they believe to be a flop. Then a screaming, name-calling session ensues. When the reviews prove encouraging, the sweetness and camaraderie return. The show was originally written by Hart as a more philosophic comedy, but after a Boston tryout that mirrored the fictitious events in the play, it was rewritten as a slam-bang farce. Insiders recognized that the vain, effusive Irene was a send-up of Gertrude *Lawrence; the Blacks, of Billy *Rose and his wife,

Eleanor Holm; and Fitzgerald, of Guthrie *McClintic. The play was Hart's only successful solo venture, aside from the wartime *Winged Victory* (1943), but appearing in a season of exceptional competition it didn't enjoy the longer run it deserved.

LIGHTNIN' (1918), a play by Winchell *Smith and Frank *Bacon. [Gaiety Theatre, 1,291 perf.] When "Lightnin'" Bill Jones (Bacon) meets young John Marvin (Ralph *Morgan) in Marvin's cabin near Tahoe, the two men take an instant liking to one another, although Marvin quickly realizes that Jones is a chronic boozer and teller of tall tales. Marvin is in trouble with some shady speculators who work for the railways, and Jones promises to lie in court to help Marvin. Jones and his wife (Jessie Pringle) own a hotel that straddles the California and Nevada line. A line has been painted across the lobby for the benefit of guests coming to procure a divorce or avoid arrest. The same speculators harassing Marvin convince Mrs. Jones to sell the hotel, but Jones refuses to co-sign the agreement. Mrs. Jones, finally fed up with Jones's drinking and prevaricating, files for divorce. However, Jones manages to expose the speculators as crooks and win back his wife. Arthur *Hornblow wrote in *Theatre Magazine*, "The authors have put into their play something—a character, in fact, that seems to be drawn from life. Mr. Bacon's impersonation of the central figure is Jeffersonian in its simplicity and understanding." Because many thought Bacon's performance was necessary to the success of the play, no road company was sent out at first. When the Smith and John *Golden production closed on Broadway, it was the longest-running show in American history, a record broken seven years later by *Abie's Irish Rose*. Bacon died, however, during the post-Broadway tour, but other actors were able to keep it on the road through 1925. A 1938 revival with Fred *Stone failed to run.

LI'L ABNER (1956), a musical satire by Norman Panama, Melvin Frank (book), Gene de Paul (music), Johnny Mercer (lyrics). [*St. James Theatre, 693 perf.] Al Capp's popular comic strip about the residents of Dogpatch, U.S.A., was given a cartoonish rendering in this lively show staged by Michael *Kidd. Easygoing Abner Yokum (Peter Palmer) is chased by the ever hopeful Daisy Mae (Edith Adams) while the government makes plans to test atomic bombs on the worthless site, and Marryin' Sam (Stubby Kaye) keeps matrimony alive through the annual Sadie Hawkins Day race. *Notable songs*: Namely You; Jubilation T. Cornpone; The Country's in the Very Best of Hands. While the satire was not as pointed as in the political comic strip, *Li'l Abner* managed to be very entertaining and afforded Mercer his only Broadway hit. **Johnny MERCER** (1909–76) was born in Savannah, Georgia, and began his career as a vocalist with celebrated big bands. Although he wrote several stage scores, he had greater success as a Hollywood and Tin Pan Alley lyricist. Mercer's other Broadway shows include *St. Louis Woman* (1946), *Top Banana* (1951), *Saratoga* (1959), and *Foxy* (1964).

LILIOM (1921). Ferenc Molnar's play, with fantastic overtones, which told of the star-crossed romance of a carnival barker and a serving girl, was first produced in America by the *Theatre Guild at the Garrick Theatre in 1921 and ran for three hundred performances. Joseph *Schildkraut and Eva *Le Gallienne were the principals. It has been revived on several occasions and was the source of the 1945 musical *Carousel.

LILLIE, Beatrice [Gladys] (1894–1989), comedienne. Born in Toronto, she became a popular London performer before making her New York debut in *Charlot's Revue* (1924) where her uproarious clowning as she led a totally disorganized brigade and sang "March with Me" made her an overnight star. She consolidated her reputation in the *Charlot Revue of 1926, Oh, Please!* (1926), *She's My Baby* (1928), *The Third Little Show* (1931), and *Walk a Little Faster* (1932). Lillie's other revue performances included *At Home Abroad* (1935), *The Show Is On* (1936), *Set to Music* (1939), *Seven Lively Arts* (1944), and *Inside U. S. A.* (1948), culminating in *An Evening with Beatrice Lillie* (1952). After the failure of *The *Ziegfeld Follies of 1957*, she succeeded Rosalind *Russell in *Auntie Mame* then played the wacky medium Madame Arcati in *High Spirits* (1964). Howard Taubman of the *Times* wrote of her performance, "Overflowing with coziness, she begins to move like a ballerina. Her hands flutter as she takes mincing little steps, then they wave broadly as the afflatus of Terpsichore possesses her. . . . And when the audience roars for more and won't let the show go on, she flutters through a devastating mockery of curtsies and fond gestures of farewell." A tiny, slender woman, who wore her hair in a mannishly short bob, she was generally recognized as the greatest comedienne of her era. No small part of her genius came from her retaining her ladylike decorum even in the coarsest, most vulgar bits. Biography: *Beatrice Lillie: The Funniest Woman in the World*, Bruce Laffey, 1990.

LINCOLN CENTER FOR THE PERFORMING ARTS (New York). Built in the 1960s and covering blocks of cityscape on Amsterdam Avenue and Broadway, Lincoln Center was the largest and most ambitious arts project in the city's history. The complex of buildings includes the new Metropolitan Opera House, the New York State Theatre, the Avery Fisher Hall, the Alice Tully Hall, and two legitimate theatres: the *Vivian Beaumont and *Mitzi E. Newhouse Theatres. The plans for the center included a home for the Repertory Theatre of Lincoln Center, founded in 1960 as a nonprofit theatre designed to offer a permanent company in seasons of classic and new plays. Robert *Whitehead and Elia *Kazan were appointed its co-directors, and the group's regular homes were to be the Beaumont and the smaller Forum (later Newhouse) Theatre. While the houses were still in the final planning stages and under construction, a training program for a core of performers was initiated in 1962; and in 1964 the company offered its first production, Arthur *Miller's *After the Fall*, at a temporary playhouse, the ANTA-Washington Square Theatre. The first two regular seasons offered a balance between new American plays and European and American classics, but the critical response was cool, so by the end of 1964 both Kazan and Whitehead resigned and were replaced by Herbert Blau and Jules Irving from the *Actor's Workshop of San Francisco. A continued lack of striking success prompted Blau's resignation in 1967 and Irving's in 1972, and for a time Joseph *Papp and his *New York Shakespeare Festival attempted to run the problematic theatres. When he and his company threw in the towel, Richmond Crinkley briefly took over management. After several dark seasons, the two playhouses were relit in 1986, but the new leaders, artistic director Gregory Mosher and executive producer Bernard Gersten, abandoned the idea of a repertory ensemble. Since the late 1980s, the theatre company, now simply called *Lincoln Center Theatre, has finally flourished. Currently run by André Bishop and Gersten, the group presents plays and musicals in its two spaces all year long and rents Broadway theatres for other offerings. New American and foreign plays, musical and play revivals, and even special, not-easily-categorized productions such as *Contact (2000) have turned Lincoln Center into one of New York's most vital theatre groups. **Gregory** [Dean] **MOSHER** (b. 1949) studied theatre at Oberlin and Ithaca Colleges and trained at Juilliard before going to Chicago in 1974 where he ran the *Goodman Theatre and directed the early works by David Mamet and others. During his five-year tenure at Lincoln Center he was able to turn the troubled institution into a critical and popular success. Since leaving Lincoln Center in 1991, he has concentrated on freelance directing and producing.

LINDEN, Hal [né Harold Lipshitz] (b. 1931), actor and singer. A native New Yorker, the genial leading man with a perennial smile and pleasant singing voice was educated at the High School of the Performing Arts, Queens College, and City College before studying acting. After summer stock and a show that closed out of town, Linden made his Broadway debut in 1958 as a replacement for the leading man in *Bells Are Ringing*. He was applauded for his Billy Crocker in the long-running Off-Broadway revival of *Anything Goes* (1962), but he did not get recognition on Broadway until he played the ambitious patriarch Meyer in *The Rothschilds* (1970). After a very successful television career, Linden returned to the New York theatre in character parts.

LINDSAY and CROUSE, playwriting team. Howard Lindsay [né Herman Nelke] (1889–1968) was born in Waterford, New York, and educated at Harvard, then began his theatrical career as an actor in 1909. He continued to act and occasionally direct all through the 1920s, but found a more successful métier when he wrote the play *She Loves Me Not* (1933), then joined Russel *Crouse (1893–1966) to rewrite the book for *Anything Goes* (1934). Crouse was born in Findlay, Ohio, and pursued a journalist career in Cincinnati and then New York. As a press agent for the *Theatre Guild he contributed to *The Gang's All Here* (1931) and *Hold Your Horses* (1933) before teaming up with Lindsay on *Anything Goes*. The show was a hit and the twosome worked again on the musicals *Red, Hot and Blue!* (1936), *Hooray for What!* (1937), *Call Me Madam* (1950), *Happy Hunting* (1956), The *Sound of Music* (1959), and *Mr. President* (1962). Their nonmusical collaborations were just as successful, in particular the record-breaking comedy *Life with Father* (1939) in which Lindsay played the title character. Among the team's other plays were *Strip for Action* (1942), *State of the Union* (1945), *Life with Mother* (1948), *Remains to Be Seen* (1951), *The Prescott Proposals* (1953), *The Great Sebastians* (1956), and *Tall Story* (1959). As producers, Lindsay and Crouse's offerings included *Arsenic and Old Lace* (1941) and *Detective Story* (1949). Although their works may have had minimal merit as dr matic literature, they were excellent, show-wise writers whose best plays were consummately theatrical.

LINGARD, W[illiam] **H**[orace] [né Thomas] (1839–1927), comic actor. The English-born comedian had established a reputation in London music halls before immigrating to America in 1868. He specialized in short, satirical character sketches and songs and was quickly recognized as the best in his line. George *Odell recalled, "His versatility was remarkable, he exactly hit off some of the foibles of the day, and his protean changes were extraordinary." His youthful, drolly pixyish face immensely enhanced his comic flair. Although Lingard frequently acted in regular plays and musicals, often with his wife, Alice Dunning Lingard, his skits and songs were in such demand that he was forced to offer them between acts when they could not be incorporated into the plays themselves. He also tried his hand successfully at managing theatres and producing plays.

LION AND THE MOUSE, THE (1905), a play by Charles Klein. [*Lyceum Theatre, 586 perf.] Under the alias of Sarah Green, Shirley Rossmore (Grace *Elliston) has written a muckraking book exposing the methods of the multimillionaire John Burkett Ryder (Edmund *Breese), who is known as "Ready-money" Ryder. Shirley wrote the book partly in revenge for Ryder's destroying the career of her father, Judge Rossmore (Walter Allen), whose decisions had gone against Ryder's monopolies. But she is also determined to clear her father's name, and to this end allows Ryder's son, Jefferson (Richard *Bennett), to court her with neither father nor son realizing she is the Sarah Green who wrote the exposé. The older Ryder asks her to write a book answering Green's charges, and Shirley agrees but insists on having access to all Ryder's papers. When she comes across the papers that clear her father, she confronts the Ryders and discloses her identity. The Henry B. *Harris production was the biggest hit of its season (its opening followed closely those of *Peter Pan and The *Girl of the Golden West, neither of which ran nearly as long), and was seen as a powerful, skillful if contrived, and not very subtly veiled portrait of Ida Tarbell and John D. Rockefeller.

LION IN WINTER, THE (1966), a play by James Goldman. [*Ambassador Theatre, 92 perf.] The English king Henry II (Robert *Preston) allows Queen Eleanor (Rosemary *Harris), whom he has long imprisoned, to join the family's Christmas festivities at which he is determined to select an heir. He favors their youngest son, John (Bruce Scott), but Eleanor favors the eldest, Richard (James Rado), who has long been her pet. The argument that ensues is conditioned as much by the couple's ambivalent love-hate relationship as by genuine political considerations. It is made more complex when all three sons and the young king of France (Christopher *Walken) unite against Henry and he has little choice but to forgive the children—and to send Eleanor back into imprisonment. A largely fictitious, often wittily anachronistic treatment of historical figures, the play received generally excellent notices but failed to find a public.

However, it has always remained popular regionally. A 1999 Broadway revival with Laurence Fishburne and Stockard *Channing met with mixed notices. The Chicago-born **James GOLDMAN** (1927–98) was also the author of *Blood, Sweat and Stanley Poole* (1961), as well as the books for the musicals *A Family Affair* (1962) and **Follies* (1971).

LION KING, THE (1997), a musical play by Roger Allers, Irene Mecchi (book), Elton *John (music), Tim *Rice (lyrics). [*New Amsterdam Theatre, still running; Tony, NYDCC Awards.] Director–costume/puppet designer Julie Taymor took the 1994 *Disney animated film and turned it into a thrilling theatrical experience, rethinking the movie in terms of ritual theatre performance. The villainous lion Scar (John Vickery) murders his brother, King Mufasa (Samuel E. Wright), then convinces the lion cub Simba (Scott Irby-Ranniar) that he is responsible for his father's death. Simba flees and Scar becomes king; but once he matures and realizes his responsibilities, the grown-up Simba (Jason Raize) returns to oust Scar and rule as the rightful lion king. *Notable songs*: Circle of Life; Can You Feel the Love Tonight; Hakuna Matata. This tribal tale is told through dance, puppetry, choral chanting, and a variety of theatrics that dazzle the eye while they feed the imagination. Critical acclaim and strong popular demand kept the Disney-produced musical at SRO for years. **Julie TAYMOR** (b. 1952) was born in Boston, the daughter of a gynecologist and a political activist, educated at Oberlin College, and studied puppetry with the *Bread and Puppet Theatre and in Bali. Taymor directed the classics in regional theatre while her puppet and mask creations were seen in such New York productions as *The Haggadah* (1980) and *Black Elk Speaks* (1981). She cowrote, staged, and designed the theatrical fable *Juan Darién*, which arrived on Broadway in 1996. Endlessly creative, Taymor uses both ancient performance techniques and modern innovative ideas to create theatre pieces that are surprisingly accessible.

LION OF THE WEST, THE; or, A Trip to Washington (1831), a play by James Kirke Paulding. [*Park Theatre, in repertory.] The giddy young Cecilia Bramble (Mrs. Sharpe), the daughter of testy old Governor Bramble (Mr. Blakely) and the cousin of the unlettered but sage new Kentucky Congressman, Col. Nimrod Wildfire (J. H. *Hackett), dreams of marrying a titled Frenchman and living in Paris. Her wishes seem to come true when she is courted by the Count de Grillon (Peter *Richings) who persuades her to elope. But the elopement is thwarted by another suitor, the upright American Mr. Roebuck (Mr. Woodhull), and a third suitor, Mr. Higgins (Mr. Collett), appears on the scene to complicate matters. After some mistaken identities and a noisy but harmless series of gunshots, Wildfire exposes the Count as a swindler and Higgins as a coward. Cecilia refuses to marry Roebuck until she can prove she deserves him. Hackett presented the play after it won a prize of $300, which he had offered for "an original comedy whereof an American should be the leading character." Many contemporaries saw in Wildfire a good-natured spoofing of Davy Crockett, but Paulding and Hackett strenuously denied this. However, the play was not totally successful, so it was immediately withdrawn for revisions, which Paulding allowed John Augustus *Stone to write. Stone retained only the basic plot and the character of the Congressman. During his 1833 trip to London, Hackett had William Bayle *Bernard provide him with yet a third similar vehicle about Wildfire, which was in two acts and was called *The Kentuckian; or, A Trip to New York*, although it was sometimes offered as *A Kentuckian's Trip to New York* in 1815. In later years, until his retirement, Hackett used this play and, apparently on some occasions, Stone's, to keep Wildfire before an adoring public. Typical of Wildfire's Americanisms was his calling lawyers catfish, "'cause you see they're all head, and they're head all mouth." Hackett played the part in "buckskin clothes, deerskin shoes, and a coonskin hat." Laurence *Hutton noted, "He had many contemporary imitators, who copied his dress, his speech and his gait." The writer **James Kirke PAULDING** (1778–1860) was a friend of Washington Irving whose diverse works cover a range of subject matter and genres. In addition to *The Lion of the West*, he wrote the comedy *The Bucktails; or, Americans in England* and published *American Comedies*, which contained plays by himself and his son, William Irving Paulding.

LITHGOW, John [Arthur] (b. 1945), actor. Born in Rochester, New York, he studied at Harvard and at the London Academy of Music and Dramatic Art. The tall, versatile, Everyman-type actor made his debut at the Antioch Shakespeare Festival in 1953 and was praised for his Broadway bow as the athlete Kenny Kendal in *The Changing Room* (1973) earning a *Tony Award. Active on Broadway, Off Broadway, and in regional theatres (as well as in films and television), Lithgow has appeared as seaman Mat Burke in **Anna Christie* (1977), the ex-radical Chris in *Division Street* (1980), boxer McClintock in *Requiem for a Heavyweight* (1985), newspaper editor Walter Burns in *The *Front Page* (1986), French diplomat René Gallimard in **M. Butterfly* (1988), and columnist J. J. Hunsecker in *Sweet Smell of Success* (2002).

LITT, Jacob (1860–1905), manager. He began his theatrical career by selling programs at the Grand Opera House in his native Milwaukee, then within a few years he was treasurer of the house. Shortly thereafter Litt acquired two local theatres and began mounting popular melodramas, which he sent on tour throughout the Midwest. With profits from these shows, he was able to buy additional theatres. He found his greatest moneymaker in the melodrama *In Old Kentucky* (1899), which major New York managements had rejected. By the time a nervous disorder forced his early retirement, he had theatres as far east as New York and was sending out not only companies of his own plays but also handling Midwestern operations for Charles *Frohman and other Broadway producers. Despite his short career, his estate amounted to well over a million dollars.

LITTLE ACCIDENT (1928), a comedy by Floyd Dell and Thomas *Mitchell. [*Morosco Theatre, 304 perf.] On the eve of his wedding to Madge Ferris (Elvia Enders), Norman Overback (Mitchell) discovers that he is the father of Isabel Drury's child. When Isabel (Katherine Alexander) tells Norman she is putting the baby up for adoption, Norman kidnaps it. Madge is willing to marry Norman anyway; so is his landlady's daughter. But Norman decides he really loves Isabel, who was his sweetheart at college. Based on Dell's novel, *The Unmarried Father*, the slight but amusing comedy produced by Crosby *Gaige was a major hit of its season.

LITTLE CHURCH AROUND THE CORNER, THE (New York). At George *Holland's death in 1870, Joseph *Jefferson and Holland's son went to arrange the funeral service at a nearby Episcopal church. Refused on the grounds that Holland was an actor, they were informed, "There is a little church around the corner where they do that sort of thing." As a result, the Protestant-Episcopal Church of the Transfiguration on East 29th Street acquired its nickname and has ever since served popularly for theatrical weddings and funerals. It was featured prominently (and was sung about) in the musical *Sally* (1920).

LITTLE FOXES, THE (1939), a drama by Lillian *Hellman. [National Theatre, 410 perf.] The Hubbards are a rapacious, hate-filled family who dominate a small Southern town at the turn of the century. Oscar (Carl Benton Reid) has married Birdie Bagtry (Patricia *Collinge) for her family's money, and now that they again need cash, Oscar and his older brother Ben (Charles Dingle) reluctantly offer their crafty sister Regina (Tallulah *Bankhead) one-third interest in a new cotton mill they plan in return for a $75,000 loan. When Regina's husband, Horace Giddens (Frank Conroy), refuses to lend the money, Oscar goads his weakling son, Leo (Dan Duryea), into stealing Horace's bonds. Since the bonds were willed to Regina, Horace says nothing. But when an argument ensues between the two that induces Horace's heart attack, Regina refuses to get his medicine and lets him die. She then demands not one-third but a three-quarters interest in the business for her silence about the missing bonds. The Herman *Shulman production boasted a superb cast, highlighted by Bankhead's finest performance. Comparing it to Hellman's earlier play *The *Children's Hour*, Richard *Watts Jr. of the *Herald Tribune* thought it a "grim, bitter and merciless study, a drama more honest, more pointed and more brilliant." It has been revived regularly, most notably on Broadway in 1967 with Margaret *Leighton as Regina, in 1981 with Elizabeth Taylor, and in 1997 with Stockard *Channing. Hellman returned to the Hubbard family in her later play **ANOTHER PART OF THE FOREST** (1946). Marcus Hubbard (Percy Waram) made his fortune during the Civil War by blockade-running, extortion, and even leading the Union troops to a massacre of Confederate soldiers. His children have turned out as ruthless and grasping as he. His eldest, Ben (Leo Genn), does not hesitate to blackmail him to get his hands on the Hubbard money, but it is the unloving daughter Regina (Patricia Neal) who is content to wait until her time comes, and she is sure it will. Kermit *Bloomgarden produced the drama at the Fulton Theatre and it won general critical approval but failed to find a large audience, running only 182 performances. Two years later composer-lyricist Marc Blitzstein turned *The Little Foxes* into the opera **REGINA** (1949) with Jane Pickens in the title role. Although the work was a commercial failure on Broadway, it has since found a place in the repertory of several opera companies. *Notable songs:* Birdie's Aria; The Best Thing of All.

LITTLE JOHNNY JONES (1904), a musical play by George M. *Cohan (book, music, lyrics). [Liberty Theatre, 52 perf.] The Yankee Johnny Jones (Cohan) comes to England to ride in the Derby. Anthony Anstey (Jerry Cohan) offers him a bribe to throw the race, but Johnny refuses, so when he actually loses the race, Anstey spreads rumors that he did so intentionally. After clearing his name, Johnny returns to America where Anstey has kidnapped Johnny's sweetheart, Goldie Gates (Ethel Levey). So Johnny must scour San Francisco's Chinatown to recover her. *Notable songs*: Give My Regards to Broadway; Life's a Funny Proposition After All; The Yankee Doodle Boy. Although most critics assailed the play as too slangy, contrived, and chauvinistic, the public adored it, and Cohan had his first of many Broadway hits. Within a few months after its original run, Cohan and producer Sam H. *Harris twice brought it back for return engagements. A largely rewritten, poorly mounted 1982 revival failed to run.

LITTLE JOURNEY, A (1918), a play by Rachel *Crothers. [Little Theatre, 252 perf.] When Manhattan society belle Julie Rutherford (Estelle *Winwood) loses both her fortune and her fiancé in quick succession, she decides to head west to live with her brother. She is nearly kicked off the train when it is discovered she has lost her ticket, but a handsome young rancher, Jim West (Cyril Keightley), lends her the money to remain aboard. He quickly grows fond of her, but she remains enamored of her old frivolous way of life. The train is involved in a horrendous wreck, in which the widowed young mother of a baby is killed. Her own close brush with death, her motherly instincts at seeing the orphaned baby, and Jim's obvious manly virtues all contrive to offer Julie new hope and a new life. Not typical of Crothers's best work, usually dealing with the interaction of women, this rather ordinary, if theatrical love story was made memorable by her subtle drawing of an essentially rootless young lady.

LITTLE KATY. See *Hot Corn*.

LITTLE MARY SUNSHINE (1959), a musical comedy by Rick Besoyan (book, music, lyrics). [*Orpheum Theatre, 1,143 perf.] Little Mary Sunshine (Eileen Brennan) runs a lodge in the Rockies, but is in danger of being evicted. The Colorado Rangers, led by Captain Jim (William James), all love her, and on their way to hunt the villainous Yellow Feather stop to help her. Eventually they capture their man and save Mary from eviction. *Notable songs*: Colorado Love Call; Little Mary Sunshine; Look for a Sky of Blue. The delightful musical spoof satirized 1920s operettas such as *Rose-Marie* and *Rio Rita*, with deadly and hilarious accuracy. The show remains popular with all kinds of theatre groups and is even enjoyed by audiences unfamiliar with its musical targets.

LITTLE MURDERS (1967), a dark comedy by Jules Feiffer. [*Broadhurst Theatre, 7 perf.] The Newquists are a rather kooky Manhattan family trying to make the best of a bad deal. The father, Carol (Heywood Hale Broun), would like to have a less feminine name; the mother, Marjorie (Ruth White), would like to have a different family; and the son, Kenny (David Steinberg), would like to be of a different sex. Only the sweet but spunky daughter, Patsy (Barbara *Cook), seems vaguely content, although she is in love with a thin-skinned liberal, Alfred Chamberlain (Elliott Gould), who thinks the best way to deal with muggers is to let them beat you. The jangle and blare around them grows increasingly hectic and menacing until Patsy is killed in her living room by a stray bullet. At that point, the Newquists decide to shoot back. Although Alexander H. *Cohen's Broadway mounting failed, it was produced with great success in England by the *Royal Shakespeare Company, and this led to a 1969 Off-Broadway revival at the *Circle in the Square that ran four hundred performances. **Jules** [Ralph] **FEIFFER** (b. 1929) is a New Yorker best known for his incisive cartoons about the anguish of contemporary life. Among his other plays are *Feiffer's People* (1968), *The White House Murder Case* (1970), *Knock Knock* (1976), *Grownups* (1981), *Eliot Loves* (1990), and *A Bad Friend* (2003).

LITTLE NELL AND THE MARCHIONESS (1867), a play by John *Brougham. [*Wallack's Theatre, 28 perf.] Nell (Lotta *Crabtree) and her Grandfather Trent (T. J. Hind) are forced from the Old Curiosity Shop by the rapacious Quilp (E. Coleman). They wander the country roads of England until the old man finds work at a small church. Eventually the grandfather's long-lost rich brother returns to help him retrieve his shop, but by that time the wear and tear has been too much for Little Nell, who dies and is lifted bodily to heaven. In a second, interwoven story, Dick Swiveller (J. C. Williamson) falls in love with the poor servant girl (also Crabtree) of Quilp's unscrupulous lawyer, Simon Brass (W. J. Leonard). He names her "The Marchioness" and, after she nurses him through an illness, marries her. Based on Dickens's *The Old Curiosity Shop*, the play was written as a vehicle for "Lotta." It became the most popular piece in her repertory, and she played it as long as she performed. Neither her Nell nor her Marchioness was totally faithful to the original, but served as excuses for her banjo playing, her clog dances, and other turns. The show's short original run is in no way indicative of its popularity, since it was a limited engagement. T. Allston *Brown noted, "Rarely in the history of New York theatricals has a summer engagement proved so profitable." Receipts averaged a then exceptional $1,100 per night, the run was extended one week, and Lotta herself realized $10,000 from the stand.

LITTLE NIGHT MUSIC, A (1973), a musical comedy of manners by Hugh *Wheeler (book), Stephen *Sondheim (music, lyrics). [*Shubert Theatre, 600 perf.; Tony, NYDCC Award.] The lawyer Fredrik Egerman (Len *Cariou) and his child bride Anne

(Victoria Mallory) have an odd marriage—she is still a virgin and is lusted after by Fredrik's grown son, the divinity student Henrik (Mark Lambert)—so Fredrik is drawn to his former mistress, the actress Désirée (Glynis Johns). But her lover Count Carl-Magnus (Laurence Guittard) is suspicious of her, so Désirée invites the Egerman family to the country manse of her mother, the aged courtesan Mme. Armfeldt (Hermione *Gingold). During a moonlit summer night, Henrik and Anne decide to run off together, the Count's jealousy brings him closer to his wife (Patricia Elliott), Mme. Armfeldt quietly dies, and Fredrik and Désirée are free to pursue their romance. *Notable songs*: Send in the Clowns; Every Day a Little Death; Remember?; The Miller's Son; Liaisons; A Weekend in the Country. Based on the 1955 Swedish film, *Smiles of a Summer Night*, the musical's score was written entirely in three-quarter time or variations thereof. Though the work displayed much of Sondheim's misanthropy, it was mellower than most of his later works and became one of his most accessible shows. The original mounting by producer-director Hal *Prince featured a superior cast, magical scenery by Boris *Aronson, and elegant period costumes by Florence *Klotz. The adult musical comedy has been frequently revived by both theatres and opera companies around the world.

LITTLE SHOP OF HORRORS (1982), a musical comedy by Howard *Ashman (book, lyrics), Alan *Menken (music). [*Orpheum Theatre, 2,209 perf.] The nerdy clerk Seymour (Lee Wilkof) brings a small plant into Mushnik's florist shop where he works and names it Audrey II, after the girl (Ellen Greene) he loves. The singing plant, which demands human blood, begins to grow and grow, preferably feeding on bits of Seymour's rival for Audrey's affections and eventually on Mushnik, Audrey, and Seymour himself. It seems the plant has hopes to take over the world. *Notable songs*: Somewhere That's Green; Feed Me; Suddenly Seymour. Based on a low-budget 1960 film of the same name, this delightful, small-scale spoof enjoyed worldwide success. Audrey II was a huge puppet manipulated by a puppeteer; its voice came from an actor off stage. The small musical remains very popular with all kinds of theatre groups across the country and was revived on Broadway in 2003.

LITTLE SHOW, THE. A series of intimate revues presented on Broadway in 1929, 1930, and 1931, the first edition featured songs by Arthur *Schwartz, Howard *Dietz, and others, and sketches by Dietz and George S. *Kaufman. The first revue starred Fred *Allen, Clifton *Webb, and Libby *Holman, and the hit songs "I Guess I'll Have to Change My Plan" and "Moanin' Low." The final edition starred Beatrice *Lillie and Ernest *Truex and offered "Mad Dogs and Englishmen," "When Yuba Plays the Rhumba on the Tuba," and "There Are Fairies at the Bottom of My Garden." The first offering established the Broadway careers of Dietz and Schwartz and introduced an era of superlative revues in the 1930s.

LITTLE THEATRE IN AMERICA. If regionally oriented amateur production is considered the essence of Little Theatre, then the first American example might be said to have been the performance by one Colonel Ornate's troops of *Los Moros y los Christianos* before an audience of probably bewildered Native Americans in 1598 in what afterward became New Mexico. As theatre later spread across the colonies in succeeding centuries, scattered amateur entertainments no doubt were offered occasionally. The controversial playing of *The *Bear and the Cub* is possibly another instance, as would be performances by General Burgoyne's troops during the Revolutionary War. Amateur groups sprang up across the country all through the 19th century from the Lobero Theatre in Santa Barbara, California, to the Comedy Club in New York City, the latter group, founded in 1885, still active today. But a concerted effort to develop such theatres did not occur until early in the 20th century when such important figures as Percy *MacKaye began trumpeting the merits of "a theatre wholly divorced from commercialism." MacKaye's plea, in his 1909 book *The Playhouse and the Play*, came precisely at the moment when silent films began to make noticeable inroads, luring away many less educated, less affluent playgoers from cheap melodrama and farce, and forcing the closing or conversion of many marginal live theatres. Although MacKaye attempted to promote the term *Civic Theatre*, the somewhat more descriptive term *Little Theatre* quickly took hold and spread. Indeed the rapidity of the spread was remarkable. Chicago was the cradle of several important little theatres, including that at the Hull-House in 1900 and the later group founded by Maurice *Browne, who is sometimes called the father of the Little Theatre movement in America. Kenneth *MacGowan was also an avid supporter of such playhouses. Historian Joseph Wesley Ziegler noted, "In the number of theatres created and the number of amateur talents working in them, the Little Theatre movement was the farthest-reaching homegrown theatre in American history. It was also the most self-consciously noble; it is no accident that even now we speak of the phenomenon in capital letters." The heyday of the movement was in the 1920s, when prosperity, a general renaissance in dramatic writing, and an awareness of that renaissance sharpened interest everywhere. As a rule the troupes presented recognized Broadway successes and occasionally the more accessible or at least undemanding of the classics. A few attempted original drama, though virtually nothing of importance emerged from these theatres. Contrary to MacKaye's hopes, they were at heart only a little less conservative, if that, than Broadway. Many of the more successful groups were able to finance the erection of attractive, well-equipped playhouses, usually seating only a few hundred patrons. In their informative study of the movement, *Curtains Going Up* (1938), Albert McCleery and Carl Glick were able to list more than five hundred community groups that had functioned or were still flourishing in the then forty-eight states. (The book also provides excellent photographs of the often-beautiful playhouses and the fine physical productions.) With the coming of sound films, followed immediately by the Great Depression and eventually World War II, interest in the movement waned. While a number of durable amateur groups continue to prosper in various localities, the sheen and the excitement that once surrounded the Little Theatre movement have long since been transferred to the fine professional regional theatres that have developed since the war. **Maurice BROWNE** (1881–1955), a sometime poet who came to America in 1919, founded the Chicago Little Theatre with his wife, Ellen Van Volkenburg, and did much to promote the little theatre in America. Browne also produced several shows in New York, including a highly praised but short-lived mounting of *Medea* (1920), with his wife in the title role. Returning to England, where he spent the rest of his career, he wrote a curiously embittered autobiography, *Too Late to Lament*, 1955.

LITTLE THEATRE MOVEMENT. See Little Theatre in America.

LITTLE TYCOON, THE (1886), a comic opera by Williard *Spenser (book, music, lyrics). [Standard Theatre, 104 perf.] General Knickerbocker (R. E. Graham) is returning home from Europe with his daughter Violet (Carrie M. Dietrich) and Lord Dolphin (E. H. Van Veghten), the monosyllabic nobleman he has decided his daughter must marry. But Violet loves Alvin (W. S. Rising), so after they arrive at the Knickerbocker estate, Alvin comes disguised as "His Royal Highness Sham, The Great Tycoon of Japan" and with his flattery gulls the social-climbing general into allowing him to wed Violet. *Notable songs*: The Cats on Our Back Fence; Love Comes Like a Summer Sigh. After a long run in Philadelphia, the musical played New York as part of its road tour.

Although Broadway critics dismissed it as typifying the Philadelphia School of Comic Opera, its original engagement was extended by popular demand. It toured or was revived regularly for about a decade.

LIVING MODELS. Living pictures or tableaux vivants had been popular in American theatre from very early on. Patriotic spectacles in particular were wont to have such finales, often with the personification of Liberty at the center of a carefully posed ensemble. It also became the custom to have the first curtain call taken in a dramatically held pose. These extravagant tableaux remained popular through the era of *Ziegfeldian revues. However, during the 1847–48 season a special variety of tableau was the rage: carefully posed reproductions of famous statues and paintings. Excuses were found to place them in all types of entertainment. As so often happens, the vogue faded when excesses, especially posing of virtually nude female figures, led to moral protests and finally to police action.

LIVING NEWSPAPER. See Federal Theatre Project.

LIVING THEATRE COMPANY (New York). Established as a repertory ensemble in 1947 by Julian Beck and his wife, Judith Malina, it first performed at the Cherry Lane Theatre and after 1951 at its own theatre on lower Sixth Avenue. From the start its repertory leaned heavily on plays that had little chance of commercial success. The choices, and often the mountings, were daring, frequently leftish in bent, and increasingly controversial. Among the writers whose plays were produced were Gertrude Stein, T. S. *Eliot, Luigi *Pirandello, and Jean Cocteau. The company's most famous production was not a revival but an original play, Jack Gelber's The *Connection (1959), one of the earliest attempts to look candidly at the growth of drug addiction. In 1961 and 1962 the troupe made two well-received visits to Europe, but growing concern with what was perceived as its increasingly confrontational, iconoclastic nature embroiled the company in legal and critical battles (many dealing with the troupe's rampant nudity) and may have speeded the onset of the financial difficulties that forced the theatre to close in 1963. The Becks later ran a similar company in Europe and then Brazil. In 1984 the company again settled in Manhattan but productions since have been sporadic at best.

LOCKE, Edward (1869–1945), playwright. Born in England, he came to America while still in his early teens and soon became an actor both in the theatre and in vaudeville. After writing some vaudeville sketches, he turned to full-length plays, several of which were done by cheaper touring companies before he reached Broadway with the successful *The *Climax* (1909). Although Locke subsequently was the author or co-author of numerous other plays, none proved nearly as popular. Among his other works were the drama *The Case of Becky* (1912) and the romance *The Dancer* (1919).

LOCKE, George E. (1817–80), actor. Known popularly as "Yankee" Locke for his impersonation of native types, he was born in Epsom, New Hampshire and made his theatrical debut in Boston where he performed for many seasons before he found his special métier and began to make a name for himself across the country. The names of the characters Locke played suggest their nature and the kind of the vehicles written around them: Jedediah Homebred, Zedediah Short, Solomon Swop, and Moderation Easterbrook. He was one of the many performers who played the major cities only briefly, finding warmer welcomes on the stages of smaller cities and towns.

LOESSER, Frank [Henry] (1910–69), composer and lyricist. Although he was born into a musical New York family, his father, a piano teacher, disapproved of popular music, so young Loesser was largely self-taught. His earliest professional work was writing lyrics and sketches for vaudeville and radio, and Broadway first heard of him solely as a lyricist when he set words to some Irving Actman melodies for *The Illustrators' Show* (1936). By the time he returned to the theatre in 1948 as both composer and lyricist for **Where's Charley?*, he had long since established himself as a songwriter in films and what was left of Tin Pan Alley. The versatile songwriter provided colorful, urban numbers for **Guys and Dolls* (1950); Italianate opera melodies and brassy Broadway ditties for *The *Most Happy Fella* (1956); delicate, rural songs for *Greenwillow* (1960); and sassy, satirical musical numbers for **How to Succeed in Business Without Really Trying* (1961). In a trade notoriously jealous of its fame and success, Loesser was known for his generosity to other songwriters and gave important boosts to the Broadway careers of Richard *Adler, Jerry *Ross, and Meredith *Willson. Biography: *A Most Remarkable Fella*, Susan Loesser (his daughter), 1993.

LOEWE, Frederick. See Lerner and Loewe.

LOFTUS, [Marie] **Cecilia** (1876–1943), actress and singer. One of the most versatile of performers, who moved successfully back and forth between vaudeville and musical comedy on the one hand and romantic drama and Shakespeare on the other, she was born in Glasgow, the daughter of popular music hall entertainers. The attractive, dark-haired woman, often known as Cissie, first called attention to herself as a mimic in her American debut at Koster and Bial's Vaudeville Theatre in 1895. Loftus's varied credits included the operetta *The Mascot* (1900); Viola in **Twelfth Night* and Hero in *Much Ado About Nothing*; Lady Sacheverell in *Richard Lovelace* (1901) and Katherine in **If I Were King* (1901), opposite E. H. *Sothern (the latter written with her in mind by her husband, Justin Huntly McCarthy); Juliet and Desdemona on tour opposite William *Faversham; and headliner engagements at the *Palace throughout the 1920s, winning applause for her imitations of the Barrymores and other popular performers. Her final appearance was in *Little Dark Horse* (1941), in which she played a tyrannical grandmother.

LOGAN FAMILY, THE. Playwright and comedian Cornelius A[mbrosius] Logan (1806–53) is generally believed to have been born in Baltimore and to have made his acting debut in Philadelphia in 1825. Noah *Ludlow notes that Logan manifested ambitions to be a tragedian, but that his "unchangeable comic" face denied him success. Much of his acting career was spent in the Midwest (called the West in his day), where he specialized in Yankee roles. He was the author of several comedies in which such Yankee characters were pivotal figures: *Yankee Land; or, The Foundling of the Apple Orchard* (1834), *The Vermont Wool Dealer* (1840), and *Chloroform; or, New York a Hundred Years Hence* (1849). Logan's daughters were also prominent performers. The eldest, Eliza (1830–72), was given a careful education by her father in the hope that she would not follow in his wandering footsteps. However, he supported her final decision to become an actress. She made her debut as Young Norval in Philadelphia's *Walnut Street Theatre when she was only eleven and her New York bow in 1850 as Pauline in *The *Lady of Lyons*. Most of her career was spent performing as a major star in the South or Midwest. She is said to have possessed an attractive, expressive face, a fine figure, and a sweet, adaptable voice. The critic for the *New York Herald* described her acting as "impulsive, electric and at times singularly impressive from the power she throws into a few brief words." She retired in 1859 when she married George Wood, who operated theatres in St. Louis and Cincinnati. Olive [Sykes] Logan (1839?–1909) made her debut as a child actress playing opposite her father. After his death she spent several seasons in important roles at

Philadelphia's *Arch Street Theatre, then left to study in Europe, where she published her first novel and travel book. Returning to America she assumed the title role in her own play, *Eveleen* (1864), which she performed in New York and on tour. Other roles included Laura Roslyn opposite Frank *Chanfrau in *Sam*, Lady Gay Spanker in *London Assurance*, and with a troupe of French actors who were appearing in New York in *500 Francs de Récompense*. Thereafter she performed only on occasion, preferring to lecture on women's rights and other topics of interest to her, and to write. Among her other plays were *Surf* (1870), *A Business Woman* (1873), *La Cigale* (1878), and *Newport; or, The Swimmer, the Singer, and the Cypher* (1879); among her books was *The Mimic World* (1871).

LOGAN, Joshua [Lockwood] (1908–88), director and playwright. Born in Texarkana, Texas, he studied at Princeton and with *Stanislavsky in Moscow, then founded the *University Players in 1928, with whom he remained until 1933. Logan's first solo directorial assignment on Broadway was *To See Ourselves* (1935), but it was his staging of *On Borrowed Time* (1938) that called attention to his talent and inaugurated a string of successes or interesting productions: *I Married an Angel* (1938), *Knickerbocker Holiday* (1938), *Stars in Your Eyes* (1939), *Morning's at Seven* (1939), *Two for the Show* (1940), *Higher and Higher* (1940), *By Jupiter* (1942), *This Is the Army* (1942), *Annie Get Your Gun* (1946), *Happy Birthday* (1946), *John Loves Mary* (1947), *Mister Roberts* (1948), *South Pacific* (1949), *The Wisteria Trees* (1950), *Wish You Were Here* (1952), *Picnic* (1953), *Fanny* (1954), *Kind Sir* (1953), *Middle of the Night* (1956), *Blue Denim* (1958), and *The *World of Susie Wong* (1958). He co-wrote and/or co-produced several of the above. At his best, Logan's direction was distinguished by a deep insight into character and a remarkable fluidity, the latter especially evident in his staging of often-cumbersome musicals. He was sometimes criticized in his later shows and films, however, for too heavy a touch. Autobiography: *Josh: My Up and Down, In and Out Life*, 1976.

LOMBARDI, LTD. (1917), a comedy by Frederic and Fanny *Hatton. [*Morosco Theatre, 296 perf.] Tito Lombardi (Leo Carrillo) is a skilled dressmaker whose simple honesty and quiet morals seem out of place in the often harsh, cynical world of fashion. Apart from his work, his one love is a chorus girl named Phyllis Manning (Sue MacMannamy). Unfortunately she is a scheming gold digger who returns his affections only so long as it serves her purposes. When Phyllis runs out on him and his business seems on the verge of bankruptcy, he looks with new eyes on his self-sacrificing, long-suffering assistant, Norah Blake (Janet Dunbar). Although many critics found the play trite and contrived, the Hattons' professional know-how, their varied pictures of theatrical showgirls, Carrillo's warm performance, and a number of scenes with scantily clad mannequins made the play exceedingly popular both in New York and on the road. Producer Oliver *Morosco called the show "as completely gratifying as anything I ever did in show business."

LONDON ASSURANCE (1841). The only enduring British comedy of the first half of the 19th century, this earliest Dion *Boucicault success tells of a lordly Belgravia fop, Sir Harcourt Courtly, whose wooing of a Gloucestershire heiress is thwarted by none other than his own son. Romping in and out of the amorous adventures is a determined horsewoman, Lady Gay Spanker. The American premiere occurred at the *Park Theatre in 1841 with a cast that included Henry *Placide as Courtly and Charlotte *Cushman as Spanker. The premiere was a landmark in the annals of the American theatre. First of all, it followed the innovation employed in its original London production by Mme. Vestris of using a box set, so that audiences appeared to be watching the action from the fourth wall of a real house. Equally important was the comedy's stand of three uninterrupted weeks, the first "long run" in American history. The play was regularly revived by J. W. and Lester *Wallack in productions in which John *Gilbert invariably played Harcourt Courtly and in which such actresses as Fanny *Davenport and Rose *Coghlan portrayed Spanker. Laura Keene's horsewoman was also admired, as was Ada *Rehan's in Augustin *Daly's 1896 revival. Thereafter the play was brought back with increasing infrequency and with little success. Even a superb *Royal Shakespeare Company production, imported in 1974, attracted few American playgoers. Yet there was praise for the Roundabout Theatre's 1997 revival featuring Brian Bedford as Harcourt.

LONERGAN, Lester (1869?–1931), director and actor. The Irishman came to America as a young man and acted in Western stock companies before graduating to important supporting roles opposite such notables as John *Barrymore, John *Drew, and Helena *Modjeska. In his later years he largely abandoned acting and was responsible for staging such successes as *Abraham Lincoln* (1919), *The Bad Man* (1920), *The *Road to Rome* (1927), and *The Command To Love* (1927).

LONG DAY'S JOURNEY INTO NIGHT (1956), a play by Eugene *O'Neill. [*Helen Hayes Theatre, 390 perf.; Pulitzer Prize, Tony, NYDCC Awards.]

On an uncomfortably hot day in their New England summer home, the Tyrones confront their pasts and each other. James Tyrone (Fredric *March) is an aging actor, famous but miserly, who wasted his talent performing in the same trashy melodrama rather than risk failure in more adventuresome plays. To save pennies he had called in a quack doctor when his wife gave birth to their third son, Edmund (Bradford Dillman). As a result of the poor treatment, Mary Tyrone (Florence *Eldridge) has been a drug addict ever since. Their eldest son, James Jr. (Jason *Robards), is a rakish, boozing ne'er-do-well, who is both protective of and jealous of his younger brother. As the day turns into night, the destructively probing conversations continue, until the rattled, drugged Mary appears in her wedding gown, reliving a happier, irreclaimable time. Louis *Kronenberger wrote, "This relentless chronicle of O'Neill's riven and tormented family, mingling the fierce thrust of unblushing theatre with the harsh, unsoftened truth, may very possibly come to seem O'Neill's most substantial legacy to the American stage." Written as a sort of autobiographical catharsis, its production violated O'Neill's stipulation that it not be performed until twenty-five years after his death. Co-producer José *Quintero directed the superior cast and the long and difficult drama is continually revived. Notable New York productions were seen in 1971 with Robert Ryan, Geraldine *Fitzgerald, James Naughton, and Stacy *Keach; in 1976 with Robards (now playing the father), Zoe *Caldwell, Michael Moriarty, and Kevin *Conway; in 1981 with Earle *Hyman, Gloria *Foster, Peter-Francis-James, and Al Freeman Jr., in 1986 with Jack *Lemmon, Bethel Leslie, Peter *Gallagher, and Kevin *Spacey; and in 2003 with Brian Dennehy, Vanessa Redgrave, Robert Sean *Leonard, and Philip Seymour Hoffman.

LONG, John Luther (1861–1927), playwright. Born in either Philadelphia or Hanover, Pennsylvania, he was a successful Philadelphia attorney who had published short stories before collaborating with David *Belasco on two tragic Oriental romances, *Madame Butterfly* (1900) and *The *Darling of the Gods* (1902). Also with Belasco he wrote *Adrea* (1904) and with Edward Childs *Carpenter, *The Dragon Fly* (1905). Long's solo efforts included the Mrs. *Fiske vehicle *Dolce* (1906), the Mrs. Leslie *Carter vehicle *Kassa* (1909), and, his last produced play, *Crowns* (1922). Long's plays usually have exotic locales, melodramatic situations, and juicy roles for women. In a sense he was an early-20th-century throwback to the 18th- and 19th-century Philadelphia tradition of gentleman-lawyer-writer.

LONG VOYAGE HOME, THE. See *S.S. Glencairn.*

LONG WHARF THEATRE (New Haven, Connecticut). Founded in 1965 by Harlan Kleiman and Jon Jory, it is situated in a former meat and produce warehouse near the waterfront. A three-quarter thrust stage was erected into an auditorium that originally seated about 440 people, but that was slightly enlarged soon after the opening. Arvin *Brown was named artistic director in 1967 and over the next thirty years he made the company one of the finest on the east coast. The emphasis was on an acting ensemble and plays that allowed for intricate human relationships. The repertory consists of new plays and revivals, several of which transferred to New York, including *The Changing Room*, *Streamers*, *The *Shadow Box*, *Quartermaine's Terms*, *American Buffalo*, *All My Sons*, A *View from the Bridge*, *Broken Glass*, and *Wit*. In 1977 a 199-seat "Stage II" was added, and in 1979 the company received the regional theatre *Tony Award. Douglas Wager and then Gordon Edelstein succeeded Brown.

LONG, William Ivey (b. 1947), costume designer. One of the busiest and most awarded designers during the last three decades of the 20th century, the Pennsylvania-born artist was educated at the College of William and Mary, Yale, and the University of North Carolina. In addition to extensive work in opera, dance, and even rock concerts, Long provided the costumes for such notable theatre productions as *Nine* (1982), *Lend Me a Tenor* (1989), *Assassins* (1990), *Six Degrees of Separation* (1990), *Crazy for You* (1992), *Guys and Dolls* (1992), *Cabaret* (1998), *Swing* (1999), *The *Man Who Came to Dinner* (2000), *Seussical* (2000), *The *Producers* (2001), and *Hairspray* (2002).

LONGACRE THEATRE (New York). Named after nearby Longacre Square, this theatre on West 48th Street retained the name even after the crossroads area was changed to Times Square. The 1,400-seat playhouse was built by entrepreneur H. H. *Frazee in 1913, and the Henry *Herts–designed house seemed very intimate for its seating capacity. Over the years the auditorium has lost three hundred seats to make it more comfortable, but the Longacre is still a compact house ideal for plays and small musicals. The *Shuberts acquired the theatre from Frazee during the Great Depression and still own it. The space was converted to a radio (and later television) studio between 1944 and 1953 but soon returned to legitimate status and quickly found tenants once again. The theatre's longest-running tenant was the musical revue *Ain't Misbehavin'* (1978).

LOOK BACK IN ANGER (1957). The John *Osborne play served as America's introduction to the new postwar school of British playwrights known as "the angry young men." The drama focuses on the raging discontent of Jimmy Porter, a working class Brit, and on his tortured relations with his wife and his best friend. The play was first produced in New York by David *Merrick at the *Lyceum Theatre in 1957, and ran for 407 performances. Kenneth Haigh, Mary Ure, and Alan Bates were the original leads. Many critics pointed out that America long had had drama of strident social protest, so that the new English school did not seem so really new. However, it soon became evident that these English playwrights did bring about a subtle change in protest plays in that the expression of the anger and not its actual causes frequently became central to the play. A popular revival at the *Roundabout Theatre in 1980 featured Malcolm McDowell, Lisa Banes, and Raymond Hardie.

LOOK HOMEWARD, ANGEL (1957), a play by Ketti Frings. [*Ethel Barrymore Theatre, 564 perf.; Pulitzer Prize, NYDCC Award.] Eugene Gant (Anthony *Perkins) is a moonstruck, sensitive youth who lives in the boardinghouse run by his domineering mother Eliza (Jo Van Fleet). His father, W. O. Gant (Hugh Griffith), is a blustering, frequently drunk, dreamer and his elder brother Ben (Arthur *Hill) is too frail to live in the real world he longs for. Eugene's own world seems shattered when Ben dies and when his affair with the Gants' boarder, Laura James (Frances Hyland), ends. As he goes off to college he can only hope to overcome his past and make something of himself. Kermit *Bloomgarden co-produced this fine adaptation of Thomas Wolfe's autobiographical novel, and the production featured a riveting cast, delicate direction by George Roy Hill, and an exceptionally atmospheric set by Jo *Mielziner. **Ketti FRINGS** [née Catherine or Katherine Hartley] (1910?–81) was born in Columbus, Ohio, and gained major attention with her novel *Hold Back the Dawn*. Better known as a screenwriter, her other Broadway efforts were failures.

LOOS, Anita (1893–1981), playwright. Born in Sisson, California, she was an actress before turning to writing and then became famous with her comic novel *Gentlemen Prefer Bondes*. Although Loos spent much of her career in Hollywood, she was represented on Broadway with a handful of plays, most notably *The Whole Town's Talking* (1932), **Happy Birthday* (1946), and her dramatization of Colette's novel *Gigi* (1951). She contributed to both the play version and the musical version of her **Gentlemen Prefer Blondes* in 1926 and 1949. Autobiography: *A Girl Like I*, 1966.

LOPEZ, Priscilla (b. 1948), actress, singer, and dancer. The animated Hispanic performer, who has shone brightly in both plays and musicals, was born in the Bronx and educated at the High School of the Performing Arts. Lopez started dancing in the Broadway chorus in 1966, then replaced others in featured roles, finally coming into her own as the Puerto Rican chorine Diana in A *Chorus Line* (1975). Her other notable performances include the Harpo Marx–like Gino in *A Night in the Ukraine* (1980), the New Yorker Lisa looking for romantic commitment in *Key Exchange* (1982), the shrewd lawyer Kate Sullivan in **Other People's Money* (1990), and a variety of wacky characters in the one-woman show *Class Mothers of '68* (2002).

LOQUASTO, Santo (b. 1944), designer. The versatile scenic and costume designer was born in Wilkes Barre, Pennsylvania, and attended the local King's College before studying design at Yale. His first professional credits were at the *Williamstown Theatre Festival and the *Hartford Stage, arriving in New York in 1970 and soon making his reputation for his sets and costumes at the *Public Theatre. Loquasto has excelled with both detailed and realistic sets, such as those for **That Championship Season* (1972), **American Buffalo* (1982), and *Cafe Crown* (1988), as well as more suggestive or abstract scenery, as with **Sticks and Bones* (1971), *The Cherry Orchard* (1977), *Bent* (1979), and **Grand Hotel* (1989). He has also designed costumes for Broadway, such as for **Ragtime* (1998), and for dance companies.

LORAINE, Robert (1876–1935), actor and manager. The handsome Englishman, whose huge repertory ranged from the heroes of Shakespearean drama and 18th-century comedy through swashbuckling melodrama and modern drawing-room comedy, first played for American audiences in 1901 as the gallant Ralph Percy in *To Have and to Hold*. From then until shortly before his death, he made numerous return visits. By far his best-known part, at least for American theatregoers, was John Tanner, which he played in the American premiere of *Shaw's *Man and Superman* (1905), a role Loraine portrayed for six months in New York, then toured the country with for two seasons.

LORD, Pauline (1890–1950), actress. Born in Hanford, California, she made her debut in San Francisco stock in 1903 and afterward toured with Nat *Goodwin and played in stock in Milwaukee and in Springfield (Massachusetts) before winning recognition in New York as the innocent Ruth Lennox who is corrupted in *The Talker* (1912). Lord next found success as two prostitutes: Sadie in *The

Deluge (1917) and Anna Christopherson in **Anna Christie* (1921). On a much different track was her portrayal of the innocent young waitress Amy in **They Knew What They Wanted* (1924). In the 1920s Lord appeared in *Trelawny of the Wells* (1925 and 1927), *Sandalwood* (1926), *Mariners* (1927), *Salvation* (1927), and replaced Lynn *Fontanne as Nina Leeds in **Strange Interlude* (1928). Her most notable parts in the 1930s were the loyal cook Abby in *The Late Christopher Bean* (1932), the embittered, unkempt wife Zenobia in **Ethan Frome* (1936), and Amanda Wingfield in the 1946 touring production of *The *Glass Menagerie*. She was an actress with a singularly identifiable style of performing, which Ward *Morehouse described as "so jerky, so halting, so gasping, so volatile, and so brilliant," and Brooks *Atkinson declared "elusive, tremulous, infinitely gifted."

LORRAINE, Lillian [née Eulallean De Jacques or Mary Ann Brennan] (1892–1955), singer. A San Franciscan who began performing professionally at the age of four, she grew to be an exquisite beauty and the reputed mistress of Florenz *Ziegfeld. Lorraine appeared in more than a dozen Broadway musicals between 1906 and 1922, including the 1909, 1910, 1911, 1912, and 1918 editions of the *Ziegfeld Follies*. Songs she introduced included "My Pony Boy" in *Miss Innocence* (1908), "By the Light of the Silvery Moon" in the *1909 Follies*, and "Row, Row, Row" in the 1912 edition.

LORTEL, Lucille (1902–98), producer. Dubbed "the Queen of Off Broadway," Lortel presented challenging new works, as well as unusual foreign plays, at the *Theatre de Lys for more than forty years. The native New Yorker studied at the *American Academy of Dramatic Arts in the 1920s then began her career as an actress. She left the theatre when she married but returned as a producer in the 1950s, first at the White Barn Theatre in Connecticut and then in Manhattan, offering such significant Off-Broadway productions as *The *Threepenny Opera* (1954), *Dames at Sea* (19), *A Life in the Theatre* (1977), **Buried Child* (1978), **Getting Out* (1978), and *Cloud Nine* (1981). The Theatre de Lys was renamed in her honor in 1981, as are the annual Lucille Lortel Awards given by the League of Off-Broadway Theatres and Producers for outstanding work Off Broadway.

LOS ANGELES (California). For many years the city played second fiddle to its northern rival San Francisco, although it was a good legitimate theatre town with such people as Oliver *Morosco running theatres and producing plays there. By the late years of the Great Depression, only the Biltmore Theatre remained as a regular touring house. However, some other playhouses, often much smaller, enjoyed long runs with locally produced plays. Among these were a record run of *The *Drunkard* and the revue *Blackouts*. Only since the 1980s has the city not only surpassed San Francisco but also become one of the most important theatre towns in America. The erection of a huge cultural center, at least one new legitimate theatre, and the conversion of some old filmhouses all hastened the growth. While the Los Angeles and San Francisco Light Opera Company is now based in the city, this once active producing organization today does little but book in large musicals. However, the other organizations, such as the *Mark Taper Forum, associated with the cultural center have occasionally mounted new works or important revivals that have later toured successfully. Among the other theatres to be found in the Los Angeles area are the Bilingual Foundation of the Arts, Fountain Theatre, *Geffen Playhouse, Ahmanson Theatre, *Odyssey Theatre Ensemble, Colony Theatre Company, Moving Arts, L.A. Theatre Works, Blue Sphere Alliance, West Coast Ensemble, and the nearby *Pasadena Playhouse, California Repertory Company at Edison Theatre, *South Coast Repertory, Ensemble Theatre Company of Santa Barbara, Alliance Repertory Company, Attic Theatre, and Hudson Theatre. The Los Angeles Critics Circle Awards have been given since 1969 to honor area theatre productions.

LOST IN THE STARS (1949), a musical play by Maxwell *Anderson (book, lyrics), Kurt *Weill (music). [*Music Box Theatre, 273 perf.] Stephen Kumalo (Todd *Duncan), a black preacher in the South African hinterlands, goes to Johannesburg to seek his straying son Absalom (Julian Mayfield). But Absalom has killed a white man and is sentenced to death. All Stephen can do is comfort Absalom's girl, Irina (Inez Matthews), and reach a compassionate understanding with the murdered man's father, James Jarvis (Leslie Banks). *Notable songs*: Lost in the Stars; Stay Well; Thousands of Miles; Trouble Man. The *Playwrights' Company presented this musical version of Alan Paton's acclaimed novel, *Cry, the Beloved Country*, which managed to find an audience despite its grim subject matter. Over the years the score has become more appreciated. The musical was revived unsuccessfully in 1972.

LOST IN YONKERS (1991), a play by Neil *Simon. [*Richard Rodgers Theatre, 780 perf.; Pulitzer Prize; Tony Award.] Widower Eddie Kurnitz (Mark Blum) leaves his young sons Arty (Danny Gerard) and Jay (Jamie Marsh) in the care of his cold, ill-tempered mother (Irene *Worth) who runs a candy store in Yonkers. Grandma not only makes life miserable for the two boys but also verbally abuses her slightly retarded daughter Bella (Mercedes Ruehl) and scoffs at her small-time crook of a son, Louis (Kevin *Spacey). Bella finally stands up to her mother and life continues on with an icy understanding between the two. Generally applauded by the press, the Emanuel *Azenberg production boasted superb performances (Worth, Ruehl, and Spacey all won *Tonys) and acute direction by Gene *Saks.

LOST PARADISE, THE (1891), a play by Henry C. *de Mille. [Proctor's 23rd Street Theatre, 138 perf.] Andrew Knowlton (Frank Mordaunt) is a rich Boston manufacturer who has turned over the day-to-day operation of his huge factory to his trusted, good-hearted manager, Reuben Warner (William *Morris), so that he may devote his time to his daughter, Margaret (Sydney Armstrong). He wants her to marry Ralph Standish (Orrin Johnson), and to further the chance takes the snobbish young man in as a partner. But the two men treat the workers so cruelly that the employees strike and Warner sides with the laborers. To Knowlton's dismay, so does Margaret. She breaks off her engagement to Standish and agrees to marry Warner, who, it turns out, was the inventor of the device that has allowed Knowlton to become rich. Based on Ludwig Fulda's *Das verlorene Paradies*, the Charles *Frohman production was told entirely in American terms and appealed to the sympathy of playgoers aware of the frequent callous and selfish abuse of American workers.

LOTITO, Louis A[nthony] (1900–80), manager. An orphan who became an usher at the *Hippodrome in his native New York to help support his family, he soon caught the eye of Charles *Dillingham and later of Vincent *Youmans, for both of whom he worked as treasurer and office manager. He next worked for Martin *Beck, and after Beck's death was asked by Mrs. Beck to run the Martin Beck Theatre. The playhouse had been a white elephant, but under his aegis became one of the most profitable in New York. As a result, in 1943 he was elected president of City Investment Corp. and ran its *Morosco, Fulton, Coronet, Bijou, and 46th Street theatres as well. Lotito's record of successes in booking was unique, but he also led the way in refurbishing worn-out playhouses. Noted for his honesty and loyalty in a profession in which both are all too rare, he was elected to serve as president of the *Actors' Fund of America.

LOTOS CLUB, THE. See Theatrical Clubs.

LOTTA. See Crabtree, Charlotte.

LOTTERY MAN, THE (1909), a comedy by Rida Johnson *Young. [Bijou Theatre, 200 perf.] Jack Wright (Cyril Scott) is a handsome, charming newspaperman who is deeply in debt. To obtain the money he needs to pay back his loans, he decides to raffle himself off. Women flock to buy chances on the likable bachelor, but in the midst of the hubbub Jack falls in love with Helen Heyer (Janet *Beecher). He and his friends buy up as many chances as possible in Helen's name to give her the best opportunity to win, but Helen learns of the schemes and is furious. Of course, all ends happily. The *Shuberts produced the very popular comedy.

LOTTERY OF LOVE, THE (1888), a comedy by Augustin *Daly. [Daly's Theatre, 105 perf.] Mrs. Zenobia Sherramy (Mrs. G. H. *Gilbert), a "strong-minded, woman's rights, female suffrage platform apostle" who was jailed in her youth for parading in bloomers, makes life so miserable for her new son-in-law, Adolphus Doubledot (John *Drew), and his bride, Diana (Sara Chalmers), that on the very afternoon of the wedding they agree upon a divorce. Two years later Adolphus has married Josephine (Ada *Rehan), daughter of the widower Benjamin Buttercorn (James *Lewis). Adolphus is horrified when Buttercorn suddenly appears with his own new bride, none other than Diana, with Mrs. Sherramy in tow. But the harridan again makes life so miserable that Adolphus and Buttercorn conspire to foist Diana on the doting Tom Dangerous (Frederick Bond), who agrees to take daughter and mama to Brazil with him. Based on Bisson and Mars's *Les Surprises du divorce*, which by coincidence *Coquelin was performing across the street during the play's run, the work was called by one of Daly's biographers "the best of Daly's adaptations from the French." At Daly's and elsewhere it held the stage for the rest of the century.

LOUDON, Dorothy (b. 1933), character actress and singer. The big-voiced comic performer, who excels at bigger-than-life characters, was born in Boston and educated at Syracuse University, Emerson College, and the American Academy of Dramatic Arts. Loudon's first jobs were in nightclubs and musical revues, later making her Broadway debut in 1962. She was very funny as the ever-pregnant Edith in the 1973 revival of *The *Women* and became a Broadway star as the cartoonish Miss Hannigan in *Annie* (1977). Other noteworthy performances include the lonely widow Bea discovering new love in *Ballroom* (1978), the befuddled TV actress Dottie Otley returning to the stage in *Noises Off* (1983), and the manipulating Dolly Levi in *The *Matchmaker* (1991).

LOUISIANA PURCHASE (1940), a musical comedy by Morrie *Ryskind (book), Irving *Berlin (music, lyrics). [*Imperial Theatre, 444 perf.] When the Yankee Senator Loganberry (Victor *Moore) is sent to investigate the corrupt Louisiana Purchase Company in New Orleans, the firm's lawyer, Jim Taylor (William *Gaxton), attempts to compromise him with the vampish Marina Van Linden (Vera Zorina) and with the coquettish Madame Bordelaise (Irene *Bordoni). But the good Senator proves incorruptible and ends up marrying one of the women. *Notable songs*: It's a Lovely Day Tomorrow; You're Lonely and I'm Lonely; Louisiana Purchase; Fools Fall in Love; What Chance Have I? Another of the many musicals of the era that reflected the day's headlines, this show was based on a story by producer B. G. *De Sylva that was a thinly veiled satire on the Huey Long machine in Louisiana. Boasting one of Berlin's finest scores, the musical nevertheless is rarely revived.

LOUISVILLE CHILDREN'S THEATRE (Kentucky). Founded by the Junior League of Louisville in 1946, the company's mission is to provide high quality, professional theatre for young audiences in the hopes of building strong family and community bonds. The noted children's theatre playwright Moses Goldberg was artistic director for many years. Today the company performs in the Bomhard Theatre and the Louisville Garden Armory Street Theatre.

LOVE IN '76 (1857), a "comedietta" by Oliver Bunce. [Laura Keene's Theatre, 10 perf.] Although her father is a Tory loyalist, Rose Elsworth (Laura Keene) loves Captain Walter Armstrong (M. V. Lingham) of the American army. When Armstrong is trapped in her home by British troops, she attempts to claim he is someone else. The ruse fails, so Rose is forced to try another ploy: she feigns affection for British Captain Arbald (Mr. Benson) and secures the promise of the British Major Cleveland (J. G. Burnett), who has his own eyes on her, that he will protect "the captain who is her husband." Suspecting another deception, however, Cleveland arranges to marry Armstrong to Rose's maid Bridget (Miss Howell). Rose, in disguise, changes places with Bridget at the ceremony and is married to Captain Armstrong. She then confronts Cleveland with his promise and threatens to question his word of honor publicly if he reneges. While Arthur *Quinn has called the comedy "the best of the Revolutionary plays," its wartime setting was hardly essential to the story. Despite its short initial run, it remained popular until the end of the century. **Oliver Bell BUNCE** (1828–90), a New York–born writer, enjoyed some

slight success with the rural comedy *The Morning of Life* (1848) but stumbled badly with the Greek revolt drama *Marco Bozzaris; or, The Grecian Hero* (1850). *Love in '76* was his only unqualified hit. Later a consultant to publishers as well as a novelist, short-story writer, and essayist, in 1872 he became editor of *Appleton's Journal,* a post he held for nine years.

LOVE! VALOUR! COMPASSION! (1994), a play by Terrence *McNally. [City Center, 321 perf.; Tony, NYDCC Awards.] Gregory Mitchell (Stephen Bogardus), a famous Manhattan choreographer, opens up his 1915 vintage summer home on a lake in upstate New York for three holiday weekends, inviting some of his closest gay friends to relax with him. But each guest brings so much emotional baggage with him that the weekends become fraught with subtle as well as overt tension. The colorful guests include the flamboyant costume designer Buzz (Nathan *Lane); the frustrated English composer John (John Glover) and his twin brother, the gentle James (Glover also); and the blind Bobby (Justin Kirk). There was little plot but a lot of Chekhov-like meanderings punctuated by plenty of in-jokes about the gay theatre world. Joe Mantello directed the *Manhattan Theatre Club production, Loy Arcenas designed the atmospheric set that included a dollhouse version of the farmhouse, and the play was popular enough to transfer to Broadway's Walter Kerr Theatre for a profitable run.

LOVERS' LANE (1901), a play by Clyde *Fitch. [Manhattan Theatre, 127 perf.] The Reverend Thomas Singleton (Ernest Hastings) has alienated many of the small minds in his backwater flock. After all, he has not only fed the undeserving poor and taken in an unruly orphan the local orphanage could not handle, but he allows a divorced woman to sing in his choir and sees nothing wrong with billiards and cards. The conservative Deacon Steele (Julian Barton) speaks for these petty churchgoers when he announces, "a hell that was good enough for our grandfathers is good enough for us." But the liberal minister is unswayed and triumphs. William A. *Brady was reluctant to produce the play, since it depended for much of its appeal on the secondary characters whom Fitch drew so cuttingly. But after a tryout in Trenton, New Jersey, he wired the author, "Great success. All the little Fitchisms going like hell."

LOWELL [Robb], **Helen** (1866–1937), actress. The New Yorker was a popular performer for fifty years, although her moments of stardom were few and her best roles were secondary parts. She made her debut in 1884 as Iolanthe in one of the many all-children casts common at the time. Lowell is especially recalled as the snubbed, pessimistic Miss Hazy in *Mrs. Wiggs of the Cabbage Patch* (1904) and Mrs. Fisher, the mother-in-law of *The *Show-Off* (1924).

LUCAS, Craig. See *Prelude to a Kiss*.

LUCE, Clare B. See Boothe, Clare.

LUCILLE LORTEL THEATRE (New York). The 299-seat playhouse on Christopher Street is considered the premiere Off-Broadway theatre because of its Greenwich Village location, ideal size, and impressive history. It was renovated in 1951 from an old movie house and named the Theatre de Lys after producer-owner William de Lys. The theatre became the center of the new Off-Broadway boom in 1954 when producer Lucille *Lortel acquired it. Her first production in the space was the long-running The *Threepenny Opera* (1954), which defined what an Off-Broadway musical hit was. Lortel also instigated a Matinee Series in 1956, which ran for years and became legendary. With its intimate orchestra seating and small balcony, the house is ideal for plays and small musicals. The playhouse was rightfully named after Lortel in 1981.

LUDERS, Gustav (1865–1913), composer. A thoroughly trained musician, he immigrated from his native Bremen in 1888, settling first in Milwaukee and then in Chicago. Luders was a theatre conductor there when he wrote his first score for *Little Robinson Crusoe* (1899). Thereafter he wrote most of his shows with either Frank *Pixley or George *Ade. His most notable musicals were *The Burgomaster* (1900), *King Dodo* (1902), *The Sho-Gun* (1904), *Woodland* (1904), *The Grand Mogul* (1907), *The Fair Co-ed* (1909), and *The Old Town* (1910), but his finest score was for *The *Prince of Pilsen* (1903). Although popular in their era, none of his songs is remembered today. Luders's range as a melodist was restricted, and he appeared not to grow artistically. Nevertheless, at his best his was a small, clear, and enchantingly sweet musical voice.

LUDLAM, Charles (1943–87), playwright and actor. Ludlam was a multitalented, off-the-wall and out-of-the-closet actor, playwright, director, and producer whose Ridiculous Theatrical Company broke boundaries and helped define the avant-garde *Off-Off-Broadway movement. He was born in Floral Park, New York, and educated at Hofstra University. He first acted professionally in New York in 1967 with the Playhouse of the Ridiculous where some of his plays were performed. But later that year he founded his own troupe and was busy for the next twenty years, the company going from obscurity to campy cult interest to citywide admiration. Ludlam usually played the leading role (male or female) in his outrageous spoofs, although as time went by he employed less camp and more of a highly theatrical style. Perhaps his Marguerite Gautier in *Camille* (1974) was the role most identified with Ludlam and his play The *Mystery of Irma Vepp* (1984) is his most revived in theatres across the country. Biography: *Ridiculous! The Theatrical Life and Times of Charles Ludlam*, David Kaufman, 2002.

LUDLOW, Noah M[iller] (1795–1886), manager and actor. One of the great pioneers of the American theatre, he was born in New York and made his debut as an actor in Albany in 1813. Ludlow acted with Samuel *Drake before he organized his own troupe in 1817 called the American Theatrical Commonwealth Company. For a decade he toured regions of the South and Midwest (then the West), many of which had never seen proper live theatre before. In 1835 he joined with Sol *Smith to form a reorganized, reinvigorated American Theatrical Commonwealth Company, which soon was managing theatres in all the major cities along the Mississippi River and in some inland towns as well. Joseph *Jefferson, who worked briefly with them, recalled the company was notorious for its "economy of organization." It was dissolved when Ludlow elected to retire after a farewell entertainment at the New Orleans St. Charles Theatre in 1853. He was considered a competent actor, especially in comic roles, but his claim to fame rests on two other achievements: his acumen and courage as a theatrical producer and theatre manager in regions largely ignored by most professional luminaries, and his superb autobiography, *Dramatic Life as I Found It*, 1880, filled with historically important and fascinating pictures of America and its playhouses.

LUDWIG, Ken. See *Lend Me a Tenor*.

LULU BELLE (1926), a play by Edward *Sheldon and Charles *MacArthur. [*Belasco Theatre, 461 perf.] Lulu Belle (played in blackface by Lenore *Ulric) is a flamboyant prostitute who pounds the pavements both of San Juan Hill and Harlem. She succeeds in luring a white barber, George Randall (Henry *Hull), away from his wife and family, only to desert him for Butch Cooper (John Harrington), a prizefighter. But Lulu leaves him, too, when the Vicompte de Villars (Jean Del Val) promises to set her up in luxury. Yet the passions she evokes overwhelm all the figures in her life: Butch winds up with a knife in his ribs, and the demented Randall follows her to Paris and strangles her in her posh apartment. Brooks *Atkinson concluded, "*Lulu Belle* is splendid showmanship; but it retains few of the elements of drama." Although "Negro" groups protested against the lurid picture the play painted of African-American life, producer-director David *Belasco's reputation and skill turned the melodrama into one of the era's biggest successes.

LUNT, Alfred [David] (1892–1980), actor and director. Considered by many the greatest leading man of his generation, he was born in Milwaukee and educated at Carroll College. He abandoned his early ambition to become an architect and made his theatrical debut with the Castle Square Theatre stock company in Boston in 1912, then toured with Lillie *Langtry and Margaret *Anglin. Broadway first saw him in *Romance and Arabella* (1917), but it was his performance as the shy, bumbling young man, *Clarence* (1919), that brought him important recognition. In 1922 he married Lynn *Fontanne and rarely thereafter performed without her. Three of his few noteworthy assignments alone was as Mr. Prior, the boozy, newly dead young man, in *Outward Bound* (1924); the flashy bootlegger Babe Callahan in *Ned McCobb's Daughter* (1926); and Marco Polo in *Marco Millions* (1928). The Lunts' first great triumph together was in *The Guardsman* (1924), followed by *The *Second Man* (1927), *The Doctor's Dilemma* (1927), *Elizabeth the Queen* (1930), *Reunion in Vienna* (1931), *Design for Living* (1933), *The *Taming of the Shrew* (1935), *Idiot's Delight* (1936), *Amphitryon 38* (1937), *The Seagull* (1938), *There Shall Be No Night*, (1940); and *The Pirate* (1942). The Lunts spent the rest of the war years playing in England, returning to appear in a series of competent, but often indifferent comedies: *O Mistress Mine* (1946), *I Know My Love* (1949), *Quadrille* (1954), and *The Great Sebastians* (1956). Only with their farewell play, *The Visit* (1958), did they again find a worthy drama. Lunt occasionally directed plays, such as *Candle in the Wind* (1941) and *Ondine* (1954). In her autobiography, Theresa *Helburn suggested that there was "always something tortured" in his manner, that, in effect, he never totally stopped playing the timorous, befuddled Clarence, while Billie *Burke in her memoirs recalled "his distinguished voice . . . and his luminous brown eyes, with their always-startled expression." John Mason *Brown wrote of the Lunts' teamwork, "They are shrewd judges of what to underscore and what to throw away. They realize that the very act of seeming to throw a phrase or a word away is in itself a form of emphasis. They are no less adroit in altering the tempo of their separate scenes than they are in changing the pace of their single sentences. What is more, their watches are always synchronized." Biography: *The Fabulous Lunts*, Jared Brown, 1986.

LUNT-FONTANNE THEATRE (New York). The musical house, named after the celebrated acting couple Alfred *Lunt and Lynn *Fontanne, was built in 1910 by producer Charles *Dillingham as the Globe Theatre. Architects Carrere and *Hastings designed the Italian Renaissance–style theatre with an entrance on Broadway even though the structure sits on West 46th Street. (The entrance has since been moved closer to the lobby on the side street.) The Globe housed many musical hits until the Depression when Dillingham lost the property and it was turned into a movie house. When the playhouse reopened as a legitimate venue in 1958, it had a remodeled interior with an 18th-century style, fewer seats, and a new name. Lunt and Fontanne starred in the first production, *The *Visit* (1958), but it was their farewell appearance and much of the Lunt-Fontanne's subsequent tenants have been large musicals.

LuPONE, Patti (b. 1949), actress and singer. The dark, exotic, mannered leading lady of musicals and plays, is one of the theatre's most distinctive players, exuding both a sensual and a chilly, distanced persona in her performances. She was born in Northport, New York, and educated at Juilliard where she later became one of the original members of the *Acting Company. LuPone was first widely noticed in 1975 for her backwoods heroine Rosamund in *The Robber Bridegroom* (1975) and became a Broadway star with her passionate performance as the ambitious Eva Peron in *Evita* (1979). Among her other outstanding New York roles were the singing evangelist Reno Sweeney in *Anything Goes* (1987), the temperamental diva Maria Callas in *Master Class* (1996), and the confused television actress Dotty Otley in *Noises Off* (2001). Two of her finest performances never made it to New York: the French bride Genevieve in the Broadway-bound *The Baker's Wife* (1976) and silent screen star Norma Desmond in *Sunset Boulevard* (1993) in London.

LUV (1964), a comedy by Murray Schisgal. [*Booth Theatre, 901 perf.] When Milt Manville (Eli *Wallach) comes across his old college buddy, Harry Berlin (Alan Arkin), about to commit suicide by jumping off a bridge, he is so casual and courteous that Harry changes his mind, climbs down, and throws away his suicide note. It turns out that Milt, locked in a seemingly hopeless marriage and anxious to wed another girl, is as unhappy as Harry. In a moment of inspiration Milt decides to solve all their problems by foisting his wife, Ellen (Anne *Jackson), on his friend. His plan works at first. Harry and Ellen wed, and so do Milt and his young girlfriend. However, after a few months Milt decides he wants Ellen back. To achieve this he plans to murder Harry. The plan misfires but Milt and Ellen are reunited and Harry is left to climb a lamppost to escape a vicious dog. Another of the many small-cast (three actors) plays of the era, this comedy was funnier and filled with more imaginative turns of plot than most. A musical version called *What About Luv?* has found some success regionally. **Murray SCHISGAL** (b. 1926) was born in Brooklyn and graduated from Brooklyn Law School. He earned recognition when his double bill *The Typists* and *The Tiger* (1963) was presented Off Broadway. None of his subsequent works matched *Luv*'s popularity, though many contained a similar kind of comic absurdity. They include *Jimmy Shine* (1968), *The Chinese* and *Dr. Fish* (1970), *All Over Town* (1974), *Twice Around the Park* (1982), and *Road Show* (1987).

LYCEUM THEATRE (New York). Although a number of Manhattan playhouses have been called the Lyceum, two are of great historical importance, and both at some time were associated with Daniel *Frohman. The earliest was built on Fourth Avenue between 23rd and 24th Streets in 1885 by Steele *MacKaye, who had recently been forced out of his *Madison Square Theatre. The new theatre incorporated many of the innovations of the older auditorium and was the first erected with electrical lighting throughout the building (supervised by MacKaye's friend Thomas Edison). However, once again MacKaye quickly lost the theatre, and within a year Frohman was in charge. Under his aegis the theatre saw the premieres of many of the best David *Belasco–H. C. *de Mille collaborations as well as *The *Prisoner of Zenda* and the New York premiere of *Trelawny of the Wells*. Unfortunately, the theatre district was moving north, and although one paper observed in 1899, "A dozen or more years have passed but no playhouse of later construction has come up to the Lyceum in excellence and beauty," the building was demolished in 1902. A year later Frohman opened his new Lyceum, still standing, on 45th Street, just east of Broadway. *Herts and Tallant designed the gray limestone structure, which boasts Roman columns on the facade and a marble staircase in the lobby. The auditorium, which seats 920 spectators, saw a long series of hits, which did not save it from the threat of demolition in 1939. Luckily it was spared and continued on its prosperous career. The house is owned by the *Shuberts and the former offices and apartment of Frohman, which sit above the auditorium, are now the home of the Shubert Archives. The Lyceum vies with the *New Amsterdam as the oldest operating theatre in New York, the two opening a month apart in 1903.

LYCEUM THEATRE SCHOOL OF ACTING. See American Academy of Dramatic Arts.

LYRIC THEATRE. See Ford Center for the Performing Arts.

LYTTON, Edward George Earle Lytton Bulwer (1803–73), playwright. The English novelist and dramatist wrote three plays that became among the most popular and enduring in American theatrical history: the romantic costume melodramas, *The *Lady of Lyon* (1837) and *Richelieu* (1839), and the comedy *Money* (1841). Several of his novels, including *Eugene Aram*, were dramatized at various times by other hands.

M

M. BUTTERFLY (1988), a play by David Henry *Hwang. [*Eugene O'Neill Theatre, 777 perf.; Tony Award.] Sitting in a French prison, René Gallimard (John *Lithgow) looks back on how he destroyed his marriage and his promising diplomatic career. A lover of Puccini's *Madame Butterfly*, he long thought of Cho-Cho-San as his "feminine ideal." This created problems when he was stationed in Beijing and fell madly in love with a beautiful Peking Opera actress, Song Liling (B. D. Wong). Yet throughout their long relationship, Gallimard never realized (or chose not to believe) that Liling was actually a spy and a man. Convicted of conspiring with the Communists, Gallimard dresses as Cho-Cho-San and commits suicide just as she had. The drama, based on an actual event in the 1960s, was filled with stimulating ideas about East-West cultural differences and the role of the male and female in each world. Vibrant performances, under the astute direction of John Dexter, helped make for a colorful, fluid, and fascinating piece of theatre, and the first Asian-American play to become a mainstream hit.

MA RAINEY'S BLACK BOTTOM (1984), a play by August *Wilson. [*Cort Theatre, 275 perf.; NYDCC Award.] Ma Rainey (Theresa Merritt), an African-American blues singer, is difficult at the best of times, and the 1920s are not the best of times, particularly for blacks in Chicago. When she arrives for a recording session, she has had a run-in with the police after an automobile accident, the producer is demanding she use a new arrangement by the young trumpet player Levee (Charles S. Dutton), and the equipment either is not functioning or has been sabotaged. Bitter arguments ensue, tensions mount, and by the time Ma stomps out, the atmosphere is so charged that a slight misstep provokes Levee to knife one of his fellow musicians. While some critics saw it as a collection of superbly delineated character studies rather than a fully realized drama, it nonetheless made for compelling theatre, especially with the sterling cast under Lloyd *Richards's direction. Dutton reprised his performance in a 2003 Broadway revival starring Whoopi Goldberg as Ma; the script was again

commended but the uneven production was not and it failed to run.

MABOU MINES (San Francisco). A determinedly avant-garde ensemble founded in 1970 by JoAnne *Akalaitis, Lee Breuer, Philip Glass, Ruth Maleczech, and David Warrilow, it specializes in original works that frequently and imaginatively employ mixed media. It is also known for its interpretations of plays by Samuel *Beckett. The troupe has toured extensively and was in residence at *La MaMa in New York for a time. Among its notable productions have been *Dressed Like an Egg* (1977), *A Prelude to Death in Venice* (1979), *Dead End Kids: A History of Nuclear Power* (1982), *Cold Harbor* (1983), *Through the Leaves* (1984), *Flow My Tears, The Policeman Said* (1988), a gender-switched *King Lear* (1990), and *Cara Lucia* (2003). Glass has often provided music for the productions. **Lee BREUER** (b. 1937) began working in theatre at the San Francisco Actors' Workshop and studied in Europe with the Berliner Ensemble and the Polish Theatre Lab before co-founding and directing for Mabou Mines. He has also staged productions for various regional theatres and taught directing and Asian and African arts at Yale.

MACARTHUR, Charles. See Hecht, Ben.

MACBETH. Shakespeare's shortest tragedy, but one of his best, was first done in Philadelphia in 1759 with the younger Lewis *Hallam in the title role. Subsequently the play has enlisted almost every great American and visiting tragedian but has rarely been a major commercial success for any of them and has come to be considered something of an actor's jinx. (As in England, American actors are superstitious about even mentioning the title of "the Scottish play" when in a theatre.) Notable early Macbeths have ranged from the formal Thomas Abthorpe *Cooper to the gruff Edwin *Forrest to the poetic Edwin *Booth. Outstanding Lady Macbeths have included Charlotte *Cushman, Fanny *Janauschek, and Emma *Waller. Among the more successful 20th-century revivals were the 1941 offering starring Maurice *Evans and Judith *Anderson and a 1988 mounting with Christopher

*Plummer and Glenda Jackson. The work remains a favorite with collegiate and festival groups.

MacDONALD, Christie (1875–1962), singer and actress. The blonde beauty, with one of the finest soprano voices of her generation, was born in Pictou, Nova Scotia, and was given her start in New York by Francis *Wilson, who featured her in his 1893 revival of *Erminie*. Between then and her retirement in 1920, MacDonald was the leading lady in a score of musicals, most notably *The Spring Maid* (1910) and *Sweethearts* (1913), which was written for her by Victor *Herbert. Among her other assignments were the heroines of *The Belle of Mayfair* (1906) and *Miss Hook of Holland* (1908). A critic described MacDonald as "dainty as a moss rose" and as one of the few operetta stars "worth fussing over."

MacDONOUGH, Glen (1870–1924), lyricist and librettist. The Brooklyn-born writer began his career as an actor and author of farces but became best known for his books and lyrics for such composers as John Philip *Sousa, Raymond *Hubbell, and Victor *Herbert. With the last he wrote *Babes in Toyland* (1903) and *It Happened in Nordland* (1904). MacDonough was also the American adapter of Johann *Strauss's last work, *Vienna Life* (1901), and of Franz *Lehar's *The Count of Luxembourg* (1912). In all he was associated with more than two dozen musicals.

MacGOWAN, Kenneth (1888–1963), producer and critic. Born in Winthrop, Massachusetts, and educated at Harvard, he was assistant drama critic for the Boston *Evening Transcript* and critic for the Philadelphia *Evening Ledger* before serving in a similar position on the New York *Globe* from 1919 to 1923. At the same time he was drama critic for both *Vogue* and *Theatre Arts*. With Robert Edmond *Jones and Eugene *O'Neill, he took over the Provincetown Playhouse in New York in 1924 and later that same year also joined the Greenwich Village Theatre. At both houses he helped produce a number of interesting revivals, notably one of *Fashion* as well as several of O'Neill's plays, such as *All God's Chillun Got Wings* (1924), *Desire Under the Elms* (1924), *The Fountain* (1925), and *The *Great God Brown* (1926). Although O'Neill had begun to move away from traditional realism in *The *Emperor Jones* (1920) before he met MacGowan, it was his meeting and ensuing friendship with MacGowan that confirmed and strengthened this drift, which was aimed at creating a theatre that would be at once both professional and idealistic and which, as MacGowan wrote, would "attempt to transfer to dramatic art the illumination of those deep and vigorous and eternal processes of the human soul." Ironically, when MacGowan later moved to Broadway and mounted more commercial ventures, he was less successful. He was also the author of several books on the theatre, including *The Theatre of Tomorrow* (1921), *Continental Stagecraft* (1922) written with Jones, *Masks and Demons* (1923), and *Footlights Across America* (1929). In later years he was an associate producer for RKO Pictures.

MacGREGOR, Edgar (1879–1957), director. For thirty years the Rochester, New York, native was one of the most successful stagers on Broadway. Early in his career he served as assistant to William *Gillette and Jane *Cowl. Although he later occasionally worked on plays, MacGregor was best known for his sharp direction of musical comedy. His numerous credits included *The Kiss Burglar* (1918), *The Gingham Girl* (1922), *Queen High* (1926), *Honeymoon Lane* (1926), *The *Desert Song* (1926), *Good News!* (1927), *Funny Face* (1927), *The *New Moon* (1928), *DuBarry Was a Lady* (1939), *Panama Hattie* (1940), and *Louisiana Lady* (1947).

MACHINAL (1928), a play by Sophie Treadwell. [*Plymouth Theatre, 91 perf.] A stenographer, simply identified as Young Woman (Zita Johann), is a cog in the machinery at the Jones Company. In her desperate search to find "somebody" to love her, she takes as a Husband (George Stillwell) a vacuous man who brings her neither change nor real love. After her marriage she meets a Young Man (Hal K. Dawson) and believes she has finally found relief from the unthinking sameness around her. She asks her husband to release her, but he refuses, so she kills him. The Woman is tried, convicted, and executed. As she dies she cries out for "somebody." The staccato dialogue and rapidly changing scenes were played out against Robert Edmond *Jones's expressionistic settings. Brooks *Atkinson wrote of the Arthur *Hopkins production, "Subdued, monotonous, episodic, occasionally eccentric, 'Machinal' is fraught with a beauty unfamiliar to the stage." The play was revived Off Broadway in 1960 and 1990, the second production being praised highly. The California-born Sophie **TREADWELL** (1890–1970) had been an actress and protégé of Helena *Modjeska before attempting to write plays. Half a dozen of her works reached Broadway, including *Gringo* (1922), *Plumes in the Dust* (1936), and *Hope for a Harvest* (1941), but *Machinal* was her only success. Biography: *Sophie Treadwell: The Career of a 20th Century American Feminist*, N. Wynn, 1982.

MacHUGH, Augustin. See *Officer 666*.

MacKAYE, Percy [Wallace] (1875–1956), playwright. One of the most curious figures in American dramaturgy, he was the son of Steele *MacKaye and was born in New York. Upon graduating from Harvard, he began teaching as well as writing poetry and plays. While scholars over the years have admired MacKaye's work, only one of his plays ever found a public: the fantasy *The *Scarecrow* (1911). The rest of his work ranges from historical drama to political satire and spectacle. Such important theatrical figures as E. H. *Sothern and Walter *Hampden saw fit to mount a few of these, always without success. Shortly before his death he completed a tetralogy, *The Mystery of Hamlet, King of Denmark; or, What We Will* (1949), which purports to show the events leading up to Shakespeare's play. His books, such as *The Playhouse and the Play* (1909), *The Civic Theatre* (1912), and *Community Drama* (1917), argue for a subsidized, noncommercial theatre and suggest why his theatre pieces today seem more like closet drama.

MacKAYE, [James Morrison] **Steele** (1842–94), playwright. One of the most important innovators in late 19th-century American theatre, he was born in Buffalo, where his father was a respected lawyer and art connoisseur. He studied art in Paris before returning home to fight in the Civil War, rising to the rank of Major before illness forced him to resign. Once again in Paris, he became the disciple of François Delsarte, who was advocating a naturalistic style of theatre, and MacKaye promoted the Delsartean school in lectures back in America. In 1872 his first play, *Monaldi,* co-written with Francis Durivage, won some critical approval but failed commercially; on the other hand, his comedy-drama, *Won at Last* (1877), was well received. Afterward MacKaye took over the old *Fifth Avenue Theatre and remodeled it with the most modern, elaborate equipment ever seen in an American playhouse, including overhead and indirect lighting and a double moving stage that allowed rapid scene changes. He reopened the house as the *Madison Square Theatre with his play *Hazel Kirke* (1880), which established a long-run record for a nonmusical play. In both writing and performance, the play was an attempt to move toward the newer principals he was espousing. But MacKaye's mismanagement cost him his theatre, so in 1885 he opened another technically inventive theatre, the *Lyceum. Here he established a school of acting that eventually became the *American Academy of Dramatic Arts. In time he lost this theatre too, but continued to write plays, most importantly the French Revolution drama, *Paul Kauvar; or, Anarchy* (1887). In all, nineteen of his plays were produced in New York (and nearly all enjoyed some commercial success), including *Rose Michel* (1875), *Won at*

Last (1877), and *The Drama of Civilization* (1887). Shortly before his death, MacKaye planned a huge, technically progressive auditorium for the Chicago Columbian Exposition, but it was never built. Otis *Skinner remembered him as "tall, spare, emotional and eloquent, looking like a more stalwart Edgar Allan Poe, holding forth to a knot of listeners on some theory destined never to be realized, some dream never to become articulate. He was always magnetic and compelling." Biography: *Epoch*, Percy *MacKaye (his son), 1927.

MACK, Andrew [né William Andrew McAloon] (1863–1931), actor and singer. The Bostonian began his career in vaudeville in 1876, using the name Andrew Williams and later found his greatest success playing romantic leads in Irish plays with music such as *Myles Aroon* and *The Last of the Rohans*. His last important assignment was as a replacement in the role of Patrick Murphy, the father, in *Abie's Irish Rose.*

MACK, Willard [né Charles Willard McLaughlin] (1878–1934), playwright and actor. The Canadian performed in vaudeville for many years before joining a stock company in San Francisco. He came to New York in 1913 with a vaudeville sketch, which the following year he expanded into his first hit play, *Kick In. Among his subsequent successes were such melodramas as *Tiger Rose* (1917), *High Stakes* (1924), *The Dove* (1925), *The Noose* (1926), and *A Free Soul* (1928). Mack's many acting assignments included originating Captain Bartlett in Eugene *O'Neill's *Gold* (1921). He also frequently served as a director and producer.

MACKINTOSH, Cameron [Anthony] (b. 1946), producer. A native of Enfield, England, he studied acting then took work as a stagehand to familiarize himself with all aspects of theatre. He began producing shows for the British provinces before hitting the big time in London with *Cats, which he brought to Broadway in 1982. Slightly earlier he had co-produced *Tomfoolery* (1981) and *Little Shop of Horrors* (1982) Off Broadway. Alone or with others, Mackintosh subsequently gave New York *Song and Dance* (1985), *Les Misérables* (1987), *The *Phantom of the Opera* (1988), *Five Guys Named Mo* (1992), and *Putting It Together* (1999). In 1990 he made headlines when he engaged in a brouhaha with *Actors' Equity over his right to cast his forthcoming production of *Miss Saigon* with its London stars, canceling the production until the union capitulated. How much of this disagreement was genuine and how much clever publicity is uncertain.

MacLEISH, Archibald. See *J. B.*

MACREADY, William Charles (1793–1873), actor and director. A great, if controversial, English tragedian, he was lauded for his forceful, albeit somewhat formal acting, and despised for his arrogance and explosive temper. His American debut came at the *Park Theatre in 1826 in one of his greatest roles, Virginius, and prompted the *Mirror* to remark, "It is said there is no actor living who unites as much power and original genius with correct taste and cultivated talents as Macready. . . . His person is tall and commanding—his carriage noble—his face, though not technically a first rate stage face, is wonderfully expressive, and his voice peculiarly fine, deep and mellow." He followed his Roman with his Damon, William Tell, Macbeth, and Coriolanus, adding Othello, King Lear, and Richelieu to his American repertory when he returned in 1843. From the start, elements of the press had attacked him personally, and his open contempt for American actors exacerbated matters. These problems came to a head on his third trip in 1848 when his rivalry with Edwin *Forrest, as much a national and class rivalry as a personal one, exploded in May 1849 with the *Astor Place Riots. Immediately thereafter he sailed for England, never to return. Mrs. John *Drew, who acted with him, recalled, "Macready was a dreadful man to act with . . . [he was] a terribly nervous actor; any little thing which happened unexpectedly irritated him beyond endurance." Biography: *The Eminent Tragedian: William Charles Macready*, Alan S. Downer, 1966.

MADAME BUTTERFLY (1900), a one-act play by David *Belasco and John Luther *Long. [Herald Square Theatre, 24 perf.] Cho-Cho-San (Blanche *Bates), a geisha, falls in love with an American naval officer, Lieutenant Pinkerton (Frank Worthing). When he leaves for home, he promises to be true and to return. The American consul, Mr. Sharpless (Claude Gillingwater), later informs her that Pinkerton has remarried. She refuses to believe it. However, when the fleet returns and the Consul's story is confirmed, she kills herself. Most historians suggest the dramatization was entirely the work of producer-playwright Belasco, who used Long's short story as his source. Whether or not this was the case, their subsequent joint efforts appear to have been more genuine collaborations. Added as an afterpiece during the run of the farce *Naughty Anthony*, the play was looked on as static and talky, but nevertheless a theatrically effective character study. The production was mostly remembered for a stunning silent sequence when Cho-Cho-San waits through the night for the dawn and the return of Pinkerton, Belasco's subtle lighting moving from dusk to moonlight to sunrise. The play might well have been totally forgotten had not Puccini later created an opera from it and years later it served as the source material for *Miss Saigon* (1990).

MADAME SHERRY (1910), a "musical vaudeville" by Otto *Harbach (book, lyrics), Karl *Hoschna (music). [*New Amsterdam Theatre, 231 perf.] Edward Sherry (Jack Gardner) and his Sherry School of Aesthetic Dancing have long been supported by Edward's archaeologist uncle, Theophilus (Ralph Herz). To please his uncle, who spends most of his time in Greece, Edward has pretended to marry and have children. When the uncle suddenly appears, Edward is forced to draft his housekeeper and some of his young pupils into acting as his wife and offspring. Theophilus is not fooled, so he takes everyone out to sea in his yacht and threatens not to return to port until he discovers the truth. Luckily, Theophilus's niece Yvonne (Lina Abarbanell) has fallen in love with Edward, and they agree to marry. Only then does Theophilus consent to return to port. *Notable songs*: Every Little Movement; The Smile She Means for You; The Birth of Passion; Put Your Arms Around Me, Honey (interpolation by Junie McCree and Albert Von Tilzer). A curious combination of musical comedy, operetta, and, in the last act when the plot was all but over, vaudeville turns, this was one of the most memorable and delightful musicals of the era. The hit song, "Every Little Movement," while first sung as part of the dancing lesson, was reprised throughout the show in different tempos and with altered harmonies to suggest the progress of several romances.

MADISON SQUARE THEATRE (New York). In 1879 Steele *MacKaye gutted what had been Augustin *Daly's first *Fifth Avenue Theatre and which had been restored only two years before after a disastrous fire in 1873. He redesigned the playhouse into one of the world's most ingenious theatres, with an elevator stage that allowed rapid scene changes, with the orchestra playing from a box above the proscenium, and with the first attempt at a primitive air-conditioning system. The house seated only about seven hundred playgoers and was so arranged as to give the impression of a drawing room. George *Odell recalled, "The exquisite interior, in which no color seemed to prevail at the expense of others . . . gave an effect of rich, simple elegance hitherto unknown in New York theatres." MacKaye's intention was to form a stock company on the order of the *Comédie Française. Although the theatre housed *Hazel Kirke*, the longest-running drama up to its time under MacKaye, its actual owners, the Mallory brothers, editors of a religious publication, squeezed out the often-impractical playwright. It then came under the management first of Daniel *Frohman, then of Albert M. *Palmer, and later of Charles *Hoyt, who temporarily called it Hoyt's Theatre. By the time of Hoyt's death, the theatre district had moved away from the area and, though the original name had been restored, bookings became difficult. The building was demolished in 1908.

MAEDER, C. F. See Fisher, Clara.

MAEDER, Frederick G[eorge] (1840–91), playwright and actor. Son of the once-popular actress Clara *Fisher, he was born in New York and made his acting debut in Portland (Maine) in 1859, playing Bernardo in *Hamlet*. He was considered a good eccentric comedian, but was best known in his own day as a prolific, if undistinguished, playwright. Many of Maeder's works seem to have been written to order for particular performers or companies. Among his works were *Help* (1871), *Lola* (1871), *Red Riding Hood; or Wolf's at the Door* (1868), *Buffalo Bill* (1872), *Life's Peril; or, The Drunkard's Wife* (1872), and *Nip, the Pretty Flower* (1873).

MAGIC SHOW, THE (1974), a musical entertainment by Bob Randall (book), Stephen *Schwartz (music, lyrics). [*Cort Theatre, 1,920 perf.] When the Passaic Top Hat, a minor New Jersey night club, hires a young magician (Doug Henning) to replace a tired old act, much against the wishes of a jealous old-timer (David Ogden Stiers), it gets more than it bargained for. *Notable songs*: West End Avenue; Lion Tamer; Up to His Old Tricks. The slim plot was merely an excuse for Henning's spectacular feats of magic, which turned the show into a long-running hit.

MAGIC THEATRE, INC. (San Francisco). Mostly known as the theatre that premiered such Sam *Shepard plays as *True West*, *Buried Child*, and *Fool for Love*, the company has concentrated on avant-garde and new works for over thirty years. It was founded in 1967 by John Lion, a graduate student at the University of California at Berkeley, who took the name from a sequence in Herman Hesse's novel *Steppenwolf*, where Harry is invited to attend "an anarchist evening at the Magic Theatre. For madmen only. Price of admission: your mind." The group first performed in a Berkeley bar, then in 1977 took up residence at the Fort Mason Center where works were presented in the thrust stage Northside Theatre and the proscenium Southside Theatre. In addition to Shepard, new plays by Terrence *McNally, Jon Robin *Baitz, David *Mamet, and others premiered there, as well as European avant-garde playwrights and performance art pieces. Lion led the company until 1990,

and his successors have broadened the repertory to include some revivals and more traditional works.

MAGUIRE, Thomas (1820?–96), manager. Called in his own day the "Napoleon" of San Francisco theatre, he was believed to have been born in New York to poor immigrant parents. Using Tammany connections, he served as a bartender in playhouses and then opened his own bar near City Hall. Maguire joined the westward trek of the 49ers, but preferred working in gambling saloons and bars to panning for gold. In 1850 he opened the tiny Jenny Lind Theatre on the second floor of the Parker House, a hotel and casino he ran in San Francisco. The theatre was the first of three to bear the same name, all of which he operated before building Maguire's Opera House, which opened in 1854 and long was the city's leading theatre. Maguire pioneered in encouraging great New York performers to come west; and, establishing the famous San Francisco Minstrels, he dominated San Francisco theatre for a quarter of a century, building or managing several other playhouses and largely determining what local audiences saw. Many historians believe his decline actually began with the erection of the Academy of Music in 1862, but he remained in San Francisco until 1878. His last important position was as manager of the *Baldwin Theatre. Maguire then returned to New York, where he tried unsuccessfully to enter the theatrical scene. When he died in poverty he was buried by the *Actors' Fund.

MAINBOCHER [né Main Rousseau Bocher] (1890–1976), costume designer. Celebrated Chicago-born designer of high fashion, he studied not only art, but also voice and piano in leading world cultural centers before embarking on his theatrical career in Paris. Mainbocher almost never designed all the costumes for a show, merely those for its star, such as Mary *Martin in *One Touch of Venus* and *The *Sound of Music*, Ruth *Gordon in *Over 21*, Tallulah *Bankhead in *Private Lives*, Ethel *Merman in *Call Me Madam*, Katharine *Cornell in *The Prescott Proposals*, Rosalind *Russell in *Wonderful Town*, and Lynn *Fontanne in *The Great Sebastians*.

MAJESTIC THEATRE (New York). The musical house on West 44th Street has long been a particular favorite of producers because of its large capacity (1,800 seats when it opened, 1,655 today) and, for patrons, for its steeply raked orchestra section that allows for excellent sightlines. The playhouse was built by the Chanin brothers in 1927 and designed by Herbert J. *Krapp in the Louis IV style. Most of its attractions over the years have been large musicals, including four Rodgers and Hammerstein shows, *Porgy and Bess* (1942), *The *Music

Man (1957), **Camelot* (1960), and **Phantom of the Opera* (1988). The Shubert-owned theatre has been renovated and remodeled over the decades, but its most pleasing elements have remained intact.

MAJOR, Clara Tree (1880–1954), actress. An English performer who immigrated to America in 1914, she immediately began to take an interest in children's theatre. After acting with the *Washington Square Players and other groups, Major devoted all her attention to the juvenile stage, with which her name became synonymous. She prepared most of her scripts herself and handled their direction. In 1948 she had six companies touring at once.

MAJORITY OF ONE, A (1959), a comedy by Leonard Spigelgass. [*Shubert Theatre, 556 perf.] Mrs. Jacoby (Gertrude *Berg), a Brooklyn housewife who lost a son fighting the Japanese, and Koichi Asano (Cedric Hardwicke), a businessman who lost a daughter at Hiroshima, meet on shipboard. At first they turn their larger, national resentments against each other, but with time they overcome their prejudices to reach perhaps more than an affectionate understanding. The *Theatre Guild and Dore *Schary co-produced the warmhearted comedy, helped to success by the ebullient Berg, who had been famous as radio's Molly Goldberg, and the distinguished British actor Hardwicke. The Jewish Repertory Theatre revived the play with interest in 1999 with Phyllis Newman and Randall Duk Kim.

MALE ANIMAL, THE (1940), a comedy by James Thurber and Elliot *Nugent. [*Cort Theatre, 243 perf.] Tommy Turner (Nugent), a professor of English, suddenly finds himself confronted by two problems: the return to campus of Joe Ferguson (Leon Ames), a former college football star and old flame of Turner's wife, Ellen (Ruth Matteson), and an editorial in the college newspaper protesting Turner's reading of a letter sent by the anarchist Vanzetti to Vanzetti's daughter before his execution. Turner's edginess about Joe leads to getting them both drunk and engaging in fisticuffs. But the letter proves reasonably harmless, and Joe soon returns home to his own wife. Richard *Watts Jr. of the *Herald Tribune* saw the Herman *Shumlin–produced comedy as "a singularly happy combination of Thurber's comic brilliance and Nugent's gift for human and likable characters." A 1952 revival, with Nugent, Robert *Preston, and Martha *Scott, outran the original production.

MALKOVICH, John (b. 1953), actor. The unconventional leading man, who specializes in threatening yet mesmerizing characters, was born in Christopher, Illinois, and educated at Eastern Illinois State and Illinois State University before going to Chicago and co-founding the *Steppenwolf Theatre where he acted and directed for seven years. Malkovich made an impressive Manhattan debut in 1982 as the dissolute Lee in **True West* and has returned to the New York stage for such intriguing portrayals as the lost son Biff in **Death of a Salesman* (1984) and the volatile Pale in **Burn This* (1987).

MALTBY, Richard, Jr. See *Miss Saigon.*

MAME. See *Auntie Mame.*

MAMET, David (b. 1947), playwright and director. Born in Flossmore, Illinois, he studied at Goddard College, then settled in Chicago where he helped found the St. Nicholas Theatre Company, which produced many of his early plays. New Yorkers first saw his work Off Broadway with the popular double bill **Sexual Perversity in Chicago* and *Duck Variations* (1975). Among his subsequent plays are *The Water Engine* (1977), **American Buffalo* (1977), *A Life in the Theater* (1977), **Glengarry Glen Ross* (1984), *Speed-the-Plow* (1988), **Oleanna* (1992), *Cryptogram* (1995), *The Old Neighborhood* (1997), and *Boston Marriage* (2002). Mamet has directed his and others' plays, as well as written and directed films. Much of his work is characterized by minimal plots, sleazy characters, and colorful, rhythmic dialogue punctuated with profanity.

MAMMA MIA (2001). This import from Australia featured pop songs by the Swedish soft-rock group ABBA (Benny Andersson, Bjorn Ulvaeus) that were forced into a contrived plot by Catherine Johnson about a bride-to-be who invites her three possible fathers to her wedding. It opened at the *Winter Garden Theatre where audiences, nostalgic for the hits of past decades, forgave the weak script and enjoyed the lively music and spirited performances.

MAMOULIAN, Rouben (1897–1987), director. Born in Russia, the son of an actress, and educated in Paris and Moscow, he worked at the Eastman School of Music before coming to New York to take employment with the *Theatre Guild where he staged highly praised mountings of **Porgy* (1927), **Marco Millions* (1928), and *Wings over Europe* (1928). All his subsequent important theatrical work was with musicals: **Porgy and Bess* (1935), **Oklahoma!* (1943), **Carousel* (1945), and **Lost in the Stars* (1949). Mamoulian was known for his excellent handling of crowd scenes and for an overall sense of theatrically rhythmic movement. He was also highly admired as a film director. Biography: *Rouben Mamoulian*, Tom Miln, 1969.

MAN AND SUPERMAN (1905). *Shaw's epic look at the battle of the sexes was first presented here by Charles *Dillingham in 1905 with Robert *Loraine and Clara *Bloodgood, running for six months. The production omitted the long act known as "Don Juan in Hell," a policy followed by most subsequent stagings. Loraine also headed the cast of a 1912 revival, Maurice *Evans starred in a highly praised 1947 revival that chalked up 294 performances, while "Don Juan in Hell" was given an all-star reading with tremendous success in 1951 with Charles *Boyer, Charles *Laughton, Cedric Hardwicke, and Agnes Moorehead. The full-length work was mounted by the *Phoenix Theatre in 1964 with Ellis *Rabb, Rosemary *Harris, and Nancy *Marchand, and by the *Circle in the Square in 1978 with George *Grizzard, Ann Sachs, and Philip *Bosco.

MAN FROM HOME, THE (1908), a play by Booth *Tarkington and Harry Leon Wilson. [Astor Theatre, 496 perf.] When Daniel Voorhees Pike (William *Hodge), a straightforward, likable lawyer from Kokomo, Indiana, comes to Italy to visit his ward, Ethel Granger-Simpson (Madeline Louis), he finds her engaged to Almeric St. Aubyn (Echlin P. Gayner), the spoiled son of the Earl of Hawcastle (Hassard *Short). Pike discovers that the Earl himself is not only more worthless than his son, he is downright treacherous. In exposing them, Pike wins the hand of Ethel and also frees Ethel's brother Horace (George Le Guere) from an equally unsavory alliance. The three agree to return home to Kokomo. Although many critics viewed the *Liebler and Co. production as excessively jingoistic, the public disagreed. Walter Prichard *Eaton seemingly summed up both sides when he observed, "We think it a pleasant and popular piece of extremely parochial jingo. We should call it as an excellent bad play." It held the stage for six consecutive seasons and was regularly revived thereafter. **Harry Leon WILSON** (1867–1939), a noted novelist and editor of *Puck* from 1892 to 1902, was born in Oregon, Illinois. This was his most successful play. He also collaborated with Tarkington on *Cameo Kirby* (1909), *Your Humble Servant* (1910), *Tweedles* (1923), and *How's Your Health?* (1929). Several of Wilson's stories were dramatized by other playwrights, including *Ruggles of Red Gap* (1915), *His Majesty Bunker Bean* (1916), and *Merton of the Movies* (1922).

MAN OF LA MANCHA (1965), a musical play by Dale Wasserman (book), Mitch Leigh (music), Joe Darion (lyrics). [*ANTA Washington Square Playhouse, 2,328 perf.; Tony, NYDCC Awards.] Writer Cervantes (Richard *Kiley), a prisoner of the Spanish Inquisition, enacts for his fellow cellmates the story of his hero, the noble madman Don Quixote (Kiley). The unworldly, idealistic Don and his servant Sancho (Irving Jacobson) set out to rid the world of evil, battling windmills, and honoring the sluttish serving wench Aldonza (Joan Deiner) as a lady and rechristening her Dulcinea. But in the end Quixote's illusions are shattered and he is destroyed, just as Cervantes goes off to meet his fate in the hands of the Inquisition. *Notable songs*: The Impossible Dream; Dulcinea; To Each His Dulcinea; What Does He Want with Me? An unflinching musical rendition of Cervantes's great classic, it was derived from Wasserman's television script and produced at the *Goodspeed Opera House before becoming the sleeper hit of the Broadway season. "The Impossible Dream" was one of the last theatre songs to enjoy widespread popularity. Kiley revived it on Broadway in 1972 and 1977, Raul *Julia in 1992, and Brian Stokes *Mitchell in 2002.

MAN OF THE HOUR, THE (1906), a play by George *Broadhurst. [Savoy Theatre, 479 perf.] Alwyn Bennett (Frederick Perry) is a rich, idealistic young man who has gotten himself elected mayor on a reform ticket. Charles Wainwright (James E. Wilson), a rapacious financier, and Richard Horigan (Frank MacVicars), the local political boss, set out to obtain a perpetual monopoly on the city's public transportation. When Bennett refuses to grant the franchise and announces he will fight it, the men determine to use every means to destroy him. Bennett's problem is compounded by the fact that he loves Wainwright's niece, Dallas (Lillian Kemble), whose fortune is tied to the success of the franchise. On Bennett's side are James Phelan (George *Fawcett), an alderman who has long opposed Horigan, and Henry Thompson (Geoffrey Stein), Wainwright's private secretary, who unbeknownst to Wainwright is the son of a man Wainwright drove to suicide. Together they succeed in frustrating the monopolists while saving Dallas's money. The "virile melodrama" was one of the big muckraking hits of its day, on the order of *The *Lion and the Mouse*, although more careful not to pattern its characters after specific, well-known figures. More than one critic found it "a valuable service to the community" in exposing political greed and corruption.

MAN ON THE BOX, THE (1905), a play by Grace Livingston Furniss. [*Madison Square Theatre, 111 perf.] Lt. Robert Worburton (Henry E. *Dixey), returning from a long tour of duty, decides to surprise his sister by substituting himself for her coachman when she leaves an embassy ball. By mistake he picks up the wrong lady, and comic complications ensue. Furniss adapted the play from a novel by Harold MacGrath. It owed its success largely to Dixey and one young actress, Carlotta Nillson.

MAN WHO CAME BACK, THE (1916), a play by Jules Eckert *Goodman. [Playhouse, 457 perf.] Disowned by his wealthy father, the dissolute Henry Potter (Henry *Hull) takes to wandering the world, living a life of increasing dissipation and, along with the dance hall hostess Marcelle (Mary *Nash), sinks lower and lower until both hit bottom in a Shanghai opium den. Emissaries from his dying father locate Henry and beg him to return home for a final visit, but they insist he must leave Marcelle behind. Henry refuses to desert her and the decision, with its moral and ethical implications, somehow revitalizes him. In the end Henry does return, with an equally reformed Marcelle, who is welcomed into the Potter household. The *Times*, comparing the play offering to serials then common in many popular magazines, called it "A little lurid, at times intensely theatrical, but interesting all the way through." The play was based on a story by John Fleming Wilson. Producer William A. *Brady later claimed the production "made millions" for him.

MAN WHO CAME TO DINNER, THE (1939), a comedy by Moss *Hart and George S. *Kaufman. [*Music Box Theatre, 739 perf.] Having slipped on the ice on the Stanleys' doorstep, the celebrated but cantankerous celebrity Sheridan Whiteside (Monty *Woolley) is forced to convalesce at their home. He is unhappy about it and determined to see the Stanleys are as unhappy as he is. Whiteside runs up telephone bills, invites convicts to lunch, broadcasts on the radio from their living room, alienates the Stanley children from their parents, and turns his nurse, Miss Preen (Mary Wickes), so misanthropic that she takes a job at a munitions factory in hopes of destroying the human race. When his secretary, Maggie Cutler (Edith Atwater), falls in love with a local newsman, Bert Jefferson (Theodore Newton), Whiteside tries (unsuccessfully) to break it up by inviting a glamorous actress, Lorraine Sheldon (Carol Goodner), to lure the newsman away. He even blackmails the Stanleys by threatening to disclose that Mr. Stanley's sister was once acquitted of a celebrated ax murder. Everyone is relieved when Whiteside is finally well enough to leave. But as he departs he slips on the ice again and is brought back into the house, bellowing his threats to initiate another six weeks of despotism. The authors made little secret that Whiteside was patterned after their friend, Alexander *Woollcott. Many felt the character of Lorraine Sheldon was modeled after Gertrude *Lawrence, while two other supporting figures, the suave Beverly Carlton and the madcap Banjo, were suggested

by Noel *Coward and Harpo *Marx respectively. John Anderson wrote in the *Journal-American* that no such richly Falstaffian character as Whiteside had heretofore been created in American literature, "No one so full of the carbolic acid of human kindness; no one with the enthusiasm, the ruthless wit, the wayward taste, disarming prejudice, and relentless sentimentality of the man so carefully undisguised as the hero." The Sam H. *Harris production was an immediate hit, and the play remains one of the most-frequently revived of all American comedies. Notable Whitesides on Broadway have included Ellis *Rabb in 1980 and Nathan *Lane in 2000. The play was turned into the short-lived musical *Sherry!* in 1967.

MANAGERS' PROTECTIVE ASSOCIATION. See Producing Managers' Association.

MANDEL, Frank (1884–1958), playwright and producer. Although the San Francisco–born writer translated or collaborated on a number of plays early in his career, it was his work in the musical theatre for which he is largely remembered. He was co-librettist of, among others, *Mary* (1920), *The O'Brien Girl* (1921), and *No, No, Nanette* (1925) before he joined with Laurence *Schwab to form a new production company. Their first offering, in conjunction with Horace Liveright, was the drama *The *Firebrand* (1924). Mandel afterward collaborated on the books for their productions of *The *Desert Song* (1926) and *The *New Moon* (1928), and with Schwab produced *Good News!* (1927), *Follow Thru* (1929), and several less-successful shows.

MANEY, Richard (1891–1968), press agent. Born in Chinook, Montana, and raised in Seattle, he later relocated to New York where he eventually became the most famous press agent of his day. Maney helped publicize many successes, from the *Greenwich Village Follies* to *My Fair Lady*, as well as such leading figures as Tallulah *Bankhead, Katharine *Cornell, and producer Billy *Rose. He was also skilled at publicizing himself, thus making his profession better known and understood by playgoers. Autobiography: *Fanfare*, 1957.

MANHATTAN PUNCH LINE (New York). Dedicated to producing new comedies, the Off-Off-Broadway company was founded in 1979 by Mitch McGuire, Faith Caitlan, and Steve Kaplan. In addition to producing plays, the group held a Comedy Institute on occasion and presented a festival of short new comedies for several seasons. The company disbanded in 1992.

MANHATTAN THEATRE CLUB (New York). Founded in 1970 by A. E. Jeffcoat, Gene Frankel,

Philip Barber, and other New York East Side residents to provide an alternative to commercial theatre, it was first situated in the old Bohemian National Hall on East 73rd Street before moving to its present location at the City Center on 55th Street. Productions are mounted in the 299-seat Stage One and the 150-seat Stage Two, as well as at the *Biltmore Theatre, the nonprofit company's new Broadway home. Lynne Meadow has been its artistic and executive director since 1972 and helped make the group one of Off Broadway's most consistently successful theatres. The repertory is almost exclusively original plays and musicals by American playwrights and New York premieres of foreign works. Among its many notable productions over the years (several of which moved to Broadway) were *Ain't Misbehavin'; Ashes; *Crimes of the Heart; Mass Appeal; Lips Together, Teeth Apart; *Frankie and Johnny in the Clair de Lune; *Love! Valour! Compassion!; Sylvia; Sight Unseen; It's Only a Play; Putting It Together; The Wild Party; Class Act; *Wit; *Proof; and The *Tale of the Allergist's Wife.

MANN, Emily. See McCarter Theatre Center.

MANN, Louis (1865–1931), character actor. The native New Yorker made his debut in German-language theatricals while still a child, then withdrew from the stage to complete his education. Mann later performed with such notables as Lawrence *Barrett, John *McCullough, and Tommaso *Salvini, and created the role of Dick Winters in Incog (1892) before recognizing that his true métier was in dialect roles. His most famous part was Karl Pfeifer, whose loyalty to the fatherland was tested, in *Friendly Enemies (1918). He often appeared in conjunction with his wife, Clara Lipman.

MANN, Theodore [né Goldman] (b. 1924), director and manager. Born in Brooklyn, he studied law and was a practicing lawyer prior to co-founding the *Circle in the Square in 1950 and its school in 1961. He has frequently directed that group's warmly received productions. On occasion he has served as co-producer on Broadway, including *Long Day's Journey into Night (1956), Hughie (1964), and The Royal Hunt of the Sun (1965).

MANNERING, Mary [née Florence Friend] (1876–1953), actress. The handsome, round-faced, dark-haired performer acted for several seasons in her native England before Daniel *Frohman brought her to America in 1896 to appear in The Courtship of Leonie. Shortly thereafter she married James K. *Hackett and scored a major success playing opposite him as the romantic niece Fay Zuliani

in The Princess and the Butterfly (1897). Two of her best roles came in 1900 when she played Rose in a revival of Trelawny of the Wells and the Revolutionary heroine Janice Meredith. Mannering continued to play leading roles in similar romantic comedies and dramas for the next decade. Her last appearance was as Domini in The *Garden of Allah (1911), after which she retired at the height of her popularity.

MANNERS, J[ohn] Hartley (1870–1928), playwright. Born in London, he began his theatrical career as an actor and continued to perform for a time even after he turned to playwriting. He came to America in 1902 as a member of the cast of his own play, The Crossways, which he had written as a vehicle for Lillie *Langtry. Manners enjoyed a modest success with Zira (1905), which he wrote with Henry *Miller. Many of his subsequent works were created as vehicles for his wife, Laurette *Taylor. By far the most successful was *Peg o' My Heart (1912), followed by The Harp of Life (1916), Out There (1917), Happiness (1917), One Night in Rome (1919), and The National Anthem (1922). Manners always professed to have serious ambitions as a playwright, but his work was usually bathed in a roseate glow and tailored to the talents of his wife. He seems never to have fully appreciated her abilities as a serious actress, or perhaps was incapable of writing the best dramas for them.

MANSFIELD, Richard (1854–1907), actor. The famous but controversial American leading man was born in Berlin, the son of an English merchant and a well-known prima donna, Erminia Rudersdorff. He was educated in England and on the Continent, then brought to America in 1872 by his mother, where he appeared in amateur theatricals before returning to London. Mansfield returned to make his professional New York debut in 1882 singing the part of Dromez in the comic opera Les Manteaux Noirs. He first won recognition a year later as the sensual, brutal roué Baron Chevrial in A Parisian Romance. After several seasons without another hit, he found success as the impecunious nobleman *Prince Karl (1886), followed by his widely popular version of Dr. Jekyll and Mr. Hyde (1887), *Richard III (1889), and *Beau Brummel (1890). After a string of failures, Mansfield realized the changing nature of his theatre and turned to G. B. *Shaw, who had never been professionally produced in America, and offered himself as Bluntschli in Arms and the Man (1894). It failed to run but he had better luck when he mounted The *Devil's Disciple (1897), playing Dick Dudgeon, and then appeared as *Cyrano de Bergerac (1898) and as Prince Karl Heinrich in Old Heidelberg (1903). The remainder of his career interspersed revivals of his more popular roles with failed attempts in new vehicles. Shortly before his death, however, he defied the wrath of conservative reviewers by appearing in the title role of *Peer Gynt*. Mansfield was an extremely short man with a pale, square-cut face and thinning brown hair, who was sensitive about his appearance. Many critics and playgoers admired his work as an exemplar of a passing romantic school, but others strongly dissented. Because of his arrogance, short temper, and treachery, his fellow actors generally detested him. With the appearance of the *Theatrical Syndicate or Trust he professed to join the other stars of his era in fighting the monopoly, only to quickly sign on with it. He also promised Edward *Harrigan, when he leased Harrigan's Theatre, to retain the name, then immediately renamed it the Garrick. His vanity was such that shortly before his death, he commissioned William *Winter to write a monumental biography of him. The work was issued in two volumes in 1910 as *The Life and Art of Richard Mansfield*.

MANTELL, Robert B[ruce] (1854–1928), actor. Born in Irvine, Scotland, he first acted in England under the name Robert Hudson, then reverted to his real name when he came to America in 1878 to play in support of Helena *Modjeska. After serving as Fanny *Davenport's leading man, most notably as Loris Ipanoff in *Fedora* (1883), Mantell became a star playing Raymond Garth in *Tangled Lives* (1886). Subsequently he played the leading roles in such similar romantic melodramas as *The Marble Heart* (1887) and *The *Corsican Brothers* (1890). After the turn of the century he appeared almost solely in Shakespearean roles, among them Hamlet, Richard III, Othello, and King John. His performances in these parts divided the critics, many of whom saw his "thundering," "roaring" style as outmoded. Nevertheless, Mantell won huge audiences, especially on the road. Biography: *Robert Mantell's Romance*, Clarence Joseph Bulliet, 1918.

MANTLE, [Robert] Burns (1873–1948), critic and editor. Born in Watertown, New York, he became a drama critic in 1898, serving on Denver and Chicago newspapers before coming to New York in 1911 as critic for the *Evening Mail*. In 1922 Mantle moved to the *Daily News*, where he remained until 1944. Although he was the author of *American Playwrights of To-day* (1929) and *Contemporary American Playwrights* (1938), he is best remembered as the originator and editor of the *Best Plays* series, an annual anthology of plays and statistics, which he continued to edit from 1920 until shortly before his death. His writings were warm and reasonable, without any of the ostentation of some of his fellow critics.

MAPES, Victor. See *Boomerang, The*.

MARBLE, Dan[forth] (1810–49), character actor. Although he entered the theatre relatively late and died young, he was for well over a decade one of the most respected and popular interpreters of Yankee-dialect characters. He was born in East Windsor, Connecticut, and had been a silversmith before paying $20 for the privilege of making his acting debut at the Chatham Theatre in 1831. Within a short time he was starring in such vehicles as *The Backwoodsman*, *The *Forest Rose*, *Sam Patch, the Jumper*, *The Stage-Struck Yankee*, and *The Vermont Wool Dealer*. Contemporary critics suggested his characterizations had a more Western tinge and were more romantic and exaggerated than those of *Hackett or *Hill. He was not a particularly handsome man, having a large-nosed and rough-hewn square face, but his popularity and financial husbanding were such that when he died he left a then not inconsiderable estate of $25,000. Biography: *Dan Marble*, Jonathan F. Kelly, 1851.

MARBLE, Scott (1845?–1919), playwright. A New York native, he began his career at *Barnum's Museum in 1865 and continued to perform until the late 1880s, when he turned to playwriting. He specialized in action-packed melodramas, such as *The Police Patrol* (1892), *The Diamond Breaker* (1893), *Tennessee's Pardner* (1894), *The Sidewalks of New York* (1895), *The Great Train Robbery* (1896), *The Cotton Spinner* (1897), and *The Heart of The Klondike* (1897). His works, like similar ones by other authors, were rarely played in New York and then only at minor houses. But Marble's plays were produced around the country until around 1910. By then films had usurped the market for his sort of entertainment, so he became one of the earliest writers of film scenarios.

MARBURY, Elisabeth (1856–1933), agent. The daughter of a famous New York attorney, she was encouraged by Daniel *Frohman to become an author's agent. Most of her early clients were foreign playwrights, such as Victorien *Sardou, Oscar *Wilde, Somerset *Maugham, and Sir James *Barrie. Marbury is believed to have been the first agent to negotiate a percentage of box office receipts for her clients. She later began to represent important American figures, including Clyde *Fitch, Rachel *Crothers, and Jerome *Kern. In connection with Kern, it was she who apparently suggested to Ray *Comstock that the small *Princess Theatre be turned into a house for intimate musicals, thus creating the stage for the Princess Theatre Musicals that helped make Kern, Guy *Bolton, and P. G. *Wodehouse famous. Autobiography: *My Crystal Ball*, 1924.

MARCH, Frederic [né Frederick McIntyre Bickel] (1897–1975), actor. Born in Racine, Wisconsin, and educated at the University of Wisconsin, he made his stage debut as the Prompter in *Deburau* in 1920. Within a few seasons he had risen to leading man in several short-lived dramas, then became a star in films. March did not return to Broadway until 1938, when he appeared opposite his wife, Florence *Eldridge, in the quick failure, *Yr. Obedient Husband*. Further failures followed before he won praise as the allegorical Mr. Antrobus in *The *Skin of Our Teeth* (1942). He subsequently distinguished himself as Major Victor Joppolo in *A *Bell for Adano* (1944), the father Clinton Jones in *Years Ago* (1946), the meddling, self-important artist Nicholas Denery in *The Autumn Garden* (1951), the bitter, tight-fisted actor James Tyrone in *Long Day's Journey into Night* (1956), and the Angel of God in *Gideon* (1961). His performance as Tyrone, which won him numerous honors, was called by Brooks *Atkinson "masterful ... a character portrait of grandeur." It was made all the more believable because, like the figure he was playing, March had a touch of the ham in him and the aura of an earlier-day matinee idol, handsome, but stern-looking.

MARCH OF THE FALSETTOS. See *Falsettos.*

MARCHAND, Nancy (1928–2000), actress. Marchand was a tall, statuesque leading lady in classic productions in New York and in regional theatre who later developed into a favorite character actress. She was born in Buffalo and educated at Carnegie Tech before going into stock in 1946. Marchand made her New York debut five years later and played supporting roles on and off Broadway before getting noticed as the cold-hearted Madame Irma in *The Balcony* (1960). Usually playing characters older than herself, she excelled at mothers, aunts, spinsters, and elderly women, both in tragic and comic pieces. Among her many noteworthy performances were her hilarious Mrs. Sneerwell in *A School for Scandal* (1962), Queen Elizabeth in *Mary Stuart* (1971), the school administrator Ceil in *And Miss Reardon Drinks a Little* (1971), the bewildered mom Ida in *Morning's at Seven* (1980), and the aristocratic matriarch Ann in *The Cocktail Hour* (1988).

MARCIN, Max (1879–1948), playwright. Born in Germany but educated in America, this journalist-turned-dramatist scored his first success with the melodrama *The *House of Glass* (1915), followed by the popular comedy, *Cheating Cheaters* (1916). But his biggest hit came a year later when he collaborated with Charles Guernon on *Eyes of Youth* (1917). Marcin's subsequent successes were *The Woman in Room 13* (1919), written with Samuel

*Shipman, *Silence* (1924), and *Badges* (1924), written with Edward Hammond. A skillful contriver of theatrically effective pieces, he often wrote to order, such as his vehicle for the boxer Jack Dempsey, *The Big Fight* (1928). In all some two dozen of his plays reached the boards.

MARCO MILLIONS (1928), a play by Eugene *O'Neill. [Guild Theatre, 92 perf.] As a young man, Marco Polo (Alfred *Lunt) is sent to China on business in the company of his father and uncle. He is so determined to succeed that he has no conception of the deep love Kukachin (Margalo *Gillmore), the Kaan's granddaughter, holds for him. He piles commercial success upon commercial success until he eventually returns to Venice, where he lives in ostentatious luxury, unaware that Kukachin has pined for his love and died for lack of it. Marco, after all, is the eternal merchant. So eternal, in fact, that as the houselights come back on and the audience prepares to leave, there is Marco, the tired businessman, rising from a front row seat and heading for the limousine that awaits him outside. Although many critics agreed with Brooks *Atkinson of the *Times* that the *Theatre Guild's "satiric pageant" was "an original, powerful and searching drama," the play's attack on pervasive, obsessive commercialism had little appeal for the tired businessmen it mocked. Revivals in 1930 and 1964 were no more successful.

MARGARET FLEMING (1891), a play by James A. *Herne. [Palmer's Theatre, 1 perf.] Philip Fleming (E. M. Bell), a successful and seemingly happily married manufacturer, is dismayed to learn that he has fathered a child by one of his mill girls. He resolves to keep the knowledge from his wife, Margaret (Katherine C. Herne), who is threatened with blindness from her own recent pregnancy. Margaret's maid, Maria (Mattie Earle), has a sister who has just had a child and is apparently dying after a troubled birth. She begs Margaret to visit the sister, and Margaret agrees. There she learns of her husband's infidelity, for the sister is Fleming's mill girl. The shock and the death of the mill girl's baby bring on the blindness that had been threatening, and Margaret deserts her husband. They meet by coincidence years later when Margaret stumbles on her own child, who is being raised by Maria. A squabble ensues, and they are hauled into the police station. There Margaret resolves to raise her own child, but never more to see Fleming. The first important American play to demonstrate *Ibsen's influence, it remains a significant milestone in American dramaturgy. Because no New York producer or theatre owner would mount or book the play, the performance at Palmer's was a special matinee. Critics were sharply divided, with the

Ibsenites strongly in favor and the anti-Ibsenites vigorously opposed. Herne later revised the play, cutting it and giving it a happier ending. Although it was afterward given several important revivals, it never won over either the public or the more traditional critics. Modern critics object not to its debt to Ibsen, but to its vestiges of traditional melodrama.

MARGIN FOR ERROR (1939), a play by Clare *Boothe. [*Plymouth Theatre, 264 perf.] Karl Baumer (Otto Preminger), the Nazi consul in New York, is a blackmailer, a thief, and a double-crosser. He has only contempt for America, a contempt that explodes into a fervent wish to break relations with the country after a Jewish policeman, Officer Finkelstein (Sam *Levene), is assigned to guard him. Despite Finkelstein's precautions, Baumer is murdered. The death is especially embarrassing to Finkelstein since he could have had several chances to stop it—for Baumer was poisoned, and stabbed, and shot. Finkelstein is eventually able to pin the poisoning on a young American Nazi, and finds reasons for looking the other way when he learns who the stabber and shooter were. When his captain appears, Finkelstein tells him of the triple methods of murder. The captain, who has known and disliked the consul, can only ask, "Did it kill him?" Burns *Mantle called the work "the first successful anti-Nazi play to reach the stage, a rare combination of melodrama and comedy."

MARGULIES, Donald. See *Dinner with Friends*.

MARION, George (1860–1945), director and actor. Born in San Francisco, where he made his debut as an actor in a local stock company, he later toured with Lew Dockstader's Minstrels before settling in New York. Turning to directing, Marion staged many of Anna *Held's early vehicles for her husband, Florenz *Ziegfeld. Joining Henry W. *Savage, he directed the producer's mountings of such successes as The *Prince of Pilsen (1903), The *County Chairman (1903), The *College Widow (1904), The *Merry Widow (1907), and Sari (1914). Although he continued to direct until the end of the 1920s, he insisted that acting was his first love, and after 1919 he regularly returned to the footlights, most notably when he created the role of Chris Christopherson in *Anna Christie (1921).

MARK HELLINGER THEATRE (New York). Few Broadway theatres have such an unusual history as this 51st Street playhouse that opened in 1930 as the spectacular movie palace, the Hollywood Theatre. Thomas W. Lamb designed the baroque structure as the flagship for the Warner Brothers empire and it boasted grand staircases, 1,600 plush seats, an entrance on Broadway, and even plans for an office building to be built above it. (A Novotel was built in the space in 1985.) While most legit theatres were becoming movie houses in the Great Depression, the Hollywood reversed the trend and started presenting live shows in 1934 as the 51st Street Theatre. Over the next two decades, the playhouse seesawed between this name and the Hollywood as it switched back and forth from legitimate theatre to films. In 1949 it was named the Mark Hellinger after a popular Broadway columnist and remained a busy venue for forty years, its most celebrated tenant being *My Fair Lady (1956). In 1989 the structure was leased for five years as a church; when the lease ran out the church purchased the Mark Hellinger and Broadway lost (for now) one of its finest houses.

MARK TAPER FORUM, THE (Los Angeles). Founded in 1967 by members of UCLA's The Theatre Group on the premise that "a creative theater makes its mark with new material," it first performed at a small theatre in the downtown district. Although its repertory has included classics and popular contemporary works, more than half of its major productions have been world premieres. Several of these afterward won acclaim on Broadway, including The *Shadow Box, I Ought to Be in Pictures, *Children of a Lesser God, *Burn This, *Angels in America, and the rewritten *Flower Drum Song. It now operates out of the 760-seat Mark Taper Theatre at the Los Angeles Music Center and on occasion at the large Ahmanson in the John Anson Ford Cultural Center in Hollywood. It also offers such special projects as the ITP (Improvisational Theatre Project) and tours local schools and community centers. Much of the company's success over the years has been through the producing and directing skills of Gordon *Davidson.

MARLOWE, Julia [née Sarah Frances Frost] (1866–1950), actress. Born in England, at the age of four, she was brought by her mother to America where the family assumed the name of Brough. It was as Fanny Brough that she made her stage debut in 1879 in one of the many juvenile troupes of *H.M.S. Pinafore that were the rage of the day. She continued to sing in comic opera for several seasons before playing Heinrich in a touring company of *Rip Van Winkle in 1882. After studying with Ada Dow and performing in a dramatic company run by Colonel R. E. J. Miles, she made her New York debut as Parthenia in *Ingomar (1887). Marlowe rose rapidly in public esteem, offering over the next few seasons her Viola, Rosalind, and Julia (in The *Hunchback). In 1896 she was Lydia Languish in the all-star revival of The Rivals, and for several years she played Shakespearean heroines opposite her first husband, Richard Taber. Following their separation she created the title role in *Barbara Frietchie (1899), then portrayed Mary Tudor in *When Knighthood Was in Flower (1901). Marlowe assumed these roles at the behest of the Theatrical Syndicate or *Trust which wanted her to gain a larger following and also to cover the financial losses her Shakespearean tours had incurred. Most of her later career was again in Shakespearean roles, this time opposite her second husband, E. H. *Sothern. An early biographer described Marlowe as "of medium height, slender and frail of aspect, with a pale and rather sallow face, great, dark, and wistful eyes, a head that seemed too big for her body, beautiful, dark-brown hair." Many critics remarked on her prominent cleft chin. Her recording of Juliet suggests a lush, musical, and fruity delivery that would be too artificial for modern tastes. Biography: *Julia Marlowe's Story*, E. H. Sothern, edited by Fairfax Downey, 1954.

MARQUIS, Donald. See *Old Soak, The.*

MARQUIS THEATRE (New York). Although three operating and two unused theatres had to be demolished to make room for this new musical house and the vast Marriott Marquis Hotel that surrounds it, the Broadway community soon learned to appreciate the fine comfort, sightlines, and acoustics in the 1,600-seat playhouse. John C. Portman and Roger Morgan designed the hotel-theatre complex with the box office and entrance at street level on Broadway but the auditorium on the third floor. It may be quite a trek to one's seat, but with escalators, elevators, and superior handicap access, the Marquis remains one of the district's most comfortable venues. The theatre opened in 1986 with the hit musical *Me and My Girl* and most of its subsequent tenants have been large musicals.

MARRE, Albert [né Moshinski] (b. 1925), director. A native New Yorker, he studied at Oberlin and Harvard. Shortly after World War II, he directed the Allied Repertory Theatre in Berlin, then became managing director of the Brattle Theatre Company in Cambridge (Massachusetts). As artistic director of the New York *City Center Drama Company for the 1952–53 season, Marre staged highly praised mountings of *Love's Labours Lost* and *Misalliance*. Subsequent successes included the musical *Kismet (1953), The Chalk Garden (1955), Time Remembered (1957), Milk and Honey (1961), and *Man of La Mancha (1965 and 1992).

MARSDEN, Fred [né William A. Silver] (1842–88), playwright. The son of a Baltimore storekeeper, he

studied law and practiced in Philadelphia before changing both his profession and his name. From 1872 on he was in constant demand as a creator of melodramas and farces for popular stars. Among his plays were *Zip (1874) and Musette (1876) for Charlotte *Crabtree; Kerry Gow (1880) and Shaun Rhue (1886) for the well-liked portrayer of Irishmen, Joseph Murphy; Cheek (1883) and Humbug (1886) for the comedian Roland Reed; and The Irish Minstrel (1886) for another Irish delineator, W. J. *Scanlan. At the time of his highly publicized suicide, he was said to hold $30,000 in contracts for new plays.

MARSH, Howard [Warren] (d. 1969), singer and actor. The handsome, if stiff-necked, tenor was born in Bluffton, Indiana, and appeared in a number of Broadway musicals between 1917 and 1930. He is best remembered for three important roles: Baron Schober in *Blossom Time (1921), Karl Franz in The *Student Prince (1924), and Gaylord Ravenal in *Show Boat (1927). Marsh introduced such song classics as "Serenade," " Deep in My Heart, Dear," "Make Believe," and "You Are Love."

MARSHALL, E[dda] G[unnar] (1910–98), actor. A commanding dramatic actor who often played the voice of conscience or the man who understands the just way, Marshall was born in Owatonna, Minnesota, and educated at Carleton College and the University of Minnesota. After touring with the Oxford Players, Marshall made his New York debut in 1938 with the *Federal Theatre Project and first caught the public's attention in 1942 as the sour stagehand Humphrey in *Jason.* He went on to play supporting roles in some of the finest plays of the 1940s and 1950s and in 1956 was the first American to play Vladimir in *Waiting for Godot. Marshall later shone as *John Gabriel Borkman* (1980) and Hardcastle in *She Stoops to Conquer* (1984).

MARSTON, Richard (1847–1917), designer. The son of a noted English Shakespearean actor, Henry Marston, he was born in Brighton and began his career as a performer. However, after coming to America in 1867 he devoted himself primarily to set design. One of his first assignments was creating new scenery for the long-running The *Black Crook. Shortly thereafter he did the sets for that spectacle's failed successor, The White Fawn (1868), as well as for plays by John *Brougham and offerings of the San Francisco Minstrels. For many years Marston served as house designer first at the *Union Square Theatre and later at the *Madison Square Theatre. Among the plays that featured his work there were *Rose Michel (1875) and A Parisian Romance (1883). Much of his subsequent work was for musicals, including The Devil's Deputy (1894),

Fleur-de-Lis (1895), *Half a King* (1896), and *A Little Bit of Everything* (1904), but he also continued designing settings for plays, such as *The Great Diamond Robbery* (1895) and Richard *Mansfield's first American mounting of *Cyrano de Bergerac* (1898). Contemporaries felt he excelled at the designing and painting of outdoor scenes.

MARTIN, Ernest. See Feuer and Martin.

MARTIN, John (1770–1807), actor. Although William *Dunlap calls him the first native American to become a professional player, he was probably deprived of that honor by the young Princeton graduate known only as *Greville. However, he almost certainly was the first American to have an extended career on his native stages. Dunlap wrote of him, "He was of fair complexion, middle height, light figure, and played the youthful characters of many tragedies and comedies in a style called respectable. . . . He laboured hard, lived poor, and died young." Martin made his debut as Young Norval in *Douglas* at the *John Street Theatre in 1791. He later played such roles as Mendoza in *Sheridan's *The Duenna,* Octavius in *Julius Caesar,* Malcolm in *Macbeth,* and in 1794 created the role of Ferdinand in *Tammany.*

MARTIN, Mary [Virginia] (1913–90), actress and singer. One of the most popular of all contemporary performers, she was born in Weatherford, Texas, and worked as a dance instructor and nightclub entertainer before making her show-stopping New York debut singing "My Heart Belongs to Daddy" in *Leave It to Me!* (1938). After a brief but successful career in films, she returned to Broadway in *One Touch of Venus* (1943) and *Lute Song* (1946). One of her most memorable roles was the spirited Ensign Nellie Forbush in *South Pacific* (1949), about which Brooks *Atkinson recalled, "Miss Martin acted . . . with insight and relish; and as a musical-stage virtuoso she made the songs express the subtle qualities of a disarming human being." Turning to comedy, she played the actress Jane Kimball in *Kind Sir* (1953). Martin then triumphed in a series of hit musicals: *Peter Pan* (1954), the governess Maria in The *Sound of Music* (1959), Dolly Levi in *Hello, Dolly!* on tour and in London, and the wife Agnes in *I Do! I Do!* (1966). Her rare Broadway flops were as the actress *Jennie* (1963) and the elderly Lidya Vasilyevna in *Do You Turn Somersaults?* (1978). Stanley *Green wrote that the attractive, wholesome performer "combined naive charm and buoyant enthusiasm with a warm and rangy soprano." Autobiography: *My Heart Belongs,* 1976.

MARTINOT, [Sarah] **Sadie** (1861–1923), actress and singer. The beautiful New Yorker began her stage career at the age of fifteen, then spent several years at the *Boston Museum where she was the first American Hebe in *H.M.S. Pinafore* in 1878. In New York she played prominent roles both in musicals and straight plays, her biggest success coming in the title role of the operetta *Nanon* (1895). Martinot was also noted for her fiery temperament and as a clotheshorse; and in an 1896 revival of *Patience,* in which she played Lady Angela to Lillian *Russell's heroine, she gained notoriety by wearing the first strapless gown seen on Broadway.

MARX BROTHERS, THE, comedians. The riotous team consisted of five brothers: Chico (né Leonard] (1887?–1961), Harpo [né Adolph] (1888?–1964), Groucho [né Julius] (1890?–1977), Gummo [né Milton] (1895?–1977), and Zeppo [né Herbert] (1901?–79). All were born in New York, the grandchildren of performers in Germany. Their mother was the sister of comedian Al Shean, of *Gallagher and *Shean fame. Pushed by their classic stage mother, they appeared in vaudeville in 1909 as "The Three (or Four) Nightingales." Gummo left the act early on, and Zeppo joined the act in the 1910s. During the 1920s they played in three successful Broadway musicals: *I'll Say She Is* (1924), *The *Cocoanuts* (1925), and *Animal Crackers* (1928). Chico portrayed a high-strung, fast-dealing Sicilian. Harpo, forever mute, hurried across the stage in a red wig, battered hat, and tattered, ill-fitting clothes, chasing girls and stealing everything he could. Groucho, dressed in a poorly tailored morning suit, walking with a deep-kneed crouch, and flourishing his cigar and a painted-on mustache and boxy eyebrows, was at the ready with a wisecrack. Zeppo, the handsomest of the group, was that act's straight man. Both Chico and Harpo had musical talents, which they incorporated into their routines, Chico playing the piano with his singular method of seemingly shooting his fingers at the keys, and Harpo performing, appropriately but often with surprising seriousness, on the harp. The team regularly disconcerted both authors and fellow players by departing from rehearsed texts to ad lib through a scene. In the 1930s they enjoyed an immensely popular film career, returning to the stage only rarely and then usually not as a team but as single performers. Groucho also had a popular radio and television quiz program. The brothers have been the subject of plays and musicals, such as *Minnie's Boys* (1970), *A Day in Hollywood—A Night in the Ukraine* (1980), and *Groucho: A Life in Revue* (1986). Autobiographies: *Groucho and Me,* 1959; *Harpo Speaks,* 1961; biographies: *The Marx Brothers,* Kyle Crichton, 1950; *Life with Groucho,* Arthur Marx (his son), 1952; *Groucho, Harpo, Chico—and Sometimes Zeppo,* J. Adamson, 1973.

MARY (1920), a musical comedy by Otto *Harbach, Frank *Mandel (book, lyrics), Louis A. *Hirsch (music). [Knickerbocker Theatre, 220 perf.] Mary Howells (Janet Velie) is secretary to rich Mrs. Keene (Georgia Caine) and in love with Mrs. Keene's son Jack (Jack *McGowan). But Jack seems totally unaware of Mary. He is determined to go West and build low-priced, portable homes that young married couples can afford. He calls them "love nests." However, while digging foundations he strikes oil instead. With his newfound wealth he returns home and realizes that he does, indeed, love Mary. Notable songs: The Love Nest; Mary; We'll Have a Wonderful Party. Although Mary's story was not one of rags-to-riches, playgoers and critics of the day lumped the show with *Irene and *Sally, and saw all three as initiating the vogue for such stories in musicals of the time, so that the era from 1921 to 1924 became known as "The Cinderella Era" on Broadway. The show's relatively short run was attributed to the number of road companies producer George M. *Cohan sent out, one of which was playing before the main company opened in New York.

MARY, MARY (1961), a play by Jean *Kerr. [*Helen Hayes Theatre, 1,572 perf.] When Bob McKellaway (Barry *Nelson) shows his fiancée, Tiffany Richards (Betsy von Furstenberg), reviews of his latest work, he is reminded that his ex-wife used to ask him why his books were so good that "a hundred thousand people wouldn't read them." It was an incessant fusillade of such barbed comments that led him to leave her. Now he must meet with her again to straighten out some income tax problems. When Mary (Barbara *Bel Geddes) appears, she is as caustic as ever. At the same time, an old friend, Dirk Winsten (Michael Rennie), arrives. He is a fading film star who is deserting Hollywood—"the sinking ship leaving the rats." Dirk's romantic interest in Mary makes Bob and his ex realize that they still love each other. Welcomed by Thomas Dash of Women's Wear Daily as "urbane, witty and sophisticated," the Roger L. *Stevens long-run hit skillfully blended a standard, syrupy plot with consistently brittle, impertinent dialogue.

MARY OF SCOTLAND (1933), a play by Maxwell *Anderson. [Alvin Theatre, 248 perf.] Because Catholic Mary Stuart of Scotland (Helen *Hayes) represents a genuine political threat to England's Protestant Queen Elizabeth (Helen *Menken), Elizabeth conspires with disaffected Scottish nobles to overthrow her. Mary is forced to flee to England, where she is captured and imprisoned and the two queens confront each other. Although she realizes that Elizabeth will have her killed, Mary

is triumphant, pointing to her son and heir, and to the rich life she has led, while noting that Elizabeth is an unloved, bitter woman. John Mason *Brown, writing about the *Theatre Guild production in the Evening Post, hailed the blank-verse tragedy as "the best historical drama that has been written by an American—a script which brings the full, flooding beauty of the English language back to a theatre in which its beauties are but seldom heard."

MARY THE THIRD (1923), a comedy by Rachel *Crothers. [39th Street Theatre, 163 perf.] In a double prologue, brief glimpses are seen of the first and second Marys (Louise Huff), mother and daughter, as they are courted by their future husbands, William and Robert (Ben Lyon). Now the granddaughter and daughter of those girls, who is also named Mary (Huff), is courted by Lynn (Lyon). However, this third Mary is an ardent flapper who is dismayed to learn that her parents are contemplating divorce and that her grandparents' marriage was not all it seemed to be. She determines to "live in sin" rather than repeat their mistakes, but in the end bows to social pressures and her own feelings for her suitor. Mary can only ask lamely, "It is one of those great eternal passions that will last through the ages—isn't it, dear?" Another of Crothers's woman's-eye views of mores and relationships, the Lee *Shubert production was welcomed for its wit and shrewd observation, although many critics were uncertain about the precise nature of its philosophic bent.

MASK AND WIG CLUB. See Collegiate Theatrical Clubs.

MASON, Jackie (b. 1931), comedian. Mason has enjoyed more success on Broadway than any other stand-up comic, triumphing in no less than six popular one-man shows that he both wrote and performed. He was born in Sheboygan, Wisconsin, the son of a rabbi, and followed in his father's footsteps until he turned to stand-up comedy in clubs in the 1950s. Among his successful one-man shows were The World According to Me (1986), Politically Incorrect (1994), Love Thy Neighbor (1996), Much Ado About Everything (1999), and Prune Danish (2002).

MASON, John [Becher] (1857–1919), actor. Born in Orange, New Jersey, he was scion to a musical family and the grandson of Lowell Mason, who wrote "Nearer My God to Thee." He made his acting debut in 1878, apprenticed at Philadelphia's *Walnut Street Theatre and the *Boston Museum, then in 1886 played Laertes to Edwin *Booth's Hamlet. Mason joined Daniel *Frohman's company in 1900 then scored some of his greatest successes playing opposite Mrs. *Fiske, including Lovberg in *Hedda Gabler* (1904), Paul Sylvaine in *Leah Kleschna* (1904), and John Karslake in The *New York Idea* (1906). In 1907 he won high praise as Jack Brookfield, who uses the powers of the occult to clear a man wrongly charged with murder, in The *Witching Hour*. Of his performance as the sympathetic Jewish physician Dr. Seelig in As a Man Thinks (1911), Walter Prichard *Eaton wrote, "Mr. Mason has the power of clearcut, fine and sincere speech. . . . With his long and sound training behind him, he projects the ideal of a character worth knowing and listening to." Turning villain, he portrayed the lustful Baron Stephen Audrey in The Yellow Ticket (1914). His last memorable role was Judge Filson in *Common Clay (1915). George *Arliss, who frequently played opposite the paternally dignified actor, remarked after his death, "John Mason would, in my opinion, have been the greatest actor in America if his private character had been as well balanced as his public performance. He had personality, great ability, and a magnificent voice. But he had no control over the frailties of his nature."

MASON, Marshall W. (b. 1940), director and manager. Born in Amarillo, Texas, Mason was educated at Northwestern before studying at the *Actors Studio. He first started directing in New York at the *Caffe Cino and other *Off-Off-Broadway spaces, then in 1969 he co-founded the *Circle Repertory Theatre where he served as artistic director until 1986. Mason is most identified with the playwright Lanford *Wilson and has directed most of his plays at the Circle or elsewhere, including The *Hot l Baltimore (1973), The *Fifth of July (1978), *Talley's Folly (1979), Angels Fall (1983), *Burn This (1987), and Redwood Curtain (1993). He also directed As Is (1985), The Seagull (1992), Cakewalk (1996), and others in New York, as well as productions regionally.

MASON, Mrs. (1780–1835), comic actress. The English performer had made a small name for herself in Dublin and Edinburgh before her American debut at the *Park Theatre in 1809. She soon gained celebrity as a brilliant comedienne, both in classics and contemporary comedies. Much married, she was also known as Mrs. Entwistle and Mrs. Crooke. She spent several highly profitable seasons at Philadelphia's *Chestnut Street Theatre and in New Orleans.

MASSEY, Raymond [Hart] (1896–1983), actor. The tall, gaunt, Canadian, who brought a singular brooding intensity to many of his best interpretations, made his professional debut in London in 1922. His first New York appearance was in 1931 as Hamlet, followed by the quick failure, The Shining Hour (1934). But Massey later enjoyed a major success in the title role of *Ethan Frome (1936). His most famous role was unquestionably in *Abe Lincoln in Illinois (1938). Brooks *Atkinson observed that he played the president "with an artless honesty that is completely overwhelming in the end." Opposite Katharine *Cornell he was Sir Colenso Ridgeon in The Doctor's Dilemma (1941), James Morell in *Candida (1942), and Rodney Boswell in Lovers and Friends (1943). After touring the war zones playing the Stage Manager in a USO production of *Our Town, he returned to Broadway as Higgins to Gertrude *Lawrence's Liza Doolittle in *Pygmalion (1946). Massey's later performances included the Captain in *Strindberg's The Father (1949), a reading of John Brown's Body on tour, Brutus and Prospero at the *American Shakespeare Festival, and the God-figure Mr. Zuss in *J. B. (1958). His son **Daniel MASSEY** (1933–98) was also a celebrated actor, but he spent much of his career in England where he was born. His New York appearances of note included the Budapest clerk Georg in the musical *She Loves Me (1963) and the German conductor Wilhelm Furtwangler in Taking Sides (1996). His sister is the British actress Anna Massey.

MASTER CLASS (1995), a play by Terrence *McNally. [*John Golden Theatre. 601 perf.; Tony Award.] The play takes the form of one of opera diva Maria Callas's famous master classes in voice in 1971. While Callas (Zoe *Caldwell) makes snide comments about other opera singers and demands passion and fervor from three student vocalists (Karen Kay Cody, Audra *McDonald, and Jay Hunter Morris), the action sometimes shifts to reveal the secrets in her heart: her ugly duckling childhood, an abortion, a failed marriage, and intimate conversations with her lover Aristotle Onassis. Although the script met with mixed reactions in the press, the production (co-produced by Robert *Whitehead) was praised for Caldwell and McDonald's performances and both won *Tony Awards.

MASTER JUBA. See Lane, William Henry.

MASTEROFF, Joe. See Cabaret.

MATCHMAKER, THE (1955), a comedy by Thornton *Wilder. [*Royale Theatre, 486 perf.] Dolly Levi (Ruth *Gordon), who is supposedly helping the rich, smug, and pompous merchant Horace Vandergelder (Loring Smith) save his niece from an elopement with an artist, is also supposedly helping the widowed Vandergelder find a new wife. To this end she has a pair of candidates she is pushing. But what Dolly is pushing most is Dolly, for she is determined that she will wed Vandergelder. She arranges for all the figures—the lovers, the candidates, Vandergelder's clerks, and, of course, Vandergelder and herself—to come together at a New York night spot. By the end of the evening she has paired everyone off to her satisfaction—which means she has gotten Vandergelder. Originally produced as *The Merchant of Yonkers* in 1938, the play was based loosely on Johann Nestroy's 1842 farce *Einen Jux Will Er Sich Machen*, whose central figure was one of the clerks. The 1938 version, which starred Jane *Cowl, failed. But Tyrone *Guthrie's madcap direction turned the revised farce into a major success for the *Theatre Guild. Co-producer David *Merrick had even better luck with the piece when he turned it into the musical *Hello, Dolly! (1964).

MATHER, Margaret [née Finlayson] (1862?–98), actress. Born in Canada but raised in Detroit in dire poverty, she came to New York and was encouraged and promoted by J. M. Hill of the *Union Square Theatre where he starred her in revivals of *Romeo and Juliet (1885) and *Leah the Forsaken (1886). An emotionally disturbed if beautiful young actress, she soon broke with Hill and toured in her own company, then retired. In 1897 she emerged from retirement to play her old roles as well as Imogene in *Cymbeline*, but died while on tour. Otis *Skinner, for a time her leading man, said she "had impulse, power, intensity, but it was all unrestrained."

MATHEWS, Cornelius (1817–89), playwright. Although he was highly respected in New York as an editor, novelist, and poet, his plays were never well received there. As a result, he took his later plays to Philadelphia for their premieres. His melodrama *Witchcraft; or, The Martyrs of Salem (1846), was highly praised in all major theatrical centers, except New York. A similar fate befell his historical drama, *Jacob Leisler* (1848), followed by the less-successful satire, *False Pretenses; or, Both Sides of Good Society* (1855).

MATTHAU, Walter [né Matuschanskavashy] (1920–2000), character actor. In the late 1940s and early 1950s, the sour-faced New Yorker won laughs in a dismaying number of flops. His first major hit came as the once-successful "playwrote" Michael Freeman in *Will Success Spoil Rock Hunter?* (1955). Matthau also scored as the sarcastic manager Maxwell Archer in *Once More with Feeling* (1958) and the bored aristocrat Benjamin Beaurevers in *A Shot in the Dark* (1961). However, his greatest stage success came as the hopeless slob Oscar Madison in *The *Odd Couple* (1965). In the 1960s, his film career took off and he never returned to the New York stage.

MATTHEWS, [James] **Brander** (1852–1929), author. Born in New Orleans, he graduated from Columbia and turned to teaching and writing after his family lost its fortune. He taught at his alma mater from 1891 to 1924, and for his last twenty-four years there was its first Professor of Dramatic Literature. Before that he had written, alone or with collaborators, several popular if now-forgotten comedies: *Margery's Lovers* (1884), *A Gold Mine* (1889), and *On Probation* (1889). In 1886 he worked with Laurence *Hutton to compile the five-volume *Actors and Actresses of Great Britain and the United States*. His writings were warm and thoughtful, giving marked evidence of his wide-ranging interests and travels. Autobiography: *These Many Years*, 1917.

MAUGHAM, [William] **Somerset** (1874–1965), playwright and novelist. The English author was one of his era's finest writers of high comedy. His first play to reach America was *Jack Straw*, which Charles *Frohman presented in 1908 at the *Empire Theatre with John *Drew as star. The producer's high reputation, coupled with the great stars he cast in the plays, gave a special, added cachet to such early works as *Lady Frederick* (1908), *Mrs. Dot* (1910), and *Smith* (1910). However, Maugham's four best works are generally considered to be the knowing comedies *Our Betters* (1917), *Too Many Husbands* (1919), *The Circle* (1921), and *The Constant Wife* (1926). His melodrama, *The Letter* (1927), was also a major success. One of the great hits of the 1920s, *Rain*, was dramatized by other writers from one of his short stories.

MAVOURNEEN (1891), a play by George H. *Jessop and Horace Townsend. [14th Street Theatre, 102 perf.] Terence Dwyer (W. J. *Scanlan) rescues his beloved Kate (Grace Thorne) from abductors, only to have her mean sister, Lady Caroline Dwyer (Helen Tracy), contrive to separate the pair and have Terence sent away. The young lovers part but promise to remain true. After ten years, during which he has made a fortune in America, Terence returns to Ireland to find Kate about to marry another man in order to save the family from bankruptcy. Terence sets matters right and takes Kate for himself. Only Scanlan's increasingly obvious insanity forced the show to end its initial run. His part was taken over on tour by Chauncey *Olcott, who played the role afterward for many years. Both men inserted numerous Irish-style ballads into the piece.

MAY BLOSSOM (1884), a play by David *Belasco. [*Madison Square Theatre, 169 perf.] When Richard Ashcroft (Walden Ramsay) is arrested as a spy during the Civil War, he begs his friend, Steve Harland (Joseph Wheelock), to tell his fiancée, May Blossom (Georgia *Cayvan), what has happened. But Steve, who covets May for himself, lets her believe that Richard has deserted her, so she marries Steve and has a child by him. Richard reappears and Steve's perfidy is revealed; but though Richard asks May to elope with him, she refuses. Both men go off to war where Richard is killed in battle, while Steve does not return until long after the war is over. By then May has decided she loves Steve. Belasco's first New York success, it was a reworking of his earlier adaptation of a novel, *Sylvia's Lovers*, and very similar in theme to his collaboration with James A. *Herne, *Hearts of Oak*.

MAY [Pettie or Petty], **Edna** (1878–1948), actress and singer. A native of Syracuse, she began her career in one of the many children's companies of *Gilbert and *Sullivan operettas. May became a star and won international celebrity when she played the lead in The *Belle of New York (1897). Although she later appeared in The Girl from Up There (1901), most of her subsequent career was in England.

MAYER, Edwin Justus. See *Firebrand, The*.

MAYO, Frank (1839–96), actor. The Boston-born performer made his professional debut in San Francisco in 1856 and within a few years had earned an excellent reputation, especially in Shakespearean roles. His first major New York appearance was as Ferdinand in The *Tempest (1869). By that time his fame was such that he received billing and pay second only to E. L. *Davenport, who played Prospero. Apparently feeling he could not be certain of a steady income in Shakespearean roles, Mayo soon turned to popular new plays, achieving his greatest success as *Davy Crockett (1873). Laurence *Hutton wrote, "Mr. Frank Mayo's performance . . . is a gem in its way. He is quiet and subdued, he looks and walks and talks the trapper to the life, never overacts and never forgets the character he represents." He played the part for the remainder of his career, only occasionally essaying other new roles or returning to his old Shakespearean repertory.

MAYO, Margaret [née Lilian Clatten] (1882–1951), playwright. Born in Brownsville, Illinois, she was an actress from 1896 to 1903, when she retired from performing to devote herself to playwriting. Her earliest successes were adaptations of novels: The Marriage of William Ashe (1905) and The Jungle (1907). However, Mayo is best remembered as the author of more original plays such as *Polly of the Circus (1907), *Baby Mine (1910), *Twin Beds (1914), and Seeing Things (1920), written with Aubrey Kennedy.

MAYTIME (1917), an operetta by Rida Johnson *Young (book, lyrics), Sigmund *Romberg (music). [*Shubert Theatre, 492 perf.] The romance of rich Ottillie Van Zandt (Peggy *Wood) and the poor workman, Richard Wayne (Charles *Purcell), is broken up by Ottillie's snobbish father, who forces her to marry her worthless cousin. As the decades pass Richard becomes wealthy and respected, while the cousin succeeds in bankrupting Ottillie. When her estate is put up for auction, Richard appears, buys it all, and gives it back to her. After they are long dead, their grandchildren fall in love and, ignoring family opposition, marry. Notable songs: Jump Jim Crow; The Road to Paradise; Will You Remember? The bittersweet romance was the biggest musical success of its season. It was said to be the favorite selection of American troops heading for Europe. The musical was able to buck the perception that operetta was a German, and therefore enemy, genre. Ironically, it was based on the German musical, Wie einst im Mai, but animosity toward the Central Powers forced the producing Shuberts to jettison Walter Kollo's score and reset the book in America. They also billed it as a "musical play," not an operetta.

McCARTER THEATRE CENTER (Princeton, New Jersey). While the professional nonprofit theatre company in Princeton was formed in 1973, the performance space on the campus goes back to 1929 when it served as the home for the *Triangle Club. For many years the house was also a popular tryout place for Broadway-bound productions, such as *Our Town, *You Can't Take It with You, and *Bus Stop. In 1960 Milton Lyon founded a theatre company in association with the university, and thirteen years later it went professional, severing its academic ties. Under such artistic directors as Ellis *Rabb, Nagle Jackson, and Emily Mann, the McCarter has earned a reputation for distinctive revivals and occasional new works. The company performs on the renovated Matthew stage, an adjustable proscenium house, and the smaller, new 360-seat Berlind stage. The McCarter won the regional theatre *Tony Award in 1994. **Emily MANN** (b. 1952) is a respected director and playwright who has staged productions for such theatres as the *Guthrie, *Brooklyn Academy of Music, *Actors Theatre of Louisville, and the *American Place Theatre. Her plays, usually written in a documentary format, include Still Life (1980), Execution of Justice (1986), and Having Our Say (1995).

McCARTHY, Joseph. See Tierney, Harry.

McCARTHY, Kevin (b. 1914), actor. The hardy leading man possesses a distinctively musical voice that makes his performances in both classics and modern plays special. He was born in Seattle and studied for a diplomatic career at Georgetown University and the University of Minnesota, but while attending the latter school he became interested in acting. McCarthy made his Broadway debut in 1938 playing minor roles in *Abe Lincoln in Illinois* and slowly worked his way to leading characters, most significantly in classic plays, such as his Trigorin in *The Sea Gull* (1954) and Vershinin in *The Three Sisters* (1964). He also shone in contemporary works, as his idealistic Protestant artist Ayamonn in *Red Roses for Me* (1955) and the ruthless Senator Ackerman in *Advise and Consent* (1960).

McCAULL, John A. (1846–94), producer. Often called "The Father of American Comic Opera," the Scottish-born lawyer practiced in Baltimore after fighting as a colonel for the Confederacy. While handling a case for John *Ford (some sources say for Emily *Melville, the singer), he found the theatre so attractive that he first specialized in theatrical cases, then entered the producing ranks. He established the McCaull Opera Comique Company, which became a leading importer of foreign comic operas (mostly now-forgotten German and Viennese works), and was so successful that several branches were soon organized. Although he was sufficiently commercial to cater to the insistent demand for European material, he also attempted to develop a native school of writing and performing. To this end he was the first important producer to mount the comic operas of John Philip *Sousa and gave major breaks to such entertainers as De Wolf *Hopper and Francis *Wilson. With Rudolf *Aronson he built the *Casino Theatre, the first legitimate playhouse erected in America expressly for the purpose of offering musicals. Wilson recalled him as "a proud man, he was swift to take offense; he could be a firm friend and a bitter enemy. His impulsiveness often warped his judgment."

McCLENDON, Rose (1885–1936), actress. The most distinguished African-American actress of her generation, she was a mature woman before critics in her native New York began to take notice of her. She first attracted attention when she played opposite Charles *Gilpin in a touring production of *Roseanne* (1924), then won high praise for her performance as a wise, aged quadroon in the musical *Deep River* (1926). McClendon's three most memorable portrayals followed in short order: the

friend Goldie McAllister in *In Abraham's Bosom* (1926), the compassionate Serena in *Porgy* (1927), and the old sibyl Big Sue in *The House of Connelly* (1931). In 1935 she helped organize the Negro People's Theatre, then found another great role as Cora Lewis in *Mulatto* (1935) before her premature death. In reviewing the play Brooks *Atkinson called her "an artist with a sensitive personality and a bell-like voice," continuing, "It is always a privilege to see her adding fineness of perception to the parts she takes."

McCLINTIC, Guthrie (1893–1961), director and producer. He was born in Seattle and studied at the University of Washington and the *American Academy of Dramatic Arts before making his acting debut in 1913. He first played for New York audiences a year later, appearing in several shows until 1918, when he joined Jessie *Bonstelle's stock company. His directing career began after he left to become Winthrop *Ames's assistant. McClintic embarked on his own when he produced and directed *The Dover Road* (1921). Subsequently he directed, and frequently produced, such popular plays as The *Shanghai Gesture* (1926), *Saturday's Children* (1927), *Brief Moment* (1931), *Winterset* (1935), *Ethan Frome* (1936), John *Gielgud's *Hamlet* (1936), *High Tor* (1937), The *Star Wagon* (1937), *Mamba's Daughters* (1939), and *Key Largo* (1939). However, he is most often associated in playgoers' minds with the work he did in conjunction with his wife, Katharine *Cornell. He directed her in *The Green Hat* (1925) and *Dishonored Lady* (1930), then beginning with The *Barretts of Wimpole Street* (1931), both directed her in and co-produced with her all her later plays. Although he was a sensitive, knowing director, he was a prissy, volatile man, who was deftly parodied as Carleton Fitzgerald in Moss *Hart's comedy *Light Up the Sky.* Autobiography: *Me and Kit*, 1955.

McCLOSKEY, James. See *Across the Continent*.

McCULLOUGH, JOHN [Edward] (1832–85), actor and manager. Born in Ireland, he was sent to live with relatives in Philadelphia after the death of his mother and soon took an active interest in amateur theatricals, including the local Boothenian Dramatic Association. He made his professional debut at the *Arch Street Theatre, then came to the attention of Edwin *Forrest, who adopted him as a protégé. The result of this apprenticeship was that McCullough's repertory and acting style were very much those of the older actor. He played many second leads to Forrest, and after the star's death, assumed the principal roles in such old Forrest standbys as The *Gladiator, Virginius,* *Jack Cade,* and *King Lear.* He managed San Francisco's *California

Theatre until financial difficulties forced him to relinquish the post in the late 1870s, so he resumed touring in his best-known roles. His last appearance was in Chicago in 1884, after which his growing mental instability forced his commitment to an institution. A large, rugged, masculinely handsome man, McCullough was highly admired for his fairness in an often-selfish profession, although his acting was seen to belong to a passing tradition. J. Rankin *Towse wrote, "His Othello was an imposing and martial figure, with authority in voice and mien and all the external indications of the 'frank and noble nature' with which Iago credited him. And his 'waked wrath' was terrible. . . . But it was only in storm and stress that it was remarkable. In detail it was crude, unimaginative, unfinished, a bold freehand sketch rather than a completed study." Biography: *John McCullough as Man, Actor and Spirit*, Susie Champney Clark, 1905.

McCULLOUGH, Paul. See Clark and McCullough.

McDONALD, Audra (b. 1971), actress and singer. The African-American performer, with an opera-quality voice and a passionate stage presence, has found success with each of her New York appearances to date. She was born in Berlin, Germany, to American parents in the military and was educated at Juilliard and the *American Conservatory Theatre School. McDonald made an impressive Broadway debut as the textile worker Carrie Pipperidge in the 1994 revival of *Carousel*, followed by highly praised performances as the young opera student Sharon in *Master Class* (1995), the tragic servant girl Sarah in *Ragtime* (1998), winning *Tony Awards for all three, and the murderous Creole lover *Marie Christine* (1999).

McELFATRICK, J. B., AND COMPANY. The leading firm of theatrical architects at the turn of the century, its New York houses included the Broadway, *Empire, *Hudson, Music Hall (later the New York), Lyric (later the Criterion), Republic, Victoria, and *Wallack's. The firm is said to have designed more than one hundred theatres across the country. The founder, John Bailey McElfatrick (1829–1906), was born in Harrisburg, Pennsylvania, and practiced for many years in St. Louis before coming to New York in the 1880s.

McEVOY, J. P. See *Potters, The*.

McGOWAN, John (1892–1977), actor, singer, and playwright. A native of Muskegon, Michigan, he began his career as a vaudeville song-and-dance man, then became a leading man in musical comedy (often under the name Jack McGowan), introducing "The Love Nest" in *Mary* (1920) and "I'll Build a Stairway to Paradise" in *George White's Scandals of 1922*. He next turned to playwriting, with his most successful endeavor being *Excess Baggage* (1927). Subsequently McGowan collaborated on the books for such musicals as *Hold Everything!* (1928), *Flying High* (1930), and *Girl Crazy* (1930).

McGUIRE, William Anthony (1885–1940), playwright. The Chicago native began his working career as a journalist, but he had started writing plays while in his teens. All his major successes came in the 1920s, including *Six Cylinder Love* (1921) and *Twelve Miles Out* (1925). In the musical theatre he wrote the librettos or sketches for nine of Florenz *Ziegfeld's shows, most memorably *Rosalie* (1928), *The *Three Musketeers* (1928), and *Whoopee* (1929). On occasion McGuire also served as director and producer.

McHUGH, [James Francis] Jimmy (1894–1969), composer. The Boston-born songwriter had a major hit with his first Broadway score for *Blackbirds of 1928*, remembered for "Diga Diga Doo," "I Can't Give You Anything But Love," and "I Must Have That Man." His lyricist was Dorothy *Fields, with whom he next wrote the scores for *Hello, Daddy* (1928) and the *International Revue* (1930). McHugh did not return to Broadway until 1939, when he scored *The Streets of Paris* (including "South American Way"), *Keep Off the Grass* (1940), and *As the Girls Go* (1948), whose superb songs are undeservedly neglected. His long Hollywood career between 1930 and 1947 produced many memorable songs, such as "I'm in the Mood for Love" and "A Lovely Way to Spend an Evening."

McINTYRE and HEATH, comedy team. James McIntyre (1857–1937) was born in Kenosha, Wisconsin, and Thomas Heath (1852–1938) in Philadelphia, the two teaming up in 1874 and touring the South where they soon learned to mimic both African Americans and stereotypical imitations of them. In their blackface comedy act, Heath, with a pillow-stuffed belly, portrayed a shabbily genteel know-it-all who was always able to lure the thin, believing, whiny-voiced McIntyre into preposterous enterprises. They appeared in several Broadway shows written especially for them, most notably in *The Ham Tree* (1905), but also in *In Hayti* (1909), *The Show of Wonders* (1916), and *Hello, Alexander* (1919). The team was the longest lived of any major two-man act, though neither man spoke to the other, except in performance.

McINTYRE, Frank (1879–1949), comedian. The bulky performer, a native of Ann Arbor, Michigan, made his debut in 1901 and for many years was a favorite in both musicals and plays. His best-known roles were the title part in The *Traveling Salesman (1908) and in the musical *Queen High (1926).

McKENNA'S FLIRTATION (1889), a farce by Edgar Selden. [*Park Theatre, 104 perf.] Timothy McKenna (William Barry), a newly rich contractor who is building tenements in the squatter area known as goat town, receives by mistake a letter apparently signed by the wife of his best friend, the milkman Michael Ryan (Hugh Fay). Thinking she is suggesting a tryst, he starts out to pursue her, getting himself and everyone else in hot water before the mistake is brought to light. Essentially a *farce-comedy replete with scattered vaudeville turns and songs, it was one of many such pieces that straddled the fence at the time between the newly emerging musical comedy and traditional farce. Barry and Fay had long been a popular two-a-day team, and author Selden was an actor who wrote vaudeville sketches.

McLELLAN, C[harles] M. S. (1865–1916), lyricist and playwright. Born in Bath, Maine, he was a newspaperman before turning his hand to the theatre, although he continued in the literary world and eventually became editor of Town Topics. His earliest theatre work was as a librettist and lyricist, and was done under the name Hugh Morton. Beginning in 1896 with In Gay New York, he created the dialogue and rhymes for some fifteen Broadway musicals, most notably The *Belle of New York (1897) and The *Pink Lady (1911). McLellan also attempted more serious playwriting, scoring a major success with his melodrama *Leah Kleschna (1904). Among his other dramas were The Jury of Fate (1906), Judith Zaraine (1911), and The Fountain (1914).

McMARTIN, John (b. 1932), actor. The dapper, sandy-haired leading man has been equally at home in dramas as in musicals over the past forty years. He was born in Warsaw, Indiana, and educated at Columbia University. McMartin made an auspicious Off-Broadway debut in 1959 as the Canadian Mountie Capt. Big Jim Warington in the popular spoof *Little Mary Sunshine. Over the years he has played such diverse characters as the neurotic Oscar in *Sweet Charity (1966), the disillusioned socialite Benjamin Stone in *Follies (1971), Don Alonso in Don Juan (1972), the failed painter Dion Anthony in The *Great God Brown (1972), the victimized town official Schill in The Visit (1973), riverboat captain Andy Hawks in *Show Boat (1995), the tipsy uncle Willie in High Society (1998), and the Narrator who also plays the Mysterious Man in *Into the Woods (2002).

McNALLY, John J. (1852?–1931), playwright. Born in Charlestown, Massachusetts, he studied law at Harvard but soon abandoned his practice to become a drama critic on the Charlestown Chronicle, the Boston Times, and finally the Boston Herald. His first theatre work appears to be Revels (1880), a *farce-comedy and a revised libretto for E. E. *Rice's *Evangeline. McNally's entire early stage career was given over to writing additional farce-comedies, and next to Charles *Hoyt, he was probably the best in the field. Among his better works were A Mad Bargain (1892), A Country Sport (1893), and the May *Irwin vehicles The Widow Jones (1895) and Courted into Court (1896). From 1896 to 1905 he was associated with the *Rogers Brothers, who were the principal rivals to *Weber and *Fields, writing for the brothers the books for all their musicals. He withdrew from the stage after writing the *McIntyre and *Heath vehicle In Hayti (1909).

McNALLY, Terrence (b. 1939), playwright. A native of St. Petersburg, Florida, and raised in Corpus Christi, Texas, he studied at Columbia. His early plays included Next (1969), Where Has Tommy Flowers Gone? (1971), and Bad Habits (1973), but it was the popular farce The *Ritz (1975) that most firmly established him. McNally was one of the most produced American playwrights during the 1980s and 1990s with many productions Off Broadway and in regional theatres. Among the noteworthy plays of that period were The Lisbon Traviata (1985), *Frankie and Johnny in the Clair de Lune (1987), Lips Together, Teeth Apart (1991), A Perfect Ganesh (1994), *Love! Valour! Compassion! (1994), *Master Class (1995), and Corpus Christi (1998). McNally also began to write librettos for musicals with The Rink (1984), followed by *Kiss of the Spider Woman (1993), *Ragtime (1998), The Full Monty (2000), and A Man of No Importance (2002). His plays tend to be about contemporary, urban, and usually gay characters in a loosely plotted tale filled with vibrant dialogue. McNally's librettos (mostly adaptations of other works), on the other hand, are tightly structured, economically plotted, and true to their source material.

McRAE, Bruce (1867–1927), actor. He was born in India, a nephew of the famed British star Charles Wyndham, and supposedly came to America intent on becoming a rancher but soon made his acting debut in 1891 in Thermidor. In 1899 he was the original Dr. Watson in *Sherlock Holmes, then portrayed Charles Brandon in *When Knighthood Was in Flower (1901). McRae was Ethel *Barrymore's leading man in, among others, Cousin Kate (1904), A Doll's House (1905), Alice Sit-by-the-Fire (1905), and His Excellency the Governor (1907). After portraying John Rosmer opposite Mrs. *Fiske in *Rosmersholm* (1907), he was the leading man in such successes as *Nobody's Widow* (1910), *Come Out of the Kitchen* (1916), *Daddies* (1918), *The *Gold Diggers* (1919), and *The *Awful Truth* (1922). A highly accomplished actor, he was perhaps better described as attractive than handsome.

McVICKER, J[ames] H. (1822–96), character actor and manager. Born in New York, he began performing in New Orleans and within a short while developed a reputation as a superior interpreter of Yankee roles. T. Allston *Brown recalled, "He was a good actor, a comedian of the purest and most acceptable type; he united unctuous humour with a gentle dignity that never forsook him, even in the broadest phases of his art." However, McVicker is best remembered for his work in Chicago, where he moved in 1857 and built his own theatre, becoming both a leading performer and producer in the city. Although he retained his Chicago base, his success was such that he eventually ran theatres in several major cities. In 1876 he added New York's *Lyceum Theatre to his chain, opening it with Edwin *Booth in *Hamlet* and himself assuming the role of the First Gravedigger.

McVICKER'S THEATRE (Chicago). The Madison Street playhouse had to be rebuilt four times during its rocky history, but for decades it was considered the most beautiful theatre West of the Allegheny Mountains. Otis Wheelock designed the structure in the likeness of an Italian palazzo; and actor-manager James H. *McVicker built it in 1857 for his stock company, though it was better known for the procession of stars who passed through. In addition to battling vaudeville and (later) movies, McVicker's suffered in other ways. It burnt down during the Chicago fire of 1871, was rebuilt in 1885 only to burn down again in 1890, and was reconstructed yet again only to be razed in 1922 and replaced by a movie house (which was torn down in 1984).

ME AND MY GIRL (1937). This musical tale about a cockney lad who inherits an earldom had book and lyrics by L. Arthur Rose and Douglas Furber, and music by Noel Gay. Its original London production in 1937 ran four years; an enlarged, revised version began an even longer run in 1985. The musical was not seen in America until that West End production opened the new *Marquis Theatre on Broadway in 1986 with its London star, Robert Lindsay. Its catchy songs, particularly "The Lambeth Walk," and its outrageous clowning marked a refreshing change from the solemnity of many contemporary musicals, and audiences kept it on the boards for 1,420 performances.

MEADOW BROOK THEATRE (Rochester, Michigan). Founded in 1967 by John Fernald, who served as its first artistic director, the nonprofit theatre performed in a 600-seat theatre located on the Oakland University campus, though it was not affiliated with the school. The company was the largest professional troupe in the state and presented a traditional repertory of classic and modern revivals when its board of trustees decided to dissolve the company in 2003. Plans are under way to institute a new performing group in the space, to be called the Meadow Brook Theatre Ensemble.

MEDCRAFT, Russel Graham. See *Cradle Snatchers*.

MEDEA. Euripides' tragedy has remained a stageworthy piece for centuries, though most stage versions in the 19th century were by French and German writers. The first major American adaptation was by poet Robinson Jeffers, and was produced successfully by Robert *Whitehead and Oliver Rea at the National Theatre in 1947 with Judith *Anderson as Medea and John *Gielgud as Jason. It ran 214 performances and for many years was the translation of choice in American productions. That same version was revived in 1982 with Zoe *Caldwell as Medea and Anderson this time playing her nurse. Other New York Medeas of note include Irene Papas in 1973, Diana Rigg in 1994, and Fiona Shaw in 2002. Michael John *LaChiusa's operatic version of the tale, *Marie Christine* (1999), played briefly at *Lincoln Center.

MEDOFF, Mark. See *Children of a Lesser God*.

MEEHAN, Thomas (b. 1929), librettist. A native New Yorker, Meehan was educated at Hamilton College then pursued a playwriting career with little success, so in 1956 he started writing for television. He also had extensive writing experience with *The New Yorker* magazine and for films, including some screenplays co-written with Mel *Brooks. Meehan's first theatre credit was the libretto for the musical hit *Annie* (1977), followed by equal success in scripting *The *Producers* (2001) and *Hairspray* (2002). For a former gag writer, Meehan's librettos are traditionally plotted and well structured.

MEGRUE, Roi Cooper (1883–1927), playwright. The New York–born dramatist served as assistant to Elisabeth *Marbury before turning his hand to playwriting. Skilled at both superficial, if theatrically effective melodrama and lightweight comedy, he enjoyed long runs with *Under Cover* (1914), *It Pays to Advertise* (1914), *Under Fire* (1915), *Potash and Perlmutter in Society* (1915), *Seven Chances*

(1916), and *Tea for Three* (1918), some written with others. On occasion Megrue directed others' plays, most notably the first *Pulitzer Prize-winner, *Why Marry?* (1917), which he co-produced.

MEISNER, Sanford. See Neighborhood Playhouse.

MELMOTH, Mrs. [Charlotte] (1749–1823), actress. The "grande dame" of tragedy on the early American stage, her maiden surname is unknown. She was said to be the daughter of an English farmer and to have run away from school to marry an English actor, Samuel Jackson Pratt, who used the stage name Courtney Melmoth. They quickly separated, but she retained his name professionally. After performing for many years in England and Ireland, she came to America in 1793, making her acting debut as Euphrasia in *The Grecian Daughter*. Although Melmoth was past her prime and growing exceedingly corpulent, she won applause for her characterization of the heroines in contemporary drama and for such classic figures as Lady Macbeth, Constance, and Mrs. Malaprop. Her fiery temper caused occasional problems, so she retired many years before her death to run a seminary for girls and a dairy farm.

MELVILLE, Emily [also spelled Emilie and Emelie] (1850–1932), actress. Only five years old when she played the Duke of York to Edwin *Forrest's Richard III in Providence, Rhode Island, the Philadelphian was a popular child star in Louisville and elsewhere on what was called the "Western" circuit. She moved to San Francisco in 1868 and for the next sixty years remained one of its most beloved actresses. Much of her early success was as the prima donna of contemporary comic operas, but Melville also earned acclaim for her Ophelia and other dramatic interpretations. As late as the 1920s she played important older parts with the Alcazar Theatre's famous stock company and at other local playhouses.

MELVILLE, Rose (1873–1946), actress. Born in Terre Haute, Indiana, she made her debut in 1889 then scored a major success in a touring play called *Zeb*, in which she appeared as the hayseed Sis Hopkins. Melville played the part so well that it was elaborated for her, then she developed a vaudeville sketch around the same yokel. In her Broadway appearances, in such musicals as *Little Christopher Columbus* (1894) and *By the Sad Sea Waves* (1899), Melville invariably portrayed Sis. She played little else until she retired sometime in the 1920s.

MEMBER OF THE WEDDING, THE (1950), a play by Carson McCullers. [*Empire Theatre, 501 perf.; NYDCC Award.] Frankie Addams (Julie *Harris), a lonely, sensitive twelve-year-old girl, lives in a small southern town with a widowed father, who ignores her, and Berenice Sadie Brown (Ethel *Waters), the warm, understanding, thrice-married "Negro" cook. Only Berenice and Frankie's bespectacled six-year-old cousin John Henry West (Brandon de Wilde) make life bearable for Frankie until her brother Jarvis (James Holden) returns from the army and asks her to be a member of his wedding party. Frankie is thrilled, then shattered when she realizes that she cannot accompany them on their honeymoon, as she had expected to do. Although John Henry dies of meningitis and Berenice leaves to get married again, the first stirrings of adolescent romance promise better days for Frankie. The play was adapted by the playwright from her novel of the same name. Although most critics had initially held serious reservations about the work, questioning the play's construction, the luminous performances made the Robert *Whitehead offering a surprise hit, capping Waters's career and launching Harris into stardom. Revivals by the *Phoenix Theatre in 1975, with Mary Beth Hurt and Marge Elliott, and by the *Roundabout Theatre in 1989, with Amelia Campbell and Esther Rolle, confirmed the play's stage worthiness.

MEN AND WOMEN (1890), a play by David *Belasco and Henry C. *de Mille. [Proctor's 23rd Street Theatre, 204 perf.] A panic brings the Jefferson National Bank to the brink of collapse, especially when bonds kept in its vault are discovered missing. Suspicion falls on young Edward Seabury (Orrin Johnson), just as he is to announce his engagement to Dora Prescott (Maude *Adams), sister of his best friend and fellow cashier, William Prescott (William *Morris). Will, too, has just become engaged, to Agnes Rodman (Sydney Armstrong), daughter of Arizona's governor, Stephen Rodman (Frank Mordaunt). Calvin Stedman (R. A. Roberts), who loves Dora, determines to pin the theft on Edward, and when Governor Rodman comes to Edward's defense, Stedman reveals that the Governor has a criminal record. This revelation forces Will to confess that he stole the bonds. Although he is not prosecuted, Will loses his job and cannot find work. Finally the sympathetic bank president, dismissing Will's actions as a youthful mistake, finds him another position and the lovers are all happily paired. Based on a then recent and celebrated case, the Charles *Frohman production was the last collaboration of Belasco and de Mille. The New York *Star* praised it as the "best they have ever written." Except for the *Herald*, most critics agreed, even if some saw little purpose in the weak ending.

MEN IN WHITE (1933), a play by Sidney *Kingsley. [*Broadhurst Theatre, 351 perf.; Pulitzer Prize.] George Ferguson (Alexander Kirkland) is a young, idealistic intern whose rich fiancée, Laura Hudson (Margaret Barker), cannot understand his self-sacrificing dedication. She is willing to buy his advancement in his profession if he will spend more time with her. But their disagreement comes to a head when Laura discovers that George has had an affair with Barbara Dennin (Phoebe Brand) who has died following an abortion. George leaves to study surgery in Vienna. The first success for both Kingsley and the *Group Theatre, much of its success was attributed to the often graphically realistic production, directed by Lee *Strasberg, and to the then fresh theme. Mordecai *Gorelik's settings were particularly memorable, and the outstanding cast also included Morris *Carnovsky, Robert *Lewis, Sanford *Meisner, Art Smith, and Ruth Nelson. Percy *Hammond of the Herald Tribune called it "an honest, tricky, and propaganda show that can be attended without a sacrifice of intelligence."

MENCKEN, H[enry] L[ouis] (1880–1956), author. The crusty Baltimore journalist was best known to theatregoers for his association with the famed critic George Jean *Nathan, with whom he edited The Smart Set and The American Merciery, and with whom he wrote two plays that never reached New York: The Artist (1912) and Heliogabulus (1920). The character of E. K. Hornbeck in *Inherit the Wind was modeled after him.

MENKEN, Adah Isaacs (1835–69), actress. Although her real name was later given variously as Ada McCord, Adelaide McCord, and Dolores Adios Fuertes, this flamboyant, controversial performer, who was the most famous of all Americans to play Mazeppa, was born in Milneburg, Louisiana, and christened Ada Bertha Theodore. Her earliest attempts to go onstage led nowhere, so she married Isaac Menken, the son of a Cincinnati manufacturer, and converted to Judaism. Adopting her new stage name (adding the letter "s" to Isaac apparently for euphonic reasons), she made her debut in 1858 in Shreveport as Pauline in The *Lady of Lyons. A year later she was acting in New York but, finding roles hard to secure, became an assistant to the famous acrobat Blondin, and also tried her hand at a vaudeville act. It was James *Murdoch who, learning of her riding skills, suggested that she attempt the role of Mazeppa, with its famous scene in which the hero (a trouser role), tied to his horse and supposedly nude, is sent on a wild ride into the hills. Menken first played the part in 1861 and performed in little else thereafter, even touring to London and Paris, where she died. Away from the stage the small but amply proportioned, dark-haired actress was a fascinating figure. Not only was she a fine rider but also an excellent shot. Menken was one of the first women to smoke in public, loved to gamble, and was much married; but her poetry and scintillating conversation won her such friends as Walt Whitman, Swinburne, and the elder Dumas. Biography: Mazeppa: The Lives, Loves, and Legends of Adah Isaacs Menken, Wolf Mankowitz, 1982.

MENKEN, Alan (b. 1949), composer. One of Hollywood's most-awarded songwriters, Menken began in the theatre and later retained a Broadway flavor in his film compositions. He was born in New Rochelle, New York, the son of a dentist, and educated at New York University. His first collaboration with librettist-lyricist Howard *Ashman was the short-lived Off-Broadway musical God Bless You, Mr. Rosewater (1979) based on a Kurt Vonnegut story. The team had much greater success with *Little Shop of Horrors (1982), and then they were hired by Disney to score animated musicals. After Ashman's death in 1991, Menken wrote additional songs with lyricist Tim *Rice for the 1994 Broadway version of Beauty and the Beast. He also composed the music for the Off-Broadway Weird Science (1992) with lyricist David Spenser and the Madison Square A Christmas Carol (19940 with lyricist Lynn *Ahrens.

MENKEN, Helen (1901–66), actress. Only five years old when she made her debut as a fairy in a 1906 production of A *Midsummer Night's Dream, the attractive New Yorker continued her career by appearing in contemporary musicals. She then spent several years in stock before playing opposite John *Drew in Major Pendennis (1916). Menken first attained major recognition when she played Miss Fairchild in *Three Wise Fools (1918), then won further acclaim as the poor waif Diane in *Seventh Heaven (1922). Her other memorable performances included the three-hundred-year-old Emilia Marty, who has the formula for eternal youth, in The Makropoulos Secret (1926); the unyielding lesbian Irene De Montcel in The Captive (1926); Dorinda in The Beaux' Stratagem (1928); Queen Elizabeth to the Mary of Helen *Hayes in *Mary of Scotland (1933); and the spinster Charlotte Lovell in The *Old Maid (1935).

MERCER, Johnny. See Li'l Abner.

MERCHANT OF VENICE, THE. Shakespeare's often-controversial play was first done at Williamsburg, Virginia, in 1752 and marked the debut of the elder Lewis *Hallam's company in America. The play held the stage actively all through the 19th century, although it was regularly performed in a truncated version, usually ending with the trial scene. Edwin *Booth and other notable performers essayed the role of Shylock, many of them emphasizing the dark undercurrents in Shakespeare's story rather than the lighter elements of the play. There was also sharp disagreement on how to portray Shylock, with many performers seeing him simply as a stereotypical villain and Jew. Numerous critics and playgoers suggested the finest of all 19th-century productions was that offered on their visits by Henry *Irving and Ellen *Terry. Irving's attempt at injecting sympathy into his portrayal of Shylock and Terry's richly warm and feminine reading of Portia redressed the balance to a large extent. In the 20th century a number of distinguished Jewish actors, including Jacob *Adler, David *Warfield, and Morris *Carnovsky, essayed the role of Shylock in order to show that Shakespeare was drawing a human figure and not a caricatured Jewish villain, but the role of Portia was generally relegated to a secondary place. Other noteworthy New York Shylocks include George C. *Scott, Dustin *Hoffman, and Ron Leibman. Two modern plays that attempted to retell Shakespeare's tale were Arnold Wesker's *The Merchant* (1977) and A. R. *Gurney's *Overtime* (1996); both were short-lived.

MERCURY THEATRE, THE (New York). Founded by Orson *Welles and John *Houseman as a repertory company in 1937, its chief aim was to offer "classical plays excitingly produced." To this end the small, slightly out-of-the-way Comedy Theatre on 41st Street was leased and renamed, and an ensemble formed, which included such later famous performers as Hiram *Sherman, Joseph *Cotten, and Martin *Gabel. During its brief but noteworthy history, the group produced a modern-dress version of *Julius Caesar*, *The Shoemaker's Holiday*, *Heartbreak House*, and *Danton's Death*. Away from its main playhouse the group produced Marc *Blitzstein's controversial *The *Cradle Will Rock*. By the end of 1938, a combination of financial problems, the desertion of leading players, and pressing demands on others from radio and films caused the group's collapse. Some historians consider the film *Citizen Kane* as the troupe's last and most enduring achievement.

MEREDITH, Burgess (1908–97), actor and director. The short, somewhat fey performer was born in Cleveland and served a theatrical apprenticeship with the *Civic Repertory Theatre in 1930. Although he remained active in the theatre for half a century, he is best remembered for three early roles: Mio, the young man who seeks death after his father is executed, in *Winterset* (1935); Van Van Dorn, who flees civilization for a night, in *High Tor* (1937); and Stephen Minch, who is allowed to return to the days of his youth, in *The *Star Wagon* (1937). He also enjoyed a long career in films, radio, and television. Autobiography: *So Far, So Good*, 1997.

MERIVALE, Philip (1886–1946), actor. The lanky, suave, slightly haughty leading man was born in India and spent several seasons acting in London before he came to America in 1914 with Mrs. Patrick *Campbell. He made his debut playing Higgins to her Liza Doolittle in *Pygmalion*. Thereafter he moved back and forth between the West End and Broadway. Among his notable American performances were Prince Albert in *The Swan* (1923); the neglectful husband Maurice Sorbier in *Grounds for Divorce* (1924); Hannibal in *The *Road to Rome* (1928); His Serene Highness, the personification of Death, in *Death Takes a Holiday* (1929); barrister Jim Warlock in *Cynara* (1931); and the Earl of Bothwell in *Mary of Scotland* (1933). In 1935 he appeared with his wife, Gladys Cooper, playing the title roles in *Othello* and *Macbeth*.

MERMAN, Ethel [née Zimmermann] (1908–84), actress and singer. The leading musical comedy queen of her era, she was born in Astoria, New York, and performed in cabarets and in vaudeville before making her Broadway debut in *Girl Crazy* (1930) where her singing of "I Got Rhythm" stopped the show and catapulted her to fame. Thereafter she appeared in *George White's Scandals of 1931* and *Take a Chance* (1932) before getting many juicy roles in Cole *Porter musicals: the evangelist-turned-songstress Reno Sweeney in *Anything Goes* (1934), former manicurist Nails O'Reilly in *Red, Hot and Blue!* (1936), nightclub singer May Daly in *Du Barry Was a Lady* (1939), saloon owner Hattie Mahoney in *Panama Hattie* (1940), and rancher Blossom Hart in *Something for the Boys* (1943). One of her greatest successes was the sharpshooter Annie *Oakley in Irving *Berlin's *Annie Get Your Gun* (1946), followed by ambassadress Sally Adams in his *Call Me Madam* (1950). After playing the Philadelphia Main Liner Liz Livingston in *Happy Hunting* (1956), Merman gave what was considered her greatest performance: the driven stage mother Rose in *Gypsy* (1959). Walter *Kerr described her Rose as a "brassy, brazen witch on a mortgaged broomstick, a steamroller with cleats, the very mastodon of all stage mothers." Her last appearances were in a 1966 revival of *Annie Get Your Gun* and as a replacement in the lead of *Hello, Dolly!* Prior to her time, Broadway's leading ladies usually had been demure innocents. The dark-haired, brassy performer with perfect projection and impeccable diction changed the nature of heroines for many musicals, usually playing tougher, more knowing, and cynical figures. Autobiography: *Merman*, with George Eells, 1978.

MERRICK, David [né Margulois] (1911–2000), producer. One of Broadway's busiest, most successful, and most controversial showmen, he was born in St. Louis where he studied then practiced law. He served under Herman *Shumlin before producing his first success, *Fanny (1954), followed by many and varied successes: The *Matchmaker (1955), *Look Back in Anger (1957), The Entertainer (1958), The *World of Susie Wong (1958), La Plume de Ma Tante (1958), *Gypsy (1959), *Take Me Along (1959), A Taste of Honey (1960), Becket (1960), Irma La Douce (1960), *Carnival (1961), Stop the World!—I Want To Get Off (1962), *Oliver! (1963), *Hello, Dolly! (1964), *Cactus Flower (1965), Marat/Sade (1965), *Promises, Promises (1968), *Play It Again, Sam (1969), and *42nd Street (1981). In all he produced more than seventy plays, many of them importations of foreign hits. His methods of publicizing his plays often made front-page news. During the run of *Look Back in Anger*, he paid a woman to climb on stage and slap an actor. For an advertisement of one of his musicals to which the critics had been lukewarm, he found a group of men with the same names as the leading Broadway theatre critics and printed the nonprofessionals' more favorable remarks with their names subscribed. Merrick remained a colorful figure to the end, still making headlines with his last failed ventures *Oh Kay!* (1990) and *State Fair* (1996). Biography: Howard Kissell, *David Merrick: The Abominable Showman*, 1993.

MERRILL, Bob. See *Carnival*.

MERRILY WE ROLL ALONG (1934), a play by George S. *Kaufman and Moss *Hart. [*Music Box Theatre, 155 perf.] At a 1934 house party on his Long Island estate, the successful playwright Richard Niles (Kenneth MacKenna) has gathered together his friends and associates, many of whom are as successful as he is. But before long the principals are reliving the important moments of the past and realizing how bit by bit they sacrificed their integrity to achieve their goals. In a relentless, backward-moving chronology going as far back as 1916, they end up at the beginning: their college years when Richard admonished to be true to themselves. Although Brooks *Atkinson saw the work as a "resolute, mature-minded drama," many critics found the Sam H. *Harris production more noble in purpose than in execution. After a modest run in New York, the play was taken on the road, where it quickly folded. A 1981 musical version of the same title boasted a superb score by Stephen

*Sondheim but had such a problematic book (by George Furth) and misguided production (staged by Hal *Prince) that it closed after sixteen performances. The tale still went backward, following a songwriter-producer, a lyricist, and a failed novelist as they traveled from 1980 to the beginning of the story in 1955. The musical became a cult favorite and there were many productions regionally and in London where it was a hit. *Notable songs*: Not a Day Goes By; Old Friends; Good Thing Going; Our Time; Now You Know.

MERRY, Mrs. [née Anne Brunton] (1769?–1808), actress. The daughter of English actor John Brunton, she came to America in 1796 after her husband, Robert Merry, was adjudged a bankrupt and threatened with debtor's prison. She made her debut as Juliet at the *Chestnut Street Theatre, then immediately became the leading actress in Philadelphia, extending her fame to New York a year later as Belvidera in *Venice Preserved*. Among Merry's other great roles were such Shakespearean ladies as Katharine, Constance, and Imogen. She married Thomas *Wignell in 1803, but he died a few weeks later so she wed the first William *Warren in 1806. *Ireland wrote of her, "Her person was rather under size, but her figure was elegant, and her action and deportment graceful and easy. Without possessing great beauty of countenance, she had highly expressive features, and, with a fine, clear articulation, her sweetness of voice struck every ear like a charm." The dates of her American career virtually parallel those of her principal rival, Mrs. *Melmoth.

MERRY WIDOW, THE (1907). Operetta had all but passed from the American scene after the earlier great epochs of French opéra bouffe, English comic opera, and Middle-European operetta had died out in the late 1880s and early 1890s. Almost single-handedly, this Franz *Lehar operetta rekindled the mode for Viennese musicals, a vogue that lasted until World War I. Moreover, it set the fashion for operettas of the period, telling stories placed in real, contemporary locales and dealing with modern mores. Heretofore, as well as in later times, most operettas were set in distant eras and exotic, often imaginary, lands. Contemporaries perceived the best of the new school as more artful and mature than new American offerings of the time. Even more important was the softer, freeflowing music of this new school. From *The Merry Widow* came such perennial favorites as "Maxim's," "Vilja," and "The Merry Widow Waltz" ("I Love You So"). This last song is frequently credited with initiating the vogue for ballroom dancing that soon became known as "the dancing craze." The original New York stars of *The Merry Widow*, presented at the *New Amsterdam Theatre in 1907, were Donald *Brian and Ethel *Jackson. Revivals followed regularly, with the most notable coming in 1943 with Jan Kiepura and Marta Eggerth in the leading roles. Recently the work has entered the repertory of several American opera companies.

MERRY WIVES OF WINDSOR, THE. Shakespeare's comedy about Falstaff's misadventures seems to have been offered to Americans first at Philadelphia's *Southwark Theatre in 1770. Later it became one of J. H. *Hackett's showcases. It has remained fairly popular ever since, although recent major mountings have been confined to festival and regional theatres. Barnard *Hughes made a delightful Falstaff in Central Park in 1974 and Brian *Murray essayed the same role in the same park with success in 1994.

MERTON OF THE MOVIES (1922), a comedy by George S. *Kaufman and Marc *Connelly. [*Cort Theatre, 398 perf.] Merton Gill (Glenn *Hunter) is so film struck that he has become the joke of the tiny Illinois town of Simsbury. When his preoccupation causes him to neglect his duties as clerk in Amos Gashwiler's general store and get fired, Gill immediately heads for Hollywood, where he is befriended by "Flips" Montague (Florence Nash), a bathing beauty in a famous slapstick series. She lands him a small part in a film, but Gill is disillusioned by the crassness and deception all about him; however, he plods on. He is finally cast in a slapstick comedy, which he plays with such serious intensity that he becomes a star and marries "Flips." Based on Harry Leon *Wilson's series in the *Saturday Evening Post,* the play was generally acknowledged to be the 1920s' best spoof of Hollywood.

METAMORA; *or, The Last of the Wampanoags* (1829), a play John Augustus *Stone. [*Park Theatre, in repertory.] The great Indian chief Metamora (Edwin *Forrest) is determined not to forsake the land of his forebears but knows he fights a losing battle. He tells his wife, Nahmeokee (Mrs. Sharpe), "The power of dreams has been on me, and the shadows of things that are to be have passed over me. When our fires are no longer red, on the high places of our fathers; when the bones of our kindred make fruitful the fields of the stranger . . . then will the stranger spare, for we will be too small for his eye to see." Yet he is willing to save the life of a white woman, Oceana (Mrs. Hilson), and aid her romance with Horatio [in some texts, Walter] (Mr. *Barry). In the end, however, the white adversaries prove too much for the Native Americans, and Metamora dies fighting and cursing

them. Written in response to producer-star Forrest's offer of a prize for a new American play, the drama proved one of his most enduring vehicles and was scarcely ever out of his repertory. After Forrest's death, numerous other actors attempted the part, with only small success.

MIDDLE OF THE NIGHT (1956), a play by Paddy *Chayevsky. [ANTA Theatre, 477 perf.] When a rich, aging, and widowed Manufacturer (Edward G. *Robinson) falls in love with his young, newly divorced receptionist, their liaison is opposed on both sides: by the Mother (June *Walker) of the Girl (Gena Rowlands), and by the Manufacturer's Daughter (Anne *Jackson). Only his Son-in-Law (Martin *Balsam) seems sympathetic. The Girl returns briefly to her former Husband (Lee Philips), a coarse, oversexed musician, before the Manufacturer and the Girl reach an understanding. Originally produced as a shorter television play, the work was expanded into a Joshua *Logan production that divided the New York critics, some seeing it as a sensitive character study, others as soap opera. The magnificent, understated performance of Robinson was the main reason for the play's success.

MIDDLETON, George (1880–1967), playwright. Born in Paterson, New Jersey, he was the author of some twenty produced plays, the best remembered of which were written with Guy *Bolton: *Polly with a Past* (1917) and *Adam and Eva* (1919). Before these he wrote *Hit-the-Trail Holliday* with Bolton in 1915, although George M. *Cohan substantially rewrote it and took full credit when the play was produced. Middleton was a founder of the *Dramatists Guild. Autobiography: *These Things Are Mine,* 1947.

MIDSUMMER NIGHT'S DREAM, A. Shakespeare's fantastic comedy was first offered at the *Park Theatre in 1826. Its popularity in the 19th century was abetted by two landmark revivals: William *Burton's sumptuous production in 1854, with himself as Bottom, and *Daly's 1888 mounting with Ada *Rehan, John *Drew, Virginia Dreher, and Otis *Skinner as the lovers, and James *Lewis as Bottom. As with Burton's production, this revival was mounted with Victorian opulence, its elaborate settings the work of Henry *Hoyt. Many of the most memorable 20th-century presentations have been importations. The lavish *Old Vic revival in 1954 was on such a scale that it was presented not at a regular playhouse but at the Metropolitan Opera House. The noted dancers Robert Helpmann and Moira Shearer were Oberon and Titania, and Stanley Holloway was an engaging Bottom. By contrast the *Royal Shakespeare

Company offered Peter *Brook's austere and modern interpretation in 1971. One commentator noted, "The fairy tale was no longer ethereal, no more spirits with gauzy wings, but an intensely physical magic. Against Sally Jacobs's glaring white three-walled setting, the actors in their orange and purple robes were psychedelically present." The fantasy remains one of the most produced of Shakespeare's works in schools, regional theatre, and festivals. There have been at least two American musical versions of the tale: *Swingin' the Dream* (1939) with a jazzy Jimmy Van Heusen score and an all-black cast that included Louis Armstrong as Bottom, and the Off-Broadway offering *Babes in the Woods* (1964) by Rick Besoyan; both were quick failures.

MIELZINER, Jo (1901–76), designer. The leading scenic artist of his era, he was born in Paris but studied in America at the Pennsylvania Academy of Fine Arts and the National Academy of Design. His first professional work in the theatre was as both an actor and designer for Jessie *Bonstelle in Detroit and as an actor and stage manager for the *Theatre Guild before creating the sets for their 1924 production of *The Guardsman*. Between then and his death, Mielziner designed the scenery, and usually the lighting, for more than four hundred Broadway plays. The word most often employed to describe his best work was "poetic." He abandoned, especially in his later years, the detailed realism that was still in vogue when he began, as well as the fashionable expressionistic turn of such men as Robert Edmond *Jones. Instead, he perfected the art of suggestive, skeletonized settings, evocatively lit. A complete list of even his finest work would include virtually all the best plays and some of the most successful musicals for the fifty years he was active, particularly after 1930. Representative of his work were his settings for *Strange Interlude* (1928), *Street Scene* (1929), *Of Thee I Sing* (1931), *Winterset* (1935), *On Your Toes* (1936), *Abe Lincoln in Illinois* (1938), *Pal Joey* (1940), The *Glass Menagerie* (1945), *Annie Get Your Gun* (1946), A *Streetcar Named Desire* (1947), *Mister Roberts* (1948), *Death of a Salesman* (1949), *South Pacific* (1949), *Guys and Dolls* (1950), The *King and I* (1951), *Tea and Sympathy* (1953), *Cat on a Hot Tin Roof* (1955), *Gypsy* (1959), and *1776* (1969). Writing of his work for *Winterset*, John Mason *Brown noted, "In his visualization of the bridge, Mr. Mielziner has provided *Winterset* with one of the finest backgrounds our contemporary theatre has seen. It is a setting of great majesty and beauty, and alive with a poetry of its own . . . simple, direct and impressive." Biography: *Mielziner: Master of Modern Stage Design*, Mary C. Henderson, 2001.

MIGHTY DOLLAR, THE (1875), a play by Benjamin E. *Woolf. [*Park Theatre, 104 perf.] The most famous salon in Washington is appropriately named Grabmoor, for it is here that the leading wheelers and dealers come to contrive arrangements that will allow them to pile up the mighty dollar. They stop their greedy machinations for a few moments to help a newly married lady, Clara Dart (Maude *Granger), when she is bothered by a former suitor, but the money grubbing continues the moment she leaves. Prominent among the figures at Grabmoor are the not particularly ethical Congressman, the Hon. Bardwell Slote (W. J. *Florence), and Mrs. General Gilflory (Mrs. Florence). Slote is given to qualifying his statements with "not by a large majority," and dropping such abbreviations as B. O. T. and P. D. Q., which he later explains mean "bully old time" and "pretty darn quick." The upstart Mrs. Gilflory has her own pet phrases to show off her learning, most notably "from Alpha to Omaha." Assailed by critics as vulgar and formless, the comedy nevertheless gave the Florences their most enduring success and added the colorful character of Slote to the body of dramatic literature.

MIKADO, THE (1885). *Gilbert and *Sullivan's comic opera about the preposterous carryings-on in the mythical Japanese village of Titipu won favor with Americans from its first major New York performance at the *Fifth Avenue Theatre in 1885 for a run of 250 performances. The cast included Courtice Pounds as Nanki-Poo and Geraldine Ulmar as Yum-Yum. Actually, the New York premiere had taken place a month earlier in an unauthorized production by Sydney *Rosenfeld at the *Union Square Theatre. An injunction was obtained and the mounting was withdrawn after its initial performance. The comic operetta has been revived a number of times, including a fine resurrection by Winthrop *Ames in 1927 that ran 150 performances. The work is also a favorite with amateur theatre groups, summer theatres, and schools. In 1939 it was the source of two jazzy black versions: *The Swing Mikado* and *The Hot Mikado*.

MILLER, Arthur (b. 1915), playwright. The New York–born dramatist studied at the University of Michigan, where he was a winner of the Avery Hopwood Award for playwriting. His first play to be produced was the short-lived *The Man Who Had All the Luck* (1944), but his subsequent dramas *All My Sons* (1947) and *Death of a Salesman* (1949) were widely lauded and continue to be frequently revived. Miller's version of *Ibsen's *An Enemy of the People* (1950) received a mixed reaction, as did his tale of the Salem witch hunt, The *Crucible* (1953), which many saw as a thinly veiled indictment of

McCarthyism. But the latter has proven to be one of the playwright's most respected and produced works. Miller's plays thereafter have been greeted with more interest than enthusiasm, yet each one contains elements of superb playwriting: the double bill of A *View from the Bridge and A Memory of Two Mondays (1955), the semiautobiographical *After the Fall (1964), the political Incident at Vichy (1964), the domestic drama The *Price (1968), the biblical comedy The Creation of the World and Other Business (1972), the Great Depression panorama The American Clock (1980), the psychological drama Broken Glass (1994), the probing The Ride Down Mt. Morgan (1998), and others. Miller began as a firmly committed leftist, whose political philosophizing sometimes got the better of his dramaturgy. However, at his best he is a master of creating potent situations, interesting characters, and powerful ideas. Autobiography: Timebends, 1987.

MILLER, Gilbert [Heron] (1884–1969), producer. The son of Henry *Miller, he was born in New York and worked for some years as an actor before presenting his first productions in London. In short order Miller became as active and important as he soon was to be in New York. Curiously, with a few exceptions, he rarely produced the same plays in both theatre centers. His New York offerings included The Constant Wife (1926), Journey's End (1929), *Berkeley Square (1929), *Tomorrow and Tomorrow (1931), The *Animal Kingdom (1932), The *Petrified Forest (1935), Victoria Regina (1935), Tovarich (1936), *Harriet (1943), Edward, My Son (1948), The *Cocktail Party (1950), the 1951 *Olivier-Leigh double bill of *Antony and Cleopatra and *Caesar and Cleopatra, and Witness for the Prosecution (1954).

MILLER, [John] Henry (1859–1926), actor and manager. Born in England, he was brought to Canada at the age of fourteen and determined to become an actor shortly thereafter, when he witnessed a performance of *Across the Continent with Oliver Doud *Byron. Joining a stock company in Toronto, he made his debut in a bit part in Amy Robsart in 1877. Miller's first New York appearance came three years later as Arviragus opposite Adelaide *Neilson in Cymbeline. He soon rose to leading roles first under Daniel *Frohman and then with Charles *Frohman at the *Empire Theatre, then left in 1897 to become a star in his own right as the brilliant composer Eric Temple in Heartsease. Subsequent successes came as Sidney Carton in The Only Way (1899), Richard Savage (1901), and Dick Dudgeon in The *Devil's Disciple (1903). In 1905 Miller took over the *Princess Theatre, where he produced and directed *Zira, which he co-authored with J. Hartley *Manners. The next year he presented The *Great Divide, assuming the role of

Stephen Ghent, and in 1910 he produced, directed, and starred in The *Faith Healer. Among his most important later roles were Neil Summer in The Rainbow (1912) and Jeffrey Fair in The *Famous Mrs. Fair (1919). Miller produced and directed numerous other popular successes, notably The *Servant in the House (1908), *Daddy Long Legs (1914), and *Come Out of the Kitchen (1916), frequently assuming leading roles in these productions during their runs, and in 1918 he built his own Broadway theatre. He was a handsome, slightly stocky man, much respected for his versatility, but also feared for his famous explosive temper. Biography: Backstage with Henry Miller, Frank P. Morse, 1938.

MILLER, Jason. See That Championship Season.

MILLER, Joaquin. See Danites, The.

MILLER, Marilyn [née Marilynn Reynolds] (1898–1936), actress, singer, and dancer. The unquestioned queen of Broadway musical comedy in the 1920s, the tiny, delicate-featured blonde beauty was only five years old when she became a member of her family's vaudeville act. She toured the world in variety for ten years before Lee *Shubert discovered her in London in 1913. Miller appeared for the Shuberts in the 1914 and 1915 editions of The *Passing Show as well as in The Show of Wonders (1916) and Fancy Free (1918), but it was Florenz *Ziegfeld who made her a star after she performed in his *Ziegfeld Follies of 1918. Except for a brief, unsuccessful attempt at *Peter Pan (1924), under the aegis of Charles *Dillingham, she spent the entire decade of the 1920s starring in Ziegfeld or Dillingham musicals: *Sally (1920), *Sunny (1925), Rosalie (1928), and Smiles (1930). Miller also starred in the revue *As Thousands Cheer (1933) before her premature death. A competent actress and singer, she was most admired for her Dresden china beauty and for her airy, traditional dancing. Her biographer disputes the generally accepted idea that her real name was Mary Ellen and insists that her given name, with its spelling modified, was the first use of a name which has since become common. Biography: The Other Marilyn, Warren G. Harris, 1985.

MILLS, Florence (1895–1927), singer. The charismatic African-American performer who became almost a legend in her own short life, with her sparkling eyes, torchy voice, and graceful stepping, was born in Washington and began performing at the age of four. Her Broadway appearances were in *Shuffle Along (1921), Plantation Revue (1922), *Greenwich Village Follies (1923), and Dixie to Broadway (1924), in which she sang "I'm a Little Blackbird Looking for a Bluebird."

MILTON [Davidor], **Robert** (1885–1956), director. Born in Russia, but brought to America while still a child, he started his theatrical career as an actor and eventually as assistant director with Richard *Mansfield, then worked for a time under Mrs. *Fiske and William *Harris. Among the shows he later directed were *The Cinderella Man* (1916), **Oh, Lady! Lady!* (1918), **Friendly Enemies* (1918), *The Charm School* (1920), *He Who Gets Slapped* (1922), **You and I* (1923), *The Youngest* (1924), *Outward Bound* (1924), *The *Enemy* (1925), *Bride of the Lamb* (1926), **Peggy Ann* (1926), and *Here Come the Clowns* (1938). Milton was an early advocate of the Stanislavsky method, and when staging nonmusicals insisted his performers create their own imaginary biographies for the characters they were playing.

MILWAUKEE REPERTORY THEATRE. An ever-growing theatre company that has moved to larger quarters on three occasions, it was founded by Mary Widrig John in 1954 as the Fred Miller Theatre Company, housed in a converted Milwaukee, Wisconsin, movie house. The space was home to the *Association of Producing Artists and the *American Conservatory Theatre for a time before Milwaukee's own resident company was established in 1964. Under such artistic directors as Tunc Yalman, Nagle Jackson, and John Dillon, the company expanded its programs and moved to the Todd Wehr Theatre in Milwaukee's Performing Arts Center, also presenting plays at the Court Street Theatre and the *Pabst Theatre on occasion. Another move was made to its current home on the east bank of the Milwaukee River: the Patty and Jay Baker Center, a converted power plant that houses the 720-seat Quadracci Powerhouse Theatre, the 218-seat Stiemke Theatre, and the 118-seat Stackner Cabaret. Under Dillon, original works were encouraged, most memorably the premieres of Larry *Shue's three plays, *The *Foreigner*, *The Nerd*, and *Wenceslas Square*.

MIME IN AMERICAN THEATRE. Mime has never played an important role in the mainstream of American theatre, and virtually all the successful mime presentations on Broadway or in other major theatrical centers have emanated from Europe. Notable examples have been Max *Reinhardt's German spectacle, *Sumurun* (1912); the visits, beginning in the 1950s, of Marcel Marceau; and the 1,326-performance run of a Swiss mime troupe Mummenschanz, between 1977 and 1980. Mime in these instances should not be confused with English-style pantomime, which flourished in America only during the lifetime of G. L. *Fox. America's only notable mime to make an impact on the theatre is Bill *Irwin whose delightful unspoken theatre pieces, such as *The Regard of Flight* (1982), *Largely New York* (1989), and *Fool Moon* (1993), push the parameters of mime a bit but have endeared many to the old art form.

MINER, Henry Clay (1842–1900), manager. The son of a noted New York civil engineer, he studied to be a pharmacist, but after serving in the Civil War chose instead careers in the theatre and politics. He became an advance agent for several performers, notably William "Buffalo Bill" *Cody, and then in 1875 began to lease and build vaudeville houses. In 1895 he attempted unsuccessfully to form a national syndicate with J. H. *McVicker and others. Miner is credited with originating "amateur nights," and his son Tom is thought to have been the first to use a hook to pull recalcitrant performers off the stage. Besides his theatres and political interests, he owned a chain of drugstores, a theatrical cosmetics firm, and was a partner in mining endeavors.

MINNELLI, Liza [May] (b. 1946), singer and actress. The daughter of Vincente *Minnelli and film star Judy Garland, she was born in Los Angeles and made her New York debut in a 1963 Off-Broadway revival of *Best Foot Forward*. She later starred as the naive artist Flora in *Flora, the Red Menace* (1965), the Las Vegas entertainer Michele Craig in *The Act* (1977), and the estranged daughter Angel in *The Rink* (1984). The film and recording star has also appeared on Broadway in concerts and as replacements during the runs of *Chicago* and *Victor/Victoria*. Widely popular, Minnelli exudes a sense of intimacy and vulnerability even in the largest venues.

MINNELLI, Vincente (1903–86), designer and director. For a brief time in the 1930s, the Chicago native was one of Broadway's most imaginative artists. His first designs were seen in the 1931 edition of the **Earl Carroll Vanities* and *The Du Barry* (1932). Subsequently he both designed and staged *At Home Abroad* (1935), *The Show Is On* (1936), *Hooray for What!* (1937), and *Very Warm for May* (1939). Minnelli also designed, but did not direct, the **Ziegfeld Follies of 1936*. His designs were known for their tasteful, if slightly exaggerated use of color. He later became a major director of musical films. Autobiography: *I Remember It Well*, 1974.

MINSKOFF THEATRE (New York). Standing on the site of the old Astor Hotel on Broadway, the 1,620-seat Minskoff is part of an office-building complex that opened in 1973. The design by Robert Allan Jacobs has the auditorium thirty-five feet above street level with escalators leading to a grand foyer and plenty of lobby space. The theatre was built by developer Jerome Minskoff who co-owns it with the *Nederlanders. The modern theatre opened with a hit revival of *Irene starring Debbie Reynolds, and musicals have continued to be the venue's primary tenants.

MINSTREL SHOWS. Although blackface performers, often billed as "Ethiopian" entertainers, had been growing in popularity for a decade, it was the 1843 appearance at the Bowery Amphitheatre of Dan Emmett, Billy Whitlock, Frank Pelham, and Frank Brower as the Virginia Minstrels that is generally allowed to have ushered in the era of American minstrelsy. The popularity of this new form of entertainment was so quick to sweep the nation that within a year a band called the Ethiopian Serenaders was performing at the White House, and other groups followed them there through succeeding administrations until shortly before the Civil War. These early groups were small, usually four to eight men, and their entertainment essentially musical. They were also in marked contrast to the formal, often imported attractions at regular theatres. In his excellent study of minstrelsy, *Blacking Up* (1974), Robert C. Toll noted that for the first time "the vitality and vigor of the folk" was brought into popular culture, adding, "It was immediate, unpretentious, and direct. It had no characterization to develop, no plot to evolve, no musical score, no set speeches, no subsidiary dialogue—indeed, no fixed script at all. Each act—song, dance, joke, or skit—was a self-contained performance that strived to be a highlight of the show." Toll also credits minstrelsy with introducing a sense of fast pacing hitherto unknown on the American stage, and which played no small part in the later development of musical theatre. A certain formality soon crept in so that early minstrel shows quickly displayed a somewhat standard two-part form, the first offering the minstrels' celebrated semicircle, with one end manned by a comic called Mr. Bones clacking an appropriate set of bones, and the other end manned by another comic called Mr. Tambo, wielding a tambourine. At the center was a master of ceremonies known as the interlocutor. For many the great attraction of this section was the balladeer. The second part was a freewheeling olio, much like prototypical vaudeville. Stump speeches constituted a popular part of this segment. Comedy sketches, often of plantation life or spoofing contemporary events and plays, were another feature of this part and with time became so important that many students see them as a third, separate section.

From the start minstrelsy helped perpetuate the stereotype of the black slave: lazy, dumbly guileful, noisy, flashily garbed, but essentially happy. Make-up exaggerated the stereotype, the blackface not resembling any real Negroid features. As early as the 1850s some African-American performers created their own minstrel shows and performed mainly for abolitionist groups. Troupes such as the Luca Family and Callendar's Georgia Minstrels were very popular during the Civil War but were taken over by white managements by the 1870s. As minstrel competition developed, the intimacy of the first shows gave way to gargantuan spectacles often featuring dozens of performers. By this time, however, the popularity of minstrelsy was waning, with vaudeville, comic opera, and musical comedy coming to replace it in the public's affection. While the shows moved away from their original emphasis on music toward an emphasis on comedy, they gave theatregoers the first enduring songs to come from American theatre. *Emmett's "Dixie" jumps to mind at once, but it should be remembered that Stephen *Foster was one of many contemporary popular composers to write actively for the minstrel stage. Laurence *Hutton suggests that while minstrels did not invent the banjo, they were its prime developers and were responsible for the instrument's long popularity. Among the great names of minstrelsy were Dan Bryant, Emmett, E. P. and George N. Christy, Lew Dockstader, "Honey Boy" Evans, J. H. Haverly, Eph Horn, Francis *Leon, and Eddie Leonard and such bands as Buckley's Serenaders, Bryant's Minstrels, [the original] Christy Minstrels, Ordway's Aeolians, the San Francisco Minstrels, and Wood's Minstrels.

By the 1880s the vogue of minstrelsy had largely disappeared. It remained alive only in a few cities, notably Philadelphia, where Sanford's Minstrels, John L. Carncross, and Dumont's Minstrels kept the tradition alive well into the 20th century. Many great performers, such as Francis *Wilson and Al *Jolson, spent part of their early careers with minstrel companies, although their fame came elsewhere.

MIRACLE WORKER, THE (1959), a play by William *Gibson. [Playhouse, 719 perf.] Having graduated from Boston's Perkins Institute for the Blind, Annie Sullivan (Anne *Bancroft) arrives at the Alabama home of Captain Keller (Torin Thatcher) to become a teacher-companion for his daughter Helen (Patty Duke), who is deaf, dumb, and blind, and also an undisciplined but iron-willed youngster. It requires all of Annie's persistence, and sometimes a touch of savagery, to begin to bring the girl around. Not until Helen is purposely drenched and manages to spell out the word "water" does Annie realize she has reached the girl. A friendship slowly develops that will in part release Helen from her lonely, dark world. The play was based on Gibson's earlier television version, which in turn had been derived from the true story of the Sullivan-Keller relationship. Robert Coleman of the *Daily Mirror* wrote, "Gibson's words are terse and eloquent, highly dramatic, but it is the frightening, harrowing, physical conflicts of his drama that terrify and grip you." Gibson's sequel *Monday After the Miracle* (1982), about the later years of Annie and Helen, was commended by some of the critics but failed to find an audience. The original play, on the other hand, remains one of the most-produced dramas by schools and amateur theatre groups.

MISS LULU BETT (1920), a play by Zona Gale. [Belmont Theatre, 201 perf.; Pulitzer Prize.] Lulu Bett (Carroll McComas) is a drudge in the home of her sister Ina (Catherine Calhoun Doucet) and brother-in-law, Dwight Deacon (William E. Holden). When Dwight's brother Ninian (Brigham Royce) visits, he jokingly flirts with Lulu. Dwight reads the civil marriage ceremony, and Lulu and Ninian respond accordingly, before Dwight realizes that he has inadvertently married them. The newlyweds go off on a honeymoon, from which Lulu returns after she learns that Ninian is already married. But Ninian follows her with assurances that his first wife has died. Based by the author on her own novel of the same name, the Brock *Pemberton production was perceived as an observant, warmly written drama of midwestern life of the time. **Zona GALE** (1874–1938) was born in Portage, Wisconsin, and educated at the University of Wisconsin. She became best known as a novelist, although she was also the author of several respected dramas, none as successful as *Miss Lulu Bett*. *The Neighbors* (1917) and *Mr. Pitt* (1924) were presented in New York, but the others were produced by amateur groups and never reached Broadway. Biography: *Still Small Voice*, August W. Delreth, 1940.

MISS SAIGON (1991). The London musical import, which updated *Madame Butterfly* to the final days of the Viet Nam War, boasted a mammoth production directed by Nicholas *Hytner and designed by John *Napier, highlighted by a spectacular scene in which a helicopter descended from above to pick up the remaining Americans during the fall of Saigon. Lea Salonga was Kim, the orphan-prostitute who falls in love with a G.I. (Willy Falk), bears his child, and years later kills herself so that the boy can go to the States with his father. The events were tied together by the Engineer (Jonathan Pryce), a conniving Eurasian who manipulates the main characters for his own benefit. *Notable songs*: The Last Night of the World; The Movie in My Mind; Why God, Why?; The American Dream. Richard Maltby Jr. adapted Alain Boublil's French book and lyrics, Claude-Michel Schonberg wrote the music, and it opened at the *Broadway Theatre for a run of 4,097 performances. The highly publicized show was given more press coverage right before opening when producer Cameron *MacKintosh threatened to cancel the production and return the $25 million in advance sales if *Actors Equity did not allow Pryce to re-create his London performance in New York. Mackintosh won, Pryce received a *Tony, and the musical was a giant hit. **Richard MALTBY JR.** (b. 1937) was born in Ripon, Wisconsin, the son of a well-known orchestra leader, and educated at Yale where he met his composer-collaborator David Shire. The team would score such musicals as *Starting Here, Starting Now* (1977), *Closer Than Ever* (1989), *Baby* (1983), and *Big* (1996). Maltby also conceived and directed the popular revue *Ain't Misbehavin'* (1978) and adapted the lyrics for *Song and Dance* (1985).

MISSOURI REPERTORY THEATRE (Kansas City). Begun by Dr. Patricia McIlrath in 1964 as a summer theatre presented by the University of Missouri–Kansas City (UMKC), the company became a full-time producer of plays in 1977. Two years later the group moved into the 733-seat Helen F. Spenser Theatre on the UMKC campus but became a separate entity, although the academic professional training program in theatre is closely associated with the university. In addition to its usual schedule of revivals and some new works, the company has been touring longer than any other professional regional theatre.

MISTER ROBERTS (1948), a play by Thomas Heggen and Joshua *Logan. [Alvin Theatre, 1,157 perf.] Lt. Douglas Roberts (Henry *Fonda) has long served the bored, unhappy crewmen of a navy cargo ship as a buffer between themselves and the cantankerous, unsympathetic Captain Morton (William *Harrigan) who seems more interested in his palm tree than in his men. The crew often releases its frustrations in mischief, such as the time Ensign Pulver (David *Wayne) attempts to blow up the Captain's quarters but blows up the laundry instead. The Captain has regularly refused Roberts's plea for a transfer, but Roberts finally succeeds, only to be killed in action. News of his death prompts the crew to move more forcefully against the Captain. Taking his own action, Ensign Pulver knocks on the Captain's door and announces, "I just threw your palm tree overboard. Now what's all this crap about no movie tonight?" Based on Heggen's novel, the Leland *Hayward production was one of the most popular plays about World War II and afforded Fonda his best (and longest) Broadway stint.

MISTRESS NELL (1900), a play by George C. Hazelton. [Bijou Theatre, 104 perf.] Nell Gwynne (Henrietta *Crossman) is an orange-vendor-turned-actress who has become the mistress of Charles II (Aubrey *Boucicault). The Duke of Buckingham (Geoffrey Stein), the king's rival for Nell's favors, and the Duchess of Portsmouth (Adelaide Fitz Allan), Nell's rival for the King's attentions, conspire to destroy her at the same time they attempt to put England under French dominion. Nell disguises herself as a man and manages to foil their treachery. The costume melodrama was one of the many romantic swashbucklers so tremendously popular at the turn of the century. Born in Boscobel, Wisconsin, **George C[ochrane] HAZELTON** (1868?–1921) was an actor and playwright, perhaps best remembered for his collaboration on *The *Yellow Jacket* (1912).

MITCHELL, Brian Stokes (b. 1957), actor and singer. The dashing African-American baritone was born in Seattle and grew up in Navy bases in Guam and the Philippines. Mitchell made his New York legitimate theatre debut in 1986 and became a Broadway star with his passionate performance as the piano player-turned-radical Coalhouse Walker in *Ragtime* (1998), then showed a lighter side of his talents as the boastful Petruchio in *Kiss Me, Kate* (1999). Mitchell was also lauded for his performances as the ex-con King in *King Hedley* (2001) and Cervantes's Don Quixote in *Man of La Mancha* (2002). He is an old-style musical theatre star in that he may be the focal point of the production but he approaches each role as a distinct character with no recurring characteristic flourishes.

MITCHELL, David (b. 1932), scenic designer. The much-awarded artist is known for his stark and intriguing sets for the *New York Shakespeare Festival as well as for several spectacular Broadway musicals. He was born in Honesdale, Pennsylvania, and was educated at Penn State University and Boston University before making his Manhattan debut with *Henry V* (1965) in Central Park. His other credits include *The *Basic Training of Pavlo Hummel* (1971), *Barnum* (1971), *Short Eyes* (1974), *Annie* (1977), *La Cage aux Folles* (1983), *Tru* (1989), and *Dream* (1997).

MITCHELL, Grant (1874–1957), actor. Born in Columbus, Ohio, he studied at Yale and at Harvard Law School, then both practiced law and served as a newspaperman before making a late decision to become an actor. After attending the *American Academy of Dramatic Arts, Mitchell made his debut in 1902 playing opposite Richard *Mansfield in *Julius Caesar.* He soon became a popular performer, most admired for his work in fast-paced comedies of the time. At his height, the actor, who bore a resemblance to the later James Cagney, won applause for such parts as business rival Rodney Martin in *It Pays to Advertise* (1914) and the dapper dresser John Paul Bart in A *Tailor-Made Man* (1917). Within a few years, however, Mitchell was reduced to prominent supporting roles, so with the coming of sound films he left for Hollywood.

MITCHELL, Julian (1854–1926), director. Probably the most prolific stager of musicals in Broadway's history, he started his career as a dancer at *Niblo's Garden. In 1884 he became Charles *Hoyt's principal director and staged many of Hoyt's later plays, including A *Trip to Chinatown* (1891). With Hoyt he learned the art of fast, fluid pacing that characterized his best work. Mitchell then moved to *Weber and *Fields, where he was often credited with establishing that team's celebrated chorus line of beauties. In 1903 he directed two of the year's biggest musical hits, The *Wizard of Oz* and *Babes in Toyland*. Florenz *Ziegfeld hired him to help stage the first *Ziegfeld Follies* in 1907, and he eventually helped mount eight more of them. Mitchell's work was also seen in The *Fortune Teller* (1898), *It Happened in Nordland* (1904), *Miss Innocence* (1908), The *Pink Lady* (1911), *Mary* (1920), *The Perfect Fool* (1921), and *Sunny* (1925). In all he staged more than eighty musicals, although in his later years he was virtually deaf.

MITCHELL, Langdon [Elwyn] (1862–1935), playwright. The son of the famous Philadelphia physician and novelist, S. Weir Mitchell, he received much of his education abroad but returned to study law at Harvard and Columbia and in 1886 was admitted to the New York bar. A year later his first play, the romantic tragedy *Sylvian*, was produced and failed, but he gave up the law all the same and continued to write plays, many of which were dramatizations of novels, such as *Becky Sharp* (1899) from *Vanity Fair, The Adventures of François* (1900), *The Kreutzer Sonata* (1906), and *Major Pendennis* (1916) from Thackeray. Only one of Mitchell's original plays is significant, but it remains one of the classic social satires of American stage literature, The *New York Idea* (1906). In 1928 he became the first Professor of Playwriting at the University of Pennsylvania.

MITCHELL, [Margaret Julia] Maggie (1832–1918), actress. Although the tiny, curly-haired, spritelike New Yorker is said to have been on stage from the time she was a child, the earliest record of her performing is as Julia in *The Soldier's Daughter* in 1851. She subsequently became a favorite at the Bowery, where she played the title role of *Oliver Twist*, and at Burton's. However, Mitchell's greatest success was as *Fanchon, the Cricket* (1862); her acting of the piquant country girl, including her famous shadow dance, made her an overnight star. Although critics were later to praise her Jane Eyre, Mignon, Pauline in *The *Lady of Lyons*, and Parthenia in *Ingomar*, it was her Fanchon that the public demanded and to which she continually returned for the next twenty-five years. Her nephew was director Julian *Mitchell.

MITCHELL, Thomas (1895–1962), character actor. Born in Elizabeth, New Jersey, he made his debut in Ben *Greet's company in 1913 and then played Shakespeare roles under the aegis of Charles *Coburn. His best early performances were dreamer Charles Bemis in *The *Wisdom Tooth* (1926) and Norman Overback in *Little Accident* (1928), which he co-authored. After a long career in films, Mitchell enjoyed success in the title role of *An Inspector Calls* (1947), as Willy Loman in the road company of *Death of a Salesman*, and in the musical *Hazel Flagg* (1953).

MITZI. See Hajos, Mitzi.

MITZI E. NEWHOUSE THEATRE (New York). The 299-seat performance space housed in the same building as the larger *Vivian Beaumont Theatre is *Lincoln Center's Off-Broadway venue. Architect Eero Saarinen and scenic designer Jo *Mielziner designed the two theatres as nontraditional playhouses, and this more intimate, thrust-stage auditorium is considered the better of the two spaces. Called the Forum Theatre when it opened in 1965, it was intended for experimental productions but for much of its early history it sat empty while financial and management problems reduced it to storage space. The Forum was renamed in 1973 after the donor Mrs. Samuel I. Newhouse and under Joseph *Papp's management, it saw some powerful productions, such as *Streamers* (1976). The little playhouse found new life again in 1986 when theatre at Lincoln Center was revitalized, and several memorable productions have been presented at the Newhouse since.

MIZNER, Wilson (1876–1933), playwright. The once famous, if controversial wit, was born in Bernicia, California, and had at one time or another hustled for a medicine show, been a professional cardsharp, and managed a celebrated prizefighter, before making his playwriting debut with *The Only Law* (1909), written with George Bronson

Howard. The play failed to run, but he later enjoyed some success when he collaborated with Paul *Armstrong on *The Deep Purple* (1911) and *The Greyhound* (1912). Mizner also claimed to have been Armstrong's collaborator on *Alias Jimmy Valentine* (1910), and his biographer states he did receive some program credit. He and his brother Addison Mizner were the subject of the Stephen *Sondheim musical *Bounce*. Biography: *Rogue's Progress*, John Burke, 1975.

M'LISS (1878), a play by Clay *Greene. [*Niblo's Garden, 16 perf.] M'liss (Kate Mayhew) is "the waif of the Sierras," a bright, attractive young hoyden who has been neglected by her drunken miner father. She is spunky enough to fight off ruffians who would attack the young man she loves, and also to win him away from a more sophisticated lady—"the pink and white thing"— in whom he seems all too interested. The play, based on a Bret Harte story, was produced in New York after Mayhew won an injunction preventing Annie *Pixley from presenting her production of the work. The victory was short-lived, for the injunction was soon lifted and it was Pixley who afterward was identified with the part and toured in it for many years. There is some question as to whether Greene wrote the version Miss Mayhew employed. Pixley's version was sometimes billed as *M'liss, the Child of the Sierras*.

MLLE. MODISTE (1905), an operetta by Henry *Blossom (book, lyrics), Victor *Herbert (music). [Knickerbocker Theatre, 202 perf.] Fifi (Fritzi *Scheff), a salesgirl in a hat shop, and Capt. Etienne de Bouvray (Walter Percival) are in love, but the romance is opposed by both Fifi's employer and by Etienne's rich, determined uncle, the Compte de St. Mar (William Pruette). An American, Hiram Bent (Claude Gillingwater), stumbles into the shop and takes a liking to the girl. She tells him of her ambition to become a singer and performs for him, so Bent agrees to pay for her schooling. A year later the stubborn Count holds a fete at which one Mme. Bellini wins applause for her fine singing. When the count learns she is none other than Fifi, he withdraws his objections to the match. *Notable songs*: The Time and the Place and the Girl; Kiss Me Again; The Mascot of the Troop; I Want What I Want When I Want It. Many critics considered this Charles *Dillingham offering the finest American musical written up to its time, admiring its solidly constructed, humorous book and its superb score, which "fit the story like a glove."

MODJESKA, Helena [née Opid] (1840–1909), actress. Born in Cracow, the daughter of a humble teacher and musician, she became a child actress in her native city, where her half brother was already a popular performer. Shortly thereafter she married a man twenty years her senior; the marriage was short-lived but, with slight respelling, it gave her her stage name. She next married a Polish aristocrat, fled with him to America when their radical political views became known, and settled in California. A need for funds forced the actress to master English quickly and return to the stage. Her debut at San Francisco's *California Theatre in 1877 as Adrienne Lecouvreur marked Modjeska as an important newcomer, and she quickly consolidated her reputation with her Ophelia, Juliet, and Camille. She returned to Adrienne Lecouvreur for her New York debut later the same year and for the next twenty-eight seasons, despite a slight paralytic stroke in 1897, her career was a series of triumphs, becoming one of the most respected and beloved of all American performers. Among her other noteworthy roles were Magda, Frou-Frou, Mary Stuart, and such Shakespearean ladies as Rosalind, Viola, Lady Macbeth, and Isabella. William *Winter admired her for "her slender, graceful figure, her pensive countenance, her sympathetic voice, her air of soft bewilderment, and her handsome dress." Otis *Skinner sounded a different note, recollecting, "The dominant characteristics of her acting were eagerness and joy . . . a joy restrained and admirable in execution; the great joy of artistry." Modjeska also was respected for the warm encouragement she gave to promising young talent. Autobiography: *Memories and Impressions of Helena Modjeska*, 1910.

MOELLER, Philip (1880–1958), director and producer. The native New Yorker was educated at New York University and Columbia before cofounding the *Washington Square Players, where he directed several productions. After that group disbanded, Moeller served in similar capacities for the *Theatre Guild. Among the many Guild plays he staged were *The Guardsman* (1924), *They Knew What They Wanted* (1924), *Ned McCobb's Daughter* (1926), The *Second Man* (1927), *Strange Interlude* (1928), *Dynamo* (1929), *Hotel Universe* (1930), *Elizabeth the Queen* (1930), *Mourning Becomes Electra* (1931), *Biography* (1932), *Ah, Wilderness!* (1933), and *End of Summer* (1936). He called himself an "inspirational" director, preferring to let himself and his actors improvise as they rehearsed. Theresa *Helburn has written, "His timing was brilliant and in comedy he was unequaled. But he had his blind spots. We used to say rather wistfully that it would be nice if Phil would read a play before he produced it."

MOGULESKO, [Zelig] Sigmund (1858?–1914), comic actor. The bantam, droll comedian was born in Romania and was established as a popular favorite there and on other European Yiddish stages before he arrived in America in 1886. He immediately became the premier Yiddish comedian of his generation. Typical of Mogulesko's virtuosity was his New York debut in *Coquettish Ladies*, in which he played a different part in each act: a young pimp, an old drunk, and a gossipy lady matchmaker. His acting was scarcely realistic, but exaggerated in the fashion of the Yiddish stage. Nonetheless, Abraham Cahan, the well-known Jewish publisher and historian, wrote, "A born genius he was, and his personality was as marvelous as his art. His talent and charm lit that foolish play with rays of divine fire. He bewitched us with his singing and his acting alike."

MOLINEUX, Roland Burnham (1866–1917), playwright. Possibly the only American convicted of murder to have a play produced on Broadway, he was arrested for having sent a bottle of poisoned Bromo-Seltzer to the manager of the Knickerbocker Athletic Club after an argument. The manager's cousin took some and died. After two mistrials Molineux was found guilty, but the verdict was appealed, and he was acquitted in a retrial after three years in prison. He then wrote books as well as a play, *The Man Inside* (1913) about political corruption and the drug trade. The play was produced by David *Belasco, but was only moderately successful. Tensions related to the production apparently proved too much for the author, for shortly after the play closed he was committed to an insane asylum where he died four years later.

MOLNAR, Ferenc (1878–1952), playwright. The versatile Hungarian dramatist, as skilled at romantic fantasy as at high comedy, came to American playgoers' attention when his early play, *The Devil* (1908), opened at two Broadway theatres on the same night. (The production with George *Arliss was by far the more successful.) Unlike many foreign dramatists, Molnar was exceptionally fortunate in the excellent translations and mountings given his plays in America. Leo *Ditrichstein starred in Belasco's version of *The Phantom Lover* (1914), Eva *Le Gallienne and Joseph *Schildkraut headed the *Theatre Guild's *Liliom* (1921), Le Gallienne also took the central role in *The Swan* (1923), the Guild staged *The Guardsman* (1924) with the *Lunts as stars, while Holbrook *Blinn headed a fine cast in *The Play's the Thing* (1926). Many other of his plays were also well received, and several of his best have had major revivals, notably *The Play's the Thing*, which saw reputable New York productions in 1948, 1973, 1978, and 1995. Molnar's works have also lent themselves to musical versions, *The Phantom Lover* becoming *The Love Letter* (1921) and *Liliom* being made into **Carousel* (1945).

MONTAGUE, H[enry] J[ames] [né Mann] (1844–78), actor. This late 19th-century Valentino was born in England and had made a name for himself in T. W. *Robertson comedies in London before Lester *Wallack brought him to America in 1874 to serve as leading man with his ensemble. George *Odell has noted, "Montague became at once the accepted matinée idol; he was handsome, gentle and gentlemanly—a perfect specimen of refined English manhood. New York had seen nothing like him before; he had the faculty of making most other leading men seem boorish, ill-dressed, and possibly a bit vulgar. . . . His photographs by Mora and Sarony were soon on every dressing-table." He played Captain Molineux in the premiere of *The *Shaughraun* (1874) and later earned praise for his performance in such contemporary successes as **Caste*, **Diplomacy*, and *The Overland Route*. As popular with his confreres as he was with the public, Montague is reputed to have suggested the founding of the club that became the *Lambs.

MONTEZ, Lola [née Marie Dolores Eliza Rosanna Gilbert] (1818?–61), actress. The famous Irish-born beauty was a notorious courtesan who had been mistress to both Franz Liszt and King Ludwig I of Bavaria before coming to America in 1851. Walter *Leman recalled her "face full of expression, fine eyes, and hair that a mermaid might envy." At first her attempts to traffic in her notoriety were commercially successful, although they met with little encouragement from critics. Montez offered herself as a dancer and an actress, including the title role in *Lola Montez in Bavaria* (1852), which purported to recount her European amours. When her allure began to wane, Montez endeavored to conquer the lecture circuit, but was less successful. She died in comparative poverty, but her legend remains richly alive.

MONTGOMERY, Dave. See Stone, Fred.

MONTGOMERY, James (1882–1966), playwright. An actor turned dramatist, he scored his biggest nonmusical success with the farce **Nothing But the Truth* (1916). However, he enjoyed a number of hits when he wrote the librettos for musicals based on some of his less-popular comedies: *Oh, Look!* (1918) derived from his 1912 *Ready Money* (1919) and **Irene* (1919) from his failed play, *Irene O'Dare* (1916). Montgomery's plays also served as a source for other librettists, most notably when Otto *Harbach turned his *The Aviator* (1910) into *Going Up!* (1917).

MOODY, William Vaughn (1869–1910), playwright. The son of a Mississippi riverboat captain, he was born in Spencer, Indiana, and educated at Harvard, where he became the class poet. He later taught both at Harvard and at the University of Chicago before retiring to devote himself to writing poetry and plays. His earliest theatrical works were blank-verse dramas, *The Masque of Judgment* (1900) and *The Fire Bringer* (1904). Neither was produced during his lifetime, although scholars have found merit in both, and only two others were enacted on stage while he was alive. *The *Great Divide* (1906), one of the milestones in the history of American theatre, was seen as an examination of a fundamental native conflict and was an early instance of what *Quinn has called the "Drama of Revolt." *The *Faith Healer* (1909), which centered on a man's attempt to regain divine curative powers, failed, possibly because Moody was too ill to make the requisite revisions. His early death is believed by many scholars to have deprived the theatre of a major voice and to have left it for Eugene *O'Neill to bring American drama to maturity a decade later. Biography: *Estranging Dawn*, Maurice F. Brown, 1973.

MOON FOR THE MISBEGOTTEN, A (1957), a play by Eugene *O'Neill. [Bijou Theatre, 68 perf.] Having buried his mother, the hopelessly dissipated James Tyrone Jr. (Franchot *Tone) wanders aimlessly in search of a mother figure. On the wretched Connecticut farm of a seedy Irishman, Phil Hogan (Cyril Cusack), James finds such a figure in Hogan's homely, but warm-hearted daughter, Josie (Wendy Hiller). Josie and her father plan to trick James into marrying her but instead, during a long night of drunken blather and confessions, James and Josie reach an understanding of each other's fatal instincts. James leaves her, wandering off on his path toward self-destruction. The play originally failed in a 1947 tryout and was coolly received when it opened on Broadway ten years later. Not until a fine revival by the *Circle in the Square in 1968 were its merits fully perceived. The revival featured Mitchell Ryan as Tyrone, W. B. Brydon as Hogan, and Salome Jens as his daughter. A 1973 revival, directed by José *Quintero and starring Jason *Robards Jr. and Colleen *Dewhurst, is recognized as the touchstone performance of the work. Less successful but still commendable were revivals in 1984 with Kate Nelligan and Ian Bannen and in 2000 with Cherry *Jones and Gabriel Bryne. While not quite top rank O'Neill, it remains a powerfully moving drama and is closely linked to the even more autobiographical **Long Day's Journey into Night* by the importance of the Tyrone figure to both works.

MOON IS BLUE, THE (1951), a comedy by F. Hugh *Herbert. [*Henry Miller Theatre, 924 perf.] After meeting on the observation tower of the Empire State Building, architect Donald Gresham (Barry *Nelson) and Patty O'Neill (Barbara *Bel Geddes) saunter off to his apartment where, on the telephone, he attempts to break off his engagement to a girl he had met earlier. This does not sit well with that girl's father, David Slater (Donald Cook), who is something of a cavalier libertine and who quickly seeks to make a conquest of Patty for himself. Nor does all of this sit well with Patty's father, who arrives to lecture the young couple and then give Donald a solid punch in the jaw. The next day the young couple again meet on the observation tower to decide their future. This small-cast, light-as-air comedy was one of the long-run hits of the 1950s.

MOON OF THE CARIBBEES, THE. See *S.S. Glencairn.*

MOONCHILDREN (1972), a play by Michael *Weller. [*Royale Theatre, 16 perf.] While the war is being waged in Viet Nam and protests occur on the streets of a college town, the inhabitants of a student apartment seem more concerned about failing relationships, kooky roommates, and their future. Originally presented as *Cancer* in London, then at the *Arena Stage, David *Merrick and others brought it to Broadway where it met with a divided press then quickly closed. The next year it was successfully produced Off Broadway, followed by many college and regional productions. The play is aimless in a Chekhovian manner and the characters are often funny, irritating, and truthful. **Michael WELLER** (b. 1942), a New York-born playwright who studied at Windham College and Brandeis, has written numerous plays that have been well received Off Broadway and at regional playhouses but have met with little success on Broadway. His other noteworthy plays include *Fishing* (1975), *Loose Ends* (1979), *The Ballad of Soapy Smith* (1984), *Spoils of War* (1988), and *Lake No Bottom* (1990).

MOORE, Grace (1901–47), singer. A native of Del Rio, Tennessee, the beautiful blonde performer, who is better known for her later work in films and opera, made her Broadway debut in *Hitchy-Koo, 1920.* After appearing in *Up in the Clouds* (1922), she introduced "What'll I Do?" in the 1923 edition of the *Music Box Revue* and "All Alone" in the 1924 edition. Her last appearance was in *The Du Barry* (1933). Autobiography: *You're Only Human Once*, 1944.

MOORE, Robert (1927?–84), director. He began his career as an actor in the late 1940s, initially using the

name of Brennan Moore, then for a decade he acted and directed at numerous regional theatres. Moore's first New York directorial assignment was a 1961 Off-Broadway revival of *The *Ticket-of-Leave Man,* but he did not gain major recognition until he staged *The *Boys in the Band* (1968). His subsequent successes included *Promises, Promises* (1968), *The *Last of the Red Hot Lovers* (1969), *The Gingerbread Lady* (1970), *Lorelei* (1974), *Deathtrap* (1978), *They're Playing Our Song* (1979), and *Woman of the Year* (1981).

MOORE, Victor [Frederick] (1876–1962), comic actor. A popular comedian, whose style was a singular amalgam of wistfulness and toughness, he was a pudgy man with a bleating voice. He was born in Hammonton, New Jersey, and made his stage debut while in his teens. Success did not come until he entered vaudeville in 1901 with his wife, Emma Littlefield. Arthur *Hopkins recalled, "The timid Moore, who even in those days, was mostly hips, would waddle to the footlights and beseech the spotlight man in the gallery, as though reluctant to remind him, 'Mister, hey, mister, spotlight, you know, mister, you know like we rehearsed—spotlight.'" Moore continued to perform the act between major Broadway appearances, such as his wily Kid Burns in both *Forty-five Minutes from Broadway* (1906) and *The Talk of New York* (1907). After featured roles in *Oh, Kay!* (1926) and *Funny Face* (1927), he was teamed with William *Gaxton in *Of Thee I Sing* (1931), playing the befuddled Vice President Alexander Throtle-bottom opposite Gaxton's suave, brash style, which complemented Moore's diffident manner. The two were coupled afterwards in *Let 'Em Eat Cake* (1933), *Anything Goes* (1934), *Leave It to Me!* (1938), *Louisiana Purchase* (1940), *Hollywood Pinafore* (1945), and *Nellie Bly* (1946). Moore's last appearances were as Gramps in a 1953 revival of *On Borrowed Time* and as the Starkeeper in a 1957 revival of *Carousel.*

MORANT, Fanny (1821–1900), actress. The attractive, if somewhat mouse-faced, performer was born in England and performed at Drury Lane before settling in America in 1853. From 1860 to 1868 she appeared with *Wallack's great company and then Augustin *Daly's new ensemble. With the group Morant played such diverse parts as the scorned Clothilde in *Fernande*; the motherly, matchmaking Mrs. Ten Eyck in *Divorce*; Mistress Page; and Mrs. Candour. Despite her seeming success she left Daly's for the *Union Square Theatre where, willingly or no, she became one of its leading character actresses. George *Odell has written, "No one ever surpassed her grand old ladies of comedy and drama."

MOREHOUSE, Ward (1899–1966), critic. Born in Savannah, Georgia, he was a student at North Georgia College when he joined a professional Shakespearean reader on tour. He subsequently worked for several Southern newspapers and for the New York *Tribune* before joining the New York *Sun*. Morehouse's "Broadway After Dark" column became one of that paper's most popular features, and in 1943 he was appointed its drama critic, a position he held until the paper folded and he became a critic and columnist for the Newhouse papers. He was also the author of one successful play, *Gentlemen of the Press* (1928), and of several eminently readable theatrical histories: *Forty-five Minutes Past Eight* (1939), *George M. Cohan: Prince of the American Theatre* (1943), *Matinee Tomorrow* (1949), and *Just the Other Day* (1953).

MORGAN, Frank [né Francis Philip Wupperman] (1890–1949), character actor. The son of a well-to-do New Yorker, he studied at the *American Academy of Dramatic Arts before making his professional debut in 1914. Despite his suave appearance he excelled at befuddled characters, playing variations of them in, among others, the musical *Rock-a-Bye Baby* (1918), *Seventh Heaven* (1922), The *Firebrand* (1924), *Gentlemen Prefer Blondes* (1926), *Rosalie* (1928), *Topaze* (1930), and the revue The *Band Wagon* (1931). His last years were spent in films. Actor Ralph *Morgan was his brother.

MORGAN, Helen (1900–41), singer and actress. The tiny, seemingly fragile torch singer was born in Danville, Illinois, and first called attention to herself in the 1926 revue *Americana*. Although she appeared in several other shows, she is remembered largely for her performance as Julie in *Show Boat* (1927 and 1932), in which she introduced "Bill" and "Can't Help Lovin' Dat Man"; and as Addie in *Sweet Adeline* (1929), in which she sang "Don't Ever Leave Me" and "Why Was I Born?" Her voice was higher than modern-day torch singers, actually a soprano voice. Chicago's often acerbic Claudia *Cassidy said of it, "She had in her voice the note of heartbreak—authentic heartbreak, worth its weight in theater gold." Biography: *Helen Morgan: Her Life and Legend*, Gilbert Maxwell, 1975.

MORGAN, Ralph [né Wupperman] (1883–1956), actor. Brother of Frank, he was less well known, although he was a more versatile performer. Originally a lawyer, he took to the stage in 1908. Among his early successes were gadabout Jack Wheeler in *Fair and Warmer* (1915) and the juvenile John Marvin in *Lightnin'* (1918). Morgan's biggest hit was as the duped husband Tony Dorning in *Cobra* (1924). After replacing Tom *Powers as family friend Charles Marsden in *Strange Interlude*, he spent many years in films, returning much later to play a number of supporting roles without much success.

MORMONS IN AMERICAN THEATRE AND DRAMA. Unlike other Christian sects, the Mormons embraced and encouraged theatre almost from their very beginnings. Even during their precarious sojourn in Illinois, their leader, Joseph Smith, promoted a "Fun House" at the Nauvoo settlement. Mormon missionaries frequently accepted work as actors, ignoring the disdain in which performers were held by many clerics. When they established a permanent home in Salt Lake City, they quickly erected a Bowery that served both for religious services and as a playhouse. The first play, The *Triumph of Innocence*, was given in 1848. Brigham Young, who had succeeded Smith as head of the church and who had led the great trek from Illinois to Utah, was himself a lover of theatre and continually urged his followers to perform in and even write plays. Young's children were among the regular performers. He oversaw the erection of several later playhouses, including the Salt Lake Theatre in 1862, a theatre long considered the finest between the Mississippi and California. Curiously, though these playhouses offered a wide-ranging dramatic fare, including religious works, Young is said to have been a special advocate of clean, homespun comedy, a genre designed to divert members from their frequently hard, harassed lives. Yet the Mormons' affection and respect for theatre counted for little among non-Mormon playwrights, actors, and producers, who either shared or pandered to the contempt in which the sect was held by most Americans of the time. In 1858 both *Burton and *Wallack offered plays centering on the group: The *Mormons; or, Life in Salt Lake City* and *Deseret Deserted; or, The Last Days of Brigham Young*. Although both plays were comedies or farces, they both clearly displayed an underlying distrust or dislike. The best-known work about the Mormons was The *Danites; or, The Heart of the Sierras* (1877) by Alexander Fitzgerald. The *Times* review described the sect as "an organized body [who] combine religion, murder, and rapine in their every-day life"—a view obviously held by many playgoers. When one of the earliest American comic operas, *Deseret; or, The Saint's Difficulties* (1880), took a tongue-in-cheek look at the group, the *Times* wailed that Mormon polygamy was deserving only of scorn and not of laughter. Typical of later works was *The Mormon Wife* (1901), which portrayed the downfall of a Mormon convert. Mormons continued to be portrayed as the blackest villains for many years; and when this characterization disappeared, they long continued as disreputable, if comic figures or at least as the butt of essentially derogatory jokes. For example, the comic villain in The *Girl from Utah (1914) was a Mormon who pursued the heroine, determined to add her to his flock of wives. Poking fun at Mormons remained a not-uncommon practice in comedies and musicals into the 1930s. By the end of World War II, the presence of Mormons on stage had all but disappeared. A later example that did consider the subject was *Angels in America (1993) in which a major character is a fallen away Mormon and his mother a comic paradox: a grumpy Mormon. As for the sect itself, the Church of the Latter Day Saints continues to present theatrics with their annual Hill Cumorah Pageant, a giant outdoor spectacle produced near Palmyra, New York, each summer.

MORNING'S AT SEVEN (1939), a comedy by Paul *Osborn. [*Longacre Theatre, 44 perf.] The Swansons and the Boltons have lived side by side in a small American town for more than fifty years. Cora Swanson (Jean Adair) and Ida Bolton (Kate McComb) are sisters, so there is particular reason for excitement when the youngster of the clans, forty-year-old Homer Bolton (John Alexander), decides to marry his thirty-nine-year-old sweetheart, Myrtle Brown (Enid Markey), to whom he has been engaged for many years. The excitement, however, is not all to the good. It makes old Carl Bolton (Russell Collins) more aware of his "spells" of introspection; causes Esther Crampton (Effie *Shannon), Cora and Ida's sister, to have a falling out with her husband David (Herbert Yost); and prompts Cora to ask yet another sister, Aaronetta Gibbs (Dorothy *Gish), a spinster who has been living with the Swansons, to move out. By the time Homer and Myrtle are ready to settle down, everything has been happily resolved: Aaronetta is to move across the yard and live with the Boltons. Although the play opened to excellent reviews, the Dwight Deere *Wiman production found only a small public. Burns *Mantle attributed the failure to the spate of fine comedies that had preceded it that season, most notably The *Man Who Came to Dinner and *Life with Father. A superb 1980 revival on Broadway confirmed the play's merits and ran over a year, making the old comedy a favorite in summer, community, and regional theatres. A 2002 mounting on Broadway was also well received.

MOROSCO, Oliver [né Mitchell] (1876–1945), producer. Born in Logan, Utah, but raised in San Francisco, he began his theatrical career there as an acrobat in a troupe headed by Walter Morosco, whose name he adopted professionally. When the elder Morosco became the lessee of several San Francisco theatres, he made his young protégé his manager. On his own he leased the Burbank Theatre in Los Angeles, and within a few years ran no fewer than six Los Angeles playhouses. To keep his theatres lit, Morosco began producing shows in 1909. Among his play hits were The *Bird of Paradise (1912), *Peg o' My Heart (1912), The *Unchastened Woman (1915), The Cinderella Man (1916), *Upstairs and Down (1916), The Brat (1917), *Lombardi, Ltd. (1917), and Cappy Ricks (1919). His musical successes, for which he often collaborated on the book and songs, included The Tik Tok Man of Oz (1912); Canary Cottage (1917), and several shows starring Charlotte *Greenwood: So Long, Letty (1916), Linger Longer, Letty (1919), and Letty Pepper (1922). Morosco also wrote a number of plays. Because of his close association with the *Shuberts, they joined him in building the *Morosco Theatre in New York, which opened with his Canary Cottage (1917). Biography: The Oracle of Broadway, edited by Helen M. Morosco and Leonard Paul Dugger, 1944.

MOROSCO THEATRE (New York). The first of many theatres designed by Herbert J. *Krapp for the *Shuberts, the Morosco was a simple, unadorned playhouse ideal for dramas because of its fine acoustics, clear sightlines, and practical proportions. The West 45th Street playhouse, which opened in 1917, was named after the West Coast producer Oliver *Morosco. It has the distinction of housing many Pulitzer Prize plays as well as major works by America's three greatest playwrights: Eugene *O'Neill, Tennessee *Williams, and Arthur *Miller. Despite fervent efforts to save it, the theatre was razed in 1982 (along with two others) to make room for the Marriott Hotel and *Marquis Theatre.

MORRIS, Clara [née Morrison] (1848–1925), actress. The Toronto-born performer began as a child ballerina in Cleveland and eventually acted opposite the great actors of her time. Working for Augustin *Daly, she won instant acclaim as the betrayed Anne Sylvester in Man and Wife (1870), followed by the Creole, Cora, in Article 47 (1872), and as the neglected, tragic heroine of Alixe (1873). Leaving Daly's ensemble system, Morris became a star in her own right with such triumphs as the title parts of *Camille (1874) and Miss Multon (1876). Modjeska recalled her as "a born actress, genuine, admirable, spontaneous, and powerful in her tragic moments, tender and gentle in the touching scenes, and always true to nature." Failing health forced her to appear less frequently after the 1880s, though she occasionally tried new plays, revived old ones, and played in vaudeville. In 1901 she published a rather self-defensive autobiography, Life on the Stage, as well as a curious book of reminiscences, Stage Confidences.

MORRIS, George Pope. See *Briar Cliff*.

MORRIS, Owen (1719?–1809), character actor. Virtually nothing is known of the early years of this performer except that he made his debut with the *American Company in 1759. Morris specialized in comic old men, including Oliver Surface and Polonius before retiring from the stage in 1790. The first Mrs. Owen Morris (d. 1767) was America's earliest Ophelia and, excluding a performance by British troops during the Revolutionary War, the earliest Lady Teazle. The second Mrs. Owen Morris (1753–1826) was a strikingly tall woman whose acting ability divided the chroniclers of her time. Nevertheless she proved a popular comedienne with the public, much admired for her Lady Teazle and her Beatrice, as well as her Ophelia. Her eccentricities were notorious, and she went to absurd lengths not to expose herself to daylight. Following the advent of Mrs. *Merry, her popularity waned rapidly.

MORRIS, William (1861–1936), actor. The Bostonian began his career at the *Boston Museum, then performed for Augustin *Daly and toured with Helena *Modjeska and Mrs. *Fiske. His noteworthy roles included the bank thief William Prescott in *Men and Women* (1890), the idealistic plant manager Ruben Warner in The *Lost Paradise* (1891), and Lt. Hawksworth in The *Girl I Left Behind Me* (1893). Subsequently he toured for over a decade as leading man in several shows. In later years Morris was a prominent character actor who remained active until the early 1930s.

MORSE, Robert [Alan] (b. 1931), actor. The perennially impish performer, he was born in Newton, Massachusetts, and made his Broadway debut as the clerk Barnaby Tucker in The *Matchmaker* (1955). His subsequent appearances were in musicals: the boy-producer Ted Snow in *Say, Darling* (1958), the Connecticut youth Richard Miller in *Take Me Along* (1959), the ambitious businessman J. Pierpont Finch in *How To Succeed in Business Without Really Trying* (1961), the musician-on-the-run Jerry in *Sugar* (1972), and the would-be actor David in *So Long, 174th Street* (1976). Morse also triumphed as writer Truman *Capote in the one-man show *Tru* (1989). He also briefly headed a road company of *Sugar Babies* in 1980 and played Cap'n Andy in the Toronto company of *Show Boat* in 1993.

MORSE, Woolson. See *Wang*.

MORTON, Hugh. See McLellan, C. M. S.

MORTON, Martha (1865–1925), playwright. From the late 1880s until shortly before World War I, this New York–born dramatist produced a steady stream of essentially romantic, comic stage pieces that were almost always welcome by both critics and audiences. She was an admirer of the German school of playwriting; and one of her first successes, *His Wife's Father* (1895), was merely a translation of a German success. Among her subsequent, more original works were *The Fool of Fortune* (1896), *A Bachelor's Romance* (1897), and *Her Lord and Master* (1902). Her brother was the playwright **Michael MORTON** (1864–1931) who was born in England but spent most of his earliest years in America. After going back to England to finish his education, Morton returned to New York in the 1880s where he found work as an actor at Daniel *Frohman's *Madison Square Theatre. Morton began his prolific career as a playwright in 1897 when Frohman mounted his farce *Miss Francis of Yale*, which Morton himself staged. It was not a success, but Morton had better luck with the William H. *Crane vehicle *A Rich Man's Son* (1899) and his dramatization F. Hopkinson Smith's novel, *Caleb West* (1900). In 1902 he moved permanently to London, although he returned on occasion to direct American versions of his London successes.

MOSCOW ART THEATRE. see International Theatre Companies Visiting America.

MOSEL, Tad. See *All the Way Home*.

MOSES, Montrose J[onas] (1878–1934), author. A scholar of world drama, the native New Yorker wrote numerous studies of American theatre that are still valuable. These works include *Famous Actor-Families in America* (1906), *The American Dramatist* (1910), *Representative Plays by American Dramatists* (3 vols. 1918–25), *The Fabulous Forrest* (1929), and *The American Theatre as Seen by Its Critics* (1934) with John Mason *Brown.

MOSES, Thomas G[ibbs] (1856–1934), designer. Possibly the most prolific and important of midwestern scenic artists in the late 19th and early 20th century, he was born in Liverpool, England, on the ship of his father, an American sea captain. In his teens he moved to Chicago and began painting scenery at *McVicker's Theatre while enrolled at the Chicago Art Institute for further training. In 1880 Moses joined the newly formed Sosman and Landis Scene Painting Studio, which eventually became the Midwest's leading set builders, becoming president in 1915. He designed scenery for hundreds of productions, not only in Chicago but for Helena *Modjeska in California and occasional New York productions as well. His forte was said to be "freely rendered rugged landscapes and woodland scenes." Unfortunately, the autobiography on which he was known to have worked for many years, *Sixty Years Back of the Curtain Line*, has yet to be published.

MOSHER, Gregory. See Lincoln Center.

MOST HAPPY FELLA, THE. see *They Knew What They Wanted.*

MOSTEL, [Samuel Joel] Zero (1915–77), actor. The hefty, cocky comedian was born in New York where he studied art at New York University. His earliest professional performances were given in small Greenwich Village nightclubs, followed by roles in several Broadway shows before calling attention to himself as Leopold Bloom in an Off-Broadway production of *Ulysses in Nighttown* (1958). He consolidated his reputation with his playing of John, the clerk who turns into a wild animal, in *Rhinoceros* (1961). Moving to musicals, Mostel starred as the clever slave Pseudolus in *A *Funny Thing Happened on the Way to the Forum* (1962) and the poor dairyman Teyve in **Fiddler on the Roof* (1964), the latter generally recognized as the high point of his career, and he returned to it for several revivals. *Newsweek* wrote that from his performance "there radiates so supple, luminous, and wide a light as to transform the stage into a scene of high, compelling art. When he sings 'If I were a rich man . . . ' he follows these words with a sighing, dream-tasting spiral of Yiddish scat-syllables which become the anthem of yearning for poor men everywhere." He was on tryout tour with *The Merchant* at the time of his death.

MOTLEY, costume designers. Founded in the early 1930s in London by Audrey Sophia Harris, Margaret F. Harris, and Elizabeth Montgomery, the company designed clothes for West End shows for a decade before beginning to offer their work to Americans in 1941. Among the plays that featured their costume designs were *A *Bell for Adano* (1944), **Anne of the Thousand Days* (1948), **South Pacific* (1949), **Can-Can* (1953), **Peter Pan* (1954), **Middle of the Night* (1956), *The *Most Happy Fella* (1956), and **Long Day's Journey into Night* (1956).

MOULAN, Frank (1875–1939), comic actor and singer. The New York–born comedian had worked with several prominent comic opera companies before scoring a huge success and becoming a star in *The *Sultan of Sulu* (1902). He went on to play in such musicals as *The Grand Mogul* (1907), *The Arcadians* (1910), *The Siren* (1911), *The Count of Luxembourg* (1912), *Her Regiment* (1917), and *Just Because* (1922). In his later years Moulan was popular in the *Gilbert and *Sullivan repertory.

MOURNING BECOMES ELECTRA (1931), a trilogy by Eugene *O'Neill. [Guild Theatre, 157 perf.] In *The Homecoming*, the New England wife Christine Mannon (Alla *Nazimova) has been having an affair with Captain Adam Brant (Thomas Chalmers) while her husband, Brigadier-General Ezra Mannon (Lee Baker), is away fighting in the Civil War. Christine's daughter, Lavinia (Alice *Brady), who hates her mother and secretly loves Brant, suspects the truth and wheedles a confession from him. The Mannons' son, Orin (Earle *Larimore), has always been more favored by his mother and is berated by the General when he returns home. This resentment leads Christine to poison her husband and make the death look natural. But Lavinia discovers the poison and pleads to her beloved dead father, "Don't leave me alone! Come back to me! Tell me what to do!" In *The Hunted*, Lavinia tells Orin what has happened and convinces her brother that they must be revenged on their mother. They follow Christine to a rendezvous she has with Brant, and when Christine departs, Orin kills Brant. Christine, on learning of Brant's death, commits suicide. The tale concludes with *The Haunted* in which Orin is plagued with a growing sense of guilt and has come to blame himself for all the family deaths. Indeed, he has come to suspect that the love he had for his mother was not entirely natural and that it has been transferred to his sister. Unable to conciliate the furies that hound him, he kills himself. Lavinia once again must don her mourning. She orders the house shut up, knowing she will live there alone for the rest of her life. "It takes the Mannons to punish themselves for being born," she concludes. The *Theatre Guild performed the five-hour resetting of the classic Oresteia in a single evening, with a dinner intermission between the first and second plays. Robert *Benchley, writing in *The New Yorker*, called it "a hundred times better than *Electra* because O'Neill has a God-given inheritance of melodramatic sense." It was revived in 1971 by the *American Shakespeare Festival and in 1972 by the *Circle in the Square.

MOWATT, Anna Cora [née Ogden] (1819–70), playwright and actress. The daughter of a prosperous New York merchant, she was born in France, and when she was seven, came to live in America, where at fifteen she was married to a well-known lawyer. Mowatt's poor health often restricted her to her home, where she took to writing to pass the time. In addition to poetry and novels, she wrote several unproduced plays. She is most remembered for her first play to be seen on Broadway, the society satire *Fashion* (1845). The success of the piece allowed her to recruit her strength and, taking advantage of her newfound health and fame, she tested her skills at acting. Mowatt's debut was as Pauline in The *Lady of Lyons (1845), and she was so successful that she spent the next two seasons touring, the second season with E. L. *Davenport as her leading man. Among her other roles were Mrs. Haller in The *Stranger, Beatrice, Lady Teazle, and Gertrude in her own Fashion. Edgar Allan *Poe wrote of the auburn-haired actress, "Her figure is slight—even fragile—but eminently graceful. Her face is a remarkably fine one, and of that precise character best adapted to the stage. . . . Her manner on the stage is distinguished by an ease and self-possession. . . . Her voice is rich and voluminous." Mowatt's second play to be produced was the costume drama Armand (1847). When Mr. Mowatt died while touring with her in England in 1851, she returned to America to attempt another tour, but her health gave out. She made her farewell at *Niblo's Garden in 1854, then three days later she remarried. Her last decade was spent largely in England. Although Fashion often has been revived and remains one of the best 19th-century American comedies, Mowatt's real importance may rest with the respectability that she as a gentlewoman gave to acting as a profession. Autobiography: Autobiography of an Actress; or, Eight Years on the Stage, 1854.

MR. WILKINSON'S WIDOWS (1891), a farce by William *Gillette. [Proctor's 23rd Street Theatre, 140 perf.] Mrs. Dickerson (Henrietta *Crosman) and Mrs. Perrin (Louise Thorndyke Boucicault) are two recently remarried widows who live in the same apartment house and strike up a friendship, which leads to the horrifying discovery that both had the very same husband and that both had married him on the very same day. When Major P. Ferguson Mallory (Thomas Burns) enters the picture to try to clear up the problem, he only succeeds in adding to the confusion. Based on Alexandre Bisson's Feu Toupinel, Gillette's Americanization laundered out many of the more risqué aspects of the original.

MRS. BUMPSTEAD-LEIGH (1911), a comedy by Harry James *Smith. [*Lyceum Theatre, 64 perf.] Mrs. Bumpstead-Leigh (Mrs. *Fiske) returns from a long sojourn in England to continue her triumphant social rise. What many of her fawning friends do not know is that she is an impostor, none other than Della Sales of Missionary Loop, Indiana, and the daughter of a man who made his fortune selling quack medicines. She travels with her mother, who is now called Mrs. de Salle (Florine Arnold), and her sister, Viola (Kathlene MacDonell), for whom she is determined to make a proper match. Her world is threatened by the appearance of bumptious Peter Swallow

(Henry E. *Dixey), who had been her suitor years before. But Mrs. Bumpstead-Leigh had not come all this way for nothing. She convinces Peter he is mistaken and finds the right man for Viola. This delightfully contrived farce, produced by her husband Harrison Grey *Fiske, was one of the versatile Mrs. Fiske's biggest successes.

MRS. LEFFINGWELL'S BOOTS (1905), a comedy by Augustus *Thomas. [Savoy Theatre, 123 perf.] Mrs. Leffingwell (Margaret *Illington) is a perfectly respectable married woman and Walter Corbin (William *Courtenay) is a proper young man-about-town who loves the equally decorous Mabel Ainslee (Fay Davis). So imagine the shock waves that rumble through society when Mrs. Leffingwell's quilted blue silk boots are discovered in Corbin's rooms. No one is more shocked than the explosively jealous Mr. Leffingwell (Louis Payne). Matters look dark for the lady and even darker for young Corbin, until it is learned that Mabel's demented brother stole the boots and planted them in the apartment. This French-like farce was considered too risqué by some of New York's stodgier critics, but the public adored the Charles *Frohman production.

MRS. WIGGS OF THE CABBAGE PATCH (1904), a play by Anne Crawford Flexner. [Savoy Theatre, 150 perf.] Mrs. Wiggs (Madge Carr Cook) is an eternally optimistic country lady who loves nothing better than helping others. She helps Bob (Thurston *Hall), a newspaper editor, persuade Lucy (Nora Shelby) to marry him, though it means Lucy must leave her beloved home and head for the big city. She helps her son Billy (Argyle Campbell) in his courtship of the orphaned Lovey Mary (Mabel *Taliaferro). She even helps her boozy, roving husband, Mr. Wiggs (Oscar Eagle), when he suddenly reappears in her life. The Kentucky-born Flexner (1874–1955) saw a half-dozen more of her plays produced on Broadway between 1901 and 1936, but none was as popular as this, which she drew from the stories of Alice Hegan Rice. The *Liebler and Co. production had toured successfully for a year before reaching New York and continued to tour for many years thereafter. Cook (1856–1933), who was born in England but spent most of her acting career here, was long identified with this role. She was the mother of Eleanor *Robson.

MUCH ADO ABOUT NOTHING. When first acted at the *Southwark Theatre in 1789, Shakespeare's comedy featured the younger Lewis *Hallam as Benedick and Mrs. Morris as Beatrice. The play proved especially congenial to Victorian temperaments, so Benedick and Beatrice found their way into the repertory of many leading performers of the era. J. W. *Wallack used Benedick for his farewell performance in 1859. Other noted artists who appeared in major revivals were Charles and Ellen *Kean, Henry *Irving and Ellen *Terry, and E. H. *Sothern and Julia *Marlowe. Ada *Rehan was also admired for her Beatrice, although her Benedick, Charles *Richman, received meager praise. Numbered among the better 20th-century revivals were a 1959 rendering with John *Gielgud and Margaret *Leighton, a 1972 *New York Shakespeare Festival production with Sam Waterston and Kathleen Widdoes set in pre–World War I America, a memorable *Royal Shakespeare Company mounting on Broadway in 1984 with Derek Jacobi and Sinead Cusack, a 1988 Central Park version with Kevin *Kline and Blythe Danner, and a Stratford Festival production from Canada in 1998 with Brian *Bedford and Martha Henry.

MULATTO (1935), a play by Langston Hughes. [Vanderbilt Theatre, 373 perf.] Colonel Thomas Norwood (Stuart Beebe) is a rich Georgia plantation owner who has fathered several children by his black housekeeper, Cora Lewis (Rose *McClendon). Two of these mulatto children, Sally (Jeanne Greene) and Robert (Hurst Amyx), seem exceptional enough that they are sent north to be educated. Sally returns home and is seduced by Norwood's vicious overseer, Talbot (John Boyd) while Robert demands to be treated as a white. When his father threatens to shoot him, he strangles Norwood. A lynch mob is formed but thwarted by Robert's suicide. Although the play was criticized as diffuse and contrived, its basic drama and McClendon's fine performance (her last) gave the work a substantial run. [James Mercer] **Langston HUGHES** (1902–67), the celebrated African-American poet, also wrote the folk musicals *Simply Heavenly* (1957) and *Tambourines to Glory* (1963) and several plays, including *Little Ham* (1936), *Joy to My Soul* (1937) and *Front Porch* (1938), though none were as successful as *Mulatto*. Hughes wrote the librettos for four operas but is more remembered for his lyrics for Kurt *Weill's musical rendition of *Street Scene* (1947). *Mule Bone*, a folk comedy he wrote with Zora Neale Hurston in 1930, was not produced until a well-received production by the *Public Theatre in 1991. Biography: *The Life of Langston Hughes*, A. Rampersad, 1986,1988.

MULLIGAN GUARDS' BALL, THE (1879), a play with music by Edward *Harrigan (book, lyrics), David *Braham (music). [Theatre Comique, 138 perf.] The Irish-American "social" group known as the Mulligan Guards, led by Dan Mulligan (Harrigan), plan a ball, but Dan is also concerned about the romance between his son Tommy (Tony *Hart) and Katy Lochmuller (Nellie Jones). Dan does not approve of the Irish marrying Germans, while Dan's wife, Cordelia (Annie *Yeamans), detests Katy's mother. The Guards discover a "Negro" organization, the Skidmore Guards, has booked the same ballroom. The Skidmores are forced to take the second floor facilities, but they stomp so wildly that the floor gives way and they come tumbling down upon the Irish. In the confusion Tommy and Katy elope. *Notable songs*: The Babies on Our Block; The Mulligan Guard; Pitcher of Beer. Originally conceived as a short vaudeville sketch, the piece was enlarged by producers Harrigan and Hart on several occasions and exists in several versions, sometimes called simply *The Mulligan Guard*. Its arrival in the 1878–79 season, along with *H.M.S. Pinafore* and The *Brook, signaled the beginnings of modern musical theatre in America.

MUNI, Paul [né Frederick Weisenfreund] (1895–1967), actor. Born in Austria but raised in Chicago, he made his stage debut in Yiddish theatre in 1908 and his bow on professional English-speaking stages 1926. Muni did not gain prominence until 1931 when he played the Jewish lawyer George Simon in *Counsellor-at-Law followed by his commanding performance in 1939 when he portrayed the wartime deserter King McCloud in *Key Largo (1939). His last important appearance was as attorney Henry Drummond in *Inherit the Wind (1955). Muni was a superb technician, although some playgoers felt he wore his technique on his sleeve. He also enjoyed a distinguished career in Hollywood. Biography: *Actor: The Life and Times of Paul Muni*, Jerome Lawrence, 1974.

MURDER IN THE CATHEDRAL (1935). T. S. *Eliot's 1935 drama about the martyrdom of Thomas à Becket was first presented in America that same year at Yale then the *Federal Theatre Project offered it to New York in 1936. Since then it has remained popular with collegiate and other groups, who often mount it in suitable churches rather than in regular theatres.

MURDOCH, Frank H. [né Hitchcock] (1843–72), playwright and actor. The nephew of actor James E. Murdoch (whose name he used on stage), he began acting and writing while still in his teens and his first play, *The Keeper of Lighthouse Cliff*, was apparently produced in California in the 1870s and may have influenced James A. *Herne's *Shore Acres. Murdoch's most famous play was *Davy Crockett, which he wrote as a vehicle for Frank *Mayo. At the time of its production he was too ill to attend to revisions; and by the time New York first saw it in June 1873, seven months after his death, Mayo had substantially revised it. His other works were the satire on drama critics, *Bohemia; or, The Lottery of Art* (1872), and the sentimental comedy *Only a Jew* (1873). Clara *Morris observed, "He had good height, a good figure, and an air of gentle breeding; otherwise he was unattractive," adding that his sensitivity about his looks often led to petulance.

MURDOCH, James E[dward] (1811?–93), actor. The son of a prominent Philadelphia family, he made his debut at the *Arch Street Theatre in 1829 playing Frederick in *Lovers' Vows*. Murdoch quickly attained a national reputation, even though he performed far more frequently in his native city than elsewhere. As the result of accidental arsenic poisoning in 1832, which led to recurring problems, he retired temporarily from the stage on several occasions, but always returned within a few seasons and did not give his final performance until 1889. He won acclaim for his Claude Melnotte in *The *Lady of Lyons* and his *Hamlet*, which many contemporaries considered the finest on the American stage until the advent of Edwin *Booth. However, he was even more admired as a comedian. Among his best comic interpretations were Rover in *Wild Oats*, Charles Surface, Orlando, and Benedick. Playgoers and critics both praised his superb elocution and unostentatious manliness. Autobiography: *The Stage*, 1880.

MURDOCK, John. See *Triumphs of Love, The.*

MURRAY, Brian [né Bell] (b. 1939), actor. He was born in Johannesburg, South Africa, made his London debut in 1959, and first came to America in 1964 as part of a *Royal Shakespeare Company tour of A *Midsummer Night's Dream*. Murray was praised on Broadway for his tragicomic portrayal of Rosencrantz in *Rosencrantz and Guildenstern Are Dead* (1967) and a decade later was highly lauded for his heartbreaking performance as the infertile would-be parent Colin in *Ashes* (1977). By then Murray was settled in New York and each season found interesting characters to play either on or Off Broadway. Among his most significant performances were the Irishman Charlie trying to deal with his dead father and his own past in *Da* (1978), the hassled director Lloyd Dallas in *Noises Off* (1983), the innocent businessman Jack McCracken deep in corruption in *A Small Family Business* (1992), various characters (male and female) in *Travels with My Aunt* (1995), the persecuted cleric Harry Henderson in *Racing Demon* (1995), the domineering businessman Ben Hubbard in *The *Little Foxes* (1997), and the charming but disturbing Man in *The Play About the Baby* (2001).

MURRAY, J. Harold (1891–1940), singer and actor. A native of South Berwick, Maine, he was a professional singer from childhood, and had appeared in vaudeville before making his Broadway debut in *The *Passing Show of 1921*. His most remembered role was the Texas Ranger, Capt. James Stewart, in *Rio Rita* (1927), but he was also featured in the musicals *Caroline* (1923), *China Rose* (1924), *Captain Jinks* (1925), *Castles in the Air* (1926), *East Wind* (1931), *Face the Music* (1932), and *Thumbs Up!* (1934). Murray has been described as a "sandy-haired, strong-featured baritone."

MURRAY, Walter (fl. mid-18th century), actor and manager. With his partner Thomas *Kean, he led a band of traveling players around the eastern seaboard in the early 1750s. At one time their aggregation was known as the Virginia Company of Comedians. Their repertory consisted entirely of the English plays then most popular in London.

MUSEUM OF COSTUME ART. Founded in 1937 by Irene Lewisohn, Aline *Bernstein, and Lee *Simonson to house their collections of costumes and their libraries on costume design, the museum grew and moved several times before being absorbed in 1946 by the Metropolitan Museum of Art.

MUSIC BOX REVUES, a series of musical revues mounted by Sam H. *Harris and Irving *Berlin at their new *Music Box Theatre in 1921, 1922, 1923, and 1924. Among the Berlin hits to emerge from the series were "All Alone," "Crinoline Days," "Everybody Step," "Lady of the Evening," and "What'll I Do?" as well as the series' theme song, "Say It with Music." The shows featured elaborate sets and costumes on a Ziegfeldian order but also intimate musical numbers and sketches, thus forming a bridge between the waning extravaganzas and the smaller, more intellectually witty revues of the late 1920s and 1930s. Among its famous comic moments were two from the 1923–24 edition, Robert *Benchley's "Treasurer's Report" and George S. *Kaufman's "If Men Played Cards as Women Do."

MUSIC BOX THEATRE (New York). This jewel of a playhouse on West 45th Street is ideal in many ways: a size (975 seats) that is both intimate yet financially practical, a location in the heart of the theatre district, and a timeless decor with a high loggia, Palladian windows, and a limestone facade. It was designed by C. Howard Crane and named by Irving *Berlin who built it with his partner Sam *Harris in 1921. The theatre opened with the first of a series of clever musical shows called the *Music Box Revues* and throughout its history the playhouse would find success with both plays and smaller musicals. Hits such as *Of Thee I Sing* (1931), *Dinner at Eight* (1932), *As Thousands Cheer* (1933), and *Stage Door* (1936) kept the playhouse solvent during the Great Depression, and it continues to be a "lucky" house for most tenants. The Music Box is co-owned by the *Shuberts and the Berlin estate.

MUSIC IN THE AIR (1932), an operetta by Oscar *Hammerstein II (book, lyrics), Jerome *Kern (music). [Alvin Theatre, 342 perf.] When Karl Reder (Walter *Slezak) writes a song called "I've Told Ev'ry Little Star," he and his fellow Bavarian villagers trek to Munich to have it published. But once there, Karl is pursued by a flirtatious prima donna, Frieda Hatzfeld (Natalie *Hall), while a composer, Bruno Mahler (Tullio *Carminati), falls in love with Karl's sweetheart, Sieglinde (Katherine Carrington) and he writes an operetta especially for her. But the romances and high hopes come to naught, so Karl, Sieglinde, and the villagers head home. *Notable songs*: There's a Hill Beyond a Hill; The Song Is You; We Belong Together; When Spring Is in the Air. Like The *Cat and the Fiddle before it, the musical was Kern's attempt to write a modern operetta without resorting to excessive European mannerisms. Many critics consider this his finest, most unified work, citing not only the beauty of the melodies but also their prevailing appropriateness of tone.

MUSIC MAN, THE (1957), a musical comedy by Meredith *Willson (book, music, lyrics). [*Majestic Theatre, 1,375 perf.; Tony, NYDCC Awards] "Professor" Harold Hill (Robert *Preston) is a "con" man who cannot read a note of music but specializes in organizing boys' bands and selling band instruments, then disappearing with the money. But when Harold comes to the Iowa town of River City, he comes up against the town librarian, Marion Paroo (Barbara *Cook), who plans to unmask him until she realizes that he is bringing new life to the town and that she is falling in love with him. But Harold is found out by the townspeople anyway and is about to be tarred and feathered until the boys' band gives a horribly cacophonous concert, which the children's doting parents think masterful. *Notable songs*: Goodnight, My Someone; Seventy-Six Trombones; Till There Was You; Trouble; Gary, Indiana; Marion the Librarian; Lida Rose. Louis *Kronenberger wrote, "If The Music Man was not cream, but only nice fresh half-and-half, it did catch the jubilant old-time energy of a small-town jamboree." The apple-pie American musical was drawn from Willson's recollections of his Iowa boyhood and the score employed numerous clever devices. He used the same basic melody in Hill's rousing

"Seventy-Six Trombones" and Marion's tender "Goodnight, My Someone" to suggest a common bond, "Rock Island" mimicked the rhythm of a moving train, "The Piano Lesson" duet was set to practicing piano scales, and the tongue-in-cheek sermonizing of "Trouble" was turned into a modern-day patter song. Long a favorite in theatres across the country, it was revived on Broadway with success in 2000.

MUSIC MASTER, THE (1904), a play by Charles *Klein. [*Belasco Theatre, 627 perf.] For sixteen years, the once-successful Viennese conductor Anton von Barwig (David *Warfield) has searched for his daughter, who was taken from him by his wife when she deserted him for an American bounder. The search has taken him to New York, where he struggles to make a living by teaching music. Von Barwig's reputation as a teacher brings to his door young society girls, one of whom is Helen Stanton (Minnie *Dupree). In time von Barwig comes to realize that Helen is his long-lost child, but when he confronts her father, Henry A. Stanton (Campbell Golan), Stanton warns him that exposing the truth would destroy Helen's chances of marrying the wealthy Beverly Cruger (J. Carrington Yates). Reluctantly von Barwig prepares to leave for Vienna, but Helen has discovered who he is and welcomes him into her home. Most critics dismissed the David *Belasco production as shallow and excessively sentimental. Arthur *Hornblow wrote in *Theatre Magazine*, "In the hands of another stage manager [read producer] and with another actor as the music master, we might have had theatricalism and unreality in place of genuineness of character and emotion." Warfield played the role for three years and returned to it at intervals as late as 1916.

MUSSER, Tharon (b. 1925), lighting designer. One of the American theatre's most prolific and skillful lighting designers, Musser has lit dozens of plays and musicals in New York and regionally. She began as a stage manager then started lighting dance concerts. Her Broadway debut was the moody lighting for *Long Day's Journey Into Night* (1956), and over the years she would demonstrate her talent for everything from brash Broadway musical lighting, as in *Mame* (1966) and *42nd Street* (1980), to delicate and subtle productions, such as The Seagull (1964) and A *Little Night Music (1973). Musser made several innovations in lighting design technique and was the first to use a computer lighting system on Broadway when she devised the lighting for A *Chorus Line (1975).

MY FAIR LADY (1956), a musical comedy by Alan Jay *Lerner (book, lyrics), Frederick *Loewe (music). [*Mark Hellinger Theatre, 2,717 perf.; Tony Award.] Coming from a performance at Covent Garden, Professor Henry Higgins (Rex *Harrison) meets a fellow scholar, Colonel Pickering (Robert Coote), and a somewhat raucous Cockney flower girl, Liza Doolittle (Julie *Andrews). Higgins casually mentions to Pickering that given a little time he could turn her into a lady, so when Liza appears later at his residence asking him to make good on his boast, Higgins accepts Pickering's wager on the affair. It is a long, hard struggle, but by the time Liza can properly enunciate "The Rain in Spain" and Higgins takes her to the Ascot races, her pronunciation is perfect, even if her conversation is not. Later she is successfully passed off as a lady at a ball; and her father, the dustman Alfred P. Doolittle (Stanley Holloway), inherits a fortune and must conform to middle-class morality. Eliza is wooed by the lovesick Freddy Eynsford-Hill (John Michael King), but she has deeper feeling for the unfeeling Higgins so she leaves to set out on her own. But Eliza soon returns, only to have Higgins ask, "Where the devil are my slippers?" *Notable songs*: I Could Have Danced All Night; Wouldn't It Be Loverly; An Ordinary Man; Just You Wait; On the Street Where You Live; Show Me; I've Grown Accustomed to Her Face. Considered by many the finest of all American musicals, the Herman *Levin production was a triumph not only for its performers and writers, but for its director, Moss *Hart, its set designer, Oliver *Smith, and its costume designer, Cecil *Beaton. Unlike *The Chocolate Soldier*, an earlier musical version of *Shaw's *Arms and the Man*, this lyric version of *Pygmalion* managed to retain all of Shaw's irreverence, wit, and intellectuality while maintaining an unerring sense of style and tone in its own contributions. Popular all over the world, the musical was revived in New York in 1964, 1968, 1976, 1981 (with Harrison), and 1993.

MY HEART'S IN THE HIGHLANDS (1939), a play by William *Saroyan. [Guild Theatre, 44 perf.] Ben Alexander (Philip Loeb), a failed poet, lives from hand-to-mouth with his son Johnny (Sidney Lumet) and his mother-in-law (Hester Sondergaard), who speaks no English. Although they are liked by many of their neighbors and are visited by Jasper MacGregor (Art Smith), an old tragedian who plays music on a golden bugle, they are eventually forced to abandon their humble shack and move on. Originally slated for only five performances, the *Group Theatre production managed a longer run, although most critics were baffled by it.

MY MARYLAND. See *Barbara Frietchie*.

MY ONE AND ONLY. See *Funny Face*.

MY PARTNER (1879), a play by Bartley *Campbell. [*Union Square Theatre, 39 perf.] Although their characters are totally disparate, warm, idealistic Joe Saunders (Louis *Aldrich) and cynical, self-serving Ned Singleton (Henry Crisp) are the closest of friends and both love Mary Brandon (Maude *Granger). When Ned violates Mary, Joe demands that Ned marry her. But Ned is murdered by Josiah Scragg (J. W. Hague), who makes it seem that Joe is the killer. Joe is tried and convicted, and before he is to be executed, he and Mary agree to wed. Joe is saved from the gallows when Wing Lee (Charles T. *Parsloe) discovers Scragg's bloodstained cuff. Set in California as civilization was brushing away gold rush crudities, the play was not as popular with the public as Campbell's *The *White Slave*. Critics, however, were in virtual agreement that this was his best work. The *Tribune* noted, "It is a very strong piece. The effort has been made to deal with elemental passions and real persons, and to paint a picture of tragedy and heroism upon the tumultuous background of a turbulent semi-civilization; and the object has been accomplished with startling force and unusual, if not even skills. . . . It is a better piece of its class than has hitherto been produced in America." The play held first class stages for nearly a decade.

MY SISTER EILEEN (1940), a comedy by Joseph A. *Fields and Jerome *Chodorov. [*Biltmore Theatre, 864 perf.] Two Ohio sisters, the acerbic Ruth (Shirley *Booth), who is determined to become a famous writer, and the sweet Eileen (Jo Ann Sayers), who dreams of becoming an actress, move to New York and take a Greenwich Village basement apartment that is constantly jolted by blasts from subway construction. Although Eileen quickly has dozens of suitors, she cannot find work, and Ruth's attempts to persuade Robert Baker (William Post Jr.), editor of *Manhatter* magazine, to publish her work come to naught. Finally Chick Clark (Bruce MacFarlane), a newspaper reporter, gets Ruth an assignment welcoming a Brazilian naval ship. Ruth invites the sailors home, where a fight ensues, the police arrive, and Eileen punches a policeman. The melee lands Eileen on the front page and also gets her an acting job, and Ruth falls in love with Baker and starts her journalism career. Based on Ruth McKenney's *New Yorker* stories, the Max *Gordon production was hailed by the *Post* as "the giddiest delight to be seen hereabouts since *You Can't Take It with You*." The comedy served as the basis for the successful musical *WONDERFUL TOWN* with Fields and Chodorov adapting their own play, Leonard *Bernstein composing the music, and Betty *Comden and Adolph *Green providing the lyrics. Rosalind *Russell was

Ruth, Edith Adams was Eileen, and George Gaynes was Baker. *Notable songs*: Ohio; A Quiet Girl; One Hundred Easy Ways; Conga! Robert *Fryer produced the show at the *Winter Garden Theatre where it ran 559 performances. The musical was revived on Broadway in 2003.

MYERS, Richard [son] (1901–77), producer and songwriter. A Philadelphia native, between 1925 and 1934 he contributed songs or whole scores to a dozen Broadway musicals, including the 1925 and 1926 editions of the *Greenwich Village Follies* and the 1934 edition of the *Ziegfeld Follies*. He also wrote incidental music for several dramas. Subsequently Myers turned to producing, and in association with others mounted such offerings as *Margin for Error* (1939), *Goodbye, My Fancy* (1948), 1949 and 1950 revivals of *Caesar and Cleopatra* and The *Devil's Disciple*, respectively, The *Moon Is Blue* (1951), The *Love of Four Colonels* (1953), and *Hotel Paradiso* (1957).

MYSTERY OF EDWIN DROOD, THE (1985), a musical comedy by Rupert Holmes (book, music, lyrics). [*Imperial Theatre, 608 perf.; Tony Award.] Charles Dickens's last, unfinished novel was turned into a musical entertainment as performed at a Victorian music hall in London. Since the murderer remains a mystery in the book, the audience was asked to vote on whom the culprit was and the show ended accordingly. *Notable songs*: Don't Quit While You're Ahead; Moonfall; Perfect Strangers; Off to the Races; Wages of Sin. This unlikely piece for American audiences was first presented by Joseph *Papp in Central Park in the summer of 1985, and it was so popular that he moved it to Broadway in the fall. Wilford Leach directed the play-within-a-play with a playful touch and George *Rose, as the Chairman, held the audience participation show together. Also outstanding were Betty *Buckley as the actress playing Drood, Howard McGillin as the villainous Jasper, Cleo Laine as the dope peddler Princess Puffer, and Patti Cohenour as the ingenue Rosabud. Holmes's score is a pastiche of Victorian tunes that are both accurate and entertaining. During the run the title was officially changed to *Drood*. **Rupert HOLMES** (b. 1947) was born in Cheshire, England, to an American father in the military and a British mother, but grew up in Nyack, New York, later studying composition at the Manhattan School of Music. Holmes has also written best-selling pop songs, as well as several theatre works, including the short-lived Broadway thrillers *Accomplice* (1990) and *Solitary Confinement* (1992), the biography play about George Burns called *Say Goodnight, Gracie* (2002), and the musical *Marty* (2002).

N

NAPIER, John (b. 1944), designer. No other British designer has found more success in America than Napier who designed the celebrated sets and sometimes costumes for some of the biggest hits of his generation: *Equus* (1974), *Cats* (1982), *Les Misérables* (1987), *Starlight Express* (1987), *Miss Saigon* (1991), *Sunset Boulevard* (1994), and others. A native Londoner, he studied at the Hornsey College of Art and the Central School of Arts and Crafts and worked in opera before finding fame as the designer for the *Royal Shakespeare Company and on the West End. Napier's most famous sets tend toward the spectacular: the rising tire in *Cats* (1982), the rotating barricade in *Les Misérables* (1987), the multilevel race track in *Starlight Express* (1987), the helicopter in *Miss Saigon*, and the Gothic mansion in *Sunset Boulevard* (1994). But his work can also be sparse and effective, as in *Equus* (1974); rustic and evocative, as in *The *Life and Adventures for Nicholas Nickleby* (1981); or moodily suggestive, as in *Jane Eyre* (2000).

NASH, Mary (1885–1976), actress. A native of Troy, New York, she studied at the *American Academy of Dramatic Arts before making her debut in 1904. After playing important supporting roles opposite Ethel *Barrymore at the *Empire Theatre, she scored major successes as Cecily Rand in *The *City* (1909), Wanda Kelly in *The *Woman* (1911), and Marcelle in *The *Man Who Came Back* (1916). Nash continued in leading assignments throughout the 1920s in such plays as *Captain Applejack* (1921), *The Lady* (1923), and *A Lady's Virtue* (1925), and was Henrietta in a 1926 revival of *The *Two Orphans*. Her sister, Florence (1888–1950), was also a popular performer.

NASH, N. Richard. See *Rainmaker, The.*

NATHAN, George Jean (1882–1958), critic. Probably the most famous and respected drama critic of his day, he was born in Fort Wayne, Indiana, and educated at Cornell and the University of Bologna. His uncle, the critic and playwright Charles Frederic Nirdlinger, obtained a post for him on the New York *Herald* in 1905, but Nathan soon quit to become critic for two magazines, *Outing* and *The Bohemian*. Two years later he moved to *The Smart Set*, where his name was first associated with that of H. L. *Mencken, the pair becoming its co-editors in 1914. From the start, Nathan railed against the shallowness and hollowness of the theatre of his day and advocated a drama of ideas and the plays of such men as *Ibsen, *Strindberg, and *Shaw. He was the first important critic to extol the genius of Eugene *O'Neill, publishing O'Neill's early work in *The Smart Set*, and in later years he championed the plays of Sean *O'Casey and William *Saroyan. But Nathan also understood that the theatre thrived by being entertaining, so he endorsed many a flippant comedy and light-hearted musical. Indeed, as the American musical became more pretentiously artful, he was one of the few critics to maintain affection for the older style. After leaving *The Smart Set*, he founded *The American Mercury* with Mencken in 1924 and co-edited it with him until 1930. He also founded *The American Spectator* in 1932 with O'Neill and others. His criticisms appeared in numerous other magazines and papers, including *Puck, Judge, Vanity Fair*, and *The Saturday Review of Literature*. Among his notable books devoted to the theatre were *Mr. George Jean Nathan Presents* (1917), *The Popular Theatre* (1918), *Comedians All* (1919), *The Theatre, The Drama, The Girls* (1921), *The Critic and the Drama* (1922), *The Testament of the Critic* (1931), *Since Ibsen* (1933), *The Theatre of the Moment* (1936), and *Encyclopedia of the Theatre* (1940). From 1943 until shortly before his death, he edited *The Theatre Book of the Year*. His will established the George Jean Nathan Award "to encourage and assist in developing the art of drama criticism and the stimulation of intelligent theatre going."

NATIONAL ASSOCIATION OF THEATRICAL PRODUCING MANAGERS. See Producing Managers' Association.

NATIONAL PLAYWRIGHTS CONFERENCE. Another branch of the Eugene *O'Neill Theater Center, it was first convened in 1965. Its purpose is to create "a situation in which, without commercial pressures, young dramatists can see their plays presented in staged readings by professional actors and directors before an audience of sympathetic critics and fellow-writers, and can discuss their comments and make revisions on the spot for a less 'provisional' performance." Among the playwrights whose early works were offered there were John *Guare, Lanford *Wilson, Lee Blessing, and August *Wilson.

NATIONAL THEATRE OF GREAT BRITAIN. See International Theatre Companies Visiting America.

NATIONAL THEATRE OF THE DEAF. The idea for a professional touring ensemble of deaf performers was first discussed in the 1950s but did not become a working reality until the *Eugene O'Neill Theater Center took it under its aegis in 1966. The group employs an effectively dramatized version of traditional deaf sign language, but also generally includes a few nondeaf performers who serve as "speakers" and elaborate on the action. The company has made numerous national and international tours, offering both classic and original plays. It no longer is affiliated with the O'Neill Center and, located in Hartford, Connecticut, continues its impressive programs.

NATIONAL THEATRES (Washington, D.C.). Shortly after a visit by Fanny *Kemble, during which she complained about the shameful quality of playhouses in the nation's capital, several Washington civic leaders, led by William W. Corcoran, decided to erect a proper theatre. A site was selected on E Street, not far from the White House, and the new theatre, called the National, opened in 1835. The auditorium was converted briefly to a circus in 1844, but, after serving as the scene of President Polk's inaugural ball, burned to the ground in 1845. Since then five other theatres, all called the National, have occupied approximately the same lot. Like the first, the next three burned—in 1857, 1873, and 1885. The fifth house, designed by J. B. *McElfatrick, opened in 1885 and closed in 1922, when the present theatre was erected. Virtually all the great performers of the American stage have appeared at one or another of these Nationals, and nearly all American presidents since Andrew Jackson have attended performances there. Apart from a stint as the circus in 1844 and service as a film house from 1947 to 1952, during which time *Actors' Equity refused to allow its members to perform there because of the house's policy of not selling tickets to African Americans, the property and the theatres built on it have accumulated a record of theatrical continuity almost unparalleled in American history.

NATIVE AMERICANS IN DRAMA. The immediacy of whites-versus-Indians wars and the proximity of many settled Indians to American 18th-century cities made Native Americans figures of interest to several early American dramatists. The first play to center on them, however, was written not in English but in French. *Le Père-Indien* was the work of LeBlanc de Villeneuve, a French officer stationed in New Orleans, and was given an amateur mounting there in 1753. Although it had no influence on later plays, its story of an Indian father who sacrifices his life for the sake of his son foreshadowed numerous pictures of noble, tragic primitives that would long characterize plays of Native American life. In 1766 the maverick Major Robert Rogers published his semihistorical if romanticized tragedy of *Ponteach*, but no record of performance survives. One reason for its failure to find a stage may have been an implicit contempt or at least condescension on the part of most whites toward Indians. This could explain why the earliest Native-American–themed plays to reach the stage and sometimes find success, although they, too, generally depicted the Indian as wronged and doomed, were couched in musical terms. *Tammany* (1794), The *Indian Princess* (1808), and *Harlequin Panattatah; or, The Genii of the Algonquins* (1809) are examples. The Indian Princess is probably the first play to deal with Pocahontas, who for decades remained a favorite of dramatists, including George Washington Parke Custis, Robert Dale Owen, and John *Brougham. But the immediate inspiration for the deluge of Indian stories that flooded American stages in the 1830s and 1840s certainly can be ascribed to John Augustus *Stone's *Metamora* (1828), which was turned into one of the raging successes of contemporary theatre by Edwin *Forrest. Perhaps because by this time most theatrical centers were far removed from Indian territory, such plays could generally offer a romanticized view of these imposed-upon natives, often fighting to the death to protect what they saw as their heritage. The lengthy list of now-forgotten works would include *Sassacus, or, The Indian Wife; Onylda, or, The Pequot Maid; Ontiata, or, The Indian Heroine; Osceola; Tuscalomba; Carabasset; Narramattah; Wacousta; Wissahickon;* and many others. Apart from *Metamora*, the most popular play on the subject during the first part of the 19th century was undoubtedly Brougham's burlesque, *Pocahontas; or, The Gentle Savage* (1855). Taking a light-hearted look at both Native Americans and settlers, it served as a sort of bridge between the basically humanistic, romanticized pictures that preceded it and the more indifferent, even negative depictions that arose after the Civil War. Native Americans in the late 19th century almost never served as heroes or heroines as they had before; they were generally minor figures or, more often, a band of drink-crazed marauders doing the villain's bidding. *Across the Continent (1871) is a typical example. The Wild West shows offered by Buffalo Bill (William *Cody) and others also fostered period perceptions. The pendulum swung back at the beginning of the 20th century with such plays as Strongheart (1905) and The *Squaw Man (1905). But a further rise in the popularity of Native-American themes in the theatre may have been discouraged by the growth at the time of silent films, which offered a greater range and freedom of action when recounting tales of the Wild West. Thereafter Native Americans rarely appeared in American drama. At best they were consigned minor roles, often comic. The wise Sitting Bull in *Annie Get Your Gun (1946) exemplifies this treatment.

Two exceptions were Arthur *Kopit's Indians (1969), which attempted to make modern audiences share the guilt for their forefathers' behavior toward Native Americans, and Christopher Sergel's Black Elk Speaks (1981), based on John Neihardt's book about the history leading up to the massacre at Wounded Knee in 1890. Both well-intentioned plays failed to find an audience in New York but enjoyed many productions in regional and amateur theatres. Theatre by and about Native Americans has not been very widespread in modern times, though ritual dramas, in which the audience were all participants, was very common throughout the hundreds of North American tribes that existed before the arrival of Europeans. These performances were built around legends and the history of the community, so the art form died out when the communities were broken up. In the 1970s attempts were made by contemporary Native Americans to revive this form of theatre. The Red Earth Theatre in Seattle and the Native American Ensemble Theatre in New York were two early groups, later joined by others. But a revived Native American theatre still was experiencing growing pains at the end of the century.

NATIVE SON (1941), a play by Paul *Green and Richard Wright. [*St. James Theatre, 114 perf.] Bigger Thomas (Canada *Lee) is an African-American youth with a long record of trouble. He has grown up both frightened by and hateful of the white society he knows he is not a part of. Despite his record, a rich white man hires him as chauffeur. By accident Bigger kills the man's daughter and, in a panic, he burns her body and flees. He is captured, tried, and sentenced to death. While awaiting execution, his fears disappear and he becomes convinced he has played a small, but noteworthy role in destroying the security of the white world. Based on Wright's novel, the Orson *Welles and John *Houseman production, according to Burns

*Mantle, "builds steadily through a series of theatrical climaxes, and though it may be argued that theoretically these are the common climaxes of a conventional melodrama concerned with the career of a tough black, criminally inclined, they take on a new stature in this particular case." Despite similarly exultant notices by most other critics, as well as Lee's bravura performance and Welles's brilliant direction, the play found a relatively limited audience.

NATURALISM. A theatrical style sometimes called "realism," it began as a rebellion against the romantic artificialities of much 19th-century theatre. Initially such early exponents as Emile Zola conceived it as simply offering an unadulterated "slice of life" with all theatrical glossing over of hard facts removed and with only limited concern, if any, about the necessity of presenting such views in "well-made" plays. However, it soon came to be perceived, at least popularly, as unswerving portrayals of the seamiest side of existence. Gorky's The Lower Depths is often cited as the classic example. Those who separate realism from naturalism often suggest that the former is more selective and therefore has to be more carefully contrived, and they offer the best plays of *Ibsen as instances. Naturalism is often seen as a heightened form of realism with all five senses involved. David *Belasco's productions with dirt on the floor and live chickens on stage were the most obvious examples. *O'Neill's sea plays or his The *Iceman Cometh and some of the "*living newspapers" of the 1930s were later examples. Some more recent New York productions that involved naturalism might include *American Buffalo (1977), *Talley's Folly (1980), and several of August *Wilson's dramas.

NATWICK, Mildred (1905–94), actress. The Baltimore native made her stage debut in her hometown in 1929 and first appeared in New York in 1932 in Carry Nation. A versatile performer, she was active for nearly forty years. Perhaps her most-remembered comic roles were the outlandish medium Madame Arcati in Blithe Spirit (1941), the looney Mme. St. Pé in Waltz of the Toreadors (1957), the harassed mother Mrs. Banks in *Barefoot in the Park (1963), and the crafty thief Ida Dodd in 70, Girls, 70 (1971).

NAUGHTY MARIETTA (1910), an operetta by Rida Johnson *Young (book, lyrics), Victor *Herbert (music). [New York Theatre, 136 perf.] Marietta (Emma *Trentini) is an independent young lady of noble origin who has fled to America to escape an unwanted marriage. Coming to Louisiana disguised as a peasant, she meets Captain Dick

Warrington (Orville Harrold) who leads his rangers in seeking out the villainous pirate, Bras Priqué. The mysterious pirate is actually the lieutenant governor's son Etienne Grandet (Edward Martindel), who has cast aside his quadroon mistress Adah (Marie Duchene) and turns his attentions on Marietta. To win her hand, Etienne reveals his pirate identity and threatens to have her sent back home. But Marietta insists she will marry only the man who can finish a snatch of song she has sung since childhood. When Dick does just that in "Ah, Sweet Mystery of Life," Etienne is captured and Dick ends up with Marietta. *Notable songs*: Italian Street Song; Tramp, Tramp, Tramp; I'm Falling in Love with Someone; 'Neath the Southern Moon. As in the two other major American musical successes of its season, *Madame Sherry* and The *Pink Lady*, this operetta employed its best melody as a sort of motif throughout the evening, although it was not fully sung until just before the finale. The American setting might be seen to have given the musical a certain, special pertinence, but was, after all, set in a distant, romantic time when New Orleans was under foreign rule. The score is generally acknowledged as Herbert's best. It is still revived on occasion and has entered the repertory of the New York City Opera and other companies.

NAZIMOVA, Alla (1879–1945), actress. The dark, intense Russian-born leading lady studied in Switzerland and in her homeland, where she soon became known in St. Petersburg. She came to America in 1905 and was performing at Orlenoff's Russian Lyceum on Third Street when Henry *Miller spotted her and convinced her to learn English and to star in his production of *Hedda Gabler*. Walter Prichard *Eaton wrote, "Her Hedda Gabler was a high-born exotic, an orchid of a woman, baleful, fascinating—and to some of us not at all like Ibsen's heroine." After seeing her in several other plays, he concluded, "She has brought something to our stage it did not possess before, something modern, subtle, exciting, the power to suggest finer shades of meaning, symbols in the dialogue." Nazimova was best known for her acting in such classic works as *A Doll's House*, *The Master Builder*, *Little Eyolf*, *The Cherry Orchard*, *A Month in the Country*, and *Ghosts*, and she created one major contemporary role: the murderous wife Christine Mannon in Eugene *O'Neill's *Mourning Becomes Electra* (1931). Biography: *Nazimova*, Gavin Lambert, 1997.

NEAFIE, J[ohn] A[ndrew] J[ackson] (1815–92), actor. Born in New York, he worked as a joiner before turning to the stage, paying Edmund *Simpson $300 for the privilege of making his debut as

Othello at the *Park Theatre in 1838. That same season he also offered his Shylock and Richard III. For a time he toured as principal supporting player to Edwin *Forrest, then served as leading man at the *Bowery Theatre. The tall, strong-voiced actor spent most of the rest of his career touring the South and what was the West of his day.

NED McCOBB'S DAUGHTER (1926), a play by Sidney *Howard. [*John Golden Theatre, 132 perf.] Carrie (Clare *Eames), daughter of Captain Ned McCobb (Albert Perry), has married into the good-for-nothing Callahan family. Her faithless husband, George (Earle *Larimore), has forced McCobb to mortgage his farm to pay for an abortion for George's mistress and has also been stealing money from the local ferry company. When George is arrested, his bootlegger brother, Babe (Alfred *Lunt), offers Carrie the money to pay off the mortgage and to provide George's legal fees in return for allowing him to store his whiskey in her barn. Carrie accepts the money but then cooperates with the authorities to rid herself of both brothers. Sharply etched character studies elevated this *Theatre Guild production above the run of contemporary melodramas. The figures of Carrie and Babe allowed Eames and Lunt to give two of their finest, most offbeat performances.

NEDERLANDER, James [Morton] (b. 1922), theatre owner and producer. The son of Detroit theatre owner David Nederlander (1886–1965), he has enlarged the family holdings until they are second nationally only to those of the *Shubert Organization. Among the Nederlander-owned theatres are the *Palace, the *Nederlander, and *Marquis Theatres. As a producer, he has presented such successes as *Winged Victory* (1943), *On a Clear Day You Can See Forever* (1967), *Applause* (1970), *Whose Life Is It Anyway?* (1979), *Peter Pan* (1979 and 1990), *Joseph and the Technicolor Dreamcoat* (1982), *Me and My Girl* (1986), *Shadowlands* (1990), and The *Will Rogers Follies* (1991).

NEDERLANDER THEATRE (New York) The 1,200-seat playhouse on West 41st Street has gone by many names during its history, and has changed ownership several times. It was built as the National Theatre in 1921 when there were still a handful of Broadway playhouses south of 42nd Street. But as the others disappeared, the National found itself outside of the Times Square district and it became a problematic house. William Neil Smith designed the theatre with a dark Italian walnut interior and a festive facade of galleries. The National was renamed the Billy Rose Theatre in 1958 when producer *Rose bought it and renovated it, only to be rechristened the Trafalgar Theatre when the *Nederlanders purchased it in 1979. The next year it was renamed the Nederlander after the organizations's founder, the late David Nederlander. Although the playhouse has had its hit plays and musicals over the decades, none ran as long as *Rent (1996).

NEEDLES AND PINS (1880), a "comedy of the present" by Augustin *Daly. [Daly's Theatre, 79 perf.] The pushy Mrs. Vandusen (Fanny *Morant) is determined to marry off her weak son Kit (John Brand) to a rich lady, although Kit loves the poor piano teacher Mary Forrest (May Fielding). She is also determined to marry off her aging sister Dosie Heffron (Mrs. G. H. *Gilbert), to anybody who will have her so that Silena Vandusen (Ada *Rehan), Mrs. Vandusen's daughter, may then be free to wed. In revealing her plans to Mr. Vandusen (Charles *Fisher) she lets slip that she knows he himself once loved a poor piano teacher named Silena and later persuaded his wife to name their daughter after his lost love. Miss Forrest comes into a huge inheritance and decides to do good deeds with her new wealth. She, too, has learned of the old romance and instructs her young lawyer, Tom Versus (John *Drew), to make Silena and Vandusen rich enough to marry, not realizing that both have long since married others. Because young Kit had been named for his father, a series of mistaken identities transpires, made all the more complicated when the characters meet at a masked ball. In the end, of course, everything is happily resolved when Mrs. Vandusen learns that Mary is now quite eligible to marry Kit. Tom marries Silena; Dosie seems to snare an elderly collector of bric-a-brac, Nicholas Geagle (James *Lewis); and Mr. and Mrs. Vandusen can finally look forward to some wedded bliss after long married years of living on needles and pins. The comedy was loosely adapted from J. Rosen's *Starke Mitteln*. Daly's biographer brother noted that it was this play "in which Miss Rehan, Mr. Drew, Mrs. Gilbert, and Mr. Lewis were first recognized as the famous quartet which for so many seasons endeared Daly's Theatre to the public."

NEGRO ENSEMBLE COMPANY (New York). With a substantial financial contribution from the Ford Foundation, the group was organized in 1967 by Robert Hooks, Douglas Turner *Ward, and Gerald Krone. Their aim was to establish "a place wherein Black theatrical talent could be continuously presented—without regard to the whims of commercial theatre." During its history the company won numerous awards and additional grants, but it also faced periods of financial strain, which often showed in their low-budget productions. Yet the quality of the acting remained outstanding and several of the original scripts premiered, such as The *River Niger (1973) and A *Soldier's Play (1981), were also superior. By the 1990s the company lost its Off-Broadway home and was presenting shows only sporadically, and in 1997 it quietly ceased operation. Yet it remains the longest-lived African-American producing organization in the history of New York theatre. **Robert HOOKS** (b. 1937) began his professional theatre career as an actor in the touring production of A *Raisin in the Sun (1959). After appearing Off Broadway in The Blacks (1962), he was acclaimed for his performance as the victimized Clay in LeRoi *Jones's Dutchman (1964). Hooks later performed in many Negro Ensemble productions before going to Washington and founding the D.C. Black Repertory Company.

NEIGHBORHOOD PLAYHOUSE (New York). Built on Grand Street in 1915 by Alice and Irene Lewisohn, it housed an amateur repertory company until 1920, when the ensemble turned professional. The new troupe offered plays by *Shaw, *O'Neill, and other contemporary dramatists, as well as a series of popular revues known as The Grand Street Follies. The company was disbanded in 1927. The surviving corporation occasionally mounted plays in later years. However, the most important offshoot of the company was the Neighborhood Playhouse School of the Theatre, founded in 1928 by the Lewisohns and Rita Wallach Morgenthau. The professional training program continues today. From 1935 to 1990 its most important faculty member was **Sanford MEISNER** (1905–97) who taught his Meisner Technique of acting based on *Stanislavsky's ideas. Meisner was an original member of the *Group Theatre who acted in or directed some of that company's early successes. He later performed with the *Theatre Guild before taking up teaching and freelance directing.

NEIL SIMON THEATRE (New York). A popular musical house located on the edge of the theatre district (West 52nd Street), the playhouse opened in 1927 as the Alvin Theatre, its name fashioned by the first syllables of the producers Alex *Aarons and Vinton *Freedley who built it. Herbert J. *Krapp designed the 1,400-seat theatre, which was in the style of the eighteenth-century English playhouses. The opening production, the *Gershwins' *Funny Face (1927), was a hit; and over the years the Alvin saw many others, from *Anything Goes (1934) and *Lady in the Dark (1941) to *Company (1970) and *Annie (1977). The theatre is owned by the *Nederlanders who in 1983 renamed it after Neil *Simon whose hit *Brighton Beach Memoirs (1983) was playing there at the time.

NEILSON, [Lilian] **Adelaide** (1848–80), actress. The English performer, whose own life was as tragic as some of the heroines she portrayed, was of illegitimate birth. A great beauty, she had slightly irregular features, which only added a certain piquancy to her dark eyes and chestnut hair, the latter sometimes dyed with a gold tinge. Neilson made several American tours between 1872 and 1879 and was called by William *Winter "the best representative of Shakespeare's Juliet, Viola, and Imogen who had appeared on the stage in our time." He wrote, "The subtlety of [her Juliet] was equaled only by its intensity, and neither was surpassed except by its reality." Her other American offering included Rosalind, Beatrice, Pauline in *The *Lady of Lyons*, and Lady Teazle. Biography: *Adelaide Neilson*, Laura Holloway Langford, 1885.

NELSON, Barry [né Robert Nielson] (b. 1920), actor. The stocky, rather beady-eyed leading man was born in Oakland, California, and made his debut in *Winged Victory* (1943). After gaining notice as the playwright Peter Sloan in *Light Up the Sky* (1948), he scored a major success as the romantically inclined architect Donald Gresham in *The *Moon Is Blue* (1951). His other long runs came as Bob McKellaway, the writer who can't help loving his exasperating ex-wife, in *Mary, Mary* (1961), and Julian, the philandering dentist, in *Cactus Flower* (1965). In 1983 he headed a road company of *42nd Street* and in 1990 led a tour of *Lend Me a Tenor*.

NELSON, Richard (b. 1938), lighting designer. A native New Yorker educated at the High School of the Performing Arts, he began designing lights professionally Off Broadway in 1955. In addition to plenty of commercial lighting and for dance companies, Nelson has lit such theatre productions as *All Over* (1971), *The *Magic Show* (1974), *Morning's at Seven* (1980), *The Caine Mutiny Court-Martial* (1983), *Sunday in the Park with George* (1984), *Into the Woods* (1987), *Cafe Crown* (1989), *No Man's Land* (1994), *The *Shadow Box* (1994), and *Golden Child* (1996).

NELSON, Richard (playwright). See *James Joyce's The Dead*.

NERVOUS WRECK, THE (1923), a comedy by Owen *Davis. [Sam H. Harris Theatre, 279 perf.] When timid, hypochondriacal Henry Williams (Otto *Kruger), recovering on an Arizona ranch from his latest nervous attack, helps Sally Morgan (June *Walker) escape an unwanted marriage, he finds himself in a heap of trouble. The pair are pursued by a posse, they run out of gas, and Henry is forced to hold up a passing motorist to get additional fuel. Then they hide in a neighboring ranch, posing as a cook and waitress. By the time Sally's father agrees not to force her to marry the man of his choice, Sally is prepared to nurse Henry through sickness and health indefinitely. Davis had based his comedy on E. J. Rath's magazine serial, *The Wreck*. Welcomed by John *Corbin of the *Times* as "a really funny farce," the play later became the source for the popular musical *WHOOPEE* (1928) with Eddie *Cantor starring as Henry. The new book by director William Anthony *McGuire added some Indians to the plot, as well as the funny, loyal nurse Mary Custer (Ethel Shutta) whom Henry weds when Sally (Frances Upton) ends up with her sweetheart (Paul Gregory). Walter Donaldson (music) and Gus Kahn (lyrics) provided the score, and the Florenz *Ziegfeld production ran 407 performances at the *New Amsterdam Theatre. *Notable songs*: Love Me or Leave Me; Makin' Whoopee; I'm Bringing a Red, Red Rose. A 1979 revival, which originated at the *Goodspeed Opera House, tampered heavily with the text and tone of the work but still proved to be delightful entertainment.

NESBITT, Cathleen [Mary] (1888–1982), actress. The beautiful, worldly English leading lady, once reputed to be the mistress of Rupert Brooke, made her American debut in 1911 with the Irish Players of the *Abbey Theatre. She reappeared regularly thereafter, but is best remembered for several later roles: Julia in *The *Cocktail Party* (1950), the kindly, knowing dowager Alicia de St. Ephlam in *Gigi* (1951), Mrs. Larrabee in *Sabrina Fair* (1953), and Mrs. Higgins in *My Fair Lady* (1956). At the age of ninety-two, shortly before her death, she repeated this last role in a 1981 revival.

NETHERSOLE, Olga [Isabel] (1866–1951), actress. The Latin-miened English performer, famous for her torrid love scenes, made her American debut in 1894 in *The Transgressor* and then toured as Camille, Juliet, and Frou-Frou. Nethersole made several other American tours before winning notoriety by creating the role of the French courtesan Fanny Legrand in Clyde *Fitch's *Sapho* (1900). Outraged editorials led to her arrest for indecency, but she was acquitted after many notables, including the archly conservative William *Winter, appeared in her defense. In later years she played in *Magda*, *The Labyrinth*, and *Adrienne Lecouvreur*, as well as taking the title role in the *New Theatre's mounting of *Mary Magdalene*. Her last American appearances were in vaudeville in 1913, where she offered a truncated version of *Sapho*.

NEVER TOO LATE (1962), a comedy by Sumner Arthur Long. [Playhouse, 1,007 perf.] Although

Harry Lambert (Paul *Ford) and his wife Edith (Maureen O'Sullivan) are well into middle age and have a grown daughter and son-in-law, they are also expectant parents. Harry is a crusty, if somewhat perturbed codger, the sort who replies to his wife's asking if he likes her new hat with "Keep it, anyway." His response to the news that he is to be a father again is one sustained howl. His family's attempts to comfort him all seem to backfire until everyone learns to live with the situation. This slight comedy was enhanced immeasurably by Ford's dourly droll performance. Not all critics felt that its humor was derived from the main situation, Henry *Hewes noting in the *Best Plays series, "The fun of the play turned out to be the running battle between the parsimonious father and his dependent but frustratedly defiant son-in-law."

NEW AMSTERDAM THEATRE (New York). Built in 1903 as the flagship of the *Erlanger empire from designs by *Herts and Tallant, this ornate house helped establish 42nd Street as New York's principal theatrical thoroughfare. Within the eleven-story structure were two theatres (a 1,750-seat auditorium and a rooftop theatre), elevators, lounges, decorative murals, and an elegant green, mother of pearl, and mauve color scheme. Although the theatre opened with A *Midsummer Night's Dream and left the legitimate fold after Walter *Huston's 1937 *Othello, it was known primarily as a musical house. Most of the *Ziegfeld Follies played there, as did The *Merry Widow, *Sally, The *Band Wagon, and other great musical hits. For many years its enclosed roof garden housed a popular cabaret, ideal for summertime fare before the advent of air conditioning. In 1937 the house started showing films, and it slowly deteriorated over the decades. In 1979 both its exterior and interior were declared landmarks, but the old house was not restored until 1992 when the *Disney corporation bought it and started to renovate the theatre as part of the redevelopment of 42nd Street. More than $50 million was spent to recreate the original colors, fixtures, and ornamentation of the New Amsterdam, and the result was proclaimed by all to be perhaps the finest theatre restoration project in the city. The theatre reopened in 1997 with a limited run of King David, then six months later The Lion King (1997) became its first new (and longest) tenant.

NEW FACES. This was a series of revues presented by Leonard [Dexter] Sillman (1908–82), a Detroit-born actor-turned-producer, as a showcase for young talent. Editions were offered in 1934, 1936, 1942, 1952, 1956, 1962, and 1968. Players who made early appearances in the show included Imogene Coca, Henry *Fonda, Van Johnson, Eartha Kitt, Paul Lynde, Maggie Smith, T. C. Jones, Madeline *Kahn, and Robert Klein. The 1952 edition was the most successful (365 performances) and probably the best of the series, offering such memorable comic numbers as "Boston Beguine," sung by Alice Ghostley, and "Monotonous," sung by Kitt. Among its best sketches were "Oedipus Goes South," in which Ronny Graham, lolling in a hammock, spoofed a pouting Truman *Capote, and "Tour of the Month," in which a bandaged Paul Lynde, on crutches, described his recent African safari with his late wife.

NEW FEDERAL THEATRE (New York). Named after the African-American branch of the *Federal Theatre Project in the 1930s, this ambitious company dedicated to works by women and minority artists, was founded in 1970 by Woodie King Jr. Working out of the Henry Street Settlement's Arts for Living Center on the lower East Side, the group collaborates with the *Public Theatre where many of its productions have moved for greater recognition. Among the New Federal Theatre's notable productions were Ntozake Shange's for colored girls who have considered suicide when the rainbow is enuf and David Henry *Hwang's The Dance and the Railroad.

NEW GIRL IN TOWN. See Anna Christie.

NEW JERSEY SHAKESPEARE FESTIVAL (Madison). The state's only professional theatre dedicated to the works of Shakespeare and the classics, it was founded by Paul Barry and Phillip Dorian in 1963 as a summer program. The company has grown and now performs in the 308-seat proscenium F. M. Kirby Theatre and in an open-air amphitheatre situated on the campus of the College of St. Elizabeth in nearby Morristown. The group's repertory is strong in Greek and Roman plays, as well as in the works of Shakespeare. The company changed its name to the Shakespeare Theatre of New Jersey in 2003.

NEW MOON, THE (1928), an operetta by Oscar *Hammerstein II (book, lyrics), Frank *Mandel, Laurence *Schwab (book), Sigmund *Romberg (music). [*Imperial Theatre, 509 perf.] Robert Misson (Robert *Halliday) is a French nobleman whose revolutionary sympathies have forced him to flee to New Orleans where he is disguised as a servant. He falls in love with his employer's daughter, Marianne (Evelyn *Herbert). With his friend Philippe (William O'Neal) and others, Robert hopes to defeat the royalists. But Robert's cover is exposed, and he believes Marianne is responsible. When he is put on a ship returning to France, Marianne follows him aboard. Robert's men, disguised as pirates, attack the ship and take him and Marianne to a settlement on the Isle of Pines. Robert studiously ignores Marianne until they all learn of the Revolution and he learns of Marianne's innocence. *Notable songs*: Softly, As in a Morning Sunrise; Wanting You; One Kiss; Stouthearted Men; Lover, Come Back to Me. Hailed by St. John Ervine of the *World* as "the most charming and fragrant entertainment of its sort that I have seen in a long time," the musical was the last traditional operetta of its era to enjoy a long run. The New York City Opera revived it in 1986, and it remains in the repertory of other groups.

NEW ORLEANS (Louisiana). The first plays presented in New Orleans were apparently those given by a company of French performers who had fled from what is now Haiti after the black revolution there and who set up in the city in 1791. Drama in English began in 1806 when a Mr. Rannie presented a double bill at Moore's Large Building. Thereafter for many years French and English theatre flourished side by side. In 1807 the first real theatre, Théâtre St. Pierre, was erected but survived only three seasons. Noah *Ludlow's visits encouraged the growth of English plays, although the city did not become a significant theatrical center until the arrival there of James *Caldwell. He erected several playhouses, including the long-famous St. Charles Theatre (which stood until 1965). These early years are covered in detail in Nelle Smither's *A History of the English Theatre in New Orleans* (1944). Subsequently the city remained an important stop for all great visiting players and supported several local stock companies. It was less affected by the Civil War than most Southern cities and continued to offer lively theatre well into the 20th century. However, today New Orleans has become a minor touring town and is one of the few large cities in the nation without a major resident theatre. But it does boast the touring house Saenger Theatre, the Southern Repertory Theatre, and Le Petit Theatre Du Vieux Carre, which claims to be the oldest continuous community theatre in the country.

NEW THEATRE (New York). Underwritten by leading New York citizens, including J. P. Morgan and Otto Kahn, and designed by *Carrère and *Hastings, the theatre was opened in 1909 with the hope that it would provide a home for a permanent repertory company offering the greatest in classic and new plays. The structure, designed in the Italian Renaissance style, seated twenty-five hundred and boasted a second theatre on the rooftop, a large orchestra pit, twin grand staircases, and a revolving stage run by electric power.

The first attraction was *Antony and Cleopatra*, with E. H. *Sothern and Julia *Marlowe in the title roles. The opening productions proved disappointing, and this, coupled with the theatre's out-of-the-way location (62nd Street facing Central Park), discouraged playgoers. Because the huge, elaborate house had large operating costs, the poor attendance forced quick abandonment of repertory plans. For a time the theatre was called the Century and served to house sumptuous *Ziegfeld and *Dillingham musicals, and later was used by Max *Reinhardt for his gigantic mountings. The theatre was demolished in 1930 and replaced by luxury apartments.

NEW YORK CLIPPER. See *Clipper*.

NEW YORK DRAMA CRITICS CIRCLE. While discussions about forming an association of local critics were initiated as early as 1927, the group was not officially organized until 1935. No small part of the impetus at that time came from dissatisfaction with the drama selections of the *Pulitzer Prize committee. The first winner of the New York Drama Critics Circle Award was *Winterset*. In later years the group added other awards, including those for best foreign play and best musical. The Circle also holds regular meetings to examine problems of contemporary theatre. It should be noted that in many years a foreign play was selected as the overall best play and that some of the American entries won awards only after a clear majority could not decide, and so a "weighted" ballot was taken. All of the American plays and musicals that won a NYDCC Award have their own entries. The complete list of winners and the year the award was given follows. 1936: *Winterset*; 1937: *High Tor*; 1938: *Of Mice and Men, Shadow and Substance*; 1939: *The White Steed*; 1940: *The Time of Your Life*; 1941: *Watch on the Rhine, The Corn Is Green*; 1942: *Blithe Spirit*; 1943: *The Patriots*; 1944: *Jacobowsky and the Colonel*; 1945: *The Glass Menagerie*; 1946: *Carousel*; 1947: *All My Sons, No Exit, Brigadoon*; 1948: *A Streetcar Named Desire, The Winslow Boy*; 1949: *Death of a Salesman, South Pacific, The Madwoman of Chaillot*; 1950: *The Member of the Wedding, The Consul, The Cocktail Party*; 1951: *Darkness at Noon, Guys and Dolls, The Lady's Not for Burning*; 1952: *I Am a Camera, Pal Joey, Venus Observed*; 1953: *Picnic, Wonderful Town, The Love of Four Colonels*; 1954: *Teahouse of the August Moon, The Golden Apple, Ondine*; 1955: *Cat on a Hot Tin Roof, The Saint of Bleecker Street, Witness for the Prosecution*; 1956: *The Diary of Anne Frank, My Fair Lady, Tiger at the Gates*; 1957: *Long Day's Journey into Night, The Most Happy Fella, The Waltz of the Toreadors*; 1958: *Look Homeward, Angel, The Music Man, Look Back in Anger*; 1959: *A Raisin* *in the Sun, The Visit, La Plume de Ma Tante;* 1960: *Toys in the Attic, Fiorello!, Five Finger Exercise;* 1961: *All the Way Home, Carnival!, A Taste of Honey;* 1962: *The Night of the Iguana, How to Succeed in Business Without Really Trying, A Man for All Seasons;* 1963: *Who's Afraid of Virginia Woolf?, Beyond the Fringe;* 1964: *Hello, Dolly!, Luther;* 1965: *The Subject Was Roses, Fiddler on the Roof;* 1966: *Man of La Mancha, Marat/Sade;* 1967: *Cabaret, The Homecoming;* 1968: *Your Own Thing, Rosencrantz and Guildenstern Are Dead;* 1969: *The Great White Hope, 1776;* 1970: *The Effect of Gamma Rays on Man-in-the-Moon Marigolds, Company, Borstal Boy;* 1971: *The House of Blue Leaves, Follies, Home;* 1972: *That Championship Season, The Screens, Two Gentlemen of Verona, Sticks and Bones;* 1973: *The Hot l Baltimore, A Little Night Music, The Changing Room;* 1974: *Candide, The Contractor, Short Eyes;* 1975: *A Chorus Line, Equus, The Taking of Miss Janie;* 1976: *Streamers, Pacific Overtures, Travesties;* 1977: *American Buffalo, Annie, Otherwise Engaged;* 1978: *Ain't Misbehavin', Da;* 1979: *Sweeney Todd, The Elephant Man;* 1980: *Talley's Folly, Betrayal, Evita;* 1981: *Crimes of the Heart, A Lesson from Aloes;* 1982: *A Soldier's Play, The Life & Adventures of Nicholas Nickleby;* 1983: *Brighton Beach Memoirs, Plenty, Little Shop of Horrors;* 1984: *Glengarry Glen Ross, The Real Thing, Sunday in the Park with George;* 1985: *Ma Rainey's Black Bottom;* 1986: *A Lie of the Mind, Benefactors;* 1987: *Fences, Les Liasons Dangereuses, Les Misérables;* 1988: *Joe Turner's Come and Gone, Into the Woods, The Road to Mecca;* 1989: *The Heidi Chronicles, Aristocrats;* 1990: *The Piano Lesson, Privates on Parade, City of Angels;* 1991: *Six Degrees of Separation, The Will Rogers Follies, Our Country's Good;* 1992: *Two Trains Running, Dancing at Lughnasa;* 1993: *Angels in America, Millennium Approaches, Someone Who'll Watch Over Me, Kiss of the Spider Woman;* 1994: *Three Tall Women;* 1995: *Love! Valor! Compassion!, Arcadia;* 1996: *Seven Guitars, Rent, Molly Sweeney;* 1997: *How I Learned to Drive, Violet, Skylight;* 1998: *Pride's Crossing, Art, The Lion King;* 1999: *Wit, Parade, Closer;* 2000: *Jitney, James Joyce's The Dead, Copenhagen;* 2001: *Proof, The Producers, The Invention of Love;* 2002: *The Goat;* 2003: *Take Me Out, Hairspray, Talking Heads.*

NEW YORK DRAMATIC MIRROR. See *Dramatic Mirror.*

NEW YORK IDEA, THE (1906), a play by Langdon *Mitchell. [Lyric Theatre, 66 perf.] Since Cynthia Karslake (Mrs. *Fiske) and John Karslake (John *Mason) are divorced, there seems to be no reason why Cynthia should not marry Judge Phillip Phillimore (Charles Harbury), who himself has been divorced recently. After all, "Marry for whim! That's the New York idea of marriage." The news

prompts the ex-Mrs. Phillimore, Vida (Marion Lea), to set her sights on John. Before long it is announced that John and Vida will marry at the same time as Cynthia and Phillip. Enter an English roué, Sir Wilfred Cates-Darby (George *Arliss), who would win both ladies away from their new amours. On the day of the wedding he invites Cynthia, an ardent horsewoman, to the races. She accepts and telegraphs Phillip that she will be late for the nuptials. The delay and Phillip's reaction to it convince Cynthia she has made a mistake. She rushes to John's home, only to learn that the wedding has taken place. Her dismay turns to relief when she discovers the bride and groom are Vida and Wilfred. She returns to John, who has kept her wedding ring just in case. Theatrical historian Edwin J. Bronner has called the work "a play of wit and substance, one of the outstanding high comedies of the American theatre." It has enjoyed numerous revivals.

NEW YORK SCHOOL OF ACTING. See American Academy of Dramatic Arts.

NEW   YORK   SHAKESPEARE   FESTIVAL. Founded in 1954 by Joseph *Papp, it was chartered by the State of New York Educational Department to "encourage and cultivate interest in poetic drama with emphasis on the works of William Shakespeare and his Elizabethan contemporaries, and to establish an annual summer Shakespeare Festival." Performances were given in various locations before the company acquired a permanent home at the Delacorte Theatre in Central Park in 1962. The productions were often refreshingly experimental and sometimes featured such notable players as George C. *Scott, Colleen *Dewhurst, and James Earle *Jones. In 1966 the organization took over the old Astor Library, not far from Washington Square, and converted it into an Off-Broadway theatre center called the **PUBLIC THEATRE.** The first of the theatres in the building opened in 1967 with the musical *Hair. Although the summer outdoor productions, which were offered free to the public except for some reserved seats, continued to emphasize Shakespearean mountings, the Off-Broadway venue presented a wide-ranging program of revivals and new plays. The large number of productions, their variety and striking percentage of successes made the New York Shakespeare Festival–Public Theatre probably the most exciting producing organization since the heyday of the *Theatre Guild. However, some of the plays wallowed in gratuitous profanity and nudity, others took aggressively confrontational stances, and many tended to be trendy and more interested in current topics than solid dramaturgy. Still, the Public became the voice for many African-American,

Hispanic, and Asian-American playwrights, and the summer Shakespeare offerings were groundbreaking in color-blind casting. Among the Festival's many offerings, besides *Hair*, were **No Place to Be Somebody* (1969), *The *Basic Training of Pavlo Hummel* (1971), the musical **Two Gentlemen of Verona* (1971), **Sticks and Bones* (1971), **That Championship Season* (1972), *A *Chorus Line* (1975), a popular *The *Pirates of Penzance* (1980), and *The *Mystery of Edwin Drood* (1985). The Public also hosts experimental theatre companies from across the country and around the world. For a short period in the early 1970s, Papp and the organization attempted to also manage the Repertory Theatre at *Lincoln Center but withdrew from the ever-problematic venue. The Public Theatre has suffered since the death of Papp in 1991. JoAnne *Akalaitis was named his immediate successor but didn't last a full season. George C. *Wolfe has been more successful in managing the large, disparate organization, though the number of plays and musicals to achieve any notoriety has been small. But the goal of both the New York Shakespeare Festival and the Public Theatre has never been to create hits; both continue to serve the New York community with valuable theatre ventures that might not exist were the organization not there.

NEW YORK SOCIETY FOR PREVENTION OF CRUELTY TO CHILDREN. See Gerry Society.

NEW YORK THEATRE WORKSHOP (New York). Founded in 1979, the company (located in a 188-seat East Village space) was first noticed when it presented a British production of *Mad Forest* (1991) and found nationwide acclaim when it premiered **Rent* (1996). The theatre group is dedicated to new works (though unusual revivals have been seen there) and offers readings and residencies in addition to its fully staged productions. Some offerings became well known by their controversial nature, such as *Quills* (1995) and *Shopping and Fucking* (1998), while *Rent* and *Dirty Blonde* (2000) were mainstream hits that transferred to Broadway.

NIBLO'S GARDEN (New York). In 1828 William Niblo (1790?–1878), an entrepreneur who had made his money as a caterer and running a stagecoach line between Boston and New York, built the small Sans Souci Theatre on the grounds of the Columbia Garden at Broadway and Prince Street. Offering light, vaudeville-like entertainments to summer patrons out for fresh air and cool drinks, it proved so successful that a year later he built a larger, more permanent structure. The whole complex was renamed *Niblo's Garden and Theatre, which New Yorkers quickly abbreviated to Niblo's Garden. To increase patronage at what was then

virtually a northern suburb, Niblo ran stagecoaches from the Battery to the theatre. As the town steadily moved toward his playhouse and older theatres burned or were demolished, Niblo's became a major stage for drama and spectacle. Niblo retired when his own theatre burned in 1846, but was persuaded to rebuild it in 1849. In 1852 he prompted the erection of the Metropolitan Hotel on the site of the garden, and the auditorium thereafter was entered through the hotel lobby. After Niblo retired permanently in 1861, William *Wheatley took over management. It was under Wheatley's auspices that *The *Black Crook* was produced there in 1866. The extravaganza's success established the theatre as New York's leading home for musical and dramatic spectacle. It was rebuilt after another fire in 1872, but it never again enjoyed its former prominence because the theatrical center had continued to move still farther north. When it was demolished in 1895 it was New York's oldest playhouse.

NICE PEOPLE (1921), a play by Rachel *Crothers. [Klaw Theatre, 247 perf.] Teddy Gloucester (Francine *Larrimore) and her friends Hallie Livingston (Tallulah *Bankhead) and Eileen Baxter Jones (Katharine *Cornell) are hedonistic flappers. Over the objections of her father and aunt, Teddy spends the night partying with the equally high living Scottie Wilbur (Hugh Huntley). When Teddy and Scottie later find themselves stranded at the Gloucester country cottage, it brings down the wrath of Teddy's father. But during that rainy night at the cottage the young peoples' idyll had been intruded upon by a stranded motorist, young Billy Wade (Robert *Ames). The serious, proper Wade wins Teddy's affections, much to her father's pleasure. Hallie and Eileen are dismayed to realize that Teddy will be marrying and settling down. They will do no such thing, not when so many attractive men and lively parties beckon. Although many critics felt the play collapsed in the last act, with its contrived happy ending, the public found the Sam H. *Harris offering an excellent study of contemporary mores.

NICHOLS, Anne. See *Abie's Irish Rose.*

NICHOLS, Mike [né Michael Igor Peschkowsky] (b. 1931), director and comedian. Born in Berlin, his family fled the Nazis and came to New York. He studied at the University of Chicago for two years, then made his Manhattan acting debut in 1960 in *An Evening with Mike Nichols and Elaine May.* Their humor, often improvised or seemingly improvised, ridiculed the foibles and frustrations of everyday life. Thereafter Nichols worked primarily as a director, staging such comedy hits as **Barefoot in the*

Park (1963), *Luv (1964), *The* *Odd Couple (1965), *Plaza Suite (1968), *The* **Prisoner of Second Avenue* (1971), *The Real Thing* (1983), and *Social Security* (1986). He also directed more serious works, such as revivals of *The* *Little Foxes (1967), *Uncle Vanya* (1973), **Waiting for Godot* (1989), and *The Sea Gull* (2001), as well as *Streamers (1976), *Hurlyburly* (1984), and *Death and the Maiden* (1992). Nichols has co-produced some New York productions, most successfully *Annie (1977), and has directed many films.

NICHOLSON, Kenyon (1894–1986), playwright. Born in Crawfordsville, Indiana, he studied at Columbia University before braving Broadway with his first collaboration, *Honor Bright* (1921). Although most of his plays were written in conjunction with other playwrights, including two with S. N. *Behrman, his first success was a solo effort, *The Barker* (1927). Nicholson's biggest hit was **Sailor, Beware!* (1933), written with Charles Robinson, with whom he later collaborated on the modest successes *Swing Your Lady!* (1936) and *Apple of His Eye* (1946).

NICK OF THE WOODS; or, The Jibbenainosay (1839), a play by Louisa H. Medina. [New Bowery Theatre,12 perf.] After the Indians have massacred his family, Reginald Ashburn (Joseph *Proctor) adopts the disguise of a pacifist Quaker and travels the wilderness seeking revenge. He becomes known by a number of names, including Bloody Nathan, Nick, and Jibbenainosay, the last meaning an avenging devil. In his wanderings Ashburn is accompanied by Telie Doe (Mrs. *Shaw), a white girl who has been kidnapped and raised by Native Americans and who turns out to be Ashburn's long-lost cousin. With time he kills numerous Indians, including Wenonga (H. Lewis), the chief who had engineered the murder of Ashburn's family. But this last battle also costs Nick and Telie Doe their lives. Based on the novel of the same name by Robert M. *Bird, the work was often viewed as a corrective to the romantic notions of Native Americans then in vogue. First produced a year earlier at the *Old Bowery, it failed to catch on until this revival. It remained popular for several decades. Louisa H. Medina (d. 1838) was an active playwright of the time. Many of her works were dramatizations of contemporary novels, especially those of *Bulwer-Lytton. She was the wife of Thomas S. *Hamblin.

NICKINSON, Isabella. See Walcot, Charles M.

NIELSEN, Alice (1876–1943), singer and actress. Born in Nashville, she decided to become a professional singer after the break-up of her first marriage. Her earliest appearance was as Yum-Yum in an 1893 Oakland (California) production of *The* *Mikado. She then was immediately hired as leading lady at San Francisco's *Tivoli Opera House. There Henry Clay *Barnabee heard her sing and signed her on as a member of the *Bostonians in 1896, scoring a major success with Victor *Herbert's *The Serenade* (1897). To capitalize on her acclaim, Nielsen promptly deserted the Bostonians to form her own company, taking several prominent members with her. Her desertion proved the beginning of the end for the long-popular troupe. Her first solo venture was her greatest triumph, Herbert's *The* *Fortune Teller (1898), followed by the operetta *The Singing Girl* (1899). Shortly thereafter she left the legitimate stage for a career in grand opera. By the time she returned to Broadway in 1917 in *Kitty Darlin'*, her small, pure voice and her youthful charm had faded, so she quietly retired a short time later.

NIGGER, THE (1909), a play in three acts by Edward *Sheldon. [*New Theatre, in repertory.] Philip Morrow (Guy Bates Post) is a patrician, dedicated Southern governor who has long advocated white supremacy. However, when he hesitates to veto a prohibition bill opposed by his cousin, the distiller Clifton Noyes (Ben Johnson), Noyes discloses an old letter that reveals that Philip is the grandson of a Negro slave. Urged on by his fiancée, Georgiana (Annie *Russell), Philip vetoes the bill and prepares to face the voters with the truth about his past. The only American play to be produced in its first season by the highly touted, but short-lived repertory company at the New Theatre, it was also one of that group's few successes. Although some strident objections were raised to the title, and several critics felt the whole racial problem was subsidiary in the play to the romantic interest, the drama was so successful that two road companies were quickly sent out.

'NIGHT, MOTHER (1983), a play by Marsha *Norman. [*John Golden Theatre, 388 perf.; Pulitzer Prize.] The widow Thelma Cates (Anne Pitoniak) lives with her divorced daughter Jessie (Kathy Bates) in a small, snug house in the country. They would seem to lead a quiet but satisfactory life. Yet Jessie, an overweight epileptic whose husband has walked out on her and whose son has turned out badly, is so unhappy that on one seemingly normal evening she announces to her mother her intention to commit suicide. At first her mother is disbelieving, but later, recognizing that Jessie has given much thought to the matter and is very much in earnest, she tries, despite her growing terror, to dissuade her. But her efforts are in vain, for Jessie calmly, rationally shoots herself with her late father's gun. Essentially a long one-act play, it

was honestly if harrowingly written. The drama was first seen at the *American Repertory Theatre before the *Shuberts presented the grim play in a Broadway house where it became an unlikely hit. Many regional productions followed, prompted somewhat by its economic two-character cast.

NIGHT OF JANUARY 16TH, THE (1935), a play by Ayn Rand. [*Ambassador Theatre, 232 perf.] At the trial of Karen André (Doris Nolan) for murder, it is revealed that she loved her millionaire employer, Bjorn Faulkner, and apparently murdered him after she learned he was bankrupt and had married another woman in return for a large loan. A sense of shock pervades the courtroom when it is announced that the body in question was not Faulkner's after all, and that Faulkner is probably hiding in South America. Karen confesses that she knew Faulkner was preparing to flee. In fact, she was going to join him. But she insists that she knew nothing about the murder. The jury is asked to reach a decision. Since the jury was selected each night from members of the audience, two endings had been written and rehearsed, depending on the verdict. While many critics dismissed the work as claptrap, audiences were seemingly intrigued by the novel way of handling the decision. **Ayn RAND** (1905–82) was a Russian-born author who came to this country in 1926 and who was best known for her novels advocating the rights of the individual, notably *The Fountainhead*. Her only other play to reach Broadway was *The Unconquered* (1940), an anti-Communist tract.

NIGHT OF THE IGUANA, THE (1961), a play by Tennessee *Williams. [*Royale Theatre, 316 perf.; NYDCC Award.] At a seedy resort on the west coast of Mexico that is run by the man-hungry Maxine (Bette Davis), her old friend, the defrocked minister Shannon (Patrick O'Neal), arrives with a busload of tourists whom he is guiding through the desert. Staying at the resort is the spinster Hannah Jelkes (Margaret Leighton) and her aged poet father (Alan Webb) and an attraction develops between the volatile Shannon and the reserved Hannah. In the end, the poet dies, Hannah moves on, and Shannon stays to revive his relationship with Maxine. Critical reaction was mostly positive, aisle-sitters agreeing that it was "one of Williams' saddest, darkest and most contemplative plays." The drama was revived in New York in 1976 with Richard Chamberlain, Dorothy Malone, and Sylvia Miles, in 1988 with Nicholas Surovy, Maria Tucci, and Jane *Alexander, and in 1996 with William Peterson, Cherry *Jones, and Marsha Mason.

NINE (1982), a musical play by Arthur *Kopit (book), Maury *Yeston (music, lyrics). [46th Street Theatre, 732 perf.; Tony Award.] Having reached a point in life where he feels he is both creatively and emotionally exhausted, the great Italian film director, Guido Contini (Raul *Julia), attempts to recruit his strengths by reexamining his past, especially his relationships with the many women in his life, including his mother (Taina Elg); Saraghina (Kathi Moss), who first taught him about sex; Liliane LaFleur (Liliane Montevecchi), his producer; Luisa (Karen Akers), his unhappy wife; and Carla (Anita Morris), his mistress. His retrospections lead to acceptance by his nine-year-old self and a resolution of sorts. *Notable songs*: My Husband Makes Movies; Be Italian; Only with You. Based on Federico Fellini's 1963 film, *8 1/2*, this pleasantly melodic, lightweight musical was enhanced by Tommy *Tune's imaginative staging and outstanding production values. The musical was successfully revived on Broadway in 2003.

NINETY AND NINE, THE (1902), a play by Ramsay Morris. [Academy of Music, 128 perf.] Refugees from a fast-spreading forest fire are huddled at a railroad station, hoping a train will come to their rescue before the fire reaches them. But no engineer can be found to run the only nearby train. Ruth Blake (Katherine Grey), whose family is among those at the station, has long loved Tom Silverton (Edwin Arden), though he appears to most people to be a drunken ne'er-do-well. With her help she gives him the confidence to drive the train and rescue the stranded victims. Although the play was looked upon as preposterously dated for most chic audiences, it played at an aging theatre and at low prices, thereby attracting a less-sophisticated audience. Morris, who was the author of other melodramas and of Irish romances, claimed the basis for the plot was a hymn of the same name.

NIXON-NIRDLINGER, Samuel F. (1848–1918), manager. Born in Fort Wayne, Indiana, and educated at Notre Dame Academy, he spent his early years in a mercantile business in South Bend, then became a traveling salesman for a notions house. In Philadelphia he met George K. Goodwin, the lessee of the *Walnut Street Theatre, who appointed him business manager. Before long Nixon-Nirdlinger owned a chain of theatres, always using Philadelphia as a home office. He is reputed to have been one of the organizers of the *Theatrical Syndicate or Trust.

NO, NO, NANETTE (1925), a musical comedy by Otto *Harbach (book, lyrics), Frank *Mandel (book), Vincent *Youmans (music), Irving *Caesar (lyrics). [Globe Theatre, 321 perf.] Balking at the restraints imposed upon her by her Uncle Jimmy (Charles *Winninger) and her Aunt Sue (Eleanor Dawn),

Nanette (Louis *Groody) runs off to Atlantic City. By coincidence Jimmy, who is a Bible publisher and a naive philanderer, has arranged to meet several of his girlfriends at the same resort. Sue and Tom Trainor (Jack Barker), Nanette's beau, have followed in pursuit. By the end of the evening, a chastened Jimmy is back with Sue, while Tom and Nanette are planning a future together. *Notable songs*: Tea for Two; I Want to Be Happy; Too Many Rings Around Rosie; You Can Dance with Any Girl at All. The musical was based on a 1920 comedy success, *His Lady Friends*. Despite its relatively short run in New York, the H. H. *Frazee show had several road companies and internationally was the biggest American musical comedy hit of the 1920s. For many years, "Tea for Two" remained the top American song standard to come from Broadway. A fairly faithful 1971 revival on Broadway was a huge success, nearly tripling the run of the original. Its bright and engaging cast included Ruby Keeler, Patsy Kelly, Jack *Gilford, Bobby Van, Helen *Gallagher, and, as Nanette, Susan Watson.

NO PLACE TO BE SOMEBODY (1969), a play by Charles Gordone. [*Public Theatre, 250 perf.; Pulitzer Prize.] Johnny Williams (Nathan George) is an African-American racketeer in a seedy world dominated by whites, whom he resents. He hopes that when his old buddy, Sweets Crane (Walter Jones), is released from prison they can take on the Mafia together. But Crane is a drained, disillusioned man when he reappears and Johnny recognizes he must go it alone. His attempt fails, so he persuades Gabe Gabriel, an effeminate would-be playwright, to kill him. Alone and dressed as a woman, Gabe is left to observe, "My black anguish will fall on deaf ears." Rejected by the *Negro Ensemble Company, the script was produced by the *New York Shakespeare Festival and became the first Off-Broadway play to win a *Pulitzer Prize. It was also the first play by an African American to earn the award. **Charles GORDONE** (b. 1925) was born in Cleveland but raised in Elkhart, Indiana. After attending Los Angeles State College, he served as an actor and director before this, his only successful play to date, was produced. A 1970 revival outran the original production.

NO STRINGS (1962), a musical play by Samuel *Taylor (book), Richard *Rodgers (music, lyrics). [54th Street Theatre, 580 perf.] In Paris, David Jordan (Richard *Kiley), a prize-winning American writer who has been suffering a long dry spell, meets the African-American model Barbara Woodruff (Diahann Carroll) and their romantic affair brings them all over Europe. But when David realizes he must return to his native country if he hopes to write again, the two realize that an interracial marriage in the States would be doomed, so they go their separate ways. *Notable songs*: No Strings; The Sweetest Sounds; Nobody Told Me; Loads of Love. Rodgers's first musical following the death of his longtime partner, Oscar *Hammerstein, it offered one of his best scores as well as some excellent lyrics.

NO TIME FOR COMEDY (1939), a play by S. N. *Behrman. [*Ethel Barrymore Theatre, 185 perf.] With the world plunging toward war, meddling, pushy Amanda Smith (Margalo *Gillmore) convinces her friend Gaylord Esterbrook (Laurence *Olivier) that he should abandon his writing of frivolous comedies and turn to more serious dramatic works. This suggestion infuriates Gaylord's wife, Linda (Katharine *Cornell), who has been the star of his plays. She snaps at Amanda, "Sleep with him if you must, but don't spoil his style." Gaylord and Amanda decide to leave their respective spouses. Linda finds Gaylord packing and slyly suggests that the situation would make a good play. Gaylord agrees, except that he cannot think of how to end the play. When Amanda calls, impatiently demanding to know what is taking him so long to pack, Gaylord realizes the perfect ending for just such a play, so he hangs up on her and remains with Linda. This *Playwrights' Company production was Cornell's first attempt at modern comedy. Richard *Watts Jr. wrote in the *Herald Tribune* of the author, "His prose style is so graceful, his wit so sprightly, his mind so tolerant and his viewpoint so modest that he becomes the most winning of the drama's counselors."

NO TIME FOR SERGEANTS (1955), a comedy by Ira *Levin. [Alvin Theatre, 796 perf.] Will Stockdale (Andy Griffith) is a garrulous, innocent hillbilly serving in the Air Force. Crotchety Sergeant King (Myron McCormick) takes an instant dislike to Will and determines to make his life miserable. He orders him to clean latrines, telling him their captain is especially fond of clean latrines. Will makes the latrines sparkle but also blurts out King's comments to the captain. Deciding he must get Will out of his squad, King gives him the answers to a classification test, only to have Will mate the answers with the wrong questions. Later Will is presumed lost when his plane flies into an atomic test. At a ceremony awarding him a posthumous medal, Will blithely turns up. He is given a second medal to keep his mouth shut. Based on Mac Hyman's novel, the military comedy was praised by Brooks *Atkinson as "ludicrous, intimate and refreshing."

NOAH, Mordecai Manuel (1785–1851), playwright. The son of a Portuguese Jew, he was born in Philadelphia where he became an avid theatre-goer, then moved to Charleston, studying law there and becoming editor of the *City Gazette*. His strongly anti-British stance led him to fight several duels, but also came to the attention of President Monroe, who appointed him consul in Tunis. His first play, *Paul and Alexis* (1812), was mounted in Charleston before his departure. On his return he settled in New York, advancing in local politics until he was appointed Supreme Court Commissioner, and actively contributing to numerous New York newspapers. Noah also became a leading advocate of establishing a special homeland for his fellow Jews, attempting at one point to convert an island near Buffalo into a Jewish city to be called Ararat. Despite these varied occupations he found time to continue writing plays, such as *The Siege of Tripoli* (1820), *Marion; or, The Hero of Lake George* (1821), *The Grecian Captive* (1822), and *The Siege of Yorktown* (1824). All these were essentially patriotic spectacles, even his history of Greco-Turkish conflict seen in terms of its similarity to America's fight for independence. His best-known work, depicting a then-recent incident, was the war drama *She Would Be a Soldier; or, The Plains of Chippewa* (1819). In the preface to his published plays Noah offers interesting pictures of the contemporary American theatre and discusses the problems confronting an American playwright in the face of the popularity of English comedies and dramas.

NOBODY HOME (1915), a musical comedy by Guy *Bolton (book), Jerome *Kern (music), others. [*Princess Theatre, 135 perf.] Vernon Popple (George Anderson) loves Violet (Alice Dovey) but cannot marry her without her aunt's consent. The aunt (Maude Odell), however, refuses, since she has heard that Vernon has been seen about town with the Winter Garden star, Tony Miller (Adele Rowland). Vernon's brother, Freddy (Lawrence *Grossmith), arrives in town and Tony, who expects to go out on tour, leases her apartment to him. The tour is canceled, and all the characters meet at Tony's apartment, where misunderstandings lead to complications that are cleared up only in time for a happy ending. The show was originally to have been merely an Americanization of the English musical, *Mr. Popple of Ippleton*, but was drastically revised after a preview showed the early adaptation would not work. The F. Ray *Comstock musical, while not without its faults, pioneered in presenting intimate, stylish shows at the tiny Princess and launched the series that became known as the Princess Theatre musicals.

NOBODY'S WIDOW (1910), a comedy by Avery *Hopwood. [*Hudson Theatre, 215 perf.] When newlywed Roxana Clayton (Blanche *Bates) finds her husband (Bruce *McRae) kissing another woman, she storms out and announces to her friends that her husband has died suddenly. But wherever she goes there is her "dead" husband quietly trying for a reconciliation. Each time she is about to melt, another incident pops up to fuel her anger. But the husband's persistence finally wins the day. Mounted by David *Belasco because Bates insisted on trying her hand at drawing room comedy, the play won critical and public acceptance but widened the breach that saw Bates leave the producer after the show closed.

NORMAN, Marsha [née Williams] (b. 1947), playwright. A native of Louisville, she was educated at Agnes Scott College and at the University of Louisville. After spending time as a schoolteacher and a journalist, she wrote her first play, *Getting Out*, which was presented by the *Actors' Theatre of Louisville in 1977 and a year later in New York. She also directed for the Actors' Theatre, which subsequently produced her plays *Third and Oak* and *The Circus Valentine*. Norman won a *Pulitzer Prize for the gripping drama *'Night, Mother* (1983), and also wrote *The Pool Hall* (1978), *Traveler in the Dark* (1984), *Winter Shakers* (1987), *Sarah and Abraham* (1988), *The Red Shoes* (1993), *The Last Dance* (2003), and others, though only a few have been produced in New York. Perhaps her finest work was her most atypical: the book and lyrics for the musical *The *Secret Garden* (1991).

NORTON, [William] Elliot (1903–2003), critic. A Bostonian who was educated at Harvard, he became a drama critic on the *Boston Post* in 1934. In 1956 he moved to the *Record American*, remaining with it after it became the *Herald American* in 1972. His almost fifty years as a major critic is one of the longest stints in American theatrical annals and gave him a renown and prestige accorded to few reviewers outside New York. Boston's annual Elliot Norton Awards for theatre were named in his honor.

NORWORTH, Jack. See Bayes, Nora.

NOTABLE NAMES IN THE THEATRE. First published in 1966 as *The Biographical Encyclopaedia and Who's Who of the American Theatre* and revised under its present title in 1976, it includes not only detailed biographies of all major, living American theatrical figures, but also excellent lists of New York productions from 1900 on, premieres in America, premieres of American plays abroad, histories of noted theatrical groups, details of all major theatres in New York, complete lists of important awards, a biographical bibliography, and a necrology. In its accuracy and thoroughness it often surpasses the older *Who's Who in the Theatre and is an essential tool for all theatrical researchers.

NOTHING BUT THE TRUTH (1916), a comedy by James *Montgomery. [*Longacre Theatre, 332 perf.] Because Robert Bennett (William *Collier) is so insistent that honesty is the best policy, his brokerage firm partners bet him $10,000 that he cannot tell nothing but the truth for twenty-four hours. He takes the bet—and nearly loses the firm all its clients. Bennett also nearly loses his lady friend, Gwendolyn Ralston (Margaret Brainerd), when he is forced to confess that she is not the first love of his life. Gwendolyn forgives him when she discovers his other heartthrob was the actress Maude *Adams. At the end of the twenty-four hours he is a richer man but is so on edge that all he can do is tell a string of lies. Based on a novel by Fred Isham, the H. H. *Frazee–produced comedy served as the source for later musicals, including *Yes, Yes, Yvette* (1927) and *Tell Her the Truth* (1932).

NOVELS DRAMATIZED ON AMERICAN STAGES. Novels and short stories have long been the source for much popular theatre. One might even suggest that since Shakespeare and other early playwrights used forerunners of these modern forms as models for their plots, examples have been seen in the American theatre from the start. By the late 18th century fresh theatricalizations of such popular novels as Walpole's *The Castle of Otranto* were offered to American playgoers. Indeed, the romantic movement lent itself handsomely to dramatization. The first major American novel to be transferred to the stage with noted success was The *Spy (1821). Other Cooper novels followed, as did many of the works of Sir Walter Scott. His *Guy Mannering*, for example, was the source for *Meg Merrilies*, long a standby of Charlotte *Cushman and others. But the more obvious examples of romantic writings were not the only works seized upon by contemporary playwrights. Traditional stories of love and adventure were also popular, as witnessed by *Briar Cliff (1826), George P. Morris's version of *Whigs and Tories*. After the decline of romanticism's vogue, newer styles of novels were adapted in turn. With one exception, none matched the popularity of plays drawn from Dickens's works. *Oliver Twist* was a favorite in several versions, and great American actresses from Cushman on won special applause for their interpretations of Nancy. William E. *Burton mounted a number of highly esteemed adaptations, including *Nicholas Nickleby* and *Dombey and Son*, with his Captain Cuttle from the latter rating as one of his most memorable achievements. The great Ameri-

can novelists of this period such as Hawthorne and Melville were ignored, but such now virtually forgotten writers as Mrs. E. D. E. N. *Southworth saw many of their works rewritten for the stage. However, by far the most successful and influential dramatizations were those of Harriet Beecher Stowe's militantly anti-slavery *Uncle Tom's Cabin, the version by George L. *Aiken establishing a number of contemporary records. Many of the most popular plays of the last half of the 19th century were also taken from novels, although again the source was generally European. They ranged widely in subject matter and treatment. Among the best known were *Fanchon the Cricket (1862), suggested by George Sand's tale of rural life, *La Petite Fadette*; the various versions of Dumas père's *Le Comte de Monte Cristo*, especially the 1872 Charles *Fechter–James *O'Neill redaction; *Dr. Jekyll and Mr. Hyde* (1887), from the story by Robert Louis Stevenson; *Trilby* (1895), adapted from DuMaurier's novel; and *Sherlock Holmes (1899), suggested by the famous Conan Doyle mysteries.

Of plays derived from American stories, the most beloved was the Dion *Boucicault–Joseph *Jefferson retelling of Washington *Irving's *Rip Van Winkle (1866). The coming of the 20th century, which saw a tremendous expansion of America as a world power and a consequent rise in its self-confidence, also saw the theatre turn increasingly to native fiction for inspiration, even if it continued to ignore the more literary or masterful writers and to prefer more broadly read authors. Thus, Stephen Crane was totally passed over, and, whereas such men as Henry *James and William Dean *Howells tried their hands at original dramas, their novels were not yet theatricalized. Instead successful plays were made from the likes of Lew Wallace's *Ben-Hur (1899) and Edward Noyes Westcott's *David Harum (1900). Not until after World War I did Broadway turn with some regularity to more important authors, although it retained its preference for less literary but widely known bestsellers. One of the earliest winners of the *Pulitzer Prize was Zona *Gale's dramatization of her own *Miss Lulu Bett (1920). Subsequent winners included The *Green Pastures (1930), taken from stories by Roark Bradford; The *Old Maid (1935), derived from an Edith Wharton novel; The *Teahouse of the August Moon (1953), from Vern Sneider's novel; *Look Homeward, Angel (1957), taken from Thomas Wolfe; and *All the Way Home (1960), adapted from James Agee's *A Death in the Family*. Parenthetically, another winner was The *Diary of Anne Frank (1955), which was based on the writings of a young Jewish girl who died in World War II. While some interesting plays such as The *Heiress (1947), from James's *Washington Square*, and *Billy Budd*

(1951), from Melville, were based on older works by acknowledged masters, most dramatizations still had recourse to contemporary efforts. To cite but a few longer-running examples: *Tobacco Road* (1933), from an Erskine Caldwell novel; *Life with Father* (1939), from Clarence Day's short stories; *Mister Roberts* (1948), from Thomas Heggen's book; The *Member of the Wedding* (1950), adapted by Carson McCullers from her own novel; *No Time for Sergeants* (1955), from Mac Hyman's novel; and *Auntie Mame* (1956), from Patrick Dennis's bestseller. A two-evening version of The *Life and Adventures of Nicholas Nickleby* was hugely successful in 1986, but a much-lauded dramatization of The *Grapes of Wrath* failed to find an audience.

Musicals, too, used novels and short stories for inspiration. One of the earliest successes in the American theatre was *Tom and Jerry; or, Life in London* (1823), taken from the work of Pierce Egan. However, it was not until much later that the musical stage followed the practice more commonly. Three notable early examples were The *Wizard of Oz* (1903), adapted from L. Frank Baum's stories; *Show Boat* (1927), from an Edna *Ferber novel; and *Porgy and Bess* (1935), taken from Dubose Heyward's novel *Porgy*, by way of the 1927 play of the same name. Both *South Pacific* (1949), taken from James Michener's *Pulitzer Prize–winning *Tales of the South Pacific*, and *How To Succeed in Business Without Really Trying* (1961), taken from Shepherd Mead's book, went on to garner their own Pulitzer Prizes. Other long-running adaptations included *Guys and Dolls* (1950), which employed some of Damon *Runyon's short stories; The *King and I* (1951), from Margaret Landon's *Anna and the King of Siam*; The *Pajama Game* (1954), based on Richard Bissell's *7 1/2 Cents*; *Damn Yankees* (1955), from Douglass Wallop's *The Year the Yankees Lost the Pennant*; *Fiddler on the Roof* (1964), based on short stories by Sholom Aleichem; *Man of La Mancha* (1965), which was a musical version of *Don Quixote*; *Mame* (1966), a lyric version of *Auntie Mame*; and The *Wiz* (1975), another version of *The Wizard of Oz*. In the 1980s foreign musicals based on novels enjoyed considerable vogue, notably *Les Misérables* (1981), The *Phantom of the Opera* (1988), and *Aspects of Love* (1990). More recently, Broadway has seen musical versions of such literary classics as *Big River: The Adventures of Huckleberry Finn* (1985), The *Secret Garden* (1991), *Jekyll & Hyde* (1997), The Scarlet Pimpernel (1997), *Ragtime* (1998), *Jane Eyre* (2000), *James Joyce's The Dead* (2000), and *The Adventures of Tom Sawyer* (2001). With rare exceptions, even the most successful stage versions of novels could not offer the depth of characterization or the range of incidents found in their sources, but on their own level of theatrical immediacy, they sometimes were among the finest and most enduring works of their epochs.

NUGENT, Elliott [John] (1899–1980), actor and playwright. A theatrical jack-of-all-trades, he was the son of vaudevillians and made his debut in Los Angeles two-a-day at the age of four. Born in Dover, Ohio, he temporarily abandoned the stage to study at Ohio State University. His first New York appearance was in a minor role in *Dulcy* (1921), then he won fame the next year when he collaborated with his father, J. C. Nugent, on *Kempy* and assumed the title role of the naive plumber of the title. The Nugents wrote another hit in 1925, *The Poor Nut*, in which Elliott played the shy student John Miller who suddenly finds himself an important campus figure. After some time in films he scored another major hit with his collaboration with James Thurber, The *Male Animal* (1940), playing the central role of the idealistic professor Tommy Turner. Nugent played Bill Page, the soldier on a weekend pass, in John *van Druten's The *Voice of the Turtle* (1943) and that same year staged the hit play, *Tomorrow the World*. His final success came when he re-created the role of Tommy Turner in a 1952 revival of *The Male Animal*. Autobiography: *Events Leading Up to the Comedy*, 1965.

NUNN, Trevor (b. 1940), director. The British director, equally successful in staging the classics as well as giant Broadway musicals, was born in Ipswich, England, and educated at Cambridge where he began directing. Nunn has long been associated with the *Royal Shakespeare Company and several of his productions for them have found acclaim in America, such as The *Life and Adventures of Nicholas Nickleby* (1981), *All's Well That Ends Well* (1983), and *Les Misérables* (1987). His other American productions of note include, *Cats* (1982), *Aspects of Love* (1990), *Sunset Boulevard* (1994), *Not About Nightingales* (1999), *Arcadia* (1995), and *Oklahoma!* (2002).

NUNSENSE (1985), a musical by Dan Goggin (book, music, lyrics). [Cherry Lane Theatre, 3,672 perf.] Five nuns, the only survivors among their order of an epidemic of food poisoning, put on an amateur show to raise money for their sisters' burials. Undistinguished, and sometimes more amateurish than it was pretending to be, this intimate musical nonetheless proved appealing to a widespread audience. Its low cost also helped it achieve a remarkable run not only Off Broadway, but also in numerous local productions around the country and overseas. There were several less-successful sequels, including a Jewish and a Country-Western *Nunsense*, as well as an all-male drag version called *Nunsense Ah-Men!*

O

OAKLEY, Annie. See *Annie Get Your Gun*.

OATES, Alice [née Merritt] (1849–87), actress. One of the notable pioneers of the American musical stage, she was born in Nashville and studied for a career in opera in Louisville and New Orleans. However, after her marriage to James A. Oates, a prominent actor at Wood's Theatre in Cincinnati, she made her stage debut in supporting roles under his aegis then toured the Midwest and West, playing increasingly more important assignments. Following the huge success of Lydia *Thompson and her English musical burlesques, Oates organized her own burlesque troupe, touring successfully for several seasons, then evolving into the Alice Oates New English Opera Company, which specialized in presenting French opéra bouffe in English. Quick to appreciate the potential of *H.M.S. Pinafore*, she added it to her repertory before it had even been presented to New York. Oates's appearances in the East were relatively rare, but she remained a star west of the Mississippi for many years.

OBIE AWARDS. The Village Voice Off-Broadway Awards, known popularly as Obies, were started by *The Village Voice* critic Jerry Talmer in 1956. The New York publication still sponsors the awards, which are determined by a panel of judges picked annually and cover a wide range of categories, including best new play, best production, and best performers. In 1969 specific categories were largely eliminated, but later were reinstated. While the Obies do not carry the clout of the major awards like the *Pulitzer Prize or the *Tony Award, they have importance because they recognize only Off-Broadway work and, consequently, provide notoriety for new plays and artists.

O'BRIEN, Jack (b. 1939), director. He was born in Saginaw, Michigan, and educated at the University of Michigan before joining the Association of Producing Artists (APA) in 1969 where he served as an assistant to Ellis *Rabb. That same year O'Brien first directed at the *Old Globe Theatre in San Diego, a theatre he managed from 1981 to 1991 and where he has staged dozens of productions over the years. At first he was known for his direction of large musicals and operas, such as the acclaimed *Porgy and Bess* for the Houston Grand Opera in 1976, but he soon enjoyed a reputation for staging classics and modern works as well. O'Brien's New York credits include *The Cocktail Hour* (1988), *Two Shakespearean Actors* (1992), *Hapgood* (1994), *The Full Monty* (2000), *The Invention of Love* (2001), *Hairspray* (2002), and the star-filled *Lincoln Center revival of *Henry IV Part One* in 2003.

O'CASEY, Sean [né Sean O'Cathasaigh or John Casey] (1880–1964), playwright. The renowned Irish dramatist, who moved from grimly realistic works into symbolism and *expressionism, was most successful in America with his earlier plays of troubled Dublin life: *Juno and the Paycock* (1926) and *The Plough and the Stars* (1927). O'Casey began to move away from his earlier style in *Within the Gates* (1934). Although his *Red Roses for Me* (1955) was a succès d'estime on Broadway, his later plays were rarely mounted there and found a better welcome Off Broadway and at regional theatres.

OCTOROON, THE (1859), a play by Dion *Boucicault. [*Winter Garden Theatre, 48 perf.] George Peyton (A. H. Davenport) will inherit the Southern plantation Terrebonne on the death of his aunt, Mrs. Peyton (Mrs. W. R. Blake), if his late uncle's mismanagement does not cause his aunt to lose her property. He would like to settle on the estate, where he has met and fallen in love with the regal octoroon Zoe (Agnes *Robertson). But the villainous Yankee overseer, Jacob McClosky (T. B. Johnston), murders the slave who is sent to pick up a letter bringing Mrs. Peyton assurances of the money she needs to save her land. McClosky also learns that on a technicality Zoe was never legally freed, and he demands she be put up for sale. Dora Sunnyside (Mrs. J. H. Allen), who loves George but understands his feelings for Zoe, offers to buy Zoe's freedom, as does a kindly overseer, Salem Scudder (Joseph *Jefferson). McClosky outbids them. Zoe takes poison rather than become McClosky's property. At the same time McClosky's murder of the slave is unmasked and he is forced to flee. George and Dora rush to Zoe's side. She tells George as she dies, "O! George, you may, without a blush, confess your love for the Octoroon." Boucicault derived the main story from Mayne Reid's novel, *The Quadroon*, and the incidents relating to the murder of the slave from Albany Fonblanque's novel, *The Filibuster*. For theatrical effect he added a spectacular scene in which a riverboat burns. Although Boucicault emphasized the absurdity of Southern racial laws by making Zoe an octoroon instead of a quadroon (that is, one-eighth instead of one-quarter black), he basically attempted to balance the rights and wrongs of sectional division. As Joseph *Jefferson noted of the play, "The truth of the matter is, it was non-committal. The dialogue and the characters of the play made one feel for the South, but the action proclaimed against slavery and called loudly for its abolition." The melodrama has enjoyed successful revivals, including a fine 1961 mounting by the *Phoenix Theatre.

ODD COUPLE, THE (1965), a comedy by Neil *Simon. [*Plymouth Theatre, 964 perf.] Felix Unger (Art *Carney), having separated from his wife, arrives bag and baggage at the apartment of his divorced friend Oscar Madison (Walter *Matthau) who takes him in. Within a short while, the obsessively neat Felix has driven the slovenly Oscar up all four walls and appears on the verge of destroying Oscar's regular poker game. But after a seemingly disastrous double date with a pair of neighboring sisters, Felix announces he will move in with one of the girls. His stay, however, has not been without its effect. As Oscar resumes his poker game he warns his fellow players not to flick ashes on the floor. Howard Taubman observed of Simon in the *Times*, "His skill—and it is not only great but constantly growing—lies in his gift for the deliciously surprising line and attitude. His instinct for incongruity is faultless. It nearly always operates on the basis of character." The much-revived comedy, a particular favorite in summer stock and community theatres, was rewritten as a vehicle for two women and presented on Broadway with success in 1985; that version also became popular across the country.

ODELL, George C[linton] D[ensmore] (1866–1949), historian. Born in Newburgh, New York, he was educated at Columbia, where he succeeded Brander *Matthews as Professor of Dramatic Literature in 1924. He is best remembered for his *Annals of the New York Stage* (1927–49), a fifteen-volume set covering the history of New York theatre from its beginnings to mid-1894. The work is detailed, accurate, and written with great personal warmth and remains the definitive study of the 18th- and 19th-century New York stage.

ODETS, Clifford (1906–63), playwright. The leading dramatist of left-wing social protest in the 1930s, he was born in Philadelphia but raised in New York. His earliest professional work in the theatre was as an actor, including several seasons with the *Group Theatre, whose theories of drama and staging he shared. When the Group mounted a special benefit performance of his explosive one-act play about a taxi drivers' union strike, *Waiting for Lefty*, its reception made him famous overnight. However, before the troupe brought the play to Broadway, it first produced his landmark domestic drama *Awake and Sing!* (1935). A confused indictment of the emptiness of the middle class, *Paradise Lost* (1935) was so coldly received that Odets temporarily abandoned Broadway for Hollywood. On his return he offered what many have considered his best play, *Golden Boy* (1937). But a falling away of his dramatic abilities became evident with *Rocket to the Moon* (1938), *Night Music* (1940), and *Clash by Night* (1941). Eight years passed before Odets returned to Broadway with a highly colored attack on Hollywood, *The Big Knife* (1949). His last two plays suggested that the dramatist could still recover some of his earlier sureness: the backstage drama *The *Country Girl* (1950) and the lighthearted Biblical Noah play *The Flowering Peach* (1954). At his best Odets was a powerful dramatist with a gift for sympathetic, memorable characterization, but his frequent rejections and returns to Broadway hint that his approach to writing was beset by the very conflict between commercialism and preachy idealism that was the essence of many of his works. Biography: *Clifford Odets—American Playwright*, Margaret Brenman-Gibson, 1982.

ODYSSEY THEATRE (Los Angeles). Founded in 1969 by Ron Sossi, who served as its artistic director, the little theatre group was housed in a Hollywood storefront before expanding its program and moving to a new three-theatre complex. In addition to classic and modern revivals, the company emphasizes innovative works and international plays.

OENSLAGER, Donald [Mitchell] (1902–75), designer. Born in Harrisburg, Pennsylvania, he studied at Harvard under George Pierce *Baker, then began his theatrical career as an actor. Oenslager turned to set design in 1924 and went on to create the scenery for such memorable productions as *Good News!* (1927), *The *New Moon* (1928), *Follow Thru* (1928), *Girl Crazy* (1930), *The Farmer Takes a Wife* (1934), *Anything Goes* (1934), *Stage Door* (1936), *Johnny Johnson* (1936), *You Can't Take It with You* (1936), *Of Mice and Men* (1937), *The *Man Who Came to Dinner* (1939), *Margin for Error* (1939), *My Sister Eileen* (1940), *Claudia* (1941),

Born Yesterday (1946), *Goodbye, My Fancy* (1948), *Sabrina Fair* (1953), *Coriolanus* (1954), *Janus* (1955), *A *Majority of One* (1959), and *A Far Country* (1961). Although much of his work for the commercial theatre was traditional, he is generally linked with the major developers of modern American stage design. Oenslager was for many years on the faculty of the *Yale School of Drama and was the author of *Scenery Then and Now* (1936).

OF MICE AND MEN (1937), a play by John *Steinbeck. [*Music Box Theatre, 207 perf.; NYDCC Award.] Farm laborer Lennie (Broderick Crawford) is a loving but infantile giant who has often killed pets accidentally with his crushing embrace. His buddy and fellow migrant worker, George (Wallace Ford), has warned him to be careful, since one day it might not be an animal that he kills. When their boss's sluttish daughter-in-law (Clare Luce) finds Lennie in a barn weeping over a dead puppy, she is sympathetic, so Lennie attempts to embrace her. But she screams and, in a panic, Lennie breaks her neck. George finds out where Lennie has run to hide and shoots him before the other men can get to him. Steinbeck based the play on his own novel, which appeared to have been written with a play in mind. The drama has seen many revivals, including a fine Broadway mounting in 1974 with Kevin *Conway and James Earl *Jones. The popular novelist **John STEINBECK** (1902–68) was born in Salinas, California, and educated at Stanford. *Of Mice and Men* was his first (and only) stage success, although he adapted some of his other stories for the stage, such as *The Moon Is Down* (1942) and *Burning Bright* (1950). *Rodgers and *Hammerstein's short-lived musical *Pipe Dream* (1955) was based on Steinbeck's novella *Sweet Thursday* and his novel *East of Eden* served as the basis for the equally short-lived musical *Here's Where I Belong* (1968).

OF THEE I SING (1931), an operetta satire by George S. *Kaufman, Morrie *Ryskind (book), George *Gershwin (music), Ira *Gershwin (lyrics). [Music Box Theatre, 441 perf.; Pulitzer Prize.] While campaigners march and sing "Wintergreen for President," the staff for presidential candidate John P. Wintergreen (William *Gaxton), recognizing that he has no real issue on which to run, decides to build his platform on love. To that end they hold a beauty contest with the winner slated to wed Wintergreen. Although the Southern belle Diana Devereaux (Grace Brinkley) wins the contest, Wintergreen has fallen in love with his secretary, Mary Turner (Lois Moran), and marries her as he wins the election. But his ditching of Miss Devereaux brings a strong protest from the French Ambassador (Florenz Ames) who protests that France has been defamed since Miss Devereaux is an "illegitimate daughter of an illegitimate son of an illegitimate nephew of Napoleon." The Supreme Court and the Senate are eventually called in to pronounce on the case and impeachment hearings against Wintergreen begin, only to be halted when Mary announces that she is pregnant. Since the government has never impeached an expectant father, Wintergreen is cleared and Miss Devereaux gets to marry a man whom everyone has ignored and whose name no one recalls: vice president Alexander Throttlebottom (Victor *Moore). *Notable songs*: Love Is Sweeping the Country; Who Cares?; Of Thee I Sing, Baby; Because, Because. The first musical to win the *Pulitzer Prize, it was hailed by George Jean *Nathan as "the happiest and most successful native music-stage lampoon that has thus far come the way of the American theatre. With it, further, I believe that American musical comedy enters at length upon a new, original and independent lease on life." While the Sam H. *Harris production was a hit, a sequel (involving all the same talents) called *Let 'Em Eat Cake* (1933) failed, as did a 1952 Broadway revival of the original musical. Yet the show remains delightfully pertinent and is occasionally produced by regional theatres, particularly in election years.

OFF BROADWAY. The term applied to a widely dispersed group of small theatres away from the principal commercial theatre center near Times Square. Many of these playhouses were established in basements, lofts, converted churches, and elsewhere, and they regularly produced plays deemed too risky for commercial production. Although such playhouses existed throughout the century (witness the *Provincetown, Greenwich Village, and *Neighborhood playhouses), the designation did not take hold until after World War II. Many of the plays first presented in these theatres were later moved to traditional Broadway houses, while others, such as *Threepenny Opera* or The *Fantasticks*, remained in their original playhouses for their entire long runs. By the 1960s Off-Broadway theatres were often providing much of the most exciting theatre in New York. Among the notable producing groups were the *Circle in the Square, *La Mama, the *Living Theatre Company, the *Negro Ensemble Company, the *Phoenix Theatre, and the *New York Shakespeare Festival. Many playwrights, such as *Beckett, *Genet, and the Americans Sam *Shepard and A. R. *Gurney Jr., have been presented in New York almost solely in Off-Broadway houses, and several playwrights, such as Tennessee *Williams, announced a preference for Off Broadway after their later plays were not well received uptown. Off Broadway has its own prestigious award, the *Obie, and an organization called the League of Off Broadway Theatres and Producers.

OFF OFF BROADWAY. By the early 1970s, theatres started springing up across Manhattan and in the boroughs that served as an alternative to Off Broadway and Broadway. Deemed the most experimental and least compromising of the three venues, Off Off Broadway often has a specific agenda: gay or lesbian plays, feminist works, ethnic theatre, deconstructing the classics, and so on. The spaces are small and mostly found in such unconventional places as church basements, community centers, former storefronts, even garages and warehouses. Many Off-Off-Broadway productions are nonunion, others are Equity-approved showcases, and some are defiantly amateur. In 1972 the Off-Off-Broadway Alliance was formed to somehow organize the many groups, but by their very nature these little theatre companies defied organization. Theatres were formed, sometimes quickly blossomed, and just as often disappeared in a year or two without a trace. It is estimated that in any one season there are more than sixty such groups in New York.

OFFENBACH, Jacques (1819–80), composer. Although born in Cologne, he achieved his fame in Paris where he became France's finest and best-known composer of *opéra bouffe. In 1867 his *The *Grand Duchess of Gerolstein* was presented in New York and initiated the American rage for the genre. Among his other works popular here were *La Belle Hélène* (1868), *Orpheus in the Underworld* (1868), *Barbe Bleue* (1868), *La Perichole* (1869), *La Vie Parisienne* (1869), and *The Princess of Trebizonde* (1871). This rash of premieres came at the same time as the success of *The *Black Crook*, **Humpty Dumpty*, and the semimusical **Fritz, Our Cousin German* and thus helped open American stages to musical theatre.

OFFICER 666 (1912), a farce by Augustin Mac-Hugh. [Gaiety Theatre, 291 perf.] Travers Gladwin (Wallace *Eddinger) returns from Europe to learn that someone is posing as him in order to steal both his famous art collection and his girl, Helen Burton (Ruth Maycliffe). To catch the thief, he borrows the uniform of Officer 666 (Francis D. McGinn) and enters his own mansion in disguise. Misunderstandings and mistaken identities ensue, and for a moment Gladwin is even arrested for attempting to steal his own art. The play was heavily rewritten by Winchell *Smith before *Cohan and *Harris presented it on Broadway. **Augustin MacHUGH** (1877–1925) was an actor and vaudevillian who wrote numerous vaudeville sketches and several other Broadway plays. His only other success was *The Meanest Man in the World* (1920),

telling of a kind-hearted lawyer who decides the best way to rise in the world is to be nasty.

OH, BOY! (1917), a musical comedy by Guy *Bolton (book), P. G. *Wodehouse (book, lyrics), Jerome *Kern (music). [*Princess Theatre, 463 perf.] Although George Budd (Tom *Powers) has just married Lou Ellen (Marie Carroll), his problems have only begun: his guardian-aunt Penelope (Edna May Oliver), who holds the family purse strings, knows nothing of the marriage and will almost certainly disapprove. Moreover, a young lady named Jackie (Anna Wheaton) has invaded his apartment and has been encouraged to remain there by his sporting friend, Jim Marvin (Hal Forde). Before all the complications have been resolved Jackie has had to pose both as Mrs. Budd and as Penelope. *Notable songs*: Nesting Time; An Old-Fashioned Wife; A Pal Like You; Till the Clouds Roll By. This was the best and most successful of William Elliot and F. Ray *Comstock's Princess Theatre musicals. It had a solidly constructed, believable, and literate book, and both its humor and songs derived from situations and characters. The musical was adventuresome in making its heroine not totally likable and in assigning love songs to comics and comic numbers to the lovers. The critic for the *Sun* typified reviewers' reactions when he exclaimed, "If there be such things as masterpieces of musical comedy, one reached the Princess last night."

OH, CALCUTTA! (1969), a revue with music devised by Kenneth Tynan, with contributions by several playwrights. [Eden Theatre, 1,314 perf.] A revue that trafficked largely in then-faddish nudity, its nature was summed up by Otis L. *Guernsey Jr. who noted, "Its clinkers of unredeemed vulgarity in a couple of unfortunate skits [including one in which a naked couple offer themselves for sexual experiment] were somewhat redeemed by the gracefulness of the dancers, in groups and pairs, in poetic movements of the naked and well-formed male and female bodies. The show had a point of view (blithely hetero) and found some humor in the image of a man and a woman, stark naked and fully lit, copulating." With some changes, the revue was revived off-Broadway in 1976 and, depending on (mostly foreign) tourists, ran for 5,969 performances in a small theatre.

***OH DAD, POOR DAD**, Mamma's Hung You in the Closet and I'm Feelin' So Sad* (1962), "a pseudo-classical tragifarce" by Arthur *Kopit. [Phoenix Theatre, 454 perf.] Madame Rosepettle (Jo Van Fleet) arrives at a Caribbean hotel accompanied by her usual ménage: the stuffed corpse of her husband, her pet piranha, and her stammering, neurotic son, Jonathan (Austin Pendleton). Into their peripatetic world comes the wide-eyed, determined prostitute, Rosalie (Barbara *Harris) who, as a "professional babysitter," tries to seduce Jonathan. But her advances throw him into a panic and he smothers her to death. Entering the disordered bedroom, Mamma looks around in dismay and asks, "What is the meaning of this?" This choice American example of the theatre of the absurd was the Off-Broadway sensation of its season and launched Kopit's career.

OH, KAY! (1926), a musical comedy by Guy *Bolton, P. G. *Wodehouse (book), George *Gershwin (music), Ira *Gershwin (lyrics). [*Imperial Theatre, 256 perf.] Because Jimmy Winter (Oscar *Shaw) spends so little time on his Long Island estate, Kay (Gertrude *Lawrence) helps her rum-running brother cache his illegal booze there. When Jimmy returns unexpectedly, he and Kay fall in love. As a result he helps Kay outwit the revenue agents and, after renouncing his numerous other promises of marriage, agrees to marry Kay. *Notable songs*: Clap Yo' Hands; Do, Do, Do; Maybe; Someone to Watch Over Me. The musical was Lawrence's first starring role on Broadway and was said to have been written with her in mind. Her singing of "Someone to Watch Over Me" while cuddled up on a sofa with a small, raggedy doll was one of the era's most memorable musical moments. The Alex A. *Aarons and Vinton *Freedley production was a resounding hit, and in 1960 it was revived successfully Off Broadway. But a 1978 mounting, slated for Broadway, folded on the road and a 1990 revised version, with an all-black cast, did reach Broadway but quickly closed.

OH, LADY! LADY!! (1918), a musical comedy by Guy *Bolton (book), P. G. *Wodehouse (book, lyrics), Jerome *Kern (music). [*Princess Theatre, 219 perf.] Just before Willoughby Finch (Carl Randall) is to marry Mollie Farrington (Vivienne *Segal), the Farrington jewels are stolen. This presents an awkward situation for Willoughby, since it is known that his valet, Spike (Edward Abeles), was once a jewel thief. However, Spike proves loyal to his master and recovers the jewels, allowing the wedding to proceed. *Notable songs*: Greenwich Village; Not Yet; When the Ships Come Home; Bill (dropped before the New York opening). Although its authors considered this the best of F. Ray *Comstock and William Elliot's Princess Theatre series, critics and the public disagreed, so the trio broke up and the series soon came to an end.

OH, MEN! OH, WOMEN! (1953), a comedy by Edward *Chodorov. [*Henry Miller Theatre, 382 perf.] Just as Alan Coles (Franchot *Tone), a successful society psychoanalyst, is about to marry Myra Hagerman (Betsy von Furstenberg), he learns from one of his patients that his bride-to-be has had a very active and not-too-selective sex life. He also discovers that the handsome movie-star husband of another patient intends to seduce Myra before the wedding, just to see if Coles "can take it as well as dish it out." Coles quickly realizes he must analyze his own reactions to this news. He does, in time for a happy ending. Although most critics agreed with Louis *Kronenberger, who wrote, "Despite what is fresh and funny, the play cannot maintain a really high level of farce," the public clearly enjoyed the Cheryl *Crawford-produced comedy.

OKLAHOMA! (1943), a musical play by Oscar *Hammerstein (book, lyrics), Richard *Rodgers (music). [*St. James Theatre, 2,212 perf.] When the handsome young cowboy Curly (Alfred *Drake) comes to ask Laurey (Joan Roberts) to ride with him to a local box social, the pair tease each other then quarrel, so Laurey agrees to be escorted by Jud Fry (Howard *da Silva), a brooding farmhand who works for her Aunt Eller (Betty Garde). Laurey immediately regrets her decision, even dreaming that Curly and Jud have a fight over her and that Curly is bested. At the social Curly outbids Jud for Laurey's box lunch, so Jud stalks off, muttering threats and Laurey and Curly make up and agree to marry. But at the wedding a drunken Jud shows up, gets into a fight with Curly, then dies when he falls on his knife. Curly is acquitted in time for Laurey and him to ride off on their honeymoon. In the subplot, the flirtatious, oversexed Ado Annie (Celeste *Holm) gives Will Parker (Lee Dixon) a hard time before agreeing to marry him and try not to look at other men, particularly the peddler Ali Hakim (Joseph *Bulof). *Notable songs*: Oh, What a Beautiful Mornin'; The Surrey with the Fringe on Top; People Will Say We're in Love; Oklahoma; Out of My Dreams; I Cain't Say No; Many a New Day; Pore Jud; Kansas City. Based on Lynn Riggs's 1931 play *Green Grow the Lilacs*, this breakaway musical, Rodgers and Hammerstein's first professional collaboration, revolutionized the American musical. It set new high standards for integration of song and story, and also was one of the first musicals to integrate narrative, dramatic ballet into the action. Agnes *de Mille's ballet, depicting Laurey's dream, played a part in advancing the narrative far more than any other earlier ballet in musical theatre. The show began not only a vogue for ballet, but also for musicals unfolding in historic American settings. The *Theatre Guild production was directed by Rouben *Mamoulian and boasted stylized scenery by Lemuel *Ayers and costumes by Miles *White. When it closed, it was the longest-running musical in Broadway history. To distinguish this and subsequent American operettas from the Viennese school, the term "musical play" came into fashion. Frequently revived by every kind of theatre group, *Oklahoma!* saw exceptional Broadway mountings in 1979 and 2002.

OLCOTT, [Chancellor John] **Chauncey** (1860?–1932), singer and actor. He was born in Buffalo and made his stage debut in 1880 as a ballad singer in a minstrel show. After spending several seasons in minstrelsy, the handsome performer turned to plays and comic opera, including an appearance as Lillian *Russell's leading man in *Pepita; or, The Girl with the Glass Eyes* (1886). However, he found his true niche starring in romantic musical plays, such as *Mavourneen* (1892), *The Irish Artist* (1894), *The Minstrel of Clare* (1896), *Sweet Inniscarra* (1897), *A Romance of Athlone* (1899), *Old Limerick Town* (1902), *Eileen Asthore* (1906), *Macushla* (1912), and *The Isle o' Dreams* (1913). Songs he introduced included "Mother Macree," "Macushla," and "When Irish Eyes Are Smiling." His last New York appearance was as Sir Lucius O'Trigger in an all-star production of *The Rivals* mounted by the *Players. Biography: *Song in His Heart*, Rita Olcott, 1939.

OLD AMERICAN COMPANY. see American Company.

OLD GLOBE THEATRE. See San Diego Old Globe Theatre.

OLD HOMESTEAD, THE (1887), a play by Denman *Thompson, George W. Ryer (uncredited). [14th Street Theatre, 160 perf.] Joshua Whitcomb (Thompson) is a New Hampshire farmer who always has a friendly welcome for neighbors and strangers alike. But he also has a problem that worries him: his son Reuben (T. D. Frawley) has gone to New York and has not been heard from for nearly a year. So Joshua decides to go and seek out Reuben. He stays in the Manhattan mansion of his old schoolmate Henry Hopkins (Walter Lennox) who has become a millionaire. They soon discover that Reuben has hit the skids and become a derelict. Joshua helps rehabilitate his son and makes him promise that he will return home for the holidays. When the holidays come, Reuben does return, a reformed man. Joshua welcomes him and all his friends, admonishing him, "Now don't let this be your last visit to the Old Homestead. Come up in June when all natur' is at her best—come on, all of you, and let the scarlet runners chase you back to childhood." Called by George *Odell "certainly the most famous of all rural plays," it grew out of a vaudeville sketch that Thompson first wrote and performed in 1875. Thompson played Josuha regularly until shortly before his death in 1911.

OLD MAID, THE (1935), a play by Zoë *Akins. [*Empire Theatre, 305 perf.; Pulitzer Prize.] When Charlotte Lovell (Helen *Menken) has an illegitimate daughter, her married cousin, Delia Ralston (Judith *Anderson), agrees to raise her as her own. Delia also prevents Charlotte from marrying her brother-in-law. Years later, Charlotte has moved in with her cousin; and the child, Tina (Margaret Anderson), has grown into an attractive woman who loves her supposed mother and has little time for her prim, dour maiden aunt. At Tina's wedding to rich Lanning Halsey (John *Cromwell), Charlotte decides to reveal the true story, but finds she cannot summon up the courage to do so. Understanding her agony, Delia quietly tells Tina to give her last kiss to Cousin Charlotte. Based on Edith Wharton's novel, the play divided New York's critics. But their division turned to unity in their dismay at the play's being awarded the *Pulitzer Prize. This dissatisfaction, coupled with the Pulitzer committee's bypassing *Winterset the next season, led to the establishment of the *New York Drama Critics Circle and its own award.

OLD SOAK, THE (1922), a comedy by Don Marquis. [*Plymouth Theatre, 325 perf.] Clem Halsey (Harry Beresford) is the village drunk and the bane of his wife, Matilda (Minnie *Dupree). She scolds him for having no willpower, but he responds, "What do you think kept me drinkin' if twasn't my will power?" When the stocks that his wife has hidden disappear, she accuses Clem of stealing them and orders him out of the house. Clem learns that his playboy son, Clem Jr. (George Le Guere), actually is the thief, and that he sold the stock at a discount to the Hawleys' cousin, Webster Parsons. Clem sees a way to right matters. The snobbish, prissy Parsons is the town's banker and a teetotaler; but he is also the money behind the local bootleggers. So Clem quietly blackmails Parsons into paying him the full price for the stocks. Alexander *Woollcott welcomed the Arthur *Hopkins–produced comedy as "a likable and amusing and mighty cheerful piece." **Don**[ald Robert Perry] **MARQUIS** (1879–1937) was an Illinois native best known as a humorous columnist. Both this play and his most famous work, ar*chy and mehitabel,* grew out of figures that originally appeared in his newspaper columns.

OLD VIC, THE. See International Theatre Companies Visiting America.

OLDMIXON, Mrs. [née Georgina Sidus] (1763?–1836), actress and singer. Using the stage name Miss George, she made a great impression on London playgoers on her debut at the Haymarket in 1783, remaining a London favorite for ten years before coming to America to play under the aegis of *Wignell at the *Chestnut Street Theatre. Critics readily hailed her as the best singing actress of the time, although her remarkably broad talents allowed her to succeed not only in contemporary ballad operas but also in such wide-ranging roles as Ophelia, Juliet's Nurse, and Mrs. Candour in *The School for Scandal*. *Ireland recalled that she "was the most brilliant and scientific vocalist in America. She had neither youth nor personal beauty to recommend her; in fact, a peculiar twist in the position of her mouth gave her face a ludicrous appearance, but she possessed great skill as a comic actress, and a thorough musical education, and, with these aids, ranked as one of the most popular artistes of the time." Portraits suggest that the "peculiar twist" may have been an exaggeratedly Cupid's bow mouth, of the sort so popular in the 1920s. Whatever her shortcomings, Oldmixon was reputed to be the highest paid performer at the Chestnut. After the opening of the *Park Theatre in New York she made numerous appearances there and in other cities as well, but she remained primarily a Philadelphia actress.

OLEANNA (1992), a play by David *Mamet. [Orpheum Theatre, 513 perf.] Carol (Rebecca Pidgeon), a college student having difficulty in a particular course, goes to John (William H. Macy), her pedantic and somewhat distracted professor, in his office. Their conversation is perfunctory yet Carol, encouraged by a feminist group on campus, later claims sexual harassment charges against John. The twosome's next meeting, in which he tries to get her to drop the charges, goes badly, and by their third conversation the embittered John (who has been denied tenure because of the scandal) lashes out and makes the claims come true. Was John the victim or was Carol? The insightful drama led to stimulating discussion Off Broadway for nearly two years.

OLIVER! (1963) One of the few West End musicals to find success on Broadway before the British invasion of the 1970s, the musical play with book, music, and lyrics by Lionel Bart opened at the *Imperial Theatre for a lucrative run of 774 performances. Charles Dickens's epic tale of the orphaned Oliver Twist was given a cursory but tuneful retelling, from his days in the orphanage to getting mixed up with a gang of pickpockets in London to discovering his true parentage and fortune. *Notable songs*: I'd Do Anything; As Long as He Needs Me; Consider Yourself; Where Is Love? The show (co-produced by David *Merrick and London's Donald Albery) benefited from a lively production and some songs that became very popular in the States. Although it has always been popular in summer stock and schools, a 1984 Broadway revival (and musical versions of other Dickens novels) failed.

OLIVER, EDITH (1913–98), critic. After graduating from Smith College, Oliver became an actress who worked in regional theatre and on radio before turning to writing and producing quiz shows. She was hired by *The New Yorker* magazine in 1948, and for the next forty years wrote theatre reviews, usually Off Broadway and experimental productions. Oliver was an astute and open-minded reviewer who was the first to recognize and champion such playwrights as David *Mamet, Christopher *Durang, and Wendy *Wasserstein.

OLIVIER, Laurence [Kerr] (1907–89), actor, director, and manager. The most acclaimed English thespian of his generation, he made early New York appearances in *Murder on the Second Floor* (1929), *Private Lives* (1931), *The Green Bay Tree* (1933), and opposite Katharine *Cornell in *No Time for Comedy* (1939). In all these appearances the dark, handsome actor had been looked upon mainly as a promising leading man. By the time he returned in 1946 with the Old Vic, he had earned an international reputation as a versatile performer. With the *Old Vic he played Hotspur, Justice Shallow, Oedipus, Puff in *The Critic*, and Astrov in *Uncle Vanya*. Olivier returned in 1951 with Vivien Leigh, his wife at the time, to offer his Caesar and Marc Antony to her Cleopatras. His next major American appearance was to portray Archie Rice, the small-time music-hall song-and-dance man, in *The Entertainer* (1958). Brooks *Atkinson noted of this performance, "He tap-dances, he sings in the nasal tones that are usual in the lower ranks of the profession; he tells blue jokes in a cheap accent and throws the usual insults at the orchestra leader. His shoulders swivel with a kind of spurious bravado. Wearing his hat at a flashy angle, swinging his stick smartly, Mr. Olivier is the very model of the worn-out, untalented music-hall performer who is on the downgrade." For his final American appearances he played the title role of *Becket* (1960) in New York, then assumed the part of Henry II on tour. Some critics have found him excessively mannered, the studied mannerisms growing with the years, but few could deny his commanding presence and power to breathe life into the classic roles. In his later years Olivier directed many productions and ran the *National Theatre of Great Britain. Autobiography: *Confessions of an Actor*, 1982.

OLNEY THEATRE (Olney, Maryland). This theatre in suburban Washington, D.C., opened in 1938 as a community group and over the years has grown to professional status and has become affiliated with Boston University, the University of Maryland, and Middlebury College. Productions are staged in the 440-seat proscenium theatre and the flexible black box Mulitz-Gudelsky Theatre in the Olney Theatre Center for the Arts. The company's presentations of classic and original works are popular enough that the group is in the process of building a new 440-seat theatre.

OLSEN and JOHNSON, comedy team. John [Siguard] Olsen (1892–1963) from Peru, Indiana, and Chic [Harold Ogden] Johnson (1891–1962) from Chicago were a zany comedy pair who first joined forces in 1914 and had established themselves as a popular vaudeville team before touring in *Take a Chance* in 1933. Their greatest Broadway success was their madcap revue *Hellzapoppin* (1938), the longest-run musical at the time of its close. The pair met with increasingly less success in their subsequent revues, *Sons o' Fun* (1941), *Laffing Room Only* (1944), and *Pardon Our French* (1950). Unlike most comedy teams, in which one of the pair was essentially a stooge who set up laughs for his or her partner, both Olsen and Johnson participated actively in the gagging. Many felt that Johnson's shrill, high-pitched laughter made him the more outrageous of the pair. They customarily closed their act or their shows with Olsen stating, "May you live as long as you like," and Johnson concluding, "May you laugh as long as you live."

OMAHA THEATRE COMPANY FOR YOUNG PEOPLE (Nebraska). A children's theatre company with an ambitious program of plays and musicals, it also offers internships for teenagers in the area of performance. The troupe goes back to 1949 when Emma Gifford started the Omaha Junior League Theatre consisting mostly of volunteer members of the local Junior League. In 1976 the company, with the help of local native Henry *Fonda, raised money for a new home, the Center Theatre. Today the troupe performs in the 2,776-seat Rose Theatre, named after Rose Blumkin who contributed substantially to the renovation of an old movie house. The company also tours nationally and has been honored by the American Alliance for Theatre and Education with the Sara Spencer Artistic Achievement Award, the highest recognition for children's theatre.

ON BORROWED TIME (1938), a play by Paul *Osborne. [*Longacre Theatre, 321 perf.] Gramps Northrup (Dudley *Digges) is fearful that after his death his young, orphaned grandson Pud (Peter Miner) will be placed in the care of his cranky, moralizing Aunt Demetria (Jean *Adair). So when the Angel of Death, in the form of Mr. Brink (Frank Conroy), comes for Gramps, the old man chases him up an apple tree and fences him in. Gramps's careless description of the incident convinces Demetria and Dr. Evans (Clyde Franklin) that Gramps has become senile, leading the doctor to certify that Demetria will thereafter be Pud's guardian. In despair, Pud runs away and climbs up the apple tree, from which he slips and falls. Gramps, seeing the lifeless Pud, releases Mr. Brink and joins his beloved grandson in death. Based on Lawrence Edward Watkin's novel, the Dwight Deere *Wiman production was described by Robert *Benchley as a "heart-warming, delightful play." A well-received 1953 revival featured Victor *Moore as Gramps, and it was also successful in 1991 with George C. *Scott and Nathan *Lane (as Death).

ON GOLDEN POND (1979), a play by Ernest Thompson. [New Apollo Theatre, 156 perf.] Ethel (Frances *Sternhagen) and Norman Thayer (Tom *Aldredge) have been spending their summers in their Maine cottage ever since they were married. Norman has always been a little crotchety and something of a hypochondriac, but now that he is turning eighty, he is sure he is dying. Their summer is made eventful by the arrival of their grown daughter (Zina Jasper), her fiancé dentist (Stan Lachow), and his teenage son (Mark Bendo) whom, after a lot of fussing, Norman finally accepts. As the summer ends the old couple pack up and leave, realizing this may be their final farewell to the summer home. This quiet, touching idyll reopened the old Apollo Theatre on 42nd Street, initiating a hoped-for rebirth of the street that had once been New York City's main theatrical block and long had been given over to grind movies. The play originally had been produced Off Broadway earlier in the season, and later became a popular entry in summer stock and community theatres. **Ernest THOMPSON** (b. 1949) was born in Vermont, and studied theatre at various universities around the country before becoming an actor and writing plays. *On Golden Pond* was his first full-length work to be mounted professionally, although an earlier play, *The West Side Waltz*, was revised and used as a vehicle by Katharine *Hepburn, first on tour and then in New York during the 1981–82 season.

ON THE QUIET (1901), a comedy by Augustus *Thomas. [*Madison Square Theatre, 160 perf.] Robert Ridgeway [in some texts, Treadway] (William *Collier) has married Agnes Colt (Louise

Allen) secretly, since Robert is still a student at Yale. Their attempts to keep the secret lead to the inevitable misunderstandings and mistaken identities, especially in the hands of a dotty English duke and Agnes's interfering brother.

ON THE TOWN (1944), a musical comedy by Betty *Comden, Adolph *Green (book, lyrics), Leonard *Bernstein (music). [Adelphi Theatre, 463 perf.] Three sailors, the romantic Gaby (John Battles), the down-to-earth but vain Chip (Cris Alexander), and the clownish Ozzie (Green) are on twenty-four-hour leave in New York. During a subway ride Gaby falls in love with a picture of "Miss Turnstiles" (Sono Osato), so the boys set out to find her. Roaming as far as the Museum of Natural History and Coney Island, Chip and Ozzie also find romance, Chip with an outspoken lady cab driver, Hildy (Nancy *Walker), and Ozzie with an anthropology student, Claire de Loon (Comden). At the end of the twenty-four-hour period, the three couples wistfully part. *Notable songs*: Lucky to Be Me; New York, New York; Come Up to My Place; Some Other Time; I Get Carried Away; Lonely Town. Derived from the *Bernstein–Jerome *Robbins ballet *Fancy Free*, this musical made its authors and choreographer Robbins important figures in the popular musical theatre. A 1971 Broadway revival failed to run; a Central Park summer mounting in 1997 was very popular but could not last when it transferred to a Broadway house.

ON TRIAL (1914), a play by Elmer *Rice (then billed as Elmer L. Reizenstein). [Candler Theatre, 365 perf.] Robert Strickland (Frederick Perry) is accused of murdering Gerald Trask (Frederick Truesdell). According to the prosecution, Strickland repaid a loan of $10,000 to Trask, then later that evening returned to the Trask home to steal the money, killing Trask when he caught Strickland in the act. The defense is not helped by Strickland's silence or by the strange disappearance of Strickland's wife (Mary Ryan). When she is finally found, she confesses that she had years before been seduced by Trask and had gone to his house the night of his murder to plead with him not to reveal her past; but, she insists, she did not murder him. The defense lawyer catches Trask's secretary, Glover (J. Wallace Clinton), in some damaging contradictions and gets Glover to admit he stole the money but also insists he did not commit the murder. The jury acquits Strickland. The play is often said to be the first important drama to make use of the cinematic technique of flashbacks and one of the earliest that, in effect, recounted a trial from beginning to end. Its novelty and expense scared off numerous major producers, but when it finally opened under the aegis of George M. *Cohan, Sam H. *Harris, and Arthur *Hopkins, the *Globe* hailed it as "the most striking novelty that has been seen for years," adding correctly, "undoubtedly it will bring about important changes in the technique of the theatre."

ON THE TWENTIETH CENTURY. See *Twentieth Century*.

ON YOUR TOES (1936), a musical comedy by George *Abbott (book), Richard *Rodgers (book, music), Lorenz *Hart (book, lyrics). [*Imperial Theatre, 315 perf.] Junior Dolan (Ray *Bolger), the son of old vaudevillians, becomes a music professor and helps a struggling Russian ballet company. But complications force him to go on in place of the lead dancer and perform opposite the Russian prima ballerina Vera Barnova (Tamara *Geva). Gangsters try to shoot him during the ballet, but they are apprehended in time for a happy ending, which includes his proposal of marriage to sweet songwriter Frankie Frayne (Doris Carson). *Notable songs*: There's a Small Hotel; On Your Toes; It's Got to Be Love; Too Good for the Average Man; Glad to Be Unhappy; Quiet Night. The production was an innovative musical, in no small measure because of the fine George *Ballanchine ballets, including the legendary "Slaughter on Tenth Avenue," which was the first to have a story and a connection with the plot of the show. The Dwight Deere *Wiman production starred Bolger in one of his finest performances and featured Monty *Woolley and Luella *Gear in secondary roles. A major revival in 1954 featured Vera Zorina and Bobby Van, while a more successful 1983 revival starred Natalia Makarova and Lara Teeter, both productions directed by Abbott who staged the original.

ONCE IN A LIFETIME (1930), a comedy by Moss *Hart and George S. *Kaufman. [*Music Box Theatre, 406 perf.] The fading of vaudeville and the coming of sound films create turmoil in the entertainment industry. The two-a-day team of Jerry Hyland (Grant Mills), May Daniels (Jean Dixon), and George Lewis (Hugh O'Connell) find themselves out of work, so they head west to give elocution lessons to the terrified actors at the Glogauer film studio. Once in Hollywood they discover uniformed pages circulating with signs announcing Mr. Glogauer's whereabouts and roomfuls of dejected playwrights who have been brought to Hollywood en masse, and who now seem likely to have nervous breakdowns from underwork. The thickheaded George is made a film director. He shoots the wrong script, forgets to order the lights turned on, and audibly cracks nuts during the shooting. But the film is hailed as a masterpiece and George as a genius, so he is made Glogauer's second-in-command. In this first of the great Hart-Kaufman collaborations, Kaufman himself assumed the role of a depressed, articulate playwright. Although *Merton of the Movies had earlier used a similar story to spoof Hollywood, it was this play that initiated a rash of satires on the film industry. A successful 1979 revival at the *Circle in the Square featured John *Lithgow, Treat Williams, and Deborah May.

ONCE UPON A MATTRESS (1959), a musical fairy tale by Jay Thompson, Dean Fuller (book), Marshall Barer (book, lyrics), Mary Rodgers (music). [*Phoenix Theatre, 460 perf.] Princess Winnifred (Carol *Burnett) arrives at the castle as a possible bride for Prince Dauntless the Drab (Joseph Bova) but first must endure a series of tests laid out by the dictatorial Queen Agavain (Jane *White). Notable songs: Happily Ever After; In a Little While; Very Soft Shoes; Shy. This tongue-in-cheek look at the Princess and the Pea story had its unpretentious charms and was so popular it transferred to Broadway and made Burnett a star. It has remained a favorite in schools and community theatres, though an admirable 1997 revival on Broadway featuring Sarah Jessica Parker failed to show a profit. **Mary RODGERS** (b. 1931) was born in New York, the daughter of composer Richard *Rodgers. She was educated at Mannes College of Music and Wellesley College before contributing songs to Off-Broadway revues. Rodgers's other theatre scores include Hot Spot (1963), The Mad Show (1966), and some contributions to Working (1978).

110 IN THE SHADE. See Rainmaker, The.

ONE OF OUR GIRLS (1885), a comedy by Bronson *Howard. [*Lyceum Theatre, 200 perf.] Kate Shipley (Helen Dauvray) is the daughter of an American father and French mother who has been cut off from her family because she married against their wishes. Now Kate comes to France to visit her mother's family and finds history repeating itself. Her cousin, Julie Fonblanque (Enid Leslie), is refusing to marry the Comte de Crebillon (F. F. Mackay) and has arranged to elope with the man she loves, Henri Saint-Hilaire (Vincent Sternroyd). Kate follows her to her rendezvous and, to avoid problems for Julie, claims it is she Henri is meeting. The situation leads to a duel in which Henri is wounded, but it also brings the Fonblanques to their senses. Julie is allowed to marry Henri, while Kate agrees to marry Capt. John Gregory (E. H. *Sothern), who has stood by her. Many critics felt the play was inferior to Howard's *Young Mrs. Winthrop and accused him of stealing the crucial scene—in which Kate risks her reputation—from *Sardou's Les Pattes de mouche. However, Howard insisted he was not familiar with the French play.

ONE SUNDAY AFTERNOON (1933), a play by James S. Hagan. [Little Theatre, 322 perf.] When the dentist Biff Grimes (Lloyd Nolan) is asked to perform an emergency extraction for Hugo Barnstead (Rankin Mansfield), he plans to kill him with an overdose of gas because years before Barnstead had framed Grimes and sent him to prison. To make matters worse, Barnstead had then run off with Grimes's attractive girlfriend, Virginia Brush (Mary Holsman). But Grimes discovers that the intervening years have turned Virginia into an overbearing shrew and that Barnstead is a miserably unhappy and troubled man while Grimes himself has long since made a good marriage. So when Barnstead arrives at his office, Grimes does not kill him. He merely extracts the tooth—without any gas whatsoever. Richard Lockridge of the Evening Sun wrote, "It is simple-hearted, and that disarms criticism. Mr. Hagan has, by the sincerity and frequent delicacy of his writing, made the story real and affecting." The day after the play opened, President Roosevelt declared a national bank holiday. Without funds the play was forced to close for a week until money could be found. It was later reported to have come within a single vote of winning the *Pulitzer Prize.

ONE THOUSAND MILLINERS WANTED FOR THE GOLD DIGGINS IN CALIFORNIA (1852). An American version of Joseph Sterling Coyne's one-act afterpiece, One Thousand Spirited Milliners Wanted for the Gold Diggings in Australia, which had premiered at London's Royal Olympic Theatre in 1852, it was first presented to New York just over a month later by William *Burton at Burton's Theatre. It told of two mischievous young men, lawyer's clerk Joe Baggs (Burton) and medical student Tom Tipton (T. B. Johnston), who decide to look over a large cross section of local young ladies by luring them to the office of Baggs's employer, Mr. Singleton (Mr. Gourlay), with promises of lucrative work out West. They trick Singleton into visiting a distant client, then dress up as two kindly spinsters. The girls jam the office, but the ruse is exposed when the men are caught smoking and wearing boots under their frocks. The angry women tie the men to chairs just as a furious Singleton returns. To keep the ladies from broadcasting what has passed, the lawyer is forced to offer a champagne party. The play gave Burton one of his biggest hits. Other versions sprang up at competing houses with almost equal success under such simpler titles as One Thousand Milliners, One

Thousand Milliners Wanted, and *Wanted: One Thousand Milliners*. Ben *De Bar toured as Baggs for many seasons, and the play held the boards as long as afterpieces remained part of bills.

ONE TOUCH OF VENUS (1943), a musical comedy by S. J. Perelman (book), Ogden Nash (book, lyrics), Kurt *Weill (music). [*Imperial Theatre, 567 perf.] When Whitelaw Savory (John Boles) tells his barber, Rodney Hatch (Kenny Baker), that Savory's statue of Venus is the most beautiful woman in the world, Hatch disagrees. After all, he is engaged to the most beautiful woman in the world, Gloria Kramer (Ruth Bond). To prove his point, he places Gloria's engagement ring on the marble statue, which promptly comes to life. The escapades of Venus (Mary *Martin) and Hatch turn Manhattan upside down, with Savory, Gloria and her mother, and a mad Anatolian all in pursuit. The fling destroys the Hatch-Kramer romance, so Hatch is especially disconsolate after Venus returns to stone. But just as he is about to walk away from Savory's art school, a young girl appears. She is the image of Venus, and Hatch is certain he has an engagement ring to fit her finger. *Notable songs*: Speak Low; That's Him; The Trouble with Women; Foolish Heart; I'm a Stranger Myself Here. With a book and lyrics among the most literate and witty of any American musical comedy, the John Wildberg–Cheryl *Crawford production was also the first musical comedy to use the briefly voguish Agnes *de Mille ballets that *Oklahoma!* had popularized fewer than seven months before. As with *Oklahoma!*'s dream ballet, the second act, "Venus in Ozone Heights," contained material that shaped and furthered the action, in this instance convincing Venus that she would be unhappy remaining earthbound. S[idney] J[oseph] **PERELMAN** (1904–79), the noted Brooklyn-born humorist, rarely had good luck on Broadway. His first efforts were sketches for the revues *The *Third Little Show* (1931) and *Walk a Little Faster* (1932), but his plays *All Good Americans* (1933) and *The Night Before Christmas* (1941) failed to run. After *One Touch of Venus*, Perelman's other major work is the literate farce *The Beauty Part* (1962), which opened in the midst of a newspaper strike and could not find an audience.

O'NEAL, Zelma [née Schroeder] (1903–89), singer and dancer. The vivacious blonde performer was born in Rock Falls, Indiana, and appeared in vaudeville before making her debut in *Good News!* (1927), in which she introduced "The Varsity Drag." She next appeared in *Follow Thru* (1929), in which she sang "Button Up Your Overcoat," and finally in *The Gang's All Here* (1931). The rest of her career was in England.

O'NEILL, Eugene [Gladstone] (1888–1953), playwright. Generally acknowledged as the greatest of all American dramatists, he was the son of the celebrated actor James *O'Neill, and, though he was born in New York, he spent most of his first seven years accompanying his mother and older brother as they followed the actor from city to city. Six years of Catholic schooling were succeeded by four at the Betts Academy and a year at Princeton, after which he left to accept work in a mail-order house, then spent time prospecting in Honduras. An attack of malaria forced his return to the United States, where he became assistant manager of a theatrical touring company. O'Neill then spent several years on a variety of ships, traveling as far as South America. He gave up sailing to accept a small role in his father's company, where he started to consider a writing career. His elder brother secretly helped him secure work on a newspaper, but with the onset of tuberculosis he entered a sanatorium and there more purposefully began writing plays. On his release he enrolled in Professor George Pierce *Baker's classes on playwriting at Harvard, then in the summer of 1916 joined the *Provincetown Players, the ensemble with which his professional career began. The young company presented his one-acts *Bound East for Cardiff* (1916), *Thirst* (1916), *Before Breakfast* (1916), *The *Long Voyage Home* (1917), *The *Moon of the Caribbees* (1918), and others. *In the Zone* (1918) was first produced by the *Washington Square Players, and by 1920 O'Neill's one-acters had clearly stamped him as the most promising of young American playwrights, a promise he moved toward fulfilling with his first full-length play, *Beyond the Horizon* (1920). This realistic drama was followed by the expressionistic The *Emperor Jones* (1920), demonstrating O'Neill's sense of experimentation that would characterize his career. Other notable works of the 1920s include *Anna Christie* (1921), The *Hairy Ape* (1922), *All God's Chillun Got Wings* (1924), *Desire Under the Elms* (1924), The *Great God Brown* (1926), *Marco Millions* (1928), *Strange Interlude* (1928), and *Dynamo* (1929). This fertile period was capped by his masterful trilogy *Mourning Becomes Electra* (1931); thereafter O'Neill worked at a slower pace, though he maintained the quality of his earlier writing. His only comedy, *Ah, Wilderness!* (1933), was followed by his "modern miracle play" *Days Without End* (1934) before the onset of Parkinson's disease prompted O'Neill to retire from the theatrical arena for many years. Nevertheless, in 1936 he was awarded the Nobel Prize for Literature.

New York did not see another new O'Neill play until The *Iceman Cometh* (1946) although he was continually writing scripts that would not see the light of day for some time. His most ambitious project was a planned cycle of eleven plays tracing the history of a single American family for over a century. Before his death he destroyed most of the material for these plays, but two survived. Sickly, embittered, and overwhelmed with the despair that had long overshadowed his life, O'Neill died in 1953 believing that his life had amounted to little. It was a brilliant 1956 revival of *The Iceman Cometh* at the *Circle in the Square that began a positive reevaluation of his art. As a result, his widow released other works, which O'Neill had hoped would not be produced for several decades. The autobiographical *Long Day's Journey into Night* was first produced in 1956 and remains, in the opinion of many, the playwright's finest work. Later that year A *Touch of the Poet, one of the surviving plays from the projected cycle, and A *Moon for the Misbegotten were given posthumous productions. In the 1960s two minor works were finally produced: the long one-act *Hughie* (1964) and the unfinished *More Stately Mansions* (1967), also part of the planned cycle. Other one-acts and fragments would surface over the years.

Although O'Neill was perceived early on as a master of stark, realistic tragedy, time has suggested that much of the power and beauty of his work came from its fundamental romanticism and even from a tinge of sentimentality that colored his tragic vision. These aspects, often touching on the supernatural, could be seen from the very start in the early one-acts. But an intellectual or instinctive sureness usually allowed O'Neill to restrain his romantic impulses and weave them effectively into the basically realistic fabric of his stories. He was almost always at his best when he had a good story to tell and allowed its transcendental implications to simply speak for themselves. His understanding of the dark, labyrinthine side of human nature and of its limitations were unmatched by any other American dramatist and, whether he realized it or not, sufficed to assure him preeminence. When O'Neill attempted to analyze and expound upon his tragic vision, his theatrical acumen sometimes deserted him, so as a rule the most profoundly philosophic of his plays have been among the least actable and therefore the least commercially successful. Nor was he always comfortable when he departed from traditional dramatic structuring and essayed experiments in symbolism, *expressionism, or other more or less-novel forms. Curiously, as has long been noted, his plays rarely read well. On the printed page they often seem prolix and turgid. But O'Neill was such a natural child of the theatre that all but a handful of his works come irresistibly alive on stage. Biographies: *O'Neill: Son and Playwright,* Louis Shaeffer, 1968; *O'Neill: Son and Artist,* Louis Sheaffer, 1973.

O'NEILL, James (1847–1920), actor. Born in Kilkenny, Ireland, he was brought to this country at about the age of five and raised in Buffalo and Cincinnati. He gave up work in a clothing store to become a super at a Cincinnati theatre during an engagement there by Edwin *Forrest in 1868. After barnstorming for several seasons, O'Neill became a leading man first at *McVicker's, then at *Hooley's Theatre in Chicago. In 1875 he began a two-year stint in New York under the aegis of A. M. *Palmer, then left for San Francisco. During his three seasons there he played numerous parts, including that of Jesus Christ in the controversial *Passion Play. O'Neill made his New York debut as Edmund Dantes in The *Count of Monte Cristo (1883), a role he would often return to and one that he would be identified with thereafter. Although he subsequently played such roles as D'Artagnan in *The Musketeers* (1899) and the title part in a revival of *Virginius* (1907), his public demanded only his *Monte Cristo,* and as a rule he obliged. He was a florid, emotive actor of a supercharged romantic school. His adherence to this older, passing style led to problems when he was called in to direct the American premiere of *Before Breakfast,* an early work by his son Eugene, who later portrayed him affectionately in *Ah, Wilderness!* and more savagely, as a mean pinchpenny, in *Long Day's Journey into Night.*

O'NEILL, Nance [née Gertrude Lamson] (1874–1965), actress. A major turn-of-the-century touring star, she was born in Oakland, California, and made her stage debut in San Francisco in 1893. She played for several seasons in New York before embarking on a tour as a star. O'Neill's repertory included Juliet, Rosalind, Viola, Parthenia in *Ingomar, Magda, Fedora, Camille, and Nancy in *Oliver Twist.* One of her few major New York triumphs was as the self-sacrificing sister Odette in David *Belasco's 1909 production of *The Lily.* With the coming of films, the road began to fade and so did her popularity. However, she remained active, often in important supporting roles, well into the 1940s.

OPEN THEATRE. See Chaikin, Joseph.

OPÉRA BOUFFE IN AMERICA. The rage for opéra bouffe exploded on American stages in 1867 with the presentation of such Offenbach operettas as *La Grande Duchesse de Gérolstein and La Belle Hélène. The initial productions were done in French with imported casts, and since they could be understood by few American playgoers, to whom their satire of French politics and society would have been meaningless in any case, they relied for their appeal on the color of the mountings, the élan of the performance, and their gorgeous melodies, which ranged from soaringly lyrical to rousing (including most Americans' introduction to can-can music). A reaction set in when they were performed in English, at which time America's Victorian morality caused many critics and theatre patrons to condemn their seeming salaciousness. Nevertheless the vogue continued for many years, abetted by the arrival of a later school of more romantic French works, such as Audran's *Olivette*. In the 20th century, revivals of these works on Broadway have been sporadic, but many of the better operettas have entered the repertories of opera companies.

ORALLOOSSA; or, The Last of the Incas (1832), a tragedy by Robert Montgomery *Bird. [*Arch Street Theatre (Philadelphia), 5 perf.] Having slain the Inca leader Atahualpa, Francisco Pizarro (Daniel Redd) feels free to tighten his stranglehold on Peru. But he has not reckoned with Atahualpa's son, Oralloossa (Edwin *Forrest). The treacherous Diego de Almagro (John R. *Scott) urges Oralloossa on, hoping to supplant Pizarro. However, after Oralloossa kills the Spanish conquistador, Almagro turns Oralloossa's fellow Incas against him. Oralloossa is slain, and his sister, Orallie (Miss Eliza Riddle), is buried alive. The new Viceroy, Vaca de Castro (Mr. Quinn), orders Almagro put to death. This blank-verse drama won one of several prizes Forrest offered for a new American play. Bird later stated he had two purposes in writing the play, "first, the portraiture of a barbarian in which is concentrated all those qualities of good and evil which are most strikingly characteristic of savage life; the second, to show how the noblest designs of a great man and the brightest destinies of a nation could be interrupted and destroyed by the unprincipled ambition of a single individual." Forrest met with only indifferent success in the title role, though he continued to revive it on occasion. It also proved a popular vehicle for Edwin *Adams until his early death.

ORBACH, [Jerome] **Jerry** (b. 1935), actor. The swarthy, lanky performer was born in the Bronx and, after graduating from Northwestern, studied with Herbert *Berghof and Lee *Strasberg. He made his New York debut as a replacement in the role of Macheath in the long-running *Threepenny Opera* in 1958, then called attention to himself when he created the part of El Gallo in The *Fantasticks (1960). Leading musical roles followed: the crippled puppeteer Paul in *Carnival* (1961) and the enterprising businessman Chuck Baxter in *Promises, Promises* (1968). Orbach's nonmusical performances included the put-upon Jewish husband Harold Wonder in *Scuba Duba* (1967) and the apartment hunter Paul Friedman in *6 Rms Riv Vu* (1972). His last major Broadway roles were the slippery lawyer Billy Flynn in *Chicago* (1975) and the Broadway producer Julian Marsh in *42nd Street* (1980). Much of his later career has been in films and television. Orbach is not a traditional leading man, yet he has an engaging stage presence. Writing in the *Times* of his *Promises, Promises* performance, Clive *Barnes describes this presence, noting that he "has the kinds of wrists that look as though they are about to lose their hands, and the kind of neck that seems to be on nodding acquaintance with his head."

OREGON SHAKESPEARE FESTIVAL (Ashland). The group was founded in 1935 by Angus L. Bowmer, whose original intention was to present the complete canon of Shakespeare's plays over a series of summer seasons. By 1958 it had performed the complete works of Shakespeare, and by 1978 the cycle had been repeated. Except for a shutdown during World War II, the festival has operated continually since its inception and enlarged both its vision and its program. It now operates three theatres, the 1,200-seat, open-air Elizabethan, the 600-seat Bowmer, and the flexible New Theatre. While nearly half its repertory remains Shakespearean, its programs today include the full range of classic drama as well as new plays of interest, offered during a season that generally runs from February through October. Since 1988 the group performs in late fall and during the winter at the Portland Center for the Performing Arts. Bowmer later wrote a history of the festival, *As I Remember, Adam* (1975). In 1983 the group received the regional theatre *Tony Award.

ORIENTAL DRAMA IN AMERICA. See Asian Drama in America.

ORIGIN OF THE CAKE WALK, THE. See *Clorindy*.

ORIGINAL CAST RECORDINGS. From the very beginnings of recorded sound in the late 19th century, prominent American theatrical figures have stood before microphones and left their voices and interpretations for posterity. However sketchily and faintly, such notables as Edwin *Booth, Joseph *Jefferson, and such early musical stars as Jessie Bartlett *Davis and Eugene *Cowles have offered examples of the readings that made them famous. As records grew more commonplace and sophisticated, increasing numbers of artists, especially from our musical stages, made recordings. Usually these were merely the best-received songs from a show and were customarily recorded with a studio orchestra. Both

Victor and Columbia for many years issued "Gems," medleys of songs from a show on a single side of a large record. The term "original cast recording," on the other hand, came to mean a virtually complete recording of a musical with its original cast and theatre orchestra. In this respect England was far ahead of America, presenting remarkable examples as far back as the turn of the century. One ironic result is that many of the great American musicals of the 1910s, 1920s, and 1930s are available only with their original London casts. The vogue for recording American casts of American shows unquestionably began when Jack *Kapp recorded the opening-night cast of *Oklahoma! for Decca in 1943. For about the next quarter of a century, every major American musical received a practically complete original cast recording. After Kapp's death, Goddard *Lieberson at Columbia Records was in the vanguard of responsible record makers, issuing not only the material from new shows but also often going back in time to re-create earlier unrecorded works. The original cast recording of *My Fair Lady is said to have sold more than six million copies, a record in its field. With the decline of the American musical in the 1970s and 1980s, and changes in record company policies, such recordings became fewer. However, in recent years a few specialty houses are reconstructing even Broadway failures and issuing them in limited pressings for what may be perceived as a "cult" market. The introduction of compact disks in the 1980s meant that recordings were no longer limited by the playing time of a record. Over the years many famous and not-so-familiar Broadway musicals have been remastered and put on CD, sometimes with material that was originally recorded but not used when the LP was first released.

ORPHEUM THEATRE (New York). The Off-Broadway playhouse is one of the few remnants of the once-flourishing Yiddish theatre district on Second Avenue. It opened in 1905 as the Orpheum Concert Gardens but the vaudeville-like programs did not sell, so it was converted into a movie house in 1911. From the early 1920s until World War II, the Orpheum housed Yiddish shows, some plays but mostly variety attractions. After serving as a neighborhood movie theatre, the playhouse was renovated in 1959 into a 399-seat legitimate theatre, and it quickly became one of Off Broadway's favorite houses. Today it mostly features limited engagement guest attractions.

OSBORN, Paul (1901–88), playwright. Born in Evansville, Indiana, the son of a minister, he was educated at the University of Michigan, then studied with Professor George Pierce *Baker at Yale. Osborn taught at both schools before seeing his first plays produced: the campus drama *Hotbed* (1928) and the melodrama *A Ledge* (1929). He scored his first hit when he turned to comedy with *The Vinegar Tree* (1930), followed by the short-lived *Oliver Oliver* (1934) and the popular fantasy *On Borrowed Time* (1938). The warm domestic comedy *Morning's at Seven* (1939) failed to run very long but decades later became Osborn's most-produced play when it was a hit on Broadway and in theatres across the country. His remaining works to reach Broadway were successful adaptations of novels: *The Innocent Voyage* (1943), *A *Bell for Adano* (1944), *Point of No Return* (1951), and *The *World of Suzie Wong* (1958). The diversity of his writing makes it difficult to characterize Osborn, but his best original works were filled with sharply and affectionately drawn figures.

OSBORNE, John (1929–94), playwright. The British dramatist, whose *Look Back in Anger* (1957) served as America's introduction to the postwar school of "angry young men," subsequently found success on Broadway with *The Entertainer* (1958), *Epitaph for George Dillon* (1958), *Luther* (1963), and *Inadmissible Evidence* (1965). Thereafter his gifts seemingly waned, and, except for the interesting but short-lived *A Patriot for Me* (1969), none of his later plays was given a major Broadway presentation.

OTHELLO. First performed in America in 1751 by Robert *Upton, this tragedy was, along with *Hamlet and **Richard III*, one of the three Shakespearean plays most favored by 19th-century classic American tragedians. One special reason for the favor seems to have been that they could alternate in the roles of Iago and Othello. For many early 19th-century Americans, Edmund *Kean's dignified but volatile Moor served as an exemplar, challenged only by the more ferocious, stentorian Moor of Edwin *Forrest. Both Junius Brutus *Booth and Edwin *Booth met marked success in either role, with the younger actor's interpretations marked by subtleties apparently foreign to his father. Among the other notable interpreters of one or both parts were Thomas Abthorpe *Cooper, G. F. *Cooke (whose Iago won praise for not being too theatrically villainous), A. A. Addams, James *Fennell, E. L. *Davenport, Lawrence *Barrett, James *Murdoch, John *McCullough, and Robert *Mantell. Most, but not all of these actors, performed the Moor in black or swarthy make-up. A notable Moor was Tommaso *Salvini, who emphasized the figure's Mediterranean emotionalism. In modern times Walter *Huston suffered a major failure when he essayed the Moor, but Alfred *Drake, better known for starring in musicals, won high praise when he offered an insinuating but carefully controlled Iago at the *American Shakespearean Festival. However, the most memorable modern revivals have both offered African Americans as the Moor. In 1943 Paul *Robeson gave a richly humane performance to the Iago of José *Ferrer and the notable Desdemona of Uta *Hagen, while a 1982 production offered James Earl *Jones as Othello and Christopher *Plummer as Iago. The American who has played Othello the most is Earle *Hyman, with hundreds of performances around the world.

OTHER GIRL, THE (1903), a comedy by Augustus *Thomas. [Criterion Theatre, 160 perf.] When the world boxing champion known as the "Kid" (Lionel *Barrymore) is taken under the wing of a fight-mad minister, Dr. Bradford (Frank Worthing), he decides he would like to marry into society and live the good life. The girl he decides to marry is Catherine Fulton (Drina De Wolfe), ignoring the fact that she is engaged to Reginald Lumley (Joseph Wheelock Jr.). Catherine proves so susceptible to his magnificent physique and rough charms that she agrees to elope. Recognizing that such a match would be a disaster, Catherine's brash friend, Estelle Kitteridge (Elsie De Wolfe), contrives to take her place. In their haste the young couple accidentally run over Reginald. Good sense prevails in the end. This broad, somewhat preposterous farce, produced by Charles *Frohman, owed much of its success to its performances and to what one critic called Thomas's ability to inject "a wealth of accurately observed and truly felt character." Elsie De Wolfe (1865–1950) became for a time a leading set designer in her native New York, after which, as Lady Mendl, she was a well-known author and interior decorator.

OTHER PEOPLE'S MONEY (1989), a play by Jerry Sterner. [Minetta Lane Theatre, 990 perf.] Lawrence Garfinkle (Kevin Conway) is a smug, uncouth corporate raider, who has set out to take over the conservatively managed, somewhat decrepit New England Wire and Cable Company. The company's chairman, Andrew Jorgenson (Arch Johnson), determines to resist. But the cunning, persistent Garfinkle slowly wins over many stockholders, and, far more surprisingly, he gains the affection of Kate Sullivan (Mercedes Ruehl), who is not only the daughter of Jorgenson's longtime assistant (Scotty Bloch) but also a sharp Wall Street lawyer brought in to fend off Garfinkle. While this incisively written drama succeeded handsomely Off Broadway, a highly praised road company quickly folded. But the play has met further success in regional theatres. It is virtually the only drama to deal with a major economic prob-

lem of the decade. Jerry STERNER (1938–2001) was a Bronx native and college dropout. He spent many years in the real estate business and as a Wall Street broker before abandoning it to work full time at playwriting. His first produced play, Be Happy for Me (1986), was a quick failure. The success of Other People's Money promised further hits, but Sterner's premature death intervened.

OUR AMERICAN COUSIN (1858). A comedy by Englishman Tom *Taylor, it originally centered on a rather bumptious Yankee, Asa Trenchard, who arrives in England, where he rescues his virtually impoverished English relatives from the treacherous financial machinations of a supposed family counselor and also marries the young girl whom he himself had inadvertently deprived of an inheritance. The play was initially offered to J. W. *Wallack, who rejected it and suggested it be submitted to Laura *Keene. She, too, at first was cool to the comedy. However, when she produced it at her theatre in 1858 with Joseph *Jefferson as Asa and E. A. *Sothern as the silly, lisping Lord Dundreary, the play became one of the biggest comedy hits of its era and helped both actors on the way to stardom. With time Sothern expanded his role until it was the most important part in the play. A comparison of an 1869 printed version and an 1870 manuscript used by Sothern shows markedly different dialogue. The play did not reach its author's native England until 1861. It held the stage in both countries for several decades and was revived with some regularity until the turn of the century. Most Americans know the play as the one being performed at the time of President Lincoln's assassination.

OUR BOARDING HOUSE (1877), a comedy by Leonard Grover. [*Park Theatre, 104 perf.] When her supposed brother-in-law, Joseph Fioretti (W. E. *Sheridan), informs the widow Beatrice Manheim (Maud Harrison) that her marriage has no legal standing, the other roomers in the Chicago boardinghouse where she stays are thrown into an uproar. Some are for evicting her, others sympathize. The most prominent among the boarders are Professor Gregarious Gillypod (Stuart *Robson), the inventor of "The Great Flying Machine," and Colonel M. T. Elevator (W. H. *Crane), an expert in the ups and downs of the grain market. The pair are friendly enemies, but they share in the general joy when Miss Manheim discovers that not only was her marriage legal after all, but also that her late husband has left her a fortune. The frame device of Miss Manheim's marital problems was merely an excuse to offer a comic selection of boarders. The show was the first to couple Crane and Robson, whose success was so great that they immediately became one of the theatre's leading comedy teams. **Leonard GROVER** (1835–1926) was born on a farm in Livingston County, New York, and began his career as an actor but soon switched to producing and managing theatres. Among the noted theatres he ran were Philadelphia's *Chestnut Street Theatre, Washington's *National Theatre, and New York's Olympic. This was his only successful play.

OUR TOWN (1938), a play by Thornton *Wilder. [*Henry Miller Theatre, 336 perf.; Pulitzer Prize.] The Stage Manager (Frank *Craven) walks onto a bare, uncurtained stage, with only a few chairs and tables as props, and narrates the events of a typical American small town, Grover's Corner, New Hampshire, in the years 1901 to 1913. The town is going about its leisurely, traditional business. Professor Willard (Arthur Allen) and Editor Webb (Thomas W. Ross) describe the town's scientific and social backgrounds, and much of the drama centers on the families of Webb and Dr. Gibbs (Jay Fassett). The first act, "Daily Life," focuses on the ordinary pursuits of the town on a May Day in 1901. The second act, "Love and Marriage," describes the courtship and marriage of Emily Webb (Martha *Scott) and George Gibbs (John Craven). The third act presents the funeral of Emily, who has died in childbirth. Offered a chance to return to relive any one special day in her life, she selects her twelfth birthday. But the return is painful, for she realizes that the living cannot appreciate how precious life's small moments really are. Moving back to the cemetery, where she finds George crying at her grave, she muses to her mother-in-law, beside whom she is buried, "They don't understand, do they?" "No, dear, they don't understand," Mrs. Gibbs responds. With that, the Stage Manager sends the audience home. One of the most original and popular of all American plays, it was praised by Richard Lockridge of the *Evening Sun* for its "rare simplicity and truth." Its vibrant humanity—its expression of a sense of "something way down deep that's eternal about every human being"—has helped establish it as an American classic, while its continued appeal can be attributed in good part to its moving depiction of simpler times and simple values. Largely because of its basic sets and optimistic message, it has long been popular with amateur theatrical groups, but noteworthy New York revivals were seen in 1959 at the *Circle in the Square, in 1969 with Henry *Fonda as the Stage Manager, in 1988 with Spalding *Gray, and in 2002 with Paul Newman.

OUTER CRITICS CIRCLE. The group was formed in 1950 by critics John *Gassner, Charles Freeman, and Joseph Kaye as an "organization of writers on the New York theatre for out-of-town newspapers, national publications and other media beyond Broadway." Its main purpose was "to recognize distinctive achievement in the professional New York theatre by the awarding of medallions and scrolls to selected theatrical participants at an annual awards event" as well as to promote the exchange of ideas and friendships among widely dispersed critics. Currently there are about seventy-five critics and writers in the organization, which awards Broadway and Off-Broadway productions each spring.

OVER THE RIVER AND THROUGH THE WOODS (1998), a comedy by Joe DiPietro. [John Houseman Theatre, 800 perf.] When Nick Cristano (Jim Bracchitta) announces that he is going to leave New York and take a job in Seattle, his four Italian-American grandparents go to great lengths, including matchmaking, to keep their grandson from leaving. The sitcom play was dismissed by most of the critics as "strained humor" and "unadulterated corn," but it was very popular with audiences Off Broadway and later in community theatres. DiPietro is also the author of the long-running Off Broadway musical revue *I Love You, You're Perfect, Now Change* (1996) and *The Thing About Men* (2003).

OVER THERE THEATRE LEAGUE. A group formed during World War I to entertain American troops overseas, much as the USO did in the next war, it was underwritten by producers and other members of the theatrical fraternity and sent out full productions of popular plays and vaudeville bills. The name of the organization came from George M. *Cohan's popular war song "Over There."

OVER 21 (1944), a comedy by Ruth *Gordon. [*Music Box Theatre, 221 perf.] When Max Wharton (Harvey Stephens), a newspaper editor who is barely young enough to be accepted by the armed forces, enters officers' candidate school, his wife, Paula (Gordon), gives up her successful career as novelist and screenwriter to be with him. Army rules and regulations sometimes make things difficult, but not nearly as much as Joel Nixon (Philip Loeb), a Hollywood producer insisting on revisions in Paula's latest script, or Robert Drexel Gow (Loring Smith), Max's demanding publisher who attempts to get him out of the army. By the time Max is transferred to Arkansas, Paula has understood that they will have to wait until the war is over to live properly again and accepts Gow's offer to replace Max as editor. Ward *Morehouse of the *Sun* insisted, "The jokes are better than the story," only to add, "But as entertainment the piece is immense." With this, her first play,

Gordon displayed a competency and versatility rare among leading actresses.

OWENS, John E[dmond] (1823–86), character actor. One of the most popular of nineteenth century performers, he was born in Liverpool and at the age of five was brought to Philadelphia where he made his stage debut in 1841 under the aegis of William *Burton. Although his rise was comparatively slow, Owens established himself in the public affection with his characterizations of Dr. Pangloss, Caleb Plummer, Paul Pry, Aminadab Sleek, and Timothy Toodle, many of which Burton had popularized earlier. However, his most famous role was the cracker-barrel Yankee Solon Shingle in the play known both as *Solon Shingle* and *The *People's Lawyer*. Others had played the part before him, but when Owens first performed it in 1856, theatregoers and critics generally agreed that his interpretation was the best. Joseph *Jefferson considered him "the handsomest low comedian I had ever seen. He had a neat, dapper little figure, and a face full of lively expression. His audience was with him from first to last, his effective style and great flow of animal spirits capturing them." Owens's wife noted his versatility when she wrote, "In *Solon Shingle* his voice ruralized into eccentricity, and in *Caleb Plummer* it sobered into pathos." Biography: *Memories of the Professional and Social Life of John E. Owens*, Mrs. John E. Owens, 1892.

P

PABST THEATRE (Milwaukee). When the Stadt Theatre, the home for Milwaukee's German-language theatre and symphony orchestra, burned to the ground in 1895, brewer Frederick Pabst built a new theatre on the site and gave it his family name. German-born architect Otto Strack designed a 1,820-seat playhouse that reflected his European background but also used the latest technology, such as hydraulic machinery backstage and an all-electric lighting system for both stage and auditorium (the first in the nation). By the end of 1895 the Pabst opened with a visiting play from Berlin and has been a local favorite ever since. In 1928 the playhouse was remodeled, the boxes were removed, the seating decreased to 1,640, and its present chandelier added.

PACIFIC OVERTURES (1976), a musical play by John *Weidman (book), Stephen *Sondheim (music, lyrics). [*Winter Garden Theatre, 193 perf.; NYDCC Award.] Commodore Perry from America appears off the coast of Japan in 1853 with the intentions of opening up the "floating kingdom" after hundreds of years of isolation. But the Japanese react with horror at the Westerners' arrival. In a series of both funny and tragic vignettes, the history of the next 120 years is revealed, showing how the secluded nation adopted Western ways and rose from a medieval civilization to a world power. *Notable songs*: Pretty Lady; A Bowler Hat; Please Hello; Someone in a Tree. The ambitious musical was made more daunting by producer-director Hal *Prince's decision to use Kabuki and other Japanese theatre techniques to tell the story. Notices were decidedly mixed but everyone marveled at Boris *Aronson's evocative scenery that meshed Asian art with Broadway panache. The musical was successfully revived Off Broadway in 1984 with a smaller, more intimate production.

PACINO, Al (b. 1940), actor. The brooding, dynamic movie star who specializes in playing anti-heroes began in the New York theatre and has returned much more often than most film stars of his stature. A native New Yorker, he briefly attended the High School of the Performing Arts before studying at the Herbert *Berghof Studio and at the *Actors Studio, then made a provocative debut Off Broadway in 1968 as the drunk prankster Murph in *The *Indian Wants the Bronx*. He was further praised the next year for his Broadway performance as the drug addict Bickham in *Does a Tiger Wear a Necktie?* (1969). Pacino's film career began in 1971, but he managed to find time for such riveting stage performances as the boxing champ Kilroy in *Camino Real* (1970); the gullible, doomed recruit Hummel in *The *Basic Training of Pavlo Hummel* (1977); a fierce *Richard III* (1979); the small-time crook Walter Cole with a big-time ego in **American Buffalo* (1981); the talkative salesman Erie Smith in *Hughie* (1996); and the Hitler-like gangster Arturo Ui in *The Resistible Rise of Arturo Ui* (2002).

PAGE, Geraldine [Sue] (1924–87), actress. Born in Kirksville, Missouri, she studied at the *Goodman Theatre School and with Uta *Hagen before coming to playgoers' attention as the frustrated spinster Alma Winemiller in a celebrated 1952 revival of *Summer and Smoke* at the *Circle in the Square. Subsequent successes included the illiterate wife Lily in *Midsummer* (1953); Marcelline, the wife of a homosexual, in *The Immoralist* (1954); the prairie spinster Lizzy Curry in *The *Rainmaker* (1954); the fading film star Princess Kosmonopolis in *Sweet Bird of Youth* (1959); the possessive Nina Leeds in a 1963 revival of *Strange Interlude;* various roles in the double bill *White Lies* and *Black Comedy* (1967); the aristocratic wife Marion in *Absurd Person Singular* (1974); the unstable Zelda Fitzgerald in *Clothes for a Summer Hotel* (1980); Mother Miriam Ruth in *Agnes of God* (1982); and the slovenly wife Lorraine in *A Lie of the Mind* (1985). Page was playing Madame Arcati in a 1986 revival of *Blithe Spirit* at the time of her death. Although she at first seemed to subscribe to the mannerisms of the Method School, she proved a versatile, wide-ranging actress, particularly noted for her Tennessee *Williams characters.

PAID IN FULL (1908), a play by Eugene *Walter. [Astor Theatre, 167 perf.] Joseph Brooks (Tully Marshall) is an attractive but basically worthless young man who has been lucky enough to marry above his station. His wife, Emma (Lillian

Albertson), deeply in love with him, is blind to his failings. Not even the warnings of her mother, Mrs. Harris (Hattie Russell), her sister, Beth (Oza Waldrop), or of James Smith (Ben Johnson), a loyal family friend who has loved Emma for many years, can open her eyes. When Brooks is caught embezzling company funds he demands that Emma plead for him with his boss, Captain Williams (Frank Sheridan), who had once been a partner of Emma's father. In fact, Brooks hints that Emma should be willing to prostitute herself if that is what it takes to exonerate him. When Emma dutifully visits Williams, the old man recognizes the shamefulness of Brooks's ploy, writes a letter exculpating Brooks, then reads Emma the riot act. When Emma returns home Brooks demands a full accounting of what occurred, ready to condemn Emma for doing what he sent her to do. His baseness now is evident even to his wife, who walks out on him. Although he felt that Walter was not always steadfast in his seriousness of purpose, suggesting, for example, that Mrs. Harris and Beth were farcically exaggerated, Walter Prichard *Eaton nevertheless agreed that the play "has a purpose above the mere trickle of a story, the rehashing of conventional situations—that is, searching for truth." For all its comic interludes, many playgoers found the grimness in the *Wagenhals and *Kemper production too unrelieved.

PAINTER, Eleanor (1890–1947), singer and actress. A native of Walkerville, Iowa, she had sung leads in opera in Germany and across the United States before making her Broadway debut in *The Lilac Domino* (1914). Her most famous role was the title part in Victor Herbert's *Princess Pat* (1915), in which she introduced "Love Is the Best of All." Painter later starred in *Glorianna* (1918), a 1920 revival of *Florodora*, *The Last Waltz* (1921), *The Chiffon Girl* (1924), and *The Nightingale* (1927).

PAIR OF SIXES, A (1914), a farce by Edward *Peple. [*Longacre Theatre, 207 perf.] George H. Nettleton (George Parson) and T. Boggs Johns (Hale Hamilton) are partners in a pharmaceutical business that has made a fortune with a "pill [that] will fill the bill." But their success has not kept them from constantly feuding. So their lawyer, Thomas J. Vanderholt (Fritz Williams), arranges for them to play a game of poker, with the loser forfeiting his say in the business for a whole year and serving during that time as the winner's butler. Vanderholt's ploy is not entirely disinterested, since he is Johns's rival for the affections of Florence Cole (Ann Murdock), so he contrives to have Johns lose. Since Johns will have to give up entirely his share of the company if he fails to keep his part of the bargain, all sorts of obstacles are thrown in the way, including Nettleton's aging, amorous maid, Coddles (Maude Eburne). In the end, however, Johns proves he is a very good loser indeed. Producer H. H. *Frazee's rollicking, fast-paced farce was turned into the musical hit **QUEEN HIGH** (1926), featuring Charles Ruggles as Johns, Frank *McIntyre as Nettleton, and Luella *Gear as Florence, with book by Laurence *Schwab and B. G. *De Sylva, lyrics by De Sylva, and music by Lewis Gensler. The show's hit tune was "Cross Your Heart."

PAJAMA GAME, THE (1954), a musical comedy by George *Abbott, Richard Bissell (book), Richard *Adler, Jerry *Ross (music, lyrics). [*St. James Theatre, 1,063 perf.] Babe Williams (Janis Paige), head of the union grievance committee at the Sleep-Tite Pajama Factory, refuses to date the factory's new superintendent, Sid Sorokin (John *Raitt), because he sits on the opposite side of the bargaining table. However, when Sid convinces the company president to give the employees a seven-and-a-half-cent raise, she relents. A subplot centers on the antics of the company's production manager, the jealous Hines (Eddie *Foy Jr.), and the flirty bookkeeper (Carol Haney). *Notable songs*: Hernando's Hideway; Hey, There; Steam Heat; I'm Not at All in Love; Once a Year Day. Based on Bissell's novel, *7 ½ Cents*, the musical was melodic and comic, with the labor-management theme downplayed into farce. The musical was an impressive debut for songwriters Adler and Ross and for co-producers Hal *Prince and Robert E. *Griffith. In his first choreographic assignment, Bob *Fosse showed the wit and imagination that led him to become a major name in American musicals. Long popular on regional stages, the lightweight musical was revived on Broadway in 1957, 1973, and 1989.

PAL JOEY (1940), a musical comedy by John O'Hara (book), Richard *Rodgers (music), Lorenz *Hart (lyrics). [*Ethel Barrymore Theatre, 374 perf.] The handsome, small-time dancer Joey Evans (Gene Kelly) arrives in Chicago and immediately begins his courtship of innocent Linda English (Leila Ernst), then drops her when he meets and beds Vera Simpson (Vivienne *Segal), a rich, callous, past-her-prime matron. She sets Joey up in an apartment where they can meet, and even builds a nightclub for him. In time Joey's selfishness and egotism pall even for the tolerant Vera. Matters come to a head when some small-time blackmailers threaten to tell Vera's husband about the sordid liaison. Vera dumps Joey, giving him back to Linda who, having wised up, refuses the offer. Having lost both women and his meal ticket, Joey sets out to find another lucrative romance. *Notable songs*: Bewitched; I Could Write a Book; Do It the Hard

Way; Den of Iniquity; You Mustn't Kick It Around; Zip. Innovative in its no-punches-pulled look at bought love, this became a landmark American musical comedy. George *Abbott produced and directed the hard-as-nails production that featured Kelly in his only starring role on Broadway. Not all critics accepted it at first. While Louis *Kronenberger hailed it as "the most unhackneyed musical show since *Of Thee I Sing*," Brooks *Atkinson moaned, "If it is possible to make an entertaining musical comedy out of an odious story, 'Pal Joey' is it . . . [but] can you draw sweet water from a foul well?" Although its initial production was highly successful, an excellent 1952 revival, prompted by the popularity that year of "Bewitched" and an increasingly open moral climate, was more popular. Segal again headed the cast, with Harold Lang as Joey. There have been several subsequent revivals.

PALACE THEATRE (New York). Built by Martin *Beck on Broadway between 46th and 47th streets, the house was opened in early 1913. By that time, however, Beck had lost it. The 1,800-seat jewel box in crimson and gold quickly became the flagship of the *Keith circuit and America's leading vaudeville house. "To play the Palace" was the ambition of all two-a-day performers. With the coming of sound films and the demise of vaudeville, it became a film house in the 1930s. A policy of vaudeville was reinstated briefly in the early 1950s. In 1965 the house was extensively renovated and redesigned by Ralph *Alswang, and opening with *Sweet Charity*, the Palace became a major home to Broadway musicals for the first time in its long history. It has continued to be a popular home for large musicals, such as *Applause* (1970), *La Cage aux Folles* (1983), The *Will Rogers Follies* (1992), *Beauty and the Beast* (1994), and *Aida* (2000).

PALMER, A[lbert] M[arshall] (1838?–1905), producer and manager. Born in North Stonington, Connecticut, he graduated from New York University Law School but never practiced law. Instead he became active in politics, in which he met Sheridan Shook, collector of internal revenue for New York, and became Shook's right-hand man. Palmer worked as a librarian and an accountant but had little connection with the theatre until Shook made him head bookkeeper, then later manager at the *Union Square Theatre, a vaudeville house at the time. Palmer quickly assembled a first-rate company and turned the theatre into a legitimate playhouse that rivaled *Wallack's as well as *Daly's flourishing new troupes. Among his successes were The *Two Orphans* (1874), *A Celebrated Case* (1878), *The Lights o' London* (1881), and *A Parisian Romance* (1883). In 1884 he took over the *Madison Square Theatre and four years later took over *Wallack's, renaming it Palmer's. His successes in this period included *Beau Brummell* (1890), *Alabama* (1891), *Lady Windermere's Fan* (1893), and *Trilby* (1895), while performers whose careers he furthered included Maurice *Barrymore, John *Drew, Richard *Mansfield, and Clara *Morris. Just before the turn of the century both his health and his theatrical judgment began to fail. Palmer's final years were spent first as Mansfield's manager and then as manager of the Herald Square Theatre for Charles *Frohman. Although his early success came largely from imported plays and from recruiting established actors from other companies, with time and growing confidence Palmer also presented new works by American authors and employed untested actors.

PAN ASIAN REPERTORY THEATRE (New York). The premiere producer of Asian-American plays on the East Coast, this group, founded by Tisa Chang in 1977, presents contemporary works by Asian-American playwrights as well as adaptations of Western classics that utilize an Asian sensibility, such as its successful *Shogun Macbeth*. The company's first hit, R. A. Shiomi's satirical *Yellow Fever* (1983), put the group in the limelight, and offerings since have been noteworthy. The troupe, operating out of two Off-Broadway theatre spaces, expanded its scope in the 1990s, presenting works about India and Southeast Asia, such as *Cambodia Agonistes*.

PANAMA HATTIE (1940), a musical comedy by Herbert *Fields, B. G. *De Sylva (book), Cole *Porter (music, lyrics). [46th Street Theatre, 501 perf.] Hattie Maloney (Ethel *Merman) is a saloon owner in the Canal Zone, where she meets and falls in love with a Philadelphia socialite, Nick Bullett (James Dunn). He agrees to marry Hattie if she can win the affection of Nick's young daughter from a former marriage. So Hattie sets about wooing little Geraldine (Joan Carroll) and eventually succeeds. *Notable songs*: I've Still Got My Health; Let's Be Buddies; Make It Another Old-Fashioned, Please. A brash, brassy musical without a truly top-drawer Porter score, producer De Sylva's excellent production, Merman's appeal, and improving economic times made it the first book musical since the Depression to run more than five hundred performances.

PAPER BAG PLAYERS. (New York) The oldest operating children's theatre company in America, it was founded by Judith Martin in 1958 as a way of bringing theatre to young children (the preferred age of the group's audiences is between four and nine) in an imaginative way. Paper Bag productions do not utilize elaborate sets and costumes but, instead, use cardboard boxes, household objects, and paper bags to create illusions and stimulate the imagination. The much-awarded group is based in New York but spends most of its time touring nationally and internationally. Martin was still running the complex operation at the turn of the century.

PAPER MILL PLAYHOUSE (Millburn, New Jersey). This ambitious theatre company, the official State Theatre of New Jersey, was founded in 1934 and located in an abandoned paper mill that dates back to 1795. The group peforms in a 1,200-seat auditorium in the original building and specializes in musical revivals, including major mountings of such large shows as *Show Boat* and *Follies* and adaptations of literary classics, such as *Great Expectations*. The artistic director, who stages most of the important productions, is Robert Johanson.

PAPP, Joseph [né Papirofsky] (1921–91), producer, manager, and director. He was born in Brooklyn and studied at Hollywood's Actors Laboratory, where he then served as managing director from 1948 to 1950. After understudying both sons in a touring company of *Death of a Salesman*, for which he was also stage manager, Papp returned to New York. There he directed and sometimes produced a number of Off-Broadway mountings. In 1954 he founded the Shakespearean Theatre Workshop, which in time evolved into the *New York Shakespeare Festival. The rest of his career was inextricably tied to that organization, presenting dozens of new playwrights, actors, directors, and designers for the first time. Papp was a volatile, passionate, controversial figure. He refused to identify left-wing artists to the House Committee for Un-American Activities, returned an NEA grant for $748,000 rather than sign an antiobscenity pledge, and once declared, "If this theatre isn't being criticized for being too extreme, there's something wrong." Critics and playgoers did not always agree with Papp's productions, but they usually admired and defended him all the same. Biography: *Joe Papp: An American Life*, Helen Epstein, 1994.

PARADE (1998), a musical play by Alfred *Uhry (book), Jason Robert Brown (music, lyrics). [*Vivian Beaumont Theatre, 85 perf.; NYDCC Award.] When a fourteen-year-old girl is found murdered in the basement of the Atlanta factory where she worked, suspicion immediately falls on Leo Frank (Brent Carver), the aloof Jewish manager of the factory from Brooklyn. The press rallies the public against the non-Christian Yankee, a string of lies is presented at his trial, and Frank is found guilty. His wife, Lucille (Carolee Carmello), convinces the governor to commute the sentence, but an angry mob storms the jail and lynches Frank from a tree. *Notable songs*: The Old Red Hills of Home; All the Wasted Time; You Don't Know This Man. Based on a true case in Atlanta in 1915, the dark musical, produced by *Lincoln Center, met with mixed notices, though there was wide praise for the cast, Hal *Prince's direction, and the score. **Jason Robert BROWN** (b. 1970) was born in Ossining, New York, the son of a salesman and a schoolteacher, and educated at the Eastman School of Music in Rochester. Brown's first score to be heard in New York was *Songs for a New World* (1995) Off Broadway, and he made his Broadway debut with *Parade*. He is also the author-composer of the two-character musical *The Last Five Years* (2001).

PARIS BOUND (1927), a comedy by Philip *Barry. [*Music Box Theatre, 234 perf.] For six years Mary (Madge *Kennedy) and Jim Hutton (Donald *Cook) have seemed the ideal young couple. Then Mary discovers that Jim has not been totally faithful to her. Back on their wedding day, Jim's divorced father, James Sr. (Gilbert *Emery), had warned them to overlook occasional strayings, lest it ruin their marriage as it had destroyed his. At first Mary is bitter and determined on divorce. But when she realizes that Jim has ignored her own flirtation with a handsome young composer, Richard Parrish (Donald MacDonald), she decides to live and let live. Brooks *Atkinson of the *Times* hailed the Arthur *Hopkins offering as "a comedy of manners, rich in quality, true in temper and buoyant in its social criticism."

PARK THEATRE (New York). Opened in 1798 as the New Theatre by Lewis *Hallam and John *Hodgkinson to replace the *John Street Theatre, it served as New York's only playhouse for a quarter of a century and for several decades thereafter remained a prestigious auditorium. Under its earliest managers it boasted a fine stock company, probably surpassed only by those in Philadelphia and Boston. Matters changed during Stephen *Price's thirty-one-year tenure, which began in 1808. It was in his time that New York became the largest American city and thus America's theatrical capital. Probably unwittingly, Price initiated the decline of the stock company by importing foreign celebrities and increasingly emphasizing the star system. Because the growing population required more performances of successes, Price also began to abandon the repertory policy. However, it was not until a year after his death that the three-week stand of *Boucicault's *London Assurance* (1841) gave New York its earliest "long run." The first American play to enjoy a similar engagement was *Fashion* in 1845. The theatre had been reconstructed after several fires, but when it burned to the ground in 1848, shortly after Thomas *Hamblin had taken over, it was not rebuilt, since by then the theatre district had moved northwards. The first permanent theatre to be built in Brooklyn was also called the Park. It was opened in 1863 and enjoyed many years of prosperity under the *Conways.

PARKE, John (1754–89), playwright and author. A Delaware soldier in the Continental Army, he wrote poetry and a biography of Horace as well as *Virginia, A Pastoral Drama on the Birth-Day of an Illustrious Personage and the Return of Peace, February 11, 1784.* In it, Washington appears as the silent Daphnis and is saluted by nymphs and shepherds. Although no record survives of a professional performance, *Quinn believed it may have been mounted by some amateur group.

PARKER, Dorothy [née Rothschild] (1893–1967), critic, poet, and playwright. Born in West End, New Jersey, the writer and wit occasionally served as a drama critic, most notably for *The New Yorker.* She became famous for her poisonously caustic dismissal of plays and performers; in one review she stated, "*The House Beautiful* is the play lousy," and elsewhere accused Katharine *Hepburn of running a gamut of emotions "from A to B." Parker also created highly praised sketches for the 1922 revue *The 49ers* and co-wrote two plays that reached New York: *Close Harmony* (1924) and *Ladies of the Corridor* (1953). Although her most lasting legacy is probably her poetry, her only lyric contributions to the theatre were a few songs in *Candide* (1956). Biography: *You Might as Well Live*, John Keats, 1970.

PARKER, Henry Taylor (1867–1934), critic. The Boston-born play reviewer, known for many years largely by his initials H. T. P., was said to have left Harvard because it failed to offer sufficient courses in drama and literature. He worked as a correspondent for several papers before becoming drama and music critic for the New York *Globe* in 1900. In 1905 he returned to Boston to assume a similar position with the *Transcript*, remaining with the paper until his death. He was one of the most distinguished critics of his era, respected for his long, thoughtful, and open-minded reviews. John Mason *Brown recalled, "This remarkable little man of fine perceptions, with his dark eyes burning quizzically in a head bent forward with a sleuthing thrust and emphatic in its nods, was a giant among critics." Biography: *H. T. P.: Portrait of a Critic*, David McCord, 1935.

PARKER, Lottie Blair. See *Way Down East.*

PARKS, Suzan-Lori. See *Topdog/Underdog.*

PARLOR, BEDROOM AND BATH (1917), a farce by C. W. Bell and Mark Swan. [Republic Theatre, 232 perf.] Although Reggie Irving (John *Cumberland) is shy and harmless, his wife, Angelica (Sydney Shields), is convinced he has had a lurid past. So that she won't be disappointed, Reggie writes himself love letters signed "Tootles" and allows Angie to find them. When this ploy seems likely to be exposed, a friend arranges for Reggie to be discovered in a hotel room with another woman. The plan almost backfires when Reggie is discovered with several women, as well as a scandal-sheet columnist and a husband who believes Reggie has alienated the affections of his wife. At least Angie is duly impressed. A. H. *Woods produced this fast-paced, uproarious farce, which was considered highly "suggestive" in its day. **Mark** [Elbert] **SWAN** (1871–1942), a native of Louisville, had a brief career as an actor before turning playwright. Over a dozen of his plays or librettos reached Broadway, but this was his most successful. **C. W. BELL** (1876–1938), a Canadian who was a lawyer and eventually a member of Parliament, also wrote several other plays and librettos that were produced in the 1910s and early 1920s.

PARLOR MATCH, A (1884), a *farce-comedy by Charles H. *Hoyt. [Tony Pastor's Theatre, 16 perf.] I. McCorker (Charles E. Evans), a not-too-principled book agent, and Old Hoss (William F. *Hoey), a tramp who was once an auctioneer's assistant, combine their dubious talents to gull Capt. William Kidd (Daniel Hart) into believing he is a natural medium at séances. With the help of Kidd's mischievous daughter, Innocent (Jennie Yeamans), they call back from the dead a motley assortment of figures who sing and dance for them and who also speak up in McCorker and Innocent's interests. Old Hoss finds time to rummage through the Kidd household in search of items for an auction, and once, fearing detection, hides in a drawer; this scene became quite famous. The typical late farce-comedy used its elementary plot as an excuse for an evening of songs, dances, and specialty acts. It toured for many years, and during its tour Hoey introduced "The Man Who Broke the Bank at Monte Carlo." An 1896 revival served as Anna *Held's American debut.

PARSLOE, Charles Thomas, Jr. (1836–98), actor. The son of a famous actor and theatrical agent, he was born in New York and began his theatrical career as a call boy at *Burton's, then later performed juvenile parts at *Wallack's and elsewhere. Parsloe's small build and youthful countenance allowed him to continue in such roles well into middle age, although he also became known for his Chinese portrayals. Among the roles he created or became well known for were Bermudas in *Under the Gaslight* (1867), Wishee-Washee in The *Danites* (1877), the title part in *Ah Sin* (1877), and Wing Lee in *My Partner* (1879).

PARSONS, Estelle (b. 1927), character actress. Born in Lynn, Massachusetts, she was educated at the Connecticut College for Women, studied law at Boston University in hopes of going into politics, then worked in television as a production assistant and writer before she started performing in the 1950s. The nasal-voiced actress made her Broadway debut in 1956 and has been active ever since, remaining loyal to the theatre even though her vehicles have sometimes been short-lived or unworthy of her talents. Among Parsons's many roles of distinction were the kind-hearted stripper Myrtle in *The Seven Descents of Myrtle* (1968), the caustic schoolteacher Catherine Reardon in *And Miss Reardon Drinks a Little* (1971), the dictatorial Sarah in *The Norman Conquests* (1975), the fascist teacher in the title of the one-woman tirade *Miss Margarida's Way* (1977 and 1990), the "baby farmer" Ruth in The *Pirates of Penzance* (1981), the aged mountain woman Grace Stiles in *Grace & Glorie* (1996), and the small-town housewife Cora Swanson in *Morning's at Seven* (2002).

PARTICIPATORY THEATRE. Performances that asked the audience to join in, whether it was to take off one's clothes at a *Living Theatre production or to come on stage and have some wine with the cast of *Godspell, were expected occurrences beginning in the 1960s. But two decades later a unique genre of participatory theatre developed and, in a few cases, found success. The first and most elaborate of these was *Tamara* (1987), an intricately plotted tale set in an Italian mansion in which audience members chose which characters they were interested in, following certain actors into certain rooms where the story would continue in pieces and they would see different aspects of the same story. Part of the evening involved a multicourse gourmet dinner with selected characters. Indeed, food seems to be the common link in all the successful participatory programs. The longest-running such show was *Tony 'n' Tina's Wedding* (1988), in which the audience attended the church service and then the reception of a fictitious Italian wedding. When the same idea was tried with the Jewish *Grandma Sylvia's Funeral* (1995) and the Irish wake *Finnegan's Farewell* (1999), the result was much less popular. Another long-running example of the genre is *Late Nite Catechism* (2000), in which the audience becomes members of a religious education class and are quizzed (and scolded) by the nun who is teaching them. *The Angel Project* (2003) even took its audience to different locations in New York City to tell its tale. Also, murder-mystery performances, in which the audience participates in discovering the identity of the culprit, have become very popular regionally. Participatory theatre may be a minor genre but one that is likely to continue for some time.

PASADENA PLAYHOUSE. Founded in 1918 by Gilmor Brown as a semiprofessional troupe, the community group prospered, built a fine new theatre, and for many years was Southern California's most exciting playhouse. Besides reviving classics it regularly offered new plays by unknown playwrights at its Laboratory Theatre and conducted a highly praised acting school. Among its outstanding productions was the first mounting of Eugene *O'Neill's *Lazarus Laughed* in 1928. It was made the official State Theatre of California in 1937 and enjoyed a reputation as one of the finest community theatres in the nation. But the organization later fell on hard times in the 1960s, and its properties were auctioned off in 1970. The theatre reopened in 1986 and, despite damage incurred during the 1991 earthquake, continues on today as a professional resident company performing in its 672-seat theatre. **Gilmor BROWN** (1887?–1960), a native of New Salem, North Dakota, began his career as an actor in Western stock companies. For a time he joined Ben *Greet's traveling ensemble before founding and running the Playhouse for thirty-one years. He also served as California state supervisor for the *Federal Theatre Project and as president of the National Theatre Conference. Biography: *Gilmor Brown, Portrait of a Man—and an Idea*, Harriet L. Green, 1933.

PASSING REGIMENT, THE (1881), a comedy by Augustin *Daly. [Daly's Theatre, 103 perf.] When members of the Excelsior Regiment of the National Guard of New York are billeted briefly at the Narragansett Pier, a number of romances blossom, including that of Telka Essipoff (Ada *Rehan), a Russian heiress, and Adjutant Paul Dexter (John *Drew). Daly adapted this slight comedy from Von Moser and F. von Schoenthan's *Krieg im Frieden*. Daly biographer Marvin Felheim has suggested that the success of the comedy, coming on the heels of *Needles and Pins, confirmed the producer in his policy of emphasizing such light entertainment.

PASSING SHOW, THE (1894), a revue presented by George *Lederer. [*Casino Theatre.] A few prototypical, tentative revues had been presented earlier by John *Brougham and others, but this was really the first American revue to employ the generic term (although it spelled it "review") and is generally acknowledged to have started the fashion for such shows. The original production, in keeping with most subsequent turn-of-the-century revues, used a thin story line to tie together its songs and sketches. In 1912 the *Shuberts revived the name *The Passing Show* and offered it as the title of a series of elaborate revues designed to buck the popularity of the *Ziegfeld Follies*. Editions were presented yearly, excepting 1920, until 1924. The mountings were popular and not without merit, yet it was widely perceived that they fell short of the *Follies* in virtually every aspect. Willie and Eugene *Howard were the most regularly featured performers in the series. Charlotte *Greenwood, Marilyn *Miller, Ed *Wynn, De Wolf *Hopper, Jefferson *De Angelis (who had appeared in the 1894 production), Fred and Adele *Astaire, Marie *Dressler, and Fred *Allen all appeared in one or more years. Among the enduring songs first sung in the series were "Pretty Baby" (1916), "Good-bye Broadway, Hello, France!" (1917), "Smiles" (1918), and "I'm Forever Blowing Bubbles" (1918). An attempt was made to revive the series in the 1940s, but the production closed on tryout. Most of the librettos for the series were written by **Harold R. ATTERIDGE** (1886–1938), a native of Lake Forest, Illinois, who graduated from the University of Chicago. After his work was seen in the musicals *A Winning Miss* (1905) and *The Girl in the Kimono* (1907), he quickly became the *Shuberts' in-house librettist, creating over forty musicals to order for the producers, beginning with *Vera Violetta* (1911). Atteridge's other works included *The Honeymoon Express* (1913), *Sinbad* (1918), *Bombo* (1921), *Make It Snappy* (1922), *The Dream Girl* (1924), *Big Boy* (1925), *Ziegfeld Follies of 1927*, and *Everybody's Welcome* (1931). Many of his librettos were constructed as vehicles for particular stars, especially Al *Jolson. For the most part unimaginative and trite, they nevertheless were professionally competent and satisfied audiences if not critics.

PASSION (1994), a musical play by James *Lapine (book), Stephen *Sondheim (music, lyrics). [*Plymouth Theatre, 280 perf.; Tony Award.] When the handsome Italian officer Giorgio (Jere Shea) is separated from his married mistress, Clara (Marin Mazzie), he is pursued by the unattractive Fosca (Donna Murphy), his captain's sickly, morose cousin. Her love for him is so unrelenting that when Clara chooses her marriage over her lover, Giorgio falls into an equally obsessive love for Fosca that ruins his career and takes his life. *Notable songs*: Happiness; Loving You; I Read; I Wish I Could Forget You. Sondheim's most somber work was produced by the *Shuberts,

*Lincoln Center, and others and was greeted with mixed notices, but applause was unanimous for Murphy's *Tony Award–winning performance.

PASSION PLAY, THE [also known simply as *The Passion*]. A play by a Jewish playwright, Salmi Morse, recounting the major events in the New Testament, it was produced in San Francisco in 1879 by Tom *Maguire, directed by David *Belasco, and starred James *O'Neill as Christ. The play divided local critics, most of whom felt it was exceedingly dull but who nevertheless attested to the emotional fervor with which many in the audience responded. Some Protestant clergy, however, were offended and succeeded in having the producer, the playwright, and the actors hauled into court and fined for violating an ordinance prohibiting the "personation of any scriptural character upon the stage." In 1883, after much protest, the play was produced in New York, where the response was much the same and the drama soon closed. Shortly thereafter, Morse committed suicide by drowning in the Hudson River. Described by one San Francisco paper as a "tall, rabbinical-looking Hebrew, scrupulously dressed in black, with reverent gray hairs, mild, benignant eyes and somewhat heavily molded features," Morse claimed to have spent twenty years in the Middle East doing research for the work.

PASTOR, Tony [Antonio] (1837–1908), producer and actor. Often considered the father of modern American vaudeville, he was born in New York, where his father was a theatre violinist. While still a youngster he sang on the temperance circuit, then gave his first professional performance as a child prodigy at *Barnum's Museum in 1846. After appearing in minstrel shows and with circuses, Pastor made his variety debut in 1861. At the time, variety still had a certain bad odor attached to it. Most theatres had bars that actively pushed the sale of liquor and attracted a relatively rough order of patrons. The ambitious, highly moral Pastor set out to change all that and quickly succeeded. When he opened his first theatre in 1865, he discouraged serving of drinks, attempted to clean up sometimes off-color acts, and solicited family trade. His methods proved so popular that he opened a larger theatre in 1875, then in 1881 opened the theatre on 14th Street, which was afterwards identified with him and where he achieved his greatest success. A small, stocky, mustachioed man, Pastor regularly appeared on his own bills, not merely to introduce the acts but also to sing his "Rhymes for the Times," comic, topical songs twitting current events and celebrities. Virtually his only failure was his attempt to approach the legitimate stage with extended pieces of a sort that *Harrigan and

*Hart had popularized. Toward the end of his career, despite his fame, he was rudely pushed aside by newer figures who were attempting to set up national chains and monopolize vaudeville. Biography: *Tony Pastor: Dean of the Vaudeville Stage*, Parker Zellers, 1971.

PATINKIN, Mandy [né Mandel Bruce Patinkin] (b. 1947), actor and singer. The magnetic performer of intense or flamboyant characters is a nontraditional leading man who can play both experimental and Shakespearean roles with equal panache. He was born in Chicago and educated at the University of Kansas and Juilliard before working several years in regional theatre. Patinkin made his New York debut Off Broadway in 1974 and three years later was noticed on Broadway as the despondent lover Mark in the drama *The *Shadow Box* (1977). But his most successful stage appearances were in musicals, such as the wry commentator Che in *Evita* (1979), the two artists named George in *Sunday in the Park with George* (1984), the sullen uncle Archibald Craven in *The *Secret Garden* (1991), and the self-destructive vaudevillian Burrs in *The Wild Party* (2000).

PATRICK, John. See *Teahouse of the August Moon, The.*

PATRIOTS, THE (1943), a play by Sidney *Kingsley. [National Theatre, 172 perf.; NYDCC Award.] Thomas Jefferson (Raymond Edward Johnson) returns from France, hoping to settle with his daughters at his Monticello retreat. But George Washington (Cecil Humphreys), buffeted by rough political opposition and particularly fearful of rising monarchist strength, urges Jefferson to become his secretary of state. Jefferson accepts reluctantly. Before long he is locked in battle with his arch rival, the Federalist, Hamilton (House Jameson), before running successfully for president in 1800. The *Playwrights' Company produced the solidly written chronicle play when World War II gave Jefferson's fight for democratic ideals added meaning. Kingsley was a sergeant in the army at the time of the production.

PAUL KAUVAR; or, Anarchy (1887), a play by Steele *MacKaye. [Standard Theatre, approx. 100 perf.] Paul Kauvar (Joseph Haworth), a commoner who has risen to high rank in the French Revolution, is repelled by its swift drift into terrorism, and he attempts to harbor, under aliases, the Duc de Beaumont (Edwin Varrey) and the Duc's daughter, Diane (Annie Robe), whom he secretly marries. The notorious and duplicitous Gouroc (Wilton *Lackaye) betrays the Duc and makes it seem that Kauvar wittingly issued the death warrant. To show his innocence Paul prepares to take the Duc's place at the guillotine. Both the Duc and Paul escape, but Paul is later captured by royalists. After disguising himself as the royalist general, whom he allows to escape, he is reunited with Diane just as news arrives of Robespierre's death and the end of the reign of terror. This summary only hints at the complications of plot in this gripping if farfetched melodrama. To some extent the play was inspired by what MacKaye perceived as the unfair trial and execution of the Chicago anarchists in 1887. It was tried out as *Anarchy*, but the title was changed to avoid charges that MacKaye was trading on headlines. George *Odell recalled, "Its reworking of old material, lovers in danger, villains, sansculottes, swirling, shouting mobs led by the customary mad woman revolutionist, fascinated the public for the best part of the season and came back, later, into the friendly domain of the combination houses. It is the remarkable handling of the mob scenes, with Lillie Eldridge as the shouting terror, Scarlotte, that I chiefly remember."

PAUL PRY (1826). A comedy by John Poole, it was first produced in New York in 1826, a year after its London premiere. Its story centered on a comically mischievous snooper and busybody who turns hero when he rescues from a well papers that incriminate more serious troublemakers. Thomas *Hilson created the part at the *Park Theatre, while subsequent interpreters included J. H. *Hackett, William E. *Burton, the younger William *Warren, and John *Brougham. The comedy retained its popularity until the early 1870s.

PAULDING, James Kirke. See *Lion of the West, The.*

PAYNE, B[en] IDEN (1881–1976), manager and director. After a distinguished career in England, associated largely with Shakespearean productions, he came to America in 1913 and worked as artistic director for little theatres in both Philadelphia and Chicago. Payne also occasionally directed for Broadway, including the 1916 productions of Langdon *Mitchell's *Major Pendennis* and John *Galsworthy's *Justice*. From 1919 to 1934 he was professor of drama at the Carnegie Institute of Technology, then later taught at several major universities, including the University of Texas. He continued in rare instances to direct Broadway plays, among them the Ethel *Barrymore vehicle *Embezzled Heaven* (1944).

PAYNE, John Howard (1791–1852), playwright and actor. Remembered today primarily as the lyricist of "Home, Sweet Home," which was part of the operetta *Clari, the Maid of Milan* (1823), he was a versatile and intriguing figure on early stages. He was born somewhere near New York and raised in Boston, where his father was a schoolmaster. Fascinated by accounts of the English child prodigy Master Betty he pressed his family to allow him to go on the stage. They demurred and sent him instead to serve an apprenticeship in a New York mercantile house. While there, at the age of fourteen, Payne began the publication of one of the earliest American theatrical journals, *Thespian Mirror* (December 1805 to March 1806). At the same time he wrote his first play, a melodramatic comedy, *Julia; or, The Wanderer,* that shocked many critics and playgoers. He made his stage debut in 1809 at the *Park Theatre as Young Norval in *Douglas. He later essayed Hamlet, Rolla in *Pizarro, and Palmyra in *Mahomet*. In Boston his leading lady was Elizabeth Poe, mother of the poet. But he soon concentrated on writing, his comedy *Lovers' Vows* and others finding success in London before they were presented in his native country. His best-known works included *Brutus (1819), *Thérèse* (1821), and *Charles the Second (1824). Payne is believed to have written between fifty and sixty plays. In 1842 he was appointed by President Tyler as consul at Tunis, where he was serving when he died. *Quinn has written, "Payne's position in our dramatic history is a peculiar one. His most significant work was done abroad and his direct inspiration was foreign." Biography: *America's First Hamlet*, Grace Overmyer, 1957.

PAYTON, Corse (1867–1934), actor. Self-advertised as "The World's Best Bad Actor," he was born in Centreville, Iowa, and at the age of sixteen organized a traveling company composed largely of members of his family. After trouping the West and Midwest for many years, he opened Corse Payton's Theatre in Brooklyn, where for nearly two decades he headed a stock company that offered a variety of plays each season at a scale of ten, twenty, and thirty cents. Among the performers who served some apprenticeship with him were Fay *Bainter, Richard *Bennett, Lillian and Dorothy *Gish, and Ernest *Truex.

PECK'S BAD BOY (1884), a play by Charles Pidgin. [Haverly's New York Comedy Theatre, 40 perf.] Young Henry Peck (William Carroll) is the bane of his neighborhood, creating mayhem wherever he might be, whether that is his own home, the local grocery and drug stores, or out on a picnic. Accompanying him on his havoc-making escapades are his "chum" Jimmy (Mollie Fuller) and his little girl friend (Florence Bates). Advertised as "Without plot, but with a purpose—to make people laugh," the play was viewed by the *Clipper* as indeed "sans plot and sans motif," but "Though the piece is the veriest nonsense, it is irresistible in its humor." Based on George Peck's "The Bad Boy Sketches," which had originally appeared in the *Milwaukee Sun*, the comedy remained a popular touring attraction for thirty years. Among the many performers who headed road companies and later went on to stardom were George M. *Cohan and Frank *Daniels.

PEG O' MY HEART (1912), a comedy by J. Hartley *Manners. [*Cort Theatre, 603 perf.] No sooner do the Chichesters learn they are bankrupt than a small silver lining appears: The late brother of Mrs. Chichester (Emily *Melville) has offered her a handsome annuity if she will look after his teenage daughter, Margaret (Laurette *Taylor). Peg arrives just as her cousin Ethel (Christine Norman) and a young philanderer, Christian Brant (Reginald Mason), are locked in a secret embrace. The family is appalled at Peg's dowdy dress and at the homely mutt she carries with her. Peg is equally taken aback by her relatives' haughty, unloving nature. Her only real friend would appear to be a young neighboring farmer, Jerry (H. *Reeves-Smith). Only after Peg prevents Ethel from foolishly eloping with Brant does the family begin to soften toward her. Before long Jerry reveals he is actually Sir Gerald Adair, her legal guardian. To his proposal of marriage the delighted Peg replies, "My father always said: 'Sure there's nothing half so sweet in life as love's young dream.'" One of the best-loved of all American plays, it is reputed to have had eight road companies, which were kept busy for three years. When it closed in New York, it was the longest-run nonmusical play in Broadway history. Taylor and the comedy returned to Broadway in 1921 for a successful run, and the play was musicalized and seen Off Broadway in 2003.

PEGGY ANN (1926), a musical comedy by Herbert *Fields (book), Richard *Rodgers (music), Lorenz *Hart (lyrics). [Vanderbilt Theatre, 333 perf.] Peggy Ann (Helen *Ford) drudges along, helping her mother run a boarding house, hoping to marry Guy Pendleton (Lester Cole), and spending much of her waking time daydreaming of a better life. She dreams of all sorts of riches and adventures, from shopping on Fifth Avenue to fending off pirates. Only Guy's proposal brings her back to reality. *Notable songs*: A Tree in the Park; Where's That Rainbow?; Maybe It's Me. The musical used the same basic story that co-producer Lew *Fields had employed in *Tillie's Nightmare*, a musical he had mounted in 1910 as a vehicle for Marie *Dressler. But the new treatment was unusually adventurous for 1926, with no splashy opening, a quiet finale with only Peggy on stage, much use of Freudian symbolism, and sets changed as the audience watched.

PEMBERTON, Brock (1885–1950), producer. Born in Leavenworth and educated at the University of Kansas, he was a journalist and drama editor for the New York *Mail* and the New York *World* before becoming assistant to Arthur *Hopkins in 1917. Three years later he produced his first play, *Enter Madame* (1920). Subsequent successes included *Miss Lulu Bett* (1920), *Six Characters in Search of an Author* (1922), *Loose Ankles* (1926), *The *Ladder* (1926), *Strictly Dishonorable* (1929), *Personal Appearance* (1934), *Kiss the Boys Goodbye* (1938), *Janie* (1942), and *Harvey* (1944).

PENN, Arthur (b. 1922), director. The Philadelphia native has worked largely in television and films but is recalled for his staging of such plays as *Two for the Seesaw* (1958), *The *Miracle Worker* (1959), *Toys in the Attic* (1960), *All the Way Home* (1960), *Wait Until Dark* (1966), *Fortune's Fool* (2002), and *Sly Fox* (2004).

PENNINGTON, Ann (1894?–1971), dancer. Both the birthplace and birthdate of the tiny (less than five feet), dimple-kneed dancer are open to question, with Camden, New Jersey, Philadelphia, and Wilmington, Delaware, all offered as native cities while her birth year is sometimes given as 1892. She appeared in amateur performances in Philadelphia before making her professional debut in the chorus of *The Red Widow* (1911). Subsequently Pennington appeared in seven editions of the *Ziegfeld Follies* between 1913 and 1924, and five editions of *George White's Scandals*. In the 1926 version of the latter she introduced "Black Bottom." She also performed in *Miss 1917*, *Jack and Jill* (1923), *The New Yorkers* (1930), and *Everybody's Welcome* (1931). During the 1940s she danced in tawdry touring companies of *The *Student Prince* and *Blossom Time*.

PEOPLE'S LAWYER, THE (1842), a play by Joseph S. *Jones. [*Park Theatre, 1 perf.] Winslow (Mr. Bellamy), an unscrupulous merchant, fires his clerk, Charles Otis (Mr. Lovell), after Charles refuses to perjure himself for Winslow's benefit. He also persuades another clerk, John Ellsley (Mr. A. Andrews), to plant a watch in Charles's pocket and to accuse Charles of theft. At his trial, Charles is defended by Robert Howard (Mr. Clarke), a crusading attorney who is known as "The People's Lawyer" and who has a special interest in this case, since he loves Charles's sister, Grace (Miss Buloid). The trial is thrown into confusion by the testimony of the kindly but fuzzy Yankee Solon Shingle (George H. *Hill), who seems to think he is to testify about his lost "barrel of apple-sarse." Pangs of guilt prompt Ellsley to confess the truth. The play was originally presented in Boston in 1839 and quickly became one of Hill's most popular

vehicles. It was also an important vehicle for Charles *Burk, who first performed Shingle at Philadelphia's *Arch Street Theatre. In 1857 John E. *Owens attempted the part and met with such success that he rewrote the play to expand the role of Shingle and, under the title of *Solon Shingle*, toured with it for a quarter of a century.

PEPLE, Edward [Henry] (1867–1924), playwright. Born in Richmond, Virginia, he turned to writing after a long career in railroading. Although well over a dozen of his plays were produced, only two were major successes: *The *Prince Chap* (1904) and *A *Pair of Sixes* (1914). Two other less popular plays are of passing interest: the Civil War melodrama *The Littlest Rebel* (1911) and the musical *The Charity Girl* (1912). The latter was shut down by the police in one city because of objections to the lyric for "I'd Rather Be a Chippie than a Charity Bum."

PERELMAN, S. J. See *One Touch of Venus*.

PERFECT CRIME (1987), a thriller by Warren Manzi. [47th Street Theatre, still running.] Author and psychiatrist Margaret Thorne Brent (Cathy Russell) and her psychiatrist husband, Harrison (Manzi), are interviewed by Inspector Archer (Perry Perkkanen), who is investigating a local murder. Archer soon becomes obsessed with Margaret, her work, her patients, and her link to the crime. When Harrison is murdered, Archer proves that Margaret did it and arrests her, even though he has fallen in love with the brilliant murderess. The little thriller opened without fanfare, gathered a few appreciative reviews and, without ever becoming a hot ticket, survived into the next century. It is estimated that Russell played Margaret over four thousand times. *Perfect Crime* holds the record for Off Broadway's longest-running nonmusical.

PERFORMANCE ART. Although the emphasis in these loosely constructed, multidimensional programs may sometimes be on music, poetry, dance, political speeches, visual art, or other forms, there is something inherently theatrical about them because they are always performed. The very nature of performance art defies strict definitions, but in each case the artist's expression of an idea must take place before a live audience. A painting viewed is considered too stagnant for the genre, but a painting being created is performance art. While many pieces are sociopolitical, outspoken, controversial, and confrontational, there is much in performance art that is personal and intimate. Some involve a "cast" of artists while others are solo projects. The creator of the art and the performer are usually the same person, even if it is scripted in a somewhat traditional manner. And even as such theatrical elements as scenery, costumes, sound effects, lighting, dialogue, and songs may be used, often performance art occurs in found spaces in an impromptu fashion rather than in traditional theatre buildings. Among the most well-known performance artists, many of whom began in traditional theatre, include Laurie Anderson, Eric *Bogosian, Chong Ping, Martha Clark, Ethyl Eichelberger, Karen Finley, Richard *Foreman, Tehching Hsieh, Holly Hughes, Alan Kaprow, Suzanne Lacy, Tim Miller, Meredith Monk, Linda Montano, Rachel Rosenthal, and Carolee Schneermann.

PERKINS, Anthony (1932–92), actor. The son of Osgood *Perkins, he was born in New York and educated at Rollins College and Columbia. After playing on summer circuits he made his debut as a replacement in the role of Tom Lee in *Tea and Sympathy* in 1954. Later he appeared as such juvenile leads as the would-be writer Eugene Gant in *Look Homeward, Angel* (1957); the wanderlust youth Gideon Briggs in the musical *Greenwillow* (1960); the awkward society crasher *Harold* (1962), and hippie journalist Andy Hobart in *The Star-Spangled Girl* (1966). After a very successful film career Perkins returned for more mature performances, including the angst-ridden Tandy in *Steambath* (1970) and the haughty playwright Jason Carmichael in *Romantic Comedy* (1979), but his finest portrayal was probably as a replacement in the role of the psychiatrist Martin Dysart in *Equus* in 1975, treating the type of psychotic youth he had so often played in the movies.

PERKINS, Osgood (1892–1937), actor. Born in West Newton, Massachusetts, he was educated at Harvard, fought in World War I, and worked in films before making his late debut in a small part in *Beggar on Horseback* (1924). For a time thereafter he drifted between larger roles in short-run plays and supporting roles in minor hits, among them Joe Cobb in *Spread Eagle* (1927). Perkins's career-making role was the cynical, gimlet-eyed newspaper editor Walter Burns in The *Front Page* (1928). Twelve years after the play closed Brooks *Atkinson wrote that he could still see Perkins "cutting through the uproar like a bright, sharp penknife, and peeling off the layers of the plot as he went along." Subsequent successes came as Michael Astroff in *Uncle Vanya* (1930), the acid-tongued secretary Samuel Gillespie in *Tomorrow and Tomorrow* (1931), novelist Kenneth Bixby in *Goodbye Again* (1932), Sganarelle in The *School for Husbands* (1933), pilot Jake Lee in *Ceiling Zero* (1935), and the fortune-hunting Kenneth Rice in *End of Summer* (1936).

PERRY, Antoinette (1888–1946), director and producer. Born in Denver, she began her career as an actress in 1905, but after her marriage to Frank Wheatcroft Freauff in 1909 she retired from the stage until 1924. Perry abandoned performing when she became a director for Brock *Pemberton and often his silent partner in production. Among the plays she staged were *Strictly Dishonorable* (1929), *Personal Appearance* (1934), *Ceiling Zero* (1935), *Kiss the Boys Goodbye* (1938), *Janie* (1942), and *Harvey* (1944). With Rachel *Crothers and Jane *Cowl she helped organize the New York *Stage Door Canteen and also served as chairman of the board and secretary of the *American Theatre Wing. In 1947 the Antoinette Perry Awards, popularly known as the *Tonys, were named after her and were first given for distinguished achievement in the theatre.

PERSONAL APPEARANCE (1934), a comedy by Lawrence Riley. [*Henry Miller Theatre, 501 perf.] While touring to promote her latest film, *Drifting Lady*, the glamorous, susceptible screen star Carole Arden (Gladys George) develops car trouble near Wilkes-Barre. A handsome young gas-station attendant, Chester Norton (Philip Ober), helps fix the car and also puts her up for the night at the home of his fiancée's parents. Carole falls madly in love with Chester and when he mentions he has an invention to improve sound films she prepares to take him back to Hollywood with her. Fearing the consequences of her behavior, her press agent, Gene Tuttle (Otto Hulette), scuttles the arrangement and leaves Chester in the arms of his local girlfriend. A basically minor comedy, producer Brock *Pemberton ended up with a hit largely because of Grace George's comic playing.

PETER PAN (1905). James M. *Barrie's whimsical tale of a boy who refuses to grow up and who takes other children to his special never-land was first offered to American playgoers in 1905 with Maude *Adams, for whom it was written, in the title role. To no small extent because it is a play to which children can be taken, it has never lost its appeal. Later Peter Pans have included Marilyn *Miller, Eva *Le Gallienne, and Jean Arthur. Leonard *Bernstein composed incidental music for this last production. A musical version, with music by Mark Charlap and Jule *Styne and lyrics by Carolyn Leigh, Betty *Comden, and Adolph *Green, was offered in 1954 with Mary *Martin as Peter and Cyril *Ritchard as Hook. It was directed and choreographed by Jerome *Robbins and ran 152 performances in the *Winter Garden Theatre. *Notable songs*: I'm Flying; Neverland; I Won't Grow Up; Tender Shepherd; I've Got to Crow. The musical was revived in 1979 with Sandy Duncan as star and ran 551 performances, the longest Broadway run of any production of *Peter Pan*. Cathy Rigby was Peter in successful revivals on tour and on Broadway in 1990, 1991, and 1998. **Carolyn LEIGH** (1926–83), the lyricist who often worked with composer Cy *Coleman, was known for her brassy, confident lyrics. Born in the Bronx and educated at Queens College, Leigh wrote for radio and television before finding success with some best-selling pop songs in the 1950s. In addition to *Peter Pan*, her Broadway musicals were *Wildcat* (1960), *Little Me* (1962), and *How Now Dow Jones* (1967).

PETERS, Bernadette [née Lazzara] (b. 1948), actress and singer. The gamine, baby-voiced performer was born in Ozone Park, New York. She was not quite eleven when she made her first professional appearance in a *City Center revival of *The *Most Happy Fella*, then two years later she played in a touring company of *Gypsy*. Fame came when she portrayed Ruby (read Ruby Keeler) in the Off-Broadway musical spoof *Dames at Sea* (1968). Although Peters has appeared in plays, she is best known for musical roles such as vaudevillian Josie Cohan in *George M* (1968), Italian waif Gelsomina in *La Strada* (1969), silent film comedienne Mabel Normand in *Mack and Mabel* (1974), artist's model Dot and her daughter Marie in *Sunday in the Park with George* (1984), transplanted Brit Emma in *Song and Dance* (1985), the Witch in *Into the Woods* (1987), struggling actress Paula in *The Goodbye Girl* (1993), sharpshooter Annie Oakley in *Annie Get Your Gun* (1999), and stage mother Rose in *Gypsy* (2003). Peters is one of the few remaining Broadway musical stars, known for her considerable acting talents and for her Broadway belt that can also be intimate and cozy.

PETERS, [Charles] Rollo, [III] (1892–1967), actor and designer. The son of the California painter Charles Rollo Peters, he was born in Paris but raised in California and later studied art in Europe. When Peters returned to America he served as designer and performer with the *Washington Square Players and, after that group was disbanded, with the young *Theatre Guild. He designed many of the company's early productions, using only odds and ends and materials from closed shows. His designs were seen in *Bonds of Interest* (1919), in which he played Leander, and in *John Ferguson* (1919), in which he portrayed Andrew Ferguson. Among his subsequent roles were Romeo to Jane *Cowl's Juliet (he also designed the sets for the 1923 production), Antony to her Cleopatra (again designing the sets), Tom Wrench in *Trelawny of the Wells* (1927), Julian Beauclerc in *Diplomacy* (1928), Newland Archer in *The Age of Innocence* (1928), and Jack Absolute in *The Rivals* (1930). Later Peters appeared in and designed the sets for revivals of *The Streets of New York* (1931) and *The Pillars of Society* (1931).

PETRIFIED FOREST, THE (1935), a play by Robert *Sherwood. [*Broadhurst Theatre, 197 perf.] Alan Squire (Leslie *Howard) is a world-weary idealist whose wanderings have brought him to the Black Mesa Bar-B-Q in Arizona. This combination of gas station and lunchroom sits near the petrified forest that seems to represent an inevitable and much-desired death to Squire. The owner's daughter, Gabby Maple (Peggy *Conklin), is an attractive young girl who dreams of romance and of studying art in Paris. She reads some French poetry to Squire, who is intrigued and not a little smitten. But their idyll is interrupted by the arrival of Duke Mantee (Humphrey Bogart) and his gang, who have decided to use the lunchroom as a hideout. Seeing some hope for the future in Gabby and feeling his own wanderings have reached the end of the road, Squire signs over his life insurance policy to the girl and goads Mantee into killing him. Historian William Torbert Leonard has written, "The desperation of the depressed thirties is reflected in Sherwood's drama of [a] lost intellectual, Squire, and the death of his era." Although Percy *Hammond of the *Herald Tribune* called the work "a delightful improbability," he concluded it was "made probable by Mr. Howard and his accomplices." When he repeated his role in Hollywood, Bogart's career was launched and for many years he was typecast in gangster roles.

PFAFF'S. Opened by Charles Pfaff at 647 Broadway in either 1858 or 1859, it was originally a small saloon that soon attracted leading intellectuals and theatrical figures. Its popularity was such that in 1864 Pfaff enlarged the premises into a full-service restaurant. As the theatre district moved northward, the restaurant relocated at 9 West 24th Street, then closed in 1887.

PHANTOM. See *Phantom of the Opera, The*.

PHANTOM OF THE OPERA, THE (1988). A British musical based on Gaston Leroux's famous novel, it has a book by Richard Stilgoe and Andrew Lloyd *Webber, lyrics by Charles Hart, and music by Webber. The West End smash hit was quickly brought to America, where it opened at the *Majestic Theatre in 1988, and repeated its London success. Michael Crawford played the disfigured man who haunts the Paris Opera House and Sarah Brightman was Christine, the singer he adores and promotes. It continues to play to substantial crowds on Broadway and in numerous road companies. A different musical version of Leroux's tale, called *PHANTOM* (1991), was written at the same time but, unable to compete with the Webber version on Broadway, opted to play in regional theatres. It has a book by Arthur *Kopit and a score by Maury *Yeston.

PHILADELPHIA. The first important American theatre center, it was the site of performances in 1749 by Thomas *Kean and Walter *Murray, possibly at the warehouse of William Plumstead and certainly in the face of stern Quaker and other puritanical opposition; this, despite the fact that Plumstead was a magistrate, councilman, and three times mayor. Indeed, the early years were a constant struggle between players and antitheatrical authorities. Plumstead's building, which stood on the waterfront between Pine and Lombard streets and which remained standing for another hundred years, was also home to the elder *Hallam when he brought his company there in 1754. *Douglass and the *American Company began regular seasons in the city in 1759. In 1766 he opened the first permanent American theatre there, the *Southwark. It was at this playhouse that he gave the first professional performance of a native play, The *Prince of Parthia, in 1767. Three later playhouses figured importantly in the city's history: the *Chestnut Street (opened in 1793), the *Walnut Street (built as a circus in 1809, converted to drama in 1811, and still in use as the oldest theatre in America), and the *Arch Street (opened in 1828). Thomas *Wignell was a major figure in the city's early theatricals, and Edwin *Forrest used the city as his base throughout most of his career. In the first half of the 19th century the city was also home to the Philadelphia School of Dramatists, a group of playwrights who usually wrote blank-verse romantic tragedies: Robert Montgomery *Bird, George H. *Boker, Robert T. *Conrad, Richard Penn Smith, and John Augustus *Stone. Although by the first third of the century the city had lost its primacy to New York, it continued to be a flourishing center. Its most famous ensemble was that run by Mrs. John *Drew during the last half of the 19th century at the Arch Street Theatre. About the same time, the Philadelphia School of Comic Opera enjoyed a heyday that lasted almost until World War I. The name was given, largely in derision by the New York press, to musicals written and produced in Philadelphia, some of which toured the country and were often well received except by New York. The school is best exemplified by the works of Willard *Spenser and by his most successful musical, The *Little Tycoon (1886). Philadelphia was also the last important bastion of traditional minstrelsy. Although as many as ten theatres were lit during the 1920s, the city had become largely a tryout and touring town. It sunk to only three occasionally used theatres in the Depression, enjoyed a small revival beginning with World War II, then languished again. Some have pointed out that the waning of theatre in Philadelphia was the result of the demise of its greatest newspaper, The Evening Bulletin; the city was left without a drama critic comparable in knowledgeability and acuity to its noted reviewer, Ernest Schier. The theatre scene did not improve until the 1970s, when Philadelphia enjoyed the fruits of the regional theatre movement. Among the many companies operating in and near the city at the turn of the 21st century are the Arden Theatre Company, Interact Theatre Company, Society Hill Playhouse, Philadelphia Shakespeare Festival, Venture Theatre, *Philadelphia Theatre Company, American Music Theatre Festival with the Prince Music Theatre, Philadelphia Drama Guild, *Hedgerow Theatre, Mum Puppettheatre, Lantern Theatre Company, Wilma Theatre, and the People's Light and Theatre Company. Add to this the area collegiate productions and tours at the Academy of Music, the Forrest and Merriam theatres, and the new Kimmel Center for the Performing Arts and the theatregoing situation is not so grim. Since 1995, Philadelphia honors outstanding theatre productions with its annual Barrymore Awards, named after the illustrious family of actors who came from there.

PHILADELPHIA STORY, THE (1939), a comedy by Philip *Barry. [*Shubert Theatre, 417 perf.] Because the marriage of the socially prominent "virgin goddess" Tracy Lord (Katharine *Hepburn) to the self-made, priggish George Kitteredge (Frank Fenton) is news, Destiny magazine assigns Mike Connor (Van Heflin), a tough special reporter, and Elizabeth Imbrie (Shirley *Booth), a wisecracking photographer, to cover the event. The pre-wedding festivities are made all the more interesting by the arrival of Tracy's first husband, C. K. Dexter Haven (Joseph *Cotten), whose subtle baiting of Tracy exacerbates her private doubts about the marriage. The night before the nuptials she drinks too much and winds up swimming nude in the family pool with Mike. This proves more than George can take, but after he leaves the wedding goes on—with Dexter once again the groom. Barry wrote the comedy with Hepburn in mind and the *Theatre Guild produced it, becoming a great success for all three. Although many critics felt it was inferior to some of the author's earlier works, the public disagreed. Often produced at colleges and in regional theatres, the play was successfully revived on Broadway in 1980 with Blythe *Danner, Edward *Herrmann, and Frank Converse. The play became the popular movie musical High Society (1956); when the film was adapted into a stage musical in 1998 with the same name, it quickly closed on Broadway.

PHILADELPHIA THEATRE COMPANY. Founded in 1974 by Jean Harrison and Robert Hedley as the Philadelphia Company, the troupe has presented revivals of classics and modern works, as well as the occasional world premiere, such as Terrence *McNally's *Master Class and David Ives's Lives of the Saints. The company performs in the elegant little Plays and Players Theatre, a 324-seat proscenium space located in the historic Rittenhouse Square district of Philadelphia, Pennsylvania.

PHISTER, Montgomery [sometimes spelled Physter] (1851–1917), critic. An important 19th-century drama critic, he was born in Maysville, Kentucky, and was educated at Yale. For most of his newspaper career he was associated with the Cincinnati Commercial Tribune, in which his thoughtful and fair criticisms were examined seriously by major performers and writers. He is said to have refused several offers to move to New York.

PHOENIX THEATRE (New York). Organized in 1953 by T. Edward Hambleton and Norris Houghton, the group took over the old Yiddish Art Theatre on Second Avenue, which it renamed and where it remained for eight years. Among its notable productions were Sidney *Howard's Madam, Will You Walk (1953), Coriolanus (1954), The *Golden Apple (1954), Phoenix '55, A Month in the Country (1956), The Littlest Revue (1956), The Duchess of Malfi (1957), *Once Upon a Mattress (1959), The *Great God Brown (1959), and The *Octoroon (1961). Financial problems forced the company to find a smaller house in 1961, where its biggest hit was *Oh, Dad, Poor Dad . . . (1962). For five years beginning in 1964 the organization joined with Ellis *Rabb and the *Association of Producing Artists, during which time its successful mountings included revivals of *You Can't Take It with You (1966) and The *Show-Off (1967). Thereafter, the group continued to produce Off Broadway until its dissolution in 1982.

PHYSIOC, Joseph A[llen] (1865–1951), designer. Born in Richmond, Virginia, and raised in Columbia, South Carolina, he began his career as a set designer in small theatres in Alabama, later moving to New York and taking a job as an assistant scene painter at the Metropolitan Opera. He also briefly tried his skills at acting. In 1894 he joined with Henry E. *Hoyt to design the sets for *De Koven's comic opera Rob Roy. Among Physioc's many later successes were *Mansfield's *Richard III (1896), Courted into Court (1896), *Beau Brummell (1900), The *Climbers (1901), The *Lion and the Mouse (1905), The *Traveling Salesman (1908), *Within the Law (1912), *Peg o' My Heart (1912), *Lightnin' (1918), *Seventh Heaven (1922), and Dracula (1927). A formal, carefully detailed painter of the old school, he found himself at odds with the more stylized set designs that began to come into vogue

shortly before World War I. Rather than adapt, he retired and spent his last years painting pictures for exhibitions.

PIANO LESSON, THE (1990), a play by August *Wilson. [*Walter Kerr Theatre, 329 perf.; Pulitzer Prize, NYDCC Award.] Boy Willie (Charles S. Dutton) drives a load of watermelons from his Mississippi home to the Pittsburgh house of his sister, Berniece (S. Epatha Merkerson). He hopes to sell the melons and also his sister's piano to purchase land his family has worked since slave days. Although she hasn't played the piano in the years following her husband's death, Berniece adamantly opposes selling an instrument built and carved with family portraits by her grandfather. Making Boy Willie's task more difficult, Berniece and others start to see the ghost of a man Boy Willie may have killed. Berniece's suitor (Tommy Hollis) holds an exorcism that brings Berniece back to the piano and brings Boy Willie to the realization that he probably must look elsewhere for his money. Besides having Wilson's usual flair for the poetic African-American vernacular and incisive characterizations, the play also boasted a disquieting sense of mystery not previously seen in his works.

PICNIC (1953), a play by William *Inge. [*Music Box Theatre, 477 perf.; Pulitzer Prize, NYDCC Award.] On a hot Labor Day morning in a small Kansas town, a cocky, muscle-bound vagrant, Hal Carter (Ralph Meeker), strays into the Owens's backyard and changes the lives of the family. He breaks the heart of the tomboy younger daughter Millie (Kim *Stanley), goads Mrs. Owens's (Peggy *Conklin) spinster sister Rosemary (Eileen *Heckart) into forcing her reluctant gentleman friend to marry her, and prompts the older daughter Madge (Janice Rule) to give up her rich boyfriend, Alan (Paul Newman), and to run away with him. The *Theatre Guild production featured a superb cast under the direction of Joshua *Logan. Louis *Kronenberger noted, "Mr. Inge's naturalistic round dance of frustrated, unfulfilled, life-hungry women catches something of the mischance and misbegottenness of life itself." Inge's earlier (and personally preferred) version of the play, called Summer Brave, was presented at the ANTA Theatre in 1975 but was considered less effective. The *Roundabout Theatre presented a fine production of the familiar version in 1994.

PICON, Molly (1898–1992), comic actress. Although the tiny, impish New York–born performer, who was raised in Philadelphia, made her first appearance in an English-language vaudeville act at a nickelodeon in 1904, most of her early career was spent on the Yiddish stage, where she became a major comic star. She also appeared at the *Palace Theatre in the late 1920s. With the decline of Yiddish theatre, she turned increasingly to Broadway, where she played character parts in such lightweight shows as *The Kosher Widow* (1959), *How to Be a Jewish Mother* (1967), *Paris Is Out!* (1970), and *Something Old, Something New* (1977). Her most successful role was as the American widow looking for a husband in Israel in the musical *Milk and Honey* (1961). Autobiography: *So Laugh a Little*, 1962.

PILGRIM, James. See *Harry Burnham.*

PINK LADY, THE (1911), a musical comedy by C. M. S. *McLellan (book, lyrics), Ivan *Caryll (music). [*New Amsterdam Theatre, 312 perf.] Before his marriage to Angele (Alice Dovey), Lucien Garidel (William Elliot) decides to have one last fling with his old flame from the demimonde, Claudine (Hazel *Dawn). The fling is complicated by the fact that someone has been stealing kisses from attractive girls in the Forest of Compiègne. The satyr is unmasked, Lucien and Claudine enjoy their time together, then Lucien returns to Angele. *Notable songs*: By the Saskatchewan; Donny Didn't, Donny Did; The Kiss Waltz; Love Is Divine; My Beautiful Lady. Although Dawn was the lead in this *Klaw and *Erlanger musical, she did not keep the hero in the end, because the mores of the time would not allow a member of her class to win in musical comedy. The show was based on *Le Satyre*, a French farce by Georges Berr and Marcel Guillemand.

PINS AND NEEDLES (1937), a musical revue with sketches by various authors, Harold *Rome (music, lyrics). [Labor Stage, 1,108 perf.] Originally mounted by the International Ladies Garment Workers' Union as a pleasant entertainment on weekends, with a cast recruited entirely from union members, this sometimes lighthearted but generally propagandistic revue, which poked fun at most of the expected left-wing bêtes noires, quickly attracted a large audience and settled down for a long run in the 299-seat Labor Stage (once the *Princess Theatre) and later at the 849-seat Windsor. Revisions in the sketches and songs kept the revue up to current events and enticed many playgoers to make return visits. *Notable songs*: Sing Me a Song with Social Significance; Sunday in the Park; Chain Store Daisy; Nobody Makes a Pass at Me.

PINTER, Harold (b. 1930), playwright. The English dramatist, whose elusive, elliptical tragicomedies are thought to reflect the influence of *Beckett and *Ionesco, received his first American mounting when *The Birthday Party* was produced by San Francisco's *Actor's Workshop in 1960, then presented on Broadway in 1967. Other major New York stagings of his works have included *The Caretaker* (1961), *The Homecoming* (1967), *No Man's Land* (1976), and *Betrayal* (1980). Several of his works have been offered frequently and successfully Off Broadway, at regional playhouses, and at collegiate theatres. Pinter is also an actor, director, and screenwriter.

PINZA, [Fortunato] Ezio (1892–1957), singer. The great Metropolitan Opera basso, who was born in Rome, came to Broadway only after his career in opera had ended, but his voice was still superior to almost any other heard in the legitimate theatre, and his good looks and personal charm overcame some minor difficulties in his pronunciation of English. He made only two appearances, both of them memorable: the French planter Emile de Becque in *South Pacific* (1949) and the French father César in *Fanny* (1954).

PIPPIN (1972), a musical comedy by Roger O. Hirson (book), Stephen *Schwartz (music, lyrics). [*Imperial Theatre, 1,944 perf.] The life of Charlemagne's son, here called Pippin (John Rubinstein), is played out in a series of vaudeville-like sketches performed largely by a group of commedia dell'arte-style clowns, who were headed by the Leading Performer (Ben Vereen). Pippin seeks greatness in war, sex, and politics but settles for compromise and reality. *Notable songs*: Magic to Do; No Time at All; Corner of the Sky; Morning Glow; On the Right Track. Originally written by Schwartz while he was still in college, the show was produced on Broadway after the success of his *Godspell. Otis L. *Guernsey Jr. noted, "In a year of little experiment and less musical appeal . . . *Pippin* was a standout entertainment and stand-in for the dormant avant garde." Bob *Fosse's stylized staging was a major factor in the show's success. Another reason was that the musical was one of the first Broadway shows to employ a large television advertising campaign to promote business.

PIQUE (1875), a play "of today" by Augustin *Daly. [*Fifth Avenue Theatre, 237 perf.] In a moment of anger Mabel Renfrew (Fanny *Davenport) renounces her fiancé, Raymond Lessing (Maurice *Barrymore), and marries Captain Arthur Standish (D. H. Hawkins), son of the puritanical Matthew Standish (Charles *Fisher). Once the young couple goes to live with the elder Standish, Arthur quickly realizes that Mabel does not love him, and his father's rigid code of behavior further exacerbates difficulties, so he leaves. Immediately thereafter the Renfrews' young child is kidnapped. The search for the stolen youngster reunites the couple and shows the elder Standish's basic valor. When Raymond weds Mabel's widowed step-mother, Mabel understands that the decision made in pique was the right one after all. With the little boy recovered, she acknowledges, "A happiness that begins tonight for me . . . will endure while heart can beat, or life can last." The first three acts were based on Florence Lean's novel, *Her Lord and Master*, while the remaining two acts were suggested by the then recent unsolved kidnapping of Charley Ross and by scenes from *Les Misérables*. Critics were sharply divided on the merits of Daly's script and production. The *Tribune* took a middle ground, calling it "not of a high order, either in literary attributes or dramatic construction" but concluding correctly that it combined "comedy, sentiment, and sensation in a way that will not fail to please the average tastes." A road company, one of the first so organized, was quickly sent on tour.

PIRANDELLO, Luigi (1867–1936), playwright. The greatest of modern Italian dramatists is best remembered in America for three surrealistic plays that question the nature of truth: *Six Characters in Search of an Author* (1922), *Enrico IV* or *Henry IV* (1922), and *Right You Are (If You Think You Are)* (1927). These are regularly revived by collegiate and regional playhouses and occasionally on and Off Broadway. Many of Pirandello's other works have been produced, but none of these has found enduring favor with American playgoers.

PIRATE, THE (1942), a comedy by S. N. *Behrman. [Martin Beck Theatre, 177 perf.] When a troupe of traveling performers comes to a small West Indies town, it is refused a license to play by the mayor. However, the license is quickly granted when the leader of the troupe, Serafin (Alfred *Lunt), lets the mayor know he has recognized him as a long-sought pirate. In short order, romance blossoms between Serafin and the mayor's wife, Manuela (Lynn *Fontanne). The romance is tempestuous, with Serafin at one point walking a tightrope to enter Manuela's boudoir. Finally the actor hypnotizes Manuela into publicly revealing the truth about her husband, who is carted off to jail. Suggested by Ludwig Fulda's German play, *The Sea Robber*, the comedy was, as Brooks *Atkinson suggested, "not out of Mr. Behrman's usual drawer." Nevertheless, a capital production by the *Theatre Guild and the *Playwrights' Company and the performances of the Lunts turned it into engaging theatre.

PIRATES OF PENZANCE, THE (1879). *Gilbert and *Sullivan's comic opera, about law and order, love, misplaced children, and the difficulties of being born on the extra day of leap year, was unusual among Savoyard works in that, in order to protect American copyrights, it was given its world premiere at New York's *Fifth Avenue Theatre in 1879. The *D'Oyly Carte production, featuring Hugh Talbot as Frederick, Blanche Roosevelt as Mabel, and J. H. Ryley as the Major General, ran just over two months. Since then it has been given numerous revivals. Memorable were those by Winthrop *Ames in 1926 and the *New York Shakespeare Festival in 1981. The latter mounting did not employ Sullivan's orchestrations, added material from other shows, and was staged in a freewheeling, untraditional manner, with rock stars Rex Smith and Linda Ronstadt in the romantic leads and George *Rose as the Major General. As a result it displeased the purists but won the support of the critics and the public and enjoyed by far the longest American run of any Gilbert and Sullivan comic opera.

PITOU, Augustus (1843–1915), manager, producer, and playwright. Often called "King of the One-Night Stands," he began his career in his native New York as an actor in a minor role in Edwin *Booth's *Hamlet* in 1867. He remained with Booth for several years before abandoning performing in favor of managing theatres and actors. At one time or another he ran such New York theatres as *Booth's, the *Fifth Avenue, and the Grand Opera House and guided the careers of performers such as Rose *Coghlan, Chauncey *Olcott, and W. J. *Scanlan. Pitou was not merely Olcott's agent but his producer and playwright as well, creating the books for and mounting such Olcott romantic musical dramas as *Sweet Inniscarra* (1897), *A Romance of Athlone* (1899), and *Old Limerick Town* (1902). However, most of the plays he produced were designed as touring shows and, without a star of Olcott's attraction, never played major New York houses. After his death his son, Augustus Jr., continued his policies for nearly a decade.

PITTSBURGH PLAYHOUSE. In 1933 a group of noted local residents joined forces to establish a playhouse in this western Pennsylvania city to offer a more wide-ranging repertory than was available at the surviving legitimate theatre. At first it used the stage of the Frick Training School for Teachers, then performed in a converted speakeasy before opening its own complex of three theatres in the Oakland section of Pittsburgh. After many years as one of the nation's most successful community theatres, the troupe attempted to go professional in the 1960s but only met with financial collapse. Reopened as an affiliate of Point Park College, the playhouse is kept busy with semiprofessional, student, and children's theatre productions.

PITTSBURGH PUBLIC THEATRE. By the early 1970s Pittsburgh, Pennsylvania, still had no fully professional theatre company, so community leaders Joan Apt and Margaret Rieck invited producer-director Ben Shaktman to run a new resident company in 1975. The group performed in the converted Carnegie Free Library and Music Hall for several years before moving into the new 650-seat O'Reilly Theatre downtown. The repertory is a mix of contemporary plays and small musicals with classics and occasional original works.

PIXLEY, Annie [née Annie Shea] (1858–98), actress. The dark-haired, plump but gamin performer was born in Brooklyn and raised in California, where she took her stepfather's name when she began a stage career. She scored successes in *The *Danites* and in the title role of an 1876 version of *Snow White and the Seven Dwarfs* called *Snowflake*. Coming to the attention of Joseph *Jefferson, she played opposite him in *Rip Van Winkle* before enjoying her most memorable hit as the hoydenish waif who was the title figure of *M'liss*. Pixley bleached her hair blonde to fight off villains in two vehicles Fred *Marsden wrote for her, *Zara* (1883) and *Eily* (1885). Later successes included the stage-struck heroine of A. C. *Gunter's *The Deacon's Daughter* (1887) and the girl who helps her sweetheart fight in the Civil War, the title part in *Kate* (1890). Most of her vehicles offered her an opportunity to sing and dance, so many critics saw her as an imitator of Charlotte *Crabtree. However, as one obituary noted, "There has been no greater favorite with American play-goers."

PIXLEY, Frank (1867–1919), librettist. Born in Richfield, Ohio, he turned to newspaper work on leaving college. After writing a few unsuccessful plays he began a collaboration with composer Gustav *Luders, which resulted in some of the most popular turn-of-the-century musicals: *The Burgomaster* (1901), *King Dodo* (1902), *The *Prince of Pilsen* (1903), *Woodland* (1904), *The Grand Mogul* (1907), and *Marcelle* (1908). Following Luders's death he retired from the stage and spent his last years writing film scenarios.

PIZARRO (1800). Richard Brinsley *Sheridan's long-popular tragedy of a noble Inca's doomed battle against the Spanish invader, its most famous scene depicted the hero, Rolla, leaping over a chasm with a young child in one hand and his defending sword in another. Sheridan had based his play on a German drama by *Kotzebue. When it was first played at the *Park Theatre in America in 1800, a year after its Drury Lane premiere, it was further revised by William *Dunlap and offered as *Pizarro in Peru; or, The Death of Rolla.*

In one version or the other it remained a major attraction for seventy years. Among the notable Rollas who followed John *Hodgkinson were James *Fennell, Thomas Abthorpe *Cooper, Edwin *Forrest, William B. *Wood, and Edward *Eddy.

PLACIDE, Henry (1799–1870), actor. The son of rope dancer Alexandre Placide, he began performing in his father's shows while still a youngster. His debut as an adult was as Zekiel Homespun in *The Heir-at-Law* at the *Park Theatre in 1823. Placide rapidly grew to be the most polished and celebrated comedian of his day, his famous roles including Bob Acres, Sir Anthony Absolute, Sir Peter Teazle, and Sir Harcourt Courtly, as well as major parts in now forgotten contemporary pieces. In 1866 *Ireland wrote of him, "He is the only one who ever trod the American stage perfectly irresistible in humor, and yet entirely free from grimace and buffoonery . . . no other actor has ever so completely exemplified our idea of what a genuine comedian should be." His sister, **Jane PLACIDE** (1804–35) was hailed as the "Queen of the Drama in New Orleans." After her debut in Norfolk, Virginia, in 1820 she moved to New Orleans and remained there, except for brief tours, until 1833, excelling in such tragic roles as Lady Macbeth and Cordelia but also demonstrating skill at comedy. She died while still at the height of her powers and popularity.

PLAIN AND FANCY (1955), a musical comedy by Joseph *Stein, Will Glickman (book), Albert Hague (music), Arnold B. Horwitt (lyrics). [*Mark Hellinger Theatre, 461 perf.] Two New Yorkers (Shirl Conway and Richard Derr) come to the Pennsylvania Dutch country of Lancaster County, where they encounter stern Papa Yoder (Stefan Schnabel) as well as two young lovers, Katie Yoder (Gloria Marlowe) and Peter Reber (David Daniels). Problems arise because Peter has left the tight community and is therefore "shunned." But, with the help of the two visitors, all ends happily. *Notable songs*: It Wonders Me; Plenty of Pennsylvania; Why Not Katie?; Young and Foolish. The musical was unusual not because of a basically trite love story but because its setting, the Amish country, was one Broadway musicals had heretofore ignored and which was now treated with a careful respect and affection. One major scene depicted a traditional Amish barn raising. Curiously, many playgoers who saw the show remembered it best for Barbara *Cook's performance in a secondary role.

PLATT, Livingston (1874–1933?), designer. Born in Plattsburgh, New York, he studied art abroad and began to design for the stage at a theatre in Bruges, then returned to America in 1911 to accept a position as set and costume designer for Mrs. Lyman Gale's Toy Theatre in Boston. Platt then came to the attention of Margaret *Anglin, who assigned him the task of creating sets and clothing for four 1914 Shakespearean revivals: *The *Taming of the Shrew*, *Twelfth Night*, *Antony and Cleopatra*, and *As You Like It*. He eschewed the cumbersome, pseudo-realistic settings then fashionable and instead designed stylized settings whose use of a double proscenium allowed virtually instant changes. These sets were lit by him with striking imagination. Platt himself noted that his aim was "to see that every space of light and shadow which surrounds the action shall heighten and amplify the significance of the action," and he added, "Too much detail often ruins a play because it distracts attention from the action of the drama itself." Among his highly praised early settings were those for *East Is West* (1918) and *Shakuntala* (1919). In later seasons his fine designs were seen in such less imaginative mountings as *Daisy Mayme* (1926), *The *Racket* (1927), *Behold the Bridegroom* (1927), *The First Mrs. Fraser* (1929), *Dinner at Eight* (1932), and *The *Pursuit of Happiness* (1933). Platt disappeared after being detained on morals charges, but whether he committed suicide or lived somewhere obscurely cannot be determined.

PLAY IT AGAIN, SAM (1969), a comedy by Woody Allen. [*Broadhurst Theatre, 453 perf.] Having been left by his wife, who wants livelier company, mousy film critic Allen Felix (Allen) is so stupefied that he can only suck on undefrosted TV dinners and turn to a fantasy world. But even in his wildest fantasies, in which no less than Humphrey Bogart (Jerry Lacy) comes to his assistance, he keeps striking out with women. His best friend, Dick (Anthony Roberts), a hustling businessman, tries to help, as does Dick's wife, Linda (Diane Keaton). When the mouse finally roars, he has a fling with Linda, bravely gives her up, and in Bogart fashion becomes his own man. The popular David *Merrick production, which offered one of the best comic views of the modern antihero, marked Allen's only Broadway appearance. **Woody ALLEN** [né Allen Stewart Konigsberg] (b. 1935) is a Brooklyn-born humorist and stand-up comic who wrote sketches for the revue *From A to Z* (1960) and a hit comedy, *Don't Drink the Water* (1966). Better known for writing, directing, and appearing in films, Allen has also been represented in the New York theatre with *The Floating Lightbulb* (1980), *Central Park West* (1995), and *Writer's Block* (2003).

PLAYBILL. In 1884 Frank Vance Strauss founded a company to print theatrical "programmes" in a magazine format that included considerable advertising. Older programs had generally consisted of only four pages, which offered only basic credits and perhaps minimal advertising. In 1911 the founder began to call his publication the *Strauss Magazine Theatre Program*. Each playhouse was given a special full-color cover, but the rest of the playbill varied little. The program's name underwent several later changes, finally adopting *The Playbill* in 1934. Four years earlier sepia had replaced colored covers, and the programs' covers began to feature photographs of stars or scenes from the play in question. The organization has also undergone numerous changes of management. Today's programs, besides credits and advertising, contain feature articles, none of them critical and all very supportive of the New York theatre scene. Since 1982 the company has also published *Playbill—The National Theatre Magazine*, a monthly that utilizes much of the same material found in the theatre playbills.

PLAYERS, THE. See Theatrical Clubs.

PLAYERS EQUAL SUFFRAGE LEAGUE. Formed in late 1913 or early 1914 by the actress Mary *Shaw, it was designed to promote women's right to vote. Margaret *Anglin, Billie *Burke, and Jane *Cowl were among its most prominent members. When the League came to Boston to spread its advocacy, Charlotte *Crabtree gave the group a huge reception and was elected vice president. A few of its members made speeches on its behalf during curtain calls, but most simply spoke at regular meetings or helped underwrite advertisements and campaign literature. The group disbanded after women were enfranchised.

PLAYMAKERS REPERTORY COMPANY (Chapel Hill, North Carolina). Established in 1975 as a professional company housed on the campus of the University of North Carolina at Chapel Hill, the group has concentrated on intimate comedies and dramas that embrace cultural diversity. The troupe performs in the 500-seat Paul *Green Theatre (named after the local playwright) and in the flexible 280-seat Elizabeth Price Kenan Theatre.

PLAYWRIGHTS' COMPANY, THE (New York). A producing company, it was founded in 1938 by Maxwell *Anderson, S. N. *Behrman, Sidney *Howard, Elmer *Rice, and Robert E. *Sherwood. Although Anderson suggested the organization was begun "to make a center for ourselves within the theatre, and possibly rally the theatre as a whole to new levels by setting a high standard of writing and production," the founders were all established writers who had long since set high standards and whose real reason for embarking on their own was their displeasure with the policies of the *Theatre Guild, which had been their principal producer. In later years Kurt *Weill, Robert *Anderson, lawyer John Wharton, and producer Roger L. *Stevens became members. Among the company's memorable productions were *Abe Lincoln in Illinois (1938), *Knickerbocker Holiday (1938), *No Time for Comedy (1939), *Key Largo (1939), *There Shall Be No Night (1940), The *Eve of St. Mark (1942), The *Pirate (1942), The *Patriots (1943), *Dream Girl (1945), *Anne of the Thousand Days (1948), *Tea and Sympathy (1953), *Sabrina Fair (1953), *Cat on a Hot Tin Roof (1955), The *Pleasure of His Company (1958), and The *Best Man (1960). By 1960 the only founders still alive were Behrman, who had left the group, and Rice, and with few new playwrights on the horizon promising a constant and worthy output, the organization was dissolved. Wharton's Life among the Playwrights (1974) provides an interesting insider's view of the group.

PLAYWRIGHTS HORIZONS (New York). Perhaps no other Off-Broadway theatre company has been more successful in introducing notable new plays and playwrights than this small but potent organization. Founded in 1971 by Robert Moss as a writer's showcase, the group was the first to feature Christopher *Durang, William *Finn, James *Lapine, and other artists, as well as premiering many works that later transferred to Broadway. Among the long list of productions developed at the company were Kennedy's Children, *Gemini, Table Settings, Sister Mary Ignatius . . . , Terra Nova, The *Dining Room, Once on This Island, Marvin's Room, *Driving Miss Daisy, *Sunday in the Park with George, Later Life, *Falsettos, The Substance of Fire, *Assassins, *James Joyce's The Dead, *Violet, *Floyd Collins, and I Am My Own Wife. Moss was succeeded by André Bishop, Don Scardino, and Tim Sanford. The company performed for many years in a small space on *Theatre Row. Its home is currently being renovated into a two-theatre complex.

PLAZA SUITE (1968), three one-act plays by Neil *Simon. [*Plymouth Theatre, 1,097 perf.] In "Visitor from Mamaroneck," the first of three playlets set in a lavish suite at Manhattan's Plaza Hotel, suburbanites Karen (Maureen *Stapleton) and Sam Nash (George C. *Scott) take the same suite at the Plaza that they had on their honeymoon twenty-four years before. But Karen discovers that Sam's secretary is his mistress, and when he leaves for a rendezvous with the girl, she is left alone with a bottle of champagne and two glasses. "Visitor from Hollywood" concerns the efforts of movie producer Jesse Kiplinger (Scott) to seduce Muriel Tate (Stapleton), his old high school sweetheart. The farcical "Visitor from Forest Hills" deals with the frantic

attempts by Roy (Scott) and Norma Hubley (Stapleton) to coerce their daughter, Mimsey (Claudette Nevis), out of the locked bathroom minutes before her wedding ceremony. The plays prompted Otis L. *Guernsey Jr. to write of Simon, "He is the Molière of the high-rise era; he knows his contemporaries intimately and he treats them affectionately, but never too gently." The successful triplet comedy prompted Simon to write the sequels California Suite (1976), London Suite (1995), and Hotel Suite (2000), none of which were as accomplished or as popular.

PLEASURE OF HIS COMPANY, THE (1958), a comedy by Samuel *Taylor and Cornelia Otis *Skinner. [*Longacre Theatre, 474 perf.] Jessica Poole's world is thrown into confusion just before her marriage to Roger Henderson (George Peppard), the son of a rich rancher. Jessica (Dolores Hart) has been raised by her mother, Katherine Dougherty (Skinner), and stepfather, Jim Dougherty (Walter *Abel). Now her roving, sybaritic father, Biddeford Poole (Cyril *Ritchard), suddenly reappears after a fifteen-year absence. He makes Jessica's life and fiancé seem hopelessly stolid. When he begs her to give up her wedding plans and travel with him she finally agrees—but only for a year. The play was one of the last literate high comedies to achieve success in New York.

PLUMMER, [Arthur] **Christopher** [Orme] (b. 1929), actor. The Canadian-born performer has appeared in numerous Shakespearean roles with festivals in Canada and abroad and won praise for his Iago in a 1981 Broadway revival of *Othello. Among his other memorable assignments have been the Earl of Warwick in The Lark (1955), the satanic Nickles in *J. B. (1958), Pizarro in The Royal Hunt of the Sun (1965), Cyrano de Bergerac in the musical Cyrano (1973), various Russians in The Good Doctor (1973), *Macbeth (1988), Spooner in No Man's Land (1994), Barrymore (1997), and *King Lear (2002 and 2004). Dashing, romantic, and yet cynical, Plummer exudes an old-school charisma on stage but never stoops to histrionic tricks.

PLYMOUTH THEATRE (New York). The *Shuberts built the 1,000-seat playhouse on West 45th Street in 1917 and leased it to producer Arthur *Hopkins, who used it to present such daring works as *What Price Glory? (1924) and *Machinal (1927). But these kinds of experiments made little money during the Depression, and the theatre reverted back to the Shuberts, who still own it today. Designed by Herbert J. *Krapp in a rather subdued but elegant style, the Plymouth is an excellent house for nonmusical plays, and it has seen many outstanding productions over the decades, including *Holiday (1928), *Abe Lincoln in Illinois (1938), The *Odd Couple (1965), and The *Life and Adventures of Nicholas Nickleby (1981).

PLYMPTON, Eben (1853–1915), actor. The handsome, virile leading man was born and educated in Boston, where he took a job as bookkeeper on the Boston Post until a breakdown in his health forced him to leave for California. There he recuperated and then made his stage debut in 1871. Plymton appeared at *Wallack's in New York but secured his career portraying André in *Rose Michel (1875). Important Shakespearean assignments followed as Sebastian and Romeo in 1877, then he won applause as Walter Dalrymple in *Our Boarding House (1878), Lord Travers in *Hazel Kirke (1880), and the rugged farmer Dave Hardy in *Esmeralda (1881). Plympton later spent several seasons playing leads opposite Mary *Anderson and supporting Edwin *Booth in several productions, including Laertes in an all-star performance of *Hamlet. Among his subsequent roles were King Philip II in *In the Palace of the King (1901), Sir Harcourt Courtly in *London Assurance (1905), and the Bishop in The Duel (1906). Otis *Skinner remembered him as "talented, forceful, but extremely temperamental and egotistical."

POCAHONTAS; or, The Gentle Savage (1855), a musical burlesque by John *Brougham (book, lyrics). [*Lyceum Theatre, in repertory.] Coming to the court of the Tuscaroras, Captain John Smith (Charles M. *Walcot) spots the Indian princess Pocahontas (Georgina Hodson) and falls in love with her, and she with him. But Pocahontas's father, King H. J. Pow-ha-tan (Brougham), has promised his daughter to the Dutchman Mynheer Rolff (Charles Peters). A game of cards settles the matter in Smith's favor. Filled with doggerel and the outlandish puns beloved of the era, this musical burlesque was offered as an afterpiece. The music, largely borrowed from others, was adapted by James G. Maeder. It continued on the bill regularly for three weeks, then frequently reappeared thereafter. For the next thirty years, until both this sort of burlesque and afterpiece went out of style, it was by far the most popular example of its genre.

POE, Edgar Allan (1809–49), critic. The famed American poet and short-story writer was the son of actors, although he was not raised by them. In 1835 he published sections of an unfinished blank-verse drama, Politian, and later he occasionally wrote theatrical criticism for various publications, including the Broadway Journal, of which he became owner. As with much of his critical writings, he argued against what he deemed superficial and foreign. However, Poe was a perceptive enough playgoer to quickly, and largely correctly, evaluate the merits of an American effort such as *Fashion.

POLLOCK, Channing (1880–1946), playwright and critic. Born in Washington, D.C., but raised in Omaha and Salt Lake City, his theatrical career began when he returned to his birthplace to become a drama critic for the Washington Post and later for the Times and the *Dramatic Mirror. After working as a publicist for Florenz *Ziegfeld, William A. *Brady, and the *Shuberts, he turned to playwriting, experiencing a quick failure with his The Game of Hearts (1903), but later that year scored his initial success with his dramatization of Frank Norris's muckraking novel, The Pit. Alone or with collaborators Pollock wrote about thirty shows that saw the footlights, ranging from sketches for several *Ziegfeld Follies and the books of musical comedies to farce and melodrama. Among his early works were *Clothes (1906), Such a Little Queen (1909), The Crowded Hour (1918), Roads of Destiny (1918), and The Sign on the Door (1919). During this period he continued to write drama criticism, some of which so antagonized his former employers, the Shuberts, that they barred him from their theatres. Pollock's career took a marked turn in 1922 with The *Fool. His remaining works could all be perceived as contemporary morality plays: The Enemy (1925), Mr. Moneypenny (1928), and The House Beautiful (1931). Critics were increasingly put off by the preachiness of his last plays and grew steadily unkind, which prompted Pollock to retire. Autobiography: Harvest of My Years, 1943.

POLLY OF THE CIRCUS (1907), a play by Margaret *Mayo. [Liberty Theatre, 160 perf.] Polly (Mabel *Taliaferro) is a circus rider who is injured in a fall and taken to the home of the local minister, the Reverend John Douglass (Malcolm Williams), to recuperate. The two grow fond of each other, but Polly leaves as soon as she has recovered. She not only feels that a romance with the minister would hurt his standing in his small town, but she wants to continue in the circus tradition that runs far back in her family. The minister has other ideas. He comes after her and persuades her to marry him. Broadway scuttlebutt of the day said that Frederic Thompson, who was both the show's producer and the star's husband, had a major share in the writing, while others suggested Winchell *Smith was a silent collaborator. The circus scenes accounted as much for the show's popularity as did the romantic story.

POLLY WITH A PAST (1917), a comedy by George *Middleton and Guy *Bolton. [*Belasco Theatre, 315 perf.] Rex Van Zile (Herbert Yost) is madly in love with a young lady who is more enamored of doing good deeds than she is of Rex. His friends persuade him to allow himself to go to seed so that the young lady can save him. To this end they enlist the aid of the comely Polly (Ina *Claire), a minister's daughter from East Gilead, Ohio, who has come to New York to study for a concert career and who has taken a job as a maid to help pay her expenses. Polly agrees to pose as Paulette Bady, a French adventuress, and to "vamp" Rex. By the time the ruse has been played out, Rex and Polly are in love. David *Belasco produced the pleasant comedy that launched Claire on her career as a high comedienne.

PONISI, Mme. [née Elizabeth Hanson] (1818–99), actress. Born in England, she went on stage while still in her teens and shortly afterward married a fellow actor, James Ponisi. In 1850 they came to America, where she made her debut at Philadelphia's *Walnut Street Theatre as Mariana in *The Wife*, then played Lady Teazle for her first New York appearance. She rapidly earned a reputation as a fine and versatile performer, playing Cleopatra to Edward *Eddy's Antony, and Lady Macbeth, Desdemona, and Cordelia opposite Edwin *Forrest. In 1855 she created the title role in *Francesca da Rimini*. Ponisi joined *Wallack's great ensemble in 1871 as the company's leading portrayer of old women and remained with the troupe until it was dissolved. Her Mrs. Hardcastle and Mrs. Malaprop were numbered among her finest interpretations, but she also continued to create new roles such as Widow O'Kelly in The *Shaughraun (1874). Ponisi had an expressive, attractive, though not beautiful face, with large, alert eyes.

PONTEACH; or, The Savages of America (1766), a tragedy by Major Robert Rogers. The English who come to America are an unpleasant mixture of indifference, callousness, and greed in their treatment of the Native Americans. Some, like the hunters Honnyman and Orsbourn, shoot the Indians for sport. The English Governors, Sharp, Gripe, and Catchum, ignore instructions to make peace with the Native Americans. Sharp says, "Must mind that good old Rule, Take care of One," while Gripe agrees, "Ay, Christian Charity begins at home; / I think it's in the Bible, I know I've read it." The result is the destruction of the well-meaning, even noble Indians, led by Ponteach [pronounced Pontiac]. Grieving over the death of his loved ones, the chief exhorts the elements to "witness for me to your new base Lords, / That my unconquer'd Mind defies them still." The first tragedy to be written with a basically American theme and to feature Native Americans, this mediocre blank-verse drama was published in 1766 but appears never to have been performed. **Major Robert ROGERS**

(1731?–95) was a Massachusetts native who fought in the French and Indian Wars, but who was noted for his sympathies for the Native Americans. He spent much of his life in England, where he also published his *Journal of the French and Indian War* and *A Concise Account of North America* (1765).

POOR OF NEW YORK, THE (1857), a play by Dion *Boucicault. [*Wallack's Theatre, 42 perf.] After depositing $100,000 with the banker Gideon Bloodgood (W. H. Norton), Captain Fairweather (William R. *Blake) learns that Bloodgood's bank is shaky, so he returns to give back Bloodgood the receipt and reclaim his money. An argument ensues in which Fairweather dies. Bloodgood keeps the money, but the receipt falls into the hands of the banker's equally treacherous clerk, Badger (Lester *Wallack). Years later, Fairweather's family is living in dire poverty in the slums, and Badger lives next door. After he attempts to blackmail Bloodgood with the old receipt, the tenement is set afire. The handsome Mark Livingstone (E. A. *Sothern), who is nearly tricked into marrying Bloodgood's haughty daughter, Alida (Mrs. John *Hoey), helps rescue the Fairweathers and the all-important paper. He confronts Bloodgood with the evidence of his crime and wins the hand of the dead captain's daughter, Lucy (Mrs. J. H. Allen). Basing his work on Édouard Brisebarre and Eugène Nus's *Les Pauvres de Paris,* Boucicault added the climactic fire scene to accommodate contemporary demands for a spectacular denouement. The play was revived frequently, usually with the title *The Streets of New York*, and was a major success in England, too, where it was known as *The Streets of Liverpool* or *The Streets of London*.

PORGY (1927), a play by Dorothy and Dubose Heyward. [Guild Theatre, 217 perf.] The African-American Porgy (Frank *Wilson) is a crippled beggar who lives and works in the Charleston tenement district called Catfish Row. He loves the beautiful but weak-willed Bess (Evelyn Ellis), who is the mistress of the vicious Crown (Jack Carter), but when Crown flees after murdering a man, she goes to live with Porgy. On Crown's return Porgy fights with him and kills him. He is taken to jail, and while he is there Bess is lured away by the drug peddler Sportin' Life (Percy Verwayne). Released from jail and finding Bess gone, Porgy leaves Catfish Row to seek her. The *Theatre Guild offering was a bold and powerful work, and the script, while overshadowed by the later musical version *Porgy and Bess*, remains one of the greatest of all American folk dramas. [Edwin] **Dubose HEYWARD** (1885–1940), the South Carolina novelist and poet, worked as an insurance agent before publishing his first poems and short stories in the early 1920s. He and his wife, the former Dorothy Hartzell Kuhns (1890–1961), dramatized two of his novels of black life: *Porgy* and *Mamba's Daughters* (1939). Heyward wrote an unsuccessful original drama, *Brass Ankle* (1931), and collaborated on the musical *Porgy and Bess* (1935). Biography: *Dubose Heyward, the Man Who Wrote Porgy*, Frank Durham, 1954.

PORGY AND BESS (1935), a "folk opera" by Dubose *Heyward, Ira *Gershwin (book, lyrics), George *Gershwin (music). [Alvin Theatre, 124 perf.] The crippled Porgy (Todd *Duncan), who rides around the Catfish Row section of Charleston, South Carolina, loves Bess (Anne Brown), the mistress of the troublesome bully Crown (Warren Coleman). When Crown kills a fellow gambler in a crap game, he flees and Bess is taken in by Porgy. But later Crown suddenly returns and he and Porgy fight, Porgy killing him with Crown's own knife. While Porgy is in jail, the glib drug peddler Sportin' Life (John W. Bubbles) woos Bess with visions of life in the big city, and they leave together for New York. Porgy is released from jail, and hearing from the neighbors about Bess and Sportin' Life, he sets out in his goat cart to retrieve her. *Notable songs*: Summertime; My Man's Gone Now; A Woman Is a Sometime Thing; I Got Plenty o' Nuttin'; It Ain't Necessarily So; Bess, You Is My Woman Now; Dere's a Boat Dats Leaving Soon for New York; I Loves You, Porgy. One of the towering achievements of the American musical theatre, the original *Theatre Guild production was not a commercial success. George Gershwin was so disappointed in what he considered his masterwork that he took up Hollywood's offer and never returned to Broadway again. Over the years the piece has gained in critical and popular favor. A major 1942 revival by Cheryl *Crawford, in which Duncan and Brown re-created their original roles, began to turn the tide. Later, Metropolitan Opera soprano Leontyne Price headed a 1953 revival. The Houston Grand Opera's production toured successfully and reached Broadway in 1976. In 1983 the Radio City Music Hall produced a gigantic mounting, which subsequently toured. There have been other lesser revivals, a film version, and in the 1984–85 season it entered the repertory of the Metropolitan Opera.

PORTER, Cole [Albert] (1891–1964), composer and lyricist. Born into a family of wealth in Peru, Indiana, he was educated at Yale and Harvard. Although he interpolated a few songs into earlier musicals, Broadway heard its first complete Porter score in the short-lived *See America First* (1915). While some songs he wrote for *Hitchy-Koo* (1919) and *Greenwich Village Follies of 1924* were noticed, it was his score for *Paris* (1928) and its hit song "Let's Do It" that launched his career. It was followed by *Fifty Million Frenchmen* (1929), *Wake Up and Dream!* (1929), *The New Yorkers* (1930), *Gay Divorce* (1932), *Anything Goes* (1934), *Jubilee* (1935), *Red, Hot and Blue!* (1936), *You Never Know* (1938), *Leave It to Me!* (1938), and *Du Barry Was a Lady* (1939). Porter's wartime musicals were mostly star-driven vehicles for Ethel *Merman or Danny *Kaye, but some superb songs could still be found in *Panama Hattie* (1940), *Let's Face It!* (1941), *Something for the Boys* (1943), *Mexican Hayride* (1944), and *Seven Lively Arts* (1944). One of his rare flops was *Around the World in Eighty Days* (1946), followed by his biggest hit, *Kiss Me, Kate* (1948). Porter's later musicals were *Out of This World* (1950), *Can-Can* (1953), and *Silk Stockings* (1955). His songs trafficked in a knowing, sometimes showy sophistication, and his generally silken melodies were combined with lyrics that ranged from suave and blasé to sexually obsessive and even raunchy. More than any other major songwriter, his songs seemed, except for some of his last musicals, to have a cavalier detachment from their shows. Biography: *Cole Porter: A Biography*, William McBrien, 1998.

PORTER, Stephen [Winthrop] (b. 1925), director. Born in Ogdensburg, New York, Porter was educated at Yale and then taught at McGill University in Montreal, staying in Canada and directing at various theatres before making his Off-Broadway debut in 1956 staging *The Misanthrope*. Throughout his career he would excel at directing the classics (particularly Shaw and Molière), working at all the major Shakespeare festivals and regional theatres in North America. Porter was artistic director of the New Phoenix Repertory Company in Manhattan in the 1970s and was represented on and Off Broadway with such productions as *Private Lives* (1969), *Harvey* (1970), *The School for Wives* (1971), *The Visit* (1973), *The Importance of Being Earnest* (1977), *Man and Superman* (1978), *Major Barbara* (1980), *Misalliance* (1981), *The Misanthrope* (1983), *The Madwoman of Chaillot* (1985), *The Devil's Disciple* (1988), *The Miser* (1990), and *Getting Married* (1991).

PORTLAND STAGE COMPANY. Begun in 1974 as a touring company called the Profile Theatre, the group evolved into the resident theatre that today performs in its own 288-seat theatre in Portland, Maine. Its repertory consists of classical and contemporary revivals, though musicals and original scripts are presented on occasion, such as *Leaving Queens*, which transferred to New York. The group is the largest professional theatre in northern New England.

POTASH AND PERLMUTTER (1913), a comedy by Montague *Glass (and Charles *Klein, uncredited).

[Cohan Theatre, 441 perf.] Mawruss Perlmutter (Alexander Carr) and Abe Potash (Barney Bernard) are partners in the garment trade. And, oy, have they got problems! Like the customer who says, "I can send a check, but you'll have to wait for the money," to which they can only retort, "Send the money and we'll wait for the check." They also must find a new designer and a new salesman. But their biggest woe comes with the news that an employee, wanted by the Russian government on a murder charge, seemingly has reneged on the $20,000 bail Abe has paid and brought them close to bankruptcy. They put aside their perpetual bickering and finagling to save their firm. As a bonus, the new designer, Ruth Snyder (Louise *Dresser), proves so wonderful that Mawruss marries her. Based on Glass's short stories in the *Saturday Evening Post*, the work was hailed in a *Times* headline as "Indescribably Enjoyable Entertainment." The A. H. *Woods production was a big enough hit to prompt the sequels *Abe and Mawruss* (1915), *Business before Pleasure* (1917), *His Honor Abe Potash* (1919), *Partners Again* (1922), and *Potash and Perlmutter, Detectives* (1926). **Barney BERNARD** (1877–1924), a short, balding, mustachioed man with very slightly crossed eyes, was born in Rochester, New York, and began his career as a Jewish-dialect comedian in vaudeville. He played in San Francisco for many years, then found growing renown in a variety of productions. His greatest success came with these Abe Potash and Perlmutter comedies, but he died at the height of his popularity.

POTTER, John S. (1809–69), manager. A Philadelphian who began a career as an actor while still in his teens, he abandoned performing to build and manage theatres. Rarely staying long in one place, he moved about the entire country, often erecting a community's first playhouse. Many of these were primitive wooden theatres, soon superseded. But he is said to have built more theatres than any other single man in American theatrical history, thus becoming a sort of theatrical "Johnny Appleseed." Among the various cities, then sometimes small towns or villages, where he constructed theatres were Natchez, Vicksburg, and Jackson, Mississippi; Dubuque, Iowa; Rochester, New York; Cleveland, Ohio; Little Rock, Arkansas; and numerous unspecified towns in California and Oregon.

POTTER, Paul [Meredith] [né Walter McEwen or McLean] (1853–1921), playwright. He was born in England, where he spent time as a journalist before a scandal forced him to change his name and leave for America. Settling first in Chicago and continuing his newspaper work, Potter then took up playwriting. His earliest works included the comedy *The City Director* (1890) and the romance *The Ugly Duckling* (1890), written with A. D. Gordon as a vehicle for Mrs. Leslie *Carter. He scored his greatest success with his dramatization of George Du Maurier's *Trilby* (1895). Virtually all of his later hits were also dramatizations, notably *The *Conquerors* (1898), **Under Two Flags* (1901), and *The Honor of the Family* (1908).

POTTERS, THE (1923), a comedy by J. P. McEvoy. [*Plymouth Theatre, 245 perf.] According to Ma Potter (Catharine Calhoun Doucet), her husband, Pa Potter (Donald Meek), is "the ablest man in his office, except on payday." She nags her bumbling, timid husband to invest in a speculative oil deal in an effort to make the fortune she feels is her due. The oil deal apparently goes sour at the same time their daughter, Mamie (Mary Carroll), elopes. Ma would make Pa's life totally miserable, but a surprise gusher in the oil fields finally gives Pa the upper hand. The play, produced by Richard *Herndon, was welcomed by Burns *Mantle as "a lifelike study of American family life." J[oseph] P[atrick] McEVOY (1894–1958) was born in New York and studied at Notre Dame. He was a journalist before turning to the theatre with this, his first produced play. Most of his other theatre works were sketches for revues, notably the series known as *Americana* (1926, 1927, 1932). He was also a novelist, and his novel *Show Girl* became the source of *Ziegfeld's 1929 musical of the same name.

POWER, Tyrone (1797–1841), actor. Born in Kilmacthomas, Ireland, he established himself as London's greatest delineator of Irish characters before coming to America in 1833. London's appraisal was quickly confirmed by American audiences. He was a tall, handsome, if slightly stocky man with light hair and striking blue eyes. T. Allston *Brown praised the "clearness and melodious softness" of his voice. Power was lost at sea in the sinking of the *President* while returning to England. Autobiography: *Impressions of America*, 1836 (reissued 1969).

POWER, [Frederick] Tyrone (1869–1931), actor. Grandson of the first Tyrone *Power, his parents were performers in London, where he was born. He came to America in 1886 and made his debut in St. Augustine, Florida, then spent time with Augustin *Daly's famous ensemble. Power's early roles included the Marquis of Steyne in Mrs. *Fiske's *Becky Sharp* (1899), Judas Iscariot in her production of *Mary of Magdala* (1902), the title role in *Ulysses* (1903), the loyal barbarian Arkissus in *Adrea* (1905), and the black sheep brother Robert in *The *Servant in the House* (1908). One of his major assignments was the title role in the musical *Chu Chin Chow* (1917). In his later career Power performed largely in prominent supporting roles in Shakespearean revivals. Although he was starred only intermittently, he formed an important link between his grandfather and grandson. Biography: *Tyrone Power*, William Winter, 1913.

POWER, Tyrone (1913–58), actor. The last in a long line of performers bearing his name, he was born in Cincinnati and made his professional debut in 1931 in Chicago, where he continued to perform for several seasons. New York first saw him as Benvolio in Katharine *Cornell's *Romeo and Juliet* (1935) and as Bertrand de Poulengy in her *Saint Joan* (1936). After a long career in films he returned to Broadway in a dramatic reading of *John Brown's Body*. He later again played opposite Cornell as the evil Richard Gettner in *The Dark Is Light Enough* (1955), then shortly before his premature death assumed a series of roles in a 1958 revival of *Back to Methuselah*.

POWERS, James T. [né McGovern] (1862–1943), comic actor. The small, red-headed, rubber-faced comedian was born in New York and spent time in vaudeville and with circuses before calling attention to himself in a series of *farce-comedies: *Dreams* (1882), *A Bunch of Keys* (1883), and *A Tin Soldier* (1886). One critic called him "a thorough genius run wild, with a face quite as grotesque as a gargoyle," and added, "This clever actor, in addition to his natural *vis comica*, has a broad sense of humor which animates both his features and his gestures." For several years Powers was a comedian with the *Casino Theatre company, then returned to farce-comedy in *A Straight Tip* (1891), *A Mad Bargain* (1892), *The New Boy* (1894), and *Gentleman Joe* (1896). With the coming to America of the English Gaiety musical comedies he became the principal comedian in many of the best importations, including *The Circus Girl* (1897), *The Geisha* (1897), *A Runaway Girl* (1898), *San Toy* (1900), *The Messenger Boy* (1901), and *Havana* (1909). Thereafter, his career began to fade, although he appeared in a number of all-star revivals such as *The Rivals* (1922, 1923, 1930); *Henry IV, Part I* (1926); and *The Beaux' Stratagem* (1928). Autobiography: *Twinkle Little Star*, 1939.

POWERS, Tom (1890–1955), actor and singer. The handsome, versatile performer was born in Owensboro, Kentucky, and studied at the *American Academy of Dramatic Arts. He made his debut in Lancaster, Pennsylvania, as Dave in *In Mizzoura* in 1911, came to New York in 1915, and the following year scored personal successes in two short-lived plays, *Mr. Lazarus* and *Mile-a-Minute Kendall*. Turning to musical comedy, Powers enjoyed a long run as George Budd in *Oh, Boy!* (1917), in which he introduced "Till the Clouds Roll By." Another

success came as the mate-swapping Leonard Chadwick in *Why Not?* (1922). Shortly thereafter, Powers joined the *Theatre Guild, performing such roles as Gregers Werle in *The Wild Duck* (1925), the Captain in *Androcles and the Lion* (1925), Napoleon in *The Man of Destiny* (1926), and Bluntschli in *Arms and the Man* (1926). His other noteworthy roles included the street cleaner Archie Inch in *White Wings* (1926), the novelist Charles Marsden in *Strange Interlude* (1928), and King Magnus in *The Apple Cart* (1930). While Powers remained active until the mid-1940s, the rest of his career was occupied largely either with failures, with road companies, or in replacing other performers, including Orson *Welles, whom he succeeded as Brutus in the *Mercury Theatre mounting of *Julius Caesar* in 1938.

PRELUDE TO A KISS (1990), a play by Craig Lucas. [*Circle Repertory Theatre, 440 perf.] At the wedding of Peter (Alec Baldwin) and Rita (Mary-Louise Parker), an uninvited Old Man (Barnard *Hughes) kisses the bride and from that point on Rita becomes morose and forgetful. When Peter later confronts the Old Man, he discovers that the senior citizen has Rita's vivacity and spirit. The Old Man, terminally ill, has exchanged personalities with Rita, and Peter must now learn to love his wife in her new form. The odd play was deemed a "charming and highly original fantasy comedy" by several reviewers. Originally produced at the *South Coast Repertory in California, *Prelude to a Kiss* was popular enough at the Circle to successfully transfer to Broadway's *Helen Hayes Theatre with Timothy Hutton as Peter. **Craig LUCAS** (b. 1951) was born in Atlanta, Georgia, the son of an FBI agent, and educated at Boston University. He began his career as an actor, appearing in a handful of Broadway musicals, then made his playwriting debut Off Broadway with the urban comedy *Blue Window* (1984). His other works include the book for the intimate musical *Three Postcards* (1987), the surreal fable *Reckless* (1988), the early Internet drama *God's Heart* (1997), and the Hollywood exposé *The Dying Gaul* (1998).

PRESBREY, Eugene. See *Raffles*.

PRESTON [Meservey], **Robert** (1918–87), actor. Born in Newton Highlands, Massachusetts, he was raised in California and studied at the theatre school of the *Pasadena Playhouse. He made occasional West Coast appearances while becoming a film actor who specialized in tough men and Western villains. In New York, his versatility was displayed when he succeeded José *Ferrer in 1951 in the revival of *Twentieth Century* and when he next portrayed Joe Ferguson in a 1952 revival of *The *Male Animal*. After a series of failures Preston scored a hit as the duped husband Gil in *Janus* (1955). Broadway stardom finally came with his mesmerizing performance as con man Harold Hill in The *Music Man* (1957), followed by the title role in Ben Franklin in Paris (1964), King Henry II in The *Lion in Winter* (1966), husband Michael in *I Do! I Do!* (1966), and moviemaker Mack Sennett in Mack and Mabel (1974). His last Broadway appearance was as a replacement in another con-man role, Foxwell J. Sly in Sly Fox (1977). Preston was a virile, handsome, full-voiced leading man whose theatrical delivery and twinkle in his eye made him unique.

PRICE, Fanny B[ayard] (1847–97), actress. A niece of William *Warren, she was born in Vicksburg, Mississippi, and made her debut in Chicago while still virtually an infant as the Child to James E. *Murdoch's Rolla in *Pizarro*. In 1864 she became leading lady in stock in Louisville, then toured for many years as a star. She almost never appeared in New York but was popular on the road as the heroine of numerous contemporary plays.

PRICE, Stephen (1783–1840), manager. One of the earliest major theatre operators in America, he was the first not to be an actor or playwright as well. In 1808, when the *Park Theatre was having financial difficulties, he bought shares in the theatre and eventually was in full control. His careful fiscal husbanding began to turn the ledgers around, but his master stroke was to import London stars, beginning with George Frederick *Cooke and Edmund *Kean. Price's policies signaled the start of purely business interests dominating the American theatre. His penchant for spectacle, however artless it might seem, also demonstrated that he knew what his public most wanted. The Park's heyday virtually coincided with Price's tenure, since at the time of his death the first important competition and the movement northward of New York's theatre district were taking their toll.

PRICE, THE (1968), a play by Arthur *Miller. [*Morosco Theatre, 429 perf.] Two estranged brothers, the policeman Victor (Pat *Hingle) and the doctor Walter (Arthur *Kennedy), meet again after sixteen years to sell the family possessions to the aged furniture dealer Gregory Solomon (Harold Gary), and recriminations about the past arise, including Walter's leaving Victor to support the family when he went to medical school. Victor's bitter wife, Esther (Kate Reid), does not help matters and, after some revelations are made that sober up both brothers, the two part with their differences still unresolved. The engrossing drama was produced by Robert *Whitehead and others and was commended for its rich characterizations,

including Miller's finest comic creation, the crusty old Solomon. It was revived on Broadway in 1979 and 1999, and John *Tillinger directed a fine Off-Broadway revival at the *Roundabout in 1992.

PRIDE OF JENNICO, THE (1900), a play by Abby Sage Richardson and Grace Livingston Furniss. [Criterion Theatre, 111 perf.] Princess Marie Ottilie (Bertha Galland) and her maid, who is also named Marie (Gertrude Rivers), come to the Bohemian castle of Basil Jennico (James K. *Hackett). The women agree to switch places so that Marie Ottilie can see if Jennico will love her even though he thinks her a commoner. He does, despite the evil plotting of Eugen von Rothenberg (Brigham Royce) and the gypsy Michel (Grace Reals). Charles *Frohman produced the play that was based on incidents in a novel by Agnes and Egerton Castle. Alone or together, Richardson and Furniss wrote several other plays produced in New York at the turn of the century.

PRIDE'S CROSSING (1997), a play by Tina Howe. [*Mitzi E. Newhouse Theatre, 137 perf.; NYDCC Award.] Aged Mabel Tidings Bigelow (Cherry *Jones) has led a full life: a spoiled upbringing by a conservative, chauvinistic family; unhappy romances and a problematic marriage to a rich, drunkard husband; and the fame of swimming the English Channel in 1928. The comedy-drama shifted from the present Mabel to scenes in the past, Jones making the transformations without wigs or makeup. While critical reactions to the script and the *Lincoln Center production were mixed, Jones was unanimously lauded for her "fluid, finely graded portrait." **Tina HOWE** (b. 1937) was born in New York, the daughter of celebrated radio newsman Quincy Howe, and educated at Sarah Lawrence. Her work was first produced in 1970, and she soon established her reputation as something of a playwright's playwright. Howe's notable plays include The Art of Dining (1979), describing events in a Jersey Shore restaurant; Painting Churches (1983), in which an artist attempts to do a portrait of her aging parents; and Coastal Disturbances (1987), examining various characters, including two in a late summer romance, on a New England beach.

PRINCE, Faith (b. 1957?), actress and singer. The wide-eyed, demonstrative performer with a powerful Broadway belt excels at smart dumb blondes (even though her hair is red). She was born in Augusta, Georgia, and educated at the University of Cincinnati, where she studied voice before performing in musicals in regional theatre. Prince made her New York debut Off Broadway in 1981 and received wide recognition eight years later for her various characters in *Jerome Robbins' Broadway* (1989). Her funny, touching Miss Adelaide in the 1992 revival of *Guys and Dolls* made her a Broadway star, and she has also triumphed in leading roles in revivals of The *King and I* (1997), *Little Me* (1998), and *Bells Are Ringing* (2001).

PRINCE, Hal [né Harold Smith Prince] (b. 1928), director and producer. Born in New York and educated at the University of Pennsylvania, he began his theatrical career as a stage manager, then joined Frederick *Brisson and Robert E. *Griffith with whom he co-produced The *Pajama Game* (1954), *Damn Yankees* (1955), and *New Girl in Town* (1957). With Griffith he produced *West Side Story* (1957) and *Fiorello!* (1959), among others. On his own Prince next produced *Take Her, She's Mine* (1961), A *Funny Thing Happened on the Way to the Forum* (1962), and *Fiddler on the Roof* (1964). He turned to directing (while still producing) with *She Loves Me* (1963), then repeated the double assignment for *Cabaret* (1966), *Company* (1970), *Follies* (1971), and A *Little Night Music* (1973). Prince moved away from producing in the 1970s and concentrated on directing such productions as *Candide* (1973), *Sweeney Todd* (1979), *Merrily We Roll Along* (1981), A *Doll's Life* (1982), *Grind* (1985), *Roza* (1987), The *Phantom of the Opera* (1988), *Show Boat* (1994), *Parade* (1998), *Hollywood Arms* (2002), and *Bounce* (2003). He has been one of the master directors of modern musicals, giving dramatic movement to even static scripts and knowingly underscoring with his staging the meanings and moods of his texts. Along with his frequent associate, Stephen *Sondheim, he has been the leading advocate of the "conceptualized musical"—a musical in which text and production are conceived from the start as an integral totality. Autobiography: *Contradictions*, 1974. Biography: *Harold Prince and the American Musical Theatre*, Foster Hirsch, 1989.

PRINCE CHAP, THE (1905), a play by Edward *Peple. [*Madison Square Theatre, 106 perf.] A dying model leaves her small daughter with the young sculptor William Payton (Cyril Scott), and Payton's fiancée, Alice Travers (Grace Kimball), assumes the child is his so she breaks off their engagement. Payton raises the girl, Claudia, into womanhood, while Alice has married another man and since become a widow. She has learned that Payton had told her the truth and, still loving him, hopes for a reconciliation. Payton is willing to be her friend but has recognized that it is Claudia he truly loves. The play, Peple's first, opened on the same night as plays by Augustus *Thomas, Clyde *Fitch, Hall Caine, and *Shaw's *Man and Superman*, and so was reviewed by critics far down in the pecking order. Nonetheless, it was recognized as a superior work. Two weeks later in its Sunday canvas of recent openings the *Times* called it "the most satisfying offering of the early season." The drama toured for several years and returned to New York in 1907. The role of Claudia was played by a different actress in each act in order to convey her growth.

PRINCE KARL (1886), a comedy by A. C. *Gunter. [*Madison Square Theatre, 122 perf.] Impecunious Prince Karl (Richard *Mansfield) has promised to marry a rich old woman but changes his mind when he falls in love with Mrs. Florence Lowell (Maida Craigin), a beautiful widow slated to inherit an even larger fortune. Karl feigns suicide and reappears as his own "foster brother," offering to serve Mrs. Lowell as a courier. She learns of his trick but mischievously pretends to be ignorant of it. Eventually she falls in love with him and reveals that her inheritance that was left her by Karl's long-lost uncle actually belongs to him. Written as a serious romance and first presented with Mansfield at the *Boston Museum, it was quickly turned by the star into an amiable farce.

PRINCE OF PARTHIA, THE (1767), a tragedy by Thomas Godfrey. [*Southwark Theatre (Philadelphia), 1 perf.] Vardanes (Mr. Tomlinson) plots to turn his father, King Artabanus (David *Douglass), against his brother Arsaces (Lewis *Hallam Jr.) because he resents Arsaces's success in war and, even more, his brother's winning the affection of Evanthe (Miss *Cheer), a captive maiden whom both Vardanes and the king covet. Vardanes succeeds in having the king imprison Arsaces, but their third brother, Gotarzes (Mr. Wall), leads an army to free him. During the ensuing battle, Evanthe hears that Arsaces has been killed, so she poisons herself. But the news of his death was only a rumor. Arsaces rushes to the dying girl, and when she expires he kills himself. His last words are "Out, out vile cares, from your distress'd abode." Gotarzes is left to restore order. The first play by an American author to be professionally produced in America, its dramatic and theatrical values are modest. The incomplete records of the period make it uncertain whether more than one performance was given, and the *American Company cast listed above is the one postulated by Seilhamer and generally accepted by later scholars. **Thomas GODFREY** (1736–63) was born in Philadelphia, the son of the inventor of a sea quadrant, and was apprenticed to a watchmaker until William Smith, provost of the College of Philadelphia, saw potential in the boy. He released Godfrey from his indentures and began his education, which included dramatic performances. Godfrey wrote *The Prince of Parthia*, his first and only play, while still in his early twenties.

At the same time Smith helped him obtain a commission in the Pennsylvania militia, and Godfrey served in the expedition against Fort Duquesne and later was promoted to lieutenant. Shortly thereafter, he moved to North Carolina, where he died of a sudden fever. His play was not mounted until after his death. Godfrey was also a poet of some repute.

PRINCE OF PILSEN, THE (1903), a musical by Frank *Pixley (book, lyrics), Gustav *Luders (music). [*Broadway Theatre, 143 perf.] The Cincinnati brewer Hans Wagner (John W. Ransome) arrives in Nice with his daughter, Nellie (Lillian Coleman), to visit his son, Tom (Albert Parr), who is serving there with the American navy. Prince Carl Otto of Pilsen (Arthur Donaldson) is booked into the same hotel. When Hans is confused for the royal guest, the prince takes advantage of the confusion to go out on the town incognito. He meets and falls in love with Nellie. By the end of the evening Nellie is on her way to becoming a princess, while both her father and brother have also made romantic attachments. *Notable songs*: The Heidelberg Stein Song; The Message of the Violet. Henry W. *Savage produced this, the best of the many Pixley-Luders collaborations, and it continued to tour successfully for over a decade. Part of its popularity may have stemmed from the fact that while it was an operetta it essentially employed the American-in-foreign-lands theme that had only recently become the rage of musical comedy.

PRINCESS THEATRE (New York). An intimate 299-seat playhouse built by the *Shuberts and others on 39th Street, between Broadway and Sixth Avenue, it was designed by William A. *Swasey. The theatre opened in 1913 as the home for one-act plays, but when this policy failed the playhouse was turned over to small musical comedies in 1915. These *Kern musicals—*Nobody Home* (1915), *Very Good Eddie* (1915), *Oh, Boy!* (1917), and *Oh, Lady! Lady!!* (1918), along with two others written for the house but presented elsewhere—established new standards for musical comedy. They offered fundamentally believable characters in tight-knit, fundamentally believable situations; they allowed both humor and songs to derive from these characters and situations and sometimes advance the action or character development; and they mounted these singularly literate, witty, and melodic works with grace and charm. The shows became known as the Princess Theatre musicals. The theatre continued to offer experimental plays in the 1920s. With the coming of the Depression it became a film house but was later rechristened the Labor Stage and served as the original home of *Pins and Needles* (1937). It then returned to showing films again before it was demolished in 1955.

PRISONER OF SECOND AVENUE, THE (1971), a comedy by Neil *Simon. [*Eugene O'Neill Theatre, 780 perf.] Mel Edison (Peter Falk) and his wife, Edna (Lee Grant), have lived in their fourteenth-floor apartment for six years, and New York City and its high-pressure way of life are beginning to tell on Mel. He can hear not only the music the German airline stewardesses keep playing next door, but he can even hear "one car driving around in Jackson Heights." When Mel loses his job because of downsizing, he goes to pieces, wandering about the apartment unshaven and in his pajamas while Edna joins the workforce. Heading for a nervous breakdown, Mel also starts to become paranoid that the city is against him. But when Edna loses her job and starts to fall apart, Mel finds the strength for both of them to face the modern world with optimism. Simon's ninth successive hit, it made a warm, human comedy out of the brutal, small materials of everyday life and even out of the seeds of tragedy.

PRISONER OF ZENDA, THE (1895), a play by Edward E. *Rose. [*Lyceum Theatre, 112 perf.] Years ago Gilbert, Earl of Rassendyll (Howard Gould), and Prince Rudolf of Ruritania (E. H. *Sothern) fought a bitter duel. Now, decades later, the families' paths cross again under different circumstances. The current Prince Rudolf (also Sothern) is about to be crowned king, but his brother, Michael, Duke of Streslau (Arthur R. Lawrence), and Rupert of Hentzau (Morton Selten) drug him to prevent the ceremony. Rudolf Rassendyll (Sothern), who is the image of the new king, is hastily enlisted to take the king's place. In doing so he falls in love with Princess Flavia (Grace Kimball), who is to be queen. Rassendyll eventually discovers that the king is being held prisoner at the castle of Zenda and there confronts the conspirators, who are quarreling over a woman. Rupert kills Michael, then flees. Rassendyll restores Rudolf to his rightful place and reluctantly renounces Flavia, who with equal reluctance accepts her destiny. Based on Anthony Hope's famous novel, the play was such a huge hit that when prior commitments required Sothern to end his New York engagement, producer Daniel *Frohman brought in a second company. The melodrama toured regularly for many seasons, including a company headed by James K. *Hackett, who mounted a major revival in 1908. The work served as the basis for the 1925 Sigmund *Romberg operetta *Princess Flavia* and for a failed Vernon *Duke musical, *Zenda*, in 1963.

PRIVATE LIVES (1931). A 1930 English comedy by Noel *Coward, it was presented in New York the next year with Coward and Gertrude *Lawrence re-creating their original London roles of a divorced couple who have married new mates and who meet by chance on their respective honeymoons and rekindle their old romance. Few contemporary comedies have retained such ongoing popularity. Major Broadway revivals have included those in 1948 with Tallulah *Bankhead and Donald *Cook, in 1969 with Tammy *Grimes and Brian *Bedford, in 1983 with film star Elizabeth Taylor and her ex-husband Richard *Burton, and a British import in 2002 with Alan Rickman and Lindsay Duncan. The comedy also remains a favorite in regional theatre and summer stock.

PROCTOR, Joseph (1816–97), actor. Although the stern-faced Philadelphia-born tragedian was praised for his performances in such roles as Macbeth (opposite Charlotte *Cushman), Marc Antony, and Damon, he elected, like several other important contemporaries, to assure his financial security by relying on a single part with which he was largely identified. That part was the title role in *Nick of the Woods*, which he first played in 1839 and returned to regularly until he retired. Otis *Skinner characterized him as "stately, formal, of the Forrest school."

PRODUCERS, THE (2001), a musical farce by Thomas *Meehan (book), Mel Brooks (book, music, lyrics). [*St. James Theatre, still running; Tony, NYDCC Awards.] Down-and-out theatrical producer Max Bialystock (Nathan *Lane) and nebbish accountant Leo Bloom (Matthew *Broderick) contrive a plan to raise more cash than they need to present a flop show on Broadway, then keep the surplus money for themselves. But all their efforts to come up with a turkey (a musical called *Springtime for Hitler*) go awry, the show is a hit, and their scheme is discovered. *Notable songs*: Springtime for Hitler; That Face; I Wanna Be a Producer; We Can Do It. A smash-hit musical comedy in the old-time tradition, *The Producers* boasted outstanding performances, a bright book and score, and lively choreography and direction by Susan *Stroman. It won a record twelve *Tony Awards and was Broadway's hottest ticket for over two years. **Mel BROOKS** [né Melvin Kaminsky] (b. 1926) was born in Brooklyn and was writing comedy sketches for television when still in his teens. He co-wrote the librettos for the Broadway musicals *Shinebone Alley* (1957) and *All American* (1962) but found more success as a writer-director-performer in Hollywood, beginning with his film *The Producers* in 1968. Although Brooks had written original songs for his movies, this was his first Broadway score.

PRODUCING MANAGERS' ASSOCIATION. A group apparently founded to deal with growing unionism in the theatre, it was long headed by Sam H. *Harris and listed virtually every major producer and theatre owner as a member. It may have been superseded by the Managers' Protective Association, although the latter may have represented simply a name change. Arthur *Hammerstein was president. A similar group, the National Association of Theatrical Producing Managers, seems to have had a broader membership, including many figures in burlesque and other theatre forms, and possibly a broader scope as well. Surviving correspondence in the *Shubert Archive shows it dealt with unions but more often with local and national legal matters and outside pressure groups. William A. *Brady is listed as president. This organization may have given way to the United Managers' Protective Association, which was headed for a time by Marc *Klaw. Both the Producing Managers' Association and the United Managers' Protective Association are listed in newspaper articles dealing with events related to the 1919 strike by *Actors' Equity. More research is required to clarify the history and purpose of these associations.

PROFESSIONAL PLAYERS, THE. This was a subscription group organized in the late 1920s in major tryout towns to promote better productions and an audience for them. The onset of the Depression and better-organized subscription series, such as those offered by the *Theatre Guild, led to its quick disbanding.

PROFESSOR, THE (1881), a play by William *Gillette. [*Madison Square Theatre, 151 perf.] Professor Hopkins (Gillette) is a handsome but unworldly pedant who finds himself pursued by a bevy of young girls, a pursuit which infuriates the Yale students who have been courting the girls. He must also confront a kidnapper and the girl he kidnapped, and a long-lost brother and sister. Called "a character study" by the author, the play was accepted by the public for what it was—a lighthearted summer comedy.

PROMISES, PROMISES (1968), a musical comedy by Neil *Simon (book), Burt Bacharach (music), Hal David (lyrics). [*Shubert Theatre, 1,281 perf.] Chuck Baxter (Jerry *Orbach) is a young executive who is willing to help his rise to the top by lending his bosses his apartment for trysts. Complications develop when one of the boss's dates attempts to commit suicide in the flat. The girl is Fran Kubelik (Jill O'Hara), and Chuck's careful nursing of her leads to a romance between the two that gives him the strength to stop cowtowing to his bosses. *Notable songs*: I'll Never Fall in Love Again; Promises, Promises; Whoever You Are; Knowing When to Leave; You'll Think of Someone. Based on the 1960 film *The Apartment*, the

David *Merrick production offered a clever collaboration of Simon with the pop songwriting team of Bacharach and David and gave Broadway one of its brightest musical comedies of the decade. This was Bacharach and David's only Broadway score, although their non-theatre song hits were heard in the short-lived Broadway revue *The Look of Love* (2003).

PROOF (2000), a play by David Auburn. [*Walter Kerr Theatre, 917 perf.; Pulitzer Prize, Tony, NYDCC Awards.] Catherine (Mary-Louise Parker) is the daughter of a brilliant mathematician who was driven to insanity and death by the realization that he could never surpass the genius of his youthful years. She has inherited some of her father's melancholia as well as his mathematical skills, and her sister, Claire (Johanna Day), wants her to leave the family home in Chicago and come back to New York with her, where mental help is waiting. But Catherine shows Hal (Ben Shenkman), the young mathematics teacher who is smitten with her, a math proof that dazzles him and she must then convince him and Claire that she is the one who wrote it. A penetrating character study as well as a gripping whodunit of sorts, the play was first presented Off Broadway by the *Manhattan Theatre Club, then transferred to Broadway, where it was a surprise hit, helped by Parker's *Tony Award–winning performance and the astute direction of Daniel *Sullivan. **David AUBURN** (b. 1969) was born in Chicago, raised in Ohio and Arkansas, and educated at Juilliard. *Proof* was his first play of note, and in 2001 he adapted a one-person musical by the late Jonathan *Larson into *Tick, Tick . . . Boom!*

PROVINCETOWN PLAYERS. Founded in 1915 in Provincetown, Massachusetts, by a group of theatre lovers headed by Susan *Glaspell and her husband, George Cram *Cook, it gave its first performances that same summer in a small theatre on a wharf in the city. Robert Edmond *Jones designed the sets. The second summer the program was much enlarged and included two plays, *Bound East for Cardiff* and *Thirst* by Eugene *O'Neill. The season was so successful that the group took over a small playhouse in New York's Greenwich Village (later moving to another one) and began the first of over a decade of seasons that would continue until 1929, with a major reorganization after 1921 that left Jones, O'Neill, and Kenneth *MacGowan in charge. At first the company offered largely one-act plays but later included full-length works. Among the major or interesting works offered by the group were John Reed's *Freedom* (1916); O'Neill's *Before Breakfast* (1916), *Fog* (1917), *The Sniper* (1917), *The *Long Voyage Home* (1917), and *Ile* (1917); Maxwell Bodenheim's *Knot Holes* (1917), written wit William

Saphir, and *The Gentle Furniture Shop* (1917); O'Neill's *The Rope* (1918), *Where the Cross Is Made* (1918), *The *Moon of the Caribbees* (1918), and *The Dreamy Kid* (1919); Edna St. Vincent Millay's *Aria da Capo* (1919); Edna *Ferber's *The Eldest* (1920); O'Neill's *Exorcism* (1920), *The *Emperor Jones* (1920), and *Diff'rent* (1920); Glaspell's *Inheritors* (1921); O'Neill's *The *Hairy Ape* (1922); a revival of *Fashion* (1924); O'Neill's *The Ancient Mariner* (1924) and *All God's Chillun Got Wings* (1924); Edmund Wilson's *The Crime in the Whistler Room* (1924); O'Neill's *Desire under the Elms* (1924); and Paul *Green's *In Abraham's Bosom* (1926). During its heyday the troupe ran the Greenwich Village Theatre as well as the **PROVINCETOWN PLAYHOUSE.** In their excellent history of the company, *The Provincetown: A Story of a Theatre* (1931), Helen Deutsch and Stella Hanau concluded simply, "The Provincetown was more a laboratory than a theater. . . . To it belonged the task of developing playwrights, of taking risks with unknown actors and designers."

PROVINCETOWN PLAYHOUSE. See Provincetown Players.

PUBLIC THEATRE. See New York Shakespeare Festival.

PUERTO RICAN TRAVELING THEATRE (New York). Miriam Colón, an actress from the *Actors Studio, founded this company in 1966 in order to present bilingual productions in parks, jails, street corners, and storefronts in an effort to bring live theatre to disadvantaged neighborhoods. Although the troupe is headquartered in a former Manhattan firehouse, the group travels to all five boroughs and several communities in New Jersey. New and old plays, both in Spanish and English, are presented, and the company also offers classes in acting and playwriting.

PULITZER PRIZE FOR DRAMA. The most prestigious of all drama awards, it was created in 1917 by Joseph Pulitzer to honor "the original American play performed in New York which shall best represent the educational value and power of the stage in raising the standards of good morals and good manners." The drama Pulitzer, given by the Graduate School of Journalism at Columbia University, is a playwright's award, given to a script and not a production, and carries much weight since there is only one category. The winner cannot be based on a previous play (eliminating most musicals from winning), and the committee can withhold the award one year if it deems no works are worthy of it. Over the years the Pulitzer's decisions have often been criticized, and displeasure with them prompted the founding of the *New York Drama Critics Circle and its awards. The script no longer need be produced in New York to win, allowing regional theatre premieres to be eligible. All of the Pulitzer winners have their own entry. They are: 1918: *Why Marry?*; 1920: *Beyond the Horizon*; 1921: *Miss Lulu Bett*; 1922: *Anna Christie*; 1923: *Icebound*; 1924: *Hell-Bent for Heaven*; 1925: *They Knew What They Wanted*; 1926: *Craig's Wife*; 1927: *In Abraham's Bosom*; 1928: *Strange Interlude*; 1929: *Street Scene*; 1930: *The Green Pastures*; 1931: *Alison's House*; 1932: *Of Thee I Sing*; 1933: *Both Your Houses*; 1934: *Men in White*; 1935: *The Old Maid*; 1936: *Idiot's Delight*; 1937: *You Can't Take It with You*; 1938: *Our Town*; 1939: *Abe Lincoln in Illinois*; 1940: *The Time of Your Life*; 1941: *There Shall Be No Night*; 1943: *The Skin of Our Teeth*; 1945: *Harvey*; 1946: *State of the Union*; 1948: *A Streetcar Named Desire*; 1949: *Death of a Salesman*; 1950: *South Pacific*; 1952: *The Shrike*; 1953: *Picnic*; 1954: *The Teahouse of the August Moon*; 1955: *Cat on a Hot Tin Roof*; 1956: *The Diary of Anne Frank*; 1957: *Long Day's Journey into Night*; 1958: *Look Homeward, Angel*; 1959: *J. B.*; 1960: *Fiorello!*; 1961: *All the Way Home*; 1962: *How to Succeed in Business Without Really Trying*; 1965: *The Subject Was Roses*; 1967: *A Delicate Balance*; 1969: *The Great White Hope*; 1970: *No Place to Be Somebody*; 1971: *The Effects of Gamma Rays on Man-in-the-Moon Marigolds*; 1973: *That Championship Season*; 1975: *Seascape*; 1976: *A Chorus Line*; 1977: *The Shadow Box*; 1978: *The Gin Game*; 1979: *Buried Child*; 1980: *Talley's Folly*; 1981: *Crimes of the Heart*; 1982: *A Soldier's Play*; 1983: *'night, Mother*; 1984: *Glengarry Glen Ross*; 1985: *Sunday in the Park with George*; 1987: *Fences*; 1988: *Driving Miss Daisy*; 1989: *The Heidi Chronicles*; 1990: *The Piano Lesson*; 1991: *Lost in Yonkers*; 1992: *The Kentucky Cycle*; 1993: *Angels in America, Part I: Millennium Approaches*; 1994: *Three Tall Women*; 1995: *The Young Man from Atlanta*; 1996: *Rent*; 1998: *How I Learned to Drive*; 1999: *Wit*; 2000: *Dinner with Friends*; 2001: *Proof*; 2002: *Topdog/Underdog*; and 2003: *Anna of the Tropics*.

PURCELL, Charles (1883–1962), singer and actor. He was born in Chattanooga and made his Broadway debut in 1908, later becoming a popular leading man in the 1910s and 1920s. Purcell appeared in *Pretty Mrs. Smith* (1914), *Flora Bella* (1916), *My Lady's Glove* (1917), *Monte Cristo, Jr.* (1919), *Poor Little Ritz Girl* (1920), *The Rose Girl* (1921), *Oh, Please!* (1926), *Judy* (1927), *Shady Lady* (1933), and other musicals, but his best-known roles were as Richard Wayne in *Maytime* (1917), in which he introduced "Will You Remember?," and the British captain Sir John Copeland in *Dearest Enemy* (1925), in which he sang "Bye and Bye" and "Here in My Arms." Purcell's last Broadway appearance was in *Park Avenue* (1946).

PURLIE. See *Purlie Victorious*.

PURLIE VICTORIOUS (1961), a comedy by Ossie *Davis. [*Cort Theatre, 261 perf.] Purlie Victorious Judson (Davis), an exuberant young African-American preacher, returns to his small Georgia hometown, hoping to acquire Big Bethel Church and convert it into an integrated house of worship. His plans are opposed by the hidebound, unreconstructed Ol' Cap'n Cotchipee (Sorrell Brooke) who resents all modern innovations, such as colleges that teach students to pronounce "nigger" as if it were spelled "negro," as well as the political leanings of his son, Charley (Alan *Alda), who is "too friendly to the Supreme Court." But Purlie's middle name was not Victorious for nothing. A delightfully funny comedy, it turned many stereotypes inside out and upside down. Davis contributed to the book of the musical version called **PURLIE** (1970), which featured Cleavon Little as Purlie, John Hefferman as the Cap'n, and Melba Moore as Purlie's love interest, Lutiebelle. Gary Geld (music) and Peter Udell (lyrics) wrote the vivacious score, and producer Philip Rose staged the musical like a swinging revival meeting. It ran 688 performances in the *Broadway Theatre. *Notable songs*: Walk Him up the Stairs; I Got Love; First Thing Monday Mornin'; New Fangled Preacher Man.

PURSUIT OF HAPPINESS, THE (1933), a comedy by Alan Child and Isabelle Louden (pen names for Lawrence *Langner and Armina Marshall). [Avon Theatre, 252 perf.] When Max Christmann (Tonio Selwart), a Hessian soldier in hiding, takes refuge on the Connecticut farm of Captain Aaron Kirkland (Charles *Waldron), he falls in love with Kirkland's daughter, Prudence (Peggy *Conklin), who is engaged to Thaddeus Jennings (Raymond Walburn), the local sheriff. A Puritan precept states, "Since in a bed a man and maid may bundle and be chaste, it does no good to burn our wood," so it does not seem untoward for Prudence to invite Max to bundle with her. Jennings catches them and demands the local minister denounce the practice of bundling. He agrees, forcing Max and Prudence to wed. Max happily realizes he has enjoyed the American right to "Life, Liberty and the Pursuit of Happiness." The only successful collaboration by Langner and Marshall, who was actually Mrs. Langner, the play served as the source for the musical **ARMS AND THE GIRL** (1950) with a book by Herbert *Fields and Dorothy *Fields. Nanette *Fabray and Georges Guetary played the lovers, but the show was stolen by Pearl *Bailey as the ex-slave Connecticut who sang "There Must Be Something Better Than Love" and "Nothin' for Nothin'." The charming score was by Morton

Gould (music) and Dorothy Fields (lyrics), and the *Theatre Guild production ran in the 46th Street Theatre for 134 performances.

PYGMALION (1914). This modern retelling of the Pygmalion-Galatea legend was first seen in America in 1914, with *Shaw's original Eliza Doolittle, Mrs. Patrick *Campbell, repeating her role. Most critics kindly overlooked the fact that she was far too old for the part, for her transition from street waif to lady was highly praised, with one critic adding, "with the deftest touch she suggests the old Eliza is not so far below the surface after all." Her Higgins was a younger Philip *Merivale. Although some critics were disturbed by her American accent, Lynn *Fontanne dominated a 1926 *Theatre Guild revival in which Reginald Mason was Higgins. The play enjoyed its longest American run when it was revived in 1945 for Gertrude *Lawrence (also rather old for the part) with Raymond *Massey as Higgins. A 1987 revival starred Peter O'Toole and Amanda Plummer, but Ivar Brogger won applause when he took over during O'Toole's all too frequent indispositions. The play also served as the basis for the most literate of all American operettas, *My Fair Lady* (1956). To many who saw the original production, the youthful Julie *Andrews and, more especially, the reptilian Rex *Harrison will probably remain the definitive interpreters of the roles.

Q

QUEEN HIGH. See *Pair of Sixes, A.*

QUINN, Arthur Hobson (1875–1960), author. The Philadelphia-born scholar studied at the University of Pennsylvania and later taught English and Drama there from 1895 to 1945. His books on theatre include *Representative American Plays* (1917), *The Early Drama* (1917), *History of the American Drama from the Beginning to the Civil War* (1923), *Contemporary American Plays* (1923), and *History of the American Drama from the Civil War to the Present Day* (1927). He also served as editor for *Harper's Plays and Playwrights Series.* His two histories of American drama, which like several others of his books were brought up to date after the first publication, remain the most complete and best study of our dramatic literature. While some of his views naturally reflect the thinking of his era, his long exposure to drama and careful training make him a generally reliable guide.

QUINTERO, José [Benjamin] (1924–99), director. Born in Panama, he studied at the University of Southern California and directed summer stock before gaining attention with his sensitive stagings at the *Circle in the Square, including a 1952 revival of *Summer and Smoke and a 1958 revival of *Children of Darkness.* However, it was his work on Eugene *O'Neill plays for which he is best remembered. These include the celebrated 1956 revival of *The *Iceman Cometh* at the Circle in the Square, the original Broadway production of *Long Day's Journey into Night* (1956), *Hughie* (1964), *More Stately Mansions* (1967), a 1973 revival of *A *Moon for the Misbegotten*, and the lauded but commercially unsuccessful 1988 revival of *Long Day's Journey into Night.* Autobiography: *If You Don't Dance, They Beat You*, 1972.

R

RABB, Ellis (1930–98), actor, director, and manager. He was born in Memphis, Tennessee, and educated at the University of Arizona, Carnegie Tech, and Yale before starting to act and direct in summer Shakespeare festivals. Rabb made his New York debut in a 1956 production of *A *Midsummer Night's Dream* and appeared mostly in classic roles throughout his acting career. In 1960 he founded the *Association of Producing Artists (APA), a repertory company for classics that gave New Yorkers some of the best revivals of the era. The APA disbanded in 1970 and Rabb became a freelance director and sometime actor.

RABE, David (b. 1940), playwright. Born in Dubuque, Iowa, he was educated at Loras College and at Villanova University, then served for a brief time as a newspaperman. His first play to be produced was *The *Basic Training of Pavlo Hummel* (1971), which described the disillusionment and death of a soldier in the Viet Nam War. It was produced by Joseph *Papp's *New York Shakespeare Festival, which mounted all his plays in the 1970s: *Sticks and Bones* (1971), *The Orphan* (1973), *Boom Boom Room* (1973)—later rewritten and retitled *In the Boom Boom Room*—and *Streamers* (1976). Rabe took a deadly view of Hollywood in *Hurlyburly* (1984), followed by the less-popular *Those the River Keeps* (1994) and *The Dog Problem* (2001).

RACHEL [née Elisa Felix] (1820–58), actress. Usually considered the greatest of French classical tragediennes, she made her American debut in 1855 as Camille in Corneille's *Horace*. The *Albion* reported, "There came in a severe classic figure, a polychrome statue, gliding past the columns, and breathing rather than articulating. . . . So deep, vibrant and magnetic were the first tones of [her] voice that they sent a thrill through the vast assembly, a thrill which at once opened communication between the genius of Rachel and her new hearers." On later evenings she presented her Phèdre, Adrienne Lecouvreur, and Andromaque, among others. Apparently she caught a cold that aggravated her tubercular condition, and her last performance was in Charleston, where she was barely able to perform. She then sailed for France, where she died just over two years afterward. Biography: *Rachel,* Joanna Richardson, 1956.

RACKET, THE (1927), a play by Bartlett Cormack. [*Ambassador Theatre, 119 perf.] When the reporters who cover an outlying Chicago police station taunt Captain McQuigg (John *Cromwell) about whether an honest, dedicated police officer would be exiled to a relatively unimportant post if he attempts to buck both political corruption and gangland boss Nick Scarsi, McQuigg evades their barbs. McQuigg knows full well that has been his own history and that Scarsi has now opened a brewery in his district. After he arrests Scarsi's younger brother, he also knows he has joined battle. Under an assumed name, Scarsi (Edward G. *Robinson) appears, demanding to see his brother's girl, Irene (Marion Coakley), who he fears can cause trouble for his brother. A policeman refuses, so Scarsi shoots him and escapes, but he is caught and brought back to the station where McQuigg declines to release him despite a judge's order. In an argument in front of State Attorney Welsh (Romaine Callender), Irene gets Scarsi inadvertently to admit the killing, but Scarsi threatens to destroy Welsh and the whole Chicago political machine if he is prosecuted. Pulling a gun, Scarsi attempts to shoot McQuigg, only to be shot instead. Burns *Mantle hailed the play as one that "bears unmistakably the stamp of authenticity in character, scene and speech and reflects vividly a phase of civic life in America." This was the first time Robinson played a gangster, and the only time on Broadway. Attempts were made by Chicago authorities to ban the play there, in the light of the success of *Chicago* and other similar plays and the bad image of Chicago that resulted.

RAFFLES, the Amateur Cracksman (1903), a play by E. W. Hornung and Eugene Presbrey. [*Princess Theatre, 168 perf.] A. J. Raffles (Kyrle *Bellew) is a highly educated, chivalrous English gentleman. For the fun of it, he is also a jewel thief. Invited to the home of a friendly lord, he thinks nothing of stealing the family diamonds, but his exquisite scruples demand he reject the advances of his host's wife and daughter. Captain Bedford (E. M. Holland) is an amateur sleuth who is determined to catch Raffles, and he nearly does. Yet after learning that Raffles has returned the lord's jewels and escaped, he can only sigh, "I'm glad of it." *Liebler and Co. produced this superb comedy-thriller based on Hornung's popular stories. It was revived regularly for more than a decade. **Eugene W[yley] PRESBREY** (1853–1931) was born in Williamsburg, Massachusetts, and made his debut as an actor in Boston in 1874. Coming to New York in 1880, he was a director for A. M. *Palmer from 1883 to 1896 and began to write plays. These ranged from light farces to romantic dramas, many of them written in collaboration with other writers or dramatizations of novels and short stories. They included *The Courtship of Miles Standish* (1895), *A Ward of France* (1897), *A Virginia Courtship* (1898), *New England Folks* (1901), and *Mary, Mary, Quite Contrary* (1905); but his biggest success was *Raffles*. As a rule, Presbrey directed all his own plays and frequently staged works by other authors as well. About the time of World War I he recognized that his sort of theatre was passing from the scene, so he became a screenwriter for the silent movies.

RAGTIME (1998), a musical play by Terrence *McNally (book), Stephen *Flaherty (music), Lynn *Ahrens (lyrics). [*Ford Center, 861 perf.] Based on E. L. Doctorow's sprawling novel about turn-of-the-century America, the musical follows three different groups of characters: an upper-class white family in which Father (Mark Jacoby) tries to maintain the old ways while Mother (Marin Mazzie) discovers her individuality and her Younger Brother (Steven Sutcliffe) becomes an anarchist; the Jewish immigrant Tateh (Peter Friedman) who rises from a peddler to a silent movie mogul; and the African-American ragtime pianist Coalhouse Walker (Brian Stokes *Mitchell) who goes on a killing rampage when he is insulted and his fiancée Sarah (Audra *McDonald) is killed. The three stories overlap and, peopled with such famous personages as Harry Houdini (Jim Corti), Evelyn Nesbit (Lynette Perry), and Emma Goldman (Judy *Kaye), form a complex panorama of an explosive time in history. *Notable songs*: Wheels of a Dream; Back to Before; Your Daddy's Son; New Music; Make Them Hear You. The ambitious musical was well received with applause for the script, score, cast, Frank *Galati's direction, Graciela *Daniele's choreography, Eugene *Lee's stunning scenic design, and Santo *Loquasto's period costumes. Produced by Livent, Inc., *Ragtime* was such an expensive production that it failed to recoup even after a nearly three-year run.

RAILROAD OF LOVE, THE (1887), a comedy by Augustin *Daly. [Daly's Theatre, 108 perf.] According to Phenix Scuttleby (James *Lewis), an aging man-about-town, the pace of modern courtship has become too rapid: "Man alive! It's railroad time with the women nowadays. If you are loaded with millions, you may court on way-freight time, or a particularly fascinating fellow may jog along on accommodation schedule." In this high-speed society, Lieutenant Howell Everett (John *Drew) pursues Viva Van Riker (Phoebe Russell) until he recognizes that she prefers the impecunious artist Benny Demaresq (Otis *Skinner). Even then he might have pressed his suit but for the appearance of a beautiful, rich widow, Mrs. Valentine Osprey (Ada *Rehan). A clause in her late husband's will diverts his estate to old Scuttleby if she remarries, unless by some wild chance Scuttleby marries first. Events and friends conspire to marry Scuttleby to Eutycia Laburnam (Mrs. G. H. *Gilbert), a country dowager who longs for "a change from the eternal birds and crickets." So all the couples are happily paired. Daly took the play from Schoenthan and Kadelburg's *Goldfische*, adapting it freely and totally Americanizing it. George *Odell recalled, "*The Railroad of Love* was the most exquisite modern comedy I ever saw at Daly's." Although it was one of his biggest successes and was revived, its runs were inevitably curtailed by the producer's practice of prior scheduling. Curiously, despite praise from such respected British figures as Ellen *Terry and Charles Dickens, it failed in London when Daly produced it there.

RAIN (1922), a play by John *Colton and Clemence Randolph. [Maxine Elliott's Theatre, 648 perf.] Joe Horn (Rapley Holmes) is a former American who has left his homeland because of Prohibition and similar puritanical ways, and who has established a hotel in Pago Pago that caters to sailors, beachcombers, and others seeking a good time. Into this hedonist band come two disparate figures: the flamboyant Sadie Thompson (Jeanne *Eagels), an American prostitute fleeing the law in Chicago, and the Reverend Alfred Davidson (Robert Kelly), who is determined to teach the depraved natives the meaning of sin and to save one and all from the devil. The pair soon lock horns, but it is not a fair fight since the missionary is brought to realize that his own motives are not entirely pure, at least where the voluptuous Sadie is concerned. In the end, Davidson commits suicide, and Sadie, preparing to leave for Australia, can only muse, "I guess I'm sorry for everybody in the world." Sam H. Harris produced the play that was taken from a Somerset *Maugham short story (known variously as "Rain" and "Sadie Thompson"). In his review for the *Times*, John *Corbin noted, " 'Rain' is not a 'pleasant' play . . . but it is strikingly original in theme, true in characterization, vigorous in drama and richly colored." For most playgoers, Eagels's electrifying performance was the evening's high point. A musical version, *Sadie Thompson* (1944), originally conceived for Ethel *Merman but finally starring June Havoc, failed.

RAINMAKER, THE (1954), a play by N. Richard Nash. [*Cort Theatre, 124 perf.] The Curry family has two problems: their farm is threatened by a severe, prolonged drought, and they have been unable to marry off plain, outspoken Lizzie Curry (Geraldine *Page). Into their midst swaggers a handsome con man, Bill Starbuck (Darren McGavin), who promises to bring rain for a fee of $100 and who courts Lizzie. Nature finally brings the rain; but by the time Starbuck leaves, he has given Lizzie sufficient confidence and poise for her to win a husband on her own. Although he felt it became too cluttered with symbolism near the end, Louis *Kronenberger praised the work as having "a bright, brisk air and an engagingly humorous smack." The play has remained popular in regional theatres and a 1999 revival from the *Williamstown Theatre Festival was well received on Broadway. Nash wrote the libretto when it was turned into the musical *110 IN THE SHADE* (1963) with a superior score by Harvey *Schmidt (music) and Tom *Jones (lyrics). Inga Swenson was Lizzie, Robert Horton was Starbuck, and the David *Merrick production ran 331 performances in the *Broadhurst Theatre. *Notable songs*: Simple Little Things; Little Red Hat; Everything Beautiful Happens at Night; Love, Don't Turn Away. N[athaniel] **Richard NASH** [né Nusbaum] (b. 1913) was born in Philadelphia and educated at the University of Pennsylvania. He wrote a number of unsuccessful plays as well as the books for the musicals *Wildcat* (1960) and *The *Happy Time* (1968).

RAISIN. See *Raisin in the Sun, A.*

RAISIN IN THE SUN, A (1959), a play by Lorraine Hansberry. [*Ethel Barrymore Theatre, 530 perf.; NYDCC Award.] Lena Younger (Claudia McNeil) lives with her son, Walter (Sidney Poitier); his wife, Ruth (Ruby *Dee); and their young son in a two-room apartment in the Chicago ghetto. Lena hopes to use the $10,000 she will receive from her late husband's life insurance policy to move her family into a house in a nice neighborhood. But the house she has her eye on is in a white part of town, and the neighbors send a representative to the Youngers to try and buy the property back. But Lena stands firm; and even after Walter loses some of the money trying to invest in a liquor store, the family prepares to move. Hansberry based her play on personal experience, her African-American family having

gone through a similar dilemma when they tried to move into one of Chicago's better neighborhoods. The play was a landmark of sorts, being the first time an African-American female playwright was produced on Broadway. The fact that it had a black director, Lloyd *Richards, was also a first. Producer Philip Rose found no New York theatre was available, so the production toured to Philadelphia, New Haven, and Chicago, getting such an enthusiastic response that it finally arrived on Broadway. Business was slow at first but gradually picked up with positive word of mouth. It remains one of the finest of American dramas and is frequently revived regionally and Off Broadway. The play was later made into the musical *RAISIN* (1973) with a score by Judd Woldin (music) and Robert Brittan (lyrics) and featuring Virginia Capers as Lena and Joe Morton as Walter. Hansberry's husband, Robert Nemiroff, produced it and worked on the libretto, which adhered to the original very closely. The musical ran 847 performances at the 46th Street Theatre, winning the *Tony Award. *Notable songs*: A Whole Lotta Sunshine; Measure the Valleys; Sidewalk Tree. **Lorraine HANSBERRY** (1930–65) was born in Chicago's South Side where her father was an early civil rights leader. She studied at the University of Wisconsin, the University of Guadalajara in Mexico, and Roosevelt University. In 1950 Hansberry moved to New York to pursue her writing career, finding success with *Raisin in the Sun* but less so with *The Sign in Sidney Brustein's Window* (1964). After her untimely death from cancer, Nemiroff, also a respected writer, completed her unfinished play *Les Blancs* in 1970 and compiled a program of her works called *To Be Young, Gifted, and Black*, which has often been produced.

RAITT, John [Emmet] (b. 1917), singer and actor. A native of Santa Ana, California, the husky, virile singer was Curly in the Chicago company of *Oklahoma!* but is remembered primarily as the original Billy Bigelow in *Carousel* (1945) and the factory supervisor Sid in *The *Pajama Game* (1954). Raitt's other New York appearances were in *Magdalena* (1948), *Three Wishes for Jamie* (1952), *Carnival in Flanders* (1953), and *A Joyful Noise* (1966).

RAJAH, THE; or, Wyncot's Ward (1883), a comedy by William Young. [*Madison Square Theatre, 190 perf.] Harold Wyncot (George Clarke), an imperious but seemingly indolent and worthless young man, has served in India where his fellow officers contemptuously nicknamed him "The Rajah." On his uncle's death, Wyncot is made his heir as well as the guardian of his uncle's adopted daughter, Gladys (Rillie Deaves). He takes over the estate and at first seems to alienate Gladys by his stern rules and pomposity. However, Gladys realizes she loves him after he puts some labor agitators (one of whom is an escaped convict) in their places and mollifies the other workmen. Originally meant as a light summer filler, the comedy succeeded beyond everyone's expectations, including those of most reviewers, the majority of whom had dismissed the play. Its popularity was increased by excellent publicity, especially the fame of its third-act setting, which included a real waterfall. Producer Daniel *Frohman sent pictures of this set, taken by B. J. *Falk, to newspapers and magazines around the country. **William YOUNG** (1847–1920) was born near Chicago, where he studied and practiced law for a time, then later became an actor with the express intention of learning playwriting from a performer's vantage point. His early blank-verse tragedies, *Pendragon* (1882) and *Ganelon* (1891), were both mounted by Lawrence *Barrett. The latter was much esteemed. His most successful plays, however, were *The Rajah* and his 1899 dramatization of *Ben-Hur*. About a dozen of his other plays were mounted, with varying success.

RAMBEAU, Marjorie (1889–1970), actress. The San Francisco native spent many seasons with stock companies in her hometown and in Los Angeles before braving New York, where her first success came in the title role of *Sadie Love* (1915). She scored an even bigger hit as detective Nan Carey in *Cheating Cheaters* (1916). Rambeau's most memorable role followed when she portrayed Gina Ashland in *Eyes of Youth* (1917). A major mistake was her rejection of the role of Sadie Thompson in *Rain* (1922), and her career soon began to fade, although she enjoyed minor successes as Edith Fields in *Daddy's Gone A-Hunting* (1921) and the ambitious divorcée Jenney in *The Goldfish* (1922). George *Middleton, who had a bitter experience with her in one of his plays, *The Road Together* (1924), wrote, "Though she lacked soul, she could assume its trappings. Beautiful, too, and eye-arresting, she impressed by the commanding way she moved about. Mistress of stage strategy, gained from hard years in stock, she could handle resourcefully almost any demand of emotion or comedy." In later years she was well known as a character actress in films.

RAND, Ayn. See *Night of January 16*.

RANDALL, Tony [né Leonard Rosenberg] (b. 1920), actor and manager. The urbane, genial leading man was born in Tulsa, Oklahoma, the son of an art dealer, and was educated at Northwestern and Columbia before studying acting at the *Neighborhood Playhouse School. Randall worked in radio before making his New York theatre debut in 1941, and his first noticeable role on Broadway was the sly reporter E. K. Hornbeck in *Inherit the Wind* (1955), followed by the leading part of Captain Henry St. James who has two wives in two ports in *Oh, Captain!* (1958). Randall was a regular in no less than six television series over the decades, yet he returned irregularly to the theatre for the next forty years. In 1991 he founded and ran the National Actors Theatre, sometimes appearing in its productions of American and foreign classics.

RANKIN, [Arthur] McKee (1841–1914), actor. The slim, handsome leading man, who grew somewhat portly with time, was born in Sandwich, Canada, and began his acting career in 1861 in Rochester, New York, using the name of George Henley. After spending several seasons in London, he returned to make his New York debut in 1866 as Hugh de Brass in *A Regular Fix*. In 1872 he became a leading man at the *Union Square Theatre, where his roles included Phyllon in W. S. *Gilbert's *The Wicked World* (1873), George de Lesparre in *Led Astray* (1873), Armand in *Camille* (1874), and Jacques Frochard in *The *Two Orphans* (1874). His greatest success came when he produced and starred as Alexander McGee in *The *Danites* (1877). Rankin returned to the play frequently for the next dozen years. Later he appeared in a variety of plays from popular contemporary melodrama to classic comedy. He also was active as a producer and theatre manager. In his last years he toured with his protégé Nance *O'Neill.

RAPHAELSON, Samson (1896–1983), playwright. Born in New York and educated at the University of Illinois, he was a journalist and short-story writer before turning to the theatre. His first play was the popular *The *Jazz Singer* (1925), followed by the less-successful *Young Love* (1928) and *The Wooden Slipper* (1934). Raphaelson's other works included *White Man* (1936), *The Perfect Marriage* (1944), and *Hilda Crane* (1950), but he is most remembered for three stylish comedies: *Accent on Youth* (1934), *Skylark* (1939), and *Jason* (1942). He was also a successful film writer who worked closely with Ernst Lubitsch.

RASCH, Albertina (1896–1967), choreographer. Born and trained in Vienna, she came to this country to dance in the *Hippodrome spectacles in 1911. After appearing in a few productions, she worked with several opera companies and toured in vaudeville before staging numbers for *George White's Scandals of 1925. Rasch first attracted major attention with her dances in *Rio Rita* (1927). Her work, largely balletic, was seen in more than two dozen subsequent offerings, including *The *Three Musketeers* (1928), *Three's a Crowd* (1930), *The *Band Wagon* (1931), *The *Cat and the Fiddle* (1931), *The

Great Waltz (1934), **Jubilee* (1935), and **Lady in the Dark* (1941).

RATHBONE, Basil (1892–1967), actor. The slim, suave, somewhat hawk-faced leading man was born in Johannesburg and spent more than a decade on English stages before making his debut as Count Alexei Czerny opposite Doris *Keane in *The Czarina* (1922). Among his subsequent roles were Dr. Agi opposite Eva *Le Gallienne in *The Swan* (1923) and Jacques Virieu in the controversial *The Captive* (1926). In later years his best-remembered roles were Romeo to Katharine *Cornell's Juliet in 1934 and the tyrannical father Dr. Sloper in The *Heiress* (1947). Although Rathbone is largely recalled as the Sherlock Holmes of many films, his only attempt to portray the sleuth onstage in 1953 was unsuccessful. Autobiography: *In and Out of Character*, 1962.

RATTIGAN, Terence (1911–82), playwright. The English writer, whose best plays were literate and dramatically effective, albeit sometimes superficial, scored his first American success in 1937 with *French Without Tears*. Numbered among his later American entries were *O Mistress Mine* (1946), *The Winslow Boy* (1947), *The Browning Version* (1948), *The Deep Blue Sea* (1952), *The Sleeping Prince* (1953), *Separate Tables* (1956), *Ross* (1961), and *In Praise of Love* (1974). Many of Rattigan's plays fell out of favor in the 1960s but have been enjoying new productions on London and New York stages since the 1990s. Biography: *Terence Rattigan*, Geoffrey Wansell, 1997.

RAYMOND, John T. [né O'Brien] (1836–87), comic actor. Born in Buffalo, New York, he ran away from home and made his debut in Rochester in 1853, afterward playing in Philadelphia and Baltimore. He toured the South before joining Laura *Keene's ensemble in 1861, calling attention to himself when he replaced Joseph *Jefferson as Asa Trenchard in *Our American Cousin*. Raymond gained stardom in 1874 as the daydreaming Colonel Sellers in *The Gilded Age*, so stealing the play that it was rewritten and retitled *Colonel Sellers*. He continued to return to the role regularly until his death. Among his other noteworthy portrayals were Ichabod Crane in Wolfert's *Roost* (1879), Ferdinand Fresh in *Fresh, the American* (1881), and the wheeling-dealing politician Gen. Limber in *For Congress* (1884). He was a slim, long-faced actor, of whom William *Winter wrote, "His humor was rich and jocund. He had an exceptional command over composure of countenance. He could deceive an observer by the sapient gravity of his visage, and he exerted that facial faculty with extraordinary comic effect."

REBECCA OF SUNNYBROOK FARM (1910), a play by Kate Douglas Wiggin and Charlotte Thompson. [Republic Theatre, 216 perf.] Prospects look bleak when ten-year-old Rebecca Rowena Randall (Edith *Taliaferro) is sent to live with her seemingly crotchety Aunt Miranda (Marie L. Day), but everything turns out joyously, thanks to her optimism and genial nature. Adapted from Wiggin's 1903 best-seller, the *Klaw and *Erlanger mounting was especially popular with children.

RED MILL, THE (1906), a musical comedy by Henry *Blossom (book, lyrics), Victor *Herbert (music). [Knickerbocker Theatre, 274 perf.] Kid Conner (David *Montgomery) and Con Kidder (Fred *Stone) are two Americans who find themselves without cash in a small Dutch village. The town's strict burgomaster wants his daughter Gretchen (Augusta Greenleaf) to marry the Governor of Zeeland (Neal McCay), so he locks her in a mill to prevent her eloping with a sea captain, Doris Van Damm (Joseph M. Ratliff). But the two Americans climb into the mill and help Gretchen escape on the mill's sail. The Governor decides to marry Gretchen's Aunt Bertha (Allene Crater) so the lovers are united, and Kid and Con, with the small change they have garnered, head for a boat to take them back to New York. *Notable songs*: Because You're You; Every Day Is Ladies' Day with Me; The Isle of Our Dreams; Moonbeams; The Streets of New York. The basic plot of Americans plunked down in an exotic land was the favorite musical comedy device of its era, but Blossom's fine book and lyrics and Herbert's melodic score made the Charles *Dillingham production the best and most beloved of its ilk. A revival in 1945, with Michael O'Shea, Eddie *Foy Jr., and Dorothy Stone heading the cast, outran the original, compiling 531 performances.

REDHEAD (1959), a musical thriller by Herbert *Fields, Sidney Sheldon, David Shaw (book), Dorothy *Fields (book, lyrics), Albert Hague (music). [46th Street Theatre, 452 perf.; Tony Award.] In Victorian London, Essie Whimple (Gwen *Verdon) fashions figures at the Simpson Sisters' Waxworks but soon finds herself in the middle of a Jack the Ripper-like murder spree. With the help of the music hall strongman Tom Baxter (Richard *Kiley), Essie uncovers the identity of the redheaded culprit and wins Tom's love along the way. *Notable songs*: Merely Marvelous; Look Who's in Love; Erbie Fitch's Twitch. A curiosity of a musical presented by Robert *Fryer and Lawrence Carr, *Redhead* tried to combine music-hall entertainment with a whodunit but ended up being another tailor-made vehicle for Verdon, directed and choreographed by Bob *Fosse.

REED, Florence (1883–1967), actress. The small, dark performer was the daughter of a minor actor-manager, Roland [Lewis] Reed (1852–1901). Born in Philadelphia, she began a long apprenticeship with New York's *Fifth Avenue Theatre stock company in 1901, then toured as E. H. *Sothern's leading lady, playing Katherine de Vaucelles in *If I Were King and Ophelia. She later appeared in *Seven Days (1909), The Typhoon (1912), and The Master of the House (1912) before scoring a major success as the Russian prostitute Marya Varenka in The Yellow Ticket (1914). After turning to musicals with Chu Chin Chow (1917), Reed enjoyed a run as Mrs. Moreland in The Mirage (1920), but her greatest triumph came as the whorehouse proprietor Mother Goddam in The *Shanghai Gesture (1926). Looking back, Ward *Morehouse recalled, "Miss Reed's recitation of the 'I survived' speech . . . remains one of the most vivid tirades ever to be delivered in the history of melodrama." She never again created so noteworthy a role, although she headed touring companies of *Mourning Becomes Electra and *Elizabeth the Queen and played the Fortune Teller in the original production of The *Skin of Our Teeth (1942). Reed continued to act until shortly before her death. Her grandfather, John "Pop" Reed, was for many decades the gas man at the *Walnut Street Theatre and gained a small foothold in American theatrical legend by bequeathing the theatre his skull to be used in performances of *Hamlet.

REEVES-SMITH, H[arry] (1862–1938), actor. The Englishman first came to America in 1887 to tour with John Sleeper *Clarke and in later years served on tours as leading man to Henrietta *Crosman and Grace *George. His memorable roles on Broadway included the title part of *Captain Jinks of the Horse Marines (1901), Peter Mottram in Mid-Channel (1910), Jerry in *Peg o' My Heart (1912), Hubert Knolys in The *Unchastened Woman (1915), and the knowing Prentice Van Zile in *Polly with a Past (1917). His last major appearance was as the elder Johann Strauss in The Great Waltz (1934).

REGINA. See Little Foxes, The.

REHAN, Ada [née Ada Crehan] (1860–1916), actress. A regal beauty and one of America's greatest performers, she was born in Limerick, Ireland, brought to America at the age of five, and grew up in Brooklyn, where she watched her older sisters adopt stage careers. It was her brother-in-law, Oliver Doud *Byron, who helped her make her debut in 1873 as Clara in his once-famous vehicle, *Across the Continent. Rehan then joined Mrs. *Drew's celebrated ensemble at the *Arch Street Theatre. A typographical error in an early program

there dropped the first letter of her surname, giving her the stage name she afterward employed. After two seasons with Drew and in companies in Louisville and Albany, she played Mary Standish in an 1879 revival of Augustin *Daly's *Pique and then played in his L'Assommoir. Her performances so impressed Daly that she joined his company and played Nelly Beers in Love's Young Dream. Under his guidance Rehan quickly became the finest and probably the most beloved of all younger comediennes. She excelled at classic comedy, including such Shakespearean roles as Mrs. Ford, Katherine, Helena, Rosalind, Viola, and Beatrice, as well as Sheridan's Lady Teazle. But she was also at home in the newer comedies Daly presented, among them the American premieres of *Pinero's The Magistrate (1885) and Dandy Dick (1887), in which she played Mrs. Posket and Georgiana Tidman respectively. Along with Mrs. *Gilbert, John *Drew, and James *Lewis, Rehan was a mainstay of Daly's ensemble. William *Winter wrote, "Her physical beauty was of the kind that appears in portraits of women by Romney and Gainsborough—ample, opulent, and bewitching—and it was enriched by the enchantment of superb animal spirits. She had gray-blue eyes and brown hair." He added, "Her acting, if closely scrutinized, was seen to have been studied; yet it always seemed spontaneous; her handsome, ingenuous, winning countenance informed it with sympathy, while her voice—copious, tender, and wonderfully musical—filled it with emotion, speaking always from the heart." After Daly's death she continued to appear largely in the roles in which he had cast her, but despite her skill and popularity, success eluded her, so she retired in 1905. Biography: Ada Rehan: A Study, William Winter, 1891.

REHEARSAL CLUB. See Theatrical Clubs.

REID, [James] Hal[leck] (1873?–1920), playwright. Apparently born in Minneapolis, he started his career as an actor but turned to playwriting, though he remained an actor virtually until his death. He soon became one of the most prolific authors of such cheap-priced touring melodramas as Alone in the World, In Convict Stripes, A Midnight Marriage, A Millionaire's Revenge, and A Wife's Secret. He remained active in the field until films destroyed the market, after which he himself became a screenwriter and a player in silent movies. His son, Wallace Reid, briefly was a Hollywood star.

REILLY AND THE FOUR HUNDRED (1890), a musical comedy by Edward *Harrigan (book, lyrics), David *Braham (music). [Harrigan's Theatre, 202 perf.] Wiley Reilly (Harrigan), an immigrant pawnbroker, has watched his lawyer son Ned (Harry Davenport) rise in society and successfully court a socially acceptable lady. But all his plans and dreams could be shattered by Herman Smeltz (Harry Fisher), a sausage tycoon who has somehow wheedled his way into the "400." Wiley knows a dark, long-kept secret about Smeltz and uses it to see that everything ends happily. *Notable song*: Maggie Murphy's Home. The first show to play Harrigan's own new theatre, it enjoyed the longest run of any of his plays, but was virtually his last success. The play propelled Ada *Lewis, who portrayed a roughneck girl, to fame.

REILLY, Charles Nelson (b. 1931), character actor and director. The bespectacled comic, who appeared in some significant 1960s musicals, is also a respected director of serious plays. A native New Yorker, Reilly attended the University of Connecticut and studied acting with Uta *Hagen and Herbert *Berghof before finding work in summer stock and then making his New York debut Off Broadway in 1956. He appeared in several revues before playing minor roles in *Bye Bye Birdie* (1960) and finding success as the obnoxious Bud Frump in *How to Succeed in Business Without Really Trying* (1961) and the lovesick clerk Cornelius Hackl in *Hello, Dolly!* (1964). Reilly also shone in two unsuccessful shows: as the antique shop assistant Roger Summerhill in *Skyscraper* (1965) and the nearsighted celestial messenger Sidney Lipton in *God's Favorite* (1974).

REINAGLE, Alexander (1756?–1809), manager and composer. The son of an Austrian musician, he was born and raised in Portsmouth, England, then at eighteen moved to Edinburgh where he studied with Raynor *Taylor. Reinagle came to America in 1786 and settled in Philadelphia. By 1791 he was a respected composer and teacher with strong ties to local theatre and so found substantial support among Philadelphians when he joined with the actor Thomas *Wignell to build what became the *Chestnut Street Theatre. The house was opened in 1794 and for the remainder of his career he was active in its management. He also adopted many English ballad operas for local audiences, composed incidental music for other plays, and wrote the score for several light operas, notably *The Sicilian Romance* (1795).

REINHARDT, Max [né Goldmann] (1873–1943), director and producer. The famed Austro-German showman first came to the attention of most American playgoers in 1912 when Winthrop *Ames imported his mounting of the Oriental pantomime *Sumurun*. In 1924 Reinhardt visited New York to re-create his production of *The Miracle*, and then in 1927 brought over his German company for a season of repertory. Following the rise of the Nazis, he moved permanently to America where he staged his version of A *Midsummer Night's Dream* in Hollywood in 1934 and *The Eternal Road* in New York in 1937. Other Broadway directorial credits included Thornton *Wilder's *The Merchant of Yonkers* (1938) and Irwin *Shaw's *Sons and Soldiers* (1943). Reinhardt's version of *Die Fledermaus* was offered to Broadway as *Rosalinda* (1942) by his son Gottfried shortly before the elder's death.

RÉJANE, Gabrielle [Charlotte] [née Réju] (1857–1920), actress. The fine French comedienne, who was also competent in more serious roles, made two extended American tours, the first in 1895 and the second in 1904. She scored a huge success as Catherine Hubscher in *Mme. Sans-Gêne*. The *Times* reported she was "a woman of medium height, lithe and graceful, certainly not young or handsome. Her small nose, round eyes, high brows, and large mouth impress spectators grotesquely. . . . Her facial play is inimitable and unique. Her motions are so swift that one can scarcely follow her." Réjane's repertory also included such once-popular French works as *Zaza*, *Divorçons*, and *Sapho*, as well as a French version of *A Doll's House*.

RELIGIOUS DRAMA IN AMERICA. Perhaps because significant religious bodies had early on succeeded in preventing the opening of theatres in colonial America and later, after playhouses had begun to appear, remained a potent source of possible repression, the separation of church and theatre was long a part of the American scene, much the same as the separation of church and state. Very little of what might be termed "religious drama" was offered to playgoers until late in the 19th century. Dramatizations of Biblical stories were virtually unheard of in the professional theatre, and even the portrayal of such figures as ministers was generally restrained and infrequent. Non-Protestant clerics were sometimes characters in tales of Renaissance Italy, but these figures often seemed to derive more from Elizabethan and Jacobean traditions than from genuine observation. (For further material on religious groups see "Jews in American Theatre and Drama" and "Mormons in American Theatre and Drama.") It may be telling that the first 19th-century success centering on a major religious figure was *Bulwer-Lytton's English drama *Richelieu* (1839), which dealt not directly with religious matters but rather with the Cardinal's attempts to influence affairs of state and of the heart. Depicting such meddlesomeness may have appealed to the strong anti-Catholic sentiments of many playgoers, although the real reason for the play's long popularity was undoubtedly the performances of Edwin *Forrest, Charles *Macready, and Edwin *Booth in the title role. One of the first important American religious plays of national interest was a version of the classic passion play, known either as The *Passion Play (1879) or as The Passion. However, this dramatization of the New Testament story by a Jewish playwright offended many Christian clergy, who lobbied for its suppression. The later arrival of such English plays as Henry Arthur *Jones's Saints and Sinners (1895) and Jerome K. Jerome's The Passing of the Third Floor Back (1909) further increased acceptance of religiously oriented works. At the same time native drama began to employ religious and Biblical figures and themes with increasing success. The most notable from a commercial standpoint was the dramatization of Lew Wallace's famous novel, *Ben-Hur (1899), which attracted huge audiences as much by its spectacle, including a celebrated chariot race, as by its religious message. Charles Rann Kennedy's simple and more thoughtful The *Servant in the House (1908) met with great critical acclaim but found only small audiences. The disillusionment and cynicism that followed World War I led to few religious works being attempted during the 1920s. Given the tenor of the age, it may be significant that Eugene *O'Neill's Dionysian study of a Biblical story in Lazarus Laughed (1927) was the playwright's only major effort not to be given a Broadway hearing. Other examples of the period were the 1924 presentation of Max *Reinhardt's decade-old pageant The Miracle, *Shaw's *St. Joan (1923), and The *Ladder (1926), the curious play that attempted to promote the Eastern idea of reincarnation.

If the hedonism and cynicism of the 1920s offered relatively infertile fields for the growth of commercial religious drama, the political and economic preoccupations of the 1930s proved equally discouraging, especially since the theatre and other arts were dominated by the often-irreligious left. Such major playwrights as O'Neill and Philip *Barry were given short shrift when they presented their religious questions in theatrical terms: O'Neill in *Days Without End (1934) and Barry in Bright Star (1935) and Here Come the Clowns (1938). Yet the most successful and memorable of all American Biblical plays was a product of this era, The *Green Pastures (1930). It was also in this period that T. S. *Eliot wrote the first of his religious dramas, *Murder in the Cathedral (1936), followed later by A Family Reunion (1947) and The *Cocktail Party (1950). By contrast with the bitter, disbelieving response to the failure of "the war to end all wars" to achieve its aim, the prosperous decades that followed World War II and that encompassed the Cold War, the McCarthy era, and several dismay-

ing, brutal hot wars, saw a variety of responses, including a reexamination of religious values and the importance of religion in private lives, and an ill-defined, sometimes wavering fascination with mysticism. The shock of the Nazi extermination of European Jewry brought forth a number of intriguing works dealing with the subject. The *Diary of Anne Frank (1955), the importation The Deputy (1964), and Arthur *Miller's Incident at Vichy (1964) were among the more interesting of such plays. Works treating Biblical subjects directly included Robinson *Jeffers's curious, failed Dear Judas (1947), which attempted to argue that Judas betrayed Jesus in order to ensure Jesus' immortality; Archibald *MacLeish's *J. B. (1958), which recounted the Job legend in modern terms; Clifford *Odets's The Flowering Peach (1954) about Biblical Noah; and Paddy *Chayefsky's The *Tenth Man (1959) and *Gideon (1961). The musical stage turned to religious themes of one sort or another with great success in the 1960s and 1970s, with such works as *Fiddler on the Roof (1964), Salvation (1969), *Godspell (1971), Your Arms Too Short to Box with God (1976), and the English products *Jesus Christ Superstar (1971) and Joseph and the Amazing Technicolor Dreamcoat (1982). English and French dramas concerning religious ideas included Becket (1960), A Man for All Seasons (1961), Luther (1963), *Amadeus (1980), and Racing Demon (1995), while native plays, such as The Runner Stumbles (1976), Mass Appeal (1981), Agnes of God (1982), Handy Dandy (1990), and Sacrilege (1995), also dealt with religion. Ironically, the most popular pieces were the ones that looked back on a religious upbringing and laughed nostalgically at it: Do Black Patent Leather Shoes Reflect Up? (1981), Sister Mary Ignatius Explains It All for You (1981), *Nunsense (1985), and Late Nite Catechism (1996).

RENT (1996), a rock musical play by Jonathan Larson. [*New York Theatre Workshop, still running; Pulitzer Prize, Tony, NYDCC Awards.] This retelling of La Boheme, reset in the East Village of Manhattan in the 1990s, turned Rudolfo into the HIV-infected composer Roger (Adam Pascal) and Mimi (Daphne Rubin-Vega) into a drug addicted, S&M dancer who also has AIDS. Roger's roommate, Mark (Anthony Rapp), is a struggling video artist trying to get over losing his girl friend, the performance artist Maureen (Idina Menzel), to an African-American woman (Fredi Walker). Other colorful characters inhabiting this tale of modern-day Bohemia include the cross-dressing Angel (Wilson Jermaine Heredia), his ex-professor lover Tom Collins (Jesse L. Martin), and the young, conniving entrepreneur Benny (Taye Diggs). The sung-through rock musical often parallels the opera's plot, though Mimi survives at the end and instead

Angel is the frail victim of disease. *Notable songs*: Rent; Seasons of Love; I'll Cover You; La Vie Boheme; Out Tonight. The musical received reams of publicity when its young composer-author died of an aneurysm following the last dress rehearsal, so all the major critics saw the little New York Theatre Workshop production Off Broadway and their rave reviews prompted a Broadway transfer to the *Nederlander Theatre. Yet there is much more than sentiment and publicity behind the show's success. One of the few musicals to incorporate rock music without softening its style for Broadway, *Rent* has found legions of young (and old) admirers of its sheer energy and powerful theatrics. **Jonathan LARSON** (1960–96) was born in White Plains, New York, and educated at Adelphi University before moving to New York where he wrote musicals seen Off Off Broadway and in workshops. One of these works was produced again after his death under the title *Tick, Tick . . . Boom!* (2001) and was a success. The three-person show, about a struggling composer-lyricist, demonstrated that Larson was much more than a one-play talent.

REPERTORIO ESPAÑOL (New York). In 1968 Gilberto Zaldívar and René Buch founded this company in order to present new and classic works from various Spanish-language drama traditions. The troupe performs in Spanish but the Latin American, Hispanic, Puerto Rican, and Cuban productions include simultaneous translations via an infrared system so its audience base is quite diverse. The company spent much of its early years touring but since 1972 is headquartered at the Grammercy Arts Theatre where it has programs encouraging new *Hispanic-American playwrights and offering English-language works in translation, such as a popular mounting of *Who's Afraid of Virginia Woolf?*

REPERTORY THEATRE OF LINCOLN CENTER. See Lincoln Center for the Performing Arts.

REPERTORY THEATRE OF ST. LOUIS. After a problematic history and three name changes, this nonprofit professional company located in a suburb of St. Louis has survived to become a notable regional theatre. It was started by Marita Woodruff and Wayne Loui in 1966 on the campus of Webster College and named the Repertory of Theatre at Loretto-Hilton. The title came from the Sisters of Loretto, who administer the college, and from Conrad Hilton, an alumnus who contributed substantially to the project. The troupe had a true rotating repertory, using drama students from Webster to offset the costs, but the program was a financial failure and was dissolved after a few seasons. By 1973 it was operating as the Loretto

Hilton Repertory Theatre and fared better, eventually changing its name once again to reflect its status as the city's premiere resident theatre. The company currently performs in a 733-seat thrust stage and in a 125-seat studio theatre, offering classic and modern revivals, small-scale musicals, and occasionally new works. Their children's theatre touring group is called the Imaginary Theatre Company.

RETURN OF PETER GRIMM, THE (1911), a play by David *Belasco. [*Belasco Theatre, 231 perf.] Peter Grimm (David *Warfield) is a kindly old man who persuades his orphan ward Katrien (Janet Dunbar) to marry his nephew Frederick (John Sainpolis) so that the Grimm line may continue. Katrien agrees out of fondness for Peter, although she loves another man and does not care for Frederick. Peter and his friend Dr. MacPherson (Joseph Brennan) have made a compact—that whoever dies first will attempt to come back to earth with a message from the dead. Peter dies and keeps his promise. In death he realizes that he made a great mistake in pressing Katrien to marry Frederick, but on his return he is unable to "get across" to the living. Only Wilhelm (Percy Helton), the ailing little son of his former housekeeper, is able to see and hear him. The others are skeptical of Wilhelm's visions, so Peter has Wilhelm reveal the ugly truth learned in death—that Wilhelm's father is Frederick. The news frees Katrien to marry the man of her choice. Little Wilhelm dies, and Peter takes him on his shoulder and carries him to the realm of the dead, to the accompaniment of the circus music the boy so loved. Although Walter Prichard *Eaton insisted the "play degenerates into mawkishness and loses its potential poetry," most critics and playgoers agreed with Adoph *Klauber of the *Times,* who called the work "a big play, and one which, more than anything its author has done, proclaims him an astonishing genius of the theatre." Warfield toured with the play for two years and revived it successfully in 1921.

REUNION IN VIENNA (1931), a comedy by Robert *Sherwood. [Martin Beck Theatre, 264 perf.] Ever since her marriage, Elena Krug (Lynn *Fontanne) has been measuring her psychoanalyst husband Anton (Minor Watson) in terms of her first love—the one that got away, Rudolf Maximilian Von Hapsburg (Alfred *Lunt). Prince Rudolf had been forced into exile and into driving a cab in Nice after the downfall of the Austro-Hungarian Empire. When Anton learns that Rudolf has returned secretly to Vienna for a reunion of old aristocrats at the Hotel Lucher, he encourages Elena to visit Rudolf in hopes that a fresh perspective will break the spell. The former lovers meet and take up their romance where they left off, but only for a while. The couple eventually accept reality and Rudolf returns to France and Elena to Anton. Although many critics complained that the play did not come alive until Rudolf first appears and the lovers meet in the second act, the scintillating dialogue and the brilliant acting of the Lunts was ample compensation and the *Theatre Guild production was a success.

REVUE IN AMERICA. Some 18th- and early 19th-century patriotic spectacles may be seen to foreshadow the opulence of later revue tableaux, while the skits and songs of minstrelsy and the mixed vaudeville bills of the later 19th century, as well as such one-man shows of skits as those produced by Charles *Mathews, all pointed unwittingly toward the future genre. Perhaps the most interesting precursor was John *Brougham's *Dramatic Review for 1868, a loosely tied together assemblage of songs and sketches. Like the earliest "reviews" a quarter of a century later, it used an English spelling for the term, the French spelling not coming into vogue until the second decade of the 20th century. Indeed, although revues were an important feature of Parisian theatre for much of the late 19th century, French influence seems to have been small. The show that unquestionably began the American fashion for revues was The *Passing Show, which opened at the *Casino Theatre in 1894 with a book and lyrics by Sydney *Rosenfeld, and music by Ludwig *Englander. That Rosenfeld was credited with a "book" instead of with sketches is significant, since virtually all early revues sewed together their songs and skits by means of some elementary plot. Not until shortly before World War I did revues abandon the idea of employing a story line. For several seasons the Casino produced a revue each summer, and for many seasons revues were considered primarily summer fill-ins. But other theatres also housed occasional revues. The vogue for revues began to grow in earnest with Florenz *Ziegfeld's *Follies of 1907 (he did not add his own name to the series until the 1911 edition). His revues soon came to feature not only better, more important stars than had heretofore been seen in these shows, but offered better, more enduring music, a new standard of extravagant yet tasteful opulence, and a line of chorus beauties that became requisite. Within a few seasons his own editions had to compete with such other annuals as the *Shubert *Passing Shows (which had no connection with the 1894 revue), *George White's Scandals, the *Music Box Revues, the *Earl Carroll Vanities, and others. George M. *Cohan was among the important figures who produced occasional revues, and he is often credited with dropping plots from these

shows. The heyday of the extravagant revue lasted from just before World War I until shortly after the war. By the mid-1920s these lavish shows began to be considered too heavy and dated. A vogue for lighter, more literate revues took their place. Although American offerings such as The 49ers (1922) helped kindle the new fashion, many see the arrival of *Charlot's Revue (1924) as signaling the crucial turning point. American revues of the very late 1920s and the 1930s in this newer style included The *Little Shows, Three's a Crowd (1930), The *Band Wagon (1931), *As Thousands Cheer (1933), Life Begins at 8:40 (1934), and At Home Abroad (1935). Other notable revues of the 1930s included the union-mounted *Pins and Needles (1937) and *Olsen and *Johnson's *Hellzapoppin (1938). In the 1940s the revue began to fade away, although the decade produced such memorable examples as Irving *Berlin's *This Is the Army (1942), using enlisted men; Call Me Mister (1946), which included mostly war veterans; and the last great revue, the uproariously funny if unmelodic Lend an Ear (1948).

Thereafter some possible internal exhaustion, coupled with the rise of television and the popularity of the more purposeful, integrated musical play, swept revues from American stages. In the last decades of the century a peculiar form of revue flourished briefly. These shows had no skits, but instead made an entire evening out of the music of an old or dead composer. Ironically, none of these shows used the music of the giants of the revue field or even of the American musical theatre. Rather they relied on important composers whose connections with Broadway had generally been brief and unsuccessful. The major successes of this form of revue have been *Ain't Misbehavin' (1978), Eubie (1978), and Sophisticated Ladies (1981), which featured the music of Fats Waller, Eubie *Blake, and Duke Ellington, respectively, and Black and Blue (1989), a potpourri of jazz-age material. The longest running of these nostalgic revues was *Smokey Joe's Cafe (1995) featuring the songs of Lieber and Stoller who never wrote for Broadway. At its height the revue of the past gave important starts to many composers and songwriters, such as George *Gershwin; De Sylva, Brown, and *Henderson; and Harold *Rome. Virtually all of Arthur *Schwartz's great songs have come from revues, while for many years Irving Berlin wrote for little else on Broadway. The form allowed many performers not adept at handling the dialogue or characterization required by book shows to shine. Perhaps the most noteworthy example was Ed *Wynn, whose revues were among the most popular of the 1920s, but who generally failed when caught in book musicals. Many historians look on Al *Jolson's so-called book shows as glorified revues and insist that he, too, shone best as a solo performer. Fanny *Brice gave her best performances in revues. Other notable stars who moved with more ease from one form to the other included Bert *Williams, Eddie *Cantor, Beatrice *Lillie, and Bert *Lahr.

REYNOLDS, James (1892–1957), designer. Born in Warrenton, Virginia, the set and costume designer was given his first opportunities on Broadway by John Murray *Anderson, for whom he created many of the stage pictures for *What's in a Name?* (1920) and the 1920, 1921, 1922, and 1923 editions of the *Greenwich Village Follies.* Concurrently he helped design the 1921, 1922, and 1923 editions of the *Ziegfeld Follies* and the 1924 edition of the *Music Box Revue.* In the mid-1920s he was Charles *Dillingham's chief designer, providing sets and costumes for, among others, *Sunny* (1925), *Criss-Cross* (1926), and *Oh, Please!* (1926). Reynolds's later work was seen in The *Royal Family* (1927), *Fifty Million Frenchmen* (1929), *Life Begins at 8:40* (1934), and *Jumbo* (1935). His designs were admired for their sumptuous beauty and skillful color coordination. He retired in the mid-1930s to devote himself to writing, painting, and lecturing.

RIALTO, THE. The name, taken from a famous district in Venice, seems to have caught hold as an expression denoting New York's theatre district in the 1870s when the principal theatres were located between Union Square and Madison Square. It remained a common term well into the 20th century. One newspaper had a regular Sunday section called "News and Gossip of the Rialto." The expression was rarely applied after the 1950s.

RICE, E[dward] E[verett] (1848–1924), producer. Born into a poor family in Brighton, Massachusetts, he left home while still in his teens to become an itinerant actor, then worked as a printer and copywriter in Boston until he married the daughter of an important theatrical manager. Soon afterward Rice joined forces with J. Cheever *Goodwin to write *Evangeline* (1874). Following its success he plunged actively into producing, and on rare occasions writing, for the musical theatre of his day. He quickly became one of American musical theatre's most important pioneers. His Rice's Surprise Party was probably the most popular band performing those prototypical musical comedies called *farce-comedies. In 1884 he produced *Adonis,* the first musical to run more than five hundred performances in New York. With the coming of English musical comedy, he established himself as one of its principal American importers, but he also continued to explore new possibilities with native talents. Rice's 1898 mounting of *The Origin of the Cake Walk; or,*

Clorindy on the roof garden of the *Casino Theatre was the first time a musical written and enacted by African Americans had been offered to white audiences. Among the major figures he either discovered or gave important boosts to were Henry E. *Dixey, Lillian *Russell, Fay *Templeton, Julian *Eltinge, and Jerome *Kern.

RICE, Elmer [Leopold] [né Reizenstein] (1892–1967), playwright. The native New Yorker studied law and began to practice before switching to the theatre. In a career that lasted more than forty years, he had more than twenty plays produced on Broadway, ranging from starkly realistic drama to comic fantasy. His earliest work leaned heavily on his experience as a lawyer, and his first drama, *On Trial* (1914), provided one of the most sensational first nights in theatre history. *For the Defense* (1919) and *It Is the Law* (1922) followed, as did a vehicle for Mrs. *Fiske written with Hatcher *Hughes, *Wake Up, Jonathan!* (1921). The *Adding Machine* (1923) was a landmark expressionistic fantasy. *Close Harmony* (1924), written with Dorothy *Parker, was well received but failed, while his mystery *Cock Robin* (1928), written with Philip *Barry, enjoyed a modest run. He earned a *Pulitzer Prize for his unflinching slice of New York life, *Street Scene* (1929), but two other plays the same year, *The Subway* and *See Naples and Die,* were unsuccessful. Rice deftly probed American expatriates in Paris in The *Left Bank* (1931), then a month later returned to the legal world with the powerful drama *Counsellor-at-Law.* For the rest of the 1930s he wrote largely well-intentioned propaganda pieces, which failed to please critics and playgoers: *We, the People* (1932), *Judgment Day* (1934), *Between Two Worlds* (1934), and *American Landscape* (1938). Of his later works, such as *Two on an Island* (1940), *Flight to the West* (1940), *A New Life* (1943), *The Grand Tour* (1951), *Not for Children* (1951), *The Winner* (1954), and *Cue for Passion* (1958), his most interesting play was *Dream Girl* (1945), written for his wife, Betty *Field. Rice directed most of his own plays, as well as those by others, including *Abe Lincoln in Illinois* (1938). He served as a regional director of the *Federal Theatre Project and was a founder of the *Playwrights' Company. Autobiography: *Minority Report,* 1963.

RICE, T[homas] D[artmouth] (1808–60), singer and dancer. The tall, slim entertainer is usually considered the first blackface performer to gain international renown. He was born in New York, where his earliest theatrical work was as a supernumerary at the *Park Theatre. Various accounts exist claiming to offer the origin of his famous "Jim Crow" song and the shuffling dance that accompanied it. The most commonly told is that he saw a crippled slave in Louisville singing a similar song and walking with a similar gait. Rice added his own words, which ran in part: "Wheel about, turn about. Do jes so,/ An' ebery time I wheel about I jump Jim Crow." Rice first performed his routine in 1828, and his success was instant and widespread. Later he incorporated the song and dance into such entertainments as *Bone Squash, The Virginia Mummy,* and *Jim Crow in London.* Although an eccentric, reclusive man, refusing to join the burgeoning minstrel ensembles, he retained his popularity until his death.

RICE, Tim (b. 1944), lyricist and librettist. He was born in Amersham, England, and educated at Lancing College before beginning his career in music broadcasting and recording. Rice first teamed up with composer Andrew Lloyd *Webber in 1968 to write the pop cantata *Joseph and the Amazing Technicolor Dreamcoat* for a boys' school, the team continuing together to write **Jesus Christ Superstar* (1971) and **Evita* (1979). Rice's musicals with other composers to play in New York were *Chess* (1988), **Beauty and the Beast* (1994), The **Lion King* (1997), and **Aida* (2000).

RICH, Frank (b. 1949), critic. A native of Washington, D.C., he studied at Harvard. He was a film critic for many years with *Time,* the New York *Post,* and other publications before he joined the New York *Times* in 1980 and was soon appointed its drama critic. Rich's reviews were marked by sometime brutal attacks on plays not meeting with his approval so that he was called "The Butcher of Broadway." The cast of a musical he alone panned is said to have taken to wearing buttons reading "Get Rich, Quick." He had even begun to attack critics who disagreed with him: yet Rich's advocates pointed out his talent for fluid writing, attention to details, and willingness to go into depth when writing about plays and productions. To the relief of many, he gave up reviewing theatre in 1993 and since writes articles on the op ed page. Rich is the author of a few books, including a thorough study of designer Boris *Aronson.

RICHARD CARVEL (1900), a play by Edward E. *Rose. [*Empire Theatre, 128 perf.] Richard Carvel (John *Drew) overcomes the machinations of a wicked uncle, kidnapping by pirates, and a spell in debtors' prison to fight alongside John Paul Jones (George Le Soir) and win the affection of Dorothy Manners (Ida Conquest). Based on Winston Churchill's popular novel, the Charles *Frohman production gave Drew a rare chance to play a swashbuckling role instead of the drawing room sophisticates that he usually portrayed. Though his performance was lauded, it was acknowledged he was really too old for the part.

RICHARD RODGERS THEATRE (New York). The 1,400-seat playhouse on West 46th Street was built by the enterprising Chanin brothers in 1924 and named (predictably) Chanin's 46th Street Theatre. The Chanin name was dropped during the Great Depression when the *Shuberts took ownership, but they also lost the structure and today it is a *Nederlander house. Herbert J. *Krapp designed the auditorium with steep orchestra seating, so that its rear section is as high as most theatres' balcony. Suitable for both plays and musicals, the house has seen more than its fair share of hits in both genres, from *The Spider* (1927) to **Lost in Yonkers* (1991), and from **Good News* (1927) to *Movin' Out* (2003). In 1990 the playhouse was renamed in honor of composer Richard *Rodgers, though of his thirty-some musicals, only *Do I Hear a Waltz?* (1965) ever played at the old 46th Street Theatre.

RICHARD III. The first of Shakespeare's plays to be produced in America, it was offered by Thomas *Kean in New York on March 5, 1750. (There is reason to believe he might have presented it in Philadelphia even earlier.) It remained a favorite of virtually all the great 19th-century tragedians, no doubt in large measure because the title part is one of the juiciest villain-heroes in all dramatic literature. Junius Brutus *Booth, George Frederick *Cooke, and Edmund *Kean all made their American debuts in the role, which was also identified with Edwin *Forrest, William *Macready, and Edwin *Booth among others. Perhaps because the role was so meaty most great performers associated with it seem to have eschewed unnecessary histrionics, although by modern standards they would probably be judged overly emotive. Thus, when the elder Booth first offered his interpretation, the *National Advocate* noted, "In the conception of the character of the crooked back tyrant, Mr. Booth seems to be perfect. He exhibited none of those stage tricks, which many, who undertake the part, substitute for their lack of judgment." The drama was superbly revived in 1920 with John *Barrymore, followed by more recent New York outings with George C. *Scott in 1957, Donald Madden in 1970, Al *Pacino in 1979, Kevin *Kline in 1983, Denzel Washington in 1990, and Ian McKellen in 1992, as well as many others in festival theatres.

RICHARDS, Lloyd [George] (b. 1923), director and manager. Born in Toronto, Canada, the pioneering artist graduated from Wayne State University and worked as an actor before directing at regional theatres. Richards was the first African American to direct a Broadway play, the legendary *A *Raisin in the Sun* (1959). After staging the musical *I Had a Ball* (1964), he moved into management; in

1969 he became the artistic director of the *National Playwrights Conference and then served as artistic director of the *Yale Repertory Theatre from 1979 to 1991. He has staged many of August *Wilson's plays, such as *Ma Rainey's Black Bottom (1984), *Joe Turner's Come and Gone (1986), *Fences (1987), The *Piano Lesson (1988), and *Seven Guitars (1996).

RICHARDSON, Ralph [David] (1902–83), actor. The excellent, if somewhat stiffly mannered English performer made his American debut as Mercutio and the Chorus in Katharine *Cornell's *Romeo and Juliet in 1935. He returned in 1946 as a member of the *Old Vic to offer his Falstaff in *Henry IV, Part I, Vanya in Uncle Vanya, Tiresias in Oedipus, and Lord Burleigh in The Critic. Richardson's later appearances were in four modern plays: The Waltz of the Toreadors (1957), Home (1970), No Man's Land (1976), and Early Days (1981); and in one classic role, Sir Peter Teazle in a 1963 revival of The School for Scandal. Biography: Ralph Richardson: An Actor's Life, Garry O'Connor, 1982.

RICHELIEU; or, The Conspiracy (1839). The play by Edward *Bulwer-Lytton centered on the 17th-century French cardinal who uses his spies and his native skills to thwart attempts to assassinate him. He also brings about an alliance with Spain and helps his ward defy the king and marry the man she loves. Edwin *Forrest was the first American Richelieu in 1839. Later Charles *Macready and Edwin *Booth were known for their interpretations. While Booth was considered the Richelieu par excellence, the play continued to be revived for many seasons after his death. Walter *Hampden staged a notable revival in 1929.

RICHINGS, Peter [né Puget] (1797–1871), comic actor and manager. Born in Kensington, England, he was the son of a naval captain who sent him to Oxford to prepare for a career in law. His family's opposition to his decision to go on the stage prompted him in 1821 to immigrate to America where he made his debut at the *Park Theatre as Henry Bertram in Guy Mannering. But Richings soon became better known as a comedian who excelled at playing fops. Among his best roles were Osric, Sparkish, Captain Absolute, and Sir Benjamin Backbite. In the 1840s he also served as manager for the National Theatre, *Walnut Street Theatre, and *Chestnut Street Theatre in Philadelphia and the *Holliday Street Theatre in Baltimore. He retired in 1868. Clara *Morris, who worked with him late in his life, remembered him as "six feet tall, high-featured, Roman nosed, elegantly dressed; a term from bygone days . . . describes him perfectly: he was an 'old Buck!' " His adopted daughter was [Mary] **Caroline RICHINGS** [née

Reynoldson] (d. 1882), born in England and brought to America while still a child. She made her professional debut as a pianist in 1847, but in 1852 turned to the lyric stage when she sang Marie in the Seguin Opera Company's mounting of The Daughter of the Regiment. She later formed her own company and continued to perform until shortly before her death. Although she sang roles that today would be largely confined to opera houses, opera in her day was part of many legitimate theatres' programs. Her repertory included a number of primitive American comic operas, such as The *Doctor of Alcantara. T. Allston *Brown wrote that she was "a thoroughly schooled and most conscientious singer, but she was mechanical and unsympathetic."

RICHMAN, Charles J. (1870–1940), actor. The Chicagoan made his debut in 1894 and two years later became leading man for Augustin *Daly, playing such roles as Orlando and Benedick as well as the heroes of contemporary pieces. Among his subsequent leads were the pacifist Kearney in The *Rose of the Rancho (1906), Burton Temple in The *Fighting Hope (1908), and the possessive Robert Stafford in *Bought and Paid For (1911). In after years he was a fine supporting actor in such plays as *Strictly Dishonorable (1930) and *Biography (1932).

RICHMAN, Harry [né Reichman] (1895–1972), singer. The brash, jaunty performer was born in Cincinnati and began his career in vaudeville as a pianist for Mae *West, the *Dolly Sisters, and Nora *Bayes. Striking out on his own he gave imitations of Al *Jolson and David *Warfield but soon developed a turn in which he sang dressed either in white tie and tails or a straw hat and blazer. His Broadway appearances were almost always in revues, notably *George White's Scandals of 1926, in which he introduced "The Birth of the Blues" and "Lucky Day," and International Revue (1930), in which he performed "Exactly Like You" and "On the Sunny Side of the Street." Much of his later career was confined to nightclubs. Autobiography: A Hell of a Life, with Richard Gehman, 1966.

RIGL, Emily (fl. late 19th century), actress. Coming to America with her then better-known sister, Betty, to dance in the original production of The *Black Crook (1866), she gave up dancing to learn elocution and acting, and soon entered Augustin *Daly's company, where she became a respected supporting player. Rigl won applause in such contemporary hits as The *Big Bonanza (1875), *Saratoga (1875), and *Pique (1875), as well as for such classic roles as Olivia in *Twelfth Night. Leaving Daly briefly, she created the role of the deserted wife Francesca in *The *Galley Slave* (1879). She remained active as late as 1907. Never a major star, she was still considered one of the best actresses of her day.

RINEHART, Mary Roberts (1876–1958), playwright. The Pittsburgh-born author best known for her mystery novels was also a successful dramatist. Her first play, written under the pen name Rinehart Roberts, was *The Double Life* (1906), but she had her first hit when she collaborated with Avery *Hopwood on the comedy *Seven Days* (1909). After writing *Cheer Up* (1912) she rejoined with Hopwood in 1920 to write two huge successes, *Spanish Love* and *The *Bat*. Rinehart's last play, an adaptation of another of her books, was the mystery *The Breaking Point* (1923). Autobiography: *My Story*, 1931.

RING, Blanche (1876?–1961), singer. The Boston-born daughter and granddaughter of performers, the tiny blonde belter of songs made her first appearance in a small role opposite Richard *Mansfield in *A Parisian Romance* in 1892, and later played in companies headed by Nat *Goodwin and Chauncey *Olcott. She attained stardom overnight after introducing "In the Good Old Summertime" in *The Defender* (1902). Ring also sang "The Belle of Avenue A" in *Tommy Rot* (1902), "Bedelia" in *The Jersey Lily* (1903), and "I've Got Rings on My Fingers" in *The Midnight Sons* (1909). In all, she appeared in two dozen musicals between 1902 and 1938, as well as in several nonmusical plays. She was also a great favorite in vaudeville, where she was one of the first to get audiences to sing along with her and where her mimicry was as celebrated as her singing. Among the other songs she made famous were "Come, Josephine, in My Flying Machine," "Waltz Me Around Again, Willie," and "Yip-I-Addy-I-Ay."

RIO RITA (1927), an operetta by Guy *Bolton, and Fred *Thompson (book), Harry *Tierney (music), Joseph *McCarthy (lyrics). [*Ziegfeld Theatre, 494 perf.] Jim (J. Harold *Murray), a captain in the Texas Rangers, falls in love with Rio Rita (Ethelind Terry), knowing full well that she is also courted by the unsavory Mexican, General Esteban (Vincent Serrano). Since Jim is searching for the bandit called "The Kinkajou," Esteban tells Rita that Jim's prime suspect is her brother Roberto (George Baxter). This cools the romance between Jim and Rita until Jim proves "The Kinkajou" is none other than Esteban himself. *Notable songs*: The Kinkajou; The Rangers' Song; Rio Rita; If You're in Love, You'll Waltz. Although the plot seemed merely a rewriting of the story of *Naughty Marietta, the fine score and sumptuous *Ziegfeld production made this

musical, which opened the Ziegfeld Theatre, one of the most memorable of its era.

RIP VAN WINKLE (1866), a play by Dion *Boucicault (and Joseph *Jefferson, uncredited). [Olympic Theatre, 35 perf.] Rip Van Winkle (Jefferson) is a dissolute, ne'er-do-well, with no illusions about his worthlessness. His guilty unhappiness is not assuaged by his scold of a wife, Gretchen (Mrs. Saunders), who finally drives him from his home. With his dog, Schneider, he retreats to a cove in the Kaatskill Mountains. There, beset by demons, he drinks himself into a stupor. When he wakes years later, he returns home, but no one recognizes him. Gretchen thinks him a beggar, gives him a penny, and takes pity on him. Not until his daughter Meenie (Marie Le Brun) realizes who he is do matters change. Rip promises to stay sober and Gretchen to be a good wife. Jefferson had played in earlier dramatizations of the story, but while in London he had Boucicault write him a new version, which he first offered there in 1865. The initial American reception was lukewarm, but Jefferson quickly made changes in Boucicault's text and polished his own performance. The play served as his vehicle for years and remained one of the most popular American stage pieces for the rest of the century.

RISTORI, Adelaide (1822–1906), actress. The great Italian tragedienne was usually perceived as the successor to *Rachel on international stages. She began the first of several American tours in 1866 as Medea, and continued her season in such roles as Mary Stuart, Phèdre, Adrienne Lecouvreur, Francesca da Rimini, and Lady Macbeth. However, her greatest role in American eyes was unquestionably her Queen Elizabeth in Giacometti's play about the English monarch. J. Ranken *Towse wrote of this interpretation, "The haughty carriage, imperious address, fierce temper, blunt humor, petty vanity, masculine sagacity, and feminine jealousy were all indicated with surpassing skill and blended into a consistent whole with finished artistry." By no means a beautiful woman (the kindest critics called her handsome), she had little delicacy or poetry in her style, excelling instead in power and grandeur. On her last visit, during the 1884–85 season, she attempted to perform in English with disastrous results. Autobiography: *Memoirs and Artistic Studies*, translated by G. Mantellini, 1907.

RITCHARD, Cyril [né Cyril Trimnell-Ritchard] (1897–1977), actor and director. His era's consummate portrayer of fops, he was born in Sydney, Australia, and made his first American appearance in *Puzzles of 1925*. However, he did not call attention to himself with American playgoers until he returned with John *Gielgud's company in 1947 to play Tattle in *Love for Love*. Among his later notable roles were the effeminate Georgie Pillson in *Make Way for Lucia* (1948), Lord Foppington in *The Relapse* (1950), Captain Hook in the 1954 musical version of *Peter Pan*, the space alien Kreton in *Visit to a Small Planet* (1957), the incorrigible playboy Biddleford Poole in *The *Pleasure of His Company* (1958), the god Pluto in *The Happiest Girl in the World* (1961), the ragged aristocrat Sir in *The Roar of the Greasepaint—The Smell of the Crowd* (1965), and millionaire Osgood Fielding Jr. in *Sugar* (1972). Although his wide, humorous eyes and curiously bleating delivery made him irresistible on stage, he was also a sought-after director. His stagings included *John Murray Anderson's Almanac* (1953), *The Reluctant Debutante* (1956), *Visit to a Small Planet*, *The Pleasure of His Company*, and *The Happiest Girl in the World*.

RITCHIE, Adele [née Pultz] (1874–1930), singer and actress. Born in Philadelphia, the beautiful but now totally forgotten musical comedy star made such a hit in her debut in *The Isle of Champagne* (1893) that she was given a major part in the first American revue, *The *Passing Show* (1894). Ritchie enjoyed her biggest success in *A Chinese Honeymoon* (1902). In all she was featured or starred in twenty musicals, including the title roles in *Glittering Gloria* (1904) and *Fascinating Flora* (1907).

RITZ, THE (1975), a comedy by Terrence *McNally. [*Longacre Theatre, 400 perf.] The Ritz is a steam bath catering to homosexuals. To it come Gaetano Proclo (Jack *Weston), a garbage man who signs himself in as Carmine Vespucci, the name of the murderous brother-in-law from whom he is attempting to hide; Michael Brick (Stephen Collins), a detective hired by the real Vespucci to follow Proclo; and the real Vespucci (Jerry Stiller), bent on killing Proclo. While pursuing their own ends, they are pursued by a collection of homosexuals all out for an hour's fun. By the end of the evening, Proclo has gotten Carmine gagged and bound and has left him to be fought over by a policeman and a pervert whose special delight is fat men. This uproarious farce makes an interesting comparison with a farce of a half century before, *Ladies' Night in a Turkish Bath*. The pieces vividly demonstrate the remarkable change in mores that has occurred, while suggesting that well-made theatrical bedlam can find a home in any social climate. Oddly, a 1983 Broadway revival of *The Ritz* closed on opening night.

RIVER NIGER, THE (1973), a play by Joseph A. Walker. [*Brooks Atkinson Theatre, 280 perf.; Tony Award.] The African-American father Johnny Williams (Douglas Turner *Ward) is a housepainter by profession and a poet by avocation but seems to have failed as both. He lives in Harlem with his no-nonsense wife (Roxie Roker) and inebriated mother (Frances *Foster), but his pride and joy is his son Jeff (Les Roberts) who has become an officer in the air force. When Jeff returns home and tells his father he is giving up on a military career, Johnny goes on a bender. He writes a long poem that attempts to find meaning in the whole of the black experience just as the police surround the house, looking for Jeff's old gang who have killed a cop. In the melee, Johnny confesses that he shot the officer so that the innocent Jeff will have a future. Originally produced Off Broadway, the play later moved to Broadway where it marked a triumph for Ward who directed and starred in his *Negro Ensemble Company's production.

RIVERA, Chita [née Dolores Conchita Figueroa Del Rivero] (b. 1933), dancer, actress, and singer. The vivacious Latin-miened performer was born in Washington, D.C., and studied at the School of American Ballet. She appeared in the choruses of *Guys and Dolls*, *Call Me Madam*, and *Can-Can* before garnering attention in *Shoestring Revue* (1955). Roles followed in *Seventh Heaven* (1955) and *Mr. Wonderful* (1956), after which she created the part of the Puerto Rican immigrant Anita in *West Side Story* (1957). Rivera starred as the wily Rosie in *Bye Bye Birdie* (1960), the gypsy Anyanka in *Bajour* (1964), taxi dancer Charity in a touring company of *Sweet Charity* (1967), murderess Velma Kelly in *Chicago* (1975), the Queen in *Merlin* (1983), Italian housewife Anna in *The Rink* (1984), in the revue *Jerry's Girls* (1985), and as Aurora and the ghostly Spider Woman in *Kiss of the Spider Woman* (1993). Her most recent Broadway appearance was as the agent Liliane LaFleur in *Nine* (2003). Rivera took years to become a bona fide Broadway star, but she remains one of the most durable and beloved of stage troupers.

RIVES, Amélie (1863–1945), playwright. The Virginia-born poet and novelist, who married the Russian Prince Troubetzkoy, wrote a number of blank-verse tragedies at the turn of the century, including *Herod and Miriamne* (1888), *Athelwold* (1893), and *Augustine the Man* (1906). At the same time she also dramatized her novelette, *The Quick or the Dead?* (1888), then years later wrote *Allegiance* (1918) with her husband. Rives's later works were a dramatization of *The Prince and the Pauper* (1920); a recounting of an old Irish legend, *The Sea-Woman's Cloak* (1925); and a light triangle comedy, *Love in a Mist* (1926) with Gilbert *Emery.

ROAD TO ROME, THE (1927), a play by Robert *Sherwood. [Playhouse, 392 perf.] Fabius Maximus (Richie Ling) cannot understand why his wife, Amytis (Jane *Cowl), is not excited over his being declared Dictator of Rome, or why she seems so intrigued by their enemy, the Carthaginian Hannibal (Philip *Merivale), whose army is pushing toward the city. When news arrives of a Roman defeat and of Hannibal's presence nearby, Amytis pretends to flee. Instead she goes to Hannibal's camp, where she does something the Roman army cannot do. She talks to him, lets him make love to her, and convinces him to withdraw. Described by Charles Brackett of *The New Yorker* as "A hymn of hate against militarism—disguised, ever so gaily, as a love song," it was rejected by most major producers until William A. *Brady Jr. and Dwight Deere *Wiman took a risk on the unknown playwright; it established Sherwood's career.

ROAD TO YESTERDAY, THE (1906), a play by Beulah Marie Dix and E. G. *Sutherland. [Herald Square Theatre, 216 perf.] An impressionable American girl, Elspeth Tyrrell (Minnie *Dupree), comes to London for a hectic tour. One night she falls asleep and dreams she is living in Elizabethan times and is kidnapped by a handsome ruffian. When she awakes she realizes that the ruffian resembles a friend of a friend. She had never before considered marrying the man, but now she does. The Lee *Shubert–produced play, which mixed a satirical look at reincarnation and a swashbuckling tale, was the source of Victor *Herbert's last musical, *The Dream Girl* (1924). **Beulah Marie DIX** (1876– 1970), born in Kingston, Massachusetts, and educated at Radcliffe, wrote numerous plays in the early years of the 20th century. Her other successful work was *A Rose o' Plymouth Town* (1902), dealing with the early American heroine Priscilla Alden.

ROAD TOURS. Before the 1870s when trains made travel more practical, most theatre outside of New York consisted of small stock companies who performed from a home base. The only forms of extensive touring before the Civil War were the regional appearances of such stars as Edwin *Forrest, Charlotte *Cushman, Junius Brutus *Booth, and George Frederick *Cooke who did not travel with a company but performed their famous roles with local actors. But the thorough railroad network that was completed by the last decades of the 19th century made touring profitable, and almost every town and small city, as well as each major metropolis, built theatres to accommodate road productions. Some of America's favorite stars, from Joseph *Jefferson and William *Gillette in the 19th century to Katharine *Cornell and the *Lunts

in the 20th century, toured extensively and became beloved favorites across the country as well as in Manhattan. Tours broke into roughly two categories: New York successes that were duplicated and sent out with first-class companies, and cheaper productions utilizing scripts that were written specifically with the road in mind. Playwrights such as Charles *Blaney, Lincoln J. *Carter, Owen *Davis, Scott *Marble, and Hal *Reid turned out dozens of these "blood and thunder" melodramas that appealed to the supposedly less sophisticated playgoers across the country. When the road started to wane in the first decade of the new century, it was this latter kind of "popular" theatre that disappeared. After 1910, the road usually meant a traveling version of a New York hit. It is estimated that there were five thousand theatres across the United States in 1900; by 1932 there were only one hundred, and a third of those were in New York City. In the decades surrounding World War II, these tours could play for several weeks or months in major cities like Chicago, Boston, and Philadelphia. Secondary tours, labeled "bus and truck," were less expensive versions of the first-class tours and tended to play split weeks in less-populous cities. But when the number of Broadway offerings shrunk in the 1960s, the road suffered. Musicals were particularly successful on tour, but so few new works originated from Broadway in the 1970s and 1980s that road producers were (and still are) often reduced to presenting old favorites, particularly if they had recently enjoyed a successful revival in Manhattan. By the end of the 20th century, the road had dwindled to major Broadway musicals playing in large houses (sometimes even converted movie palaces) for short runs in major cities. Nonmusical plays rarely tour unless a name performer is attached to it, and "bus and truck" companies tend to play college campuses and arts centers where the overhead is much smaller than at the traditional "road houses." The rise of the regional theatre network in the last four decades of the century may have contributed to the decline of the road. Yet these resident theatres rarely produced the large and spectacular Broadway musicals on which tours continued to depend. The future of the road seems to be Broadway's brassiest works visiting America's biggest urban markets.

ROBARDS, Jason, Jr. (1922–2000), actor. The dark, somewhat weather-beaten-looking performer was the son of another famous actor. Born in Chicago, he studied at the *American Academy of Dramatic Arts and with Uta *Hagen and began appearing professionally in the late 1940s. However, acclaim first came with his performance as Hickey in a 1956 *Circle in the Square revival of *The *Iceman Cometh.*

Brooks *Atkinson wrote, "His unction, condescension and piety introduce an element of moral affectation that clarifies the perspective of the drama." Robards subsequently distinguished himself in other Eugene *O'Neill roles, including James Tyrone Jr. in the original Broadway production of *Long Day's Journey into Night (1956), Smith in Hughie (1964), and James Tyrone Jr. in a 1973 revival of A *Moon for the Misbegotten. He displayed his versatility in such other roles as the ne'er-do-well Julian Berniers in *Toys in the Attic (1960), the genial William Baker in *Big Fish, Little Fish (1961), the nonconforming Murray Burns in A *Thousand Clowns (1962), and the guilt-ridden lawyer Quentin in *After the Fall (1964). In 1983 he scored as Martin Vanderhof in a revival of *You Can't Take It with You. He re-created the role of Hickey in a 1985 revival of The Iceman Cometh, then played James Tyrone Sr. and Nat Miller in 1988 revivals of Long Day's Journey into Night and *Ah, Wilderness! Robards's later performances of note included the grumpy teacher Jacob Brackish in Park Your Car in Harvard Yard (1991), the mysterious Hirst in No Man's Land (1994), and the wasted eye surgeon Mr. Rice in Molly Sweeney (1996), his last New York appearance. Also popular in films, the grainy-voiced actor was as distinctive as he was enthralling.

ROBBINS, Jerome [né Rabinowitz] (1918–98), choreographer and director. Born in New York, he studied ballet with Anthony Tudor and other famous dancers before dancing in several Broadway musicals in the late 1930s. It was only after he attained success as a choreographer and dancer with the Ballet Theatre that Robbins returned to the theatre to devise the dances for *On the Town (1944), which had been inspired by his ballet Fancy Free. His "Mack Sennett Ballet" for *High Button Shoes (1947) remains the comic masterpiece among all dances created for Broadway musical comedies. This was followed by his choreography for Look, Ma, I'm Dancin' (1948), Miss Liberty (1949), *Call Me Madam (1950), and The *King and I (1951). In 1954 he co-directed The *Pajama Game, then starting with *Peter Pan (1954) Robbins served as director for all the shows he choreographed: *Bells Are Ringing (1956), *West Side Story (1957), *Gypsy (1959), and *Fiddler on the Roof (1964), as well as the nonmusical *Oh Dad, Poor Dad . . . (1962) and uncredited work on A *Funny Thing Happened on the Way to the Forum (1962). If he was often the wittiest of choreographers, he was also brilliantly adept at creating the starkest of dance dramas, as witnessed by his work for West Side Story. Other examples of his great variety included the imaginatively stylized "Small House of Uncle Thomas" ballet in The King and I and the folkloristic Jewish dances in Fiddler on the Roof. His later years were devoted to major ballet companies, but he returned to the theatre when he restaged his past dances for the retrospective Jerome Robbins' Broadway (1989). Biography: Dance With Demons: The Life of Jerome Robbins, Greg Lawrence, 2001.

ROBERTA (1933), a musical comedy by Otto *Harbach (book, lyrics), Jerome *Kern (music). [*New Amsterdam Theatre, 295 perf.] When all-American fullback John Kent (Ray Middleton) inherits the exclusive Paris dress shop "Roberta" from his Aunt Minnie (Fay *Templeton), he and his pal Huckleberry Haines (Bob *Hope) go to Europe to take charge. John allows his aunt's young assistant Stephanie (Tamara) to run the shop, and soon a romance blossoms between the two. The appearance of John's old flame, Sophie (Helen Gray), nearly destroys the affair, but John recollects that Sophie deserted him before and could do it again. He settles for Stephanie, who turns out to be a Russian princess. Notable songs: Smoke Gets in Your Eyes; The Touch of Your Hand; Yesterdays; You're Devastating. Derived from Alice Duer Miller's novel, Gowns by Roberta, the musical exemplifies the ability a single hit song once had to turn a potential failure into a success. Critics lambasted the Max *Gordon show, especially its dull book, but the raging popularity of "Smoke Gets in Your Eyes" turned its fate around.

ROBERTS, Florence (1871–1927), actress. Although born in the East, she was raised in California and made her debut at San Francisco's *Baldwin Theatre in 1889. Shortly thereafter she became the leading lady at the Alcazar Theatre when its stock company was the finest in the state and played such classic roles as Juliet, Ophelia, Portia, Rosalind, Parthenia in *Ingomar, Camille, and La Tosca, as well as leads in many now-forgotten plays. Roberts also made successful star tours of the West but rarely played New York. After World War I she toured South Africa, played in a few silent films, and then retired.

ROBERTS, James (1835–92), designer. Born in Bath, England, he learned his trade as a scene painter in London theatres before coming to America in 1860. A meeting with Augustin *Daly in 1869 led to his becoming Daly's chief set designer, and his work was seen in such memorable productions as Man and Wife (1870), *Saratoga (1870), and the 1872 revival of The Merry Wives of Windsor. Injuries sustained in the burning of Daly's *Fifth Avenue Theatre left Roberts's hearing permanently impaired and his health weakened. He thereafter usually created only one or two sets for a production. Nevertheless he continued to be the house set designer until his death, so had a hand in all of Daly's triumphs of the time. His specialty was realistic interiors.

ROBERTS, J[ames] B[ooth] (1818–1901), actor. The squat, heavy-set, stern-faced performer was born in Newcastle, Delaware, and made his debut at the *Walnut Street Theatre playing Richmond to Junius *Booth's *Richard III* in 1836. Critics were laudatory. When he played Sir Giles Overreach in New York in 1857, the *Tribune* wrote, "Mr. Roberts may be cited as a fine actor, with an ever-present intellectuality coloring and shaping his delineations. . . . [He] has some merits to which older actors were strangers. We mean particularly his ability to speak naturally. Without being positively graceful, he is easy; without a commanding stature, he commands universal attention." Nevertheless, he found but small favor with New York audiences, although he remained an important star on the road. Among his major classical roles were Richard III, King Lear, Othello, Iago, and Jaffier.

ROBERTS, Tony (b. 1939), actor and singer. The lightweight comic actor of plays and musicals was born in New York, the son of radio and television announcer Ken Roberts, and educated at Northwestern before making his Broadway debut in 1962. Among his many notable performances were the dense ambassador's son Axel Magee in *Don't Drink the Water* (1966), the Wall Street trader Charley in *How Now, Dow Jones* (1967), the busy executive Dick Christie always tied to the phone in *Play It Again, Sam* (1969), the musican-on-the-run Joe forced to perform in drag in *Sugar* (1972), the gay Parisian entrepreneur Toddy in *Victor/Victoria* (1995), and the socially conscious allergy doctor Ira in *The *Tale of the Allergist's Wife* (2000).

ROBERTSON, Agnes (1833–1916), actress. Born in Edinburgh, she began to perform when she was thirteen and soon became the ward of the famous English actor Charles *Kean. After marrying Dion *Boucicault, she traveled with him to America where she made her debut in 1853 as Maria in his *The Young Actress.* Her American career was tied inextricably with his. Among her important roles were Grace in several revivals of *London Assurance,* the Rachel-like figure *Violet* (1856), the heroic Jessie Brown in *Jessie Brown; or, The Siege of Lucknow* (1858), Dot in a 1859 dramatization of *The Cricket on the Hearth,* the doomed heroine Zoe in *The *Octoroon* (1859), and the secretly wed heroine Eily O'Connor in *The *Colleen Bawn* (1860). In late 1860 Robertson returned to England and thereafter appeared in America only on rare occasions. *Odell described her as "one of the most simple, artless and captivating artistes ever seen on our stage; in guileless Scotch and Irish peasant girls she has probably never been surpassed."

ROBERTSON, T. W. See *Caste.*

ROBESON, Paul (1898–1976), actor and singer. Born in Princeton, New Jersey, and educated at Rutgers (where he was a champion athlete) and Columbia (where he received a law degree), the dynamic African-American performer made a number of noteworthy appearances on Broadway, including the roles of lawyer Jim Harris in *All God's Chillun Got Wings* (1924) and the tormented Brutus Jones in a 1925 revival of *The *Emperor Jones.* Jerome *Kern and Oscar *Hammerstein are said to have written the role of Joe in *Show Boat* with him in mind, but he did not sing it until the London premiere and played it in America only in the 1932 revival. Robeson's greatest success came when he played Othello to José *Ferrer's Iago in 1943; the production became the longest-running Shakespearean revival in history. Robeson was a powerful, athletic figure with a deep, resounding voice in both speaking and singing. Always a controversial figure because of his outspoken views on discrimination, he was a Communist sympathizer in the 1950s and, consequently, shunned by many. After spending some years in Russia, Robeson returned to America and lived in seclusion the last decades of his life. Autobiography: *Here I Stand,* 1971; biography: *Paul Robeson,* Martin B. Duberman, 1988.

ROBIN HOOD (1891), a comic opera by Harry B. *Smith (book, lyrics), Reginald *De Koven (music). [Standard Theatre, 40 perf.] The Sheriff of Nottingham (Henry Clay *Barnabee) wrongfully deprives Robert, Earl of Huntington (Tom Karl), of his lands and gives them and the Earl's fiancée, Maid Marian (Caroline Hamilton), to his own friend, Guy of Gisbourne (Peter Lang). Robert becomes an outlaw and assumes the name of Robin Hood. When he is captured through treachery, the Sheriff intends to force him to witness the marriages of Marian to Guy, and of Annabel (Lea Van Dyke), the betrothed of Alan-a-Dale (Jessie Bartlett *Davis), to the Sheriff himself. But before the wedding can take place Robin Hood is rescued by his band, who carry a pardon from the king. *Notable songs:* Brown October Ale; Oh, Promise Me; Tinkers' Chorus. Generally acknowledged as the first great masterpiece of the American musical stage, the work was revived regularly for nearly half a century. The reasons for its early success were varied and probably did not include the reused scenery and costumes initially employed by the producing group the *Bostonians. Indeed, Smith recalled that the first mounting, because of the reused material, cost just over one hundred dollars. But the solid and, for the time, witty libretto; the songs, which were among the earliest classics of the American musical theatre; and the excellent singing and acting of the company all played a part. Smith has suggested an additional reason, noting most contemporary comic operas were created as show pieces for prima donnas while this operetta carefully balanced the men's and women's roles. "Oh, Promise Me," with a lyric by Clement Scott, was interpolated after opening and was one of the earliest theatre songs to retain its popularity for decades. It was the wedding song of choice for more than forty years.

ROBINSON, Bill (1878–1949), dancer. The beguiling African-American tap dancer, known affectionately as "Bojangles," began his career by performing for pennies on street corners while still a child in his native Richmond, Virginia. At seventeen he became part of a vaudeville act, and within a few seasons he was doing a solo turn, featuring his relaxed, self-assured stepping. His Broadway appearances were in *Blackbirds of 1928, Brown Buddies* (1930), *Blackbirds of 1933, The Hot Mikado* (1939), *All in Fun* (1940), and *Memphis Bound* (1945). Biography: *Mr. Bojangles,* James Haskins, 1988.

ROBINSON, Charles. See *Sailor, Beware!*

ROBINSON, David G. (fl. mid-19th century), actor and manager. Known affectionately as "Doc" or "Yankee" Robinson, but not to be confused with Fayette Lodawick *Robinson, who was also addressed as "Yankee," he was born between 1805 and 1809 in East Monmouth, Maine. He is said to have attended Yale and to have been graduated as a physician in the early 1830s. Later he toured with his family in his own temperance play, *A Reformed Drunkard,* before moving to San Francisco around 1847 and setting himself up as a doctor and also opening a drug store. In 1850 Robinson built one of the city's first playhouses, the 280-seat Dramatic Museum on California Street, and began to present his own burlesques, including *Seeing the Elephant,* a spoof of gold-rush prospectors, and *Who's Got the Countess?,* a send-up of Lola *Montez. At the same time he wrote and performed in satires on local politics. These proved so popular that when he ran for alderman, he was elected. After the Museum burned, he erected and managed several other theatres. Robinson also guided the career of his young daughter, Sue Robinson, who was briefly acclaimed as a child prodigy or "fairy star." However, by the mid-1850s his luck and popularity deserted him. He has been described as a "tall, angular man with hawklike eyes and an acid wit."

ROBINSON, Edward G. [né Emanuel Goldenberg] (1893–1973), actor. The stocky, gruff actor was born in Bucharest but was raised in New York. He studied at City College of New York, Columbia, and the *American Academy of Dramatic Arts before making his professional debut in Binghamton, New York, in 1913. Ten years later he joined the *Theatre Guild's acting ensemble, appearing with them in such plays as *Peer Gynt* (1923), *The *Adding Machine* (1923), *Androcles and the Lion* (1925), and *Ned McCobb's Daughter* (1926). Robinson was considered an actor of great range, depth, and promise, but shortly after creating the role of the gangster, Nick Scarsi, in *The *Racket* (1927), he left for a long career in Hollywood and returned only to tour in *Darkness at Noon* in 1951 and to create the role of the Manufacturer in *Middle of the Night* (1956). Autobiography: *All My Yesterdays,* with Leonard Spigelgass, 1973; biography: *The Edward G. Robinson Encyclopedia,* Robert Beck, 2002.

ROBINSON, Fayette Lodawick (1818–84), actor and manager. Known popularly as "Yankee" Robinson, but not to be confused with San Francisco's David G. *Robinson, who often was given the same nickname, he was born near Avon Mineral Springs, New York. He began his career in 1835 when he joined a small traveling tent show, later establishing his own tent troupe, which he called Robinson's Athenaeum. His versions of *The Drunkard* and similar shows proved exceedingly popular with rural and small-town audiences. Robinson also established a circus with which, according to his obituaries, he "gained a reputation second only to Barnum." He was a rather homely, balding man with a huge goatee.

ROBSON, Eleanor [Elise] (1879–1979), actress. Born in England, she was brought to America as a child by her mother, who had remarried after her father's death and who acted under the name of Madge Carr *Cook. After graduating from a seminary on Staten Island in 1897, she went to join her mother, who was playing in San Francisco, and found herself thrust on stage to replace an ailing performer in *Men and Women. Robson played in stock for several seasons before creating the role of Bonita in *Arizona* (1899). Impressed by her great beauty and fine acting, George C. *Tyler cast her as Constance in Browning's *In a Balcony* (1900) and she remained under Tyler's aegis for the rest of her career. Among her memorable interpretations were her Juliet in 1903 and her Kate Hardcastle in 1905, but she is best recalled for her sweet-natured, innocent drudge Mary Ann in *Merely Mary Ann* (1903). She retired after her marriage to August Belmont III, becoming a celebrated socialite and philanthropist. In the latter capacity she was long associated with the Metropolitan Opera. Autobiography: *The Fabric of Memory,* 1957.

ROBSON, Stuart. See Crane, W. H.

ROCKET TO THE MOON (1938), a play by Clifford *Odets. [*Belasco Theatre, 131 perf.] Ben Stark (Morris *Carnovsky) is a young dentist badgered by his pushy, shrewish wife, Belle (Ruth Nelson), who believes he can make more money for himself and have more celebrity as a specialist. Belle's rich father, Mr. Prince (Luther *Adler), is caught in the middle. He wants the best for his daughter and has offered to set his son-in-law up as a specialist, but he himself was unhappily married and longs for the life he never had. He suggests that Ben have an affair with his dental secretary, Cleo Singer (Eleanor Lynn). Ben does, but the affair turns out badly and Ben returns to his wife. When many critics assailed the *Group Theatre offering for its weak last act, Odets rewrote the work, but despite much fine dialogue and character observation, the play never fully succeeded.

RODGERS, Mary. See *Once Upon a Mattress.*

RODGERS, Richard [Charles] (1902–79), composer. He was born in New York and educated at Columbia, where he wrote music for college shows. The first part of Rodgers's remarkable career was collaborating with lyricist Lorenz *Hart on the songs and occasionally the books of imaginative musical comedies. Their work for Broadway was heard initially in *Poor Little Ritz Girl* (1920), but success did not begin to come until they wrote "Manhattan" for the first *Garrick Gaieties* (1925). Other musicals with Hart included *Dearest Enemy* (1925), *Garrick Gaieties of 1926, The Girl Friend* (1926), *Peggy-Ann* (1926), *Betsy* (1926), *A *Connecticut Yankee* (1927), *Present Arms* (1928), *She's My Baby* (1928), *Chee-Chee* (1928), *Heads Up!* (1929), *Spring Is Here* (1929), *Simple Simon* (1930), *America's Sweetheart* (1931), *Jumbo* (1935), *On Your Toes* (1936), *Babes in Arms* (1937), *I'd Rather Be Right* (1937), *I Married an Angel* (1938), *The *Boys from Syracuse* (1938), *Too Many Girls* (1939), *Higher and Higher* (1940), *Pal Joey* (1940), and *By Jupiter* (1942). After breaking with Hart he joined Oscar *Hammerstein and largely abandoned musical comedy for the musical play. Their *Oklahoma!* (1943) revolutionized American operetta writing, just as their next success, *Carousel* (1945), explored new ways of integrating song and character and their disappointing *Allegro* (1947) experimented with new ways of storytelling. The subsequent Rodgers and Hammerstein musicals were *South Pacific* (1949), *The *King and I* (1951), *Me and Juliet* (1953), *Pipe Dream* (1955), *Flower Drum Song* (1958), and *The *Sound of Music* (1959). After Hammerstein's death, Rodgers's luck soured although he continued to compose fine music, most notably when he set his own lyrics to his melodies for *No Strings* (1962). Hs later scores, with various lyricists, were *Do I Hear a Waltz?* (1965), *Two by Two* (1970), *Rex* (1976), and *I Remember Mama* (1979). Rodgers sometimes co-produced his shows and those by others, such as *I Remember Mama* (1944), *Annie Get Your Gun* (1946), *Happy Birthday* (1946), and *John Loves Mary* (1947). From the start Rodgers's music was both traditional and inventive. One notable point was his steady return to the waltz at a time when many composers neglected it. Perhaps his most remarkable effort in this style was "The Carousel Waltz." Because of the types of musicals for which he was writing and because of his lyricist, his material with Hart tended to be lighter and jauntier. Working with Hammerstein, both his sentimental and humorous moments tended to become more heavy-handed. But his gift for incomparable melody never deserted him, nor did his willingness to attempt musicals on fresh, challenging themes. Few theatre composers were more popular than Rodgers; his songs still are performed in various venues perhaps more than any of his contemporaries. His enticing use of melody and harmony, his endless variety, and his ability to capture a mood or an entire culture in a few notes are among the talents that make Rodgers one of the greatest musical artists America ever produced. Autobiography: *Musical Stages,* 1975; biographies: *Richard Rodgers,* William Hyland, 1998; *Somewhere for Me: A Biography of Richard Rodgers,* Meryle Secrest, 2001.

ROGERS, Major Robert. See *Ponteach.*

ROGERS, Will[iam Penn Adair] (1879–1935), comedian. The famed cowboy humorist was born in Olagah in Indian Territory (present-day Oklahoma) and began his theatrical career with a traveling Wild West Show. He turned to vaudeville in 1904 and made his New York debut a year later. In 1912 Rogers made his first appearance in a Broadway show, *The Wall Street Girl.* However, playgoers recalled him best for his appearances in the 1916, 1917, 1918, 1922, and 1924 editions of the *Ziegfeld Follies,* where he spun out his witty, homey philosophy and comments while toying with a lariat. His last Broadway appearance was in *Three Cheers* (1928). Shortly before his death in a plane crash, he had appeared as Nat Miller in a 1934 West Coast production of *Ah, Wilderness!.* Rogers was also very popular in films and on radio and in the newspapers. The 1991 musical *The Will Rogers Follies* was an entertaining if simple-minded retelling of his life. Autobiography: *Autobiography of*

Will Rogers, Donald Day, editor, 1949; biography: *Will Rogers: His Life and Times,* R. Ketchum, 1973.

ROGERS BROTHERS, THE [né Gus (1869–1908) and Max (1873–1932) Solomon]. The brothers, both of whom were born in New York, began to perform together in 1885 and soon became favorites at *Tony Pastor's, with their "Dutch" dialect routines. When *Weber and *Fields rose to popularity but refused to cooperate with the *Theatrical Syndicate or Trust, Abe *Erlanger set out to make the Rogers Brothers their rivals. They were starred in *A Reign of Error* (1899) and then in an annual series of musicals with such titles as *The Rogers Brothers in Wall Street* (1899) and *The Rogers Brothers in Washington* (1901). The series continued until Gus died. Although Gus was considered the lesser of the pair, Max's career quickly faltered.

ROLLO'S WILD OAT (1920), a comedy by Clare *Kummer. [Punch and Judy Theatre, 228 perf.] Rollo Webster (Roland *Young), the amiable heir to an air-brake fortune, has no real interest in running the business. His only ambition is to play Hamlet, so he uses his money to mount his own production of the play. For Ophelia he casts a pretty young lady named Goldie MacDuff (Lotus Robb) who has taken to the stage solely to support herself and who has lost out on a chance for a part in *The Midnight Frolics* because she cannot stay awake that late. At the first performance, Goldie-Ophelia interrupts Rollo-Hamlet to tell him his grandfather is dying. Rollo rushes offstage to be with his grandfather, and leaves his stage manager to come before the audience to ask if there is another Hamlet in the house. Finally, Rollo's dresser is hurried into costume, only to discover the costumes have not been properly sewn. At home Rollo makes another discovery: his grandfather is very much alive and had resorted to a ruse to keep Rollo from making a fool of himself. All that is left for Rollo to do is to propose to Goldie, which he does. Alexander *Woollcott hailed the comedy as "a kind of airy and capricious nonsense which was familiar enough in the best of Oscar Wilde." The play remained popular with amateur groups for several decades.

ROMANCE (1913), a play by Edward *Sheldon. [Maxine Elliott's Theatre, 160 perf.] Harry Putnam (George Le Soir), who is reluctant to tell his grandfather, Bishop Armstrong (William *Courtenay), that he is engaged to an artist, is surprised when the bishop tells him his own history. The bishop recounts how, many years before, the rage of New York had been the great diva Margherita Cavallini (Doris *Keane), and how, as the new rector of St. Giles, he had been invited to meet her at a fashionable soiree where he fell in love instantly. Later Armstrong was revolted to learn she had been a man's mistress, but his love was such that he forced himself to overlook her past. Cavallini, however, realized their worlds were far apart, and though she loved him, walked out of his life to allow him to continue his calling. As the bishop finishes his story, he is brought the evening paper, which announces Cavallini's death. After Harry has gone, he pulls from his pocket some faded violets and a woman's handkerchief. One of the greatest successes of its decade, it held the stage with some regularity for more than a dozen years. A musical version, *My Romance* (1948), failed, despite a pleasing Sigmund *Romberg score.

ROMBERG, Sigmund (1887–1951), composer. The Hungarian was slated to become an engineer, but when he was sent to Vienna, he took work at the Theatre-an-der-Wien and studied with Richard Heuberger. Coming to America in 1909, Romberg accepted odd jobs until he could establish his own small dance band and publish some songs, which came to the attention of the Messrs. *Shubert, who signed him as their house composer in 1914. His first song hit was "Auf Wiedersehn," which was one of his additions to Eysler's score for *The Blue Paradise* (1915). In 1916 alone he wrote music (mostly tinny ragtime melodies) for at least six Shubert shows, but he did not begin to gain real recognition until he was allowed to compose a score entirely in his own middle-European idiom for *Maytime* (1917), followed by his redactions of Schubert melodies for *Blossom Time* (1921). Romberg enjoyed four huge successes in the 1920s: The *Student Prince* (1924), The *Desert Song* (1926), *My Maryland* (1927), and The *New Moon* (1928). With the coming of the Great Depression and the rise of Nazism, the vogue for German-style operettas waned, and Romberg had little success in the 1930s. However, he scored a final success in 1945 with a bit of nostalgic Americana, *Up in Central Park*. After Romberg's death his underrated score for *The Girl in Pink Tights* (1954) was offered to Broadway. In all he composed songs for nearly sixty Broadway musicals. Romberg was often accused of borrowing themes from classic compositions, and his music often seems less original and less passionate than that of his principal rival, Rudolf *Friml. Nevertheless, the pair was almost solely responsible for the great outpouring of gorgeous, memorable melodies in the final American heyday of traditional operetta. Biography: *Deep in My Heart,* Elliott Arnold, 1949.

ROME, Harold [Jacob] (1908–93), composer and lyricist. Born in Hartford, Connecticut, he studied both law and architecture at Yale, then accepted work as a draftsman before he began composing songs for summer camp shows. Rome's first Broadway score was for the long-running union revue *Pins and Needles* (1937), followed by the revues *Sing Out the News* (1938) and *Call Me Mister* (1946). His book musicals (for which he continued to write both music and lyrics) included *Wish You Were Here* (1952), *Fanny* (1954), *Destry Rides Again* (1959), and *I Can Get It for You Wholesale* (1962). Stanley *Green has written, "The ability to express in songs honest emotions of those who are least articulate has been one of his most distinguishing characteristics. For Rome is, essentially, a people's composer and lyricist who ... provides the common man with uncommon musical expressions."

ROMEO AND JULIET. *Shakespeare's greatest love story was first unveiled for New Yorkers in 1754 with Mr. Rigby and Mrs. *Hallam heading the cast, and it has retained its popularity ever since. Although the leading 19th-century actors often played Romeo, the fashion for "trouser roles" at the time allowed Charlotte *Cushman and other celebrated actresses to assume the part as well. Adelaide *Neilson and Julia *Marlowe were among the most admired Juliets. Curiously, a rare old recording made by Marlowe and E. H. *Sothern of their reading of the balcony scene suggests that performances of the period might have been too lush for modern tastes. In later years Ethel *Barrymore, Jane *Cowl, and Katharine *Cornell found varying luck in the part. One reason for Barrymore's failure may have been that she assigned the part of Romeo to a minor actor, McKay Morris, thus turning the play into a one-star vehicle and upsetting its balance. Cowl and Cornell were craftier, hiring Rollo *Peters and Basil *Rathbone, respectively. All these artists were no longer truly young, so that they incorporated a change, begun by Ellen *Terry, of making Juliet eighteen or nineteen years old instead of fourteen. As his wife's director, Guthrie *McClintic also restored many important cuts, including the "Gallop apace, you fiery-footed steeds" speech that had been dropped at least since Neilson's day. Laurence *Olivier and Vivian Leigh presented their version in 1940. The musical *West Side Story* (1957) was suggested by the play, but set its action in contemporary New York and had the lovers associated not with rival families but with rival street gangs. Perhaps the most unusual treatment of Shakespeare's play of late was Off-Broadway's *R & J* (1998) in which four prep-school boys, wearing their uniform shirts, ties, and V-neck sweaters, played all the male and female roles. The sleeper hit ran ten months, the longest New York run of *Romeo and Juliet* on record.

ROOM SERVICE (1937), a farce by John Murray and Allen Boretz. [*Cort Theatre, 500 perf.] Gordon Miller (Sam *Levene), a penny-ante producer, has a play, a director (Philip Loeb), a cast of twenty-two actors, and the promise of a theatre but no money. He sells a ten-percent interest in the show to Joseph Gribble (Cliff Dunstan), the manager of the White Way Hotel, in return for lodging his entire entourage. But when the bills mount up, the hotel attempts to oust the company. Miller has his not-very-bright playwright, Leo Davis (Eddie *Albert), pretend he is too ill to move. The ploy is threatened with exposure, so Miller and Binion announce Davis has committed suicide, and they stall for time by claiming they must attend to the funeral. In desperation the hotel helps finance the play, which becomes a smash hit. The farce was originally produced by Sam H. *Harris, who withdrew from it during tryouts. George *Abbott took over, helped rewrite it and directed it. Richard *Watts Jr. of the *Post* welcomed *Room Service* as "the funniest play that New York has seen in years and years." A 1983 revival closed before reaching New York, but a 1985 Off-Broadway mounting was well received.

ROONEY, Pat[rick James], **Jr.** (1880–1962), singer. The tiny, pixieish performer, a native New Yorker, was the son of another famous vaudevillian, the first Pat Rooney (1844–92), who was also known for his song-and-dance routines. The younger Rooney and his wife, Marion Bent (1879–1940), became one of vaudeville's most-popular teams. Among his most applauded numbers was "The Daughter of Rosie O'Grady," to which he did a clog dance while nonchalantly keeping his hands in his pockets. He also appeared with his wife in musical comedy and revues, notably in *Love Birds* (1921). After arthritis forced his wife to retire, Rooney continued to perform alone. One of his memorable appearances was in *Guys and Dolls* (1950), in which he introduced "More I Cannot Wish You." His son, Pat Rooney III (1909–79), occasionally performed with him and sometimes did a solo song-and-dance act.

ROSE, [William Samuel] **Billy** [né Rosenberg] (1899–1966), producer and lyricist. The feisty, bantam, theatrical jack-of-many-trades was born in New York and began his theatrical career as a lyricist writing the words for such hits as "A Cup of Coffee, a Sandwich, and You" for *Charlot's Revue of 1926* and the title song for *Great Day* (1929). Turning producer, he brought to Broadway *Sweet and Low* (1930) and a reworked version, *Billy Rose's Crazy Quilt* (1931), *The Great Magoo* (1932), *Jumbo* (1935), *Carmen Jones* (1943), and *Seven Lively Arts* (1944). Rose also owned the National Theatre, which he renamed the Billy Rose, and the *Ziegfeld

Theatre, which he eventually sold to developers. Besides regular theatre work, he ran "Aquacades" at the New York and San Francisco World's Fairs and several popular nightclubs. Biography: *Only a Paper Moon: The Theatre of Billy Rose,* Stephen Nelson, 1987.

ROSE, Edward E[verett] (1862–1939), playwright and director. Born in Stanstead, Quebec, and educated at Harvard, at the turn of the century he became the most prolific and respected adapter of novels for the stage, but he was less successful as a rule when he tried his hand at original drama. Among his most successful redactions were *The *Prisoner of Zenda* (1895), *Under the Red Robe* (1896), *David Harum* (1900), *Richard Carvel* (1900), *Janice Meredith* (1900), *Alice of Old Vincennes* (1901), and *Penrod* (1918). Nearly fifty of his works reached the boards. Rose also was a successful director, his hits including *The *Pride of Jennico* (1900) and *Alias Jimmy Valentine* (1910).

ROSE, George [Walter] (1920–88), character actor. The English performer made his American debut with the *Old Vic in 1946 but first gained major attention when he portrayed the Common Man in *A Man for All Seasons* (1961). Among his later roles were the conquistador-narrator Martin Ruiz in *The Royal Hunt of the Sun* (1965), Alfred P. Doolittle in 1968 and 1972 revivals of *My Fair Lady,* the effeminate Henry in *My Fat Friend* (1974), the knowing servant Hawkins in *The Kingfisher* (1978), Captain Hook in *Peter Pan* (1979), Major-General Stanley in *The *Pirates of Penzance* (1981), the Reverend Ernest Lynton in a revival of *Aren't We All?* (1985), and the music hall Chairman in *The *Mystery of Edwin Drood* (1985).

ROSE-MARIE (1924), a musical play by Otto *Harbach, Oscar *Hammerstein (book, lyrics), Rudolf *Friml, Herbert *Stothart (music). [*Imperial Theatre, 557 perf.] Rose-Marie La Flamme (Mary Ellis) works at Lady Jane's, a small hotel in the Canadian Rockies, and is courted by both the trapper Jim Kenyon (Dennis *King) and the villainous Ed Hawley (Frank Greene), who manages to throw blame for the murder of the Indian Black Eagle (Arthur Ludwig) on his rival. The truth was that Black Eagle had found his wife, Wanda (Pearl Regay), with Hawley, and Wanda had killed her husband when he attacked Hawley. A clever trader, Hard-Boiled Herman (William Kent), tricks Wanda into a confession, so Rose-Marie and Jim are free to wed. *Notable songs*: Indian Love Call; The Mounties; Rose-Marie; The Door of Her Dreams; Totem-Tom-Tom. The Arthur Hammerstein–produced musical sparked the revival of traditional operetta after World War I,

during which the genre was perceived as German and therefore enemy entertainment. The excellence of the writing and the freshness of the setting coupled with the long-dormant appeal of operetta allowed this musical a singular success. It was the biggest international musical hit of the decade, offering not only several American road companies but also running 851 performances in London and establishing a Paris long-run record of 1,250 performances. Oddly, it has been revived less frequently than the other operetta hits of the 1920s.

ROSE MICHEL (1875). Steele *MacKaye's adaptation of Ernest Blum's French drama was first played at the *Union Square Theatre in 1875. The story told of the dilemma of the heroine who must choose between revealing that her husband is a murderer and destroying the happiness and forthcoming marriage of her daughter. Rose *Eytinge played the title role and the drama was one of the biggest hits of its decade, revived occasionally for the rest of the century.

ROSE OF THE RANCHO, THE (1906), a play by David *Belasco and Richard Walton *Tully. [*Belasco Theatre, 327 perf.] Lawless Americans are seizing Spanish land in California and, if necessary, killing the Spaniards who own the property and have developed it. Kearney (Charles *Richman) has been sent from Washington to investigate matters and has fallen in love with Juanita (Frances *Starr), the half-American daughter of one of the old Spanish landowners, who loves Kearney, rejecting family pleas to marry a Spaniard. Her family's property is being menaced by the vicious Kinkaid (John W. Cope), who succeeds in making it appear that Kearney is helping him seize the land. This turns Juanita against Kearney for the moment, but when the truth comes out, she is free to marry him. The production was one of producer Belasco's many triumphs of theatricality—that is, of brilliantly detailed production and clever appeal to immediate emotion—over form and substance.

ROSE TATTOO, THE (1951), a play by Tennessee *Williams. [Martin Beck Theatre, 306 perf.; Tony Award.] In a small village on the Gulf Coast, the passionate and devout Sicilian-American, Serafina della Rosa (Maureen *Stapleton), lives with an idealized memory of her late husband, a truck driver. But, for all the defenses she builds, the truth about her husband's many infidelities are eventually brought home to her and threaten to destroy her until Alvaro Mangiacavallo (Eli *Wallach) comes into her life. He too is a truck driver, and his warmth and ebullience help restore Serafina's zest for life. Happy again, she even encourages a budding romance between her daughter Rosa (Phyllis Love) and a young sailor, Jack Hunter (Don Murray). The play had been written with Italian film star Anna Magnani in mind, but she refused to play it on stage, though she eventually made the film version. Many critics were disturbed by Williams's growing penchant for symbolism, which was woven through the work, but the play has successfully held the stage in regional theatres and in a fine mounting at the *Circle in the Square in 1995 featuring Mercedes Reuhl and Anthony LaPaglia.

ROSEDALE; or, The Rifle Ball (1863), a play by Lester *Wallack. [*Wallack's Theatre, 125 perf.] Lady Florence May (Mrs. *Hoey) is a widow whose late husband stipulated in his will that if she remarried without the consent of his uncle, Col. Cavendish May (H. F. Daly), she would forfeit her inheritance, half of which would go to her young son and half to the Colonel. The Colonel plots to kill the child and either to push Florence into remarrying without his consent or to break her heart. To this end he connives with the black-guard Miles McKenna (John *Gilbert). Meanwhile, Elliot Grey (Wallack), a former suitor of Lady Florence, has become a soldier of fortune since being rejected, but remains loyal and loving. Matthew Leigh (Charles *Fisher), a local doctor, also loves Florence. Years before, Matthew's baby brother had been stolen by gypsies, so when McKenna tells him he is that same younger brother and now has a criminal record, Matthew breaks off his suit. McKenna and the Colonel then kidnap Florence's son but Elliot Grey retrieves the child and reveals that he, Elliot, is Matthew's real lost brother. So Matthew and Florence are free to wed. This complicated, often preposterous and action-filled melodrama was one of Wallack's biggest successes, remaining in the company's repertory until the end. That such a piece could have so vast an appeal to audiences in New York's most elite play-house suggests that the difference between Bowery melodrama and many of Wallack's plays was one of degree not kind. Even after Wallack's company disbanded, the play was revived regularly for the rest of the century.

ROSENFELD, Sydney (1855–1931), playwright. A curious figure in Broadway theatrical history, he was born in Richmond, Virginia, and later claimed he was smuggled through enemy lines during the Civil War so that he might attend school in New York. He apparently began his theatrical career by adapting foreign plays but soon turned his hand to any sort of writing that might turn a profit. Alone or with collaborators he wrote such diverse fare as the burlesque *Well-Fed Dora* (1884); W. H.

*Crane's vehicle The *Senator (1890); the libretto for the first major revue, The *Passing Show (1894); the book and lyrics for the operetta The Mocking Bird (1902); and the book for the popular Elsie *Janis musical, The Vanderbilt Cup (1906). Rosenfeld was often accused of plagiarism and in one celebrated case was stopped from mounting a pirated production of The *Mikado in 1885. He continued to produce and write actively until the end of World War I. In all, about fifty of his works reached Broadway. He was also editor of the popular humor periodical *Puck*.

ROSENTHAL, Jean (1912–69), lighting designer. The American theatre's dean of lighting design, Rosenthal pioneered many of the practices and techniques that are considered standard today. She was also responsible for developing the role of the theatrical lighting designer as separate from scenic and costume artists. Rosenthal was particularly noted for her use of light to depict mood and evoke emotions in her designs. Her credits include more than two hundred plays and musicals (from *Federal Theatre Project productions in the 1930s to *Dear World* in 1969), operas, and ballets (including many works with Martha Graham), as well as architectural and industrial design.

ROSS, Jerry. See Adler and Ross.

ROSTAND, Edmond (1868–1918), playwright. The romantic French dramatist is known in this country primarily for one work, his masterpiece, *Cyrano de Bergerac (1898). His *L'Aiglon* is recalled largely as a vehicle for Sarah *Bernhardt, who included it in her American tours. Much was expected of his *Chanticleer*, which Charles *Frohman offered in 1911 with Maude *Adams as star, but the production was a costly failure. Also, it was Rostand's *Les Romantics* that provided the basic plot for the long-running musical The *Fantasticks (1960).

ROUND UP, THE (1907), a drama by Edmund Day. [*New Amsterdam Theatre, 155 perf.] When guilt at having stolen his best friend's wife becomes too much for Jack Payson (Orme *Caldara), he heads out into the desert to seek that former buddy. Dick Lane (Wright Kramer) is now a mining engineer who has sought to forget his bitterness by accepting work in dangerous and forsaken places. Just as the men meet, a band of Apaches attacks the encampment. The two men fight side by side until Lane is killed and the Indians routed, after which Payson can return home with a somewhat clearer conscience. A rather strange story, since the man who comes out best was the less likable of the two and since the woman in question never appears, the *Klaw and *Erlanger production found much of its appeal from the performance of Maclyn *Arbuckle as Sheriff "Slim" Hoover, who is resigned that "nobody can love a fat man." **Edmund DAY** (1866–1923), a New Yorker, was an actor-turned-playwright whose works included a farce-comedy, *The Head-Waiters* (1902), a melodramatic vehicle for boxer Jim Corbett, *Pals* (1905), and a comedy for Lillian *Russell, *The Widow's Might* (1909).

ROUNDABOUT THEATRE COMPANY (New York). After many years of presenting low-budget revivals in a variety of inhospitable venues, this company became one of New York's most potent producing groups on and Off Broadway in the 1990s. Founded in 1965 by Gene Feist to present seasons of revivals of notable plays, the group first performed in a church, then in the basement of a supermarket before finding a home in a converted cinema. In 1984 the company moved to the old Tammany Hall building off Union Square. Jane *Alexander, Jim *Dale, Anthony Hopkins, Philip *Bosco, and Irene *Worth are among the distinguished performers who have appeared in a broad range of plays, including Shakespeare and classical Greek drama, but emphasizing 19th- and 20th-century British works. By the late 1980s the company boasted the largest list of regular subscribers in New York and was sending productions regularly to Broadway. It next occupied the Criterion Center in Times Square, making its shows bona fide Broadway entries, though the company remained a nonprofit venture. In 2000 the Roundabout moved into its permanent Broadway home, the restored Selwyn Theatre on 42nd Street, now called the *American Airlines Theatre, while still presenting shows Off Broadway at the *American Place Theatre and the former discotheque Studio 54. The repertory still consists almost exclusively of play and musical revivals, some of which enjoyed long runs, such as the 1998 mounting of *Cabaret*.

ROW AT THE LYCEUM, A; or, Green Room Secrets (1851), a play by John *Brougham. [Brougham's Lyceum, 21 perf.] As the audience enters it finds actors and others associated with the blank-verse tragedy, *Horror on Horror's Head; or, The Liar and the Slave*, about to begin a rehearsal. Just as the session starts, one of the performers (Mrs. Brougham) objects to the smallness of her part. Her complaint brings her to the attention of a man in the audience (Brougham), who jumps up, claims she is his wife, and demands she leave the stage. From the gallery come the shouts of a fireman (W. J. *Florence) who threatens to whip the protester if he touches his wife. A ruckus ensues, stopping the rehearsal. Both the supposed husband

and fireman run on stage, where the police grab them. At this point all the performers turn to the audience, while one of them recites an epilogue confessing that the row at the Lyceum was all a joke. A refreshing bit of zany nonsense, quite untypical of the theatre of its day, the one-act play was, however, typical of the adventurous, wide-ranging, and free-spirited producer Brougham, who was also a pioneer of musical revue.

ROWE, George Fawcett (1834–89), actor and playwright. Little is known about the man who was advertised as being "from the London and Australian theatres" when he made his New York debut in 1866. As a performer his most successful roles were as the comic upstart Digby Grant in *Two Roses* (1872), Wilkins Micawber in *Little Em'ly* (1874), and Hawkeye in his own dramatization of Cooper's *Leatherstocking; or, The Last of the Mohicans* (1874). Rowe's other writings ranged from his burlesque for Lydia *Thompson, *Mephisto and the Four Sensations* (1873), to his adaptation of *Feuillet's melodrama *The Sphinx* (1874) for Clara *Morris.

ROYAL FAMILY, THE (1927), a comedy by George S. *Kaufman and Edna *Ferber. [Selwyn Theatre, 343 perf.] The Cavendishes are the greatest acting family in America, presided over by the aging Fanny Cavendish (Haidee Wright). Her daughter, Julie (Ann Andrews), is the leading contemporary actress, while Julie's daughter, Gwen (Sylvia Field), is a promising ingenue. Both Julie and Gwen are toying with marriage and with abandoning the theatre. Fanny's dashingly handsome son, Tony (Otto *Kruger), could have been the greatest performer of all, but he prefers the celebrity that comes with being a film star and wild affairs with women, so his escapades keep him perpetually on the run. Fanny's brother Herbert Dean (Orlando Daly) is a fine farceur and former matinee idol who is fighting the ravages of age and of a faltering career. Hovering over the family is the great producer Oscar Wolfe (Jefferson *De Angelis). For all their complaints about their lives, the call of the theatre is irresistible, so Julie leaves her own problems to rush off to meet a curtain and Fanny quietly dies while planning yet another tour. Jed *Harris produced this uproarious send-up of the *Barrymore and the *Drew families that infuriated Ethel *Barrymore, but Brooks *Atkinson of the *Times* felt the authors had "toyed entertainingly and absorbingly with the madness of show folk and the fatal glamour of the footlights." The play has enjoyed numerous revivals, most memorably a 1975 production directed by Ellis *Rabb that featured Rosemary *Harris, Eva *Le Gallienne, George *Grizzard, and Sam *Levene.

ROYAL NATIONAL THEATRE of Great Britain. See International Theatre Companies Visiting America.

ROYAL SHAKESPEARE COMPANY. See International Theatre Companies Visiting America.

ROYAL [Dewar], **Ted** (1904–81), orchestrator. He was born in Skedee, Oklahoma, and after attending the University of Kansas continued his musical studies in Houston and New York. His orchestrations were first heard on Broadway in *Too Many Girls* (1939), and later in such shows as *Du Barry Was a Lady* (1939), *Panama Hattie* (1940), *Pal Joey* (1940), *Mexican Hayride* (1944), *Annie Get Your Gun* (1946), *Brigadoon* (1947), *Where's Charley?* (1948), *Guys and Dolls* (1950), *House of Flowers* (1954), and *Mr. Wonderful* (1956).

ROYALE THEATRE (New York). With 1,100 seats and plenty of backstage space, the playhouse on West 45th Street has served well for both plays and musicals over the decades. It was designed in a Spanish style by Herbert J. *Krapp and built by the Chanin brothers in 1927, though they lost ownership during the Great Depression. For a time in the early 1930s, the house was managed by John *Golden, who renamed it after himself, and in the late 1930s it was a radio studio. From Gilbert and Sullivan operettas to such three-character plays as *Art* (1998) and *Copenhagen* (2000), the Royale has been a suitable house for just about every kind of theatre. Today the *Shuberts own it.

ROYCE, Edward (1870–1964), director and choreographer. Born in Bath, England, he began his theatrical career as a set designer, but later took up dancing and became a choreographer, then finally turned to directing musical comedies. He was brought to this country at the suggestion of his friend Jerome *Kern, and his first New York assignment was creating the dances for *The Doll Girl* (1913), for which Kern supplied interpolations. His many subsequent successes, as director and sometimes also as choreographer, included *Oh, Boy!* (1917), *Leave It to Jane* (1917), *Going Up!* (1917), *Oh, Lady! Lady!!* (1918), *Apple Blossoms* (1919), *Irene* (1919), *Sally* (1920), *Good Morning, Dearie* (1921), *Orange Blossoms* (1922), *Kid Boots* (1923), and *The Merry Malones* (1927).

ROYALE, Edwin Milton. See *Squaw Man, The.*

RUBY, Harry. See Kalmar and Ruby.

RUNYON, Damon. See *Guys and Dolls.*

RUPERT, Michael (b. 1951), actor and singer. The likable leading man of musicals, who started on Broadway as a teenager, has an everyman look and demeanor even though he often plays colorful neurotics. He was born in Denver and trained at the *Pasadena Playhouse, making an impressive Broadway debut in 1968 as the French-Canadian youth Bibi Bonnard in *The *Happy Time.* As an adult performer, Rupert is most associated with the character of Marvin, the difficult homosexual who leaves his wife and moves in with his male lover in *March of the Falsettos* (1981). He continued his Marvin characterization in *Falsettoland* (1990) and reprised both musicals as *Falsettos* (1992).

RUSSELL, Annie (1864–1936), actress. Born in Liverpool but raised in Canada, she made her first appearance in Montreal, playing opposite Rose *Eytinge in *Miss Multon* in 1872. Her New York debut was in 1879 as Josephine in a traveling juvenile company of *H.M.S. Pinafore.* Russell continued to play with various tours, including one that took her to South America and Australia, before scoring a major success as *Esmeralda* (1881). Among her later roles were the title part in a dramatization of Tennyson's *Lancelot and Elaine,* called simply *Elaine* (1887), and, after a long retirement because of illness, the title role in Bret Harte's *Sue* (1896) and Winifred in *The *Girl and the Judge* (1901). In her final active years Russell organized the Old English Comedy Company, in which she assumed such roles as Kate Hardcastle, Beatrice, Lydia Languish, and Lady Teazle before retiring in 1918. George *Odell later wrote of this frail, darkish woman, with a slightly lugubrious face, "All who saw Miss Russell know how sweet she was either in comedy or in pathetic plays, and will recall gratefully her charm, her grace, her exquisite voice, her genuine dramatic power."

RUSSELL, Lillian [née Helen Louise Leonard] (1861–1922), singer and actress. The first great prima donna of the modern American musical stage, known to her admirers and the press as "Airy Fairy Lillian," she was born in Clinton, Iowa, where her father was the owner and editor of the local newspaper. She grew up in Chicago and then New York, where she studied singing with Leopold Damrosch. Her professional debut was in the chorus of E. E. *Rice's 1879 production of *H.M.S. Pinafore.* One year later Tony *Pastor hired her, gave her her stage name, and featured her in his vaudeville. It was in his travesties of *Olivette, The *Pirates of Penzance,* and *Patience* that Russell caught the eyes and ears of New York's critics and playgoers. Her performance in the *Patience* parody led to her being cast in the Bijou Theatre's regular 1881 production of the comic opera, although her first major assignment had come several months earlier when she played the leading feminine role in Audran's *The Grand Mogul* (also known as *The Snake Charmer*). Between then and 1899 she appeared as the star of no fewer than twenty-four musicals, many of them written expressly for her. These included *Polly* (1885), *Pepita* (1886), *Dorothy* (1887), *The *Grand Duchess* (1889), *La Cigale* (1891), *Princess Nicotine* (1893), *La Périchole* (1895), *The Tzigane* (1895), *An American Beauty* (1896), and *The Wedding Day* (1897). In her prime, Russell was a gorgeous, well-proportioned, if ample, blue-eyed blonde. "Her voice," wrote one of her biographers, "while never rich, was at least a clear, full-throated, lyric soprano of true pitch and impressive quality." At the same time she was notorious for not pay-ing bills, for not honoring contracts, and for walking out both on her shows and her several husbands. When her popularity began to wane slightly, she joined Weber and Fields in their famous music hall, remaining with them until 1903. It was in their 1902 production *Twirly-Whirly* that she sang "Come Down, Ma Evenin' Star," the only song she was ever to record. A musical version of *The School for Scandal* was written for her in 1904 and called *Lady Teazle*. Except for an appearance in the 1912 *Weber and *Fields reunion with *Hokey Pokey,* it marked her last performance in a musical. She continued to act in vaudeville and in nonmusical plays until shortly before her death, but it was commonly accepted that she was living on her reputation. Biography: *Lillian Russell: A Biography of America's Beauty,* Armond Fields, 1999.

RUSSELL, Sol Smith (1848–1902), comic actor. The lanky, bright-eyed comedian was born in Brunswick, Missouri, and made his stage debut at the age of twelve in Jacksonville, Illinois. He toured for many years both as an actor and as a monologist, whose most celebrated turn was the spoof of a European lecturer. Russell spent some time with Augustin *Daly's ensemble beginning in 1874, but was best known for three roles that he played around the country for many years: the seeming ne'er-do-well Tom Dilloway in

Edgewood Folks (1880), the inventive, itinerant beggar Noah Vale in *A Poor Relation* (1889), and the dedicated bookworm David Holmes in *A Bachelor's Romance* (1897).

RUSSELL, Rosalind (1912–76), actress. The tall, classy comedienne was born in Waterbury, Connecticut, and studied at the *American Academy of Dramatic Arts, then played in stock before making her New York debut in the 1930 edition of the *Garrick Gaieties. Minor roles followed, after which she went to Hollywood, where she became a major film star. Russell returned to the stage in 1951 to tour as the love-struck witch Gillian in *Bell, Book and Candle*. Her two major Broadway assignments were the caustic Ruth Sherwood in *Wonderful Town* (1953) and the wildly unconventional guardian of a young boy, the title role in *Auntie Mame* (1956).

RYAN, Dennis (d. 1786), actor and manager. Very little is known about this early theatre pioneer. With his wife he performed in New York in 1783, then later that year headed a company that played in Baltimore and toured the South. In keeping with the times, he played everything from Iago and Falstaff and Young Marlow in *She Stoops to Conquer* to numerous roles in long-forgotten contemporary works.

RYERSON, Florence. See *Harriet*.

RYSKIND, Morrie (1895–1985), librettist. Born in New York, where he studied at Columbia, he began his theatrical career by writing sketches and lyrics for *The 49ers* (1922) and *Merry-Go-Round* (1927). With George S. *Kaufman he wrote the book for *Animal Crackers* (1928), then helped revise Kaufman's book for *Strike Up the Band* (1930). Ryskind shared a *Pulitzer Prize with Kaufman and Ira *Gershwin for his work on *Of Thee I Sing* (1931) and afterward rejoined them for *Let 'Em Eat Cake* (1933). Although he later wrote the book for the hit *Louisiana Purchase* (1940), his other theatre work was all on failed musicals. Ryskind was also a writer of screenplays.

S

S.S. GLENCAIRN (1924), four short plays by Eugene *O'Neill. [Provincetown Playhouse, 105 perf.] The four one-acts, each of which had been seen earlier in various venues, were combined and given the title of the tramp steamer where the characters worked. In **BOUND EAST FOR CARDIFF** (1916), seaman Yank (Sidney Machet) is critically injured in a fall. Although his shipmates attempt to offer him solace, they all recognize that he is dying. Yank can only respond that "this sailor life ain't much to cry about leaving" and in the end death comes to him as a vision of "a pretty lady dressed in black." **IN THE ZONE** (1917) concerns Smitty (E. J. Ballantine), whose mates on the *S.S. Glencairn* see him furtively remove a little black box from his suitcase, and they conclude he may be a spy. They bind and gag him, then rummage through his belongings until they find the box. Its contents prove to be letters from an old sweetheart who left him because of his drinking. In the atmospheric piece **THE MOON OF THE CARIBBEES** (1918), the ship is anchored off a West Indies island and the crew await the arrival of the Negress Bella (Mary Johns), with her girls and her smuggled rum. When the girls arrive, one of them, Pearl (Ruth Collins Allen), flits teasingly between Yank and the more reticent Smitty. Eventually a fight ensues, and one sailor is stabbed to death. The women are finally made to leave the ship, and the sailors, alone on the deck, have nothing to do but listen to the lonely singing coming from the island. Generally considered the finest play of the group, **THE LONG VOYAGE HOME** (1917) is set in Fat Joe's sleazy bar on the London waterfront, where the crew of the *S.S. Glencairn* is drinking. Olson (Walter *Abel) tells the others of his joy to be finished with the sea and of his plans to go home to Sweden. But his joy is short-lived, for he is given a mickey and shanghaied aboard the *Amindra,* bound for Cape Horn. The *Amindra,* he notes before he passes out, is the "worst ship dat sail to sea." The quartet of plays represents O'Neill's finest writing before he successfully essayed longer dramas.

SABRINA FAIR (1953), a comedy by Samuel *Taylor. [National Theatre, 318 perf.] The Larrabees are extremely rich Long Islanders with two eligible sons, the wayward David (Scott McKay) and the misanthropic Linus Jr. (Joseph *Cotten). They also have a chauffeur, Fairchild (Russell Collins), whose brilliant daughter, Sabrina (Margaret *Sullavan), has just returned from a stint in Paris. David and several other local boys court her, but she recalls that as a child it was Linus Jr. whom she loved. Linus seems unreceptive, but he has not bargained on Sabrina's charm and insinuating ways. Whether he wins her or she wins him is moot. To add icing to the cake, Linus Sr. (John *Cromwell) discovers that Fairchild has been quietly playing the stock market and is a very rich man in his own right. Brooks *Atkinson welcomed the *Playwrights' Company production as one written "with taste and good humor about agreeable people."

SACKLER, Howard. See *Great White Hope, The.*

SADDLER, Frank (1864–1921), orchestrator. Born in Franklin, Pennsylvania, and educated in Munich, he was one of the first in his field who was not also an active composer or conductor, although early in his career he led pit bands at burlesque theatres. George *Gershwin called him "the father of modern arranging." He is credited with bringing to the musical comedy orchestra pit the elegant, polished sound that had usually been heard only in the best operettas. Up to the time of his death he orchestrated almost all of Jerome *Kern's shows, including *Very Good Eddie* (1915), *Oh, Boy!* (1917), *Oh, Lady! Lady!!* (1918), *The Night Boat* (1920), and *Sally* (1920). Saddler also arranged the music for the *Hippodrome extravaganzas presented by Charles *Dillingham as well as his *Watch Your Step* (1914), *Stop! Look! Listen!* (1915), *Jack o' Lantern* (1917), and *Tip Top* (1920).

SAG HARBOR (1900), a play by James A. *Herne. [Republic Theatre, 76 perf.] Two brothers, Ben (Forrest Robinson) and Frank Turner (Lionel *Barrymore), both love Martha Reese (Julie A. Herne). Although she loves Frank, she marries the older Ben out of a sense of obligation. Two years later Frank reappears and almost persuades Martha to elope with him. Only the intervention of Captain

Dan Marble (Herne), who recounts the disastrous results of a similar elopement, dissuades the couple. *Liebler and Co. presented Herne's last play, and it was deemed by many to be merely a rewriting of his early *Hearts of Oak*, albeit Herne publicly denied this. Critics admired Herne's warm performance but were sharply divided on the merits of the drama.

SAILOR, BEWARE! (1933), a comedy by Kenyon *Nicholson and Charles Robinson. [*Lyceum Theatre, 500 perf.] When the crew of the USS *Dakota* arrives in the Canal Zone, the men decide to see if their leading man with the ladies, Chester "Dynamite" Jones (Bruce MacFarlane), can win the cold heart of Billie "Stonewall" Jackson (Audrey *Christie), the celebrated nightclub hostess at the Idle Hour Cafe. Bets are placed both by the sailors and the girls at the club, and "Dynamite" and "Stonewall" are brought together. For a while an immovable object confronts an irresistible force, until Billie learns that the sailors have called off their bets. Despite a large cast and an elaborate, expensive-to-run production, this rowdy but funny comedy presented by Courtney Burr became one of the most profitable successes of the Depression. **Charles** [Knox] **ROBINSON** (1909–80), a New Yorker, also wrote *Mahogany Hall* (1934), *Swing Your Lady* (1936), and *The Flying Gerardos* (1940), but his other successful work was the Walter *Huston vehicle *Apple of His Eye* (1946).

ST. JAMES THEATRE (New York). Although it is large (over 1,600 seats) and has two balconies, the beloved playhouse on West 44th Street feels intimate, and both artists and patrons have long favored it for musicals. It was designed in a simple but elegant Georgian style by the architectural firm Warren and Whetmore with interiors by John Aingraldi. The house was built in 1927 by theatre mogul Abraham *Erlanger, who named it Erlanger's Theatre. From the start it was a popular playhouse, yet it went through a succession of owners over the decades and today is *Jujamcyn property. Among the musical classics to open there were *Oklahoma! (1943), The *King and I (1951), *Hello, Dolly! (1964), and The *Producers (2001). In 1932 Erlanger's was renamed the St. James Theatre after a revered playhouse in London.

SAINT JOAN (1923). Winifred *Lenihan was the first American Joan in the *Theatre Guild's 1923 production of *Shaw's play. Although some critics felt her performance was too undisciplined and frenetic to be totally satisfying, Lawrence *Langner, looking back over several decades, insisted her "courage, fervor and youth" made her the best Joan he had ever seen. Katharine *Cornell headed

the cast of a 1936 revival with supporting players Brian Aherne, Tyrone *Power, Arthur *Byron, Charles *Waldron, and Kent Smith. John Anderson of the *Journal* observed, "Her performance is enkindled by the spiritual exaltation of a transcendent heroine." In 1951 Uta *Hagen starred as the maid, giving a determined, totally believable performance that paid only small attention to the mystic aspects behind the story. Less successful was a 1956 *Phoenix Theatre revival in which Siobhan McKenna made Joan into a fanatic, not very intelligent Irish serving girl, but years later Diana *Sands in 1968, Lynn Redgrave in 1978, and Maryann Plunkett in 1993 shone in the role.

ST. LOUIS MUNICIPAL OUTDOOR THEATRE (St. Louis). Known locally as "The Muny Opera," it was opened as a huge (11,000 seats) amphitheatre in the city's Forest Park in 1919 with a production of *Robin Hood. Since then it has mounted an annual summer season of revivals, with occasional new musicals on the bill. Major stars have often appeared with the group. Since 1982 it has sponsored a "Broadway Series" that offers touring musicals during the colder months at the Fox Theatre, a converted film house.

SAKS, Gene [Jean Michael] (b. 1921), director and actor. A native New Yorker, he was graduated from Cornell, then spent several years studying acting, later performing on and Off Broadway for more than a decade before turning to directing in the early 1960s. Among his major directorial assignments have been *Enter Laughing* (1963), *Half a Sixpence* (1965), *Generation* (1965), *Mame (1966), *Same Time, Next Year (1975), *California Suite* (1976), *I Love My Wife* (1977), *Brighton Beach Memoirs (1983), *Biloxi Blues (1985), *Broadway Bound (1986), *Rumors* (1988), *Lost in Yonkers (1991), *Jake's Women* (1992), and *Barrymore* (1997). Something of a Neil *Simon specialist, Saks is probably the best stager of comedies of his generation.

SALLY (1920), a musical comedy by Guy *Bolton (book), Jerome *Kern (music), Clifford Grey and others (lyrics). [*New Amsterdam Theatre, 570 perf.] Sally Rhinelander (Marilyn *Miller), an orphan and a dishwasher at the Elm Tree Alley Inn, is befriended by her co-worker "Connie" (Leon *Errol), the exiled Duke Constantine of Czechogovinia, and by the rich young bachelor Blair Farquar (Irving Fisher). She later substitutes for a dancer at a party Blair has thrown, which leads to a fight between her and Blair, but also to a contract to dance in the *Ziegfeld Follies*. Sally is a big hit, and she and Blair are reconciled. *Notable songs*: Look for the Silver Lining; Whip-Poor-Will; Wild Rose; The Church 'Round the Corner. Hailed by Charles

Darnton of the *World* as "nothing less than idealized musical comedy," the Florenz *Ziegfeld show was one of its era's biggest and most beloved successes and established the beautiful, light-footed Miller as the leading female musical star of her day. A 1948 revival—without Miller, Ziegfeld's flair, and Joseph *Urban's great designs—failed.

SALOMY JANE [also known as *Salomy Jane's Kiss*] (1907), a play by Paul *Armstrong. [Liberty Theatre, 122 perf.] When Salomy (Eleanor *Robson) is molested by an insistent suitor, a stranger (H. B. *Warner) shoots the man. Although she learns that the stranger shot the man for personal reasons, she helps him escape a lynch mob. Armstrong based the play on a Bret Harte story.

SALVATION NELL (1908), a play by Edward *Sheldon. [Hackett Theatre, 71 perf.] Nell Saunders (Mrs. *Fiske) is a scrubwoman at Sid McGovern's seedy bar on Tenth Avenue and is loved by the ne'er-do-well Jim Platt (Holbrook *Blinn). When Al McGovern (John Dillon) makes advances to Nell, a fight ensues and Jim kills Al. After Jim is taken away by the police, Myrtle Odell (Hope Latham), a prostitute who is a habitué of the bar, attempts to persuade Nell to adopt her trade. Nell refuses the offer and instead comes under the guidance of Major Williams (David Glassford) of the Salvation Army. With her newfound fervor, Nell attempts to reform Jim when he is released from prison. He is appalled and offended at first, but her goodness and perseverance finally win him over. Sheldon's first success and one of Fiske's most memorable vehicles, *Theatre Magazine* wrote of it, " 'Salvation Nell' is from the heart of the times. . . . The intent is not to entertain us with the disagreeable or to make us acquainted with vice for our amusement. It is all incidental to the pity and sympathy which it should evoke."

SALVINI, Tommaso (1829–1916), actor. The distinguished Italian tragedian made five American visits between 1873 and 1889. He had a majestic figure and a mobile face with a large forehead, dark, striking eyes, and an aquiline nose. His voice has been described as "one of the most powerful, flexible, and mellifluous organs ever implanted in a human throat." Salvini made his debut in his greatest role, Othello. His performance was so violent that when he later played opposite American performers many actresses refused to be his Desdemona. He always performed in Italian while the others played in English. The most memorable of these bilingual productions were several in which he co-starred with Edwin *Booth, playing Othello and the Ghost to Booth's Iago and Hamlet. Among his other roles were Hamlet, Macbeth, King Lear, Coriolanus,

Ingomar, and Paolo. His son Alessandro (1860–96) enjoyed some American success. Autobiography: *Leaves from the Autobiography of T. Salvini*, 1893.

SAME TIME, NEXT YEAR (1975), a comedy by Bernard Slade. [*Brooks Atkinson Theatre, 1,453 perf.] In 1951 George (Charles Grodin), a businessman from New Jersey, and Doris (Ellen Burstyn), a California housewife, meet and enjoy one night in bed together in a motel. Although both are married, they find the affair so pleasant that they agree to meet each year in February for a brief tryst. During each annual rendezvous they grow to know each other better, exchange confidences, and even fall in love, but never, apparently, seriously consider divorce and marriage. The meetings keep up for twenty-four years and, despite all the changes each has gone through, promise to go on indefinitely. The comedy was recognized as one of the better of the many one-set, two-character plays forced on the theatre by the crushing economics of the day. **Bernard SLADE** (b. 1930) was born in St. Catharines, Ontario, Canada, and raised in England but returned as a teenager to work in stock and television. He is the author of two other Broadway hits, the Jack *Lemmon vehicle *Tribute* (1978) and *Romantic Comedy* (1979), and the short-lived *Special Occasions* (1982).

SAM'L OF POSEN; or, The Commercial Drummer (1881), a play by George H. *Jessop. [Haverly's 14th Street Theatre, 96 perf.] Samuel Plastrick (M. B. Curtis) is a Polish immigrant who would like to give up his work as a traveling salesman and settle down, especially after he meets Rebecca Heyman [in some programs Dreyfus] (Gertie Granville), whose uncle was a friend of his father back in the old country. Rebecca and her friend Jack Cheviot (Nelson Decker) obtain work for him at the jewelry store owned by Jack's uncle, Mr. Winslow (Welsh Edwards). Jack leads a dissipated life but wants to reform and marry Ellen (Carrie Wyatt). Unfortunately, another nephew of Winslow's, Frank Kilday (Frank Losee), implicates Jack in a crime of which Jack is really innocent, so Winslow fires Jack, Rebecca, and Samuel. The determined Samuel sets out to get the goods on the real criminal, Frank, which he does in time for a happy ending. Curtis is said to have commissioned Jessop to write a play in which the central figure was a good Jew. With Edward Marble, Curtis later rewrote the play and took credit for it. He continued to play the title role for over a dozen years.

SAMUEL FRENCH, INC. For many decades the leading licenser of plays to amateur theatres, it was founded in the early 1850s by Samuel French (1821–98), who in the late 1830s started peddling cheap editions and pulp literature, eventually adding plays. In 1854 he initiated the series known as French's American Drama and shortly thereafter bought out his major competitor, William Taylor and Co., for whom he had served briefly as an agent. He moved to England in 1872 to open a London branch, leaving his sons in charge of his American enterprises. In the 1920s the company bought out the American Play Company, an important source for licensing plays run by Elisabeth *Marbury, *Edgar Selwyn, and others. French soon had branches in all major English-speaking theatrical centers. For many years it offered services in allied fields, such as makeup and costuming, but they have long since been abandoned. In recent times the company has begun to license musicals as well. Its "acting editions" provide detailed stage directions as well as helpful information on scenery, props, and other matters.

SAN DIEGO OLD GLOBE THEATRE. A long and checkered history accompanies the replica of Shakespeare's Globe Theatre built in San Diego in 1935 as part of the California Pacific International Exposition. The structure was meant to be temporary, but a group of citizens raised money to make the building the permanent home of the San Diego Community Theatre. Popularly called the Old Globe, the group changed its name to that in 1958. Craig Noel, a member of the company for a decade, became artistic director in 1947 and presented summer Shakespeare productions in association with San Diego State College, the troupe now calling itself the San Diego National Shakespeare Festival. A fire destroyed the old structure in 1978, but a zealous board of directors saw it rebuilt into an impressive 580-seat house with a strong resident company headed by Noel and Jack *O'Brien. Today the company performs in the replica as well as in the 612-seat outdoor Lowell Davies Theatre and the 225-seat Cassius Carter Centre Stage. The repertory is large and varied, including classic revivals with new plays and musicals. Under O'Brien's leadership the theatre has found national attention, sending several works to Broadway, including *Into the Woods, Jake's Women, a popular revival of *Damn Yankees, Play On!, and The Full Monty. The Old Globe won the regional theatre *Tony Award in 1984.

SAN DIEGO REPERTORY THEATRE. Starting out in California as a street theatre troupe called Indian Magique, it became a professional resident theatre in 1976 under the leadership of producing director Sam Woodhouse and artistic director Douglas Jacobs. The company moved to its current home, the Lyceum Theatre in Horton Plaza, in 1986. The repertory is traditional, though some new

works, such as It Ain't Nothin' But the Blues, have garnered attention and transferred to New York.

SAN FRANCISCO (California). While the city did not join the theatrical ranks until relatively late, it soon became an exciting and major center. Shortly after the 1849 gold rush, eccentric impresarios such as David "Doc" *Robinson came to the fore, but they were quickly replaced by more durable figures: Thomas *Maguire was a major manager; Mrs. *Judah a popular actress. Lawrence *Barrett and John *McCullough also spent significant portions of their careers there, while David *Belasco received his earliest training in the city's playhouses. Among the famous theatres were the raffish *Bella Union, the *Tivoli Opera House, the *Baldwin, and the *California. New theatres were quickly built after the 1906 earthquake. Among the important figures and organizations to emerge were Homer *Curran, Edwin *Lester, and their San Francisco Light Opera Company. After World War II the city saw the rise of the *Actor's Workshop and the *American Conservatory Theatre as well as numerous interesting Off-Broadway style groups, including the *Magic Theatre, Inc., Eureka Theatre Company, New Conservatory Theatre Center, *San Francisco Mime Troupe, Lorraine Hansberry Theatre, Theatre Rhinoceros, the traveling Jewish Theatre, and nearby *Berkeley Repertory Theatre and Marin Theatre Company. San Francisco is still an active touring center, with road shows playing in the Orpheum, Golden Gate, and Curran Theatres.

SAN FRANCISCO MIME TROUPE. Although this California company began doing silent mime plays, it soon evolved into a "collective" of artists more interested in avant-garde performance pieces and highly stylized dramatics that "mimic" more than mime. The troupe was founded in 1962 by R. G. Davis, who had studied pantomime in Paris. By the late 1960s the group's agenda was defiantly political, yet it often used satire and commedia dell'arte theatrics in performances about very serious topics. They have no artistic director but instead work as a committee in devising scripts and performance ideas. Much of the time is spent touring, and many of the performances are outdoors. The unique company won a *Tony Award in 1987 for its excellence in regional theatre.

SANDERSON, Julia [née Julia Sackett] (1887–1975), singer and actress. The doll-faced beauty, who was the leading musical star between the heydays of Lillian *Russell and Marilyn *Miller, was born in Springfield, Massachusetts, and was the daughter of a popular actor, Albert Sackett. She made her debut as a child in Philadelphia with Forepaugh's Stock Company. After serving a five-year apprenticeship there she appeared in the chorus of several musicals before her big break came as De Wolf *Hopper's leading lady in a 1904 revival of *Wang. Important roles followed in both New York and London before she achieved stardom with her performance in *The Arcadians* (1910). Sanderson's other successes included *The Siren* (1911); *The Sunshine Girl* (1913); *The *Girl from Utah* (1914), in which she introduced "They Didn't Believe Me"; *Sybil* (1916); *Rambler Rose* (1917); and *The Canary* (1918). In many of these shows she was co-starred with Donald *Brian and Joseph *Cawthorn. So popular was the trio that George M. *Cohan saluted them with the song "Julia, Donald and Joe" in *The Cohan Revue of 1916*. After playing in *Hitchy Koo, 1920*, she joined her husband, Frank Crumit, in her last Broadway success, *Tangerine* (1921). Sanderson later toured in prominent roles in *No, No, Nanette* (1925) and *Oh, Kay!* (1927), then played with Crumit in vaudeville before retiring from the stage. Although she had a fine voice and was exceptionally comely, she lacked the verve and exploitive sex appeal of her contemporaries, either Lillian Russell or Marilyn Miller.

SANDS, Diana (1934–73), actress. She was an attractive, stylish African-American player who managed in her short life to break barriers, playing classical roles usually denied blacks and getting cast in contemporary roles written for white women. A native New Yorker, she was educated at the Performing Arts High School and trained at the Herbert *Berghof Studio. Sands made an impressive Broadway debut in 1959 as the radical daughter Beneatha in the original *A *Raisin in the Sun*. She was lauded for her bereaved Juanita in *Blues for Mister Charlie* (1964), then made Broadway history by being cast as the call girl Doris in *The Owl and Pussycat* (1964), a role written with no indication of race. Sands's other noteworthy performances include a vibrant *Saint Joan* (1968) at *Lincoln Center, the wacky Red Cross worker Ruth in *We Bombed in New Haven* (1968), and the outspoken New Yorker Gloria in *The Gingham Dog* (1969).

SARATOGA; or, Pistols for Seven (1870), a comedy by Bronson *Howard. [*Fifth Avenue Theatre, 101 perf.] Bob Sackett (James *Lewis) is engaged to the lovely belle Effie Remington (Fanny *Davenport), but he has also, in one manner or another, promised himself to the widow Olivia Alston (Fanny *Morant), the newly wed Lucy Carter (Clara *Morris), and the popular little flirt Virginia Vanderpool (Linda Dietz). Attempting to escape from the mess he has gotten himself into, Bob takes off for Saratoga, where, to his horror, he is confronted by the four women as well as by Lucy's wildly jealous husband, Frederick (J. Burnett), and the elder

Vanderpools (William *Davidge and Mrs. *Gilbert). One of the finest of American 19th-century comedies, this broadly farcical piece produced by Augustin *Daly was also one of the first American works to achieve widespread international popularity. It was done in England as *Brighton* and in Germany as *Seine erste und einzige Liebe*.

SARDI'S RESTAURANT (New York). Long the favorite eatery in New York theatrical circles, it was founded in 1921 by Eugenia and Vincent Sardi in the basement of a brownstone on West 44th Street. The brownstone was torn down in 1926 to make way for what is now the *St. James Theatre, so the *Shuberts built the Sardis a new restaurant slightly to the east on the same street. The walls of Sardi's are covered with celebrated caricatures of theatrical figures and were done first by Alex Gard and, after his death in 1947, by Don Bevan and Richard Baratz. It has become a traditional gathering place where actors and others associated with a new show await the early reviews. Vincent Sardi Jr. sold the restaurant in 1986. It closed briefly in 1990, then reopened, and has again become a popular nightspot.

SARDOU, Victorien (1831–1908), playwright. One of the most successful French dramatists of his day and an exponent, like *Scribe before him, of the "well-made" play, he saw many of his most successful Parisian works find a welcome in America. Among the best received were *Ferreol* (1876), *Diplomacy* (1878), *A Scrap of Paper* (1879), *Divorçons* (1882), *Fedora* (1883), *La Tosca* (1888), *Gismonda* (1894), and *Madame Sans-Gêne* (1895). Most closely identified with his work in America was Fanny *Davenport, who re-created here many of the roles written for Sarah *Bernhardt. One curious play of his was *L'Oncle Sam*, which the French government attempted to ban, surprisingly, as too derogatory of Americans. Augustin *Daly agreed to produce it in New York but found no success; since no Americans took serious offense, a Parisian mounting followed the 1873 New York premiere.

SARGENT, Epes (1813–80), playwright. The Boston journalist, novelist, and author of tracts on spiritualism was also for a brief time a successful playwright. His best-known work was *Velasco* (1837), which was first performed by James E. *Murdoch in Boston and later produced in New York, Philadelphia, and London. Its story, which Sargent said was based on the career of Rodrigo Diaz (El Cid), told of star-crossed lovers whose romance is destroyed by jealous or vengeful outsiders. Sargent's other tragedies were *The Bride of Genoa* (1837) and *The Priestess* (1855), and his comedies included *The Candid Critic*, *The Lampoon*, and *Change Makes Change*. From 1839 to 1847 he lived in New York, where he was an editor of the *Mirror*. During this time he befriended Anna Cora *Mowatt, and it was at his suggestion that she wrote her famous comedy *Fashion*. He also aided Mowatt in launching her career as an actress.

SARONY, Napoleon (1821–96), photographer. The most famous of 19th-century theatrical photographers, said to have photographed over thirty thousand actors or actresses, he was born in Quebec, where he studied lithography under his father. Coming to New York in 1833, he eventually co-founded the lithographic firm of Sarony and Major, which pioneered in the modern theatrical poster. He sold the company after his wife's death and went to Europe to study painting but soon found an even greater interest in the new art of photography. While in England he photographed Adah Isaacs *Menken in scenes from *Mazeppa*. The popularity of these photographs established him in his new career. Sarony returned to America in 1865 and quickly became by far the leading figure in his field. He did not like to photograph actual productions, preferring that performers pose formally in his studios.

SAROYAN, William (1908–81), playwright. The eccentric, spirited author was born in Fresno, California, where his Armenian parents were fruit farmers and where he worked at odd jobs before gaining fame as a short-story writer. He came to playgoers' attention with *My Heart's in the Highlands* (1939) but became famous with his much lauded *The *Time of Your Life* (1939), which won the *Pulitzer Prize, although Saroyan noisily rejected it. His later works included *Love's Old Sweet Song* (1940); *The Beautiful People* (1941); *Across the Board on Tomorrow Morning* and *Talking to You* (1942); *Hello, Out There* (1942); *Get Away Old Man* (1943); and *The Cave Dwellers* (1957). Wolcott *Gibbs called the writer "the most completely undisciplined talent in American letters," and Brooks *Atkinson, in a preface to Saroyan's published plays, noted, "When he writes out of general relish, usually in isolated scenes, [he] is at his best and made a definite contribution to the mood of these times, [but] when he permits himself to discuss ideas he can write some of the worst nonsense that ever clattered out of a typewriter." Biography: *A Daring Young Man*, John Leggett, 2002.

SATURDAY'S CHILDREN (1927), a play by Maxwell *Anderson. [*Booth Theatre, 310 perf.] After Bobby Halevy (Ruth *Gordon) nabs the man of her dreams, Rims O'Neill (Roger Pryor), she quickly realizes how unrealistic her ideas of married life were. Financial problems, family interference, and

a certain immaturity all converge to destroy the marriage. Bobby leaves Rims and takes a room in a boardinghouse that forbids men to call on lady tenants. Rims, still deeply in love, climbs a fire escape to visit Bobby and convinces her that though Saturday's child must struggle for a living, life is worthless without love. Percy *Hammond of the *Herald Tribune* called the work a "hushed little comedy" and admired "the quiet speed with which it tells its story."

SAVAGE, Henry W[ilson] (1859–1927), producer. Born in New Durham, New Hampshire, he was educated at Harvard and had become a prosperous Boston real estate agent until a client who ran the Castle Square Opera House failed and he was forced to assume its management. He turned it into one of the nation's most successful stock companies, eventually sending out several branch companies. Moving to New York, Savage produced a series of notable turn-of-the-century hits, including *The *Sultan of Sulu* (1902), *The *County Chairman* (1903), *The *Prince of Pilsen* (1903), *The *College Widow* (1904), *The *Merry Widow* (1907), *Madame X* (1909), *Excuse Me* (1911), and *Sari* (1914). He often prefaced his name with "Colonel," although his claim to that distinction was a matter of dispute.

SCANLAN, W[illiam] J[ames] (1856–98), actor and singer. A puckish performer with a fine Irish tenor voice, he was born into a poor family in Springfield, Massachusetts, and while still in his teens formed a vaudeville act with William Cronin. After the act disbanded in 1877 he toured with Minnie Palmer before achieving success as the Irish spy Carroll Moore in *Friend and Foe* (1882). The role brought him to the attention of Augustus *Pitou, under whose aegis he starred in similar parts in such plays of Gaelic romance as *Shane-Na-Lawn* (1885), *The Irish Minstrel* (1886), *Myles Aroon* (1888), and *Mavourneen* (1891). Scanlan composed many of the songs he introduced, including "Peek-A-Boo," which was one of the most popular ditties of its era. Like several great stars of his day, he had to be forcibly removed from the stage when he became insane as the result of paresis.

SCARBOROUGH, George [Moore] (1875–1951), playwright. Born in Mount Carmel, Texas, he was educated at Baylor University and the University of Texas to become a lawyer but elected instead to write for the theatre. While waiting to find a producer he served as a newspaperman and as a federal Secret Service agent, later putting his experience to use in several of his melodramas. Over a dozen of his plays reached Broadway, his most notable successes including *The Lure* (1913), *At Bay*

(1913), *The Heart of Wetona* (1916), *Moonlight and Honeysuckle* (1919), and *The Son-Daughter* (1919).

SCARECROW, THE (1911), a play by Percy *Mac-Kaye. [*Garrick Theatre, 23 perf.] With the aid of a Yankee version of the Devil known as Dickon (Edmund *Breese), the 17th-century witch Goody Rickby (Alice Fisher) turns a scarecrow into a man she names Lord Ravensbane (Frank Reicher). To retaliate against Justice Merton (Brigham Royce), who once had been her lover, she sends Ravensbane to Merton's home, where the young man becomes betrothed to Merton's niece Rachel (Beatrice Irwin). Richard Talbot (Earle Brown), her former fiancé, exposes Ravensbane. At the same time, however, Ravensbane has developed a heart and a conscience. Realizing the damage he has done, he purposely destroys the brimstone-burning pipe that has kept him alive. His dying lament is, "Oh, Rachel, could I have been a man—!" Based on Hawthorne's tale "Feathertop," the play was first presented by the *Harvard Dramatic Club in 1909. Its commercial production by Henry B. *Harris was a failure, but the odd and engaging piece remained popular with collegiate and amateur groups. It was given a fine Off-Broadway revival in the 1953–54 season.

SCENE (and Lighting) DESIGN IN AMERICAN THEATRE. Although the decorative aspects of theatre are essential to the complete enjoyment of a play and to the understanding of our theatre's history, no full-scale study of American set design and set designers, along with costumes, lighting, and their creators, has yet been published. Only individual artists have been researched and documented. Until such a complete history appears, only a cursory outline of developments can be offered, and this must of necessity neglect the almost wholly uncharted developments and figures away from New York. Virtually nothing is known about the scenery employed in the very earliest American theatricals, although it can be assumed that it was a possibly primitive version of the wing-and-drop or wing-and-shutter variety used in English playhouses. The first relatively sophisticated settings probably appeared when the elder Lewis *Hallam and his company sailed from England to establish a traveling company in the colonies. There is reason to believe that Hallam brought much of his scenery with him and that it had previously been used at London's Goodman's Fields Theatre. A notice printed in the *Virginia Gazette* at the time of Hallam's arrival nonetheless claimed "the Scenes, Cloaths, and Decorations, are entirely new, extremely rich, [and] being painted by the best Hands in London, are excelled by none in Beauty and Elegance." Despite the period settings of some of the plays Hallam offered, his costumes were undoubtedly contemporary, in the fashion of the time, and his generalized settings, which had to be used in various plays, lit by candlelight. If we cannot be certain of the quality of Hallam's scenery, we can be even less certain of what it represented. Within a few decades most playhouses retained at least five basic settings—a rich interior, a simple interior, a garden, a woodland scene, and a street scene—but whether the limited space available to Hallam and the exigencies of frequent travel allowed him the luxury of even these few settings is unknown. Certainly after the revolution, when Lewis *Hallam Jr. headed the Old American Company, a temporary decline in quality may have become evident. In 1787 the New York *Advertiser* complained, "Frequently where the author intended a handsome street or beautiful landscape, we only see a dirty piece of canvas . . . nor is it uncommon to see the back of the stage represent a street while the side scenes represent a wood." Yet the final years of the 18th century saw the emergence of the first great American set designers with the work of the European-trained Charles *Ciceri in Philadelphia and New York and Monsieur *Audin in Charleston. Indeed Ciceri, who worked in Paris and London before coming to America, is credited with bringing here the first transparent scrim. At the same time, so far as American theatre was concerned, the hesitant introduction of architecturally conceived scenery, as opposed to mere painted flats, may have occurred in Boston in 1797 with the production there of John Daly *Burk's *Bunker Hill,* in which the hill was "raised gradually by boards extended from the stage to a bench." The English-born John Joseph *Holland, long connected with New York's *Park Theatre, is sometimes credited with being the first American set designer to attempt historical accuracy in his work, but it was not until two decades after his death that a burgeoning movement toward realism ushered in two major developments. The first was the box set, which allowed playgoers to imagine themselves as viewing a room from an invisible fourth wall. This new treatment of interiors received instant and widespread attention because it was introduced in conjunction with the most successful play of the era, Dion *Boucicault's *London Assurance* (1841). Five years later the visit of Charles *Kean, far more than Holland's tentative efforts, established the notion that theatrical period pieces should be accurately set.

The older tradition of standard settings built in the wing-and-drop style received a further blow with the erection of Edwin *Booth's ill-fated theatre in 1869. Booth dispensed with the exaggeratedly raked stage, which made realism difficult; with proscenium doors, which had been used for entrances and exits that were difficult or at least artificial by the wing-and-drop designs; and with the huge apron in front of the proscenium. None of these changes originated with Booth, but the actor's distinguished reputation gained them immediate acceptance.

The 19th century also saw the two major basic changes in lighting come about. The introduction of gas lighting is believed to have taken place at Philadelphia's *Chestnut Street Theatre in 1816, although the expense of installing the gas works, which required an elaborate distillation of coal, prevented gas from becoming commonplace for nearly two decades. For example, the first New York house to convert was the Chatham in 1825. The first practical spotlight, known as the limelight, the calcium light, the oxyhydrogen light, or the Drummond light, while perfected in Europe in the 1840s, came into general usage here only about the time of the Civil War. There is reason to believe it was first employed in New York in the 1866 production of The *Black Crook. Primitive electric lighting began to gain a foothold in the 1880s and grew into a standard method of illumination far more rapidly than gas had. These brighter methods of lighting gradually helped eliminate the exaggerated makeup and acting that darker stages had required.

Although architecturally conceived scenery became increasingly frequent throughout the 19th century and into the early 20th century, most scenic effects were achieved by careful painting, and set designers were therefore usually known as scene painters, a term not necessarily demeaning. A partial list of the great American scene painters during these years would include Ernest *Albert, D. Frank *Dodge, Philip *Goatcher, the *Grain family, Ernest *Gros, George *Heister, George *Hielge, Henry E. *Hoyt, Richard *Marston, Thomas G. *Moses, Joseph *Physioc, James *Roberts, Russell *Smith, Edward G. *Unitt, William *Voegtlin, and Charles *Witham. That these men worked largely in New York, Chicago, and Philadelphia suggests not that these cities excelled in set design but that our knowledge of scenery and scene painters elsewhere is sadly scant.

The movement away from realistically painted flats and toward more stylized, suggestive, and architecturally conceived sets, usually enhanced by imaginative lighting, began to gain prominence around the time of World War I. Many historians agree that it was the work of Robert Edmond *Jones for the 1915 production of The Man Who Married a Dumb Wife that "sounded the note that began the American revolution in stage scenery." Other designers of distinction whose work from the 1930s on have been notable and influential included Boris *Aronson, Lemuel *Ayers, Watson Barratt, Howard *Bay, Norman *Bel Geddes, Aline *Bern-

stein, Stewart *Chaney, William and Jean *Eckart, Ben Edwards, Frederick *Fox, Mordecai *Gorelik, David Hays, George *Jenkins, Jo *Mielziner, Donald *Oenslager, Livingston *Platt, Lee *Simonson, Oliver *Smith, Cleon *Throckmorton, and Joseph *Urban. Their work was often made even more attractive by the artistry of modern lighting designers, though some of these designers created their own lighting effects. Indeed, with the increasing use of transparent scrims and skeletonized settings, lighting frequently became an integral part of the stage picture rather than serving merely to illuminate it. In a few avant-garde instances lighting served as the primary scenery. Recent seasons have seen such technically elaborate scenery, especially in imported English musicals, that computers have been needed to control it. By the last decades of the 20th century, the busiest and most accomplished scenic designers included John Lee *Beatty, John* Conklin, David Jenkins, Marjorie Bradley *Kellogg, Heidi *Landesman, Peter Larkin, Eugene *Lee, Ming Cho *Lee, Santo *Loquasto, David *Mitchell, Douglas *Schmidt, Robin *Wagner, Tony *Walton, and the British Bob Crowley and John *Napier. Among the noteworthy lighting designers during the last decades of the 20th century are Martin Aronstein, Ken *Billington, Peggy *Eisenhauer, Abe *Feder, Jules *Fisher, Paul *Gallo, John J. Gleason, David Hersey, Tharon *Musser, Richard *Nelson, Jean *Rosenthal, Thomas *Skelton, and Jennifer *Tipton.

SCHARY, Dore. See Sunrise at Campobello.

SCHEFF, [Friedrike Jaeger] **Fritzi** (1879–1954), singer. The tiny, fiery prima donna with the hourglass figure was born in Vienna, where her mother was a leading singer with the Imperial Opera. She studied and sang in Europe before being brought to the Metropolitan Opera House in 1901. Two years later Charles *Dillingham persuaded her to leave the opera stage and starred her in Victor *Herbert's Babette. Scheff subsequently played the principal roles in five other musicals, the most famous being Herbert's *Mlle. Modiste (1905) in which she introduced "Kiss Me Again." After several seasons in vaudeville her career began to fade, although she remained on stage virtually until her death. Except for occasional revivals of Mlle. Modiste and a 1908 Herbert operetta, The Prima Donna, she thereafter played mostly supporting roles.

SCHENCK, Joe. See Van and Schenck.

SCHILDKRAUT, Joseph (1896–1964), actor. The swarthy, dashingly handsome son of the famous German and Yiddish actor Rudolf Schildkraut, he was born in Vienna and studied for the stage both in Germany and at the *American Academy of Dramatic Arts. His first American appearances were under his father's aegis in German-language performances at the Irving Place Theatre in 1910. After acting for Max *Reinhardt and other famous producers in Europe, Schildkraut had his first American success as the feckless carnival barker *Liliom (1921), followed by his lauded performance as the roguish artist-lover Benvenuto Cellini in The *Firebrand (1924). In the 1930s he was an important member of Eva *Le Gallienne's *Civic Repertory Theatre and appeared in films before returning to Broadway as the mild-mannered murderer *Uncle Harry (1942). Schildkraut's last major role was as Mr. Frank in The *Diary of Anne Frank (1955). Autobiography: My Father and I, 1959.

SCHISGAL, Murray. See Luv.

SCHMIDT, Douglas (b. 1942), scenic designer. He was born in Cincinnati and educated at Boston University before beginning his design career in regional theatre. Schmidt is known for his keen sense of detail and ways of evoking mood, but his work has been very eclectic, as seen in such varied Broadway productions as *Grease (1972), Veronica's Room (1973), Over Here! (1974), Frankenstein (1981), *Porgy and Bess (1983), and *42nd Street (2001).

SCHMIDT, Harvey. See Jones and Schmidt.

SCHNEIDER, [Abram Leopoldovich] Alan (1917–84), director. He was born in Karkov, Russia, but raised and educated in America, where he studied at the University of Wisconsin and Cornell and with Lee *Strasberg. He first major directing job in New York was in 1948 with A Long Way from Home, followed by such notable Broadway assignments as The Remarkable Mr. Pennypacker (1953), Anastasia (1954), *Who's Afraid of Virginia Woolf? (1962), The Ballad of the Sad Café (1963), *Tiny Alice (1964), A *Delicate Balance (1967), *Moonchildren (1972), A Texas Trilogy (1976), and Loose Ends (1979). Because much of the most exciting contemporary theatre was on regional stages, Schneider spent a large part of his career directing at college theatres and other important playhouses away from Manhattan. He mounted many productions for the *Arena Stage, ranging from Shakespeare and Chekhov to world premieres, and was made an associate director of the organization in 1971. He was also a director of John *Houseman's *Acting Company. Off Broadway he figured importantly in staging many of Samuel *Beckett's plays, including the American premieres of *Waiting for Godot (1956), Endgame (1958), and Happy Days (1961). Autobiography: Entrances, 1986.

SCHOENFELD, Gerald. See Shuberts.

SCHWAB, Laurence (1893-1951), producer and librettist. Born in Boston and educated at Harvard, he first found success when he co-produced the musical The Gingham Girl (1922). Subsequent productions, often mounted in collaboration with Frank *Mandel, included Captain Jinks (1925), *Queen High (1926), The *Desert Song (1926), *Good News! (1927), The *New Moon (1928), *Follow Thru (1929), Take a Chance (1932), and May Wine (1935). Schwab also served as co-librettist for most of these musicals.

SCHWARTZ, Arthur. See Dietz and Schwartz.

SCHWARTZ, Jean (1878–1956), composer. Born in Budapest but brought to America at the age of ten, he began his musical career as a song plugger for a sheet-music firm. Like most composers of the time he heard his earliest songs sung as interpolations in others' scores: "Rip Van Winkle Was a Lucky Man" from The Sleeping Beauty and the Beast (1901), "Mr. Dooley" from A Chinese Honeymoon (1902), and "Bedelia" from The Jersey Lily (1903). Between 1904 and 1928 Schwartz wrote the greater part or the entire score for about thirty Broadway musicals, including many of The *Passing Shows. His 1910 revue Up and Down Broadway left behind "Chinatown, My Chinatown." Almost all of these songs were written with lyricist William Jerome (1865–1932), but his most enduring hit was an interpolation in the 1918 *Jolson extravaganza, Sinbad, "Rock-A-Bye Your Baby with a Dixie Melody," for which Joe Young and Sam Lewis provided words.

SCHWARTZ, Maurice (1890–1960), actor and manager. Born in Sedikor, Russia, he came to America in 1901 and four years later gave his first professional performance with a Yiddish theatre in Baltimore. He acted in various cities before joining David *Kessler in New York in 1912. When World War I made German-language plays unpopular, he took over the Irving Place Theatre and turned it into the *Yiddish Art Theatre, an organization he headed until 1950. Called the "John Barrymore of the Yiddish Theatre," he was an actor of the old school. Dark-haired and with piercing eyes, he had a flamboyant style, a rumbling voice, and, according to Yiddish theatre historian Nahma Sandrow, "distinctive rapid gabbling inflections." Although Schwartz made infrequent appearances on English-language stages, it was largely for his work in Yiddish that he was admired. Among his most noted roles were his Shylock and his aging Hassidic rabbi in Yoshe Kalb.

SCHWARTZ, Stephen (Lawrence] (b. 1948), composer and lyricist. A New Yorker who was educated at Juilliard and Carnegie Tech, his career started propitiously with three musicals that each ran over a thousand performances: *Godspell (1971), *Pippin (1972), and The *Magic Show (1974). Despite the commendable songs in The Baker's Wife (1976), Working (1978), and Rags (1986), Schwartz's later theatre career has been uneven. His Children of Eden, first produced in London in 1991, has enjoyed many regional productions in America. His most recent project is Wicked (2003). Also a very successful songwriter for films, Schwartz's work is very eclectic, his songs ranging from rock to vaudeville camp to highly romantic.

SCOTT, George C[ampbell] (1927–99), actor. Born in Wise, Virginia, and educated at the University of Missouri, he first gained prominence as an imprisoned nobleman in the *Circle in the Square's 1958 revival of Children of Darkness. Among his subsequent assignments were the Judge Advocate Lt. Col. Chapman in The Andersonville Trial (1959), the tough old farmer Ephraim Cabot in *Desire under the Elms (1963), Southern businessman Ben Hubbard in The *Little Foxes (1967), three hassled New Yorkers in *Plaza Suite (1968), Dr. Astrov in Uncle Vanya (1973), Willy Loman in *Death of a Salesman (1975), swindler Foxwell J. Sly in Sly Fox (1976), egotistical actor Garry Essendine in Present Laughter (1982), Gramps in *On Borrowed Time (1991), and defense attorney Henry Drummond in *Inherit the Wind (1996). For the *New York Shakespeare Festival he essayed Antony, Richard III, and Shylock. Although the hard-faced actor was often perceived as a serious dramatic performer, and he showed great skill in such parts, much of his success came from his often overlooked abilities as a comedian. Scott also enjoyed an impressive film career.

SCOTT, John R. (1808–56), actor. Born in Philadelphia, where he was active in amateur theatricals, he made his professional debut at New York's *Park Theatre in 1829, playing Malcolm to Junius *Booth's Macbeth. He rose quickly to become a favorite both at the *Arch Street Theatre in Philadelphia and at the *Bowery in New York. Although he played such classic tragic parts as Othello, Hamlet, and Sir Giles Overreach, Scott was most admired for his romantic leads in the new melodramas of the day, but he never won favor at the most prestigious houses. *Ireland wrote of him, "Possessing a fine personal appearance and great natural abilities, he might, with proper caution in personal habits and a closer application to study, have ranked among the very highest of our actors." In the latter part of his career he was apt to disappoint his audiences by his sudden disappearances.

SCOTT, Martha (1914–2003), actress. She will always be remembered as the original Emily Webb in *Our Town (1938), a role with which she made her Broadway and Hollywood debuts. Scott was born in Jamesport, Missouri, and educated at the University of Michigan before going into stock. She never received the chance to originate another great role like Emily, usually acting in short-lived plays or replacing others in long-run hits. But she later developed into a fine character actress. Her last Broadway appearance was as the saintly old Rebecca Nurse in the 1991 revival of The *Crucible.

SCRIBE, [Augustin] Eugene (1791–1861), playwright. The leading French dramatist of the first half of the 19th century, he reacted to the overblown, romantic melodramas of his day by devising the "well-made" play in which essentially middle-class problems were presented in neat, economically contrived plots and with prosaic, commonplace dialogue. While these plays were theatrically effective, many detractors felt they merely substituted taut construction for vitality and depth. Although a number of his works were translated and met with varying success in America, he was best known and largely remembered here for a single drama, Adrienne Lecouvreur.

SCUBA DUBA (1967), a comedy by Bruce Jay Friedman. [New Theatre, 692 perf.] Harold Wonder (Jerry *Orbach) is an ultraliberal Jewish intellectual whose liberalism is sorely tested when his wife, Jean (Jennifer Warren), runs off with "a spade frogman," Foxtrot (Cleavon Little). Harold seeks reassurance by lugging around his version of a personal security blanket, a scythe; by inviting over an attractive bikinied neighbor; and by conversations with his psychiatrist, Dr. Schoenfeld (Ken Olfson), and his very Jewish mother (Stella Longo). When Jean brings Foxtrot home Harold storms out, telling his wife that he is going shell-hunting with some girls. The Bronx-born **Bruce Jay FRIEDMAN** (b. 1930) studied at the University of Missouri before finding fame as a novelist and a magazine humorist. His particular brand of dark, racial comedy can be seen in his two other notable plays: Steambath (1970) and Have You Spoken to Any Jews Lately? (1995).

SEABROOKE, Thomas Q. [né Thomas James Quigley] (1860–1913), actor. A native of Mount Vernon, New York, he made his debut in 1880 and for the next several years appeared in dramas and a few comedies before he won popularity as star of such musicals as The Isle of Champagne (1894) and Tabasco (1895). His greatest success came in the imported English musical A Chinese Honeymoon (1902). Thereafter, his vogue waned, although he remained a headliner in vaudeville.

SEASCAPE (1975), a play by Edward *Albee. [*Shubert Theatre, 65 perf.; Pulitzer Prize.] On a deserted stretch of beach, the late-middle-aged couple Charlie (Barry *Nelson) and Nancy (Deborah Kerr) are discussing their "pleasant" marriage when two human-sized lizards, Leslie (Frank *Langella) and Sarah (Maureen Anderman), enter from the sea, having taken a giant step in the evolutionary process and are considering becoming land creatures. After a bizarre but articulate discussion by the foursome, the lizards decide to return to the water, but Nancy suggests that one day they shall return because change is inevitable. Widely mixed notices forced the play (produced by Richard *Barr and others) to close before it was awarded the *Pulitzer Prize.

SEASON IN THE SUN (1950), a comedy by Wolcott *Gibbs. [*Cort Theatre, 367 perf.] Tired of writing glib articles for *The New Yorker*, George Crane (Richard *Whorf) flees with his wife, Emily (Nancy Kelly), to the supposed quiet and privacy of Fire Island, where he proposes to dedicate himself to becoming a serious novelist. But quiet and privacy are not what George finds. Instead, his summer cottage turns into a way station for a motley assortment of kooks and bores. In desperation, George returns to the relative sanity of New York City. The comedy was one of the rare successful attempts by a modern critic at playwriting.

SEATTLE REPERTORY THEATRE. After many years of difficulties, this nonprofit theatre in Washington found national recognition in the 1990s and became a favorite place to test original works before sending them on to Broadway. The company was founded in 1963 by Stuart Vaughan and was housed in a building remaining from the Seattle World's Fair. The troupe struggled with financial difficulties for over a decade, but by 1974 its subscription base and reputation in Seattle were secure and the company added a second performance space, Stage 2. Daniel *Sullivan became artistic director in 1981 and helped revitalize the theatre, instituting a New Plays program and expanding the repertory. In 1983 the group moved into the 850-seat Bagley Wright Theatre at the Seattle Center and added the 140-seat PONCHO Forum space for new works. By the 1990s the Seattle Rep was sending such works as Wendy *Wasserstein's *The *Heidi Chronicles, The *Sisters Rosensweig,* and *An American Daughter* to Broadway, as well as plays by Neil *Simon and other established playwrights. The company received the 1990 *Tony Award for outstanding regional theatre.

SECOND MAN, THE (1927), a comedy by S. N. *Behrman. [Guild Theatre, 178 perf.] Clark Story

(Alfred *Lunt), a novelist and carefree hedonist, proposes to marry the rich, understanding Mrs. Kendall Frayne (Lynn *Fontanne), but his plans are sidetracked when Monica Grey (Margalo *Gillmore) tells him she is pregnant. Seeming to accept his fate, he ruefully tells Monica's disappointed suitor, Alistin Lowe (Earle *Larimore), how dreary the prospect of marriage to Monica appears to him—"Her talk is not small. It is infinitesimal." Inevitably Monica and Clark recognize they are wrong for each other. She is reconciled with Alistin, while Clark agrees to let Mrs. Kendall keep him in luxury. Although many critics complained about the slight plot of the *Theatre Guild's offering, most agreed with John Mason *Brown, who hailed the play's "shimmering dialogue."

SECOND STAGE (New York). Dedicated to producing plays of the recent past that did not get the recognition they were due, this company was founded by Carole Rothman in 1979. The goal of producing works ahead of their time or ones that suffered from inadequate original productions allows the company a wide field to choose from. The Second Stage brought attention to such works as *Painting Churches* (1983), *Coastal Disturbances* (1987), *Reckless* (1988), *Spoils of War* (1988), and *The Good Times Are Killing Me* (1991), most of which were new to most audiences. The company has also supported emerging playwrights and has presented early, forgotten works by well-known writers, such as August Wilson's *Jitney* (2000) and Stephen *Sondheim's *Saturday Night* (2000). In recent history the company has premiered new works as well, most memorably *The Waverly Gallery* and *Metamorphoses*.

SECRET GARDEN, THE (1991), a musical play by Marsha *Norman (book, lyrics), Lucy Simon (music). [*St. James Theatre, 706 perf.] Frances Hodgson *Burnett's beloved tale, about the morose orphaned girl Mary Lennox (Daisy Eagan) and the new life she discovers when she brings her dead aunt's garden back to life, was presented as a lovely chamber piece accented by Heidi *Landesman's ingenious sets and held together by masterful direction by Susan Schulman. Mandy *Patinkin was Mary's gloomy Uncle Archibald; John Babcock was his bedridden son, Colin; Alison Fraser the understanding maid Martha; Rebecca Luker the ghost of Aunt Lily; and John Cameron Mitchell the Yorkshire conjurer Dickon. *Notable songs*: Lily's Eyes; Winter's on the Wing; Where in the World; Race You to the Top of the Morning.

SECRET SERVICE (1896), a play by William *Gillette. [*Garrick Theatre, 176 perf.] Lewis Dumont (Gillette), a Northern agent posing as the

Confederate officer Captain Thorne, comes to Richmond, where he wins the affection of loyal Virginian Edith Varney (Amy Busby). Benton Arrelsford (Campbell Gollan) of the War Office suspects that Thorne is a spy, but Thorne cleverly confounds all of Arrelsford's attempts to expose him. However, Edith has come to realize Thorne's real position, so she offers him a means of escape. He rejects the chance, yet he is sufficiently shamed that he revokes forged orders that he has telegraphed to Confederate lines and which would have prompted an unnecessary retreat. When he is arrested and sent to prison, Edith promises to wait for his release. A gripping, soundly constructed melodrama, in which, as *Quinn noted, "Not a word is wasted and not an action," it was originally tried out with Maurice *Barrymore as Dumont. Withdrawn for revisions by producer Charles *Frohman, it later gave Gillette one of his greatest successes. The melodrama was frequently revived until the time of World War I, though a splendid *Phoenix Theatre mounting in 1976 with John *Lithgow and Meryl Streep was well received.

SEDLEY-SMITH, W. H. See *Drunkard, The*.

SEESAW. See *Two for the Seesaw*.

SEGAL, Vivienne (1897–1992), actress and singer. The petite, chubby-faced beauty was born in Philadelphia, where she studied for a career in opera and appeared with local opera companies. Her father, a prominent Philadelphia physician, bought her the leading role in *The Blue Paradise* (1915). Paying for entry into the theatre was nothing new, but most performers who bought their way in had little talent and soon disappeared. Segal was not only lovely to look at and listen to but proved a good actress and superb comedienne, so she remained at the top for her entire career. Among the musicals in which she played leading roles were *Miss 1917*, *Oh, Lady! Lady!!* (1918), *The Little Whopper* (1919), *The Yankee Princess* (1922), *The *Desert Song* (1926), *The *Three Musketeers* (1928), *The Chocolate Soldier (1931)*, and *I Married an Angel* (1938). Her later (and perhaps her most memorable) roles were the sly, hedonistic Vera Simpson in *Pal Joey* (1940 and 1952) and the comic murderess Morgan Le Fay in the 1943 revival of A *Connecticut Yankee*.

SELDES, Gilbert (1893–1970), author and critic. The distinguished writer was born in Alliance, New Jersey, and was graduated from Harvard. He earned widespread recognition with his book *The Seven Lively Arts* (1924), which was one of the earliest serious studies of popular entertainment and in which he insisted that Al *Jolson and Fanny

*Brice were the equal of more traditional stars such as John *Barrymore and Ethel *Barrymore. Seldes also wrote numerous articles and reviews as well as several plays, including an adaptation of *Lysistrata*, which was produced on Broadway in 1930. In his later years he became more interested in radio and television and served as professor and dean at the University of Pennsylvania's Annenberg School of Communication.

SELDES, Marian (b. 1928), actress. The tall, stately performer, known for her durability and dedication, is perhaps the busiest player of her generation, appearing in over fifty New York productions over a period of fifty years. She was born in Manhattan, the daughter of Gilbert *Seldes, and studied dance at the American Ballet School and acting at the *Neighborhood Playhouse School. Seldes's professional acting debut in 1947 was in a Greek tragedy, and for much of her early years she played dramatic parts, but over time her talent for comedy was also displayed. Of Seldes's many stage roles, the most prominent were the spoiled divorcée Julia in A *Delicate Balance* (1966), the bitchy Upper East Sider Marian in *Father's Day* (1971), the hyperventilating playwright's wife Myra in *Deathtrap* (1978), the elegant but fading Fanny Church in *Painting Churches* (1983), the middle-aged character called B in *Three Tall Women* (1994), the outspoken grande dame Madame Desmermortes in *Ring Round the Moon* (1999), the enigmatic Woman in *The Play about the Baby* (2001), and the demonstrative Carlotta Vance in *Dinner at Eight* (2002). Autobiography: *The Bright Lights*, 1984.

SELF (1856), a comedy by Mrs. Sidney F. *Bateman. [Burton's Chambers Street Theatre, 18 perf.] Mrs. Apex (Mrs. A. Parker) lives far beyond her means, as does her unscrupulous son by her first marriage, Charles Sanford (Mr. Morton). Mary (Mrs. E. Davenport), her stepdaughter, on the other hand, has lived prudently and saved $15,000. Charles forges Mary's name to a check of that amount, and when Mr. Apex (Charles *Fisher) later attempts to cash a check Mary has given him, the check bounces. Mary realizes what has happened but refuses to betray her stepbrother. Furious, Mr. Apex orders her out of the house. It requires the thoughtful ministrations of her uncle, the retired banker John Unit (William Burton), to bring the family to its senses. His philosophy takes into account that "after all, our labours are prompted by that great motive power of human nature—Self!" The comedy, which owed a clear debt to the earlier *Fashion, was filled with clever minor characters, who sported such names as Cypher Cynosure and Mr. Promptcash, but it was the character of Unit, not unlike that of Trueman in

Fashion, which stole the show. After producer-actor Burton relinquished the role, John E. *Owens toured in it for many years.

SELWYN, Arch[ibald] (1877?–1959), producer. He appears to have been the son of a Polish-Jewish immigrant whose surname was actually Simon, and he was probably born in Toronto. He came to New York after his older brother Edgar *Selwyn gained success as an actor, then held a series of odd jobs before working in the box office of the Herald Square Theatre. Later he formed a play brokerage business with Edgar, and then the brothers merged with Elisabeth *Marbury and John Ramsay to form the larger *American Play Company. The brothers' other firm, Selwyn and Company, was a major producer whose hits included *Within the Law* (1912), *Under Cover* (1914), *Fair and Warmer* (1915), *Why Marry?* (1917), *Tea for Three* (1918), *Wedding Bells* (1919), *Smilin' Through* (1919), *The Circle* (1921), Jane *Cowl's *Romeo and Juliet* (1923), *Charlot's Revue* (1924), and *Dancing Mothers* (1924). After splitting with his brother he continued to produce alone, although whatever success he had was with importations such as *This Year of Grace* (1928) and, with Florenz *Ziegfeld, *Bitter Sweet* (1929). The Selwyns also built three New York theatres (the Apollo, the Selwyn, and the Times Square) as well as two bandbox playhouses in Chicago.

SELWYN, Edgar (1875–1944), producer and actor. A theatrical jack-of-all-trades, he was born in Cincinnati to a poor, peripatetic Jewish family whose last name apparently was Simon. He made his stage debut in 1896 in *Secret Service*, then played several years in stock. With his swarthy good looks he began to rise but not fast enough to suit him. He turned his hand to playwriting to create his own romantic vehicles, among them *Pierre of the Plains* (1908) and *The Arab* (1911). Then he abruptly abandoned acting, although he continued to write. By this time, however, he was joined by his brother Arch *Selwyn, and the pair entered into a career of play brokering, producing, and theatre building. After their company was dissolved he went his own way, producing alone or with others such hits as *Gentlemen Prefer Blondes* (1926), *The Barker* (1927), and *Strike Up the Band* (1930) before he retired in 1941.

SENATOR, THE (1890), a play by David D. Lloyd and Sydney *Rosenfeld. [Star Theatre, 119 perf.] Silas Denman (J. G. Padgett) and his daughter, Mabel (Lizzie Hudson Collier), come to Washington to press a claim dating back to the War of 1812. Sympathetic Senator Hannibal Rivers (William H. *Crane) agrees to help, since the money will allow Mabel to wed the Austrian diplomat Count Ernst von Strahl (Henry Bergman). But Rivers soon learns that von Strahl is a faithless philanderer. With the help of a rich, coquettish widow, Mrs. Hilary (Georgiana Drew *Barrymore), he exposes the Count while Mrs. Hilary also lures away a crucial senator who would stop the claim. Winning the claim proves too much for old Denman, who suffers a fatal stroke. But Rivers's actions earn him Mabel's hand, while Mrs. Hilary is rewarded with the hand of an officer she has had her eye on. Lloyd died before completing this play, so Rosenfeld was called in to finish it. The role of Rivers was one of Crane's best interpretations. Contemporaries ranked the character with Barnwell Slote of *The *Mighty Dollar* and Colonel Sellers as one of the great pieces of American comic writing.

SEPARATE ROOMS (1940), a comedy by Joseph Carole, Alan Dinehart, Alex Gottlieb, and Edmund Joseph. [Maxine Elliott's Theatre, 613 perf.] When gossip columnist Jim Stackhouse (Dinehart) learns that Pam (Glenda Farrell) has been reluctant to fulfill her marriage obligations to his brother Don (Lyle Talbot), he blackmails her into becoming a more loving wife. Although dismissed by most critics as a negligible work, the play used cut-rate tickets and a sexually exploitive ad campaign to become one of the biggest hits in a season of hits. **Alan DINEHART** (1890–1944), a native of St. Paul, was a popular performer on vaudeville and legitimate stages and in films who usually played gruff, authoritative figures. Among his many Broadway appearances were those in *Lawful Larceny* (1922), *Rose Briar* (1922), *Applesauce* (1925), *The Marriage Bed* (1929), and *Alley Cat* (1934).

SERBAN, Andrei (b. 1943), director. The internationally known director, who uses minimalism, nontraditional music, and avant-garde approaches to classic texts, was born in Bucharest, Romania, where his productions first attracted attention. Serban immigrated to the States in 1969 but continues to stage controversial productions around the world. His American credits include *The Good Woman of Setzuan* (1975) at *La Mama, *Agamemnon* (1977) and *The Cherry Orchard* (1977) at *Lincoln Center, *The Marriage of Figaro* (1982) at the *Guthrie Theatre, *King Stag* (1984) at the *American Repertory Theatre, *Cymbeline* (1998) in Central Park, and *Hamlet* (1999) at the *Public Theatre.

SERIOUS FAMILY, THE (1849). Morris Barnett's free English adaptation of the French comedy *Un Mari en Champaigne* was first presented by William E. *Burton in 1849 and immediately became one of his greatest hits. Burton portrayed Aminadab Sleek, a comic, cowardly spouter of pious sentiments who is finally routed by young love. The play remained in his repertory for the rest of his career. Although William *Davidge and others later played the role with some success, by the 1880s the play was rarely mounted.

SERVANT IN THE HOUSE, THE (1908), a play by Charles Rann Kennedy. [Savoy Theatre, 80 perf.] Everyone in the home of the Reverend William Smythe (Charles Dalton) mentions that the new butler, the strange and singularly humble Manson (Walter *Hampden), looks familiar. But they are more concerned about the arrival of Smythe's detested brother-in-law, the Bishop of Lancashire (Arthur Lewis), who is virtually deaf and blind and preoccupied with worldly success. The vicar's brother Joshua, long out of touch and now supposedly an important figure in the church, is also expected. The third arrival is to be another long-lost brother, Robert (Tyrone *Power), who took to drink after his wife's death and is now a common laborer. When Robert shows up, the family behaves badly and it remains for the butler Manson to quietly bring the family closer together and teach them the true meaning of their religion. Amazed at Manson's healing powers, the vicar asks him, "In God's name, who are you?" Manson replies, "In God's Name—your brother." Henry *Miller produced the modern morality play, and Walter Prichard *Eaton called it "not a sermon or a tract, but a statement of applied or ethical religion in terms of the drama, a play with its own dramatic appeal and human significance." Almost inevitably, a play such as this had little broad appeal. **Charles Rann KENNEDY** (1871–1950), the grandson of the famous classical scholar of the same name, was an English-born actor and playwright who made his first American appearance as the Doctor and Messenger in a 1903 revival of *Everyman*. While the fact that his American debut was in a medieval morality play may have been mere coincidence, it remains significant that most of his plays had markedly religious bents. Among his other works were *The Winterfeast* (1908), *The Terrible Meek* (1912), and *The Army with Banners* (1918). In later years he produced and played in an annual festival of Greek plays at Millbrook, New York.

SEVEN DAYS (1909), a comedy by Mary Roberts *Rinehart and Avery *Hopwood. [Astor Theatre, 397 perf.] James Wilson (Herbert Corthell) has not told his rich Aunt Selina (Lucille La Verne) about his divorce from his wife, Bella (Hope Latham), so when Selina suddenly appears he is forced to palm off his friend Anne Brown (Florence *Reed) as his wife. Anne is an odd girl, a psychic who is convinced (correctly as it turns out) that there is a burglar in the house. Suddenly a policeman appears and announces that James's cook is in the hospital with a communicable disease. Therefore, everyone in the house is under a seven-day quarantine. Bella suddenly arrives and she, too, is confined. For the next week the group attempts to do household chores and learn to cook, ending up knowing each other all too well. This slight farce, produced by *Wagenhals and *Kemper, was one of the biggest hits of its era and was later made into the musical *Tumble In* (1919).

SEVEN GUITARS (1996), a play by August *Wilson. [*Walter Kerr Theatre, 187 perf.; NYDCC Award.] The title refers to seven residents of Pittsburgh's Hill District in the late 1940s, six of whom gather after the funeral of Floyd Barton (Keith David) to mourn, joke, sing, and reminisce about the promising blues singer who was on the brink of a notable career. In flashbacks we see Floyd trying to convince his side men Canewell (Ruben Santiago-Hudson) and Red Carter (Tommy Hollis) to go to Chicago with him to cut a record. Floyd also tries to sweet-talk his ex-lover Vera (Viola Allen) into joining him, despite his past infidelity. He is successful in the second effort, but when he needs cash for the trip, Floyd takes part in a robbery and then is murdered by the half-crazed old Hedley (Roger Robinson) when he tries to bury the money in the yard. Jack Kroll in *Newsweek* described the play as "a kind of jazz cantata for actors" and the acting, under the direction of Lloyd *Richards, was exemplary, particularly Santiago-Hudson, who won a *Tony Award.

SEVEN KEYS TO BALDPATE (1913), a comedy by George M. *Cohan. [Astor Theatre, 320 perf.] Baldpate is a summer hotel, normally closed in the winter. But when writer William Hallowell Magee (Wallace *Eddinger) bets the owner that he can write a work in twenty-four hours if left alone there, the owner agrees to open the closed hotel for him. As he starts to write, Magee finds he is not alone. Come to the hotel are a gun-toting man, a pretty young newspaper reporter with whom Magee falls in love at first sight, an adventuress, and some politicians and a railroad magnate looking to make a secret deal. Shots and screams galore seem to interrupt Magee's work. But when the twenty-four hours are up, Magee has finished his piece. Were the interruptions a joke staged by the owner of the hotel, or were they simply the story that Magee was writing? Based on the novel by Earl Derr Biggers, the play remained a favorite with summer stock and other similar groups for decades.

7-20-8; or, Casting the Boomerang (1883), a "comedy of to-day" by Augustin *Daly. [Daly's Theatre, 49 perf.] *Portrait of a Lady*, picture #728 at the annual Academy exhibition, so lovingly depicts a beautiful woman and her huge dog that both Courtney Corliss (John *Drew), a handsome young man-about-town, and the remote Lord Lawntennis decide to seek her out. The Englishman sends an effervescent Italian opera impresario, Signor Tamborini (William Gilbert), to do his legwork. Corliss's and Tamborini's search brings them to the country estate of Launcelot Bargiss (James *Lewis), whose daughter Flos (Ada *Rehan) is indeed the lady of the picture. Flos, who fears she will "die of the blues" if she cannot escape her dreary isolation and live in New York City, is immediately taken by Courtney. He suggests she not be afraid of a little adventure, that the follies of youth are the happy memories of old age, and that we all cast little boomerangs that come home to haunt us and eventually amuse us. At the same time Mrs. Bargiss (Mrs. G. H. *Gilbert) has submitted to a shady publisher all the love poems her husband had sent her when they were courting, unaware that he lifted them from Shakespeare and other great poets. Courtney persuades the family to spend a season in New York, where Bargiss is eventually caught having a fling on the town and where he must buy up all copies of his supposed works to save his reputation. When it turns out that Lord Lawntennis is actually seeking to purchase the dog in the painting, Flos and Courtney are free to wed. Based loosely on Schoenthan's *Die Schwabenstreich*, the play was the first major success of Daly's second troupe and saved the company from probable bankruptcy. Although prior commitments shortened the original run, Daly revived and toured the work regularly. The title was derived from the small theatre at 728 Broadway (by then *Harrigan and *Hart's Theatre Comique), which Daly had used briefly after his *Fifth Avenue Theatre had burned.

SEVEN YEAR ITCH, THE (1952), a comedy by George Axelrod. [Fulton Theatre, 1,141 perf.] Richard Sherman (Tom *Ewell) is a nervous paperback book publisher who finds that his wild imagination leads to thoughts of infidelity when he becomes a summer bachelor. These thoughts are given a nudge by a flowerpot that nearly lands on him from a balcony above his. The flowerpot belongs to the girl (Vanessa Brown) upstairs and serves as an excuse for their meeting. But despite Richard's Walter Mittyish dreams of conquest, the voice of his conscience and his own comic apprehensions keep him on the straight and narrow. Brooks *Atkinson hailed the Courtney Burr–Elliott *Nugent production as "original and funny" and it had a long life in summer theatres, still revived today on occasion. The New York–born **George AXELROD** (1922–2003) wrote only one other popular play, *Will Success Spoil Rock Hunter?* (1955), a spoof of Hollywood told in terms of the Faust legend. He was also co-producer of **Visit to a Small Planet* (1957) and later directed several comedies.

SEVENTEEN (1918), a play by Hugh Stanislaus Stange and Stannard Mears. [*Booth Theatre, 225 perf.] Teenager Willie Baxter (Gregory *Kelly), living in a small Indiana town at the turn of the century, is so smitten one summer with the visiting baby-talking Lola Pratt (Ruth *Gordon) that he steals his father's evening clothes in order to court her, leading to romantic and family complications. Stuart *Walker produced the gentle comedy based on Booth *Tarkington's famous novel of puppy love. The same story served as the basis for the musical *Seventeen* (1951) with a book by Sally Benson and a delightful score by Walter Kent (music) and Kim Gannon (lyrics). Kenneth Nelson was Willie and the musical ran 180 performances at the *Broadhurst Theatre. *Notable songs*: Summertime Is Summertime; Reciprocity; After All, It's Spring.

1776 (1969), a musical play by Peter *Stone (book), Sherman Edwards (music, lyrics). [46th Street Theatre, 1,217 perf.; Tony, NYDCC Awards.] In the spring and summer of 1776, delegates have gathered in Philadelphia to work on a Declaration of Independence. Much of the give-and-take is seen through the eyes of the waspish John Adams (William *Daniels), who writes about it to his beloved Abigail (Virginia Vestoff). Thomas Jefferson (Ken *Howard) and Benjamin Franklin (Howard *Da Silva) also play prominent roles. By the time the Declaration is signed, they and their associates have all had to compromise, particularly on the slave issue, but a new nation is created. *Notable songs*: Sit Down, John; Momma Look Sharp; Molasses to Rum; He Plays the Violin. This unusual musical relied on the intelligence of its book and score, fine acting, and an elegant mounting to turn a history lesson into engaging musical theatre. It remains popular with amateur and collegiate groups and was successfully revived in New York by the *Roundabout Theatre in 1997.

SEVENTH HEAVEN (1922), a play by Austin Strong. [*Booth Theatre, 704 perf.] Diane (Helen *Menken) is saved from her brutal sister Nana (Marian Kerby), who would force her into prostitution, by the sympathetic sewer cleaner Chico (George Gaul). He takes her to his shabby seventh-floor walk-up (his seventh heaven), where the two quickly fall in love. When war breaks out and Chico is called into the army, they pledge their loyalty. Diane goes to work in a munitions factory and when the war ends, she is led to believe that Chico has been killed, so she takes up with another man, Brissac (Frank *Morgan). Chico returns, but since he has been blinded, he does not see Brissac. The lovers are reunited, and Diane can only agree with Chico's assessment of himself—that he is "a most remarkable fellow." Many critics felt this highly sentimental drama was immeasurably strengthened by Menken's performance, but the John *Golden show toured successfully for several seasons without her. A musical version failed on Broadway in 1955. **Austin STRONG** (1881–1952) was born in San Francisco but was raised in Samoa (his step-grandfather was Robert Louis Stevenson). Nearly a dozen of his plays reached Broadway, most notably *A Good Little Devil* (1913) and *Three Wise Fools* (1918).

SEX (1926), a play by Jane Mast. [Daly's Theatre, 375 perf.] Margie LaMont (Mae *West) shares her apartment with a blackmailing gigolo. When he drugs a rich socialite, Margie rescues her. But the woman, fearing for her reputation, accuses Margie of theft. So Margie gets even by seducing the woman's son. Not only was the show panned by critics, but many newspapers refused to accept its advertisements. As a result the producer flooded New York with posters boldly plugging the title. The show was still playing to good business when it was raided by the police. West was hauled into court and sentenced to ten days in the workhouse. Jane Mast was to have been Miss West's pen name. An Off-Off-Broadway revival in 2000 proved that the controversial play was more than a curiosity.

SEXUAL PERVERSITY IN CHICAGO (1975), a play by David *Mamet. [St. Clements, 273 perf.] The hustling Bernie (Robert Townsend) is always coaching Danny (Robert Picardo) about sex and how to use women, but Danny ignores his advice and moves in with Deborah (Jane Anderson), looking for a meaningful relationship. But the romance falters and soon Danny is back with Bernie, the two of them once again reducing women to sexual objects. After its 1974 premiere in Chicago, Mamet's first success played Off Off Broadway, then transferred to the larger Cherry Lane Theatre, gaining the attention of the critics and public and launching Mamet's career.

SEYMOUR, William [Gorman] (1850?–1933), director. Born in New York City to actor parents, he began performing while still a child and subsequently worked with most of the great players of the last half of the 19th century. Seymour started to direct while serving a stint at the *Boston Museum late in the century, then moved on to become a principal stager for Charles *Frohman and for *Liebler and Company. His courtesy to actors and his willingness to follow a playwright's ideas won

him wide respect. At the time of his death he was called "the dean" of Broadway's directors.

SHADOW BOX, THE (1977), a play by Michael Cristofer. [*Morosco Theatre, 315 perf.; Pulitzer Prize, Tony Award.] At a hospice for the terminally ill, three patients await death in separate cottages. Joe (Simon Oakland) is a family man who is determined that he and his wife and son enjoy their last weeks together. Brian (Laurence Luckinbill) is a bisexual author who would like to reach an understanding with his ex-wife (Patricia Elliott) and his male lover (Mandy *Patinkin). Felicity (Geraldine *Fitzgerald) is an aging woman who finds solace in pretending that a long-dead daughter is still alive. Like many of the best modern works, this play was presented at important regional theatres (the *Mark Taper Forum and the *Long Wharf Theatre) before reaching New York. California director Gordon *Davidson staged the play beautifully in an impressive forest setting designed by Ming Cho *Lee. Otis L. *Guernsey Jr. observed that the work was "remarkable more for texture and tone than momentum," adding, "Cristofer handled his subject—not death itself, but life before death— with emotional maturity, with a touch of gallows humor but no trace of morbidity." The play received many regional productions and was revived at the *Circle in the Square in 1994. **Michael CRISTOFER** [né Procaccino] (b. 1944) was born in Trenton, New Jersey, and raised there and in Princeton. He dropped out of Catholic University to become an actor, appearing in such New York productions as *Lincoln Center's *The Cherry Orchard* (1977), *Conjuring an Event* (1978), *No End of Blame* (1981), and the *Roundabout Theatre's *Hamlet* (1992). Cristofer also wrote *Black Angel* (1982), *The Lady and the Clarinet* (1983), and *Amazing Grace* (1998), none of which found success in New York.

SHAFFER, Peter [Levin] (b. 1926), playwright. An English dramatist whose works have often met with remarkable success in America, he has been represented on Broadway by *Five Finger Exercise* (1959); the double bill *The Private Ear* and *The Public Eye* (1963); *The Royal Hunt of the Sun* (1965); a second double bill, *Black Comedy* and *White Lies* (1967); *Equus* (1974); *Amadeus* (1981); and *Lettice and Lovage* (1990). Shaffer's plays often return to the theme of a mediocrity (conquistador Pizarro, psychiatrist Dysart, composer Salieri, etc.) confronted with an inspired, passionate opposite (Incan ruler Atahuallpa, horse-worshipping youth Alan, prodigy Mozart, etc.). His twin brother **Anthony SHAFFER,** also a playwright, has been represented on Broadway by the very popular *Sleuth* (1970) and the less successful *Whodunnit* (1982).

SHAKESPEARE, William (1564–1616). The Elizabethan playwright's work came to American stages relatively early, although there have since been notable peaks and valleys in his popularity with playgoers and producers. The first Shakespearean play performed on an American stage was probably *Richard III*, which Thomas *Kean acted in New York in 1750 and may have played earlier in Philadelphia. Kean and his partner Walter *Murray did not use Shakespeare's actual text but rather Colley Cibber's version. Indeed, the use of Restoration and 18th-century redactions of virtually all of Shakespeare's plays was commonplace as much in America as in London until well into the last half of the 19th century. For the remainder of the 18th century and the very early years of the next, the Shakespearean repertory of the time was presented as part of the regular season by the stock companies that dominated the various American theatrical centers. However, with the appearance of noted tragedians such as *Cooper, *Cooke, and Edmund *Kean, and the rise of the star system, the great actors began to tour. They generally toured alone, accepting whatever supporting casts and scenery local playhouses offered. Not until after the Civil War did great tragedians such as Edwin *Booth and Lawrence *Barrett begin to travel with specially selected companies and their own scenery. These touring ensembles peaked at the turn of the century, notably with the company headed by Julia *Marlowe and E. H. *Sothern. The productions of the great itinerant ensembles, as well as those mountings by distinguished stock companies from *Burton's through *Daly's, were, according to modern standards, top-heavy with elaborate scenery. In the 20th century the rise of a more blatant commercialism on Broadway, the growth of an audience not steeped in older traditions, and perhaps simply a surfeit of Shakespeare caused a gradual dropping off of productions. Thereafter, most noted productions were mounted as occasional vehicles for special stars. To some extent collegiate playhouses compensated for this falling away. About the time of World War I, Shakespearean productions also discarded their sumptuous settings, relying thereafter primarily on more suggestive sets and imaginative lighting. These changes came about as much for aesthetic reasons as for commercial ones. In the 1930s and beyond Shakespearean festivals were established from Oregon to Connecticut, and many of the rarely performed works, no longer deemed profitable in mainstream theatres, were offered here along with the more famous plays. Starting in the 1950s there was an increase in the number of productions, the result of what would become the *New York Shakespeare Festival in Manhattan and the development of regional theatres across the country, most of which would include one of the Bard's works on a regular basis. Today the only Shakespeare productions on Broadway are those boasting stars or coming from a renowned international troupe, such as the *Royal Shakespeare Company. In an ambitious move, producer Joseph *Papp offered the entire canon beginning in 1988 and not completed until 1997, six years after his death.

The following Shakespeare plays each have their own entry: *Antony and Cleopatra, As You Like It, Hamlet, Henry IV, Julius Caesar, King Lear, Macbeth, Merchant of Venice, The Merry Wives of Windsor, A Midsummer Night's Dream, Much Ado About Nothing, Othello, Richard III, Romeo and Juliet, The Taming of the Shrew*, and *Twelfth Night*. As for the other works, a thumbnail history in America follows.

All's Well That Ends Well had been performed on rare occasions by collegiate and regional theatres, but the New York Shakespeare Festival gave it its professional premiere, as far as the city was concerned, when it included it in the 1966 season in Central Park. In 1983 the Royal Shakespeare Company offered a critically acclaimed mounting, set at the time of World War I, that marked its first appearance in a Broadway theatre. *The Comedy of Errors* was first done at the *Park Theatre in 1804, but its most memorable American revival was the free-wheeling version offered with William H. *Crane and Stuart *Robson in 1878 and again in 1885. It has been performed intermittently since but is probably most familiar to playgoers through the *Rodgers and *Hart musical version, *The *Boys from Syracuse* (1938), which employed only a single line of the text. Perhaps even more removed was a *Lincoln Center production in 1987 that retained Shakespeare's text but was performed by the juggling Flying Karamazov Brothers as a one-ring circus. *Coriolanus* was presented initially at Philadelphia's *Southwark Theatre in 1767 and it remained popular with all the classic tragedians, including Edwin *Forrest and John *McCullough, and is still revived with some regularity. Christopher *Walken was particularly praised as the Roman emperor in a 1988 Public Theatre mounting. *Cymbeline* had its American premiere at the Southwark Theatre in 1767 with Miss *Cheer as Imogen and the younger *Hallam as Posthumus. Never very popular, it nonetheless provided successful vehicles for Adelaide *Neilson and Viola *Allen but has rarely been revived in modern times. Cooper was apparently the first American *Henry V* at the Park Theatre in 1804. One of the least popular of the plays for many years, it saw new life in the 1960s and 1970s when presented as an antiwar piece. The three parts of the history *Henry VI* have been presented in America only on collegiate and festival stages or the occasional mounting by a visiting company. The pageant play *Henry VIII* was first offered to New York in 1799. Although infrequently done, it was part of the season mounted in 1946 by the *American Repertory Theatre with Victor Jory as Henry, Eva *Le Gallienne as Katharine of Aragon, and Walter *Hampden as Cardinal Wolsey. *King John* was first mounted at the Southwark Theatre in 1768 with *Douglass in the title role, but it has never been popular with American playgoers, although such celebrated performers as McCullough and *Modjeska have starred in revivals.

Love's Labours Lost was not produced in New York until Daly's celebrated 1874 mounting, and it continues as one of the plays least-often resurrected. The earliest known American presentation of the dark comedy *Measure for Measure* is in 1818 in New York with performances by Mr. and Mrs. John *Barnes. Adelaide Neilson headed a memorable 1880 mounting, although critical reaction to the play itself as "repulsively immoral" may explain the relative infrequency of Victorian stagings. The changing moral climate in the 1950s and 1960s was probably a factor in the increasing revivals of *Measure for Measure,* especially at Canada's Shakespeare Festival and some intriguing productions at the Public Theatre. Stagings of *Pericles* have pretty much been confined to collegiate and festival theatres. *Richard II* was first offered to New York by James W. *Wallack in 1819. It is one of the rare Shakespearean plays that has proved far more popular in the 20th century than it was earlier. Noteworthy among contemporary revivals was Maurice *Evans's 1937 production, to which he returned on several later occasions. *The Tempest* was first presented in 1770 at the Southwark Theatre in Dryden's redaction, and it was many years before a faithful rendering was presented. A movement toward textual accuracy was seen in one of the great 19th-century productions, that of William E. *Burton in 1854 with Charles *Fisher as Prospero and Burton as Caliban. Besides restoring much, although not all, of the original text, Burton employed music by Arne, Purcell, and, somewhat anachronistically, Halévy and emphasized pictorial spectacle. By contrast, a notable modern version, staged by Margaret *Webster in 1945 with Arnold Moss as Prospero and Canada *Lee as Caliban, while rearranging the original text at some major points, offered relatively lean, suggestive settings and costumes and employed modern music by David Diamond. More recent New York Prosperos of note have been Sam *Waterston in 1974, Frank *Langella in 1989, and Patrick Stewart in 1995. *Timon of Athens* was a surprise success for the National Actors Theatre in 1993, with Brian *Bedford giving a commanding performance in the title role. *Titus Andronicus* and *Troilus and Cressida* have been almost wholly in collegiate and festival theatres, although the *Old Vic offered the latter in

its 1956 visit. Ellen and Charles *Kean were the first performers to offer Americans *The Two Gentlemen of Verona,* which they acted during their 1846 visit. Daly staged a major revival in 1895. While rarely mounted since, except at collegiate and festival productions, it provided the source of a successful musical of the same name (minus the "the") in 1971. Produced by the New York Shakespeare Festival, it employed rock music; some highly objectionable, scatological lyrics; and a mixture of modern, skeletonized settings with period costuming. *The Winter's Tale* was called *Florizel and Perdita* when it was first presented in 1795. Its most successful 19th-century revival was that of Mary *Anderson, who assumed the roles of both Hermione and Perdita. A 1946 *Theatre Guild revival was short-lived.

SHAKESPEARE & COMPANY (Lenox, Massachusetts). A vital group that looks into new ways to make Shakespeare's plays come alive for today's audiences, it was founded in 1978 by Tina Packer, who continues on as artistic director, and acting-vocal expert Kristin Linklater. The company has performed the Bard's works and stage adaptations of literary classics in the modified-thrust Founders' Theatre located at the Mount, author Edith Wharton's estate. The troupe has purchased land in Lenox and is currently developing an International Center for Shakespeare Performance and Studies with productions to be staged in an authentic reconstruction of the Rose Playhouse.

SHAKESPEARE THEATRE, THE (Washington, D.C.). In 1932 the Folger Shakespeare Library opened in the Capitol Hill district of Washington, and it included a 243-seat re-creation of an Elizabethan playhouse on a reduced scale. The unique space saw concerts, lectures, and other events before it became the home of the Folger Theatre Group in 1970. Despite highly commended productions of Shakespearean and other classic works, the theatre was frequently in financial distress. It was ready to close in 1985 when Michael Kahn was hired as artistic director and, under the new name Shakespeare Theatre at the Folger, the little company thrived for a while. In 1992 the group dropped "at the Folger" from its name and moved to a 451-seat performance space in the city's Pennsylvania Quarter arts district. Productions by the company continue to be of high quality and have found enthusiastic audience support.

SHAME WOMAN, THE (1923), a play by Lula *Vollmer. [Greenwich Village Theatre, 276 perf.] For twenty years, ever since she was seduced by Craig Anson (Edward Pawley), Lize Burns (Florence Rittenhouse) has been shunned by her North

Carolina hillbilly neighbors as a "shame woman." She has lived in an isolated cabin with only her adopted daughter, Lily (Thelma Paige), for company. Lonely and heartsick, she has never had the courage to tell Lily of her past or to warn her not to wander carelessly among the hills. However, learning that Lily has been meeting a man at night, Lize finally forces herself to tell Lily her history, which causes Lily to run from the room and kill herself. When Anson calls at the cabin, Lize finds out he was Lily's seducer. She kills him with a potato knife to prevent him from boasting of his latest conquest and from disclosing that Lily, too, had become a "shame woman." John *Corbin of the *Times* saw the work as "an exposition, truly epic in its length and its dead seriousness, of the wrongs women suffer at the hands of predacious men."

SHANGHAI GESTURE, THE (1926), a melodrama by John *Colton. [Martin Beck Theatre, 331 perf.] At the "Far-Famed House of Mother Goddam," a Shanghai brothel, the proprietress entertains the head of the British-China Trading Company, Sir Guy Charteris (McKay Morris). Mother Goddam (Florence *Reed) reminds Sir Guy of several things he has forgotten: that they were once lovers, that he had promised to marry her, and that he had sold her to some cruel Chinese junkmen when he fell in love with an English girl. As Sir Guy and his friends look on, Mother Goddam now sells a young girl to similar junkmen, then reveals that the girl was a daughter she had had by Guy. When the daughter, Poppy (Mary Duncan), returns to the brothel as a dope addict and a prostitute, Mother Goddam strangles her. Originally written as a vehicle for Mrs. *Fiske who was dismissed by director Guthrie *McClintic during the tryout, the play was lambasted by many critics. George Jean *Nathan called it "a pâté of box-office drivel." But its lurid story and Reed's memorable performance made it a major hit.

SHANNON, Effie (1867–1954), actress. Born in Cambridge, Massachusetts, she began a stage career that was to span seventy years when she appeared as a child extra in John *McCullough's production of *Coriolanus* in Boston in the early 1870s. Her first important assignment followed shortly, when she portrayed Eva in *Uncle Tom's Cabin*. Billed as La Petite Shannon, she grew up to be a tall, slim beauty. After her first New York assignment in 1886 in *Tangled Lives*, Shannon played for a time for Augustin *Daly, including Titania in his 1888 mounting of A *Midsummer Night's Dream*. A year later she created the role of Jenny Buckthorn in *Shenandoah*, and in the 1890s she supported Rose *Coghlan and Lillie *Langtry. Stardom came when she played opposite her husband, Herbert *Kelcey, in *The Moth and the Flame*

(1898), followed by another success as Indiana Stillwater in *Her Lord and Master* (1902). In 1907 she was Blanche in the first American performance of *Shaw's *Widowers' Houses*, after which she toured for two years as Marie-Louise in *The Thief*. Shannon's other notable later performances included the stern maiden aunt Miss Harrington in *Pollyanna* (1916), the dual roles of the German and American wives in the war play *Under Orders* (1918), the first American Hesione Hushabye in *Heartbreak House* (1920), Mrs. Hardcastle in *She Stoops to Conquer* (1924), Mrs. Winslow in *The Youngest* (1924), Trafalgar Gower in *Trelawny of the Wells* (1927), and Esther Crampton in *Morning's at Seven* (1939). In 1942 Shannon replaced Jean *Adair as sweet murderer Martha Brewster in *Arsenic and Old Lace* and played the role until her retirement two years later.

SHARAFF, Irene (1910–93), designer. The Boston-born costumer studied in America and in Paris before serving as assistant to Aline *Bernstein at the *Civic Repertory Theatre. Working alone or with distinguished collaborators, she later created the stylish, color-splashed costumes for such shows as *As Thousands Cheer* (1933), *Life Begins at 8:40* (1934), *Jubilee* (1935), *Idiot's Delight* (1936), *On Your Toes* (1936), The *Boys from Syracuse* (1938), *Lady in the Dark* (1941), The *King and I* (1952), *Candide* (1956), *West Side Story* (1957), *Funny Girl* (1964), *Sweet Charity* (1966), and the 1973 revival of *Irene*. The *Theatre Development Fund annually honors costume achievement with the TDF/Irene Sharaff Award, named after her.

SHAUGHRAUN, THE (1874), a play by Dion *Boucicault. [*Wallack's Theatre, 143 perf.] Robert Ffolliott (J. B. Polk) is a rich young Irishman who is under sentence of death for his Fenian sympathies. Robert's fiancée, Arte O'Neal (Jeffreys Lewis), lives on one of his estates with his sister Claire Ffolliott (Ada Dyas). Corry Kinchela (Edward Arnott), who hopes to win Ffolliott's lands, plots to have him captured, but his plans are momentarily frustrated when Captain Molyneaux (H. J. *Montague), the British officer sent to arrest Robert, falls in love with Claire. When Robert is eventually arrested, Kinchela learns that a pardon is in the offing, so he suggests to Robert that he flee, planning to kill him during his escape. Robert's best friend, Conn, the Shaughraun (Boucicault)—"the soul of every fair, the life of every funeral, the first fiddle at all weddings and parties"—helps Robert make good his escape. Kinchela shoots Conn, leaving him for dead, and takes Arte and Claire captive. Playing dead, Conn learns the girls' whereabouts. They are rescued and Kinchela arrested. Robert and Arte, and Molyneux and Claire, are free to wed. Called by *Odell "that best of all Boucicault Irish plays," it was also his most financially successful and enjoyed the longest run of any play at Wallack's in the 1870s. Boucicault and others revived it regularly. Historian Jack A. Vaughn has written, "It is skillfully structured to provide its implausible, sensational situations with a maximum of credibility, and it contains several scenes of genuine humor and Gaelic charm. The role of Conn is one of the better acting parts of the period." A "shaughraun" was a wanderer or vagabond. The show was revived with tremendous success in London in 1988 by the *National Theatre.

SHAW, George Bernard (1856–1950), playwright. The most famous and possibly the most controversial of 20th-century English dramatists was described by the *Times* in its review of the first major American production of *Arms and the Man* as "the eccentric and able London socialist, essayist, music critic, Ibsenite, and wearer of gray flannel clothes." With occasional shadings of difference, critical opinion of Shaw in America has remained much the same ever since. Especially in early years his subjects offended many playgoers and critics, dealing as they did with such matters as prostitution, religious hypocrisy, slum landlordism, profiteering, and, of course, socialism. In these early years his most noted exponents included Richard *Mansfield and Arnold *Daly, while in after seasons the *Theatre Guild regularly offered even his minor plays. The last several decades have witnessed fewer Shaw works on Broadway but a marked increase Off Broadway and in regional venues. *Caesar and Cleopatra, Candida, The Devil's Disciple, Man and Superman, Pygmalion,* and *Saint Joan* each has its own entry. A thumbnail history of some other Shaw works in America follows.

The short comedy *Androcles and the Lion*, twitting early Christians, was hissed at its 1913 London premiere but received a cordial welcome when Harley Granville-Barker presented it in New York in 1915 with O. P. *Heggie as Androcles. The major American revivals occurred in 1925, when the Theatre Guild presented it with Henry Travers as the hero and such superior players as Romney Brent, Clare *Eames, Tom *Powers, and Edward G. *Robinson in supporting roles, and in 1946 when the *American Repertory Theatre offered it with Ernest *Truex in the lead. *Arms and the Man*, Shaw's beguiling spoof of militarism, was his first play presen-ted in America. Mansfield played the antihero Bluntschli in 1894, and William *Winter thought his performance "a delicious piece of mystification, crisp in speech and diversified by airy nonchalance and whimsical humor." Never one to proclaim Shaw, Winter admitted the script "causes thought as well as mirth." A major revival was in 1925 when the Theatre Guild presented Alfred *Lunt and Lynn *Fontanne in the leads. Howard

*Lindsay recalled Lunt's Bluntschli as "cold, precise, hard and . . . probably one of the greatest high-comedy performances any actor, American or British, has given in our time." Of Shaw's most accessible works, *Arms and the Man* has often been seen in New York since the 1920s but has not enjoyed any outstanding productions. Many Americans know the play best through its musical version, the Viennese operetta *The Chocolate Soldier*. *The Doctor's Dilemma,* a comedy about egocentricity and medical ethics, was first produced in New York by Arnold Daly in 1915. The first major revival was by the Theatre Guild in 1927 with a remarkable cast that included Helen *Westley, Dudley *Digges, Earle *Larimore, Fontanne, and Lunt as Dubedat. Many critics felt the acting was superior to the play. A change in emphasis came in 1941 when Katharine *Cornell revived the work, playing Jennifer Dubedat with support from Raymond *Massey and Bramwell *Fletcher. The *Phoenix Theatre mounted the play in 1955 with Roddy MacDowall as the doomed artist. The Theatre Guild's 1920 mounting of *Heartbreak House* provided that play's belated premiere. This look at a modern Armageddon seems to have spoken eloquently to a world where a major war is always looming and so has been offered a number of fine revivals. Orson *Welles, dressed to resemble Shaw, played Shotover in the *Mercury Theatre's 1938 mounting, while Maurice *Evans assumed the role in a 1959 production and Rex *Harrison played it in an abridged but superb 1983 revival at the *Circle in the Square.

Grace *George presented and starred in the 1915 American premiere of *Major Barbara,* the play about big business and warmongering, offering a notable cast of famous or soon-to-be-famous theatrical names, including Clarence *Derwent, Guthrie *McClintic, Ernest Lawford, John *Cromwell, Mary *Nash, and Conway Tearle. It was welcomed at the time as "a provocative, often richly amusing and continuously stimulating comedy." Major revivals have included a 1928 Theatre Guild presentation; an exceptionally successful 1956 production, which ran seven months, with Glynis Johns and Charles *Laughton in the leads; and a well-acted Broadway revival in 2001 with Cherry *Jones as Barbara. *Mrs. Warren's Profession,* the play about prostitution that prompted court action in 1905, both during its New Haven tryout and in New York, starred Arnold Daly, who was also the producer, and Mary *Shaw. Both were arrested but were acquitted of charges of presenting an immoral play. However, the work proved more sensational than durable, revivals being infrequent and short-lived. Uta *Hagen headed a fine 1985 revival. As the fate of *Mrs. Warren's Profession* suggests, the initial success or notoriety of a Shaw play was no reliable indicator of its future vogue. Several plays that were huge successes at their first American presentation have since been largely neglected, while other works, often branded as minor, have enjoyed tremendous success later on, thanks on occasion to an unusual production or the appearance of a major star. An example of the former would be *Fanny's First Play*, which ran eight months in New York when it was premiered there in 1912 but which has never had a major revival outside of the Shaw Festival in Canada. By contrast such plays as *The Apple Cart* and *The Millionairess*, dismissed or totally ignored at first, enjoyed newsworthy and relatively successful mountings when produced with Maurice Evans (1956) and Katharine *Hepburn (1952) respectively.

SHAW, Irwin (1913–84), playwright. Born in New York and educated at Brooklyn College, the writer briefly gave promise of becoming an important dramatist, coming from his early antiwar play *Bury the Dead* (1936) and the character study *The *Gentle People* (1939). His other theatre works included *Siege* (1937), *Retreat to Pleasure* (1941), *Sons and Soldiers* (1943), *The Assassin* (1945), *Patate* (1958), and *Children from Their Games* (1963). Although Shaw's sympathies fell in line with the leftish sentiments of many playgoers and critics, his later writings were wanting in terms of theatrical effectiveness. He finally abandoned the theatre to become a popular novelist.

SHAW, Mary (1860?–1929), actress. The Boston-born scion of an old New Hampshire family, she made her debut at the *Boston Museum in 1878 and afterwards performed in important supporting roles with *Modjeska, Mrs. *Fiske, Julia *Marlowe, and many other major stars. However, she is remembered largely for her early advocacy of *Ibsen and *Shaw. She was the first American Mrs. Warren in *Mrs. Warren's Profession* (1905) and won critical acclaim for her Hedda Gabler and Mrs. Alving. Her playing of Mrs. Warren led to her arrest and subsequent acquittal on morals charges. Shaw was also a celebrated lecturer on theatre. That she never achieved widespread popularity despite critical praise may have been because the public was daunted by her intellectual approach to theatre.

SHAW, Oscar [né Schwartz] (1889–1967), actor and singer. Born in Philadelphia and educated at the University of Pennsylvania, the pleasant-looking song-and-dance man with the slicked-down black hair and the toothy grin began his theatrical career as a chorus boy in *The Mimic World* (1908). During the next four years he appeared in important secondary roles in musicals. After some time in England, he was noticed as Dick Rivers in *Very Good Eddie* (1915), in which

he introduced "Some Sort of Somebody." He was rarely idle for the next seventeen years, his hits including *Leave It to Jane* (1917), *Two Little Girls in Blue* (1920), *Good Morning Dearie* (1920), *Music Box Revue* (1924), *Oh, Kay!* (1926), *The Five O'Clock Girl* (1927), and *Flying High* (1930). In 1932 Shaw toured as John T. Wintergreen in the road company of *Of Thee I Sing*, after which his career faded away. His last roles were in nonmusicals, the most important being his replacement of Dennis *King as the lead in *Petticoat Fever* (1935).

SHE LOVES ME (1963), a musical comedy by Joe *Masteroff (book), Jerry *Bock (music), Sheldon *Harnick (lyrics). [*Eugene O'Neill Theatre, 301 perf.] The Budapest bachelor Georg Novack (Daniel Massey), a clerk at Maraczek's Parfumerie, has been writing to a girl he knows only as "Dear Friend," so when Amalia Belash (Barbara *Cook) obtains employment in the same shop and the two constantly quarrel, he has no reason to suspect she is his correspondent. But Georg discovers the truth after a rendezvous at the Café Imperiale that goes awry, and he leaves the restaurant without disclosing his identity. When Amalia reports in sick for work and Georg appears at her apartment, she is furious at first, thinking he is checking on her excuse. But a gift of ice cream alters matters and soon she sees Georg differently. By Christmas Eve Georg has identified himself to her and they walk away from the store in a happy embrace. *Notable songs*: Dear Friend; Ice Cream; She Loves Me; I Resolve; Tonight at Eight; Will He Like Me? A musical version of Ernst Lubitsch's film *The Shop Around the Corner* and the Hungarian play on which that film was based, Miklos Laszlo's *Parfumerie*, the show failed to chalk up a long run despite almost universally glowing notices. Stanley *Green suggested that the reason for the failure may have been that this charming bonbon was "too gentle, too intimate, and too free from Broadway razzle-dazzle to attract the customers." Hal *Prince produced and directed the charming piece, which boasted a sterling cast and one of the decade's finest scores. The musical became a cult show among aficionados, but after a *Roundabout Theatre revival in 1993 that was popular enough to transfer to Broadway, *She Loves Me* has seen many more mountings across the country.

SHE LOVES ME NOT (1933), a comedy by Howard *Lindsay. [46th Street Theatre, 360 perf.] Escaping from the police after witnessing a gangland murder, the nightclub dancer Curley Flagg (Polly Waters) seeks refuge in the Princeton dorm room of Paul Lawton (John Beal), where Paul and his friends cut Curley's hair, give her men's clothes, and introduce her as a younger brother. They even try to get Curley work in films. The result is that the campus is invaded by the press, film crews, and an odd assortment of curiosity seekers, and the college authorities almost expel the boys. When order is restored, they are allowed to continue their education, Curley lands a major movie contract, and Paul finds romance with the dean's daughter. Based on a novel by Edward Hope, the play was greeted by Richard Lockridge of the *Sun* as "a jovial six-ring circus." Many critics felt the performance of Burgess *Meredith as Buzz Jones, Paul's buddy, was the highlight of the evening.

SHE WOULD BE A SOLDIER; or, *The Plains of Chippewa* (1819), a play by Mordecai M. *Noah. [*Park Theatre, in repertory.] When her father insists she marry the bumpkin farmer Jerry Mayflower (John *Barnes), Christine (Catharine Leesugg) disguises herself as a man and runs away to be with her sweetheart, Lenox (James Pritchard), who is fighting with the American army in the War of 1812. Entering the army camp she is seized as a spy and condemned to death. Blindfolded and placed in front of a firing squad, Lenox recognizes Christine and stops the execution. Jerry rushes in but, realizing the lengths Christine has gone to be with Lenox, accepts the inevitable. He adds, "Miss Crissy, you look very pretty in pantaloons, and make a fine solger, but after all, I'm glad to have escaped a wife who wears the breeches before marriage." Written with Leesugg in mind, the play remained popular for many years and was seen in New York as late as 1848. Richard Moody noted, "For its sincerity of tone, its brightness and charm, its democratic spirit, and its praise of the Indian, Noah's play ranks a full step above ... other dramas dealing with similar historical events."

SHEAN, Al. See Gallagher and Shean.

SHELDON, Edward [Brewster] (1886–1946), playwright. The son of wealthy Chicagoans, he was educated at Harvard, where he was one of the first important pupils of Professor George Pierce *Baker. His first produced play was the hard-hitting drama *Salvation Nell* (1908), followed by the equally powerful plays *The *Nigger* (1909) and *The *Boss* (1911). Sheldon's subsequent works were softer and more commercial, though often quite accomplished: the comedy *Princess Zim-Zim* (1911), the gypsy melodrama *Egypt* (1912), the political exposé *The High Road* (1912), the extremely popular *Romance* (1913), the dramatizations *Song of Songs* (1914) and *The Garden of Paradise* (1914), the Italian *The Jest* (1919), and the Hungarian *The Czarina* (1922). With the onset of the illness that left him blind and hopelessly paralyzed for the rest of his life, he resorted to collaborations for his final

works. The three most successful were *Lulu Belle* (1926), written with Charles *MacArthur, and two written with Margaret Ayer Barnes: the comedy *Jenny* (1929) and the thriller *Dishonored Lady* (1930). Although throughout his career Sheldon willingly sacrificed depth for theatrical effectiveness, his best plays remain gripping theatre and would probably still be stageworthy if prejudices against his apparent claptrap could be set aside. Biography: *The Man Who Lived Twice*, Eric Wollencott Barnes, 1956.

SHENANDOAH (1889), a play by Bronson *Howard. [Star Theatre, 250 perf.] The outbreak of the Civil War means that two West Point friends, Kerchival West (Henry *Miller) of New York and Robert Ellingham (Lucius Henderson) of Virginia, must take opposing sides. Both men become colonels in their respective armies. Before the war, each man was in love with the other's sister: Madeline West (Nanette Comstock) and Gertrude Ellingham (Viola *Allen). When Robert is taken prisoner and Gertrude is arrested as a spy, they are brought before West, who finds Gertrude surprisingly hostile. But West is stabbed by another Confederate, Thornton (John E. *Kellerd), who, in order to save himself, tells General Haverhill (Wilton *Lackaye) that West has been the lover of Haverhill's wife. Since West has a locket with Mrs. Haverhill's picture, the charge seems believable, but West reveals he obtained the locket from a young soldier, Lt. Bedloe (G. W. Bailey). Bedloe turns out to be Haverhill's son, fighting under an assumed name. Taken prisoner, he is exchanged for Robert. The men go back to fighting, and not until the war is over are the lovers reunited. This summary gives some indication of the complexity of the plot, which many critics assailed. Nevertheless, the Charles *Frohman production was a major hit, the first for the young producer and one that launched his long, distinguished career.

SHENANDOAH (1975), a musical by James Lee Barrett, Philip Rose (book), Peter Udell (book, lyrics), Gary Geld (music). [Alvin Theatre, 1,050 perf.] The Anderson family has determined to stay out of the Civil War, preferring their peaceful life on a farm in Virginia's Shenandoah Valley. But after the youngest son Robert (Joseph Shapiro) is kidnapped by soldiers, Charlie Anderson (John *Cullum) and his other sons decide they have no choice but to join the bloody struggle. *Notable songs*: Next to Lovin'; Violets and Silverbells; Freedom; We Make a Beautiful Pair. The musical was based on the 1965 film rather than the 1889 play of the same name. It originated at the *Goodspeed Opera House, then opened on Broadway to divided notices so the show resorted to cut-rate tickets. Although it rarely enjoyed a sellout week, discounted ticket offers and good word-of-mouth helped it to enjoy a long run and even send out a road company. It was revived briefly in 1989.

SHEPARD, Sam (né Samuel Shepard Rogers Jr.) (b. 1943), playwright. Born in Fort Sheridan, Illinois, and reared in California, he is one of the more prolific of late 20th-century playwrights. Shepard was first produced Off Off Broadway in 1964 and has since written over thirty plays, which have been offered in New York and in regional theatres. He was first noticed for his early short works *Icarus's Mother* (1965), *Chicago* (1966), *Red Cross* (1967), *La Turista* (1967), *Forensic and the Navigators* (1967), and *Action* (1975). Among his notable full-length plays are *The Tooth of Crime* (1972), **Buried Child* (1978), *The Curse of the Starving Class* (1979), **True West* (1980), **Fool for Love* (1983), *A *Lie of the Mind* (1985), *The States of Shock* (1991), *Simpatico* (1994), and *Eyes for Consuela* (1998). In Shepard's plays imaginative language composed of slang, scientific jargon, B-movie dialogue, and rock and roll idioms, and a stage peopled with farmers, devils, witch doctors, rock stars, spacemen, cowboys, gangsters, and other American stereotypes demonstrate his interest in popular American culture and the folklore of the American Southwest. He has also had a successful career as a film actor.

SHEPARD, Thomas Z[achary] (b. 1936), record producer. A native of Orange, New Jersey, he studied at Juilliard, Oberlin, and Yale Graduate School of Music, then worked for many years at Columbia Records. It was there that Shepard made recreations of such old shows as **Lady in the Dark* and later supervised original cast recordings of newer musicals such as **Company* and the revivals of **No, No, Nanette* and **Irene*. Moving to RCA, he put on disk, among others, **Sweeney Todd*, the complete **Porgy and Bess* and **Ain't Misbehavin'*. His aim was "to create a theatrical illusion while in the context of the best musical performance possible."

SHERIDAN, Richard Brinsley (1751–1816), playwright. He was the earliest English playwright whose works were presented in America while they were still new to the London stage and that have retained their popularity ever since. The initial representations of his most enduring works, *The Rivals* and *The School for Scandal*, were given here during the Revolutionary War by British soldiers and their friends in 1778 and 1782 respectively. Professional productions followed shortly thereafter. Throughout the 19th century the plays remained special favorites with the great ensemble houses such as **Wallack's and **Daly's in New York, Mrs. **Drew's in Philadelphia, and the **Boston Museum. Late in the century Mrs. Drew and Joseph **Jefferson

toured in a famous all-star company of *The Rivals*. In the early years of the 20th century major professional revivals, including those headed by Kyrle **Bellew and Ada **Rehan, were few and far between and short-lived. Later the **Players briefly mounted several all-star productions. Curiously, important back-to-back revivals of *The School for Scandal* were offered in 1962 and 1963 by the **Association of Producing Artists (APA) and an English troupe headed by John **Gielgud and Ralph **Richardson. *The Duenna* and *The Critic* keep a fitful hold on American stages, the latter having a memorable revival by the **Old Vic on its 1946 visit. One of Sheridan's most popular works in his lifetime was his adaptation of **Kotzebue's *Die Spanier in Peru* as **Pizarro*. It was frequently performed in America for many decades, either in Sheridan's actual version or **Dunlap's redaction, but has long since faded from view.

SHERIDAN, W[illiam] **E**[dward] (1840?–87), actor. Born in Boston, where he made his debut at the **Howard Athenaeum in 1858, he became a leading portrayer of villains and tragic figures in Cincinnati until the outbreak of the Civil War. After the war, despite a badly injured arm, he continued to be an important actor, his notable roles including Othello, Shylock, and Sir Giles Overreach. Sheridan also was the first American Beamish McCloud in **Arrah na Pogue* (1865). Following a long San Francisco engagement, he left for a tour of Australia, where he died. Otis **Skinner remembered the virile actor with dark, deep-set eyes as "a man of splendid power, with one of the most intriguing voices I ever listened to." Others remarked on his voice's striking resonance.

SHERLOCK HOLMES (1899), a play by William **Gillette. [**Garrick Theatre, 256 perf.] Alice Faulkner (Katherine Florence) holds letters written to her late sister by a member of royalty. She believes that her sister died of a broken heart from the man's faithlessness and is determined to use the letters against him. But Madge (Judith Berolde) and James Larrabee (Ralph Delmore), two blackmailers, also want the letters and are holding Alice prisoner. Sherlock Holmes (Gillette) is called into the case and by arranging a fake fire manages to discover the whereabouts of the letters and to free Alice. But the Larrabees have called in Professor Moriarty (George Wessells) to aid them. One by one Holmes foils his designs, although it seems that when Moriarty lures Alice and the detective to a shabby, gloomy gas works, he has caught them in his vise. Holmes throws the place into darkness and tricks the villains as to his whereabouts with a lighted cigar. He convinces Alice to give up the letters to the proper authorities, and she finds herself falling in love with Holmes. The Charles **Frohman offering, based on short stories of Sir Arthur Conan Doyle (whom some early programs listed as co-author), was Gillette's greatest success. For many years he alone was identified with the role, which he returned to regularly as late as 1931. A richly Victorian revival by the *Royal Shakespeare Company, with John *Wood in the title role, ran for 471 performances on Broadway in 1974.

SHERMAN, Hiram (1908–89), character actor. The Boston native was educated at the University of Illinois and studied acting at the *Goodman Theatre School. After working professionally in stock in Chicago, the chubby actor went to New York, making his Broadway bow in 1936 in the *Federal Theatre Project's farce *Horse Eats Hat*. When the Project was discontinued, Sherman remained with director Orson *Welles and performed in some *Mercury Theatre productions such as the modern-dress *Julius Caesar* (1937) and the Elizabethan farce *The Shoemaker's Holiday* (1938). He was in the company of the legendary first production of The *Cradle Will Rock* (1937) and played Shakespearean clowns in productions at the 1939 World's Fair. Sherman was frequently seen on television but returned to Broadway regularly. His last role was one of his best: the Wall Street tycoon Wingate in the musical *How Now Dow Jones* (1967).

SHERWOOD, Robert E[mmet] (1896–1955), playwright. Born in New Rochelle, New York, he attended Harvard, where he was active on the *Lampoon* (which his father had co-founded) and with the *Hasty Pudding Club and studied theatre history under George Pierce *Baker. After spending World War I with the Canadian Black Watch, Sherwood returned home disillusioned with the governments that had brought the conflict about. After serving in various capacities at *Vanity Fair*, *Life*, and *Scribner's* and earning a reputation as one of the earliest serious critics of film, he found success with his first play, the antiwar comedy The *Road to Rome* (1927). *The Love Nest* (1927), *The Queen's Husband* (1928), and *This Is New York* (1930) failed to run, and his wartime romance *Waterloo Bridge* (1930) found a better reception in London than in New York. Nevertheless, the rest of the 1930s proved his heyday with such memorable works as *Reunion in Vienna* (1931), The *Petrified Forest* (1935), *Idiot's Delight* (1936), *Abe Lincoln in Illinois* (1938), and *Tovarich* (1936). Sherwood's biographer has suggested that with his Lincoln play he purged himself of his war-bred disillusionment and a negative streak that had heretofore run through his works. How this purgation affected his writing is moot, but he wrote only one other play of lasting merit, *There Shall Be No Night* (1940). His last works were *The Rugged Path* (1945),

the musical *Miss Liberty* (1949), and the revision of Philip *Barry's unfinished *Second Threshold* (1951). One of the founders of the *Playwrights' Company, he turned to politics in his last active years, serving as a speechwriter for FDR and writing a history of Roosevelt's relationship with Harry Hopkins. Biography: *The Worlds of Robert E. Sherwood*, John Mason *Brown, 1965.

SHEVELOVE, Burt [on George] (1915–82), director and librettist. He was born in Newark, New Jersey, and began in the New York theatre in 1948, writing sketches and directing small musical revues. Shevelove found success as the co-author of A *Funny Thing Happened on the Way to the Forum* (1961), scripted the Stephen *Sondheim musical *The Frogs* (1974) at Yale, then stumbled badly with his libretto for the Cole *Porter musical *Happy New Year* (1980). He was also a respected director who staged the Broadway musicals *Hallelujah, Baby!* (1967), *No, No, Nanette* (1971), and *So Long, 174th Street* (1980).

SHIPMAN, Samuel [né Shiffman] (1883–1937), playwright. The New York–born writer began his career by translating Jacob *Gordin's *The Kreutzer Sonata* for English-language production in 1904. Over the next thirty-three years he had a hand, usually as collaborator, in some thirty plays to reach the boards. The most successful were the comedy *Elevating a Husband* (1912), the wartime play *Friendly Enemies* (1918), an Asian-set *East Is West* (1918), the mystery *The Woman in Room 13* (1919), the revenge drama *Lawful Larceny* (1922), the social indictment *Crime* (1927), and the murder mystery *Behind Red Lights* (1937).

SHOESTRING REVUE. Produced in 1955 and 1957 by Ben *Bagley, these Off-Broadway musicals lacked memorable melodies but were among the wittiest revues ever offered to Broadway and gave important boosts to the careers of Beatrice *Arthur, Dody Goodman, Arte Johnson, Chita *Rivera, and one great comedienne who was to die very young, Dorothy Greener.

SHORE ACRES (1893), a play by James A. *Herne. [*Fifth Avenue Theatre, 244 perf.] Nathan'l Berry (Herne) is a kindly old man who has largely let life pass him by. His brother, Martin (Charles G. Craig), has inherited "Uncle" Nat's land and long ago wed the girl Nat had courted. Unlike Nat, Martin is narrow-minded, unsentimental, and greedy. He would even sell to developers the piece of land on which their mother is buried. While Martin opposes a marriage between his daughter, Helen (Katherine Grey), and a young physician, Sam Warren (David M. Murray), Nat can see nothing wrong in encouraging the youngsters to elope. They do so by boat, but a storm arises and the ship is in danger of being wrecked on the nearby rocks. Martin is the keeper of Berry Light but is so angry at the youngsters that he refuses to light the beacon. After a fight, Nat succeeds in lighting it and saving the ship. When the newlyweds are safely home, Nat offers his pension money to keep the property in the family, and Martin is shamed into admitting how wrong he has been. With the others gone, Nat slowly turns out all the lights at Shore Acres and puts the house to bed. Written as *The Hawthornes* and tried out as *Shore Acres Subdivision* and *Uncle Nat*, the work did not succeed until it played a long run at the *Boston Museum before coming to New York, where most critics extolled the drama. The *Mercury* observed, "Mr. Herne's play marks an epoch in the drama of the American stage." Herne toured in the play for five years; for many playgoers and reviewers the high moment of the drama was at the end, with Herne's quiet, five-minute pantomime of making the house safe for the night. Several modern scholars have noted that *Chekhov's use of a similar conclusion for *The Cherry Orchard* was nine years later.

SHORT, [Hubert] **Hassard** (1877–1956), director and actor. Born in England, he began his theatrical career as an actor in 1895 and six years later came to America, where he continued to perform until 1919, his roles including important parts in *Peg o' My Heart* (1912) and *East Is West* (1918). Short abandoned acting to try his skill at directing and designing, quickly becoming an important figure behind the scenes of many Broadway musicals. He made innovative use of moving stages (including elevators), mirrors, perfume sent through the auditorium, and colored lights. He was sometimes credited with replacing footlights with lights hung from the auditorium. Among the forty musicals on which he worked were the *Music Box Revue* (1921, 1922, 1923), *Sunny* (1925), *Three's a Crowd* (1930), The *Band Wagon* (1931), *As Thousands Cheer* (1933), *Roberta* (1933), *The Great Waltz* (1934), *Jubilee* (1935), *Lady in the Dark* (1941), *Mexican Hayride* (1944), *Make Mine Manhattan* (1948), and his last show, *My Darlin' Aida* (1952).

SHOW BOAT (1927), a musical play by Oscar *Hammerstein (book, lyrics), Jerome *Kern (music). [*Ziegfeld Theatre, 575 perf.] When Cap'n Andy (Charles *Winninger) and his wife, Parthy Ann (Edna May Oliver), bring their show boat *Cotton Blossom* into town for a performance, their daughter, Magnolia (Norma Terris), meets and falls for a handsome professional gambler, Gaylord Ravenal (Howard *Marsh). Magnolia seeks advice from the African-American workhand Joe (Jules *Bledsoe), who tells her only the river knows what's to be and it "don't say nothin'." The boat's leading lady, Julie

(Helen *Morgan), begins to understand Magnolia's situation, but when Julie is accused of having Negro blood she is forced to leave, taking her husband (and the troupe's leading man) with her. Magnolia and Gaylord are pressed into assuming the lead roles on the show boat, eventually getting married (much against Parthy's wishes) and going off together. Years later, living in Chicago, Gaylord's gambling luck has run out so he deserts Magnolia and their young daughter, Kim. Magnolia applies for a job singing at a nightclub where Julie, now a drunkard, works. Julie recognizes Magnolia and sacrifices what is left of her own career to help Magnolia begin hers. On New Year's Eve Magnolia is a hit and goes on to become a famous entertainer. More years pass and Magnolia and Kim (also Terris) are visiting the *Cotton Blossom* when they meet up with the aging Gaylord. To his relief he is welcomed by Magnolia and the two are reunited as they joyfully watch their daughter launch her own career. *Notable songs*: Ol' Man River; Make Believe; Can't Help Lovin' Dat Man; You Are Love; Bill; Why Do I Love You?; Life upon the Wicked Stage. One of the greatest and best loved of all American operettas, the musical was based on Edna *Ferber's popular novel and presented by Florenz *Ziegfeld in a memorable (and atypical for him) production. *Show Boat* was recognized at once as a masterpiece and has never fallen out of favor. The 1932 revival included Paul *Robeson, for whom the part of Joe was originally intended. A 1946 revival, which opened just after Kern's death, included the composer's last new song. Several other Broadway revivals followed, including ones in 1966, 1983, and 1994. There have also been three film versions. With hindsight, it has become obvious that this show was the precursor of the modern American "musical play," the American operetta genre that resorted to the American past for its material and employed American musical idioms in its songs.

SHOW BOATS. Although their origins are uncertain, these floating playhouses, which brought theatre to towns along the great rivers of the United States, are a singularly American phenomenon. Possibly the earliest figure of note in their development was Samuel *Drake, who in 1815 took his family of actors and other performers from Pittsburgh to Kentucky by means of the Allegheny River. However, while Drake's band gave performances along the way, he seems not to have actually used his small boat for these theatricals but rather selected sites ashore. It remained for the young actor-manager Noah *Ludlow, who had first worked and traveled with Drake, to take a flat-bottomed boat with a small enclosed space at one end to travel down the Cumberland and Mississippi Rivers offering plays on board in 1817. But he, too, preferred where possible to stage his plays on land. Credit for conceiving and running a boat specifically designed to present plays seemingly goes to William B. Chapman Sr. (1764–1839), who launched his earliest venture, apparently called the *Floating Theatre*, around 1831. It was described by Ludlow as "a large flatboat with a rude kind of house built upon it, having a ridge-roof, above which projected a staff with a flag attached, upon which was plainly visible the word Theatre." The boat, or at least the enclosed structure on it, was about 100 feet long and 14 feet wide. The enclosure had a shallow stage at one end and benches running the width of the auditorium. Like Drake before him, the core of Chapman's company was his own family. They traveled annually from Pittsburgh to New Orleans, stopping mainly at smaller towns and plantations that lacked even the semblance of a permanent playhouse. As a rule, stands were for one night only. When the ship reached New Orleans, Chapman would sell it rather than attempt the difficult northward passage and, returning north, commission another ship for use the following season. After Chapman's death in 1839, his widow sold the latest boat to Sol *Smith, who operated it briefly and then joined Ludlow in a famous managerial partnership. By the 1830s show boats had spread to other waterways and sometimes presented more than melodramas, comedies, and primitive olios. In the late 1830s and early 1840s one Henry Butler plied the Erie Canal with his combination museum and theatre. Not surprisingly, his repertory leaned heavily toward nautical comedies and dramas, such as *Black-Eyed Susan*. In 1845 New Yorkers and Brooklynites could enjoy entertainments on a vessel at first called the *Great North River Opera House*, which was moored at the foot of Spring Street and which was described as "a floating dramatic temple—with galleries, boxes, pit, scenes, and machinery, as well as with commodious cabins, for the dressing rooms of the artistes." It was said to have been a large, converted "Man-of-War Built Steamship" and to have seated two thousand playgoers. When Manhattan drama buffs tired of it, it was moved to a pier at Fulton Street in Brooklyn. Spaulding and Rodgers' *Floating Circus Palace*, built in Cincinnati in 1851, featured clowns and equestrians and other animal acts on an unusually short, wide vessel. The offerings were done in arena style and presented olios and dramas as well as circuses.

The Civil War disrupted the spread of this entertainment form, but after the conflict it made a quick comeback. One of the first was the *Will S. Hays*, built in 1869 by the famous clown Dan Rice. Even more elaborate and enduring were the five vessels known as *French's New Sensation*, all constructed and operated by Captain Augustus Byron French. The first was launched in 1878 and the second a few years later. Since Mrs. French was the only woman on the Mississippi to hold both a pilot's and a master's license, the couple was able to run two ships concurrently. Despite French's celebrated flamboyance, he maintained a strict discipline among his small company and presented no play capable of provoking controversy or offense. This, combined with the relative luxury of his boats, gave these crafts a new cachet and respectability. Two other celebrated Mississippi captains were E. A. Price and E. E. Eisenbarth, who later became curiously linked in the romantic story of these boats. Eisenbarth was believed to be the first to name a boat the *Cotton Blossom* and the first to attempt an opera aboard ship. Price built the long-popular *Water Queen* in 1885. It was his boat that was used in the famous 1936 film version of *Show Boat*, although Edna *Ferber had called the boat in her story the *Cotton Blossom*. Members of the Bryant family were also well-known owners and captains, and Billy Bryant's *Children of Ol' Man River* (1936) provides one of the most interesting stories of life on these vessels. The romanticized picture of show boats with huge side or rear paddle wheels and towering smokestacks is historically inaccurate, since most show boats were not self-propelled but were pushed along by small tug boats. (The 1994 Broadway revival of *Show Boat* was the first to realize this concept on stage.) The show boats themselves were customarily three decks high, the first two decks being enclosed and containing not only the long, narrow auditorium, but living quarters for the company. The top deck was open except for a sort of cupola, which served various functions on different vessels. The repertory remained conservative and with time came to appear absurdly out of date to more sophisticated city theatregoers. However, admissions more or less matched those of small-town theatres with a 50-cent top ticket prevailing until the Civil War and many charging $1 thereafter. The quality of acting in these plays undoubtedly left much to be desired, and the boats, unlike *minstrel shows, *vaudeville, or *burlesque, seem to have failed to produce any great stars of their own or even have served as a training ground for stars in other fields. However, the frequent employment of an olio between the acts or before and after the main attraction remains unexplored as a possible source for the later burgeoning of variety or vaudeville. The boats began to go into a sharp decline with the development of larger cities and, even more so, with the coming of films. The coup de grâce came with the Depression. A few surviving boats remain moored at city docks, where they serve as dinner theatres or more or less as living museums.

SHOW-OFF, THE (1924), a play by George *Kelly. [Playhouse, 571 perf.] The Fishers, a lower-middle-class Philadelphia family, are dismayed that their daughter Amy (Regina Wallace) is in love with the likes of Aubrey Piper (Louis John Bartels), a nut who, with his patent leather shoes, his cheap, slick toupee, and a carnation in his buttonhole, is convinced he is "The pride of old West Philly!" When Amy marries him despite the grumbling of her father (C. W. Goodrich) and the barbed warnings of her mother (Helen *Lowell), she learns quickly that he is not the good provider he boasted of being. Matters come to a head when Aubrey, in a borrowed car, hits both a trolley and a policeman. His brother-in-law, Frank (Guy d'Ennery), is forced to bail him out and later pay his fine. At the same time Mr. Fisher dies of a stroke. Just as the future looks bleak, Amy's brother, Joe (Lee *Tracy), is awarded $100,000 for a rust-proofing invention. He acknowledges that Aubrey inadvertently gave him the lead that made the invention possible. Moreover, the family is amazed to learn that Aubrey secretly confronted the people with whom Joe was dealing and bulldozed them into doubling their offer. To his awed wife, Aubrey remarks, "A little bluff goes a long way sometimes." Mrs. Fisher, however, is not awed. She can only exclaim, "God help me, from now on." Expanded from a vaudeville sketch that Kelly had created, the play was the biggest hit of its season and was hailed by Heywood *Broun as "the best comedy which has yet been written by an American." The *Pulitzer Prize jury selected it for its annual award but, to virtually everyone's surprise, was overridden by Columbia University officials who gave the award to *Hell-Bent for Heaven. Of the many revivals of the comedy, a 1967 mounting with Helen *Hayes as Mrs. Fisher was the most memorable.

SHOW SHOP, THE (1914), a play by James *Forbes. [Hudson Theatre, 156 perf.] Max Rosenbaum (George Sidney), a shoestring but eternally optimistic Broadway producer, learns that his leading lady and leading man have walked out on him on the eve of the dress rehearsal for his new play. He hastily signs Bettina Dean (Patricia *Collinge) as his leading lady, even though his sour-tongued director Wilbur Tompkins (Ned A. Sparks) warns him that Bettina's notorious mother (Zelda Sears) will always be on hand. Jerome Belden (Douglas *Fairbanks), a handsome young man-about-town, loves Bettina, but Mrs. Dean, recalling that marriage destroyed her chance to become a star, will not hear of it for her daughter. To be with Bettina, Jerry offers to underwrite the play and assume the role of leading man. The play is so bad it folds out of town, but Mrs. Dean insists that there will be no marriage until her daughter becomes a star on Broadway. Jerry then pays Rosenbaum $5,000 to produce another play, with the stipulation that it

must flop but also that it must play at least one night in New York with Bettina as star. To make certain it fails Rosenbaum again casts Jerry as his leading man. The play is called *A Drop of Poison*, but Mrs. Dean orders it renamed *Dora's Dilemma* after Bettina's role. Although Jerry's performance is as bad as the play, the critics love it. Taking the bull by the horns, however, Bettina and Jerry announce they are leaving the show and marrying. Since Mrs. Dean has realized her wish, a compromise is reached that allows the youngsters to marry but to stay with the play for its run. Called by Walter Prichard *Eaton "the most pungent, amusing, and yet the most kindly satire of stage life and the shams of theatrical production, yet written by an American," this neglected gem is a superbly written comedy, rich in backstage lore and especially in its marvelous portrait of the classic stage mother.

SHRIKE, THE (1952), a play by Joseph Kramm. [*Cort Theatre, 161 perf.; Pulitzer Prize.] Despondent over his failure to obtain work as a theatrical director, Jim Downs (José *Ferrer) attempts to kill himself and is committed to the psychiatric ward. Taking advantage of her legal status, his vicious, estranged wife, Ann (Judith Evelyn), determines to keep him there until he comes back to her. She quietly turns the doctors against him and agrees to his release only after he promises to abandon a warm, loving girl with whom he has been having an affair. Trapped, he reluctantly accepts Ann's terms. Although the play seems to be largely forgotten today, it was a gripping melodrama and superbly acted.

SHUBERT ALLEY (New York). A famous theatrical thoroughfare between 44th and 45th Streets, just west of Broadway, it was created by the space between the back of the Astor Hotel and the *Shubert and *Booth Theatres. The alley was fenced off for many years, used by actors in the two theatres as a cool place to spend intermission and, at one end, served as a terminal for a New Jersey bus line. To hide the unsightly alley from pedestrians on the sidewalks, a row of large theatre posters were put on the fence. The posters stayed even after the buses left and the walkway was open to pedestrian traffic. After the demolition of the hotel and the erection of a skyscraper in its place, the famous alley was widened and, still featuring a row of posters, remains a popular site with players.

SHUBERT THEATRE (New York). Officially the Sam S. Shubert Theatre, the famous West 44th Street playhouse was named after the Shuberts' eldest brother, who got them started in show business. It was designed by Henry B. *Herts in the Venetian Renaissance style to be the flagship of the growing Shubert empire. Its structure (with the attached *Booth Theatre) stretches a full city block and includes offices above and *Shubert Alley below. The theatre opened in 1917 and quickly established itself as a favorite musical house. Its longest tenants have been *A *Chorus Line* (1975) and the 1996 revival of *Chicago*.

SHUBERTS, THE. [Levi] **Lee** (1873?–1953), **Sam**[uel] **S.** (1876?–1905), and **J**[acob] **J.** (1878?–1963) [né Szemanski] were born in Shervient, Lithuania, and brought to America in 1882 and settled in Syracuse, New York. Lee and Sam soon had odd jobs at local theatres, and Sam shortly became box-office treasurer at one. When Sam purchased the area-touring rights to the Charles *Hoyt play *A Texas Steer* in 1894, the brothers' careers were launched. By 1900 Sam and Lee were ready to tackle New York, although this meant bucking the *Theatrical Syndicate, or Trust and its boss Abe Erlanger. They leased the old Herald Square Theatre, made a precarious agreement with *Erlanger, and booked in *Arizona* (1900). The play's success put their house on a firm footing. Within a few years, joined by brother J. J., they would break Erlanger's monopoly and become the largest theatre owners in New York and elsewhere, as well as the most active producers in America. When Sam was killed in a train wreck, Lee took over management. Many had felt that Sam was the driving force behind the brothers, but Lee proved as good an executive. From the start J. J. was the least of the trio, left to attend to the staging of productions and to import his beloved operettas. Their first production, *The Brixton Burglary* (1901), was not a success, but their second, the musical *A Chinese Honeymoon* (1902), was, and between then and 1954 "The Messrs Shubert," as their billing read, produced 520 plays on Broadway. Their emphasis was largely on musicals, since, if successful, they promised the greatest return. A brief sampling of their productions, musical and nonmusical, includes *Heidelberg* (1902), *Widowers' Houses* (1907), *The Passing of the 3rd Floor Back* (1909), *The *City* (1909), *Little Eyolf* (1910), *The *Passing Show* (first edition, 1912), *Ruggles of Red Gap* (1915), *Peter Ibbetson* (1917), *Maytime* (1917), *Sinbad* (1918), *He and She* (1920), *Blossom Time* (1921), *Bombo* (1921), *The *Student Prince* (1924), *Countess Maritza* (1926), *Life Begins at 8:40* (1934), *At Home Abroad* (1935), *The Show Is On* (1936), *Hellzapoppin* (1938), and *Dark of the Moon* (1945). Among their principal New York houses were the *Shubert, the *Winter Garden, and the *Princess. Although the brothers' tactics were often deemed crass and ruthless, they could be seen as responding to the tactics of the Trust and other unethical managers. Typically, in later years, they often gave substantially reduced rents to struggling, worthwhile attractions and kept many theatres in the legitimate fold that might otherwise have been lost to movies or burlesque. The vast collection of records, manuscripts, and other materials left behind by the brothers has been reorganized into the Shubert Archive, housed in the *Lyceum Theatre. The brothers' various companies were restructured in 1973 as the Shubert Organization. The new company has been headed by two native New Yorkers, Bernard B. Jacobs (1916–96), a graduate of New York University and Columbia Law School, and Gerald Schoenfeld (b. 1924), a graduate of the University of Illinois and New York University Law School. The Shubert Organization owns and operates sixteen Broadway houses, as well as others in cities such as Chicago, Boston, Los Angeles, and Philadelphia, and has co-produced dozens of productions, including *Amadeus* (1980), *Dreamgirls* (1981), *The *Life and Adventures of Nicholas Nickleby* (1981), *Little Shop of Horrors* (1982), *Glengarry Glen Ross* (1984), *Sunday in the Park with George* (1984), *Big Deal* (1986), *Once on This Island* (1990), *Passion* (1994), *Bring in da Noise, Bring in da Funk* (1996), and *Dirty Blonde* (2000). Biography: *The Boys from Syracuse: The Shuberts' Theatrical Empire*, Foster Hirsch, 1998.

SHUE, Larry. See *Foreigner, The*.

SHUFFLE ALONG (1921), a musical comedy by Flournoy Miller, Aubrey Lyles (book), Eubie Blake (music), Noble Sissle (lyrics). [63rd Street Theatre, 504 perf.] Two partners in a Jimtown grocery store, Steve Jenkins (Miller) and Sam Peck (Lyles), become opposition candidates for mayor. Each promises the other that if elected he will make his partner chief of police. Jenkins wins and keeps his word, but Peck soon realizes he has nothing to do. Noisy fights and public charges of corruption follow, so before long Harry Walton (Roger Matthews) announces he will run as a reform candidate. He ousts the partners, who ramble off seeking new worlds to conquer. *Notable songs*: I'm Just Wild About Harry; Love Will Find a Way; Bandana Days. Although there had been a number of turn-of-the-century black musicals, most starring Bert *Williams and his partner George Walker, the vogue for such shows had died off until the raging popularity of this show set off a new boom that survived into the 1930s. Its superb, rhythmic dancing was a major attraction and set a pattern that caused most African-American musicals of the decade to be looked upon primarily as dancing shows. Except for *Blackbirds of 1928*, none of the period's similar musicals matched its success. The Baltimore-born composer [James Hubert] **Eubie BLAKE** (1883–1983) and his lyricist-singer partner **Noble SISSLE** (1889–1975) spent 1915–19 with the famous African-American conductor James Reese

Europe. After Europe's murder, the pair enjoyed success as a vaudeville act that shunned traditional black stereotypes. After *Shuffle Along*, the team's songs were heard in *Elsie* (1923) and *The Chocolate Dandies* (1924). With Andy Razaf, Blake wrote the songs for **Blackbirds of 1930*, then was reunited with Sissle on two failed attempts to recapture the appeal of their first hit: *Shuffle Along of 1933* and *Shuffle Along of 1952*. A revival of ragtime and interest in early African-American music in the 1970s brought Blake renewed attention, and in 1978 a retrospective revue, *Eubie!*, further rekindled his popularity as a performer and raconteur. His songs were also featured in the musicals *Doctor Jazz* (1975) and *Bubbling Brown Sugar* (1976). Biography: *Eubie Blake*, Al Rose, 1979.

SHUMLIN, Herman (1898–1979), producer and director. Born in Atwood, Colorado, he worked in New York for the **Clipper* and **Billboard*, then served with Laurence Schwab and Frank *Mandel and with Jed *Harris before embarking on an independent career as producer and director. Among his notable productions were *The *Last Mile* (1930), **Grand Hotel* (1930), *The *Children's Hour* (1934), *The *Little Foxes* (1939), *The *Male Animal* (1940), *The Corn Is Green* (1940), **Watch on the Rhine* (1941), *The Searching Wind* (1944), **Inherit the Wind* (1955), and *The Deputy* (1964). Lillian *Hellman, whose plays he produced, wrote that he "has made many an actor into a star, and many a star into a decent actor. The theatre, for him, is not a place to show off. . . . He is one of the few directors who believes in the play; he is one of the very few who has the sharp clarity, the sensitivity, the understanding, which should be the director's gift to the play."

SIBERIA (1883), a play by Bartley *Campbell, [Haverly's 14th Street Theatre, 40 perf.] After the assassination of Czar Alexander II, radicals and Jews come under attack in Russia. Sara (Georgia *Cayvan) and Marie (Blanche Mortimer) are the daughters of a Christian mother, but since their father is Jewish they find it prudent to flee. They wander across Russia, encountering both friendship and betrayal. Although most critics agreed that the play's complicated plot forbade retelling, they were divided on the work's merits. Among those who approved, the *Tribune* observed that Campbell "handled [his] materials so as to arouse and maintain interest in a story that is extravagant and [in] persons who are radically commonplace." Each act built to a melodramatic climax. This and its topicality kept the work on the boards for a quarter of a century.

SIDE MAN (1998), a play by Warren Leight. [*Classic Stage Company, 485 perf.; Tony Award.] This memory play about itinerant musicians in the waning days of the Big Band era was narrated by Clifford (Robert Sella), the son of restless jazz trumpeter Gene (Frank Wood) and the bitter alcoholic Terry (Edie Falco). The play switches back and forth in time, showing the uneasy courtship of Gene and Terry, their tempestuous marriage, and eventual break up. Much of the "sorrowing but trenchantly humorous family drama" centered on the side men, Gene's cronies who were portrayed colorfully and unsentimentally. The play opened quietly Off Off Broadway, then was picked up by Off Broadway's *Roundabout Theatre, eventually playing at the *John Golden Theatre on Broadway. **Warren LEIGHT** (b. 1957) was born in New York and educated at Stanford before making his professional writing debut providing sketches and lyrics for the musical revue *Mayor* (1985). He is also the author of *Glimmer, Glimmer, and Shine* (2001).

SIEDLE, Mrs. Caroline (1867?–1907), designer. Probably the first woman in America to receive widespread recognition as a costume designer, she was born in England but little is known of her early history. She began to attract attention to her work in the mid-1890s, and until her early death she specialized in creating the colorful costumes for the period's musicals. Siedle designed many of Lillian *Russell's productions as well as such successes as **El Capitan* (1896), *The *Wizard of Oz* (1903), **Babes in Toyland* (1903), *It Happened in Nordland* (1904), *The *Red Mill* (1906), *The Rich Mr. Hoggenheimer* (1906), and *A Parisian Model* (1906). On her death, Julian *Mitchell remarked, "Without her assistance I should never have been able to carry out the musical comedy color schemes which have made beautiful stage pictures. Her taste was always good, and her ability to design amounted to genius."

SIGNATURE THEATRE (New York). This little theatre company, now located in a space on *Theatre Row with only 160 seats, has received much attention since it was founded by James Houghton in 1991. Its goal is unique and revealing: to dedicate each season to the work of one established playwright, to revive past works, and to premiere new ones by the chosen writer who works with the company throughout the season. Featured playwrights have included Lee Blessing, Edward *Albee, Sam *Shepard, John *Guare, Arthur *Miller, Maria Irene *Fornés, Romulus Linney, Adrienne Kennedy, Horton *Foote, Lanford *Wilson, and Bill *Irwin. The company has received numerous special awards for its enterprising program of presenting the work of American playwrights.

SILSBEE, Joshua (1813–55), comedian. He was born somewhere in New York State or in Litchfield,

Connecticut, and did not turn to acting until 1839 when he made his debut in Natchez, Mississippi. For several years he played in towns along the Mississippi River and in Cincinnati, specializing in juveniles and fops. However, his greatest success came when he began portraying Yankee characters much like those played by G. H. *Hill and Dan *Marble. By the time Silsbee made his New York debut in 1843, his characterizations of Lot Sapsago, Deuteronomy Dutiful, Jonathan Ploughboy, and other similar roles were his stock in trade. In 1850 he went to England, where for a brief time he became the most popular exponent of stage Yankees. One critic noted, "Faithfully as he performs the Yankee character, his performances are permeated with the natural humor of the man. His looks, gestures, and action—even the arch twinkle of his eye—impress the spectator with ludicrous emotions, and his inflexible countenance, rigidly innocent of fun while his audience are in roars of laughter, gives an additional zest to the humor." He returned to America in 1853 but died in California while on a transcontinental tour.

SILVER CORD, THE (1926), a play by Sidney *Howard. [*John Golden Theatre, 112 perf.] Mrs. Phelps (Laura Hope *Crews) is a pathologically possessive mother determined to destroy the engagement of her son Robert (Earle *Larimore) to Hester (Margalo *Gillmore), as well as the marriage of her son David (Eliot Cabot) and his wife, Christina (Elizabeth Risdon). When Christina accuses her of being little more than a civilized cannibal, she responds, "I would cut off my hands and burn out my eyes to rid my son of you." She succeeds in driving Hester to suicide and cowing Robert, but with Christina's encouragement David breaks his mother's "silver cord." Gilbert Gabriel of the *Sun* called the *Theatre Guild production "a play for the mature, the unafraid; and to them it guarantees an evening of excitive truths and rare dramatic instinct." While many critics compared the piece favorably with George *Kelly's study of a selfish spouse, *Craig's Wife*, it failed to find the large public of the earlier play.

SILVER SPOON, THE (1852), a comedy by Joseph Stevens *Jones. [*Boston Museum, in repertory.] Having been elected by his "feller townsmen" to represent Cranberry Center in the "Gineral" assembly, Jefferson S. Batkins (William *Warren) comes to the state capital to assume his post and fight for his country neighbors against the big city "klinks"—his reading of "cliques." He decides to stay with Ezra Austin (W. H. *Smith), whose aunt, Hannah Partridge (Mrs. Thoman), he had courted long ago and whom he proposes to court again. At the same time, young Glandon King has returned from Europe for the reading of his father's will. The document announces that since Glandon has been given everything he wanted in life, his father's money goes to establish a college, and Glandon's sole reward is a silver spoon. A shady lawyer, Simon Feedle (Mr. Curtis), attempts to break the will and establish his law clerk, Tom Pinfeather (C. H. Saunders), as a second son of the late Mr. King. The ploy is exposed and a later will is discovered in which King announces that if Glandon has made no effort to break the first will, then the entire estate is his. Glandon's proposal of marriage is accepted by Austin's daughter, Sarah (Mrs. Wulf Fries), while Hannah agrees to become Mrs. Batkins. Despite its title, this most popular of all Boston 19th-century comedies really centered on Batkins, whose gaffes cause endless embarrassment and whose innocence gets him into several awkward situations. Much of the comedy came from a confused speech Batkins hopes to make to the assembly and which he tries out on anyone who will listen. The play remained in Warren's and the Boston Museum's repertory until Warren's death and was popular in stock until shortly before World War I.

SILVERMAN, Sime (1873–1933), critic. Born in Cortland, New York, but raised in Syracuse, he was the son of a banker who tried unsuccessfully to have his son follow in his footsteps. Instead, young Silverman went to New York, where he became a critic, writing as "The Man in the Third Row" for the *Daily American* and later as "Robert Speare" for the *Morning Telegraph*. After being fired when a vaudeville act he had panned canceled its annual Christmas ad, he borrowed $1,500 and in 1905 started his own theatrical paper, *Variety*. Under his guidance as editor and publisher it soon became the most important American theatrical trade journal. Silverman demanded absolute impartiality and attempted to report news as fully as possible. He also originated much of the curious slang for which the paper became known. Later he founded *The Times Square Daily*, an extended gossip sheet, which led to the *Daily Variety* around the time of his death. Biography: *Lord Broadway: Variety's Sime*, Dayton Stoddart, 1941.

SILVERS, Phil[ip] [né Philip Silver] (1911–85), comedian. The Brooklyn-born comic, who specialized in smart-alecky bunglers, began performing as a child and had appeared in vaudeville and burlesque before making his Broadway debut as Punko Parks in *Yokel Boy* (1939). By the time he returned to the theatre as the con man Harrison Floy in *High Button Shoes* (1947), he had won recognition in films. He later starred as TV clown Jerry Biffle in *Top Banana* (1951), schemer Hubie

Cram in *Do Re Mi* (1960), and as the wily slave Pseudolus in *A *Funny Thing Happened on the Way to the Forum* (1972). Silvers was most known for his years in television.

SIMON, [Jovan Ivan] John (b. 1925), critic. A native of Yugoslavia, he was educated at Harvard. He has served as drama critic for such periodicals as the *Hudson Review* and *New York* magazine. Simon has also taught at several universities and has published numerous books, most about films. He is often perceived as the most vitriolic of contemporary critics, but his writing is fluid and masterful.

SIMON, [Marvin] Neil (b. 1927), playwright. The most successful popular dramatist of his era, he was born in the Bronx and educated at New York University. Early in his career he was a radio and television script writer, then turned to the stage by writing sketches for summer camp revues. His sketches were seen on stage in *Catch a Star* (1955) and *New Faces of 1956* before finding success with his first full-length play, *Come Blow Your Horn* (1961). After writing the book for the musical *Little Me* (1962), Simon then enjoyed a string of hits unparalleled in American stage history: *Barefoot in the Park* (1963), *The *Odd Couple* (1965), *Sweet Charity* (1966), *Plaza Suite* (1968), *Promises, Promises* (1968), and *Last of the Red Hot Lovers* (1968). He had less success with *The Star-Spangled Girl* (1966) and *The Gingerbread Lady* (1970) but had back-to-back hits with *The *Prisoner of Second Avenue* (1971) and *The *Sunshine Boys* (1972). From that point on, Simon's theatre career was a matter of hit-or-miss with some estimable plays in both categories: *The Good Doctor* (1973), *God's Favorite* (1974), *California Suite* (1976), *Chapter Two* (1977), *They're Playing Our Song* (1979), *I Ought to Be in Pictures* (1980), *Fools* (1981), and the autobiographical trilogy consisting of *Brighton Beach Memoirs* (1983), *Biloxi Blues* (1985), and *Broadway Bound* (1986). His later efforts include *Rumors* (1988), *Lost in Yonkers* (1991), *Jake's Women* (1992), *Laughter on the 23rd Floor* (1993), *The Goodbye Girl* (1993), *London Suite* (1995), *Proposals* (1997), *The Dinner Party* (2000), *45 Seconds from Broadway* (2001), and *Rose's Dilemma* (2003). Simon, a shrewd observer of human foibles and a master of the surprise one-line joke, often makes remarkably effective comedies out of potentially unpleasant themes. Much of his success depends on these qualities, since his plays rarely offer major plot twists. While Simon's more serious efforts have met with mixed reactions, they usually employ the same skill and vivid characterizations. Many of his plays have been made into popular films, often with his own screenplays. Autobiographies: *Rewrites*, 1996; *The Play Goes On*, 1999.

SIMONSON, Lee (1888–1967), designer. The New York–born scenic artist, who studied at Harvard under George Pierce *Baker, did his earliest commercial set designs for the *Washington Square Players. After serving in World War I he became one of the founders of the *Theatre Guild and did many of the group's most noteworthy sets. Simonson also usually lit his own sets and often created the costumes for the same productions. Among his memorable achievements were his designs for *Liliom* (1921), *He Who Gets Slapped* (1922), *R. U. R.* (1922), *Peer Gynt* (1923), *The *Adding Machine* (1923), *The *Road to Rome* (1927), *Marco Millions* (1928), *Dynamo* (1929), *Hotel Universe* (1930), *Elizabeth the Queen* (1930), *End of Summer* (1936), *Idiot's Delight* (1936), and *Joan of Lorraine* (1946). His associate, Theresa *Helburn, wrote, "He could perform miracles with light and he has produced some of the most interesting experimental sets seen on the American stage." His creations ranged from the expressionistic settings for *The Adding Machine* and the realistic *Dynamo* to the virtually bare stage for *Joan of Lorraine*. He also wrote *The Stage Is Set* (1932) and *The Art of Scenic Design* (1950). Autobiography: *Part of a Lifetime*, 1943.

SIMPSON, Edmund Shaw (1784–1848), actor and manager. Born in England, his debut occurred at Towchester in 1806 in *The *Stranger*. While performing in Dublin three years later he was signed by Thomas *Cooper and Stephen *Price to appear at the *Park Theatre, and his American bow was in *The Road to Ruin* (1809). He was greeted with "the warmest approbation" and quickly established himself as a versatile performer. Among his early roles were Charles Teazle, Jaffier, and Richmond, which he played to the Richards of both Edmund *Kean and Junius Brutus Booth. In 1812 Simpson was appointed acting manager of the Park, and in 1815 he became Price's partner in the theatre. He was injured during a performance in 1828 and was permanently crippled, yet he continued to perform until 1833, after which he played only on special occasions. Following Price's death in 1840, he attempted to run the theatre alone, but the theatre district had moved northward and the Park encountered continual financial problems. Shortly before his own death he sold out to *Hamblin. Whatever the failures of his last years (and they were overcome briefly by the successful premieres of *London Assurance* and *Fashion*), he remained a popular and respected figure with New York playgoers and critics.

SINN, Col. William E. (1834?–99), manager. He was born in the Georgetown section of Washington, D.C., and spent several years as a traveling salesman before going into partnership with his brother-in-law Leonard B. *Grover in 1861. Within a few years they had several theatres in the D.C. area as well as in Cincinnati. On his own he took over Philadelphia's *Chestnut Street Theatre in 1864 and the Front Street Theatre in Baltimore in 1869. However, Sinn was most successful after moving his base to Brooklyn in 1875, quickly turning the Park Theatre there into the city's leading house. Although he never served in any army, he was made a colonel in the Confederate forces for his help in enlisting men during the Civil War.

SINNERS (1915), a play by Owen *Davis. [Playhouse, 220 perf.] Mary Horton (Alice *Brady) leaves her small New Hampshire town and her widowed mother (Emma Dunn) to seek her fortune in New York. She quickly falls in with the wrong company and accepts their immoral ways. Learning that her mother is dying, Mary returns home, where she is determined to keep from her simple, pious mother the truth about her behavior. But the arrival of some of her big city friends does not help matters. Although many critics considered the William A. *Brady offering little better than the cheap melodramas Davis had written for A. H. *Woods, Davis himself felt it was one of the dramas that marked his emergence as a more serious writer.

SISSLE, Noble. See *Shuffle Along*.

SISTERS ROSENSWEIG, THE (1992), a comedy by Wendy *Wasserstein. [*Mitzi E. Newhouse Theatre, 556 perf.] The three Rosensweig sisters were born and bred in a very ethnic Brooklyn neighborhood, but each has come far in the world. Sara (Jane *Alexander) is an international banker who has been married a few times and now finds herself attracted, against her better judgment, to the Jewish furrier Melvyn Kant (Robert Klein). Gorgeous Teitelbaum (Madeline *Kahn) is famous in Boston for giving advice on her radio show. Pfeni (Frances McDormand) is a renowned travel writer in a dead-end romance with the bisexual stage director Geoffrey Duncan (John Vickery). The three sisters meet at Sara's posh London flat to celebrate her fifty-fourth birthday and reminisce about their ongoing relationship with their feminism and Jewishness. Daniel *Sullivan directed the outstanding cast (Kahn won a *Tony Award), and the comedy was so popular that *Lincoln Center transferred it to Broadway's *Ethel Barrymore Theatre for a healthy run.

SIX-CYLINDER LOVE (1921), a comedy by William Anthony *McGuire. [Sam H. Harris Theatre, 430 perf.] Having lived beyond their means, Richard Burton (Donald Meek) and his wife, Geraldine (Eleanor Gordon), are facing eviction. To pay moving costs they will have to sell their new car. But they don't have to look far for a buyer as there are newlyweds next door. In no time Marilyn Sterling (June *Walker) is convinced that she wants nothing more than a new car, so her doting husband, Gilbert (Ernest *Truex), buys the Burtons' auto. Before long the Sterlings are living wildly beyond their means, and when Mr. Stapleton (Burton Churchill), Gilbert's staid boss, pays a sudden visit, his unfavorable impression of their mode of living costs Gilbert his job. Gilbert sells the car and convinces Mr. Stapleton to give him back his job. But Gilbert suddenly finds a new expense item in his ledgers: Marilyn will soon need a baby carriage. Burns *Mantle noted, "Somewhat extravagant as to story, its characters are purposely exaggerated to give it a farcical trimming, and thus punctuate its proceedings with laughter. The basic dramatic situations, however, and the impelling motives that inspire its principal characters, are sincerely and convincingly human." The Sam H. *Harris production was one of the most popular comedies of its era.

SIX DEGREES OF SEPARATION (1990), a play by John *Guare. [*Mitzi E. Newhouse Theatre, 485 perf.; NYDCC Award.] A sophisticated Manhattan couple, Flanders (John Cunningham) and Ouisa Kittredge (Stockard *Channing), are entertaining a businessman when a beaten and bloody African-American youth (James McDaniel) stumbles into their swank apartment, claiming to be a friend of their children away at college. He says that his name is Paul, the son of film star Sidney Poitier, and that he has been robbed of his money and his college thesis. The Kittredges take him in for the night, and he charms them by cooking a creative dinner and revealing his considerable knowledge of art, literature, and their children. But when Ouisa discovers Paul in bed with a hustler and both flee, the couple starts to question everything the youth told them and soon discover that he is a fraud who has worked his way into some of their friends' homes the same way. Paul also tricks a struggling young couple (Paul McCrane and Mari Nelson) out of their savings and has a brief affair with the boy, which leads to his suicide. Paul is arrested by the police and seems to disappear into the justice system, but the Kittredges are still haunted by the young man who affected them so deeply so quickly. Reviews were enthusiastic, Douglas Watt in the New York Daily News calling the play "a magic carpet ride . . . endlessly stimulating and funny." Channing's performance and Jerry *Zaks's direction were particularly praised. After six months, *Lincoln Center moved the production upstairs into the *Vivian Beaumont Theatre, where it ran nearly a year.

SKELLY, Hal [né Joseph Harold Skelley] (1891–1934), comic actor. Born in Allegheny, Pennsylvania, he performed in circuses before joining the original Chicago production of The *Time, the Place and the Girl in 1908. Further appearances followed in circuses, musical comedy touring troupes, and with Lew Dockstader's minstrels. After playing the lead in the road tour of So Long, Letty, he made his New York debut in Fiddlers Three (1918). Throughout the 1920s Skelly was a leading comedian in other musicals, but he is best recalled for his role in a nonmusical play, in which he portrayed the failing performer Skid in *Burlesque (1927).

SKELTON, Thomas (b. 1927), lighting designer. Born in Bridgetown, Maine, and educated at Middlebury College, he apprenticed to Jean *Rosenthal before making his Manhattan design debut in 1958. In addition to many dance and regional theatre productions, Skelton has lit such New York productions as *Oh, Dad, Poor, Dad (1963), Coco (1969), *Purlie (1972), *Death of a Salesman (1975), *Shenandoah (1975), *Richard III (1979), *Show Boat (1983), The *Iceman Cometh (1986), and A Few Good Men (1989).

SKIDDING (1928), a comedy by Aurania Rouverol. [Bijou Theatre, 448 perf.] Marion Hardy (Marguerite Churchill) decides to break off her engagement and begin a political career by helping her father, Judge Hardy (Carleton Macy), in his own campaign. The campaign is a success, but so is Judge Hardy when he makes Marion realize she will be happy in marriage as well. Largely dismissed by the critics, the comedy far outran many better plays in an excellent season. It served as the basis for the Andy Hardy movies so long popular in Hollywood.

SKIN OF OUR TEETH, THE (1942), a play by Thornton *Wilder. [*Plymouth Theatre, 359 perf.; Pulitzer Prize.] Mr. and Mrs. Antrobus (Fredric *March and Florence *Eldridge) live in a modern home in Excelsior, New Jersey, with their malevolent son, Henry (Montgomery Clift), their giddy daughter, Gladys (Frances Heflin), and their pet mammoth and pet dinosaur. Although the advancing Ice Age is threatening to destroy their home and world, the Antrobuses survive to no small extent because Mr. Antrobus is inventive enough to create the wheel and the alphabet (while his wife discovers sewing and cooking), and he is enlightened enough to encourage art and learning. Nor can he be seduced by their aggressive maid, Sabina (Tallulah *Bankhead). Eons later, on the boardwalk at Atlantic City, Mr. Antrobus is elected president at the convention of the Ancient and Honorable Order of Mammals. A cassandric fortune-teller (Florence *Reed) spouts gloom and doom as the murderous

Henry continues to attack those he hates; Sabina, made a beauty queen, still determines to lure Mr. Antrobus away from his wife; and a deluge arises to engulf the world. Mr. Antrobus manages to get pairs of animals aboard an ark before the waters destroy them. Yet the flood has scarcely passed when a great war decimates civilization. Not even this can discourage Mr. Antrobus, who determines to build a better new world. At this point Sabina begins the same scene she had at the play's opening, only to stop and add, "This is where you came in. We have to go on for ages and ages. You go home. The end of the play isn't written yet." Wilder's modern allegory, which juxtaposed biblical events with such modern phenomena as the Miss America Pageant, baffled many tryout critics but was an instant success in New York. Students have seen in it strong influences not only of expressionist and epic theatre but also of James Joyce's Finnegans Wake. The original production was aided immeasurably by Bankhead's tour-de-force performance, which allowed her to be both siren and liaison with the audience, by Elia *Kazan's fluid direction, and by Albert *Johnson's surrealistic settings and his use of projection screens. The play remains one of the few effective stage allegories and is still revived with some regularity. Major mountings have included a 1945 English production, a 1955 New York production, an international tour in 1961 assisted by the State Department, and a Central Park revival in 1998.

SKINNER, Cornelia Otis (1901–79), actress. The regal-looking daughter of Otis *Skinner was born in Chicago, began to act while a student at Bryn Mawr, and made her professional debut in her father's production of Blood and Sand (1921). After appearing in several other plays, Skinner first presented her bill of one-woman character sketches in 1925, then toured with it for several seasons. She returned to these sketches at frequent intervals throughout her career. Among her noteworthy regular roles were the embittered actress Julia Lambert in Theatre (1941), the diplomat's wife Emily Hazen in The Searching Wind (1944), Mrs. Erlynne in a 1946 revival of Lady Windermere's Fan, and mother-of-the-bride Katherine Dougherty in The *Pleasure of His Company (1958). Skinner was also the author of a number of plays and books.

SKINNER, Otis (1858–1942), actor. The son of a Cambridge, Massachusetts, minister, he made his debut at the Philadelphia Museum in 1877, then performed with the stock company at the *Walnut Street Theatre for two seasons, making his first Manhattan appearance when the troupe visited New York. After playing small roles opposite Edwin *Booth and Lawrence *Barrett he spent four seasons with the famous company of Augustin *Daly. In 1889 he joined Helena *Modjeska and Booth to play such roles as Claudio, Bassanio, Laertes, and Macduff, later touring with Modjeska as her leading man. Skinner embarked on a career as star in 1894 and played such notable parts as the Count of Grammont in *His Grace de Grammont* (1894); Lanciotto in his celebrated 1901 revival of *Francesca da Rimini;* the swaggering bully Col. Philippe Bridau in *The Honor of the Family* (1908); the scampish, conniving beggar Hajj in *Kismet* (1911); the fun-loving Italian Antonio Camarado-nio in *Mister Antonio* (1916); and the doomed bull-fighter Juan Gallardo in *Blood and Sand* (1921). Writing of Skinner's Hajj, Walter Prichard *Eaton noted, "Mr. Skinner is, in this country, the man of destiny for the part—abounding energy, triumphant clarity of speech, romantic swagger, physical pic-turesqueness, all are his." George *Middleton char-acterized him as "flamboyant and scene-filling, like rich claret running over everything." In his later years Skinner frequently returned to his older hits, besides starring in a number of classic revivals. Alone or with his wife, Maud, he was also the author of numerous books on theatre, including *Mad Folk of the Theatre* (1928), *One Man in His Time* (1938), and *The Last Tragedian* (1939). Autobiogra-phy: *Footlights and Spotlights*, 1924.

SKULNIK, Menasha (1892?–1970), character actor. The diminutive, doleful-looking comedian, famous for his ludicrous shrugs, was born in Warsaw and spent many years on European Yid-dish stages before coming to America in 1930. Long a favorite of Yiddish audiences here, he made his English-language stage debut as the harassed executive Max Pincus in The *Fifth Season (1953), then scored another success as the biblical Noah in *The Flowering Peach* (1954). Skulnik later toured in several popular shows, but his subse-quent Broadway appearances were all in failures.

SKYSCRAPER. See *Dream Girl.*

SLADE, Bernard. See *Same Time, Next Year.*

SLEUTH (1970). Anthony *Shaffer's two-character thriller, in which a husband (Anthony Quayle) confronts his wife's lover (Keith Baxter) and who together play a series of deadly games, was presented on Broadway in 1970, only nine months after its London premiere. Although it ran only half as long as the London original, its 1,217 performances made it the second-longest stand of any London play in New York.

SLEZAK, Walter [Leo] (1902–83), actor and singer. The son of the famed opera singer Leo Slezak, he

was born in Vienna and had a successful career there in musicals before being brought to this coun-try to appear in the musical *Meet My Sister* (1930). Actually, Lee *Shubert had seen Oscar Karlweis in a show, but when an emissary was sent to engage him, Slezak was substituting and was signed by mistake. The pudgy, beady-eyed actor proved a surprise success and was seen in numerous plays and musicals, the most memorable being *Music in the Air* (1932), in which he introduced "I've Told Every Little Star"; *I Married an Angel* (1938); *My Three Angels* (1953); and *Fanny* (1954). He was long popular in films. Autobiography: *What Time's the Next Swan?*, 1962.

SLOANE, A[lfred] **Baldwin** (1872–1925), com-poser. The most prolific songwriter for musical comedies at the turn of the century, he wrote the scores for no fewer than two dozen Broadway musicals between 1896 and 1912. He was born in Baltimore, where his songs were first heard in amateur productions. Coming to New York he began interpolating melodies into others' scores and soon was invited to create his own. His biggest hit was "Heaven Will Protect the Working Girl," which Marie *Dressler introduced in *Tillie's Nightmare* (1910), but none of his songs found enduring popularity. Among Sloane's shows were *The Mocking Bird* (1902), *The *Wizard of Oz* (1903), *Lady Teazle* (1904), and *The Summer Widowers* (1910). He composed only rarely after 1912, but he did provide much of the music for the 1919 and 1920 *Greenwich Village Follies*. His last score, for *China Rose* (1925), was heard after his death.

SMITH, Anna Deavere (b. 1950), actress and playwright. The African-American performer was born in Baltimore and educated at Beaver College and *American Conservatory Theatre, where she became a member of the acting company. Smith made her Manhattan debut in 1976, but much of her career has been traveling to different cities with the solo performances that she writes. The most memorable of these programs were *Fires in the Mirror* (1992), about the racial strife in Crown Heights, Brooklyn; and *Twilight: Los Angeles, 1992* (1994), about the riots following a controversial trial verdict. David Richards in the *New York Times* described Smith as "the ultimate impressionist: she does people's souls."

SMITH, C[harles] **Aubrey** (1863–1948), actor. The British performer, who in his last years per-sonified English gentlemen in films, had a long career on American stages. His many appearances included supporting or leading roles in *The Light That Failed* (1903), *The Morals of Marcus* (1907), *The Runaway* (1911), and *The Constant Wife* (1926), but his most successful appearance came as Basil Winterton, who brings together all his illegitimate children, in *The Bachelor Father* (1928).

SMITH, Cecil (1906–56), critic and author. After studying at Harvard he served for many years on the faculty of the University of Chicago. At the same time, he was music critic and sometime drama critic for the *Chicago Tribune*. Smith was also associated with other publications, including *Theatre Arts Monthly*, of which he was associate editor and for which he generally wrote about musicals. His *Musical Comedy in America* (1950) was the first serious study of the whole history of our musical theatre and remains a perceptive, eminently readable work. It was brought up to date by Glenn Litton in 1981.

SMITH, Edgar [McPhail] (1857–1938), librettist and lyricist. The Brooklyn native was the author of some 150 works to reach Broadway. He began his career as an actor, then briefly turned playwright, collaborating on several works with Augustus *Thomas. However, he found his true métier when he was hired by the *Casino Theatre in 1886 to translate and adapt the foreign musicals the theatre was importing. In 1897 he moved to *Weber and *Fields, where he wrote many of their celebrated burlesques, among them *The Con-Curers* and *Cyranose de Bric-a-Brac* in 1898. Two of his biggest hits were introduced by Fay *Templeton in *Fiddle-Dee-Dee* (1900): "I'm a Respectable Working Girl" and "Ma Blushin' Rosie," both with music by John Stromberg. Smith also wrote or adapted *Old Dutch* (1909), *Tillie's Nightmare* (1910), *La Belle Paree* (1911), *The Blue Paradise* (1915), and *Hello, Paris* (1930), his last show.

SMITH, Dr. Elihu Ubbard (1771–98), playwright. The New England–born physician and author wrote one of the earliest American comic operas, *Edwin and Angelina; or, The Banditti* (1796), a musical dramatization of Oliver Goldsmith's "The Hermit." He also wrote several admired theatrical prologues. However, his promising career was cut short when he died while attending his patients in a yellow fever epidemic.

SMITH, Harry B[ache] (1860–1936), librettist and lyricist. The most prolific writer in the history of the American theatre, he was, by his own count, the author of some 300 librettos and 6,000 lyrics. Broadway saw 123 of his shows, while many others were mounted in Chicago and elsewhere. He was born in Buffalo but grew up in Chicago, then spent many years in a variety of capacities with Chicago newspapers and magazines, although he also gained some acting experience as a member of the Chicago Church Choir Opera Company. His friendship with Reginald *De Koven led the pair to conclude they could write American comic operas the equal of *Gilbert and Sullivan's. Their initial effort, *The Begum* (1887), had only small success, but with *Robin Hood* (1891) they created the first enduring work of our lyric stage, although, oddly, Smith did not write the lyric for "Oh, Promise Me," that operetta's biggest hit song. Smith later provided the books and often the lyrics for such musicals as *The Serenade* (1897), *The *Fortune Teller* (1898), *The Singing Girl* (1899), *The Casino Girl* (1900), *The Little Duchess* (1901), *The Office Boy* (1903), *Babette* (1903), *The Free Lance* (1906), *The Rich Mr. Hoggenheimer* (1906), the *Ziegfeld Follies* (1907–10, 1912), *The *Girl from Utah* (1914), *Watch Your Step* (1914), *Stop! Look! Listen!* (1915), *Angel Face* (1919), *Countess Maritza* (1926), and his last, *Marching By* (1932). Although his work seems lackluster and often stilted when compared with later writers, Smith was a pioneer who was respected by his contemporaries for his excellent humor and style. He was also the earliest American lyricist to be honored with a published collection of his lyrics. Autobiography: *First Nights and First Editions*, 1931; biography: *Harry B. Smith: Dean of American Librettists*, John Franceschina, 2003.

SMITH, Harry James (1880–1918), playwright. Born in New Britain, Connecticut, he studied biology at Williams College and Harvard, then taught at Oberlin. He abandoned teaching in 1906 to become an associate editor at the *Atlantic Monthly* and, at the same time, started to write plays. His first to be produced was the popular *Mrs. Bumpstead-Leigh* (1911), followed by *Blackbirds* (1913), *A *Tailor Made Man* (1917), and *The Little Teacher* (1918). Smith's promising career was cut short when he was killed in an accident while serving with the Canadian Red Cross.

SMITH, Lois [neé Lois Arlene Humbert] (b. 1930), actress. The durable dramatic player was born in Topeka, Kansas, and educated at the University of Washington and studied acting with Lee *Strasberg at the *Actors Studio. After some experience in stock, Smith made her Broadway debut as high schooler Jeannie in *Time Out for Ginger* (1952), followed by other juvenile roles, most notably the daughter Laura opposite Helen Hayes in *The *Glass Menagerie* (1956). She often returned to regional theatres, where she played a wide range of classical and contemporary characters. Of her many later, more mature roles in New York, special mention should be made of her determined Ma Joad in *The *Grapes of Wrath* (1990) and her slovenly Hallie in *Buried Child* (1996).

SMITH, Oliver [Lemuel] (1918–94), designer. Born in Waupaun, Wisconsin, and educated at Pennsylvania State University, he first designed sets for Broadway in 1942 with *Rosalinda*. His work was then seen in dozens of musicals and comedies, such as *On the Town* (1944), *Brigadoon* (1947), *High Button Shoes* (1947), *Gentlemen Prefer Blondes* (1949), the 1952 revival of *Pal Joey*, *In the Summer House* (1953), *My Fair Lady* (1956), *Auntie Mame* (1956), *Candide* (1956), *Visit to a Small Planet* (1957), *West Side Story* (1957), The *Sound of Music* (1959), *Camelot* (1960), *Mary, Mary* (1961), *Barefoot in the Park* (1963), *Hello, Dolly!* (1964), The *Odd Couple* (1965), *Plaza Suite* (1968), The *Last of the Red Hot Lovers* (1969), the 1975 revival of The *Royal Family*, and *Lunch Hour* (1980). As the list suggests, his creations covered a wide range of periods and plays, all done with style and imagination. He won numerous honors, including seven *Tony Awards, and co-produced a half dozen shows as well.

SMITH, Queenie (1902–78), singer and dancer. A native New Yorker, the petite, bouncy performer was trained for ballet and had danced at the Metropolitan Opera before making her Broadway debut in *Roly-Boly Eyes* (1919). Between 1922 and 1932 she played major supporting roles or leads in eleven musicals. Her most notable role was the title part in *Tip-Toes* (1925), in which she introduced "Looking for a Boy," "That Certain Feeling," and "These Charming People."

SMITH, Richard Penn (1799–1854), playwright. The grandson of the provost of the University of Pennsylvania and the son of a noted minister, he was a distinguished Philadelphia lawyer and the most active of the gentlemen playwrights who comprised the Philadelphia School of Dramatists. His playwriting covered the period 1825–36, his first play to reach the boards being *Quite Correct* at the *Chestnut Street Theatre in 1828, followed by The *Eighth of January* (1829); The *Disowned; or, The Prodigals* (1829); *A Wife at a Venture* (1929); The *Sentinels; or, The Two Sergeants* (1829); and *William Penn* (1829). Many students consider his The *Triumph at Plattsburg* (1830) the best play about the War of 1812, although it seems not to have been a success. Smith's other works included The *Deformed; or, Woman's Trial* (1830); *The Water Witch* (1830); *Caius Marius* (1831); *Is She a Brigand?* (1833); *The Daughter* (1836); and *The Actress of Padua* (1836). Although he was highly respected by contemporaries, even the discovery of the complete text of *Caius Marius* cannot change the judgment of his modern editors, Ralph H. Ware and H. W. Schoenberger, who concluded, "Smith was a practical playwright who always wrote with a view to stage presentation. A fairly competent craftsman, he had little originality, for thirteen of his plays are based upon either native or foreign inspiration." Biography: *The Life and Writings of Richard Penn Smith*, Bruce W. McCullough, 1917.

SMITH, Robert B[ache] (1875–1951), librettist and lyricist. The younger brother of Harry B. *Smith, he was born in Chicago, then began his career with a brief apprenticeship with *Weber and *Fields, where he wrote the lyric for "Come Down, Ma Evenin' Star" in *Twirly-Whirly* (1902). Alone or with collaborators, Smith worked on such shows as *Fantana* (1905), *The Spring Maid* (1910), *Sweethearts* (1913), *Angel Face* (1919), and his last show, *The Girl in the Spotlight* (1920).

SMITH, Russell (1812–96), designer. The most famous Philadelphia scenic designer of the 19th century, he was born in Glasgow and brought to America in 1819 after his parents' political views made them unwelcome in Scotland. He spent much of his childhood in Pittsburgh, where he began his theatrical career as an actor. However, Smith soon recognized that painting was his major interest and began to create sets as well as study painting under James R. Lamdin, eventually becoming set designer for the Pittsburgh Theatre in 1833. Two years later he relocated to Philadelphia's *Walnut Street Theatre, remaining in that city for most of his career. He supplied scenery, drop curtains, and some interior decoration not only for the Walnut, but for the *Chestnut Street Theatre, the Academy of Music, and the *Arch Street Theatre. Smith excelled at painting atmospheric outdoor sets, although he designed many other types of settings as well. Biography: *Russell Smith, Romantic Realist*, Virginia E. Lewis, 1956.

SMITH, Sol[omon Franklin] (1801–69), actor and manager. He was born on a farm in Norwich, New York, but raised in nearby Solon and at the age of twelve ran away, walking three hundred miles to join his brothers in business in Boston. In 1819 he ran away from the business and made his acting debut in Vincennes, Indiana. By 1823 Smith had his own company, which lasted four years, then joined the company of J. H. *Caldwell, who was offering plays in cities along the Mississippi. He also performed at the *Park Theatre in New York and in Philadelphia under *Wemyss. In 1835 Smith entered into partnership with Noah *Ludlow, and for the next sixteen years they dominated what was then the western extremes of the American theatre, building the first major theatre in St. Louis and offering plays up and down the Mississippi. The partnership was dissolved in 1853. As an actor he excelled at low comedy and was especially admired for his Mawworm in *The Hypocrite*. He made only rare appearances after 1853, declining William *Burton's invitation to act in New York and another manager's offer of $10,000 to tour for a year as Mawworm and other similar figures. Smith became a lawyer and was later elected to the State Convention of Missouri, which was designed to bring about that state's secession from the Union. His son, Mark (1829–74), was a popular actor, specializing in old men's parts. Autobiography: *Theatrical Management in the West and South for Thirty Years*, 1868.

SMITH, Winchell (1872–1933), playwright and director. The brilliant theatrical jack-of-all-trades was born in Hartford, Connecticut, and, as an usher at the Herald Square Theatre, was encouraged by Richard *Mansfield to become an actor. After making his debut in 1896 as the telegraph operator Lt. Foray in *Secret Service*, he continued to act for a decade. In 1903 he was Arnold *Daly's silent partner in the first American production of *Candida*. However, Smith was best known as a playwright, almost always in collaboration with others, and as a director. His only important solo venture was The *Fortune Hunter* (1909), but his team ventures included *Brewster's Millions* (1906), *Polly of the Circus* (1907), The *Boomerang* (1915), *Turn to the Right* (1916), and *Lightnin'* (1918). Besides directing many of his own plays, he staged such works as The Last of Mrs. Cheyney* (1925), The *Wisdom Tooth* (1926), and The Vinegar Tree* (1930). Although Smith continued to direct until shortly before his death, he had long since abandoned playwriting, recognizing, "The theater's gone on ahead of me. . . . I'm out of date." Ward *Morehouse called him "a shrewd showman . . . with an extraordinary sense of the theater, an actor-director-playwright who became the most astute play-fixer of the stage for the period of two decades."

SMITH, W. H. See *Drunkard, The*.

SMOKEY JOE'S CAFE (1995), a musical revue by Jerry Leiber, Mike Stoller (music, lyrics). [*Virginia Theatre, 2,036 perf.] Pop songs from the 1950s and 1960s, such as "Fools Fall in Love," "Treat Me Nice," and "Hound Dog," were the appeal in this spirited revue that was small in scale (nine singers, seven musicians) but a giant at the box office, going on to become the longest-running Broadway revue on record. Jerry *Zaks directed the production that featured thirty-five songs from the Leiber-Stoller catalogue, none of which were written for the theatre but nevertheless were now, as one number stated, "On Broadway."

SOBEL, Bernard (1887–1964), publicist and author. Born in Attica, Indiana, he earned degrees from several universities and taught before turning to the theatre. Although he wrote plays and served as drama critic for the *New York Mirror* in the early 1930s, he was better known as the publicist for such leading theatrical figures as Florenz *Ziegfeld, Charles *Dillingham, A. L. *Erlanger, and the *Shuberts and for writing numerous books on the theatre, among them *Burleycue: A History of Burlesque* (1931), *The Theatre Handbook* (1940), *Broadway Heartbeat* (1953), and *A Pictorial History of Vaudeville* (1961).

SOCIETY OF AMERICAN DRAMATISTS AND COMPOSERS. An organization founded in 1890 by Bronson *Howard, David *Belasco, and others to assure authors fair treatment from producers, to attempt to set a standard for royalties, and to fight play and song piracy. The group had only small success in dealing with producers, but it lobbied effectively in Congress and in state legislatures for better copyright laws. Play piracy largely disappeared as a result of its efforts and the new laws. Its other aims were later achieved by the *Dramatists Guild.

SOCIETY OF STAGE DIRECTORS AND CHOREOGRAPHERS. With actors, authors, and almost all other theatrical branches formed into unions it was only a matter of time before the stagers of plays and musicals banded together. This group was founded in 1959 and in 1962 was recognized by the *League of American Theatres and Producers. While many professional directors do not belong to the union and it does not carry the clout of the other labor groups in theatre, the society has effectively managed to allow directors to protect their work and to share in royalties.

SOLDIER'S PLAY, A (1981), a play by Charles Fuller. [Theater Four, 468 perf.; Pulitzer Prize.] When the African-American Sergeant Vernon C. Waters (Adolph Caesar) is shot dead at a Louisiana army base, the Ku Klux Klan is suspected of the killing. To the resentment of some white officers, the black officer Capt. Richard Davenport (Charles Brown) is sent to investigate. In a series of interviews and flashbacks we see the vicious Waters raving against whites and, even more strongly, against "lazy, shiftless Negroes." It turns out that Waters was murdered in cold blood by the cool renegade Melvin Peterson (Denzel Washington), hoping that the whites would be blamed. The whole incident is brushed aside by the chief of staff as "the usual, common violence any commander faces in Negro military units." The *Negro Ensemble Company production, astutely directed by Douglas Turner *Ward, was one of the troupe's greatest critical and commercial accomplishments.

Charles FULLER (b. 1939) was born in Philadelphia. Several of his other plays were produced Off Broadway by the Negro Theatre Ensemble, including *In the Deepest Part of Sleep* (1974), *The Brownsville Raid* (1976), and *Zooman and the Sign* (1981). Long interested in the history of African Americans, in the 1990s Fuller created a series of six plays about the fight for Negro rights in the years following the Civil War.

SOLID GOLD CADILLAC, THE (1953), a comedy by Howard Teichmann and George S. *Kaufman. [Belasco Theatre, 526 perf.] When a sweet little old lady named Laura Partridge (Josephine *Hull) turns up at a huge corporation's stockholders' meeting and begins to ask embarrassing questions, the executives try to shut her up by giving her a job writing letters to other stockholders. Her letters are so warm and homey that by the next meeting she has enough proxies to take over the company. Her first order of business is to quietly fire the corrupt officials who had hoped to silence her. Most critics felt the Max *Gordon offering was held together by Hull's beguiling performance. Kaufman's biographer, Malcolm Goldstein, observed of the play, "No one could deny that this was a slim plot and that it resounded with echoes of a score of plots concocted by Kaufman in the past." The play marked the farewells to Broadway of Gordon, Hull, and Kaufman.

SOLO PERFORMANCES. Ever since Aeschylus added the second actor, theatre has thrived on the dramatic possibilities of two or more characters on stage at the same time. So it is surprising to find playwrights and actors returning to solo dramas two thousand years later and exploring the theatrics of a lone performer. Most one-man shows in the distant past were more in the form of a dramatic lecture, such as the celebrated speaking tours by Mark Twain and Charles Dickens in the 19th century, though both authors also acted out scenes from their novels. Hal *Holbrook and Emlyn Williams successfully re-created those famous performances in the 20th century, giving the two most popular solo performances of the 1950s and 1960s. Also in the last century, some performers specialized in evenings of monologues, most memorably Ruth *Draper and Cornelia Otis *Skinner. But the risky economics of theatre and the desire by talented performers to brave an entire evening on their own led to some very satisfying one-person shows beginning in the 1970s. Most of these involved the re-creation of historical and liter-ary people, such as Henry *Fonda's portrayal of *Clarence Darrow* (1974) and Julie *Harris's portrait of Emily Dickinson in *The Belle of Amhurst* (1976). These and other solo plays were written and directed by others, so the performer was in effect in a traditional play; it just happened to have only one character. But in the 1990s solo performances started to change. The performer became the author and sometimes even the subject. Anna Deavere *Smith created her own script from interviews with real people, then played all the characters in one-person programs such as *Fires in the Mirror* (1992) and *Twilight: Los Angeles, 1992* (1994). Eric *Bogosian portrayed a whole gallery of oddball people in his self-written pieces. Others, such as John Leguizamo and Charlayne Woodard, played themselves, writing and performing autobiographical programs in which they re-created scenes from their youth and portrayed all of their family members as well as neighbors, friends, and enemies. By the end of the century, solo performances came in many forms. Playwrights turned to writing one-person shows and producers presented them because they were economically viable. Even a Broadway production could turn a quick profit on a solo performance if the lone performer had box office appeal. Among the many other actors to find recent success in such shows were Rob Becker, Sandra Bernhard, Margaret Cho, Olympia *Dukakis, Eve Ensler, Amy Freed, Sherry Glaser, Spalding *Gray, Danny Hoch, Barry Humphries, Mark Linn-Baker, Priscilla *Lopez, Jackie *Mason, Christopher *Plummer, Mark Setlock, Claudia Shear, Frank Gorshin, Torah Feldshuh, and Patrick Stewart.

SOLON SHINGLE. See *People's Lawyer, The.*

SONDHEIM, Stephen [Joshua] (b. 1930), composer and lyricist. The most daring and often demanding theatre songwriter of his era, he was born in New York and given his precollege education at the George School in Newtown, Pennsylvania. There he met James Hammerstein and befriended his father, Oscar *Hammerstein II, who became a sort of mentor to Sondheim. After majoring in music at Williams College, Sondheim continued his studies with Milton Babbitt. His first score (music and lyrics) was written for *Saturday Night,* a Broadway-bound musical that was aborted on the death of its producer; the show would not be performed until forty years later. Sondheim's lyrics were first heard on Broadway in *West Side Story* (1957), followed by his lyrics for *Gypsy* (1959). The popular A *Funny Thing Happened on the Way to the Forum* (1962) marked his Broadway debut as both a composer and a lyricist, followed by the unsuccessful cult favorite *Anyone Can Whistle* (1964). After providing lyrics only for *Do I Hear a Waltz?* (1965), Sondheim hit his stride with a series of musicals in the 1970s that were not always commercially successful but never less than fascinating: *Company*

(1970), *Follies (1971), A *Little Night Music (1973), *Pacific Overtures (1973), and *Sweeney Todd (1979). In 1981 his *Merrily We Roll Along was harshly received and had a brief run but in later years was produced frequently. *Sunday in the Park with George (1984) won a *Pulitzer Prize and his *Into the Woods (1987) enjoyed a long run. *Assassins (1991) was highly praised during its limited run and has found life in regional and college theatres, while *Passion (1994) was more awarded than it was popular. He also contributed lyrics to the revised *Candide (1973) and songs for the Yale production of The Frogs (1974). Compilation shows based on his songs include Side by Side by Sondheim (1977), Marry Me a Little (1980), and Putting It Together (1993 and 1999). His most recent project is the biographical musical Bounce (2003). Although many of Sondheim's songs have become favorites among theatregoers, only "Send in the Clowns" has enjoyed the kind of wide-ranging celebrity possible in the days of Rodgers and Hammerstein. Nevertheless, he is one of the most musicianly of contemporary composers and he is tirelessly experimental in the many forms theatre music can take. His forte, however, is his brilliant lyric writing, and only the most elegant, decorous work of Alan Jay *Lerner equals it among contemporaries. Sondheim is an exceedingly clever rhymer and a superb, if misanthropic, wit. This wit and misanthropy have combined with his musicianship to make his musical comedies unique, while they have given his operettas a style and tone closer to the comic opera masterpieces of *Gilbert and Sullivan than anything since the heyday of the Savoyard works. Biography: Stephen Sondheim: A Life, Meryle Secrest, 1998.

SONG OF NORWAY (1944), an operetta by Milton Lazarus (book), Robert *Wright, George *Forrest (music and lyrics based on musical themes by Edvard Grieg). [*Imperial Theatre, 860 perf.] Norwegian Edvard Grieg (Lawrence Brooks) dreams of being a great composer, and these dreams are shared by his friend Rickard (Robert Shafer) and Grieg's sweetheart, Nina (Helena Bliss). Grieg is lured to Italy by the great prima donna Louisa Giovanni (Irra Petina), but he finds he cannot create amid all the glitter and excitement and so returns to Norway and his beloved Nina to write his music. Notable songs: Freddy and His Fiddle; Now!; Strange Music; Hill of Dreams. Edwin *Lester produced this, the last successful pseudo-biography musical in the tradition of *Blossom Time (1921). The work was revived in 1981 by the New York City Opera but is rarely done by theatre companies.

SONNECK, Oscar [George Theodore] (1873–1928), historian. One of the most important figures in initiating studies of the early American musical stage,

he was born in Jersey City, New Jersey, but was raised by his widowed mother in Germany. Sonneck returned to America at the turn of the century and in 1902 was appointed the first chief of the music division of the Library of Congress. His Early Opera in America (1915) offered much valuable material on 18th-century American comic opera, while additional material could occasionally be gleaned from his other books.

SONNECK SOCIETY, THE. Founded in 1975 at the instigation of Irving Lowens, who became its first president, the organization is devoted to the promotion of American music. The group was named after Oscar *Sonneck. Its publications include a Society newsletter. Several of its members have contributed important studies in the field of musical theatre, the results of which have been offered as papers at the Society's meetings and sometimes published in the newsletter or elsewhere. The group is associated with Society for American Music.

SOPHISTICATED LADIES (1981), a musical revue by Donald McKayle (concept), Duke Ellington (music). [*Lunt-Fontanne Theatre, 767 perf.] Thirty-six numbers by Ellington were performed in this sleek, stylish revue that took the form of a classy nightclub floor show. Michael Shumin directed and co-choreographed the musical numbers and the talented cast featured Gregory *Hines, Judith Jamison, Hinton *Battle, Phyllis Hyman, and Gregg Burge.

SOTHERN, E[dward] A[skew] (1826–81), character actor. The tall, lanky performer, one of the best eccentric comedians of his era, was born in Liverpool. Using the name Douglas Stewart, he had appeared on English stages before making his American debut in Boston in 1852 as Dr. Pangloss in The Heir-at-Law. He joined *Wallack's celebrated ensemble in 1854 and began using his real name. However, success and fame did not come until 1858, when he grudgingly accepted the part of Lord Dundreary in Laura *Keene's mounting of *Our American Cousin. The critic Henry Austin *Clapp later recalled, "I think the funniest small thing I ever noted at a theatrical performance was his delivery of one of Dundreary's speeches in connection with Sam's 'letter from America.' The passage began, 'Dear Bwother,' Mr. Sothern reading the opening words of the epistle; then he made one of his pauses, and with a characteristic click and hitch in his voice, commented—'Sam always calls me his bwother—because neither of us ever had a sister.' . . . the actor's voice became instantly saturated with mock pathos, and the sudden absurd demand for sympathy reached the amazed auditor with soul-tingling effect." Sothern soon expanded the role until it virtually dominated the play. Among his other notable parts were the title roles in a play about Dundreary's relative, *Brother Sam* (1862), and in *David Garrick* (1864), as well as the failed actor Fitzaltamont in *The Crushed Tragedian* (1877). Biography: *A Memoir of Edward Askew Sothern*, Thomas Edgar Pemberton, 1889.

SOTHERN, E[dward] H[ugh] (1859–1933), actor. Smaller and more handsome than his father, E. A. *Sothern, he proved a versatile leading man and became one of the great Shakespeareans of his day. He was born in New Orleans and educated in England, where he planned a career as a painter. However, deciding to follow his father's profession, he made his debut in New York in 1879 as a cabman in his father's *Brother Sam*. He then toured with John *McCullough before becoming a member of Daniel *Frohman's *Lyceum Theatre company. During his ten years there his many successes included the befuddled auctioneer Jack Hammerston in *The Highest Bidder* (1887) and the title role in *Lord Chumley* (1888), but his greatest success came in the dual roles of the real Prince Rudolf and his look-alike impostor in *The *Prisoner of Zenda* (1895). While at the Lyceum he married Virginia *Harned, and the two played together for many years, including his first important Shakespearean production, *Hamlet* (1900). However, his fame reached its pinnacle when he co-starred with his second wife, Julia *Marlowe, in a series of Shakespearean seasons, beginning in 1904 with *Romeo and Juliet*. His major roles included Benedick, Shylock, Antony, and the one numerous critics felt was his best, Malvolio. Sothern continued to act occasionally after Marlowe retired in 1924. While Ludwig Lewisohn wrote, "He speaks the verse as verse and yet as authentic human speech. He conveys an impression of complete naturalness while never slurring the iambic pattern of his text," a surviving recording of the balcony scene from *Romeo and Juliet* suggests a lush, formal style that would not be popular today. Autobiography: *The Melancholy Tale of "Me,"* 1916.

SOUND OF MUSIC, THE (1959), a musical play by Howard *Lindsay, Russel *Crouse (book), Richard *Rodgers (music), Oscar *Hammerstein (lyrics). [*Lunt-Fontanne Theatre, 1,443 perf.; Tony Award.] When the lively Maria (Mary *Martin), a postulant at an Austrian convent, seems an unlikely candidate for her religious order, the Mother Abbess (Patricia Neway) arranges for her to serve as governess to the seven children of the stern, widowed naval officer Captain Georg von Trapp (Theodore *Bikel). Maria wins the children's love immediately and inadvertently falls for the Captain himself. He

is opposed to the Nazis, so when they order him to report for duty, the whole family flees to the safety of the West. *Notable songs*: The Sound of Music; My Favorite Things; Edelweiss; Do-Re-Mi; Climb Ev'ry Mountain; The Lonely Goatherd; Sixteen Going on Seventeen. Written shortly before Hammerstein's death and thus this great partnership's last work, the musical, which was based on Maria von Trapp's autobiography *The Trapp Family Singers*, was condemned by such staunch detractors of operetta as Brooks *Atkinson. The public, however, adored it. A 1965 film version broke records, helping the show to remain a favorite in theatres across the country. A 1998 Broadway revival was well received by audiences and the critics.

SOUSA, John Philip (1854–1932), composer. Born in Washington, D.C., to a Portuguese father and Bavarian mother, he began his musical training while still in grammar school. After seven years as an apprentice to the U. S. Marine Band and further studies with George Felix Benkert, Sousa worked with various theatre orchestras, primarily in Philadelphia, where he began to compose comic opera scores. In 1880 he became the bandmaster for the Marine Band and gained his greatest fame as a bandleader and composer of marches. His first musicals, mounted by John *McCaull, never played New York. His best-known works, for which he sometimes served as librettist and lyricist, were *El Capitan* (1896), *The Bride Elect* (1898), *The Charlatan* (1898), *Chris and the Wonderful Lamp* (1900), and *The Free Lance* (1906). He also occasionally orchestrated others' scores, offered interpolations to other shows, and in 1915 appeared with his band in the *Hippodrome extravaganza *Hip Hip Hooray*. Although Sousa sometimes had difficulty writing music for singers, his work was eminently theatrical and often memorably melodic. He is probably the only composer of his era, aside from Victor *Herbert, whose work could enjoy a major revival. Indeed, his *The Glass Blowers* (1913) has recently been successfully mounted by opera companies. Autobiography: *Marching Along*, 1928.

SOUTH COAST REPERTORY (Costa Mesa, California). Begun as a summer theatre in 1964 by Martin Benson and David Emmes, who continue to head the group today, the theatre consistently grew in scope as it occupied a small space in Newport Beach, then a converted marine hardware store, before finding a permanent home in Costa Mesa in 1967. Five years later the company became fully professional and was successful enough by 1976 to build a new two-theatre complex that houses a 507-seat main stage and a 161-seat flexible space. The South Coast Repertory dedicates much of its money and energy on original scripts and works new to the area. They also run a Summer Conservatory as well as a Youth Conservatory. The repertory is more challenging than most regional theatres, and the company has seen some of its productions transfer to New York, most memorably *Collected Stories* and *Golden Child*. In 1988 the group won a *Tony Award for distinguished achievement by a regional theatre.

SOUTH PACIFIC (1949), a musical play by Oscar *Hammerstein (book, lyrics), Joshua *Logan (book), Richard *Rodgers (music). [*Majestic Theatre, 1,925 perf.; Pulitzer Prize, Tony, NYDCC Awards.] The high-spirited Nellie Forbush (Mary *Martin), an American nurse serving in the Pacific in World War II, has fallen in love with the older French planter Emile de Becque (Ezio *Pinza), but she wonders how two such different people can be right for each other. Her doubts become greater when she learns that Emile has two Polynesian children by his deceased wife. Paralleling this relationship is an affair between Lt. Joseph Cable (William Tabbert) and the native girl Liat (Betta St. John), the daughter of the crafty black marketeer Bloody Mary (Juanita *Hall), who has engineered the little romance. Just as Nellie cannot override her instinctive prejudices, Cable breaks off with Liat and goes on a dangerous mission with Emile. Cable is killed, but the planter returns to embrace a welcoming Nellie, who is willing to cast aside her doubts. *Notable songs*: Some Enchanted Evening; There Is Nothin' Like a Dame; Younger Than Springtime; A Wonderful Guy; Bali Ha'i; I'm Gonna Wash That Man Right Outa My Hair; You've Got to Be Carefully Taught; Happy Talk. Based on James A. Michener's *Tales of the South Pacific*, this was one of the greatest and most successful of modern operettas. However, its plea for racial understanding caused problems when it attempted to tour the South. Revivals have been plentiful, though not on Broadway.

SOUTHWARK THEATRE (Philadelphia). Sometimes called the South Street Theatre, it was the first permanent playhouse erected in America. Because of prejudices against theatricals it was built just outside what was then the center of the city. The structure, largely of brick, was painted red and was lit by oil. Opened in 1766 by *Douglass and his *American Company and later managed by his successors, Lewis *Hallam Jr. and John *Henry, it housed the first performance of a professionally produced American play, *The *Prince of Parthia*, in 1767. It remained in use as a playhouse until 1821. The building had served for many years as a distillery before it was demolished in 1912.

SOUTHWORTH, E[mma] D[orothy] E[liza] N[evitte] (1819–99), novelist. She was once a popular writer of sentimental and melodramatic novels usually set in the South. Her works lent themselves to dramatizations that became for a short while the rage of lesser theatres. The most successful was *The Hidden Hand* (1859), but others included *The Bride of Evening* (1858), *The Doom of Deville* (1859), and *Rose Elmer, or; A Divided Heart* (1860).

SOVEY, Raymond (1897–1966), designer. Born in Torrington, Connecticut, and educated at Columbia, he began his theatrical career as an actor but soon switched to set designing. His work was seen in such shows as *The *Butter and Egg Man* (1925), *Gentlemen Prefer Blondes* (1926), *Coquette* (1927), *The *Ladder* (1928), *The *Front Page* (1928), *Little Accident* (1928), *Strictly Dishonorable* (1929), *Strike Up the Band* (1930), *Green Grow the Lilacs* (1931), *Counsellor-at-Law* (1931), *Her Master's Voice* (1933), *The *Petrified Forest* (1935), *Yes, My Darling Daughter* (1937), *Our Town* (1938), *Tomorrow the World* (1943), *Over 21* (1944), *State of the Union* (1945), *Gigi* (1951), *Witness for the Prosecution* (1954), and *The Great Sebastians* (1956). A versatile artist, he was particularly noted for his elegant interiors.

SPACEY, Kevin [né Fowler] (b. 1959). Actor and manager. The smiling, affable performer, who often surprises with his riveting, intense performances, was born in South Orange, New Jersey, and was educated at Los Angeles Valley College and Juilliard before starting his career as a stand-up comic in clubs. Spacey made his New York legit debut in 1981 and was soon noticed for his sensitive but seething Oswald in *Ghosts* (1982). His subsequent performances of note include the bitter alcoholic Jamie Tyrone in *Long Day's Journey Into Night* (1986), the small-time hood Louie in *Lost in Yonkers* (1991), and the guilt-ridden salesman Hickey in *The *Iceman Cometh* (1999). In 2003 Spacey was named artistic director of London's *Old Vic Theatre Company.

SPELVIN, George. This name was given to a character or an actor in a play to hide his real identity. It was employed as early as 1886 by Charles A. Gardner in his *Karl, the Peddler*. William Collier jokingly credited Spelvin as co-author of *Hoss and Hoss* (1893). Its use was most widely popularized by Winchell *Smith, who first employed the name for a performer in *Brewster's Millions* (1906). The success of the play prompted Smith to revive the name in many of his subsequent shows. John *Golden also used the name in several of his productions. At one time *Theatre Arts Monthly* gave the name to a critic who wrote on other critics. The name "Harry Selby" has sometimes been similarly employed. In England the false name used for similar occasions is "Walter Plinge."

SPENSER, Willard (1852–1933), composer and lyricist. A native of Cooperstown, New York, he settled after his marriage in a suburb of Philadelphia and soon became the leader of what was called the Philadelphia School of Comic Opera. *The *Little Tycoon* (1886) and *Princess Bonnie* (1895) were among the most popular musicals of the late 19th century. None of his subsequent shows reached New York, but several were major hits in Philadelphia. These later works included *Miss Bob White* (1901), *Rosalie* (1906), and *The Wild Goose* (1912).

SPEWACK, Samuel (1899–1971) and **Bella** [neé Cohen] (1899–1990), playwrights. He was born in Russia, raised in America, and served for several years as a journalist after attending Columbia. She was born in Bucharest, raised in New York, and also was a journalist for several New York papers and a theatrical press agent before joining with her husband to write approximately a dozen plays or musicals that reached Broadway. Most successful were *Boy Meets Girl* (1935); *Leave It to Me!* (1938), based on their 1932 comedy *Clear All Wires* (1932); *Kiss Me, Kate* (1948); and *My Three Angels* (1953). On his own, Samuel Spewack wrote *Two Blind Mice* (1949) and also directed many of their plays. The team was known for their satirical tone and lively dialogue.

SPIALEK, Hans (1894–1983), orchestrator. Born in Vienna, he studied music there and also in Russia while he was a prisoner of war. He later composed and conducted before coming to America in 1924. Spialek soon became one of Broadway's most distinguished orchestrators. Among the 147 shows he worked on were *The *New Moon* (1928), *Fifty Million Frenchmen* (1929), *The New Yorkers* (1930), *On Your Toes* (1936), *Babes in Arms* (1937), *The *Boys from Syracuse* (1938), *Du Barry Was a Lady* (1939), *Pal Joey* (1940), *Panama Hattie* (1940), and *Something for the Boys* (1943). His elegant arrangements were heightened by what he called his attempt to convey the exciting "atmosphere of being in a theatre." When he reconstructed his orchestrations for the 1983 revival of *On Your Toes*, his work was widely hailed for its disarming simplicity and appropriateness to the music.

SPIRIT OF THE TIMES, THE. A weekly, founded in 1831 as *The Spirit of the Times and Life in New York*, it soon shortened its name and was billed as "A Chronicle of Turf, Agriculture, Field Sports, Literature and the Stage." While offering detailed accounts of New York theatricals, it also maintained correspondents in other important theatrical centers. Publication ceased in 1861. A similar periodical, *Wilkes' Spirit of the Times*, was issued from 1859 to 1902.

SPY, THE; *or A Tale of the Neutral Ground* (1822), a play by Charles Powell Clinch. [*Park Theatre, in repertory.] The itinerant peddler Harvey Birch (R. C. Maywood) is believed by many to be a Loyalist spy, although he is actually serving secretly in Washington's intelligence. Out of his good nature he performs acts of kindness for many friends he knows to have Loyalist sympathies and even helps the British captain Henry Wharton (Jacob Woodhull) escape execution. In the end Birch is shot, but before he dies a letter signed by Washington is found on him and his true position is recognized. Based on James Fenimore Cooper's then popular novel, the play (opening ten weeks after the book's publication) was probably the very first successful American dramatization of an American novel. Clinch remained faithful to the original, except for the dramatic ending, which he added. It held the stage for several decades and its success prompted the dramatization of more Cooper novels, as well as other authors' works. C[harles] P[owell] **CLINCH** (1797–1880), the son of a New York businessman, was an associate of the Knickerbocker writers and served briefly as a drama critic. *The Spy* was his first play, followed by *The Expelled Collegian* (1822), *The Avenger's Vow* (1824), and *The First of May in New York* (1830). Thereafter, he abandoned playwriting, devoting the rest of his long life to business and politics.

SQUALL, THE (1926), a play by Jean Bart. [48th Street Theatre, 444 perf.] Fleeing from her gypsy band, Nubi (Suzanne Caubet) takes refuge in the home of Juan Mendez (Horace Braham), pleading, "Me Nubi. Nubi good girl. Nubi stay." With the gypsies gone, she goes about seducing all the men at the Mendez home. The show was propelled into a long run with major assistance from *Leblang's Ticket Office agency and from Richard *Maney's excellent press work. Maney had a field day with critic Robert *Benchley's response: "Me Benchley. Benchley bad boy. Benchley go." Bart later wrote several less successful plays.

SQUAW MAN, THE (1905), a play by Edwin Milton *Royle. [*Wallack's Theatre, 222 perf.] Captain James Wynnegate (William *Faversham) loves Diana (Selene Johnson), his cousin's wife. When it is learned his cousin has stolen funds from a charity, James agrees to immigrate to America so that it will appear he is the culprit. He settles in the West, takes the name Jim Carston, and soon falls in love with and marries the Native American Nat-u-ritch (Mabel Morrison), who once saved his life. But when Lady Diana comes to America to tell Wynnegate that his innocence has been recognized and that he is now Earl of Kerhill, Nat-u-ritch understands that she is in his way. She kills herself to give her husband and their young son a chance for a better life. The *Liebler and Co. production was one of the major successes of its day and was revived with some frequency as late as 1921. It served as the source for an important early silent film and afterwards was made into the unsuccessful musical *The White Eagle* (1927). **Edwin Milton ROYLE** (1862–1942) was born in Lexington, Missouri, and educated at Salt Lake City's Collegiate Institute, Princeton, the University of Edinburgh, and Columbia Law School. He abandoned law to become an actor and performed in his first play, *Friends* (1892), with his wife, Selma Fetter Royle (1860–1955). In his later works he displayed a wide variety of skills, writing the farce *My Wife's Husbands* (1903), the musical comedy *Marrying Mary* (1906), and the poetic tragedy *Launcelot and Elaine* (1921). However, Royle is remembered largely for *The Squaw Man*. In all, more than thirty of his plays were produced.

STADLEN, Lewis J. (b. 1947), character actor. An energetic comic often in scene-stealing supporting roles, Stadlen has the polish and panache of old-time vaudeville comedians even though he is several generations removed from them. He was born in Brooklyn and trained at the *Neighborhood Playhouse and the Stella *Adler Studio before making a rollicking Broadway debut in 1970 as the young Groucho *Marx in the musical *Minnie's Boys;* his imitation of the famous comic was so well received that Stadlen later toured as Marx in a one-man show. Among his many merry performances in New York were the frustrated nephew Ben Silverman in *The *Sunshine Boys* (1972), a variety of hilarious characters in the revised *Candide* (1974), the Spanish "date" Manolo in the female version of *The *Odd Couple* (1985), the wisecracking television sketch writer Milt in *Laughter on the 23rd Floor* (1993), the Harpo Marx–like clown Banjo in *The *Man Who Came to Dinner* (2000), the big-time Borscht Belt comic Mickey Fox in *45 Seconds from Broadway* (2001), and as a replacement for the scheming Max Bialystock in *The *Producers* in 2003.

STAGE DOOR (1936), a play by George S. *Kaufman and Edna *Ferber. [*Music Box Theatre, 159 perf.] While boarding at the Footlights Club, a home for aspiring young actresses, Terry Randall (Margaret *Sullavan) finds her loyalty to the theatre sorely tested. Her fiancé, the radical playwright Keith Burgess (Richard Kendrick), is tired of living "on bread and cocoa for days at a time," so he abandons her and the stage for a lucrative film offer, as does a sexy but untalented fellow resident. Another girl commits suicide after being fired from a part. But it is a motion picture scout,

David Kingsley (Onslow Stevens), who urges Terry to have the courage of her convictions. She does, thereby winning a juicy role and David as well. Most critics compared the Sam H. *Harris mounting unfavorably with earlier Kaufman-Ferber collaborations, *The *Royal Family* and *Dinner at Eight,* but enjoyed reading certain parts as identifiable caricatures, such as Keith Burgess, who mirrored the history of playwright Clifford *Odets.

STAGE DOOR CANTEEN (New York). This cabaret and dining room was established during World War II to entertain soldiers free of charge. It was founded by the *American Theatre Wing and the USO (United Service Organization). The first and principal one was established in the basement of the 44th Street Theatre. Broadway performers and others passing through New York offered their services gratis, not merely entertaining but often serving as waiters and dishwashers. Irving *Berlin saluted it in his all-soldier show, *This Is the Army* (1942), with the song "I Left My Heart at the Stage Door Canteen." Similar, smaller establishments were opened in other major theatrical centers, and Los Angeles copied the idea with the popular Hollywood Canteen.

STAGE WOMEN'S WAR RELIEF. An organization founded during World War I by Rachel *Crothers, Jane *Cowl, and others, it allowed actresses and other women of the theatre to assist in the war effort. It provided free tickets for soldiers and made similar charitable contributions. The group disbanded at the end of the war.

STAGG, Charles and Mary (fl. early 18th century), actors. A husband and wife, they were listed as "actors" on a 1716 petition to erect a theatre in Williamsburg, Virginia. Nothing is known of their origins, if they did in fact perform in Williamsburg, or what happened to them afterwards. If they were professionals, their appearance on the American theatrical scene little more than a decade after Anthony *Aston marks them as two of America's earliest recorded performers.

STAHL, Rose (1870–1955), actress. The thin-faced, nasal-voiced performer, with tangled blonde hair and hazel eyes, was born in Montreal and made her acting debut with a Philadelphia stock company. She continued with various stock groups and in minor roles on Broadway before turning to vaudeville, where she caused a stir in a playlet called "The Chorus Girl." Its author, James *Forbes, expanded the work into a full-length play, *The *Chorus Lady* (1906). For nearly five years she played Patricia O'Brien, a feisty, slangy chorine who saves her sister's virtue. Her only other success was the title salesgirl in *Maggie Pepper* (1911) before she faded from the scene.

STAIR and HAVLIN. A large chain of theatres extending from the East Coast to Kansas City and situated primarily in smaller cities and towns, it was run by E. D. Stair, J. H. Havlin, and their silent partner, George H. Nicolai. The chain, which flourished in the early years of the 20th century, specialized in offering action-packed melodrama and knockabout farce. Many of the attractions were proprietary, although the company often bought out Broadway hits after the plays had toured major theatrical centers.

STANGE, Stanislaus (1862–1917), librettist and lyricist. Born in Liverpool, he came to America in 1881 and embarked on a career of acting and playwriting. His biggest success was his dramatization of the novel *Quo Vadis?* (1900). However, Stange was most in demand as a lyricist and librettist, working often with Julian *Edwards. At least eighteen of his musicals reached New York, among them *Madeleine* (1895), *Brian Boru* (1896), *The Wedding Day* (1897), *The Jolly Musketeer* (1898), and his best work, *When Johnny Comes Marching Home* (1902). He enjoyed his longest run with his adaptation of Oscar Straus's Viennese favorite, *The Chocolate Soldier* (1909), which he also directed.

STANISLAVSKY, Konstantin (1863–1938), director, actor, and author. The famous Russian theorist, who co-founded the *Moscow Art Theatre, promoted theories of realistic, psychologically probing acting that discarded the seemingly artificial conventions of the past. He came to the United States in 1923 with his company and offered a superb example of his theory put to practice, as well as giving interviews that shed further light on his ideas. Also, Stanislavsky's books were soon translated into English and widely read in America. The acting of several ensembles in the 1930s, such as the *Group Theatre and the later "Method" technique advocated by Lee *Strasberg, were clearly and often admittedly influenced by Stanislavsky's theories. Frequently overlooked was the fact that Stanislavsky rose to prominence just as sophisticated electric lighting was making stages brighter and thus minimizing the need for the heavy makeup and exaggerated gestures that had prevailed until then. For better or worse, most modern acting and directing are descended from Stanislavsky. Autobiography: *My Life in Art*, translated by J. J. Robbins, 1924.

STANLEY, [Patricia Kimberly] Kim [née Reid] (1925–2001), actress. The tall, attractive blonde, whose somewhat high voice and jittery mannerisms exemplified the modern "method school" of acting, was born in Tularosa, New Mexico. She attended the universities of New Mexico and Texas before studying acting at the *Pasadena Community Playhouse and at the *Actors Studio. Stanley acted in several Off-Broadway productions and then replaced Julie *Harris in *Monserrat* (1949) before scoring her first major success as the lovesick tomboy sister Millie in *Picnic* (1953). Among her important later roles were the flashy nightclub singer Cherie in *Bus Stop* (1955), the innkeeper's daughter Sara Melody in *A *Touch of the Poet* (1958), Freud's patient Elizabeth von Ritter in *A Far Country* (1961), and Masha in a 1964 revival of *The Three Sisters*. After suffering a nervous breakdown, she retired from the stage to teach acting.

STAPLETON, Jean [neé Jeanne Murray] (b. 1923), character actress. The bony, precise performer, forever remembered for her years on television, enjoyed a busy theatre career before, during, and after her glory days on the tube. She was born in New York and educated at Hunter College, after which she worked as a secretary while studying acting at the American Apprentice Theatre, the American Actors Company, and the *American Theatre Wing. Stapleton was featured as the baseball fan Sister in *Damn Yankees* (1955) and as the answering service owner Sue in *Bells Are Ringing* (1956). While she played supporting roles on Broadway in the 1960s, Stapleton performed a variety of major characters in stock, particularly at the Totem Pole Playhouse in Pennsylvania. She returned there for many summers even after she became famous on television. When Stapleton reappeared on Broadway in 1986, she was a bona fide stage star in *Arsenic and Old Lace* (1986), though later she preferred the more intimate Off-Broadway venue, where she acted in several dramas by Horton *Foote.

STAPLETON, [Lois] Maureen (b. 1925), actress. Described by *Vogue* as having "big show-girl eyes, a small mouth, the skill of a Japanese tumbler, a radiance, and a voice that combines harridan and chamber music with layers of cello and violin," she was born in Troy, New York, and studied acting with Herbert *Berghof. She made her New York debut in 1946 in *The Playboy of the Western World* but rose to stardom as the emotional widow Serafina in *The *Rose Tattoo* (1951). Subsequent notable roles included the sex-starved storekeeper Lady Torrance in *Orpheus Descending* (1957), the possessive sister Carrie Berniers in *Toys in the Attic* (1960), three different worried New Yorkers in *Plaza Suite* (1968), and the alcoholic singer Eva Mears in *The Gingerbread Lady* (1970). Stapleton also shone in several revivals, among them Lady Anne in *Richard III* (1953), Masha in *The Seagull* (1954),

Amanda in The *Glass Menagerie (1965 and 1975), and Birdie in The *Little Foxes (1981). She has made many television and film appearances as well.

STAR WAGON, THE (1937), a play by Maxwell *Anderson. [*Empire Theatre, 223 perf.] When Martha Minch (Lillian *Gish) berates her husband of thirty-five years, Stephen (Burgess *Meredith), for not making enough money, he shrugs off her complaint. Stephen is a clever inventor whose boss, Duffy (Kent Smith), is ready to fire him for inventing a tire that will not wear out. But Stephen also has a more interesting invention: a time machine he calls his star wagon, which he uses to go back into his youth with Martha and relive the chance he had to marry a rich girl, Hallie Arlington (Jane Buchanan). The visit convinces Martha and him that they made the right decisions. After all, look at the man who married Hallie—none other than crotchety old Duffy! This likable Anderson fantasy, produced by Guthrie *McClintic, was assessed by Mary McCarthy in the Partisan Review as "richer in period comedy than in metaphysics. It is entertaining and quite harmless."

STARR, Frances [Grant] (1881–1973), actress. The soft-eyed beauty, probably the loveliest of David *Belasco's great stars, was born in Oneonta, New York, and spent many years in stock after making her debut in 1901. Spotting her in a minor comedy, Belasco hired her as a replacement in The *Music Master, then raised her to stardom as Juanita, who saves her family's land from ruthless speculators, in The *Rose of the Rancho (1906). Her most memorable role was the kept woman Laura Murdock in The *Easiest Way (1909). Of her performance, one critic wrote, "The suggestion of abject hopelessness at the end is indescribably affecting, and its impressiveness is embodied in the frail personality and remarkably sensitive playing of Miss Frances Starr, whose performance has a tremendous emotional depth hardly to be expected in so delicate an organism." Subsequent roles for Belasco included Dorothy with a dual personality in The Case of Becky (1911), the unworldly nun Marie-Odile (1915), the governess Anne Churchill in Little Lady in Blue (1916), the poor but noble Sally in Tiger! Tiger! (1918), and the seamstress Connie Martin in Shore Leave (1922). After Starr left Belasco her career faltered, although she kept busy until she retired in the early 1950s. Her most important role in that period was Mrs. Brown, the heroine's dying mother, in *Claudia (1942).

STATE OF THE UNION (1945), a comedy by Howard *Lindsay and Russel *Crouse. [Hudson Theatre, 765 perf.; Pulitzer Prize.] Having been out of power for so long, the Republicans are desperate to find a candidate who will win them the White House. Led by James Conover (Minor Watson), they pick an idealistic industrialist, Grant Matthews (Ralph *Bellamy). For him to win it will be necessary for his wife, Mary (Ruth Hussey), to campaign with him, since rumors are rife that Grant has been having an affair with the publisher Kay Thorndyke (Kay Johnson). Conover is quick to assure Mary that there will be no problems. After all, there is only one fundamental difference between the Democrats and the Republicans, "They're in—and we're out!" But a problem arises when Grant's idealism is too much for the political bosses, and rather than compromise his beliefs, Grant withdraws. The comedy was said to have been suggested loosely by the career of Wendell Willkie. To keep the Leland *Hayward production up to the minute, especially when certain headlines had to be read, the authors nightly wired all companies minor changes in the script.

STEEL MAGNOLIAS (1987), a play by Robert Harling. [*Lucille Lortel Theatre, 1,126 perf.] Truvy (Margo Martindale), whose motto is "there is no such thing as natural beauty," runs a hairdressing salon in a small Southern town. Over the period of a few years, the lives of some of her clients are glimpsed with humor and sentiment: the cranky spinster Ouiser (Mary Fogarty), the football-loving gossiper Clairee (Kate Wilkinson), the upper-class mother M'Lynn (Rosemary Prinz), and her diabetic daughter, Shelby (Betsy Aidem), whose marriage, motherhood, and death frame the story. Described by Mel *Gussow in the New York Times as "an amiable evening of sweet sympathies and small-town chatter," the comedy-drama was a major Off-Broadway hit and remains very popular in regional and community theatres.

STEIN, Joseph (b. 1912), librettist. The New York native studied at City College of New York and began his career by contributing sketches to Broadway revues in 1948. Alone or with collaborators he later wrote the books for such musicals as *Plain and Fancy (1955), Mr. Wonderful (1956), The Body Beautiful (1958), *Take Me Along (1959), Juno (1959), *Fiddler on the Roof (1964), Zorbá (1968), The Baker's Wife (1976), King of Hearts (1978), Carmelina (1979), and Rags (1986). He also successfully dramatized Carl Reiner's comic novel Enter Laughing (1963), which he later adapted into the short-lived musical So Long, 174th Street (1976).

STEINBECK, John. See Of Mice and Men.

STEPPENWOLF THEATRE COMPANY (Chicago). Perhaps no other theatre expresses the "Chicago style" of acting than this troupe, founded in 1976 by Jeff Perry, Terry Kinney, and Gary Sinise. The emphasis has always remained on acting, though many new works have also premiered there. By the mid-1980s the company was getting national recognition, in no small part due to some of its actors who became famous: Sinise, Kinney, Glenne Headly, John *Malkovich, Laurie Metcalf, John Mahoney, and Joan Allen. Among the productions that have transferred to New York were *True West, Balm in Gilead, Orphans, *Burn This, The *Grapes of Wrath, and One Flew over the Cuckoo's Nest. After performing in three different spaces over the years, the Steppenwolf moved into its three-theatre complex in 1991. The company received a *Tony Award in 1985 for regional theatre excellence and the National Medal of Arts from President Clinton in 1998.

STERNHAGEN, Frances (b. 1930), character actress. The matronly but lively Sternhagen became a recognized performer late in her career, although she had been giving splendid performances for decades. She was born in Washington, D.C., and educated at Vassar College and Catholic University before studying acting at the *Neighborhood Playhouse. She made her New York debut Off Broadway in 1955 and played supporting roles for years, failing to receive wide notice until the 1970s with such memorable performances as Mavis Parodus Bryson in The Sign in Sidney Brustein's Window (1972), various Russian characters in The Good Doctor (1973), the religious mother Dora Stang in *Equus (1974), and the cheerful senior citizen Ethel Thayer in *On Golden Pond (1978). Later roles of note included the American tourist Margaret Civil in India in A Perfect Ganesh (1993), the practical Aunt Lavinia in The *Heiress (1995), and the worried mother Ida losing her grown son in *Morning's at Seven (2002).

STERNER, Jerry. See Other People's Money.

STETSON, John (1836–96), producer and manager. The impresario was born in Charlestown, Massachusetts, and gained early fame as an athlete who went professional. After publishing a controversial Boston magazine, he turned to the theatre and he took over numerous playhouses, including the *Howard Athenaeum, Olympic, Globe, and the Park in Boston; and the Globe, *Booth's, the *Fifth Avenue, Standard, and the Star in New York. Stetson worked closely with *Harrigan and *Hart in their first years as a team and afterwards managed such stars as Tommaso *Salvini, Lillie *Langtry, Helena *Modjeska, and James *O'Neill. He also produced shows, including several of the original importations of *Gilbert and Sullivan. Writing of the "big, bass, blustering" impresario, Otis *Skinner

remarked, "His usual manner was that of a war tank—he went through things as if they stood in his way. One look at his aggressive face, square jaw, and clouded dead eye was enough to cause timid ones to step aside." Unlike many other noted theatrical producers and theatre owners who made and lost fortunes, Stetson died a very wealthy man.

STEVENS, Ashton (1872–1951), critic. Born in San Francisco, he began his reviewing career there in 1894 with the News-Letter. After working on several other local papers and a three-year stint on the New York Evening Journal, he went to Chicago for most of his career—the Herald and Examiner from 1910 to 1932, then on the Herald-American until his death. An outspoken, often acerbic critic, Stevens fought "dullness" not only in plays but in drama criticism and among audiences as well, once writing that "dull people don't like Mrs. *Fiske's acting."

STEVENS, Emily (1882–1928), actress. The talented niece of Mrs. *Fiske was born in New York and made her stage debut in a small role in her aunt's mounting of *Becky Sharp in 1900. She continued with Fiske for nearly a decade, playing such increasingly important roles as Claire Berton in *Leah Kleschna (1904) and Grace Phillimore in The *New York Idea (1906). Among her later roles were Emily Griswold, who reforms her corrupt, power-hungry husband, in The *Boss (1911); the spoiled wife Lily Wagner in *Today (1913); the selfish wife Caroline Knolys in The *Unchastened Woman (1915); the hedonistic wife Mathilde Fay in Fata Morgana (1924); and Hedda Gabler (1926). Although Stevens specialized in neurotic, disagreeable women, the theatre world was shocked when the beautiful actress committed suicide at the height of a brilliant career.

STEVENS, Roger L[acey] (1910–98), producer. He was born in Detroit and studied for a time at the University of Michigan. Having made a considerable fortune in real estate, he entered the producing lists in 1949 with a mounting of *Twelfth Night. In 1951 he became a member of the *Playwrights' Company, and in 1954 formed the Producers Theatre and co-founded the *American Shakespeare Festival. Stevens was also associated with the *Phoenix Theatre for many years, and in 1971 he became the head of the *Kennedy Center in Washington. Besides the plays produced with the groups mentioned above, he co-produced such productions as *Tea and Sympathy (1953), *Bus Stop (1955), A *View from the Bridge (1955), *Cat on a Hot Tin Roof (1955), *West Side Story (1957), Under the Yum Yum Tree (1960), *Mary, Mary (1961), and Finishing Touches (1973).

STEWART, Ellen. See La Mama Experimental Theatre Club.

STEWART [Rubin], **Michael** [né Rubin] (1929–87), librettist and lyricist. The Yale-educated New Yorker came to playgoers' attention with sketches for revues in the 1950s. He subsequently wrote the books for such musicals as *Bye Bye Birdie* (1960); *Carnival!* (1961); *Hello, Dolly!* (1964); *George M!* (1968); *Mack and Mabel* (1974); *The Grand Tour* (1979); *42nd Street* (1980); *Bring Back Birdie* (1981); and *Harrigan 'n Hart* (1985). Stewart also provided both book and lyrics for *I Love My Wife* (1977) and *Barnum* (1980).

STICKNEY, Dorothy (1903–98), character actress. She was born in Dickinson, North Dakota, the daughter of a country doctor, and trained for the stage at an acting school in Minneapolis. Stickney toured for several years before making her Broadway debut in 1926, soon getting attention for her small but juicy roles, such as the suicide victim Molly in *The *Front Page* (1928). She reached star status by the time she played Granny in *On Borrowed Time* (1938), then found the role of her career: the delightfully scattered Vinnie Day in *Life with Father* (1939), co-written by her husband, Howard *Lindsay, who played Father. She reprised the character in the less-successful sequel *Life with Mother* (1948) and in a 1967 Broadway revival. Stickney always found a sweet, eccentric quality in even her darkest characterizations.

STICKS AND BONES (1971), a play by David *Rabe. [*Public Theatre, 366 perf.; Tony, NYDCC Awards.] Ozzie (Tom *Aldredge) and Harriet (Elizabeth *Wilson) are typical Americans with two typical American sons, David (David Selby) and Rick (Cliff De Young). But when David returns from the Vietnam War blind and emotionally numb, he proves an embarrassment to his family, especially when he keeps talking to a Vietnamese girl whom he insists follows him around but whom no one else can see. Not knowing what else to do with David, Ozzie and Harriet convince him to commit suicide. Rick lends him a razor and even helps his brother cut his wrists. Then Rick rushes to take one last photograph of David for the family album. The play was praised by Douglas Watt of the *Daily News* as a "serious and strikingly original antiwar play . . . a powerful human document." Ozzie and Harriet Nelson and their sons Rick and David were performers in an early television series about an apple-pie American family. The *New York Shakespeare Festival production was so popular Off Broadway that it transferred to Broadway for a long run.

STILL ALARM, THE (1887), a play by Joseph *Arthur. [14th Street Theatre, 16 perf.] The romance between Jack Manley (Harry Lacy) and Elinore Fordham (Blanche Thorne) is looked at askance by the villainous John Bird (Nelson Wheatcroft), who is not above trying to burn the lovers alive. But the New York Fire Department comes to their rescue in time for a happy ending. Its famous scene of horses and engines setting out from the firehouse and of the rescue from a burning building made it one of the most popular plays of the era, especially with backwater audiences. Although New York critics sneered, the play chalked up a run of 104 performances when it returned to Manhattan in March 1888.

STOCK COMPANIES IN AMERICA. In the sense that they were more or less permanent companies of players, the first American troupes, such as those of David *Douglass and Lewis *Hallam, and possibly even the players associated with Thomas *Kean and Walter *Murray, could loosely be called stock companies, as could the ensembles attached to the earliest established theatres. However, for a number of decades all these companies, because of the relative smallness of American cities and therefore the limited coterie of playgoers, had to perform in repertory fashion, giving a different play with each successive performance and only returning to a play once several others had been mounted. By later definition a stock company was an organized group of players that would perform a single play for a limited run before proceeding to the next work. Thus stock companies in this sense could develop only after the growth of larger cities and a notable increase in the number of playgoers. As such, traditional stock ensembles did not really begin to develop until the 1840s, with William Mitchell's band of burlesque artists an interesting early example. William *Burton soon established noteworthy troupes in Philadelphia and New York. The heyday of American stock companies may be said to have begun when the *Wallack family established its first ensemble and opened its first New York theatre in 1852. Augustin *Daly, A. M. *Palmer, and, for a time, the old *Lyceum Theatre under Daniel *Frohman followed over the next several decades. Whether Wallack's or Daly's marked the apogee is moot, but time has been kinder to the memory of Daly's great players such as John *Drew, Mrs. *Gilbert, James *Lewis, and Ada *Rehan. All these companies offered schedules of new plays interspersed with mountings of major revivals of older classics, but the emphasis was generally on comedy or romantic escapist drama, and very few of the more innovative, significant serious plays of the time first premiered at their houses, although there were notable exceptions. Away from New

York, great companies flourished in larger cities such as Philadelphia, most notably at the *Arch Street Theatre under Mrs. *Drew, and in Boston at the great *Boston Museum. With the growing practice of open casting for each new mounting, a practice pushed by the Frohman brothers and many of their contemporaries, and the increasing emphasis on stars relied on by many of these same producers, the great stock companies began to fade away in the 1890s. A few fine stock troupes continued to thrive briefly away from New York in the early years of the 20th century. These included the companies headed by George *Fawcett in Baltimore and by Henry *Jewett in Boston. However, by the 1910s stock companies were no longer in the first rank of American theatrical organizations. Nevertheless, many continued to thrive in outlying parts of New York City and elsewhere in America. They usually offered troupes of second-class actors and newcomers anxious to learn the trade. Their bills consisted largely of plays that had been popular a season or two before in "first-class" houses, although some more venturesome groups regularly tried out new plays. An excellent example of this sort of stock company was run for many years by Jessie *Bonstelle in Buffalo and Detroit. The Depression and sound films dealt the final death blow to such ensembles, although in later years *summer stock troupes flourished seasonally.

STODDART, J[ames] H[enry] (1827–1907), character actor. Born in Yorkshire, England, he was the son of a moderately popular actor and first played children's roles opposite his father. Stoddart performed mainly in Scotland and the north of England before coming to America, where he made his debut with *Wallack's company in 1854 as Mr. Sowerberry in *A Phenomenon in a Smock Frock*. The slim, handsome, if somewhat gaunt-faced, actor was immediately recognized as a superior low comedian. His performance of Don Whiskerandos in *The Critic* was hailed by the English comedian Charles Mathews as the best he had ever seen. A fiery temperament saw Stoddart move back and forth from Wallack's to Laura *Keene's to *Palmer's and back again. His performance as the rascally innkeeper Pierre in *Rose Michel* was so successful that he largely abandoned comic roles for more villainous ones. It was his refusal to play the Baron Chevrial in *A Parisian Romance* (1883) that gave Richard *Mansfield his start. Although his prominence later diminished, Stoddart continued to act until he was struck by a train, ending an American career of over half a century. Autobiography: *Recollections of a Player*, 1902.

STONE, [Val] **Fred** [Andrew] (1873–1959), comic actor. Born in Valmont, Colorado, he was raised in

Topeka and, with his brother, joined a circus as an acrobat for several years. While a member of Haverly's minstrels he met **Dave** [David Craig] **MONTGOMERY** (1870–1917), a native of St. Joseph, Missouri. When the minstrel troupe was disbanded, the pair went into vaudeville as grotesquely made-up acrobatic clowns. Their first Broadway appearance was in *The Girl from Up There* (1901). Subsequently they starred in *The *Wizard of Oz* (1903), *The *Red Mill* (1906), *The Old Town* (1910), *The Lady of the Slipper* (1912), and *Chin-Chin* (1914). By the time of Montgomery's death they were indisputably America's most popular musical comedy team. On his own, Stone appeared in *Jack o' Lantern* (1917), *Tip Top* (1920), *Stepping Stones* (1923), *Criss-Cross* (1926), *Ripples* (1930), and *Smiling Faces* (1932). All but the last two were huge hits. Later he appeared with only small success in a number of straight plays. Whether alone or with Montgomery, much of Stone's humor came from his comic acrobatics. His wife, Allene Crater, and daughter Dorothy were also popular performers. Autobiography: *Rolling Stone*, 1945.

STONE, John Augustus (1800–34), playwright and actor. This once admired dramatist was born in Concord, Massachusetts, and made his debut as an actor in Boston in 1821 as Old Norval in *Douglas*. Despite his youth, Stone specialized thereafter in old men's parts. Without ever becoming a star he played in New York regularly from 1822 to 1831 and then moved to Philadelphia. Responding to Edwin *Forrest's 1828 offer of a $500 prize for "the best tragedy, in five acts, of which the hero, or principal character, shall be an aboriginal of this country," Stone wrote *Metamora; or, The Last of the Wampanoags* (1829), which gave Forrest one of his greatest successes. His other plays included *Tancred, King of Sicily; or, The Archives of Palermo* (1831), *The Demoniac; or, The Prophet's Bride* (1831), a revision of J. K. *Paulding's *The *Lion of the West* (1831), *The Ancient Briton* (1833), and *The Knight of the Golden Fleece; or, The Yankee of Spain* (1834). Several other plays are said to have been performed, but only the scantiest records of them survive. In ill health and despondent, Stone committed suicide by drowning in the Schuylkill River. Although one obituary noted, "Mr. Stone has contributed more, both as author and performer, to raise the character of the stage, than any other native American," his work retains only historical interest.

STONE, Peter (1930–2003), librettist. He was born in Los Angeles, the son of a writer-movie producer, and educated at Bard College and Yale. Although he wrote a few plays and many television and film scripts, he is most known in theatre for his librettos for Broadway musicals. His credits include *Kean* (1961), **Skyscraper* (1965), **1776* (1969), *Two By Two* (1970), *Sugar* (1972), *Woman of the Year* (1981), *The *Will Rogers Follies* (1991), and **Titanic* (1997). Stone was also a reliable play doctor, rewriting such musicals as **My One and Only* (1983) and **Grand Hotel* (1989) and penning the revised libretto for **Annie Get Your Gun* (1999).

STOPPARD, Tom [né Thomas Straussler] (b. 1937), playwright. Perhaps the most brilliant (if not widely accessible) modern English playwright, he was first represented on Broadway by *Rosencrantz and Guildenstern Are Dead* (1967). His later works to reach New York included *Jumpers* (1974), *Travesties* (1976), *Dirty Linen* and *New-Found-Land* (1977), *Every Good Boy Deserves Favour* (1979), *Night and Day* (1980), *The Real Thing* (1984), *Artist Descending a Staircase* (1989), *Hapgood* (1995), *Arcadia* (1994), *The Invention of Love* (2001), and *Indian Ink* (2003). Several of his other plays have been popular with little theatres and elsewhere, although they have been denied the benefit of Broadway's approval. His best plays show a marked influence of the theatre of the absurd but, unlike most examples of the school, also manifest a traditional theatrical construction, superior character development, and gymnastic, witty dialogue. Biography: *Tom Stoppard: A Life*, Ira Nadel, 2002.

STOTHART, Herbert (1885–1949), composer. The Milwaukee native wrote part or all of the scores for a dozen Broadway musicals in the 1920s. However, the most memorable songs to come from these shows were often by his collaborators. Stothart's work included *Always You* (1920), *Tickle Me* (1920), *Wildflower* (1923), **Rose-Marie* (1924), *Song of the Flame* (1925), *Golden Dawn* (1927), and *Good Boy* (1928). He also served as a conductor and orchestrator before leaving for Hollywood, where he was involved in many film musicals.

STRAIGHT, Beatrice (1918–2001), actress. The accomplished leading lady possessed a soft but deeply featured face that made her ideal for tragic heroines. She was born in Old Westbury, New York, the daughter of a banker-diplomat, and educated in private schools in Manhattan and in England, later studying acting with Michael Chekhov. Straight soon attracted attention with her dramatic supporting roles, such as her Lady Macduff in Michael Redgrave's **Macbeth* (1948), then in leading parts, such as the governess Miss Giddens, who finds that her two charges are haunted in *The Innocents* (1950). Perhaps her most recalled performance was the Puritan wife Elizabeth in the original *The *Crucible* (1953). Later in her stage career Straight won plaudits for playing tragic mothers in revivals of *Ghosts* (1973), **All My Sons* (1974), and **Hamlet* (1979).

STRANG, Lewis C[linton] (1869–1935), critic and author. Born in Westfield, Massachusetts, and educated at Boston University, he took work at the *Boston Journal*, where he eventually became its drama critic. Later he held a similar position on the *Washington Times*. At the turn of the century he churned out a spate of books that still hold interest for theatrical historians: *Famous Actresses of the Day* (1899 and 1902), *Famous Actors of the Day* (1899 and 1901), *Prima Donnas and Soubrettes of Light Opera and Musical Comedy in America* (1900), *Celebrated Comedians of Light Opera and Musical Comedy in America* (1901), and *Players and Plays of the Last Quarter Century* (1902).

STRANGE INTERLUDE (1928), a play by Eugene **O'Neill. [**John Golden Theatre, 426 perf.; Pulitzer Prize.] Nina Leeds (Lynn **Fontanne) has turned against her father, Professor Leeds (Philip Leigh), for persuading her fiancé, Gordon, not to marry her until the war was over. When Gordon dies in battle, Nina continues to hold on to his memory despite the subtle overtures made by the writer Charles Marsden (Tom **Powers), who is too shy and too attached to his mother's apron strings to confess his affection openly. Nina weds the weak Sam Evans (Earle **Larimore), whom she has little feeling for, and soon finds herself pregnant. When Sam's mother (Helen **Westley) reveals to her that the family has had a tendency toward insanity, Nina has an abortion. She keeps this a secret from Sam and shortly afterwards has a child by Dr. Edmund Darrell (Glenn **Anders), who has always loved her. After their son, whom she names Gordon, is born, Edmund asks Nina to divorce Sam and marry him, but she refuses. Years later Gordon (John J. Burns) has grown up preferring Sam to his real father or his increasingly possessive mother. Realizing she has lost both Edmund and Gordon, she is stunned when Sam's death removes him, too, from her life. Only the loyal Charles remains, so she marries him. Charles urges her to regard the past as an interlude. She agrees, concluding, "Our lives are merely strange dark interludes in the electrical display of God the Father!," and she congratulates Charles, "who, passed beyond desire, has all the luck at last." The action of the nine-act play, in which O'Neill consciously drew on Freud, frequently stopped to allow the characters to probe their inner thoughts in extended soliloquies. "The effect," wrote Joseph Wood **Krutch, "is to combine to a remarkable extent the vivid directness of the drama with the more intricate texture of the modern novel." Because the **Theatre Guild production was four hours long, the curtain rose at 5:15 and had a long intermission for dinner at 7:00. Although it quickly became the season's conversation piece, it was banned in several important cities, most notably in Boston. A major revival was mounted in 1963 with Geraldine *Page as Nina, and a British revival in 1985 with Glenda Jackson was very popular in New York.

STRANGER, THE (1798). William *Dunlap's adaptation of *Kotzebue's *Menschenhass und Reue* was first presented at the *Park Theatre in 1798 and initiated the popularity of the German playwright in America. Its air of melancholy and mystery provided American playgoers with their introduction to theatrical romanticism. The story recounted the heroic actions of a Stranger who comes to a castle where a Mrs. Haller is staying. She has been unfaithful to her husband, and they have long been separated. Although she is courted by Baron de Steinfort, Mrs. Haller refuses all offers of marriage. The Stranger turns out to be Mrs. Haller's husband. At first he is reluctant to be reunited with her, but the entreaties of their children eventually prevail. Thomas Abthorpe *Cooper was the first American Stranger. The play remained in favor until the Civil War era. Later actors who essayed the title role included James William *Wallack, Thomas *Barry, and James *Murdoch.

STRASBERG, Lee [né Israel Strassberg] (1901–82), director. Born in Poland, he was brought to America at the age of seven and soon developed an interest in theatre, working at a settlement playhouse and later studying at the American Laboratory Theatre. After a time as an actor with the *Theatre Guild he joined Harold *Clurman and Cheryl *Crawford in founding the *Group Theatre. However, for many his main influence was his work at the *Actors Studio. Strasberg came to the organization in 1948, a year after its inception, and quickly became its guiding force. There he advocated the "method school" of acting, a style influenced by *Stanislavsky's theories and which encouraged performers to respond as much to their own inner feelings as to the requirements of the text or dramatic effectiveness. Although the result was that the American theatre was beset with much undisciplined and inelegant acting, a number of fine performers emerged from his classes. These included Anne *Bancroft, Julie *Harris, Geraldine *Page, Kim *Stanley, and Maureen *Stapleton. His daughter Susan Strasberg became a well-known actress.

STRAUSS, Johann (the younger) (1825–99), composer. Son of the famous "Waltz King," he became the leading composer of late 19th-century *Viennese operetta. Although he is best known today for *Die Fledermaus* and *The Gypsy Baron,* in his day he was more popular for such now-forgotten works as *The Merry War* (1882), *The Queen's Lace Handkerchief*

(1882), and *Prince Methusalem* (1883). Even *A Night in Venice* (1884) had only a short run. However, under a number of titles such as *Champagne Sec* and *Rosalinda, Die Fledermaus* enjoyed Broadway revivals throughout the first half of the 20th century.

STREAMERS (1976), a play by David *Rabe. [*Mitzi E. Newhouse Theatre, 478 perf.; NYDCC Award.] An army barracks seems like a microcosm of 1965 America. Among the soldiers are Billy (Paul Rudd), an idealist who sees himself as a typical American; Roger (Terry Alexander), an African American who has made a precarious peace with an alien society; Richie (Peter Evans), a young man disturbed by homosexual problems; and Martin (Michael Kell), a boy so upset with army life he is prepared to commit suicide. Into their midst comes Carlyle (Dorian Harewood), a bitter, vicious, trouble-making black man. The others recognize they must purge him to save their society, but they fail. Carlyle goes on a murderous rampage, and Billy is one of his victims. The play was perceived as an allegory of the American scene of the time, when large cities were subject to burning, rioting, and looting and the dilemma this presented for many Americans. The drama was presented at *Lincoln Center by the *New York Shakespeare Festival when Joe *Papp was running both organizations.

STREET SCENE (1929), a play by Elmer *Rice. [Playhouse, 601 perf.; Pulitzer Prize.] A row of old New York brownstones has become a street of tenements housing a wide variety of people. Among them are an Irish couple, Frank (Robert Kelly) and Anna Maurrant (Mary Servoss), their daughter, Rose (Erin O'Brien-Moore), and younger son, Willie (Russell Griffin). Rose is attractive and is courted by two men, the flashy, prosperous Harry Easter (Glenn Coulter) and her serious but affectionate Jewish neighbor, Sam Kaplan (Horace Braham). When Frank discovers his wife having an affair with the milkman Steve Sankey (Joseph Baird), he kills them both. Left alone with a brother to raise, Rose rejects proposals from Harry and from Sam (whom she prefers). She is determined to bring up Willie so that he can be freed from the life she and her parents have known. John Anderson of the *Evening Journal* wrote, "It is a play which builds engrossing trivialities into a drama that is rich and compelling and catches in the wide reaches of its curbside panorama the comedy and heartbreak that lie a few steps up from the sidewalks of New York." In 1947 Rice adapted his play into a superb opera version of the same title with music by Kurt *Weill, lyrics by the poet Langston *Hughes, and a cast headed by Anne Jeffreys, Brian Sullivan, and Polyna Stoska. The musical version only ran 148 performances in the Adelphi Theatre but later became part of several opera companies' repertories. *Notable songs*: What Good Would the Moon Be?; Somehow I Never Could Believe; Moon-Faced, Starry-Eyed; Remember That I Care.

STREETCAR NAMED DESIRE, A (1947), a play by Tennessee *Williams. [*Ethel Barrymore Theatre, 855 perf.; Pulitzer Prize, NYDCC Award.] The faded Southern belle Blanche Du Bois (Jessica *Tandy), who lives with illusions of past elegances, comes to visit her sister, Stella (Kim *Hunter), and brother-in-law, the coarse, brutish Stanley Kowalski (Marlon Brando) in their shabby apartment in the French Quarter of New Orleans. The visit becomes more permanent when it is revealed that Blanche lost the family home and has no money or job. Tensions between Stanley and Blanche mount, but Stella, who is pregnant and expecting to deliver any day, loves them both and tries to keep peace. Blanche starts dating Stanley's lonely, kindly coworker Harold "Mitch" Mitchell (Karl Malden), but Stanley breaks up the relationship when he tells Mitch about what he has found out about Blanche's past: She was no better than a whore back in her hometown and was fired from her teaching job for trying to seduce one of her students. When Stella goes to the hospital to have the baby, the rivalry between Stanley and Blanche climaxes when he rapes her. Blanche suffers a nervous breakdown and is sent to an asylum. To the doctor who comes for her, she remarks, "Whoever you are—I have always depended on the kindness of strangers." Brooks *Atkinson wrote of Williams and his drama, "Out of poetic imagination and ordinary compassion, he has spun a poignant and luminous story." The original production was made especially memorable by Jo *Mielziner's glowingly imaginative setting, Elia *Kazan's taut yet sympathetic direction, and the tender, understanding portrayal of Tandy. But for many playgoers the evening's high point was Brando's rough-hewn strength and magnetic performance, a triumph of the method acting style. The drama has been revived continually in regional theatres and in New York, most memorably in 1973 with Rosemary *Harris and James Farentino. **Marlon BRANDO** (b. 1924), a native of Omaha, had appeared in *I Remember Mama* (1944), *Truckline Café* (1946), and *Candida* (1946), among other plays, before making this, his final stage appearance. Since then his work has been confined to films.

STREETS OF NEW YORK, THE. See *Poor of New York, The.*

STREISAND, Barbra. See *Funny Girl.*

STRICTLY DISHONORABLE (1929), a comedy by Preston Sturges. [Avon Theatre, 557 perf.] When

Isabelle Parry (Muriel Kirkland), a sweet Southern belle, is deserted by her churlish escort, Henry Greene (Louis Jean Heydt), at a New York speakeasy, she finds herself there with only two other men, Count Di Ruvo (Tullio *Carminati), a Metropolitan Opera star known affectionately as Gus, and the avuncular Judge Dempsey (Carl Anthony), who lives above the nightclub. Anxious for some fun, she accepts Gus's offer to spend the evening with him, even though he assures her his intentions are strictly dishonorable. But as the evening progresses Gus finds himself falling in love. When Henry returns contritely, he is asked to wait in the car. Isabelle tells Gus that she, too, is in love. Not willing to miss his opportunity, Gus says his only condition is that he wants four sons and seven daughters. The Judge offers to tell Henry not to wait any longer. This charming, graceful comedy was the only Broadway success by **Preston STURGES** [né Edmond P. Biden] (1898–1959), although many critics had admired his *The Guinea Pig* (1929). After two more failures, *Rapture* (1930) and *Child of Manhattan* (1932), he became a famous Hollywood writer and director. He returned to the theatre in the 1950s with two unsuccessful musicals, *Make a Wish* (1951) and *Carnival in Flanders* (1953).

STRIKE UP THE BAND (1930), a musical comedy by Morrie *Ryskind, George S. *Kaufman (book), George *Gershwin (music), Ira *Gershwin (lyrics). [Times Square Theatre, 191 perf.] Horace J. Fletcher (Dudley Clements) wants his country to go to war over a Swiss tariff on chocolates. He is even willing to underwrite the war, so long as it is called the Horace J. Fletcher Memorial War. But when his daughter's fiancé, Jim Townsend (Jerry Goff), threatens to reveal that Fletcher uses Grade B milk in his chocolates, Fletcher becomes an ardent pacifist. However, by then the war is out of control and only won when the Americans decode the Swiss yodeling signals. Delighted with the outcome, the Americans decide to go to war with Russia over a tariff on caviar. *Notable songs*: I've Got a Crush on You; Soon; Strike Up the Band. Originally produced in 1927, the musical was withdrawn after its tryout. Ryskind rewrote Kaufman's original book, softening many of the original script's sharpest barbs and framing the story as a dream. Much of the fun came from the antics of Bobby *Clark and his sidekick Paul McCullough, although their roles were not crucial to the main plot.

STRINDBERG, [Johann] **August** (1849–1912), playwright. Although the Swedish dramatist's plays have never been popular in commercial theatre, they have been performed with some frequency by experimental and collegiate playhouses. The best known are probably *Miss Julie* and *The*

Father, which, despite a paucity of notable American productions, have exerted a major influence on American dramaturgy. Strindberg's use of both realism, naturalism, and, later, of expressionism had a notable effect on the writings of Eugene *O'Neill and other American dramatists.

STRITCH, Elaine (b. 1925), actress. The "gritty-voiced blonde" from Detroit had appeared in a number of plays before calling attention to herself when she sang "Civilization" in the 1947 musical revue *Angel in the Wings*. After singing "Zip" in a 1952 revival of *Pal Joey*, she toured in the Ethel *Merman role in *Call Me Madam*. She was later seen in the 1954 revival of *On Your Toes*, as the hard-nosed road house operator Grace in *Bus Stop* (1955), silent screen star Maggie Harris in *Goldilocks* (1958), cruise ship entertainment director Mimi Paragon in Noel *Coward's *Sail Away* (1961), the caustic wife Joanne in *Company* (1970), the sour Parthy in *Show Boat* (1994), the alcoholic Claire in *A *Delicate Balance* (1997), and in her one-woman autobiographical program *At Liberty* (2002). Stritch has also spent many years performing in London.

STROMAN, Susan (b. 1960), choreographer and director. Born in Wilmington, Delaware, and educated at the University of Delaware, Stroman began choreographing musicals in regional theatre in 1987 and was first noticed in Manhattan for her clever dances in the Off-Broadway revue *And the World Goes Round* (1991). Soon she was one of the most sought-after choreographers in New York, providing dances for *Crazy for You* (1992), *Show Boat* (1994), *A Christmas Carol* (1994), *Big* (1996), *Steel Pier* (1997), and *Oklahoma!* (2002). By the end of the 20th century Stroman was a recognized director-choreographer as well, with such Broadway productions as The *Music Man* (2000), *Contact* (2000), The *Producers* (2001), and *Thou Shalt Not* (2002).

STRONG, Austin. See *Seventh Heaven*.

STROUSE, Charles. See Adams and Strouse.

STUDENT PRINCE, THE (1924), an operetta by Dorothy *Donnelly (book, lyrics), Sigmund *Romberg (music). [Jolson Theatre, 608 perf.] When Prince Karl Franz (Howard *Marsh) leaves his father's palace to attend school at Heidelberg, his old tutor Dr. Engel (Greek Evans) is assigned to accompany him. Once there, the Prince readily joins the other students in their camaraderie and falls in love with the beer-garden waitress Kathie (Ilse Marvenga). But after Karl Franz's father dies, he knows he must assume the throne and marry the girl who has been selected for him, Princess Margaret (Roberta Beatty), although she, too, loves

someone else. Karl Franz returns briefly to Heidelberg to say farewell to Kathie and to promise to remember forever their happy times together. *Notable songs*: Deep in My Heart, Dear; Golden Days; Serenade; Drinking Song. Although the title was correctly *The Student Prince in Heidelberg*, hardly anyone called it that. The show was Romberg's biggest success and the quintessential example of both his work and period operetta. Along with *Rose-Marie*, which had opened earlier in the same season, it sparked a five-year revival of traditional operetta. The *Shubert production also started a vogue for full-voiced male choruses, as witnessed in the "Drinking Song." The musical continued to tour season after season until the late 1940s and has been revived occasionally since.

STUDIO ARENA (Buffalo). This group started in 1927 as an educational theatre program called the Studio Theatre School, but it did not turn professional until 1965 under the leadership of Neal DuBrock. Its performance space is not in true arena style but instead is a 637-seat thrust stage with an amphitheater that wraps around it and gives the performance space an intimate audience-actor relationship. They also have a second, smaller space for new and more experimental works. Under such artistic directors as David Frank and Gavin Cameron-Webb, the company has presented a varied repertory of plays and has engaged in cooperative programs and productions with other League of Resident Theatres (LORT) theatres.

STUDIO THEATRE (Washington, D.C.). Perhaps the most experimental theatre group in the nation's capital, it was founded in 1978 by Joy Zinoman, Russell Metheny, and Virginia Crawford as a showcase for challenging original scripts, innovative revivals, and performance art pieces. The company performs in two spaces, the Mead and Milton Theatres, each seating two hundred patrons and plans to open a new venue in 2004.

STUDLEY, J[ohn] B. (1831–1910), actor. The Bostonian made his professional debut in Columbia, South Carolina, in 1848. Thereafter, he played seasons as leading man in many important companies around the country before acting opposite Charlotte *Cushman and essaying a memorable Bill Sykes in her mounting of *Oliver Twist*. A melodramatic actor of what was increasingly perceived as an old school, he proved absolutely right as the villainous Byke in *Under the Gaslight* (1867) and as the drunken Wolf in *Horizon* (1871). His later career typified that of many admired second-rankers, with major supporting parts and occasional leads in first class New York houses and starring roles in touring shows and at minor Manhattan theatres.

STURGES, Preston. See *Strictly Dishonorable*.

STYNE, Jule [né Julius Kerwin Stein] (1905–94), composer. Born in London but brought to America at the age of eight, he proved a child prodigy on the piano, giving recitals with the Chicago and Detroit symphonies and entering the Chicago College of Music at thirteen. He later abandoned classical music in favor of becoming a pianist in a dance band and eventually organized his own band. After many years of composing for Hollywood films and Tin Pan Alley, Styne turned to Broadway and enjoyed a smash hit with his second try, *High Button Shoes* (1947). Working with a variety of lyricists he scored *Gentlemen Prefer Blondes* (1949), *Two on the Aisle* (1951), *Hazel Flagg* (1953), *Peter Pan* (1954), *Bells Are Ringing* (1956), *Say, Darling* (1958), *Gypsy* (1959), *Do Re Mi* (1960), *Subways Are for Sleeping* (1961), *Funny Girl* (1964), *Fade In—Fade Out* (1964), *Hallelujah, Baby!* (1967), *Sugar* (1972), and *The Red Shoes* (1993). He also produced a number of Broadway shows, most memorably the 1952 revival of *Pal Joey*. Styne's traditional but melodic and eminently theatrical music will probably be seen as the last set squarely in the school of great American composers that began with the musical comedy songs of Irving *Berlin and Jerome *Kern. He was unquestionably the most prolific and successful of composers to appear on Broadway just after World War II. Biography: *Jule: The Story of Composer Jule Styne*, Theodore Taylor, 1979.

SUBJECT WAS ROSES, THE (1964), a play by Frank D. Gilroy. [Royale Theatre, 832 perf.; Pulitzer Prize, Tony, NYDCC Awards.] When Timmy Cleary (Martin Sheen) returns from the war, his father, John (Jack Albertson), and his mother, Nettie (Irene Dailey), find themselves fighting each other to win his love and respect. After two days together, Timmy tells his parents that he is leaving to strike out on his own. Scarred from the family infighting, John and Nettie grudgingly agree. A small-cast, largely actionless play typical of its day, its winning so many awards, especially after two seasons in which no *Pulitzer award was given, testified to the hollowness of American playwriting at the time. **Frank D[aniel] GILROY** (b. 1925) was educated at Dartmouth and Yale. His early play, *Who'll Save the Ploughboy?* (1962), won him some recognition. After the surprise success of *The Subject Was Roses* Gilroy directed several films, but none of his later plays found favor, including the prequel *Any Given Day* (1993), which looked at John and Nettie Cleary before Timmy was born.

SUBWAY CIRCUIT. This was the name given to a group of theatres, some within Manhattan but most of them in the other boroughs, that regularly offered touring shows after their Broadway runs and on rare occasions served as tryout theatres. They had disappeared by the 1950s.

SUGAR BABIES (1979), a musical revue by Ralph G. Allen. [*Mark Hellinger Theatre, 1,208 perf.] A collection of traditional burlesque skits and familiar musical numbers, the show was an affectionate look back at the raunchy glories of the Minsky era. The revue's stars, Hollywood favorites Mickey Rooney and Ann Miller, may have been a bigger attraction than the burlesque material, for the road company headed by two top Broadway figures, Carol *Channing and Robert *Morse, quickly folded. Yet when Rooney and Miller took the show on the road it was remarkably successful.

SULLAVAN, Margaret (1911–60), actress. The throaty-voiced blonde beauty was born in Norfolk, Virginia, and after several years in amateur and stock productions made her Broadway debut in 1931 in *A Modern Virgin*. She is best remembered for four roles: the aspiring actress Terry Randall in *Stage Door* (1936); Sally Middleton, who finds love with a soldier on wartime leave in The *Voice of the Turtle* (1943); Hester Collyer, a woman in love with an unloving man in *The Deep Blue Sea* (1952); and the chauffeur's daughter Sabrina Fairchild in *Sabrina Fair* (1953). Sullavan was trying out in what promised to be another success when she committed suicide. She was also popular in films. *Haywire*, a book by her daughter Brooke Hayward about her and Brooke's father, producer Leland *Hayward, was published in 1977.

SULLIVAN, Arthur. See Gilbert and Sullivan.

SULLIVAN, Daniel (b. 1940), director and manager. He was born in Wray, Colorado, and educated at San Francisco State University, staying after graduation to work in local theatres. Sullivan was assistant director for *Hair* (1968) and *An Enemy of the People* (1971) on Broadway before he started directing Off Broadway and at *Lincoln Center. But much of the 1970s was spent in regional theatres, in particular at the *Seattle Repertory Theatre, where he served as artistic director in the 1980s. His Seattle production of *I'm Not Rappaport* (1985) brought Sullivan back to Manhattan, where he has staged such critical successes as The *Heidi Chronicles* (1988), The *Sisters Rosensweig* (1992), *Dinner with Friends* (1999), A *Moon for the Misbegotten* (2000), *Proof* (2000), *Major Barbara* (2001), and *The Retreat from Moscow* (2003).

SULLIVAN, HARRIS and WOODS. A firm founded in 1899 by P. H. "Paddy" Sullivan, who provided the financing, A. H. *Woods, and Sam H.

*Harris, it was for a number of years a principal producer of cheap, touring melodramas. The firm disbanded after both Woods and Harris elected to pursue independent careers on Broadway.

SULTAN OF SULU, THE (1902), a musical comedy by George *Ade (book, lyrics), Alfred G. Wathall (music). [*Wallack's Theatre, 192 perf.] Ki-Ram (Frank *Moulan) leads an idyllic life as the Sultan of Sulu until sailors from the American navy arrive to claim the island for Uncle Sam. Determined to maintain his trouble-free ways, Ki-Ram courts the lady judge-advocate whom the American government has sent. But when the judge realizes that Ki-Ram is merely offering her a place in his harem, she issues several decrees, which assure an end to Ki-Ram's bliss. Luckily a legal technicality is discovered that allows Ki-Ram to resume his own lackadaisical ways. Notable songs: Since I First Met You; The Smiling Isle. One of the few Chicago-originated musicals to win acclaim in New York, it initiated the rage, which lasted for several seasons and culminated with The *Red Mill, for musical comedies centering on the contrast between American and foreign ways of life. Other examples included The Isle of Spice, The Yankee Consul, The Sho-Gun, It Happened in Nordland, and Fantana.

SUMMER AND SMOKE (1948), a play by Tennessee *Williams. [*Music Box Theatre, 100 perf.] Alma Winemiller (Margaret Phillips), the prim daughter of the local minister, is at once repelled and fascinated by her handsome, amoral neighbor, Dr. John Buchanan Jr. (Tod Andrews). She sets about to give him higher moral standards, while he takes it upon himself to teach her the realities of life and sex. Both are all too successful, for John becomes high-minded and spiritual, while Alma dwindles into the town prostitute. One of Williams's best-constructed and imaginative plays, it was first seen in Texas in a production directed and produced by Margo *Jones. When it moved to Broadway the play was coolly received and failed to run. A successful 1952 revival at the *Circle in the Square, with Geraldine *Page as Alma, prompted a critical re-evaluation. Williams's revised version of the play, called The Eccentricities of a Nightingale, was seen briefly on Broadway in 1976 with Betsy Palmer as Alma. Critics could not agree if it was superior or inferior to the original and audiences stayed away. Yet both versions have seen several revivals.

SUMMER STOCK. As early as the first half of the 19th century, summer playhouses on the outskirts of growing American cities began to attract playgoers seeking entertainment as they escaped from city heat and crowds. Many began in parks or gardens where citizens came for light refreshment and cooling breezes. In New York, Chatham Garden had a popular theatre in the 1820s, and a decade later *Niblo's Garden offered shows as well as food and drink. One of the oldest summer playhouses, operating up until 1994, was *Elitch's Gardens Theatre, founded in Denver in 1890. Almost all these theatres were opened with the idea of presenting light olios for summer, but several of the more successful soon started to offer regular plays, particularly comedies. Although their development was assisted by the spread of trolleycar lines to outlying reaches around the turn of the century, it was really the arrival of the automobile several years later that spurred the greatest growth. One of the earliest summer theatres to gain widespread recognition was the *Provincetown Playhouse, which opened on a wharf in Provincetown, Massachusetts, during World War I. However, it was atypical in many ways. Most notably, it was dedicated to serious new drama and not to the rehashed escapist material that soon came to characterize most summer stock. Second, it soon opened a New York branch for winter seasons. Third, it was built on a wharf. Many early summer stock theatres were begun in converted barns or mills and often self-consciously retained a distinct rustic ambiance for many years. One result was the name popularly given to summer stock—straw-hat theatre—which reflected its barnlike origins as much as it did the fashion of wearing straw hats in summer. Other examples, atypical in their dedication to serious theatre, were the *Hedgerow Theatre in Moylan, Pennsylvania, and the playhouse at Williamstown, Massachusetts. Far more on the order of what the public came to think of as summer theatres were such long-successful operations as the Bucks County Playhouse in New Hope, Pennsylvania; the Westport Country Playhouse in Westport, Connecticut; the Cape Playhouse in Dennis, Massachusetts; the North Shore Players in Marblehead, Massachusetts; and the Boothbay Playhouse in Boothbay, Maine. Even if much of their fare consisted of frothy comedies, most of the better straw-hats offered occasional serious dramas and tryouts of new plays. Many also lured stars, either Broadway stars in between major assignments or Hollywood names who did not want to commit themselves to a full New York season or feared the more demanding standards of New York critics. Other houses did not use stars but employed a genuine, if seasonal, stock company. These theatres were built on essentially traditional lines, but huge open-air amphitheaters such as the one at Jones Beach, near New York, and that of the St. Louis Municipal Outdoor Theatre, also thrived, although they specialized in musicals. The *Paper

Mill Playhouse, a regular enclosed conversion in Milburn, New Jersey, because of its proximity to New York, was able to extend its seasons, usually of musicals, to an almost year-round operation. The heyday of the straw-hats was between the two World Wars and for a short period thereafter. One postwar development was the rise of tents, generally offering musicals in-the-round. Economic and other considerations then began to affect playhouses, closing some and forcing others to rely on packaged tours, usually featuring high-priced names. Most of the tents gave way to permanent structures, with large concrete parking lots that retained little of the bucolic atmosphere once so carefully fostered. However, a number of the old, traditional playhouses still flourish.

SUNDAY IN THE PARK WITH GEORGE (1984), a musical play by James *Lapine (book), Stephen *Sondheim (music, lyrics). [*Booth Theatre, 604 perf.; Pulitzer Prize, NYDCC Award.] Parisian artist Georges Seurat (Mandy *Patinkin) is determined to finish his painting, *A Sunday Afternoon on the Island of La Grande Jatte*, even if it means his friends and associates will ridicule him and even if in the process he must neglect and lose his mistress, Dot (Bernadette *Peters). Years later his American great-grandson, George (Patinkin), is also an artist, hoping to find meaning and purpose working in multimedia while trying to play the funding game with museums and sponsors. But he is encouraged by his grandmother Marie (Peters) to pursue his art. Visiting the drearily overdeveloped Grande Jatte after her death, he finds solace in her memory and in notes once scribbled by Dot, who appears to George and inspires him to continue on. *Notable songs*: Sunday in the Park with George; Color and Light; Children and Art; Finishing the Hat; Putting It Together; Sunday; Move On. With its French-influenced music, intricate lyrics, and intriguing ideas about the creative process, the musical was more a succès d'estime than a hit. Yet for many it was Sondheim's most personal and moving work. Lapine directed the lovely production, a high point being the replication of the Seurat painting at the end of the first act.

SUNNY (1925), a musical comedy by Otto Harbach, Oscar *Hammerstein (book, lyrics), Jerome *Kern (music). [*New Amsterdam Theatre, 517 perf.] Sunny Peters (Marilyn *Miller) is an American circus performer working in England, where she meets and falls in love with fellow American Tom Warren (Paul Frawley). When Tom has to return to the States, Sunny decides to follow him but realizes she cannot afford the fare. Her ex-husband, the circus owner Jim Deming (Jack *Donahue), suggests they remarry, sail back together, then get a divorce. Sunny prefers to stow away. She is caught, but everything ends happily. *Notable songs*: D'ye Love Me?; Sunny; Who? One of the best and most successful 1920s musical comedies, the Charles *Dillingham production marked Kern's first association with Harbach and Hammerstein, who would become his principal collaborators.

SUNRISE AT CAMPOBELLO (1958), a play by Dore Schary. [*Cort Theatre, 558 perf.; Tony Award.] Franklin D. Roosevelt (Ralph *Bellamy) has taken a swim that has left him tired and achy. Within a few hours he can no longer move parts of his body. His wife, Eleanor (Mary Fickett), his mother, Anna (Roni Dengel), and his long time political associate Louis McHenry Howe (Henry Jones) all recognize that he has polio. They gather together to help Roosevelt, who is depressed and even terrified when he thinks of his helplessness should a fire break out. Although Anna wants him to retire, for three years she and the others persist in their encouragement and aid until Roosevelt has so recruited both his strength and his spirit that he is able to go to New York to nominate Al Smith (Alan Bunce) at the 1924 Democratic Convention. One of the many contemporary plays centering on the problems of the handicapped, the *Theatre Guild mounting gained added interest from its portraits of historical figures. **Dore SCHARY** (1905–80), a native of Newark, New Jersey, had been a journalist and a Hollywood executive before embarking on a theatre career. He produced this play, as well as *A *Majority of One* (1959), *The Unsinkable Molly Brown* (1960), and others.

SUNSET BOULEVARD (1994). As in the celebrated 1950 film, this London hit musical was a dark tale about the silent screen has-been Norma Desmond (Glenn *Close) and the gigolo-screenwriter (Alan Campbell) whom she loves, then murders. *Notable songs*: With One Look; As If We Never Said Goodbye. Andrew Lloyd *Webber wrote the music, Don Black and Christopher Hampton penned the book and lyrics, and the expensive production opened at the *Minskoff Theatre for a run of 977 performances (and won the *Tony Award) without ever realizing a profit. John *Napier's sets were both lavish and grotesque, and the performances, particular Close's Norma, were also oversized. Patti *LuPone had originated the role of Norma in London, and the publicity over her being dropped for the Broadway production was as theatrical as the show itself.

SUNSHINE BOYS, THE (1972), a comedy by Neil *Simon. [*Broadhurst Theatre, 538 perf.] Willie Clark (Jack Albertson) and Al Lewis (Sam *Levene) were an old vaudeville team who fought and separated many years earlier. Willie now lives alone, largely in pajamas, in a small New York hotel. Al lives with his daughter in New Jersey. CBS wants to do a nostalgic program about the history of comedy and wants to reunite Lewis and Clark. It falls to Al's nephew, Ben Silverman (Lewis J. *Stadlen), to persuade the old men to forget their animosities and perform together again. This proves a hard task, but Ben finally succeeds. But during a rehearsal at the studio Willie has a heart attack. Recuperating back home, he finally agrees to move to the Actors' Home. Then Al pays him a visit and announces that he, too, must move to the Home. The quarreling can continue on. Hailed by T. E. Kalem of *Time* magazine as "a cripplingly funny show," this affectionately savage comedy was Simon's tenth consecutive success. A 1997 revival with Tony *Randall and Jack Klugman was also a hit.

SUN-UP (1923), a play by Lula *Vollmer. [*Provincetown Playhouse, 356 perf.] Widow Cagle (Lucille La Verne), a North Carolina mountain woman whose son is fighting in World War I, discovers that the stranger (Eliot Cabot) she has been harboring is not only a deserter but is the son of the man who killed her moonshining husband. When she learns that her son has died in the war, the widow determines to kill the deserter. However, as she is about to pull the trigger, the voice of her son warns her that his own death came from such blind hatred and that killing the stranger will serve no purpose. She changes her mind and even refuses to turn the man over to the sheriff. Instead she will spend her remaining years alone, but in peace. She tells her son's voice, "I'm a knowin' God A'mighty is a takin' keer of ye." Although Vollmer worked for the *Theatre Guild, she was unable to get that company to produce the play. Minor producers finally took a chance with it, but its fine reviews and immediate success prompted Lee *Shubert to move it to the *Princess Theatre. The play was revived Off Broadway in 2003.

SUPERSTITION (1824), a tragedy by James Nelson *Barker. [*Chestnut Street Theatre (Philadelphia), in repertory.] In a duel to protect the honor of Mary Ravensworth (Mrs. John *Duff) from the unwanted attentions of George Egerton (Francis C. *Wemyss), Charles Fitzroy (William Wood) wounds Egerton but walks away unscathed. Rather than pleasing Mary's father, the Reverend Ravensworth (Mr. Darley), the news angers him, since Charles and his mother, Isabella (Mrs. Wood), have not shown the proper respect for his clerical office. Matters are made worse when the village is attacked by Indians. Charles and a man called the Unknown (John *Duff) lead the attack against them, defeat them, and again walk away unharmed.

Charles and his mother are then perceived as devils, and at their trial Ravensworth testifies against them. Charles is executed and his mother dies of grief. The Unknown turns out to be William Goffe—one of the men who had sentenced King Charles I to death—and also Isabella's father and Charles's grandfather. Mary is left to denounce her father for his cruelty. One of the first important American plays based on domestic history, the blank-verse drama skillfully wove together the various events, all conspiring inexorably against the hero. One student of American drama, W. J. Meserve, has called the work "the single outstanding American play written during the first quarter of the nineteenth century." It sometimes was given the subtitle *The Fanatic Father.*

SUSAN AND GOD (1937), a play by Rachel *Crothers. [*Plymouth Theatre, 288 perf.] Selfish, vain Susan Trexel (Gertrude *Lawrence) becomes a convert to the Oxford movement and sets about to reform the world. She arrives as a guest at the home of Irene Burroughs (Vera Allen), promptly crimping Irene's affair with Michael O'Hara (Douglas Gilmore). She then sets to work on her own alcoholic husband, Barrie (Paul McGrath,) and her "girl scout gone wrong" daughter, Blossom (Nancy Kelly). For a time Susan does succeed in keeping Barrie on the wagon, but when she accuses him of having an affair with another woman, he slips off. Susan is made to recognize that being meddlesome is not being religious and that real faith comes from within. Although many critics felt there was not sufficient story line and that Lawrence was left to carry the play, Richard Lockridge wrote in the *Evening Sun*, "It doesn't need proving that Miss Crothers, theme or no theme, can write dialogue that humor glints on, and handle her situations and characters with a suave dexterity enchanting to watch." The author returned to the theatre for this, her last play, after five years of writing for films.

SUTHERLAND, Evelyn Greenleaf [née Baker] (1855–1908), playwright. Born and educated in Boston, she began to write for the stage comparatively late in life. The *Theatre of Arts and Letters mounted the one-act *Drifting*, her collaboration with Emma Sheridan Fry, in New York in 1892. Of her full-length plays, the three best known are *Beaucaire* (1901), written with Booth *Tarkington and based on his novel about a duke masquerading as a barber; A Rose o' Plymouth Town (1902), written with Beulah Marie *Dix and recounting the story of Priscilla Alden; and her biggest hit, again with Dix, The *Road to Yesterday (1906), in which the heroine's dreams take her back to adventurous times three hundred years earlier.

SWAN, Mark. See *Parlor, Bedroom and Bath.*

SWASEY, William A. [fl. early 20th century] architect. He designed several important New York theatres, including the 48th Street, 44th Street, *Princess, 39th Street, and *Winter Garden.

SWEENEY TODD, or the Demon Barber of Fleet Street (1979), a musical thriller by Hugh *Wheeler (book), Stephen *Sondheim (music, lyrics). [Uris Theatre, 557 perf.; Tony, NYDCC Awards.] Bitter at his imprisonment and at the world in general, Sweeney Todd (Len *Cariou) returns to London and sets up as a barber. But he is no ordinary barber. He slits his customers' throats and turns their bodies over to his friend, Mrs. Lovett (Angela *Lansbury), who bakes them into pies. He even succeeds in murdering the venal judge who sent him to prison, but when he learns he has also inadvertently murdered his long-lost wife his mind snaps completely, and he pushes Mrs. Lovett into her own oven. He in turn is murdered by a young boy Mrs. Lovett had taken in off the streets. *Notable songs*: The Ballad of Sweeney Todd; Johanna; A Little Priest; Not While I'm Around; Worst Pies in London. The musical was based on Christopher Bond's 1973 play, *Sweeney Todd*, which in turn was derived from George Dibdin Pitt's 1847 melodrama, *The String of Pearls,* long a favorite at the *Bowery Theatre. Hal *Prince staged the mammoth production using Brechtian techniques, a constructivist set by Eugene *Lee, and bold, bigger-than-life performances. For many it was Lansbury's crowning performance. Both critics and playgoers were sharply divided over the musical's merits: some considering it a superbly artful, venturesome work; others, a gruesome joke. Over the years the challenging piece has caught on and it is now revived in theatres and opera houses across the country.

SWEET ADELINE (1929), a musical play by Oscar *Hammerstein (book, lyrics), Jerome *Kern (music). [Hammerstein Theatre, 234 perf.] When Addie Schmidt (Helen *Morgan), who sings at her father's Hoboken beer garden, loses her beloved Tom Martin (Max Hoffman Jr.) to her own sister Nellie (Caryl Bergman), she leaves New Jersey to seek a stage career. Her climb is aided by James Day (Robert Chisholm), who also makes her forget Tom. *Notable songs*: Don't Ever Leave Me; Here Am I; 'Twas Not So Long Ago; Why Was I Born?; Some Girl Is on Your Mind. Written as a vehicle for Morgan after her success in *Show Boat*, the Arthur *Hammerstein offering started out as a smash hit only to have its run curtailed by the onset of the Depression.

SWEET BIRD OF YOUTH (1959), a play by Tennessee *Williams. [Martin Beck Theatre, 375 perf.] Under the name of Princess Kosmonopolis, the boozy, drug-addicted, fading screen star Alexandre Del Lago (Geraldine *Page) comes to a small Gulf Coast town with her handsome gigolo, Chance Wayne (Paul Newman). Wayne had grown up in the town and had left after giving the political boss's daughter a case of venereal disease. Boss Finley (Sidney *Blackmer) has not forgotten and has determined to be avenged. Suddenly Alexandre discovers she has made a huge success in a new film and appears on the verge of a major comeback. She walks out on Chance, telling him, "You've gone past something you couldn't afford to go past; your time, your youth, you've passed it. It's all you had, and you've had it." Recognizing the truth of what she has said, Chance decides not to follow her but to stay and await Finley's men who are coming to castrate him. Louis *Kronenberger recorded, "At its best, *Sweet Bird of Youth* has force and fascination. But far too often everything seems excessive, with a fuming and rioting depravity." Cheryl *Crawford produced the drama, which proved to be one of Williams's last commercial successes. The play was given a memorable revival in 1975 featuring Irene *Worth and Christopher *Walken.

SWEET CHARITY (1966), a musical comedy by Neil *Simon (book), Cy *Coleman (music), Dorothy *Fields (lyrics). [*Palace Theatre, 608 perf.] Charity Hope Valentine (Gwen *Verdon) is a dance hall hostess at the Fandango Ballroom. She longs to settle down with a man, but the men in her life simply love her and leave her—when they bother loving her at all. One steals her purse and throws her in a lake; another, jilted by his date, shoves her in a closet when his date returns. Finally, she is trapped in an elevator with Oscar (John McMartin), who seems to her to be the man she has waited for. But when he learns what she does for a living, he, too, walks out on her. Yet somehow Charity continues on with hope for better things. *Notable songs*: Baby, Dream Your Dream; Big Spender; If My Friends Could See Me Now; I'm a Brass Band; Where Am I Going? Based on Fellini's 1957 film *Nights of Cabiria*, the musical served as the first attraction when the Palace was turned into a legitimate theatre. Curiously, although the show had a better book and more memorable songs than many musicals of the time, with Verdon performing the dynamic choreography of her husband, Bob *Fosse, it was often perceived as essentially a dance show. A successful 1986 revival starred Debbie Allen.

SWEET INNISCARRA (1897), a play by Augustus *Pitou. [14th Street Theatre, 104 perf.] Gerald

O'Carroll (Chauncey *Olcott), an Irishman raised in London, comes to the small Irish town of Inniscarra, where he falls in love with the local schoolteacher, Kate O'Donoghue (Georgia Busby). Her father objects to their romance and attempts to have Gerald shanghaied, but Gerald escapes and returns to Inniscarra in time to prevent Kate from being forced into an unwanted marriage. This play, interlarded with a few Irish-style songs, was typical of the romantic dramas in which Olcott and his competitors trafficked so profitably for many years. As the working-class Irish deserted the theatre for films, this sort of play disappeared.

SWEET KITTY BELLAIRS (1903), a play by David *Belasco. [*Belasco Theatre, 206 perf.] Kitty Bellairs (Henrietta *Crosman) is an Irish lass determined to rise to the top of society in 18th-century Bath. When she and her arch rival, a former queen of Bath society (Edith Crane), are both forced to hide behind the bed curtains in the room of Kitty's soldier sweetheart (Charles Hammond), it is Kitty who comes forth to disclose herself, thereby saving her rival from scandal. Calculation or selflessness, it wins Kitty both acceptance and a man. Derived from Agnes and Edgerton Castle's *The Bath Comedy*, the play was later turned into a 1917 Rudolf *Friml operetta, *Kitty Darlin'*.

SWEETHEARTS (1913), an operetta by Harry B. *Smith (book, lyrics), Fred de *Gresac (book), Victor *Herbert (music). [*New Amsterdam Theatre, 136 perf.] Sylvia (Christie *MacDonald) was found as a baby by the laundress Dame Paula (Ethel De Fre Houston), who raised her as one of her daughters. While traveling incognito, Franz (Thomas Conkey), the heir-presumptive to the throne of Zilania, meets Sylvia and falls in love with her. But his hopes seem thwarted when Lieutenant Karl (Edwin Wilson) comes courting. Karl, however, proves to be a lothario, and so is rejected. At the same time, a search has been going on for a long-lost Zilanian princess, who turns out to be Sylvia. Franz and Sylvia wed and promise to rule Zilania fairly together. *Notable songs*: Angelus; The Cricket on the Hearth; Every Lover Must Meet His Fate; Jeannette and Her Little Wooden Shoes; Pretty as a Picture; Sweethearts. One of the best of Herbert's operettas, it was successfully revived in 1947 with Bobby *Clark as the principal comedian.

SYDNEY, Basil (1894–1968), actor. The distinguished English leading man first came to America with Granville Barker in 1914. He made several other trips in the 1920s and 1930s but is most remembered in America for his Hamlet, which he played in 1926 in modern dress. Sydney's other Shakespeare roles in New York include Romeo, Petruchio, and Prince Hal, as well as Harry Domin in *R.U.R.* (1922), Giannetto Malespini in *The Jest* (1926), and Rawdon Crawley in *Becky Sharp* (1929).

SYRACUSE STAGE. A professional nonprofit theatre affiliated with Syracuse University in New York, it was founded in 1974 by Arthur Storch, who served as its artistic director for two decades. The company presents a traditional repertory of play and musical revivals, with some original works produced on a regular basis. Its educational outreach program includes a teen playwriting contest, school performances, and its continued association with the university. Robert Moss is the theatre's current artistic director.

T

TAB SHOWS. The name given to traveling shows, often they were drastically cut-down versions of Broadway musical comedies or revues but just as often original compilations. Tabs toured in the smallest towns and frequently played carnivals. The name was later applied to live shows given in conjunction with film showings.

TAILOR MADE MAN, A (1917), a comedy by Harry James *Smith. [Cohan and Harris Theatre, 398 perf.] John Paul Bart (Grant *Mitchell), a drudge in a tailor's shop, dreams of marrying Tanya Huber (Helen MacKellar), his boss's daughter, and of becoming a great and famous man. But Tanya has an arrogant, snobbish fiancé who has written a book in which he says that with proper clothes and charm any man can reach the top. John appropriates some evening clothes left at the shop and heads out to conquer society. He is soon lionized, courted by an heiress, and given a cushy Wall Street job. Of course, John is eventually exposed and sent back to the tailor shop. By that time, however, Tanya has fallen in love with him, so his future is not totally unpromising. Although Smith and producers George M. *Cohan and Sam H. *Harris openly acknowledged that the play was based on a German work by Gabriel Dregley, the adaptation and production were good enough to overcome wartime prejudices against almost anything German.

TAKE ME ALONG. See *Ah, Wilderness!*

TAKE ME OUT (2003), a play by Richard Greenberg. [*Walter Kerr Theatre, 356 perf.; Tony, NYDCC Awards.] After selling out its brief run at the *Public Theatre in 2002, this fanciful meditation about the art and beauty of baseball moved to Broadway, where it found an audience, in no small part because of its extensive use of male nudity. When Darren Lemming (Daniel Sunjata), star player for the Empires, casually mentions his homosexuality during a press conference, the league is in an uproar, and the team's chances of winning the pennant are threatened. Darren hires the mousy accountant Mason Marzac (Denis O'Hare) to sort out his troubled finances. In helping the baseball player, Marzac, an overlooked gay man on the outside of life, is transformed as he becomes enveloped in the great American pastime. Although critics pointed out some weak plotting and the undeveloped secondary characters in the piece, the drama soared in its poetic passages about baseball and how it relates to life. **Richard GREENBERG** (b. 1958) was born in East Meadow on Long Island, the son of a film executive, and was educated at Harvard, Princeton, and Yale. He was first noticed for his one-acts *Life under Water* (1985) and *The Author's Voice* (1987), then gained recognition for *Eastern Standard* (1988), a caustic look at a group of Yuppies confronting a homeless woman and AIDS. His other plays include *The Maderati* (1987), *The American Plan* (1990), *The Extra Man* (1992), *Night and Her Stars* (1995), *Hurrah at Last* (1999), and *The Violet Room* (2003). Greenberg's works are very contemporary and often deal with the mores of young urbans in a tragicomic manner.

TALE OF THE ALLERGIST'S WIFE, THE (2000), a comedy by Charles *Busch. [*Ethel Barrymore Theatre, 777 perf.] Upper-class New Yorker Marjorie Taub (Linda *Lavin), a failed novelist and frequent patron of the arts, is in deep depression until her old friend Lee Green (Michele Lee) comes into her life. The globe-trotting, influential Lee is everything Marjorie is not, and her company revitalizes her. But neither Marjorie's allergist husband, Ira (Tony *Roberts), her mother (Shirl Bernheim), nor anyone else has actually seen Lee, and they suspect she is a figment of Marjorie's imagination. But it turns out Lee is more than real, and her manipulation of the Taubs' money and even their sex life has a positive effect. The comedy was so popular Off Broadway at the *Manhattan Theatre Club that the company transferred it to Broadway, where it was a popular attraction for two years.

TALIAFERRO, Edith (1893–1958), actress. Born in Richmond, Virginia, the daughter of theatre people, she made her debut at the age of three in *Shore Acres*. She was active on the stage for over forty years, scoring by far her biggest success in 1910 in the title role of *Rebecca of Sunnybrook Farm,* playing it for three years. Her sister Mabel (1887–1979) had an even longer career, making her debut at the age of two in *Blue Jeans* and continuing to act regularly into the 1950s. Her greatest hit was as the dainty acrobat *Polly of the Circus* (1907).

TALLEY'S FOLLY (1980), a play by Lanford *Wilson. [*Brooks Atkinson Theatre, 277 perf.; Pulitzer Prize, NYDCC Award.] After a long absence, the St. Louis accountant Matt Friedman (Judd *Hirsch) comes calling again on Sally Talley (Trish Hawkins) at her rural Missouri home. Her bigoted family has told Matt that since he is a Jew he is not welcome, and one member of the family has even threatened to shoot him. Moreover, they have hinted at some dark secret in Sally's past. After a moonlit night of arguing, joking, and wooing down at the dilapidated Victorian boathouse (the family's folly of the title), Sally confesses to Matt that an earlier disease left her unable to bear children and her former fiancé called the wedding off when he found out. Unconcerned and still in love, Matt asks Sally to elope and she agrees. The *Circle Repertory Company's production of the brief, two-character play was so popular that it moved to Broadway, complete with Marshall W. *Mason's sterling direction of the two players, John Lee *Beatty's rustic setting, and Dennis Parichy's naturalistic lighting. The romantic piece was part of Wilson's trilogy about the Talley family. **THE FIFTH OF JULY** (1978) had been seen earlier at the Circle Theatre Off Broadway, where it ran 158 performances. Many years after the events of *Talley's Folly* and on the same rural homestead live Kenneth Talley Jr. (William Hurt), who lost both legs in Vietnam and now teaches at the high school, and his male lover, Jed (Jeff *Daniels), who is planning and building an elaborate garden on the property. Visiting them for the Fourth of July weekend is Sally (Helen Stenborg), an elderly widow who has returned with Matt's ashes, which she plans to sprinkle in the lake where he once wooed her. Also gathered are some relatives and an odd assortment of friends who while away the day after the holiday with talk, jokes, arguments, and discussions on whether to sell the old house or not. The Chekhovian character study was described by Otis L. *Guernsey Jr. as "a not-very-tightly structured study of human spirit in the aftermath of stress." After the success of *Talley's Folly*, it was revived on Broadway in 1980 and ran for 511 performances. A 2003 Off-Broadway production was also well received. The third play of the trilogy, *A Tale Told* (1981), was not as popular. Showing what occurred in the family home while Matt was courting Sally in *Talley's Folly*, it was seen Off Broadway for 30 performances. Wilson later revised the script and it was produced as *Talley & Son* in 1985.

TAMIRIS, Helen [née Becker] (1905–66), choreographer. The native New Yorker studied with Michael Fokine, danced for the Metropolitan Opera, and founded her own company before coming to the Broadway stage late in her career. She received recognition with her "Currier and Ives Ballet" in *Up in Central Park* (1945), followed by such musicals as *Show Boat* (1946), *Annie Get Your Gun* (1946), *Park Avenue* (1946), *Inside U. S. A.* (1948), *Touch and Go* (1949), *Flahooley* (1951), *Fanny* (1954), and *Plain and Fancy* (1955).

TAMING OF THE SHREW, THE. Initially offered in Garrick's version, *Catherine and Petruchio*, at Philadelphia's *Southwark Theatre in 1766 with Miss *Cheer and the younger *Hallam in the title roles, *Shakespeare's comedy continued to be produced in this and similar versions, and usually with similar titles, for over a hundred years. Later casts included Mrs. Mason and Thomas Abthorpe *Cooper, Mrs. Darley and William *Macready, Mrs. Sharpe and William B. *Wood, and Ada Clifton and Edwin *Booth. Augustin *Daly presented the first more or less faithful version, under its correct title, in 1887 with John *Drew and Ada *Rehan in the leading roles. He offered the play as high comedy, not farce, and mounted it with sets of carefully painted realism and opulence. Julia *Marlowe and E. H. *Sothern and Alfred *Lunt and Lynn *Fontanne were later hailed as the dueling lovers. The great American musical *Kiss Me, Kate* (1948) was derived from the comedy, offering brief snatches of it as well as using lines in its lyrics, especially its finale, but framing it as a play within a play and setting the frame, which told a similar story, in modern times. Alfred *Drake and Patricia Morison were the original leads. More recent productions of Shakespeare's original must deal with the antifeminist tone of the comedy, and many stagings tend to get gimmicky to avoid modern parallels, such as a popular 1990 mounting in Central Park with Morgan *Freeman and Tracey Ullman that was set in the Wild West.

TAMMANY; or, The Indian Chief (1794), a musical by Mrs. [Anne Kemble] Hatton (book), James Hewitt (music). [*John Street Theatre, in repertory.] The Indian Chief Tammany (John *Hodgkinson) loves an Indian maiden (Mrs. Hodgkinson). After she is kidnapped by the invading Spaniards led by Ferdinand (John *Martin), Tammany rescues her. Pursued by the Spaniards, they take refuge in a cabin, which the Spaniards set afire, killing the lovers. The earliest produced stage work about Native Americans, it reached the boards at the time of widespread sympathy for the French Revolution. According to George *Odell, "The piece was consequently turned into a symbol of republicanism, and as such was patronised by the hot-heads of New York, to the utter rout of the aristocrats." Hatton (1757?–96?) was the sister of the famous English performers John Philip Kemble and Mrs. Siddons. She was also the official poet of New York's Tammany Society. James Hewitt (1770–1827) was a violinist, composer, conductor of the orchestras at the John Street Theatre and later at the *Park Theatre, and in later years one of the first important music publishers in America.

TAMS-WITMARK. See Aborn, Milton.

TANDY, Jessica (1909–94), actress. The slim, sharp-voiced leading lady was born in England and first appeared on Broadway in *The Matriarch* (1930). She made only occasional New York appearances thereafter until she won wide acclaim for her performance as Blanche DuBois in *A *Streetcar Named Desire* (1947). Among her subsequent roles were the suicidal divorcée *Hilda Crane* (1950), the loving wife Agnes in *The *Fourposter* (1951), the shy Mary Doyle courted by the Devil in *Madam, Will You Walk?* (1953), the troubled wife Agnes in *A *Delicate Balance* (1966), the card-playing senior citizen Fonsia Dorsey in *The *Gin Game* (1977), the elderly backwoods widow Annie Nations in *Foxfire* (1982), and the liberal Lady Elizabeth Milne in *The Petition* (1984). *Variety* wrote of her performance in *Foxfire*, "Everything about the character, her confusion, simplicity, love of her husband and son, pride in her offstage grandchildren, is played with crystalline expressiveness and excitingly precise detail." Tandy appeared with her husband, Hume *Cronyn, in the last six plays. The couple performed regularly at major regional playhouses, most notably the *Guthrie Theatre, where she assumed such diverse roles as Queen Gertrude, Madam Ranevskaya, and Linda in *Death of a Salesman.

TANGUAY, Eva (1878–1947), singer. The highest-paid performer in the heyday of vaudeville, she was known as the "I Don't Care Girl," after her most famous song. Born in Marbleton, Quebec, Canada, she appeared in stock and in Broadway plays before turning to two-a-day in the early 1900s. She was a hoydenish, frizzy-haired blonde, celebrated for her animated delivery and her outlandish, often wildly feathered costumes. Although Percy *Hammond once compared her brassy singing to "the wail of the prehistoric diplodocus," her public clamored for more. Tanguay's popularity was such that E. F. *Albee and B. F. *Keith were rarely able to restrain her from singing risqué songs that other stars could not get away with. Her numbers had such titles as "It's Been Done Before but Never the Way I Do It," "Go as Far as You Like," and "I Want Somebody to Go

Wild with Me." When vaudeville died in the 1930s she retired and lived a virtual recluse, all but blind by the time she died in obscurity.

TARKINGTON, [Newton] **Booth** (1869–1946), playwright. The famed Indiana novelist first achieved theatrical success when he dramatized his novel *Monsieur Beaucaire* (often known simply as *Beaucaire*) with Evelyn Greenleaf *Sutherland in 1901. With Harry Leon *Wilson he wrote *The *Man from Home* (1908) and *Cameo Kirby* (1909), and for Otis *Skinner he wrote *Mister Antonio* (1916). Tarkington's other collaborations included *The Country Cousin* (1917) and *Tweedles* (1923), while on his own he penned *Clarence* (1919), *Intimate Strangers* (1921), and *Colonel Satan* (1931). Several of his novels were dramatized by others, including *Seventeen* (1918), *Penrod* (1918), and *The Plutocrat* (1930). Tarkington was much admired for his warm, homey humor, but like his novels, there was an underlying melancholy present as well. Biography: *Gentleman from Indiana*, J. Woodress, 1955.

TAVERN, THE (1920), a play by George M. *Cohan. [Cohan Theatre, 252 perf.] The quiet of a small country inn is disrupted by the arrival of several people who report that bandits are active at a nearby crossroads. The arrivals include a Vagabond (Arnold *Daly), a Woman (Elsie Rizer), and a Governor (Morgan Wallace) and his family. Both the Woman and the Governor's daughter (Alberta Burton) fall in love with the dashing Vagabond. But the evening becomes increasingly menacing until a sheriff and an attendant from a local asylum come to claim some escapees, including the Vagabond. Producer-author Cohan based his farcical spoof of melodrama on a turgid, seriously conceived play by Cora Dick Gantt, to whom he gave credit in early playbills. Alexander *Woollcott noted, "Something of the still echoing laughter started by the hermit in 'Seven Keys to Baldpate' is recalled by the fun he brings to 'The Tavern.'" Cohan assumed the leading role in several revivals, and the piece continued for decades to find some favor in summer stock and with amateur groups.

TAYLEURE, Clifton W. See *East Lynne.*

TAYLOR, Charles A[lonzo] (1864?–1942), producer and playwright. Born in South Hadley, Massachusetts, he is said to have run away from home after reading about the life of P. T. Barnum. Taylor tried a number of odd jobs before writing his first play. Within a short time he was a successful turn-of-the-century producer and author of cheap touring blood-and-thunder melodramas, many of which were written for his wife, Laurette *Taylor. His titles included *The Escape from Chinatown, Escape from the

Harem, *From Rags to Riches*, and *Stolen by Gypsies*. Biography: *Blood and Thunder*, Dwight Taylor, 1962.

TAYLOR, [Joseph] Deems (1885–1966), composer and critic. The distinguished native New Yorker was known to playgoers for his score to the musical *The Echo* (1910), as well as his incidental music to such works as *Liliom* (1921), The *Adding Machine* (1922), and *Beggar on Horseback* (1924). He also wrote operas, including *Peter Ibbetson*, which were commissioned by the Metropolitan Opera. Taylor was the author of many books on music and the other arts.

TAYLOR, Laurette [née Loretta Cooney] (1884–1946), actress. One of the greatest, yet, in a way, most tragic of all American performers, she was born in New York and began her theatrical career as a child in vaudeville, where she was billed as "La Belle Laurette." She later played many years in various stock companies as well as touring in plays by her first husband, Charles A. *Taylor, before her first success as the Hawaiian princess Luana in The *Bird of Paradise* (1912). Even greater acclaim fell to her for her winsome performance in the title role of *Peg o' My Heart* (1912), written by her second husband, J. Hartley *Manners. Afterwards she wasted her enormous, if sometimes undisciplined talent, starring in minor vehicles that Manners wrote for her. Following his death she virtually retired from the stage, becoming reclusive and alcoholic, but returned for occasional revivals. The most notable was a 1938 mounting of *Outward Bound*, in which she played Mrs. Midgit. Her last Broadway appearance was generally acknowledged as not only her greatest but as one of the most memorable performances of her generation: Amanda Wingfield in The *Glass Menagerie* (1945). She continued in the role until shortly before her death. Theresa *Helburn summed up the actress's unique aura, observing, "Her inner radiance fell like moonlight on an audience without the use of any stage tricks that I could detect. In my day there has been no such radiant personality as hers." Taylor was a short, slim redhead with wide hazel-blue eyes and high eyebrows. Biography: *Laurette*, Marguerite Courtney, 1955.

TAYLOR, Mary [Cecilia] (1836–66), actress. "Our Mary," as she was known affectionately to her admirers, was born in New York, where her father played in the *Park Theatre orchestra. She was about two years old when she made her debut at the National Theatre as Cupid in *Zazezizozu* and by the mid-1840s was a popular performer at both the Olympic and the *Bowery Theatres. Her notable roles included Prince Ahmed in *The Magic Arrow* (1844) and Eliza Stebbins in *A *Glance at New York* (1848). She retired at the time of her marriage in 1851. The buxom beauty, who must be considered the Shirley Temple of her day, did not totally delight all her audiences. Joseph N. *Ireland, who saw her, recalled, "Miss Taylor's two great and unfailing charms were her delicious voice and the perfect ease with which she went through every work allotted her. As a vocalist, she was lacking in feeling and expression; as an actress, she had been so thoroughly drilled into pert sauciness of manner in the Olympic burlesques, that it clung to her in every character."

TAYLOR, Raynor (1747?–1825), composer. The English actor-turned-composer came to America in 1792 and settled in Philadelphia where, according to one historian, "As a specialty he cultivated burlesque olios or 'extravaganzas' which came dangerously near being music hall skits." Among his works were his "mock Italian opera," *Capocchio and Dorinna*, and his "comic burletta," *Old Woman of Eighty Three*, both from 1793. His most important theatrical work was his music for the "New Grand Romantick Drama" *The Ethiop; or, The Child of the Desert* (1814). One scholar, Victor Fell Yellin, has written, "His overture to *The Ethiop* is perhaps the finest theatrical overture that has survived from the Federal period."

TAYLOR, Samuel (1912–2000), playwright. Born in Chicago, he was raised in San Francisco and attended the University of California. Taylor was a writer for radio and a play reader before The *Happy Time* (1950), his dramatization of Robert Fontaine's novel, gave him his first success. His other memorable comedies were *Sabrina Fair* (1953), the story of a chauffeur's daughter and a rich man; and The *Pleasure of His Company* (1958), in which a playboy father returns home to complicate his daughter's wedding plans. He also wrote the book for the musical *No Strings* (1962).

TAYLOR, Tom (1817–80), playwright. The English-born journalist-turned-dramatist enjoyed tremendous success in America with both his domestic comedies and exciting melodramas. His biggest hits included the controversial *Still Waters Run Deep* (1855); the comedy *Our American Cousin* (1858), which was being performed when Lincoln was shot; *The Overland Route* (1860); and the early detective play The *Ticket-of-Leave Man* (1863).

TAYMOR, Julie. See *Lion King, The*.

TEA AND SYMPATHY (1953), a play by Robert *Anderson. [*Ethel Barrymore Theatre, 712 perf.] At the New England boys' school he attends, Tom Lee (John Kerr) is considered an "off horse," a boy whose shyness sets him apart from others and even leads to suspicion of homosexuality. Neither the sanctimonious, aggressively masculine headmaster, Bill Reynolds (Leif Erickson), nor Tom's own father, Herbert Lee (John McGovern), helps matters. Tom's problems are brought to a head when he is cast as a girl in a school play. The only person who understands him and is willing to provide more than the customary tea and sympathy is Reynolds's wife, Laura (Deborah Kerr). She berates Reynolds for persecuting Tom to hide his doubts about his own masculinity, then discreetly offers herself to the boy, remarking, "Years from now—when you talk about this—and you will—be kind." Louis *Kronenberger saw the play as "a full-fashioned theatre piece, a thoroughly effective matinee drama," and the *Playwrights' Company production was also one of the first American plays to directly address homophobia and the prejudices that arise from it.

TEA FOR THREE (1918), a comedy by Roi Cooper *Megrue. [Maxine Elliott's Theatre, 300 perf.] Because he knows so many men who find his Wife (Margaret Lawrence) attractive, the Husband (Frederick Perry) becomes unreasonably jealous. Aware of this, the Wife and the Friend (Arthur *Byron) meet for lunch and determine to teach her spouse a lesson. They arrange for the Husband to catch them in a compromising but actually innocent situation. When the Husband demands that he and the Friend draw lots and the loser to commit suicide, the Friend loses. Only after he believes the Friend dead does the Husband recognize the absurdity of his jealousy. When the Friend reappears, very much alive, the Husband invites him to continue his harmless tête-à-têtes with the Wife at will. The *Times*, while acknowledging the *Selwyn and Co. play was not of great substance, concluded, "It has a very rare virtue of doing what it intends with neatness and a certain finality of skill which keeps the attention of the audience throughout and insures an evening of genuine entertainment."

TEAHOUSE OF THE AUGUST MOON, THE (1953), a comedy by John Patrick. [Martin Beck Theatre, 1,027 perf.; Pulitzer Prize, Tony, NYDCC Awards.] Captain Fisby (John Forsythe) is under orders to bring democracy to a postwar Okinawan village, whether the locals want it or not. He attempts to establish some free enterprise, but the only thing the islanders can produce are cricket cages, for which there is no export market. When one wily resident, Sakini (David *Wayne), transforms Fisby's plans for a schoolhouse into a teahouse, where some stronger spirits may also be served, all hell breaks loose. Fisby's frightened,

befuddled superior, Col. Wainwright Purdy III (Paul *Ford), arrests Fisby and orders the teahouse destroyed. The demolition is no sooner complete than Purdy discovers the teahouse has been hailed in Washington as a shining example of "American 'get-up-and-go.'" Luckily, Sakini and his friends have only dismantled and hidden the building materials, so the edifice is hastily reassembled to await the visit of the congressmen and news photographers. Based on a novel by Vern Sneider, this ingratiating comedy, which some felt was really held together by Wayne's superb characterization, nonetheless walked away with all the season's awards. It was the source of the failed musical *Lovely Ladies, Kind Gentlemen* (1970). **John PATRICK** (1907–95) was born in Louisville and attended both Columbia and Harvard. Although he had several other plays produced on Broadway, his only other success was *The Hasty Heart* (1945). Among Patrick's other plays were *The Curious Savage* (1950) and *Everybody Loves Opal* (1961), both of which were very popular with amateur and summer stock groups.

TEAL, Ben (1857?–1917), director. The San Francisco native served an apprenticeship in his home town as actor and assistant director under young David *Belasco. In 1889 he wrote *The Great Metropolis* with George H. *Jessop, which he also staged. This was the first play to be produced by A. L. *Erlanger, and shortly thereafter Teal became the head staff director for *Klaw and Erlanger. He staged many of the firm's musical extravaganzas as well as the series of musical comedies the organization produced for the *Rogers brothers. His most memorable nonmusical success was *Ben-Hur* (1899), but he also directed many other works, including *Sweet Nell of Drury Lane* (1900) and *The Wanderer* (1917).

TELLEGEN, Lou (also billed as Lou-Tellegen) [né Isidor Louis Bernard van Dammeler] (1881–1934), actor. The Dutch-born matinee idol played for many seasons on European stages before making his American debut opposite Sarah *Bernhardt on her 1910 tour. He settled permanently in America in 1914, and for the next seven years he played in numerous romantically melodramatic vehicles, often having a hand in their writing. After a career in films, Tellegen made several unsuccessful attempts at a comeback on stage, then committed suicide. Autobiography: *Women Have Been Kind*, 1931.

TEMPEST, Marie [née Mary Susan Etherington] (1864–1942), singer and comedienne. The London-born performer was a West End favorite for over fifty years. A small, lithe, and graceful woman with a cute turned-up nose, she starred in many important late 19th-century English musicals. Her American debut in 1890 was in one of these, *The Red Hussar*. For the next five years she played largely in America, appearing in the American premiere of *Der Vogelhändler*, known here as *The Tyrolean* (1891), and in two comic operas written for her by Reginald *De Koven, *The Fencing Master* (1892) and *The Algerian* (1893). She also toured in several other of her English roles. In 1900 Tempest abandoned the musical stage to concentrate on comedies. Her subsequent American appearances were rare, most notably in *The Marriage of Kitty* (1903) and as Becky Sharp in *Vanity Fair* (1911). Biography: *Marie Tempest*, Hector Bolitho, 1936.

TEMPLETON, Fay (1865–1939), actress and singer. She was one of the most beloved of all American performers, her career spanning sixty-four years from her 1869 appearance as Cupid in vaudeville to her portrayal of Aunt Minnie, the aged dress shop owner, in *Roberta* (1933). She was born in Little Rock, Arkansas, the daughter of a singer and a theatrical manager and editor. Her New York debut was as Puck in Augustin *Daly's 1873 mounting of *A *Midsummer Night's Dream*. Afterwards she rarely left the stage and by the 1880s was featured in a succession of comic operas. Templeton later starred in such musicals as *Hendrik Hudson* (1890) and *Excelsior, Jr.* (1895). She had grown a little plump by the time she added her exuberant clowning and throaty-voiced singing to *Weber and *Fields's burlesques in 1898, remaining with them for five seasons. One of her greatest successes came as Mary in George M. *Cohan's *Forty-five Minutes from Broadway* (1906). Although Templeton ostensibly retired in 1910, she returned on occasion to play in the Weber and Fields 1912 reunion, as Buttercup in several revivals of *H.M.S. Pinafore*, and in vaudeville.

TEN NIGHTS IN A BARROOM (1858), a play by William W. Pratt. [National Theatre, 7 perf.] Joe Morgan, the village drunkard, is encouraged in his boozing and other irresponsible ways by Simon Slade, the evil owner of the Sickle and Sheaf bar. Even the plea of his little daughter, Mary ("Father, dear father, come home"), cannot drag Morgan away for long. In a barroom brawl Mary is accidentally struck by a glass thrown at her father. The shock helps Morgan reform, Slade is killed by his own son, and the village votes to close the saloon. This prohibitionist drama, based on a story by T. S. Arthur, was never popular in major cities, but was second only to *Uncle Tom's Cabin* on rural circuits.

TENT SHOWS. In the early 19th century entertainment in tents began to appear in regions that could not support full-time playhouses. The trend was given widespread popularity when it was taken up by religious groups, including the Millerites in the 1840s and, far more importantly, the Chautauqua Movement in the 1870s and thereafter. The latter interwove vaudeville turns and didactic plays with the group's lectures and preachings. But numerous other troupes, unaffiliated with any religious sect and usually totally secular, toured the country, especially Southern, Midwestern, and Western regions, offering minstrel shows, vaudeville, drama, comedy, and musicals. These groups did not use the circular seating arrangements common to circuses but built stages at one end of the tent and seated audiences in traditional fashion. It was because of their popularity that performers such as Sarah *Bernhardt had no difficulty obtaining tents or audiences when they defied the *Theatrical Syndicate and were denied regular stages. There were as many as four hundred tent companies touring when the practice peaked around 1920. Something of the nature of many of their plays can be deduced from the most popular character in them, a redheaded young country bumpkin named Toby, who seemed stupid and lazy but often proved surprisingly sly.

TENTH MAN, THE (1959), a play by Paddy *Chayefsky. [*Booth Theatre, 623 perf.] About to banish demons from Evelyn Foreman (Risa Schwartz), the granddaughter of one of their members, the old men who belong to a shabby orthodox synagogue find they have only nine worshipers in attendance. Jewish religious law requires a minyan, or quorum of ten. So they convince a clean-cut young man who happens to be passing by to join them. He is Arthur Brooks (Donald Harron), who turns out to be possibly even more troubled than Evelyn. The exorcism expels his devils, but not the girl's. Arthur, however, has fallen in love with Evelyn and believes his love will cure her. Some critics felt the play's ending was contrived, but Brooks *Atkinson noted, "Although 'The Tenth Man' aspires to lofty areas of mysticism, it always has its feet on the ground." A 1989 revival at *Lincoln Center failed to please.

TEN-TWENT'-THIRT'. The name was given to popular-priced theatres and touring companies in the late 19th and very early 20th century. These companies toured small towns and poorer large-city neighborhoods, offering shows for which the best seats were thirty cents and the cheapest were a dime. Many important theatrical figures and ardent playgoers received their first taste of theatre from these outfits, which were also a training ground for future stars.

TERRY, Ellen [Alice] (1848–1928), actress. A highly polished performer whose regal beauty and radiant personality overcame whatever shortcomings she possessed as an actress, she made her American debut in 1883, playing Queen Henrietta opposite Henry *Irving in *Charles I.* Among the other roles she essayed on this and several subsequent tours with Irving were Jeanette in *The Lyons Mail,* Ophelia, Beatrice, Viola, and her most famous portrayal, Portia. William *Winter wrote, "Ellen Terry embodied Portia . . . the essential womanliness of that character was for the first time in the modern theatre adequately interpreted and portrayed." After leaving Irving she later toured, most successfully in 1907 as Lady Cecily Wayneflete in *Captain Brassbound's Conversion.* In after years Terry traveled as a lecturer on Shakespeare. She wrote an autobiography, *The Heart of Ellen Terry* (1928), and, following her death, her correspondence with G. B. *Shaw was published.

TESORI, Jeanine. See *Violet.*

THAT CHAMPIONSHIP SEASON (1972), a play by Jason Miller. [*Public Theatre, 844 perf.; Pulitzer Prize, Tony, NYDCC Awards.] Four former high school basketball players have come to the home of their old coach (Richard A. Dysart) for a reunion. Their championship season would seem to have been but the beginning of successful careers for them, but appearances are deceiving. George Sikowski (Charles *Durning) has become a corrupt but ineffective politician; Tom Daley (Walter McGinn), a cynical alcoholic; Phil Romano (Paul Sorvino), a ruthless, lecherous strip miner and womanizer; and James Daley (Michael McGuire), a failed high school administrator with futile dreams of success in politics. The absence of the fifth player on the team also says something about their victory; he refuses to come because he believes they won the championship unfairly. All the same, the coach manages to summon up memories of their one day of triumph in order to continue on. The *New York Shakespeare Festival production of this mordant, unflinching look at middle-American life boasted a superb cast under the careful direction of A. J. *Antoon. It was so successful Off Broadway that Joe *Papp moved it to Broadway, where it won all the major awards. A 1999 revival by the *Second Stage proved the work to be still very stageworthy. **Jason MILLER** (1940–2001) was born in Scranton, Pennsylvania, and was a film and stage actor as well as a playwright. His only other play to receive a major production was the short-lived *Nobody Hears a Broken Drum* (1970).

THAYER, MRS. [Edward] [née Agnes Diamond] (d. 1873), actress. The English-born performer made her American debut as Mrs. Palmer Fisher in Kentucky theatres in 1820 and shortly thereafter moved to Philadelphia, where she married Thayer. She rarely played New York, but until her retirement in 1865 she was a favorite at Philadelphia's *Chestnut Street and *Arch Street Theatres. Both T. Allston *Brown and her obituaries referred to her as "the Clive of the American stage," and Brown added that she "is the beau ideal of comedy . . . and wears Thalia's mask with infinite glee and grace." Mr. Thayer (1798–1870) was a Bostonian who was said to have been university educated and to have served in the navy and as a lawyer before becoming an actor in 1821. He played opposite his wife with distinction until their retirement.

THEATRE ARTS. A magazine founded in Detroit in 1916 with Sheldon *Cheney as editor, it was first issued as a quarterly. It later became a monthly, edited first by Edith J. R. *Isaacs and then by Rosamund *Gilder. In its heyday it featured erudite yet popular articles on all aspects of theatre and avoided the more gossipy commonplaces of other such magazines. It also regularly offered complete scripts to plays and musicals and superbly reproduced photographs. In 1948 it combined with *The Stage* (a magazine that had grown out of a *Theatre Guild house organ). Publication was discontinued in 1964.

THEATRE COLLECTIONS. Although American collections of theatrical or "performing arts" materials have proliferated in recent years—at least on a major public scale—they appear to have existed for almost as long as the American theatre itself. However, most early collections were those of amateurs. Many of these were dispersed on the deaths of the collectors, but a handful of relatively late ones were bequeathed to public collections that began to take important shape at the beginning of the 20th century. One older, semipublic collection of note is the library at the *Players. By the 1930s between sixty and seventy significant collections were acknowledged. The first major collegiate theatrical collection may well have been that at Harvard, founded in 1901 at the urging of Professor George Pierce *Baker. Developing over the years, it remains probably the most important academic collection. Other important academic collections include the William Seymour Theatre Collection at Princeton, the Hoblitzelle Theatre Arts Library at the University of Texas at Austin, and the Wisconsin Center for Film and Theatre Research at the University of Wisconsin at Madison. By far the greatest collection at a public library is that of the New York Public Library for the Performing Arts at *Lincoln Center. The Library of Congress also has an outstanding collection. An example of a small but nonetheless notable collection is that at the Free Library in Philadelphia. Another outstanding assemblage is the *Shubert Archive, housing the vast collection of the Shubert brothers and located at the *Lyceum Theatre in New York. A 1981 publication, *Theatre and Performing Arts Collections*, edited by Louis A. Rachow, offers detailed discussions of several important collections and a long but necessarily incomplete list of others. Much significant material remains in the hands of private collectors, some of whom have opened their holdings to scholars on a quasi-public basis.

THEATRE COMMUNICATIONS GROUP. Calling itself "the national organization for the nonprofit professional theatre," it was founded in 1961 to serve the needs of the growing regional theatre movement. It assists with casting, job placement, management, and research problems and also issues numerous publications, such as its magazine, *American Theatre* (which concentrates on regional theatre and gives short shrift to Broadway); reissues of out-of-print plays; and other works covering a wide range of theatrical matters.

THEATRE DEVELOPMENT FUND. A nonprofit corporation founded in 1967 "to stimulate the production of worthwhile plays in the commercial theatre." The most visible manifestation of this stimulus is the *TKTS booth in Times Square, at which cut-rate tickets for Broadway and Off-Broadway shows are sold. It also offers a "Theatre Access Program" to help handicapped playgoers obtain transportation and special seating. Finally, the Fund sponsors banquets and lectures that honor theatre artists, such as the annual TDF/Irene *Sharaff Award in costume achievement.

THEATRE GUILD, THE (New York). The most exciting and responsible producing organization of the 1920s and 1930s, it began as an outgrowth of the defunct *Washington Square Players. The group was formally organized in 1919 with a board consisting of, among others, Lawrence *Langner, Philip *Moeller, Rollo *Peters, Lee *Simonson, and Helen *Westley. Later important additions to the board were Dudley *Digges and Theresa *Helburn. The first production was *Bonds of Interest* (1919), but the group's success was signaled by its second mounting, *John Ferguson* (1919). Other early productions included *Jane Clegg* (1920), *Heartbreak House* (1920), *Mr. Pim Passes By* (1921), *Liliom* (1921), *He Who Gets Slapped* (1922), *Back to Methuselah* (1922), and *R. U. R.* (1922), all of which were foreign works. Not until its production of Elmer *Rice's The *Adding Machine* (1923) did the group begin to mount American works as aggressively as it had mounted imported ones. Among its

subsequent productions of note, both American and European, were *Saint Joan* (1923), *The Guardsman* (1924), *They Knew What They Wanted* (1924), The *Garrick Gaieties* (1925), *Ned McCobb's Daughter* (1926), The *Silver Cord* (1926), The *Second Man* (1927), *Porgy* (1927), *Marco Millions* (1928), *Strange Interlude* (1928), *Dynamo* (1929), *Hotel Universe* (1930), *Elizabeth the Queen* (1930), *Mourning Becomes Electra* (1931), *Reunion in Vienna* (1931), *Biography* (1932), *Both Your Houses* (1933), *Ah, Wilderness!* (1933), *Mary of Scotland* (1933), *Days Without End* (1934), *Valley Forge* (1934), *Porgy and Bess* (1935), *End of Summer* (1936), and *Idiot's Delight* (1936). By the mid-1930s political, artistic, and financial disagreements had resulted in the formation of two major breakaway organizations, the *Group Theatre and the *Playwrights' Company. Thereafter, both the Guild's daring and its success waned, although over the next few years it produced The *Philadelphia Story* (1939), The *Time of Your Life* (1939), *There Shall Be No Night* (1940), and The *Pirate* (1942). It was on the verge of financial collapse when the success of *Oklahoma!* (1943) saved it, but it was never again so important a producer. Its later offerings included the *Robeson-*Ferrer *Othello* (1943); *Carousel* (1945); The *Iceman Cometh* (1946); *Come Back, Little Sheba* (1950); and *Sunrise at Campobello* (1958), as well as several other hits. By the 1970s the Guild existed only on paper, its productions so infrequent that most thought the group was gone. Its last official offering was as co-producer of the unsuccessful musical *State Fair* (1996). In its heyday the Guild was the principal producer of such playwrights as George Bernard *Shaw, Eugene *O'Neill, Maxwell *Anderson, and Robert *Sherwood and greatly advanced the careers of such players as Lunt and *Fontanne. Its pioneering subscription plan guaranteed audiences in New York and elsewhere the best in modern theatre, and in turn assured the Guild a loyal, knowledgeable group of playgoers.

THEATRE MAGAZINE. Founded in 1900 as a pictorial quarterly called *Our Players*, it changed its name to *The Theatre* in May of 1901 when it became a monthly edited by Arthur *Hornblow. Subsequently it was known as *Theatre Magazine* or simply *Theatre*. It became the finest of popular monthlies devoted to the theatre, as opposed to the more intellectual *Theatre Arts*, and survived for exactly thirty years, closing after its April 1931 issue.

THEATRE OF ARTS AND LETTERS, THE. An attempt during the 1892–93 season by a group of minor authors, headed by Henry Burton McDowell, to establish subscription audiences in New York, Boston, Washington, and Baltimore and to present plays of literary merit, it folded after its first season.

THEATRE ROW (New York). A group of small theatres on the south side of 42nd Street between Ninth and Tenth Avenues, it was established in the mid-1970s with the loose idea of creating a convenient complex of nonprofit *Off-Broadway (and *Off-Off-Broadway) playhouses. Although the idea of being totally nonprofit has not been adhered to strictly, the playhouses constitute the largest cluster of Off-Broadway theatres in New York and are situated just below the main theatre area. With the redevelopment of the theatre district on 42nd Street, several of the little spaces on Theatre Row were also renovated or are in the process of being redone. Among the current ones are the Acorn, Judith Anderson, Samuel Beckett, Chashama, Harold Clurman, Douglas Fairbanks, John Houseman, Kirk, Lion, Little Shubert, *Manhattan Punch Line, Peter Norton, and *Playwrights Horizons theatres.

THEATRE UNION, THE. A nonprofit producing company formed in 1932 to mount plays of social significance at popular prices, its largely left-wing dramas were offered primarily at the *Civic Repertory Theatre. It disbanded in 1937 following the failure of its last production, John Howard *Lawson's *Marching Song.*

THEATRE WORLD. An annual survey of plays produced in New York and elsewhere, it was first issued for the 1944–45 season with Daniel Blum as the original editor. Since his death, John Willis, who was his assistant, has been editor. Unlike the *Best Play* series, it does not offer synopses of plots or detailed excerpts from any works. Instead it provides at least one photograph of each major production. It also features biographies and has continued to present useful obituaries, a feature *Best Plays* unfortunately has long since dropped. Some librarians suggest it is less unwieldy and therefore easier to use than *Best Plays*, even if in some respects it is not as thorough. Since its beginning, the publication has given out Theatre World Awards each season, honoring a handful of actors making impressive New York debuts.

THEATREWORKS/USA (New York). Although headquartered in Manhatttan, this company spends most of its time bringing theatre pieces for young people to schools, arts centers, civic centers, and theatres across the nation. Founded in 1961, the company has grown over the years and today is the nation's largest and most prolific professional troupe of its kind. The repertory consists of original theatre pieces and adaptations of classic tales and literature, many of them musicals. Each year the theatre's many companies reach most of the fifty states.

THEATRICAL CLUBS. Social clubs made up of members of the theatre profession or recommended theatre observers have long been popular in London. In New York the first such organization, though not strictly a theatrical one, was the Lotos Club, founded in 1870 in response to a New York mayor's plea for a suitable place to entertain foreign visitors. The club soon broadened its aim "to let in such businessmen as were lovers of literature and art." It has been called "The Godfather of the Arts." Since 1947 it has been housed in a one-time Vanderbilt residence. Many famous theatrical personalities have either been members or have been honored by the organization. The first true theatrical society was the Lambs Club, founded in 1874 by a group of men, most of whom were members of the cast of The *Shaughraun, as a supper club and named it after a similar London society. Until that time most actors had used either Union Square or public bars as meeting places. The club was incorporated in 1877 and moved to its first permanent home shortly thereafter. In short order the members became famous for their camaraderie and conviviality. Their president was known as their Shepherd, their vice president as the Boy. In 1904 the club moved into impressive new quarters on 44th Street just east of Broadway, complete with its own theatre, all designed by Stanford White. One of the group's most famous functions was the *Lambs' Gambols*, in which members performed for no fee and whose proceeds were offered to charity. During the club's heyday, several of these *Gambols* toured the country. Financial difficulties forced the club to sell its building in 1974, and the organization now operates on a more restricted scale.

The most distinguished of American theatrical clubs is the Players, incorporated in 1888. Noteworthy theatrical figures such as Lawrence *Barrett, Edwin *Booth, Augustin *Daly, John *Drew, Joseph *Jefferson, and A. M. *Palmer were among the charter members, but founders also included Mark Twain and General William Tecumseh Sherman, since the group, which was patterned after London's Garrick Club, was aiming to bring together not only professionals but others interested in the theatre. Booth purchased a large house on Gramercy Park, in which he retained a small apartment until his death, and bequeathed the building to the club. He served as its first president and was succeeded by such celebrated men as Jefferson, Drew, Walter *Hampden, Howard *Lindsay, Dennis *King, Alfred *Drake, and José *Ferrer. The club possesses a fine collection of theatrical memorabilia and a superb library, named for Hampden. For many years its members mounted an annual revival of a classic play, which was presented in a regular Broadway house. Although that policy has been discontinued, the club still offers productions for members on its own small stage and at frequent intervals has black-tie "Pipe Nights" in honor of some celebrated theatrical figure.

The Friars Club was organized in 1904 as the Press Agents' Association, or the National Association of Press Agents, by Charles Emerson Cook, Channing *Pollock, John W. Rumsey, and several other men, and it rapidly became a popular theatrical club, and so changed its name and constitution in 1907. Although the name has no real connection with the theatre, the club has been consistent in its nomenclature, calling its clubhouse a monastery and its chief officer an abbot. Its clubhouses were first situated in the heart of the theatre district, but the last of these was disposed of during the Depression. A new clubhouse was established in 1948, away from the main theatre area, and in 1956 the club moved to its present building on East 55th Street. The organization has regularly mounted celebrated shows known as *Frolics*, giving the proceeds to charity. George M. *Cohan served as abbot for nearly twenty years, while later abbots have included George *Jessel, Milton Berle, Joe E. Lewis, Ed Sullivan, and Frank Sinatra. As the record of leadership indicates, the club has drifted away from primarily legitimate theatre membership. A Los Angeles Friars was organized with permission of the New York club. None of these organizations allowed women at first.

Four women's theatrical clubs were established in Manhattan as well. The Twelfth Night Club was founded in 1891 to provide financial assistance and moral support for actresses. The Professional Women's League, started the following year, also helped actresses. The Charlotte *Cushman Club, started in 1907, and the Rehearsal Club, begun in 1913, provided inexpensive lodgings and home-style food for young actresses. Losses were underwritten by a philanthropic board of directors. The latter club inspired the background for several plays, most notably *Stage Door* (1936). The inflation of the 1970s, combined with a changing canon of conduct, prompted its closing in 1980, but the Cushman Club continued into the 1990s, leaving behind the Charlotte Cushman Foundation that makes theatre-related gifts.

THEATRICAL COMMONWEALTH, THE. This was the name first taken by a group of actors and other theatre figures who banded together in 1805 after William *Dunlap's financial failure and attempted to assure themselves an income. The group apparently fell apart with the resumption of production at the *Park Theatre. In 1812 a group of Philadelphia performers, unhappy with conditions in theatres there, used the name in their attempt to mount their own productions, but they failed. A year later in New York still another band of disgruntled actors, who were displeased with policies at the Park or who could not even get work there, appropriated the term. They took over an old circus building, converted it into a theatre, and began offering their own attractions in the fall of 1813. For a brief time the company's excellent mountings gave the Park serious competition, but the group disbanded in early 1814, shortly after the death of Mrs. Twaits, one of its leading actresses and the wife of its manager.

THEATRICAL SYNDICATE, THE [also known as The Theatrical Trust]. Formed in 1895 at a secret meeting which included A. L. *Erlanger, Charles *Frohman, William *Harris, Al *Hayman, Marc *Klaw, Samuel F. Nixon-Nirdlinger, and Fred *Zimmerman, its ostensible purpose was to bring order to the chaotic booking practices then prevalent in the theatre. Within a short time, however, the group monopolized virtually all major American playhouses and dictated terms to producers, actors, and other theatrical figures. A few stalwart opponents, notably Mr. and Mrs. *Fiske and Sarah *Bernhardt, bucked the group and were often reduced to playing in rundown auditoriums or in tents. David *Belasco later joined the Trust's adversaries. However, despite often violent opposition in the national press, the group maintained a practical stranglehold on the American theatre until its monopoly was broken by the organization built by the *Shubert brothers in the early years of the 20th century. By the time of World War I, the Shuberts had supplanted the Syndicate as the dominant force in American theatre, forming a mini-monopoly of their own.

THERE SHALL BE NO NIGHT (1940), a play by Robert E. *Sherwood. [Alvin Theatre, 181 perf.; Pulitzer Prize.] The Nobel Prize–winning scientist Dr. Kaarlo Valkonen (Alfred *Lunt) and his American-born wife, Miranda (Lynn *Fontanne), are reluctant to believe that the Russians will invade his beloved Finland. Nor can they see much purpose in resistance, should the Russians invade. But when war breaks out and their son, Erik (Montgomery Clift) enters the army, Kaarlo joins the medical corps. He concludes that this war will not be the end of civilization, but rather "the long deferred death rattle of the primordial beast." While many critics felt the acting turned a thin but well-meant play into an exciting evening, John Mason *Brown wrote, "No one can complain about the theatre's being an escapist institution when it conducts a class in current events at once as touching, intelligent and compassionate as *There Shall Be No Night*." After the Russian defeat of the Finns, Sherwood changed the locale of the play to Greece and made the Germans the villains.

THESPIAN ORACLE, THE. The earliest known American periodical devoted to theatre was first published in Philadelphia in January 1798 and seems to have survived only for a single issue. Not until 1805 did two somewhat longer-lived journals appear: *The Theatrical Censor in Philadelphia* and John Howard *Payne's *The Thespian Mirror* in New York.

THEY KNEW WHAT THEY WANTED (1924), a play by Sidney *Howard. [*Garrick Theatre, 192 perf.; Pulitzer Prize.] Tony (Richard *Bennett), an aging Italian winegrower in the California Napa Valley, proposes by letter to a San Francisco waitress, Amy (Pauline *Lord), who waited on him once. Fearing she would consider him too old and too ugly, he sends her a photograph of his hired hand Joe (Glenn *Anders). When Amy arrives at Tony's vineyard, she is shocked to learn the truth and soon finds herself having an affair with Joe before he leaves town. Tony is forgiving, even offering to adopt the baby Amy will have. His goodness melts Amy's disdain, and she agrees to marry him. The *Theatre Guild presentation offered what were generally acknowledged as some of the finest performances of the era. It was adapted into the musical **THE MOST HAPPY FELLA** (1956) by Frank *Loesser, who wrote the book, music, and lyrics. Amy was renamed Rosabella (Jo Sullivan), Robert Weede played Tony, and Art Lund was Joe. The musical struck many critics as a not altogether successful amalgam of musical play, musical comedy, and opera. The most operatic music was given to Tony; Rosabella and Joe were given songs typical of modern operetta or musical play; while the lighter songs were assigned to the secondary, comic roles. Yet the show offered something for everyone, and it has enjoyed many revivals regionally, by opera companies, and on Broadway. *Notable songs*: Big 'D'; Standing on the Corner; The Most Happy Fella; Happy to Make Your Acquaintance; Somebody, Somewhere; Warm All Over; My Heart Is So Full of You.

THEY'RE PLAYING OUR SONG (1979), a musical comedy by Neil *Simon (book), Marvin *Hamlisch (music), Carole Bayer Sager (lyrics). [*Imperial Theatre, 1,082 perf.] Vernon Gersch (Robert Klein), a successful composer, and Sonia Walsk (Lucie Arnaz), an equally successful lyricist, are thrown together for a projected collaboration that turns into a bumpy romance. *Notable songs*: If He Really Knew Me; They're Playing Our Song; Just for Tonight. The musical carried Broadway's slimming process to an almost anorexic extreme with only two principals and a chorus of six who acted as the principals' alter egos. Even the score, of only nine songs (many regularly reprised) was smaller than

customary. The popular show quickly dated and has all but disappeared.

THIRD DEGREE, THE (1909), a play by Charles *Klein. [Hudson Theatre, 168 perf.] A bogus art collector commits suicide after his old, long-married flame refuses to visit him. The woman's alcoholic son, Howard Jeffries Jr. (Wallace *Eddinger), is seen coming from the house, and the police, after a brutal interrogation, force a confession of murder from the innocent young man. His parents, whom he alienated by marrying a poor girl, will not come to his aid, but his loyal wife, Annie (Helen Ware), secures a leading attorney, Richard Brewster (Edmund *Breese), who unearths the suicide note and forces the police to make their error public. As he had with The *Lion and the Mouse, Klein successfully mingled social commentary derived from the muckraking of the time (in this instance the campaign against wanton police brutality) with gripping theatre.

THIRTEENTH CHAIR, THE (1916), a play by Bayard *Veiller. [48th Street Theatre, 328 perf.] Mrs. Crosby (Martha Mayo) is pleased when her son, Will (Calvin Thomas), announces his engagement to Helen O'Neill (Katherine La Salle), although Helen is reluctant to talk about her own mother. Only Edward Wales (S. K. Gardner) expresses any reservations about the betrothal. But the matter is put aside since Mrs. Crosby has engaged a medium, Rosalie La Grange (Margaret *Wycherly), to hold a séance in which it is hoped a murdered friend will identify his murderer. During the séance Wales is stabbed to death, although no knife can be found. Suspicion falls on Helen, especially after it becomes known that she is actually Rosalie's daughter. Rosalie then traps the real murderer in a second séance. Thirty years after its premiere, John *Chapman noted that the play "remains the best of all the shriek-in-the-dark dramas," adding, "Who will ever forget the first spine-curling thrill of seeing that nasty skewer stuck in the ceiling, or the chunk with which it fell down and stuck, quivering, in the tabletop?"

THIS IS THE ARMY. Proceeds from this 1942 revue with an all-soldier cast and with songs by Irving *Berlin went to service charities. *Notable songs*: American Eagles; I Left My Heart at the Stage Door Canteen; I'm Getting Tired So I Can Sleep; This Is the Army, Mr. Jones; Oh, How I Hate to Get Up in the Morning. Berlin himself sang this last song, as he had in a similar all-soldier revue of World War I, *Yip, Yip, Yaphank* (1918), whose score had also included his "Mandy." Other services mounted shows during both wars but without the enormous success of these two army revues.

THOMAS, A[lbert] E[llsworth] (1872–1947), playwright. Born in Chester, Massachusetts, and educated at Brown, he served with several New York newspapers before becoming a dramatist. Thirty of his plays (written alone or with others) were produced, beginning with *Her Husband's Wife* (1910). His longest runs included *Come Out of the Kitchen* (1916), *Just Suppose* (1920), *The Champion* (1921), *The French Doll* (1922), and *No More Ladies* (1934).

THOMAS, Augustus (1857–1934), playwright. Born in St. Louis, he tried the law, railroading, and journalism before writing his first play, *Editha's Burglar* (1889) co-authored by Edgar *Smith. Shortly thereafter, Thomas supplanted Dion *Boucicault as the play doctor and adapter for the *Madison Square Theatre. His first totally original success was *Alabama* (1891), which signaled Thomas's interest in plays based on American themes. Among his more notable achievements were *In Mizzoura* (1893), *Arizona* (1900), *The *Witching Hour* (1907), *As a Man Thinks* (1911), and *The *Copperhead* (1918). Besides these more-or-less realistic dramas, he also wrote several popular comedies, the best of which were *The *Earl of Pawtucket* (1903) and *Mrs. Leffingwell's Boots* (1905). Thomas served as president of the *Society of American Dramatists for many years and after the death of Charles *Frohman became active in the firm that the producer left behind. Not counting his early translations and adaptations, some three dozen of his plays were produced. As a writer he was sometimes criticized for working too hastily and unevenly but was lauded for his determination to make American drama reflect American themes and interests. Autobiography: *The Print of My Remembrance*, 1922.

THOMAS, John Charles (1891?–1960), singer. Although better known for his later career in opera and on radio, the stocky baritone from Meyersdale, Pennsylvania, made his Broadway debut in *The *Passing Show of 1913* and later played leads in *The Peasant Girl* (1915), *Step This Way* (1916), *Her Soldier Boy* (1916), and *The Star Gazer* (1917). After heading a road company of *Maytime*, he scored his biggest hit in *Apple Blossoms* (1919).

THOMASHEFSKY, [Baruch] Boris (1868–1939), actor, producer, and playwright. Born in Kiev, Russia, he came to America with his parents in 1881, after his father was expelled for antigovernment leanings. He worked in a shirt factory before starting out in the budding Yiddish theatre of the time. Within a few years he had developed into a handsome matinee idol. Besides winning fame as a performer, he eventually ran his own theatre, wrote plays, and produced his own shows. He was less

inclined than Jacob *Adler and other contemporaries to the loftiest theatre, often preferring claptrap and romantic operettas. Even as an old man he insisted on playing young lovers. His attempts to perform in English on regular Broadway stages met with no success. Autobiography: *My Life* (in Yiddish), 1937.

THOMPSON, [Henry] Denman (1833–1911), actor and playwright. One of many 19th-century players who made a career largely of a single role, he was born in Beechwood, Pennsylvania, but raised in New England. He performed as a circus acrobat and in stock before creating a vaudeville sketch about a kindly country man named Joshua Whitcomb, whom he first portrayed in the mid-1870s. His success was such that a play, *Joshua Whitcomb* (1878), was written around the character. He toured with it for about a decade. In 1887 he wrote with George W. Ryer *The *Old Homestead* (1887), which told how Josh goes to the big city to save his son. It quickly became one of the most popular plays of its era, and Thompson played it until just before his death. On rare occasions he essayed other parts, sometimes in plays he was credited with writing, but none was the least successful, so he soon returned to playing Josh. He was a stocky, red-haired (if balding), slightly jowly man with a friendly, avuncular face, who performed Josh in baggy pants, an ill-fitting vest, thick glasses, and a large straw hat.

THOMPSON, Ernest. See *On Golden Pond*.

THOMPSON, Fred (1884–1949), playwright. Between 1913 and 1944 the London-born librettist, working alone or with collaborators, wrote some fifty musicals. Most were for the West End, but in the 1920s he had a hand in eleven Broadway offerings, including *Lady, Be Good!* (1924), *Tip-Toes* (1925), *Rio Rita* (1927), *The Five o'Clock Girl* (1927), and *Funny Face* (1927). All but the last were written with Guy *Bolton. Shortly before his death he again worked with Bolton on *Follow the Girls* (1944).

THOMPSON, Lydia (1836–1908), actress. A yellow-haired beauty whose ample proportions pleased an overstuffed era, she caused a sensation in New York in 1868 when she arrived from her native London with her troupe of British blondes to perform a series of burlesque musicals such as *Ixion; or, The Man at the Wheel* and *The Forty Thieves*. The most shapely of the girls, including Thompson, regularly assumed the trouser roles in these offerings, so as to show off their legs. Although the more prudish and finicky critics found some of her entertainments salacious, most observers admired her comic flair and graceful, dainty movements. Her success initiated the rage for extended burlesques that flourished in America until the retirement fifty years later of *Weber and *Fields. Thompson continued to make regular trips between the West End and Broadway, her last American appearance coming in 1894 in *The Crust of Society*. Biography: *Lydia Thompson: Queen of Burlesque*, Kurt Ganzl, 2002.

THOMPSON, Sada (b. 1929), actress. She was born in Des Moines, Iowa, and studied theatre at Carnegie Tech before making her professional debut in 1947 in Massachusetts. Thompson first acted in New York in an Off-Broadway revival of *Under Milkwood* (1953), followed by many other roles in various Manhattan venues. She was praised for her Emilia in *Othello* (1964) and Dorine in *Tartuffe* (1965) but didn't become a name in New York until 1970, with her chilling performance as the bitter Beatrice in The *Effect of Gamma Rays on Man-in-the-Moon Marigolds*. Thompson was similarly lauded for playing three very different sisters and their mother in *Twigs* (1971). Much of the rest of her long career has been in regional theatre.

THOMPSON, Woodman (1889?–1955), designer. The Pittsburgh-born scenic artist created the sets for some seventy shows and is best remembered for his colorful work on Winthrop *Ames's revivals of *Gilbert and Sullivan operettas in the 1920s, including *Iolanthe* (1926) and The *Pirates of Penzance* (1926). However, he also designed other important productions, such as *Beggar on Horseback* (1924), *What Price Glory?* (1924), The *Firebrand* (1924), The *Cocoanuts* (1925), The *Wisdom Tooth* (1926), The *Desert Song* (1926), The *Barretts of Wimpole Street* (1931), Katharine *Cornell's *Romeo and Juliet* (1934), and *The Magnificent Yankee* (1946). Thompson taught set design at Columbia for many years until shortly before his death.

THORNE, Charles R[obert] (1814?–93), actor and manager. The son of a New York merchant, he made his debut at the *Park Theatre in 1829 and continued to perform for fifty years. He was also active in management, on various occasions running not only the Chatham Garden and National Theatre in New York and the *Baldwin Theatre in San Francisco, but touring with his wife, Ann Maria Mestayer Thorne (d. 1881), and his company through South and Central America. For a time he managed a troupe that performed along the Erie Canal. His son was **Charles R[obert] THORNE JR.** (1840–83), who began performing while still a child in his parents' company. On reaching maturity his good looks and dashing personality prompted producers to cast him in revivals in such roles as the detective Hawkshaw

in The *Ticket-of-Leave Man* (1873), Armand in *Camille* (1875), and Raphael in *The Marble Heart* (1877). Among the parts he created on the American stage were the tight-lipped, virtuous Chevalier de Vaudrey in The *Two Orphans* (1874) and John Strebelow in The *Banker's Daughter* (1880). The illness that led to his death forced him to retire while still much in demand.

THOROUGHLY MODERN MILLIE (2002), a musical comedy by Richard Morris (book), Dick Scanlan (book, lyrics), Jeanine *Tesori (music). [*Marquis Theatre, still running; Tony Award.] Would-be flapper Millie Dillmont (Sutton Foster) arrives in Manhattan during the Roaring Twenties with the ambition of getting a secretarial job with a rich, handsome boss whom she will marry. But instead she falls for the penniless Jimmy Smith (Gavin Creel), and after a series of adventures, including the uncovering of a white slave operation run by her landlady Mrs. Meers (Harriet Harris), Millie forsakes her employer Trevor Graydon (Marc Kurdisch) and accepts Jimmy, who turns out to be an heir in disguise. *Notable songs*: Thoroughly Modern Millie; Jimmy; Forget About the Boy. Based on the 1967 film musical, the unpretentious show (originally seen at the *La Jolla Playhouse) recalled the Cinderella musicals of the 1920s. Two original songs from the movie were added to some old favorites (such as "Ah, Sweet Mystery of Life") and to new pastiche numbers by Tesori and Scanlan that cleverly evoked the era. Michael Mayer's ingenious direction and Rob Ashford's spirited choreography were also roundly applauded.

THREE FACES EAST (1918), a play by Anthony Paul Kelly. [Cohan and Harris Theatre, 335 perf.] German espionage headquarters enlists the aid of a beautiful girl known as Fraulein Helene (Violet Heming) to take the place of a murdered Englishwoman. She is to go by U-boat to make contact with the mysterious Franz Boelke (Emmett Corrigan), who hopes to blow up the cabinet during a meeting. The Germans' plans are thwarted, and Boelke is exposed after it is revealed Helene is actually an English counterspy who even finds time for a romantic fling. Co-producer George M. *Cohan's extensive rewriting and swift-paced direction, coupled with wartime prosperity, accounted in large measure for the success of this thriller. The Chicago-born Anthony Paul Kelly (1895–1932) was primarily a screenwriter, whose only other Broadway play was *The Phantom Legion* (1919), another war drama.

THREE MEN ON A HORSE (1935), a farce by John Cecil Holm and George *Abbott. [Playhouse, 835 perf.] Having had a tiff with his wife, Audrey

(Joyce Arling), the meek-mannered greeting-card writer Erwin Trowbridge (William Lynn) finds solace at a bar, where he happens to mention that, while he does not bet, he invariably picks winners at the races. Three small-time racketeers latch on to him and win one race after another. Since Erwin's inspiration comes only when riding on a bus, this means they do a lot of traveling. But after they become doubtful of one of his choices and force him to place a bet, his inspiration deserts him. So do the racketeers. He returns to his wife and to writing corny couplets. Robert *Benchley said the play was "distinctly low in tone, broad in method, and ostensibly mad in design, but there is an underlying comic truth running through it, even in minor roles, which made it consistently funny to me, and sometimes more than funny." One of the best modern American farces, often revived in all venues, it was also the basis for two musicals, *Banjo Eyes* (1941) and *Let It Ride!* (1961). **John Cecil HOLM** (1904–81) was a Philadelphia-born actor, director, and playwright. His biggest success, apart from this play, was his book for the musical *Best Foot Forward* (1941).

THREE MUSKETEERS, THE (1928), an operetta by William Anthony *McGuire (book), Rudolf *Friml (music), P. G. *Wodehouse, Clifford Grey (lyrics). [Lyric Theatre, 319 perf.] With his friends Aramis (Joseph Macaulay), Athos (Douglass R. Dumbrille), and Porthos (Detmar Poppen), the dashing D'Artagnan (Dennis *King) comes to Paris, where he soon falls in love with Constance Bonacieux (Vivienne *Segal). However, when the villainous Richelieu (Reginald Owen) threatens to expose the fact that Queen Anne of France (Yvonne D'Arle) has given some precious jewels to the Duke of Buckingham (John Clark), D'Artagnan makes a hurried trip to England to recover them. Once they are safely in the Queen's hands, he can resume his lovemaking and dueling. *Notable songs*: Ma Belle; March of the Musketeers; My Sword and I; Your Eyes. Friml's last success was sumptuously mounted by Florenz *Ziegfeld, with superb Joseph *Urban settings. It has enjoyed intermittent revivals. A clumsily revised and ineptly mounted 1984 revival was short-lived.

THREE OF US, THE (1906), a play by Rachel *Crothers. [*Madison Square Theatre, 227 perf.] Rhy Macchesney (Carlotta Nillson) and her two younger brothers own "The Three of Us" mine. Rhy's fiancé, Stephen Townley (Frederic Truesdell), learns of an even richer lode and passes on the information to Rhy. The older of Rhy's two brothers, Clem (John Westley), who has no love for mining and wants to go East, overhears the conversation. He sells the scuttlebutt to a speculator,

Louis Berresford (Henry Kolker), who quickly buys the property. For a time Stephen thinks Rhy betrayed him, but he later learns better. Of this, her first success, one critic noted, "Miss Crothers has gone straight ahead without any resort to the commonplace trickery of the stage. Her people have hearts, and she gets to these hearts. They have brains and minds; they act on natural and not fictitious impulse."

THREE TALL WOMEN (1994), a play by Edward *Albee. [Promenade Theatre, 582 perf.; Pulitzer Prize, NYDCC Award.] In a posh bedroom, a perky twenty-six year old girl labeled C (Jordan Baker) and the more cynical, middle-aged B (Marian *Seldes), talk with the aged, slightly dotty A (Myra Carter), to whom the bedroom belongs. But A soon has a stroke and is put to bed, and her look-alike enters, at which point it becomes clear that A, B, and C are the same woman at different epochs in her life. They discuss her first affair; her marrying a tiny, horsey man with a glass eye for his money; and her cold, if dutiful, son. A concludes that life's happiest moment is when you know life is finished. Calling it a "welcome showcase for actresses," *Best Plays* observed, "This is a play not of plot but of nuance, Albee being more interested in how time and experience change our voices." *Three Tall Women* was first seen in Europe and regionally in the States before this Vineyard Theatre presentation Off Broadway.

THREE WISE FOOLS (1918), a play by Austin *Strong. [Criterion Theatre, 316 perf.] Judge James Trumbull (William Ingersoll), Dr. Richard Gaunt (Harry Davenport), and the banker Thomas Findley (Claude Gillingwater) are three middle-aged bachelors who share a Washington Square home. They also share memories of a sweetheart, now dead, who rejected them in favor of a man later convicted of a crime he did not commit. Into their lives comes Miss Fairchild (Helen *Menken), daughter of their old flame. She appears to rejuvenate their humdrum existence until some escaped convicts appear on the scene, and the girl attempts to take the blame for the crime her father supposedly committed. The men are shattered and turn against the girl before Gordon Schuyler (Charles Laite), a nephew of one of the men, sets matters aright. Gordon proposes to Miss Fairchild. After all, he may be wise, but he is no fool. The show opened to divided notices and was ready to close until co-producer John *Golden erected one of Broadway's first huge signs in front of the theatre and turned unsold seats over to *Leblang's Ticket Agency. Within a week or two the show became a sellout. Strong acknowledged that the play was heavily rewritten by co-producer Winchell *Smith.

THREEPENNY OPERA, THE (1928). A modern, markedly satiric redaction of John Gay's *The Beggar's Opera*, it had a libretto by Bertolt *Brecht and music by Kurt *Weill. The story centered on the outlaw Macheath, his wooing of Polly Peachum, his betrayal, near-execution, and reprieve. Originally presented in Berlin in 1928 as *Die Dreigroschenoper*, an adaptation by Gifford Cochran and Jerrold Krimsky failed on Broadway in 1933. A second adaptation, this time by Marc *Blitzstein, was offered Off Broadway at the Theatre de Lys in 1954. When this acclaimed production closed after a limited engagement of 95 performances, the critical cry for its return was such that it was revived six months later at the same theatre and ran for 2,611 performances, an Off-Broadway record at the time. The cast included Lotte *Lenya, Weill's wife, as the prostitute Jenny, in a role she had created in the original German production; as well as Scott Merrill as Macheath; Jo Sullivan as Polly Peachum; and Beatrice *Arthur as Lucy Brown. The action was transferred from the 18th century to Victorian times. This production helped rekindle an interest in the works of both Weill and Brecht. The play's best-known song, "The Ballad of Mack the Knife," remained popular for decades, Weill's curious, jazz-influenced melodies and orchestrations prompting similar instrumentation in later musicals, most notably in *Cabaret*. A third translation, one by Ralph Manheim and John Willett, was offered by the *New York Shakespeare Festival in 1976. A major 1990 revival, in yet another translation, was poorly received.

THREE'S A FAMILY (1943), a comedy by Phoebe and Henry Ephron. [*Longacre Theatre, 497 perf.] After quarreling with her husband, Eugene (Francis de Sales), Kitty Mitchell (Katherine Bard) moves with her new baby into her parents' small apartment. Kitty is barely unpacked when her brother, Archie Whitaker (Edwin Philips), appears with his pregnant wife. Since the Whitakers are already bedding down Mrs. Whitaker's sister and two live-in maids, the place becomes awkwardly crowded. It takes aged Dr. Bartell (William Wadsworth), who is partially blind and totally befuddled (and who has resumed his practice only because of the wartime shortage of doctors), to bring some order out of the chaos. Although most critics dismissed the John *Golden offering as trite and unoriginal, wartime prosperity and the public's search for escape turned it into a major hit. Phoebe [née Wolkind] (1916–71) and Henry Ephron (1912–92) were a New York husband and wife team whose only other stage success was *Take Her, She's Mine* (1961).

THROCKMORTON, Cleon (1897–1965), designer. Born in Atlantic City, he studied at Carnegie Tech and at George Washington University before embarking on a career as a landscape and figure painter. After a few years he turned to the theatre, assisted on the designs for *The *Emperor Jones* (1920), and later created the sets for *All God's Chillun Got Wings* (1924), *S.S. Glencairn* (1924), *In Abraham's Bosom* (1926), *Burlesque* (1927), *Porgy* (1927), *Another Language* (1932), *Alien Corn* (1933), and others. By his retirement in the early 1950s he had designed sets for over 150 plays. Throckmorton also drew up architectural plans for such summer theatres as the Cape Playhouse in Dennis, Massachusetts, and the Westport (Connecticut) Country Playhouse.

THURBER, James. See *Male Animal, The*.

TICKET-OF-LEAVE MAN, THE (1863). Tom *Taylor's English play, about a parolee whose trusting disposition leads to misadventures, was first played in New York in 1863, six months after its London premiere. The play was a huge success, with W. J. *Florence in the principal role of Bob Brierly. Numerous revivals followed for the rest of the century.

TIERNEY, Harry [Austin] (1890–1965), composer. Born into a musical family in Perth Amboy, New Jersey, the composer pursued his studies at the Virgil Conservatory of Music in New York before embarking on a career as a concert pianist. His growing interest in popular music, however, led him to sail for England in 1913. There he worked for a London music publisher, interpolated songs into West End shows, and eventually wrote his first score. Returning to America, he again began by interpolating songs into others' shows. It was then he met and teamed up with lyricist **Joseph McCARTHY** (1885–1943), who was born in Somerville, Massachusetts, and had began interpolating his songs into Broadway shows shortly before World War I. Among his early hits was "You Made Me Love You" (music by Jimmy Monaco), which was introduced by Al *Jolson in *The Honeymoon Express* (1913). In 1918 McCarthy wrote the lyrics to Harry Carroll's melodies for *Oh, Look!* including the still-popular "I'm Always Chasing Rainbows." The first Tierney-McCarthy score heard on Broadway was for the most successful musical up to its day, *Irene* (1919). Six more Broadway shows by the team followed in the 1920s, with the longest runs going to *Kid Boots* (1923) and *Rio Rita* (1927). Their last show was *Cross My Heart* (1928). In the 1930s Tierney composed several operettas, but none reached New York.

TIGER ROSE (1917), a play by Willard *Mack. [*Lyceum Theatre, 384 perf.] Rose Bocion (Lenore

*Ulric) is a French-Canadian "hellcat." She is loved by all the men in the neighborhood, including the moony Pierre Le Bey (Pedro De Cordoba) and the villainous Mountie Constable Devlin (Mack). But she loves only Bruce Norton (Calvin Thomas). When Bruce commits a murder, actually justifiable, he becomes a fugitive, hunted by Devlin, who would use the circumstances to have his way with Rose. She, however, resists, and helps hide Bruce until all the facts can be brought to light. A good, if unexceptional melodrama, the play was made into a long-running hit by producer David *Belasco's spectacular staging, which offered a frightening onstage thunderstorm.

TILLER, John (1852?–1925), choreographer. The famed British dance master was born in Manchester, England, and at an early age established a celebrated dancing school. He sent many bands of "Tiller Girls" to dance in American musicals, especially in the 1910s and 1920s. In these years in particular they specialized in precision routines that many critics dismissed as glorified acrobatics. His girls appeared in the 1922 and 1924 editions of the *Ziegfeld Follies, in *George White's Scandals of 1923, and in several musical comedies produced by Charles *Dillingham. After Tiller's death his associate Mary Read continued his policies.

TILLINGER, John [né Joachim] (b. 1939), director. He was born in Iran, the son of an American engineer stationed there, and studied theatre at the Bristol Old Vic School in London. Tillinger made his New York acting debut in 1966 but later turned to directing and was soon noticed for his productions at the *Long Wharf Theatre. He became known as a New York director with his staging of A. R. *Gurney's The Golden Age (1983), and he would direct several of that playwright's later works. His Manhattan credits include The Lisbon Traviata (1985), The Perfect Party (1986), What the Butler Saw (1989), Lips Together, Teeth Apart (1991), Broken Glass (1994), Sylvia (1995), The Exact Center of the Universe (2000), and Comic Potential (2000). Tillinger is a masterful director of contemporary plays who never imposes a personal stamp on his productions but serves the playwright diligently.

TIME OF THE CUCKOO, THE (1952), a play by Arthur *Laurents. [*Empire Theatre, 263 perf.] A lonely American spinster, Leona Samish (Shirley *Booth), comes to Venice to look at the sights of the Old World and, not incidentally, to look for romance. She finds it with a suave, handsome Italian, Renato de Rossi (Dino Di Luca). But the idyll is shattered when Renato proves both a sponger and a married man, yet Leona returns home with a better sense of herself. Louis *Kronenberger saw this small but delicately made play as "one with shrewd comments and effective scenes, one where, in terms of love, there is much to be said on both sides; or where—in line with Hebbl's requirement for sound drama—all the people seem in the right." A beautifully staged and acted revival at *Lincoln Center in 2000 featured Debra Monk as Leona. Laurents later adapted his play into the musical **DO I HEAR A WALTZ?** (1965), making few changes to the story or characters. Richard *Rodgers (music) and Stephen *Sondheim (lyrics), in their only collaboration together, provided a lovely score, but the tale did not play as well this time around, much of the blame being put on Elizabeth Allen, whose Leona did not compare favorably with Booth's or Katharine *Hepburn's (who had played it in the 1955 film Summertime). The musical managed a run of 220 performances in the 46th Street Theatre; it was Rodgers's only show in the theatre that was later named after him. Notable songs: Do I Hear a Waltz?; Moon in My Window; We're Gonna Be All Right; Someone Like You.

TIME OF YOUR LIFE, THE (1939), a play by William *Saroyan. [*Booth Theatre, 185 perf.; Pulitzer Prize, NYDCC Award.] At a run-down San Francisco bar, the open-hearted, openhanded Joe (Eddie *Dowling) encourages one and all to be their own eccentric selves. He finds employment for a would-be dancer, Harry (Gene Kelly), and fosters the romance between his sidekick Tom (Edward Andrews) and the good-hearted streetwalker Kitty Duval (Julie *Haydon). An old Indian fighter, Kit Carson (Len Doyle), spins wild yarns of his imaginary past and kills the vicious detective Blick (Grover Burgess), who seeks to destroy the serene world of the contented castaways. After a pinball addict, Willie (Will Lee), strikes the jackpot, Joe muses, "In the time of your life, live, so that in that good time there shall be no ugliness or death for yourself or for any life your life touches." John Mason *Brown called the work "at once gleeful and heartbreaking, tender and hilarious, probing and elusive." The *Theatre Guild offering was the first play to win both major drama awards. Revivals have been plentiful, particularly in regional theatres.

TIME, THE PLACE AND THE GIRL, THE (1907), a musical comedy by Will M. *Hough, Frank R. *Adams (book, lyrics), Joe *Howard (music). [*Wallack's Theatre, 32 perf.] After a drunken brawl, Tom Cunningham (George Anderson) and Johnny Hicks (Arthur Deagon) are forced to take refuge in a sanatorium, where Tom discovers an old flame, Margaret Simpson (Violet McMillan), and Johnny finds a new one, Molly Kelly (Elene

Foster). An infectious outbreak forces the authorities to quarantine the sanatorium, and the enforced stay gives Tom and Johnny time to pursue their courtships successfully. *Notable songs*: Blow the Smoke Away; Waning Honeymoon. The musical was a Chicago show that had established a new long-run record of over four hundred performances in that city and had toured the country profitably. Its short New York run typified the city's response to most Midwestern shows.

TIMES, THE; or, Life in New York (1829), a comedy by "a gentleman of this city." [*Park Theatre, in repertory.] This apparently lost play was written as a vehicle for J. H. *Hackett, giving him the popular character of Industrious Doolittle. According to the *Mirror,* the comedy consisted of "a dozen or so of scenes thrown cleverly though loosely together, exhibiting the manners and habits of the worthy inhabitants of this city. . . . There is a pretended English baronet . . . a Frenchman, two Broadway dandies (a black and a white), a plain merchant and his fashionable wife, a talking speculating Yankee, and a brace of young ladies and young gentlemen." George *Odell viewed it as an important precursor to plays such as *A *Glance at New York* and the later *Harrigan and Hart shows, while Arthur *Quinn saw it as foreshadowing *Fashion.* It was, most certainly, in the tradition of *Tom and Jerry,* which had been offered at the same theatre six years earlier.

TIN PAN ALLEY. This term, said to have been coined by composer Monroe H. Rosenfeld, described the cluster of publishing houses on two blocks of 28th Street between Fifth Avenue, Broadway, and Sixth Avenue. Many younger composers, who later became important to the American musical theatre, received their start there, often as song pluggers. Soon the term referred to the music business in general. A not-too-subtle distinction developed between a "Tin Pan Alley composer" and a "Broadway composer." The former largely wrote songs published separately or designed for vaudeville singers, while the latter offered whole scores for musicals. The term Tin Pan Alley remained with music publishing for decades after the center of activity shifted from 28th Street to the Brill Building on upper Broadway.

TINNEY, Frank (1878–1940), comic actor. The diminutive, baby-faced comedian was born in Philadelphia, where he made his first appearance at the age of four, performing in blackface. Although he rarely used a dialect, he continued to employ blackface for much of his career. He became a favorite in vaudeville, where his act consisted of patently corny jokes, confidences to the

audiences, and joking with the conductor. His turn had a carefully contrived looseness and ingenuousness. He also appeared in such musicals as the 1910 and 1913 editions of the *Ziegfeld Follies, *Watch Your Step* (1914), *The Century Girl* (1916), *Tickle Me* (1920), *Daffy Dill* (1922), and the 1923 edition of the *Music Box Revue.* In 1923 he was involved in a notorious scandal and two years later suffered the mental breakdown that prompted his retirement from the stage.

TINY ALICE (1964), a play by Edward *Albee. [Billy Rose Theatre, 167 perf.] The world's richest woman, Miss Alice (Irene *Worth), bequeaths $2 billion to the Catholic Church with the stipulation that the strange lay brother Julian (John *Gielgud) be sent to her home to accept the money. Julian, who confesses he has spent six years in a mental institution, is seduced by Alice, and dies, exclaiming, "God, Alice . . . I accept thy will." Although Albee remarked that the play "is an examination of how much false illusion we need to get through life," most critics were baffled by the work. It provoked acrimonious discussion and still does when the play is revived.

TIP-TOES (1925), a musical comedy by Guy *Bolton, Fred *Thompson (book), George *Gershwin (music), Ira *Gershwin (lyrics). [Liberty Theatre, 194 perf.] When Al (Andrew Tombes) and Hen Kaye (Harry Watson Jr.) of the vaudeville act The Three K's are stranded in Palm Beach with the girl in their act, Tip-Toes (Queenie *Smith), they wangle some money and set Tip-Toes up in local society, where she is wooed and won by a handsome young glue magnate, Steve Burton (Allen *Kearns). *Notable songs*: Looking for a Boy; Sweet and Low-Down; That Certain Feeling; These Charming People; When Do We Dance? Although Ira Gershwin was later to claim this was the first show in which he honed his skills as a lyricist, Alexander *Woollcott concluded, "It was of course [George] Gershwin's evening, so sweet and sassy were the melodies . . . so fresh and unstinted the gay, young blood of his invention."

TIPTON, Jennifer (b. 1937), lighting designer. She was born in Columbus, Ohio, and educated at Connecticut College and Cornell before apprenticing with Thomas *Skelton and making her New York design bow in 1969. Tipton has designed for dance companies, regional theatres, and avant-garde performance pieces. Among her memorable theatre productions are *Our Town* (1969), *The Cherry Orchard* (1977), *The *Pirates of Penzance* (1981), *Sophisticated Ladies* (1981), *Alice in Wonderland* (1982), *Hurlyburly* (1984), *Singin' in the Rain* (1985), *Jerome Robbins' Broadway* (1989), *La Bête*

(1991), *In the Summer House* (1993) The *Hairy Ape* (1997), and *James Joyce's The Dead* (2000).

TITANIC (1997), a musical play by Peter *Stone (book), Maury *Yeston (music, lyrics). [*Lunt-Fontanne Theatre, 804 perf.; Tony Award.] As the world's largest ship crosses the Atlantic in 1912, characters from the staff and passenger list are featured before and during the famous sinking. The more interesting personages included Captain Smith (John Cunningham), ship designer Thomas Andrews (Michael Cerveris), White Star owner J. Bruce Ismay (David Garrison), stoker Frederick Barrett (Brian d'Arcy James), social-climbing second-class passenger Alice Beane (Victoria Clark), and three hopeful Irish immigrants, all named Kate. *Notable songs*: In Every Age; Lady's Maid; The Proposal; Still. The $10 million production (produced by the *Kennedy Center and others) met with lackluster notices but strong word of mouth, and the lack of new and exciting competition helped the musical run over two years, still failing to show a profit.

TIVOLI OPERA HOUSE (San Francisco). Sometime between 1872 and 1875, Joseph Kreling converted an old mansion into a beer garden, offering musical entertainment. The enterprise was so successful that in 1878 he built a larger, more formal café and theatre, changing the name from the Tivoli Beer Garden to the Tivoli Opera House. The main floor, however, remained for many years given over to tables and service of beverages, so technically this could not be considered the first legitimate theatre designed exclusively for the performance of musicals. (That honor belongs to New York's *Casino Theatre.) Nevertheless, for most of its history the Tivoli was the principal producer of musicals west of the Mississippi. It mounted not only East Coast successes but also a number of importations not seen in the East, as well as original musicals. Although some of its artists, such as composer-conductor William *Furst, comedian Edwin Stevens, and soprano Alice *Nielsen, went on to national fame, many favorites, such as Ferris Hartman, Annie Meyers, and Arthur Cunningham remained merely local stars. By the turn of the century the theatre's vogue had passed, and, like so many other houses, it was destroyed in the 1906 fire.

TKTS BOOTH (New York). This is the name given to the box offices set up by the *Theatre Development Fund in a large trailer in Times Square that offer cut-rate tickets to Broadway shows. The arrangement began in 1973 and quickly became a major factor in increasing theatre attendance in New York. Shows generally turn over unsold tickets for sale on the day of the performance. The arrangement is highly reminiscent of that run for many decades by *Leblang's Ticket Office. Some grumbling has surfaced to suggest that the seemingly high prices of contemporary Broadway tickets have purposely been pegged that way with the sale of these lower-priced seats in mind and that by generally lowering prices, especially for balcony seats, the same end could be achieved. However, most producers and theatre owners have been reluctant to argue with success. For example, in the 2002–2003 season, 12.5% of total box office for Broadway and Off Broadway, a total of $63 million, was handled through the TKTS booth. The arrangement, under various names, has spread to theatrical centers in other cities.

TO THE LADIES (1922), a comedy by George S. *Kaufman and Marc *Connelly. [Liberty Theatre, 128 perf.] Leonard Beebe (Otto *Kruger), a salesman for the Kincaid Piano Company, is something of a dreamy visionary, unlike his quiet, down-to-earth wife, Elsie (Helen *Hayes). When Mr. and Mrs. Kincaid (George Howell and Isabel Irving) visit the Beebes, they are most impressed with Elsie, who arranges with Mrs. Kincaid to wangle Leonard a promotion. The plan is to have him speak at a company banquet, but when he becomes tongue-tied, Elsie must make the speech for him. It wins him the promotion. Despite generally welcoming notices, the George C. *Tyler and A. L. *Erlanger production was only a modest success in New York and proved somehow too arcane to have any appeal on the road.

TOBACCO ROAD (1933), a play by Jack Kirkland. [Masque Theatre, 3,182 perf.] The Lesters are a shabby, worthless family of sharecroppers who have lost the land their ancestors had long farmed in a desultory fashion. Jeeter Lester (Henry *Hull) is the shiftless head of the family. He has sold his oldest daughter for seven dollars, and when her husband, Lov Besney (Dean Jagger), comes to complain that she will not consummate the marriage, Jeeter allows his other daughter, Ellie May (Ruth Hunter), to run off with Lov. His son, Dude (Sam Byrd), marries a neighbor who has enough money to let him buy an old car. When Dude's mother, Ada (Margaret *Wycherly), berates her son, he runs her over and kills her. Jeeter seems indifferent to all this, just sitting on his stoop and rubbing dirt with his hand. Based on the novel by Erskine Caldwell, the play was assailed by almost every critic. Richard Lockridge of the *Sun* typified much of the revulsion when he referred to the work as "a play that achieves the repulsive and seldom falls below the faintly sickening." To the surprise of the show-wise, the play became the longest-running drama up to its time. Recent revivals tend to play the old play for laughs. **Jack KIRKLAND** (1902–69) was born in St. Louis and was represented on Broadway as author and/or producer of ten plays. His only other success was *I Must Love Someone* (1939), a fictionalized account of the famous Florodora girls, written with Leyle Georgie.

TOBIN, Genevieve (1899–1995), actress. The native New Yorker began her career in 1912 and within a few seasons was being touted by many critics as a successor to Maude *Adams. Although her career never lived up to its earliest promises, she won praise as the immigrant Patricia O'Day in *Little Old New York* (1920), chorine-turned-star Polly Brown in *Polly Preferred* (1923), Cordelia in *King Lear* (1923), the assertive Nancy Blake in *The Youngest* (1924), and the American tourist Looloo Carroll in *Fifty Million Frenchmen* (1929).

TODAY (1913), a play by George *Broadhurst and Abraham S. Schomer. [48th Street Theatre, 280 perf.] When Frederick Wagner (Edwin Arden) fails in business, his spoiled, spendthrift wife, Lily (Emily *Stevens), cannot accept the fact that she must give up the luxuries she has enjoyed. To ensure that she need not, Lily secretly goes to work in a fashionable brothel. Her husband has become the agent for the landlord who owns the building in which the brothel is located, and when he arrives there on a professional visit he discovers his wife's wiles. A confrontation follows, after which he leaves her. While many critics agreed with Adolph *Klauber of the *Times*, who dismissed the work as "an indecent, vicious play," enough of the playgoing public was titillated to turn the work into a major success.

TODD, Michael [né Avrom Goldbogen] (1907–58), producer. The flamboyant showman was born in Minneapolis and first called attention to himself with his productions at the 1933 Chicago World's Fair. His first Broadway offering, *Call Me Ziggy* (1937), was a three-performance failure, and he did not begin to make a name until his mounting in 1939 of *The Hot Mikado*. Todd enjoyed a long run with *Star and Garter* (1942) and with such subsequent musicals as *Something for the Boys* (1943), *Mexican Hayride* (1944), *Up in Central Park* (1945), *As the Girls Go* (1948), and *Michael Todd's Peep Show* (1950). Most of his musical productions were perceived as glorified burlesque, with an emphasis on scantily clad, beautiful girls and gaudy sets and costumes. Among his nonmusical offerings were *Pick-Up Girl* (1944), Mae *West's vehicle *Catherine Was Great* (1944), and Maurice *Evans's *Hamlet* (1945). Biography: *A Valuable Property*, Michael Todd Jr. and Susan McCarthy Todd, 1983.

TOM AND JERRY; or, Life in London (1823). W. T. Moncrieff's dramatization of Pierce Egan's story was first played at the *Park Theatre in 1823. The play took its leading figures on a tour of the city, interspersed with song and dance. Its popularity gave rise to numerous similar, loosely constructed entertainments, but more importantly, in the opinion of many students, it planted the seeds for later musical comedy and revue.

TOMORROW AND TOMORROW (1931), a play by Philip *Barry. [*Henry Miller Theatre, 206 perf.] Gail (Harvey Stephens) and Eve Redman (Zita Johann) are a childless couple who live in a small American town where Gail's father had founded a college. When the noted Dr. Hay (Herbert Marshall) comes to teach at the school, the college authorities ask the Redmans to house him. Before long, Eve has had not only an affair with the doctor but has borne his child, although she leads Gail to believe the baby is his. Years later, the boy suffers an emotional trauma after an accident, and Eve summons Hay. He manages to cure the boy, something other doctors had failed to do. Hay begs Eve to come with the boy and live with him, but she remains true to her faithful, uncomprehending husband. Burns *Mantle hailed the Gilbert *Miller production as "sensitively and delicately wrought in both character and situation."

TOMORROW THE WORLD (1943), a play by James Gow and Arnaud d'Usseau. [*Ethel Barrymore Theatre, 500 perf.] Emil Bruchner (Skippy Homeier), whose liberal father was killed by the Fascists, is a young boy who was raised and thoroughly indoctrinated into the Nazi philosophy. He is brought to America by his uncle, Michael Frame (Ralph *Bellamy), a university professor. Emil spews hatred, tries naively to spy for the Germans, and in a particularly vicious moment slashes an old family portrait. But Frame, his sister Jessie (Dorothy Sands), and, most of all, a compassionate schoolteacher, Leona Richards (Shirley *Booth), eventually make him see the error of his ways. This was one of the war's more literate propaganda pieces. James Gow (1907–52), who was born in Creston, Iowa, and Arnaud d'Usseau (1916–90), who was born in Los Angeles, were primarily film writers. Their only other stage success was *Deep Are the Roots* (1945).

TONE, Franchot (1905–68), actor. Born in Niagara Falls, New York, the lanky, somewhat swarthy leading man studied at Cornell, then made his professional debut with a stock company in Buffalo. Broadway first saw him in *The Belt* (1927), followed by such major roles as the unhappy publisher Tom Ames in *Hotel Universe* (1930), cowhand Curly McClain in *Green Grow the Lilacs* (1931), aristocrat Will Connelly in *The House of Connelly* (1931), racketeer Harold Goff in *The *Gentle People* (1939), the psychoanalyst Alan Coles in **Oh, Men! Oh, Women!* (1953), and the dissipated young James Tyrone in *A *Moon for the Misbegotten* (1957). He was long popular in films as well.

TONY AWARDS. Officially the Antoinette Perry Awards, they were established by the *American Theatre Wing in 1947, a year after the death of *Perry, and have been offered ever since for "distinguished achievement" in the theatre. There are numerous categories, some of which have changed over the years, and only Broadway productions are considered. Special awards are also given regularly. Apart from the *Pulitzer Prize and the *New York Drama Critics Circle Award for best plays, these are the most respected of all theatrical honors. More so than the other honors, the Tonys carry the most clout at the box office. The televised ceremony itself is often seen as a national advertisement for Broadway, and sometimes nominations are determined with the broadcast in mind. Shows that have closed and cannot benefit from the free advertising, for example, are frequently overlooked, while less-accomplished offerings that are still running are favored. Like all of the major awards, the Tonys have been surrounded by controversy on many occasions. Much of the grumbling is more a matter of money than aesthetics since so much business rides on the Tonys. The awards have even changed the structure of the theatre season, producers all trying to get their productions opening in the late spring right before the nominations are determined. All of the American works that won the Tony for best play and best musical have their own entry. All the winners in these two categories, American or not, are herein listed. 1948: *Mister Roberts*; 1949: *Death of a Salesman, Kiss Me, Kate*; 1950: *The Cocktail Party, South Pacific*; 1951: *The Rose Tattoo, Guys and Dolls*; 1952: *The Fourposter, The King and I*; 1953: *The Crucible, Wonderful Town*; 1954: *The Teahouse of the August Moon, Kismet*; 1955: *The Desperate Hours, The Pajama Game*; 1956: *The Diary of Anne Frank, Damn Yankees*; 1957: *Long Day's Journey into Night, My Fair Lady*; 1958: *Sunrise at Campobello, The Music Man*; 1959: *J. B., Redhead*; 1960: *The Miracle Worker, Fiorello!* and *The Sound of Music* (tie); 1961: *Becket, Bye Bye Birdie*; 1962: *A Man for All Seasons, How to Succeed in Business Without Really Trying*; 1963: *Who's Afraid of Virginia Woolf?, A Funny Thing Happened on the Way to the Forum*; 1964: *Luther, Hello, Dolly!*; 1965: *The Subject Was Roses, Fiddler on the Roof*; 1966: *Marat/Sade, Man of La Mancha*; 1967: *The Homecoming, Cabaret*; 1968: *Rosencrantz and Guildenstern Are Dead, Hallelujah, Baby!*; 1969: *The Great White Hope, 1776*;

1970: *Borstal Boy, Applause*; 1971: *Sleuth, Company*; 1972: *Sticks and Bones, Two Gentlemen of Verona*; 1973: *That Championship Season, A Little Night Music*; 1974: *The River Niger, Raisin*; 1975: *Equus, The Wiz*; 1976: *Travesties, A Chorus Line*; 1977: *The Shadow Box, Annie*; 1978: *Da, Ain't Misbehavin'*; 1979: *The Elephant Man, Sweeney Todd*; 1980: *Children of a Lesser God, Evita*; 1981: *Amadeus, 42nd Street*; 1982: *The Life and Adventures of Nicholas Nickleby, Nine*; 1983: *Torch Song Trilogy, Cats*; 1984: *The Real Thing, La Cage aux Folles*; 1985: *Biloxi Blues, Big River*; 1986: *I'm Not Rappaport, The Mystery of Edwin Drood*; 1987: *Fences, Les Misérables*; 1988: *M. Butterfly, The Phantom of the Opera*; 1989: *The Heidi Chronicles, Jerome Robbins' Broadway*; 1990: *The Grapes of Wrath, City of Angels*; 1991: *Lost in Yonkers, The Will Rogers Follies*; 1992: *Dancing at Lughnasa, Crazy for You*; 1993: *Angels in America (Pt. 1), Kiss of the Spider Woman*; 1994: *Angels in America (Pt. 2), Passion*; 1995: *Love! Valour! Compassion!, Sunset Boulevard*; 1996: *Master Class, Rent*; 1997: *The Last Night of Ballyhoo, Titanic*; 1998: *Art, The Lion King*; 1999: *Side Man, Fosse*; 2000: *Copenhagen, Contact*; 2001: *Proof, The Producers*; 2002: *The Goat, Thoroughly Modern Millie*; 2003: *Take Me Out, Hairspray*.

TONY 'N' TINA'S WEDDING (1988), an interactive comedy by Artificial Intelligence. [Washington Square Church/Carmelita's, approx. 4,650 perf.] The most successful of the *participatory theatre presentations, this "play" allowed the audience to be guests and participants in what Mel *Gussow described as "an intentionally tacky duplication of an Italian-American wedding ceremony" complete with church service and followed by a reception at a nearby restaurant. The Off-Off-Broadway group called Artificial Intelligence scripted the largely improvised event, which most critics and newspapers ignored until it had been running for a few years. Performance schedule was uneven and accurate records were not kept as the little show changed locations, but the nuptial oddity sent dozens of Tonys and Tinas off to wedded bliss for sixteen years.

TOO MANY COOKS (1914), a comedy by Frank *Craven. [39th Street Theatre, 223 perf.] After Alice Cook (Inez Plummer), a pretty Irish stenographer, agrees to marry Albert Bennett (Craven), a genial young clerk, they decide to build a cozy home on a plot Albert has bought with his savings. However, they make one horrendous error: They invite their families and friends to watch the bungalow rise. Alice's mother, father, two aunts, an uncle, two brothers, and two sisters all put in appearances, suggesting ways to change the house plans. So do Albert's uncle and friend. The suggestions lead the young couple into arguments and eventually into breaking off the engagement. As if that is not enough, the carpenters go on strike, so that Albert must finish the shingling alone. With no wife to share his home, he puts the crookedly shingled cottage up for sale. As he is about to leave he looks longingly at a single rose blooming on the small bush Alice had planted. Just then, Alice returns. The pair is reconciled, and they conclude they will live happily ever after with all the comforts of home but with relatives allowed only on rare occasions. Walter Prichard *Eaton noted the William A. *Brady offering was written "in the bald vernacular" and concluded that it "is funny, it is wholesome, it is true—and, best of all, it is unconsciously and thoroughly American." The comedy was the source of the hit 1922 musical *Up She Goes*, which Craven adapted from his own play, with music by the *Irene* team of Joseph *McCarthy and Harry *Tierney, starring Donald *Brian and Gloria Fay.

TOO MUCH JOHNSON (1894), a comedy by William *Gillette. [Standard Theatre, 216 perf.] Whenever the philandering Augustus Billings (Gillette) entertains his French mistress in New York, he tells his wife (Maud Haslam) and his suspicious mother-in-law, Mrs. S. Upton Batterson (Kate Meek), that he is going to inspect his plantation in Cuba. Of course, he has no plantation, but the ladies insist on joining him on one of his trips. They also find an incriminating letter in his coat pocket. Luckily, it's addressed to one Mr. Johnson, who, Billings quickly remarks, is his overseer. In Cuba, Billings manages to "borrow" a friend's hacienda, and the party even meets a cantankerous man named Johnson (Ralph Delmore). By the final curtain Billings has squirmed his way out of a series of uncomfortable situations. Based on a French play, *La Plantation Thomasin*, the Charles *Frohman production was one of Gillette's biggest hits and one of his few attempts at comedy.

TOODLES, THE (1848), a play by William E. *Burton. [Burton's Chambers Street Theatre, in repertory.] Timothy Toodle (Burton) is a lovable, easy-going man with a peculiar wife (Mrs. *Vernon). She has a penchant for buying useless things at auctions in the belief that she will sometime find use for them. For example, she brings home a doorplate with the name of Thompson on it, suggesting that if they ever have a daughter and if that daughter marries a man named Thompson and he spells his name with a "p," then the doorplate will come in handy. Determined to put an end to such wasteful expense, Toodle attends an auction and brings home a coffin, in case his wife dies before he does. Based on a sentimental old play, *The Broken Heart; or, the Farmer's Daughter*, it took that piece's comic relief for its main theme

and made the principal story of the old play its subplot. It gave Burton one of his greatest successes, which he continued to play in until his death. Other comedians also found applause with the work, notably John Sleeper *Clarke.

TOPDOG/UNDERDOG (2001), a play by Suzan-Lori Parks. [*Public Theatre, 145 perf.; Pulitzer Prize.] The two African-American brothers Lincoln (Jeffrey Wright) and Booth (Don Cheadle), so named as a joke by their parents, have always been rivals. The younger Booth admires and is jealous of his brother, once a three-card monte hustler but now a freak attraction at a carnival where patrons pay to "shoot" him as he sits dressed as Abraham Lincoln. When Booth tries to imitate Lincoln's monte techniques, tensions mount and Booth ends up shooting his brother for real. Because of some enthusiastic reviews for the lively two-hander and high praise for Wright's performance, producer George C. *Wolfe transferred *Topog/Underdog* to Broadway's *Ambassador Theatre the next year. The African-American playwright **Suzan-Lori PARKS** (b. 1963) was educated at Mount Holyoke College and was first produced in New York in 1989. She has consistently presented new works that explore the black experience, usually in exaggerated allegory form. Her other plays include *The America Play* (1994), *Venus* (1996), and two works that use *The Scarlet Letter* as a reference point for contemporary tales: *In the Blood* (1999) and *Fucking A* (2003).

TOPSY AND EVA (1924), a musical comedy by Catherine Chisholm *Cushing (book), Duncan Sisters (music, lyrics). [Sam H. Harris Theatre, 165 perf.] This lighthearted song and dance version of *Uncle Tom's Cabin*, with the emphasis, as the title suggested, on Topsy (Rosetta Duncan) and Eva (Vivian Duncan), opened in Chicago, where it was a surprise hit and ran forty-six weeks before coming to New York. Despite its relatively short New York run it was exceptionally popular on the road and toured for much of the rest of the decade. The sisters revived it as late as the 1940s. Its hit song was "Rememb'ring." **Rosetta** (1900–59) and **Vivian DUNCAN** (1902–86), a sister singing and dancing act, were Los Angeles natives who were given their start in vaudeville by Gus *Edwards. They played two-a-day for many years and appeared in several Broadway shows but are best remembered for *Topsy and Eva*.

TORCH-BEARERS, THE (1922), a comedy by George *Kelly. [48th Street Theatre, 135 perf.] Paula Ritter (Mary *Boland) is a devotee of the rising little theatre movement, and so is delighted to be cast at the last minute to replace another amateur whose husband died of a heart attack after watching his wife try to act. Paula's own husband, Fred (Arthur Shaw), is none too happy with his wife's obsession. Nor does he care for the director, a haughty, dictatorial, frustrated actress named Mrs. J. Duro Pompinelli (Alison Skipworth), who has never gotten over the small success of her book, *Technique in Acting as Distinguished from Method*. During the performance everything goes wrong, so Paula reluctantly agrees to Fred's request that she abandon the stage. Stark *Young called it a play "of real wit," prophesying, "The chances are that Mr. Kelly, if he remembers what is joyous, will be our best writer of comedy." Despite its merits and excellent notices, the play had only a modest run, but it long remained a favorite of the very groups it satirized. A well-received Off-Off-Broadway revival in 2000 featured Marian *Seldes, Faith *Prince, and Joan Copeland.

TORCH SONG TRILOGY (1982), three one-act plays by Harvey Fierstein. [Actors Playhouse, 1,222 perf.; Tony Award.] In *The International Stud*, Arnold (Fierstein), a female impersonator, thinks that with Ed (Joel Crothers), a man he picks up in a gay bar, he may have found the love he has been looking for. But in *Fugue in a Nursery*, Ed is now engaged to Laurel (Diane Tarleton), who invites Arnold and his new lover, Alan (Paul Joynt), to Ed's farm, where things do not quite work out. Several years later, in *Widows and Children First!*, Ed's marriage is on the rocks and he seeks to reestablish his relationship with Arnold, who, in turn, has taken in the gay teenager David (Matthew *Broderick), whom he plans to adopt. The arrival of Arnold's mother, Mrs. Beckoff (Estelle Getty), complicates matters for everyone, but by the end each has learned to accept the others. Each of the plays had been previously seen Off Off Broadway. Put together they made for a compassionate, if darkly funny, view of the homosexual lifestyle. The long evening was successful enough to transfer to Broadway's Little Theatre for a very long run. **Harvey FIERSTEIN** (b. 1954), a native of Brooklyn, became a female impersonator at fifteen, then studied at the Pratt Institute. He made his legit acting debut in an Andy Warhol play in 1971. He also wrote *Spookhouse* (1984), *Safe Sex* (1987), and the musicals *La Cage aux Folles* (1983) and *Legs Diamond* (1988). Fierstein has acted in plays by other writers as well, most memorably in *The Haunted Host* (1991) and *Hairspray* (2002).

TORN, Rip [né Elmore Rual Torn] (b. 1931), actor and director. The intense, unpredictable actor has always managed to find bold and unusual parts and has also directed experimental theatre projects. He was born in Temple, Texas, and educated at Texas A. and M. College and the University of Texas before working as an oil field roustabout and architectural draftsman. Torn eventually went to New York, where he studied acting with Sanford *Meisner and Lee *Strasberg, and made an auspicious Broadway debut in 1956, as a replacement for Brick in *Cat on a Hot Tin Roof*. He shone in another Tennessee *Williams role, the dangerous young Tom in *Sweet Bird of Youth* (1959), eventually taking over the lead role of drifter Chance Wayne. Among his other memorable stage performances were the farmer Eben Cabot in love with his young stepmother in *Desire under the Elms* (1963), the small-town bigot Lyle Briten in *Blues for Mister Charlie* (1964), a gritty Tom in *The *Glass Menagerie* (1975), the Howard Hughes–like recluse Henry Hackamore in *Seduced* (1979), and the failing businessman Will Kidder in *The *Young Man from Atlanta* (1995). He sometimes performed with his actress-wife, Geraldine *Page.

TORTESA, THE USURER (1839), a play by Nathaniel Parker *Willis. [National Theatre, 6 perf.] The usurer Tortesa (James W. *Wallack) so loves Isabella (Virginia Monier), the daughter of Count Falcone (Mr. T. Matthews), that he buys up and gives Falcone all the mortgages on the Count's lands. But Isabella loves a young painter, Angelo (E. S. Conner), and plays dead rather than marry Tortesa. Impressed, Tortesa relinquishes his claim on her, stating, "She's taught me that the high-born may be true." Although George *Odell dismissed this blank-verse as "a very silly tragicomedy," it remained popular for about a decade.

TOUCH OF THE POET, A (1958), a play by Eugene *O'Neill. [*Helen Hayes Theatre, 284 perf.] Cornelius Melody (Eric Portman), who keeps an inn near Boston, is a tyrannical, boozy Irishman living off memories of his past importance. As a young soldier he fought with Wellington at Waterloo. "Con" dominates his submissive wife, Nora (Helen *Hayes), and even his more forthright, aggressive daughter, Sara (Kim *Stanley), and he regards his neighboring Yankees as beneath contempt. So when Sara falls in love with Simon, the son of a rich New Englander, and the family rejects Sara as a possible suitor, Con sets out to avenge the slight with a duel. Instead, he is beaten and humiliated. Returning home, he shoots his beloved old mare, thereby severing a last small link with his past. Destined as part of the eleven-play cycle that O'Neill never finished, the play "has substance, a point of view, human principle and theatre," as Brooks *Atkinson observed. A 1977 Broadway revival with Jason *Robards, Geraldine *Fitzgerald, and Kathryn Walker, directed by O'Neill specialist José *Quintero, managed a run of 141 performances.

TOWER BEYOND TRAGEDY, THE (1950), a poetic drama by Robinson Jeffers. [ANTA Theatre, 32 perf.] Clytemnestra (Judith *Anderson) has long hated her husband, Agamemnon (Frederic Tozere), and while he is away at war she falls in love with Aegisthus (Philip Ruston). On Agamemnon's return, Clytemnestra and Aegisthus murder him. She, in turn, is slain by her son, Orestes (Alfred Ryder), to avenge his father's death. The play, which was based on Aeschylus's *Oresteia* and Jeffers's own poem on the Electra legend, had first been staged a year earlier in California. Despite many glowing notices, it failed to find a public. The famed American poet [John] **Robinson JEFFERS** (1887–1962), who was born in Pittsburgh, was best known to playgoers for his modern translation of *Medea*, which Judith *Anderson performed to great acclaim in 1947. In 1954 Washington's *Arena Stage mounted his version of the Phaedra story, *The Cretan Woman*. Biography: *The Stone Mason of Far House*, Melba Bennett, 1966.

TOWSE, J[ohn] Rankin (1854–1933), critic. Born in Streatham, England, and educated at Cambridge, he began his theatrical career as a spear-carrier in London productions, then came to America in 1869, taking a job with the New York *Evening Post*. Five years later he was made the paper's drama critic, a position he held for fifty-four years until his retirement in 1927. Like his close friend William *Winter, he was an archconservative and highly pedantic. Although Towse leaned over backwards to be fair, it became clear with the passing years that he found less and less sympathy with modern theatre. On his retirement he issued a violent denunciation of what he considered the theatre's descent into immorality and cheapness. His memoirs, *Sixty Years of the Theatre* (1916), extolled the palmy days of Edwin *Booth and the *Wallacks.

TOYS IN THE ATTIC (1960), a play by Lillian *Hellman. [Hudson Theatre, 556 perf.; NYDCC Award.] Carrie (Maureen *Stapleton) and Anna Berniers (Anne Revere) are two spinsters who live in genteel poverty and who have few pleasures in life except their ne'er-do-well brother, Julian (Jason *Robards). When he marries and seems on the verge of making an illicit fortune, the sisters become frightened of losing him. The battle between the sisters and Julian's wife, Lily (Rochelle Oliver), drives the sisters apart, destroys Julian's scheme to get rich, and crushes Julian as well. No one gives any credence to his promise to start again. The Kermit *Bloomgarden production was Hellman's last hit before she abandoned the theatre. It displayed her knife-sharp insight into human rapacity and sexual longing.

TRACY, Lee (1898–1968), actor. The exuberant, redheaded performer was born in Atlanta, Georgia, and made his debut as Joe in *The *Show-Off* (1924). He is best remembered for two early roles: Roy Lane, the spunky hoofer, in *Broadway* (1926); and Hildy Johnson, the even spunkier newsman, in *The *Front Page* (1928). His last important assignment was as Arthur Hockstader, the sharp-tongued ex-President, in *The *Best Man* (1960).

TRACY, Spencer. See *Last Mile, The*.

TRAVELING SALESMAN, THE (1908), a comedy by James *Forbes. [Liberty Theatre, 280 perf.] Beth Elliott (Gertrude Coghlan) runs the depot at Grand Crossing. Although the local citizenry thinks she is "jest as smart as a steel trap," she is naive enough to hope that no one will bid against her when her family property is auctioned off for back taxes. Bob Blake (Frank *McIntyre), a traveling salesman, arrives in town and is immediately taken with Beth, and she with him. But a group of sharpies who are determined to buy the Elliott property make it appear that Bob has cheated Beth out of the land. By the time she realizes Bob is innocent, she has accepted the crooks' check, thereby apparently sealing a deal. However, when Bob learns that no married woman in the state can execute a deed without her husband's signature, an obvious and happy way out is found. Much of the earlier acts of the play were devoted to vignettes of contemporary small-town life and developed the plot at what today would seem an unacceptably leisurely pace. Yet the charm of the piece and the excellent Henry B. *Harris production made it one of the major successes of its time.

TREADWELL, Sophie. See *Machinal*.

TREASURE ISLAND (1915), a play by Jules Eckert *Goodman. [Punch and Judy Theatre, 205 perf.] Young Jim Hawkins (Mrs. Charles Hopkins) finds himself sailing to a faraway island in search of buried treasure. Mounted at a bandbox theatre as a Christmas treat for children, the adaptation of Robert Louis Stevenson's famous novel proved a huge success.

TREE, Ellen (1805–80), actress. The romantic English leading lady made her American debut at the *Park Theatre in 1836 as Rosalind. Many considered her a great beauty, albeit some, such as *Ireland, complained of her elongated neck and slightly stooped shoulders. Similarly, her acting divided critics, many considering her art not yet fully developed. Nevertheless, in the three years she remained here she proved a major attraction for playgoers as Lady Teazle, Letitia Hardy in *The*

Lyons Mail, Julia in *The *Hunchback*, and Marianna in *The Wife*. After marrying Charles *Kean she made two later visits, in 1845 and 1864. Whatever beauty she had possessed had faded, but her acting had noticeably matured. On these returns she offered her Beatrice, Ophelia, and Portia, as well as leading roles in numerous popular contemporary pieces.

TREE, Herbert Beerbohm [né Herbert Draper Beerbohm] (1853–1917), actor and manager. The esteemed English thespian made several American visits, the first in 1895 and the last in 1916. However, he never won the admiration accorded him in London. Here his productions were seen as overblown and his acting as shallow. Tree thought Americans and especially American drama critics savagely rude, and he despised American unions. With something of the wit of his brother, Max, he remarked, "The man of property is subject to the will of the property-man." Biography: *Beerbohm Tree: His Life and Laughter*, Hesketh Pearson, 1956.

TREE GROWS IN BROOKLYN, A (1951), a musical play by Betty Smith, George *Abbott (book), Arthur *Schwartz (music), Dorothy *Fields (lyrics). [Alvin Theatre, 267 perf.] Handsome Johnny Nolan (Johnny Johnston) is a ne'er-do-well whose marriage to sweet, adoring Katie (Marcia Van Dyke) can only come to an unhappy end. Yet the shiftless Johnny makes an understanding father to his troubled teenage daughter, Francie (Nomi Mitty). At the same time, Aunt Cissy (Shirley *Booth) keeps dreaming of her long-lost love, a gentleman of singular refinement even if he was a bigamist. But when she encounters him again after many years, her dreams, too, are shattered. *Notable songs*: Make the Man Love Me; He Had Refinement; I'll Buy You a Star; I'm Like a New Broom; Look Who's Dancing. The musical version of Smith's best-selling novel had uncommonly fine songs and a brilliant, wistfully comic performance by Booth, who stopped the show nightly with "He Had Refinement." But it also had a long and unnecessary ballet and the misfortune to open in a season of stronger than usual competition. The musical has become a cult favorite, particularly for its score.

TRENTINI, Emma (1881?–1959), singer and actress. The petite, fiery prima donna was reputedly born in the slums of Mantua and was singing in a Milanese cabaret when Oscar *Hammerstein discovered her and signed her to appear with his Manhattan Opera Company. He then starred her in his mounting of Victor *Herbert's *Naughty Marietta* (1910). Herbert's biographer, Edward N. Waters, using, in part, comments of contemporary critics, noted, "Her vocalization was 'uncommonly brilliant,' her high notes were clear and birdlike,

and her manner was 'sprightly, magnetic and vivacious.'" However, her success made her so arrogant and difficult to deal with that Herbert refused to write another operetta for her. That assignment fell to young Rudolf *Friml, in whose *The *Firefly* (1912) she starred. Trentini later appeared in *The Peasant Girl* (1915) and in vaudeville, but having alienated virtually everyone who might have helped her, she left for London and then her homeland, where she died in relative poverty.

TRIAL OF MARY DUGAN, THE (1927), a play by Bayard *Veiller. [National Theatre, 437 perf.] A *Follies* beauty, Mary Dugan (Ann Harding), is on trial for the murder of millionaire Edgar Rice. Her defense seems to be faltering until her young brother, Jimmy (Rex Cherryman), a lawyer just beginning his career, insists he himself replace her present lawyer, Edward West (Cyril Keightley). Mary admits to affairs with several men but wins favor with the jury when she reveals that the money she received was used to provide Jimmy's education. After it is determined that Rice was stabbed to death by a powerful, left-handed man, Jimmy provides the reason for her initially weak defense. Rice, it seems, was murdered by attorney West, who loved Mrs. Rice, so decided to frame Mary. *Time* remarked that the play "moves more swiftly than the law with all its ruthless directness. Its plot has the fascinating features of a front-page murder story."

TRIANGLE CLUB, THE. See Collegiate Theatre Clubs.

TRILBY (1895), a play by Paul M. *Potter. [Garden Theatre, 208 perf.] Three artists, known as the Laird (John Glendinning), Taffy (Burr McIntosh), and Little Billee (Alfred Hickman), use a pretty model, Trilby O'Ferrall (Virginia *Harned), for work in their Latin Quarter atelier. But after a fight with Billee, Trilby leaves and is befriended by the strange genius Svengali (Wilton *Lackaye), who uses his hypnotic powers to turn the girl into a great opera singer. Billee recognizes her at a performance and asks her to abandon Svengali and marry him, but she refuses. However, when Svengali suddenly dies, Trilby's voice deserts her. She is reunited with Billee briefly, but her exertions under Svengali's influence, coupled with the traumatic release from them, prove too much and she withers and dies. Based on the novel by George du Maurier, the adaptation was one of the greatest and more memorable successes of its era. The play was frequently revived, including a notable restaging in 1938 by Walter *Hampden. It also provided the source for a musical that closed during its tryout, *The Studio Girl* (1927).

TRIMBLE, John (1803?–67), architect. A leading mid-19th-century builder of theatres, he was born in New York and turned to the theatre only after brief stints in the navy and as a carpenter. It was as a carpenter that he took work at the *Bowery Theatre and later at the National. When the National burned he found himself unemployed, so he began to design and erect playhouses. Trimble built thirty-four auditoriums as far south as Charleston, South Carolina, and as far west as Buffalo. His New York City theatres included the Olympic, the *Broadway, the 1845 rebuilding of the burned-out Bowery, Brougham's Lyceum, Laura *Keene's, and Christy and Wood's. He continued to work until shortly before his death, although in his last years he was beset by increasing blindness.

TRINITY REPERTORY COMPANY (Providence, Rhode Island). One of the nation's leading regional theatres, it was founded as the Trinity Square Repertory Company in 1964 and performed for many years in a converted church before opening two new stages at a renovated film house during the 1973–74 season. It presents a varied bill of classics and new plays, with which it has also toured both nationally and in Europe. Adrian *Hall was the artistic director from 1965 until 1989, and during his tenure new plays were commissioned and superb revivals transferred to New York. The company received the 1981 *Tony Award as outstanding regional theatre. ("Square" was dropped from the name in 1986.)

TRIP TO CHINATOWN, A; or, An Idyl of San Francisco (1891), a musical comedy by Charles H. *Hoyt (book, lyrics), Percy *Gaunt (music). [*Madison Square Theatre, 657 perf.] To assuage the concern of their guardian Uncle Ben (George A. Beane), a group of young people who really plan a night on the city tell him they are going sightseeing in Chinatown. They have enlisted the aid of a chaperone, Mrs. Guyer (Anna Boyd), but her letter of acceptance reaches Ben, who thinks she is inviting him to an assignation. He goes to the restaurant that she has mentioned and at which the young ones have booked a table. There he gets drunk, finds he has forgotten his wallet, but luckily misses the couples and Mrs. Guyer. When he would scold them for deceiving him, they let him know they are aware of his own little escapade. *Notable songs*: The Bowery; Reuben and Cynthia; After the Ball (an interpolation by Charles K. Harris). For nearly thirty years, until *Irene*, this held the record as Broadway's longest-run musical. Its loose construction allowed for frequent changes in songs and minor principals. Loie *Fuller, for example, danced in it for a time. The immense success of "After the Ball," which was added by

the manager of a road company playing in Milwaukee, furthered the musical's success. With this show, more than any other, *farce-comedy imperceptibly became musical comedy.

TRIP TO NIAGARA, A; or, Travellers in America (1828), a play by William *Dunlap. [*Bowery Theatre, in repertory.] The English Mr. Wentworth (John Fisher) and his sister, Amelia (Mrs. Hughes), come to America on a visit with a fellow Englishman, John Bull (W. B. Chapman), and an Irishman, Dennis Dougherty (Henry *Wallack). Wentworth likes nothing he sees, but his sister seems delighted by both the land and its citizens. Bull would like to marry Amelia, and she agrees, provided he can get her brother to stop being critical. Bull succeeds and Wentworth proclaims, "When the film of prejudice is removed from the eye, man sees his fellow man of every clime a brother . . . we shall have reason to bless our Trip to Niagara." The play was one of the first to give credit in its programs and advertisements to its designers. In a way, though not common practice at the time, this was only natural since even Dunlap confessed he had written the work as a "running accompaniment to the more important product of the Scene-painter." The panoramic effects made this one of the earliest important American spectacles and gave Dunlap, ironically, his biggest commercial success. The theatre reused the panoramas for other plays.

TRIUMPH AT PLATTSBURG, THE (1830), a play by Richard Penn *Smith. [*Chestnut Street Theatre (Philadelphia), in repertory.] In order both to elude the British and to find his missing daughter, Elinor (Mrs. Roper), Major McCrea (Mr. Foot) dons the clothes of André Macklegraith (Mr. Maywood) and poses as the half-wit son of Mrs. Macklegraith (Mrs. Turner). Elinor has fled after marrying British Captain Stanley (Mr. Rowbotham), whom she now believes has deserted her. Her arrival at the mill threatens to expose her father, but he escapes. He encounters Stanley, who proves his affections for Elinor are genuine. Set against the background of the War of 1812, this well-constructed but extremely short comedydrama was turned into a full evening's entertainment by the inclusion of such spectacular scenes as "a view of the Arrival and Capture of the British Fleet." For all its brevity, many scholars consider it the best of Smith's historical plays.

TRIUMPHS OF LOVE, THE; or, Happy Reconciliation (1795), a comedy by John Murdock. [New Theatre (Philadelphia), in repertory.] Set loosely against the background of the Whiskey Rebellion and the troubles with Algiers, it directed much of its social satire against the inbreeding of the Quakers, as exemplified by the Friendly family. The play has minimal literary merit. Its importance rests with its being the first professionally produced play in America to deal with the Society of Friends as well as the first to have an African American in its cast of characters: the slave Sambo whom George Friendly frees during the story. As was the practice at the time, the character was portrayed by a white actor in blackface. **John MURDOCK** (1749–1834) was said to be a Philadelphia barber, but he must have been a fairly affluent and versatile one, since he had published at his own expense not only this play but two others that he wrote: *The Politicians; or, A State of Things* (1798), a plea for strong government; and *The Beau Metamorphized* (1800), a farce.

TRUE WEST (1980), a play by Sam *Shepard. [*Public Theatre, 24 perf.] California screenwriter Austin (Tommy Lee Jones) is preparing a "true-to-life Western" for Hollywood when he is visited by his slob of a brother, Lee (Peter Boyle), a petty thief and drifter who moves in and trashes the house. But over time the two brothers begin to exchange personalities, Lee becoming a driven writer and Austin slipping into a slovenly and derelict manner. The sibling rivalry climaxes in a deadly fight, but both survive to continue forging new personalities. Seen earlier at San Francisco's *Magic Theatre, the play's Manhattan production was fraught with problems (both director and playwright disavowed Joe *Papp's mounting) and it quickly closed. *True West* was not widely acclaimed until a 1982 revival at the Cherry Lane Theatre, featuring John *Malkovich and Gary Sinise as the brothers, which ran 762 performances. A 2000 Broadway revival at the *Circle in the Square, with film actors John C. Reilly and Philip Seymour Hoffman, was also a hit. It remains Shepard's most produced play.

TRUEX, Ernest (1889–1973), character actor. The small, raspy-voiced performer, whose stage career spanned over seventy years, was born in Rich Hill, Missouri, where he made his first appearance as a child prodigy in 1894. He played many years in stock before his New York debut in 1908. Truex's small stature and youthful looks were responsible for his being cast in young-boy roles even when he was in his twenties. Among his notable performances were Charles MacLance in *A Good Little Devil* (1913), the boy detective Barney Cook in *The *Dummy* (1914), the hen-pecked Eddie in the musical *Very Good Eddie* (1915), the pressured husband Gilbert Sterling in *Six-Cylinder Love* (1921), the duped Johnny Quinlan in *The Fall Guy* (1925), Kinesias in a 1930 revival of *Lysistrata*, the mystery writer Wallace Porter in *Whistling in the Dark* (1932), and the hapless homebuilder Newton Fuller in *George Washington Slept Here* (1940). Although Truex continued acting for another quarter-century, including roles with the *American Repertory Theatre in 1946, he never again was in a long-run success.

TRUST, THE. See Theatrical Syndicate, The.

TUCKER, Sophie [née Sonia Kalish] (1884–1966), singer. Long billed as "The Last of the Red-Hot Mamas," the buxom, brash, blonde performer gave her birthplace as either Russia or Poland. She was still a babe in arms when her parents brought her to America, but within a few years she was singing for customers in her parents' Hartford, Connecticut, restaurant. By 1906 Tucker was performing in vaudeville, later appearing in the [*Ziegfeld] *Follies of 1909* and reaching the *Palace Theatre in 1914. Among the songs she made famous were "After You've Gone," "My Yiddishe Mama," and "Some of These Days," which became her theme number. Vaudeville historians Charles and Louise Samuels wrote that she "had the biggest, brassiest voice of all. The beat in her voice made your heart pound with it, and in syncopated time." From 1919 to 1941 Tucker appeared in half a dozen Broadway musicals, most notably as the ambitious Mrs. Goodhue in *Leave It to Me!* (1938). She continued to perform until her death, playing mostly nightclubs in her last years. Autobiography: *Some of These Days*, 1945.

TULLY, Richard Walton (1877–1945), playwright. He was born in Nevada City, California, and educated at the University of California. His first work, *The Strenuous Life*, was mounted briefly in Los Angeles by Oliver *Morosco but never brought East. However, the men later collaborated again to score a major success with *The *Bird of Paradise* (1912). Its popularity prompted one of the most famous lawsuits in American theatrical history. A schoolteacher, Grace Fendler, sued, claiming the drama was plagiarized from her *In Hawaii*. She was awarded $608,000, but an appellate court reversed the decision and made her pay all legal costs. Tully's other successes were *The *Rose of the Rancho* (1906), *Omar the Tentmaker* (1914), and *The Flame* (1916). He also directed some of his own plays, as well as directing and occasionally producing others' works, notably *Poor Little Rich Girl* (1913), *The Masquerader* (1917), and *Keep Her Smiling* (1918). Recognizing that his brand of melodramatic romance had lost its appeal to playgoers, Tully worked for a while in films and then became a noted rancher and breeder of horses.

TUNE, Tommy (b. 1939), actor, choreographer, and director. A native of Wichita Falls, Texas, the lanky, attractive if slightly effete theatre jack-of-all-trades made his Broadway debut in the chorus of *Baker Street* (1965). He was featured in *Seesaw* (1973), then served as choreographer and co-director for *The *Best Little Whorehouse in Texas* (1978). Tune then went on to direct and choreograph *A Day in Hollywood/A Night in the Ukraine* (1980), *Nine* (1982), *My One and Only* (1983), *Stepping Out* (1987), *Grand Hotel* (1989), *The *Will Rogers Follies* (1991), and *The Best Little Whorehouse Goes Public* (1994). Off-Broadway he staged such long-running plays as *The Club* (1976) and *Cloud 9* (1981). He frequently returns to performing, usually in concerts or specialty shows.

TUNICK, Jonathan (b. 1938), orchestrator. A New Yorker who studied at Juilliard, he has, usually alone but sometimes with others, orchestrated such shows as *Promises, Promises* (1968), *Company* (1970), *A *Little Night Music* (1973), *A *Chorus Line* (1975), *Pacific Overtures* (1976), *Sweeney Todd* (1979), *Nine* (1982), *Baby* (1983), *Into the Woods* (1987), *Titanic* (1997), and *Marie Christine* (1999). His work exemplifies the best in the modern Broadway sound, using not only contemporary harmonies and instrumentation, but also electronics, which have pervaded the musical theatre during the last several decades. Tunick is the first theatre orchestrator to receive a *Tony Award.

TURN TO THE RIGHT! (1916), a play by Winchell *Smith and John E. Hazzard. [Gaiety Theatre, 435 perf.] When Joe Bascom (Forrest Winant) is released from prison after serving time for a crime he did not commit, he returns to the peach farm owned by his widowed mother (Ruth Chester). He does not tell his family where he has passed the last year, nor does he tell them the truth about the two friends he brings with him, his prison mates Muggs (William E. Meehan) and Gilly (Frank Nelson). Although one was an expert at opening safes and the other was a pickpocket, both are determined to go straight. However, when they learn that the devious Deacon Tillinger (Samuel Reed) is using legal technicalities to take the farm from Mrs. Bascom, they resort to their old ways for one final time. They open the deacon's safe, take precisely the money he is demanding, pay it to him, pick his pocket, then return the money to the safe. Mrs. Bascom is shown how to make enough income from her fruit jams to remain solvent, and Joe and his buddies all win the hands of local girls. This clean, homey comedy was one of the biggest hits of its era. It was co-producer John *Golden's first success, and he noted in his 1930 autobiography that it "has been playing continuously for 15 years." A 1981 musical version failed on the West Coast despite President Ronald Reagan's attempt to have a Los Angeles critic promote it.

TWELFTH NIGHT. Shakespeare's barbed attack on prudery and hypocrisy apparently was first presented to Americans in Boston in 1794. The work did not always sit well with Victorian morality, but there were notable productions in the 19th century, including Ellen *Tree's 1837 revival; her 1845 revival with her husband, Charles *Kean; William *Burton's 1851 mounting; and several productions at *Wallack's and *Daly's. Among the important 20th-century productions were those in 1905 with Julia *Marlowe and E. H. *Sothern (with many critics considering his unctuous Malvolio a high point of his career) and in 1940 with Helen *Hayes and Maurice *Evans. The successful rock musical, *Your Own Thing* (1968), was a skillful lyric version, while *Music Is* (1976) and *Play On!* (1997), also based on *Twelfth Night*, were quick failures.

TWENTIETH CENTURY (1932), a comedy by Ben *Hecht and Charles *MacArthur. [*Broadhurst Theatre, 152 perf.] In desperate need of a success to recoup both his fortune and his reputation, the flamboyant, egomaniacal producer Oscar Jaffe (Moffatt Johnston) books a compartment on the famous train the Twentieth Century Limited. He hopes not only to elude his persistent creditors, but also to sign the screen star Lily Garland (Eugenie Leontovich), who is in the neighboring compartment. Oscar feels Lily owes him a favor, since he had taken her when she was merely Mildred Plotka and made her his star and his mistress. His plan is to have her play Mary Magdalene in his production of The Passion Play. A check from a fanatically religious millionaire, Matthew Clark (Etienne *Girardot), would seem to assure his production. Although the check proves worthless when Clark is shown to be a harmless mental case, Jaffe manages to sign Lily in the midst of one of their tempestuous battles. Percy *Hammond wrote, "Show business gets a cruel razzing from *20th Century* . . . in which those impish bad boys of the Drama kick it urgently on its pants and inspire, thereby, much hilarity." The play was a reworking of Charles Bruce Millholland's unproduced comedy *The Napoleon of Broadway* that used David *Belasco for its model for Oscar. When Hecht and MacArthur took over they added some touches of Jed *Harris to their leading figure. The play was successfully revived in 1950 with Gloria Swanson and José *Ferrer. Later it became the basis of the musical *ON THE TWENTIETH CENTURY* (1978), written by Betty *Comden and Adolph *Green (book and lyrics), with music by Cy *Coleman, and with John *Cullum and Madeleine *Kahn as Jaffe and Lily. (The religious fanatic was turned into a woman, Letitia Primrose, played with relish by comedienne Imogene Coca.) A high point of the evening was Robin *Wagner's scenery re-creating the famous old train, which led *Variety to begin its notice, "It's ominous when an audience leaves a musical whistling the scenery." Yet the score, a merry pastiche of operetta, was tuneful and the Hal *Prince–staged evening a good deal of fun. It ran 449 performances at the *St. James Theatre. Notable songs: On the Twentieth Century; Our Private World; Repent; We've Got It All; Never.

TWIN BEDS (1914), a farce by Salisbury Field and Margaret *Mayo. [Fulton Theatre, 411 perf.] Complications begin when an intoxicated Italian tenor, Signor Monti (Charles Judels), wanders by mistake into the room of Blanche (Madge *Kennedy) and Harry Hawkins (John Westley), a floor below his own. By the time Blanche comes home Signor Monti is all but undressed. She persuades him to put his clothes back on, only to find the all-too-efficient maid Norah (Georgie Lawrence) has removed them for cleaning. Naturally, Harry arrives and is furious. But when he warns Monti that a scandal could follow with Monti's picture in the papers, the befuddled tenor can only thank him for offering him some much-needed publicity. Signora Monti (Ray Cox), an Amazonian harridan, also enters and also misunderstands. They are screaming at each other when the curtain falls. Greeted as one of the best comedies in years, the play was threatened with bad business by the outbreak of the war. Producer William *Harris Jr. arranged one of the wildest publicity campaigns Broadway had ever known, including dray wagons and trucks with the name of the show plastered on their sides, which conveniently broke down at well-traveled intersections. The play soon caught on and became one of the era's most popular comedies.

TWO FOR THE SEESAW (1958), a play by William *Gibson. [*Booth Theatre, 750 perf.] Having had a falling out with his wife in Omaha, lawyer Jerry Ryan (Henry *Fonda) finds himself lonely and adrift in New York. He calls a young girl for a date and she turns out to be a warm-hearted but aggressively bohemian Jewish girl, Gittel Mosca (Anne *Bancroft). A romance ensues, but in the end different backgrounds and different interests send them on their separate ways. The romantic piece was one of the best of the many two-character plays that inundated Broadway in this period. It later became the source for the musical SEESAW (1973) that director-choreographer Michael *Bennett adapted (using an early libretto by Michael *Stewart) into a glitzy dance show. Ken *Howard and Michele Lee were

the unlikely couple with Tommy *Tune stealing the show with a big production number that he also staged. The contemporary-sounding music was by Cy *Coleman, and Dorothy *Fields, in her last Broadway outing, did the surprisingly modern lyrics. The troubled musical went through a trying preview period, then met with mixed notices, struggling on for an unprofitable 296 performances at the Uris Theatre. Notable songs: Nobody Does It Like Me; It's Not Where You Start, It's Where You Finish; Welcome to Holiday Inn.

TWO GENTLEMEN OF VERONA (1971), a musical comedy by John *Guare (book, lyrics), Mel Shapiro (book), Galt MacDermot (music). [*St. James Theatre, 627 perf.; Tony, NYDCC Awards.] This updated, musicalization of Shakespeare's The Two Gentlemen of Verona was given a rock score when presented by the *New York Shakespeare Festival in Central Park. The sly show, which used ethnic humor, slang mixed with Elizabethan verse, and plenty of anachronisms, proved so popular that producer Joe *Papp moved it to Broadway with success. The multiracial cast included Raul *Julia, Clifton Davis, Jonelle Allen, and Diana Davila. Notable songs: Who Is Sylvia?; Night Letter; Bring All the Boys Back Home.

TWO MRS. CARROLLS, THE (1943), a play by Martin Vale. [*Booth Theatre, 585 perf.] Geoffrey Carroll (Victor Jory) is a psychopathic artist living with his wife, Sally (Elisabeth *Bergner), in the south of France. While Sally mysteriously weakens, the unfaithful Geoffrey has an affair with Cecily Harden (Irene *Worth). Geoffrey's first wife, Harriet (Marjory Clark), visits Sally and warns her that Geoffrey had once tried to kill her with a slow-working poison. Sally alerts her friend, Guy Pennington (Richard Stapley), who locks Geoffrey in the house and calls the police. Geoffrey takes a lethal dose of his own poison. Martin Vale was the pen name for Marguerite Vale Veiller, the widow of Bayard *Veiller. The play was first produced in England but failed when the English version was tried out in America. Seven years later this rewritten version succeeded.

TWO ORPHANS, THE (1874). Called by George *Odell "one of the greatest theatrical successes of all time in America," Hart Jackson's translation of Cormon and *D'Ennery's Les Deux Orphelines was first performed at the *Union Square Theatre in 1874. The work centered on two sisters, one of them blind, who come to Paris where they are accidentally separated. The blind girl falls into the clutches of a vicious harridan, while her sister is carted off by a lecherous nobleman. They suffer a variety of harrowing experiences before they are happily reunited. Kate *Claxton and Kitty Blanchard played the title roles. The work held the boards almost continually for the rest of the century and was given a major revival as late as 1926, when Fay *Bainter and Mary *Nash assumed the leading roles.

TWO TRAINS RUNNING (1992), a play by August *Wilson. [*Walter Kerr Theatre, 160 perf.; NYDCC Award.] At a dingy coffee shop in Pittsburgh in 1969, the African-American regulars talk about two significant events planned for the same day: the funeral of a prominent local preacher and a protest rally spurred by the recent assassination of Malcolm X. Yet the patrons are more involved in their own everyday problems and concerns: the neighborhood's gentrification, the return of an ex-con (Larry Fishburne) who woos the bitter waitress Risa (Cynthia Martells), and the local eccentric Hambone (Sullivan Walker) who keeps ranting about a ham he was once promised but never received. Lloyd *Richards directed the strong ensemble cast (Fishburne won the Tony), and the script was deemed "the most comic of the Wilson saga so far . . . [his] most delicate and mature work."

TYLER, George C[rouse] (1867–1946), producer. One of the American theatre's busiest showmen, he was born near Chillicothe, Ohio, and had served as a reporter and editor for several Ohio newspapers before becoming the manager of James *O'Neill. In 1897 he joined with Theodore Liebler to form *Liebler and Co., which was soon one of the leading turn-of-the-century producers. Among its many notable productions were The *Christian (1898), *Sag Harbor (1900), The *Squaw Man (1905), The *Man from Home (1908), *Alias Jimmy Valentine (1910), and The *Garden of Allah (1911). The firm also brought to this country Mrs. Patrick *Campbell, *Duse, and *Réjane. A series of failures at the time of World War I brought about the dissolution of the company. For a time Tyler was associated with *Klaw and *Erlanger, then in 1919 embarked on a career as an independent producer. His productions included *Clarence (1919), *Dulcy (1921), *To the Ladies (1922), *Merton of the Movies (1922), Young Woodley (1925), and The Plough and the Stars (1927). In the middle and late 1920s he mounted a series of important revivals, including, in 1928 alone, She Stoops to Conquer, *Diplomacy, The Beaux' Stratagem, *Jim, the Penman, and *Macbeth. These were well received for the most part, but they were coupled with his presentations of unsuccessful new plays. Shortly thereafter, he retired from the theatre. In just short of forty years he had mounted over two hundred plays, but like so many other producers of his era, he died insolvent. Autobiography: Whatever Goes Up, 1934.

TYLER, Royall. See Contrast, The.

U

UHRY, Alfred (b. 1936), playwright. He was born in Atlanta and educated at Brown University before making his Manhattan playwriting debut as co-author of the libretto for the short-lived musical *Here's Where I Belong* (1968). Uhry's libretto for *The Robber Bridegroom* (1974) was much more successful, and his play *Driving Miss Daisy* (1987) ran Off Broadway for three years, winning the *Pulitzer Prize. His comedy-drama *The *Last Night of Ballyhoo* (1997) was a hit on Broadway, and his script for the dark musical *Parade* (1998) at *Lincoln Center was highly praised. Much of Uhry's work is set in the American South in the past, often dealing with Jews in a narrow-minded society.

ULRIC, Lenore [née Leonora Ulrich] (1892–1970), actress. A dark, volatile performer, at her best conveying sultry, impassioned women, she was born in New Ulm, Minnesota, and learned her trade in stock in Milwaukee, Chicago, and elsewhere. Ulric first gained national recognition when she toured in 1914 as the doomed Hawaiian princess in *The *Bird of Paradise,* and her New York debut came a year later in *The Mark of the Beast* (1915). Although the play was a quick failure, it brought her to the notice of David *Belasco, with whom she worked for the next fourteen years, playing the deceived Indian maiden Wetona in *The Heart of Wetona* (1916), Rose Bocion in *Tiger Rose* (1917), Lien Wha in *The Son-Daughter* (1919), and the saucy chorine *Kiki* (1921). Alexander *Woollcott said of her performance, "The relish and the fire and the comic spirit with which she undertakes the embodiment of the naïve, ignorant, aspiring, ardent little Parisian chorus girl is a joy to behold." By now a full-fledged star, Ulric continued under Belasco as the disguised Turkish princess Carla in *The Harem* (1924), the doomed Harlem prostitute *Lulu Belle* (1926), and the destructive siren in the title role of *Mima* (1928). After leaving Belasco she enjoyed one last success as the harlot Dot Hunter in *Pagan Lady* (1930). Thereafter, Ulric continued to be busy but was never again a star. Among her later roles were the Moorish whore Anita in *The *Fifth Column* (1940) and Charmian to Katharine *Cornell's Cleopatra in 1947.

UMPIRE, THE (1905), a musical comedy by Will M. *Hough, Frank R. *Adams (book, lyrics), Joseph *Howard (music). [LaSalle Theatre (Chicago), 300 perf.] Johnny Nolan (Cecil *Lean) is a baseball umpire who makes such an outrageous call in a crucial game that he is forced to flee all the way to Morocco. There he participates in a football game, where he not only redeems himself but wins the hand of the center, who turns out to be a young lady, Maribel Lewton (Florence Holbrook). *Notable songs*: Cross Your Heart; I Want a Girl Like You; You Look Awful Good to Father. The first American musical to deal with baseball and football, the show established a Chicago long-run record (broken the next year by *The *Time, the Place and the Girl*). In fact, its run was longer than that of any musical in New York the same season, except for the *Hippodrome extravaganza. The show established the primacy of the tiny LaSalle as Chicago's principal home for locally written musicals, a primacy that lasted nearly a decade. *The Umpire* apparently never played New York.

UNCHASTENED WOMAN, THE (1915), a play by Louis Kaufman Anspacher. [39th Street Theatre, 193 perf.] Caroline Knollys (Emily *Stevens) is a selfish and unscrupulous woman. Caught making a false declaration at customs, she attempts to bribe Emily Madden (Willette Kershaw), a woman official, whom she knows to have once been the mistress of her husband, Hubert (H. *Reeves-Smith). When she fails, she makes public the illicit liaison. Caroline also attempts to steal a young artist, Lawrence Sanbury (Hassard *Short), from his wife, Hildegarde (Christine Norman). Although Hildegarde wins back Lawrence, Hubert and Emily force Caroline to issue a statement recanting her charges. In the end Caroline gives no hint that she is remorseful or will change her ways. The success of this uncompromising look at a despicable woman surprised many. Walter Prichard *Eaton saw the Oliver *Morosco offering as "a character study of a frivolous and selfish woman, gaining its appeal from that study rather than from mere narrative excitement, or farcical situation, or machine-made slang." **Louis K[aufman] ANSPACHER** (1878–1947), born in Cincinnati

631

and educated at New York's City College and at Columbia Law School, was primarily known as a lecturer. After acting for a few years, Anspacher saw over a dozen of his plays produced, from *Tristan and Isolde* (1904) to *The Rhapsody* (1930). However, he is remembered only for *The Unchastened Woman*.

UNCLE HARRY (1942), a play by Thomas Job. [*Broadhurst Theatre, 430 perf.] Harry Quincey (Joseph *Schildkraut) is a mild-mannered bachelor, dominated by his two spinster sisters, Lettie (Eva *Le Gallienne) and Hester (Adelaide Klein), who call him "Uncle" Harry. Furious at their destroying his chance to marry Lucy Forrest (Beverly Roberts), he tricks Lettie into buying some poison and then has her serve it unwittingly to Hester in some cocoa. Lettie is sentenced to die for the murder. To Harry's dismay, Lucy will now have nothing to do with him. Remorsefully, he confesses the crime, but the authorities believe he is merely trying to save his sister. He visits Lettie in prison, where she refuses to reveal the truth. Harry thus is doomed to a life of loneliness and disgrace. Richard Lockridge of the *Sun* called the work, "An admirably sinister murder play, slightly diabolical in its ingenuity and warranted to make the timid look hereafter with uneasy suspicion on all quiet little men."

UNCLE TOM'S CABIN (1853), a melodrama by George L. Aiken. [Purdy's National Theatre, 325 perf.] The slave George Harris (J. J. Prior) tells Eliza (Mrs. J. J. Prior) he is fleeing to Canada. Eliza then learns that she and her young son are to be put up for sale, so she informs Uncle Tom (J. Lingard) that she, too, must run away. She escapes by crossing an icy river. St. Clare (J. B. Howe) has bought Uncle Tom, who had saved the life of Little Eva (Cordelia *Howard). Eva is brought up with a small black girl, Topsy (Mrs. G. C. Howard), who has no conception of her origins and insists, "I 'spect I growed." The kindly Uncle Tom warns St. Clare that his drinking will cause problems, but St. Clare does not heed his advice. Although Harris and Eliza are reunited, St. Clare is stabbed to death by the overseer Simon Legree (N. B. Clare) before he can sign the papers freeing Uncle Tom and the other slaves. Legree proves a cruel master, but he is shot dead while resisting arrest for St. Clare's murder. Little Eva dies and is carried to heaven on the back of a milk-white dove. Although numerous dramatizations of Harriet Beecher Stowe's famous novel were offered, all unauthorized, this was by far the most popular and had established a long-run record of one hundred nights in Troy, New York, before coming to Broadway. One modern editor, Richard Moody, dismissed

the tendency of many writers and critics to look on the work disdainfully, noting, "The forces of right and wrong on the slavery issue—not the struggle between North and South—are clearly and vigorously exposed. The language has an irresistible strength and vitality, and the rich panorama compels us to sense the magnitude of a vicious and pervasive evil." The most popular theatre work of its era, it played a major role, along with the original novel, in stoking the fires of abolition. Aiken's version was said to be the first play offered on Broadway as an entire evening, without an afterpiece or any other entertainment. In one version or another it continued to tour the country for decades. There were forty-nine troupes in 1879 and no fewer than a dozen companies still active in 1927. The first year not to see a full tour is believed to be 1930. Between this version and the many others touring the country, the play probably was seen by more Americans than any other in the history of our theatre. Many actors and families made careers of performing the work; they were known as "tommers" and their trade as "tomming." **George L. AIKEN** (1830–76) was born in Boston and made his first stage appearance in *Six Degrees of Crime* in Providence, Rhode Island, in 1848. While never an important actor, he seems, unlike many of his colleagues, to have been constantly employed and often was assigned major roles, although in second string companies. His play *Helos the Helot* (1852) won one of the many prizes given at the time to encourage native drama. Most of Aiken's other works were mounted either at the *Bowery or at *Barnum's *American Museum, a testimony to their melodramatic nature. Numbered among them were *Ups and Downs of New York Life* (1857), *The Doom of Deville* (1859), *Harry Blake* (1860), and *The Earl's Daughter* (1861). Aiken dramatized *Uncle Tom's Cabin* at the request of his cousin, George C. Howard, who ran the Troy (New York) Museum. Howard wanted the piece as a vehicle for his wife, who was to play Topsy, and his daughter, Cordelia *Howard, who was to play Little Eva. Aiken is said to have completed his writing in a single week.

UNDER COVER (1914), a play by Roi Cooper Megrue. [*Cort Theatre, 349 perf.] A man known as Steven Denby (William *Courtenay) has smuggled a valuable necklace into the country, then hides it in his room at the home of friends he is visiting. Inspector Daniel Taylor (De Witt C. Jennings) is determined to retrieve the jewels and threatens to jail the sister of Denby's fiancée, Ethel Cartwright (Lily Cahill), for a crime the sister inadvertently committed if Ethel does not help trap Denby. Appearing to walk into the trap, Denby turns the tables by disclosing his real identity and the significance of the jewels. A tautly made thriller, it used the then novel device of having much of the action of the fourth act take place while the action of the third act was supposedly going on.

UNDER THE GASLIGHT

UNDER THE GASLIGHT (1867), a play by Augustin *Daly. [New York Theatre, 47 perf.] Laura Cortlandt (Rose *Eytinge) is jilted by her lover, Capt. Ray Trafford (A. H. Davenport), when he discovers she is merely an adopted daughter and actually of humble parentage. Laura runs away from home but is hauled into court, where the villainous Byke (J. B. *Studley) claims she is his child and so is given custody of her. He attempts to take her to New Jersey but is stopped by a one-armed ex-soldier, Snorkey (J. K. Mortimer), and Capt. Trafford. In the tussle Byke throws Laura into the river, but she swims to safety and returns to the family who adopted her. The furious Byke then decides to rob the Cortlandt home. Snorkey overhears his plans, but Byke catches him and ties him to the railroad tracks, knowing an express train will pass by shortly. Laura happens on the tethered man and releases him just before the train comes, then returns home to settle down with Trafford. The famous railroad track scene was said to have been borrowed by Daly from an 1865 English play, *The Engineer*. Although Daly was able to patent the effect, it soon became a staple of cheap melodrama and later of early films.

UNDER THE RED ROBE (1896), a play by Edward E. *Rose. [*Empire Theatre, 216 perf.] When Gil de Berault (William *Faversham) twice violates the strictures against dueling imposed by Cardinal Richelieu (J. E. Dodson), the powerful religious leader demands that either Berault betray the brother of his sweetheart, Renée de Cochefort (Viola *Allen), or forfeit his life. The clever Berault manages to get the best of the Cardinal and live. Based on a novel by Stanley Weyman, the play was offered by Charles *Frohman in London before he brought it to New York. It was the source of the 1928 musical *The Red Robe*.

UNDER TWO FLAGS (1901), a play by Paul M. *Potter. [Garden Theatre, 135 perf.] Cigarette (Blanche *Bates) is a spunky camp follower, or vivandière, in the bleak French-occupied mountains of North Africa. To defend her country and win her man, she will even fight off a host of Bedouins or ride her horse Cochise through a dust storm in the Chellelah Gorge. Needless to say, she wins her sweetheart. Although other dramatizations of Ouida's novel had been touring the country for several years, this Charles *Frohman–David *Belasco production was the first to play in a major New York house.

UNION SQUARE THEATRE (New York) Briefly one of the most famous of New York theatres, it was situated in the middle of the block between Broadway and Fourth Avenue, on 14th Street, part of the old Morton House. H. M. Sims designed the house for Sheridan Shook, who opened it in 1871 as a variety theatre. When vaudeville failed to attract, he turned over management in 1872 to A. M. *Palmer, who established a fine stock company there, and for the next eleven years the house vied with those of *Daly and *Wallack in prestige. While the other two were best known for comedy, the Union Square enjoyed most of its great successes with the romantic dramas of the time. Among the theatre's major hits, all French in origin, were Sardou's *Agnes*, Clara *Morris in *Camille*, and *The *Two Orphans*. After Palmer moved his company farther north in 1883 the house's reputation began to fade. Destroyed by fire in 1888, the theatre was rebuilt, but the heart of the theatre district had moved away, and before long the theatre was again a vaudeville house. It was later home to burlesque and to films. The shell of the old theatre, complete with stagehouse, remains on the site. It is not to be confused with an Off-Broadway house, also called the Union Square Theatre, located on 17th Street.

UNITED MANAGERS' PROTECTIVE ASSOCIATION. See Producing Managers' Association.

UNITED SCENIC ARTISTS OF AMERICA. In 1885, the Protective Alliance of Scenic Painters of America was organized with Harley Merry as president and Richard *Marston as chairman. The history of this group is obscure, but it may have given rise to the United Scenic Artists of America, whose New York local was founded in 1912 with the stated purpose "to promote fraternal feeling among its members, regulate working hours, obtain just compensation for the working day and for overtime and to cope with such other problems of mutual interest to its members as may from time to time arise." In 1918 it became affiliated with the Brotherhood of Painters, Decorators and Paperhangers of America (now the Brotherhood of Painters and Allied Trades). Regardless of its name, the union covers lighting and costume designers as well.

UNITT, Edward G. (fl. late 19th and early 20th century), designer. One of the busiest set designers of his day and a favorite of both Daniel *Frohman and Charles *Frohman, he kept a studio for many years in the former's *Lyceum Theatre. His work was extremely versatile and difficult to characterize. Among Unitt's memorable settings were those for *Aristocracy* (1892), *Under the Red Robe* (1896), *The Little Minister* (1897), *The *Conquerors* (1898),

The Liars (1898), **Barbara Frietchie* (1899), E. H. **Sothern's *Hamlet* (1900), **David Harum* (1900), **Captain Jinks of the Horse Marines* (1901), **If I Were King* (1901), *Quality Street* (1901), *The *Girl with the Green Eyes* (1902), *The *Red Mill* (1906), *A *Grand Army Man* (1907), and *The Blue Bird* (1910).

UNIVERSITY PLAYERS. This was a group founded by Bretaigne *Windust and Charles Leatherbee in 1928 as the University Players Guild. Productions, mostly revivals, were given each summer through 1932 at Falmouth, Massachusetts. In its last year the company changed its name to the Theatre Unit, Inc., and after a season at Falmouth played briefly in Baltimore. Among its many young figures who afterwards became famous were Henry *Fonda, Joshua *Logan, Myron McCormick, Mildred *Natwick, Kent Smith, James Stewart, and Margaret *Sullavan. Norris Houghton later wrote the history of the company in *But Not Forgotten*.

UNKNOWN PURPLE, THE (1918), a play by Roland West and Carlyle Moore. [Lyric Theatre, 273 perf.] The brilliant but socially naïve inventor Peter Marchmont (Richard *Bennett) spends years in prison after his unfaithful wife (Helen MacKellar) and her lover, James Dawson (Earle Brown), steal his latest invention and frame him for a crime he did not commit. On his release he determines not only to be revenged but to reclaim his young son, whom his wife has kept from him. To this end Marchmont invents a device that, when pressed in his hand, makes him invisible, leaving only an eerie purple light to suggest his whereabouts. Under the purple cloak of invisibility he wins retribution. Apart from Bennett's superb performance, which delicately balanced both the gently loving and cruelly vindictive aspects of the hero, most critics were intrigued by the curious nature of the play. It profitably combined the universally popular "crook play" with a then much rarer element of science fiction and added to these the suddenly voguish flashback device. Critics named various older plays and went as far back as Jules Verne for the inspiration of the science fiction portions of the play, but to a man they credited **On Trial* (1914) as the source for the flashbacks.

UP IN CENTRAL PARK (1945), a musical play by Herbert *Fields (book), Dorothy *Fields (book, lyrics), Sigmund *Romberg (music). [*Century Theatre, 504 perf.] Rosie Moore (Maureen Cannon), the daughter of a Tweed Ring politician, loves the muckraking reporter, John Matthews (Wilbur Evans), but after he writes an article exposing Mr. Moore and his cronies, Rosie breaks off their romance and marries another man. Luckily, when

she comes to her senses, she learns her new spouse is a bigamist, so she can still marry John. *Notable songs*: April Snow; The Big Back Yard; Close as Pages in a Book; When You Walk in the Room; Carousel in the Park. A solid Romberg-Fields score and Helen *Tamiris's memorable "Currier and Ives Ballet" helped make this show a smash hit. However, producer Michael *Todd brought it back to New York just as Brooks *Atkinson returned to his post at the *Times*. Atkinson perceived it as superannuated operetta and led a virulent attack on it, after which it fell out of favor.

UP IN MABEL'S ROOM (1919), a farce by Wilson Collison and Otto *Harbach. [Eltinge Theatre, 229 perf.] As a shy, worrying newlywed, Garry Ainsworth (John *Cumberland) is loath to have anything disturb his bride, so when he remembers that he once gave a silk undergarment to an old flame, Mabel Essington (Hazel *Dawn), he decides he must get it back immediately. He visits Mabel in her room, but has no sooner arrived than just about everybody he does not want to see appears. "An amusing farce of the lingerie genre," as one critic put it, the comedy was one of a number of similar pieces that producer A. H. *Woods mounted in these years.

UP SHE GOES. See *Too Many Cooks*.

UPSTAIRS AND DOWN (1916), a comedy by Frederic and Fanny *Hatton. [*Cort Theatre, 320 perf.] At a giddy Long Island weekend party, the hostess, Nancy Ives (Christine Norman), begins to wonder about the amorality and immorality of her social set. Her guests are petty, selfish, and self-deceiving. Elizabeth (Mary Servoss) and her sister, Alice Chesterton (Juliet Day), are good examples— lying and backbiting each other in their efforts to attract the same man, Terrence O'Keefe (Courtney Foote). Deciding she would be happier in a blue collar world, Nancy heads for the servant quarters. But there she finds the same meanness and backstabbing among the staff headed by the family valet, Louis (Leo Carrillo). At least the rich people upstairs have the advantages of comfort and elegance. Although the Oliver *Morosco offering vacillated between social satire and standard Broadway farce, it delighted playgoers not troubled by a wavering sense of tone.

UPTON, Robert (fl. mid-18th century), manager. Although he has been called "the first advance agent and business manager in America," little is known about his history. He was sent by the elder Lewis *Hallam to America in 1751 to prepare for the coming of the Hallam troupe. Instead he set up his own company, with himself and his wife as leading performers, and in 1751–52 gave a brief New York season. The repertory included the first known American mounting of *Othello, as well as Venice Preserved, *Richard III, and The Provoked Husband. The season failed, so rather than confront Hallam he sailed for England in 1752. Thereupon he disappears from the records.

URBAN, Joseph (1872–1933), designer and architect. One of the greatest of all scenic artists, he was born in Vienna, where he later studied at the Art Academy under Baron Carl Hassauer and at the Polytechnicum. Urban first came to America to create the Austrian Pavilion for the 1904 St. Louis Fair. The Boston Opera Company brought him back in 1911 to design its sets, but it was his work on The Garden of Paradise (1914) that brought him to the attention of Florenz *Ziegfeld and launched his Broadway career. Although he designed sets for James K. *Hackett's Shakespearean revivals and other plays, it was his work on musicals for which he became famous. Urban created the sets for all the *Ziegfeld Follies from 1915 to 1931, as well as such shows as *Sally (1920), *Sunny (1925), *Rio Rita (1927) *Show Boat (1927), The *Three Musketeers (1928), *Whoopee (1928), and *Music in the Air (1932). He was the first major designer to carefully coordinate colors and to employ subtle lighting to enhance his color schemes. Typical of the work of "Unfailing Urban" was his opening set for Rosalie (1928), in which a brown arch framed a brown village rising to a bluish-brown sea. His (and Ziegfeld's) favorite color was blue, and he gained fame for what became known as "Urban blue." He also designed several theatres, most notably the egg-shaped, boxless *Ziegfeld Theatre, with its magnificent murals and gilt stage. Away from the theatre he served as architect for numerous homes and buildings and also earned a reputation as an illustrator of children's books. Biography: Joseph Urban, Randolph Carter, Robert Reed Cole, 1992.

URINETOWN (2001), a musical satire by Greg Kotis (book, lyrics), Mark Hollmann (music, lyrics). [American Theatre of Actors, 965 perf.] Because of a severe water shortage, citizens are forced to use public pay-per-use conveniences owned by the corrupt Caldwell B. Caldwell (John *Cullum). When his daughter, Hope (Jennifer Laura Thompson), falls in love with the insurrectionist Bobby Strong (Hunter Foster), who is leading a revolt against the "pay-to-pee" ordinance, Caldwell arranges for Bobby's death. But Hope picks up the cause, leads the rebels against her father, and brings down Caldwell and his monopoly. Notable songs: Look at the Sky, Don't Be the Bunny. The "uniquely outrageous" little musical was so popular Off Broadway that it transferred to the *Henry Miller Theatre, where it filled the small Broadway house for over two years.

UTAH SHAKESPEARE FESTIVAL (Cedar City, Utah). One of the most atmospheric summer festivals in the nation, the group was founded in 1961 by Fred C. Adams and gave its first performances in the summer of 1962. Performances are in the 819-seat outdoor replica of the Globe called the Adams Shakespeare Theatre, surrounded by a park in which Renaissance activities abound. There is also the indoor 769-seat Radall L. Jones Theatre. Now under the direction of Cameron Harvey, the repertory is primarily Shakespeare with occasional modern plays and musicals. The company received the 2000 *Tony Award for regional theatre excellence.

V

VAGABOND KING, THE. See *If I Were King.*

VAGINA MONOLOGUES, THE (1999), a mono-drama by Eve Ensler. [Westside Theatre, 1,0001 perf.] Ensler interviewed dozens of women about their genitalia and fashioned their comments into a one-woman program she began performing herself in 1996, bringing it Off Broadway three years later. From testimonies of rape victims to comic recounting of sexual adventures to a graphic but poetic description of giving birth, the monologues were expectantly shocking, reflective, and moving. After two months Ensler was succeeded by a series of celebrities (usually three women performing together) who kept the show on the boards for three years. The flexible, low-cost play has been very popular with feminist groups and women's centers across the country.

VALLEY FORGE (1934), a play by Maxwell *Anderson. [Guild Theatre, 58 perf.] George Washington (Philip *Merivale) has grown short-tempered watching his men starve and die in the cruel winter at Valley Forge and receiving no real aid from a narrow-minded, greedy Congress. When his old sweetheart, Mary Philipse (Margalo *Gillmore), braves the storms to visit him, he agrees to a meeting with British General Howe (Reginald Mason) to arrange for a surrender. But when Howe arrives, Washington recognizes that the bravery of his own men demands he fight to the finish. Supposedly written after several critics had complained that Anderson was more interested in English Elizabethan history than in his own, the play won generally laudatory notices, but the *Theatre Guild production could not find a public. Its imaginary meeting of Washington and Howe paralleled a similarly fictitious meeting of Mary and Elizabeth in Anderson's *Mary of Scotland.*

VAMPIRE LESBIANS OF SODOM (1985), a satire by Charles *Busch. [*Provincetown Playhouse, 2,024 perf.] This campy spoof of vamps (and vampires), from the ancient days of Sodom to the Hollywood of the 1920s up to contemporary Las Vegas, featured the exotic Madeleine Astarte (Busch) as she finesses her way through history. The comedy was prefaced by a curtain raiser titled *Sleeping Beauty or Coma* about the cutthroat fashion industry and the swinging mod scene of London in the 1960s. The double bill presented by Theatre in Limbo was deemed "bizarre and wonderful" by the press, and audiences made it the longest-running Off-Broadway nonmusical to date.

VAN and SCHENCK, comedy team. Gus Van [né August Van Glone] (1888–1968) and Joe Schenck [né Joseph T.] (1891?–1930) were childhood friends in their native Brooklyn and worked together as trolley-car conductor and motorman before entering vaudeville in 1910. Schenck played the piano and sang with his tenor voice in close harmony with Van, who excelled at dialect numbers. They were generally acknowledged as the best two-man "piano act" in vaudeville. The team also appeared in Broadway musicals, including *The Century Girl* (1916) and the 1919, 1920, and 1921 *Ziegfeld Follies.* In their first *Follies* appearance they sang "Mandy," with which they were thereafter identified. Following Schenck's death, Van continued with a solo act.

VAN DAM, Rip (1660?–1749), manager. He was the proprietor of what was possibly the first New York theatre. According to a newspaper account, dated December 11, 1732, "On the 6th instant, the New Theatre in the buildings of the Hon. Rip Van Dam, Esq. was opened with the comedy of the *Recruiting Officer.*" He served for a time as governor of the province of New York and had conducted a city census a year before this playhouse opened. His building was still used for occasional theatrical purposes as late as 1750.

VAN DRUTEN, John (1901–57), playwright. The London-born dramatist originally planned a career in law, which he practiced and taught for a time. He was well known for such plays as *Young Woodley* (1925), *There's Always Juliet* (1932), and *The Distaff Side* (1934) prior to his coming to America. Van Druten's best-received American works were *The *Voice of the Turtle* (1943), **I Remember Mama* (1944), **Bell, Book and Candle* (1950), and **I Am a Camera* (1951). He was at his best as a witty, urbane observer of modern society. Autobiography: *The Widening Circle*, 1957.

VAN ITALLIE, Jean-Claude (b. 1936), playwright. Born in Brussels, Belgium, and becoming an American citizen in 1952, Van Itallie brought a unique point of view when writing about the United States in the 1960s and 1970s. He was educated at Harvard and the *Neighborhood Playhouse and began writing plays in the early 1960s, first getting noticed for his one-act *Motel* (1965) at *La Mama. Much of his work was written in cooperation with the Open Theatre, an experimental group that premiered a number of his works, such as *The Serpent* (1969). Van Itallie has also created successful adaptations of plays by Anton *Chekhov.

VANDENHOFF, John M. (1790–1861), actor. The striking, deep-voiced tragedian was considered a major rival to William Charles *Macready when he made his American debut in 1837 as Coriolanus. Among his other noteworthy roles were Macbeth, Pierre in *Venice Preserved*, Shylock, Brutus, and Hamlet. Although the *Knickerbocker* complained of his "over-weening desire to impress his audience with the astonishing consequence of every movement portrayed, and every syllable expressed," he found general acceptance during his several visits between his debut and 1844. James *Murdoch felt he was "the finest tragedian of the classic school of acting ever seen on the American stage." His son, **George VANDENHOFF** (1820–84), was also an actor who performed in England before making his American debut at the *Park Theatre in 1842 as Hamlet. A tall, manly actor, he remained a popular performer, largely in Shakespearean roles, until his retirement in 1856. Joseph *Ireland noted, "Although lacking the passion and intensity requisite for the loftiest assumptions of drama, Mr. Vandenhoff possessed all the accomplishments and elegances of mind and person demanded for the highest grades of genteel comedy and a wide range of serious parts somewhat subordinate to the standard of Shakespeare's subtlest creations." He was also admired for his Hotspur, Falconbridge, and Benedick. After his retirement he practiced law for a time. Autobiography (George Vandenhoff): *An Actor's Notebook; or the Green-Room and Stage*, 1865.

VANITIES (1976), a play by Jack Heifner. [Westside Theatre, 1,785 perf.] This bittersweet comedy follows the lives of three Texas cheerleaders, viewing them first as high school seniors obsessed with being popular, then in college as sorority girls trying to stay close despite outside pressures, then as young adults filled with disillusionment and compromise. While most critics dismissed the play

as "lightweight and obvious," audiences responded to the nostalgic tone of the piece and made it one of the longest Off-Broadway runs on record. The play was also popular in colleges and regional theatres for a while.

VARESI, Gilda. See *Enter Madame*.

VARIETY. The leading contemporary theatrical journal, it was founded in 1905 by Sime *Silverman and has been published weekly ever since. As its title indicated, its original emphasis was on vaudeville, but it rapidly branched out to cover all aspects of what it called "show biz." It publishes weekly reports on the grosses and attendance at all major stage productions, and devotes several pages to news of legitimate theatre, albeit since the 1960s it has had to give far more coverage to films and television. Its theatrical reviews have generally been the most accurate in predicting the success or failure of shows, and at the end of each theatrical season it offers a detailed record of the year's statistics. *Variety* has long been famous for such headlines as "Wall Street Lays an Egg" and "Stix Nix Hix Pix," the latter reflecting its distinctive verbal shorthand that also included such terms as "legits," "filmusicals," and "b.o." for box office figures. *Daily Variety* is published on the West Coast. In 1987 the trade sheet was purchased by England's Cahners Publishing Co.

VAUDEVILLE IN AMERICA. In this country the term "vaudeville" has almost never had the same connotation as it had in the original French. Instead, it was borrowed rather late to indicate an entertainment consisting of short, variegated acts, some musical, some comic, all offered on the same bill. Small olios (another term for this sort of entertainment) appeared early in American stage history, usually as divertissements on the extended bills offered in the late 18th and the first half of the 19th century even in the best legitimate theatres. Nonetheless, most see the real seeds of modern vaudeville in the "free concert saloons," "free-and-easies," and Western "honky-tonks" that sprang up in the years just before the Civil War. To lure customers (almost exclusively male, except for prostitutes), these establishments provided a series of acts whose tilt, both in its comedy and lyrics and in the presentation of its occasional dancing, was rough and often salacious. In the 1870s and 1880s attempts were made to clean up the nature of the bills so as to attract a more widespread, higher class audience. Although several impresarios apparently began to incorporate such changes at about the same time, the most famous was Tony *Pastor, who was hailed as the leader in the field and whose vaudeville house in New York was considered to offer the pinnacle in such entertainment. Like others, he banned the sale of intoxicating drinks, discouraged rowdiness, and removed any performer whose act was in any way offensive. About the same time, the term "vaudeville" began replacing the term "variety," which had been accepted for several decades. (A similar transition was occurring concurrently in the British equivalent, the music hall.) The heyday of American vaudeville was the first quarter of the 20th century. The huge national circuit established by B. F. *Keith and E. F. *Albee was paramount in the field. Keith, like Pastor before him, carefully guarded the morals of his patrons, while his partner Albee established an often vicious near monopoly that frequently played havoc with competition and imposed salary and other dictates on performers. Other notable managers included Alexander Pantages, S. Z. Poli, F. F. Proctor, and Martin *Beck. Beck built the *Palace Theatre in New York, which quickly became two-a-day's most prestigious auditorium. Historian Don B. Wilmeth has noted that "at its height, ten people attended a vaudeville show to every one who patronized other forms of entertainment; as many as ten to twenty thousand vaudeville acts were competing for bookings." For many people, vaudeville indicated modes of dress and established certain canons of behavior. Thus, while managers insisted on removing offensive acts, certain religious and racial stereotypes were allowed to persist since they were not perceived as truly offensive. Yet for all its tremendous popularity and despite the enormous salaries paid headliners, vaudeville was never to have quite the cachet that attached to the legitimate stage. As a result, many performers used variety merely as a stepping stone. Lillian *Russell and *Harrigan and *Hart were among the earliest to leave the field to find even greater glory in the theatre. The loose structure of many musical comedies of the period allowed artists who were essentially vaudevillians to find occasional homes there. May *Irwin, Marie *Cahill, Blanche *Ring, and, to a lesser extent, Eva *Tanguay were all vaudeville headliners who found a welcome in book musicals. George M. *Cohan moved from vaudeville to exceptional success on Broadway. The growth of the even more loosely structured revue proved a further lure. But traffic was not all one way. With the coming of his children, a leading musical comedy star, Eddie *Foy, left book shows to create one of the greatest acts in two-a-day, Eddie Foy and the Seven Little Foys. Other legitimate stars used vaudeville to fill in between shows, while the genre afforded a haven for many fading stars who found the road receptive and loyal after more fickle Broadway audiences had lost interest in them. A few notable vaudevillians, such as Harry Lauder, never ventured afield. The coming of radio and then sound films, both major family entertainments, precipitated the demise of two-a-day. Most historians generally mark the showing of feature films at the Palace in 1932 as the end of traditional vaudeville, although it persisted, especially as *Tab Shows were presented along with feature films throughout the 1930s in some large cities. Attempts to revive big-time vaudeville at the Palace in the 1950s failed.

VEILLER, Bayard (1869–1943), playwright. The Brooklyn native had served as a police reporter and as a theatrical press agent before turning dramatist. Although nearly twenty of his plays were produced, he is best remembered for three superior thrillers: *Within the Law (1912), The *Thirteenth Chair (1916), and The *Trial of Mary Dugan (1927). Autobiography: The Fun I've Had, 1941.

VERDON, [Gwyneth Evelyn] Gwen (1926–2000), dancer and actress. The slim redhead, whose performances suggested both sexuality and vulnerability, was born in Culver City, California, where she learned dancing from her mother, Gertrude, as well as several noted dance teachers, including Jack *Cole, whom she assisted on choreographing Magdalena (1948). Verdon helped him again and also danced in the revue Alive and Kicking (1950), then recognition came when she danced in *Can-Can (1953). Thereafter, she was starred in a series of musicals choreographed by Bob *Fosse, to whom she was married for a time: *Damn Yankees (1955), *New Girl in Town (1957), *Redhead (1959), *Sweet Charity (1966), and *Chicago (1975). She was the only major musical star of the post-war theatre whose fame rested on dance, though she could interpret a song and play an engaging character with panache.

VERNON, Mrs. [née Jane Marchant Fisher] (1796–1869), comic actress. One of America's greatest comediennes, she was born in Brighton, England, and first appeared on stage at London's Drury Lane in 1817. With her brother, John Aubrey Fisher, and her future husband, George Vernon, she made her American debut at the *Bowery Theatre in 1827 in The Heir at Law. Her sister, Clara *Fisher, made her debut the same evening at the *Park Theatre. For a time she was overshadowed by her sister and brother but eventually surpassed them both in popularity and achievement. Through the years Vernon moved through a wide range of characterizations, first at the Park and the *Broadway and finally with William *Burton and with Lester *Wallack. She was a tall woman with a slightly pinched but expressive face. Summing up, late in her career, Joseph *Ireland wrote, "In early life, Mrs. Vernon was better capable of personating Lady Teazle, and Letitia Hardy, than many actresses who were recognized as stars. . . . In burlettas and burlesques of any kind, she gave a more heightened effect, a more brilliant and fantastic coloring than any actress . . . [for] antiquated dowagers, and spinsters in the last stages of desperation . . . she still maintains her well-earned position of superiority." She was said to have been an extremely intelligent woman, who often quietly helped direct the plays in which she appeared.

VERY GOOD EDDIE (1915), a musical comedy by Philip Bartholomae, Guy *Bolton (book), Jerome *Kern (music), Schuyler Greene (lyrics). [*Princess Theatre, 341 perf.] Little Eddie Kettle (Ernest *Truex) and his battle-ax bride, Georgina (Helen Raymond), are about to leave on their honeymoon aboard a Hudson River steamer, as are two other newlyweds, Percy (John Willard) and Elsie Darling (Alice Dovey). For different reasons, Percy and Georgina have to go ashore briefly, and the boat sails without them. Eddie is left to look after Elsie not only on board but at an inn where they are to lodge for the night. When a storm arises, Eddie has to comfort Elsie. By the time Percy and Georgina rejoin them the next day, Eddie is a changed man and not about to take orders from anyone. *Notable songs*: Babes in the Wood; Some Sort of Somebody; Thirteen Collar; Nodding Roses. The first of the *Princess Theatre musicals to become a smash hit, it was successfully revived, first at the *Goodspeed Opera House and then on Broadway in 1975, where it ran for 304 performances. The Goodspeed revived it again in 2003 with success.

VICTORY GARDENS THEATRE (Chicago). During the first three decades of its existence, this company has produced more world premieres than any other group in the city. Founded in 1974 by eight Chicago artists, the company has emphasized new plays from the beginning. Under the leadership of Marcelle McVay and Dennis Zacek (who continues to be artistic director), dozens of American playwrights have seen their work first staged there, including Steve Carter, Jeffrey Sweet, Lonnie Carter, Rick Cleveland, and James Sherman. The troupe received the regional theatre *Tony Award in 2001.

VIDAL, Gore (b. 1925), playwright. Born in West Point, New York, the caustic but brilliantly witty writer, while better known as a novelist, has also written several superior plays. His biggest successes were the thought-provoking sci fi comedy *Visit to a Small Planet* (1957) and the political drama *The *Best Man* (1960). Vidal's other works were *Romulus* (1962), *Weekend* (1968), and *An Evening with Richard Nixon and . . .* (1972). Biography: *The Apostate Angel*, Bernard F. Dick, 1974.

VIENNESE [and German] OPERETTA IN AMERICA. There have been two basic schools of Middle-European operetta that have enjoyed popularity in America. The earliest was exemplified by the works of such composers as von Suppé, Millöcker, and *Strauss. The success of Suppé's *Fatinitza* in 1879 inaugurated the era, although it reached its peak as far as most Americans were concerned with the great Strauss operettas. Curiously, most of what today are perceived as Strauss's masterpieces— works such as *Die Fledermaus* and *The Gypsy Baron*—were not the most popular with contemporary audiences, for whom such pieces as *The Merry War*, *The Queen's Lace Handkerchief*, and *Prince Methusalem* had more appeal. Despite their success their influence on American lyric theatre styles was minimal. *Die Fledermaus* has since been revived on Broadway under a number of titles such as *The Merry Countess* (1912), *A Wonderful Night* (1929), *Champagne, Sec* (1933), and *Rosalinda* (1942); but for the most part revivals of these works have been confined to the repertories of opera companies. By the turn of the century the initial vogue had died along with its creators. However, in 1907 the widespread success of *Lehar's *The *Merry Widow* resurrected the demand for Viennese-like operetta, albeit for a less pyrotechnic style given over to eminently danceable ballroom waltzes. Oscar Straus's *A Waltz Dream* and *The Chocolate Soldier*, Lehar's *The Count of Luxembourg*, and Emmerich *Kalman's *Sari* were among the notable works from this period, which flourished from 1907 to 1914, when ill feelings stemming from World War I put a sharp but temporary end to it, and which was alive again briefly in the 1920s. Before the war these works were considered the best on the modern musical stage and were copied in such American pieces as *The *Pink Lady*. Victor *Herbert's great works sometimes betrayed a small debt to these examples as well, although he displayed French, Irish, and other influences alongside the Germanic ones. Victor Jacobi and Fritz Kreisler's *Apple Blossoms* played a large part in reviving interest after the war, as did the works of two naturalized Americans, Sigmund *Romberg and Rudolf *Friml. The most successful importation of the era was Kalman's *Countess Maritza*. Thereafter, despite occasional revivals, the genre went through a period of disdain, although *The White Horse Inn*, with music by Benatsky and Stolz, was a hit in the 1930s. Recently, especially with some opera companies' addition of operetta to their repertories, interest has again begun to wax, albeit very slowly.

VIEW FROM THE BRIDGE, A (1955), a play by Arthur *Miller. [Coronet Theatre, 149 perf.] Eddie Carbone (Van Heflin), a Brooklyn longshoreman, has an unnaturally strong affection for his niece,

Catherine (Gloria Marlowe). Furious when she is attracted to Rodolpho (Richard Davalos), a handsome young illegal immigrant, Eddie tries to convince her that the boy is a homosexual. When this ploy fails, he informs the immigration authorities, who arrange to deport the boy and his brother. Having broken both a moral and family code, Eddie kills himself. Originally presented as part of a double bill with the play *A Memory of Two Mondays*, it was later enlarged and revised by Miller. This longer version was successfully presented Off Broadway in 1965 and far outran the original production. It was also successfully revived in 1983 with Tony Lo Bianco as Eddie and in 1998 with Anthony LaPaglia.

VINCENT, Mrs. J. R. [née Mary Ann Farley] (1818–87), actress. The most beloved of 19th-century Boston actresses, she was born in Portsmouth, England, and made her debut in *Cowes* in 1835, later that year marrying the comedian James R. Vincent. The couple came to America in 1846 to play at Boston's National Theatre, then, after her husband's death, joined the *Boston Museum, where she became a favorite and continued to perform until just a few days before she died. The heavyset, kind-faced actress appeared in 444 different roles at the Museum, including Portia, Gertrude, Mrs. Malaprop, Lady Teazle, Nancy Sykes, Widow Racket in *The Belle's Stratagem*, Widow Melnotte in *The *Lady of Lyons,* and Helen in *The *Hunchback.* On her death virtually all Boston papers referred to her as "dear old Mrs. Vincent." Biography: *Fiftieth Anniversary of the First Appearance on Stage of Mrs. J. R. Vincent . . . Fifty Years of an Actress' Life*, 1885.

VIOLET (1997), a musical play by Brian Crawley (book, lyrics), Jeanine Tesori (music). [*Playwrights Horizons, 32 perf.; NYDCC Award.] The Southern girl Violet (Lauren Ward) is marked with a facial scar she's had since her father had an accident with his ax. In 1964 she sets out from Spruce Pine, North Carolina, by bus to attend a revivalist meeting held by a televangelist in Oklahoma with the hopes of getting cured. On the journey she befriends two servicemen, the good ol' boy Monty (Michael Park) and the African-American Flick (Michael McElroy). The faith healing at the revival does not remove the scar, but she does find the strength to overcome her prejudices and fall in love with Flick. *Notable songs*: Raise Me Up; On My Way; Let It Sing; Down the Mountain. Based on Doris Betts's novel *The Ugliest Pilgrim*, the chamber piece was praised by the press and plans were made to move to a commercial venue until a pan in the all-powerful *New York Times* scuttled the transfer. The work has since been slowly finding recognition in regional houses. **Jeanine**

TESORI (b. 1961) was born in Manhasset, New York, and studied music at Barnard College. She arranged dance music and orchestrations for several musicals on and Off Broadway and conducted orchestras before *Violet* revealed her composing talents. She also wrote the music for the Broadway hit *Thoroughly Modern Millie* (2002).

VIRGINIA STAGE (Norfolk, Virginia). Before this company was founded and took up residence in 1979, the historic Wells Theatre had been a failed opera house, then a legit touring facility that saw the likes of Maude *Adams in *Peter Pan. But during the Depression it was a movie house, then a burlesque theatre, and finally an X-rated cinema. The Virginia Stage found enough success with its revivals of plays and small musicals that in 1986 a major renovation of the old theatre was completed. The current artistic director is Charlie Hensley.

VIRGINIA THEATRE (New York). This playhouse on West 52nd Street has not only gone through several name changes, but the space itself has been reconfigured on three occasions. The illustrious *Theatre Guild built the structure in 1924 to house its ambitious productions and had set designers Lee *Simonson and Norman *Bel Geddes work with architect C. Howard Crane on its Italian Renaissance design. Yet the space itself was a failure: there were only 914 seats so ticket sales could not begin to cover expenses, and there was so much room backstage devoted to storing productions in repertory that dressing rooms and other essential places were inadequate. Called the Guild Theatre, the playhouse was home to some impressive Guild productions, but soon the company used better Broadway theatres and leased its own house to others. During the 1940s the theatre was a radio studio, then in 1950 it was remodeled for more seats and became the home of the *American National Theatre and Academy, renamed the ANTA Playhouse. Productions by the nonprofit group and commercial ventures occupied the ANTA for three decades, then it was bought by *Jujamcyn, renovated once again into a 1,200-seat venue for musicals, and named the Virginia Theatre after owner James Binger's wife.

VIRGINIAN, THE (1904), a play by Owen Wister and Kirke *La Shelle. [Manhattan Theatre, 138 perf.] In a rough and tumble Wyoming of wild cowpunchers and ruthless cattle thieves, the Virginian (Dustin *Farnum) is a model of rectitude and courtesy. He can put a foul-mouth ruffian in his place by warning him, "When you call me that, smile!" But he also has a way with the gentler sex, so when he courts Molly (Agnes Ardeck), a schoolteacher from Vermont, she agrees to marry him.

One of the many dramatizations of the novels popular at the time, the stage version lacked sufficient action and life according to many critics. Its success came largely from Farnum's performance. This collaboration in dramatizing his novel was the only major theatrical venture for the Pennsylvania-born author Wister (1860–1938).

VISIT TO A SMALL PLANET (1957), a comedy by Gore *Vidal. [*Booth Theatre, 388 perf.] Dressed as a proper gentleman of the 1860s, Kreton (Cyril *Ritchard), a creature from a planet far out in space and whose hobby has been studying little, backward Earth, lands in Manassas, hoping to catch a glimpse of the Civil War. Unfortunately his timing is a bit off, so he arrives at the modern home of the celebrated television commentator Roger Spelding (Philip Coolidge) just as Spelding is hosting his old friend, the bureaucratic, cliché-ridden General Tom Powers (Eddie Mayehoff). Kreton becomes intrigued with civilization's improvements—such as giant battleships and hydrogen bombs—and sets about trying to start another world war. To his disappointment, he fails. Heading back home, he decides to see if his time machine will still let him witness the Civil War and promises to return "one bright day in 1861. The Battle of Bull Run. . . . Only next time I think it'll be more fun if the South wins." Brooks *Atkinson hailed the comedy as "a topsy-turvy lark that has a lot of humorous vitality."

VIVIAN BEAUMONT THEATRE (New York). One of Broadway's two nonproscenium theatre spaces, this flexible performance space at *Lincoln Center was co-designed by architect Eero Saarinen and scenic designer Jo *Mielziner to house the Repertory Theatre of Lincoln Center. It features a semicircular auditorium and an acting area that can shift from a thrust stage to a modified proscenium. Seating was also changeable (from 1,083 to 1,140 seats, depending on the configuration), and the backstage was twice as large as traditional playhouses. The modern, simply decorated theatre was named after donor Mrs. Vivian Beaumont Allen and opened in 1965. From the start there were complaints about the theatre's acoustical deficiencies and the problems encountered with the thrust stage. Over the years the auditorium has been remodeled, but only a few of its many difficulties have been resolved. Yet every once in a while a production plays at the Vivian Beaumont that seems to thrive on the awkward space, such as Joseph *Papp's The *Threepenny Opera (1976), Andrei *Serban's The Cherry Orchard (1977), *Six Degrees of Separation (1990), and the musical revivals *Anything Goes (1987) and *Carousel (1994).

VOEGTLIN, Arthur. See Voegtlin, William T.

VOEGTLIN, William T. (1835–?), designer. Born in Basel, Switzerland, he came to America in 1850 and began to work as a scene painter in New Orleans. He rapidly made a name for himself there and in San Francisco before coming to New York about 1870. In that year Voegtlin designed the ornate sets for the first major revival of The *Black Crook, and his work established him as a leading creator of extravagant scenery, although he often designed less flamboyant productions as well. He spent much of his later career at *Niblo's Garden and the Grand Opera House, both homes to spectacles, and later worked at Booth's Theatre. His work was seen in such offerings as Heartsease (1870), *Kit, the Arkansas Traveller (1871), Connie Soogah (1875), Hiawatha (1880), and Margaret *Mather's *Romeo and Juliet (1885). His son was **Arthur VOEGTLIN** (1858?–1948), who was born in Chicago and planned to become a more serious painter before following his father's profession. His earliest designs were seen in Charles *Hoyt's *farce-comedies, including A *Trip to Chinatown (1891), and in later musicals and dramas. However, he was best remembered for his work at the *Hippodrome, where he designed all that theatre's great spectacles from its opening in 1905 until 1918. He was generally credited with devising the Hippodrome's huge water tank and the underwater tunnel through which performers disappeared.

VOGEL, Paula. See *How I Learned to Drive*.

VOICE OF THE TURTLE, THE (1943), a comedy by John *Van Druten. [*Morosco Theatre, 1,557 perf.] Olive Lashbrooke (Audrey Christie), an actress with a male friend in every city, stops briefly at the apartment of another actress, Sally Middleton (Margaret *Sullavan), to await a date who is to meet her there. But just before the date arrives, another male friend calls to ask Olive to go out with him, and she agrees. This leaves Sally to entertain the man Olive has stood up, Bill Page (Elliott *Nugent), a soldier on leave. Before his weekend pass expires, Bill and Sally have fallen in love. The first small-cast play (only three characters) to become a smash hit, the Alfred *de Liagre Jr. production set a precedent that later economics forced other playwrights to abuse. The *Roundabout Theatre revived the play with success in 1985.

VOKES, Rosina (1854–94), actress. The daughter of a London costumer, she and her brother and sisters—Fred[erick Mortimer] (1846–88), Jessie (1851–84), and Victoria (1853–94)—came to America in 1871 along with Fawdon Vokes, who was not a member of the family and whose real name was Walter Fawdon (?–1904). They made their New York debut in 1872 in *The Belles of the Kitchen*, an early forerunner of modern musical comedy. During several visits between their debut and 1875, the Vokeses regaled playgoers with similar shows such as *The Right Man in the Wrong Place* and *Fun in a Fog* but always returned to their popular *Belles of the Kitchen*. From the first, Rosina had been considered "infinitely the cleverest, the most bewitching" of the group, so when she reappeared in America in 1885 with her own company, she was instantly welcome. One paper wrote, "She is still young, agile, slender, and graceful; the piquant prettiness of her face and the droll charm of her manner still exert a strong influence upon the susceptible spectator." Until shortly before her early death she continued to tour in made-to-order vehicles with titles such as *The Tinted Venus, My Milliner's Bill, My Uncle's Will*, and *A Lesson in Love*.

VOLLMER, Lula (1898–1955), playwright. A pioneer in the American folk-play, she was born in Keyser, North Carolina, and educated at what later became Asheville College. After graduation she went to New York to try to sell her play **Sun-Up*. Although she worked for the *Theatre Guild as a box-office clerk, the Guild joined other producers in rejecting the work, which was finally mounted by a minor producer in 1923. It told the story of a vengeful mountain woman, and Vollmer waived her royalties for the play, giving them instead to help educate Southern mountaineers. In the same year she also won praise for her backwoods drama *The *Shame Woman* (1923). None of her subsequent plays was a commercial success, although several had considerable merit. Among the more noteworthy were *The Dunce Boy* (1925), *Trigger* (1927), and *The Hill Between* (1938).

VOSKOVEC, George [né Jiri Voskovec] (1905–81), actor. He was born in Prague and educated at the University of Dijon and Charles University in his hometown. Voskovec was an experienced actor and director who ran his own company in Czechoslovakia before coming to America in 1940 and working in regional theatre, making his Broadway debut in *The Tempest* in 1945. During the war he wrote and broadcast many radio programs for the *Voice of America*, then returned to his homeland after VE Day to continue his theatre activities. But Voskovec was back in New York by 1954 and for the next twenty-five years appeared in many plays, often in supporting but potent roles.

W

WAGENHALS and KEMPER, producers and managers. Lincoln A. Wagenhals (1869–1931) and Collin Kemper (1870–1955), two Ohio men who both had worked briefly as actors, went into partnership in 1893 when they acquired a theatre in Binghamton, New York. Within a few seasons they were managing such notables as Arthur *Byron, Helena *Modjeska, Henry *Miller, Annie *Russell, and Frederick *Warde. In 1906 they became the first lessees of the new Astor Theatre. Among their successful productions in this period were *Clothes (1906), *Paid in Full (1908), *Seven Days (1909), and The Greyhound (1912). After a temporary separation, Wagenhals and Kemper had success with Seeing Things (1920), Spanish Love (1920), The *Bat (1920), and Why Men Leave Home (1922). They retired permanently in the mid-1920s.

WAGNER, Robin [Samuel Anton] (b. 1933), designer. The San Francisco native studied at the California School of Fine Arts and created his earliest scenic designs for theatres in his hometown. In New York he worked for a time under Ben Edwards and Oliver *Smith, then served as designer for Washington's *Arena Stage from 1964 to 1967. By the 1970s Wagner was among the busiest set designers on Broadway with such memorable productions as *Hair (1968), The *Great White Hope (1968), *Promises, Promises (1968), *Jesus Christ Superstar (1971), Sugar (1972), *Seesaw (1973), A *Chorus Line (1975), *On the Twentieth Century (1978), *42nd Street (1980), *Dreamgirls (1981), *Jerome Robbins' Broadway (1989), *City of Angels (1989), *Crazy for You (1992), *Angels in America (1993), Victor/Victoria (1995), The Life (1997), Saturday Night Fever (1999), The *Producers (2001), *Flower Drum Song (2002), and Wicked (2003). Wagner's sets are known for their sense of movement, whether it is simply revolving mirrors, as in A Chorus Line, or the gliding towers of lights in Dreamgirls or the complex train units in On the Twentieth Century.

WAINWRIGHT, Marie (1853–1923), actress and singer. The Paris-trained performer from an old Philadelphia family made her debut in New York as Juliet in 1877, then spent several years with the *Boston Museum, where she was the first American Josephine in *H.M.S. Pinafore and the first American Countess Zicka in *Diplomacy. Thereafter, Wainwright served as leading lady to Lawrence *Barrett, then headed her own company. She continued to act until her death, in later years assuming important secondary roles in such plays as Marie-Odile (1915) and Dear Brutus (1918).

WAITING FOR GODOT (1956). Samuel *Beckett's absurdist "tragicomedy" told of two seedy men who joke, complain, and consider suicide while waiting for a blurry figure they called Godot. When he fails to appear they decide to leave, but stand perfectly still. This baffling play had its New York premiere at the *John Golden Theatre in 1956 and enjoyed one of the longest runs (fifty-nine performances) of any work of the theatre of the absurd, thanks in large measure to remarkable acting by Bert *Lahr and E. G. *Marshall. Lahr's performance was all the more remarkable in that he is reputed never to have understood a word he was speaking, but he had lots of company across the footlights. Often revived across America, Waiting for Godot enjoyed a nine-month run in an Off Broadway revival in 1971 and a star-studded, limited-run mounting at *Lincoln Center in 1988 was a hot ticket.

WAITING FOR LEFTY (1935), a play by Clifford *Odets. [*Longacre Theatre, 168 perf.] At a meeting of a taxi drivers' union, members await the return of their committee man, Lefty Costello. The union is addressed by several people who urge them not to strike but then is harangued by agitators, who depict capitalism as corrupt and smothering. After a series of flashbacks to different people affected by the company, news arrives that Lefty has been killed, tensions explode, and the drivers go on strike. At a time when many Americans were being polarized politically, this play was one of the most effective propaganda pieces for the left. It was initially offered by the *Group Theatre at a series of special matinees. One of its producers, Cheryl *Crawford, noted, "Never before or since have I heard such a tumultuous reaction from an audience. The response was wild, fantastic. It raised the roof." The play was later moved to Broadway.

Although it was tremendously popular for a time with radical groups, it is now perceived as too simplistic to have lasting merit.

WALCOT, Charles M[elton] (1816–68), comic actor. One of the most adept and popular of mid-19th-century comedians, he was born in London and trained there as an architect. He came to America in 1837 and, after marrying an actress, decided to try his own luck on stage. Walcot made his debut in 1842, then joined William Mitchell at the Olympic, displaying his comic flair not only in his acting but in numerous burlesques he wrote for the company. When Mitchell's group disbanded, he played briefly with William *Burton, then joined *Wallack's ensemble. There he excelled in such classic roles as Charles Surface and Bob Acres. He also took the title part in his highly successful burlesque, *Hiawatha; or, Ardent Spirits and Laughing Waters* (1856). Walcot was a handsome, blue-eyed man with a conspicuously high forehead. His son, Charles Jr. (1840–1921), who was born in Boston and inherited his father's good looks, made his stage debut under the name of Charles Brown. With his wife, the former Isabella Nickinson (1847–1906), he was long a favorite in romantic roles at Philadelphia's *Walnut Street Theatre. From 1887 on, the couple played older parts with Daniel *Frohman's Lyceum Theatre company.

WALDRON, Charles D. (1874–1946), actor. Although never a star, this performer from Waterford, New York, enjoyed a career of nearly half a century playing both leads and major supporting roles. After making his debut in 1898, he spent almost a decade learning his trade in stock companies from New York to San Francisco. He returned to New York in 1907 as the Northerner Lt. Burton in *The *Warrens of Virginia.* His biggest hit came in the title role of *Daddy Long Legs* (1914), followed by his Gray Meredith in *A Bill of Divorcement* (1921), the father Dr. Besant in *Coquette* (1927), the father Edward Moulton-Barrett in *The *Barretts of Wimpole Street* (1931), the Yankee farmer Aaron Kirkland in *The *Pursuit of Happiness* (1933), and the conservative Southern Senator Langdon in *Deep Are the Roots* (1945).

WALKEN, Christopher [né Ronald Walken] (b. 1943), actor. The edgy film star known for his slightly psychotic characters is also a seasoned Shakespearean actor, as witnessed by his many classic roles in regional and New York theatre. He was born in Queens and was educated at the Professional Children's School and at Hofstra, later studying at the *Actors Studio. Walken was on television as a child performer, then made his Broadway debut in 1959 as the teenage son David in *J.B.*

His many memorable performances include the teenager Alan visiting his estranged father in *Lemon Sky* (1970), a sensitive *Hamlet (1975), the drifter Chance Wayne in *Sweet Bird of Youth* (1975), a powerful *Coriolanus* (1988), a quiet, steady Iago in *Othello (1991), the slimy Hollywood casting agent Mickey in *Hurlyburly* (1984), and Dubliner Gabriel Conroy in *James Joyce's The Dead* (1999).

WALKER, Don[ald John] (1907–89), orchestrator. Born in Lambertville, New Jersey, and educated at the University of Pennsylvania, he orchestrated over one hundred Broadway musicals, beginning with *May Wine* (1935). His work was heard in, among others, *Leave It to Me!* (1938), *By Jupiter (1942), *Carousel (1945), *Finian's Rainbow (1947), *Gentlemen Prefer Blondes (1949), *Call Me Madam (1950), *Wish You Were Here (1952), *Wonderful Town (1953), The *Pajama Game (1954), *Damn Yankees (1955), The *Most Happy Fella (1956), The *Music Man (1957), *Fiddler on the Roof (1964), *Cabaret (1966), and *Shenandoah (1975).

WALKER, George. See Williams, Bert.

WALKER, June (1899?–1966), actress. The petite blonde gave several different birth dates and places in interviews but was most likely born either in Chicago or New York. Her first Broadway assignment was in the chorus of *Hitchy-Koo, 1918*. Among her notable roles were the flighty Marilyn Sterling in *Six-Cylinder Love* (1921), reluctant bride Sally Morgan in *The *Nervous Wreck* (1923), gold-digging flapper Lorelei Lee in *Gentlemen Prefer Blondes* (1926), illegitimate daughter Antoinette Flagg in *The Bachelor Father* (1928), Oklahoma farm girl Laurey Williams in *Green Grow the Lilacs* (1931), and "canawler's" daughter Molly Larkins in *The Farmer Takes a Wife* (1934). Much of Walker's subsequent career was in failures or as a replacement for leading ladies in long-running successes. Her last important original assignment was the Mother in *Middle of the Night* (1956).

WALKER, Nancy [née Anna Myrtle Swoyer] (1921–92), comic actress. The extremely short, sour-faced comedienne was born in Philadelphia and made her stage debut as the wallflower at a college prom in *Best Foot Forward* (1941). After appearing as a man-hungry taxi driver in *On the Town* (1944), she was starred in such musicals as *Barefoot Boy with Cheek* (1947), *Look, Ma, I'm Dancin'* (1948), *Along Fifth Avenue* (1949), *Phoenix '55, Copper and Brass* (1957), and *Do Re Mi* (1960). In nonmusicals she scored a major success as Julia Starbuck in a 1956 revival of *Fallen Angels* and appeared in 1968 with the *Association of Producing Artists as Charlotte Ivanovna in *The Cherry*

Orchard and Julia in *The *Cocktail Party*. Brooks *Atkinson said of her, "Next to Beatrice Lillie, Nancy Walker is the funniest woman in the theatre. . . . She can destroy a drawing-room comedy just by walking silently across the stage." Another critic said that when she struck an attitude the attitude struck back. Unfortunately, she was rarely lucky in her choice of vehicles and so disappeared from the stage while still at the height of her comic powers. Much of her later career was in television.

WALKER, Stuart (1888–1941), manager and actor. Born in Augusta, Kentucky, he began his career in 1909 as an actor but soon became assistant director to David *Belasco. Five years later he served a brief tenure with Jessie *Bonstelle, then in 1915 established his Portmanteau Theatre. He also ran companies in such cities as Cincinnati, Indianapolis, Chicago, Louisville, and Baltimore. Walker's ensembles were essentially progressive stock companies and he, like Bonstelle, is credited with the solid early training of many later stars. His last years were in films.

WALL, Thomas (fl. mid-18th century), actor. This performer and sometimes manager first appears in American records when he performed with David *Douglass's *American Company in Charleston in 1766. He was advertised as being "From the Theatre Royal, Drury Lane and the Haymarket London." He continued to play (usually secondary roles) with the company for many seasons not only in Charleston but at Philadelphia's *Southwark Theatre and New York's *John Street Theatre. In 1781 Wall built a theatre in Baltimore in partnership with Adam Lindsay. During his two years as manager he took on such leading roles as Richard III, but he appears to have overreached, since after relinquishing the managerial reins to Dennis *Ryan he remained to again play lesser parts. Eola Willis, in her *The Charleston Stage in the XVIII Century*, suggests he may have been the same Thomas Llewellyn Lechmere Wall who left behind a valuable collection of playbills covering forty years. George O. Seilhamer, who adds that he may also have used the name John Wall, noted, "Wall was not a great actor, but he was an ambitious one, and to him and his partner, Lindsay, not to Hallam and Henry, as has always been asserted, was due the revival of the drama in the United States when the dark hours of the War for Independence were over."

WALLACH, Eli (b. 1915), actor. The Brooklyn-born performer, who never lost his borough accent or mannerisms, made his Broadway debut in 1945 and soon afterwards acted with the *American Repertory Theatre. He first won major attention as the passionate truck driver Alvaro Mangiacavallo in *The *Rose Tattoo* (1951). In later years he appeared with his wife, Anne *Jackson, in such shows as *Rhinoceros* (1961), *The Typists* and *The Tiger* (1963), **Luv* (1964), *The Waltz of the Toreadors* (1973), *The *Diary of Anne Frank* (1978), *Twice Around the Park* (1982), and *The Flowering Peach* (1994). Wallach also gave memorable performances in *Major Barbara* (1956), *Staircase* (1964), *Cafe Crown* (1988), *The *Price* (1992), *Visiting Mr. Green* (1997), and *Down the Garden Paths* (2000). An advocate of the Method school of acting, Wallach is also a superb craftsman in creating characters.

WALLACK, Henry [John] (1790–1870), actor. The eldest son of Mr. and Mrs. William Wallack, who were popular performers in London, he came to America in 1819 and made his debut at Baltimore's *Holliday Street Theatre. After time there and at Philadelphia's *Chestnut Street Theatre, he moved to New York in 1821, performing at the Anthony Street Theatre, the Chatham Garden Theatre, and the *Bowery Theatre, for a time attempting unsuccessfully to manage the former. After some years back in England, Wallack returned in 1837 to manage the National Theatre for his brother James *Wallack. When the *Broadway Theatre opened in 1847 with *The School for Scandal*, he played Sir Peter Teazle, and he continued to perform, with occasional sojourns to London, until 1854, when he marked his farewell by playing Sir John Falstaff. He was a versatile, accomplished actor, although he was never identified with any special roles and never won the fame accorded to other members of the family.

WALLACK, James William (1794–1864), actor and manager. The younger brother of Henry *Wallack, he was slated for the navy but chose to continue his family's acting tradition. He had played opposite Edmund *Kean and other leading figures before making his American debut at the *Park Theatre in 1818 as Macbeth, followed by his Rolla, Coriolanus, Romeo, Hamlet, and Richard III. For the next thirty-three years he shuttled between America and England, often appearing at Philadelphia's *Arch Street Theatre and New York's National Theatre, which he managed for a time. It was at the latter that he offered the premiere of **Tortesa, the Usurer* (1839). George *Odell has written that during these seasons, "Wallack really first showed New York what was meant by perfect stage-management, with an eye to every detail, however slight." He settled permanently in New York in 1851 and the following year opened his theatre and organized the company that was a leading American ensemble for the next thirty-five years, first under him, then under his son Lester

*Wallack. Although his repertory covered a full range of classic and modern, tragic and comic, his forte was comedy. With rare exceptions, he ignored native works, preferring the safety of English and Continental writing. Wallack retired from acting in 1859 but continued to operate his theatre (including a new one built in 1861) until shortly before his death. His contemporary, James H. *Hackett, described him thus: "His figure and bearing . . . were very distingué; his eye was sparkling; his hair dark, curly, and luxuriant; his facial features finely chiselled; and, together with the natural conformation of his head, throat, and chest, Mr. Wallack presented a remarkable specimen of manly beauty." Biography: *A Sketch of the Life of James William Wallack*, Anonymous, 1865.

WALLACK, James William, Jr. (1818–73), actor. Despite his name, he was the son of Henry *Wallack and was born in London shortly before his parents immigrated to America. In 1822 he made his debut as the child in *Pizarro* at Philadelphia's *Chestnut Street Theatre. His first New York appearance seems to have come ten years later at the *Bowery Theatre as a peasant in *Hofer, the "Tell" of the Tyrol.* For a time he acted in his uncle's company at the National. Although he inherited the Wallacks' good looks, rugged build, and fine, deep voice, he was generally judged as little more than adequate in comedy. Tragedy was his strong point, and he was admired for his Iago, Othello, Macbeth, and Richard III. Besides such classic roles he won applause as Fagin and, shortly before his retirement in 1872, as Mathias in *The Bells.* More than any other member of his family he spent most of his career away from New York, spreading the Wallack name to all the major American theatrical centers. He toured as far west as California, for a time in association with E. L. *Davenport. *Ireland remarked on his "elegance of mien, picturesqueness of attitude, and spirited declamation."

WALLACK, [John Johnstone] Lester (1819–88), actor and manager. The son of James William *Wallack, he was the only major member of the Wallack family born in America. However, despite his birth in New York, he acknowledged his English background by serving his theatrical apprenticeship in England and in Ireland. His American debut did not occur until 1847 when he appeared at the *Broadway Theatre as Sir Charles Coldstream in *Used Up.* His contemporary, W. J. *Florence, described him as "tall, straight as an Indian, graceful and distinguished in appearance. Piercing black eyes, an abundance of jet black hair, shapely limbs, small extremities, and, withal, a figure that permitted a perfect fitting of tastefully chosen clothes, were among the advantages that he once possessed and which made him almost Hyperion." For a time he played under William *Burton, where he won applause as Sir Andrew Aguecheek and Charles Surface. When his father formed the ensemble that was to be one of America's great companies for over three decades, he joined it and within a few years took over its management. Wallack played nearly three hundred roles with the company, including Orlando, Benedick, and Marlow as well as leading parts in such contemporary works as *Ours, *Diplomacy, A Scrap of Paper*, and his own dramatization of *Rosedale.* His tenure was praised for the excellence of his productions and his actors' performances but was also criticized for his failure to mount many classics and his dismissal of native American works. (He once told Bronson *Howard that he might accept an early draft of Howard's Civil War play *Shenandoah* if it were reset in the Crimea.) With the rise of Augustin *Daly in the 1870s, Wallack's star began to fade slightly; however, he remained an honored figure until his retirement in 1887. Autobiography: *Memories of Fifty Years*, 1889.

WALLACK'S THEATRE (New York). The famous playhouse on Broadway at 13th Street was one of three theatres that bore the Wallack name. An earlier house was built on lower Broadway in 1850, and a later one at 30th Street was erected in 1880. But for nearly twenty years Wallack's meant the revered structure at Union Square that opened in 1861 and, under the astute management of Lester *Wallack, presented the finest British actors in the best English plays. Critics compared the large and comfortable playhouse favorably with the Drury Lane in London. The house was renamed the Star Theatre after Wallack's death in 1888, and it was demolished in 1901.

WALLER, Emma (1820–99), actress. The English-born tragedienne made her American debut as Ophelia at Philadelphia's *Walnut Street Theatre in 1857. The following year her first New York appearance came as Marina in *The Duchess of Malfi.* She excelled at many of the same roles that Charlotte *Cushman played so well, and some critics maintained she copied Cushman's style, although she is said never to have seen her fellow actress perform. Her greatest interpretations included Meg Merrilies, Lady Macbeth, Julia in *The *Hunchback,* and the already mentioned Marina. Like Cushman she also appeared in many men's roles, including Hamlet and Iago. T. Allston *Brown noted, "Her Lady Macbeth was a wonderful performance, and I doubt if its equal has ever been seen on the American stage." Much of Waller's career was spent away from New York, including a season managing a theatre at Troy,

New York. *Winter recalled, "She was a woman of stately presence; her countenance was singularly expressive; she possessed dark, piercing eyes, a pallid expression, and a voice of unusual depth and compass." She retired in 1878 but continued to teach for many years.

WALNUT STREET THEATRE (Philadelphia). The oldest active playhouse in America, it was built as a circus in 1809 and converted to legitimate theatre two years later as the Olympic. Despite occasional dark periods and use as a burlesque house, its history has been distinguished. For many years it was a major rival to the city's *Arch Street and *Chestnut Street Theatres and for much of the 19th century housed an important stock company. The theatre also hosted performances by Edwin *Booth, Edwin *Forrest and others, was the first American theatre to install gas footlights in 1837, and in 1855 introduced a primitive air conditioning system. In the 20th century it served as a venue for major tryouts and tours, operating as a *Shubert house between 1941 and 1969. In 1968 the building was declared a National Landmark, and a major renovation restored the theatre to its 1928 look. The Walnut Street Theatre Company was founded in 1983 by a group of community leaders organized by Ed Rome and Bernard Havard. The repertory is conservative, emphasizing comedies and musicals, which has resulted in one of the largest subscription bases in the nation.

WALSTON, Ray (1914–2001), character actor. The thin, red-headed comic played wisecracking sidekicks and other colorful parts but was mostly remembered on Broadway for one musical role: the devilish Mr. Applegate in *Damn Yankees* (1955). He was born in New Orleans and worked as a reporter and a printer before turning to acting at a community theatre in Houston, Texas. Walston made his Broadway debut in 1945 in the cast of Maurice *Evans's *Hamlet*, followed by many secondary roles in comedies and dramas. In the 1960s he was very popular on television.

WALTER, Eugene (1874–1941), playwright. The Cleveland native served as a newsman and theatrical advance agent before writing his first play, followed by some two dozen others to reach Broadway. The best were a pair of melodramas that were perceived as bringing a fresh note of stark realism to the theatre of their time: *Paid in Full* (1908) and The *Easiest Way* (1909). Although Walter never lived up to the promise of these early plays, several later works were not without merit: *The Trail of the Lonesome Pine* (1912), *Fine Feathers* (1913), and *Just a Woman* (1916). He also wrote the book *How to Write a Play* (1925).

WALTER KERR THEATRE (New York). Despite a checkered history that saw it reduced to a porn movie house and a massage parlor for a time, this playhouse on West 48th Street has survived and today is a very desirable house for nonmusical plays. The 1,000-seat theatre was designed by Herbert J. *Krapp in the Italian Renaissance style and built by the *Shuberts in 1921 as the Ritz Theatre. During the 1930s it was used by the *Federal Theatre Project and was called the WPA Theatre, then in 1939 it was renamed CBS Theatre No. 4 and was used for radio broadcasts. In the 1940s and 1950s it fluctuated from legit to radio and television and then to movies, reaching its low point in the 1960s. The Ritz returned as a legit house in 1970, and in 1983 it was bought by *Jujamcyn, which renovated it and kept the space busy with small productions. In 1990 a more extensive restoration returned the theatre to its original luster, and it was renamed once again, this time after critic Walter *Kerr.

WALTON, Tony [Anthony John] (b. 1934), designer. The English-born scenic (and sometime costume) designer has enjoyed a successful career on both sides of the Atlantic. On Broadway his work has been seen in such shows as A *Funny Thing Happened on the Way to the Forum* (1962), *Pippin* (1972), *Chicago* (1975), The Act (1977), A Day in Hollywood—A Night in the Ukraine (1980), *Sophisticated Ladies* (1981), Woman of the Year (1981), The Real Thing (1984), *I'm Not Rappaport (1985), The *House of Blue Leaves (1986), Social Security (1986), *Anything Goes (1987), *Lend Me a Tenor (1989), *Six Degrees of Separation (1990), Conversations with My Father (1992), *She Loves Me (1993), Steel Pier (1997), Side Show (1997), *Kiss Me, Kate (1999), The *Man Who Came to Dinner (2000), and The *Producers (2001). Walton's style is eclectic, from lavish interiors to minimalist conceptual sets. He has also designed extensively for film, television, opera, and ballet.

WANG (1891), a musical comedy by J. Cheever *Goodwin (book, lyrics), Woolson Morse (music). [*Broadway Theatre, 151 perf.] Wang (De Wolf *Hopper) is the conniving Regent of Siam. This scarcely bothers the young prince, Mataya (Della *Fox), who is more concerned with his own courtship of Gillette (Anna O'Keefe). But Gillette's mother, La Veuve Frimousse (Marion Singer), is convinced that Mataya wants Gillette only for her money since, as the widow of a former French consul, Frimousse has managed to get her hands on the entire treasury of Siam. But the ever resourceful Wang engineers a marriage, not only between Mataya and Gillette but between himself and the widow, relieving her of the money at the same time. *Notable songs*: Ask the Man in the Moon; A Pretty Girl. One of the biggest hits of its time, it owed much of its success to Hopper's broad clowning as well as to the charm and singing of Fox in a typical trouser role of the period. [Henry] **Woolson MORSE** (1858–97) was born in Charlestown, Massachusetts, educated at the best private schools and at the Boston Conservatory, and then trained abroad. His musical *Cinderella at School* came to the attention of Augustin *Daly, who brought it to New York in 1881. Before Morse's early death he wrote the scores for six other Broadway musicals besides *Wang*, among them such once popular, if now forgotten, successes as *The Merry Monarch* (1890), *Dr. Syntax* (1894), and *Lost, Strayed or Stolen* (1896). While some of his songs were widely sung in their day, none remains popular.

WANTED: ONE THOUSAND MILLINERS. See *One Thousand Milliners,. . . .*

WARD, Douglas Turner (b. 1930), actor, playwright, director, and manager. The multitalented African-American artist was born in Burnside, Louisiana, and educated at Wilberforce University and the University of Michigan before studying acting in New York with Paul Mann. Ward made his professional debut Off Broadway in 1957 and his Broadway bow in the cast of *A *Raisin in the Sun* (1959). His twin bill of the one-acts *Happy Ending* and *Day of Absence* (1965) launched Ward's playwriting career and he acted in the latter, playing the Mayor who wakes up one morning to find that all the "Negroes" in his town have disappeared. In 1968 Ward and Robert Hooks founded the *Negro Ensemble Company, the most famous and long-lasting black theatre group in New York theatre history. Ward wrote and directed many of the company's productions over the years, sometimes acting in them as well. Among his many captivating performances were the former hoofer Russell B. Parker making ends meet in his barbershop in *Ceremonies in Dark Old Men* (1969), the Harlem house painter Johnny Williams who dreams of writing one perfect poem in *The *River Niger* (1973), the wrongly discharged Sergeant Major Saunders in *The Brownsville Raid* (1976), and the illiterate short-order cook Louie in love with an educated woman in *Louie and Ophelia* (1986).

WARD, Winifred (1884–1975), scholar and author. More than any other person, Ward shaped the form and direction that children's theatre would take in America in the 20th century. She set down the principles that differentiated theatre for children from traditional adult plays and elaborated her ideas in four textbooks on the subject. Ward taught courses in children's theatre at North-western and founded a company in Evanston, Illinois, dedicated to the genre. She also established the professional organization, the American Alliance for Theatre and Education, in 1950. Ward's teachings were picked up and developed by Sara Spenser, Charlotte *Chorpenning, Clare Tree *Major, and other important figures in the children's theatre movement.

WARDE, Frederick [Barkham] (1851–1935), actor and manager. A somewhat curious figure in the American theatre, he was born in Oxfordshire, England and, after rejecting his family's plan for him to become a lawyer, made his stage debut in 1867. He came to America in 1874, where he was seen as an actor of great promise and given important assignments opposite John *McCullough, Charlotte *Cushman, Edwin *Booth, Lawrence *Barrett, and other leading contemporaries. In 1881 he organized his own company and toured in a repertory of Shakespeare and such aging favorites as *The *Gladiator, The *Lady of Lyons*, and *Virginius*. Warde had little interest in modern works and his scholarly bent prompted him to begin lecturing on theatre in 1907, continuing to do so after he retired in 1919. He also wrote *The Fools of Shakespeare* (1913). Autobiography: *Fifty Years of Make-Believe*, 1920.

WARFIELD, David [né Wollfeld or Wohlfelt] (1866–1951), character actor. The San Francisco–born performer began his theatrical career as an usher at the city's Bush Street Theatre, later advancing to a super and a bit player. By the 1890s he had moved to New York, where he soon became a favorite of audiences at the *Casino Theatre and then with *Weber and *Fields, portraying comic, usually long-bearded, Jews. He was surprised when David *Belasco (whom he knew from his San Francisco days) approached him to star in a more serious role, the Lower East Side peddler and auctioneer Simon Levi in *The *Auctioneer* (1901). Warfield triumphed in the role, as he did as Anton von Barwig in *The *Music Master* (1904). He played the part for three years, then appeared as the aging Civil War veteran Wes Bigelow in *A *Grand Army Man* (1907). Another major success was his portrayal of the title role in *The *Return of Peter Grimm* (1911). The *Times* hailed the performance of the stocky, square-faced actor as "tremendously appealing, tender, and natural," continuing, "His playing is marked throughout by directness, simplicity, understanding, and the economy of means, which in combination spell the great art of acting." For the next eleven years he played in this and in revivals of his earlier successes, but when he decided to retire at the height of his fame in 1922 he essayed the one last role he was determined to play, Shylock. Critics were divided, and though he toured with the work for two seasons it was one of his rare commercial failures.

WARNER, H[enry] B[yron] [né Lickfold] (1876–1958), actor. The slim, suavely handsome leading man was born in London and followed his father onto the stage. He was established as a West End principal player when he left for America in 1905 to play leading roles opposite Eleanor *Robson. His greatest success came as the ex-criminal Lee Randall in *Alias Jimmy Valentine* (1910). Warner's other Broadway runs were as the bachelor He in *Sleeping Partners* (1918), the would-be painter Maitland White in *You and I* (1923), and the accused murderer Jim Warren in *Silence* (1924). His last years were spent in films, in which he was very popular.

WARREN, Mercy Otis (1728–1814), playwright. The sister of James Otis and the wife of James Warren, who was president of the Provisional Congress of Massachusetts, she did her share for the Revolution by writing two political satires: *The *Adulateur* (1773) and *The *Group* (1775). Both were printed and widely read, but neither appears to have been performed. In 1790 she published a pair of blank-verse tragedies, *The Sack of Rome* and *The Ladies of Castile*. Other plays, notably *The Blockheads* (1776), have been attributed to her, though most modern scholarship finds the attributions suspect. Biography: *First Lady of the Revolution: The Life of Mercy Otis Warren*, K. Anthony, 1958.

WARREN, William (1767–1832), character actor. The heavy-set, puffy-faced performer was born in Bath, England, and had been playing some time in the provinces when *Wignell hired him to perform with his company at Philadelphia's *Chestnut Street Theatre. Arriving in America in 1796, an outbreak of plague in Philadelphia forced him to make his debut in Baltimore. Philadelphia first saw him as Friar Laurence, and he quickly established himself as a favorite, later taking over management of the theatre with William *Wood. Among his notable roles were Sir Anthony Absolute, Sir Toby Belch, Brabantio, Sir John Falstaff, and Sir Peter Teazle. Although he excelled at comedy, he was a fine judge of all young talent, comic or serious, and it was he and Wood who gave Edwin *Forrest his first major opportunity. Warren was married three times, each time to actresses, and had six children, all of whom had careers in the theatre. He retired in 1829 but later made several special appearances. One of his sons was **William WARREN [Jr.]** (1812–88), considered by many of his contemporaries to be the greatest 19th-century American comedian. Shortly after his father's death he made his debut at Philadelphia's *Arch

Street Theatre as Young Norval in *Douglas*. He then played in various cities over the next fourteen years, including brief engagements in New York and in London. In 1846, tired of a roving life, he settled in Boston and was enlisted as a member of the *Howard Athenaeum company before going to the *Boston Museum, where he continued as its leading comedian until his retirement shortly after celebrating his semicentennial as an actor in 1882. During his stint there he gave over thirteen thousand performances in nearly six hundred plays. His most admired interpretations included Sir Peter Teazle, Sir Lucius O'Trigger, Polonius, Tony Lumpkin, Touchstone, and numerous comic roles in contemporary pieces, such as Jefferson Scattering Batkins in *The *Silver Spoon*. He was a large, tall, jowly man, with penetrating, heavy-lidded eyes and a large shock of curly black hair. Although the noted Boston critic Henry Austin *Clapp complained that "the one fault of his style was a slight excess in the use of stentorian tones," most critics undoubtedly would have agreed with an obituary which noted, "His range as a comedian was unequaled, and to the interpretation of every variety of character he brought that exquisite sensibility and clearness of insight, that mobility of nature and fullness of understanding which made his work vital, natural and satisfying." Autobiography: *Life and Memoirs of William Warren*, 1882.

WARRENS OF VIRGINIA, THE (1907), a play by William C. *de Mille. [*Belasco Theatre, 190 perf.] Although the Civil War has separated Lt. Burton (Charles D. *Waldron) of the Union Army from his Southern fiancée, Agatha Warren (Charlotte Walker), Burton succeeds in wangling permission to visit her. However, his commander requires him to travel with plans purporting to show future Northern movements. Of course, the plans are false and are designed to fall into the hands of the Confederates. The trick works, and the forces led by Agatha's father, Gen. Warren (Frank Keenan), are routed. Agatha learns of the ploy and refuses to have anything further to do with Burton. The ending of the play only hints that a reconciliation may occur when the war is over. Typical of the sentimental, romantic, and pro-Southern Civil War dramas of the era, the play owed much of its success to producer David *Belasco's staging and to Keenan's performance of the Lee-like general.

WARS IN AMERICAN DRAMA. Given its basic importance in establishing this country, the Revolutionary War has inspired few plays of merit and most of these have found but small acceptance from playgoers. Because of the scant opportunities for production, including the fact that British troops held several of the major theatre centers, contemporary dramas such as The *Adulateur, The *Fall of British Tyranny, or The *Group have been classified as "pamphlet plays," read rather than performed, although several of them seem to have had some circulation and helped steel patriotic resolve. As the war receded in history certain figures found special appeal for dramatists, among them Ethan Allen, Benjamin Franklin, Nathan Hale, Francis Marion, and Israel Putnam. But by far the most popular figures were George Washington and two men associated with treasonous behavior, Benedict Arnold and Major André. As a rule, Washington figured primarily in spectacles and other plays designed to reinforce patriotic sentiment. On the other hand, the real drama, even tragedy, of André's story gave rise early on to *Dunlap's *André (1798). The *Widow's Son (1825) focused on war-bred hatred and hysteria. Between the turn of the century and the coming of the Civil War dozens of dramas, comedies, and spectacles treating the Revolution were mounted. In his History of the American Drama, *Quinn offers a partial list of more than fifty plays mounted between 1826 and 1860, most of which have not survived. Among the most interesting are *Briar Cliff (1828), Putnam, the Iron Son of '76 (1844), *Love in '76 (1857), and *Horseshoe Robinson (1858). Generally, the more famous, successful works did not deal directly with the ramifications of the Revolution nor its more celebrated incidents, which were usually left to spectacles. Indeed, the most popular of such plays tended to be lighthearted pieces merely set against the background of the war. In later years interest in the war waned. Later 19th- and early 20th-century examples include James A. *Herne's The Minute Men of 1774–75 (1886) and two Clyde *Fitch efforts, Nathan Hale (1898) and Major André (1903). Subsequently, the Revolutionary War was dealt with in such scattered plays as Maxwell *Anderson's serious but failed *Valley Forge (1934) and the popular comedy The *Pursuit of Happiness (1933). Significantly the most successful modern treatments have been on the musical stage, notably the fluffy but melodic *Dearest Enemy (1925) and the more purposeful *1776 (1969). The War of 1812 suggested little to dramatists, the most notable works being Robert Penn *Smith's two offerings, The *Eighth of January (1829) and The *Triumph at Plattsburg (1830), while the Mexican-American War produced nothing of interest, unless the plays about Davy Crockett, who figured in the Texas battles that led up to the war, are considered.

By its very nature, the Civil War long remained of supreme interest to American playwrights. Although both Northern and Southern dramatists were prolific during the war, their immediate response produced nothing of such lasting value or contemporary popularity as the novel and its dramatization that many felt were major factors in polarizing opinions before the war, *Uncle Tom's Cabin. Most plays of the moment were flag-waving affairs. The works that came directly after the conflict and reflected the continuing interest in the battles were of no lasting significance either. Probably the first important Civil War drama was Dion *Boucicault's commercially unsuccessful Belle Lamar (1874). Its story (a Southern lady—married to a Union officer—who chooses regional loyalty over personal affection) established a pattern for the basic dilemma to be portrayed in many of the dramas that followed, as did its use of a spy as a pivotal figure. In short, slavery, slave economics, and secession (the issues fundamental to the war) were passed over in favor of romantic and melodramatic themes that employed the war itself largely as background. *Belasco's May Blossom (1884) was a further harbinger of the outpouring of Civil War themes that began with *Held by the Enemy (1886) and continued through the era of the Spanish-American War up to the time of World War I, with such works as *Shenandoah (1889), *Secret Service (1895), The *Heart of Maryland (1895), The Reverend Griffith Davenport (1899), *Barbara Frietchie (1899), the musical *When Johnny Comes Marching Home (1902), The *Warrens of Virginia (1907), and The *Copperhead (1918). If the fundamental issues behind the war were taken for granted or glossed over in most of these plays, they did receive a somewhat more probing examination in plays dealing with Reconstruction, such as *Alabama (1891) and The New South (1893). The most notable of later plays to employ the war was Eugene *O'Neill's *Mourning Becomes Electra (1931), which used the conflict as a background for the retelling of the Greek legends. Much of the later theatrical employment of the war was in musicals, including *My Maryland (1927), which was based on Barbara Frietchie; *Shenandoah (1975), which was not based on the earlier play of the same name; and The Civil War (1999).

During U.S. involvement in World War I, American dramatists produced nothing of enduring merit. The initial response appears to have been confined largely to patriotic tableaux in the extravagant revues of the era and in such entertainments as Irving *Berlin's all-soldier revue, Yip Yap Yaphank (1918). One of the most popular plays about the war, *Friendly Enemies (1918), appeared several months after the armistice and dealt not with the battlefield but with divisions on the home front. However, most agree the best American play about the Great War was Maxwell *Anderson and Laurence Stallings's salty, cynical comedy *What Price Glory? (1924). In the 1920s and 1930s the war served as the setting for such pacifist pleas as The *Enemy (1925) and *Johnny Johnson (1936). These plays signaled the unromantic, basically antiwar stance that would underlie much subsequent writing about that war. The *Petrified Forest (1935), for example, looked at the world-weariness that grew out of the war and the Depression.

The approach of World War II inspired such interesting plays as *Idiot's Delight (1936), *There Shall Be No Night (1940), Hemingway's The *Fifth Column (1940), and *Watch on the Rhine (1941), but during the war itself most serious drama, such as The *Eve of St. Mark (1942) and A *Bell for Adano (1944), was solid but unexceptional. *Tomorrow the World (1943) looked at the difficulties of eradicating Nazi ideology, while The Searching Wind (1944) was more concerned with prewar diplomatic bungling. The most successful wartime works were such fluffy comedies as The *Doughgirls (1942) and *Dear Ruth (1944). Possibly the best American play about the war, A Sound of Hunting (1945), appeared shortly after the war and failed. Another late, worthy, but unsuccessful play was Arthur *Laurents's Home of the Brave (1945). By far the most successful plays about the war came years afterwards and lightened their undercurrents of seriousness with comedy or romance. Most notable were *Mister Roberts (1948) and the musical *South Pacific (1949). Other memorable plays about the Second World War were *Command Decision (1947), The Caine Mutiny Court-Martial (1954), and A *Soldier's Play (1982).

If the Korean War promoted nothing of real note, the Vietnam War, the first war in our history actively opposed by a substantial number of thoughtful citizens, called forth a wealth of provocative theatre. The war coincided with what many saw as breakdowns in our society, with massive protests, with widespread rioting and looting as protests against racism, and by the beginnings of the worst inflation in American history. Dramas relating to the war reflected the turmoil. One of the most successful was the musical *Hair (1968), which featured nudity and a variety of protest songs and unpleasant themes, such as drug addiction, racism, and sexual promiscuity, in its portrayal of a young man who must decide whether to serve in the war. The savagely satiric MacBird! (1967) was another interesting work. Probably the most important dramatist to deal with the war was David *Rabe, who began writing about it while the conflict continued and followed with more material after the war. His plays included The *Basic Training of Pavlo Hummel (1971), *Sticks and Bones (1971), and *Streamers (1976). Although often not as craftily plotted as earlier war stories, they portrayed in superb theatrical terms the chaos, rage, and disintegration generated by the war. Dramas about veterans suffering from psychological effects of the Vietnam War also found fertile ground. The most memorable were The

Speed of Darkness (1991) and Redwood Curtain (1993), though neither was a hit.

WASHINGTON SQUARE PLAYERS (New York). When, in 1914, an intellectual group known as the Liberal Club rejected the idea of a dramatic branch, several disappointed members banded together to organize their own theatrical company. The founders included Edward Goodman, Lawrence *Langner, Philip *Moeller, and Helen *Westley. They patterned their organization after one founded in Chicago by Maurice *Browne and named it for the area in which it originated. In 1915 they began to offer one-act plays at the tiny Bandbox Theatre, a year later moving to the larger Comedy Theatre, where they eventually presented a number of full-length plays. Although the Players attempted to emphasize American writing and did produce such short works as Eugene *O'Neill's *In the Zone and Elmer *Rice's Home of the Free, many of their most admired mountings were of such foreign offerings as Maeterlinck's Aglavaine, *Chekhov's The Seagull, and *Shaw's Mrs. Warren's Profession. The group was dissolved in 1918 but during its brief history gave important starts to the careers of such later significant figures as Katharine *Cornell, Rollo *Peters, and Lee *Simonson. Many of its prime movers formed the *Theatre Guild shortly afterwards.

WASSERSTEIN, Wendy (b. 1950), playwright. She was born in Brooklyn, the daughter of a textile manufacturer, and educated at Mount Holyoke College, CCNY, and Yale. Her first play to gain attention was Uncommon Women and Others (1977), a funny but disturbing look at the residents of an exclusive girls school. Her subsequent works of note include Isn't It Romantic (1981), about the trials and tribulations of two urban single women; the *Pulitzer Prize–winning The *Heidi Chronicles (1988); The *Sisters Rosensweig (1992); An American Daughter (1997), in which a renowned physician is attacked by the press; and Old Money (2000), which explores two generations of wealth. One of the most successful women playwrights of her era, Wasserstein concentrates on characters and themes that she has experienced firsthand: intelligent, wealthy women dealing with their role in the modern world and, sometimes, coming to terms with their Jewish heritage.

WATCH ON THE RHINE (1941), a play by Lillian *Hellman. [Martin Beck Theatre, 378 perf.; NYDCC Award.] The widowed Washington matron Fanny Farrelly (Lucile Watson) soon will have a crowded household, for not only is she entertaining the Roumanian Count de Brancovis (George Coulouris) and his wife (Helen Trenholme), but she is expecting to welcome her daughter, Sarah (Mady *Christians), Sarah's husband, Kurt Mueller (Paul Lukas), and their children. She has not seen them for many years since Kurt is a German and the Muellers lived in Germany until Kurt's antifascist sympathies forced him into exile. The homecoming is marred by the Count, who recognizes Kurt and threatens to blackmail him. Kurt kills him, then decides he must return alone to Germany to continue the fight against Nazism. Writing in *PM*, Louis *Kronenberger observed, "It is a play about human beings and their ideological ghosts; a play dedicated to the deeds they are called upon to perform, not the words they are moved to utter. It is a play whose final crisis, though peculiar to one man's life, is yet central to our own."

WATCH YOUR STEP (1914), a musical comedy by Harry B. *Smith (book), Irving *Berlin (music, lyrics). [*New Amsterdam Theatre, 175 perf.] The plot, which dealt with the attempts of some heirs to meet the terms of a musical comedy will, was so slight that many critics perceived the show as a revue. Smith acknowledged its slightness in his often quoted credit, "Plot (if any) by Harry B. Smith." The show's importance rests with its music. Berlin provided a score almost entirely in a ragtime idiom. Coming just four months after Jerome *Kern established the pattern for the modern ballad with "They Didn't Believe Me" in *The *Girl from Utah*, this score consolidated the vogue for show songs written in a totally American style, most often deriving from black musical tradition. With Irene and Vernon *Castle in leading roles, it also promoted both the contemporary "dance craze" and show songs created as much for ballroom dancing as for singing. *Notable songs*: Simple Melody; Syncopated Walk.

WATERS, Ethel (1896?–1977), singer and actress. The warm, versatile African-American performer was born in Chester, Pennsylvania, and spent years in both black and white vaudeville before making her Broadway debut in *Africana* (1927). After musical appearances in *Blackbirds of 1930* and *Rhapsody in Black* (1931), among others, she received star billing in the celebrated revue *As Thousands Cheer* (1933), in which she sang "Heat Wave" and "Suppertime." Waters also triumphed in *At Home Abroad* (1935), in which she introduced "The Hottentot Potentate" and "Thief in the Night." She first demonstrated her dramatic skills as the vengeful, illiterate mother Hagar in *Mamba's Daughters* (1939). Returning to the musical stage she won applause for her singing of "Taking a Chance on Love" and the title song in *Cabin in the Sky* (1940), followed by the revue *Blue Holiday* (1945). For many her most memorable performance came as Berenice

Sadie Brown, the surrogate mother to a young tomboy, in *The *Member of the Wedding* (1950). Brooks *Atkinson wrote, "Miss Waters gives one of those rich and eloquent performances that lay such a deep spell on any audience that sees her . . . it has exalted spirit and great warmth of sympathy." Her last important appearance was in *At Home with Ethel Waters* (1953). Autobiography: *His Eye Is on the Sparrow*, 1951.

WATERSTON, Sam (b.1940), actor. The dark, thoughtful leading man was born in Cambridge, Massachusetts, and educated at Yale and the Sorbonne, training at the American Actors Workshop in Paris and with Herbert *Berghof and Frank Corsaro in New York. After some experience in stock, Waterston made his Broadway debut in 1963. Later that year he performed for the first time at the *New York Shakespeare Festival, where he often returned and gave his finest performances, such as Prince Hal in *Henry IV* (1968), Benedict in *Much Ado About Nothing* (1972), *Hamlet* (1972 and 1975), and Prospero in *The Tempest* (1974). Other provocative performances include the tramp Vladimir in *Waiting for Godot* (1978), the preoccupied shrink Oliver DeVreck in *Lunch Hour* (1980), the American diplomat John Honeyman in *A Walk in the Woods* (1988), and the title president-to-be in *Abe Lincoln in Illinois* (1993). Mel *Gussow in the *New York Times* described his Benedict as "sharp-tongued and headstrong, never losing sight of the character's propulsively romantic nature. . . . Waterston leaps at it with enormous grace and agility."

WATKINS, Harry (1830?–94), playwright and actor. A minor 19th-century dramatist and performer, he kept a vivid, gossipy, and eventually embittered journal, which he maintained from 1845 to 1863 and which was edited and published in 1938 by Maud and Otis *Skinner as *One Man in His Time*. It affords unique glimpses of theatrical life both in backwaters and in New York.

WATKINS, Maureen Dallas. See *Chicago*.

WATSON, Billy [né Isaac Levie or Levine] (1866–1945), singer, comic, and producer. He was born on New York's Lower East Side and made his debut as an entertainer in 1881. He did so well as a "Dutch" comedian in burlesque and vaudeville that he soon had his own theatre. He rejected David *Belasco's offer to head the main road company of *The *Music Master*, instead playing for many years in *Krausemeyer's Alley*, in which he played a Jewish father who objects to his son's marrying an Irish girl. When Anne *Nichols was sued for plagiarism after the opening of *Abie's Irish Rose*, she used the text of *Krausemeyer's Alley* to prove the basic theme was public property. However, Watson's greatest fame came as the producer of *Billy Watson's Beef Trust*, a comic burlesque show that featured a line of chorus girls all weighing over 190 pounds and dressed in striped tights. He retired from the stage in 1925, returning only for rare revivals of *Krausemeyer's Alley*.

WATTS, Richard, Jr. (1898–1981), critic. Born in Parkersburg, West Virginia, and educated at Columbia, he had long served as the film critic for the *Herald Tribune* before succeeding Percy *Hammond as that paper's drama critic in 1936. After spending the war years in China he became the theatre critic for the New York *Post*, a position he held until a few years prior to his death. For the *Post* he also conducted a pithy column called "Random Notes on This and That." The noted press agent Richard *Maney described him as "urbane, sensitive and waspish."

WAY DOWN EAST (1898), a play by Lottie Blair Parker, revised by Joseph R. *Grismer. [Manhattan Theatre, 152 perf.] After being seduced and losing the child of that liaison, Annie Moore (Phoebe Davies) wanders aimlessly until she finds refuge as a servant in the New England farm of Squire Bartlett (Odell Williams). Ignorant of her past, the Bartletts prove sympathetic. But when the Squire learns her history he drives her from his home in the midst of a raging snowstorm. Annie loses her way and nearly dies before she is rescued by the Bartletts' son, David (Howard Kyle). He has come to love her and finally persuades his parents that she is worthy to be his wife. Although the William A. *Brady–Florenz *Ziegfeld production was little more than a compilation of settings and motifs popular in melodrama of the period, it was praised for its restraint and honesty. The play became one of the greatest successes of the American stage and held the boards for nearly two decades. Davies, who was Mrs. Grismer in private life, played the role over four thousand times. **Lottie Blair PARKER** (1868–1937) was born in Oswego, New York, and began her theatrical career as an actress, eventually playing opposite John *McCullough, Mary *Anderson, and Dion *Boucicault. She wrote about a dozen produced plays, including *White Roses* (1892) and *Under Southern Skies* (1901), but none was as popular as *Way Down East*.

WAYBURN, [Edward Claudius] Ned (1874–1942), director and choreographer. Born in Pittsburgh, he started his theatrical career as an usher at Chicago's Grand Opera House. For a time he turned actor, but in 1901 he began to direct and choreograph Broadway musicals. Over the next thirty years Wayburn staged no fewer than sixty shows in New York and Chicago. Except for the *Ziegfeld Follies*, six of which he staged between 1916 and 1923, few are remembered today. The list includes *Mr. Bluebeard* (1903), *The Ham Tree* (1905), *The *Time, the Place and the Girl* (1907), *Old Dutch* (1909), *The *Passing Show of 1912*, *The Century Girl* (1915), *The Night Boat* (1920), *Two Little Girls in Blue* (1921), and his last show, *Smiles* (1930). Wayburn is credited with inventing theatre tap dancing in 1903 by replacing his dancers' clogs with shoes with bits of metal nailed to the soles. Later he founded his own dance school and wrote *The Art of Stage Dancing* (1925). He flourished long before directors were given to conceiving musicals as totally integrated efforts. Rather than concern himself with overall style and tone, he was preoccupied largely with creating stage pictures and with pacing. After he gave Ira *Gershwin and Vincent *Youmans the tempo and meter he wanted for each song in *Two Little Girls in Blue*, Gershwin concluded, "Obviously to Wayburn neither the play nor the numbers were the thing— only tempo mattered."

WAYNE, David [né Wayne James McMeekan] (1914–95), character actor. The versatile performer was born in Traverse City, Michigan, and made his first professional appearance in Cleveland in a 1936 revival of *As You Like It*. Wayne played in several major Broadway and touring productions before scoring a huge success as the leprechaun Og in *Finian's Rainbow* (1947), followed by such memorable performances as the roustabout Ensign Pulver in *Mister Roberts* (1948), the wily Sakini in *The *Teahouse of the August Moon* (1953), the eccentric Uncle Daniel in *The Ponder Heart* (1956), the unctuous Mr. Finnegan in *The Loud Red Patrick* (1956), the temperamental Jack Jordan in *Say, Darling* (1958), the hypochondriacal George Kimball in *Send Me No Flowers* (1960), and Private Meek in *Too True to Be Good* (1963). In 1964 Wayne joined the *Lincoln Center Repertory Company and appeared in important roles in *After the Fall*, *Marco Millions*, *But for Whom Charlie*, and *Incident at Vichy*. His last major Broadway appearance was as the bon vivant Granpère in *The *Happy Time* (1968).

WEAVER, Fritz (b. 1926), actor. The tall, introspective leading man, who has played many stern, emotionless characters, was born in Pittsburgh, educated at the University of Chicago, and trained at the Herbert *Berghof Studio before making his debut in regional theatre in 1952. Weaver started performing Off Broadway two years later, then made an auspicious Broadway bow as the scowling servant Maitland in *The Chalk Garden* (1955). Subsequent performances of note include Peer Gynt and King Henry IV (both in 1960), Sherlock Holmes in the musical *Baker Street* (1965), a stern

Henry Higgins in *My Fair Lady (1968), the much-hated, much-abused schoolteacher Jerome Malley in Child's Play (1970), college professor Niles Harris recovering from a nervous breakdown in Angels Fall (1983), and the opinionated financier Messerschmann in Ring round the Moon (1999).

WEBB, Clifton [né Webb Parmalee Hollenbeck] (1893–1966), actor, dancer, and singer. The slim, dapper, somewhat epicene performer was born in Indianapolis and began acting professionally when still a young boy, goaded on by Mrs. Hollenbeck, who was to become one of Broadway's most famous stage mothers. He left the theatre to study painting and then to work under Victor Maurel to prepare for an opera career, which was short lived. By 1911 Webb was a song and dance man in The Purple Road. Later he played in, among others, Dancing Around (1914), See America First (1916), Love o' Mike (1917), Listen Lester (1918), and As You Were (1920). After a stint in London, Webb returned to create the role of the sporting youngblood Victor Staunton in Meet the Wife (1923). He played a major supporting role in the musical *Sunny (1925) but reached stardom with the revue The *Little Show (1929) in which he sang "I Guess I'll Have to Change My Plan." He shone in the subsequent revues Three's a Crowd (1930), Flying Colors (1932), and *As Thousands Cheer (1933), in which he introduced "Easter Parade." His last musical appearance was in You Never Know (1938). Two Noel *Coward comedies marked his farewell to the stage. In both instances Webb played the parts Coward had written for himself in London: the astral bigamist Charles Condomine in Blithe Spirit (1941) and the egomaniacal actor Garry Essendine in Present Laughter (1946). In his later years he was popular in films.

WEBBER, Andrew Lloyd (b. 1948), composer. The London-born son of musical parents, he first achieved American recognition when his popular recording of the rock musical Jesus Christ Superstar, remembered for its title song and "I Don't Know How to Love Him," was dramatized in 1971. Subsequent shows to play in America have included Joseph and the Amazing Technicolor Dreamcoat, which was first presented in America in 1977 but did not settle in for a long Broadway run until 1982; *Evita (1979), whose hit was "Don't Cry for Me, Argentina"; *Cats (1982), with its hit song "Memory"; Song and Dance (1985); Starlight Express (1987); The *Phantom of the Opera (1988); Aspects of Love (1990); *Sunset Boulevard (1994); and By Jeeves (2001). Most of his more successful shows have relied heavily on spectacle, but he has also been more successful than any of his contemporaries in transferring modern musical idioms, notably rock, to the popular stage. Webber is also an important producer and theatre owner in England. Biography: Andrew Lloyd Webber: His Life and Works, Michael Walsh, 1989.

WEBER, Joe. See Fields, Lew.

WEBSTER, Jean. See Daddy Long-Legs.

WEBSTER, Margaret (1905–72), actress and director. She was born in New York, the daughter of two famous players, Ben Webster and Dame May Whitty, and spent most of her early years on British stages. American audiences first saw her work when she directed *Richard III in 1937 and first saw her act when she appeared as Masha in a 1938 revival of The Sea Gull. Webster subsequently directed several American Shakespearean productions, scoring her greatest success in 1943 with her staging of *Othello. This production, which starred Paul *Robeson and José *Ferrer and in which she played Emilia, ran 295 performances, a still unbroken record for a Shakespearean mounting. She staged a highly praised revival of The Tempest in 1945 before joining Eva *Le Gallienne and Cheryl *Crawford to found the *American Repertory Theatre, directing and performing in several of its offerings during its short existence. From 1948 to 1950 she toured with her Shakespearean company. Although Webster's stagings were usually lauded for their understanding of Shakespeare's characters and for their theatrical effectiveness, she regularly caused controversy for tampering with Shakespeare's texts: She eliminated the Clown in Othello, while in The Tempest she made an epilogue of the famous fourth act speech that begins with "Our revels now are ended." Her theories and reminiscences were blended in her book Shakespeare Without Tears (1942).

WEIDMAN, Jerome (1913–98), librettist. A native New Yorker, who was educated at New York University Law School, Weidman made his Broadway debut as co-author of the libretto for the *Pulitzer Prize–winning musical *Fiorello! (1959). He also co-wrote Tenderloin (1960) and adapted his own novel about the garment industry into the musical I Can Get It for You Wholesale (1962). His son **John WEIDMAN** (b. 1946) is also a librettist. He was born in New York and educated at Harvard, where he wrote for the humor magazine Lampoon, and Yale to pursue a law career as well. But he soon turned to writing and was first represented on Broadway as the librettist for *Pacific Overtures (1976), the experimental Stephen *Sondheim musical about the opening of Japan. Weidman's other credits include the revised libretto for *Anything Goes (1987); the bold, conceptual script for Sondheim's *Assassins (1991); Big (1996); *Contact (2000); and Bounce (2003).

WEIDMAN, John. See Weidman, Jerome.

WEILL, Kurt (1900–50), composer. The German-born composer came to America in 1935 as a refugee from Nazism, accompanied by his wife, Lotte *Lenya. American playgoers had already heard his unique, often jittery and staccato jazz-influenced music in an earlier production of The *Threepenny Opera (1933), which had a short run on Broadway. Shortly after his arrival his incidental music for Max *Reinhardt's The Eternal Road (1937) was played in the New York production of the play. Weill's American musicals were *Johnny Johnson (1936), *Knickerbocker Holiday (1938), *Lady in the Dark (1941), *One Touch of Venus (1943), The Firebrand of Florence (1945), *Street Scene (1947), Love Life (1948), and *Lost in the Stars (1949). At the time of his death he was working with Maxwell *Anderson on Raft on the River, a musicalization of Huckleberry Finn. A 1954 revival of Threepenny Opera became one of the most successful of all Off-Broadway offerings and revived interest in his work, especially after "The Ballad of Mack the Knife" became widely popular. However, attempts to present his other German musicals have not met with success, although opera companies have staged such works as The Rise and Fall of Mahagonny. Weill was a unique composer, mixing European influences with Broadway razzamatazz and coming up with a distinctive sound of his own. He was also a master of the haunting, melancholy ballad, as seen in song standards like "September Song" and "Speak Low." Biography: Kurt Weill on Stage: From Berlin to Broadway, Foster Hirsch, 2002.

WEITZENKORN, Louis. See Five Star Final.

WELCOME STRANGER (1920), a comedy by Aaron *Hoffman. [Cohan and Harris Theatre, 309 perf.] When kindly Isidor Solomon (George Sidney) opens a clothing store in a small New England town he finds himself confronted with local anti-Semitism. By his good deeds and thoughtfulness he wins over the townspeople one by one. However, the local mayor remains rabidly against him until Solomon offers his fellow citizens an explanation for the mayor's determined stance. The proof Solomon offers, written in Yiddish, is the birth notice and other early material about the mayor, who had long hidden his own Jewish background. One of the earliest attempts to confront American anti-Semitism, the Sam H. *Harris offering was greeted by Alexander *Woollcott as "an almost continuously amusing piece of theatrical entertainment."

WELLER, Michael. See Moonchildren.

WELLES, [George] Orson (1915–85), actor, director, and producer. Born in Kenosha, Wisconsin, the exceptionally talented jack-of-all-trades began performing while still a child. After some acting stints in Europe, he called attention to his abilities in 1933 when he performed opposite Katharine *Cornell as Mercutio, Marchbanks, and Octavius Moulton-Barrett in The *Barretts of Wimpole Street (1934). For the *Federal Theatre Project he staged highly admired productions of many plays, including an all-black *Macbeth (1936), and Dr. Faustus (1937), taking the lead in the latter. In 1937 Welles founded the *Mercury Theatre with John *Houseman, directing most of the company's productions, among them an acclaimed modern-dress *Julius Caesar (1937), in which he appeared as Brutus. Subsequently, along with many members of the Mercury company, he moved to Hollywood, where he created such memorable films as Citizen Kane and The Magnificent Ambersons. He also precipitated panic in many quarters with his 1938 radio broadcast War of the Worlds. Thereafter, however, his work on Broadway was intermittent. The best was his and Houseman's production of *Native Son (1941), which Welles directed. In 1946 he adapted, directed, and played Dick Fix in a musicalization of Around the World in Eighty Days, and in 1956 he directed and starred in *King Lear. Few artists of such brilliance and diversity have appeared on the American theatre scene, but he became an example of one who either burnt himself out early or wasted his talents on futile efforts. Biography: Orson Welles, The Road to Xanadu, Simon Callow, 1995.

WEMYSS, Francis Courtney (1797–1859), actor and manager. The native Londoner, son of a British naval officer and an American mother, appeared on English stages for several years before coming to America in 1822 to join the company at Philadelphia's *Chestnut Street Theatre. He was an accomplished, if unexceptional, comedian, who in keeping with the diversity required by the stock companies of the day often assumed dramatic roles. He was acting in one of these, Duncan to *Macready's Macbeth, at the time of the *Astor Place Riots. Wemyss eventually became manager of the Chestnut Street Theatre and later of houses in Baltimore, Pittsburgh, and New York, including *Barnum's *American Museum. Much admired for his offstage courtliness and integrity, he was a secretary of the Dramatic Fund. However, Wemyss is best remembered as the author of the autobiographical Twenty-Six Years of the Life of an Actor and Manager (1847) and as editor of The Acting American Theatre, a series of volumes of early American plays.

WEST, Mae [Mary Jane] (1892–1980), actress and playwright. The blonde, busty, Brooklyn-born performer who came to epitomize a bawdy, if somewhat tongue-in-cheek, sexuality, began acting in stock at the age of five. From 1911 to 1921 she appeared in a number of Broadway musicals even as she headlined in vaudeville. West specialized in leeringly risqué songs, although when one of E. F. *Albee's agents or the police were known to be in the theatre, she is said to have offered the lyrics with a childish innocence, which suggested she did not know the meaning of what she said. West caused a furor and ultimately was jailed for her performance as Margie LaMont, the prostitute, in her own play *Sex* (1926). Her next play, *The Drag* (1927), was considered so off-color that it was banned in New York. West scored a major success as a barroom hostess, the title role of her play *Diamond Lil* (1928), which was revived in 1949. Several other plays failed, but she enjoyed one final hit, apart from the 1949 revival, when she portrayed the famed Russian empress in her play *Catherine Was Great* (1944). West's curtain speech during its run was "Catherine had 300 lovers. I did the best I could in a couple of hours." Her highly popular films during the 1930s helped lead to a tightening of Hollywood's moral codes. Autobiography: *Goodness Had Nothing to Do with It*, 1959. Biography: *Mae West: An Icon in Black and White*, Jill Watts, 2001.

WEST SIDE STORY (1957), a musical play by Arthur *Laurents (book), Leonard *Bernstein (music), Stephen *Sondheim (lyrics). [*Winter Garden Theatre, 734 perf.] The Puerto Rican Sharks and the American-born Jets are rival street gangs in New York City's West Side neighborhoods. Tony (Larry Kert), a founder of the Jets who has more or less drifted away from them, falls in love with Maria (Carol Lawrence), the sister of the Sharks' leader, Bernardo (Ken LeRoy). When Tony tries to stop a fight between the groups, Bernardo kills Tony's friend Riff (Mickey Calin) so, in a fury, Tony kills Bernardo. When Bernardo's girl friend, Anita (Chita *Rivera), in a rage, tells the Jets that Maria has been killed by a Shark for her involvement with a white boy, Tony comes out of hiding, only to be shot by Maria's fiancé. Before Tony dies, he and Maria are briefly reunited and humble both gangs by the consequences of their hate. *Notable songs*: I Feel Pretty; Maria; Tonight; Gee, Officer Krupke; Somewhere; I Feel Pretty; Something's Coming; America. A modern version of the *Romeo and Juliet* story, it was devised at the suggestion of Jerome *Robbins, whose direction and choreography caught, as one critic observed, the "tautness and malevolence" of the work. The extensive dance sections of the show revealed new ways choreography and drama could be integrated. Also, the Bernstein-Sondheim score was unique in its use of opera

forms translated into theatre terms, as in the complex "Tonight Quintet." Although the Robert E. *Griffith–Hal *Prince production was initially a success, *West Side Story* soon became even more popular across America, overseas, on film, and in revivals on Broadway.

WESTERN, [Pauline] **Lucille** (1843–77), actress. Born in New Orleans, the daughter of performers, she began her stage career in Boston at the age of five, playing alongside her younger sister Helen (1844–68). For many years they toured together as child stars. Helen had barely reached maturity at the time of her death and Lucille was to live only nine years more, but she became a major attraction in that time. Her most famous role was the loving mother Lady Isobel Mount Severn in *East Lynne* (1863). She was also admired for the strong, emotional roles she portrayed in such plays as *Green Bushes*, *Camille, The *Stranger*, and *Oliver Twist*. Although Western had a slightly pinched face and a pointed nose, she was judged a great beauty. Clara *Morris wrote of her, "She was a born actress . . . in all she did there was just a touch of extravagance—a hint of lawless, unrestrained passion."

WESTLEY, Helen (1879–1942), character actress. The Brooklyn native made her debut in 1897 and acted in stock for many years before becoming a founder first of the *Washington Square Players and then of the *Theatre Guild. She never became a star but continued throughout her career to play important featured roles, among them Mrs. Clegg in *Jane Clegg* (1920), Mrs. Muskat in *Liliom* (1921), Mrs. Zero in The *Adding Machine* (1923), Ftatateeta in *Caesar and Cleopatra* (1925), Mrs. Evans in *Strange Interlude* (1928), Aunt Eller in *Green Grow the Lilacs* (1931), Frau Lucher in *Reunion in Vienna* (1931), Mrs. Wells in *They Shall Not Die* (1934), and Grandma in *The Primrose Path* (1939). Theresa *Helburn praised her sure instinct in helping the Guild select plays, and noted, "She had a theatrical appearance and manner, and dressed rather like a femme fatale—coal-black hair and black, slinky dresses, a little like Charles Addams's young witch."

WESTON, Jack [né Morris Weinstein] (1915?–96), character actor. The roly-poly, balding comic usually played incompetent or overwhelmed characters. He was born in Cleveland and studied acting at the *Cleveland Playhouse as a boy. After dropping out of high school and serving in World War II, Weston moved to New York and did odd jobs while training at the *American Theatre Wing. Both his theatre and television careers began in 1950, but he didn't find an attention-getting role on stage until he played the hapless Gaetano Proclo who hides in a gay steam bath to escape hit men in *The *Ritz* (1975). Weston also shone as various visitors in *California Suite* (1976), the unfaithful husband Sam in *Cheaters* (1978), and the seedy talent agent Jerry Wexler in *The Floating Light Bulb* (1981).

WEXLEY, John. See *Last Mile, The.*

WHAT A LIFE! (1938), a comedy by Clifford Goldsmith. [*Biltmore Theatre, 538 perf.] Henry Aldrich (Ezra Stone) is a mischievous, fun-loving high school student who shows no promise of following his father to Princeton. He is nearly expelled after his drawing of a bespectacled whale, labeled Mr. Bradley, falls into the hands of the school's principal—Mr. Bradley (Vaughn Glaser). When his mother promises him money to go to the junior prom if he passes his history test, he blithely copies another student's answers. Later he is falsely accused of stealing the school band's instruments and hocking them. He finally does manage to get to the prom, though he has to borrow the carfare from his date. Welcomed by John Mason *Brown as "a veritable Utopia of farce," the George *Abbott production was one of the biggest successes of its day and later became a popular radio program, with Stone again as Henry Aldrich.

WHAT PRICE GLORY? (1924), a play by Maxwell *Anderson and Laurence Stallings. [*Plymouth Theatre, 435 perf.] Captain Flagg (Louis *Wolheim) and First Sergeant Quirt (William Boyd) are career soldiers and longtime friendly enemies. Quirt is put in charge of Flagg's company while the Captain is given a leave in Paris. In Flagg's absence, Quirt has a fling with Charmaine (Leyla Georgie), the local village girl whom Flagg considers his own. When, on Flagg's return, Charmaine's father announces that his daughter has been ruined, Flagg demands Quirt marry the girl. The plans are set aside on orders for the company to return to the front. Quirt is wounded and, while convalescing, briefly resumes his affair. But a second call comes to head for the front. Flagg leaves, yelling to Charmaine to put her money in real estate, while Quirt, equally unconcerned about the girl, follows, shouting, "Hey, Flagg, wait for baby!" In its day the Arthur *Hopkins offering was judged a breakaway landmark in the stage's battle for honesty and genuinely reflected speech. Alexander *Woollcott noted in the *Sun*, "No war play written in the English language . . . has been so true, so alive, so salty and so richly satisfying," while Heywood *Broun of the *World* called it "far and away the most credible of all war plays." It has remained the finest American drama about World War I, although its outspokenness now seems tame and its realism streaked with a touch of romance.

WHEATLEY, Sarah [née Ross] (1790–1872), actress. The wife of the Irish-born actor Frederick (d. 1836), she was born in Nova Scotia and made her debut at the *Park Theatre in 1805. A comely woman, with large, beautiful eyes, she was not at first deemed a superior actress. With time, however, Wheatley endeared herself to playgoers for her portrayals of elderly females. Among her notable parts were Mrs. Malaprop and Juliet's nurse. Insisting she never cared for acting, she retired from the stage in 1843 and was never lured back. Three of her children became prominent: Julia as a singer, Emma (1822–54), an actress, and **William WHEATLEY** (1816–76) as an actor and noted manager. He was born in New York and made his debut at the age of ten opposite *Macready. For many years he acted at Philadelphia's *Walnut Street and *Chestnut Street Theatres, then managed that city's *Arch Street Theatre, first with John *Drew and later alone. His greatest success came when he took over *Niblo's Garden in 1862. The huge returns there from his production of The *Black Crook permitted him to retire in 1868.

WHEATLEY, William. See Wheatley, Sarah.

WHEELER, A[ndrew] **C**[arpenter] (1835–1903), critic. The once famous newspaperman and writer, who wrote under a string of pseudonyms, was born in New York and educated at City College of New York. He began his newspaper career on the staff of the then young *New York Times*, but turned briefly to playwriting when he lived for a time in Kansas and Iowa. After serving with papers in Milwaukee and Chicago he returned to New York shortly after the Civil War and under the name "Trinculo" became drama critic for the *New York Leader*. Under the byline "Nym Crinkle," Wheeler wrote highly caustic but widely informed play reviews for the *World* and the *Sun*. He also wrote as "Nym Crinkle" for numerous magazines but used other names as well. Rumor suggested he was an uncredited collaborator on several famous plays of his era, including The *Still Alarm* (1887) and *Blue Jeans* (1890).

WHEELER, Hugh [Callingham] (1912–87), playwright. The London-born dramatist had been an established novelist before turning to the theatre. His first produced play, *Big Fish, Little Fish* (1961), was a highly praised study of the parasitic people surrounding an easygoing man. He had less success with his *Look, We've Come Through* (1961) and *We Have Always Lived in the Castle* (1966). Turning to musicals, he wrote the book for A *Little Night Music* (1973), revised the book for the 1973 revival of *Candide* and did some play doctoring on the musicals *Half a Sixpence* (1965), *Irene* (1973), *Pacific

Overtures (1975), and *Meet Me in St. Louis* (1989). But Wheeler's crowning achievement is his book for the musical thriller **Sweeney Todd* (1979).

WHEN JOHNNY COMES MARCHING HOME (1902), a musical by Stanislaus *Stange (book, lyrics), Julian *Edwards (music). [New York Theatre, 71 perf.] Although the Southern belle Kate Pemberton (Zetti Kennedy) loves Union colonel John Graham (William G. Stewart), she is not above attempting to steal documents that will help her side. John catches her but is forgiving. Reconciliation is helped along when it is learned that John is a Southerner's long lost son. *Notable songs*: Fairyland; My Own United States. Often cited as Stange and Edwards's best work, it was revived regularly for at least twenty years. Its story is one of many that painted a romanticized picture, quite sympathetic to the Confederacy.

WHEN KNIGHTHOOD WAS IN FLOWER (1901), a play by Paul Kester. [Criterion Theatre, 176 perf.] The self-willed Mary Tudor (Julia *Marlowe), sister of Henry VIII (Charles Harbury), is ordered by her brother to marry Louis XII of France. Since she loves a commoner, Charles Brandon (Bruce *McRae), she refuses, telling the King's messenger, "Say to the King my brother that I will see him and his Kingdom sunk in hell before I'll marry Louis of France." She then persuades Charles to elope, but the two are captured, and Mary is forced to marry the French monarch. When Louis soon dies, she flees to England and finally marries Charles, whom Henry names Duke of Suffolk. The Charles *Frohman mounting was based on Charles Major's popular novel. Marlowe was condemned by many critics for playing in this entertaining hokum, but her Shakespearean tours had often proved unprofitable, and she later wrote, "My first season of *Knighthood* made me a fortune sufficient to render me independent for the rest of my life. The second season I more than doubled it. Freedom [to concentrate on Shakespeare] was mine." **Paul KESTER** (1870–1933) was born in Delaware, Ohio, a cousin of William Dean *Howells, and was only twenty-two when he collaborated with Mrs. *Fiske on the romantic vehicle *Countess Roudine* (1892). His later plays were of a similarly romantic, often highly sentimental nature and were usually written with specific stars in mind. Among his other successes were *Sweet Nell of Drury Lane* (1901) and *Dorothy Vernon of Haddon Hall* (1903). When styles of dramaturgy changed at the time of World War I, Kester attempted to change with them. However, he had only one later success, *The Woman of Bronze* (1920). Noting that he "flourished in an era of different proportions," George *Middleton recalled, "He could and did write only for stars—good or

limited. He deliberately restricted his skill to their exploitation."

WHEN LADIES MEET (1932), a comedy by Rachel *Crothers. [*Royale Theatre, 191 perf.] Novelist Mary Howard (Frieda Inescort) has written a book about a woman who loves a married man and about what happens when that woman meets the man's wife. Her book turns out to be a preview of her own life, for Mary loves her publisher, Rogers Woodruff (Herbert Rawlinson), and does meet his wife, Claire (Selena Royle), at the home of Bridget Drake (Spring Byington). At first neither woman realizes who the other is, but when the realization finally dawns on them they recognize they have more feelings in common than either of them has with Rogers. Mary quickly falls out of love. Bridget assumes Rogers will now return to Claire. Mary, however, ruefully informs her, "She doesn't want him now. That's what I've done to her. I'll never forget her eyes—what she saw." John *Golden produced Crothers's observant study of women interacting, and it was praised by the *Post* for being "as rich in its humor as it is warm in its sympathy."

WHERE'S CHARLEY? See *Charley's Aunt.*

WHIFFEN, Mrs. Thomas [née Blanche Galton] (1845–1936), actress and singer. The native Londoner studied voice with her mother, Mary, who was an opera singer, and later completed her education in France. She performed for a time in England before coming to America in 1868 with her aunt's *opéra bouffe company. In 1879 she was the first New York Buttercup in **H.M.S. Pinafore.* Subsequently she abandoned the musical stage and spent many seasons with the ensembles at the *Madison Square Theatre, Daniel *Frohman's *Lyceum, and Charles *Frohman's *Empire Theatre. Among the roles Whiffen created at the Empire were Mrs. Mossop in *Trelawny of the Wells* (1898) and Mrs. Jinks in **Captain Jinks of the Horse Marines* (1901). After leaving Charles Frohman she played opposite Mary *Mannering, Eleanor *Robson, Margaret *Anglin, and Henry *Miller, including the role of Mrs. Jordan in *The *Great Divide* (1906). She continued to perform actively until she was well into her eighties, one of her last roles again being Mrs. Mossop in a 1928 revival. Not unattractive, despite a low forehead, huge eyes, and a prominent chin, she was probably the last in a long line of New York's "dear old ladies"—actresses, sometimes quite young at the start, who specialized in playing lovable or cantankerous old women. Autobiography: *Keeping Off the Shelf*, 1928.

WHITE CARGO (1923), a play by Leon Gordon. [Greenwich Village Theatre, 702 perf.] Longford

(Richard Stevenson) comes to a West African plantation resolved to avoid the boredom, alcoholism, and trafficking with native girls that are rampant among the white overseers there, but with time he falls for a local half-caste, Tondeleyo (Annette Margules). In keeping with his strict code he insists on marrying her. She, however, eventually becomes bored and attempts to poison him. Longford is forced to return home, just more "white cargo" for the passage north, while his friends make Tondeleyo drink the poison she has prepared. Dismissed by most critics as turgid and trashy, the Earl *Carroll offering went on to become one of the decade's biggest hits. (Some sources give the number of its performances as 864.)

WHITE, George [né Weitz] (1890–1968), dancer, producer, and director. A New York native, he ran away from home to become a dancer, appearing in vaudeville and, between 1910 and 1918, in several Broadway musicals, including two editions of the *Ziegfeld Follies. In 1919 White launched his own series of revues, *George White's Scandals, and mounted thirteen editions, the last coming in 1939. He often appeared as a dancer in his own shows, which he regularly directed and wrote material for as well. His other productions included Runnin' Wild (1923), which introduced "The Charleston," Manhattan Mary (1927), and *Flying High (1930).

WHITE, Jane (b. 1922), actress. The African-American performer, who has played Greek and Shakespeare characters, is mostly remembered for her most atypical role: the funny, domineering Queen in the musical *Once Upon a Mattress (1959). A native New Yorker and the daughter of NAACP executive Walter White, she was educated at Smith College before studying acting with Herbert *Berghof, Uta *Hagen, and Peter Frye. White made her Broadway debut in 1945 as the Southern innocent Nonnie Anderson who has an affair with a white boy in Strange Fruit. Yet most of her subsequent roles have been in the classics, in which the question of her race was not an issue.

WHITE, Miles [Edgren] (1914–2000), costume designer. He was born in Oakland, California, and studied at the University of California and several local art schools before creating the clothes for Right This Way (1938). His designs were later seen in such shows as Best Foot Forward (1941), The *Pirate (1942), *Oklahoma! (1943), *Bloomer Girl (1944), *Carousel (1945), *High Button Shoes (1947), *Gentlemen Prefer Blondes (1949), Bless You All (1950), the 1952 revival of *Pal Joey, Hazel Flagg (1953), and *Bye Bye Birdie (1960).

WHITE, Onna (b. 1922), choreographer. The Nova Scotia–born dancer performed in several musicals before creating the choreography for a 1955 revival of *Guys and Dolls. She later created the dances for numerous Broadway shows, most notably The *Music Man (1957), *Take Me Along (1959), Irma La Douce (1960), Half a Sixpence (1965), *Mame (1966), *1776 (1969), and 70, Girls, 70 (1971).

WHITE SLAVE, THE (1882), a play by Bartley *Campbell. [Haverly's 14th Street Theatre, 40 perf.] At his death, Judge Hardin (Welsh Edwards) would free his housekeeper, Nance (Etelka Wardell), and her quadroon daughter, Lisa (Georgia *Cayvan). But Hardin's adopted son, Clay Britton (Gus Levick), who has acted as his foster father's manager, has squandered the estate and must reluctantly sell everything and everyone to William Lacy (Frank Roberts). Lacy, a villainous man who boasts, "I never deal in anything except horses and niggers," has been quietly engineering Britton's downfall, and when the young man becomes aware of the treachery he attempts to rescue Lisa. Lacy sends him to jail and warns Lisa that unless she loves him he will reduce her to the lowest of his slaves, with "a hoe in your hand, rags upon your back." Lisa responds, "Rags are royal raiment when worn for virtue's sake." More complications follow before Lisa is shown to be the white child of Judge Hardin's long dead daughter. Lacy is finally sent to prison for a murder he committed, and Lisa and the repentant Britton are free to wed. Most critics damned the play, seeing it as an inferior rewriting of *Boucicault's The *Octoroon but also acknowledged that it would undoubtedly appeal to the public. Helped by the almost instant fame of its celebrated "royal raiment" line, the work became Campbell's biggest success and was mounted regularly as late as 1918.

WHITE WINGS (1926), a comedy by Philip *Barry. [*Booth Theatre, 27 perf.] Archie Inch (Tom *Powers) is proud that he is the latest in a long line of street cleaners, or white wings, who clean up after horses. He is so proud, in fact, that he threatens to break off his romance with Mary Todd (Winifred *Lenihan), whose father invented the automobile, which is doing away with the need for horses. He vows that he will never take another job until the last horse is gone. Mary has no choice but to shoot the last horse, called Joseph (played by George Ali, who specialized in portraying animals). So Archie becomes a taxi driver whose first task is to cart off the bodies of Joseph and of his own grandfather, Major Inch (Albert Tavernier). Although most major critics were delighted with the Winthrop *Ames–produced fantasy, the public stayed away until the closing notice was posted.

By then it was too late to move the play to another theatre.

WHITEHEAD, Paxton (b. 1937), actor, manager, and director. The tall, thin British artist did not perform in New York until the 1960s but has been a favorite character actor ever since, particularly in comic roles. He was born in East Malling, England, and studied at the Webber-Douglas School of Dramatic Art before acting at the Stratford Memorial Theatre and with other English companies. Whitehead first came to America in 1961 and appeared sporadically in New York while acting and directing in regional theatres, particularly at the Shaw Festival in Canada, where he was artistic director during the 1970s. Among Whitehead's laudable performances were a melancholy Sherlock Holmes in *The Crucifer of Blood* (1978), the jolly King Pellimore in **Camelot* (1980), the obtuse method actor Freddy in *Noises Off* (1983), and various British and American characters in *London Suite* (1995) and *Suite in Two Keys* (2000).

WHITEHEAD, Robert (1916–2002), producer. He was born in Montreal, educated in Canada, and first came to Broadway's attention when he produced the highly successful mounting of **Medea* in 1947. He subsequently served as managing director for **ANTA, as a founder of The Producers' Theatre, and as a director of the Repertory Theatre of **Lincoln Center. Sometimes with these groups, sometimes with other partners, and sometimes alone he offered such memorable productions as *The *Member of the Wedding* (1950), *The *Time of the Cuckoo* (1952), **Bus Stop* (1955), *A *View from the Bridge* (1955), *The Visit* (1958), *A *Touch of the Poet* (1958), *A Man for All Seasons* (1961), **After the Fall* (1964), *Finishing Touches* (1973), *A Texas Trilogy* (1976), and *Lunch Hour* (1980). In 1982 he directed his wife, Zoë **Caldwell, in another revival of *Medea*, then staged her one-woman show, *Lillian* (1986). Approximately fifty Broadway productions bore his stamp.

WHITING, Jack (1901–61), singer, dancer, and actor. The Philadelphia-born song and dance man made his debut in the **Ziegfeld Follies of 1922*, then for more than three decades played leading or major supporting figures in two dozen musicals. Among his assignments were *The Ramblers* (1926), **Hold Everything!* (1928), *America's Sweetheart* (1931), *Take a Chance* (1932), *Hooray for What!* (1937), *Very Warm for May* (1939), *Beat the Band* (1942), *Hazel Flagg* (1953), and *The *Golden Apple* (1954).

WHITNEY, Fred C. (1861–1930), producer. Born and raised in Detroit, where his father, Clark J. Whitney (1832–1903), was a prominent theatre

manager, he went on to mount a number of plays, including a 1900 dramatization of *Quo Vadis?* But Whitney was best known for his musical productions, such as *The Fencing Master* (1892), *The Algerian* (1893), *Rob Roy* (1894), *Brian Boru* (1896), *A Normandy Wedding* (1898), *Dolly Varden* (1902), **When Johnny Comes Marching Home* (1902), *Love's Lottery* (1904), *The Chocolate Soldier* (1909), and *The Spring Maid* (1910). His brother was Bert C. Whitney (d. 1929), who operated theatres and presented productions in Chicago, Toronto, Montreal, and other cities.

WHOOPEE. See *Nervous Wreck, The*.

WHORF, Richard (1906–66), actor and designer. A sullen-looking but versatile theatrical figure, he was born in Winthrop, Massachusetts, and made his debut in Boston in 1921 as the Artful Dodger in *Oliver Twist*. In the 1930s and early 1940s he was a principal supporting player to the **Lunts in such plays as *The *Taming of the Shrew* (1935), **Idiot's Delight* (1936), *Amphitryon 38* (1937), *The Seagull* (1938), and **There Shall Be No Night* (1940). However, he is best remembered as George Crane, the writer looking for a peaceful place to work, in **Season in the Sun* (1950), and the irresponsible business partner Johnny Goodwin in *The *Fifth Season* (1953). In 1949 Whorf played Richard III, also designing sets and costumes for the production. He designed numerous other productions, including *Old Acquaintance* (1940), *There Shall Be No Night*, and *Ondine* (1954). Furthermore, he also directed several plays, including the musical **Seventeen* (1951), and many television shows.

WHO'S AFRAID OF VIRGINIA WOOLF? (1962), a play by Edward **Albee. [Billy Rose Theatre, 664 perf.; Tony, NYDCC Awards.] Martha (Uta **Hagen) is a frustrated, foul-mouthed woman married to a quiet college professor, George (Arthur **Hill). She has long held it against him that he has not been a success like her father, who is president of the college. Late one night they invite a young couple new to the college, Nick (George **Grizzard) and Honey (Melinda Dillon), to stop by for a drink. Under the influence of alcohol and under the guise of "fun and games" the small gathering explodes into a session of jokes, reminiscences, seduction, and sadomasochism. By the time the younger couple is ready to leave, George has publicly destroyed Martha's most cherished illusion— that the childless couple has a son. Alan **Schneider directed the outstanding cast, demonstrating how fireworks can come from such a small, powerful production. Although somewhat baffled by the meaning of the long play, Henry **Hewes praised the work as "an inexorable emotional contest between two recognizably real and thoroughly intelligent human beings." It was Albee's first full-length work and, in the opinion of many, still his finest play. Revivals regionally have been frequent, and it reappeared on Broadway in 1976 with Ben *Gazzara and Colleen *Dewhurst as George and Martha.

WHO'S WHO IN THE THEATRE. A basic reference book, it was first published in England in 1912 and updated for many years by its longtime editor, John Parker (1875–1952). It included biographies of living English and American theatrical figures, dates and lengths of long runs in London and New York, as well as other matters of interest. Since Parker's death others have assumed editorship. In 1978 the Gale Research Company of Detroit published a four-volume *Who Was Who in the Theatre*, which included the biographical entries of all figures who had died by 1976 and thus been dropped from the regular series. The company also now publishes the standard *Who's Who in the Theatre*.

WHY MARRY? (1917), a comedy by Jesse Lynch *Williams. [Astor Theatre, 120 perf.; Pulitzer Prize.] Ernest Hamilton (Shelley *Hull) is a brilliant young scientist who does not yet earn enough money to consider marrying. His fiancée is his lab technician, Helen (Estelle *Winwood), who is a modern woman, willing to wed and work, but she fears marriage would distract Ernest from his research. Goaded on by her unhappily married brother, John (Edmund *Breese), Helen therefore decides simply to live with Ernest—with no commitments. This does not sit well with her family, especially Uncle Everett (Nat *Goodwin), although Everett's own wife is in Reno getting a divorce. But after his wife agrees to return to him, Everett convinces the young lovers that "bad as marriage is, until we reform it, it is the best we have to offer you." This witty, epigrammatic comedy, which many contemporary critics perceived as America's answer to G. B. *Shaw, was the first play to win a *Pulitzer Prize. Williams wrote a follow-up called *Why Not?* (1922) about switching mates.

WIDOW BEDOTT (1880), a comedy by David Ross Locke. [Haverly's Lyceum Theatre, 56 perf.] Widow Bedott (Neil *Burgess) is a small-town busybody, always willing to chat and meddle while she bakes pies in her kitchen. She also is determined to marry again, and has chosen Elder Shadrack Sniffles (George Stoddart). Before he realizes what is happening, Sniffles is ready to take the widow to the altar, much to the annoyance of Widow Jenkins (Nellie Peck). Supposedly Lincoln's favorite humorist, Locke made this drama-

tization of his *Widow Bedott Papers* specifically for Burgess, the era's most famous female impersonator. Although others played the role, none surpassed his interpretation, to which he returned regularly for nearly a decade.

WIDOW'S SON, THE; *or, Which Is the Traitor?* (1825), a tragedy by Samuel *Woodworth. [*Park Theatre, in repertory.] Furious that his mother has been called a witch and himself branded a traitor, Captain William Darby (John H. Clarke) does in fact betray Fort Montgomery to the British during the Revolutionary War. His mother, Margaret (Mrs. Battersby), is shamed by his actions and offers to spy for Washington. Her work proves excellent, and she finally has the bitter satisfaction of knowing that William has been killed by the British, and not by her fellow Americans. Although the play was apparently a failure, it has remained of interest to students of American drama, even if they cannot agree on its merits. Arthur *Quinn called it "one of the best conceived and constructed plays of its kind," adding, "The play pictures well the bustle and confusion that marked the irregular warfare of that period of the Revolution, and the constant danger in which the characters move keeps the interest of the auditor stimulated." On the other hand, George *Odell, while calling it "a harrowing tale," concluded it "is an extremely poor, extravagant, ill-constructed thing."

WIFE, THE (1887), a play by David *Belasco and Henry C. *de Mille. [*Lyceum Theatre, 239 perf.] Helen Truman (Georgia *Cayvan) loves Robert Gray (Henry *Miller) but rejects him when she learns he has jilted Lucile Ferrant (Grace Henderson). On the rebound, she marries John Rutherford (Herbert *Kelcey), who is in despair when he discovers the truth. However, he resolves to win her love and does. The *Herald* called it "a good play of American life, serious in its purpose, yet with its emotional scenes relieved by pleasant comedy . . . well written and quick in action, the interest never being allowed to flag." Obviously influenced by Bronson *Howard's The *Banker's Daughter*, the play was written to order to accommodate Belasco's Lyceum ensemble and marked the first in a series of successful collaborations by Belasco and de Mille.

WIGNELL, Thomas (1753–1803), actor and manager. The English-born performer was brought to America in 1774 by his cousin, the younger Lewis *Hallam. However, the outbreak of the Revolution forced him to sail almost immediately for Jamaica, and he did not begin to earn a name for himself until his return in 1785. Wignell soon became a favorite with the Old American Company at the

*John Street Theatre in such roles as Joseph Surface, Prospero, and Laertes. William *Dunlap described him as "a man below ordinary height, with a slight stoop of the shoulders . . . his comedy was luxuriant in humour, but always faithful to his author. He was a comic actor, not a buffoon." However, much of his importance rests with his work behind the scenes. He is said to have been the man who encouraged Royall *Tyler to write The *Contrast (and was its first Jonathan). In 1793 Philadelphia's *Chestnut Street Theatre was built for a company he recruited, and with Alexander *Reinagle he ran the theatre until his death. Under his aegis it was the leading playhouse in the city and its ensemble often considered the finest in the country.

WILDE, Oscar [Fingal O'Flahertie Wills] (1854–1900), playwright. The Irish dramatist and wit was a figure of notoriety and some derision when he first visited America in 1882. His visit coincided with the production here of *Gilbert and *Sullivan's Patience, in which he was satirized, bolstering both the popularity of the musical and his own renown. His early play Vera (1883) was mounted during his stay here but failed. He is best recalled for his Lady Windermere's Fan (1893), which was first presented here with Julia *Arthur and Maurice *Barrymore in leading roles, and The Importance of Being Ernest (1895), whose original American cast included Henry *Miller, William *Faversham, and Viola *Allen. A Woman of No Importance (1893) and An Ideal Husband (1895) are sometimes resurrected. His controversial Salome (1906) was not given a professional performance until after his death; then decades later Al *Pacino played King Herod twice, in a *Circle in the Square production in 1992 and in a popular staged reading in 2003. Notable revivals of other Wilde works have included Cornelia Otis *Skinner's 1946 presentation of Lady Windermere's Fan, John *Gielgud's 1947 staging of The Importance of Being Ernest, and Peter *Hall's mounting of An Ideal Husband in 1996, which was held over for 309 performances, the longest New York run on record for a Wilde play. The man himself has shown up as a character in a handful of plays, including Diversions and Delights (1978), Oscar Remembered (1981), Gross Indecency: The Three Trials of Oscar Wilde (1997), The Judas Kiss (1998), The Invention of Love (2001), and A Man of No Importance (2002).

WILDE, Percival (1887–1953), playwright. The prolific dramatist and author was born in New York and educated at Columbia. Although few of his works were produced on Broadway and none was a commercial success, he is reputed to have had more plays performed regularly by amateur theatres than any other contemporary dramatist.

Among his popular titles were The Aftermath, The Lady of Dreams, and The Reckoning. Of his many textbooks, the best known was probably The Craftsmanship of the One-Act Play.

WILDER, Thornton [Niven] (1897–1975), playwright. The popular, broad-ranging writer was born in Madison, Wisconsin, and educated at Yale and Princeton. He had won fame for his excellent novels (especially the popular The Bridge of San Luis Rey) before writing some notable one-act plays such as The Long Christmas Dinner and The Happy Journey to Trenton and Camden. Although an earlier full-length play, The Trumpet Shall Sound (1926), dealing with a Christ-like figure in New York, was a failure, as were several later long plays, three of his full-length works are among the most interesting in the modern American theatre: the small-town drama *Our Town (1938), the expressionistic The *Skin of Our Teeth (1942), and the merry farce The *Matchmaker (1954), a rewriting of his earlier The Merchant of Yonkers (1938). He also wrote a 1932 translation of Lucrèce for Katharine *Cornell and in 1937 made an adaptation of A Doll's House for Ruth *Gordon. Despite the diversity of themes and forms, his best plays all offered thoughtful, perceptive views of essentially ordinary people and seem to grow richer over time. Biography: Thornton Wilder: An Intimate Portrait, Richard H. Goldstone, 1975.

WILDHORN, Frank. See Jekyll and Hyde.

WILL ROGERS FOLLIES, THE (1991), a musical comedy by Peter *Stone (book), Cy *Coleman (music), Betty *Comden, Adolph *Green (lyrics). [*Palace Theatre, 983 perf.; Tony, NYDCC Awards.] The musical bio of the celebrated cowboy comic was told in the form of a *Ziegfeld Follies extravaganza, which helped mask the fact that there was hardly any plot to speak of. Keith Carradine was a personable Will *Rogers and Cady Huffman shone as a kind of mistress of ceremonies, but the focal star was Tommy *Tune, who directed and choreographed the lavish production. Notable songs: Willamania; Give a Man Enough Rope; Our Favorite Son; My Big Mistake.

WILLARD, E[dward] S[mith] (1853–1915), actor. The English performer, celebrated for his portrayal of villains, made his mark in America as the vengeful potter Cyrus Blenkarn in The Middleman (1890), a role to which he returned on many subsequent visits and offered on his farewell tour in 1905. That he was equally skilled in comedy was demonstrated in 1892 when he played the absent-minded Professor Goodwillie in *Barrie's The Professor's Love Story. Willard's other popular vehicles included John Needham's Double (1892) and The Cardinal (1902).

WILLARD, J. C. See *Cat and the Canary, The.*

WILLIAMS, Barney [né Bernard Flaherty or O'Flaherty] (1823–76), comic actor. Born in Cork, Ireland, the comedian came to America as a youngster and made his first appearance in New York as a super in 1836. He spent some time in minstrelsy before finding his true métier as lovable, heavy-drinking Irishmen. Contemporaries credited his wife, the former Marie Pray (1828–1911), with prompting his change of roles. She usually played pert Yankee women opposite him, and together they toured successfully for many years in such vehicles as *Rory O'More, The Emerald Ring, Connie Soogah,* and *The Fairy Circle.* *Ireland noted, "in the conventional stage Irishman of low life, the ranting, roving, blarneying blade, or in the more dull and stupid grade of bogtrotters, he has gained a popularity on our stage unequaled by any rival."

WILLIAMS, [Egbert Austin] Bert (1874–1922), comic actor. The greatest of African-American comedians and one of the finest of all comics, he was born in the West Indies and was brought to the United States while still a youngster. Williams played for a time in minstrelsy, then in 1895 joined with George Walker (d. 1911) to form an act in which Walker played the sharp-dealing dandy and Williams his downtrodden patsy who dressed shabbily, walked with a slow shuffle, and had a lugubrious delivery that often packed a hidden punch. Together they appeared in four Broadway shows: *The Gold Bug* (1896), *In Dahomey* (1903), *Abyssinia* (1906), and *Bandanna Land* (1908). At a time when racial bigotry was rampant even among leading drama critics, *Theatre Magazine* proclaimed him "a vastly funnier man than any white comedian now on the American stage." After Walker's death from paresis, Williams appeared in *Mr. Lode of Koal* (1909) and in eight editions of the *Ziegfeld Follies,* beginning in 1910. He was also popular in vaudeville and was identified with such songs as "Nobody" and "The Darktown Poker Club." Although he was an intelligent, handsome, light-skinned man, he was forced to black up for his appearances and was never permitted to abandon the stereotypical black he portrayed so hilariously. Biography: *Nobody: The Story of Bert Williams,* Ann Charters, 1970.

WILLIAMS, Hattie (1870?–1942), actress and singer. The vivacious Boston beauty made her debut in 1893 and subsequently appeared in several Charles *Hoyt farces. She then won applause in *Vivian's Papas* (1903) and *The Girl from Kay's* (1904). Subsequently Williams starred in such musicals as *The Rollicking Girl* (1905), *The Little Cherub* (1906), *Fluffy Ruffles* (1908), and *The Doll Girl* (1913), as well as in several farces. She retired at the height of her success.

WILLIAMS, Jesse Lynch (1871–1929), playwright. Born in Sterling, Illinois, and educated at Princeton, he began his career as a writer of short stories. He worked for a time on newspapers and used his experiences to write his first produced play, *The Stolen Story* (1906). Later he won the first *Pulitzer Prize for drama for his study of young love, *Why Marry?* (1917). Five years later *Why Not?* (1922) told of two married couples who decide to exchange mates. His last play was *Lovely Lady* (1925), in which an amorous widow attempts to destroy a happy marriage. Williams also wrote several popular novels.

WILLIAMS, John D. (1886?–1941), producer. The Boston native worked for a time with *Erlanger and Charles *Frohman. Then, after the latter's death, he embarked on an independent, somewhat brief, career that nevertheless established him as one of our most thoughtful producers. His mountings included *Justice* (1916), *Our Betters* (1917), *The *Copperhead* (1918), *Sleeping Partners* (1918), *Beyond the Horizon* (1920), *Gold* (1921), *The Assumption of Hannele* (1924), *L'Aiglon* (1927), and *Pagan Lady* (1930). He also directed plays on occasion, notably *Rain* (1922).

WILLIAMS, Tennessee [né Thomas Lanier Williams] (1911–83), playwright. Considered by many to be the leading dramatist of his age, he was born in Columbus, Mississippi. His father was a violent, aggressive traveling salesman; his mother, the high-minded, puritanical daughter of a clergyman; his elder sister, a young woman beset by mental problems that eventually led to her being institutionalized. His family thus provided him with the seeds for characters who would people so many of his plays. He attended several universities before graduating from the State University of Iowa. During this time some of his early works were produced at regional and collegiate playhouses while he held numerous odd jobs. Williams's first play to receive a major production was *Battle of Angels* (1940), which folded on the road. Success came with his *The *Glass Menagerie* (1945), followed by such popular dramas as *A *Streetcar Named Desire* (1947), *Summer and Smoke* (1948), *The *Rose Tattoo* (1951), *Cat on a Hot Tin Roof* (1955), *Sweet Bird of Youth* (1959), *Period of Adjustment* (1960), and *The *Night of the Iguana* (1961). During these years he had a number of failures, including *You Touched Me!* (1945), *Camino Real* (1953), and *Orpheus Descending* (1957), but in later years they would be re-examined, and some would find favor. Although he continued to write and be produced, the plays that followed *The Night of the Iguana* were neither critical nor commercial successes. His preoccupation with social degeneracy and homosexuality, which had heretofore been contained by his sense of theatre and poetic dialogue, overcame these saving restraints and lost him a public for the newer works. Among these later works were *In the Bar in a Tokyo Hotel* (1969), *Small Craft Warnings* (1972), *Outcry* (1973), *Vieux Carré* (1978), and *Clothes for a Summer Hotel* (1980). Fifteen years after his death, an early work titled *Not about Nightingales* was uncovered and, when it was produced on Broadway in 1999, proved to be a critical success. Williams's strengths in playwriting were in his vivid characterizations and glistening dialogue. His subject matter was sometimes crude or brutal, but his writing remained elegant and poetic. Biography: *The Kindness of Strangers: The Life of Tennessee Williams*, Donald Spoto, 1985.

WILLIAMSTOWN THEATRE FESTIVAL. In the opinion of many the premiere summer theatre in America, the group from Williamstown, Massachusetts, has an international reputation for superb revivals, new translations of foreign works, and original scripts. The theatre also receives much publicity because of the many famous actors who use the festival to return to the stage away from the commercial demands of New York. The group was founded by Ralph Renzi and David C. Bryant in 1955, and for decades it was run by the Yale professor Nikos Psacharopoulos. Performances are in the 520-seat Adams Theatre and the 96-seat Nikos Stage, located on the campus of Williams College. Since the death of Psacharopoulos in 1989, Peter Hunt has been artistic director. The company won the 2002 *Tony Award as outstanding regional theatre.

WILLIS, N[athaniel] P[arker] (1806–67), playwright. Famous in his own day primarily as a poet, short story writer, and editor, he was born in Portland, Maine, but raised in Boston and educated at Yale. In 1837 he won a contest held by Josephine *Clifton for the best blank-verse tragedy to suit her talents. His play, *Bianca Visconti*, was a romantic tale of doomed love, and it remained popular for several decades. However, *The Kentucky Heiress*, a comedy written for Clifton and also presented in 1837, was a failure and now appears lost. His other success was *Tortesa, the Usurer* (1839), written for James *Wallack.

WILLSON, Meredith [né Robert Meredith Reiniger] (1902–84), composer, lyricist, and librettist. Born in Mason City, Iowa, the noted conductor and musician performed for several seasons as a flutist in the band of John Philip *Sousa. Later he

was prominent in radio, arranging and conducting the music for top shows. Willson turned to the theatre relatively late in life and wrote book, music, and lyrics for the hugely successful *The *Music Man* (1957), which reflected his Iowa boyhood. He also created the lyrics and music for *The Unsinkable Molly Brown* (1960) and *Here's Love* (1963).

WILSON, August (b. 1945), playwright. He was born in a working-class neighborhood in Pittsburgh and was a high-school dropout. In his twenties he started to write poetry, only later turning to drama. Wilson's earliest plays were mounted at regional theatres, then the *Eugene O'Neill Memorial Theater Center and the *Yale Repertory Theatre took an interest in his works and he received widespread recognition. His subsequent plays attempted to illustrate aspects of African-American life in different decades of the 20th century, most of them set in Pittsburgh. His first success in New York was *Ma Rainey's Black Bottom* (1984), followed by *Fences* (1987), *Joe Turner's Come and Gone* (1988), The *Piano Lesson* (1990), *Seven Guitars* (1996), *Two Trains Running* (1992), *Jitney* (2000), *King Hedley II* (2001), and *Gem of the Ocean* (2003). Wilson's plays are mostly character studies with little plot but explosive situations and dialogue, creating a musical tone that is uniquely African American. He is the most prodigious, awarded, and successful playwright of his race in the history of the American theatre.

WILSON, Elizabeth (b. 1921), character actress. The versatile performer has usually been cast as mothers, aunts, or spinsters, yet she has managed to find variety and humanity in her characterizations. She was born in Grand Rapids, Michigan, and studied acting at the *Neighborhood Playhouse. Wilson had extensive experience in stock before she made her Broadway debut as one of the schoolteachers in *Picnic* (1953). Among her many outstanding performances were the hassled Manhattan mother Marjorie Newquist in *Little Murders* (1969), the distant mother Harriet of a damaged Vietnam War vet in *Sticks and Bones* (1971), the overlooked niece Sonya in *Uncle Vanya* (1973), the calculating Mrs. Peachum in The *Threepenny Opera* (1976), the interfering Aunt Helen in *Taken in Marriage* (1979), the disapproving spinster Aaronetta in *Morning's at Seven* (1980), and the retired actress Bonita Belgrave in *Waiting in the Wings* (1999).

WILSON, Francis (1854–1935), comic actor. The Philadelphia-born comedian began performing while still a youngster and spent time in minstrelsy before acting in plays. However, the pinnacle of his career came when he joined the company of the newly opened *Casino Theatre in 1882, scoring his greatest success as Cadeaux in *Erminie (1886). James *Huncker wrote of his portrayal of the lovable rogue, "A secondary role became a stellar one, thanks to Mr. Wilson's racy interpretation . . . with a comic force undeniable . . . as full of the joy of life as Sam Weller, and of original sin as the Artful Dodger." Wilson played the part nearly thirteen hundred times, both in the original production and in several revivals. In 1889 he formed his own production company and over the next thirteen years appeared in eleven musicals, including The Oolah (1889), The Lion Tamer (1891), Half a King (1896), The Strollers (1901), and The Toreador (1902). Except for revivals of Erminie, he then abandoned musicals. Most notable among his later successes were his Sir Guy De Vere in When Knights Were Bold (1907) and Thomas Beach in his own play, The Bachelor's Baby (1909). Besides writing other plays, Wilson was the author of numerous books on the theatre, including works on John Wilkes *Booth and Joseph *Jefferson. Autobiography: Francis Wilson's Life of Himself, 1924.

WILSON, Frank (1886?–1956), actor. One of many performers remembered for a single role, he was born in New York and studied at the *American Academy of Dramatic Arts. The African-American actor had been understudy and replacement to the leads in *All God's Chillun Got Wings and *In Abraham's Bosom before creating the part of the kindly cripple *Porgy (1927). Wilson played the role in New York, on tour, and in London for over two years, but thereafter found few important parts and was often reduced to portraying servants.

WILSON, Harry Leon. See Man from Home, The.

WILSON, John C[hapman] (1899–1961), producer and director. Born in New Jersey and educated at Yale, he spent many years as a stockbroker before his friendship with Noel *Coward led him into the theatre. With Coward, the *Lunts, and the *Theatre Guild, he co-produced a number of works, including Design for Living (1933) and Tonight at 8:30 (1936), sometimes as a silent partner. Embarking on his own, Wilson later produced such shows as Blithe Spirit (1941), Lovers and Friends (1943), *Bloomer Girl (1944), O Mistress Mine (1946), Present Laughter (1946), and The Winslow Boy (1947). He directed many of his own productions as well as those of other producers, notably *Kiss Me, Kate (1948) and *Gentlemen Prefer Blondes (1949).

WILSON, Lanford (b. 1937), playwright. Born in Lebanon, Missouri, he began writing plays while attending the University of Chicago. Coming to New York he soon earned attention for his work presented Off Broadway and Off Off Broadway.

His first plays to reach a regular playhouse were The Gingham Dog (1969) and Lemon Sky (1970), but in 1973 his picture of life in a dingy hotel, The *Hot l Baltimore, began a run of 1,166 performances, an Off-Broadway record for a nonmusical by an American. He later wrote three plays about the same Missouri family, The *Fifth of July (1978), *Talley's Folly (1980), and A Tale Told (1981). Other noteworthy works include Balm in Gilead (1965), Rimers of Eldritch (1966), The Mound Builders (1975), Serenading Louie (1976), Angels Fall (1983), *Burn This (1987), Redwood Curtain (1993), Book of Days (2002), Rain Dance (2003), and many oft-produced one-acts. As a rule Wilson's best work blends the careful structural formality of older schools of playwriting with the preoccupations of modern authors, many of his works having a seemingly loose Chekhovian flavor to them.

WILSON, Mary Louise (b. 1936), character actress. The pinch-faced, wiry player with a distinctive sharp voice has a talent for playing outspoken women. She was born in New Haven, Connecticut, and educated at Northwestern before making her Manhattan debut in 1959. Wilson was first noticed as the strident Communist Ada in Flora, the Red Menace (1965), followed by many memorable supporting performances, including the cynical writer Nancy Blake in The *Women (1973), the stripper Tessie Tura in *Gypsy (1974), the obnoxious actress Kitty in The *Royal Family (1975), the wisecracking journalist Liz Imbrie in The *Philadelphia Story (1980), fashion magazine czarina Diana Vreeland in Full Gallop (1995), and Berlin landlady Fraulein Schneider in *Cabaret (1998).

WILSON, Robert (b. 1941), director and designer. Born in Waco, Texas, the son of a lawyer, Wilson studied business at the University of Texas and design at Brooklyn's Pratt Institute. His background in painting and architecture would surface in his experimental theatre pieces that often border on *performance art. Wilson's works are always very visual, usually very long (Stalin ran twelve hours and KA MOUNTAIN lasted one week nonstop), and often utilize original contributions by avant-gardists like composer Philip Glass and choreographer Lucinda Childs. His noteworthy productions include A Letter to Queen Victoria (1974), Einstein on the Beach (1976), the CIVIL warS (1984), Alcestis (1986), and The Days Before: Death, Destruction & Detroit III (1999).

WIMAN, Dwight Deere (1895–1951), producer. Born in Moline, Illinois, the heir to a manufacturing fortune, he studied drama under Monty *Woolley at Yale. After a brief fling in films, he joined with William A. *Brady Jr. to produce such plays as *Lucky Sam McCarver* (1925), 1926 revivals of *Little Eyolf* and *The *Two Orphans*, *The *Road to Rome* (1927), and *The *Little Show* (1929). Following the partnership's dissolution he produced, occasionally with associates, such memorable productions as *The Vinegar Tree* (1930), **Gay Divorce* (1932), **She Loves Me Not* (1933), **On Your Toes* (1936), **Babes in Arms* (1937), **On Borrowed Time* (1938), **I Married an Angel* (1938), **Morning's at Seven* (1939), **By Jupiter* (1942), and *The *Country Girl* (1950).

WINCHELL, Walter [né Wincheles] (1897–1972), journalist. The most influential Broadway columnist of his day, he was born in New York and received some of his early training as a child vaudevillian. His staccato writing and similar delivery during his radio broadcasts, his often explosive innuendos, and curious "Winchellisms," such as "infanticipating" for "pregnant," earned him a huge following, and he was credited with saving a number of Broadway shows, most notably **Hellzapoppin*, from probable failure. Biography: *Winchell*, Bob Thomas, 1971.

WINDUST, Bretaigne (1906–60), director. He was born in Paris and educated at Princeton, where he was a member of the Theatre Intime. He later served as stage manager for the original production of **Strange Interlude*, then co-founded the *University Players in 1928. Windust spent several years as an actor before directing **Idiot's Delight* (1936). His elegantly stylish, carefully paced mounting earned him numerous subsequent assignments, including *Amphitryon 38* (1937), **Life with Father* (1939), **Arsenic and Old Lace* (1941), **State of the Union* (1945), **Finian's Rainbow* (1947), and *The Great Sebastians* (1956).

WINGED VICTORY (1943), a play by Moss *Hart. [44th Street Theatre, 212 perf.] Centering on the air force career of three men—Allan Ross (Mark Daniels), an Ohio bank teller, Pinky Scariano (Don Taylor), a barber, and Irving Miller (Edmund O'Brien), a young man from Brooklyn—the story follows them through their basic training, to their tour of duty on a bomber they name "Winged Victory," and into the battle in which Pinky is seriously injured but seems likely to survive. The stirring propaganda piece was produced by the U. S. Army Air Forces for the benefit of the Army Emergency Relief Fund and featured a huge cast, many of whom later went on to stardom. The play earned millions of dollars for the relief fund in its limited engagements around the country.

WINGLESS VICTORY, THE (1936), a play by Maxwell *Anderson. [*Empire Theatre, 110 perf.] To the horror of his sanctimonious New England family, Nathaniel McQueston (Walter *Abel), captain of the ship *Wingless Victory*, returns to port with a wife, the dark-skinned Malayan princess Oparre (Katharine *Cornell). She is accepted grudgingly only because Nathaniel is so rich. However, with time she recognizes she will never be truly welcome and that she stands in Nathaniel's way and so kills herself and her children. The play, which opened less than a month before Anderson's **High Tor*, was viewed by many as old-fashioned melodrama in the guise of blank-verse tragedy. Stark *Young of the *New Republic* dismissed it as "semitosh from start to finish."

WINNINGER, Charles [né Karl Winninger] (1884–1969), character actor. A native of Athens, Wisconsin, the heavyset, outgoing comedian began performing at the age of five and had appeared with circuses, in vaudeville, and on a show boat called the *Cotton Blossom* before he made his Broadway debut in the 1910 musical *The Yankee Girl*. Over the next quarter-century he appeared in a dozen musicals, introducing "I Want to Be Happy" in **No, No, Nanette* (1925) and creating the role of Cap'n Andy of the *Cotton Blossom* in **Show Boat* (1927). After a long career in films he appeared in the 1951 revival of **Music in the Air*.

WINSLOW, Herbert Hall (1865–1930), playwright. Between *Town Lots; or, A Paper City* (1888) and *He Loved the Ladies* (1927), the prolific, wideranging dramatist, who was born in Keokuk, Iowa, wrote approximately one hundred produced plays. Most were written as vehicles for lesser touring stars, and only a handful of his works ever reached New York. Typical of his output was *The Vinegar Buyer*, which was written in 1902 for Ezra Kendall, a popular vaudevillian, and toured for several seasons. A stereotyped period comedy of rural life, it was immensely popular with smalltown audiences, but when it braved New York it was waved away as "a series of vaudeville jokes strung out through three acts."

WINTER GARDEN THEATRE (New York). Opened in 1911 by the *Shuberts, it was built on the east side of Broadway at 50th Street on the site of the old American Horse Exchange. William A. *Swasey designed the unusually wide auditorium that seated proportionately far more in the orchestra than in most Broadway houses. Although the Shubert offices were long located in or near the Sam S. *Shubert Theatre, this house was often called the producers' flagship. In the 1910s and 1920s it was home to many Al *Jolson musicals, as well as to the annual **Passing Shows*. In the 1930s it housed several superior revues. Among its later hits were *Mexican Hayride* (1944), **Wonderful Town*

(1953), *Peter Pan* (1954), *West Side Story* (1957), *Mame* (1966), *42nd Street* (1980), *Cats* (1982), and *Mamma Mia* (2001).

WINTER, William (1836–1917), critic. The most influential and widely read theatre critic of his era, he was born in Gloucester, Massachusetts, and educated at Harvard. He came to New York in 1859 to become literary editor of *The Saturday Press*, then served as drama critic for the *Albion*. In 1865 he was appointed the *Tribune*'s critic, a post he held until his retirement in 1909, after which he contributed articles to various magazines. His early criticism was learned, basically sound, and open-minded, but with the rise of realism in the 1880s he became increasingly unaccepting of new theatrical movements and was the often shrill leader of the anti-Ibsenites. Winter came to conclude that morality was all-important, and that no play, however meritorious, was worthy of patronage if it violated his rigid canons of right and wrong. He wrote numerous books on theatre, including *Other Days* (1908), *Old Friends* (1909), and *The Wallet of Time* (1913), as well as biographies of David *Belasco, Edwin *Booth, Joseph *Jefferson, Richard *Mansfield, and Ada *Rehan. His penchant for composing memorial odes to dead actors earned him the nickname "Weeping Willie." Typical both of his style and of his later, crotchety views were his comments in his Mansfield biography, "The Ibsen movement . . . impressed me, from the beginning, as unhealthful and injurious. The province of art, and especially of dramatic art, is beauty, not deformity; the need of the world is to be cheered, not depressed; and the author who avows, as Ibsen did, that he goes down into the sewers,—whatever be the purpose of his descent into those insalubrious regions,—should be left to the enjoyment of them."

WINTERSET (1935), a play by Maxwell *Anderson. [Martin Beck Theatre, 195 perf.; NYDCC Award.] Mio (Burgess *Meredith) is certain that his anarchist father, Bartolomeo, was unjustly sentenced to death for the murder of a paymaster. He visits Judge Gaunt (Richard *Bennett), who presided over the trial, but recognizes that the jurist has become mentally deranged. Mio concludes that his best hope for bringing the truth to light is Miriamne (Margo), whose brother witnessed the crime. Mio and Miriamne fall in love, and when the gangsters who were the real culprits kill Mio, she threatens to reveal the truth, and she, too, is killed. Gilbert W. Gabriel exemplified the generally enthusiastic response to this blank-verse play when he wrote in the *American*, "It is, to date, Anderson's masterpiece. This, underneath all its full-flower eloquence, is melodrama, right, tight, trig melodrama, and

immensely exciting melodrama, too." One of the most memorable aspects of the Guthrie *McClintic production was Jo *Mielziner's stunning scenery, in particular a street scene overshadowed by the Brooklyn Bridge. The play was Anderson's second attempt to dramatize the Sacco-Vanzetti story. His earlier collaboration with Harold Hickerson, *Gods of the Lightning* (1928), had failed.

WINWOOD, Estelle (1883–1984), actress. In a career that spanned seventy years, this performer moved from a beautiful leading lady and comedienne to a fine character actress. She was born in Lee, England, made her professional debut in 1898, and came to America in 1916. Her early roles included the scandalous Helen in *Why Marry?* (1917), as well as leading parts in such Somerset *Maugham plays as *Too Many Husbands* (1919) and *The Circle* (1921). Winwood later played important roles in such works as *Ten Little Indians* (1944) and *Lady Windermere's Fan* (1946), then scored one of her most memorable triumphs as the loony Mme. Constance in *The Madwoman of Chaillot* (1948). Winwood appeared on Broadway up until 1966 and in films until 1976.

WISDOM TOOTH, THE (1926), a comedy by Marc *Connelly. [Little Theatre, 160 perf.] Charley Bemis (Thomas *Mitchell) is an industrious, frugal senior clerk at the office in which he works, but he is so readily and so often browbeaten by his associates that he comes to look on himself as a mere carbon copy of a man. After Sally Field (Mary Philips), who also lives at Charley's boarding house, berates him for his timidity, Charley falls asleep and recalls his youth, including a circus in which none other than Barnum and Bailey had praised him. The dream gives him the strength to be the man he long has wanted to be. True, his standing up to his boss costs him his job, but then he may do more with an admiring Sally than play cribbage. This John *Golden mounting was Connelly's first solo effort following his split with George S. *Kaufman, and the play's comedy delighted critics even if its loose construction did not. After a slow start, it caught on, thanks in no small part to Mitchell's excellent performance.

WISE, Thomas A. (1865–1928), character actor. The burly performer was born in Faversham, England, but came to America while still young and made his debut in Dixon, California, later touring with Joseph *Grismer and then with William *Gillette. He is best recalled for such roles as Amos Bloodgood in *Are You a Mason?* (1902), the muckraking senator William Langdon in *A *Gentleman from Mississippi* (1908), and Falstaff in a 1916 revival of *The Merry Wives of Windsor*. With Harrison Rhodes, his collaborator on *A Gentleman from Mississippi*, he wrote several other less successful plays.

WISH YOU WERE HERE. See *Having Wonderful Time*.

WIT (1998), a play by Barbara Edson. [Union Square Theatre, 545 perf.; Pulitzer Prize.] Dr. Vivian Bearing (Kathleen Chalfant), a recognized English literature scholar, narrates her own eight-month chronicle of treating and succumbing to ovarian cancer, telling the tale with candor and wryness. Sometimes clinical, sometimes poetic (there is much talk about and quoting of John Donne), the drama was a tour de force for Chalfant, who was acclaimed for giving a "towering and heartbreaking performance." **Kathleen CHALFANT** (b. 1945) was born in San Francisco and educated in the classics at Stanford University. She acted with distinguished regional theatres, then began appearing Off Broadway in 1972. Despite many superb performances over the years, Chalfant did not find success until 1993, when she played the sour Mormon Hannah Pitt and other characters in *Angels in America.

WITCHCRAFT; or, the Martyrs of Salem (1847), a play by Cornelius *Mathews. [*Bowery Theatre, 5 perf.] Gideon Bodish (James E. *Murdoch) comes to the defense of his morose, memory-haunted mother, Ambla (Mrs. Wilkinson), when she is placed on trial for witchcraft. The court is heavily influenced by the testimony of Susanna Peache (Mrs. Sergeant), who loves Gideon and who believes that Ambla had used her occult powers to discourage the romance. After Ambla is executed, Susanna realizes that she has lost Gideon and so commits suicide. Jarvis Dane (J. A. J. *Neafie), a rival suitor of Susanna, kills Gideon to avenge her death. This often poignant and gripping blank-verse tragedy was first presented at Philadelphia's *Walnut Street Theatre, where it was a major success. Although it failed in New York, it was popular in other cities across the country, and, apparently, in Europe as well. Whether Mathews was familiar with a similar, earlier play, *Superstition, is unknown.

WITCHING HOUR, THE (1907), a play by Augustus *Thomas. [Hackett Theatre, 212 perf.] Although Jack Brookfield (John *Mason), a professional gambler, was long ago rejected by Helen Whipple (Jennie A. Eustace), he remains loyal and loving enough to help her when her son Clay (Morgan Conan) is convicted of murdering a man who taunted him about his curious fear of cat's-eye jewels. A retrial is arranged. Brookfield knows that Clay has been railroaded by district attorney Frank Hardmuth (George Nash), Clay's rival for the hand of Viola Campbell (Janet Dunbar), so Brookfield releases to

the newspapers material to show Hardmuth's complicity in a governor's murder. Believing in the powers of telepathy, Brookfield is sure that the sympathy of readers will be passed on to the jury in Clay's retrial. After Clay is acquitted, Hardmuth attempts to shoot Brookfield, who employs hypnosis to force Hardmuth to drop his gun. The *Shubert production was hailed by William *Winter as "the most interesting drama in years—the play of the century." Despite its somewhat preposterous acceptance of the amazing powers of telepathy and instant hypnosis, this is generally acknowledged as Thomas's best play. His interest in the occult grew out of his association with the celebrated mind reader Washington Irving Bishop.

WITHAM, Charles W. (1842?–1926), designer. One of the leading scenic artists of the last half of the 19th century, he was born in Portland, Maine. No records survive showing where he studied, but the technical excellence of his later drawings suggests a thorough schooling. Edwin *Booth appointed him to design and paint all the architectural scenes for Booth's Theatre, including his *Hamlet, *Julius Caesar, The *Merchant of Venice, and *Richelieu, all of which demonstrated a notable historical accuracy. Witham left Booth in 1873 to work with Augustin *Daly, creating primarily modern interiors but also the sets for Dion *Boucicault spectacles. Edward *Harrigan made him his chief set designer in 1881, and the plays about New York lowlife allowed Witham to move sharply toward realism in his work, which thereafter displayed a marked asymmetry.

WITHIN THE LAW (1912), a play by Bayard *Veiller. [Eltinge Theatre, 541 perf.] Falsely accused of theft by her employer Edward Gilder (Dodson Mitchell) and sentenced to three years in prison, Mary Turner (Jane *Cowl) warns Gilder she will be avenged. Four years later Mary is out of jail and has organized a group of criminals whom she keeps operating just within the law. She also weds Gilder's son Richard (Orme *Caldara) and advises the elder Gilder, "Four years ago you took away my name and gave me a number. Now I've given up that number and I've got your name." Against Mary's orders, her gang attempts to rob Gilder's home. One is killed, but when the others confess, they establish Mary's innocence. Mary and Richard realize they do love each other, and even the elder Gilder is apparently reconciled. Originally a failure when William A. *Brady produced it with his wife, Grace *George, as star, the play was rewritten, recast, and restaged by Holbrook *Blinn and presented by the *American Play Company. To *Variety it was "a great big elemental problem play, put before the public so that it cannot fail to be understood."

WITTOP, Freddy (1921–2001), costume designer. Born in Holland, he was a dancer and ran his own dance company that toured Europe and America in the 1950s before turning to design. His Broadway credits included *Carnival* (1961), *Hello, Dolly!* (1964), *On a Clear Day You Can See Forever* (1965), *George M!* (1968), *Dear World* (1969), *A Patriot for Me* (1969), *The Three Musketeers* (1984), and *Wind in the Willows* (1985). Wittop was also a busy costume designer for dance companies and opera houses.

WIZ, THE. See *Wizard of Oz, The*.

WIZARD OF OZ, THE (1903), a musical comedy by Frank Baum (book, lyrics), Paul Tietjens, A. Baldwin *Sloane (music). [Majestic Theatre, 293 perf.] When little Dorothy (Anna Laughlin) and her cow Imogene (Joseph Schrode) are whisked away from her Kansas farm by a wild cyclone and taken to the faraway land of Oz, they are joined by a Scarecrow (Fred *Stone), a Tin Man (Dave *Montgomery), and a Cowardly Lion (Arthur Hill) as they travel to visit the Wizard, who will help them return to Kansas. Of course, it is all a dream. Based on the famous children's book by Baum, he was forced to minimize the part of the lion to spotlight its two stars. No major songs emerged from the original score, but two interpolations, "Sammy" (James O'Dea/Edw. Hutchinson) and "Hurrah for Baffins Bay" (Vincent Bryan/Theodore Morse), were briefly popular. Decades later an original, highly successful all-black musical, **THE WIZ** (1975), employed the same story but used a contemporary, ethnic point of view. William F. Brown adapted the Baum book and Charlie Smalls provided the tuneful, Motown-like score. Stephanie Mills played Dorothy; Hinton *Battle, the Scarecrow; Tiger Haynes, the Tinman; Ted Ross, the Lion; and Andre *de Shields, the Wizard. *Notable songs*: If You Believe; Ease on Down the Road; Home; Be a Lion; He's the Wizard. The show ran 1,672 performances in the *Majestic Theatre (but not the same Majestic as in 1903).

WODEHOUSE, P[elham] G[ranville] (1881–1975), lyricist and librettist. After making a name for himself as a novelist and humorist, the writer, who was born in Guildford, England, came to America and served as drama critic for *Vanity Fair*. In 1916 he wrote lyrics for *Miss Springtime*, then joined composer Jerome *Kern and librettist Guy *Bolton to work on the book and lyrics for the *Princess Theatre shows. His 1917 credits included *Have a Heart*, *Oh, Boy!*, *Leave It to Jane*, *The Riviera Girl*, *Miss 1917*, and *Kitty Darlin'*. Among his later contributions were those as lyricist and/or co-librettist for *Oh, Lady! Lady!!* (1918), *Sitting Pretty* (1924), *Oh, Kay!* (1926), *Rosalie* (1928), and *Anything Goes* (1934), although his shipwreck plot had to be jettisoned after the sinking of the *Morro Castle*. Wodehouse may well be considered the first truly great lyricist of the American musical stage, his easy, colloquially flowing rhymes deftly interwoven with a sunny wit. Biography: *P. G. Wodehouse*, Frances Donaldson, 1982.

WOLFE, George C. (b. 1955), director, playwright, and manager. The multitalented African American was born in Lexington, Kentucky, and educated at Pomona College and New York University before making his Off-Broadway writing debut as lyricist and librettist for *Paradise!* (1985). Wolfe's *The Colored Museum* (1986), a satirical look at racial stereotypes, brought him acclaim, but he would soon be better known for his directing credits and was named a resident director at the *New York Shakespeare Festival, becoming artistic director in 1993. In addition to staging many classics and new works, Wolfe also wrote the librettos and staged the Broadway musicals *Jelly's Last Jam* (1992) and *The Wild Party* (2000) and directed the innovative dance piece *Bring in da Noise, Bring in da Funk* (1996).

WOLHEIM, Louis [Robert] (1881–1931), actor. Born in New York, he had served as a mining engineer and a teacher at Cornell University before his friends John *Barrymore and Lionel *Barrymore persuaded him to join them in *The Jest* (1919). A huge, strapping man with a conspicuous broken nose, he is best remembered for two exceptional portrayals: Yank, the primitive coal stoker who dreams of a better life, in *The *Hairy Ape* (1922), and Captain Flagg, the foul-mouthed career soldier, in *What Price Glory?* (1924).

WOMAN, THE (1911), a play by William C. *de Mille. [Republic Theatre, 247 perf.] Illinois Representative Jim Blake (John W. Cope) has only contempt for the public he serves. "The public," he snarls, "makes me sick." He also fears that public and what will happen when it wakes up to his corruption. Blake is especially anxious to push through a bill allowing railroads to inflate their stocks. To this end he feels he must besmirch his idealistic opponent, Matthew Standish (Cuyler Hastings), by disclosing Standish has been unfaithful to his wife. But first he must determine who the woman is. Knowing that when he broaches the matter Standish is certain to call the woman, Blake attempts to bribe a telephone operator, Wanda Kelly (Mary *Nash), to give him the number Standish calls so he can trace it. Wanda has heard Blake tell his scheme to his cronies and is loath to help. But she plays along by being evasive. Standish does call the woman but so does another man shortly thereafter. Wanda realizes that the woman is Blake's own daughter. She not only finds a means to keep anyone from being hurt but wins the affection of Blake's more amiable son, Tom (Harold Vosburgh), in the process. One of the most successful of the muckraking melodramas of its age, it was greatly enhanced by producer-director David *Belasco's brilliantly paced and strikingly realistic production. Adolph *Klauber called it "a naturally developed series of situations, curiously well knit, and consistently cumulative in their emotional effect."

WOMAN'S WAY, A (1909), a play by Thompson Buchanan. [Hackett Theatre, 112 perf.] When Howard Stanton (Frank Worthing) confesses to his wife, Marion (Grace *George), that he is in love with the widowed Mrs. Blakemore (Dorothy Tennant), Marion invites her to a dinner party. There Howard learns that Mrs. Blakemore is not the angel he thought her to be. This slight but pleasant comedy, produced by William A. *Brady, owed much of its success to George's engaging performance.

WOMEN, THE (1936), a comedy by Clare *Boothe. [*Ethel Barrymore Theatre, 657 perf.] Bitchy Park Avenue wife Sylvia Fowler (Ilka *Chase) persuades Mary Haines (Margalo *Gillmore) to use her gossipy manicurist Olga (Ruth Hammond), knowing full well that Olga will reveal the affair Mary's husband, Stephen, is having. Mary heads for Reno, falling in with a motley crew of would-be divorcées. She is eventually joined by Sylvia, seeking her own divorce. Most of the women are catty, self-serving, and as unfaithful as the men they condemn. Eventually Mary learns that Stephen's remarriage has been unsuccessful. She is prepared to take him back and also prepared to deal with her lady friends, announcing, "I've had two years to sharpen my claws." Although several important critics disliked the Max *Gordon offering—Brooks *Atkinson complaining of its "stingingly detailed pictures of some of the most odious harpies ever collected in one play"—the comedy of manners, with an all-female cast, was one of the biggest comedy hits of the decade. Broadway revivals in 1973 and 2001 revealed that the play still held the stage very well.

WONDERFUL TOWN. See *My Sister Eileen.*

WOOD, Audrey (1905–86), agent. Considered by many to have been the preeminent playwrights' agent of her day, she was born in New York, daughter of the first manager of the *Palace Theatre. In 1937 she and her husband, William Liebling (1894–1969), founded Liebling-Wood, Inc., with Liebling representing actors' interests. Almost immediately their labors for clients bore fruit with *Room Service. After the agency was dissolved in 1954, Wood worked alone. Among her clients were Tennessee *Williams, William *Inge, Robert *Anderson, and Arthur *Kopit.

WOOD, John (b. 1930), actor. The tall, gaunt British performer, who brings a dark shadow of menace to his many comic roles, has made only sporadic appearances on Broadway but usually earns raves. He was born in Derbyshire, educated at Oxford, and appeared with the Old Vic and on the West End before making his New York debut playing the confused pawn Guildenstern in *Rosencrantz and Guildenstern Are Dead* (1967). On subsequent visits Wood also shone as *Sherlock Holmes* (1974), the senile civil servant Henry Carr in *Travesties* (1975), the con man *Tartuffe* (1977), the scheming mystery writer Sidney Bruhl in *Deathtrap* (1978), a replacement for the diabolical Salieri in *Amadeus* (1981), and the seasoned traveling Player in *Rosencrantz and Guildenstern Are Dead* (1987), twenty years after his Broadway debut in the same play.

WOOD, Mrs. John [née Matilda Charlotte Vining] (1831–1915), comic actress and manager. Born in Liverpool, the comedienne made her American debut in Boston in 1854 and first appeared in New York as Don Leander in *The Invisible Prince* at the Academy of Music in 1856. That same season she scored a popular success as Minnehaha in *Hiawatha*. Later she managed a theatre in San Francisco, then took over the Olympic from Laura *Keene, running it for three years before sailing back to England. However, Wood returned at intervals into the mid-1870s. She was considered a superb performer in burlesque, although some American critics found her voice thin and her face immobile. She was, nevertheless, a vivacious actress who won over most audiences, and the American papers continued to follow her English career with interest.

WOOD, [Margaret] Peggy (1892–1978), singer and actress. The beautiful, versatile performer was born in Brooklyn and made her stage debut as a member of the chorus of *Naughty Marietta* (1910). She quickly rose to more important assignments, scoring a memorable success in *Maytime* (1917), in which she introduced "Will You Remember?" Wood starred in several more musicals before playing Portia in a 1928 mounting of *The *Merchant of Venice*. After several major roles in London musicals, she returned to New York and appeared in such shows as *Champagne, Sec* (1933); as writer Mildred Watson Drake in *Old Acquaintance* (1940); and as the second wife Ruth Condomine in *Blithe Spirit* (1941). But Wood is probably best remembered for her eight-year stint as Mama in the television series *I Remember Mama.* Autobiography: *How Young You Look*, 1940.

WOOD, William [Burke] (1779–1861), actor and manager. Born in Montreal, he worked as an accountant and as a lawyer's assistant before attempting his own business venture, which went bust and landed him in debtor prison. Wood then made his acting debut in 1798, was soon performing in Philadelphia, and was made treasurer of the *Chestnut Street Theatre, which he eventually took over in conjunction with the elder William *Warren. The pair also managed theatres in Baltimore, Annapolis, and Washington. All the time Wood continued to act, excelling at comedy, until his retirement in 1846. Autobiography: *Personal Reflections of the Stage*, 1855.

WOODRUFF, Henry [Ingott] (1870–1916), actor. The son of a prosperous New York businessman, he made his debut in the famous 1879 juvenile company of *H.M.S. Pinafore* and subsequently acted with Daniel E. Bandmann, Adelaide *Neilson, and other celebrities. In 1893 he was Charley Wykeham in the first American production of *Charley's Aunt*. Woodruff then left the stage to attend Harvard, later resuming his career and displaying his versatility in important roles in Shakespearean revivals, musical comedies, and contemporary farce and drama. His slightly pudgy, boyish good looks and comic skills helped him score his biggest success as the nobly self-sacrificing collegian Brown in *Brown of Harvard* (1906). In 1909 he starred in the Chicago musical *The Prince of Tonight*, in which he introduced the standard "I Wonder Who's Kissing Her Now." For several years before his early death he toured in vaudeville.

WOODS, A[lbert] **H**[erman] [né Aladore Herman] (1870–1951), producer. One of his era's most successful and colorful showmen, he was born in Budapest and brought to this country as an infant. After growing up on New York's Lower East Side he tried various odd jobs in the garment trade and then became an advance agent for a traveling show. Woods's first productions were cheap touring melodramas on the order of *The Bowery after Dark* and *Bertha, the Sewing Machine Girl*. Many of these were mounted by *Sullivan, Harris and Woods, the firm he founded with P. H. Sullivan and Sam H. *Harris. In 1909 he braved Broadway with *The Girl from Rectors*, and during the next thirty-four years produced over one hundred shows, including *Potash and Perlmutter* (1913), *Kick In* (1914), *Common Clay* (1915), *Cheating Cheaters* (1916), *Business Before Pleasure* (1917), *Eyes of Youth* (1917), *Parlor, Bedroom and Bath* (1917), *Friendly Enemies* (1918), *Up in Mabel's Room* (1919), *Ladies' Night* (1920), *Lawful Larceny* (1922), The *Shanghai Gesture* (1926), The *Trial of Mary Dugan* (1927), and *Five Star Final* (1930). He leaned heavily toward the lurid melodrama that had given him his start, as well as to bedroom and ethnic comedy. Woods also built the Eltinge Theatre and named it after one of his most profitable stars, female impersonator Julian *Eltinge. In his heyday Wood was famous for sitting in front of his theatre, smoking his big cigar, and calling all visitors "sweetheart."

WOODWORTH, Samuel (1785–1842), playwright. The peripatetic editor, publisher, and poet was born into a poor family in Scituate, Massachusetts, and was largely self-taught. He worked on many popular periodicals in Boston, New Haven, Baltimore, and New York, serving as editor of the *New York Mirror* in 1823. It was after this stint that he wrote most of his plays: the comic opera *The Deed of Gift* (1822), *Lafayette; or, The Castle of Olmutz* (1824), the "pastoral opera" *The *Forest Rose; or, American Farmers* (1825), the melodrama *The *Widow's Son; or, Which Is the Traitor?* (1825, the spectacular thriller *The Cannibals; or, The Massacre Islands* (1833), and the farce *Blue Laws; or, Eighty Years Ago* (1833). His last work, *The Foundling of the Sea* (1833), was written in response to G. H. *Hill's search for a play containing a prominent Yankee character. In 1836 Woodworth abandoned all literary interests and went to work for the navy but was paralyzed a year later by a stroke. Except possibly for *The Widow's Son* there is little of enduring merit in his plays, and posterity will recall him, if at all, as the lyricist of "The Old Oaken Bucket."

WOOLF, Benjamin E[dward] (d. 1901), playwright and librettist. He was born in England and brought to America at an early age, apprenticed to an engraver in his teens, and later became a violinist in the orchestra his father conducted at Burton's Theatre. He later moved to Boston, where he conducted the orchestra at the *Boston Museum. Woolf's poetry was published in book form, and his paintings were exhibited at important Boston galleries. Oddly, he seems never to have composed music for public performance. Instead, between 1860 and the mid-1890s he wrote over thirty plays and librettos for Boston production. Playgoers around the country knew him best for two works: his libretto for one of the earliest full-fledged American comic operas, *The *Doctor of Alcantara* (1862), and his comedy about American politics and materialism, *The *Mighty Dollar* (1875). His nephew, Edgar Allen Woolf (1881–1943), was also a playwright and librettist.

WOOLLCOTT, Alexander (1887–1943), critic. Born in Phalanx, New Jersey, and educated at Hamilton College, he served as a police reporter for the *New York Times* before becoming one of its drama critics in 1914. With time off for World War I, he remained at the paper until 1922, when he wrote for the *Herald*, then the *Sun*, and finally the *World*. His fellow critic, John Mason *Brown, called him "a sizzling mixture of arsenic and treacle," and said "he was as warm in his resentments as in his enthusiasms . . . his daily reviews . . . may not have been criticism but they were performances, Woollcott performing so that the emotions of a first night were captured in print with an immediacy unmatched in our time." He wrote paeans of praise on Mrs. *Fiske and the *Marx Brothers but detested many of Eugene *O'Neill's best plays. His books, often filled with theatrical criticism and reminiscences, included *Mrs. Fiske* (1917), *Mr. Dickens Goes to the Play* (1923), *Enchanted Aisles* (1924), *The Story of Irving Berlin* (1925), *Going to Pieces* (1928), *While Rome Burns* (1934), and *Long, Long Ago* (1943). With George S. *Kaufman he wrote two failed plays, *The Channel Road* (1929) and *The Dark Tower* (1933). In his last years he devoted himself largely to radio and to writing magazine articles but also took time to appear in *Brief Moment* (1931) and *Wine of Choice* (1938), and in 1940 headed the road company of *The *Man Who Came to Dinner*, playing Sheridan Whiteside, a character drawn after his own image. Biography: *Smart Aleck*, Howard Teichmann, 1978.

WOOLLEY MAMMOTH THEATRE COMPANY (Washington, D.C.). Dedicated to the production of new works, the theatre was founded in 1980 by Howard Shalwitz and Roger Brady. Operating out of various locations, including a Jewish community center and space in the *Kennedy Center, the troupe has presented dozens of original comedies and dramas. The company is currently engaged in raising funds for its new 250-seat home in downtown Washington.

WOOLLEY, Monty [Edgar Montillion] (1888–1963), actor and director. Born in New York, he spent many years teaching drama at his alma mater, Yale, before becoming a professional director and actor. He staged several classic revivals, then turned to the musical theatre to direct such shows as *Fifty Million Frenchmen* (1929), *The New Yorkers* (1930), and *Jubilee* (1935). In 1939 he won applause appearing in the musical *On Your Toes* but, with his pointed beard and sour hauteur, is best recalled as Sheridan Whiteside, the bellowingly cantankerous celebrity, in *The *Man Who Came to Dinner* (1939).

WOOSTER GROUP, THE (New York). A small artists' collective that explores alternative, experimental theatrical byways, its genesis was the Performance Group, founded in 1967 by Richard Schechner. A splinter group, working with Spalding *Gray and Elizabeth LeCompte, began operating

in 1975, and this offshoot has been known as the Wooster Group since 1980. It often performs in a flexible 150-seat space called the Performing Garage. Among its productions have been *Sakonnet Point*, *Point Judith*, *LSD (Just the High Points)*, and *Brace Up!*, as well as such unusual revivals as *The *Hairy Ape* performed as a circus in the crumbling Selwyn Theatre and *The *Emperor Jones* with a white woman playing the black Brutus Jones. The ensemble has toured extensively and is also involved with film and video. **Elizabeth LeCOMPTE** (b. 1944) was born in New Jersey and studied art at Skidmore College before beginning her theatre career as an actress. As a co-founder of the Wooster Group, she began writing as well as directing avant-garde pieces that grew out of improvisations with actors. Her notable works include the trilogy *Three Places in Rhode Island* (1978); *L.SD* (1984); a deconstruction of Arthur *Miller's The *Crucible*; and *Brace Up!* (1991 and 2003), a vaudeville version of *The Three Sisters*.

WORLD OF SUZIE WONG, THE (1958), a play by Paul *Osborn. [*Broadhurst Theatre, 508 perf.] Robert Lomax (William Shatner), a young artist living in Hong Kong, finds Suzie Wong (France Nuyen) very attractive, even after he realizes she is a prostitute. Although Susie is willing to discuss her profession in detail and continue to ply her trade, Lomax prefers to paint her portrait and reform her. Kay Fletcher (Sarah Marshall) would lure Lomax away to a more respectable life, but Lomax will not listen. Osborn based his work on the novel by Richard Mason, and David *Merrick produced it with success. To many critics both the play and its production harked back to such *Belasco mountings as *Lulu Belle. Although several reviewers dismissed the work as sophomoric, audiences found it vastly entertaining.

WORM, [Conrad Henrik] A[age] **Toxen** (1866–1922), press agent. A native of Denmark, at the turn of the century he was a press agent whose clients included James *O'Neill. He served the *Shuberts as a manager from 1910 until shortly before his death but was better known as one of the most imaginative publicists of his era. Worm originated the once famous "Masked Hostess" who was a greeter in Shubert enterprises, and he created such stunts as having the chorus girls of *The Red Petticoat*, a musical which dealt with a lady who runs a barber shop, offer free manicures to men in the audience.

WORTH, Irene (1916–2002), actress. Born in Nebraska, the actress made her professional debut on tour with Elisabeth *Bergner in *Escape Me Never* in 1942. Her New York debut came the following year in *The *Two Mrs. Carrolls*. Thereafter, she spent most of her career in London, although she returned for a number of memorable New York appearances: the other woman Celia Coplestone in The *Cocktail Party (1950), the mother-in-law Albertine Prine in *Toys in the Attic (1960), the enigmatic title seductress in *Tiny Alice (1964), the faded movie star Princess Kosmonopolis in *Sweet Bird of Youth (1975), Madame Ranevskaya in The Cherry Orchard (1977), Winnie in *Beckett's Happy Days (1979), Ella Rentheim in John Gabriel Borkman (1980), Miss Madrigal in The Chalk Garden (1982), Volumnia in Coriolanus (1988), and the hardened Grandma Kurnitz in *Lost in Yonkers (1991). Worth was a classy, commanding performer who never failed to get rave reviews in London, New York, and regional festivals. Writing of her performance in The Cherry Orchard, Clive *Barnes of the Times noted that "the range and cadences of her voice have the serenity of accepted sadness, and she moves across the stage as if it were the living room of her heart."

WRIGHT and FORREST, composers and lyricists. Robert [Craig] Wright (b. 1914) was born in Daytona Beach, Florida, and attended the University of Miami before working in various musical capacities. His career-long collaborator, George Forrest [Chichester Jr.] (1915–99) was born in Brooklyn and teamed up with Wright, scoring films in Hollywood and for West Coast theatrical productions. They came east to contribute material to the *Ziegfeld Follies of 1943 and soon had two Broadway hits: *Song of Norway (1944) and *Kismet (1953), for which they wrote lyrics to their rearrangement of the music of Grieg and Borodin, respectively. Both musicals were first mounted in California. Several of their other musicals, for which they sometimes provided original music, were successful on the West Coast but failed when they were brought east: Gypsy Lady (1946), Magdalena (1948), The Great Waltz (1949), and Anya (1965), all using classical pieces for the music. The team's original scores were heard in the short-lived Kean (1961) and the popular *Grand Hotel (1989).

WYCHERLY, Margaret [née De Wolfe] (1881–1956), actress. The slim, sad-eyed performer was born in London but raised in Boston. After studying at the *American Academy of Dramatic Arts, she made her debut in 1898 opposite Madame *Janauschek in What Dreams May Come. She spent time with Jessie *Bonstelle's company and in stock in San Francisco before returning to New York, where she played in several classic revivals and in new plays by Yeats and *Shaw. Among her notable later roles were the medium Madame LaGrange in The *Thirteenth Chair (1916), written by her husband, Bayard *Veiller; the

title role of the deceived wife in Jane Clegg (1920); the Mother in Six Characters in Search of an Author (1922); Daisy Devore in The *Adding Machine (1923); the domineering mother Mrs. Hallam in *Another Language (1932); and the downtrodden mother Ada Lester in *Tobacco Road (1933). In later years she replaced Laurette *Taylor in The *Glass Menagerie and shortly before her death played the Dowager Duchess of York in *Richard III.

WYNDHAM, Charles (1837–1919), comic actor. The great English comedian served as a doctor for the Confederate Army during the Civil War, then later won applause with Lester *Wallack's ensemble in such roles as Charles Surface. Shortly thereafter, he organized his own company and toured the country until he sailed for England in 1873. Although he soon became one of London's most popular actor-managers, Wyndham made a number of subsequent, if brief, tours in America. A tall, handsome man with a husky voice, he made his last appearance as Tom Kemp in The Mollusc (1909). One critic noted, "Sir Charles's mastery of the art of make-up is shown to distinct advantage in the piece. Although he is 72 years of age, he easily deceived the audience into believing that Tom Kemp is under 40. His delivery is remarkably virile, and his personality vigorous." Biography: All on Stage: Charles Wyndham and the Alberys, Wendy Trewin, 1980.

WYNN, Ed [né Isaiah Edwin Leopold] (1886–1966), comedian. The Philadelphia native was the son of a well-to-do hat manufacturer who hoped his son would take over the business. Instead he became a professional vaudevillian at the age of fifteen, for several seasons performing in an act known as the Rah Rah Boys. By the time Wynn made his Broadway debut in The Deacon and the Lady (1910), he had finely honed the tricks that became his trademarks: the lisp, the fluttering hands and squeaky giggle, the preposterous inventions, the zany clothing, and the outrageous puns. (He once appeared as a show boat impresario who had "bred his cast upon the waters"). Among his subsequent shows were the 1914 and 1915 editions of the *Ziegfeld Follies, The *Passing Show of 1916, Doing Our Bit (1917), Sometime (1918), The Ed Wynn Carnival (1920), The Perfect Fool (1921), The Grab Bag (1924), Manhattan Mary (1927), Simple Simon (1930), The Laugh Parade (1931), Hooray for What! (1937), Boys and Girls Together (1940), and Laugh, Town, Laugh (1942). Wynn also directed and produced many of these shows and wrote much of their material. His son was the popular character actor Keenan Wynn (1916–86), who made many films.

Y

YALE REPERTORY THEATRE (New Haven, Connecticut). The company has its roots in the Yale School of Drama, which was established in 1924, following a generous grant by Edward S. Harkness and which succeeded in luring Professor George Pierce *Baker away from Harvard to become its head. The repertory theatre was founded in 1966 by Robert *Brustein, who remained its director until 1979, when he was followed by Lloyd *Richards, Stan Wojewodski Jr., and James Bundy. The group presents not only new plays, especially those of American dramatists, but also freshly rethought versions of classics. Among the many productions to continue on to New York were *We Bombed in New Haven, Wings, A Lesson From Aloes, Master Harold . . . and the Boys, A Walk in the Woods, *Fences,* and *The Triumph of Love.* The company performs in a 489-seat semithrust theatre converted from a church. In 1991 it received the outstanding regional theatre *Tony Award.

YALE SCHOOL OF DRAMA. See Yale Repertory Theatre.

YANKEY IN ENGLAND, THE (1814), a comedy by David Humphreys. This work was produced by amateurs in 1814 but seems not to have been performed professionally. It deals with an American Whig and a Tory who become an admiral and a general after the Revolution, and who find themselves in London, where they meet a French count and countess. The countess is an adventuress who has a "Yankey" servant named Doolittle who is a typical comic Yankee, bumptious, naïve, and yet cunning. However, when the countess's schemes go awry and she prepares to swallow poison, another, more sensible, Yankee named Newman sets matters to right. The play is the first to transplant the traditional stage Yankee to foreign parts, a device that was revived with contemporary variations in American musical comedy ninety years later. **David HUMPHREYS** (1752–1818) was a Connecticut-born, Yale-educated gentleman-author who served as Washington's aide-de-camp and later was a Federal official. He wrote essays, poems, and one other known play, the romantic drama *The Widow of Malabar* (1790).

YEAMANS, Annie [née Griffiths] (1835–1912), actress. Best remembered as Cordelia Mulligan in the *Harrigan and *Hart plays, the tiny, small-mouthed performer was born on the Isle of Man. As a child she was taken to Australia, where her parents hoped to find theatrical success. She performed for many years as a bareback rider in a circus and married an American clown who was also a member of the troupe. Together they toured Asia, but coming to San Francisco her husband died, so she took herself and their children to New York. Although not in the original casts, Yeamans performed with G. L. *Fox in *Humpty Dumpty,* acted in Augustin *Daly's *Under the Gaslight,* and played Aunt Ophelia in *Uncle Tom's Cabin.* She first performed opposite Edward Harrigan in 1877 and continued to be his leading lady for eighteen years. Richard Harding *Davis wrote of her Cordelia, "We could never replace her coquetry or her brogue or her red wig and her bashful wiggle and shiver of pleasure when she is told how beautiful she is. She makes such an excellent foil to Harrigan with her excited, bustling garrulousness, the opposite at every point to the star's calm, easy confidence." After Harrigan's retirement, Yeamans appeared in such plays as *The Great Train Robbery* (1895), *Why Smith Left Home* (1899), and *Under Cover* (1903), as well as in several musicals. Her daughters were also popular actresses, especially Jennie Yeamans [née Eugenia Marguerite Yeamans] (1862–1906).

YEARS AGO (1946), a comedy by Ruth *Gordon. [Mansfield Theatre, 199 perf.] After watching Hazel *Dawn in *The Pink Lady,* Ruth Jones (Patricia Kirkland) decides to become an actress. To the consternation of her father, Clinton (Fredric *March), she rejects his plan for her to become a physical education teacher and also rejects the suit of Harvard student Fred Whitmarsh (Richard Simon). At first only Mrs. Jones (Florence *Eldridge) encourages her. But when Clinton, an ex-seaman, comes to recognize his daughter's determination, he pawns his prize telescope to help pay her way. Originally written with a contemporary setting and tried out as *Miss Jones,* this semiautobiographical comedy was rewritten, recast, retitled, and presented by Max *Gordon.

Of its Broadway version, Ward *Morehouse wrote in the *Sun*, "The play has atmosphere and character. It has been written with an understandable affection."

YELLOW JACKET, THE (1912), a play by George C. Hazelton and J. Harry *Benrimo. [Fulton Theatre, 80 perf.] When Chee Moo (Saxone Morland) bears the emperor an ugly baby, both she and her son, Wu Hoo Git, are given to a farmer to be put to death. The farmer spares them, and, while Chee Moo soon dies, Wu Hoo Git (George Relph) grows up to be a handsome young man. Guided by the spirit of his dead mother and by his beloved Suey Sin Fah (Grace A. Barbour), he bests his rival stepbrother and secures the yellow jacket that signifies he is emperor. Much of the story is told by a Chorus (Signor Perugini), while a dour, cigarette-smoking Property Man (Arthur Shaw) moves makeshift scenery about. Hailed by Walter Prichard *Eaton as "a triumph for all concerned," the play was supposedly derived from several real Chinese plays and designed to show American playgoers what Chinese drama was like. Over the next twenty years it was given important revivals, several of which outran the original production.

YES, MY DARLING DAUGHTER (1937), a comedy by Mark Reed. [Playhouse, 405 perf.] When young Ellen Murray (Peggy *Conklin) decides to spend a weekend with her handsome fiancé, Douglas Hall (Boyd Crawford), her mother (Lucile Watson) is outraged. This comes as a shock to Ellen since her mother was once one of Greenwich Village's most notorious bohemians, an advocate of free thinking and free love. Ellen spends the weekend with Doug, but she also agrees to marry him, thereby satisfying everyone. This light, amusing comedy, produced by Alfred *de Liagre Jr. was what the theatre called a "sleeper."

YESTON, Maury (b. 1945), composer and lyricist. Born in Jersey City, New Jersey, and educated at Yale and Cambridge, Yeston returned to Yale as a faculty member then ran the celebrated BMI Music Theatre Workshops in the 1970s. His first Broadway musical was *Nine* (1982), then he contributed half of the songs for *Grand Hotel* (1989). Yeston's *Phantom* has been produced regionally since the 1980s and his score for *Titanic* (1997) was heard on Broadway.

YIDDISH ART THEATRE (New York). Founded in 1918 by Maurice *Schwartz at the Irving Place Theatre, it eventually moved to a fine, new theatre built for it on Second Avenue. Yiddish theatre historian Nahma Sandrow, noting Schwartz's insistent pragmatism, observed that the organization

was "as close to traditional Yiddish theatre as to austere revolutionary art theatre principles." One result was that even in its first season a breakaway group called the Jewish Art Theatre was formed by Jacob *Ben-Ami and others. But the splinter group was short-lived while the original organization, by presenting a mixture of classics and trivial material, survived until 1950. Some of the productions were translated and performed on Broadway, and the company also toured on occasion.

YIDDISH THEATRE IN AMERICA. This unique form of community theatre came to America with the Jewish immigrants from Europe, where the art form had a stronghold in several cities. The first notable Yiddish production in New York was Avrom Goldfadn's *Koldunye; or, The Witch* in 1882 at the Bowery Theatre. Soon there were Yiddish theatres not only in Manhattan but also in Detroit, Boston, Chicago, and other cities. Most were located in the Jewish sectors and had a neighborhood feel to them, the local stars becoming favorites and the issues addressed (and often the jokes) tailored to the immediate community. The theatres were usually associated with local synagogues, social fraternities, and even labor unions. By World War I there were more than a dozen resident Yiddish theatres in New York, as well as troupes that toured from city to city. The plays were of two types: original dramas and comedies about either the old country or immigrant life in America, and Yiddish versions of the classics (particularly Shakespeare's works). Among the early Yiddish stars were David Kessler, Boris *Thomashefsky, Jacob *Adler, Sigmund Mogulesko, Stella *Adler, and Keni Liptzin. While some of these performers were known for their broad, florid acting style, others employed the ideas of Stanislavsky years before English-speaking actors used his methods. By the 1920s more and more Jewish immigrants became educated and assimilated into the world outside the neighborhoods and started attending English-speaking theatre. The Yiddish theatres began to decline, though some left-wing groups in the Great Depression remained active and there was even a Yiddish branch of the *Federal Theatre Project. But Jewish actors, playwrights, and audiences kept moving to Broadway, and it was the job of the *Yiddish Art Theatre, the Irving Place Theatre, *ARTEF, and the *Folksbiene Theatre to keep the old traditions alive. During the Nazi control of Europe and the Stalinist purge of Russia, Yiddish theatres all but disappeared in the old country. It dwindled in America as well until the late 1970s, when an interest in the old form and a renewed sense of tradition resurrected some Yiddish productions in various venues. Since fewer Americans spoke the old language, many were translated and found new life with Jewish theatre groups. Some of these productions, such as *The Golden Land* and *Kumi-Leml,* appealed to mainstream audiences as well. It is unlikely that the Yiddish theatre will ever become a strong neighborhood entertainment as in the past, but it is just as unlikely that it will pass out of existence.

YIP, YIP, YAPHANK. See *This is the Army.*

YORDAN, Philip. See *Anna Lucasta.*

YOU AND I (1923), a comedy by Philip *Barry. [Belmont Theatre, 174 perf.] Maitland White (H. B. *Warner) gave up his beloved painting career when he married so that he could support his family as a successful businessman. Eventually, however, the urge to return to his art proves too much. He paints a portrait, which turns out to be only good enough to be sold for advertising purposes. He muses, "There is no such hell on earth as that of the man who knows himself doomed to mediocrity in the work he loves." But he can persuade his son, Roderick (Geoffrey Kerr), who is prepared to give up his own dream of becoming an architect in order to marry Veronica Duane (Frieda Inescort), not to repeat his mistake. This Harvard Prize play, known originally as *The Jilts,* was Barry's first work to receive a professional production when it was presented by Richard G. *Herndon. Theatrical historian Edwin J. Bonner has called it "an intriguing tragicomedy studded with epigrammatic wit."

YOU CAN'T TAKE IT WITH YOU (1936), a comedy by Moss *Hart and George S. *Kaufman. [*Booth Theatre, 837 perf.; *Pulitzer Prize.] Philosophic, seventy-five-year-old Martin Vanderhof (Henry Travers) is the patriarch of a wacky New York City household. His daughter, Penelope Sycamore (Josephine *Hull), writes plays that she never finishes, while her husband, Paul (Frank Wilcox), manufactures fireworks in the cellar. One of Vanderhof's granddaughters, Essie (Paula Trueman), practices ballet in the living room while her husband, Ed (George Heller), plays his xylophone and runs his printing press. Another granddaughter, Alice (Margot Stevenson), invites the parents of her rich fiancé, Tony Kirby (Jess Barker), to the house for dinner. The Kirbys arrive a night early, and in the middle of the mayhem, Paul's fireworks explode. The cops arrive, and, declaring Ed's printed material anarchist, everyone is hauled off to jail. Vanderhof has also been hounded by the government for never having paid any income tax, but when the government learns that Vanderhof's wife years before had buried a homeless milkman using Vanderhof's name, it concludes he is legally dead and not liable. Sam H. *Harris produced the

popular attraction, one of the greatest in all American farces. It has remained a favorite of amateur and summer stock groups and was given major New York revivals in 1965 and 1983. This last revival, which emphasized the sentimental aspects of the play, was staged by Ellis *Rabb and starred Jason *Robards Jr. and Colleen *Dewhurst.

YOU KNOW I CAN'T HEAR YOU WHEN THE WATER'S RUNNING (1967), four one-act plays by Robert *Anderson. [*Ambassador Theatre, 756 perf.] In *The Shock of Recognition*, playwright Jack Barnstable (George *Grizzard) gets more than he bargained for when he auditions Richard Pawling (Martin *Balsam), an overeager actor, for a part that requires nudity. *The Footsteps of Doves* takes place in a furniture store where Harriet (Eileen *Heckart) and her husband, George (Balsam), are shopping for twin beds after years of sharing a double. But George thinks the switch is bad for their marriage. Before long he strikes up a friendship with a younger woman who thinks double beds are the only way to go. In *I'll Be Home for Christmas*, Chuck (Balsam) and Edith (Heckart) realize, as they fight over how to raise their children, just how empty their marriage has become. The final playlet, *I'm Herbert*, is a scattered and hilarious conversation between Herbert (Grizzard) and Muriel (Heckart), an elderly couple, who try in vain to remember accurately their earlier marriages and love affairs. A diverse, diverting collection of short plays, it enjoyed one of the longest runs of any such bill.

YOUMANS, Vincent [Millie] (1898–1946), composer. Born in New York, where his father and grandfather were well-known hatters, he originally considered a career in engineering but soon turned to music. A stint in the navy in World War I, during which time John Philip *Sousa played one of his compositions, confirmed him in his decision. Youmans served as a song plugger and inserted interpolations into a failed revue before writing much of the score for *Two Little Girls in Blue* (1921). In 1923 he collaborated on *Wildflower* and *Mary Jane McKane*, then a year later wrote his first complete score for *Lollipop*. The biggest musical comedy success of the 1920s was his *No, No, Nanette* (1925), whose songs included "I Want to Be Happy" and "Tea for Two." *Oh, Please!* (1926) offered "I Know That You Know," while from the far more successful *Hit the Deck!* (1927) came "Hallelujah" and "Sometimes I'm Happy." Thereafter Youmans decided to abandon musical comedy writing and return to operetta. He had also co-produced *Hit the Deck!* and ambitiously attempted to produce other offerings. But his subsequent shows proved failures and drove him to bankruptcy. *Rainbow* (1928) was followed by *Great Day* (1929), which despite its short run left behind its title melody as well as "More Than You Know" and "Without a Song." Youmans's last shows were *Smiles* (1930), *Through the Years* (1932), and *Take a Chance* (1932). Especially in his early years, his identifying signature was his employment of the shortest themes, often two to four notes, repeated with variations in harmony and in tempo. In later years Youmans's musical line was frequently longer, but he never fully discarded his early technique. After writing the music for the film *Flying Down to Rio*, he contracted tuberculosis. This, his heavy drinking and partying, coupled with a curious intractability in negotiations, all combined to remove him from the scene and hastened his death. Biography: *Days to Be Happy, Years to Be Sad*, Gerald Bordman, 1982.

YOUNG, John H. (early 1860s?), designer. The Michigan-born scenic artist served an apprenticeship under Thomas G. *Moses. Coming to New York, he established himself quickly as a versatile artist capable of designing for the whole range of theatrical productions. His sets were seen in such mountings as Augustin *Daly's 1889 revival of *As You Like It*; *The Man Without a Country* (1894); *Under the Polar Star* (1896), which included his highly lauded depiction of an iceberg; *Cymbeline* (1897); *Way Down East* (1898); *The *Auctioneer* (1901); and *The Pit* (1904). Producers of musicals also sought after Young, and he created the settings for many of *Weber and *Fields's famous entertainments. Other musical credits include *Babes in Toyland* (1903), *It Happened in Nordland* (1904), *George Washington Jr.* (1906), the *Follies of 1907*, and *The Candy Shop* (1909).

YOUNG MAN FROM ATLANTA, THE (1995), a play by Horton Foote. [Kampo Cultural Center, 24 perf.; *Pulitzer Prize.] In the 1950s, grocery wholesaler Will Kidder (Ralph Waite) has just moved into his new $200,000 home when he is let go by the company for whom he has worked for nearly forty years. He decides to start his own business and hopes to use the money he gave his wife, Lily Dale (Carlin Glynn), and his late son, Bill, who committed suicide. But Will soon learns that both wife and son gave all their money to Bill's roommate, a young man from Atlanta, and Will is left to face a troubled and uncertain future. Since the young man never appears, audiences were left to decide whether he was a blackmailer or a sponging lover. Although it garnered mixed notices, the drama won the Pulitzer probably as recognition for Foote's long and dedicated career. A Broadway production featuring Rip *Torn and Shirley Knight was mounted at the *Longacre Theatre in 1997 but only lasted eighty-eight performances. **Horton FOOTE** (b. 1916) was born in Wharton, Texas, and at the age of sixteen began his acting career as an apprentice at the *Pasadena Playhouse. Foote's first plays were produced in the early 1940s, and by the 1950s he scripted several films and television dramas. In the 1970s he began his nine-play cycle *The Orphans' Home*, based on his ancestors, about a Texas family from 1902 to 1928. Among his many other plays are *Only the Heart* (1942), *The Chase* (1952), *The Trip to Bountiful* (1953), *The Widow Clare* (1986), *Lily Dale* (1986), *Talking Pictures* (1994), and *When They Speak of Rita* (2000). Foote is known for his well-made, solid, traditional form of playwriting that, in its quiet way, is sometimes very powerful. Autobiography: *Beginnings*, 2002.

YOUNG MRS. WINTHROP (1882), a play by Bronson *Howard. [*Madison Square Theatre, 190 perf.] Douglas Winthrop (George Clarke) is as preoccupied with business as his wife, Constance (Carrie Turner), is with playing the social game. When Douglas, claiming the call of business, asks his wife not to go to a ball and instead to remain home with their ailing child, she agrees. Then she hears rumors questioning Douglas's fidelity, so she changes her mind. Douglas, in fact, has gone to the home where the ball is being held, but on legitimate matters. While they are away the child dies, and this leads to the couple's separation. The kindly family lawyer, Buxton Scott (Thomas Whiffen), brings about a reconciliation and makes both husband and wife see the excessiveness and consequences of their preoccupations. One of the first important American plays to deal with materialism and social climbing without satire, it was praised by the *Times* as "a play which tells what we understand; which has a genuine purpose, though not a didactic heaviness, and which hoes to its mark simply, directly, and effectively." It remained a favorite in stock at least until World War I.

YOUNG, Rida Johnson [neé Ida Louise Johnson] (1866–1926), lyricist and librettist. The Baltimore native pursued an acting career before working for the music publisher Isidore Witmark. Turning to playwriting, she saw her first work, *Lord Byron*, produced in 1900 by James Young, whom she later married. Her best-known works were *Brown of Harvard* (1906), *The *Lottery Man* (1909), *Naughty Marietta* (1910), *Captain Kidd Jr.* (1916), *Maytime* (1917), and *Little Old New York* (1920). All in all Young wrote nearly thirty plays and musicals and penned such famous songs as "Ah! Sweet Mystery of Life," "I'm Falling in Love with Someone," and "Will You Remember?"

YOUNG, Roland (1887–1953), comic actor. The short, suave, thinly mustached comedian was born in London and had performed for some time on West End stages before making his American debut in 1912. He earned applause in numerous supporting roles, including those in two plays, *Good Gracious Annabelle* (1916) and *A Successful Calamity* (1917), written by his future mother-in-law, Clare *Kummer. After he scored a major success in the musical *Buddies* (1919), Kummer wrote *Rollo's Wild Oat* (1920) for him. In 1924 Young played the imaginative composer Neil McRae in the expressionistic play *Beggar on Horseback*. His last success was as would-be singer Ned Farrar in Kummer's *Her Master's Voice* (1933). He was long popular in films.

YOUNG, Stark (1881–1963), critic and author. The noted American writer was born in Como, Mississippi, and educated at the University of Mississippi and at Columbia. After teaching English for several years he joined the staff of the *New Republic*, then served as drama critic for the *Times* during the 1924–25 season. He later served on the staff of *Theatre Arts* while continuing to review plays for the *New Republic*. Young wrote a number of unsuccessful original plays as well as admired translations of Chekhov. On rare occasions he also directed plays, including Eugene *O'Neill's *Welded* (1924). Among his books were *The Flower in Drama* (1923), *The Theatre* (1927), and a highly acclaimed historical novel, *So Red the Rose* (1934).

YOUNG, William. See *Rajah, The*.

YOU'RE A GOOD MAN, CHARLIE BROWN (1967), a musical comedy by Clark Gesner (book, music, lyrics). [Theatre 80 St. Marks, 1,597 perf.] A day in the life of Charlie Brown (Gary Burghoff), a boy "with what you call a failure face," is spent in the company of his dog Snoopy (Bill Hinnant), who thinks he is the German ace known as The Red Baron; Linus (Bob Balaban), who forever needs his security blanket; Linus's sister Lucy (Reva Rose), a battle-ax in the making; and the pianist Schroeder (Skip Hinnant), who loves Beethoven. They deal in their own special ways with such juvenile concerns as baseball, sibling rivalry, unrequited love, and school. *Notable songs*: Happiness; You're a Good Man, Charlie Brown; The Book Report; Suppertime. Derived from Charles M. Schulz's comic strip *Peanuts*, this low-budget musical became one of Off Broadway's biggest successes and remains popular with school and other amateur theatre groups, as well as in professional stock. A Broadway revival in 1999 suffered from a too-elaborate production in a bigger house and failed to run.

YURKA, Blanche [neé Jurka] (1887–1974), actress. Considered one of the finest tragedians of her day, Yurka excelled in Greek, Shakespeare, and modern dramas. She was born in the Bohemian section of Czechoslovakia and came to America as an infant, growing up in St. Paul, Minnesota. When her family moved to New York in 1898, she studied for an opera career at the Metropolitan Opera's school, and she sang there briefly before going onto the legitimate stage. Yurka appeared in several Broadway productions in the 1910s but found fame in the 1920s for her tragic roles, such as Gertrude to John *Barrymore's *Hamlet* (1922), Gina in *The Wild Duck* (1925), and Hedda Tesman in *Hedda Gabler* (1929). Other notable New York performances during her long career included *Electra* (1932), Helen in *Troilus and Cressida* (1932), Queen Elizabeth in *Gloriana* (1938), and Jocasta in *Oedipus the King* (1945). Her last New York appearance was as The *Madwoman of Chaillot* Off Broadway in 1970. Yurka was a strong advocate for the new *Actors Equity Association and served as one of its officers many times. Autobiography: *Bohemian Girl*, 1970.

Z

ZAKS, Jerry (b. 1946), director. Born in Stuttgart, Germany, he was educated in America, including Dartmouth and Smith College, and began his career as an actor before turning to directing. After working Off Broadway and in regional houses, he called attention to himself with three fine revivals at *Lincoln Center: The *House of Blue Leaves* and The *Front Page*, both in 1986, and *Anything Goes* in 1987. Among his other successful stagings have been *Wenceslas Square* (1987), *Lend Me a Tenor* (1989), *Six Degrees of Separation* (1990), *Assassins* (1991), *Guys and Dolls* (1993), A *Funny Thing Happened on the Way to the Forum* (1996), *Laughter on the 23rd Floor* (1992), *Smokey Joe's Cafe* (1995), *The Cripple of Inishmann* (1998), The *Man Who Came to Dinner* (2000), *Epic Proportions* (2000), A Bad Friend (2003), and *Little Shop of Horrors* (2003). Equally adept at big musicals as intimate dramas, Zaks is usually at his best with fast-paced farces.

ZIEGFELD, Florenz, Jr. (1867–1932), producer. The most famous of all American showmen, still synonymous with glamour and opulence, he was born in Chicago, where his father ran a musical conservatory. As director of musical events for the 1893 Columbian Exposition, the elder Ziegfeld sent his son to Europe to secure talent. Instead of hiring distinguished musical figures, the young Ziegfeld signed on music-hall performers and circus acts. In 1893 he also became manager of the strongman Eugene Sandow, and his promotion of the muscle man established his own name, too. Ziegfeld's first Broadway production was an 1896 revival of A *Parlor Match*, which featured his first wife, Anna *Held. His subsequent productions, mostly vehicles for Held, were *Papa's Wife* (1899), *The Little Duchess* (1901), *The Red Feather* (1903), *Mam'selle Napoleon* (1903), *Higgledy Piggledy* (1904), and A *Parisian Model* (1906). Even in these early productions he began to earn a reputation for offering a chorus line of beautiful girls in sumptuous costumes. His next production was the *Follies of 1907*, which initiated the famous series called the *Ziegfeld Follies*. His other musical productions included *The Soul Kiss* (1908), *Miss Innocence* (1908), *Over the River* (1912), A *Winsome Widow* (1912), *The Century Girl* (1916), *Miss 1917*, *Sally* (1920), *Kid Boots* (1923), *Annie Dear* (1924), *Louie the 14th* (1925), *No Foolin'* (1926), *Betsy* (1926), *Rio Rita* (1927), *Show Boat* (1927), *Rosalie* (1928), The *Three Musketeers* (1928), *Whoopee* (1928), *Show Girl* (1929), *Bitter Sweet* (1929), *Simple Simon* (1930), *Smiles* (1930), a 1932 revival of *Show Boat*, and *Hot-Cha!* (1932). Although he was often accused in his day of being indifferent to great comics or great show songs, his roster of brilliant clowns and the numerous still-popular melodies that came from his shows belie the accusations. He also produced a number of nonmusical plays, including *Rose Briar* (1922) for his second wife, Billie Burke. Ziegfeld's personal extravagances were as well publicized as his shows—among them his penchant for sending long telegrams to people within reach of his phone. His productions were the costliest of their day and were praised not merely for their richness but for their tasteful visual beauty, especially those designed by Joseph *Urban. The producer's excellences so overshadowed those of his associates in contemporary eyes that, for example, the original production of *Show Boat* was hailed by most critics as a Ziegfeld show and not a *Kern or *Hammerstein show. Writing of the earlier *Sally*, Alexander *Woollcott concluded, "It is of none of these, not of Urban, nor Jerome Kern, not of Leon Errol, not even of Marilyn Miller that you think as you rush for the subway at ten minutes to midnight. You think of Mr. Ziegfeld. He is that kind of producer. There are not many of them in the world." Through much of his career he was associated with two of New York's almost legendary theatres, the *New Amsterdam, where most of his *Follies* played, and the *Ziegfeld, which he opened in 1927. Biography: *Ziegfeld*, Charles Higham, 1972.

ZIEGFELD FOLLIES. The greatest and longest-lived series of extravagant revues, the first edition was mounted by Florenz *Ziegfeld on a shoestring budget as the *Follies of 1907*. (The producer did not add his name to the series until 1911.) Annual editions were produced through 1925, with versions also in 1927 and 1931. From 1922 on the revues were advertised as "Glorifying the American Girl," which was truth in advertising. Writing during the series' heyday, George Jean *Nathan observed, "Out of the vulgar leg-show, Ziegfeld has fashioned

679

a thing of grace and beauty, of loveliness and charm; he knows quality and mood. He has lifted, with sensitive skill, a thing that was mere food for smirking baldheads and downy college boys out of its low estate and into a thing of symmetry and bloom." After his death the *Shuberts bought the rights to the name and produced editions in 1934, 1936, and 1943. These editions were successful even though it was conceded they lacked the tasteful, imaginative opulence of Ziegfeld's own mountings. A 1957 edition was a quick, dismal failure. Among the great stars presented in the *Follies,* many of whom Ziegfeld discovered and developed, were Nora *Bayes, Fanny *Brice, Eddie *Cantor, Ray *Dooley, Leon *Errol, W. C. *Fields, Marilyn *Miller, Ann *Pennington, Will *Rogers, and Bert *Williams. Song hits from the shows include "Shine On Harvest Moon," "By the Light of the Silvery Moon," "Row, Row, Row," "Hello, Frisco," "A Pretty Girl Is Like a Melody," "My Man," "Second Hand Rose," "Mr. Gallagher and Mr. Shean," and "Shaking the Blues Away." From the first the productions were known for their eye-filling costumes and sets, but not until Joseph *Urban was signed on, beginning with the 1915 edition, did the series reach its legendary apotheosis. His stylish designs and carefully coordinated colors were instantly recognized as the finest work the American musical stage had yet seen. Settings often depicted exotic, color-rich lands, and musical numbers were regularly given themes. Thus, in "A Pretty Girl Is Like a Melody" mannequins paraded dressed as "Barcarolle," "Elegy," and other classic styles. From 1917 through 1925 Ben Ali *Haggin's lavish tableaux vivants were also a feature. Among the many great Ziegfeld beauties were Marion Davies, Paulette Goddard, Lillian Lorraine, Mae Murray, Drucilla Strain, and Avonne Taylor.

ZIEGFELD THEATRE (New York). Possibly the finest theatre ever built in New York, it was financed by William Randolph Hearst and designed by Joseph *Urban and Thomas *Lamb. The auditorium, located at Sixth Avenue and 54th Street, was egg-shaped, with no boxes but with a gilt, undecorated proscenium and a gilt stage whose apron extended unusually far. Its walls and ceiling, which seemed virtually as one, were covered with Urban's playful murals done in rich, burnished colors. Public rooms and backstage facilities were exceptionally spacious. Florenz *Ziegfeld opened it in February 1927 with his production of *Rio Rita,* followed by such memorable shows as *Show Boat* (1927), *Bitter Sweet* (1929), and the *Ziegfeld Follies of 1931.* After his death the house became a cinema, until Billy *Rose restored it to the legitimate fold in 1944. Its notable later offerings included *Brigadoon* (1947), *Gentlemen Prefer Blondes* (1949), and *Kismet* (1953). It was torn down in 1967 to make way for a skyscraper.

ZIMMERMAN, J. Fred (1841?–1925), manager. One of the founders of the notorious *Theatrical Syndicate or Trust, he began his career as treasurer of Washington's *National Theatre. Later his firm of *Nixon and Zimmerman developed what was then a virtual monopoly of Philadelphia theatres, including the Chestnut Street Opera House, the Broad Street Theatre, the Forrest, and the Garrick. Curiously, the only three major legitimate theatres never controlled, or run only briefly by him, were the city's three most historic houses, the *Chestnut Street (which was not the same as the Opera House), the *Arch Street, and the *Walnut Street.

ZINDEL, Paul. See *Effect of Gamma Rays . . .*

ZIP; or, Point Lynne Light (1877), a play by Frederick *Marsden. [*Park Theatre. 8 perf.] Zip (Charlotte *Crabtree) is a young girl who lives with a lighthouse keeper she believes to be her father. He is murdered by men who are determined to sink a passing ship and who black out the lighthouse and set up a false beacon. Zip foils their plans and learns that one of the passengers whom she has saved is her real mother. She is taken off to England to confirm her inheritance. A new set of villains try to deprive her of it, but once again she triumphs, even finding a sweetheart along the way. One of "Lotta" Crabtree's most popular vehicles, and typical of most of them, the story gave her plenty of opportunities to sing, dance, and play her banjo. It remained in her repertory until she retired.

ZIPPRODT, Patricia (1925–99), costume designer. Born in Evanston, Illinois, she studied at Wellesley College, the Chicago Art Institute, and New York's Fashion Institute. Among the shows for which she created costumes were a *Visit to a Small Planet* (1957), *Oh Dad, Poor Dad . . .* (1962), *Fiddler on the Roof* (1964), *Cabaret* (1966), *Plaza Suite* (1968), *1776* (1969), *Pippin* (1972), *Chicago* (1975), *Alice in Wonderland* (1982), *Don Juan* (1982), *Brighton Beach Memoirs* (1983), *Sunday in the Park with George* (1984), a 1986 revival of *Sweet Charity,* a 1988 mounting of *Macbeth, Shogun* (1990), *My Favorite Year* (1992), the 1993 revival of *My Fair Lady,* and *Picasso at the Lapin Agile* (1996). A superb and versatile costumer, Zipprodt also developed some unique techniques in costume construction, such as using layers of dyes and paint in the *Fiddler on the Roof* clothes, subtly adding color to drab peasant wear. The annual Patricia Zipprodt Award is given for "innovative costuming" in New York.

ZIRA (1905), a play by J. Hartley *Manners and Henry *Miller. [*Princess Theatre, 128 perf.] Seeing a chance for a better life, Hester Trent (Margaret *Anglin) takes the place of a woman she believes has died. This leads to complications, especially when the other woman turns up alive, but also leads to a happy romance. Based on Wilkie Collins's *The New Magdalen*, which had already been dramatized with marked success in 1873, the new version produced by Miller was reset in contemporary South Africa during the Boer War.

ZOO STORY, THE (1960), a one-act play by Edward *Albee. [*Provincetown Playhouse, 582 perf.] Jerry (George Maharis), a shabbily dressed, aggressively hostile young man, accosts Peter (William Daniels), a mild-mannered publisher, who is sitting quietly on a park bench, and begins to pour out his history and feelings. This includes telling of a dog at his boardinghouse whom kindness could not move and with whom cruelty allowed him to establish an impersonal modus vivendi. It soon becomes evident that Jerry is determined to die, by his own hand or by someone else's. His death wish is realized when he gets Peter to stab him with a knife. Presented earlier in Berlin, this talky, then suddenly dramatic, play established Albee as a promising writer. It was revived in 1963 with Albee's *The American Dream*, and since has been a staple in colleges and experimental theatres.

ZORICH, Louis (b. 1924), character actor. A seasoned performer with a warm and easygoing persona, Zorich was born in Chicago and educated at Roosevelt College and the *Goodman Theatre School, arriving in New York in 1959 where he played supporting roles for years. Zorich was first singled out in 1969 for his worldly wise Cardinal Ragna in *Hadrian VII*, but still he continued to be cast in secondary parts. In 1971 he and his wife, actress Olympia *Dukakis, founded the Whole Theatre Company in New Jersey.